ĀGAMA AND TRIPITAKA

A Comparative Study of
Lord Mahavira and Lord Buddha

VOL. II — LANGUAGE AND LITERATURE

ĀGAMA AND TRIPITAKA

A Comparative Study of Lord Mahavira and Lord Buddha

VOLUME- II

LANGUAGE AND LITERATURE

ACHARYA SHRI NAGRAJJI, D. Litt

Introduction by

Late UPADHYAYA SHRI AMARMUNIJI

A Glance by

Late DR. PRABHAKER MACHWAY

Ex-Director

Bhartiya Bhasha Parishad, Calcutta

Ex-Chairman, Sahitya Academy, New Delhi

CONCEPT PUBLISING COMPANY, NEW DELHI-110 059

ISBN 81-7022-731-3 (Vol. II)
ISBN 81-7022-730-5 (Set)

First Published -2003

Published and Printed by
Ashok Kumar Mittal
Concept Publishing Company
A/15-16, Commercial Block, Mohan Garden
New Delhi-110059 (India)

Phones: 5351460, 5351794
Fax: 091–(11)–5357103
E-mail: publishing@conceptpub.com

PREFACE

The subject-matter of Ist volume of '*Agama Aur Tripitaka—Ek Anushilan*' is 'History and Traditions' and the subject-matter of the second volume is 'Language and Literature'. The place of Ardh Magadhi Prakrita of Agamas and Pali language of Tripitakas in the modern philology and the linguistic family, they belong to, have been discussed in the initial chapter of this book. The modern shape of linguistic science has considerably advanced and is under regular process of evolution. Without properly understanding the present shape of philology, we would be simply deluding ourselves by claiming that we are correctly evaluating the characteristics of Prakrita and Pali languages. Consequently, the topic of modern philology has to be elaborately discussed in this book, which has been done probably for the first time so far canonical literature of Jaina religion is concerned. Today, everything and every subject can gain international recognition, provided they are deliberated upon and discussed in right direction with greater aptitude and in accordance with distinguished universal standard. In case, the significance of Prakrita and Pali dialects is confined to the fact that they had been used in accomplishment of religious attitudes, then their scope will be considerably limited to Jaina and Bodh Communities only. Such languages, if approved by philologists, as forming part of linguistic groups, having international recognition, they are freed from the bondage of small sects or communities and gain recognition of their existence and inability.

While discussing Aryan languages, Sanskrit inevitably comes into picture. I have also discussed it from philological view point. Like Agamas Aur Tripitaka canonical literature. I have also dealt with Vedas, Brahman treatises, Aranyakas and Upanishads etc. Under the topic of Agamas, I have discussed all the 45 Agamas and ignored the sectarian view whether the total number of Agamas is 32 or 45. Although, religious scriptures of Digamber Sect are not Agamas, yet their language is also Sorseni Prakrita. They are held equally in high esteem by their followers like Agamas. I have, therefore, also discussed them in detail.

I have tried my best to rise above the schism of Jaina, Bodh, Digamber and Swetamber Sects and discussed all matters without least bias or prejudice. How far I have been successful and remained sincere to my attempt, is a matter to be judged and appreciated by the learned readers. I have due regard for all the religious preceptors and teachers belonging to Jaina, Bodh, Digamber and Swetamber Sects. Thus considerations of high and low, big and small have never dominated my mind while elucidating the facts. Such has been my nature and sensibility.

A Language and script are interdependent. Hence a full chapter has been devoted for discussion relating to the origin and evolution of script-writing. While discussing on the nature of Prakrita dialects in relation to inscriptions on stones and pillars, I have given an elaborate account of all the stone and pillar inscriptions in a separate chapter. I have summarily thrown light on the instant points of differences respecting Bhadrabahu I and II, Chandragupta I and II, Yapniya Sangh, Swetamber and Digamber Sects so that the contentious issues may also be explained and critically discussed. In nutshell my aim has been to make this book useful not only for the learned scholars but also for common people of average intelligence.

Writing of this second volume was started in Samvat year 2030 during my sojourn at Churu during 4 months of rainy season. At that time, my intimate colleagues, Muni Sri Mahendra Kumarji I and II were not with me. Muni Sri Mahendra Kumar I was at Calcutta while Muni Sri Mahendra Kumar II was at Delhi with Acharya Muni Sri Nagrajji. Necessity is the mother of invention. By chance, Sri Sohanlal Hirawat, a literateur and social worker, happened to invite Dr. Chagan Lalji Shastry. He stayed with me for about 2 to 3 months. He extended his valuable cooperation in my literary pursuits which was really praise-worthy.

Writing of this volume was over in about 2 to 3 years. Written material was regularly sent to Muni Sri Mahendra Kumarji I at Calutta and Varanasi respectively for editing. The editing of the book was almost over before my departure from the place.

The first volume of this book had been published in Samvat year 2026 while the second volume is under publication in Samvat year 2039. There are several reasons for this long gap. We had shifted to Delhi in Samvat year 2027. There we remained awfully busy for 3 years continuously in celebrations of 2500th aniversary of final salvation of Lord Mahavira and the incidents of Churu and Raipur, in connection with the published book *Agni-Pariksa* that we could not even think to take up writing of Part II. The writing of this volume was almost over during my stay at Churu and next year at Sardulpur in rainy seasons. It has been the practice in my life to develope contacts with the public and strive for their welfare during my stays in Metropolitan cities and to undertake literary pursuits in small villages and towns for self-satisfaction and happiness.

The same year in Samvat 2031, Muni Sri Mahendra Kumarji I had appeared in different positions at Varanasi. The social friction was at its climax which was going on for past several years. All the conditions had grown critical and uncertain. Hence in that awkward and untoward situation, publication of the book was neither feasible nor I like it. After two years of the said march of events, I had to move out and take up long journey to Calcutta. In Samvat year 2035 at Calcutta, the publication of the book was commenced by Arhat Prakasan, in presence of Muni Sri Mahendra Kumarji I. It took a long period of 4 years in finishing publication of the book. The main reason for this inordinate delay was frequent break-downs of electricity at Calcutta. It is however, a matter of great consolation that the long-awaited work will be available to the readers soon. However, it would have been much soothing if the volume was ready during life time of late Muni Sri Mahendra Kumarji I, after printing.

Erudite scholar, Upadhyaya Sri Amar Maniji and renowned philosophist, Dr. Prabhakar Machway have really graced me by writing 'Introduction' and 'A Glance' respectively in appreciation of my book for which I am really indebted to them.

I also express my gratitude to all those pre-eminent writers whose books have been referred to by me in this volume.

I have now almost detached myself from worldly obligations. While all other important matters are looked into by my sincere colleagues, Muni Sri Manmalji and Muni Mani Kumarji. I am, therefore, confident that the proposed third volume of 'Agama Aur Tripitaka-Ek Anushilan' will also be soon accomplished.

ACHARYA SHRI NAGRAJJI

Loharıwala Bhawan,
Calcutta,
Deepavali, Samvat 2039

A GLANCE

Dr. Muni Sri Nagrajji is pre-eminent scholar of Jaina philosophy and history. 'AGAMA AUR TRIPITAKA—EK ANUSHILAN' is a unique treatise of its kind, written by him. I had the privilege to make a critical appreciation of it. After 12 years since then, he has written this voluminious book-styled 'VISHWA BHASHA PRAVAH (FLOW OF WORLD LANGUAGES). Because of his wider outlook, it has assumed the shape of concise encyclopaedia of history and advancement of Indian philology.

Its initial portion deals with linguistic philosophy. Besides references of Yask, Panini, Katyayan and Patanjali, Muni Sri has produced relevant illustrations and conclusions from Greek, Latin and Hebrew languages. He has referred to Vedic, Bodh and Jaina ideologies with critical evaluation, which has been done by him on the basis of rational and authentic material. Hence, there is no question to differ with him. Muni Sri has himself placed before us all relevant repudiations and vindications in support or against, wherever necessary. I really feel much astonished to witness such unceasing efforts and long perseverance of a single individual. This is the soothing consequence of his lone and concerted efforts in selecting the material.

In the next portion, the short-sighted attitude of religious doctrinaires towards languages has been exposed with analytical and critical comments by Munisri. Although, the view of grammarians of Dravadian languages are missing, a thorough investigation of Aryan languages in India has, however, been made in this volume.

There are divergent views of different scholars with regard to geographical, historical and cultural backgrounds of ancient languages. Whether Aryans and cultural backgrounds of ancient languages. Whether Aryans belonged to India or they migrated from other parts of the world—is one such controversial point. Many of our concepts have been borrowed from Western scholars who decided the chronology of principal events to suit their own interests. In order to relieve ourselves, we should revert to our own basic fountains of information. Unfortunately, even now, the heads of philology departments of leading universities in India seek guidance from America, England, Germany and Russia. There may be a few heads of linguistic departments who are really authentic scholars of ancient Indian and Asian languages. The conversants of Pali, Prakrita and Apbhransha dialects are all the more rare.

In view of the above, the material contained in the third, fourth, fifth and sixth Chapters of this Volume, written by Muni Sri, is most important. There were only a few authoritative scholars of these subjects in India and they are no longer alive. The scholars, namely—Pt. Sukhlalji, Dr. Gune, Rahul Sankritayan, Prof. Upadhye, Dr. Vasudeva Saran Agrawal, Dr. Suniti Kumar Chatterjee, Prof. T. Meenakshi Sundaram Pillai, who are alive, are specialized in one or two branches of linguistic science only. The scholars, with universal outlook and of international repute with prominence in Pali and Prakrita scripts do not exceed more than a dozen in the whole country. Muni Sri is decidedly leading most amongst them.

Major part of the discussion is of the same standard as termed 'Descriptive and Historical Linguistics' in Western Glossary. From the seventh chapter onward. Munisri has devoted himself towards progress of science of writing. However, it has not surpassed the accomplishments of Sri Gauri Sanker Hirachand. Ojha and Sri C. Siva Ram Murti in this regard.

However, the most brilliant and fundamental part of this voluminous book is its eighth chapter which is of great significance. Herein, Munisri has made a comparative and meaningful discussion on Digamber and Shwetamber beliefs with regard to divine language (Ardh Magadhi, Prakrita) and Agama Scriptures. Munisri has exercised his talents and made best use of his collective information and experience relating to phonology, morphology, semantics and syntax with critical evaluation. I came across several new informations, after going through this chapter. The renowned scholar and grammarian, of Prakritas, Dr. Pixel, has opined that 'Uttradhyan' and 'Dasavaikalika' are the best guides to undertake study of Prakritas from linguistic viewpoint. Munisri has made his own founding in the same context.

As a matter of fact, philology is not confined to the construction of words or postmortem of syntactical formation only. It is the applicability of the language that matters and not its grammar. It is said "The conventions are stronger than the holy scriptures". There is cultural, social, political, geographical and historical background behind formation of each word or sentence. After due analytical research, it is found that no idea or thought is exclusive, unalterable or everlasting. It is produced, nourished and changed from time to time, consciously or unconsciously by mankind. Munisri is an erudite and prudent scholar of ancient and modern sacreds knowledge miscellaneous. Hence, the magnificence and superiority of thoughts, contained in this grand volume are a rare gift to Hindi language. The books of English, German, French and Russian languages, available on this subject, are of no significance for only Hindi knowing readers. It is also essential to go through the books thoroughly, available on this subject, in other Indian languages. Then only, we shall be in a position to arrive at new inferences.

For instance, let us consider over group of Darad languages (languages spoken in territories leading Kasmira). In Kasmira, there are two different opinions regarding ('Ka' 'Sher') in Kasmiri language. Besides the influence of Paisachi Prakrita and Sanskrit, Pahalvi, 'Pasto' and old Persian dialects on one hand and Tibetan-Mangole dialects on the other have influenced old Kasmiri language. Several phonetic sounds and words have been borrowed in their original form from Middle East countries.

I feel really grateful to Muni Sri Nagrajji that I could have a glimpse of this unique work. This book is worthy to be acquired and is easy to be followed. The modern Indian philologists will find this book highly beneficial for studying and teaching. I would like to emphasize the significance of this book of Munisri in the words that the libraries which are equipped with books on Indian linguistic science will be enriched by including this book with them.

Calcutta
8-11-1982

PRABHAKER MACHWAY

INTRODUCTION

Whenever a worthy son of Saraswati, the goddess of knowledge, takes up even an abstruse and profoundly deep subject and discusses it with his thoughtful consideration and wisdom, the subject is not only conveniently followed by learned scholars but it is readily understood by people of average intelligence as well. Just as the phenomenal world, overed by darkness, is illuminated by the rays of sun similarly, even a most difficult and unintelligible subject, enunciated by erudite sholars with their deep insight is easily understood.

The wise and celebrated thinker, Muni Sri Nagrajji is, undoubtedly, a gifted son of goddess Saraswati. There is not the slightest exaggeration about it. I am not applying these attributes, simply because he happens to be very close to me. His deep and profound study, incusitive nature and authenticity in writing is such that all considerate, liberal and genuine thinkers are inspired to comment accordingly.

Munisri does not deal with any subject merely for demonstration or exposition. He does not pick up his pen just because he intends to write. In concistency with his name Nagraj (Meru mountain), he ascends to all heights and with the best of his talents and ability, he ponders over the subject deeply and appropriates it to himself before its real essence is made known to others. Just as his study is extensive and multifarious, so is his deep concentration, mental contemplation and reflection to elucidate the sujbect. It is indeed a rare harmonions and beautiful combination that the bright and brilliant personality of an eminent scholar is manifested before the people. Accordingly, in the words of renowned poet, Murari, Munisri is like a self-absorbed large and stout mountain of Mandrachal in the ocean of knowledge. He is not like the brave monkey of *Ramayana* period (legendary Hanuman) who crossed the ocean by taking a long leap with a flying speed without going deep into it—

"Avdhi laughati eva vanarai bhataih,
Kintwasya gambhirtam,
Apatal-nimagna-pivartanur,
Janati Manthahaah"

Long ago, I happened to go through the first volume of "Agama Aur Tripitaka-Ek Anushilan", a masterpiece work, written by Muni Sri. While it was quite voluminous in size, it was equally unique in its contents. The said treatise has been highly spoken of by leading intellectuals. Consequent upon the same, he had been awarded honorary D.Litt. degree by Kanpur University. The book really presents a comparative study of confluence of Jaina and Bodha religions, the two contemporaneous expositions of ascetic culture in a rare scholarly manner. He has unfolded many historical events, with utmost neutrality, which were, hitherto lying unknown so much so that an eminent scholar like Pt. Sukhlalji and others were greatly impressed and they have highly commended and spoken of the accomplished book of Munisri.

The second volume titled 'Language and Literature' is under publication by M/s Arhant Prakashan, Calcutta and it has been written as elaborately as its Ist Part. Consequently, it is being published also as Ist volume of 'Agama Aur Tripitaka-Ek Anushilan'. In the present volume one can also witness the rare intelligence and miraculous performance of Muni Sri. Herein also, the scholarly and analytical mode of expression finds manifestation; his comparative and investigative style of presentation is unique which impresses the intellectuals and literary geniuses. Although, Munisri has attained old age, it appears that his bright conceptual and vivid imaginative power is ever fresh. It is found as brilliant as his Ist volume-Nay, it is all the more splendid than before.

The detailed index of the subjects, dealt with in this work constitutes a book in itself. The profound analyical discussions of the growth and advancement of linguistic science from the ancient period to the modern age in India Greece and Europe has been made in such a simplified manner that it can be understood not only by intelligentia class but also by people of average intelligence.

Writing on a universal footing regarding literary accomplishments, touching multifarious dimensions will amount to greatest concentration though and contemplation. There is an interesting description of Vedic literature, Vadic Sanskrit and its close resemblance with Prakrita language. Jaina literature, various Prakrita scripts and Buddhist literature, Pali Script and its expansion, all these subjects present a thought provoking material to add to our knowledge, Muni Sri deserves all acclamation and applanse from the readers of his book.

Muni Sri has really performed a miracle while elucidating science of writing. The ancient Brahmic script and expansion of many other scripts born from it—Kharosth Script and its derivation (This ancient script was prevalent in north-west frontier region of India) roughly between 4th century B.C. to 3rd century A.D. I and its representation in Jaina and Boddh literature, profoundly deep and extensive discussion on the stone inscriptions during Ashoka regime and belonging to the earlier period, is so authentic and thought-provoking that the conscious students and readers get imbibed in it over head and ears. What is the benefit of vague and shallow writing which neither removes the shallowness of the readers nor adds to their knowledge.

I donot wish to comment upon the subjects, dealt with in this book. They will be ascertained by the readers from the book itself. It may not be worthwhile to interrupt the curiosity of the readers by lengthening the introductory or initiatory comments. I shall, therefore, request the inquisitive readers with due humility to go through this book of Munisri minutely from the beginning till end by sparing adequate time at their disposal. Such unique and authentic discussion on language and literature is rarely available elsewhere—more so in our national language Hindi.

Some of the concepts and determinations, incorporated in the book, may not be convincing to higher intellectuals. Infact, it is not essential that each and every concept and belief of the author may be acceptable to all. However, I must emphasize that critical appreciation of each subject has been made so nicely that it binds the curious readers and comples them to give full consideration to it. No doubt, it is the essential feature to judge the accomplishments of the author which is obvious from the writings of Muni Sri.

What more! I heartily applaud Muni Sri that he has made his finest contribution to the literary world, may be belated, by writing this magnificent book on such a significant subject 'Language and Literature'. This is a historic piece of writing, which will continue to provide insperations to the future generaton of scholars and intellectuals and they will be greatly enlightened by scientific and analytical discussion on the subject, made by the author.

UPADHYAYA AMARMUNIJI

Virayatan, Rajgarh,
30-7-1982

CONTENTS

1

THE FLOW OF WORLD LANGUAGES

The language of *Agamas* is *Prākrita* (Ardh Māgadhi) while that of *Tripitakas* is Pāli. There is marvellous uniformity in both the languages. The source of origin of both dialects is also the same. The process of evolution and growth has also been similar in a big way. There is also wonderful similarity in the developed shapes of both the languages. Whatever dissimilarity is found, there may be several reasons for it. In order to understand the similarities and dissimilarities in their totality, it would be essential to review the origin and course of development and growth of the two languages minutely.

There is a long history of evolution and expansion of linguistics. The evolution of languages is closely linked with the intellectual and emotional advancement of mankind. People had spared no efforts for gaining achievements in the fields of culture, philosophy, literature and science. Consequently, an acceptable and dignified shape was accomplished amongst various cultures, philosophical beliefs, literary dispositions and social achievements in the universal context. The history of rise and fall in relation to the above fields can be easily traced out since there is a close tie between practice and theory in the life of human beings. The significance of action is self-evident. It is revealed like rays of Sun. For expansion, it requires an infinite space like an open sky. Language is a medium of speech and there is a great need to undertake analytical investigation in the field of linguistic science.

Wonderful Resemblance in Different Languages

It is really surprising that there is a close affinity between languages spoken in India—such as Hindi, Bengali, Gujarati, Marathi, Punjabi and Rajasthani with French, English, etc. spoken thousands of miles away, although in external shape they are apparently quite different from them. However, it is equally surprising to note that Tāmil, Telugu, Kannaḍa and Malyālam, spoken in Southern India, have fundamentally nothing in common with languages spoken in Northern India.

The ancient languages of India—Sanskrit, Prākritas and Pāli—have close affinity with ancient languages of West-Greek, Latin and German etc. There is an astounding similarity between various languages of the world, although they are in use thousands of miles away from each other and at first glance they appear to be alien with no apparent similarity. It looks as if since ancient times, there has been some sort of mutual harmony and communication between various human races of the world. These facts come to be true while undertaking a comparative and analytical study of the forms, growth and expansion of various languages. The above considerations led to profound study of languages in a critical manner and the modern philology and linguistic science are the accomplishments thereof.

Offshoots of Linguistic Science

In science of philology, linguistic elements have been critically discussed from different viewpoints and they are being investigated even now. Phonology, morphology, semantics, syntax, etymology of words are principal components of languages.

Phonology: The chief ingredient of linguistic science is phonetic sound. The sound, when given a systematized shape, constitutes a word. Words when conjugated form a sentence. The language is accomplished by unison of sentences. Consequently, phonology is an indispensable part of philology. Phonology includes vocal chords and sound chords. Sound is articulately produced by organs of speech, comprising of oral and nasal cavities, palate, throat, lips, teeth, cerebrum and tongue, etc. The utterance of sound from the said limbs, phonetic waves, contact and clash with these waves of organ of hearing and picking up of the sound in the shape of a word explicitly by the listener and subjects like alterations in phonetic sound, evolution of sound, the effects and indications of sound form part of phonology.

Morphology: The form of the word, fit to be used in a sentence is called 'Roop'. The word Pada (a complete or inflected word) is also used for it. Pāṇini, the renowned Sanskrit grammarian, has written 'Suptihantaṁ Padaṁ'. He has defined that an inflection, suffixed to a word, gives it the sense of an adjective, pronoun or a verb and it is termed as a Pada. Gautama, the author of *Nyāya Sutra* (Jurisprudence), has defined 'Te Vibhaktyantāḥ Padaṁ'. The words inflected at the end are Padas.

The words without inflections (the crude form of a substantive, a noun in its uninflected state) before receiving the case terminations or root words are not used in their original shape. The different inflections are affixed to signify different meanings. The root words or crude forms of nouns are usable only after affixing inflections. The renowned Sanskrit poet, Kavirāj Viśwanāth, has defined 'Pada' as those alphabetical letters or conjugation of letters, which are usable and decidedly carry a definite meaning are called 'Padas'. Under morphology, there is a comparative and analytical study of inflected words in the shape of nouns and verbs as also their analysis, growth, indeclinations, prefixes and suffixes etc.

Semantics: There is an absolute relativity between a word and its meaning. A meaningless word has, absolutely, no utility in accomplishment of a language. A word is an external body while meaning is its soul. The purpose is not achieved by mere talks of outer frame. Along with it, critical appreciation of the soul is all the more important. There is a long history of words and their related meanings. When we make an evaluation of the various conditions and factors, helpful in establishing co-ordination between words and their meanings, it is simply astonishing. The interpretation given by the grammarians that the words are like the fabulous cow in heaven, which satiate all desires, further supports the view, The poly-semantic words provide utmost satisfaction to the users of these words. The method of expression may be different but basically the sense is the same what has been stated above. *For example*, let us take the word 'Jugupsā' (Intense aversion). The present meaning of the word is hatred or abhorence. However, if we unfold the old history of the word, we will find that at one stage, the word meant an inner desire to protect others. With passage of time, there was a change in its meaning. The users of this word might have later considered that what was designed to be given protection, must be kept, in hiding. Consequently, the word 'Jugupsā' began to be used in the sense of concealment. A human being is by nature ever curious and contemplative. New changes and turning points are obtained in the course of contemplation. Accordingly, there was a change again in the sense of the said word. Probably, it might have been considered over that we conceal only henious things. Good objects need not be concealed. As a result of the said consideration, the meaning of the word 'Jugupsā' again changed from concealment to aversion or contempt. In fact, the architects and users of the words are human-beings. The different categories of experiments, made by human-beings, have consistent relation with their state of mind.

Under the above heading, we undertake to discuss and make critical study of the relation between words and their meanings. Certain philologists of the modern era do not consider semantics as an ingredient of linguistic science. They try to connect it with philosophy. In fact, certain old Indian philosophers have also incidentally discussed the relation between a word and its meaning. However, when an independent analysis of linguistic science is aimed at to be done thoroughly, semantics will have to be treated as a part of this science. A critical evaluation of a language will be incomplete without considering over it. Under semantics, it will be essential to understand the significance of meanings of words from all viewpoints—whether narrative, critical evaluation, comparative and historical viewpoints. Various aspects, namely change in meaning, expansion in meaning, diminution in meaning or exaltation in meaning, form part of linguistic science.

Syntax: The main purpose of a language is to enable us to express our feelings and to obtain views of others in their correct form. In other words, a language is the source of expression and medium of conversation. Phonetic sounds, root-words and inflected words are basic ingredients of a language. When the sentences are fit to form a language, they are used to accomplish the external body of the language. The inflected words, when used in a sentence, give their desired meanings. In a sentence, the words or Padas have their local significance. Hence, in order to obtain a desired meaning, the proper placement of a word, has its own significance. *For example*, I go to school. In the said sentence of English, the verb 'go' is located in second place. Again 'Go to school'. The word 'go' has also been used in this sentence. Herein 'go' has been placed in the beginning. However, the meaning of the verb 'go' is different now with the change of its place in the sentence. In the earlier sentence, the verb 'go' has been used to denote ordinary present tense but in the latter, it implies an order. There are various other topics connected with syntax, which have their own significance in construction of a sentence. All such related subjects are being discussed under this heading.

Etymology: The origin and history of the words are discussed under this head. There are various types and categories helpful in origination of the words. On having a critical study of them, we come across several other factors. The composition of words has a close relation with the cultural and social life of mankind. In ancient times, the study of linguistic science could not be undertaken in a systematic and elaborate manner. Some attempts were made in this direction in India and Greece, though to a limited extent only. Whereas in Greece, this subject was not dealt with minutely, the Indian scholars and intellectuals had penetrated deep, into the subject to the conditions and opportunities, then available.

There is a great historical significance of Vedic literature in the vast ocean of world literature. In order to maintain the genuineness of Sanskrit language, used in composition of Vedas, the scholars accomplished another six scriptures, namely, (1) Sikṣā (Education); (2) Kalpa (sacred rules and precepts); (3) Vyākarṇa (Grammar); (4) Chhand Sāstra (prosody); (5) Jyotiśha (Astrology) and (6) Nirukta (Etymology), regarded as auxiliaries to the Vedas[1] and designed to aid in the correct pronunciation and interpretation of vedic texts and the right employment of the metres in ceremonials.

Phonology is closely connected with the texts of Vedas. Numerous laws and rules were framed for correct pronunciation of Vedic texts and for maintaining the phonetic voice of systematically arranged texts of the Vedas intact. The books, having specific mention of these guidelines are known as Prātiśākhyās (grammatical treatises laying down rules for phonetic changes of words in any branch of the Vedas). The word 'Prātiśākhyā is derived from the word Prātiśākhā (a school or branch). There are different branches of each Veda. The rules for correct pronunciation of Vedic texts relating to all such branches have been laid down in different grammatical treatises. The creation of Prātiśākhyās (grammatical treatises) was world's ancient contribution towards advancement of linguistic science. The main object of introducing the said Prātiśākhyās (grammatical treatises) was to impart systematic knowledge of the time required to pronounce a prosodical or syllabic instant, accent, laying important guidelines for correct pronunciation, the maintenance of conventional methods of pronunciation of Vedic texts, minute and subtle analysis of phonetic voices and providing knowledge of organs of sound. Besides the said grammatical treatises, there are a few other books containing rules of correct pronunciation of vedic *Mantras* which are comparatively smaller in size. This auxiliary branch of the Vedas is closely related with linguistic science. The answers to numerous questions relating to phonology are incorporated in the said subordinate branch of the Vedas. The systematic methods for pronouncing Vedic Padas or individual words by proper phonetic changes in accute, grave and mixed tones (lying between high and low) are also minutely related with phonology.

Kalpa is a technical word to signify modes for performance of religious ceremonies. The fourth subordinate branch 'Nirukta' (etymology and explanation of Vedic words) is most important from viewpoint of linguistic science. The great scholar and sage, Yāsk was the author of Nirukta (which contains glossarial explanation of obscure words, especially those occurring in the Vedas) He is believed to have lived in eighth century B.C.

Views of Grammarians

Etymologist Yāsk : Yāsk has no doubt, made great contribution in enriching Indian

1. Śikṣā Vyākarṇaṁ Chhando niruktaṁ-Jyotiṣaṁ tathā |
Kalśpascheti Ṣhaḍangāni Vedasyāhūrmanīshiṇaḥ ||

literature by authoring Nirukta (Etymology). The etymological explanations given by him of obscure words, appearing in Vedic texts, are really authentic and valuable. There were two forms of Sanskrit language in vogue during life-time of Yāsk Vedic and classical. By Vedic language, he meant—Sanskrit language used in Vedas. He attributes a few other names as well, such as—'Nigam' (Vedas); 'Chhandas' (the sacred texts of the Vedic hymns) and 'Rik' (word used for Vedas). For classical Sanskrit, he uses the word language only. According to him, Vedic Sanskrit is original or basic, while classical languages are its off-shoots.

The modern philologists believe that there was a primordial language, belonging to Indo-European family which gave birth to Vedic Sanskrit and similar other languages, belonging to the same group as also languages pertaining to East and West. It was not practically possible for Yāsk to have an access to those languages, under the prevailing conditions of his age, he was living in. There were geographical constraints also. The modes of conveyance were rare and there was dearth of other suitable conditions and favourable environments. It was, therefore, not possible for him to have an access to the languages, in vogue outside India, while providing etymological interpretations of words. At that time, although many secondary dialects were also spoken and Yāsk had, himself, given indications to that effect, yet his work of giving etymological explanation of words in the field of linguistic science was confined to those languages only which were in vogue in his life time and were within his reach. Whatever work had been done or accomplished was really commendable, keeping in view the conditions, then prevailing. The magnificent work, done by him, will continue to have unique place in the history of philological advancement in the world.

Yāsk had with him a list of Vedic words contained in 5 chapters called 'Nighantu' (the glossary of Vedic words, explained by Yāsk in his Nirukta) Yāsk has given etymological interpretation of each and every word, appearing in the vocabulary of Vedic words, separately in Nirukta. The author of Nirukta (Etymology) has really done his best in explaining the words, contained in the said vocabulary of Vedic words which was really a great achievement. Yāsk has repeatedly quoted extracts of Vedic texts or verses in support of his explanations to prove their genuineness. It was the first attempt of its kind in the field of semantics in the world. In India, the subjects, forming part of semantics, had already been widely discussed before the time of Yāsk. He, himself, has quoted the views of his preceding scholars, namely—Audumbarāyan, Vārśāyaṇi, Gārgya, Gālava and Śhakṭāyan etc. as also of his contemporary scholars. For instance, Yāsk has held that a Pada comprises of 4 parts—Noun, Verb, preposition prefixed to roots and indeclinable particle. While dealing with the topic, he has quoted the opinion of his preceding scholar, Achārya Audumbarāyan about variable and invariable nature of a word. According to Yāsk, an action is influenced solely by the sentiment or emotion. In this regard, after quoting the views of Achārya Vārshāyaṇi in respect of change of emotion or deviation from natural state of emotion, he has given his own views. Infact, the explanations of Yāsk are based on analytical research and investigation. His method of ascertainment and determination has provided great inspiration to the subsequent philologists.

Yāsk's potentiality is further established by the fact that he showed no insistence to define obscure words and he politely admitted that they were not clear to him. While considering over the etymology of the words, he has made observations here and there regarding their origin and composition of language. First of all, he held that a noun is made from a root word. Although, the said opinion calls for critical evaluation yet it has its own significance. Later on, renowned grammarian, Pāṇini also endorsed this theory.

An illustration may be useful to understand the method of providing etymological interpretations of words by Yāsk. While defining the word Achārya (A preceptor or a teacher of a school of thought), he writes. Who is an Achārya? One who acts as a spiritual guide and preaches the manner of conducting oneself or is skilled in giving explanations, who acquaints a resident pupil with the knowledge of material world or who develops the talents of a resident pupil is called an Achārya.

While explaining the etymology of the word 'Śhamśān (Burial ground), Yāsk writes: Where the dead body is laid down, where it sleeps, perpetually, the place is called 'Shamśān'.

Great Grammarian Pāṇini: After Yāsk, renowned grammarian Pāṇini is respectfully remembered for further promoting linguistic science. Pāṇini, while composing Sanskrit grammar, also made a profound and critical appreciation of morphological construction of words. He also referred to his preceding grammarians, namely, Āpshāli, Kāśakritśan etc. A distinguished grammarian prior to Pāṇini was Indra. The Taittiriya branch of Yajurveda holds Indra as the foremost grammarian. Therein it is written: "The deities (divine beings) entreated Indra— Please explain the language to us, governed and refined by grammatical rules".[1]

Indra did accordingly. Indra's class of grammarians continued to prevail before and after the life-time of Pāṇini. The Grammatical treatises, now available, belong to this very class of grammarians. The renowned commentator, Katyāyan (who wrote explanatory rules on Pāṇini's Sūtras) also belonged to the said category of grammarians.

Pāṇini incorporated the gist of valuable research work done by his predecessors in Asthādhyāyi (The 8 chapters of Pāṇini's Sūtras). In some of his references, he has given introduction of Northern and Eastern classes of grammarians also. Śri Somdeva has mentioned in his book '*Kathāsaritsāgar* that the name of Pāṇini's preceptor was Upadhyāya Varśa. Katyāyani, Vyādi and Indra Dutta were his fellow disciples Pāṇini has, undoubtedly, made great contribution to the fields of grammar, and philology by writing 'Maheśwar Sūtras' (grammatical formulas). There are some singular features of Maheśwar Sūtras. In them, the vocal cords and effort of the mouth in the production of articulate sounds and their classification accordingly, constitute an excellent example of phonology.

The main remarkable feature of Pāṇini has been his ability in simplifying the study of an intricate and complicate language like Sanskrit merely on the basis of his 14 *Sūtras* (Formulas) by comprehension of several letters or affixes into one syllable effected by combining the first letter or in the case of several *sūtras*; with

1. Bāgwe Prāchya Vyākritavadat | Te devā Indramabravamniamā no vācham Vyākurviti | Tamindro madhyatoavakramya Vyākarot||

the final letter of the last member. Even after the lapse of 2500 years, there is not the slightest variation in the language and its standard and refined shape has remained undisturbed. He, however, did not agree with morphological classification, made by Yāsk, in the form of nouns, verbs, prepositions, prefixes to roots and indeclinables suffixed. Pāṇini has divided a word in two parts—SUBANT and TINGANT Till now, whatever divisions of words have been made from grammatical and philological viewpoint, the said classification of Pāṇini was most significant. Pāṇini has made 'remarkable contributions, to the study of phonology by dealing with the subjects like coming in contact by touching, or slightly touching (applied to the semi-vowels), covered or open, aspirate sound made in the pronunciation of aspirates, weak aspiration in pronunciation of unaspirated letters of the alphabet the soft sound heard in articulation of the soft consonants and hard sound of aspirated consonants, the parts of the throat from which certain sounds are issued such as guttural, palate, cerebrum, teeth and lips, etc.

The comparative analysis of Vedic Sanskrit and classical Sanskrit is Pāṇini's most glaring contribution. It is clear from his narration that considerable change had already taken place between Vedic Sanskrit, called Prosody (Metrical Science) and classical Sanskrit, called 'language' by his time. In nutshell, it can be safely believed that Pāṇini was the best grammarian of the world. There is no similar grammatical treatise available in any other language of the world as 'Aśṭadhyāyi' (Eight chapters of Pāṇini's Sūtras), written by Pāṇini. Besides, making the study of grammar convenient and concise, he gave it a philosophical character as well. His Sutras (aphoristic rules) helped in making the study of grammar quite interesting and easier to be followed:

Western scholar, Mr. Bloom Field, father of the modern linguistic science, remarks in his book, *Language' about Pāṇini*. "This grammar (Aśṭadhyāyi) of Pāṇini which dates from somewhere around 350 to 250 B.C. is one of the greatest monuments of human intelligence. No other language (besides Sanskrit) to this day has been so perfectly described."

Mr. John B. Carole, professor of Harvard University, writes—"Western scholars were for the first time exposed to the descriptive methods of the Hindu grammarian, Pāṇini, influenced either directly or indirectly by Pāṇini, began to produce descriptive and historical studies of languages."

Katyāyan: A Critic : Several other grammarians came to the fore after Pāṇini. Kātyāyani is the most renowned amongst them. He is stated to be the fellow student of Pāṇini by the author of *Kathāsaritsāgar*. However, it does not appear believable. Kātyāyani lived during fifth or fourth century B.C. Katyāyani criticised the aphoristic rules of Pāṇini. He pointed out flaws in them and produced his own flawless formulas, as alleged by him. However, the scholars were of the opinion that the flaws, pointed out by Kātyāyan, were not the defects or shortcomings in any way. There was a gap of 150 years between the life-times of Pāṇini and Katyāyani. The variations that occurred in the language in between this period, led Katyāyan to believe that they were wrong, faulty or defective. It is, however, true that several new facts were ascertained regarding advancement and growth of linguistic knowledge by explanatory rules of Kātyāyan on Pāṇini's Sūtras, in relation to semantics and phonology.

Great Commentator, Patanjali: After Kātyāyan, Pātanjali comes to the fore. His life time dates to second century B.C. He was follower of Pāṇini. He wrote the great commentary on the Sūtras of Pāṇini, the purpose of which was to corroborate the grammatical rules of Pāṇini and to refute the explanatory rules of Katyāyan. The rules framed by Pātanjali are known as 'Isṇṭi' (A term used with reference to Pātanjali's additions to Katyāyan's Vartikās).

The significance of Pātanjali's great commentary does not lie in framing of new rules but his philosophical style of discussing linguistic science and languages. He carried out minute and critical investigation important on subjects like nature of phonetic sounds, parts of speech, relation in between articulation of sounds and semantics relating to philology. Simple, elegant and charming words, used by Pātanjali in dealing with the subjects of grammar and linguistics was really a remarkable method. His style of expression is highly graceful as well as logical. Besides the renowned commentary, 'Śāririk, Bhāsya', authored by pre-eminent scholar, Śanker, there is no other work, matching the great commentary of Pātanjali in the entire Sanskrit literature.

Subsequent Era of Grammatical Treatises

After Great Commentator, Pātanjali, many successive grammarians, belonging to Pāṇinis line, gained prominence, amongst whom the names of Jayāditya and Vāman (Ist half of seventh century) Bhartihari (seventh century); Jainendra Budhi (Ist half of eighth century); Kayyaṭa (eleventh century); Hardutta (twelfth century) are worth-mention. They authored several independent grammatical treatises and commentaries, pursuing the line of Pāṇini, in which several aspects of linguistics and rules of grammar have been profoundly discussed and elaborated. Later on, the grammarians, following the line of Pāṇini, introduced and started the tradition of writing Kaumudies. Lot of books had already been written concerning grammatical rules that it was found essential to adopt a new style to enable the readers to understand those rules easily without least inconvenience. Kaumudi type books fulfilled the requirement. Vimal Saraswati (fourteenth century); Shamçandra (fifteenth century); Bhatoji Dixit (seventeenth century) and Varad Raj (eighteenth century) were prominent writers of this nature. *Sidhant Kaumudi*, written by Bhatoj Dixit and *Laghu Kaumudi*, written by Varad Raj, are most popular books and prescribed even now for students of Sanskrit.

There were a few other branches of grammarians also, besides Pānini, in India, amongst which, branches of Jainendra, Śāktāyan, Hemcandra, Kātantra, Sāraswat and Bopadeva are most prominent.

Discussion on Linguistics in Relative Treatises other than Grammars

Besides grammatical treatises, in other Sanskrit works also, such as Jurisprudence, Poetics and philosophy, views have been incidentally expressed in regard to linguistics. Nādia in Bengal, had been the renowned centre of logicians and followers of Nyāya system of philosophy. The said logicians of that place have discussed psychological aspects of linguistics in their books. Śri Jagdish Tarkālankār (a rhetorician) has argued on the significance of words from philosophical viewpoint in his book—*Shabda-Shakti-Prakāśika*. It throws some light on semantics. In poetic compositions the names of *Kāvya Prakāś*; *Dhwanyālok*, *Chanḍrālok* and *Sāhitya Darpan* are worth mention. While commenting upon the significance of words and rhetorics, the chief elements of linguistic science—words and their meanings etc. have been minutely discussed.

Out of all systems of Indian philosophy, Mimāṁsā system of philosophy is most important. Although the subjects discussed in this philosophy chiefly relate to the correct interpretation of the rituals and ceremonial rites but the method adopted by the learned scholars in their comments over them is extremely logical. They have deeply deliberated over nature of words, their meanings, parts of speech, nature of a sentence etc.

This is a brief account of investigative work done by Indian scholars concerning linguistic elements. In ancient India, when means for undertaking critical and scientific study of a subject were extremely limited; when the research techniques had not been developed, as available now, whatever attempts had been made were quite appreciable. It was an extraordinary work of its kind in the world.

Analytical Study of Linguistics in Greece and Europe

The prominence gained by India in Eastern Countries in the sphere of advancement of ancient culture, literature and philosophy is similar to what had been achieved by Greece in Western countries. There was some contemplation upon linguistic elements in Greece also after researches made by India. However, it was of elementary nature as compared to India. It was only at preliminary stage. Yet it was the first attempt in this field, made by a western country, hence, it had its own historic significance.

Hints given by Socrates: Socrates was an eminent philosopher of Greece (dating from 469 to 399 B.C.). His primary subject of discussion was philosophy (knowledge of truth). Objectively, he did not write anything on the subject of linguistics. However, while discussing other subjects he did make certain reflections on this topic as well. The issue for determination before Socrates was whether the relation between a word and its meaning was inherent? In other words, if the existing name of an article was replaced by another name, will it be improper? Socrates was of the opinion that there was no natural or spontaneous relation between an article and its name or between a word and its meaning. It was only an assumption made by mankind. Had there been some sort of inherent relation between an article and its name, it would have been universal and found everywhere. The variation in time and space would have made no difference. In that case, the word of anyone particular language would have been used in the same sense in all other languages of the world. That is to say, there would have been one common language of each and everybody in the world.

Plato: Linguistic Elements: After Socrates, his disciple Plato (dating back 429 to 347 B.C) grew to be an eminent scholar and thinker. He too had nothing to do with linguistic science like his teacher and spiritual guide. He has only incidentally expressed his views, wherever, he found it necessary, with regard to linguistic elements, which do have their significance in the composition of history of linguistic science. He classified phonetic sounds and divided Greek phonics in two parts—voiced and unvoiced. It was the first-ever attempt of classification of phonetic sounds in Europe.

Plato has also discussed the relation between an idea and medium of speech. According to him, the only difference between an idea or thought and language lies in the fact that a thought is a silent conversation of soul, but when it is expressed with phonetic sounds, produced from the cavities of the mouth, it is known as language. In nutshell, according to Plato, there is basically no difference between a thought and a language. It lies only externally, in the shape of silent and vocal expressions.

Plato has also further discussed in respect of parts of speech and nature of words. He has also thrown some light on aim, predication, the voice of a verb such as active and passive voices, and etymological interpretations of words etc. which signify, how far Greeks had advanced in their efforts of considering and deliberating upon linguistics.

Poetry of Aristotle: The third eminent philosopher, poetic genius and thinker was Aristotle of Greece. Philology was also not his primary subject. However, incidentally, he deliberated upon and expressed his views on linguistics also. One of the leading works of Aristotle is 'Poetics' in which he has mainly discussed poetic genres—tragedy and comedy etc. In the second part of his book, 'Poetics' besides making critical evaluation of the style, he has thrown some light on linguistics also. Although, it is not connected with linguistic science directly, yet it is significant. According to him, alphabetical letters are the product of indivisible phonetic sounds. They are classified in vowels; semi-vowels (as standing between vowels and consonants and being formed by a slight contact of the vocal organs), consonants of any of the five classes of letters. He has also discussed on long and short, aspirated and unaspirated letters. The interpretation of vowels, given by him, can be considered scientific from certain viewpoints. According to him where the tongue and lips are not used in utterance of a phonic, it is a vowel..

The assertion, predication, nouns and verbs etc. have also been discussed by Aristotle. He has also thrown light on Kāraks (Denoters of relation subsisting between a noun and verb in a sentence or between a noun and other words governing it) and the names of these cases, which was the first attempt of its kind in Europe. Plato had made only preliminary discussion on parts of speech in a sentence, but the credit goes to Aristotle for determining eight parts of speech. The latter also discussed about types or genders (masculine, feminine and common genders) and their characteristics

Greek, Latin and Hebrew

Subsequently, Greek grammarians made further moves on the subject of linguistics. Amongst them, the first grammarian was Thrax (second century B.C.) As soon as, mutual contacts began to develop between Greece and Rome, exchange of mutual understanding and learning also started. Consequently, Romans adopted the Greek style for study of linguistics and started composition of grammatical treatises for study of Latin language. The first authentic grammar of Latin language was written by a scholar, named Laurentious Vāl. That was the time when faith in Christian religion was growing. Hence an arrangement had started for undertaking regular study of old testaments in Greece and Rome. It was then, the scholars were in a position to undertake a comparative and minute study of Greek, Latin and Hebrew languages as well.

Since old Testaments had been written in Hebrew language, the latter was believed to be the most ancient and mother of all other languages. Consequently, European scholars had started exploring words of other languages which had either the same meanings or conformed with those of Hebrew language. The dictionaries were composed, containing all such words. Efforts were on to prove that origin of all such words from Hebrew language was quite possible. In this background, the erstwhile scholars felt inclined to undertake critical study of Arabian and Syrian languages as well.

Fifteenth century is considered to be the age of rise and resurgence of various sciences and arts in Europe. People had turned curious for further growth and expansion of their literature and culture. Regular campaigns and substantial efforts had started at all levels. People of different countries had started concentrating their minds and energies for enrichment of their respective languages. Resultantly, comparative study of languages was undertaken to the extent, it was possible. A few achievements, made by the scholars of linguistics in this regard, were as under:

(a) It appeared to the scholars that Greek and Latin languages had a common source of origin;
(b) It was an encouraging idea from viewpoint of classification of languages of the world in various groups or families may be in a small way; and
(c) It also struck to the scholars that most probably the words had been composed from root letters.

The extent of interest developed for study of linguistics in Europe at that time is evident from the very fact that an eminent philosopher Libriz also devoted his mind to this subject. The ruling elite of that era was also greatly influenced. Accordingly, Peter, the great, got compiled a glossary of comparative words. Katherine II, Queen of Russia also proclaimed an order and invited Mr. P.S.Pallas (dating 1741 to 1811 A.D.) for accomplishing a comparative glossary of identical words. Accordingly, he collected a list of 285 comparative words from various languages of European and Asian Continents. Some more additions were made in its second edition. The identical words of nearly eighty languages were further incorporated in the second edition of glossary.

It is a brief account of undertaking critical study and investigation on linguistics in West. Certainly it proved to be highly inspiring to the next generation of philologists in one or the other way.

GIST: In both Eastern and Western parts of the world, the basic foundation for further research on linguistics had already been laid down, with the result attempts for minute and profoundly deep study of various aspects of linguistic science had continued and were still going on. Linguistic science had now established itself as an independent and one of the prominent subjects to be studied by mankind. Although, lot of research work had already been done on philology, yet it was an extensive subject which extends to the whole universe. With more and more profoundly deep and analytical study of ancient and modern languages of the world from scientific and historical viewpoints, it will, no doubt, be a grand achievement in the field of linguistic science on one hand and on the other, various facts, hitherto unmanifested, will also come to light relating to cultural advancement, social development, political and administrative changes, ups and downs occurring, from time to time, in many parts of the world.

Shape of Modern Linguistic Science

Western Scholars: For about past two centuries, minute and systematic study of various subtle aspects related with linguistics is regularly going on in the field of philology as it is generally understood now. Certainly, the main credit goes to European Scholars for taking up critical and analytical study of both Western and Eastern languages. Especially, the efforts put in by these scholars to the study of Indo-European languages are really marvellous and thought provoking.

No doubt, Western scholars have shown great zeal and aptitude for research and investigation. Western genius, Sir William Jones can be called a living embodiment of it. He was Hon'ble Chief Justice of highest court in India at Calcutta in 18th Century. He developed curiosity to minutely go through Indian Jurisprudence, administration of law and justice so that he could be in position to accord true justice to them, consistent with their respective traditions and beliefs. In order to achieve this end, study of Sanskrit was essential. Sir William Jones developed a sincere desire to study Sanskrit. He started finding out an eminent scholar of Sanskrit who could teach the subject. It was not easy. No competent and able scholar was willing to teach him. It was a stereotyped notion amongst Brahman scholars in those days that how could a divine language be taught to a heretic? After a lot of persuasion, a scholar agreed, however, subject to fulfilment of certain conditions. The room in which he would coach, would have to be washed daily with sacred water of Ganges before starting to teach. Silken clothes would have to be provided to him to be put on before coaching. Mr. William Jones would also be wearing silken clothes while studying and he would have to sit on floor.

Sir William Jones gladly accepted all these pre-conditions. One could very well imagine the dignity of the office of Chief Justice of a highest Court in India in those days. However, the said foreign dignitary ignored all formalities, attached with his office on the face of his keen and earnest desire to acquire knowledge. He began studying with strict adherence to all arrangements insisted upon by his respected teacher. The zeal, faith and devotion with which Mr. William Jones undertook study of Sanskrit language, was, infact, exemplary for other students. It was no less significant that a foreigner, for whom Sanskrit was an alien language and it was not the divine language of his own religion, devoted himself to the attainment of knowledge of such a profound subject with such uncommon zeal, inner urge and dedication. Sir William Jones acquired deep knowledge of various branches of Sanskrit language with his deep devotion, long perseverance and enterprise. He made thorough study of Yagvalkya's traditional code of Hindu Law and celebrated commentary on Yagvalkya's Smriti (the body of traditional or memorial law—civil or religious) and other explanatory literature (commentaries etc).

No doubt, Sir William Jones acquired comprehensive knowledge of Indian Society, its customs, modes and manners but it led to one more achievement which is remarkable from linguistic viewpoint. Sir William Jones was also well-versed in many other ancient Western languages—Greek, Latin and Gāthik, etc. While making critical study of various branches of Sanskrit literature, he came across many words which had minute resemblance with Greek and Latin words from viewpoint of phonology and construction. He felt accordingly surprised and developed keen interest. He discovered many words of Sanskrit language which had close resemblance with the words of Greek, Latin and other Western languages. After profound study and investigation he arrived at the conclusion that the basic source of origin of Sanskrit, Latin, Greek, Gāthik, Kāltik and old Persian languages appeared to be one and the same as far as their root letters, words and grammatical rules were concerned.

In 1796, Sir William Jones laid foundation of Royal Asiatic Society at Calcutta, On that occasion, he remarked. "The Sanskrit language, whatever be its antiquity, is of a wonderful structure, more perfect than the Greek, more copious than the Latin and more exquisitely refined than either".

The name of Sir William Jones will top the list of all those scholars who paved the way for comparative and critical study of linguistics. The system of undertaking analytical study of linguistics had started from that very time and it continued to go ahead accomplishing new heights. This type of investigation had started in several countries of the world and is still continuing. It is really wonderful and very much encouraging that many western scholars not only made deep study of ancient and modern languages of India but they also made comparative and critical evaluation of these languages from philological viewpoint, which would always provide inspiration and enlightenment to learned scholars, researchers and students of linguistic science.

Primordial Beliefs

The burning question which is not new but remains unanswered from primordial times is as to how and when a language came into existence and what course of development, it passed through, to reach its present stage. Infact, it is extremely difficult to reply this question since origin of linguistics is as old as human race itself. The human race is existing from eternity and so is language. However, learned and intelligent persons are inquisitive by nature and how can they remain contented with this vague reply? It has been the curiosity of mankind to know, how a language (medium of speech), so closely connected with day-today life, came into existence and how it passed through various phases of expansion and development. The human beings have remained anxious to have its true and correct reply. Accordingly, numerous efforts were made and different views and opinions came to the fore. However, a sustained reply, acceptable to all, concerning origin of language, has not been found till now. It is, therefore, desirable to give full consideration to the investigations made hitherto, on the subject in brief. First of all, it will be in the fitness of things to review the ideas of the learned scholors, belonging to different religions. There are different types of people, seeking satisfactory solution to the problem. They have their prejudices, pre-conceived notions and intense desire for their own publicity too. The followers of almost all religions of the world have expressed their views on origination of languages.

Beliefs of Vedic Scholars: Those who have their faith in Vedas, are of the opinion that Vedas were not composed by human beings. They are God-gifted. God created this universe, bestowed life to human beings and gifted medium of speech. The minds of seers and sages were illumined with knowledge which manifested itself in the shape of Vedic hymns and Mantras. Their language is metrical, called Vedic Sanskrit, which is eternal and God-gifted. Hence it is called a divine language. All other languages of the world have been derived from it. It is a God-gifted language to mankind.

The pre-eminent Sanskrit grammarian and author of *Aṣṭadhyāyi* (The eight chapters of Pāṇini's Sūtras), Pāṇini, has also tried to extablish that Sanskrit is a divine language though in a different manner. He has written about (अ इ उ ण)[1] etc. aphoristic rules of grammar. "In order to elevate seers, namely, Sanak etc., or in other words to impart knowledge of rules of the grammar, Lord Sivā (Name of the third god of the sacred Hindu Trinity, who is entrusted with the work of destruction, as Brahman and Viṣṇu are with the creation and preservation of the world) played on his *Damru* (a musical instrument) fourteen times, after completing his celestial dance *Tāṇḍava* (The frantic or violent dance of Lord Sivā), thus introducing 14 rules of the grammar".[2] The whole grammar is based on the said fourteen aphoristic rules.

Minute Contemplation made by Yask: It would be useful to quote, Yāsk, predecessor of Pāṇini, (dating 800 B.C.) about his views regarding the science of words. They do throw some light on the origin of a language. While discussing on morphological construction of a word and its four ingredients—noun, verb, prepositions prefixed and indeclinables suffixed, Yāsk has also incidentally discussed the significance of a word. He writes: "A word is a small unit with a limited sense. Hence it was considered necessary to name the articles in order to identify them in day today course of life."[3] He has not given his own views regarding origin of linguistics. Probably, he might not have considered it necessary. Possibly, he might have certain pre-notions or assumptions in this regard.

---

1. (1) अइउण (2) ऋलृक (3) ऐओङ् (4) ऐऔच् (5) हयवरट (6) लण् (7) ञमङणनम् (8) झभज् (9) घढ़धष् (10) जबगड़दश (11) खफछठथचटतव् (12) कपय् (13) शषसर (14) हल्।
2. Nritāvasāne Naṭrājrājo, nanād dhakkāṁ navapancạvāram | Udhārtukāmaḥ Sanakdisidhānetadvimarśe Śivasūtrajālam || — *Niruktā*, 1, 2
3. Aṇiyastvācạcạ śabdena Sangyā-Karṇaṇaṁ Vyavahārarthaloke |

People must have a medium for mutual exchange to carry on their day-today business. Mere gestures cannot meet the requirements. Therefore, people would like to invent different words to name different articles. For this purpose, they compose new words. When etymologists talk of naming articles by different words, it clearly reflects that fundamentally they did not believe in the divine nature of a language. Had there been a god-gifted language, then there must have been corresponding words to name the articles. Resultantly there would have been no necessity at all for people to give suitable names to articles. There is no imperfectness in a divine language. Necessity to name articles arises only when there is no accomplished language at the disposal of mankind. Yāsk appears to have emphasized to this effect.

Yāsk's emphasis that words, an essential ingredient of a language, have been composed by mankind, is really unique contribution to philology. Even his successor, Pāṇini, an eminent grammarian, could not rid himself from old stereotyped notion regarding origin of languages, although, his predecessor, Yāsk had given his opinion to the above effect three centuries earlier. It clearly reflects that Yāsk had a greater aspiration and zeal for research and investigation.

During the life time of Yāsk, Sanskrit language was in prominence which was considered as God-gifted language and is being treated as such even now. Yāsk has, however, substantiated divine nature of Sanskrit language in a really impressive way. He writes: "Names of articles, used by human beings, are accepted as such by celestial bodies." It follows that the deities also understand the language of mankind in the same sense. It, obviously, follows that the language of human beings is itself a divine language. Yāsk here purports to mean that the words-divine language appear accordingly for Sanskrit language.

Beliefs of Buddhists: The entire canonical literature of Bodh religion, in the shape of Tripitakās, is written in Māgadhi Prākrita, which subsequently came to be known as Pāli (a Middle Indo-Arāyan language used by Buddha for his teachings and by his followers in subsequent Buddhist tradition). Amongst Buddhists, authenticity of Ceylonic tradition is unchallenged. It was in Ceylon that Vinay, Sutta and Abhidhamma Pitakas were reduced to writing for the first time. Under Ceylonic tradition, it is believed that most prudent and defied saint, Lord Buddha delivered his discourses in Māgadhi Prākrita (Pāli). According to them, Māgadhi was the primordial language of the universe. Achārya Budhghosh has boldly asserted: "Māgadhi was the original and primordial language of all living-beings."[1]

A similar reference is found in 'Chūlvansa', an enlarged portion of 'Mahavansa'. As directed by Revat Sthavira (a senior Buddhist monk), Acārya Budhghosha proceeded to Ceylon. There he translated all Ceylonic religious tales in Māgadhi Prākrita. It had been stated therein. "All Ceylonic religious stories were translated in Māgadhi—a primordial language of all living-beings."[2]

Regarding Māgadhi or Pāli language, Burmese hold the same belief, totally, conforming with Ceylonic faith. Not only this, almost all followers of Bodh religion, having faith in Tripitakas believe that Māgadhi or Pāli, in which their religious

1. Māgadhikāya Savvasattānaṁ Mūlbhasāya—Visudhimagga
2. Parivattesi Savvāpi Sihalathakathātadā |
Savvesaṁ Mūlbhāṣāya Māgdhāyāya Nirutiyā || — Chūlvansa Chapter 37

scriptures have been written, was the first-ever language of the world.

Jaina Beliefs: Jaina tradition held the same view in respect of the language of their Agamic scriptures. All the Āgamas including 12 Angas (Auxiliary works forming part of Āgamas) have been written in *Ārdha Māgadhi Prākrita*. The Jaina religionists believe that Jaina Āgamas contain religious discourses, delivered by Lord Mahāvira himself, and compiled by his senior most diciples, known as Gandhers. According to them, *Ārdha Māgadhi Prākrita* was primordial language of the world. In the commentary on 'Sutrakritanga Niryukti', it appears. "The said *Ārdha Māgadhi Prākrita* is imbued with inherent virtues of the soul enshrined in the human body and other living beings[1] *Ardhā Māgadhi Prākrita* is a language of gods as is believed by the followers of Jaina religion. It is laid down. "Ardh Māgadhi Prākrita is the language of sages and seers, endowed with super-natural powers, hence a divine language."[2]

While Tirthankers (Sanctified religious teachers of the Jainas) delivered religious discourses, it is stated that besides celestial bodies and human beings, the animals and birds also formed part of the audience. The religious preachings of Tirthankers had been made in *Ardh Māgadhi Prākrita*. The main characteristic of Tirthankers' utterances was that once it was heard by audience it turned into their own respective dialect and easily understood by them. The organic world (animals and birds etc.) also listened to the religious discourses of Tirthankers and what they heard, was converted to their own respective dialect or speech and easily understood by them. So to say, the said Ardh Māgadhi Prākrita was not confined to divine bodies and human-beings alone but extended over to animals and birds too.

Views of Prākrita Scholars

Besides authors of Jaina canonical literature and commentators, certain Jaina and non-Jaina scholars of Prākritas also have expressed similar sentiments. Renowned rhetorician of eleventh century, Nami Sādhu while defining Prākritas, states "Prākrita dialects being free from grammatical constraints, are spontaneous and easy for conversing for all living-beings. The literal meaning of the word Prākrita (Prāk-Krit)= `Previously done' which meant that it was a primordial language. A *Prākrita* dialect is simple and easily understood even by children and ladies and a basic source of origin of all other languages."[3]

Ājaḍa, commentator of *Saraswati Kanthābharan*, written by King Bhoj, had made a similar remark. According to him, "Prākrita language is spontaneous and part of one's own nature. It is a medium of speech, easy to be followed by all living beings. It is refined and grammatically perfect and can be easily used by children, shepherds and ladies. Being basic source of origin of all other languages, Prakrita is their very nature. It is the original source of all other languges in the

---

1. Jīvassa Sābhaviyagunehiṁ te Pāgat bhāsāye |
2. Āris Vayaṇo sidhaṁ devāṇaṁ adhamāgahā Vāni |
3. Sakalgajjantūnāṁ Vyākarṇādibhirnāha Sanskāraḥa Sahajo Vacaṇ—Vyāpāraḥ Prakritih tatra Bhavam Saiva vā Prākritaṁ. . . .Prāk-Kritaṁ Prākritaṁ . . . . Bālamahitadisubodhaṁ Sakal Bhāṣā nibandhan-bhūtaṁ Vacaṇ-Muaṇyate|

same way as nature is the source of entire material world.[1]

Eminent poet, Vākpati, while stating the qualities of Prākrita, writes in his renowned poetry 'Gauḍavaho' : "Just as all rivers drop in ocean and come out in Vapoury shape, similarly, all languages enter into prakrita and again emerge out of it."[2]

Beliefs of Roman Catholics

Similar is the faith of Christians about their language. Roman Catholics and protestants are the two sects of the said religion. Roman Catholic sect is comparatively older. Their popular religious treatise is Old Testament, which has been written in Hebrew language. According to Christians, God, first of all, had gifted the well accomplished language to Adam and Eve. They firmly believe that it is the primordial (first ever) language of the world, Nay—it is the source of origin of all other languages. Celetial bodies converse in this very language.

In order to substantiate the view that Hebrew was the source of origin of all other languages, many words of other Western languages Greek, Latin etc. were compiled which resembled with parallel words of Hebrew language. In this way, attempts were made to establish origin of many words of other European languages from Hebrew language. For this, uniformity in phonetic sound and similarity in meanings were made the basis for their investigation. Anyway, attempts had begun in a systematic manner to undertake comparative study from philological viewpoint, which did provide an inspiration to scholars of subsequent period to take up extensive study of linguistic science.

Opinions of Followers of Islam

Islamic follwers also believed that their language was primordial and source of origin of all other languages. According to them, the verses of *Quran*, written in Arabic language were God-gifted.

Since ancient times, Egyptians also had similar views for their own language. After spread of Islam, Egyptians began to consider that Arabic language was primordial and God-gifted.

During past centuries, how far dogmatic and stereotyped notions had been harboured by mankind at the instance of fundamentalists, towards a medium of speech, may be evident from an example of Egypt. Telephone device had already been invented Cable-lines started to be laid down in all leading countries of the world. It was contemplated to instal telephone lines in Egypt as well. The Egyptians were wonder-struck to learn that telephonic talks would be audible exactly in the same voice from places, hundreds of miles away. The scholars of Islamic law in Egypt opposed it tooth and nail. They argued that human voice could never reach

1. Sakalbālgopālāngnāhridayasancāri nikhil Jagjantunāṁ Sabdaśāstrikrit viśeṣasanskāraḥ Sahajo Vacaan yāpāraḥ Samastetarbhashāiśeṣavnāṁ mūl-kārnatvāt Prakritirivaprakritiḥ tatra bhavā Saiva vā Prakritiḥ visesā.
2. Sayalāo iyaṁ Vayavisanti Etto ya nenti vāyāo
Enti Samuddaṁ Chiyanenti Sāyarāo caiya jalāiṁ || 93||

from such remote places. In case, it did, it could be a satanic voice and not of a human being. In other words, Satan would pick up human voice and carry it onward.

Masses had unflinching faith in the said Islamic scholars. By adhering to their Judgment, people declined to hear Satanic voice and did not agree to allow installation of telephone cables. Those at the helms were at their wits end, what to do? They were persuaded repeatedly but all in vain. Finally, They showed their concurrence subject to fulfilment of a condition. According to them, the verses of *Quran* were divine and pronounced by God. They could be recited by a human-being and not by a Satan. So, if a person recited *Quran* verses and they were correctly heard through telephone, they would believe that it was a human voice. It was done accordingly. Thereafter, the Egyptians agreed for installation of cables.

Even an eminent philosopher and metaphsician, Plato, believed that the names of the articles, found in the world, were all God-gifted. In nutshell, though in a different manner, Plato also opined that a language was divine and God-gifted. Accoding to him a language was only a coordination of nouns and verbs. Conscious and inquisitive scholars or guides were not contented with the views of different sects having sectarian faiths, with regard to the origin of a language. They expressed their coolness over such parochial outlooks. All the aforesaid linguists, having bias for their own sects or religions, claimed ancientness and divine nature of their scriptural languages. If it was assumed that the languages were inborn or God-gifted, then there ought to have been near total uniformity between all languages of the world, leaving aside minior variations subject to the time and space. However, there were fundamental differences in the languages of the world—why? No satisfactory replies were forthcoming to this and similar other doubts.

Primordial Language of Mankind—Certain Experiments

Masses sincerely believed that all newly born children had their own distinct language. However, as they grow, they pick up the language of the family, society or the country, they come in contact with. Gradually, the impression on their memory is changed and they start speaking the customary language of their country without least inconvenience. The original and inherent language of the newly-born children is forgotten and the artificial language is adpoted which is spontaneously picked up and spoken by them.

From time to time, certain experiments were carried out to arrive at the truth. According to Herodotáus, a famous writer of fifth century B.C. King Psammitochos of Egypt made an experiment in this regard. As evidenced by history, it was the first experiment of its kind to ascertain the source of origin of a language. It was assumed that the experiment would enable to ascertain certain facts about aboriginal human race as well, besides revealing the primordiality or original source of a language. It was so decided that spontaneous language, spoken by children, would be deemed to be oldest and original language of the world. Similarly, the tribe, found speaking the said language, would be considered as aboriginal community of the world.

The experiment was made thus—Two newly-born children were taken up. The visitors were strictly warned not to speak a word before them, Strict order was also issued to the attendant, prohibiting him not to utter a single word before them while looking after and feeding the children regularly. The process continued and the children grew up with passage of time. They were, however, found unable to speak anything. Only one single word 'Bekos' was heard to have been spoken by the children which belonged to Frizian language. It literelly meant bread. The attendant, who feeded them, was Frizian. It was believed that while feeding the children, the word 'bekos' might have heen unconsciously uttered by the servant which was picked-up by the children.

A similar experiment was made by Fredrick II in 12th century but with no result. Subsequently, in 15th century, James IV, king of Scotland, carried out similar experiment but all in vain. In India, during 16th century, Emperor Akbar undertook an experiment. Every possible precaution was taken and the result was anxiously awaited. However, all were stunned to find that all the children remained dumb and they failed to utter a single word.

Outcome of Experiments: From the said experiments, it was explicitly clear that no language of the world was God-gifted and no child was born with any distinct language of its own. It was only an indication of extreme superstition with no logical truth. There was another significant point. Had there been a divine or God-gifted language, it would have been fully accomplished in all respects from the very beginning. However, it is a historical fact that the languages have undergone drastic changes in their shapes during past centuries. When the modern shape of a language is compared with the centuries old structure of that language, it is evident that it had passed through regular process of development, growth and expansion and its form had completely changed with the passage of time. Undoubtedly, the scholars have done tremendous research and investigation to that effect which speak for themselves and are quite extensive.

In 18th century, Mr. J.G. Herder, a renowned scholar, wrote a research article on origin of languages in the year 1772. He also contemplated upon the alleged divine nature of a language in a critical manner and advanced rational arguments to refute the said theory. However, he did not plead any substantial theory of his own regarding source of origin of a language. Of course, he refuted the theory of divine nature of a language but simultaneously he added that it was not the product of mankind. The existence of a medium of speech was the basic necessity of mankind. Hence it came into existence spontaneously and flourished on its own without any effort of the people.

To know what is unknown is the fundamental nature of intellectuals and scholars. The concept that a language was divine and god-gifted could not satisfy the curiosity of mankind. They applied their minds to find out a definite answer and they spared no pains to exercise their talents. This is the only method for enhancement of the scope of knowledge. How far one succeeded in its attempt is a matter for critical research and investigation. Nevertheless, it can be safely asserted that the attempts, so made from time to time, provided great encouragement and inspiration to the inquisitive scholars for going ahead. In nutshell, it may be added that whatever, efforts have been made, hitherto, were more or less based on surmises only to find out the source of origin of a language since no substantial, ground or base was, there wherefrom one could proceed in the right direction to ascertain the source of origin of linguistics.

A Few Fundamental Theories

Theory of Determination

According to an opinion, people used to meet their day today requirements by making physical gestures in the absence of a medium of speech. But it did not serve their purpose. The requirements of life were growing rapidly. The means of subsistence were increasing and becoming manifold. The developing phase of society was giving birth to new ideas. However, there was no medium with human society for revelation of these ideas. Everyone was feeling dejected. People assembled. They were all anxious to trace out a medium for mutual exchange and conversation. Some phonetic sounds or words were set to indicate the names of articles and denote verbal activities and with their help, they began to express themselves and serve their day-today requirements. As the process to construct words started, it provided inspiration to frame more and more new words for mutual exchange. In linguistic science it is called as 'theory of determination.' Prof. Russoue was an ardent supporter of the said theory. It is also called 'theory of symbolism', gesticulation or theory of agreement, since it was agreed to use the words in symbolic manner or by making indicatory signs.

It is, no doubt, a fine piece of imagination but not a rational plea. In case, there was no language at all for communication, a question, obviously arises, how they decided and managed to assemble. Even for assembling, one has to explain its motive. How did they manage in the absence of a language? Even if people gathered, how did they afford to exchange their views? Only after mutual discussion, one is able to arrive at some conclusion. Acceptance of phonetic sounds or words to name the articles and verbal activities, would also be impossible with-out existence of a language.

Another important point is that if they could manage to assemble and accept certain phonetic voices and words to name the articles and verbal activities, there must have been a language in vogue, howsoever incomplete, undeveloped and imperfect, it might be. In the absence of even such a language, all this would not have been possible to be accomplished. However, if existence of some form of language was admitted, then there was no need at all to gather and explore new words or phonetic sounds for naming articles. In that case, the existing imperfect language could have been develpoed and refined.

Theory of Metal

A strange and typical idea also came to the fore regarding origin of language. It is known as theory of metal in philology. According to it, all the articles found in the world, have their own typical sound. *For example*, if we strike a bronze flat plate with a stick, it will produce a clanking sound. However, on striking a brass plate, the sound produced will be different from that of bronze plate. Altogether different sound will be produced on striking an iron sheet or box. Similarly, varying sounds will be created by striking on paper, wood, glass, cloth, leather and stone etc. Why is it so? Why is this dissimilarity in sound? According to this theory, every article has its own typical sound, which is obtained by contact, clash, collision or a strike. Not only this, the introducers of the said theory further believed that each and every human being had a strange inherent power in it. When they come in contact with or clash or touch different articles, they also produce resembling sounds, consistent with the sounds, produced by these articles. Thus, the phonetic sounds, produced by human-beings from time to time, constituted metal sounds. Initially, the metal sounds were numberless and all of them could not be preserved. Gradually, many of them disappeared. Many of the metal sounds were identical in nature. According to the theory of 'survival of the fittest', only a few of them could survive. Only four to five hundred root letters were saved from being omitted. From the said root letters, words, tending to be nouns and verbs, were constructed, leading to the accomplishment of a language. The propounders of the said theory believed that there was a mystic harmony between phonetic sounds of metal sounds and meanings attached to them. By using the word mystic here, the purport, could be that the relation between sounds and respective meanings attached to them was based on mere guess and supposition and was not subjected to any critical investigation.

The propounders of the above theory also opined that the capability of phonetic expression, found in human-beings, during primordial times, disappeared with passage of time, since the said characteristic was no longer needed after accomplishment of a language. Hence it vanished gradually and the said ability was not found in the modern human-beings.

Professors Hess, Stynthāl and Maxmuler: Prof. Hess of Germany had, first of all, propounded the above theory but he did not elaborate it in writing. He had merely referred to it in one of his lectures. Later on, Dr. Stynthāl reduced it to writing in a systematic manner and placed it before learned scholars for contemplation. Prof Stynthāl was not only an authority on linguistic science and grammar but he was also a renowned logician and psychologist. In the field of philology, he held the view that critical study of linguistic science was impossible without taking help of psychology. In one of his works, he elaborately described that there was an inherent link between grammar, philosophy and psychology. He authored several other works relating to the psychological aspect of a language.

Initially, Prof. Maxmuler found the theory of metal sounds as agreeable and dealt with it in his books. He was a distinguished scholar of sanskrit and more particularly of Vedas. Although, his primary subjects were philosophy and literature yet he also dealt with philology. He greatly admired the richness of Indian scholarship and learning. He was foremost among intellectuals who acquainted the world with excellence of India in the spheres of culture, literature, philosophy, and linguistics. His style of critical investigation was really interesting. In 1861, he delivered a few lectures on philology. He elaborated the subject of linguistics, a dry and obscure one, in such a fine and charming manner that the studious readers and students grew anxious to acquire greater knowledge of the subject. Prior to it, the study of linguistic science was confined to learned scholars only.

Ordinary people had no access to the subject. It was really creditable on the part of Prof. Maxmuler that as a result of his laudable efforts, even ordinary persons were curious to read the subject.

In the beginning, Prof. Maxmuler also considered that the theory of Metal sound was consistent and, accordingly, he discussed it in his books also. But subsequently, he changed his opinion and showed his reluctance to support the theory. It is evident that till then no settled opinion had been formed regarding origin of languages. The above theory was, probably, welcomed as a new concept by scholars, and after pondering over it, they accepted its relevance as well. However, their appreciation of the theory could not last long.

If we minutely consider, the said theory was merely imaginary and had lost in the wilderness. No doubt, imagination breeds new ideąs, but here we are not concerned with any poetic imagination. A linguistic theory must base itself on a solid ground. The process of growth and development of a language must have a scientific base. How it was, how it happened and how it is so, are the questions which must be answered in relation to a medium of speech. In poetry, however, such questions have no relevance. The renowned poetic genius, Aristotle, has stated, while discussing tragedy and comedy, that what is virtually not in existence and is created by virtue of pure imagination or emulation is poetry. Hence poetic compositions have nothing to do with universal realities. However, it is not the case with linguistic science. The imaginative thoery of formation of words from phonetic sounds, created by metals is, therefore, not relevant.

Something more is to be added regarding root letters. The words, which tend to accomplish a language, are not composed from root letters alone. Prefixes and suffixes are also necessary which find no mention in this theory. The root letters are found in Indo-European and Semitic groups of languages but there are numerous other linguistic families where there is not the slightest indication of root letters. Even if the theory of root letters was admitted, the problem of finding out source of origin of other languages in the world, would remain unsolved.

There is one more significant point worth noting regarding acceptance of the theory of root letters. The languages, which contain roots, were, infact, accomplished earlier, while the roots were discovered much later. Therefore, they are not real but imaginary. In order to give systematic shape to the construction of a language, by grammarians and philologists, it was agreed to compose words by applying prefixes and suffxes to roots. It could be called a methodical process to accomplish a language in a more refined and polished form. This procedure was adopted by grammarians and linguists after profound study and investigation. Prof Maxmuler, an eminent and erudite scholar, had initially accepted the theory of roots but later rejected it completely. The reason being that the said theory did not lay down a convincing ground with regard to the origin of a language.

Views Expressed by Yāsk: Regarding composition of words from roots, Yāsk has explained in his celebrated commentary that the nouns and verbs have been formed from roots. It was etymological interpretation of words. The great grammarian, Śākṭāyan had the similar opinion. However, learned scholar, Acārya Gārgaya and certain other grammarians did not agree that all the words had been accomplished from roots. They argued that the words which are comprised of vowels, roots, suffixes, elisions and augmentations or which have been composed in consistency with grammarian rules are stated to be born or accomplished from roots. However, where the words are not applied with such prefixes or suffixes, they only signify nouns and are merely conventional. They have no etymological derivation: Just as गो (cow); अश्व (horse); पुरुष (Male); हस्ती (elephant).

"If all the words were composed from roots, then all the living-beings, performing similar nature of work, should be named with one and the same noun. *For example*, all the living beings which reach across the road, running fast, should be named 'horse'. Similarly, whatever, is fed through beak, should be named `grass' which is not so. The difficulty is that an atricle is subjected to various uses and processes, so it should be called by different names as per each process, it had undergone, which would be somewhat cumbersome. *For example,* a pillar in a house is inserted in a big hole, hence it should also be named as दरशया (Sleeping in a hole-since it is pierced in a hole). However, it is not possible.

"There is one more problem. In case, all the words had been accomplished from roots, then in whatever forms, they should have been composed, from roots, having identical meanings, as per rules of the grammar, should have been named accordingly so that it would have been more convenient to determine their meanings. Accordingly a पुरुष (person) would have been named 'पुरिशय'; an 'अश्व' (horse) as 'अठय' and 'तृण' (grass) as `Tardan' (तर्दन). However, it is not the case.

"After a word is set with a specific meaning and used as such, then the etymological derivation of the said word is considered, as from which root, it had been composed. If it was not the case, the etymological origin of a word ought to have been ascertained earlier before it came to be used or came to be in vogue. For instance, let us take the word 'पृथ्वी' (earth) since it was spread, hence it was named as 'पृथ्वि'. But this interpretation leads us to many ifs and buts. Who had spread this earth? There must have been a base wherefrom it was spread. However, earth itself forms a base to stand upon. A person, who would spread, must have a base to stand upon. Otherwise, it could not perform the act of spreading. It is, thus, evident that etymological derivation of a word is tried to be explored only after a specific meaning of the word is set. But in practice we find that there is no conformity between the meaning of a root, from which the word was composed and the meaning of the accomplished word as it is generally understood.

"When the meaning of a word is not understood or when the meaning of a word is inconsistent with the root, from which it had been composed, then in order to establish its origin or derivation, Śākṭāyan co-ordinates its constituents from different `Padas' (morphological constructions). *For example*, with a view to compose the word `Satya' (truth), he took 'इण' (meaning activity or movement) and the letter `ya' of the word `Ayan' is placed at the end while the basic root word `Sat' is prefixed. In this manner, the word `Satya' had been accomplished but there is no spontaneity in analysing the construction of a word like this.

"Existence of activity or an inclination to act is substantial *i.e* substance is there prior to an action. For manifestation of movement, vibration, agitation or swinging a verbal activity is essential." On the basis of such activity, performed subsequently, the substance occurring earlier could not be named. Let us take the word 'अश्व' (horse) *for example*. According to etymological interpretation, a specific living-being, because of its fast running, would be named 'अश्व' that is to say, the name would be given to a living-being after seeing its action of fast running. However, the fact is otherwise. Immediately after the birth of a horse-baby, it is named as such even though it is unable to walk. Hence there is no consistent relation between the name of substance (here a living-being) and its etymological interpretation.

The significance of the theory of composition of words from roots and the origin of language from such words has been the subject of discussion and argumentation in India, thousands of years ago. On one hand, it gives an indication of critical investigation made in this sphere by genius scholars of India and on the other it clearly reflects that they had spared no pains in undertaking profound study of a subject in which people generally took meagre interest and did not exhibit eagreness to penetrate deep into the subject of composition of words and accomplishment of a language.

Although, Yāsk was not disheartened in any way by the arguments of Gārgya. He did his best to establish the theory of construction of words from roots by refuting all his pleas, the detailed narration of which is uncalled for here. However, the arguments of Gārgya could not be refuted altogether and held void. Even now, after expiry of thousands of years, whenever, the theory of composition of words from roots, advocated by Yāsk, is subjected to critical investigation, the contentions of Gārgya are found facing us like an impenetrable fort. In the context of Prākrita and Pāli languages, while considering them from philological viewpoint, the topic of roots, although not fully relevant, has been discussed here so that we could be acquainted with the line of reasoning put forward by Gārgya, thousands of years ago. Whatever theories had been advanced in regard to origin of language, their critical evaluation would be desirable in the present context.

Theory of Imitation: The origin of a language is not based on any solitary ground. Its formation is due to numerous factors. Amongst them, there is the theory of imitataion. Birds and animals are close companions of mankind. Each has its own distinct speech. The utterances of animals and birds, when they are cheerful, are obviously, different from those, made by them, while they are overawed with fear or pain. There could be other feelings as well when they might make varied utterances, although the difference might not be quite explicit. In a way, it could be called the dialect of animals and birds. The humanity, devoid of any medium of speech of its own, heard the utterances of animals and birds and tried to pick up the sound.

The sound produced by an animal or bird was heard and a conforming name was given to the bird or animal consistent with its sound. Besides them, they discovered numerous other phonograms which were consistent with their activities and mental dispositions. *For example*, when human-beings heard the sound of a cat, he picked up the word 'Miyaoo' (mewing) and adopted it. He began to use this word to indicate a cat. In Hindi, the word is used as such. The phrase "Myaoom̐ kā Mum̐ha Kaun Pakde" (who is to bell the cat and face the hazard) is sufficient to prove it. In Chinese language. the word, 'Maoo' is used for a cat in place of 'Miyaoo'. In Egyptian language, the word 'maw is used to signify a cat. Its use may be found in other countries as well with slight variation in their respective language. The words 'काक' (crow), 'घुग्घु' (owl), 'मेंमें' and 'बेबे' (Bleating of goats and sheeps), 'हिनहिनाना' (Neighing of horses), 'दहाड़ना' (growling), 'फड़फड़ाना' (Fluttering of wings), 'झीं-झीं' (sound of crickets), are some of the words of the said nature. The verbs were accomplished from 'मेंमें' as 'मिमियाना' (Bleating of goats), 'बे बे' as 'बिबियाना' (Bleating of sheeps). The country-side children are found, calling a motor as 'पों पों' (sound of a horn) and 'फटफटिया' (sound produced by a motor cycle, hence named accordingly). The word 'भोंपू' (horn) was another example of a word, composed on the basis of a sound produced by horn. English word 'Cuckoo' is of similar nature. The renowned etymologist Yāsk, has defined the word 'काक' (crow) 'काक इति शब्दानुकृति' (meaning thereby that the bird which utters 'ka-ka' is Kak (crow) which also lends support to the said theory). In this connection, Sanskrit words appearing below, need to be examined and considered. It is believed that all or most of these words have been composed on the basis of sound produced or utterance made by respective bird or animal, such as— 'घूक' (owl), 'खंजन' (wagtail), 'खंजरीट' (wagtail), 'कंक' (peacock), 'वृक' (wolf), 'कुकुटट्' (cock), 'चटका' (sparrow) 'पिक' (cuckoo), 'काक' (crow), 'क्रौंच' (curlew), 'कोक' (Male ruddy goose), 'कुरर' (osprey), 'चोरी' (cricket), 'झिल्लिका' (cricket), 'झीरुका' (cricket) 'मयूर' (Peacock), 'केकी' (Peacock), 'भृंग' (Large black bee).

However, some philologists did not subscribe to this theory. Their main argument was that had the word (names of birds), shown above, been composed on the basis of sounds uttered by them, then the names of the birds would have been identical in all the languages of the world since there was no apparent distinction in the sounds of birds and animals of all the countries of the world. Consequently, there ought to have been no diversity in the words composed in imitating the utterances of the birds and animals. However, the fact is otherwise. There was no similarity in the words found in different languages for the birds and animals. However, if we deeply consider, we will find that the dissimilarity is not real. Absolute consistency and uniformity is not possible in imitating the utterances of birds and animals. There is a definite effect on the vocal organs of living-beings in different countries as per their environments and climatic conditions. It is, therefore, quite natural to find slight variations in the utterances in each country. It is equally impossible to imitate the utterances or sounds identically. Besides it, the imitation cannot be as perfect as original one. Hence, it is neither possible nor essential that the word obtained must be totally consistent with the sound or utterance. The imitation of a sound depends on the capability of an imitator and is possible to a limited extent only. The composition of a word on the basis of sound is not absolute. It may have slight resemblance only. The eminent philologist, sweet, was also of the opinion that the words composed on imitation of sounds were not necessarily in perfect consonance with them.

Prof. Maxmuler, however, felt that this theory was incongruous. He sarcastically named the theory as 'Bow-Wow'. In English, barking by dogs is called 'Bow-Wow'. The British also give this name, to their puppies. On the north-east bank of

'Pāpuvā river, the dogs are called 'Bow-Wow' on the basis of their barking sound. Infact, Prof. Maxmuler had made this satire on the basis of the word, found in use, in coastal language near 'Papuvā' river. However, the theory is not altogether worthless. No doubt, there are a lot of words in most of the languages of the world which had been composed on the basis of sounds or utterances as discussed above. At the same time, the linguists who advovate that a language is accomplished exclusively from the words, composed on imitation of sounds, are also wrong. Besides the words, obtained from phonetic sounds, there are a lot of words which have nothing to do with them. They are rather several times in number than the words composed on the basis of imitating sounds. It is equally worth-knowing that there are certain languages in the world, which are devoid of words, based on phonetic sounds, such as 'Athvaskan' language of North America.

Theory of Reverberation: Besides the theory of imitation, the theory of reverberation (sounding conformably to a continuous tinkling echo produced by the sounds of bells, anklets etc) also finds mention in linguistics. With contact, collision, clash, falling of water, metallic articles, wood, leaves, vegetation, metallurgical and mineralogical articles and inanimate objects, varying sounds are produced, which lead to the formation of words in accordance with the theory of reverberation. Here the word reverberation has been used in place of imitation. If we minutely look to their meanings, there is difference between the two. The phonetic sounds, uttered by birds and animals, and imitated by human beings, is called an imitation. The water flows and resounds 'Nad-Nad' (musical sound produced by flowing water), it is reverberation. In accordance with this theory, words like 'Nada' or Nadi' (river) have been composed from the root 'Nad'. Leaves fall down from trees, producing sound like 'Pat-Pat'. On the basis of this sound, the root 'Pat' and the word 'Patra' (Leaf) have been obtained. From barking of the dog, the root 'buk' (an imitative word formed from the cry of dog) is obtained. 'Kal-Kal' (sound of flowing water of stream); 'Chal Chal' (sound of water flowing out). 'Jhan-Jhan' (tinkling sound) 'Khatpat' (wrangling sound) are some of the Hindi words and 'Mur-mer'(grumbling), an English word, are all of the similar nature. Such words are found in almost all languages of the world. It is also evident that there is no fundamental difference in theories of imitation and reverberation. The gross difference lies only in the nature of articles, producing varying sounds, which is but insignificant. There are some other formations of words, based on immitation of sounds which are also explained under the said theory. For instance, from the scenes of burning lamps and shining stars, the words *jagmagāhat* (refulgence, gleaming) and *chamchamāhat* (glittering, sparkling) had been obtained. All such words are covered by the theory of imitation and reverberation. In nutshell, there is a category of words which have been composed either on imitation of utterances of birds and animals; from reverberation of sounds produced by articles or on visibility of scenes. Infact, these are only varying forms of imitation. Thus the theory of reverberation also has its own role in composition of words and accomplishment of a language.

Theory of Expression of Emotions (Interjectional Theory)

According to this thoery, it is believed that in the primordial age, there was emotional supremacy in mankind as against supremacy of wisdom. The animals are also controlled by emotional urge. They are devoid of thinking and reasoning power. They are only full of emotions. The primordial human-beings were not rated higher than animals so far prudence and wisdom were concerned. The living beings may lack faculty of reasoning and discretion but they are decidedly full of emotional sentiments. The excess of joy, depression, anger hatred, jealousy and uncertainty fills mankind with intense emotions. While primordial human-beings were thus influenced by emotions, spontaneously some words used to emanate from their mouths. Since it was an expression of inherent reaction, hence no attempts had to be made for sudden eruption of interjectional words such as 'Oh', 'Ah' 'Uf' (Alas); 'छि' (Pish); 'धत' (what a surprise! how done it!) etc.

In sanskrit, the words 'आ' (Pain or regret); 'धिङ्' (sign of reproachment and revilement); 'बत' (A particle expressing regret, pity, joy or satisfaction) 'हन्त' (A word expressing, pity, grief or regrief); 'साभि' (Blamable, contemptible); 'जोषं' (calmness and contentment), 'अलं' (Sufficient for, no use of—having a prohibitive force)' 'हूँ' (An interjection of calling contempt, pride, grief)' 'हा' (A particle expressing dejection, pain, anger or reproach): 'अहह' (An exclamation implying sorrow, wonder or surprise) 'हिररुङ' (An interjection expressive of inhibition); 'आहो', 'उताहो' (An interjection expressing doubt or alternative); 'अहा, ही' (An interjection expressing of surprise); 'ऊं' (An interjection of interrogation, abuse, arrogance, envy); are manifestations of sudden feelings. The interjectional theory may also be relevant regarding origin of a language to some extent.

Similarly, in English, use of interjections Ah, Oh, Alas (implying surprise, fear and regret) Rish (contempt); Pooh (feeling of disdain or contempt); Fie (showing disgust) is made accordingly.

In English grammar, they are called interjections. Hence the above theory is called interjectional theory. The purport of this theory being that utterance of such interjectional expressions was an initial step to the composition and evolution of the words. New words were accomplished later on from the said interjectional expressions, leading to the composition of a language. Amongst propounders of the said theory, the name of Mr. Kandilek is worth mention.

Dr. Bholanath Tiwari, however, writes "There are several hurdles in acceptance of the above theory. Firstly, the interjectional words are not similar in different languages. Had these expressions been made spontaneously by human-beings in primordial times, then all of them would have uttered identical words. In the whole world, dogs bark in the same typical manner to indicate their sufferings. However, the human-beings do not express their grief or joy in one and the same words. It appears that only by coincidence the aforesaid emotions have been linked with the interjectional words, uttered by mankind. They are purely accidental. Besides this, these interjectional words throw no light as to how a full-fledged language was accomplished. Such interjectional words do not exceed the number of forty or fifty in any one language, `Benafi' had rightly remarked that interjectional words were uttered only where a medium of speech was not available. They do not form part of a langluage. However, even if such words were treated as part of language, at the most it could be claimed that the above theory enabled to ascertain the source of origin of a few words only.

On minute consideration, it may be reasonably argued that the said interjectional words did play a limited role in partial accomplishment of a language but it could not be inferred that all the words of a language were obtained from the said interjectional expressions.

Partial, validity of this theory cannot be denied. Possibly, primordial human-beings might have spontaneously uttered varying sounds under intensity of various emotions. In the absence of a medium of speech, there was no apparent relation between emotions and utterance of phonetic sounds. People living inside the same state or region produced identical sounds in expression of similar emotions does not appear to be compatible. There was no disciplined civic life for want of a medium of speech. Hence it is not inconceivable that for expression of a particular emotion, people might be uttering different interjectional sounds. With gradual development and improvement of phonetic utterances or words, the diversity in sounds of expression of the same emotion was found inconvenient. It was realized that one common word should be determined for expression of the same emotion to avoid inconvenience.

While deliberating upon the utterances of animals and birds, Dr. Tiwari agrees that in different lands, alien to each other, no diversity in their sounds was found. However, his comments that had the interjectional expressions, made by human-beings, been inherent and natural, then they would have been identical throughout the world, need to be reviewed and closely examined. While dealing with linguistics, human beings and animals could not be treated at par. The utterances of animals are restricted and confined within a limited range. There were same state of affairs even thousands of years ago and they made similar utterances even then. However, the human race is inquisitive and industrious. How far the mankind has advanced and taken long strides in the field of linguistics, is self evident in as much they are using thousands of languages now. It was only an expansion of the process of evolution, the seed of which was there even in primordial mankind.

Although, an authentic information could be provided by physiologists only, yet roughly it is believed that there was no conformity in ligaments relating to larynx in the vocal chords of human-beings on one hand and dogs or other animals on the other. A few-birds, namely parrots and cuckoos do copy the utterances of human-beings on being taught. It appears, there may be slight resemblance in vocal organs of the said birds with human-beings. However, the position of other birds and animals is, obviously, different.

How far was it possible that people, living in different countries, would have made similar interjectional utterances? As a result of diverse climatic conditions, there are, obvious, variations in vibration, stimulation, contraction and expansion of larynx in human-beings. It should also be kept in mind that under what perspective circumstance, environment or nature of dominant emotion, a specific person made sudden utterance of interjectional sound. In spite of generalogical uniformity amongst people, living thousands of miles away, there are numerous other diversities found in them. Under the circumstance, how could there be no effect upon utterance of interjectional sounds?

It could also not be claimed with certainty that people living within the boundaries of the same country, uttered a similar interjectional word in expression of a similar emotion. It is quite possible that different people might have made different interjectional utterances at different occasions in expression of the same emotion. All of those interjectional expressions have not survived. Only a few of them are now found. In nutshell, though the number of interjectional expressions, now found in a language, are barely few, but they do have a decided role in accomplishment of a language.

Dr. Bholanath Tiwari has thrown light on certain other probabilities relating to this theory. He purports to say that although the interjectional expressions were limited in number and the exchange of views, made through them might have been imperfect, yet it is quite likely that by way of constant use of such interjectional words, they might have learnt to produce some other phonetic sounds or expressions. The repetition of the process must have helped in evolvement of a language. Dr. Tiwari's assumption that utterance of interjectional words might have prompted to the expression of some other phonetic sounds, needs further comprehension. The fact remains that other phonetic sounds are the outcome of miscellaneous crude and precise articles or subtle feelings which have absolutely nothing to do with the above theory. Sudden burst of interjectional expressions and deliberate manifestation are two different things. There is no consistent relation between the two. It appears that the introduction and evolvement of other phonetic sounds, is a consequence of certain other factors and processes.

Gestural Theory: The gestural theory holds an important place amongst all other theories determined with regard to origin of a language. First of all, Dr. saye, an eminent scholar of Pālinatian language, gave an indication of this theory. Darwin, Propounder of 'Theory of Evolution', had also discussed it. He chose six languages which were alien to each other. He made a comparative study of those languages and on the said basis, he proved the genuineness of the Gestural theory. The examination and determination of this theory continued till now. Near about 1930, Mr. Richard again referred to this theory. In his book. *Human Speech*, he has described it as (oral Gestural Theory) and he has invited attention of linguistic scholars towards it. The significance of this theory is established from the very fact that the learned scholars of Icelandic language, Mr. Alexander Johnson, also deliberated upon it, almost during the same period. He has produced critical evaluation of Indo European languages and while discussing gestural theory, he has admitted its importance . Thereafter, he discussed this theory more elaborately in some of his other books. Whereas, he chose Indo-European languages to base his arguments for consideration and critical examination, on one hand, on the other he also referred to Hebrew (old), Turkish, Chinese and a few other languages. Mentioning of Johnson's conclusions will be really useful for further consideration of the subject under discussion.

Johnson's Inferences: Johnson believed that there were 4 steps leading to the accomplishment of a language. According to him, the first step was expression of phonetic sounds revealing internal feelings. When the feelings of hunger, thirst, passion, joy, grief, fear and anger overtook a person, it was keen to express them but it had no language or medium of speech at its disposal. Just as monkeys and other animals display their feelings by making typical utterances, similarly, human-beings produced phonetic sounds from their mouths. This was an initial step leading to the linguistic development. These phonetic sounds became symbolical for expression of respective feelings.

The above-noted founding of Johnson is different from interjectional theory, discussed earlier. Whereas under the former, sudden burst of phonetic voices owing to preponderance of emotional feelings had been discussed, under Johnson's theory it is stated that as soon as a person is overwhelmed with feelings of inevitability, restlessness, intolerance and sexual cravings etc. it utters certain phonetic sounds, which form the subject-matter of his discussion.

The second step leading to the linguistic advancement is that of imitative words. Imitation of utterances of birds and animals and reverberation of the sound of inanimate objects also appear to be the purport of Johnson's inference.

Emotional Indications: Gestures : Johnson discusses emotional indications or gestures as his third ladder to linguistic advancement. Although, basically the process of emotional gentures is also imitation, yet the said imitation is different from the imitation of the sounds produced by inanimate objects, birds and animals. The said imitation is of the gestures or motion of the various limbs of the body such as tongue etc. and more especially of hands. Jonson calls it as unconscious imitation, which probably means that an imitator himself is not conscious of such sort of imitation. He, probably, means to say that when a certain feeling is born in mind there is a peculiar vibration or movement in the limbs of the body. In the state of wrath and audacity, a person stands erect and assumes an unyielding Posture; its lips tremble through excessive emotional strain; in case it is overawed with fear, it shrinks and hides itself; it spreads its arm when in an elating union posture; it raises arms to indicate the state of resolute determination, takes a vow or is in an attacking posture. While in challenging posture, it strikes its palms on any article lying infront. Such movement of bodily limbs goes on, indicating one's intentions or bodily gestures suited to disclose internal feelings when vocal chords of a person utter phonetic voices unconsciously which lead to the origin of words. Probably, this is what Mr. Johnson wishes to convey.

Manifestation of Subtle Feelings: Regarding origin of words, expressing subtle feelings, Johnson states that with the mental growth of mankind successively, it began to utter certain sounds or words gradually for manifestation of its subtle feelings also. Thus, it is the final ladder out of the aforesaid four ladders leading to the accomplishment of a language.

Johnson has made an attempt to deal with several aspects of a language elaborately. He has also dwelt upon how the vowels and consonants had evolved. He has also deliberated upon the relation of phonology with semantics. *For example*, according to him, if the initial letter of a root is ṛ or r, the said root word must signify an activity or movement, because in utterance of ṛ or r, the tongue is required to make a rapid movement or run. He has also made similar other observations and given analytical explanations. Johnson has drawn attention to a specific point that a primordial person found many curves over its body and following them it found new words, expressive of internal sentiments.

Purpose of Emotional Indications or Gestures: Johnson had stated about emotional indications or gestures while dealing with the third ladder, stepping towards evolvement of a language or leading to linguistic advancement. This, however, needs further minute consideration. A person utteres certain phonetic sounds as a result of moving various limbs of the body, especially hands etc. to disclose internal feelings is not believable. The relation of a particular phonetic voice with the vibration or movement of a respective limb of the body cannot be easily believed. *For example,* if a person starts gnashing its teeth in anger or raises its hand in attacking posture, how these emotional gestures could be represented by utterance of any phonetic sound. Phonetic sounds have their own independent part to play. Moreover, no sound is uttered while making any bodily movement and therefore, no question arises for imitation of the said sound. Johanson has tried to coordinate the utterance of phonetic sounds with movement of bodily limbs, an altogether novel idea in itself, could not be considered as rational or logical.

An Initial Letter of a Root Word : Having Specific Meaning : Incoherent

The theory of initial letters of root words, carrying any specific meanings, is also found incorrect on minute investigation. Mr. Johnson had stated that the root words commencing with initial letter ṛ or r signified an activity. If it was so, then there were other parallel root words which too implied an activity or movement, however, they did not begin with initial leter ṛ or r—what about them? Sanskrit root 'Gama' (going, moving, reaching) signified a bodily activity but its initial letter was 'Ga' in utterance of which, no part of the vocal organ runs or moves fast as in the case of letter ṛ or r. How then the veracity, of Johnson's finding will be justified? Like Gama, there must be many other root words in Sanskrit which signified certain physical activity, yet they did not begin with initial letter ṛ or r. Similarly, there were many root words which did begin with initial letter ṛ or r, yet they did not signify any physical movement. Sanskrit root word 'राज्' (to shine, to appear beautiful) began with initial letter r but did not signify any bodily movement. Similar instances could be found in Greek and other languages also.

As discussed earlier, root words applied with prefixes and suffixes and obtained in the shape of nouns and pronouns as per rules of the grammar, was an attempt after the language had already evolved. When it was promptor necessary to clean and refine a language, then steps were taken to make critical examination of the words, used therein. Probably it was the prompter for accomplishing grammatical and etymological sciences. These treatises owed their accomplishment to reasoning and logical competence of learned scholars. However, it was hard to believe that ancient scholars had acquired such reasoning faculty. Infact, rational and intuitional development of mankind was the consequence of incessant and regular efforts, hard work and perseverance for thousands of years.

Coordinating views of Sweet

Sweet was an eminent linguist of 19th century. He made an attempt to find out the source that led to the origin of a language. He was of the opinion that the origin of a language was not due to any one singular factor. According to him, numerous factors, causes and conducts, when co-ordinated, helped in accomplishment of a language. He classified elementary vocabulary of words into three categories. According to him, the first category of words were based on the theory of imitation. In the second category, he included the words, obtained on expression of emotional feelings and the symbolic words were placed by him in the third category. He believed that such symbolic words were in abundance in the initial shape of a language.

Words: Meanings: Spontaneous: Symbolic

According to sweet, symbolic words were those which had no meanings of their own. Incidentally, specific meanings are attached to or are implied by such symbolic words. The words continue to be used as such, having acquired the specific meanings in a language. *For example*, there is a child who looks at its mother. It desires to speak and its lips open. Sound of 'Ma-Ma' (mother) abruptly comes out. Till then, the phonetic sound of 'Mama' carried no meaning. By chance, the said sound is repeatedly uttered by the child in the presence of its mother. Its utterance is spontaneous and easy. Mother assumes the utterance as an address to herself. Thus, the word adopts a symbolic meaning of mother. The same method is applied to obtain the word 'Papa' (Father), words— माता, पिता, भ्राता (Brother) 'in Sanskrit. Meter, Phrater, Pater in Greek; Mater, Pater, Frater' in Latin, 'Mother, Father, Brother in English: 'Mather, Pidar, Brader' in Persian and माता, पिता, चाचा (uncle),, काका (paternal uncle), दादा (grand-father), भाई (brother), बाई (A Lady), दाई (Nurse) in Hindi were, infact, symbolic words of similar type. In most of the said spontaneous utterances the initial letter is labial. As soon as a child desires to utter, its lips open. The voice, coming out from its mouth, is generally labial, since for a child it is effortless to do so.

Sweet has also incorporated certain pronouns in the category of symbolic words. Although their accomplishment was purely by chance, yet they were adopted as such with their symbolic meanings. For instance, let us take Sanskrit pronoun 'Twam' (you). It is 'To' in Greek: 'Tu' in Latin, 'तू' in Hindi and 'Thou' in English. Similarly, 'इदं' (This) and 'अदस्' (That) are used as pronouns in Sanskrit. This and That in English and 'dies and das' in German languages are used. Sweet has also considered over the origin of many verbs on the basis of the theory of symbolism

Gist: Critical Examination: In regard to the source of origin of a language, it was an initial attempt of mankind. It is quite possible that initially many words of symbolic nature might have been accomplished. They might have been also used as such. The words which might not have been found fit in manifestation of the desired meanings or were not easy to be pronounced or being heard, they might have got obliterated with the passage of time. On the other hand, the words which were found fit and compatible, might have been incorporated and formed part permanently of the language. Just as the principle of 'survival of the fittest' applies to all animate and inanimate objects, so it applies to the choice of words as well. In a language also the fittest and most suitable words survive and rest get obliterated with the lapse of time. The symbolic words which have survived in a language, are only a few now as against those ascertained originally.

Three categories of words, visualized by sweet, do have their relevance, may be to a limited extent, in structure or linguistics. However, it must be stated that sweet's attempt to establish consistency of various roots, nouns and pronouns with the theory of symbolism, does not appeal to the mind. Moreover, besides the words, explained by sweet to have been accomplished under the said three categories, there are still a lot of words, may be several times in number, which remain unexplained. They are not covered by any of the aforesaid three categories relating to theories of imitation, interjectionism, and symbolism. As discussed earlier, the words obtained by way of imitation and interjectionism were only a limited few. Similarly, symbolic words were also small in number and they only reflected mutual relations in a family, beyond which there was no trace of symbolic words.

Many other words, resembling with symbolic and other categories of words, were obtained, leading to the regular evolvement of a language. Such an assumption also does not appear to be coherent. *For example*, let us ponder over symbolic words. Children have a limited sphere. Their relations are confined to the family and they have minimum requirements. They are only concerned with eating, drinking, clothing and covering their bodies while sleeping which are infact, their primary needs. In the said perspective, the symbolic voices or words, uttered by the children, have scant informative value. They only signify a few articles or indistinct feelings. They are not supposed to make subtle or refined expressions.

Origin of Linguistics: Determination: Frustration

In this way, several views emerged in regard to the origin of a language. They were contemplated upon, discussed and modified from time to time but no tangible result was achieved. It had an adverse reaction on the minds of pre-eminent scholars. They thought, it would be entirely useless to continue efforts to ascertain the source of origin of a language, since the research and investigation, made hitherto had yielded no result.

Mr. Edgar Stuvint, Professor, Columbia University writes : "After much futile discussion and argumentation for and against, the linguists have reached the conclusion that the data with which they are concerned, yielded little or no evidence about the origin of human speech."

Renowned scholar of Italy, Mr. Morio Pai has expressed the similar view. He writes, "If there is one thing on which all linguists are fully agreed, it is that the problem of the origin of human speech is still unsolved."

American linguist, Mr. J. Kendryes repeats the same view when he writes, "...The problem of the origin of language does not admit of any satisfactory solution."

The above-noted views of prominent scholars are really pessimistic. Inspite of making constant endeavour for a long time, the desired objective is not achieved and it is bound to create slight frustration. There are two possible consequences of such a frustration. Firstly, when one loses all hopes, it is rarely possible for such a person to restart the work with the same fervour and zeal. However, in the second category, although frustration is there, yet the wise persons, having an undaunted courage or spirit treat their dejection as a temporary sojourn for relaxation and again resume their work with greater devotion and enthusiasm.

Ban on further Research: Strange Decision

It was almost a century ago, when the linguists, having failed to find a definite answer, how the medium of speech came into existence, felt greatly irked and disgusted. Even after concerted efforts, when they did not succeed in finding an explanation to the origin of human speech, they turned, averse from further pursuing the subject. Some began to plead that the subject of origin of a language was beyond the scope of linguistic science. It was part of ethnology. According to them, the subject—how a language (human speech) came into existence was also attached to ethnology, a science dealing with all aspects of human development. A few others believed that it formed part of ancient history. Some scholars opined that linguistics was an independent science and the subject of origin of human speech was attached to it. There ought to be solid data and basis for consideration and critical examination. Science has nothing to do with mere surmises and conjectures. Practically, no material data is available for undertaking research and investigation. When a language or medium of speech came into existence, nobody can decidedly say. Possibly, it might have originated lacs of years ago, the calculation of which can be made on only imaginary grounds. For want of sufficient material to be examined in a scientific manner, the subject, how a language came into existence, should not be treated as part of linguistic science. There was no use, whatsoever, to think on these lines and must keep efforts continuing.

The above-noted views created a stir and an excitement amongst the linguists of the world . In 1866, a linguistic council was established at Paris, the laws and bylaws of which had been framed. Amazingly, the council strictly banned further contemplation over the question of origin of human speech. That is to say, the founders of the council put a blanket ban on further consideration of the subject, how a language came into existence. In this way, finding an answer to the problem was stopped and the chapter was closed once for all. The proposers of the ban were not ordinary people. They were renowned philologists of world repute. Perhaps, they might have thought that why the learned scholars should waste their energies and time in carrying on their futile attempts when no result was foresighted.

Investigation and Research did not Stop

However, it was equally surprising that inspite of imposed restrictions, attempts continued to find out the answer to the question, how the human speech came into existence. Not only this, after almost every decade, a new formula was evolved to solve the problem. It is quite natural. A human-being is, obviously, curious and contemplative by nature. The curiosity for quest is not checked by imposing a ban. It always keeps genuine thinkers and prudent scholars busy in their efforts to continue their research and investigation in order to achieve their cherished goal.

The word science is analogous with physics. Physics is based on cause, effect and tradition. The cause transforms into action. No work is possible in the absence of the requisite data. If data is there, the work is not hindered. It is an accepted rule. When the said technical definition of physics is taken into consideration, philology is not a science in that sense. However, it is also not entirely based on assumptions. For that matter, it is not an art as well. It is neither an art nor science, then what is it? The linguists have pondered over the said aspect as well.

Mind is full of sentiments. They flash in the mind. An idea, fancy or imagination is conceived and a number of words come out spontaneously. It is poetry. It is the product of emotions, being touched or affected by prevailing sentiments. Hence it is lovely, charming and sweet. However, it is not the reality of material world. It is only visionary truth. In this view of the matter, it is an art. Beauty and charm are its main ingredients while truth and reality are secondary. Philology has nothing to do with it. Although, like physics, it has no causal material or data to depend upon, it is not also devoid of it entirely nor it is fanciful, or existing only in fancy. Words form a language. They are uttered by mouth. However, like an idea, fancy or imagination, they do not come out inconsistently. Words are formed by letters. The sounds uttered from gullet, larynx, oral cavities and other vocal chords, after coming in contact or clashing with breath or air, rising up from navel, give rise to root letters and the entire process is based on an extremely minute and prescribed system of cause, effect and tradition in a scientific manner. The channelization of the whole process is so mechnical and well arranged that there is not the slightest deviation from it. It can be considered a perfect scientific and methodical system with no fault at all.

Though, the development of a language is not based on a flawless causal data or material, as in the case of accomplishment of words, yet there is a systematic order, causativeness and firm basis. It is because of these characteristics that it is known as linguistic science. Although it is distinct from physics, yet it is fit, having cause, effect and tradition, to undertake critical examination and investigation.

Why such a Frustration? When we consider philology as a science (a distinct knowledge), then all aspects related to philology, must be studied minutely and in a critical manner. Besides going through historical evidence concerning its development and growth, the subject of origin of human speech must also be considered. Only because, necessary material or data was not available for research and investigation, hence the issue of the origin or birth of a language should be left out for ever and excluded from the ambit of linguistic science, is not a wise step. The true scientists or researchers do not give up a subject, merely because requisite material or data is not at their disposal. If the work of investigation is taken up regularly without pause, necessary data or information will also be available. If the information or data is not in hand now, why should we think that it will not be available, in future as well. In the present context, the saying of renowned dramatist, Sri Bhavabhūti is, most opportune which may be quoted here: "कालो ह्ययं निरवधिर्विपुला च पृथ्वी:" meaning thereby that the time is infinite and the earth is too vast and extensive. Nobody knows when and where somebody may be born in this universe, capable of accomplishing a most difficult and arduous task. The sturdy-minded and resolute persons, who remain committed to their work and are confident about their future, they do succeed in their mission one day. To give up the pursuit and forsake the work will belie all future hopes. Keeping the above point in mind, it will be worth-while to carry on some more contemplation on the origin of human-speech.

Manifestation of Human Speech

With the progress of mankind in various spheres of life, accomplishment of a medium of speech was also found within reach. Human-beings, filled with emotional sentiments and under intensity of feelings, were too eagre to pour out their innerself. Proverb goes—'Necessity is mother of invention.' Accordingly, medium of exchange, whatever was its shape then, came into existence. It is a brief introduction of phonetic sounds, uttered by human-beings, as a result of imitation of utterances of birds and animals; interjectional and gestural expressions, culminating in primitive form of language.

परा (a remote sound); पश्यन्ती (a particular sound); मध्यमा (a medial sound); बैखरी (Articulate utterance or production of sound)

In foregoing pages, a preliminary discussion was made on systematic order of production of sound through vocal organs. Now detailed discussion on the subject is called for. Under Vedic tradition, power of speech had been classified in four kinds—'परा' (remote sound); 'पश्यन्ति' (A particular vocal sound); 'मध्यमा' (Middle or central vocal sound) and 'बैखरी' (Articulate production of sound). The renowned commentator, Pātanjali has quoted a line[1] from Rigveda at the very outset of his commentary which throws light on the subject.

Mahāmahopādhyāya Pt. Durga Prasad Dwivedi, an eminent scholar and commentator of 'Sāhitya Darpaṇa', has made fine briefings of 'परा', 'पश्यन्ति' etc., various forms of utterances of sounds, while dealing with an alphabet or sound. He writes: "The soul in all its senses external and internal, directs the internal organ (heart, the seat of thoughts and feelings) to make utterances of sounds for composition of words, having desired meanings, so as to be able to speak. The heart directs the heat located in navel. The heat vibrates the air (breath). The pulsated air produces a subtle sound which is known as remote voice or speech. Thereafter, the air is pushed upwards to the hub region and after contact of the air with that region, a sound is produced which is called as 'Pashyanti' voice or speech; Both these utterances are of minute nature. They are perceptible to the gods or ascetics only. They are not audible by ordinary people. The said air (breath) then flows round to the heart region and after coming in contact with that region, the sound produced is called as speech from central organ. Sometimes, even ordinary people could hear and pick up the sound after perfectly concentrating their mind, of course, in an extremely low voice. Thereafter, the air reaches the

1. Guhā triṇi nihitā nengayānti turiyaṁ vāeho manuṣhyā vadanti | —Rigveda; 1/164/45.

mouth and draws near the throat (voice-box). It clashes with the cerebral. The air is pushed back from that portion and after passing through oral cavities, strikes with anyone of the eight parts of the throat from which certain sounds (such as nasals, gutturals etc.) emanate. The sound, thus produced, is called articulate utterance or speech".

In Pāṇini's teachings as well, the mediums of articulation of sound have also similarly been explained.[1]

What has been analysed and discussed above is a scientific process, as to how the sounds are produced by vocal organs inside our body. They can not be explained by the material or data, related with physics, because the process of articulation of sound prior to 'Vaikhri speech' is too subtle and audible only to celetial bodies. However, in spite of all this, it is based on such cause, effect and tradition that the whole process is no less scientific. Although, the process, illustrated above, is not fully acceptable to all uptil now from viewpoint of linguistic science, yet it is most viable explanation regarding origin of words leading to the accomplishment of a language. It means—when the soul directs the heart, the seat of thoughts and feelings, to make utterance of sounds for accomplishing words, having desired meanings, so as to be able to express our inner feelings, the heart stimulates internal organs to act. Thereafter, the fire in navel and the air vibrating there are set in motion. It is a minute organic process. It is universally known and an acknowledged fact that air (breath) plays an important role in producing a phonetic sound. However, in order to make the air move upwards, it is necessary to put pressure on and push it. The sole object of fire (heat) existing in the first ganglion of the body, is to force the air to move to the hub region. Thereafter, the air (breath) moves upward vertically from the region of the navel. The fact remains that the root cause of utterance of audible sound (sound within the range of hearing) lies in the moving of the air (breath) upward. The breath moving verticle clashes with the vocal chord.

Organic Shape of Vocal Chord and its Technique

Inside throat, parallel to feeding pipe, the portion of the wind pipe, which is slightly below the glottis, is known as vocal chord. Outside the throat, there is a stiff protruded portion, known as 'Kanthmaṇi or *ghāṇṭi* (laryngitis) which looks harder and more protruded in physically weak persons. That is the place where vocal chord is located inside. The said part of the wind pipe is bit thick. Applause to the nature that it provides what and where is needed. There are two resilient veils made from subtle membrane. They are called as vocal cords. The middle open part of vocal chord is called 'glottis'. While we breathe or make an utterance, the air passes through the said glottis. A person produces varied sounds by virtue of the said vocal cords. That is to say, with the contact or clash of air, the aforesaid two elastic veils adopt different forms. Sometimes, they draw closer and sometimes they move apart. There is a sequence even between closeness or remotness of the veils. How much a veil gets stretched or shrinked and how much the other veil

1. Atmā budhyā sametyārthān mano yuṅkte vivakṣayā
Manaḥ kāyāgnimāhanti sa preryati mārutaṁ ||

spreads or draws closer. Thus, diverse positions of veils-stretching, shrinking and viberation leads to the manifestation of different phonetic sounds. Just as different wires of a Veena (The Indian lute) with touch and stroke of the fingers produce varied sounds. Similar is the position of vocal chord which also passes through a regulated and systematic process.

The phonetic sounds, coming out of vocal chord and passing through oral cavities, contact vocal organs inside mouth—larynx, palate, cerebrum, teeth, lips and nose and they clash with breath. According to the subtelety of phonetic sounds, viberations or ripples are created in the breath. The said ripples, carrying along the phonetic sounds make them audible.

Creation of Most Subtle and Non-Elemental Form of Phonetic Sound

The process of utterance of sound, starting from initial ganglion of the body and coming out through oral cavities of the mouth, has to pass through various formations which is, no doubt, an extremely minute process. The gist of what has been explained above, while considering over **'परा'**, **'पश्यन्ति'**, **'मध्यमा'** and **'वैखरी'** (modes of articulation of sound) is that phonetic sounds are uttered leading to the accomplishment of words, having desired meanings, for expression of our inner feelings. The subtle form of speech is obtained then and there, which is known as 'Parā' speech. Parā speech means the remote or inaudible sound which can be heard by heavenly bodies only. Thereafter, the air, rising upwards, comes in contact with hub-region and the sound articulated therefrom is still in subtle form—though it may be comparatively bit loud. The said subtle voice moves up with the air and clashes with the heart region. The abstract form of sound moves vertically to attain tangibility. Thus the subtle sound is transformed into slightly crude form of a word. However, as aforesaid, the said sound is neither distinct nor easily audible. It is a medial form between subtle form and concrete form of sound. It appears to have been called 'Madhyama' (a middling form of sound). The subsequent form of utterance is 'Vaikhri' (Articulate sound) which is fit for mutual exchange by mankind. Manifestation of 'Vaikhri' speech means—adoption of concrete shape by the phonetic sounds in the shape of words.

Though, the subject appears to be quite intricate and confused, yet, in nutshell, it may be stated that in articulation of sound, the functional element is air or breath inside our body. The most subtle and inaudible sound originating from contact with initial ganglion and moving up after clashing with hub region, reaches heart region and after the air strikes with heart region, partly manifested and partly unmanifested form of sound is produced. Thereafter, the air further moves up and after coming in contact with elastic membrances of the vocal chord, the said membranes appear in different forms-pulled tight and stretched fully, shrinked, drawn close, half drawn, partially drawn or slightly drawn near each other, enabling the phonetic sound to manifest itself in the shape of letters, leading to the accomplishment of vowels and consonants and finally culminating in words forming a speech.

The process, enunciated above, regarding manifestation of speech is really significant and entirely scientific in nature. It is illustrative of the fact that Indian intellectuals and scholars took a long dip and penetrated deep into the subject concerning origin of human speech.

Views as per Jaina Philosophy: As per Jaina philosophy, there are 3 types of human tendencies—mental, vocal and physical. When a person is absorbed in mental concentration, it invites atomic particles which attract good or bad actions. The said particles are, though, concrete, yet in most subtle form. The atoms will be attracted as per the nature of our mental pronings.

The nature of mental inclinations is the prime ingredient for attracting similar atoms. After contemplation, the process for vocal expression starts for which a medium of speech is needed. After close application, the mind manifests itself through speech for which a language is needed accomplished from words. Atoms are invited as per nature of mental tendencies which in turn attract deeds or actions. The said atomic particles activate the process of articulation of sound. The behaviour of invited atomic particles varies according to their nature which is but natural. Consequently, consistent with our feelings and sentiments, the phonetic sounds of various types are articulated through vocal organs, leading to the accomplishment of words and culminating in a medium of speech.

Line of Distinction Between Gross and Subtle Forms

As already discussed above, the phonetic sounds or crude forms of words obtained by way of imitation of utterances of birds and animals and by interjectional and symbolic expressions was a natural process for accomplishment of a speech. The time for manifestation of subtle feelings might have come in the life of people when they had grown mentally developed considerably.

In that case, obtaining a medium of speech through process of 'Para' and 'Pashyanti' etc. or as per Jaina philosophy atoms are invited as per nature of mental tendencies which in turn attract actions or deeds. The said atoms activate the process of articulation of sound. Consistent with our feelings, the phonetic sounds are articulated, leading to the accomplishment of words and culminating in a medium of speech. Thus the process of origin of words, indicative of most precise feelings, is really enlightening.

Obviously, a question may arise here—when the phonetic sounds or words were obtained through process of 'Para' and 'Pashyanti', etc., leading to the origin of a medium of speech, or as per Jaina tradition, the atoms are attracted which activate the process of articulation of phonetic sounds, leading to the composition of words and finally origin of human speech, why then there is so much diversity in words and languages, spoken by the people, throughout the universe.

The fact remains that the people in the world donot live in similar environments, climatic conditions and social orders. There are lot of dissimilarities in living conditions. Then how could the vocal organs and the sounds, articulated through them, remain unaffected?

Another important point worth consideration is that the aforesaid process of accomplishing a human-speech was primarily related with the introduction of words, having subtle meanings, which signifies that the words implying gross sentiments had already come into existence by then, in various languages of the world. It is quite natural that the languages must be incorporating words having subtle meanings of the same type as the crude and unrefined words, they were having already. There might have been similar other factors that led to the composition of languages differently in various parts of the world.

An Epilogue: The above discussion is only an indecisive reflection, given a scientific tenor. Infact, the history of origin, growth and expansion of linguistics is long and complicated one. The human-race has spared no pains in linguistic development and give the languages, the modern refined shape. Mutual association, coming in contact with birds and animals, proximity with nature, creative work and other useful material were at the disposal of mankind which provided great stimulation and impetus to the scholars to proceed with their unfailing zeal and enthusiasm. The well flourished languages, now available are also a part of overall achievements, made by humanity. These languages contained miscellaneous knowledge and knwledge of various other branches and are the source of keeping valuable information intact for hundreds and thousands of years.

Morphological Classification of Linguistics

Each language has its own form. Each has its own distinct style of composition. The classification made according to the form of a language is called morphological classification. There are two categories of languages in the world—compound and non-compound languages.

Compound Languages: The languages which have combination of semanteme with connecting elements, are called compound languages. The sentences constructed from inflected words (complete words) build a language. There are two ingredients of a complete word —interpretation (semanteme) and a link connecting the words. The meaning indicated by a word is its semanteme but what connects the words in a sentence is called a link or connecting element. Without connecting link of words, no sentence can be constructed. Different words will always have different meanings. No apparent co-ordination is found in their meanings. *For example*, let us take few words of Sanskrit—'Asmad' (A pronominal base from which several cases of the first personal pronoun are derived); 'Yusmad' (The base of second personal pronoun); 'Vastra' (A garment) and 'Dā' (A root word-meaning to give, grant or impart). Each word has its own distinct meaning yet there is no consistent relation between them. However, as soon as they are arranged in a sentence after applying inflections, prefixes or suffixes, there is relativity and consistency in their meanings and a sentence formed from these words displays a specific sense. In order to obtain express meaning of each word, inflections and suffixes are essential to be affixed to the words. This is exactly what is knwon as connecting element. "वयम् युष्मभ्यम्, वस्त्राणि अद्म" are inflected forms (the forms derived from applying inflections-declensions or conjugations) to Sanskrit root words: "अस्मद्, युष्मद्, वस्त्र and दा" respectively. There is a methodical style for morphological construction of words.

There are certain languages including Sanskrit in the category of languages, having compounded words, in which it is not at all necessary to arrange inflected and suffixed words in a specific order. Thus the aforesaid sentence "वयं युष्मभ्यं वस्त्राणि अदम्" could be altered by arranging words in any other sequence without having least effect upon its sense or signification, such as "वस्त्राणि अदम युष्मभ्यं वयम्", "अदम वस्त्राणि युष्मभ्यं वयम्" and "युष्मभ्यं वयं वस्त्राणि अदम." However, in other compound languages, it is not possible. Alongwith semanteme and relativity, placing of subject, object and verb etc. in a specific order was equally important. The grammatical constraints have to be abided. We shall translate the above sentence in English as 'we gave you the clothes'. These words can not be arranged in a different order at will like Sanskrit. Similar is the case in Hindi.

Non-Compound or Elemental Languages : Where there is no combination of semantemes with connecting elements, they are called non-compound languages. The words, constructing such languages are not affixed with inflections, prefixes or suffixes. It is sufficient to place the words in a particular order so as to give expressed meaning or sense. By changing placement of such words and arranging them in a different order, altogether different meanings are obtained.

In the category of non-compound languages, Chinese language is worth mention. For instance, there are three words in Chinese language, namely, "न्गो, त, नि" The meaning of the word 'न्गो' is I; that of 'त' is to beat and 'ni' is used for `you'. In order to obtain meaning of the sentence as 'I beat you', the words will be placed in Chinese language as 'न्गो त नि'. However, in order to obtain the meaning 'you beat me', the words will be placed in a different order as "नि त न्गो". It means that the subject (Doer), whose activity is desired to be signified, is placed at the beginning of a sentence. Similarly, when a personal noun or pronoun is placed in a sentence after the verb, it is said to be an objective case. The subject and object are indicated by placing them in a specific order. It means there is no change in the original shape of a word in non-compound languages. Inflections, prefixes and suffixes are never added to such words.

Let us take another illustration of Chinese language 'त लइ' means "He comes". It is a sentence signifying present tense.If it is desired to be converted in past tense; there will be no change in the shape of the verb `Lai'. Only the word `लिओन' will be placed after the verb `Lai'. The word 'लिओन' literally means having completed'. Thus the sentence will read `ta lai lion', thereby indicating that he had completed the activity of coming. That is to say he came. The meaning of the word 'लिओन' is to complete. However, by placing it in the as `Ta lai lion, it establishes a relation. If the word `Liao' substitutes the word `Lion' which literally means complete or completeness, then also it will indicate past-tense. It is explicit from the above illustrations that different words, without any alteration in their shape, serve the purpose of both semanteme and connecting link, only by placing them in a particular sequence or order. However, tones and indeclinations are also significant in revelation of correct meanings.

There are only a limited number of non-compound languages in the world. The Chinese language is prominent amongst them. In Sudanese language of Africa also, there is a significance of placing words in a specific order. In Anamese language, there is greater emphasis on pronunciation and accent while in Burmese, Siamese and Tibetan languages, the affixture of indeclinable words is significant.

Classifications and Sub-classifications of Compound Languages

There are three categories of compound languages namely—Entwined compound languages; loose compound languages (having no pun) and Joined and punned compound languages.

When semanteme and connecting elements are so entwined or tied together that they cannot be distinguished, they are said to be entwined compound languages. Such as from 'शाली' (Rice) to 'शालेय' (Rice-field); from 'उपग' (Near a cow) to 'औपगव' (Protector of cows); from 'पृथ्वी' (Earth) to 'पार्थिव' (Relating to the earth, terrestrial); from 'वायु' (air) to 'वायव्य' (pertaining or belonging to the air); from 'शुल्कशाला' (A toll station or custom house) to 'शौल्कशालिक' (A superintendent of toll or customs officer); from 'वत्स' (son) to 'वात्स्य' (pertaining to son or younger relatives or near ones in general); from 'मृदु' (soft, tender) to 'मार्दव' (Softness, mildness) from 'विनता' (Name of mother of Aruṇa and Garuḍa—a large meat-eating bird— 'वैनतेय' (Name of Garuḍa); from 'नदी' (river) to 'नादेय' (River born, aquatic, marine); 'बृहस्पति' (Name of the preceptor of Gods) to बार्हस्पत्य (Relating to preceptor of deities, a pupil of Brahspati ; from 'मुद्ग' (a kind of kidney—bean; or lid) to 'मौदगीन' (Fit for being sown with beans); from 'तुला' (A pair of scales) to 'तुल्य' (of the same kind or class, of like appearance); from 'दिति' (Name of a daughter of Dakṣā, wife of Kaṣyapa and mother of the demons) to 'दैत्य' (Sons of Diti-demons); from 'कुशाम्ब' (A resident of Kauśāmbi) to 'कौशाम्बी' (Name of the capital of the Vatsa kingdom—It was near the modern Kosam, about 50 miles above Allahabad); from 'गौ' (cow) to 'गव्य' (consisting of cattle or cows); and from 'अग्नि' (Fire) to 'आग्नेय' (Fiery, belonging to Agni) etc.

It is evident that semantemes and connecting elements have altogether been entwined and so mixed up that in this category of compound languages, the connecting elements are involved (as a sentence) so exchanged or enlarged (developed) within semantemes. Thus the separate identities of semantemes and connecting elements become extinct.

Loose Compound Languages: Under this category, although there is combination of semanteme and connecting element in complete inflected words, used in such languages, yet they do not lose their separate identities and they donot get mixed as sesamum and rice. They donot get completely mixed up and form one identity. Such is the state of semantemes and connecting elements in loose compound languages. Dravidian languages fall under this category. In order to elucidate the point, one illustration of each 'Kannaḍa' and `Tamil' languages are desirable to be given below:

It has been stated above that semantemes and connecting elements donot get completely mixed up and they donot lose their identities. It means that with a view to denote number and case of a word, the inflection or suffix is applied to it at the end which remains unchanged. In such inflected and suffixed words the semanteme remains definitely unchanged. The forms of the word 'Sewak' (employee) in Kannaḍa language are produced hereunder:

Case	*Singular number*	*Plural number*
Subjective case	Sewak-Nu	Sewak-ru
Objective case	Sewak-Nannu	Sewak-rannu
Instrumental case	Sewak-Nind	Sewak-rind
Dative case	Sewak-Nige	Sewak-Rige
Possessive case	Sewak-Na	Sewak-Ra
Locative case	Sewak-Nalli	Sewak-Ralli

In Kannaḍa language, in order to denote subjective case, word 'Nu' in singular number and 'Ru' in plural number are placed with the noun. In order to show objective case, the word 'Nannu' in singular number and 'Rannu' in plural number are placed. Similarly, in instrumental case, 'Nind' represents singular number and 'Rind' plural number; in dative case, the word 'Nige' represents singular number and 'Rige' plural number; in possessive case 'Na; represents singular number and 'Ra' plural number; in locative case, 'Nalli' represents singular number and 'Ralli' plural number. The aforesaid symbolic words or case terminations have been put after the word 'sewark' of Kannaḍa language to represent the singular and plural numbers.

The words expressing both semanteme and connection have been placed in their original shape in each case which is self evident.

Now the symbolic words used to manifest singular number and plural number in each case of the Tamil word 'Kovel' (Temple) are shown below:

Case	*Singular number*	*Plural number*
Subjective	Kovel ·	Kovel-gala
Objective	Kovel-Ei	Kovel-gala-ei
Possessive	Kovel-Udīya	Kovel-gala-Udīya

In Tamil language, the word 'gala' represents plural number. In order to convert singular number into plural number, the word 'gala' is placed after the original word in singular number. In Tamil language, 'Aei' in objective case and 'Udiya' in possessive case are case-terminations. In other cases as well, the case terminations are placed after the original word to represent singular number. However, if they are to be converted in plural number, the word 'gala' is placed after the original word and, thereafter the respective case-termination is added. From the above forms of the Tamil word 'Kovel', it is quite clear. The nature of loose compound languages is thus clear by the above illustrations.

Punned Compound Languages: While discussing Entwined compound languages, it was stated that the semanteme and connecting element were so intermixed that outwardly it was not possible to ascertain their distinct identities. In punned compound languages as well, the semanteme and connecting element unite together. Slight change or deviation from the original state in semanteme is also observed, yet the connecting element does not get mixed with semanteme totally like entwined compound languages. Although, the semanteme and its relation with the words of the language is not obtained at the first glance in Punned compound languages as well yet the reflection of connecting element is definitely found. *For example*—from the word 'karma' (deed or action) to 'karmaṇya' (skilful, clever); from 'kaṇth' (Throat) to 'kanthya' (Relating to or being at the throat, guttural); from 'Saṁvatsar' (A year of Vikramaditya's era) to Saṁvatsārika (annual, yearly); from 'Pāṇini (Name of a celebrated grammarian) to 'Pāṇiniya' (Relating to or composed by Pāṇini, the great grammarian); from 'Dharma' (Religion) to 'Dharmik' (Righteous, Virtuous); from 'Nikat' (Near, close by) to "Naiktika" (Adjecent, contiguous); from 'Dadhi' (coagulated milk, curd) to 'Dādhik' (Made from or mixed with coagulated milk); from 'Dhanusha' (A bow) to 'Dhānuska' (An archer, a bowman) from 'Akṣa' (a dice-board) to 'Ākṣika' (one who plays at dice; one who gains by gambling); from 'Udūpa' (A boat) to 'Audupika' (crossing in a boat); from 'Dhenu' (A cow) to 'Dhainuk' (A herd of cows) etc. In the above illustrations, although the meanings of the words have undergone slight change, yet the connecting element (relation) has not entirely been omitted or disappeared. Partly it is there.

In Arabic language, there is a root word क्-त्-ल्. From this said root word, complete words are obtained, such as 'कतल' (murder); 'कातिल' (A murderer); and 'किल्ल' (A Foe). Like the above illustrations of Sanskrit words there is union of semanteme and connecting element in Arabic words also. However, the connecting element is somewhat identified. This is also an example of punned compound language.

Linguistic Groups on the Basis of Morphological Classification

On the basis of morphological classification of world languges, they are categorised in several groups as per vocabulary, connecting elements and similarity in phonetic sounds. The alliance of languages with their respective group, can be ascertained only after undertaking a comparative and historical study of linguistics. This is a matter entailing a profoundly deep study for quite a long time. Such detailed examination had been possible of only a few linguistic groups. There are hundreds of languages in the world. Their linguistic groups with which they were allied can be ascertained only after prolonged research and investigation. Nevertheless, the scholars have spared no pains to identify the respective groups of languages inspite of various constraints.

After expiry of two decades in 19th century, German scholar. Wilhelm Phan Hamboldat, elaborately dealt with the subject. He classified world languages in thirteen families, while other scholars determined the number of such linguistic groups differently on the basis of studies made by them. Partiz suggested that there were only 10 linguistic families. Fredrick Muler and other linguists suggested that there were as many as one hundred groups. However, a few scholars are of the view that almost one hundred linguistic groups are in existence in America alone. On the other hand, Royce believed that all the linguistics of the world belonged to one and the same family. According to Grey, world linguistics are classified in 26 groups. The views of Indian philologists also differ with regard to the number of linguistic groups.

The above figures of linguistic families, infact, create excitement and curiosity. Determining the number of linguistic groups from one to one hundred is quite fantastic and bewildering. It clearly reflects that a thorough survey of world linguistics has not been made so far. Hence the above assumed figures are only imaginary and based on mere surmises.

According to Dr. Bholanath Tiwari, the principal linguistic groups could grossly be determined as under:

1. Indo-European; 2. Semitic; 3. Hemitic; 4. Bhurāl Altāic; 5. Chinese or mono-syllabic languages; 6. Dravadian; 7. Malaya-Pālinītian; 8. Bāntu; 9. Bushman; 10. Sunḍānese; 11. Australian Pāpuvana; 12. Red Indian; 13. Caucasian and 14. Japanese-Korean.[1]

Classification of Linguistics on Geographical Grounds

There is one more system of classification of linguistics and it is geographical. It means that the regions and territories of the world have been classified on the basis of language found in use there. It is more intelligible classification. It must be borne in mind that it is not necessary at all that in any one particular territory or region, the languages, pertaining to one specific group are in vogue only. Languages belonging to different families may be in vogue. As a result of different linguistic groups, dissimilarities in the languages are quite natural. However, it is equally true that on account of geographical proximity, there is exchange of phonetic utterances and words mutually. Thus on geographical grounds, the linguistic groups have been classified in four territorial groups, namely— (1) African territorial group; (2) Euresian territorial group; (3) Atlantic oceanic territorial group; and (4) American territorial group.

Linguistic Groups

The world linguistics are classified in several groups. Just as people have their families, so is the case with linguistics or languages. There is a single group of all such languages which have a common source of origin, growth and expansion. In linguistic science, it is called a group of languages. The point may be more clear by the following illustration. Let us assume that a particular community of people is living in a specific territory of the world. It has its own medium of speech which enables the people to carry on the work in day-today course of life. With the passage of time, the population of the said territory multiplies. People may have realised that they are not faring well for want of adequate resources, and therefore, they must migrate to some other territory and settle there.

Another reason could be that they might have developed an ambition to conquer an additional piece of territory for better living. Whatever, be the case, a large number of people might have left their original place of living and moved collectively in a specific direction. After covering a long distance, they might

1. Some scholars believe that there were two separate groups of linguistics mentioned against serials number 7,11 and 14 as shown above.

have come across a suitable site for living and made a halt there. The language of that part of the territory is, obviously, different from their own medium of speech. It is rather incumbent upon a person or community to establish contacts, as early as possible, with the people originally residing there. One cannot help developing contacts with the original residents of that area to meet its day-today requirements relating to living means, social relationship, subsistence and mutual dealings. Hence the migrating community incorporates such phonetic utterances and words in its own medium of speech which may be part of the language used by the people of that territory. In this way, a new mixed language comes into existence which is slightly different from the original language of the migrating community. However, its fundamental shape is not lost. Whatever, difference occurs, is confined chiefly to the outer form of the language. The in-coming community starts using the said newly accomplished language. The original residents of that territory also begin to understand the words of the new language and it does influence the basic shape of the language of old residents as well.

The wheel of the time keeps on revolving. The population further multiplies and the migrants, settled there, find it difficult to carry on. They again decide to migrate to another territory. Many people leave the first migrated place and move on collectively in search of a new territory. After covering some distance, they again come accross a suitable place and stop there in order to settle. Again there is recurrence of the similar position. A new language is accomplished after exchange of words from either language of new migrants and those originally living there. The new language is adopted by both sections of the people for day-today dealings and transacting business in daily course of life. This facilitates mutual exchange of views and carry on their work without least inconvenience or interruption.

Let us now ponder over the characteristics of the new language which is used by the new settlers as well as old inhabitants of the region. There was a language, used by the ancestors of the new settlers at their original first place of living. The second language was accomplished at the first place of halt. As stated above, the said new language, no doubt, slightly differed but was not totally alien to the basic or original language of the migrants. The language accomplished at the place of second stay, had also not completely changed when compared with the original language of the first migrating people or the language developed at the place of their first dwelling. Ofcourse, it differed considerably from the language used at the original place of living and slightly from the language accomplished at the place of first residence. The fact remains that while dwelling at new places, people do incorporate new phonetics and words in their original language but they can not relinquish their old language altogether. Hence the original language does not lose conformity altogether with the subsequent languages, accomplished at new dwelling places.

Let us divert our attention again to the original place of living, wherefrom the first batch had migrated. Possibly, after sometime, another batch of migrants might have left in the opposite direction. People from the second batch might have left again after the first stay in search of another suitable place. In this way, new mixed languages might have come into existence at places, wherever, they took shelter and made their new dwellings.

On penetrating deep into the subject, it is found that two series of languages were accomplished by each batch of migrants who left from their original centre of living. The dwelling places of both the batches of migrants were different, the environments were different, people were different and the languages varied from each other at those places where migrants had settled, and as a result of mutual association, new languages had cropped up. Accordingly, it is quite natural that there was consistent relation between the languages which had evolved and been accomplished at new dwelling places, situated in opposite directions, although the external forms of the languages differed from each other. Nevertheless, newly accomplished languages at places in opposite direction, could not have absolute uniformity. The original place of all migrants, being one, there was likelihood of uniformity in phonetics, composition and morphological construction of words, and in syntax which thoughtless evident in external forms of languages, accomplished at two different places, yet there was consistency in their internal spirit.

At one time, the original language being one, became source of origin and accomplishment of new languages in two opposite directions. They further expanded in many branches and sub-branches at places here and there, far and wide. All such languages collectively, formed one linguistic family or group. It takes not only hundreds but thousands of years in further expansion of such linguistic groups. It is really fantastic that while undertaking critical evalution of a particular linguistic group, from historical viewpoint, we come across many unfolded layers of human civilization and culture, having evolved in between this long period of hundreds and thousands of years. The users of a language are human-beings. More the people are mentally enlightened and conscious, their awareness attains greater heights which finds its expression through human speech. Thus a language obtains a refined and well-accomplished shape after passing through many evolutionary phases which is a substantial proof of human perseverance, strong will and advancing steps towards progress by mankind. A deep and profound study of linguistic groups, as stated above, might disclose several unique feats and bring to light-many excellent aspects of human culture and civilization, contemplations over philosophy, social progress and literary achievements.

Main factors in Support of Affinity between Different Languages, Belonging to the Same Group

Vocabulary (words and their meanings); methods for morphological construction of words, grammatical inflections and phonetics are the main ingredent for consistent relationship and uniformity between languages, belonging to the same group. There is a long history of subsequent origin, growth and development of languages, pertaining to the same group. After crossing many lands, the migrants halted and settled at suitable places and after lapse of hundreds of years, they were able to accomplish a new language. By then, the phonetic sounds of words, composing that language, considerably change. Thereafter, it may be too difficult to believe that such and such languages belonged to the same group along with the said newly accomplished language. However, keeping in view other factors, the inherent similarities could be easily found inspite of apparent dissimilarities in phonetic utterances.

In the vocabularies of various languages, belonging to the same group, a lot of dissimilarities appear, because of variations in time, space and human-beings. For instance, let us take French and Hindi. Although, both languages belong to the same linguistic group, yet the words of both languages considerably differ and no apparent similarities are found in them. On the contrary, if the people, using the languages, pertaining to different groups, are living close to each other, they will obviously, exchange the words and the words of two languages will get mixed up. In such circumstances, uniformity will be achieved to a certain extent in the vocabularies of both the languages, inspite of the fact that they belonged to different groups. *For example*, we may take up Marathi and Kannaḍa languages which belong to different groups. However, many words can be found resembling with each other in both the languages, simply because their users live in close proximity.

The elements which invariably help in establishing consistency and unifomity in languages, belonging to the same group, are grammatical rules, governing them and the style of composition of words. The languages, belonging to one and the same group, undergo regular process of development and growth which is but natural. During the course of evolution, the languages are bound to undergo variations. However, these changes have very slow and nominal effect upon grammatical construction or arrangement of words.

Indo-European Group

Under morphological classification of linguistics, Pāli and Prākritas belong to Indo-European family while as per classification on geographical grounds, they relate to Euresian territorial group. Before deliberating upon these languages, it will be appropriate to make brief consideration upon Indo-European group.

Amongst all the linguistic groups in the world, maximum investingation and analytical research has been done from philological viewpoint on Indo-European group. Sanskrit is affiliated with this group. While undertaking study of Sanskrit, the European scholars felt greatly inclined to carry on an investigation in the field of linguistic science as well. The scholars now call Indo-European group as Indo-Hitti group. Nevertheless, it is still popularly known as Indo-European group, since it has been so named for a considerably long time. It is treated as most significant amongst all linguistic groups in the world. People conversing in the languages of this group exceed all, which are used in the major part of the world. It is better known for advent, development, growth and exaltation of culture, civilization and literary achievements. The said linguistic group is spread over from Britain and British islands on the west to Northern India on the east. The central territories of Eurāl-Altaic and Bask are not included in it. They do not belong to the said linguisitc group. Infact, no acceptable name has been attributed to this group so far with the result the name of the said group continues changing from time to time.

Various names of Indo-European Linguistic Group : Initially, the said Indo-European linguistic group was known as 'Indo-Germanisch' group, since Indian languages were in use on eastern side and German languages on the west. However, on Western side, the said group was not confined to Germany only but on further west of Germany, the languages of Keltik Branch, an offshoot of Indo-European group were also in use. Consequently, the name of 'Indo-Germanisch' was not favoured by the scholars and it was forsaken. Nevertheless, German scholars still call it as 'Indo-Germanisch' group. According to them, it was the only appropriate name which had been left out to reduce the significance of Germany.

Certain scholars called this linguistic group as 'Aryan-group' as well. They assert that the languages, pertaining to the said group, were used by Aryans. However, after further investigation, it was realised that the word 'Aryans' did not represent all the people using the languages of this group. Later on, the scholars were of the opinion that the word 'Aryans' symbolized the people, residing in India and Iran only. Hence it was considered irrelevant to name the entire linguistic group as 'Aryan group.' The relevance of this name could be for Indo-Iranian branch of languages, which was only an offshoot of Indo-European or Indo-Hitti linguistic group.

Sanskrit has been the prominent language of this group. Accordingly, various scholars, chiefly Indians, believed that Sanskrit alone was the principal language of the said group and it was the basic source of origin of all other languages, belonging to this group. According to them, it was more appropriate to call it 'Sanskrit group'. However, it was not supported by other scholars of the world.

Basis for the Suitability of the Name of Indo-European Linguistic Group : Several names had been proposed from time to time but from philological viewpoint, the name of Indo-European group alone has survived. The langauges, pertaining to the said group, are in use from Europe to India. It was, therefore, named accordingly. The English, French and Dutch languages, forming part of Indo-European group, are in use in several territories of America, Australia and Africa. Therefore, teachnically it may not be correct to say that languages of the said group are in vogue from Europe to India only. Nevertheless, the name of Indo-European linguistic group is alone popular and supported more than any other name.

Implied Meaning of Indo-Hitti Group

The name of Hitti language was revealed in the last decade of 19th century after excavation of Bogāzukoi town of Asia Mines, where certain inscriptions on pillars were traced out. Excavation was again taken up during first decade of 20th century wherein besides the said pillar inscriptions, some additional paintings and manuscripts etc. were also found. On the basis of the said material, the scholars arrived at the conclusion that Hitti langauge had been in use during the period ranging from 2000 to 1500 B.C. The linguists did a lot of research and investigation for determination of its linguistic group. Finally, it was the consensus that Hitti was an ally of Indo-European family. It means that originally two groups of languages came into existence-one pertaining to Indo-European linguistic group and the other Anātoliyan branch of linguistics.

Iranian, Persian, Sanskrit, Prākrita, Pāli, Apbhransha (one of the middle Indo-

Aryan languages) Hindi, Bāngla, Gujarāti and Marāthi etc. belonged to Indo-European linguistic group, while Hitti, Lydian, Lysian, Heroglaphic, Hiṭṭiṭe, Paleik and Luvian languages formed part of Anātoliyan branch of linguistics. Accordingly, the scholars had substitued the word Hitti by revising the name of Indo-European group to Indo-Hitti group.

The philologists believe that the primordial language from which the languages, belonging to the aforesaid two branches, had come into existence, was in use prior to 2400 B.C. However, certain other scholars opine that the ancient Indo-Hitti language was in vogue during the period ranging from 2900 to 2400 B.C. It means that these scholars admit presence of ancient Indo-Hitti language 500 years earlier.

Wiros : A New Concept: The use of languages, pertaining to Indo-Hitti linguistic group or Indo-European linguistic group, having originated from the then primordial language, had covered in extensive territorial parts of the world. A specific name had been conceived for the said ancient language. According to the scholars, the basis for the said assumption were the words 'VIR' in Sanskrit 'UIR; or 'VIR' in Latin; 'FER' in Irish and 'VIR' in German languages. The people inhabiting the said primordial territorial parts who used the language, were accordingly named 'WIROS'.

The sum and substance of the above discussion is that the problem of naming the linguistic group is lying still unsolved. Dr. Bholanath Tiwari has put forward a proposal which may be mentioned here. He suggests that while we call the people, using the primordial language, as WIROS, similarly, we can name the group of the languages having born and come into existence from the said primordial language, as `Wiros Group of Linguistics'. This name is more appealing and consistent than others. However, the name of INDO-EUROPEAN linguistic group has become so popular that no other name gains momentum, howsoever, befitting it may be.

Original Habitat of Aryans: Many world scholars have made profound study and deeply pondered over as to which was the original land where the WIROS language was in use and the people, using it, lived, after undertaking study of climatology, linguistic science, ancient literature, geography archaeology and astrology etc. There is a lot of controversy amongst the scholars over it. Inspiteof their sincere efforts, no unanimous opinion has been formed so far regarding the territory where the WIROS language was in vogue and where people, using it, decidely lived. Undoubtedly, the path for taking up analytical research and investigation is vast and arduous. It needs absolute dedication and long perseverance. Let us believe that the present and ensuing generations of scholars will spare no pains and shall not rest till consensual solution to the problem is found out.

The concept of WIROS is not very old. It was suggested only a short time ago. Prior to that, the people, primordially living, were called Aryans and the said name is still popular.

Primordial Place of Living—India: An Opinion

It is also the belief that WIROS (Aryans) primordially belonged to India. According to this view, Aryans had not migrated to India from elsewhere. On the contrary, it is believed that they might have migrated to foreign lands from India. India is a vast country. A particular territory or region has to be identified where the Aryans lived in ancient days.

They are mostly Indian scholars who believe that Aryans were original inhabitants of India. However, there is yet no consensus regarding identity of the territory where Aryans lived. Sri L.D. Kalla believed that Kashmir or Himalayan territory was the primordial place of their living. According to the renowned intellectual and erudite scholar, Mahamahopādhyaya Dr. Gangānāth Jha, Aryans lived in ब्रह्मर्षि देश (Name of a territory in India). As stated in 'Manusmriti' (The code of laws ascribed to the first Manu): "Kurukṣetra, Matsya (Name of the region lying to the west of Dholpur), Pāncāl (Name of celebrated region which lay between the streams of the Yamuna and Ganges and is, therefore, called Gangetic Doab) and 'Sorsena' (Name of the territory around Mathura) were the constituents of 'Brahmarshi Desha." In accordance with the said interpretation, the adjoining area of Kurukṣetra land in the vicinity of Alwar and Vairāth, etc, territory around Mathura, also called *Brajbhumi* and central land between or in the midst of Panjab, Jammu and Himachal should be considered as constituting 'Bramharshi Desha.'

According to eminent historian, Mr. D.S. Trivedi, Multan region, situate on the coast of or located in the valley of Devika river, was, infact, the *bonafide* territory where Aryans lived. Some scholars, give etymological interpretation of the word 'Multan as 'Mul-Sthan' (original place of living). According to them, being the actual abode of Aryans, the name of the territory came to be known as 'Multān'.

Another pre-eminent scholar of history, Mr. Avināsh Chandra Das, has advocated in his book *Rigvedic India* that Himalayan territory, the fountain—head of river Saraswati or the coastal region of river Saraswati was the primordial place where Aryans lived.

Saraswati and Drashadvati (Name of the river flowing into the Saraswati and forming the eastern boundary of Aryāvarta) rivers belong to vedic era. There is a mention of the said rivers in 'Rigveda' and 'Tāndya Brahman'.[1] They flowed in northern parts of Panjab and Rajasthan. During those days, their coastal areas were most fertile and prosperous.

Regarding existence of the aforesaid rivers up to Northern Rajasthan, it is mentioned in District Gazeteer of Chūru: "We are told that in the ancient times, two Vedic rivers—Saraswati and Drashadwati flowed in the contiguous areas of the district Ganganagar, which testifies to the presence of the Aryans in this part of Rajasthan.

Recent archaeological excavations, carried out in the adjoining district of Ganganagar at Rangmahal, Kālibanga, Badopāl, Nohar etc. indicate that the Indus valley civilization extended up to this area.

There is no trace of both these rivers now. Sir Monier Williams, M.W.A. K.C.I.E., has defined Saraswati river in his Sanskrit-English Dictionary: "A well-known small river (held very sacred by the Hindus); identified with the modern

1. Rigveda, 3/23/4.

Sursooty and formerly marking with Drishadavati river—one of the boundaries of the region called Arya-Desha and its sacred district called Brahmavarta."

In Rigveda 7, 95, 2, this river is represented as flowing into the sea, although later legends make it disappear underground and join the Ganges and Yamuna at Allahabad."

Vaman Shivaram Āpte writes in his dictionary[1] that river Saraswati had disappeared in the sands of Rajasthan desert.

Sir M. Monier Williams defines Drishadavati river: "Name of a river which flows into the Saraswati."[2]

Āpte writes about the said river: "A name of the river which flows into Saraswati and forming the eastern boundary of the Aryavarta."[3]

From the above consideration, it is evident that in ancient India, Aryans lived on the coast of Saraswati river. However, it is not an established fact that the said region alone was the actual place where Aryans primordially lived.

From excavations, carried out at Rang Mahal and Kalibanga etc. in the district of Sri Ganganagar of Rajasthan, and the material obtained therefrom, the archaeological scholars and experts must feel an urge to undertake profound study and investigation of Indus Valley civilization, extended up to the said area or territory. It is quite possible that many new layers may be unfolded and the facts, still unknown, may come to light with regard to ancient culture of Aryans.

Certain scholars in India, amongst whom the name of Dr. Sampurnanand may be quoted, have expressed almost indentical views, consistent with the above opinions, on the basis of Vedas, Puranas and allied scriptures. Although they donot point out any specific territory, yet they advance a strong and forceful argument that since there was no reference, whatsoever, in any of the treatises about their migration to India from elsewhere, why they should not be agreed to be *bonafide* inhabitants of India.

Comments: The founders and supporters of the above opinion are highly erudite scholars, and intellectuals. No doubt, they had made minute study of Indian canonical literature, yet their argument regarding basic abode of Aryans is not in consonance with the views expressed by several renowned scholars of the world who had carried out profound study and investigation in the fields of philology and gathered historical evidence regarding relentless struggle made by human society for its progress and development. It is quite possible that there might have been slight effect of sentimentalism upon their minds while advancing the above argument. Undoubtedly, India had achieved, tremendous progress and taken long strides in the spheres of culture philosophy, literature, arts and architecture in its ancient days. Yet its exaggerated description may hamper true investigation and adversely affect their neutrality in forming a correct opinion. This is the matter for impartial consideration and critical examination.

Let us minutely examine those aspects also which belie and fail to justify the *bonafides* of the above belief. If we look at the vast area where the linguistics pertaining to Indo-European group are in use, it will be found that they had not

1. Āpte : *Sanskrit-Hindi Dictionary*, page 1087.
2. *Sanskrit-English Dictionary*, page 492 by Sir Monier Williams, M.W.A., K.C.I.E.
3. Āpte : *Sanskrit-Hindi Dictionary*, page 471.

spread within the precincts of our country only but they had extended to Europe or close to the corridors of Asia and Europe. In view of the above, should we imagine that the Aryans (WIROS) had migrated and continued their journey towards western countries and that many new languages had been accomplished during their stay or dwelling at different places. However, the said idea, does not appeal to the mind. There ought to be an objective or an incentive for Aryans to travel to such remote places. The lands in India have been extremely fertile. The pupulation was also limited in those days. Subsistence was not a problem then.Thus, inspite of such favourable conditions, people moved to such distant countries in Europe and settled there, does not appeal to the mind. Moreover, there is no mention, whatsoever, in ancient literature of this country regarding undertaking an expedition or going out of India. On the contrary, it is more convincing that a batch of the migrants might have moved from West towards East and during the course of their long journey, they might have halted at certain places and presumably, some of them might have settled at each place of encampment. Finally, the remaining group of migrants might have arrived in North Western territory of India and decided to settle. Later on, some of them might have shifted to other regions of the country.

In India, the linguistics relating to Indo-European, Dravadian and Āgneya groups are in vogue. In Northern India, right from Panjab to Assam and in central India, languages—Panjabi, Hindi, Rajasthani, Maithli Bhojpuri, Banglā, Orriya, Assamese, Marathi etc. all belonging to Indo-European family are in use. In Bengal, Bihar, certain territories of Madhya Pradesh, hilly tracts of Khāsi Jayanti and in Ganjam distirct of Tamilnadu, Munda dialects (spoken by aboriginal of the said regions) such as Kanavari, Kherwari; Kuku, Khadiya, Juang, Sabar and Gadwā etc. are in use which belong to Āgneya group. In South, besides Andhra, Tamilnadu, Kerala and Karnataka etc. as also in Laksạdweep, and Sri Lanka too, languages, pertaining to Dravadian family (Tamil, Telugu, Malyalam, Kannaḍa, Tulu, Kudagu, Toḍā etc.) are in use. Thus, it implies that one language in one particular state and the other in another state, pertaining to Dravidian family, are spoken. *For example,* Telugu in Andhra; Tamil in Tamilnāḍu as also by Tamilians settled in Sri Lanka; Malyalam in Kerala and Kannaḍa in Karnataka are used.

Had Aryans originally lived in India, obviously languages of their own linguistic group, would have been popular throughout the length and breadth of the country. However, it was not the case which, obviously, meant that Dravidians must have already been residing in India who were using the languages, pertaining to their own group, which must have acquired somewhat polished form by then. Thereafter, the Aryans might have arrived in India and various languages, belonging to their own linguistic group, might have gradually expanded and spread to entire Northern India.

After excavations in Mohan Jo-Daro and Harappa, many new disclosures have been made. The period dates back prior to the composition of *Rigveda.* On the basis of material discovered, the scholars have carried out a lot of investigation. They have drawn the inference that. Mohan-Jo-Daro's were the ruins of a well-flourished and rich civilization of the past, prior to the arrival and settlement of Aryans in India. The people attached with the said civilization, had their own acomplished language, culture and a well disciplined life style. From the material found and results arrived, it appears that the culture and civilization, connected with Mohan-Jo-Daro, might have belonged to Dravadians. They might have their own accomplished languages which are now found in the shape of Tamil, Telugu and Kannaḍa etc.

On the basis of results obtained after undertaking critical study of geology, climatology, philology and anthropology, it is believed that the original habitat of Aryans must be considered somewhere outside the existing boundaries of India. Renowned scholor and historian, Lokmānya Bal Gangadhar Tilak also subscribes to the opinion that the original habitat of Aryans was somewhere outside India.

Original Habitat:Outside India : Since it is an important subject, it has been profoundly deliberated upon and it is still being discussed. Here it may be in the fitness of things to refer to the varied opinions of scholars of the world which have their own significance. According to Prof. Maxmuler, an eminent Sanskrit and Vedic scholar. Aryans originally lived near plateau of Pāmir and neighbouring Central Asia; Doctor Ladham, an erudite scholar of Scandenavian languages, suggests Scandenavia; while Mr. Sergi, renowned anothropologist of Italy, believes that Aryans lived primordially in the vicinity of Plateau of Asia Miner; Sri Lokmanya Tilak suggests near North Pole; according to Sir Desai, near Bālkan Lake in Russia; as per Dr. Giles—near Karpetian mountain in Hungry; Mr. Hert considers near the coast of Vishchulā river in Poland; Mr. Nehring believes that Aryans originally lived in South Russia; Mr. Mach and others suggest near coast of Western Bāltik river; Prof. Schrader, a renowned scholar of Yugoslavian languages, considers the habitat near estuary of Volga river in South Russia; while Dr. Brandestein considers South of Eural mountain ranges (South West Russia) as original habitat of Aryans.

Certain scholars have suggested Germany, Lithuvānia, Mesopotamia, Russian Turkistan, Persia, and South East coast of Bāltik sea etc. to be primordial habitats of Aryans. According to an old Indian mythological concept, Tibet was the original habitat of human race. It was the initial abode of mankind. From here, they had spread over the whole universe. According to the said belief, Tibet is a modified form of Sanskrit, word 'Triviṣtap',[1] (Three worlds). The literal meaning of the word 'Triviṣtap' is 'Associated with three worlds.' While Tibet was believed to be the place of origin of the entire human race, it, obviously, followed that it was also the primordial place where Aryans originally lived. Amidst divergent opinions, it is not an easy task to arrive at an authentic or credible inference regarding actual habitat of Aryans.

A Thorough Analytical Investigation:Founding : As soon as we carry out an impartial investigation, we agree at one point atleast. We had commented earlier also that rationalism and emotionalism are antonyms. Emotionalism breeds illusion. Delusion, leads to biased attitude, having a leaning towards a particular trend. It is but natural. The sense of judgment is impaired. There does appear slight partisan attitude of the scholars in determination of original abode of Aryans.

The view of Indian scholars that Aryans were the *bonafide* inhabitants of India was based on their study of Indian literature (in its wider sense). Prof.

1. त्रयानां विष्टपानां समाहार : त्रिविष्टयम्

Schrader declared that Yugoslavian territories where slav languages were spoken, were the actual habitat of Aryans. Prof. Schrader was a distinguished scholar of Slavian languages. His findings were based on his constant study and investigation made on the basis of his own native languages. He quoted extracts from the books of slav languages in support of his findings. Similarly, Dr. Ladham was an authority on Scandenavian languages. He did his best to extablish Scandenavia as primordial abode of Aryans on the basis of his study of Scandenavian literature, relating to the subject. All the aforesaid scholars spared no pains to establish that their own respective country was the original habitat of Aryans. It does give us reflection of slight attachment with their own country.

Miscellaneous aspects relating to propagation and expansion of linguistics, pertaining to Indo-European family in both Eastern and Western countries, various circumstances and situations, consistency and similarity in phonetic sounds, geographical conditions, history of successive growth and development of linguistics etc. have already been elaborately discussed. Ultimately, many philologists expressed their concurrence with the opinion of Mr. Brandestein, so much so that even Dr. Suniti Kumar Chatterji, renowned Indian philologist, also subscribed to the view of Mr. Brandestein. Accordingly, southern region of Eural mountain-range (in South West Russia) was believed to be the primordial abode of Aryans. Although, Dr. Battkrishna Ghosh, an eminent philologist and a few other scholars disagree with several aspects of his opinion, yet majority of the scholars have expressed their concurrence in favour of the opinion of Mr. Brandestein.

Departure from Original Habitat : Let us give serious thought and consider over the matter, after agreeing that Southern territory of Eurāl mountain-range was the original habitat of Aryans or the so called WIROS people. According to Mr. Brandestein, Aryans or WIROS lived as a compact unit undividedly at one and the same place. In the course of time, a batch of Aryans had started towards South-East direction whom we might treat as ancestors of Indo-Iranian people. Nothing could be decidedly said whether they directly reached Iran or made a halt somewhere on their way. In this connection, the views of Dr. Babu Ram Saxena, an eminent linguist of India, are worth analytical discussion. "As per historical evidence, appearance of Aryan race is comparatively much posterior or recent as against other races such as Egyptians, Summerians, Akkadians, Aserians and Chinese etc. It is believed that Primeval Aryans had, first of all, come in contact with contemporary civilized communities of Northern Mesopotāmia in 22rd or 23rd century B.C. Their presence and continuance in Mesopotāmia in or about 20th century B.C. was certain. There is an explicit reference about Aryans found in Bogazkoi stone inscriptions in or about 14th century B.C."[1] In all probability, Aryans might have taken their first shelter in Mesopotāmia.

Split of Aryans in Two Groups: The immediate effect of the first expedition was split of Aryans or WIROS at their original place of living. The Aryans who had left towards South-East direction formed one group, and those remained behind formed the other group. Again, Aryans who were left behind or majority of them might have started in search of new abodes for settling towards West, South-West or any other direction and might have continued their journey. By virtue of travelling

1. *Samanya Bhasha Vigyan*, page 325.

in different directions and settling in various regions, they might have been able to accomplish new languages.

Settling in Iran : Change in their Original Language

The batch of migrants, proceeding towards South-East and subsequently to East direction, arrived and settled in Iran. Thereafter, the change in the shape of their original language began to take place. Iran was the modified form of the word 'आर्यणाम' which appeals to the mind. Probably, 'आर्यणाम' became the popular name of that country after settling of Aryans in that territorial part.

While dealing with the subject of linguistic groups or families, it was stated that the migrants borrow many words from the language of the people, originally inhabiting the said place and thus a mixed language is accomplished. This is what happened in Iran also.

Indo-Iranian Branch of Indo-European Linguistic Family : The new language, that was accomplished after Aryans settled in Iran, formed part of Aryan branch or Indo-Iranian branch of linguistics relating to Indo-European family. It was considered a significant offshoot of Indo-European linguistic group. The great scriptural work 'Rigveda'* was accomplished in this very language which was treated as the oldest composition in the universal literature. Almost all leading intellectuals in the world accept its superiority and excellence from linguistic viewpoint beside its ancientness. In addition to this, morphological construction of words and sentences and the literary compositions obtained in the languages, forming part of Indo-Iranian linguistic branch, were really excellent. The process started of undertaking profound and multifarious study as also analytical investigation made by Western scholars in the field of linguistic science was primarily based on the languages pertaining to Aryan Branch. During the course of minute research and investigation in respect of the languages, belonging to the Aryan linguistic branch, the attention of Western scholars was attracted to the phonetical, morphological and syntactical similarities, miraculously found in various languages of the world. This fact finds support from what has been stated above while familiarizing with the brief sketch of Sir William Jones, Hon'ble Chief Justice of High Court at Calcutta, then the highest Court in India.

After arrival and settling of Aryans in Iran, a new language had been accomplished which enabled the settlers to converse with the original inhabitants of Iran on one hand and simultaneously made it convenient for the old residents to deal with the new settlers.

As soon as a language acquires its standard shape, the scholars start writing in that language. It is believed that large number of books had been written in Iranian language as well but the said accomplished literature is no longer available to the scholars of the world. The Greek emperor, Alexander had invaded. Iran in 323 B.C. Besides complete destruction, plundering and looting the properties, the libraries in Iran were also reduced to ashes. In the year 651 A.D., Arabs had invaded Iran. While the invaders had totally destroyed the country and looted its wealth, they also did not spare the libraries which were set on fire.

* It will be discussed in the next chapter as per demand of the context.

During the course of the said two invasions, the literary treasure accomplished by genius scholars and intellectuals, had altogether been destroyed after having fallen prey human frenzy and insanity. With a feeling of distress, one might ask why the invaders reduced the libraries of invaded country to ashes? It was not only the solitary loss of an invaded country but the entire world which is deprived of the benefits of most significant literary and cultural accomplishments. However, one could not help, when the people turn lunatic there is no end to destruction and arson. Whatever, little could be saved was merely a religious scripture 'Avesta' belonging to the Parsi Community and stones got inscribed by kings of 'Hakhmāni' dynasty in the year 600 B.C.

The period of composition of Avesta is believed to be in the 7th century B.C. This is the oldest literary treatise, now available. The language of 'Rigveda' resembles with that of 'Avesta'. Like 'Rigveda' there are religious prayers in 'Avesta' too. The language in which 'Avesta' had been written, is known as Avesti. Avesti was the official language of 'Vactriya' kingdom also for sometime. Hence it was also named as 'Old vactriyan language.'

Avesti and Ancient Persian: There were two branches of linguistics in Iran—Avesti and old Persian. There was not much gap in between the period of growth and active use of both the languages. It is possible that old Persian language was posterior to 'Avesti'. The Western territory of Iran was called Persia. The old Persian language was in use there. It is believed that since the language was used in old Persia, it might have come to be known as Persian. No literature was available now, written in old Persian language. Certain pillar inscriptions have been found which were got inscribed by the rulers of 'Aikmenian dynasty' probably sometime in 5th or 6th century B.C.

Origin of Pahalvi:When 'Avesti' was no longer in use or had ceased to be popular, it was replaced by mediaeval Persian or Pahalvi. The mediaeval Persian or Pahalvi had originated from old Persian language. It could otherwise be held that Pahalvi was a developed form of old Persian language itself.

As a consequence of 'Avesti' language becoming obsolete, 'Avesta' was no longer easy to be understood or followed. A commentary had been written on it in Pahalvi language, which is known as 'Zendenda'. The literal meaning of 'Zend' itself is commentary. The original book 'Avesta' and its commentary 'Zend' were combinedly known as 'Zendāvestā'. The period, when commentary had been written in Pahalvi language, could not be described exactly. However, this much could be said decisively that by the end of third century B.C., Pahalvi language was already in use. Some coins, relating to 3rd century B.C. had been found on which there were inscriptions in Pahalvi language. The coins manifested oldest form of Pahalvi language.

No literature is available, relating to the intervening period in between the time of ancient persian and mediaeval Persian languages that is to say before transformation of old Persian into Pahalvi language. The literary compositions, in Pahalvi Script, were accomplished in 3rd Century B.C. prior to it, no literature in Pahalvi script was available.

Two Shapes of Pahalvi Language: 'Huzwaresh', 'Pajand': Two forms of Pahalvi language are available—one in which there is exceeding use of Arabian words (Pertaining to Semetic family) because of contemporary influence of Islam and the script of the said form of Pahalvi is also Arabian. The said form of Pahalvi language is called 'Huzwāresh.' The other form of Pahalvi is free from the influence of Arabian words relating to Semetic branch of linguistics. It is named as 'Pājand' or Pārsi language. It is the mother-tongue of Pārsi Community, residing in India. Primarily, Parsis live at Bombay. They have been living in close proximity with Gujarāti community and there is an obvious influence of Pājand over Gujarāti language.

Modern Persian : An Improvement or Deformation

The third transformation (new form) is modern Persian which is now in use in Iran. The famous epic *Shāhnāma* was written by great poet, 'Firdausi' (Dating 940 to 1020 A.D.) in Persian language, prevalent now. In the said epic, Arabic words have been scantly used. However, subsequently, there was continuous influx of Arabic words in the modern Persian language. For sometime now, the literary circles in Iran are under influence of a new wave of nationalism. The Arabic words, used in Persian literature, are being picked out one by one and alternatively Iranian words, pertaining to Aryan linguistic branch, are being substituted.

Feelings of nationalism are alright, but to be swept away by them is not good. The traditional shape of the literature is impaired. Whatever, be the circumstances, the Arabian words, belonging to Semetic branch of linguistics having been once used and incorporated in Persian literature, had become its indispensable part. Continuance of such words in a language, throws light on rise and fall of linguistics in the world on one hand, and racial onslaughts on the other. In this way, was it not an attempt of destroying the very utility and significance of literary accomplishments by ruining their original beauty and elegance?

Pashto or Afghanian Language: As a result of regional or territorial diversities, several dialects of a language are composed for use which gradually come into existence. They are again reshaped subsequently. There are many dialects of the modern Persian language also. There are divergent opinions of the scholars as to which of them have originated from 'Avesti' language and which are the products of Persian language. The discussion on this topic is not required here. Pashto holds a significant place amongst all the aforesaid dialects. It is also known as Afghani or Afghanistani dialect. A few scholars believe that the source of origin of Pashto is from 'Avesti' language, but it is not universally recognized. Pashto is official language of Afghanistan. No literature had been composed in any of the dialects of Iraninan language. If there was any, it was almost insignificant. Only Pashto is an exception. The literary compositions had started from 16th century in Pashto. There is considerable influence of Indian phonetic sounds and syntactical constructions over Pashto. In a way, it may be treated as an intermediary dialect in between Iranian and Indian languages.

Dard-linguistic branch of Indo-Iranian Group of Linguistics

There is another important linguistic branch of Iranian group, which is prevalent between Plateau of Pamir and North-West Punjab, which are now the constituents of Pakistan. They are now popularly known as languages of Dard branch. The languages of the said branch may also be considered as intermediary dialects between Iranian and Indian languages. There is only slight variation in Pashto and dialects of Dard branch in as much as Pashto has a tilt towards Iranian Group of languages while those of Darad branch have a tilt towards Indian languages.

In Sanskrit, the word 'Darad' (दरद) literally means a mountain or a precipice. Since languages of Dard Branch were in vogue at hilly places, may be—they had been named accordingly. The words pertaining to Darad languages are also found in Indian languages—such as Panjabi, Sindhi and Marathi etc. It may not be out of place to mention here that the users of languages, belonging to Darad branch, might have lived in the states of Punjab, Sindh and Maharashtra etc. Lest how the words of Darad languages, spoken hundreds of miles away, could have mixed with Indian languages? How various languages came in contact with or influenced by other languages, was an indication of objective awareness in mankind and creative talents, found in them, which spoke volumes.

It was believed in ancient India that languages of 'Darad' branch formed part of Indian linguistic group. They were categorised as part of 'Paishāchi' Prākrita (Lowest form of a Prākrita dialect). However, as a result of further study and critical evaluation, this opinion could not sustain for long and has been totally rejected. Now the linguists are almost unanimous that languages of Darad branch belonged to Iranian linguistic family.

Kashmiri Dialect: Many scholars considered 'Kashmiri dialect' as an offshoot of 'Darad branch', in view of morphological and syntactical construction of words and similarities in phonetic voice etc. However, the most accredited philologist of India, Dr. P.D. Gune and several others opined that it belonged to Indian linguistic family. They have also been stating that Kashmiri dialect had evolved from 'Paishāchi Apbhransh' (one of the lowest forms of Prākrita languages).

Reason for Influence of Sanskrit over Kashmiri Dialect

There is an obvious influence of Sanskrit over Kashmiri dialect. The primary reason being that in ancient India, Kashmir had been an undisputed centre of great learning and scholarship in Sanskrit language. Whereas, the studious scholars used to live at Kāshi in pursuit of higher learning in Sanskrit, they also used to go to Kashmir for further enrichment of their knowledge. Sanskrit Institute of Kashmir had earned great repute and celebrity in those days. Many eminent literateurs, happened to live there who wrote master-piece and authoritative books, forming part of Sanskrit literature on almost all topics. They enriched Sanskrit literature with most outstanding works. Not one or two but hundreds of erudite scholars were there, amongst whom the names of Vaman (enjoying the support of king Jayapiḍa, ruler, during the period 779 to 819 A.D.), author of *Kāvyālankār Sūtra*, *Udbhat* (dependent on king Jayapida), author of *Bhāmhālankār*, and *Alankar-Śar-Sangrāh*; Ratnākar (enjoying the support of kings Jayāditya and Avanti Verma dating 850 A.D.), author of classical poetry, 'Harvijaya;' Bhatt Shivaswāmi (enjoying patronage of king Avanti Verma), author of *Kappnābhudaya*, Abhinava Gupta (near about 1000 A.D.), author of *Dhavanyālokalochan*, *Pratyabhigyavād* and *Abhinava Bharati* and several other analytical books; Kṣemendra, disciple of Sri Abhinava

Gupta, (Middle of 11th century A.D.), author of '*Bhārat Manjari*', *Brahatkatha Manjari*, *Dashāvtar-Charit*, *Padyakadambari*, and *Auchitya-Vichar-Charcha* etc; Somdeva (1063 to 1081 A.D.), author of '*Kathāsarit Sāgar*'; *Kalhaṇa* (1150 A.D.), author of renowned historical book *Raj Tarangini*; Jalhaṇa (1150 A.D.), author of poetic book *Sompāl Vilāsa*; and Mainkh (under patronage of King Jaya Singh, who ruled from 1129 to 1150 A.D.), author of famous poetry *Srikanth Charit* are worth mention.

Thousands of Sanskrit books on miscellaneous subjects were written in Kāshmir. There had been a congenial atmosphere in the entire state for accomplishing writings in Sanskrit. Although, the propagation and use of Sanskrit was mainly confined to highly educated gentry, yet it was bound to have its impact on the speech of common people as well. Kashmiri, being the dialect of the region, having pre-dominance of Sanskrit on it, some of the Indian scholars were naturally interested in declaring Kashmiri dialect as part of Indian branch of linguistics. However, so far its shape, system of composition and phonetic settings are concerned, its alliance with Darad branch of linguistics appears to be more consistent.

Literary Accomplishments in Kashmiri Dialect

It is believed that the process of literary compositions in Kashmiri dialect had started in 14th Century A.D. Prior to it, Kashmiri was only medium of conversation. The medium for literary accomplishments was Sanskrit language. Sanskrit, enjoying royal recognition, was used in day today official work. In 14th century, there was a renowned poetess, Lalla who wrote her poetic compositions (poems) in Kashmiri dialect. Sir George Abraham Griyason*, author of *Linguistic Survey of India*,

---

*. Sir George Abraham Griyason was an Administrative officer in Bihar. He developed keen interest to undertake study and critical examination of Indian languages. He spared no pains to acquire knowledge of various Indian languages and dialects from wherever it was possible. His vast and comprehensive knowledge, relating to linguistics, could be established by the very fact that he had acquired full knowledge of hundreds of languages and dialects. First of all, he started reading the languages and dialects of Bihar. He wrote seven grammatical books on languages, papular in Bihar which were published during the period 1883 to 1887. In the field of linguistic survey, he had done a tremendous job. His extraordinary achievement in this sphere was his masterpiece book, titled *Linguistic Survey of India*, which he had started writing in 1894 and after putting in straneous efforts, continuously for 33 years, he was able to finish the book in 1927. The said illustrious book had been published in 20 volumes. The grammatical rules with illustrations, wherever necessary, relating to almost all Indian languages and dialects are contained in it. He has enumerated the number of Indian languages and dialects as 179 and 544 respectively, which relate to the Aryan, Dravadian, Agneya and Tibetan-Burmese (mono-syllabic) linguistic families. It is believed that such authentic and full-fledged survey in the field of linguistics has not been carried out in any other country of the world.

At the commencement of his book, Mr. Griyason has given an elaborate introduction in which he has produced a historical account of Aryan languages in India. Besides the said illustrious work, he continued his analytical research in the field of linguistics. In 1906, an exploratory book on 'Pishach' (one of the lowest Prākrita dialects, generally used in plays) and in 1911, another book in two volumes, relating to Kashmiri dialect, were published. The said works are treated as most authentic and credible. He also composed a dictionary of Kashmiri dialect which was published in 4 volumes in the year 1924. A foreigner, coming from thousands of miles away from India, to serve as an administrative officer, undertook such commendable work and carried out research and investigation on linguistics in India on such an extensive scale, was really praise-worthy and highly inspiring for other scholars.

managed to get the poetic compositions of Lalla, poetess, published in London. Literature in Kashmiri language continued to flourish. Consequently, Kāshmiri literature is now quite rich and flourished. There are several sub-languages or dialects of Kashmiri language. Some dialects are spoken in adjacent lands of Punjab which have obtained new shapes because of combination of Punjabi words. They have not been able to sustain their old forms and obtained peculiarly new forms.

Use of Urdu in Kāshmir: Primarily Urdu is used now in Kashmir. Original Kashmiri language appears to have been almost neglected. After Kashmir was occupied and merged in Moghul dynasty by emperor Akbar, use of Urdu language might have started. Prior to it, there was exclusive use of Kashmiri language. Subsequently, Urdu received greater recognition and the use of original form of Kashmiri language became too meagre. Now the people in Kashmir are again feeling concern for their traditional language and restoring its use. The fact that Kashmiri language belongs to Darad branch of Iranian linguistic group, yet there is an apparent influence of Sanskrit over it, is quite clear from the above discussion.

It has been the persistent effort of mankind to lead a comfortable life with happiness enjoying all amenities. This very aspiration has provided great impetus and stimulus for undertaking daring expeditions, arduous adventures and acts of heroism. The Aryans or WIROS originally lived in southern territory of Eural mountain Range i.e. in South Western part of Russia. There are large plains in that region. Agriculture had not prospered till then. According to Brandestein, Aryans or WIROS lived on hills, having dried cliffs, totally unsuitable for agricultural production. There was no greenery or vegetation there. There were only clusters of plants (kinds of Shrubs) namely 'Gulma' and 'Bānjh'. Rapid growth of population and limited resources for subsistence, might have prompted Aryans to migrate. With full of spirit and courage, they might have left their original habitat. They might have come across horses in Southern plains of Eural mountain-range. They might have trained them and used them for carrying loads. Complimentary or laudatory references have been made for horses in Rigveda. Cows have not been given so much significance as the horses in the hymns of 'Rigveda'. Presumably Aryans might have come accross cows at a later stage and realized their importance. As per learned scholars, bullocks, camels and donkeys were primarily used those days in Mesopotamia. The said animals could not, however, match with horses in agility and speed. Consequently, Aryans kept on advancing successfully with their horses without any challenges or interruptions. Another factor that contributed to their success was their organizational solidarity.

Regarding social set up and routine of life of Aryans, Dr. Babu Ram Saxena writes: "It is the general opinion of scholars that cattle-breeding and hunting were the main sources of livelihood of Aryans (WIROS). They picked up the work of cultivation after coming in contact with the erstwhile local people, inhabiting Southern territories of India. It was then, they came to appreciate the significance of cows and bullocks. Fruit-bearing trees were also absent in their original abodes in Russia. They learnt increasing use of fruits from the said communities, living in South. The social system of Aryans was patriarchal. Polygamy was not in practice. After communion of several families, one lineage was accomplished. Their intelligence was relatively of high order. Their organisation and unity was strong.

There was self-restraint and sobriety in reciprocal behaviour amongst males and females. Due respect was shown to the ladies. The girls were married with the approval of the parents and elder brothers. In the religious sphere, they had faith in divine powers of unperceived celetial bodies, various images of divine powers had been conceived. Far away from this terrestrial globe, paradise was the abode of celetial bodies, having supernatural powers. Heaven, father, sun, earth and cows were a few of the deities whom they worshipped, unlike too many deities worshipped by Egyptians and Sumeri communities. Obviously, Aryans, who were well-organized, sober, temperate, possessing healthy bodies, minds and souls, full of heroism, wherever they reached, they established their excellence, and supermacy of their language over other communites.[1]

Aryans, having physical, mental and moral uprightness, arrived in India via Iran. Regarding their arrival and stay in Iran, we have already discussed above. In India, first of all, they arrived and dwelt in Punjab (land of five rivers) and the territory surrounded by Saraswati and Drashadwati (Name of a river flowing into the Saraswati river) rivers.

Had Aryans Arrived in India in One Single Lot?

There is one more point to be considered here. Divergent opinions have been expressed by the scholars regarding arrival of Aryans in India. Some believe that they had arrived in India in one single lot and later kept on settling in other parts of the country. However, others opine that they arrived in India in two or more batches and gradually settled in various parts of the country. The first and foremost group of Aryans had settled in Western territories and they continued moving ahead in central and eastern territorial parts of the country. Therefore, the subsequent batches might have settled in remote eastern areas comprising Magadh, Videh (lying to the north east of Magadh), Anga (This town stood on the Ganges about 24 miles west of a rocky island, and is considered to be situated very near the modern Bhagalpur) and Gauda (Near Northern Bengal) and other territories.

There is another mute point whether Aryans, who arrived in India, belonged to one particular race or different races?

While dealing with the topic of Aryans' arrival in India, Dr. Suniti Kumar Chatterji writes: "It does not appear that Aryans, who landed in India, belonged to one and the same race so far as their physical constitution was concerned. Presumably, there were two sects of Aryans, having varying constitutions. One of them were `Nordic' who had migrated from Northern lands. They possessed tall physiques, having white or fair-complexions, golden hair, blue eyes, straight noses and tall heads. Most of the scholars believed that they were the genuine Indo-Europeans or Aryans. The other category of migrants belonged to Alpine mountjans or central Europe. They were comparatively smaller in size, having reddish brown, yellowish or dark hair with flat heads. There are also diverse opinions whether the migrants, belonging to Alpine mountain range, actually spoke Aryan languages or not. However, in certain parts of India, mainly in Gujarat and Bengal, the Aryans

1. *Samanya Bhasha Vigyan*, page 327.

belonged to the said category who had migrated from Alpine range of mountains. It appears that Nordics or migrants from Northern regions, possessing tall physiques and large heads, had settled in Punjab, Rajasthan and Northern parts of India. Sub-Communities, speaking Aryan languages, had arrived in India in different batches on various occasions. Slight variations had occurred in the mediums of spech of the said sub-groups, communities or lineages of Aryans. However, besides the various mediums of conversation as stated above, a specific language had been accomplished for undertaking poetic or literary compositions, an illustration of which may be found in `Rigveda'. Aryans had their first dwelling in northern parts of Punjab. Thereafter, the Aryans had spread to the Eastern territories. From Sindh and Punjab, they proceeded to Gangetic and Yamuna plains via territory lying between two rivers, Saraswati and Drashadwati: With the spread of Aryan languages, the use of Dravadian and Astrick languages (Belonging to Agneya linguistic group) was gradually getting minimised."[1]

A few other scholars have expressed similar views regarding arrival of Aryans in India *i.e.* they arrived in this country in several batches on different occasions. As per George Griyanson, Aryans arrived in India at least on two occasions.

Aryans had their own Common Language When Arrived in India

According to Dr. Chatterjee, Aryans of two lineages—One categorised as 'Nordics' had migrated from Northern territories and the other category of migrants, belonging to Alpine mountain range or central Europe, had arrived in India. It might be correct but there is definitely a hitch in accepting the said version. People, belonging to two distinct races, where mediums of speech also must have been alien to each other, arrived in this country. How far it was possible that there was only slight variation in the languages of the two groups of migrants who originally belonged to two different lands, at a long distance from each other, and with two separate linages. This is the point to be minutely considered. However, there could be a probability. The aforesaid two branches of Aryans might have lived together for a reasonable span of time, in Southern territory of Eural mountain-range *i.e* in South-West zone of Russia, treated by us as original habitat of Aryans and they might have accomplished a mixed language. Nevertheless, out of the aforesaid two branches of Aryans, which of them originally lived in the territory, referred to above, and which branch of the people, subsequently joined them, is practically unknown. History does not suggest anything in this regard.

It is an analytical description of the language, used and spoken by Aryans. It will be more consistent to believe that Aryans who arrived in India from foreign lands, had basically one language. There could be slight variation in the dialects or mediums of speech of the people, belonging to different batches or families but they were insignificant.

Rhythmic Sound of Vedic Hymns : First of all, Aryans arrived in Punjab where natural conditions were attractive and captivating. Lands were fertile. Rivers full of clean and pure water flowed. Aryans must have picked up farming and

---

1. *Bharat Ki Bhāshāyen Aur Bhasha Sambandhi Samasyaen* pages 33-35.

cultivation after coming in contact with various communities, inhabiting different regions in between the departure from Southern plains of Eural mountains, original abode of Aryans, and their final arrival in India. They were hard-working and perseverants. They might have engaged themselves in the work of cultivation and the agricultural lands must have bloomed with abounding crops. Such lovely and charming atmosphere must have fascinated Aryans which is found reflected in the hymns of Rigveda. The seers and scholars of Rigveda have established godliness in sun, moon, earth, air, fire, heaven, dawn in the morning and are overwhelmed with joy by singing their praise and eulogy. भूमिः माता पुत्रोऽहं पृथिव्याः (Earth is my mother and I am her son) is an expression of their internal happiness and joy.

Linguistic Similarities Found in Rigveda and Avesta

The language in which Rigveda had been accomplished, was a refined and literary form of Aryans speech. There is a lot of similarity in Rigveda and Avesta from linguistic viewpoint which will be self evident from the comparative forms of the words of both the languages, reproduced below:

Vedic Sanskrit	*Avesta (Iranian Group)*
Anu (A prefix to verb)	Anu
Asi (A sword)	Ahi
Asthi (Bone)	Asti
Ritum (Season)	Ratūm
Kafaṁ (Mucus)	Kafaṁ
Krituh (A sacrifice)	Khraṭush
Jānuh (Knee)	Zānu
Dadāmi (I give)	Dadāmi
Dirghaṁ (Long in time or space)	Daregam
Nabhas (Sky, atmosphere)	Nabahā
Bharati (Fills)	Bariti
Bhūmi (A territory)	Būmi
Yaja (To sacrifice)	Yaza
Vasiṣta (Name of a celebrated sage)	Bahishta
Sakhā (A friend)	Hakha
Saptāha (A week)	Haftā
Anya (Another)	Anya
Asur (A demon)	Ahur
Āpah (One of the demi Gods called Vasu)	Apa
Ojas (Bodiliy strength)	Ojaḥ
Kṣatrāt (A warrior)	Khshthrāt
Gāthā (A narrative or tale)	Gāthā
Janghā (Thigh)	Jangā
Dahati (Burns)	Dazhaiti
Dhāryat (Sustains)	Dāryat
Putra (Son)	Puthra
Bhavati (happens)	Bavaiti
Bhrātā (Brother)	Brātā

Rinakti (Expulsion) Harinakhti
Vishwa (Universe) Vispa
Sapta (Seven) Hapta
Sindhu (Ocean) Hindu

Extract from 'Yasna' 108, pertaining to Avestā, and their adaptation in Sanskrit, done by Dr. Batkrishna Ghosh to establish the resemblance of Sanskrit with Avesti language, are produced below:

Avestā:— Yo yatha puthraṁ taurunaṁ haobhaṁ bandaen tā mashyo|

Sanskrit:—Yo yathā putraṁ taruṇaṁsomaṁ vandeta martayaḥ

(Just as the sons, on growing youths like a moon, pay obeisance to thier dead ancestors)

Aveasta:— Frā Ārvyā tanubaryā Haomo bīsite baen Shrijāi.

Sanskrit:— Pra Ābhyāstanubhyah Somo Vishte bheshjāya.

(For those, who are accustomed to take extract of Soma juice, it is like a medicine for them).

On having a minute examination it will be clearly established that there were good deal of similarities in both the aforesaid languages from phonetic, etymological, morphological and syntactical viewpoints.

Original Phonetic Sounds of Indo-European Linguistics

There are frequent changes in the shape of a language. Original phonetics of Indo-European languages had undergone considerable changes by the time of accomplishment of Vedic Sanskrit. In order to elucidate the point, a comparative study of the phonetics of both the languages is essential. The original phonetics of Indo-European languages are supposed to be as follows:

कवर्ग (Four soft palatal consonants)

(a) क्, ख्, ग्, घ्

(b) क्, ख्, ग्, घ्

(c) क्व्, ख्व्, ग्व्, घ्व्

Four soft palatal consonants in languages of Indo-European family were in three shapes. Certain scholars consider that the first shape of कवर्ग (Palatal consonants) is commonly found, while some other scholars opine that they are soft palatal consonants and only partial help of the palatal is taken in their pronouncement. The four consonants were, accordingly pronounced as क्य, ख्य, ग्य, and घ्य, Dr. Chatterji, however, does not agree with it. He does not consider them as palatal consonants. He treats them as advanced velar consonants. The second shape of palatal consonants resembles with Arabic *ka*-quadrivalent consonants. The European scholars consider them as velar consonants. However, according to Dr. Chatterjee they are back vellar or Uvular consonants. In pronouncing 3rd form of कवर्ग (*Ka*-quadrivalent consonants), partial help of lips was also taken. In utterance of the 3rd form of कवर्ग consonants, the palatal sound was quite audible, while that of व् was extremely minute, almost inaudible.

Dr. Chatterjee and certain other linguists also include the fifth letter ङ in all the three forms of कवर्ग ('Ka'-pentad consonants). However, many of the other scholars believe that the consonant न itself is adopted as the fifth consonant with the aforesaid three shapes of कवर्ग consonants.

तवर्ग (Four dental consonants) : त्, थ्, द्, ध्,

पवर्ग (Four consonants of the labial class) *i.e.* प्, फ्, ब्, भ्,

ऊष्म (The ūshman consonant स्).

If the ūshman consonant स् appears between two vowels, it will be pronounced as ज़ with voiced sound.

Intermediate consonants (The Semi-Vowels— य्, र्, ल्, व्, न्, म्)

Intermediate Vowels— इ, ऋ, लृ, उ, नृ, मृ,

Vowels (short) अ, ऍ, ओ,

Vowels (long) आ, ए, औ,

Vowels (Mixed short Vowels)— अइ अऋ, अलृ, अऊ, अनृ, अमृ,

ऍइ, ऍऋ, ऍलृ, ऍउ, एनु, एमु,

ऑइ, ऑऋ, ऑलृ, ऑउ, ऑनृ, ऑमृ

Vowels (mixed long Vowels)— आइ, आऋ, आलृ, आउ, आनृ, आमृ

ऐइ, ऐऋ, ऐलृ, ऐउ, ऐनृ, ऐमृ

औइ, औऋ, औलृ, औउ, औनृ, औमृ

In consonants, the two nasal phonetic sounds were म् and न्. The scholars are of the opinion that amongst the palatal consonants in 3 shapes, as shown above, the pronunciation of letter न् appearing before कवर्ग consonants was made as ञ while in other two forms the letter न appearing before कवर्ग consonants was pronounced as ङ. However, when the letters न् and म् appeared at specific place in the words, then they were pronounced as नृ and मृ respectively.

Regarding intermediate consonants and intermediate vowels, as stated above, it is added that the consonants य, र, ल, and व were transformed into vowels इ, उ, ऋ, and लृ, as per their placement in words. Then they were called as intermediate vowels. As a matter of fact, इ, उ, ऋ, and लृ were not basically treated as intermediate vowels in the primitive form of language but they had turned as vowels as per their placement in words.

There are divergent opinions amongst philologists regarding the phonetic sound of the letter ह. Certain scholars believe that this phonetic sound was not found in Indo-European languages, while others are of the opinion that the letter ह did appear as found in 'Hittaita' or 'Hitti' group of languages. Although, letter ह is pronounced with elevated sound, while others opine that it is both, voiced as well as unvoiced consonant.

Phonetic Sounds of Vedic Sanskrit : Their Characteristics

The phonemes of Vedic Sanskrit are as follows:

Basic vowels— अ, आ, इ, ई, उ, ऊ, ऋ, लृ, ए, ओ,

Joint vowels— ऐ (अ+इ) औ (अ+उ)

Guttural letters— क, ख, ग, घ, ङ,

Palatal letters— च, छ, ज, झ, ञ,

Cerebral or lingual letters— ट, ठ, ड, ढ, ण, ळ, and ळ्ह

Dental letters— त, थ, द, ध, न,

Labial letters— प, फ, ब, भ, म,

Labio dental letter— व,

Intermediate letters य, र, ल, व, (a term applied to the semi-vowels) as standing between vowels and consonants and being formed by slight contact of the vocal organs.

Pure nasal sound which is marked by a dot above the line and always following the preceding vowel. ं

Ushman or letters' sound clashing with vocal chord— श, ष, स, and ह

Uttered from the root of the tongue. ᳵ

A term applied to the visarga before क and ख and also to ऋ, लृ, and the guttural class of consonants. ᳵ

The aspirate Visarga before the letters प, 'फ'. ᳶ

On comparing the phonetic sounds of Vedic Sanskrit with those of Indo-European linguistics it appears that considerable changes had taken place from the time of original shapes of Indo-European languages till accomplishment of Vedic Sanskrit. A few illustrations of the said changes are given below:

* Whereas there were 3 categories of कवर्ग (soft palatal consonants) in Indo-European languages, they were reduced to only ine in Vedic Sanskrit.
* Consonants चवर्ग (Second pentad of palatal consonants) and टवर्ग (Third pentad of Cerebral consonants), which were absent in Indo-European languages, had appeared in Vedic Sanskrit.
* The Ūshman phonetic sound was only स in linguistics of Indo-European family which got expanded to श, ष, स and ह in Vedic Sanskrit.

In the table of phonetic sounds of Vedic Sanskrit, given above, the letters ए and ओ have been shown as basic vowels while letters ऐ and औ have been shown as joint vowels. There is a point to be noted here. In Sanskrit grammar, the letters ए, ऐ, ओ, and औ all the four letters, were treated as joint vowels and used as long vowels. They were pronounced as ए= अइ; ओ=अउ; ऐ=आइ and औ=आउ. However, the learned scholars, who are well-versed in the Vedas, donot agree with it. According to them, both ए and ओ were basic vowels and, infact, they were used as both short and long vowels. The joint vowels were ऐ and औ only which were pronounced as अइ and अउ respectively.

Cerebral Consonants : Characteristic

Vedic Sanskrit has a speciality. A class of cerebral or lingual consonants (uttered from inside head or cerebrum appear in Sanskrit language but the said consonants (Hindi) are not found in any of the languages, pertaining to Indo-European family.

How the said cerebral consonants found place in Vedic Sanskrit, a few scholars believe that these phonetic sounds (letters) were there in the languages, belonging to Dravidian family. Prior to arrival and settlement of Aryans in India, Dravidians were already living here, as per historical evidence (which is agreed to by the historians as well). Newly coming Aryans developed their contacts with old inhabitants of this country. Consequent upon the same, there was exchange of words in day today course of their dealings. Some words were, obviously, admitted in their respective language from the other. There was amalgamation of phonetic sounds as well. *For example*, it is believed that the Sanskrit words मीन (fish) and नीर (water) have been derived from languages of Dravidian family. In the same way, Sanskrit words were appropriated in Dravidian languages also. During the said process of appropriation, it is quite possible that the Cerebral Consonants might have been included in Vedic Sanskrit from Dravidian group of linguistics.

In cerebral Consonants, two letters ळ (la) and ळ्ह (lha) have also appeared which imply that the letter ळ (la) is unaspirated (in pronouncing of which little effort is required) while 'ळ्ह' (lha) is an aspirated letter (in pronouncing of which hard breathing or aspirate sound is meeded.

Intermediate letter व् (a term applied to the semi-vowel as standing between vowels and consonants and being formed by a slight contact of the vocal organs) and Labio-dental letter व् are two different phonetic sounds. In English, the phonetic sound of the letter 'V' is identical with that of labio-dental letter व्. It is the soft sound heard in the articulation of a soft consonant फ् In Vedic Sanskrit, the labio-dental letters य and व् were also in use.

ह् and ह् two forms of the letter ('ha') have appeared. The first form 'ह' is commonly used while the other form ह. is a sort of symbol in writing, representing a distinct hard aspiration and marked by two perpendicular dots (:), which is a substitute (That which takes the place of a thing or is substituted for it). The ordinary form of the letter ह is a soft sound (heard in the articulation of a soft consonant), while ह. is its unvoiced form (hollowness of sound with which all hard consonants and the Visarga are pronounced). The use of letters, uttered from the root of the tongue a term particularly applied to the Visarga before letters. क and ख् and the aspirate Visarga appearing before the letters प and फ is also found in Vedic Sanskrit.

It is the brief description of articulation of words and letters in Vedic Sanskrit, and forms the basis for studying all the phonetic sounds pertaining to the languages, belonging to Indo-Aryan linguistic family.

2

THE ANCIENT INDO-ARYAN LANGUAGES

Chronological Order of Indo-Aryan Languages

After arrival and settling of Aryans in India, the growth and development of Aryan languages, have been classified by the linguists in three periods from chronological viewpoint:

1. Period of ancient Indo-Aryan languages (Ranging form 1500 to 500 B.C.).
2. Mediaeval period of Indo-Aryan languages (From 500 A.D. to 1,000 A.D.).
3. Modern period of Indo-Aryan languages (From 1000 A.D. to present 20th century).

The above chronological division is accepted by majority of the scholars with slight variation of one hundred to two hundred years.

The philologists classify vedic Sanskrit and classical Sanskrit as belonging to the ancient period of Indo-Aryan languages. For Vedic Sanskrit, the word 'Chhandas' (poetic language) has also appeared. The said word has been frequently used by Pāṇini. He has used the word 'language' for classical Saṁskrit. Generally, the word Sanskrit is now used for both Vedic and classical forms. Certain linguists believe that Sanskrit was used dating back to 2000 B.C. Prof. Maxmuler, however, differs and he reckons this period even earlier than it. All the Vedas had been composed in Sanskrit. Although, the shape of the language is not strictly uniform in all Vedas, yet there are no major variations too. There are only slight variations, here and there, in the wordings and the method of their use.

The pre-eminent grammarian, Pāṇini, had further refined and perfected Vedic Sanskrit by virtue of prescribing grammatical constraints and by imparting it a systematic shape. Thereafter, all canonical literature, accomplished in India, was written in classical Sanskrit.

Vedic Literature (in a Wider Sense)

Vedas are considered to be most ancient amongst entire canonical literature, written in Indo-Aryan languages. The word 'Veda' is obtained from Sanskrit elementary (root) word 'विद' which literally means knowledge, understanding or learning. Sāyana, the renowned scholiast on Vedas, has explained the meaning of the word 'Veda' in *Taitriya Saṁhita* (Taitriya School of the Yajurveda-Krishna Yajurveda):

इष्टप्राप्त्यनिष्ट परिहारयोरलौकिक मुपायं यो ग्रन्थों वेदयति स वेदः It means that the holy scripture which prescribes the unique remedy, how to achieve the desired goal and how to get rid of the calamities—is known as 'Veda'. They are four in number. They can be classified into two categories—*Karma Kanda* (that department of the Vedas which relates to ceremonial acts and sacrificial rites and the merits arising from due performance thereof); and *Gyan-Kanda* (the inner or esoteric portion of Vedas which refers to true spiritual knowledge or knowledge of the Supreme Spirit as distinguished from the knowledge of Ceremonial rites). The treatises, relating to religious rituals, include Saṁhitā Bhāg (code of conduct), Brahmnas (That portion of the Vedas which states rules for the employment of the hymns at the various sacrifices, their origin and detailed explanation with sometimes lengthy illustrations in the shape of legends or stories) and Āranyakas (Religious and philosophical writings, connected with the Brahmnas, which were either composed in forests or must have been studied there), while in *Gyan-Kanda* are included 'Upnishadas' (knowledge derived from sitting at the feet of the preceptor) but according to Indian scholars, it means 'to destroy ignorance by revealing the knowledge of the Supreme Spirit and cutting off the bonds of worldly existence.' They are said to have been the source of the six Darshans or systems of philosophy, particularly of Vedanta philosophy). They will be analytically discussed in detail in ensuing chapters.

Rigveda

Rigveda is oldest amongst whole Vedic literature. This fact is well established by its language, composition and style etc. The language used in 'Rigveda' is oldest as compared to all other literary compositions, obtained in Indo-European languages. It is a versified composition and the verses are called Vedic hymns or metres. In this sacred treatise 'Gayatri' metre (with 6 syllables in a quarter or a Pada): 'Anushtapa' metre (There are several varieties of this metre but that which is most in use has 8 syllables in each Pada); Brahti metre (with 9 syllables in a quarter); 'Pankti' metre (with 10 syllables in a quarter or Pada); Trishtup metre (with 11 syllables in a quarter); and Jagati (with 12 syllables in a quarter); etc. have been used, majority of these verses have been composed in stanzas of 4 lines each. A few of them are composed in 3 lines stanzas also. Many of these metrès contain prayers and are precatory. Besides them, there are verses concerning Yajnas and systems of philosophy as also philosophical ideas.

Rigveda is divided in ten parts. They are called 'Mandalas' (the whole collection being divided in 10 Mandalas). Another method has also been applied for division of Rigveda. It divides it into 8 parts and each part is called as 'Ashṭaka' (A division of Regveda—it has been divided into 8 Ashṭakas). The latter method of division of Regveda has received greater recognition. It is stated that initially there were 5 branches of Rigveda, styled as—1. Shākal (The recension or traditional text of the Rigveda as represented by Shakalās); 2. Vāshkala; 3. Ashvalāyana Sūtras (a celebrated work called the Ashwalāyana Sūtras); 4. Shankhyāyan (A school or traditional recension of the Rigveda) and 5. Mānḍukeya. Now only one school or traditional recension of Rigveda as represented by Shakalas is available.

Western scholars are of the opinion that the composition of whole Rigveda had not been accomplished at only one place. According to them, the divisions No. 2 to 7 called Mandalās of the Rigveda had been composed in Punjab. The remaining first, eighth, ninth and tenth divisions of Rigveda had been composed after Aryans had moved further towards East. The reason being advanced for it, suggests that in the former compositions, the words, such as river Ganges, lions and rice donot find mention since they were non-existent in Punjab. However, in the subsequent divisions of Rigveda, the said words are found mentioned since they were all existent in East.

Yajurveda

In Yajurveda, some of the verses have been derived and included from Rigveda, while others have been composed. There is an elaborate and systematic discussion on Vedic hymns, their recension as enjoined by rules at the time of yajnas, performed by Aryans, such as *Vājpeya* (Name of a particular sacrifice); *Rājsūya* (a great sacrifice performed by a universal monarch in which the tributory princes also take part at the time of his coronation as a mark of his undisputed sovereignty) and *Ashvamedha* (In Vedic times, this sacrifice was performed by kings, desirous of offspring, but subsequently it was performed by kings and implied that he who instituted it, was a great conqueror and king of kings. A horse was turned loose to wander at will for a year, attended by a guardian; when the horse entered a foreign country, the ruler was bound to either submit or to fight. After the successful return of the horse, the rite called Ashvamedha was performed amidst great rejoicings) as also other Yagnas with significance of each. It is composed in both prosaic and poetic forms. Especially, its explanatory portion is in prosaic form. It is divided in two chief branches, namely—(1) *Shukla Yajurveda*, and (2) *Taitriya* or *Krishna Yajurveda*. Although, great scholiast, Pātanjali, has advised that there were 101 branches of Yajurveda but they are generally not-available now.

Shukla Yajurveda

As believed under Vedic tradition, this branch of Yajurveda had been manifested by sun. The sun is resplendent, bright and luminous. Accordingly, it was named as 'Shukla Yajurveda'. Another argument given for prescribing this name is that the Vedic hymns have been compiled in most appropriate and systematic manner in it. Because of the said clarity and the hymns placed in systematic order, it had been named as Shukla Yajurveda. Those hymns had been incorporated in it which were recited or sung at the time of performance of Vedic Yajnas. Shukla Yajurveda is further divided in two branches, namely, (1) Kanva (followed by a descendant or follower of Kanva), and (2) Mādhyandina (a branch of Shukla or white Yajurveda, followed by the Madhyandinas).

Krishna Yajurveda

Krishna Yajurveda has been produced in the reverse order. While the Vedic hymns have been arranged in an orderly and systematic manner in Shukla Yajurveda, they have not been produced in accordance with any system, rule or precept, in Krishna Yajurveda. Probably on account of lack of systematic arrangement of hymns and for want of clarity and unambinguity, it might have been named as 'Krishna Yajurveda'. There is another distinct feature of Krishna Yajurveda. Like Shukla Yajurveda, all Vedic hymns, meant for recitation at the time of performance of respective yajna, are incorporated in it; simultaneously there is an elaborate discussion and critical appreciation of all important yajnas as well which has added to its significance.

Krishna Yajurveda is further divided into four branches, namely—'Kāṭhak Saṁhita' (Kāthak School of Yajurveda); 'Kapishṭhalkaṭh Saṁhita' (Kāpishṭhal Kaṭh school of Yajurveda); Maitrayani Saṁhita (Maitrayani School of Yajurveda) and Taittiriya Saṁhita (Taitiriya school of Yajurveda). Sri Mahidhar, an author of commentary on Vedas, has written a very interesting and exciting story in the 'Introduction to Yajurveda commentary'. As cited therein, Vaishampāyan, the famous disciple of renowned sage, Vyās, had taught all the four Vedas to his pupils including Yāgyavalkya. One day, it so hapened that Vaishampāyan grew very much annoyed with Yāgvalkaya and ordered—"Whatever I have taught to you, you must relinquish it." On hearing this, Yāgvalkaya too was very much agitated. Whatever he had learnt, he vomitted it. On being instructed by their preceptor, Vaishampāyan, the other disciples turned into partridges and ate what had been puked out. The sacred knowledge, thus vomitted, is contained in Taitriya Saṁhita (Taitiriya school of Yajurveda).

Certain scholars in India believe that Ravana was an authority on Vedas. He had written commentary on Vedas. The portion of Yajurveda, dealt with by him in his commentary, came to be known as Krishna Yajurveda (Taitriya or black Yajurveda).

Sām Veda

Sāmveda, primarily deals with music. Most of the hymns, contained in Sām Veda have been derived from Rigveda. Independent hymns are extremely limited. They are only 75. Samveda has been compiled with concilliatory songs[1], meant to entreat divine powers while performing Yagnas. Hence the texts of Hymns have been repeatedly mentioned time and again. The total number of Mantras is 1810 in Samveda. If the Mantras, repeated again and again, were excluded the remaining ones would number only 985,' slightly more than half, *i.e.* 585 Mantras in the former half and 400 Mantras in the latter half.

Sāmveda is divided into two parts. Its former half portion is called 'Archika' (an epithet of Sāmveda) and the latter half is called 'Uttrarchika' (subsequent collection of the hymns of Sāmveda). The word 'Archika' is morphological

---

1. Yaṁ Brahmā Varuṇendrarudamārutaḥ stuṇvante divyahaistvai
Vandahai Sāng pādakrimopnishdairgāyanti yaṁ Sāmagaḥa|
Dhayanāvasthittadagtena mansāpashyanti yaṁ yogino
Yasyantaṁ na viduḥ surāsuragaṇaḥ Devaya tasmai namaḥ ||

construction from Sanskrit root word 'Rick' or 'Richa' which literally means collection of hymns relating to Sāmveda. The latter half portion of Sāmveda, known as 'Uttrarchika, has its own significance. In the said portion, the hymns have been arranged in a fine systematic order. All the Mantras, to be recited in a particular Yajna, have been compiled together at one place. It relieves from the botheration and inconvenience of tracing them out from the entire lot at the time of performance of a Yajna. The hymns relating to each yajna, are obtained in a collective form at its respective place. Similarly, Mantras, meant for entreating a specific divine-being, have been collectively arranged at one place. In case, several Mantras are incorporated in a single verse, such verses have been collected at one place. This considerably facilitates the work of pin-pointing the Mantras and reciting them in correct perspective and order.

Most significant guiding instructions, relating to music, have been incorporated in Sāmveda which acquaint us with rules concerning correct singing and recitation of Vedic hymns; conversion of short syllables into long in prosody and dropping of syllable instants for exigence of metres at the time of recitation of sacred texts; repetition of words with a view to maintain rhythmic harmony, relaxation and modulation of voice and regulation of the process, useful for correct singing and recitation of Vedic texts. Scholars believe that for all-round development of Indian music, Sāmveda formed the basis and had been the primary source of help.

It is a traditional belief that there were 1000 Shākhās of Sāmveda. However, two Shākhās in complete form and the third in an incomplete form are now available. The name of the first Shākhā is "Raṇāyaniya" which is complete. The second Shakha is titled 'Kaurthum' which is in complete and only its seventh chapter is available now. Remaining portion has been destroyed completely. The third Shākhā of Sāmveda is known by the name of "Jaimniya" which is also available in complete form.

Atharvaveda

Mantras incorporated in Atharvaveda, relate to annihilation of enemics, killing and destroying of adversaries and ruining one's enemies by magical spells. On the other hand, it also contains prayers for self-protection from calamitous sinful, unfortunate and inauspicious occurrences. Mantras for one's own safety and well-being on one hand as also evil and ill effects for others on the other have been included in this Veda. Consequent upon the same, Mr. Winternitz has held it to be a collection of Mantras meant for priests, practising sorcery and conjuration. However, besides the above contents, there are a few Mantras for recitation at the time of sacramental and religions ceremonies as also there are some Mantras for ceremonious praise and eulogy of deities.

Atharvaveda is also known as 'Atharvāngirā', 'Bhrigvangira and "Brahmaveda". Probably, the word 'Angira' signifies the priests, who, by using magical formulas of Atharvaveda, destroy the enemics of their clients. The literal meaning of the word Atharva is a priest-particularly the class of priests who are well-versed in the performance of the rites enjoined by the said Veda. There are two Shākhās of Atharvaveda, namely, 'Shaunak' and 'Paiplād. However, the first Shākhā is primarily in use.

Certain scholars believe that Atharvaveda is an embodiment of demonic craft since the Mantras, contained in it, are wielded to seek disasters, calamities and devastation for others. Consequently, it is not being considered at par with other three Vedas. Infact, amongst genuine Vedas, only three-Rigveda, Yajurveda and Sāmveda had a reckoning. The said tradition was followed for a long time. This fact, finds support by the following couplet, derived from the famous *Mahimnaḥ Stotra* (A hymn of praise and eulogium to divine powers; A doxology), written by Acharya Pushpadant:

"Trayi Sānkhyaṁ Yogaḥ Pashupatimantaṁ Vaishṇavamiti,
Prabhinne prasthāne parmidmadaḥ pathyamiti cha |
Ruchinaṁ Vaichitrayadrajukuṭilnānāpath jivaṁ,
Nrināmeko gamyāstavamasi payasamarṇava iti ||

As per Western scholars, Atharva Veda had been composed after accomplishment of other three vedas, more probably after Aryans had reached Bengal where sorcery and conjuration were already practised. It was after considerable time when it was also treated as Veda.

Brahmana Treatises

Brahmanās constitute that portion of the Vedas which states rules for the employment of the hymns at the various yajnas, their origin and detailed explanation with sometimes lengthy illustrations in the shape of legends or stories. They are distinct from the Mantra portion of the Vedas. The Vedic scholars have elaborately dealt with the rituals of various yajnas in Brāhmana treatises. The topics relating to *Yajman*[1] (A person who performs a yajna and pays its expenses or who employs a priest to perform yajna for him); *Hota*[2] (The offerer of oblations). *Udgata*[3] (The priest who chants the hymns of Sāmveda; *Adhvayu*[4] (An officiating priest, whose duty was to measure the ground, build the altar and light the fire and while doing all this, to repeat the Mantras of Yajurveda) and *Brahma*[5] (one of the four, priests employed at a same yajna, well conversant with the sacred texts of all the four Vedas) and others, who specialize in peformance of yajnas, have been elaborately dealt with. There is a profound and minute description of performances by the aforesaid four specialized priests; preparation of altar, presence of all the accomplishers of the yajna; use and employment of different mantras meant for respective yajna; fitness and propriety of the Mantras with various yajnas; the elaborate explanation of the Mantras etc., have been discussed in the said Brahmana treatises. Legends and stories have also been given, wherever necessary, with sometimes lengthy illustrations. Later on, the said illustrations in the shape of legends or stories might have formed part of *Purāṇās* (well-known sacred works;

1. A house-holder who performs yajna.
2. An invocator of divine powers by recitation of vedic hymns in loud and explicit voice.
3. One who is well conversant with the method of eulogising deities by singing mantras of Samveda.
4. One who prepares oblation and other articles regioned for performance of a yajna and recites Vedic hymns with low voice and offers oblation to the deities as specially desired.
5. A learned scholar of all the four Vedas, having profound knowledge of performance of prescribed acts or rites. He supervises the acts and performance of all other priests and corrects then, as and when necessary.

these are 18 and they contain the whole body of Hindu mythology).

Each of the four Vedas has its own Brāhmana or Brāhmnas which are the theological portions of the Vedas. The said treatises, no doubt, play significant role in elaboration of the meanings of Vedic hymns. The purport of the Vedic Mantras could be followed correctly with the assistance of Brahmana treatises only.

Āranyaks

Āranyakas are also a class of religious and philosophical writings (connected with the Brāhmanās) which have been either composed in forests or must have been studied there. They too belong to that department of the Vedas which relates to ceremonial acts and rites concerning Yajnas and the merit arising from due performance thereof. Whereas, in Brahman treatises, there is deep analytical narration of the methods and manners relating to the performance of Yajnas; in Aranayaks, there are explanations by stating the good results arising from the proper observance of the rules, methods and manners, concerning Yajnas, and the evils arising from their omissions and also by adducing traditional instances in support thereof. In Aranyakas, there are references of Vedic hymns which lay down rules and make a specific mention of the guide-lines for performance of Yajnas.

It is believed that the Sages, observing celibacy, pondered over the deep and profound subjects, relating to Vedic Yajnas, in forests, hence, the said sacred works recommending precepts by stating the good results arising from their proper observance and the evil, arising from their omission and also by adducing, historical instances in their support, were called 'Āranyakas' or as defined in the extract "Āranya eva pāthyāt Āranyakamitiryate", they were taught in forests, hence they were named as 'Āranyakas'. Accordingly, their significance is admittedly for *Vanprasthis* (those who renounce worldly lives). For abandoning worldly life, there is provision for staying in forests, where a person undertakes spiritual endeavours for attaining perpetual happiness after relinquishing worldly pleasures. However, it is seldom possible to abruptly get rid of mental allurements for house-hold life. The Āranyakas provide enlightenment to *Vanprasthis* and pave their way for spiritual accomplishments so that they might gradually advance towards achievement of eternal Spirit. Like Brahman treatises, the language and style of composition of Āranyakas are also easy, concise, activating for religious performances. There are different Āranyakas relating to each Veda.

Upnishads

These Upnishads (sacred ancient books of Hindus) relate to inner or esoteric portion which refers to true spiritual knowledge or knowledge of the Supreme Spirit as distinguished from the knowledge of rituals in Vedic literature. Although, mentioning of rituals, relating to Vedic Yajnas, is not strictly prohibited in these sacred books, yet as stated in the quotation—"Swargakayoyajet", the fruit of Yajnas is barely confined to attainment of paradise. However, the achievement of divine abode is not eternal. After decay of propitious deeds one has to descerd again to this mortal world from abode of Heaven.[1] It means that inspite of performance of rituals, pertaining to Yajnas, the state of transmigration is not done away with. One does

1. Kṣine puṇye Martyalokaṁ Vishanti.

not achieve perpetual happiness. The transcedental happiness which one gets in Heaven is also sensuous. The sensual pleasures only lead to distress and not true happiness. Beyond transmigration (birth and death), material well-being, adversity, prosperity, enjoyment and luxury, there is a mental state which is known as state of supreme pleasure (bliss) in Upnishads. It can be accomplished only through spiritual knowledge. One does not get freedom[1] from worldly attachments without spiritual knowledge. This is the gist and essence of Upnishads which has been critically discussed and evaluated from all viewpoints.

How much significant, it was considered to obtain knwoledge of Upnishads, will be evident from an example of *Chhāndogya Upnishada*. Once divine sage, 'Narada', well-versed in many disciplines, approached Sanat Kumar and requested him—"Kindly teach me and impart me true spiritual knowledge." Saying this, he sits near his feet like a disciple."

Sanat Kumar replied—"You first tell me what you already know. Thereafter, I shall preach you and sermonize."

Narada replied—"My Lord! I have already studied Rigveda, Yajurveda, Sāmveda and Atharvaveda. I have read history and gone through Purānās, which are treated as fifth Veda. I have also studied grammar; rules for performance of obsequal oblation in honour of the manes; performance of ceremonies in honour of the departed spirits of dead relatives; mathematics, science of production; science of infinite treasury; science of logics; science of morality; etymology of divine language (Sanskrit); theology; pedagogy of Rigveda, Yajurveda and Samveda; grammatical treatises containing rules for the phonetic changes, which the words in any branch of Vedas undergo; Vedic religious rituals; prosody; physical science; art of archery; art of snake-charming. Sanskrit (divine language); dancing; singing, playing on musical instruments; science of craft etc."

"My Lord! inspite of having studied all these sciences, I am merely well-versed in pronouncing Mantras and knower of their literal meanings. I have not yet attained self realization. I have learnt from Sages like you that a spiritualist is able to make self conquest and free himself from sorrow and grief. My Lord! I am afflicted with sorrow. Please help me to salvage myself from grief."

Sanat Kumar replied-"What you have learnt is merely an appellation of knowledge."[2] (You have only learnt the names of various disciplines).

After introductory dialogue, the great spiritualist, Sanat Kumar, preached divine knowledge for self-realization to Narada.

A reference from 'Vrahadāraṇyakopnishada' reads—Yāgyavalkya is keen to renounce worldly life. He had two wives—Maitreyi and Kātyāyani. Yāgyavalkya addressed. Maitreyi—"I wish to give up family life and renounce the world. Let

---

1. Rite Gyananna Muktiḥ.
2. Om avihi bhagava iti hāpsasāda Sanat Kumaraṁ and Nāradast hīvācha Yadhaittha Tena Nopasida tatast Ūrdhvam Vaksyāmiti sa hovācha!
Rigvedam Bhagvodhyemi Yajurveda Sāmveda Atharvavedanam Chaturthmitihāspurānam panchaṁ Vedānām Vedaṁ pitrya Rashi daivam nidhiṁ Vākovākyamekāyanam Devavidyām Brahmavidyaṁ Bhūtvidyaṁnaksatravidyaṁ Sarpadevajanavidyametada Bhagvodhyemi.
So hain bhagvo Mantravidevāsmi nātmavichhūta hyeva me bhagvaddrishaibhyastarit Slaokmātma viditi Sohaṁ bhagvah sochāmi taṁ mā bhagwānchhokasya Pāraṁ tāryatviti ta howacha yadwai kinehetadadhyagiṣṭhā nāmaivaitata

—*Chhandogya Upnishada*, 7th Chapter 1st Volume 1-3

me partition your share as against Kātyāyani."

Maitreyi asked "My Lord! even if the entire earth full of worldly riches is owned by me, will it make me immortal?"

Yāgvalkya replied—"It is impossible. It will only mould your life to be in consistence with other resourceful people. Wealth and riches cannot leade to attain immortality."

Maitreyi added—"What is the use of that wealth which cannot help in attaining immortalization. Kindly guide me how to achieve immortality."[1]

Realising the immense curiosity of Maitreyi and her eagreness to learn, Yāgvalkya preches her divine knowledge for self realization which forms significant part of the said Upnishada.

According to a reference appeared in "Muṇḍakopnishada", "One renowned and leading house-holder, named Shonaka, possessing a large prosperous family, approached `ANGIRA' and requested him to teach-what one should necessarily know to become an all out and well accomplished scholar?"

Angira replied "According to theologists, there are two branches of knowledge worth attainment—one spiritualistic and the other materialistic. Rigveda, Yajurveda, Samveda, Atharvaveda, theoretical and practical knowledge of grammar, etymological science, prosody and astrology constitute and are part of materialistic knowledge while spiritual knowledge leads to attainment of imperishable eternal spirit."

Upnishadas impart teaching of spiritual knowledge. A number of subjects relating to 'Brahma' (The Supreme Being, regarded as impersonal and divested of all Quality and action).'Jiva' (The soul enshrined in the body and imparting to it life, motion and sensation), 'Prakriti' (The original source of the material world) and their characteristics have been elaborately discussed in Upnishadas. Under Vedic fold, Upnishadas are considered as most significant from viewpoint of metaphysical and true philosophical knowledge. These Upnishadas are held in equal esteem by all communities, reposing faith in Vedic traditions. It must, however, be borne in mind that followers of different creeds add slight mixture of their own sectarian views while explaining the texts of these Upnishadas.

Western scholars were also greatly impressed by metaphisical and philosophical knowledge contained in these Upnishadas. Prof. Maxmuler comments in this regard:- "The Upnishadas are main exponents of Vedant philosophy, a system in which human speculation, seems to me, have reached its very acme."

Prof. Shopenhar comments: "In the world, there is no other study so beneficial and so elevating as that of Upnishadas. They are a product of the highest wisdom. It is destined sooner or later to become the faith of the people."

It has been a significant tradition to study Vedic Mantras (Metres) and retain

---

1. Maitreyiti howacha Yagvalkyo udyasyanava arehamasmātsthanadasmi Hant tenyā Katyānyataṁ Karvāniti.

   Sā hovācha Maitreyi, Yāntu ma iyain bhagoh sarvā prithvi vittena purṇā syāthathain tena mritāsyāmiti neti howaca yāgvalkyo yathaivopakaraṇavatain jivitaṁ tathaiva te jivrit vsyādmiritatvasya tu nāsāsti vitteneti.

   So hovāca Maitreyi yanāhaṁ namrita syaṁ kimhaṁ tena kuryā yadeva Bhagvānveda tadeva me bruhiti.

   — *Vrahadaranyakopnisada*, II Chapter, IV Brahmana, 1-3.

them in memory. There have been Brahman reciters of Vedas who kept all the four Vedas—from beginning to end, thoroughly committed to their memory to the very letter and phonetic sounds correctly. Some of them can be found even now. Some of the generic attributes of Brahmanas such as Dwivedi, Trivedi and Chaturvedi etc. might have been given to them because of their perfection in respective number of Vedas. A disciple used to study and attain knowledge of Vedas by attentively listening to the teachings of his preceptor. The word Shruti is used as synonym for Vedas which is an indication to this effect that the knolwedge of Vedas used to be acquired through hearing by revelation.

In olden days, it was a unique practice to learn by heart and retain the sacred knowledge in memory after listening it from the preceptor. It has been finely argued in *Chhāndogya Upnishada*,[1] how a person full of strength and vitality, purity and goodness, moved ahead in pursuit of knowledge and finally attained perfection in it. It has been cited therein—"When a person is full of vigour and disposed to truth, then only he is able to stand up and gather strength to rise. By thus moving a head and determining for making further progress, he developes an aptitude for hard work. He then appears before his preceptor and sitting at his feet, he observes certain ceremonies for initiation. He prostrates before his reverred teacher. Thus, like a resolute and determined pupil, he minutely follows the ideal life of his preceptor. Therafter, he listens most attentively to the teachings of his guru. He ponders over deeply and meditates upon the lectures of his guide and mentor. After meditation, he reposes full faith in the teachings of his *Guru*. Thus, he becomes a full-fledged intellectual. The completion of studies is over after performance of certain ceremonies. Experience and practice further enable to attain perfection in knowledge and then he is accredited as a full-fledged and celebrated intellectual."[1]

After sitting close to the feet of preceptor, rendering service to him, viewing him with respect, listening, meditating, attaining knowledge and perception and thus proceeding step by step, a pupil was able to obtain wisdom and scholarship. In order to become a learned and well accomplished person, a pupil was required to undergo the long process in olden days with complete faith, humility, service, hard labour and emotional dedication.

Methodical Recitation of Vedic Hymns

Vedic scholars undertook several measures in order to safeguard against any error in correct recitation of Vedic Mantras so that they remained intact in memory of Vedic students for a very long time—say from one generation to another. Their introduction of certain methods for correct recitation of Vedic Mantras was really excellent. They determined five methods for recitation of Vedas—(1) Saṁhita Pāth (recitation of the continuous texts of the Vedas); (2) Pada-Pāth (An arrangement

---

1. . . . Sa Yadā balo bhavati, ath uthātā bhavati | Uttisthana paricaṛita bhavaṭi | paridaran upsattā bhavati | Upsidan Dristā bhavati | Śrotā bhavati, Bhanta bhavati | Bodhā bhavati | Karta bhavati | Vigyātā bhavati

— *Chhāndogyā Upnishada*, VIII Volume page 1

of the Vedic text in which each word is written and pronounced in its original form and independently of phonetic changes)' (3) Kram-Pāth (Particular manner of reciting Vedic texts, leaving at each time one word and taking up another); (4) Jatā Pāth (A particular manner of reciting Vedic texts), and (5) Ghan-Pāth (A particular manner of reciting Vedic texts).

Saṁhita Pāth: Recital of Ved Mantras in their original form as arranged therein, is called Saṁhitā Pāth.

Pada-Pāth: Recital of Vedic Mantras after segregating them into separate words is called Pada Path. For instance, let us take कखग as symbolizing a Mantra. Pronouncing कखग in its co-ordinated form will be called Saṁhita Path, while pronouncing क, ख, ग, separately will be called Pada Path. The difference in two methods is explicit. In Saṁhita Pāth, all the words of a Mantra, are recited combinedly in their original co-ordinated shape, while in Pada Pāth they are segregated and pronounced separately. There are different rules for effecting change in phonetic sound in the beginning and at the end of each word after they are separated. It is absolutely essential for reciters of Vedic texts to adhere to these rules. Then only, the recitation will be correct. After total adherence to the rules governing recitation of words separately, re-recitation of Vedic Mantra will be perfectly correct by employing the first method of Saṁhita Pāth, as it was earlier before segregation of the words' under Pada Pāth.

Kram Pāth: Under Pada Pāth, each Pada or word was recited separately only once. However, under this method, the first word will be recited alongwith the next word. This process will go on applying successively. For instance let us take कखगघ as symbolic of a Vedic Mantra. As per the method of Pada Pāth, each word was pronounced separately such as क,ख,ग,घ. However, under Kram Pāth, the preceding word will join the next word and be read accordingly just as कख, खग, गघ.

Jatā Pāth: By making further combinations from the above three joint words under Kram Pāth as shown above, the method of Jata Pāth is obtained. *For example*, according to the method of Jatā Pāth, initially the first and second words will be combined, next second word with the first word thirdly, the first word again with the second word fourthly second word with the third word; fifthly, third word with second word and lastly second word again with the third word will be recited jointly. For the sake of illustration, these combinations will be made as कख, खक, कख, खग, गख and खग respectively.

Ghan-Pāth:- Under Jatā-Pāth, combinations—each of two words were made. According to the method of Ghan-Pāth, two combinations of two words each and three combinations of three words each—in all five combinations of Padas of a Vedic Mantra are made. In a symbolic manner, these combinations can be illustrated as कख, खक, कखग, गखक and कखग,

Saṁhita Pāth (recitation of a Vedic Mantra in its exact original shape) was classified into four shapes as per above-cited four methods. The process has been so systematic and regulated that after recitation of a Vedic Mantra in different styles as shown above, it could be re-recited in its original shape of Saṁhita Path without least difficulty. The said methodical process was, no doubt, abstruse and called for repeated practice and exercise, yet it proved extremely helpful in maintaining absolute correctness and consistency in pronunciation for thousands of years. Consequently, it is a fact that thousands of years old language or glossary of Sanskrit words, in which the Vedic Mantras were composed, remained intact without least change or alteration, whatsoever. From philological viewpoint, it is no less significant.

Utterance of Phonetic Sounds of Mantras

In order to maintain the phonetic utterance of Vedic Mantras absolutely intact and genuine, the regulation of phonetic sound is most important context of Vedic literature. As per Vedic system, the accents have been held of three types: 'Udātta' (accute accent): 'Anudātta' (lower accent) and 'Swarit' (having circumflix accent—the third or mixed tone lying between high and low sound). The vocal organs-larynx and palate etc. exist inside the mouth. There are two upper and lower regions of each vocal organ. Hence they are stated to be with regions. The breath or air, moving inside the body, comes in contact with or clashes against vocal organs and produces phonetic sound. When the said sound is created by the upper regions of the vocal organs, then the sound is comparatively louder. This is known as Udātta (accute or loud accent).[1] When the sound is produced from the lower region of the vocal organs, then the phonetic sound is said to be 'Anudātta' (lower accent).[2] When the sound produced is between high and low tones or in other words, when it is produced from the contact of the air (breath) with middle region of vocal organs, it is called 'Swarit' (having circumflex accent *i.e.*, the third tone between high and low).[3]

There are separate signs for each phonetic sound. Some Vedic texts are found with the said signs. They help in maintaining the pronunciation of Vedic Metres to be absolutely intact and genuine. Special emphasis is laid for pronouncing Vedic Mantras with correct phonetic sound. On the other hand, incorrect pronunciation of Vedic Mantras is not only considered a misdemeanour but highly undesirable too. The story of Vritra, king of demons, amply reflects upon the evil consequences of pronouncing Vedic Mantras incorrectly and against grammatical rules concerning true accent of phonetic sound.

Vritrā, king of demons, performed a Yajna with the aim of causing death to Indra, king of heaven. In between offering oblations, the Mantra to be repeatedly pronounced was "इन्द्र शत्रुर्वध स्व" which literally meant that the strength of enemy of Indra (Vritra, king of demons)[4] be multiplied. Shukra, the religious teacher of demons, was offering oblations by repeating this Mantra. In the course of pronouncing the said Mantra, a grave error occurred. In the compound word 'Indra

---

1. Uchachairuddataḥ "Asthadhyāyi 1/2/29"
Talvādisu Sabhāgesu Sthanaisurdhava bhāge nishpānnojud āttasangyaḥ Syāt.
2. Nichairanuddātah "1/2/30"
Talvādishu Sabhāgeshu sthānesvadhobhāge nishpanno s cạ anudāttasangyaḥ syāt !
3. Samaharaḥ Swaritaḥ "1/2/31"
Udāttānudattave varnadharmo Samahiyate yatra soacha swarit saṇgyaḥ .
4. Inderasya Satruḥ Shātiyatā.

Ṣhatru' (Enemy of Indra) there is 'Tatpurush Compound' (Name of a class of compound in which the first member determines the sense of the other member or in which the last member is defined or qualified by the first without losing its original independence). As a rule, the last letter of the second word should be pronounced with accute accent[1] but the oblator elevated the phonetic sound of the last letter of the preceding word. This changed the nature of compound word 'Indra-Ṣatru' from 'Tatpurush' to Bahuvrihi (one of the four principal kinds of compounds in Sanskrit. In it, two or more nouns in apposition to each other are compounded, the attributive member, whether a noun or an adjective, being placed first and made to qualify another substantive, and neither of the two members separately, but the sense of the whole compound qualifies that substantive. This compound is adjectival in character, but there are several instances of Bahuvrihi compounds which have come to be regarded and used as nouns) as soon as the sound of the last letter of the previous word was elevated, since in Bahuvrihi compound the accent of last letter of the preceding word is elevated.[2] Thus the very effect of the Mantra reversed altogether. The etymological interpretation of the compound 'Indrashatruh' became-Indra is the destroyer of enemy (Vritra, who was enemical to Indra).[3]

With the change of character of the compound, the very effect of the Mantra got entirely reversed. Under 'Tatpurush compound', the two compounded words-'Indrashsatru' originally meant that Vritra, the king of demons, aimed at destroying his enemy, Indra (king of heaven). However, as a result of change in the character of compound from Tatpurush to Bahuvrihi, Indra became the destroyer. Thus the fruit of enhancement in the strength was achieved by Indra and not Vritra. Vritra was killed in the battle. The power of Indra got increased and he became victorious. What has been stated above, will be corroborated by the following couplet

Mantro Hinaḥ swarto Varṇato Vā,
Mithyāprayukto na tamarthamāh. |
Sa Vāgvajro Yajmanaṁ hinasti,
Yathendrashatruḥ Swartoaparāghāt || [4]

If the Mantra is devoid of correct phonetic sound and character or the use of correct phonetic sound and character might be lacking or there might be wrong and incorrect use or application of these two, the Mantra will not yield the desired fruit. The incorrect use of phonetic voice in a Mantra would make it adamantine (like a fatal weapon). It even causes death to the sponsor or performer of the Yagna. The fault or error committed in correct use of the substantive accent, while pronouncing the compound word 'Indraśatru', caused death to the sponsor, Vritra.

It is explicitly evident from the above narrative that the Vedic scholars were resolutely determined to maintain accuracy and not to allow any lapse or deviation

1. Samāsāsya /6/1/223¯Ant Udāttaḥ Syāt.
2. Bahuvrihau Prakrityā Pūrvapadam "6/2/1" Udāttaswaritayogipūrvapadam Prakrityā syāt.
3. Indraḥ Shaturasya sa Indra-shatruḥ.
4. Pāṇiniya Shikshā, 52.

in correct pronunciation of the Mantra with due emphasis on correct utterence of phonetic sound.

The Phases of Evolution of Vedic Sanskrit

It is believed that excluding the Ist and Xth divisions, Rigveda is decidedly most ancient composition from linguistic viewpoint. The ancientness between Rigveda and Avestā should be determined by comparing with other divisions of the Rigveda, excluding Ist and Xth divisions. The language of the first and tenth divisions of the Rigveda, appears to be comparatively of much later period.

Western Scholar, Prof. Āntwān Maiyaye, and others opine that the oldest shape of Vedic Sanskrit relates to the period of arrival of Aryans in the territory adjoining Punjab. According to the said scholars, the second shape of Vedic Sanskrit relates to the period when Aryans had moved to Central India. Meanwhile, they had already established contacts with people, who were originally inhabiting those territorial parts respectively and the influence of their languages was inevitable on the language of Aryans. One could imagine the third shape of Vedic Sanskrit which evolved after Aryans had procceded further from Central India and reached Eastern territories. The scholars believe that this period might date back to eighth or ninth Century B.C.

Classical Sanskrit

Vedic or classical—these two words have been found in ancient literature, signifying a specific meaning. Vedas had become synonymous with performance of religious rituals, traditions etc. representing Godly or divine knowledge. The adjective Vedic was used for the said superhuman learning and knowledge. On the other hand, for all activities relating to mortal world or connected with this universe or earth, the adjective-classical was applied. The same formula applied with the language. There was a language which was the medium of Vedic rules and precepts; used for performance of religious functions and rituals and for attainment of divine knowledge, was known as Vedic language and which has already been discussed extensively. However, the urgency was felt for a language which was free from excessive use of figurative words; it was lucid and simple, easy to be understood, besides being equally efficacious for learned scholars. The language used as medium of speech by the public was already in existence. Only it was to be given a respectable status by giving it a refined and cultured shape, which was done by great grammarian, Pāṇini.

Like three forms of Vedic Sanskrit, as discussed above, it obviously, appears that there might have been three shapes of local dialects also, used as medium of speech by general masses. The scholars are of the view that the shape of Vernacular dialect on which the classical Sanskrit is based, might have been the initial form of the language, used by the people in Northern India. It is quite possible that subsequently classical Sanskrit might have been influenced by other two forms of local dialects also, spoken in Central and Eastern regions in India. The great commentator, Pātanjali, writes in this connection. "That the field relating to the use of words is too extensive. Different words spoken at different places have assumed their specific meanings. Just as the word `Shavati' (going, approaching) signifying movement is found in use in Kamboj region Valleys of Hinduskush'a mountain only. Instead, Aryans used its modified form `Shava' only a participle of `Shavati'. The word `Hammati' in Saurashtra (Gujrāt) and `Ranhati' in Eastern and Central India are used in the sense of movement. In Eastern parts of India, the word `Dāti' is used to express the meaning of cutting while in North its participled form `Dātra' is in vogue."[1]

The great commentator has pointed to the various territorial parts in India and people living there, by naming Kamboj (Name of the territory, surrounded by Hindookash mountain which separates Giljit valley from Balkh and probably extended upto little Tibet and Ladakh); Eastern, central parts, Saurastra and Northern regions in India, while he has separately mentioned about Aryans. He has given illustrations and elaborately discussed how the same verbs were used differently by the people inhabiting different regions. Here a curiosity arises as to what the great commentator is trying to establish by distinguishing Aryans from other communities. He argues about uses of the same words differently by the people, inhabiting the aforesaid regions. The discussion here relates merely to the use of words differently. The language of all those territories was the same to which the great Commentator is referring. It seems probably that the great Commentator used the word Aryans to signify those people who liked to use refined and standard form of the language as against prevailing standard of the mediums of speech in those days. Probably, they might have been the inhabitants of North Western, region from geographical consideration who used the said polished standard of language. From generic viewpoint, they were all Aryans and spoke Aryan language. Whatever, variations were there in the formations from root words in different regions, the local dialects of those areas must have influenced Sanskrit as well and our analysis over the point, given above, stands vindicated.

The classical Sanskrit came into existence after the local dialects were given a refined shape by Pāṇini. Later on, it came to be known as Sanskrit only. Whether, the name Sanskrit grew popular from the life time of Pāṇini and onwards or it had already been in use even prior to him, cannot be said decisively. The use of word Sanskrit in the sense of a language is found first of all in *Balmiki Ramayana*. There is a reference in 'Sunder Kānd' (a section of *Ramayana*) that legendary Hanumān was anxious to decide in which language, he should converse with Sitaji. The same is illustrated in the following couplet:-

> Ahaṁ hyatitanushchaiva Vānārashcạ Visheshtaḥ |
> Vāchaṁ chaudaharisyami manusimih Sanskritāṁ ||[2]

1. Etasminschāti mahati shabdasya prayogvishye te shabdāstatra tatra niyatvishyā drishyante | Tadyathā Shavatirgatikarmā Kambojesveva bhāshito bhavati, Vikārmenmāryā bhashante Shava Iti| Hammatiḥ Surāstreshu, Ranhatiḥ prāchỵamadhyeshu gamimeva twāryāḥ prayunjate, Datirlavanārthe prachayeṣhu, datramudichayeshu

— *Mahabhashya*, Ist Ahnik, Page 33

2. *Ramayana*, in Sunder Kānd, Chapter 30, verse 17.

My body is very small and particularly being a monkey, it will be in the fitness of things to speak in Sanskrit, a language befitting mankind.

It is to be considered here whether the word 'Sanskritaṁ' connected with the word 'Vāchaṁ' has been used as proper noun or as qualitative adjective. The words "Mānushiṁ Sanskritam Vāchaṁ "also mean—refined classical language. What is the reality, can not be explained with certainty. However, the word Sanskrit does appear in the literal construction of the couplet.

The words 'Laukik Sanskrit' have been translated in English as classical Sanskrit. The words 'Lok' and 'Class' are not synonymous. Since Sanskrit has been the refined and polished language of a highly educated class, namely, Brahmans, it is quite possible that the word 'Laukik' might have been translated accordingly in English. Considering that the word classical used with Sanskrit was not appropriate, some scholars have started calling it 'Shrenya Sanskrit' (a language arranged in a systematic manner) in place of 'Laukik Sanskrit'.

Vedic and Classical Sanskrit

A Few Distinguishing Features : While making an elaborate discussion on Aryan languages, a comparative study had been made of Indo-European and Vedic Sanskrit phonetic sounds. The phonetic voices of classical Sanskrit are only slightly at variance with those of Vedic Sanskrit. Diversities between vedic and classical Sanskrit can be better explained by the following illustrations

In Vedic Sanskrit, ळ (ḷa) and 'laṭ' were gutturo/labial class of consonants but they were not found in classical Sanskrit.

The phonetic sound of consonant 'व' of Vedic Sanskrit (a dentilabial consonant) is similar to that of 'V' in English. The latter disappeared in classical Sanskrit. The consonant 'व' used in classical Sanskrit is palatal.

In Vedic Sanskrit, 'Anuswār' (nasal sound which is marked by a dot above the line) was considered as a pure nasal sound. There have been diverse opinions regarding 'Anuswar', whether it was a vowel or consonant. Some scholars treated it as a vowel, while others held that it was a consonant. However, in classical sanskrit, it was treated like a nasal vowel.

In Vedic Sanskrit, there were numerous formations from the same root words. It was, however, not the case in classical Sanskrit. For instance, we find two forms इमसि and इमः used in Vedic Sanskrit while only इमः meaning as now or as here) in classical Sanskrit. There are many similar other illustrations. In Vedic Sanskrit, two formations स्मसि and स्मः are found while only स्मः is available in classical Sanskrit. There are four formations इष्टये ईष्टे, ईशे and ईशतेः in Vedic Sanskrit, while in classical Sanskrit, we find in use of ईष्टे. There are 3 formations obtained from root word श्रुः namely, श्रुद्धि, शृणुहि and श्रणोधिः in 'Lot Lakar' (a technical term used by Pāṇini to denote the imperative mood or its terminations) in second person, singular number, while in classical Sanskrit only one single formation श्रृणु is found in use. In Vedic Sanskrit, both the forms शेये and शेते were found in use while in classical Sanskrit, only one form शेते is used. In nutshell the practice of using several alternative forms of each root word in Vedic Sanskrit, disappeared in classical Sanskrit. Whereas, there was abundant use of inflections to the crude forms of nouns in Vedic Sanskrit, the practice ceased in classical Sanskrit.

In Vedic Sanskrit, the words ending in अ masquiline gender, nominative case, plural number, by affixing जस inflection, two forms were accomplished as मर्त्याः मर्त्यासः; ब्राह्मणाः, ब्राह्मणासः, देवाः: देवासः। However, in classical Sanskrit, only one form of each word namely मर्त्याः ब्राह्मणाः, देवाः was found in use. Similarly, the words ending in alphabetical letter अ masculine gender, instrumental case, plural number, by affixing भिस inflection, two forms of each word—देवोभिः, देवैः and पूर्वेभिः, पूर्वैः were accomplished in Vedic Sanskrit but only one single form of each word देवैः and पूर्वैः was used in classical Sanskrit. In Vedic Sanskrit, two forms of the word. अग्नौ and अग्ना etc. were formed in locative case, while only one form of the word अग्नौ was in use in classical Sanskrit. In Vedic Sanskrit, a verb had eleven लकार (A technical term used by Pāṇini to denote the mood or its terminations). Amongst them, it had an additional लेटलकार (to denote subjunctive mood or its terminations) also—such as—भवाति, पताति, तारिषत, etc. However, लेट लकार was not used in classical Sanskrit. There are only ten लकार in classical Sanskrit. There was the practice of formation of inflected nouns or verbs by suffixing तुमन (an infinitive). There were other suffixes as well implying the sense of 'Tuman', such as—from तवै. पातवै; from ध्यै गमध्यै from असै जीवसै etc. while only formation by suffixing तुमन् inflection was noticed in classical Sanskrit, such as— गन्तुम, मन्तुम, चलितुम्, अध्येयतुम् etc. In Vedic Sanskrit, in Lot Lakar (a technical term used by Pāṇini to denote imperative mood or its terminations) second person, plural number, four suffixes त, तन, थन, तात are applied. By inflecting these suffixes, we derive the words शिणोत, सुनोतन, यतिष्ठन, कृणुतात, However, in classical Sanskrit, only one suffix त is found, just as शिणुत.

In Vedic Sanskrit, several words are obtained by suffixing the inflection यु, just as युज्यु, देवयु, वाजयु etc. In classical Sanskrit, such inflected words almost disappeared. Only one or two words, such as दस्यु (a class of demons, enemies of gods and men and killed by Indra—the king of heaven) are found. In Vedic Sanskrit amongst the root words, which are seen in both आत्मने पद (one of the two voices in which roots are conjugated in Sanskrit and the terminations of this voice) and परस्मैपदः (one of the two voices in which verbs in Sanskrit are conjugated) only a few are found in classical Sanskrit under 'Atmnepada' category only. In Vedic Sanskrit, त्वद pronoun (a form of the second personal pronoun occurring as the first member of some compounds) is also used while in classical Sanskrit only तद (That) pronoun is found. In Vedic Sanskrit, the inflected forms of the word सर्वास्ती were in vogue, which is supported by the formation स्वस्तये (the averting of evil by the recitation of Mantras or performance of expiatory rites). In classical Sanskrit, however, the word स्वास्ति is treated as an indeclinable[1] from which no forms are

1. Sadrishaṁ trishu lingeṣhu sarvāsu caṇ vibhaktishu |
Vachaneṣhu cha Sarveshu yanna vyeti tadavyayaṁ ||

obtained. In Vedic Sanskrit, three accents of phonetic sounds—उदात्त (accute accent); अनुदात्त (low accent); and स्वरित (having circumflex accent, between high and low) are in use, while they are not used in classical Sanskrit. In Vedic Sanskrit, there is melodiousness like Greek language, but it is absent in classical Sanskrit. In Vedic Sanskrit, the use of the forms इय and इव is also noticed in place of य and व. The matching forms वीरियम and तुवम् are also found in Vedic Sanskrit as against वीर्यम् and त्वम respectively in classical Sanskrit. In Vedic Sanskrit, the suffix कत्वान is applied which is absent in classical Sanskrit. In Vedic Sanskrit, in locative case, singular number, the inflection ङि disappears. *For example*, the word व्यौमन (sky) used in Vedic Sanskrit, is changed to व्योमनि in classical Sanskrit. In Vedic Sanskrit the prefixes are placed slightly away from verbs. *For example*, प्र (a prefix meaning forward) placed in the beginning, away from the verb, as—प्र वभ्रवै शिवतिमाय शिवतीचे. However, in classical Sanskrit, they are placed immediately before the verb. In Vedic Sanskrit, the nature of compound words changes as soon as there is change in phonetic accent. *For example,* if the preceding word is aspirated, it is known as 'Bahuvrihi Compound' (Where two or more nouns in apposite to each other are compounded), but if the last word is aspirated, it turns into 'Tatpurusha Compound' (a class of compounded words in which the first member determines the sense of the other member or in which the last member is defined or qualified by the first without losing its original independence). For instance, इन्द्रशत्रु. In Vedic Sanskrit, there are 64 alphabetical letters but in classical Sanskrit, they are only 50.

There might have been numerous causes for obtaining a new morphological shape in the form of classical Sanskrit from ancient form of Vedic Sanskrit. One of the possibilities could be that Vedic Sanskrit had identified itself with Rigveda Sanskrit, which did not entertain any modifications. On the other hand, the contemporaneous Aryan languages, which were used as medium of speech in different regions with slight variations, continued changing and evolving with the wheel of time. That is to say, they were regularly in the process of evolution which is a life line for the growth and development of a language. It was, however, not the case with Vedic Sanskrit. Consequently, it continued getting alien from masses. Nevertheless, it had its great significance in the literary field for the country, and, therefore, its study and teaching was not held up. However, even for accomplishment of a literary form of the language, a simple, concise and intelligible shape of Vedic Sanskrit was essential, which was obtained in the form of classical Sanskrit.

It is obvious from the above differentiating points between Vedic and classical Sanskrit that classical Sanskrit is but simplified form of Vedic Sanskrit. Whereas, there was abundance of formations and alternative forms in Vedic Sanskrit, they either became extinct or abridged in classical Sanskrit. The descendants of the learned scholars who had an appreciation for Vedic Sanskrit, appropriated themselves with this new language. It was adopted by Aryans who had settled far and wide in India, for their literary pursuits.

Possibly, the language of the masses, popular in North or North-West regions, might have been the basis for evolving in the shape of classical Sanskrit. Consequent upon the same, it is considered special contribution of North in standardizing and refining the language. It is believed that the pronunciation and use of Sanskrit language in North was more appropriate and scholarly. For acquiring knowledge of Sanskrit language, students generally move to North. Similarly, the people eager for obtaining knowledge of Sanskrit, eagerly and attentively listened to the teachings of the scholars, whosoever visited them from North.

We have discussed above regarding correct use of language by people living in North. The fact is corroborated by the stone inscriptions found in North-West region, got inscribed by emperor Ashoka. There was a time when Kashmir was the most renowned centre of Sanskrit education. Highly reputed works of Sanskrit literature had been accomplished there. The above explanation is supported by this fact.

Medial Shape: The details of variations between Vedic and classical Sanskrit, discussed above, did not occur all atonce. The changes gradually took place which culminated in accomplishment of refined shape of classical Sanskrit with due grammatical constraints. The process of transformation look place in three phases. The first shape of Indo-Aryan language *i.e.* Vedic Sanskrit is found in Rigveda as well as other literary compositions of the same standard. In them, abundant formations from root words and sufficient alternative forms etc. can be found.

In Brahmaṇa treatises, the second form evolved in vedic Sanskrit is noticed. Names of एतरेय ब्राह्मण (Name of a Brahmaṇa treatise connected with Rigveda) and शतपथ ब्राह्मण (a well known Brahmana treatise attached to the Shukla Yajurveda) can be cited in this regard. From critical study of Brahmana treatises, it is evident that the use of abstruse words has been avoided as far as possible. Whereas, the classification as per root words belonging to the same rule and called after the first word of that series is not found in the first shape of Vedic Sanskrit, the same is witnessed in the second shape of Sanskrit in a systematic style.

Amongst the main changes that took place in the first and second linguistic shapes of Sanskrit, a few of them are illustrated here. In the first shape of Sanskrit, there were two inflected forms of words ending in letter अ with masculine gender, nominative case, plural number such as देवाः and दंवासः; but only one inflected form देवाः was found in Brahmanas. Similarly, in the first linguistic shape of Sanskrit, there were two inflected forms in Instrumental case as देवैः and देवेभिः but it was restricted to only one form देवैः in Brahmana treatises. The use of लेटलकार (A technical term used by Pāṇini to denote the Vedic Subjunctive mood or its terminations) is absent in Brahmaṇās. Several inflections suffixed, carrying the sense of तुमन were in use in the first shape of Sanskrit language. They have, however, disappeared in Brahmaṇas. Only the root word तुम is found. There is absolute similarity of the inflected forms of words and their meanings relating to लङ्ग लकार (A technical term used by Pāṇini to denote the imperfect tense or its terminations) as appeared in Brahmaṇas with those shown in Pāṇini's grammar.

The Sanskrit language used in composition of Brahmana treatises appears to be of transitional period while Vedic Sanskrit was gradually in the process of transformation to classical Sanskrit. This fact is amply supported by the above illustrations. However, it is equally worth-knowing that scholars of Brahmana treatises had followed Vedic Sanskrit in the use of words, application of inflections and formations from root words till then.

The third phase of evolution of Indo-Aryan language (Sanskrit) is obtained in 'Nirukta' (etymological compositions which contain glossorial explanations of obscure words especially those occurring in Vedas), authored by Yask, a great sage and exponent of etymological interpretations of Vedic Padas. Brahmana treatises are considered forming part of Vedas. However, it is not the case with 'Nirukta'. Rules followed for etymological formation of words (of Vedic Sanskrit) do not apply to Nirukta. Ofcourse, it has been composed in Sanskrit which is most ancient form of classical Sanskrit from linguistic viewpoint. On having a minute and critical study of 'Nirukta', it is found that many etymological formations of words, appeared in it, are missing in subsequent literature. Dr. Indra Chandra Shastry has produced below[1] : a few such words:

उपजन (आसपास)	Close by, near about
उपेक्षितव्य (परीक्षितव्य या प्राप्तव्य)	Worth being examined or due to be acquired.
कर्मन (अभिप्राय)	Purpose, Intention.
यथो (यथा)	Namely; *for example.*
उपदेशाय ग्लपयन्त (अध्यापन में असमर्थ)	Unable to teach.
शिशिक्ष राज्येन (राज्य पर आरूढ किया)	Seated on the throne.
बिल्म (विविधता)	Diversity; variation.
नैघण्टुक (गौण)	Secondary; subsidiary.
अनिर्वाह (ब्रह्मचर्य)	Celibacy.

A few techincal words which are not found in subsequent literature:-

निवृत्ति स्थान	(Weak terminations)
उपजन	(Prepositions)
उपबन्ध (आगम)	Anything handed down and fixed by tradition. The addition or insertion of a letter
नामकरण (संज्ञाओं से आने वाले प्रत्यय)	The technical name for an affix or suffix.

From the time of etymologist, Yāsk, and onwards, a change in the style of Sanskrit is quite apparent. It can be evaluated in two shapes (1) Pre-eminence of verbs, and (2) Pre-eminence of nouns.

Style having Pre-eminence of Verbs: Nouns and verbs are two main components of a sentence. A person keeps itself busy in one or the other activity. It remains associated with performance of one or the other act every moment. When the activeness of a person is desired to be expressed in writing, it is done

1. *Bharat ki Arya Bhāshāyen*, page 73-74.

by use of separate verbs having specific meanings. There the primary aim is the exposition of meaning, hence the sentences are small and clearly intelligible so that their sense may be clear without any difficulty. This is called a style of verbal pre-eminence. The style of verbal eminence was in vogue in Sanskrit literature during the eras of Yāsk and Pāṇini. In the literature accomplished during that period, the sentences are small. Verbs have been frequently used. Style of composition is simple and easy to be understood.

Style with Pre-eminence of Nouns: When the exposition of a feeling is considered more necessary, as a consequence of performance of an action, then the significance of the use of verbs is greater in a sentence. However, when the significance of the performer of an act becomes primary and its performance is given secondary importance, then the use of verbs in the aforesaid style is restrained or the use of verbs is made like an adjective to qualify the subject.

In the formation from a verbal root word, generally two elements are existent—an activity and the manner of its performance. *For example,* let us take the verbal root word 'दृश–दृश प्रेक्षणे' Here the use of the root word दृश has been made in the sense of प्रेक्षण the literal meaning of the word प्रेक्षण is not merely ईक्षण which means—seeing ordinarily, while प्रेक्षण means—seeing in a distinguished style. What is purported to mean here that the root word दृश besides meaning an act of seeing, there is a sense of seeing excellently or viewing minutely also. If the sense of excellence or minute made secondary, the word दृश loses its very significance. In that case, ordinary verbs like करोति अस्थि or भवति can meet the requirements. Consequently the use of correct verbs in a sentence becomes insignificant or their existence or non-existence in the sentence make no difference. Resultantly, their significance in a sentence becomes subordinate, or after losing their significance, they become unessential. It is called a style having supermacy of nouns. Even by converting the verbal root word in an adjective or in an ordinary verb, the sentence carries the sense. The inflections are also transformed into adjectives. Attention is drawn to a few examples given below:

Sentences having pre-eminence of verbs.	Sentences having supermacy of nouns
नरो रथमारूरूक्षत	नरो रथमारूढ
तेमन्यन्त	तैर्मतम्
स यन्त्रे चालयति	यन्त्र चालकः सः
अहं ग्रन्थपठम्	अहं ग्रन्थं पठितवान्
स क्रीडति	स क्रीडां करोति
अहं विवदामी	अहं विवादं करोमि
धर्म आचार्य्यते	धर्म आचरितो भवति
पुस्तकं पठ्यते	पुस्तकं पठितं भवति
स भाषते	स भाषणं करोति
ते स्तुन्वन्ति	ते स्तुतिं कुर्वन्ति
शास्त्रस्य वार्त्ता	शास्त्र सम्बन्धिनी वार्त्ता

कुम्भकारेण कृतःघटः	कुम्भकारकर्तृकः घटः
रोगेण कृता पीड़ा	रोगकर्तृका पीड़ा

In subsequent Sanskrit literature, the latter style has been predominantly followed. This led to greater use of compounded words. The entire sentence began to be summarised in an adjectival form.

In ancient Sanskrit literature, there was pre-eminence of verbs. The said style was followed in Brahmana treatises, forming part of Vedic literature. The styles of Yāsk and Pāṇini have already been discussed above. Even in the great commentary of Pātanjali, the style, having pre-eminence of verbs, has been predominantly followed. However, it is equally important to know that thereafter the style, having pre-dominance of nouns had begun to replace the old style of verbal predominance. This, however, establishes the unique significance of Sanskrit language in maintaining the exactness of the meaning even if the words are placed differently in a sentence.

The style, having pre-eminence of verbs was chiefly, evolved in philosophical and logical works as well as commentaries; while historical books, *Purānas* (well-known sacred books—18 in number, are supposed to have been composed by Vyās and contain the whole body of Hindu mythology) and Smirities (the body of traditional or memorial code of Hindu Laws) etc; were composed in the style, having pre-dominance of nouns. In commentary of Vatsāyayan over 'Nyaya Sūtras' (formulas of Nyaya philosophy by Gautama); Shabar commentary, authored by Jaimini on 'Mimānsā Sūtras' (one of the six chief systems of Indian philosophy, concerning itself mainly with the correct interpretations of Vedic rituals) besides several, other commentaries, written on 'Shrot Sutras' (a class of aphorisms', based on Vedas, ascribed to Sānkhyāyan and Kātyāyan), use of nominal style (having pre-eminence of nouns) is found. There is simplicity and vivacity in the style of composition. However, by the time of accomplishment of 'Navya-nyāya' (neo system of logics and jurisprudence), the said nominal style had turned abstruse and unintelligible. The use of verbs was curtained considerably. The inflections relating to nominative and ablative cases were mostly affixed such as 'Iyam Prithvi' (This earth); 'Gandhavatvāt' (scented and fragrant air); 'Ayamagni' (That fire); Dhumvatvāt (smoky air) etc. That is to say, the medium of conversatiton (human speech) became confined to use of mostlty adjectives and abstract nouns. The use of indeclinable particles also became very rare.

The Sanskrit scholars, primarily logicians (followers of Nyaya system of philosophy) even now prefer to adopt this style in religious debates. Ofcourse, exhibition of scholarship is there in the style but it has no utility for the masses. The artificiality and lack of spontaneity in language is quite obvious because of anxiety to exhibit scholarship at the cost of simplicity and straight-forwardness in style.

Vast Literature in Sanskrit

There are two great works—*Ramayāna* and *Mahābhārata*—accomplished in between the period of transformation from Vedic Sanskrit to classical Sanskrit. They are considered as great historical epics. Many prominent poetic and dramatic compositions such as *Kumar Sambhava*; *Sishupāl Vadh*; *Kirātārjuniya*; *Abhigyān Shākuntala*; *Uttar Ramcharit*; and *Anardharaghava* (Name of a drama in seven acts, authored by Mr. Murari Mishra) have derived their theme from them. Their language is very much in conformity with that of classical Sanskrit. However, old forms of words, simplicity and straight-forwardness in style, unrestricted use of inflected forms of root words, irrespective of any consideration of inflectional differences of 'Atmanapada' (one of the two voices in which roots are conjugated in Sanskrit) and 'Paraismaipada' (one of the two voices in which verbs in Sanskrit are conjugated) are a few aspects which show resemblance of these works with Vedic Sanskrit as well. From linguistic viewpoint, both these epics can be considered as connecting link between Vedic and classical Sanskrit. Both *Rāmāyana* and *Mahābhārata* present a vivacious picture of erstwhile Indian culture, folk life, social traditions and ethical values.

Words like history, legendary tales and Pūrānas (ancient or legendary history) are in use since Vedic period. In Vedic literature, the stories of 'Pururavā and Urvashi' (a famous Apsara or nymph of Indra's heaven who became the wife of king Pururavā) and "Shunaḥ Shesh" (Name of a Vedic sage, son of Ajigarta—In the Aitreya Brahmana, it is related that King Hariśachandra, being childless, made a vow that on obtaining a son; be would sacrifice him to the God Varuna. A son was born who was named Rohita, but the king put off the fulfilment of the vow under various pretexts. At last Rohita purchased for one hundred cows sunahsepha, the middle son of Ajigarta as a substitute for himself to be offered to Varuna, but the boy praised Vishnu, Indra and other deities and escaped death. He was then adopted by Vishvamitra in his own family and called by the name of Devarta etc. are found which are reflective of the taste of scholars in composition of eventful stories.

There is an accepted interpretation of history since ancient times. According to the said definition, the works which contain the past eventful stories as well as teachings concerning four ends of human existence *i.e.* attainment of spiritual or moral uplifitment, worldly prosperity, sensual pleasures and final emancipation etc. constitute the history, *Rāmāyana* and *Mahābhārata* are found fulfilling all these requirements. It is evident from the quotation reading "इतिहासपुराणाभ्यां वेदं समुपबृहयेत" that historical events and Pūrānas (legendary tales) have admittedly contributed to the enrichment and growth of Vedic culture founded on spiritual knowledge.

Rāmāyana: Through the biography of 'Maryada Purshottam Rama' (An epithet of Rama, the best amongst mankind with propriety of conduct), an attractive portrayal of ideal rule, dutifulness, justice, morality, ethics, tenderheartedness, compassion, sacrifice, service, dedication, affection and an exemplary household life has been given. It was authored by the sage Valmiki who was emotionally moved to hear the heart rending cry of a female curlew, while the male curlew enjoying sexual activity, was killed by a fowler and, spontaneously, he composed a condolence verse-शोक=२ लोकतत्व भागतः ।[1] Abruptly he utters the following

1. *Rāmāyana*, Balkand 2, 40.

words:

मा निषाद । प्रतिष्ठास्त्वमगमः शाश्वतोः समाः ।
यत्क्रौंचमिथुनादेकमवधीः काममोहितम् ।[1]

The said words spontaneously came out in grief in the shape of a 'Anustapa' Verse (a class of metre consisting of 4 padas of 8 syllables each, the whole stanza consisting of 32 syllables).

Mahābhārata is, infact, a grand encyclopaedia, comprising of several poetic works, written by different poets. Rāmāyana is not the composition of that nature which is an accomplishment of a single intellectual. It is believed that after accomplishment of Vedic literature, it was the first poetic creation by a human-being. Accordingly, the Rāmāyana had been written by first ever poet, Valmiki and it was his first endeavour. It has been fully established by the scholars after critical examination and thorough investigation that Ramayana is one of the greatest epics, having rhetorical poetic form and there has been an excellent manifestation of poetic skill in this holy book. The delicacy of style, use of simple and popular glossary, incorporation of figures of speech, where best suited, complete assimilation of all poetic sentiments and minute characterization are some of the fundamental characteristics of Rāmāyana. It is believed that there is hardly any other collection of folk poetry of this nature in the entire universal literature.

Regarding the body and size of Rāmāyana, Valmiki has himself stated as under:

चतुर्विंशत्सहस्राणि श्लोकानामुक्तवानृषिः ।
तथा सर्गशतान् पंच षट काण्डानि तथोत्तरम् ।[2]

The sage Valmiki composed 24,000 verses and classified them into 500 cantos and six sectional divisions.

There are more than 24,000 verses in Rāmāyana, available now. The number of cantos is 645. It clearly indicates that certain changes have decidedly taken place here and there in the basic contents of Rāmāyana. Some portions have been interpolated, a few cantos have been removed and a few others have been newly added. Hence Rāmāyana, available now, cannot be treated as original one which had been actually written by Valmiki. However, it must be emphasized that major portion of Rāmāyana is original and only a small portion has been interpolated or added afresh. Decidedly, the contents of Rāmāyana have not been so much disturbed as those of Mahābhārata. Some portion may be detected to have been interpolated while making a critical evaluation but the major portion of the original Rāmāyana is bound to remain undisturbed.

There are divergent views of Western scholars with regard to the bonafides of Rāmāyana. Prof. Bevar believes that it is based on Buddhist treatise 'Dasarath Jātaka' and English novel '*Iliyada*', written by Homer. Prof. Jacobi claims its consistency with the legendary tale of Indra and Vritra, appearing in Rigveda.

1. *Rāmāyana*, Balkand 2, 15.
2. *Rāmāyana* 1, 4, 2.

According to Mr. Talasvayaz wheeler, Rāmāyana is based on the adventurous victory achieved by the founders of Vijayanagar dynasty in South in 13th century A.D. Mr. Lasen is of the view that Rāmāyana is a versified manifestation of the first expedition undertaken by Aryans for battle and victory achieved in South. As a matter of fact, these opinions are only one-sided and mere reflections of immature study. Indian scholars have written a lot in this regard. Hence any further consideration of the subject is no more desirable now.

Mahābhārata

Mahābhārata has been attached greater significance than Rāmāyana by eulogizing that it is the fifth Veda in India. In fact, no other composition is treated so authentic as a Vedic text under Vedic tradition. By considering Mahāhbhārata as fifth Veda, the Indian scholars have offered their greatest tribute to it. It has been claimed in Mahābhārata itself that what has been propounded in it with regard to the four ends of human existence *i.e.* spiritual and moral uplift; attainment of prosperity, sensual pleasures and final emancipation, the same has been repeated elsewhere, may be in a different manner:;यदिहास्ति तदयन्त्र यन्नेहास्ति न तत् क्वचित्[1] what does not find place in Mahābhārata, will not be found elsewhere atleast in India.[2] This should not be mistaken as mere exaggeration. *Gita*, being only a small component of Mahābhārata holds a unique place in world literature and this is enough to establish its significance. Vyasdeva, author of Mahābhārata, has himself called it heroic history: जयो नामेतिहासोऽ यं श्रोतव्यो विजिगीषुणा.[3] It appears that in olden days Mahabharata, itself, might have been studied as history, Vyas also calls it a poetical composition. While particularly addressing Brahma (The first deity of the sacred Hindu Trinity, to whom is entrusted the work of creating the world), he says: कृतं मयेदं भगवन्! काव्यं परमपुजितम् (Brahma replied to him : त्वया च काव्यमित्युक्त तस्मात् काव्यं भविष्यति।)

Eminent poetic scholar, Acharya Anandvardhan, considered Mahābhārata to be a great epic which provided material for composition of many other epics under the tradition of figurative poetry. He has quoted extracts from Mahābhārata repeatedly, wherever, necessary, which are really heart-touching and overwhelmingly emotional and after explaining their inherent-meanings in a critical manner, he has established that although illustrations of all types of poetical sentiments can be found in Mahābhārata, yet the predominant sentiment is that of quietism.

Mahābhārata is, undoubtedly, the greatest epic amongst all historical works available in the world, keeping in view its qualities and elaborateness. The learned scholars compare Vyas with European authors—Homer and Dante but even if 'Iliyad and Adisi', the two works of Homer are combined, Mahābhārata will still be found 8 times voluminous in size. There are 18 sections in Mahābhārata. The biggest section is 'Shantiparva' (relating to settlement of differences and reconciliation), There are 14,000 *verses* in the said section. 'Harivansha' can be

1. *Mahābhārata*, Ādi Pārva, 62-26
2. Yanna Bharate tanna Bharate.
3. *Mahābhāratā*, Ādi Pārva 62-22.

considered its supplement or 19th section. There is detailed representation of Kauravas and Pāndavas in Mahābhārata while that of Lord Krshna and Yādavas is contained in Harvan's. After including Harivansha, there are one lac *verses* in Mahābhārata. It is, undoubtedly unique, voluminous and a gigantic accomplishment. Therefore, in the course of emphasizing the appropriateness of its name, it has been stated: महत्वाद भारवत्वाच्च महाभारतमुच्यते.[1]

The difficult and obscure subjects relating to philosophical, political, social and economic problems have been elaborately discussed in Mahābhārata. It incorporates and deals with methods and manners concerning 4 castes and stages of life, duties alongwith other poignant topics relating to four ends of human existence, namely—moral and spiritual upliftment, attainment of prosperity, sensual pleasures and final emancipation. The old forms of words have been used in abundance. The language is straightforward with obvious flow. Although poetic charm of Rāmāyana is not there, yet the elegance of words and popular sayings are excellent which are repeatedly found and which give the very impression of Rāmāyana. The chief characteristics of the style of Vyasa are elaborateness and clarity. The obvious qualities of bodily strength and straightforwardness are clearly perceived in the characters of Mahābhārata. The major portion of Mahābhārata is full of dialogues. Undoubtedly, Vyas has no match in composing dialogues.

There is another distinguishing feature of Vyasdeva. He has a deep insight into portrayal of strange diversities in human character. There is a reference. Ashwatthāmā beheaded all the five sons of Draupadi (common wife of 5 Pāndavas). She cries with loud shreiks as a consequence of unbearable agony and enormous grief on account of gruesome murder of all her sons. Arjuna traces out Ashwatthāmā and after tethering him like an animal drags him all along to produce him before Draupadi. While Arjun was about to decapitate him, Draupadi falls at his feet and readily forgives Ashwatthāmā.

There are innumerable illustrations of human sensitivity, emotional delicacy, generosity etc. in Mahābhārata that even adamantine and cruel persons get emotionally moved on reading or hearing them. The eminent poet, Vyāsa, belonging to an extremely religions and peace-loving country, has given his vital message at the end of Mahābhārata in the following words:

न जातु कामान्न भयान्न लोभाद्,
धर्म त्यजेनजीवितस्यापि हेतो: ।

One should not forsake the path of spiritual endeavour even on the face of adverse conditions, allurement of sensual pleasures or under the grip of fear and temptation—nay even at the cost of one's own life.

In Mahābhārata, now available, there are certain prosaic pieces as well. They are found in different sections of Mahābhārata. There are three prosaic picces (compositions not meterical, yet framed with due regard to harmony) in 'Adi Parva' (the first section of Mahābhārata); and seven pieces in each 'Vanparva' (section regarding Pāndavas leading the life in wood) and 'Shantiparva' (section relating to quietism or reconciliation). There are three prosaic portions in 'Aushāsan Parva'

1. *Mahābhāratā*, Ādi Pārva, 1,300.

(name of 13th section of Mahābhārata—so called, because it lays down precepts of advice). Thus, there are 20 prosaic portions in all. The style and language of prosaic pieces are of divine nature. Mostly, they are in the shape of episodes, narrated by sages. It is evident from the language that the said prosaic pieces, repeated by holy persons, are most ancient episodic references. On the basis of their ancientness, the Western scholars are of the opinion that Mahābhārata is older than Rāmāyana. However, the point worth consideration is that many series of events, related in Rāmāyana, are either referred to or reproduced at several places in Mahābhārata. In case, Mahābhārata had preceded Rāmāyana, how could it then be practicable? Therefore, it may not be inconsistent to believe that the said prosaic pieces had been written much earlier but added to Mahābhārata later on.

It is believed after long analytical scrutiny and examination that considerable material has been added to Mahābhārata subsequently. Vyasa had composed this great epic incorporating historical events concerning Kauravas. (relating to the Kurus) and Pandavas (five sons of King Pandu). Initially, Vyasa had titled the book as 'Jaya' (victory). It appears that from Chapter 65 of 'Adi parva' (Initial or first section) Vyasdeva had started writing Mahābhārata (A celebrated epic which describes the rivalries and contests of the sons of Dhritaraśtra and Pandu). The earlier portion of Mahābhārata appear to have been composed later on. In the Chapter 65, there is a mention of the origin of 'Chhatriyas' (warrior class or the regal caste in the traditional Hindu caste hiararchy). With the passage of time, there was regular addition to Mahābhārata so much so that it became practically impossible to trace out the portions which had genuinely been written and composed by Vyas. Vyas further expanded his work after the end of Kauravas and Pandavas. This could be considered as first edition of the celebrated epic.

Parikṣata was the son of Abhimanu and grandson of Arjuna. He died of snake-bite as a consequence of imprecation by sage 'Shringi'. Janmejaya was the son of King Parikṣata. He performed a Yagna to destroy the very progeny of snakes. It is believed that sage Vyasa had also participated in that Yagna. Janmejaya had entreated him to kindly describe the events of war between his ancestors, Pandavas and Kauravas. Vyasa, himself, did not like to narrate the contents of his great epic 'Jaya' but directed his disciple, Vaishampāyan, to do so on his behalf. Vaishampāyan obeyed the instructions of his preceptor. In the course of narration of the epic Janmejaya asked certain questions to satisfy his inquisitiveness Vaishampāyan spared no pains to satisfy him. It appears that the answers given by Vaishampāyan did not form part of the original texts of Mahābhārata, as written by Vyasa. It is, however, not evident whether Vaishampāyan exercised his own talents in providing answers or he obtained the information from elsewhere. The answers given by Vaishampāyan either got mixed or were added to the original work of Vyāsa. In this way, another edition of Mahābhārata was accomplished, which was, obviously, more extensive than the previous one. The enlarged edition, that came into existence through Vaishampāyan, was styled as 'Bharat Saṁhita'. It is related in Ādi parva (first section of Mahābhārata) as under:

चतुर्विंशतिसाहस्त्रीं चक्रे भारतसंहिताम्,
उपाख्यानैर्विना तावद् भारतं प्रोच्यते बुधैः।[1]

Besides episodes, there are 24,000 verses in 'Bharat Saṁhita'. It leads us to infer that in the original epic, styled 'Jaya', composed by Vyasa, the number of *verses* must have been less than 24,000 but it could not be much less. Vaishampāyan might have added only a small portion. Sometime later, another incident took place. Holy seer Shaunika sponsored a Yajna which was to continue for 12 years in 'Nemisāranya' (Name of a sacred forest celebrated as the residence of certain sages to whom Sautiji related the Mahābhārata). Many scholars, well-*versed* in recitation of Vedas, intellectual and learned seers and sages had participated in that Yajna. Amongst participants, there was one sage, named Sauti, son of Saint 'Romharshan'. The said sage, Sauti, had also participated in the yajna, performed by Janmejaya for sacifice of snakes, and he had also listened to the recitation of the texts of Mahābhārata by Vaishampāyan. Sauti reproduced the texts of Mahābhārata, which had been related by Vaishampāyan. Berides them, he repeated the episodets and short tales also. While reproducing the text of Mahābhārata wherever it was found necessary or while the questions were asked, he expressed his own impressions as well.This led to the accomplishment of the third edition which includes 'Harivansha'. Sauti composed and added a new portion at the commencement of Mahābhārata which could be considered as a preface; a foreword or an index of the subjects discussed therein. In this way, whole body of Mahābhārata contained one lac *verses*. Sauti also gave a new shape to the section-wise division of Mahābhārata. It was originally divided in 100 sections. Sauti re-arranged it in 18 larger sections, after undertaking a critical examination of the holy book. Sections were further sub-divided in chapters. Thus a large and voluminous epic of Mahābhārata was accomplished. The saying महत्वा भारवतवाच्च महाभारत मुच्यते might have become popular on accomplishment of the massive third edition.

A question may obviously arise as to why such a huge shape was given to 'Mahābhārata', which made it quite difficult to even identify the original texts, written by Vyasa. If the basic part cannot be identified, it may not be beneficial in any view of the matter. This badly affects the uniform flow of the language. However, it all happened. There could be several factors responsible for it. Possibly, one such idea might have been that Mahābhārata must turn into an encyclopaedia incorporating sacred miscellaneous knowledge, ethology and morality etc. Therefore, knowingly all those topics might have been taken up to be discussed and included in it for achieving the above aim. Then only the saying 'यदिहास्ति तत् सर्वत्र यन्नेहास्ति न तत् क्वाचित्' could have been justified. There could be another reason as well. With the lapse of tune, some portion of the original Mahābhārata might have been destroyed. In order to make it up, the learned scholars might have composed and added to it, a number of *verses* and chapters. How much portion had actually been destroyed and how much replacement was considered essential, had become

1. *Mahābhārata*, Ādi Parva, 1, 78.

secondary and insignificant. In the said process, it is quite possible that several wanted and unwanted portions might have been added to it. However, one soothing result was that the objective of giving Mahābhārata, a shape of grand encyelopaedia, incorporating all important subjects relating to sacred miscellaneous knowledge, science of morality and ethology, dutyfulness, knowledge of truth and principles of philosophy and religion etc. had been accomplished. Nevertheless, it also resulted in unprecedented damage to the elements of linguistic science, so much so that the fundamental texts of Mahābhārata have lost sight of and it has now become quite diffiicult to identify them clearly.

There has not been a long gap in between the period of accomplishment of 3 editions of Mahābhārata as per eventualities, refered to above, which led to further additions and enlargement of it. Hence it should not be believed that there was any fundamental change in the standard or precision of language. However, if the said process of enlargement, actuated by the aforesaid events, would have stopped thereafter, it was alright, but it is found that this process, had continued even thereafter, with the result, the addition of new material and enlargement of the sacred book, was carried on uninterruptedly. After making a profound and critical investigation of the large range of subjects treated therein, it is obtained that the topics relating to ascetic culture (austerities to be performed by religious mendicants) such as non-violence total indifference to worldly objects, detachment, endurance etc. Knowledge of the Supreme Spirit (manifested as the individual self) have also been dealt with in it. The significance of Mahābhārata in Sanskrit canonical literature will remain for ever. There is a lot of material contained in it in order to be able to make comparative study and analytical research in regard to linguistics, philosophy and culture.

On the basis of Ramāyana and Mahābhārata as also the illustrious literature accomplished in Sanskrit, thereafter, has unique significance of its own in world literature from all angles. Right from the period of Rāmāyana and Mahābhārata, till the life time of Moghul Emperor, Shahjahan, there has been an unbroken sequence of literary accomplishment in Sanskrit of an extremely high standard. To an extent, the practice is going on unceasingly even now.

Was Sanskrit Language— A Medium of Expression?

There are two divergent opinions of learned scholars whether Sanskrit was the medium of speech amongst the masses or not. As per Western scholars-Harnly, George Griyason and Baiver, Sanskrit was not used as the medium of conversation amongst common people. On the contrary, Dr. Sir Ramkrishna Gopal Bhandarker and Dr. P.D. Gune have admitted that Sanskrit language was, onetime, the medium of speech amongst general masses. They have strongly refuted the opinion of Western scholars who donot agree to it. According to them, there are rules in Sanskrit grammar which can only apply to the language used for mutual conversation relating to the acts of invocation, salutation introduction and exchange of views etc. They do realise that there is slight distinction between the shapes of a language used in accomplishment of literary compositions and that used in mutual conversation in as much as the literary language is more polished and bound by grammatical rules while the one used by people at large in mutual conversation is comparatively less constrained and bound by rules. However, inspite of this, there is not too much difference so that they could be considered as two separate forms of sanskrit language.

The fact that the nature of Sanskrit, which was given a refined shape by Pāṇini, was the same, used as medium of speech by common people, does not appeal to mind. It could be possible only when a conforming or closely resembling vocabulary was used as medium of conversation which was very close to Sanskrit. However, it is not worth believing. A language, free from constraints of grammarian rules and used at free will could never be treated as Sanskrit. In such a case, its refined and cultured shape will no longer be able to survive. As a matter of fact, the nature of language, used in accomplishment of literary works alone could remain within the constraints of grammatical rules. It is practically not possible for the language of general masses to observe any such constraints. The conversational language is always disposed towards growth and development oriented. The evolution of language is also termed as change of its form or nature. Its literal sense is deviation from the natural state which only means transformation to a different shape but not a low form of the language.

It is explicit from the shape and appearance of Sanskrit that it has been a superior and civilized language. Undoubtedly, the section of highly learned scholars must have been using it while conversing with each other. Even now, it is experienced that as and when the scholars assemble and converse mutually they generally use this refined language. There is also a directive for Vaids in Aryurvedic literature to use Sanskrit, whenever they happen to assemble and converse with each other.

Ofcourse, Sanskrit was grammatically refined language but it was not far removed from the language, used for mutual conversation. Thus it appears plausible that in olden days, the masses could conveniently follow Sanskrit vocabulary, spoken by the learned intellectuals but they, themselves, were not able to reply in Sanskrit. A positive proof of this is found in Sanskrit dramas, written in later era. In these dramas, there is a specific provision for use of a language by different characters. Wandering religious mendicants, Brahmanas, Kings, Judges, Ministers, Chiefs of army and characters belonging to higher status of families spoke Sanskrit language wsile delivering their dialogues. On the other hand, ladies, depressed classes, labourers, peasants, male and female slaves, shopkeepers etc. belonging to second category of characters (People of ordinary and lower status who are generally called now as ordinary people or common masses) were directed to speak in their own Prākrita dialects. When an attendant or servant character converses with a king, he listens to the commands given by the king in Sanskrit and replies to him in his own *Prākrita* dialect. Had he not been in a position to follow the talks of the king in Sanskrit, how could he be able to reply? Thus it is clear that during the days of popularity of Sanskrit the language spoken by the common people was not Sanskrit but it was very much close to it.

In Sanskrit dramas, the use of Prākrita dialects is not less in any way but on the contrary their use is even more frequent than Sanskrit. The number of characters speaking in Sanskrit is also lesser than those speaking in Prākrita dialects. For instance, there are in all 30 characters in, Sanskrit drama 'Mrichhakatika', written by Shudraka, amongst whom only four[1] characters converse in Sanskrit while remaining 26 speak in Prākrita dialects. Sometimes, in certain dramatic performances the characters normally conversing in Prākrita dialects, are casually shown speaking in Sanskrit as well wherever the situation so demands. *For example*, in Sanskrit drama 'Chārudatta', written by Bhas, wife of hero, Chārudatta being a high-born lady, is shown speaking in Sanskrit also although, primarily she delivers her dialogues in Prākrita dialect only. From the above arrangement in dramas, it is evident that normally Prākrita dialects formed part of the conversation by common people, while Sanskrit was used by characters of higher origin and status and that too rarely and with great effort.

The popular language, used by the common people remains in vogue but such a language is not uniform everywhere. Subject to variance in territories, castes, communities and professions, etc,. the shape of the language undergoes change and that too in different ways. Acārya Bharat, the renonwed dramatist, has given a detailed account of respective prakrita, to be spoken by characters of different categories in a drama. For further elucidation of the subject under discussion, its mention here is essential. Bharat has categorised the respective Prākrita dialect of characters, belonging to different categories as under:

Characters	*Prakrita Dialect to be Spoken*
1. An attendant (servant) Prince, Seth (a wealthy person)	Ardh Magadhi
2. Cunning (A crooked fellow)	Avantija (now known as Ujjaini)
3. Keepers of elephants, horses, goats and camels etc. and people residing near stables.	Abhir or Shabari (a low form of Prakrita dialect).
4. Khas (Inhabitants of mountaneous region in North India; Sakar (The brother of a kings concubine, usually represented as a strange mixture of pride, folly and vanity) Ghoshaka (A crier, proclaimer) and people of the similar nature	Khāsi (a dialect spoken in Khas region of North India)
5. Pulkas (Name of a mixed tribe in India)	Chāṇḍāli (lowest form of Prakrita dialect spoken by outcastes).
6. Gamblers, Town-watchmen, wrestlers.	Dravadian language spoken in South.
7. Forest-dwellers (Woodmen)	Drāmaḍi
8. Watchmen (keeping watch on the diggers of tunnel in the palace); horse-keepers or riders; distressed hero (A hero involved in difficulties)	Magadhi

1. Hero Chārudatta Viṭṭa Aryaka and a robber, named Sharvilaka belonging to Brahmana Community.

9. Jesters etc.	Prāchayā (The Eastern dialect-language spoken in the east of India.
10. Northerners	Vahinik
11. Emberers, (those who prepare coal for sale) hunters, carpenters (Partly foresters)	Shakāri dialect
12. Heroine and her friend	Shorseni Prākrita

The names of various dialects given above, are, infact, different shapes of Prākrita dialects spoken at different places by different castes and communities as also different professionals. Even now, it is found that a language spoken in the same state is spoken with slight variations by the people, belonging to different territories, professions, classes and communities. Within the precincts of the same town or village, the style, accent and manner of pronunciation by Brahman community is somewhat different from that of the trading class. The Harijan communities (depressed classes) use the same dialect in their own typical style and slightly at variance from others.

The purport of the above discussion is that the variations shown above in the use of dialects by different characters in the dramatic performances is sufficient proof of the fact that there was, no doubt, an explicit difference in the dialects used by the eminent and distinguished persons of the society on one hand and that spoken by ordinary people in those days on the other. The civilized and polished gentry must be feeling proud while speaking in Sanskrit language since this language received royal patronage for a very long period. The kings having regard for Vedic texts (Vedas, Brahmnas, Aranayaks and Upniṣadas etc.) believed in divinity of Sanskrit language in which the Vedas and other religious scriptures had been accomplished. Consequent upon the same, it was honoured as state official language. The copper plates on which grants of land were generally inscribed; gift-deeds and writings of admiration in praise of somebodies—all were scribed in Sanskrit. With colonies and embassies, established by Indian emperors in other countries, the contact language was Sanskrit. It had influenced local languages of those countries as well to a certain degree. It is why, we find Sanskrit words mixed with the languages of Tibet, China, Japan, Korea, Afghanistan and group of East islands.

There had been accomplishment of literary compositions in Sanskrit without any interruption since it was the recognized language of distinguished and eminent literateurs. Consequently, brilliant and genious scholars of Sanskrit had produced such unique and rare literary works which are considered as most accomplished pieces of world literature. Sanskrit produced such laureate poets like Kālidas, Māgh, Bhārvi and Sriharsha who were unparallel in the history and had their own distinct characteristics.

3

MIDDLE INDO-ARYAN LANGUAGES

Prākritas

As per chronological order, determined by the philologists concerning period of evolution of Indo-Aryan languages, the period of Prākritas dates back to 500 B.C. However, this determination had, probably, been made when Sanskrit had already accomplished a literary shape. Although, there is perfect unanimity and belief regarding ancientness of Vedic Sanskrit, yet it does not appear feasible that it was ever used as a medium of speech by people at large. Sanskrit language was meant only for accomplishing literary compositions by sages, scholars and priests. It is quite possible that numerous dialects, having consistency and resemblance with Vedic Sanskrit might have been in vogue. The great commentator, Pātanjali, had elaborately disucussed regarding use of different forms of the same word in different regions of the country in his commentary. Probably, this supports the view that after coming in close contact with regional dialects, either some words of Vedic Sanskrit might have adopted different shapes or certain specific forms of words of Vedic Sanskrit might have been adopted and included in their dialects. This also may not be considered unbelievable that any one of the said dialects, itself, might have adopted the shape or literary form of prosodical Vedic Sanskrit after having been perfected and refined in due course of time.

Certain scholars are of the view that composition of Vedas had started after arrival of second batch of Āryans in India. Āryans of the second batch arrived in Central India enroute Punjab and coastal regions of Saraswati and Drasadwati rivers. During the course of migration and settlement, some portions of Vedas were composed in Punjab and coastal valley of Saraswati and Drashadwati rivers while major portions of Vedas were composed in Central India. As already stated above, a major portion of Atharva veda, which is considered to have been written much later, was composed in an Eastern part of India.

There is absolutely no indication of having accomplished any literary works—at par with Vedas by the first batch of Aryans who had been diriven away by the second batch of Aryans from Central India. Consequently, there is no literature found in and around Central India in any of the dialects spoken or used by the people, having lived there. Hence there is no way to find out the characteristics of those ancient dialects, nor there is any material for arriving at any conclusion to that effect. There must have been some other forms of those dialects in pre-Vedic age also which might have been found in vogue and spoken by people at large in Western, Northern, Central and Eastern regions in India and subsequently refined during Vedic era after coming into contact with Aryans. Sir George Griyason has named the said local dialects, concurrent with Vedic period or in use prior to it, as Primary Prakritas. The period of the said primary Prākritas is considered from 2000 to 600 B.C. It is believed that these primary Prākritas had considerable similarity in pronunciation, phonetic sounds of vowels and consonants as also use of inflections etc. with Vedic Sanskrit. Having gone through the process of growth and development, the later Prākritas had obtained literary form as apparent from the shape of subsequent Prākritas.

The great commentator, Pātanjali, has discussed and laid stress regarding usefulness and significance of grammar and grammatical constraints at the very outset of his commentary. While emphasizing the importance of refraining from use of malevolent words and instead using correct forms of words, he has quoted the following verse:

"यस्तु प्रयुक्ते कुशलो विशेषे, शब्दान् यथावद् व्यवहार काले।
सोऽनन्तमाप्नोति जयं परत्र वाग्योगविद् दुष्यति चापशब्दैः।।[1]

It means that a person who is conversant with the use of correct and appropriate words or is proficient in so doing, he enjoys eternal happiness, exaltation and supreme bliss in heaven. On the contrary, one who makes use of bad or ungrammatical words (in form or meaning), he is liable to suffer ill consequences on account thereof.

While stating about wrong and ungrammatical words, he further writes that each and every word has its incorrect forms (whether formed against the rules of grammar or used in a sense not strictly Sanskrit) such as 'Gāvo, 'Gauṇi' and 'Gopotalika' in place of Sanskrit word 'Gau' (cow).[2]

Here the word 'Apbhranśa' has not been used for those languages or dialects which were spoken from 5th to 10th centuries A.D. in Western, Eastern, Northern and Central territories of India, which were, infact, developed forms of ancient Prākritas. Here the word 'Apbharanśa' (lowest form of Prākrita) has been used for the incorrect words of local dialects other than Sanskrit which could be deemed as Prākritas of that period. It appears that the use of local dialects was made extensively by then. It is quite possible that the words of those local dialects might have started mixing with Vedic and classical Sanskrit. Hence the preceptors and scholars might have made concerted efforts to check infiltration of incorrect words, who were strongly in favour of maintaining orginality and correctness of Vedic Sanskrit. The analytical discussion of Patanjali in his commentary also hints to this effect.

Pātanjali further states— "It is said that there were two sages named `Yarvānaḥ and Tarvānaḥ'. They had intuitive perception of religion. They were well conversant with highest knowledge of spiritualism and worldly wisdom. Whatever was conceivable, they had already become aware of. They had also realised the Supreme Truth. Such respectful seers, who ought to have pronounced the words "Yad vā nah: Tad vā nah" actually pronounced "Yarvanaḥ Tarvanaḥ". However, they were very cautious not to pronounce words incorrectly while performing yajnas. The demons had incorrectly pronounced the Mantras with the result, they had to suffer

1. *Mahabhāsya,* Pratham Āhnika, page 7.
2. Ekaikasya Shabdasya bahvo-apbhranshāḥ, Adyāyagaurityetasya shabdasya Gāvi, Gauni, Gopotalitetyvāmadyo apabhransāh.

— *Mahābhāsya,* Ist Ahnika, page 8.

defeat.[1]

What Pātanjali probably means to emphasize here is that even highly learned preceptors, belonging to Vedic tradition, did use some words of local Vernaculars in their day today conversation. He is even prepared to ignore it. However, he lays stress on the point that wrong and incorrect pronunciation of Vedic Mantras must not be allowed in any case since it renders a disastrous situation. It is manifestly clear when he says that the intellectuals were very much perturbed to find that the successive growth of local dialects and their excessive use was so rapidly growing that it was feared that it might not interfere with correct pronunciation of Vedic Mantras relating to religious rituals concerning Yajnas. He even lays down that in case vulgar or impure words were uttered by an oblator, while offering oblations, then he should perform yajna to please goddess Saraswati with a view to seek atonement.[2]

Pātanjali writes at one place . . . "The interpretations which have not been approved or accepted in religious commandments in order to have correct knowledge of vowels and consonants in regular order or sequence, the collection of indicatory forms of words (any word or part of a word, such as an affix, augment etc. with its anubandhas which show what particular grammatical rules are to be applied) is favoured so that incorrect use of 'षष' in place of 'शश'; 'पलाष' in place of 'पलाश' and 'मञ्जक' in place of 'मञ्चक' may not start."[3]

Pātanjali deals with another point. It is in respect of those words which had not been brought in use in Saskrit literature during his life time or even prior to him, although the said words formed part of Sanskrit vocabulary. He has selected four words 'ऊष', 'तेर', 'चक्र', 'पेच' by way of illustration. He has also mentioned that the forms 'ऊषिता' in place of 'ऊष'; 'तोर्णा' in place of 'तेर'; 'कृतवन्तः in place of 'चक्र' and 'पक्ववन्तः' in place of 'पेच' had appeared in Sanskrit literature.[4]

While avoiding to criticize regarding disuse or wrong use of the above forms of words, he further states: "It is quite possible that the forms of Sanskrit words, which are considered to have been disused, might be in use in other countries or regions which we may not be knowing. We must try to find out where those forms of Sanskrit words were in use. The area using Sanskrit glossary is too extensive. This terrestrial globe consists of 7 islands (all situated round the mountain

---

1. Evaṁ hi Śruate—Yarvāṇastarvāno nām Rishyo babhuvuḥ pratyakṣadharmānaḥ parāvaragyā Vidit – Veditavya adhigatyāthātathyāḥ | Te tatra bhavanto yādha na iti prayoktavye yarvānastarvānaḥ iti prayuinjate yāgye punaḥ karmaṇi nāpnhāsante, Taiḥ punrasurairyāgye karmanyāpbhāsitaṁ tataste parābhūtāḥ.

—*Mahabhāṣya*, Ist Arnika, pages 37-38.

2. Yāgyikāḥ pathanti Āhitāgnirapaśabdaṁ prayujya prāścittiyaṁ Śaraswati mistiṁ nirvapeta

— *Mahabhāṣya*, I Ahnika, page 14.

3. . . . Yani taharyagrahṇāni pratipavikani, eteśāmapi swarvarṇānupūrvi gyānārth updesaḥ kartavyaḥ शशः षष iti mā bhūt पलाशः पलाष iti mā bhūt, मञ्चको मञ्जक iti mā bhūt

— Same, page 48

4. Aprayogaḥ khalvapyeṣām shabdānām nyayyaḥ | kutaḥ prayoganyatvat/1 Yadeshāṁ sabdanamarthe nāyanehabdānprayunjate Yadythā ushetyasya sabdasyārthe kwa yuymushita tertyasyarthe kwa yuyam kiṁah cakretasyarthe kwa yuyam kutvantah pecetyaryarthe kwa yuyam pakrantite

— *Mahābhāṣya*, 1st Ahnika, page 31

Meru like the petals of a lotus flower, and each island being separated from the other by a distinct ocean. The central one is 'Jambudweep' in which is included India) and 3 `Lokas' (Three worlds—Heaven, earth and lower region under earth). There are four Vedas and six members of the Vedas (certain classes of works regarded an auxiliary to the Vedas and designed to aid in the correct pronunciation and interpretation of the text.and the right employment of Vedic Mantras in ceremonials). There are many other works interpreting mystic doctrines and disclosing Supreme Truth and real nature of human soul as being identified with the Supreme Spirit pervading the universe.There are 101 sub-divisons of Yajur-Veda which are quite distinct from each other. There are 1000 customary courses of Sāmveda. The sacred texts handed down by tradition or repetition of the collective body of Rigveda are of 21 types. Atharva-Veda is divided in nine ways. The treatises in the shape of questions and answers, history, *Purānas* (ancient Hindu mythological scriptures—18 in number) and Ayurveda (The science of Indian medicinal system) etc. are various other scriptures which have been composed in Sanskrit. Without going through such magnificent collection of books with regard to the use of Sanskrit words, it would be sheer audacity on our part to declare that such and such forms of words had been out of use or had become obsolete.[1]

Two points are explicit from the above discussion of Pātanjali. Firstly, certain Sanskrit words were getting mixed with local dialects and losing their original form. Then how could their grammatically shaped correct form could remain intact? He lays great stress on the point that slightly changed or simplified form of words may not be used in Sanskrit compositions, for in that case the originality and genuineness of the language would not remain intact. The comparative illustrations of inaccurate forms of words, found in use, are clear refelctions to that effect such as शश= षष; पलाश= पलाष; मञ्चक=मञ्जक; etc.

Secondly, a few words of Sanskrit language might have got mixed with local vernaculars to such an extent that they began to be used with spontaneity and they might have been adopted as *bonafide* words of those local dialects, with the passage of time. It had an adverse reaction on the scholars and they completely stopped the use of such deformed words in Sanskrit compositions. Instantly, the Sanskrit scholars declared them to be the words of local dialects or they might have decided to overlook them completely.

These things might have reacted on the mind of Patanjali. He has, therefore, spared no efforts to allay the misconceptions, if any, as a result of avoiding the use of such incorrect words. How far he was anxious to maintain the accuracy of words, sentences and their usage as per established practice, is amply evident from his statement that the knowledge of traditional letters and words (which are said to have been revealed by Lord Siva to Pāṇini) is propitious and a source of promoting happiness. He writes that collection and repetition of traditional letters

1. Sarve Khalvapyete sabdā desantereshu prayujyante. Na caivoplabhayante, Uplabdhan yatnaḥ kriyatāṁ Mahañchabdasya prayagavisayah, Saptdwipā vasumati, triyo lokaḥ Catvāro Vedaḥ Sangaḥ sarhasyāh, bahudha bhinna ekādaśamadhiviaryusākhah, sahasravartmā Samvdaḥ Ekvinśatidhābeāhvricayam navadhātharvno Vedaḥ, Vakovākyam. Itihāsaḥ Puranaṁ, Vsidyakabhityātāvānchabdasa prayogvisayah. Etavantaṁ Shabdasya prayogvisantmanaunisanya Sanlyaprayukta iti Vacamani Kervaloni Sāhasamatra meva meave— *Mahabhāṣya*, Ist Ahnik, Pages 32-33

leads to reading and recitation of correct sentences. In other words, the collection of sentences forms human speech or language. The traditional collection of letters is a pious and sacred work, adored by flowers, is fruit-bearing and glorifying like moon and stars. It should be considered as spiritual knowledge consisting in words like knowledge of the Supreme Spirit or the spirit itself. The spiritual knowledge consisting in words is as good and rewarding as that obtained from the study of all the Vedas. The parents of the students, engaged in the study of spiritual knowledge *i.e.* Vedas are crowned with glory in Heaven."[1]

Normally, the linguists believe that Prākritas belong to the mediaeval period of Indo-Aryan languages. They determine this period ranging from 500 B.C. to 1000 A.D. However, some other scholars determine it from 600 B.C.. to 1100 or 1200 A.D. Broadly speaking, these figures almost conform with each other. While determining the history of growth and development of linguistics, it is barely possible to make an accurate and exact estimation of the period. The period of Middle Indo-Aryan languages is also considered the period of Prākritas. This period is further sub-divided into three parts-initial era of Prākritas; second era of Prākritas and third era of Prākritas. The initial era of Prākritas is believed from 500 B.C. to the beginning of Christian era. In this period, there was prominence of Pali (a middle Indo-Aryan language used by Buddha for his teachings and by his followers in subsequent Buddhist scriptures) and Prākrita used in stone and rock inscriptions. The second era of Prākritas is believed to be ranging from start of Christian era to 500 A.D. The language, commonly used during this period is called Prākrita which included several forms of Prākritas. Their individual forms had already come into distinct existence. The third era of Prākritas ranges from 500 A.D. to 1000 A.D. The language, commonly in use in this period, is known as 'Apbhranṣa' which was, infact, a developed form of Prākritas, obtained in later years.

Pt. Hargovind Das T. Seth has also referred to this period of Prākritas in the 'Introduction' of his book *Paiasaddamhaṇnavo* which he believes to be the period of Prākritas of second stage. He too has divided the period of Prākritas into three stages. Since the said classification is signifcant to be comprehended in the present context, it is being produced hereunder:

Initial Era (400 B.C. to 100 A.D.)

(a) Pali language in which subsequent Buddhist scriptures, namely—Tripitakas, relating to Hinyan Sect of Baudhas, Mahavansha and Jatakas etc. were accomplished.
(b) Paiṣāchi and Chūlika Paiṣāchi.
(c) Ardh Magadhi Prākrita in which Jaina Agamas were accomplished.
(d) Jaina-Maharaṣṭriyan language in which Angas in aphoristic style (forming part of Agamas); collections of ancient aphorisms and old Jaina scripures such as 'Paumchariu' etc.

---

1. So a yamakṣarasmāmnāyo Vākyasamāmunāyaḥ puṣpitaḥ phalitaścandratārakavat pratimandito veditavṣyo brahmarāṣiḥ. sarvavedapunyaphalavaptiścāsya gyāne bhavati mātapitrau Chasya swargē loke mahiycte.

— *Mahābhāshya*, IInd Ahnik, Page 113

(e) Prākrita language in which stone inscriptions of emperor Ashoka period and those of the subsequent period were inscribed.

(f) Language in which the dramatic compositions of Ashvaghosh had been accomplished.

Middle Era (From 100 A.D. to 500 A.D.)

(a) Shorseni, Māghadi and Māhārāstriyan Prākritas, in which dramatic plays, authored by 'Bhās' and published at Trivendrum (Kerala) as also subsequent dramatic plays, authored by Kālidasa etc. were written.

(b) Mahārāstrian Prākrita in which the poetic works, namely 'Setbandhu' and 'Gāthā' Saptasati' were written.

(c) Māhārāstrian, Shorseni', 'Magadhi', 'Paiśāchi' and 'Chulika Paiśāci' Prākritas, the characteristic features and illustrations of which appear in grammars of Prākrita dialects.

(d) Shorseni' Prākrita of Digamber Jain Scriptures and Jain Māhārāṣṭrian, Prākrita of scriptures of Swetāmber sect which subsequently came into existence.

(e) 'Apbhraṇsha' Prākrita, specified in the grammar, written by 'Chaṇḍa' and used in accomplishement of 'Vikramovanshiya'.

Last or Remaining Period from (500 A.D. to 1000 A.D.)

Apbhraṇsha dialects of subsequent period pertaining to differnt regions.

The above period-wise classification of Prākritas, made by Pt. Hargovind Das T. Seth produces an elaborate picture of the kinds of various Prākritas.

Various names Obtained for Prakrita Language

Various names for Prākrita language are found in religious scriptures and literary works, such as 'Pāiya'. 'Pāia', 'Pāuya'; 'Pāuḍa'; 'Pāgaḍa'; 'Pāgata'; 'Pāgaya'; 'Pāya'; 'Pāgaya' and 'Pāyada' etc. In 'Sthānānga Sūtra[1] (the third Anga forming part of Jaina Agamas), the word 'Pāgata' has appeared. Achārya Hemchandra has used the word 'Pāgaya' in his commentary on 'Visheṣavashyaka Bhāsya'[2], written by 'Ksmā Śramana' Jinbhadragani. In Sattaka (a kind of minor drama in Prākrita dialect). styled *Karpuramanjari*,[3] written by Rajshekhar, the word 'Pauya' is found used for Prākrita. In Prākrita poetry, styled *Gaudavaho*,[4] the author, Vākpatirāj, had used the word 'Payaya' for Prākrita. All the aforesaid words have been used to mean Prākrita language. Achārya Bharat, author of *Nātyaśāstra*.[5] (a work on dramatic representation) has named the language as Prākrita.

---

1. Sthānānga Sūtra, sthan 7. aphorism 553.
2. Commentary on narrative 1466 of viśesāvasyaka Bhaṣya.
3. Karpur Manjari, Act 1, Verse 8.
4. Gaudvaho, Verse 92.
5. *Nātya Shāstra*, Chapter 17, Verse 1.

Source of Origin of Prakritas

The philologists generally believe that in the course of growth and development of Aryan languages, Sanskrit came into existence from Vedic language and Prākrita language had its origin from Sanskrit. Thus the linguists admit the existence of Prākrita after the era of Sanskrit. However, detailed investigation is called for in this regard.

Views of Grammarians

Eminent grammarian of Prākrita language, Achārya Hemchandra has stated while defining the word Prākrita "प्रकृति संस्कृतम् तत्र भवं तत्र आगतं वा प्राकृतम्" what is refined or higly polished speech and what is the natural form is Sanskrit language. Therefore, the language, originated from Sanskrit, is Prākrita. Markandeya defines in his book *Prākrita-Sarvasva*. "प्रकृतिः संस्कृतम्, तत्र भवं प्राकृतमुच्यते।" He explains that Sanskrit is original, pure and natural form of language, hence the language, having its origin from Sanskrit is Prākrita. In *Prākrita-Chandrika*, it has been defined as "प्रकृतिः संस्कृतम् तत्र भवत्वात् प्राकृतम् स्मृतम्" Original and perfect language is Sanskrita, hence the language originating from Sanskrit is Prākrita, Narsingh has defined Prākrita in his book *Saḍabhāṣā-Chandrikā*—as "प्रकृते संस्कृतायास्तु विकृततः प्राकृति मता–" which means that like nature Sanskrit is the original source and what is enolved from it is Prākrita. In *Prākrita Sanjivni*, it has been interpreted as: प्राकृतस्य सर्वमेव संस्कृत योनिः" The basic source of origin of Prākrita is Sanskrit only. Dhanik, an eminent authority on dramatic science, writes in his book *Daśarūpak* as "प्राकृतिः आगतम् प्राकृतम्, प्रकृतिः संस्कृतम्"which means that what has been obtained from nature (the original source of the material world) is Prākrita and the nature is Sanskrit itself (Perfect and highly polished language). Singh Devagani writes is his commentary on Vāgbhaṭalankar as प्रकृतेः संस्कृतात् आगतं प्राकृतम्" . It has been explained that the language which had its origin from Sanskrit—a synonym for nature (Sanskrit having natural form and grammatical purity) is Prākrita. Premchand 'Tarkvagisha' (Master of the science of logic), a commentator of 'Kāvyādarśa' writes as संस्कृतरुपायाः प्रकृतेः उत्पन्नत्वात् प्राकृतम्". It means that the language having born from Sanskrit, which is synonymous with nature is called Prākrita. Narain, while discussing regarding origin of Prākrita and Apbhransha dialects, writes in his book *Rasik-sarvasva*, as संस्कृतात प्राकृतामिष्टम् ततोअपभ्रंशभाषणम्" which means that Prākrita had its origin from Sanskrit and Apbhraṇsa is a modified form of Prākrita.

From the aforesaid views of Prākrita grammarians and certain commentators of poetical compositions, it is almost clear that they were unanimous in their comments that Prākrita had its origin from Sanskrit. First of all, it is worth consideration that the literal meaning of the word Sanskrit itself is a perfect, refined and highly polished language. In that case, how another language say Prākrita could have its source of origin from it? Either the aforesaid grammarians of Prākritas and poetic scholars had not given a serious thought to the matter from linguistic viewpoint or they actually purported to mean something else.

The real interpretation of the word 'Prākriti' is the original source of the material world or natural disposition or temperament. Infact, the word Prākrita should mean either a language of the common people or a natural language. The said interpretation will be found more consistent at the time of analysing the opinion of certain other scholars in the ensuing chapters.

In case, the above scholars, virtually believed that Sanskrit was the source of origin of Prākrita or with the said view in mind, they considered Sanskrit as the very nature of Prākrita then the matter needs to be further deliberated upon. It is an admitted fact that Sanskrit language had been perfectly regulated and conditioned by grammatical rules. In the wake of such constraints, the basic and fundamental shape of a language, no doubt, remains intact but its expansion and growth is altogether stopped. There is no occasion, whatsoever, for origin of any new language from it, since a language (sanskrit) which was once a medium of speech by general masses, assumed a refined and polished shape. If a great intellectual like Āchārya Hemchandra, who, in accordance with his religious faith, has opined that Prākrita was the primordial language of the universe then how far it was logical for him to hold that Prākrita owed its origin to Sanskrit. Āchārya Hemcandra and other grammarians have portrayed Sanskrit as the very nature of Prākrita, which appears to have a specific sense. The said grammarians and commentators of poetical compositions, as a matter of fact, belong to much later age when Prākrita dialects were no longer in use. They belong to an era when the use of Apbhransha dialects (modified form of Prākrita dialects) had already ceased and had lived near about the period of origin and growth of modern languages. By that time, reading and studying of Prākritas had almost stopped, so much so that in order to be able to understand the words of Prākrita dialects, one had to take help of the shadow Sanskrit (carrying an overall impression of original Sanskrit). Sanskrit was the medium for studying ancient languages. The main reason being that although Sanskrit was never adopted as source of human speech for the use of common people, yet the fact remains that it continued to remain intact as a refined and higly polished language, right from the advent of the peried of Aryan languages till several centuries ahead. From this viewpoint, popularity and significance of Sanskrit had not lessened, so much so the Prākritas which were one time most popular dialects of the masses, had become extinct with the passage of time and in order to comprehend them, the scholars had to depend upon a refined language like Sanskrit. Probably, the grammarians of Prākritas had to face a similar situation. Consequent upon the same, they had an impression that Sanskrit was the source of origin of Prākritas, so much so that even Jaina scholars and Jaina monks, whose entire canonical literature is basically composed in Ardh Māgadhi Prākrita, preferred to take help of Sanskrit shadow (carrying only an overall impression of the original language) and commentaries.

Some more facts may be worth-knowing regarding grammar of Prākritas, authored by Āchārya Hemchandra. As a matter of fact, he did not write any independent grammar of Prākritas of his own. He had composed an extensive grammar of Sanskrit, styled 'Sidhahemashabdānushāsan'[1] Almost all the subjects concerning Sanskrit grammar have been discussed in the initial seven chapters of his grammar. In the eighth chapter, there is discussion on Prākrita grammar. It clearly manifests that analytical discussion on grammatical rules governing Prākritas was not the primary aim of the author. Looking to the course of events, rolling onward and trend of his time, he might have also found it convenient to deal with Prākrita dialects through medium of Sanskrit. He might not have liked to deal with the Prākrita dialects straight away, since they were no longer in use as medium of speech. The study of Prākritas, as an independent subject, had almost stopped. It had become conditional to the study of Sanskrit. Consequently, he found it more convenient and in consistency with the prevailing times to adopt Sanskrit as a suitable medium for study of Prākrita dialects. To study the methods and processes of transformation from Sanskrit forms of words to Prākrita forms of words was the only practical way to study Prakrita dialects. Infact, it was in this context that Āchārya Hemchandra claimed that Sanskrit was the original source or cause of origin of Prakritas, which is quite explicit from the above discussion.

Āchārya Hemchandra was not confused in regard to the origin of Prākritas. In the first memorial *verse* of his poetic grammar, styled 'Kāvyanushāsan', he writes:

"Akritrimsevadupadam, parmārthabhidhāyiniṁ |
Sarvabhāṣāparinataṁ, Jainiṁ vachamupasmahe ||

---

1. There is an eventful story with regard to the composition of grammar by Āchārya Hemchandra. Sri Sidhrāj Jaisingh, king of Gujarat, was anxious to establish a grand institute for imparting Sanskrit education in Gujarat State, of the same standard and repute as in Kasmir, Kashi and Mithila. He called upon the learned scholars of his state to accomplish a new grammar which should be a unique work of its kind. Sidhraj Jaisingh had developed a keen urge after he got critically examined the books of a big library, which was captured and taken possession of by him along with other properties after achieving victory over Malwa region. Sidhraj happened to find a grammatical treatise, written by King Bhoj, ruler of Dhar region, which was higly spoken of by intellectuals. It aroused literary rivalry in king Sidhraj. Consequently, he called upon the learned scholars of his kingdom to accomplish a grammar of the same repute and significance. In the royal . Court of Sidhraj, Acharya Hemchandra held the highest position. He really possessed creative talents and was a true genius. He was an authority on several subjects. The said narrative had appeared in 'Prabhāvakacharita' as evident from the following verse:

   Sarve Sambhuya Vidvano, Hemchandran Vyalokyan |
   Mahabhaktya Ragyasavabhyachārya prarthi (Tastatah) ||
   Shabdavyūt pattikricachatraṁ nirmayasmanmanoatham |
   Pusyasva maharse! tvaṁ bina twāmatra kaḥ prabhuḥ ||
   Yaso mam tava khyatih, punyam ca muninayaka |
   Viśvalokopkārāya, kuru Vyakarnaṁ navaṁ ||

   — *Prabhavakcarita* 12, 81, 82, 84

   The said grammatical treatise, authored by Acharya Hemchandra was higly admired in Gujrat and at other places. The following couplet is most significant in this regard:
   Kiṁ stumah Śabdapādhai Hemchandrajater matṁ Ekṁapi hi yenedrik Kritaṁ Śabdānuśāsnaṁ ||
   Renowned Jaina scholar, Jinamaṇḍala, has expressed similar sentiments in the following couplet:
   Jayasinghdevavachanāt nirmitam Sidhahem vaganaim
   Nihsefsa Saddalakkhananihana mimina munimdenaim
   (Jayasingh devavachanat nirmitaiṁ Sidhahema vyakarnaim |
   Nihsh'easaabdalaksana nidhanmanena Munindrena ||)

He further elaborates his own explanation in 'Alankārchāūdamaṇi' in the following verse:

Akritrimāṇi-asanskritāni ateva swādūni mandahiyāmapi peśalānipadāniyasya miti vigraḥ |

— Tatha Surnartirashchāṁ Vichitrāsu Bhasāsu parinatāṁ gataṁ Sarvabhāsaparinatāṁ ||
Ekrūpāpi hi Bhagwantoadharmāgadhi bhāshā
Varidvimuktapārishada Ashryanuruptaya parinamti |"

In order to support his viewpoint, he further quotes the following verse:

Devā Devīṁ nara nāriṁ Śabrāśchāpi Śābrim
Triyanchoapi hi Tairaschi menire Bhagvadagiraṁ ||

It is evident from his own comment that he did not consider Sanskrit a spontaneous language. On the contrary, Prakrita dialects were natural, spontaneous and original languages. Therefore, how could an intellectual of his standard could establish that Prākritas had their origin from Sanskrit while be believed that Sanskrit was not a spontaneous language.

Eminent logician and poet, Āchārya Sidhsena Diwaker, who was the predecessor of Āchārya Hemchandra, had stated similarly "Akritam-swadupadairjanaṁ Jinendrah Sākṣādivapāsī bhāsitaiḥ[1]. Ācārya Hemcandra has followed the same line. Not only this, he has shown his full concurrence with the words, used by Acharya Sidhasena and adopted them as such.

While commenting upon verse No 12[2] appearing in chapter No 2 of his annotation, the renowned rhetorician, Nami Sadhu has defined the word Prākrita "Sakaljagasjantunāṁ Vyakarnadibhirnāhit Sanskārah Sahajo Vachan Vyāpārah prakritiḥ, tatra bhavaṁ Saiva dā prākritaṁ I

Prak Pūrva Krit Prākritaṁ Bālmahilādi subodhaṁ sakalbhāṣā nibandhabhutaṁ vacaṇmuchayate |"[3]

Nami Sadhu has also stated that although the rainy water dropped by clouds is similar in appearance every where, yet it adopts different forms in accordance with the shapes of land. Similarly, the Prākritas adopt various forms. The same are transformed into Sanskrit after having been refined and bound by grammatical rules as laid down by Pāṇini.[4]

In the course of his above analytical discussion, Nami Sadhu lays stress on one more point which is equally significant. He says that the original author, Acārya Rudrat, while making critical evaluation, has first referred to Prākritas and thereafter to Sanskrit.[5] From this, it is evident that by referring in this manner,

---

1. Dwātrṁishadadwātrishikā 1/18
2. प्राकृत–संस्कृत–मागध्–पिशाच भाषाश्च शोरसेनीच
   षष्ठोत्र भूरिभेदो देश विशेषादपभ्रंशं ||
3. Paiasaddaınhannuo upādghat, page 24
4. Meghnir mukta jalamivaikasuearupaṁ Tadeva vimedānāpnoti ....Paṇinyādi Vyākarnoditsśahda lakṣoṇena Sanskarnāt Sanskritmueṣyate.
5. . . . Ateriva Śastrākritā Prākritmādau nirdistaṁ tadnusanshritadini |

he means to emphasize that Prakritas are compratively older than Sanskrit. From linguistic viewpoint, his views are important and are fit to be given serious consideration, since they are somewhat inconsistent with the opinions of above-cited grammarians and commentators of poetical works. Nami Sadhu was a predecessor to all of them.

Non-Jain scholars like Rajshekhar have also expressed similar views. It is believed that he lived in 9th Century. In Bal-Ramayaṇa[1], he writes on an occasion:

"Yad yonih kil Sanskritasya sudrishaṁ jihvasu Yanmodate,
Gadyaṁ Curṇapadaṁ padaṁ ratipatestat Prākritaṁ Yadvachah,
Taṁallataṁalalitāṁgi pasya nudto dristernimeṣavritam ||

Prākritaṣ, which are the source of origin of Sanskrit, which have the previlege to be spoken by young ladies, having fascinating eyes, on hearing of which, listening to the words of other languages, appears to be unpleasant and distasteful, the prosaic compositions of which are full of elegant words and pleasing to the heart like pride of Cupid, the God of love. Prākrita language is spoken by the people of Gujrat. Oh! handsome lady, behold such people with unblinking eyes.

While describing the characteristics of Prākritas, Rajshekhar has held Prākritas as source of origin of Sanskrit, which is most significant from viewpoint of linguistic science.

What Vākpatiraj has stated regarding significance and characteristics of Prākritas in his book *Gaudavaho*, has already been discussed above. He has held Prākritas as source of origin[2] of all other languages. He has made another comment which is worth consideration from philological viewpoint. He states: "The charm and loveliness of Sanskrit is enhanced and illuminated by the effect and shadow of Prākritas. In adding to the and refining of Sanskrit, Prākritas have played a prominent role."[3]

The significance of Sanskrit language lies in its excellence and refined shape. From this popular saying, it is evident that Sanskrit has been refined, polished and cleansed in an excellent manner. The instrumental cause for it are Prakritas. In other words, Prākritas are a cause and Sanskrit their effect. The prior existence of the cause is obvious as against its effect.

We shall have to ponder over the comments of Rajśekhar and Vākpatirāj. They were not members of Jain community but were followers of Vedic tradition. Jaina scholars, being aware that all their religious scriptures had been reduced to

1. Bāl Rāmāyaṇa, 48-49.
2. Sayalāo imam Vāyā Visanti etto ya Nenti Vāyāo |
Enti samidduṁ chiya nenti Sāyarāo Chchiya jalaiṁ ||
— *Gaudavaho Kav Praśansā,* 93
(Saklā etad Vāeo Viśanti etaścā niryānti Vāeaḥ |
Āyānti Samudraṁeva niry anti. Sagradwa jalāns ||
Prakrita language is an inlet and outlet of all other lauguages. The water flows into the sea and vapours out ot it.
3. Ummilai Lāvaṇṇaṁ Payayaeachāyāe sakkyavayanaṁ |
Sakkayasakkārukkarisaṇeṇa payayassa vi pahawo || — *Gaudaudo*, 65
(Ummikhyate Lāvaṇyam Prākritcachāyyā Sanskrit padanam |
Sanskrit Sanskaṙotkarśanena Prakritasyāpi Prabhāvaḥ ||

writing in Ardh Magadhi Prākrita, could advance any pleas for sustenance of or magnifying the significance of their language. However, when non-Jaina scholars attribute such importance to Prakritas, then we could not ignore or overlook their assessment. From what both the aforesaid scholars have stated, they have truely depicted the significance and utility of Prākritas.

Opinion of Acharya Sidharshi

Acharya Sidharshi, an eminent writer of narratives on a variety of topics in Sanskrit literature, has discussed about linguistic science in his renowned Sanskrit work, styled 'Upmitibhavaprapancākatha' which will be found much helpful in the present context. He writes: "Sanskrit and Prākritas are two principal languages. Amongst them, Sanskrit occupies the place in the minds of vainly proud persons while Prākritas are easy to be taught to even young children and sweet in sound. Even then the vainly proud persons have no appreciation for Prākritas. In such an event, when a remedy is available (I am fully competent to write a book in Sanskrit), I must see that I act in the manner so as to provide utmost happiness and satisfaction to each and everybody. Keeping the said aim in my mind, I shall undertake to write the book in Sanskrit."[1]

From the above, it is evident that Āchārya Sidharṣi believes that Sanskrit language is found in the minds of proud persons. According to him, Prākritas are easy to be grasped even by small children and are pleasant to hear. As shown in the dictionary, the literal meaning of the word 'Durvigdha'[2] is pedant (one who over-rates himself as a scholar and is vainly proud of his ability) or a conceited scholar. Ordinarily, the use of the word is not made in an auspicious or good sense. Rather, it is used in a despicable sense to mean vanity or vain glory. Although, Āchārya Sidharṣi sincerely believed that Prākritas were easy to be followed and were popular languages meant for the service of the people at large, yet he realised that composition of a book in Prākrita language would not be hailed by those, proud of their scholarship. The reason is obvious. He lived in tenth or eleventh Century when use of Prākrita dialects had almost ceased and the authors or writers, inspite of recognizing the significance of Prākrita dialects, preferred to write in Sanskrit. Probably, the object in doing so, was that their work received due recognition by scholars and intellectuals. They, therefore, felt elated to write in Sanskrit, which had already acquired the status of a lingua franca. Secondly, the notion that Prākrita dialects were, one-time, most popular languages of the people at large, was only a reflection of bygone days. By that time, Prakritas too had become unintelligible like Sanskrita. However, inspite of the fact that Sanskrit was an abstruse language, the opportunities for its reading and studying were available as before, but the same facilities were not there for

---

1. Saṁskrita Prākritā ceti bhāshe pradhnmarhatah Tathāpi Sanskritā tāvaddavidagdhahudi Sthitā |
Bālānā mapi Sadbodhkārni karnapeśalā.
Tathapi Prākrita bhaṣā na teṣāmapi bhāste
Upāya sati kartaoyaṁ sarvesaṁ citranjanaṁ
Atatastanurodhena Sanskritāyaṁ Kariṣyate.
— Upmitibhave prapanca kathā Prathām Prastave 51-53
2. Gyānlauadurvidaghadaṁ Brahmāpi taṁ naraṁ na raujsyat.
— *Bhartriharinitiśataka*, 3

the study of Prākritas. Thus there was an aim to write in Sanskrit language but there was absolutely no significance or advantage to write in a Prākrita dialect. There were certain obvious reasons and circumstances responsible for the alienation of Prakrita dialects from day today use by the masses so much so that in order to study and follow Prakrita dialects, help of Sanskrit was not only considered desirable but indispensable.

In holding Sanskrit as real source or origin of Prākritas, the grammarians have allowed themselves to be influenced by the course of events so much that the aforesaid comments of Āchārya Sidharshi seem to be true. The course of events, rolling onward like a stream, became so deep-rooted that people began to believe firmly that Sanskrit was primarily the source of origin of Prākritas.

Pt. Hargovind T Seth, after having a critical study and thorough review of the observations, made by above-noted scholars, has given the etymological interpretation of the word Prākrita which is worth reading. He writes: "Prākritya swābhāven sidhaṁ Prakritaṁ" or "Prakritināṁ sādhāranajanānāmidaṁ Prakritaṁ".[1] The said interpretation appears to be quite relevant and appropriate.

Native Words of Prakritas: An Opinion

The words comprising Prākrita dialects have been classified into three categories:

(1) Tatsam (words of Sanskrit origin, used as such in later languages);
(2) Tadbhava (words of sanskrit origin which have assumed and are used in a modified form in later languages);
(3) Deshya (Native forms of words, used in Prākrita dialects).

Tatsam[1] : Here the word 'Tat' has appeared for Sanskrit. The words which are used in similar forms in both Sanskrit and Prakrita dialects are called Tatsam. Such as—Ras (sentiments); Vāri (water); Bhār (load); Sār (gist, essence); Phal (reward); Parimal (fragrance)' Naval (new); Vimal (clean); Jal (water); Nir (water); Dhaval (white); Harina (deer); Āgam (A sacred scripture); Īhā (desire); Gana (community); Gaja (elephant); Timir (darkness); Torana (An arched gateway); Taral (fluid); Saral (simple); Haraṇa (abduction); Bharaṇa (feeding); Karaṇa (instrumental); Charaṇa (steps) etc.[2]

Tadbhava : By way of assimilation of letters, omissions, additions or alterations, the modified forms of words which are considered to have originated from Sanskrit words, are said to be Tadbhava words[1]—such as Dharma > Dhamma (religion); Karma>Kamma (deeds); Yaksa > Jakkha (A class of demi-gods); Brahmana > Bamhana (The first of the four castes of Hindu society); Ksatriya> Khattiah (The second and warrior class of Hindus); Dhayan> Jhana (meditation); Drishti>Ditthi (sight); Raksati>Rakhai (Defends); Prachati>Pucchai (To interrogate);

1. *Paiyasaddamahannavo*; Ist edition's Preface page 23.
2. Tatsama words which appear in Prakrita dialects, have not been derived from Sanskrit. Either they belong to that form of ancient classical language or Prakrita of first standard, from which Vedic Sanskrit and the Prākritas of the second standard had their origin. Consequently, those words continued to be used in later languages also. From Vedic Sanskrit, these words had been derived in classical Sanskrit.

Asti>Atthi (Existent); Nasti>Natthi (Non-existent) etc.

Deshya (Native) : There is a large number of words, used in Prākrita dialects, which neither resemble with the words of Sanskrit language nor they appear to have been derived from it. The grammarians have called such words as native or local words. The consistent relation of such words is not established from any other source, whatsoever; Just as—Ūaa=Pashya (seeing); Bhunḍa=Shūkar (pig); Tomari=Lata (A creeping plant); Khuppai=Nimajjati (Bathig); Hutta=Abhimukh (facing towards); Phunṭā= Keshabandha, (A hair band); Biṭṭa=Putra (son); Dāl=Shākhā (branch of a tree); Tankā =Janghā (Thigh); Dhayan=Grah (Home); Jhaddappa=Shīghra (prompt); Chukkai=Bhrashyati (falls down); Kandoṭṭa=Kumuda (A lily flower); Ghadha=Stupa (A monument); Bichaḍa=Samūha (Group).

It will be desirable to have further deliberation upon native or local words of Prākrita dialects. It will help in determining the source of origin of Prākritas which is still controversial to a certain extent. In case, Prakritas had their origin from Sanskrit, then the local words of Prakrita dialects must have resemblance with atleast a few words of Sanskrit. However, it is not so although certain grammarians, having regard for Sanskrit language, have attempted to establish several nouns and root words of native Prakrita dialects by substituting[2] them in place of Sanskrit nouns and root words.

An attempt to this effect is noticed in grammar of Prakritas, authored by Āchārya Hemchandra. A few illustrations, relating to them, are given hereunder:—

Vriksiptayo Ruchcaḥ Chhūdhau ||2/127 "Vrishipt-yoryathasankhaṁ rukh Chudha Ityadesau Va bhavatah" 'vrikaha' and 'Cudha' words have alternatively been substituted in place of Sanskrit words `Vriksh' and 'Kṣipta' respectively. *For example*—vriksah=Rukkho (Tree); Ksiptaṁ=chhudhaṁ (Thrown) and Utkshptaṁ= uchchhūdhaṁ (Thrown upwards).

Mārjārasya Manjarvanjarau 2/132

"Marjarshabdasya Manjar Vanjar Ityadeshou va bhavatah." Prākrita words mainjar and Vanjar have alternately been substitued in place of Sanskrit word `Mārjāra'. Such as marjarah=Manjaro,Vanjaro (a cat).

Trastasa hittha-Taṭṭhau" 2/136/, "Trastasabdasya hitth Tatthya itydesho vā bhavatah". Prakritā words Hittha and Tattha have alternately been suggested as substitues in place of Sanskrit word Trasta. Such as trastṁ=Hittam, Taṭṭhaṁ (frightened).

Adhaso Heṭṭhaṁ" 2/141/ "Adhas Śabdasya hettha ityayamādeśo bhavati". Prakrita word heṭṭha has been suggested as subsitute in place of Sanskrit word Adhas. Just as Adhah=Hetthaṁ (Below, down).

Gauṇādayaḥ" 2/174/ "Gonadayaḥ Śabdā Anuktaprakritipratyayalopā-

---

1. One thing more happened. The aforesaid words which were derived in the later Prakritas from the first standard of Prākritas; which continued to maintain their original forms came to be known as Tatsam words. However, Prakritas were in their evolving process. Forms of certain words got modified, although they had been derived alike from both Sanskrit and Prakritas of first standard. They continued to maintain their original forms in Sanskrit since it was regulated and bound by grammarian rules. However, it was not practicable in Prākrita dialects. The said modified forms of words were called Tadbhava words. Therefore, the sense of the word Tadbhava is not the same as is generally understood. Tadbhava words have not been derived from Sanskrit words.
2. Mitravadāgamaḥ, Śatruvadādeśshaḥ |

gamarvarṇāvikārā bahulaṁ nipātyante." Words like Gauna etc. whose forms, suffixes, omissions, additions and transformation of one alphabet or Syllable into another, have not been elaborated, are accomplished by use of indeclinables. Such as Goh=Gauṇo; (cow); Gavo, Gāvah = Gavio; Balivardha = Baillo (Guardian, Master); Apah = Āāu (Name of one of the 8 demigods called vasus); Pancāpancāshat=Pancāvaṇṇa, Panapanna (Fifty- five); Vyutsargah=Viusagau (derived from the nature); Vyutsarjanaṁ=Vosirnaṁ (creation); Bahir maithunaṁ Vā=Bahidhā (outside sexual enjoyment); Apasmāraḥ=Bamhalo (Loss of memory); Utpalaṁ=Kandutthaṁ (A lotus or water lily); Dhikdhik=chi chi (what a pity); Sthasakaḥ=Chacchikaṁ (perfuming or smearing the body with fragrant unguents); Nilya=Nihelnaṁ (Residence, house, a place of refuge); Janaṁ=Janmanaṁ (Birth); Ksullakah=Khuduo (Malicious, wicked); Kutuhalaṁ=Kuddaṁ (Eagerness); Visnu=Bhattio (The second deity out of trio-entrusted with preservation of the world); Shamsanaṁ =Karasi (A cemetry); Asurāh=Agayā (A demon or an enemy of the gods); Pauśyaṁ Rajaḥ=Tingicchi (Supporting or nourishing a person appearing insignificant); Dinaṁ=Allaṁ (A day); Samarthaḥ=Pakkalo (capable); Paṇḍakah=Nelaccho (To collect or pile up); Karpāsah=Palahi (The cotton tree); Vali=Ujjalo (A fold of skin on the upper part of the belly especially of females regarded as a mark of beauty); Tāmbulaṁ=Jhasuraṁ (The areca nut); Punshchali=Chinchai (Tail); Śākhā=Sāḥuli (Branch) etc.

Kathervajjara-Pajjaropal-Pisuna-Sangh-Bolla-Chava-Jampa-Sisa-Sāhāh" 4/2| "Katherddhatorvajjaradyo Daśādeśā Vā bhavanti." Ten Prākrita words have been suggested to be alternatively substituted for the Sanskrit root word `Katha' (To relate, to communicate). Such as Vajjarai; Pajjarai; Uppālai; Pisuṇai; Sanghai; Bollai; Chavai; Jampai; Sisai; Sāhai; Uvvukai iti Tutpūrvakasya bukka Bhashne ityasya I Ete. Chānaairdeśiru pathitā api Usmābhirdhātvā Desikrita Vividheshu pratyeṣu pratisthantāmiti tathā Cha-Vajjaritau Kathitah, vajjariuna kathyitva, vajjarnaṁ Kathnaṁ, Vajjaranto Kathyan, Vajjariadhvaṁ-Kathyitavyamiti Roopsahasrāni sidhyanti, Sanskrit Dhātuvacchha pratyayalopāgamvidhiḥ.

"Dukkhe Ṇivvaraḥ" |4/4/ 'Dukhviṣyasya Kathernivvar ityādeśo vā bhavati'. For narrating grief, Sanskrit root word 'Kath' is substituted by Prakrit word nivvar. Such as nivvaraḥ-narrates the grief.

Pijjahdalla-paṭṭa-ghoṭṭā" /4/11/ 'Pibterete chatvār adesa vā bhavanti. The Sanskrit root word 'pib' (That which drinks) is substituted by four derivatives of Prakrita words alternatively. Such as-Pibti=Pijjai, Dallai, pattai, ghottai.

Nirdraterohirondhau /4/12/ `Nipūrvasya drāteḥ ohir ungh ityādeśo vā bhavatah. Sanskrit word `Nidra' (sleep) is in alternative substituted by two Prākrita words ohīr and Ūngh. Such as: Nidrāti=Ohirai, Unghai.

The grammarians made an attempt to mould Prakrita nouns and verbs in the shape of Sanskrit words by way of suggesting them as alternative substitutes. This was, infact, a far-fetched imagination which could not be considered a proper course.

From the above-noted illustrations of Acharya Hemchandra, two conclusions are drawn. Firstly, like other Prakrita grammarians, he could not avoid making a far-fetched imagination of suggesting Prakrita words aṣ substitutes in place of Sanskrit words. Secondly, what has already been stated above, respecting the style of composition, purpose, method of narration etc. in Prākrita grammar of Āchārya Hemchandra, it can be further added in continuation of the same context that Āchārya Hemchandra also tried to reach the bank of the river of Prakrita language by taking help of Sanskrit bridge. Although, there was no ground, whatsoever, etymological support or source of origin to justify that Prākrita words were grammatically correct, yet in his ill-attempt, he did not spare even native words or root-letters of Prākrita language and believed that no manipulations should be spared in that regard. Probably, the idea of substitution of a word or a letter' of Prākritas for Sanskrit word or letter, mooted by Ācārya Hemchandra is the consequence of similar far-fetched imagination of his.

In his second formula, appeared in the fourth chapter of Prākrita grammar, Āchārya Hemchandra, while quoting Prākritas alternative words, matching Sanskrit root word 'Katha', asserts that while his preceding grammarians had considered these Prākrita substitutes as purely local or native words of Prakrita dialects he was striving to establish their grammatically correct forms by applying suffixes. It was evident from the argument of Āchārya Hemchandra that his predecessors merely read out native words and roots of Prākrita language without bothering to establish accuracy of those forms. Āchārya Hemchandra has only shown 10 forms of native words, carrying the same meaning as that of Sanskrit root 'Katha' (To relate, To narrate) by way of an illustration. There must have been many other local forms of words which the old grammarians might have treated them as native words of Prakrita language. These were the actual state of affairs. The process of substitution of Prakrita words in place of Sanskrit roots, was a design to mould Prakrita language entirely on the pattern of Sanskrit, which was, however, uncalled for from linguistic view-point. If an attempt is made to mould the original form of a langauge as per grammatical rules, it is bound to create confusion. However, it could not be helped since the demand of the age was such.

On having a glance over Sanskrit dramas, the fact is more conspicuous. As already stated above on demand of the context—that in dramas of both Sanskrit and Prakrita languages, the male characters, belonging to well-to-do or status families, delivered their dialogues in Sanskrit while ordinary characters (Females, children and servants etc.) spoke in Prākrita dialects. The said old tradition in dramas proved that a Prākrita was the medium of speech of common people. It may, however, be mentioned here that in subsequent dramatic plays, the dialogues in Prākrita dialects had originally been composed in sanskrit and, thereafter, they were rendered in Prākrita dialects. It is all the more painful that the reflected image of Prākrita dialects in Sanskrit relating to dramatic composition, has been printed in bold letters while the original Prākrita dialogues have been printed in smaller types. The reason is obvious. A Prākrita language was always considered as less significant or secondary. According to the authors of the said dramatic plays, the main rehearsable portion was the reflected image in Sanskrit and not the original Prākrita dialogues.

The dialogues composed in Prākrita dialects are not spontaneous but they appear to be imaginary. The use of Prākrita dialects in dramas had become only formal, merely to maintain the old tradition. Infact, whenever, a writer decided to undertake composition of a literary work, he, immediately, made up his mind to try in Sanskrit.

Origin of Native Words

Various scholars have deliberated upon the source of origin of native dialects and examined the matter from different angles. According to some of them, the first batch of Aryans, which had settled in Central India, after arriving via Punjab and valleys of Saraswati and Drashadvati rivers and subsequently driven away by the Aryans of Second batch, had occupied the territories around Central India. The Aryans of the first batch who had arrived in Central India via Punjab, had accomplished Vedic literature.

The Aryans who had occupied the territories around Central India, had their mediums of speech in regional Prākrita dialects. The variations in dialects in each region or territory was quite natural. Thus the Prākritas, used by Aryans living in Central India, only partially resembled with the Prākrita dialects of those living around Central India. The dialects, used by Aryans, living in Central India, must have been very close to prosodic form of Sanskrit in as much as it must have been a standard and developed form of an ancient popular-language of the area. The local dialects in use outside Central India were comparatively far removed from prosodic shape of Sanskrit, because of territorial separation, and they had no obvious relation with Vedic tradition. The native words obtained in Prākrita literature, had their source of origin from regional dialects, in vogue outside Central India. The ancient or erstwhile forms of local dialects could not be the source of origin of Vedic language. The words obtained from the said native dialects, which came to be known as indigenous words, had no matching or corresponding words in Sanskrit.

Local Dialects: Widely Spoken

The word, native or local dialect is most ancient. In olden days, the local popular dialects or Prākritas of different regions and territories were called native dialects of those areas. There is a reference of soldiers and councillors of King Skanda in the great epic, *Mahābhārata*: "The said soldiers and courtiers of the king had covered their bodies with leather skins of various qualities. They spoke several dialects. They were well conversant with their native and local dialects and they called themselves as masters or lords[1] during mutual conversation.

Similarly, in a work on dramatic representation, there is a topic regarding use of Vernacular dialects. It has been cited therein: "I shall now deal with the alternatives or substitutes to the local dialects. Else, the users of Vernacular dialects should do so at their own initiative."[2]

Kam Sūtra (Name of an erotic work by Vatsāyana also reads: "The person, who neither excessively speaks in Sanskrit nor converses too much on a variety of topics in native dialects, alone is admired and regarded by majority of the people in the world."[3]

---

1. Nānā-charmābhirāchhannā nānābhāshāṣcha Bharat |
Deshbhāshāsu. Jalpantoanyonyabhishworah || — *Mahābhārat*, Shālyaparva 45, 103
2. Ata Ūrdhva pravakṣyāmi Deshabhāshāvikalpa |
Athvāçchhandataḥ Kāryā Deshlahashpryoktribhi || — *Nātyā Shāstra* 17,24-26
3. Nātyantaṁ Sanskritenaiva Nātyantaṁ Deshbhashyā |
Kathaṁ Goshthishu Kathyaṁ loke baharnato bhavet ||
— *Kām Sutra* 1,4,50.

Under Jaina tradition, there are numerous references of regional and local dialects. *For example,* while describing about Megh Kumar, princely son of emperor 'Shrenika', it has been cited: 'Then the said Megh Kumar. . . . had acquired proficiency in 18 regional dialects." [1]

There is another reference in *Gyātridharmakatha Sūtra* (A renowned Jaina Scripture forming part of Agamas) which reads: "There lived a courtesan, named Devaduttā, in Champā town (Name of an ancient city on the banks of Ganges, capital of the Angas and identified with the modern Bhagalpur). She was well-conversant with 18 Vernacular dialects."[2]

There are numerous other contextual references in Jaina literature. Such as— ". . . The said strong-willed young boy. . . was well-verse in 18 Vernacular dialects."[3]

". . . The said resolute and determined boy—was proficient in 18 native dialects."[4]

There was a prostitute, named Kāmodhrita, in Vānnjyagrām (a mercantile centre) who . . . was well proficient in 18 Vernacualr dialects."[5]

It is believed from the above extracts that native dialects, which were Prākritas of the first standard in the words of Pt. Hargovinddās T. Seth and Primary Prākritas according to Sir George Griyason, have been called as local or Vernacular dialects. In this connection, certain Western scholars have expressed the view that the indigenous words and roots, found in Prakrita dialects, have been admitted from linguistics, belonging to Dravadian and Āgneya families, which are non-Aryan linguistic groups. The fact remains that prior to the arrival of Aryans in India, the people, chiefly speaking languages pertaining to Dravadian and Agneya linguistic groups, were inhabiting the country. With the advancement of and capturing territories in India by Aryans, they (non-Aryans) were constrained to shift to other safer places. Subsequently, the Aryans[6] too reached there. After clash for superiority, the people of both Aryan and non-Aryan communities stabilised there. As a result of living together, development of mutual relations and contacts, was natural. Consequently, a few words of non-Aryan languages got mixed with the Aryan dialects (or erstwhile Prākrita dialects).

From the extract of Mahābhārata, already produced above, concerning native dialects, the fact stands corroborated on minutely pondering over the said reference.

---

1. Tateṇaṁ se Meghkumāre —Athārahsavihippagār Desi bhāshāvisāre --hotthā
— *Gyātridharmakāthā Sutra*, chapter 1
2. Tattha Ṇaṁ champāe nayariye Devaduttā nām ganiyā parivasai addhā —atthārasdesi bhāshā visāryā
— *Gyātridharmakāthā Sutra*, 38.92
3. Tae ṇaṁ dradhapaiṇṇe dārae —attharasavhadesippagārbhāsha Visaārye |
— *Raj Praśhniya Sūtra*, page 148
4. Tae ṇaṁ dadhapaiṇṇe dārae ---athāras desibhāsāvisāriye
— *Auppatik Sūtra*, Quotation 109
5. Tattha Nam Vāniyagāme kāmajhyā ṇaṁ guinya hotyā—Athāras desibhāsāvisāriyā
— *Vūpāk Sūtra*, page 21, 22
6. Most probably, they were the Aryans of first batch who had been ariven away from Central India by the Aryans of the second batch and the former had slipped to the territories around or in the vicinity of Central India. If had already been discussed above where the context so demanded.

It is quite evident from the appearance, dresses, conduct and demeanour of those soldiers and courtiers[1] that, most probably, they belonged to non-Aryan tribes. King Skand (name of Kartikeya. Skand is also called Gangaputra) is highly spoken of in Hindu Scriptures as commander of divine forces and conqueror of demons (enemies of the gods). It is believed that he might have organised various groups of aboriginal tribes. The author of *Mahābhārata*, after having given an elaborate account of the warriors of the various tribes, emphasizes that they were all well-conversant with their native dialects.

It is quite possible that as a result of mutual association and contacts amongst Aryans and non-Aryans, the regional dialects might have obtained specific shapes. Most probably, the said dialects in their changed form, might have come to be known as native languages.

Pt. Hargovinddas T. Seth, however, disapproves of this view that certain words of Tamil, Kannaḍa, Munda and similar other languages, belonging to Dravadian and Agneya linguistic groups had been admitted in Prākritas or Vernacular dialects. He, probably, purports to mean that had it been so, a few words and roots of native dialects (Prākritas) ought to have been found in non-Aryan languages also, which is however not so.

There is one more point to be considered in this regard. Instead of assuming that certain words of non-Aryan languages had been admitted in regional Prākritas (chiefly Prākritas spoken in territories, situated in the vicinity of Central India on all sides), it should be conceived that many new words had been accomplished as a consequence of coming in contact of regional Prākritas with non-Aryan languages. The shape of the said accomplished words neither had an apparent similarity with non-Aryan languages nor had any consistency with native dialects (Prākritas). Infact, nothing definite could be said regarding phoneticism and morphological construction of the aforesaid new words. The sole pupose of undertaking such

---

1. Nānāveshdharāshchaiva nānāmālyātulaipanā |
Nānāvastradharāshchaiva charmavāsas eva cha ||
Ushṇishiṇo mukuṭinaḥ Sugrivāshcha suvarchasaḥ |
Kiritinaḥ panchshikhāstathā Kānchan murdhjāḥ ||
Trishikhā dwiishikhāshchaiva tathā saptashikhāḥ pare |
Shikhaṇḍino mukutino mundāshcha jatilāstathā |
Chitramālādharāh Kechit Kechit Rāmānanāstatha |
Vigrahaharasa nityamajeyāh sursuttmaiḥ ||
Krishṇā nirmāswaktrāshcha dirghprishthāstanudarāḥ |
Sthulprishṭhā hrisvaprishṭha pralambodarmehnaḥ ||
Mahābhujā hrisvabhujā hrisvagātrāshcha vāmanā |
Kubjāshcha hrisvajanghāshcha hastikarṇa shirodharāḥ ||
Hastināsā Kūrmanāsā Vriknāsāstathāpare |
Dirghochchhvāsā Dirghajanghā Vikrālā hriyadhomukhāḥ ||
Mahādanshtrā hrisvadanshtrā shchaturdathrāstatha pare |
Vārṇendra nibhāshchānye bhimā Rājan Sahasrashaḥ ||
Suvibhaktsharirāshcha diptimantaḥ swalankritah |
Pingakṣā Shankukaṇāshcha Raktanāśāshcha Bhārat ||
Prithudanṣtra Mahadanshtrascha Sthulaushtha harimurdhjaḥ |
Nānā Pādaushthadanstrāshcha nānāhastshirodharāh ||

—*Mahābhārat*, Shalya Parva, 145, 93-102

minute study of indigenous and native words and languages was to elucidate the origin and growth of dialects (Prākritas) of the country since the subject is still under the grip of uncertainty, it needs further investigation.

Likeness in Vedic and Prakrita Languages

Prākritas or literary forms of Prākritas had been evolved from native dialects or in other words from ordinary forms of Prākritas, in the same manner as evolution of Vedic or prosodic Sanskrit. On analytical research and investigation, we find similarities and some sort of resemblance between Vedic Sanskrit and Prākrita language which is not, however, found between Prākrita and classical Sanskrit. *For example* in place of 'Rikar'(The letter ऋ (ri) and its sound in Sanskrit), there are 'Akār'[1] (The letter (a) and its sound).आकार (Ākār)[2] (the vowel a and its sound); 'Ikār'[3] (the vowel 'i' and_its sound) and 'Ukār'[4] (the vowel 'u' and its sound) are found in Prākrita. The tendency of using 'Ukār' in place of 'Rikar' is found in Vedic literature as well. Just as in Rigveda 1. 46. 4, the use of word Kuth has been found in place of 'krit'. Similar other uses may also be found.

In Prākrita, the last consonant is eliminated[5] in all cases—such as Yāvat (as many or as much)=Jāva; Tāvat (so much, that much, so many) = 'Tāva; 'Yashas' (Fame, reputation, glory, renown) =Jaso; 'Tamas' (darkness) = 'Tamo'. Similar trend is seen here and there in Vedic literature also. *For example*—'Pashchāt' (subsequently)= 'Pashchā' (Atharvaveda Saṁhita 10.4.11); 'Uchchāt' (To rise upwards)='Uchchā' (Taittriya Saṁhita 2.3.14);'Nīchāt' (Low, downward)= Nichā (Taittriya Saṁhita 4.5.61).

The words having two or more consonants conbined, namely 'Y','r', 'v', 'sh' and 's; etc. disappear in Prakrita language and the short vowel, preceding the said letters, turns into a long vowel[6] -such as 'Pashyati' (sees or beholds)=Pāsai; 'Kashyapaḥ' (A tortoise)=Kāsvo 'Avashyakaṁ' (Necessary)= Āvasaya; 'Shyāma' (A cow)=Sāma; 'Vishramyati' (Takes Rest)='Vīsmai'; 'Vishramaḥ' (Rest Repose)= Visāmo; 'Mishram' (Mixed, conbined)=Mīsaṁ. 'Saṁsparshah' (contact, touch)= Sāṁphāso; 'Pragalbha' (Bold, Daring)= 'Pagalbha'. 'Durlabh' (Difficult to be attained or accomplished)='Dūlaha'. Formations of similar nature are found in Vedic Sanskrit as well. *For example*, 'Apragalbha' (Bashful, modest)=Apgalbha

---

1. Ritot 11/8/1/126
   Āderrikārasya atuaṁ bhavati — Siddhaimshabdānushasnaṁ
2. Ātkrishā- mriduka, mridutiwe vā 1/8/1/127 — Siddhaimshabdānushasnaṁ
3. Itkripādau 1/8/1/128
   Kripā ityādishu Shabdesu āderritb ituaṁ bihauwti
4. Uddatvādau 1/8/1/132-
   Ritu ityādisu shaledesu Āderrit Itwaṁ bhavati
5. Antyavyanganasya 1/8/1/11
   Shabdānāṁ yad Antyavyanjanaṁ tasya lug bhavati — Siddhaimshabdānushasnaṁ
6. Lupta य–र–व–श–ष–सा Dirghaḥ 118/1/43
   Prākritalakśanshāluptā yādyā upard agho
   Bā yeshāṁ shakānsākānsakārānaṁteshā-madeh swarasya Dirgho lihavati.
   — Siddhaimshabdānushasnaṁ

(Taittriya Saṁhita 4.5.61); 'Triyacha' (A group or collection of three)=Tricha (Shatpath Brahmana 1.3.3.33); 'Durlabha' (Scarce)=Dūlabha (Rigveda 4.9.8); 'Durnāsha' (Misfortune, calamity)=Dūṇāsha (Shukla Yajurveda Pratishakhya 3.43).

In Prākrita language, the preceding long vowel to joint consonants in a word turns into a short[1] vowel, such as—'Tamrama' (water)=Tambam, Virhagni (The fire of separation) Virhaggi; 'Āsyaṁ (Belonging to the mouth or face)=Assam; Munindraḥ (The lord of the Sages, a great sage)= Munindo; Tirthaṁ (A holy place, place of pilgrimage) = Titthaṁ; 'Chūrnah' (Aromatic powder) = Chunnau' etc. Similar acceptations are found in Vedic Sanskrit also. *For example*, 'Rodsipra' (Heaven and earth) = Roḍsipra (Rigveda 10.88.10); Amātra (Boundless, immeasurable) = Amatra (Rigveda 3.36.4).

'Da' in Sanskrit turns into 'Da'[2] in Prākrita in several cases. Just as—Dashnaṁ (Ten) = Dasanaṁ 'Drishtaḥ' (seen observed) = Dattho; 'Dagdhaḥ' (Burnt, consumed by fire) = Daddho; 'Dotā' (Litter, Palanquin) = Ḍola; Daṇda (A stick, staff) = Ḍanḍo; 'Daraḥ' (Fear, terror, dread) = Daro; Dāhaḥ (conflagration) = Dāho; 'Daṁbha' (Arrogance, ostentation) = Daṁbbho;'Darbhah' (A kind of sacred grass—Kusa grass) = Ḍabbo; 'Kadnaṁ' (Insignificant, mean, bad) = Kaḍanaṁ; 'Dohadaḥ' (The longing of a pregnant woman) = Ḍohalo. Similar instances are found hither and thither in Vedic Sanskrit as well. For instance—'Durdabha' (Indomitable)= Dūḍabha (Vajasneya Saṁhita 3.36); Purodāsa (An oblation)=Purodāsh (Shukla Yajurveda Prātishakhya 3.44).

In Prākrita, the letters ख, घ, थ, भ, and ध of Sanskrit words turn into ह.[3] *For example*, Sādhuḥ (A good or virtuous man)=Sāhu; 'Badhiraḥ' (Deaf)=Bahiro; 'Bādhte' (To oppress, to torment, to harass)=Bāhai; Indradhanuḥ (Rainbow)= Indahaṇu; Sabhā (An assembly or conclave)=Sahā. Such illustrations can be found in Sanskrit literature as well. Such as 'Pratisanghāya=Pratisaṁhāya (Gaupath Brahmana 2.4).

In Sanskrit words ending in 'a', masculine gender, nominative, case singular number, the last letter 'a' is turned into 'O' in all Prākritas excepting Magadhi Prakrita. Such as-Mānushah (A man, human being)=Manaso; 'Dharmaḥ' (Religion, Virtue)= Dhammo; It is also Sometimes found in pronouns 'Etat' (this) and 'Tat' (that) such as Saḥ=So;Eshaḥ (Running or hastening towards)=Eso. In Vedic Sanskrit also, sometimes 'Au' appears in nominative case, singular number—such as 'Saṁvatsarau Ajāyat' (Rigveda Saṁhita 10.190.2); So Chit (Rigveda Saṁhita 1.191.10-11).

---

1. Hrisvaḥ Sanyoge 118/1/84
Dīrghasia yathādarshnaṁ Saṁyoge pare hrasvo bhavati — *Sidhhemshabdanushāsnaṁ*
2. Dashan – Dasta – Dagdha = Dola, Danda—Dar — Dāh — Daṁbh
-- Dabhaṁ — Krandan-Dohade— Do wadah /8/1/217
Eṣu dasya dō vā bhavato — *Sidhhemshabdānushāsnaṁ*
3. Kha-gha-the—adha bhām, 1/8/1/187
Swarāt paresāmsaṁyuktānāmnādibhutānām kha gha tha dha
bha itye teshām varṇānām prāyo ho bhavati — *Sidhhemshabdānushāsnaṁ.*

In ablative case[1], the forms of Sanskrit words ending in 'a', are made like Devāt, Narāt, Dharmāt etc. The last letter 't' in all these Sanskrit words is substituted[2] by Chh. In certain cases, the last letter त् disappears. In words ending in vowel आ (ā) of oblative case, singular number, the last letter त् disappears and the words terminate in vowel आ (ā). Such as:—'Dvāt=Devā; Narāt=Narā; Dharmāt= Dhammā. In Vedic literature too, a few words are similarly found in ablative case where the final letter त disappears and terminate in vowel आ (a). *For example*—Uchchat=Uchcha; Nichat=Nicha and Pashchat=Pashcha.

In Prākrita language, words of oblative case, plural number, the termination 'bhis' is found substituted by 'hi'. Such as—'Devehi'. In Vedic Sanskrit also, similar formations, are obtained, such as—'Devebhiḥ'; 'Jyeshthebhiḥ; 'Gambhirebhiḥ' etc.

In Prākrita language, there are singular and plural numbers only. There is no dual number. Although, in Vedic Sanskrit, the numbers are three, yet there are numerous instances, where formations in plural number have appeared for dual numbers. Such as—इन्द्रावरणौ = इन्द्रावरुणा (Indra, lord of gods with Varunah, the regent of the ocean); मित्रावरुणै=मित्रावरुणा: (Name of an Aditya, usually associated with Mitra; Mitra and varuṇa); नरौ' (a male) नरा:; सुरथों=सुरथा: (god, deity); रथितमौ = रथियतमा: (a war chariot).

Most eminent German grammarian of the modern age, Dr. Pischel, has opposed the argument that Sanskrit was the source of origin of Prakrita language in his illustrious book "Comparative grammar of the Prakrita language".[3] He has produced illustrations of words from both Vedic Sanskrit and Prakrita languages, exemplifying similarity with each other. A few of such illustrations are given below :

Prakrita language		*Sanskrit language*
तण		त्वन (A form of the second personal pronoun)
आए	(Formation of feminine gender, genitive case, singular number	आयै

1. Swaujasamoṭchhasṭāthy āmbhisange bhyaṁgabhyambhyasuga Sosāmanga yossupa.
— *Asthadhyai*, 4/1/2
Su au jas iti prathmā aṁ ot shasiti divitya. Tā bhyām bhis iti tritya `ङ bhyam bhyas itc Chaturthi 'ङसि' bhyān bhyās iti Panchami 'ङस' Ausa ām iti shashthi ङि. औ, स, सुप् iti saptaṁi.
2. 'ङसेस' त्तौ–दो–दु–हि–हिन्तो–लुक: || 3/1/8
Atah Parasya ङसे त्तै ' दौ दु हि हिन्तो लुक ityate ṣadādeśā bhavanti, such as—Yatsāt-vachhto vachhāo, vachhāu, vachchhahi, vachchhāhinto, vachchhā.
3. . . This Sanskrita was not the basis of Prākrita dialects, which on political or religious grounds, was raised to the status of a literary medium. But the difficulty is that it does not seem useful that all the Prakrita dialects sprang out from one and the same source. Atleast they could not have developed out of Sanskrit, as is generally held by Indian scholars and Hobber, Lassen, Bhandarkar and Jacoby. All the Prakrita languages have a series of common grammatical and lexical characteristics with the Vedic language and such are significantly missing from Sanskrit.
— From comparative grammar of the Prakrita language by Dr. Pischel.

एहि	(Formation in Instrumental case, Plural number)	एभिः
बोहि	(Signifying an order or command)	बोधि
ता, जा, एत्य		तात, यात, इत्या
'अम्हे		अस्मे
बग्गूहि		बग्नुभिः
सद्धि		सध्रीम
घिसु		घ्रस
रूक्षव		रूक्ष

It is established after the above discussion that Prākritas had come up from native dialects or languages, which might be in vogue prior to Vedic age, just as Vedic Sanskrit had come into existence from any one of the said local dialects.

Forms of Prākritas

Prākritas were enlivened dialects. Since these dialects were spoken in different regions, dissimilarities in their forms was obvious. The literary and refined forms of Prākritas, obtained from the said native dialects, were bound to differ. In this way, diverse forms of Prākritas had come into existence as a consequence of regional or geographical diversites. The said Prākritas were generally named as per names of the regions or territories, they belonged to.

Achārya Bharat[1], while dealing with Prākritas in his renowned work on dramatic representation, has referred to seven forms of Prākritas, namely. Magadhi, Avantya, Prāchyā, Shorseni, Ardha Magadhi, Vahnika and Daksinātya. The reputed grammarian, Varurichi, author of the most ancient Prākrita grammar, styled *Prākrita Prakāsh*,[2] has stated that there were four forms of Prākritas, namely—Maharashtri, Shorseni, Magadhi and Paishachi. 'Chanda'[3] has used the names of Maghadhikā and Paishāchiki for Magadhi and Paishāchi respectively.

Dandi, a most eminent poetic scholar (a connoisseur of poetry) has also referred to the nature of Prākritas in his book *Kavyādarsha*[4]. He has named them as- Maharashtri, Shorseni, Gaudi and Lāti.

Besides 4 forms of Prākritas, suggested by Varuruchi, Achārya Hemchandra has added another three names of Prākritas—Ārsha, Chūlika, Paishāchi and Apbhransh. Āchārya Hemchandra has called Ardha Magadhi as an Arsha language

---

1. Māgadhyavantijā prāchyā Sursenyarth māgadhi |
Vāhnikā Daksinātyā cha Sapta bhāshā Prākirtitā — *Natya-Shastra*, 17-18
2. *Prākrita Prakāsh* 10.1-2.11-1,12-32
3. Paishāchikyaṁ ramayorlanau | Magadhi kayam Rasayaurlashau
— *Prākrita Lakshan* 3.38.39
4. Mahārāstrāshrayaṁ bhashaṁ Prakrishtaṁ Sagarah Sūktiratnanaṁ
Setubandhadi yanmanthaṁ Sharseṁ cha Gaudi Cha Lāti Chānyā cha Tādrishi |
yātī Prakritamityevamvyawaharesh Sanridhaṁ —*Kāuyādarosh* 234-235

(used by a Rishi only; relating or belonging to sages; a holy or divine language).

Grammarians—Trivikram, Laxmidhar, Singhraj and Narsingh have also expressed their concurrence with the classification of Prākritas, made by Āchārya Hemchandra, with the only difference that excepting Trivikram, none else has claimed Aridh-Magadhi to be a divine language. The fact remains that Āchārya Hemchandra, being an accredited scholar of Jaina sect, held Ardh Magadhi in great esteem (Being official language of Jaina Agamic Scriptures). Hence he called it as the divine or holy language used by or belonging to sages and seers.

Mārkandeya has classified Prākritas into 16 divisions and sub-divisions. He has splitted them in four classes, namely—1. Bhāshā (Languages); 2. Vibhasha (Alternative languages); 3. Apbhransh (one of the lowest forms of the Prākrita dialect pertaining to the middle Indo-Aryan group of languages) and 4. Paishacha (one of the lowest forms of Prākrita dialect). The split of the dialects is shown below:-

(1) Bhāshā (Vernacular or native dialects)—Maharashtri, Shorseni, Prachya (the eastern dialect, spoken, in the east of India) and Avanti (native dialect of Ujjaini) as also Magadhi (one of the four principal kinds of Prākritas).
(2) Vibhasha (Sub-dialects)—Shākāri (one of the lowest forms of Prākritas, spoken by the Shākār characters); Chāṇḍāli, Shabri, Ābhirika (The dialect of Abhiras herdsmen) and Takki.
(3) Apbhraṅsha—Nāgar, Brāchada and Up-nāgar;
(4) Paishācha—Kaikaya, Shorsena, and Pānchāl (Prākrita dialect spoken by five guilds *i.e.* carpenters, weavers, barbers, washermen and shoemakers).

In the work on dramatic representation, the sub-dialects have been stated to be Shakar, Ābhir, Chāṇḍāl, Shabar and Dramil. Dramil is said to be the dialect of weak and indigent characters as also spoken by foresters and wood-cutters.

Mārkandeya, while dealing with the topic of Prakrita dialects and sub-dialects, has quoted a few verses from *Prākrita Chandrikā* in which there is a reference of 8 dialects, 6 sub-dialects, 11 Paishāchi dialects and 27 Apbhransh dialects. Eight dialects being Maharashtri, Āvanti, Shorseni, Ardh Maghadi, Vāhniki, Māgadhi, Prāchya and Dakṣinātya. Out of the said six sub-dialects, two sub-dialects, namely Dravidian and Odraj (the modern Orissa); Out of eleven Paishāchi dialects, ten Paishāchi dialeacts, namely—Kanchideshiya, Pāndhya, Pānchāl, Gauda (North Bengal), Māgadha, Brachada, Dakshinatya, Shorsena, Kaikaya, and Dravid and out of 27 Apbharansha dialects, 23 Apbhransha dialects, namely Brāchada, Lat, Vaidarbha, Barbar, Āvantya, Pānchāl, Takka, Mālava, Kaikaya, Gauda, Udra, Haiva, Pāndaya, Kauntal, Singhal, Kalinga, Prāchaya, Kārnāt, Kanch, Dravid, Gurjar, Ābhir, and Madhyadeshiya (spoken in Central India), have been named as per the name of their respective region. The Prākrita dialects were named as per names of territories, they belonged to. There is no need to feel surprised at such a long list of dialects and sub-dialects. A single language of a state adopts varied forms in different territorial parts and the said sub-dialects are given names as per the name of the respective territory. Although, there is no marked difference in the forms of the said sub-dialects when compared with the principal language of the state, yet the difference is there in the sub-dialect of each territory—may be to a slight extent only. *For example*, let us consider over Rajasthani language. Rajasthani is the principal language of the entire state, yet its form in Bikaner varies with that of Jodhpur; the dialect of Jaisalmer further varies. Similarly, the sub-dialects spoken in Chittor, Dungarpur, Banswārā, Ajmer, Marwar, Kota, Bundi, territory of Harauti, Jaipur or territory of Dhūndhada, Alwar section, Bharatur and Dholpur division are different. Each dialect or sub-dialect has a slight different shape in the said territories. Although, the people, inhabiting the same state, constitute one single unit from political and administrative viewpoint,yet in different regions, there are visibly, regional, social, cultural and geographical diversities which do have their effect on the dialects of different parts. Thus in spite of being a single principal language or dialect of the whole state, slight defference is observed in the sub-dialect, spoken in each territory. Numerous forms of Pishāch and Apbhransha dialects have been cited above which only reflects that they are spoken or are in vogue in different regions of the state.

Various forms of Prākritas or Prākrita dialects well be elaborately discussed in the ensuing chapters. Here only a reference has been made to them.

Evolution, Expansion and Background of Prākritas

The divergence in the nature of life-style and culture, observed in the Eastern and Western parts of the country is there from ancient times. The episodes of continuous warfare between Lord Krishna of Western region and Jarāsandh of Eastern region are contained in *Pūraṇās* (well-known sacred works incorporting tales of the past events and legendary history) and are well-known. The topics relating to arrival of Aryans in India, their moving ahead and settling in Eastern, Western and Central parts of India, have been elaborately dealt with, wherever the context so demanded. However, further contemplation is desirable in this regard.

After their arrival in India, the Aryans had settled in Western and Central regions. Some of them had been driven away to Eastern territories as well but probably they might not have reached the places in the vicinity of Māgadha. If at all they did, they might have occupied a small territory only. It appears that they had not covered much distance beyond Kaushal (Modern Ayodhya along the banks of river Sarayu) and Kashi (a celebrated city on the Ganges, the modern Vārānasi). The ramanants of Vedic culture with dominance of Yajnas and sacrifices, belonging to ancient Vedic era, were not traceable in eastern territories of India including Magadha. It is believed that Vedic culture had an access to eastern regions including Magadha after passage of long time, probably, only a few centuries before the era of Lord Mahāvira and Lord Buddha.

Prior to the permeation and spread of Vedic culture, the territory of Magadha was considered inauspicious. The renowned etymologist, Yāsk, has opined that Magadha was inhabited by non-Aryans. The word Kikata (a bard of Magadha tribe) has appeared in Rigveda which has been considered as a synonym for Magadha in the literature of subsequent era. Similar reflections are found in the literature, accomplished during the period of composition of Brahmanas (that portion of the Veda which states rules for the employment of the hymns at the time of performance of various Yajnas, their origin and detailed explanation, with sometimes lengthy illustrations in the shape of legends and stories), from which it is evident that the Aryans, settled in Western Zone, treated Magadha as a forbidden area. In 'Shatpath Brahmaṇa, people inhabiting eastern territories, were considered to be demons or enemical to the gods. Probably, Aryans used the words 'demonical beings for non-Aryans since they had a feeling of hatred and disliking for them.

Aryans of the first batch, who had formerly settled in Central parts of India, were driven away by the Aryans of the second batch the former had shifted to the areas around Central India mostly towards eastern territories and they re-settled there. It is quite possible that the Aryans of the first group might have developed hostile views for the Aryans of the later batch, who had forced them to flee. Persumably, the former Aryans might have developed intimacy with the original population of eastern zone. The said feeling of rapprochement might have led to the establishment of matrimonial relations and thus a new mixed clan might have come into existance, which might have maintained aloofness from the Aryans of Western Zone in cultural and religions spheres. The word 'Vrātya' (A man of the first three classes of Hindu Community, who had lost his caste owing to non-performance of the principal Sanskaras or purificatory rites especially investiture with the sacred thread; an outcast) has appeared in Vedic literature. Probably, the said word has been used for the Aryans, settled in eastern zone who had established affinity with the original residents of that area. The Scholars have given different interpretations of the word 'Vrātya'. One such interpretation is that those who had no faith in performance of Vedic Yajnas and showed respect to, the Vagrant Sadhus were called 'Vrātyās' (Inferior or low persons). There is a provision for purification and expiation of 'Vrātyās' under Vedic tradition. If they so desired, they were required to perform Yajnas, seeking atonement. It is cited in `Vrātyā-stome' (a Yajna performed to recover the rights forfeited by non-performance of the due Saṁskaras). After performance of the said Yajna, the expelled (outcast) Aryans were admitted in the institution of caste hierarchy.

A few centuries, preceding to the era of Lord Mahāvira and Buddha, the Aryans from Western and Central parts of India, who considered themselves undefiled and chaste, might have arrived in Magadha, Anga (an important kingdom, situated on the right bank of the Gangas. Its capital was Champā, also called Angpuri. It is identified with the territory near modern Bhagalpur in Bihar) and 'Banga' (Eastern Bengal including also the sea-coast of Bengal. It seems to have included at one time Tripura and Gāro hills). The systematic method to perform Yajna for atonement of sins and for readmission of outcast Aryans in the institution of caste hierarchy find mention in 'Vratya-stom' which is sufficient to corroborate the above statement.

The Aryans, settled in West, although treated the inhabitants of eastern territories as expelled from their race, yet they did not consider them as boycotted from linguistic viewpoint. In Brahmana treatises, it is cited that Vrātyās consider Vedic Sanskrit as difficult to be uttered[1] although there is no difficulty, whatsoever, in its speech. What has been stated for Vratyas in relation to Vedic Sanskrit, is infact, an indication to the effect, that they appreciated a language which was

1. Aduruktavākyam durnktamāhu —Tāndhya Mahabrahmaṇa Panchvishbrahmana.

convenient and easy in utterance. Undoubtedly, the said simplicity and easiness is there in Prakrita language as compared to Sanskrit. In this connection, Bevar is of the view that it was a pointer to Prakrita dialects. Elision of consonant clusters from compound sentences and similar other changes have been introduced in Prakrita dialects only to enable their pronunciation and utterance made easy and convenient.

Explaining the significance of grammatical rules by discouraging use of malevolent words, the great commentator, Pātanjali, has stressed how the demons had to face defeat as an ill-consequence of incorrect utterence of Vedic haymns. He has censured them for pronouncing 'Hailayaḥ'[1] in place of the correct word 'Aryaḥ'. It clearly means that they had a tendency to speak consonant 'la' in place of 'ra' which is a characteristic of Māgadhi Prakrita. This also reflects that the growth and expansion of Māgadhi Prākrita had already taken place in eastern region long ago. The inscription on copper plate found at 'Sahgaura' in Gorakhpur district of Uttar Pradesh in treated is most ancient inscription in Brāhmi Script (A widely used ancient Indian script which formed the source of evolution of Devanagiri and all other indigenous Indian scripts). It is believed to be of 4th century B.C.. The place is located in an eastern region of India. In the said inscription, the use of letter '*l*' is found in place of 'r'.

Presumably, the Aryans, settled in Western parts of India, must have set out on a large scale to eastern territories for preaching the significance of Yajnas. They might have achieved partial success also in their endeavour which might have been confined to the upper class only. However, their propaganda failed to find favour with the general masses.

The era of lord Mahāvirā and Buddhā was marked by an extensive revolutionary compaign against ancient Hindu institution of religions Yajnas and sacrifices, their prescribed rites or practices, the body of religious ceremonies, commanded by Hindu law or convention (the cult of religious rituals), external purificatory rites, and superiority by birth etc. Their preachings impressed not only the ordinary masses but the well-to-do and royal families were equally influenced by their movement. Besides, Lord Mahāvira and Buddha, there were a few other contemporary religious teachers who had declared themselves as Tirthankers (sanctified teachers or saints of Jaina religion). Prominent amongst them were M/s Puran Kashyapa, Makhali Goshala, Ajit Keshkambli, Pakudha Kāchchāyan, and Sanjaya Velatthiputta etc. In Buddhist literature, they have been considered as promptors of inactivity (neglect of duty), fatalism, excisionism, interactionism, distractionism. Although, they had their own distinct manners and morals, yet they all practised mandicancy and represented ascetic culture. While Brahmana or Vedic culture believed in supremacy of Yajnas or sacrifices, there was greater likeness and appreciation for self renunciation, indifference to the worldly desires or passions and concentration of mind in ascetic culture. The scholars have defined the word 'Shraman' multifariously. According to certain scholars, the main pillars

1. Tesurā Helyo hailya iti kuvantaḥ paravabhuvuh |
Tasmād Brahmanen na malechchhita ve napbhashit ve |
Malechchho ha vā eva yadapashabdaḥ —*Mahābhāshya*, Ist 'Ahnik', Page 6

of religions mendicancy are hard labour (mortification of the body), uprightness, calmness and tranquility, consequently greater emphasis has been laid on observance of religious austerities, ex-communication of racial and inborn superiority and showing complete indifference to worldly objects. However, all the aforesaid spiritual guides were unanimous in their opposition to performance of Yajnas or orthodox rituals. These were the conditions which greately contributed to the growth and enrichment of Prākrita dialects. Lord Mahāvira and Buddha delivered their religious discourses in the local dialects. It is quite possible that other religious heads also might have imparted their lectures in popular native dialects, yet no literature of their sects was available to substantiate this fact now.

There could, possibly, be two reasons why Lord Mahāvira and Lord Buddhā had preferred to deliver their sermons in native dialects. One of them could be that they had to propagate their views and ideology to largest number of the people for their maximum happiness and welfare and prevail upon them to oppose existing traditions or performance of orthodox rituals, yajnas and sacrificial rites, which had become the order of the day. It was possible though a native language only. Another ground might be that there was over sensitivity with regard to the superiority and sanctity of Sanskrit language, which was patronized by Hindu priests for performance of Yajnas and sacrificial rites. The great sanctified religious teachers, Lord Mahāvira and Lord Buddhā might have considered it unrealistic to impart their lectures in Sanskrit, which was a step in right direction to satisfy the popular urge of that time.

After the great religious teachers, Lord Mahāvira and Lord Buddha, had adopted native dialects (Prākritas) as medium of their preachings, it was bound to provide impetus to the rapid growth and development of the Prakrita dialects. Magadha had already eastablished itself as a powerful dynasty in Southern Bihar by then. In Northern Bihar, a few republics had emerged, relating to Vajji Sangh. Similar were the conditions in the foothill of Kaushala (a territory along the banks of Saryu or Gogra river). Lord Mahāvira belonged to Lichhavi, while Buddha belonged to Malla republic, located within the territory of Kaushala region. From then onwards, Māgadhi Prakrita and other Prakrita dialects had begun to flourish. Māgadhi (Prakrita) had become official language of Magadha dynasty which had spread far and wide around Magadha (the territory of South Bihar. Its old capital was Rajgarah and consisted of five hills). The progress and eminence of Prākritas did not remain confined to the eastern territories only. They were gaining popularity in Western lands also. People began to study Prākritas and the area of their use continued expanding. Prākritas were already the medium of speech for mutual exchange in Western parts also. Subsequently, they began to be used for all other purposes of public interest. Besides the religious field, where the preachings were already made in Prākritas, they become the source of literary accomplishments as well. The pioneers of Vedic culture and admirers of Sanskrit language began to apprehend that subjects their supremacy and predominance in religious and literary circles might not get jeopardized. The increasing use of Prakritas and their growing popularity and acceptance left an adverse effect upon the future of Sanskrit. Till then use of Sanskrit language was mainly confined relating to priesthood, performance of orthodox rituals and ceremonial rites, prescribed precepts and rules, pertaining to Yajnas and performance of purificatory ceremonies only. It was at that time that canonical and literacy works began to the written in Prākrita language, covering a large number of subjects of great significance, namely—folk ethics, economics, politics, morality, social order, public welfare (serving popular interests) etc. Prakritas were gaining momentum since they were highly popular amongst the people and considered fit for contemplatioin on philanthropic issues. Thus in the folk literature, accomplished in Sanskrit, the very soul and spirit is that of Prākrita, while its external body is that of Sanskrit. Mahābhārata may be taken as an example. The voluminous size of Mahābhārata continued expanding from time to time. Various topics relating to ascetic culture, ideology and philosophy of life, discussed therein, are glaring examples and pointer to that effect. It is a significant topic for research and investigation by scholars from both philological and cultural viewpoints.

Sanskrit literature accomplished on the above popular subjects, was welcomed by the people, speaking Vernacular dialects (Prākritas). During this process, slight variations had taken place in the shape of Sanskrit as well. Although, Sanskrit is a grammatically well-knit language so much so that there is no occasion for any major alteration in the forms of its words from roots. However, when a language is rendered fit to be used by the people, who generally speak their own language or languages, slight changes are bound to take place which may make it easy for them to pick up the language with ease and convenience. The words having similarity and based on likeness are used more fraquently. The dictionary of such a mixed language also becomes affluent with new words. There are new interpretations of the words, here and there and new meanings are adopted. Use of contradictory words and alternatives get minimised. At the same time, it is also observed that as soon as people, begin making use of any refined and flourished language, it is bound to have an effect upon their own native and indigenous dialects.

In spite of the above, the movement, launched by Lord Mahāvira and Buddhā and gaining momentum day by day by delivering their religious discourses in local dialects, sanskrit, although, becoming simpler and more popular, could not be an alternative to the local dialects. Thereafter, whatever literary works had been accomplished in Sanskrit, they fed and satiated the hunger of intellectuals and scholars only. Their utility and significance for the common masses was only nominal. Because of long compounded sentences and composition of words, obscure and unintelligible conjunctions, figures of speech, depending for their charmingness on sound of words and high-sounding verbosity Sanskrit literature became considerably complicated and difficult to be understood. How could average readers comprehend such complicated literature ?

In view of the above discussion, further consideration on various aspects of Prākrita dialects is being made in the ensuing chapters.

4

PALI LANGUAGE AND THE BUDDHIST CANONICAL LITERATURE

The period of Middle Indo-Aryan languages or Prākrita dialects is believed to be from 5th century B.C. to the commencement of Christian era. Pāli and Prākritas found inscribed on rocks and stones during the said period, have been taken up. The language in which the preachings of Lord Buddha have been reduced to writing in the shape of Tripitakas (Three collections of Buddhist scriptures) and wherein the relative and highly useful literature, based on Buddhist doctrines, have been accomplished by Buddhist monks and scholars, is called Pāli. However, the use of the word Pāli implying a language, is not very old. In the Buddhist scriptures the word Pāli, has nowhere appeared to signify the language, in which they had been written. It was after 14th centuary A.D. when the word Pali came to be used in the sense of a language, for the first time.

Historical Background for Adopting the Word Pāli

Āchārya Budhaghosha (4th-5th century A.D.) has used the word Pāli for the first time to signify the language in which the teachings of Lord Buddha and original Tripitakas (Three Buddhist scriptures) have been compiled. The same has appeared in his work 'Visudhimagga' and 'Atthakathas' (Buddhist Tales and legendary stories).

He has also used the word Pāli ın the sense of a language in his works 'Dighnikāya Atthakatha' (Sumangal vilasini); Sāmañjaphal sutta, Vanna, Dhammapada Atthakatha (Atthasalini) and Puggalpañati Atthakatha Acharya Budhaghosh has also used the word Pāli for the texts of Tripitakas. Infact original Tripitakas or texts if Tripitakas are one and the same. The difference lies only in the manner of narration. Whenever, Āchārya Budhaghosha considered it necessary to draw our attention to variant texts of Tripitakens, he has used the word Pāli in the sense of texts. *For example*, in 'Sāmañjaphalsuttavanna' of Sumangal Vilasini, a pada "Mahachcharajānubhāven has appeared. Acharya Budhaghosha has transformed it in Sanskrit as 'Mahatā Rajānu bhāvena'. 'Mahachchā' is also another reading for 'Mahaçcha'. In order to point it out, he has stated 'Mahaccha iti pi Pāli in his book, which means that the word Pāli has been used for text.

In the 4th century a Buddhist canonical book *Deepvansha* had been written in Ceylon.This book slightly precedes the life time of Āchārya Budhaghosha. Therein the word Pāli has been used for Buddha teachings. Subsequent to the period of Āchārya Budhaghosha. Buddhist literateurs and authors have been found, using the word Pāli in the sense of both Buddhist teachings and texts of Tripitakās which virtually mean one and the same thing. *For example*, Acharya Dharampāl who lived in 5th-6th century A.D. wrote a book, named *Paramatthadīpani*, incorporating narratives and legendary tales, relating to certain treatises of `Khuddakanikāya'. Therein, he has used the word Pāli for original Tripitakās (three collections of Buddhist teachings). In Chūlvansh, composed in 13th century A.D., the word Pāli has appeared for Buddha preachings Chūlvansh is an enlarged portion to Mahavansha (accomplished in 5th century A.D.). Later on, the word Pāli has appeared in *Sadhamasangaha* (composed in 14th century A.D.) also, implying the same sense (Buddha teachings).

Right from 4th century to 14th century A.D. the word Pāli is found to have been used for both Buddha preachings and texts of Tripitakās. The canonical literature, relating to the period prior to 4th century A.D., and other allied literature of that period however, donot suggest that the word Pāli was synonymous with Buddha teachings. Hence it is essential to discuss here as to how and on what basis, Acharya Budhaghosha used the word Pāli either in the sense of texts of Tripitakās or Buddha preachings. After all, what was the source or tradition, followed by the author of 'Deepvansh' and Āchārya Budhaghosha, leading to the use of word Pāli in both the above senses. This is the point worth consideration. The changes donot take place abruptly in phonetic sounds, morphological constructions and meanings of the words. There is always a motive and tradition behind them from linguistic point of view, which are, though, not apparent outwardly, yet on minute study, the real motive and source of the same are obtained.

Definition : Analysis of the Word Pāli

Certain scholars who have carried out analytical research mainly on Sanskrit, Pāli and Prākritas relating to Indology, have attempted to define and analyse the word, Pāli, in several ways. In Sanskrit, the literal meaning of the word 'Pāli' is an edge or point of anything a line or row. Pt. Vidhushekhar Bhattāchārya has accepted this very definition of the word and has tried to establish consistency of the said meaning with teachings of Lord Buddha and texts of *Tripitākas* (three collections of Buddha preachings). In Pāli literature, the word Pāli has also been used in the sense of a line or row, besides Buddha teachings. Sri Bhattacharya while elaborating the said point, has stated that the word Pāli, having the sense of a line was adopted as such later on to mean a line of Buddhist scripture. Accordingly, author of *Deepvansh* and Āchārya Budhaghosh had adopted and used this word in the sense of Tripitakas or texts of Tripitakas. Shri Bhattāchārya believes that the sequence of transformation of the word 'Pankti', must have been like this—Pankti-Panti-Paṭti-Paṭthi-Palli and Pāli.

The scholars have made full consideration over the point. The renowned monk, Jagdish Kashyapa has criticized the said view in his work *Pāli Mahāvyakarana*[1] (The great Pāli grammar). He has pointed out that there were three improbabilities in it. He considered it incongruous to believe that the word 'Pāli' or 'Pankti' meant the line of a Buddhist scripture. He argues that a line could always be of a writen scripture. The *Trpitakas* (three collections of Buddhist teachings) had not been reduced to writing prior to first century B.C. Hence the assumption that the

1. *Pāli Mahāvyākarṇa*, page 8 (Arrangement of Matter).

word Pāli has been used for the lines or texts of Buddha scriptures prior first century B.C. or before the Tripitakas were reduced to writing, does not appeal to the mind. He believes that the word Pāli was never used in the sense of a line of Buddhist scriptures. Had it been so, there must have been some consistency in their meanings. If the compounded words 'Udān Pāli' (highly reputed language= the word 'Udān' is used as an expression of praise and joy by Buddhist saints) were substituted by the compound words 'Udān Pankti' they ought to have carried sense'. However, there was no consistency between the meanings of the two compounds. From grammatical viewpoint he also draws our attention to the fact that in case the word 'Pāli' meant a 'Pankti' (line), then its use in plural number should also have been found but it is not so.

Dr. Bharat Singh Upadhyaya writes in this connection —'Regarding objections raised by monk, Jagdish Kashayapa, it could partly be argued in reply to his first objection that till the Tripitakas were reduced to writing, the word Pāli or Pankti might have been used to mean a line of recited text and after they were reduced to black and white, the word Pāli must have been used for the written line of Buddhist scripture only.

The concept of Dr. Upadhyaya with regard to the meaning and use of the word, Pankti, causes concern and requires further consideration. An unwritten scripture, still retained in memory, might consist of narratives, tales, stories, verses and padas but not lines. There is no constraint or limit of number of letters to be written in a line. A line may be bigger or smaller as per size of the paper.

Buddhist Monk, Jagdish Kāshyapa

Buddhist monk, Jagdish Kāshyapa, while giving etymological interpretation of the word 'Pāli' has suggested that the said word was synonymous with 'Pariyāya' (having the same meaning). The word Pariyāya has frequently appeared in Tripitakas—by itself or along with the word 'Dhamma' (religion). Monk, Jagdish Kāshyapa, has made it clear by giving numerous illustrations that the word 'Pariyaya' had been used in the sense of Buddha teachings or utterances. The said word 'Pariyāya' had transformed into 'Paliyaya' with the passage of time. In stone inscription of Emperor Ashoka, found at Bhābru the use of the word 'Paliyāya' is obtained. There is a message in the said stone inscription, intended for religious mendicants—'Bhante' (a term of respect applied to a Buddhist) these were religious preachings of Lord Buddha. I wish that all male and female mendicants as also Upasakas (worshippers of Buddha, who have not yet renounced the wordly life as distinguished from the Bhikshus), should listen and adhere to them'.[1]

The initial portion of the word 'Paliyāya' *i.e.*'Pāli' appears to be a prefix. Its first letter 'pa' had transformed to the latter 'pā' with the lapse of time. Thus, the word 'Paliyāya' had transformed into 'Pāliyaya'. In the process of shortening the syllable the latter part disappeared and the former part 'Pali' had only survived. Its use became synonymous with three collections of Buddha teachings (Tripitakas).

---

1 Imāni bhante Dhammapaliyāyāni etāni bhante dhammapaliyāyāni ichchhāmi kiṁ ti bahuke bhikhupāye chā bhikhuniye chā abhikhinaṁ sunyu chā updhāliyeṣhu chā Haiyaṁ bhaiva upāsaka chā upasikā chā |

Buddhist Monk Sidhārtha

Buddhist monk Sidhārtha, believed that the word Pāli was used for the texts of Buddhist scriptures. He opines that the word 'Pāth' (texts) had special significance under Vedic tradition. Infact, there was a systematic and scientific tradition of recitation of Vedic texts in the shape of 'Samhita Path' (the continuous texts of Veda); 'Pada Pāth' (an arrangement of the Vedic text in which each word is written and pronounced in its original form and independently of phonetic changes); 'Krim Path' (A particular manner of reciting Vedic texts leaving at each time one word and taking up another); 'Jata Path' (a particular manner of reciting Vedic texts thus the words नमः रुद्रेभ्यः repeated in this manner would stand thus नमो रुद्रेभ्यों नमो नमो रुद्रेभ्यः) and 'Ghan Pāth' (a particular manner of reciting Vedic texts ; thus the Padas नमः रुद्रेभ्यः ये repeated in this manner would stand thus; नमो रुद्रेभ्यो रूद्रेभ्यो नमो नमों, रुद्रेभ्यों ये ये, रुद्रेभ्यो नमों नमो रुद्रेभ्यो ये,. Religious Monk Sidhārtha, pleads that even during the age of Lord Buddha, Brahmans, who were reciters of the Vedas, used the word 'Vedic texts'. Whereas, Ksatrias (Warrior class of Hindu society); Vaish (merchant class) and Shūdras (the fourth or the last of the four principal tribes of Hindūs). Joined the religious organisation of Lord Buddha, Brahmanas (the first of the four original castes of the Hindus) also joined it. There is always an effect of the caste tradition of each caste or community, which is not necessarily converted or replaced with the change in religious faith and belief. Brahmanas, initiated in Bodh religion, who were earlier using the word Path for Vedic texts, began to use it similarly, for the texts of Buddhist preachings.

The devoted resident pupils (who stayed in the abodes of their spiritual preceptors) and followers of Buddhism used many attributives for Lord Buddha to express their respect for him, the epithets like 'Vedagya' (well conversant with Vedas) and 'Vedantagya' (A follower of Vedant philosophy) are also found to have been used for him. It is quite possible that Brahmana resident pupils might have used the said attributives for Lord Buddha, out of their extreme faith and reverence for him. Religious monk, Sidhartha has introduced many other words, which had their origin from Vedic tradition but, subsequently, they had been adopted in their new forms by Buddhist organisation. For instance the words 'Samhita' (collection of texts or verses); 'Tantra' (The regular order of the ceremonies and rites) and 'Pravachana' (expounding religious teachings) etc. are primarily words of Vedic tradition. They were admitted in Buddhist organisation in altered forms as 'Sahita' in place of Samhita; 'Tanti' for Tantra and 'Pāvachan' for Prāvachan. Buddhist Monk, Sidhartha pleads that it was very likely that the Vedic word 'Pāth' might have also been adopted in changed form, consistent with Buddhist tradition. It is one of the rules of Pāli grammar which regulates that all cerebral consonants ट, ठ, ड, ढ, ण turn into ल (la) in Pāli script. According to Sidhārtha, Sanskrit word 'Pāth' might have changed to 'Pāli' and, thereafter, to 'Pāli' in accordance with the same rule. Ofcourse, from philological viewpoint, it could not be considered an impossibility. The practice of a change in the last vowel of word is observed in both Pāli and Prākrita scripts. The consonant 'la' in Pali is not a semi vowel (as standing between a vowel and consonant) but matches with the phonetic sound of cerebral consonant ळ (la) used in Vedic Sanskrit. In some of the modern languages, the said phonic has totally disappeared, while in certain other languages, the cerebral consonant ल 'la' has been evolved into ड 'ḍa' . Avoiding further discussion on the point, there is no need to differentiate the pronunciation of consonants ळ ḷa or ल la. On the basis of the unreal resemblance or depending upon the false similarity, the difference between Pāli or Pāli was overlooked. Thus the use of the word Pāli started in place of Pāli in the sense of Buddha teachings.

The systematic history of evolution of Pāli language as put forward by Buddhist Monk Sidhartha, appears to be credible from linguistic viewpoint. Just as the opinion, held by monk, Jagdish Kashyapa, bears examination on the basis of rules governing change in phonetic sounds, similarly, the view of Buddhist monk, Sidhartha, is also consistent with the rules governing change in phonetic sounds. While exposing the untenability of arguments of Buddhist monk, Sidhartha, Dr. Bharat Singh Upadhyaya writes— 'He suggests that `Pāl' is the changed form of the word 'pāth' and the word Pāli or Pāli is its derivative. In order to prove anthenticity of the said argument, it is necessary that the use of the word Pāl was found in Pāli literature. Then only the source of derivation of the word pāli could be established. No such illustration has been provided by Bhikshu Sidhartha in his article. Out of the examples, given by him from the legends written by Acharaya Budhaghosha, only the phrase 'इति पि पाठो' (It is the text) appears to have been written by Āchāraya Budhaghosha.[1]

The criticism of the views of Bhikshu Sidhartha, made by Dr.Upadhyaya, appears to be correct. No purpose is served by merely establishing the derivation of a word on the basis of grammatical rules. Reliable historical proof is absolutely necessary to establish how the specific form of a word came to be used in a particular sense. However, it is possible that in the process of transformation of the word Pāth to Pāḷi or Pāli, the first changed form of the word Pāth, might have been paḷ, which might not have appeared in Pāli literature or only rarely appeared. The use of the derivative 'Pāli' might have started without any long intervening period. The said derived form 'pāli' might have begun to be mostly used. However, all these are mere probabilities. Infact, the opinion of Bhisksbu Sidhartha appears hardly believable.

Dr. Maxvelsar

About half a century ago, renowned German scholar, Dr. Maxvelsar, had propounded a new theory. He believed that the etymological derivation of the word Pāli was from 'Pāṭli'. The original word could be 'Pādli' in place of 'Pāṭli'. He enunciates that the native dialect of Pātliputra (Patna region) might have been Patli, and for obtaining brevity, the intervening letter 't' might have been obliterated, resulting in the accomplishment of the word 'Pāli' Pāṭliputra was a central city of Magadha dynasty. Its old capital was Rajgrha and its next capital

1. *Pāli Sāhitya kā Itihās*, page 6.

was Pāṭliputra. Hence 'Pāli' the language of Pāṭliputra could be adopted as official language of Magadha dynasty.

Has Pāṭli been the name of any language ? Whatever literature is available, the word Pāṭli has, nowwhere, appeared for any specific language. Had the local language of Patliputra region been popular by the said name, there must have been a mention to that effect somewhere or the other. Infact, the opinion of Dr. Maxvelsar is not based on any solid foundation. Hence this theory is not taken seriously by the scholars. It is a mere piece of imagination or sheer display of the strength of his intellect. Dr. Thomas has strongly refuted this theory by advancing various arguments.[1]

A few scholars have pleaded that the word 'word 'Pāli' was a derivative of 'Pālli'. The literal meaning of the Sanskrit word Pālli is a small village, a hut, a house or a camp. Thus, they have trid to hold that Pālli was the language of a village or countryside. It appears that they have thus tried to establish that Palli was a vernacular or native dialect of the common people. Most probably they believed that the order of transformation might have been from Pālli to Pālli and from Pālli to Pāli. However, it also appears to be only fanciful. There are no historical or traditional evidence in support of this contention. Hence the plea did not find favour with the learned scholars and intellectuals.

Opinions of Bhandārker and Wāketnāgal

According to Dr. Bhandarker and Wāketnāgal, Pāli was the oldest Prākrita dialect. Hence the word Pāli had been formed by derivation from the word Prākrita itself. The order of formation is—Prākrita>Pākata>Pāada-Pāala>Pāl>Pāli. When traced to its etymology, as a word the said formations are more conjectural than real. Infact, the word Prākrita does not signify one particular language. There are numerous forms of Prākrita dialects subject to territorial or regional variations. Pāli is only one of the types of Prākrita dialects. There could be slight justification, if an attempt had been made to link the etymology of the word Pāli with that particular kind of Prākrita dialect. However tracing its derivation directly from the word Prākrita cannot be sustained without any historic or scientific support.

Rajwāḍe: Rajwāde has tried to trace the origin of the word Pāli from Sanskrit word 'Prakata' (clear, evident, manifest) and considered the order of transformation as—Prakata>Pāada>Pāala>Pāli which could be further expanded as Prakata>Pāada-Pāala>Pāl>Pāli. The said etymological derivation is also not very convincing, like one conceived from the word Prākrita. Hence no credence has been shown by the linguistists to such imaginary thoughts. Moreover, there was no consistency whatsoever between the meanings of the two words 'Prakata' and 'Pāli'. It could be a mere far-fetched imagination and nothing more.

Prāleya: Prāleyaka: Pāli: A few scholars have traced the etymology of the word Pāli with Prāleya (snow, frost or dew) or Prāleyaka (a hail-stone) There are several meanings of the word 'Praleya or Praleyaka'.[2] One of the meanings is

1. *Indian Historical Quarterly*, December, 1928, pages 429-30.
2. Hail, snow frost dew snow-mountain Himaovat, frosty-rayed the moon.
—*Sanskrit-English Dictionary*, p. 702 by Sir Monier Williams.

snow-clad mountain' also. However, while analysing the said opinion, Dr. Bholanath Tewari and Dr. Bharatsingh Upadhyaya have held that the actual meaning of the word 'Prāleya or Prāleyaka' is a neighbour. However, this does not appear to be a customary meaning of the word. By imagining that Pali was the native dialect of hilly area, on the north of Magadha or mountainous region of Magadha dynasty itself (Rajgariha etc.), a remote consistency could be established between the words Pāli and Prāley or Praleyaka and the etymology of the word Pāli could be remotely considered from Prāley-Prāleya-Pāli which however, does not appeal to the mind.

Critical Evaluation: A critical review of the views and opinions of various scholars regarding etymological derivation of the word Pāli is desirable. There is renowned dictionary styled *Abhidhan Dipika*, related to Buddhist tradition. Therein the literal sense of the word Pāli has been given as Tanti-Tantra' (system or technique): Buddha teachings and 'Pankti' (a line or row). It has been cited therein that what supports or accords protection is Pāli. Simultaneously a question has been posed as to whom it supports? What it protects for? While answering the questions, it is cited "Attham Pāti" which means that it protects the very aim purport or preserves Buddha teachings. How Pāli language preserved Buddha teachings? It could be stated in reply that Tripitakas (3 collections of Buddha scriptures) were compiled and reduced to writing in Pāli script. Thus Pāli preserved the said scriptures. There could be another answer as well. During the period of king Vatthagamini ruler of Ceylon (Now Sri Lanka), a well known follower and promoter of Bodh religion, the three Buddhist scriptures were reduced to black and white in Pāli script. Thus Pāli is synonymous with Buddha teachings and it also literally means a line. Since Buddha teachings were compiled in the shape of 3 scriptures in Pāli, hence Pāli had become identified with Buddha preachings and since they were reduced to writing in Pāli script, it had become synonymous with the lines of Buddhist writings.

The etymological interpretation of the word 'Pāli', given by the author of *Abhidhan Dipika* is important, keeping in view the history of its derivation. However, a significant point has been ignored. The aforesaid author has not made any specific mention of the word 'Pariyāya'. He has only cited that the synonym of the word 'Pariyāya' were texts of Buddha tachings. Presumably, he might have omitted to consider over the relation between the words 'Pariyāya' and Pāli from linguistic viewpoint.

From the discussion made in foregoing pages, concerning the use of the word 'Pāli' in the sense of a language, it is evident that till the 14th century, nowhere it is found recorded that Pāli was the language in which the teachings of Lord Buddha had been reduced to writing. It could not be emphatically claimed when and how the word Pāli came to be used for a Prākrita dialect. In this connection, Dr. Bharat Singh Upādhyaya has expressed the view—"Initially", the word Tanti had been used as synonym, for original Tripitakas or any one of the said Pitakas in the implied sense of Pāli, such as 'Vinaya-tanti' *i.e.* 'Vinay-Pali'. Thereafter, the composite word 'Tanti Bhasha' became identified with the language of Tripitākas in Ceylon (Sri Lanka). Lateron, its synonymous compound word 'Pāli Bhasha' also began to be used. Pāli Bhasha came to be identified with the language in which

Buddha teachings had been reduced to black and white. Afterwards, the word Pāli, itself, began to be used to mean a language. Now the word Pāli signifies a language in which the Tripitakas (Three collections of "Buddha teachings) and other allied canonical literature (That from which one derives his material for writing have been written.[1]

The sequence of adoption of the word Pāli for a language, given by Dr. Upādhyaya is really significant. The use of composite word 'Tanti Bhasha' or 'Pāli-Bhāsha" made in Buddhist literature, provides relevance to the current meaning of Pāli. Dr. Upādhayaya has made it clear that the words 'Tanti-Bhasha' or 'Pāli-Bhāsha' signified the language in which Buddha teachings had been recorded. It is quite possible that the word 'Bhāsha' might have been dropped with the passage of time and the word Pāli alone might have survived and continued to be used as such.

Fundamental Shape of Pāli Language

There are diverse opinions of scholars regarding fundamental shape of Pāli language. Several names have been found or have appeared for the language in which the Tripitikas had been reduced to writing as 'Magadhi'—'Māgadha Bhasha' 'Māgadhā-Nirukti' and 'Magadhik Bhasha' etc. It is explicit from the use of these words that it was the native dialect of Magadha region. Under Ceylonic tradition as well, it is believed that it was Māgadhi, local dialect of Magadha territory. It is further believed under the said tradition that it was none else but Māgadhi in which highly prudent and deifed saint, Lord Buddha, had delivered his religious discourses. There was, a similar mention in *Kachchān Vyākarna* (a grammar) also. It has been cited therein that Magadhi was the prime language of the world in which Lord Buddha had delivered has sermons. Acharya Buddhaghosha has also subscribed to this opinion. He has stated in his work 'Samanta Pāsādika' that the language in which highly intellectual and sanctified religious teacher had imparted his lectures, was none else but Māgadhi. A person, obviously, developes affection and attachment with the language in which the scriptures relating to its religious conviction, have been written. In other words, the said attachment intensely grows to the extent of intentness and devotion. Resultantly, in place of appreciating the reality or actual state of things, a person starts pouring words of praise and eulogy. Acharya Buddhaghosha, besides being an erudite scholar, was also a preceptor of Buddhist religion and philosophy. Therefore, out of great respect and regard, he goes to the extent of declaring that Māgadhi was the prime and principal language of all living beings. This has already been stated while discussing the primitiveness of each spiritual language of the world.

Ceylonic Tradition: Even now it is staunchly believed in Ceylon that the language, known as Pāli, is the same which was the medium of speech in Magadha during the era of Lord Buddha. Under Ceylonic tradition, it is decisively belived that the language in which Lord Buddha delivered his discourses and reduced to writing in the shape of Tripitakas was none else but Māgadhi. It is also added

1. *Pāli Sāhitya Kā Itihās*, page 10.

with feeling of pleasure and contentment that Buddhist legends, written in 12th century, had also been reduced to black and white in Māgadhi.

There is a renowned treatise, styled Chūlbagga written in 13th century. It was an enlarged edition of 'Mahāvansh'. There is a reference there.[1] A senior Buddhist monk, Revata, instructed Acharya Budhaghosh to proceed to Ceylon and translate Ceylonic legendary tales in Māgadhi. It had been further cited that Āchārya Buddhaghosha had complied with the instructions of Buddhist monk, Revata. It was mentioned therein that all the Ceylonic tales had been translated in fundamental language of the world, Māgadhi. Slightly earlier, in 12th century, the learned scholar, Mogglān had authored *Pāli Vyākarana* (grammar of Pāli language). He had stated in the preface of the book that he would be writing the science of words or grammar relating to Māgadhi dialect.

Burmese Tradition: Regarding form of language in which Tripitakas and other canonical allied literature had been written, the belief of Ceylonic tradition has been endorsed by Burmese tradition also.

Ceylon and Burmah are treated as prominent centres of the followers of 'Thervād'. Under Burmese tradition as well, it is believed that Lord Buddha had delivered his religious discourses in Māgadhi which was the primary and *bonafide* language of the world. The teachings of Lord Buddha are obtained in the shape of Tripitakas (Three collections of Buddhist preachings). In 19th century, a work on Jurisprudence, styled 'Mohvichhedini' had been accomplished in Burmah in Pali language which is considered superb in Burmese Pali literature. It has similarly been held in the said book.[2]

What has been stated above, is only one of the various opinions, expressed by the scholars regarding the form of language, in which Lord Buddha had delivered his lectures. Views of other scholars are also produced hereunder so that thorough review and critical investigation could be carried out on the subject in the light of observations made by other philologists.

Prof Rayas Davids: Prof Rayas Davids had carried out a lot of research work on Pali.In nutshell, he opines that Lord Buddha belonged to Kaushal region (the territory along the banks of river Saryu, signifying the area, north of Ayodhya, comprising Gauda and Bahraich). His mother tongue was, obviously, the same, which was customary in the then Kaushal region. It is but natural that a religious preceptor always sermonizes in his own mother-tongue. Hence the language, now known as Pāli, was, infact the medium of speech, commonly used in Vth-VIth century A.D. in Kaushal region. Prof. Rayas Davids further states that within the period of almost one hundred years, after final salvation of Lord Buddha, his teachings had been prmarily compiled in the territory of Kaushal, itself.

Ujjaini Dialect and Pāli: There is an opinion that the source of origin of Pāli was Ujjaini dialect, spoken in modern Ujjain territory (situated on the banks of Sipra river. It is the Western part of Mālwa region). The propounders of the said theory are Western Guard[3] and Prof. E. Kuhan.[4] They have advanced two arguments

1. *Chūlleagga*, Chapter 37, Narrative pages 229-30.
2. *The Pāli literature of Burmah*. Pages 88-89 (London, 1909)
3. *History of Pāli literature*, Vol l pages 50-56 (Preface by Dr. Law)
4. *Buddhistic Studies*, page 233, edited by Dr. Law.

in support of their view. Firstly, Pāli had considerable resemblance with the script, inscribed on the stone inscription of Lord Asoksa, found at Girnār in Saurashtra (Gujarat) state . Secondly prince Mahendra, son of Emperor Asoka, who had propagated Bodh religion in Ceylon and had carried with him the aforesaid 3 collections of Buddha Preachings, reduced to writing in Pāli, had lived in his childhood at Ujjaini. Obviously, the language of said region was his mother-tongue in which three collections of Buddha teachings had been compiled.

Pāli and dialect of Vindhya Region: Another opinion regarding origin of Pāli language is that it had been evolved from the language of Vindhya region. The exponent of this view is Mr. R.O. Frank. The plea[1] given by him is that Pāli considerably resembled with the languge of the stone inscription of Lord Ashoka, found at Girnār.

M/s Wester Guard and E. Kuhan had also advanced a similar argument, holding that Pāli had its origin from Ujjaini language. The qustion, obviously, arises whether the dialects of Vindhya and Ujjaini regions were identical or they had considerable resemblance with each other? Mr. R.O Frank had also stated that the form of Pāli language greatly matched with the script of stone inscriptions, found in central India. Ofcourse, he has pointed out certain dissimilarities of the two languages also. Vindhya region is also a part of Central India. Possibly the language of Vindhya region mighty have greatly influenced the language of Ujjaini territory, Western part of Central India. This very fact might have induced Mr. R.O. Frank to believe that Pāli had its origin from the language of Western territory of Vindhya region.

Stain Cono: Mr. Stain Cono[2] has also subscribed to the view that Pāli had its origin from the dialect of Vindhya territory. However, the reason deduced by him were quite different. According to Stain Kono, Pāli greatly matched with Paishāchi Prākrita (one of the lowest forms of Prākrita dialects). Another argument, advanced by him, is that Paishāchi, Prākrita was in vogue in Vindhya region in the vicinity of Ujjaini.

The plea of Mr.Stain Cono that Paishachi Prākrita was spoken in Vindhya region in the vicinity of Ujjaini territory has failed to convince the philologists. The fact remains that Paishāchi dialect was never the medium of speech in Ujjaini or Mālwa region. Most eminent linguist, Sir George Griyason, has opined that Paishāchi dialect was spoken by the people in the lands of Kaikeya and East Gandhar (Name of the territory between India and Persia, the Modern Kandhar). The opinion of Stain cono was virtually contrary to that of Mr. Griyason. As a matter of fact, the views of Mr. Griyason receive greater sanction by intellectuals and are rational as well.

Consistency of Pāli with language of Kalinga: It is also opined that Pāli had evolved from the language, spoken in Kalinga region (A territory, lying to the South of Orissa and extending to the mouths of Godavari and bordering modern Āndhra Pradesh). The exponent of this theory is Dr. Olden Verga.[3] He appears to believe that since Kalinga was close to Ceylon, the propagation of Bodh religion

---

1. *Pāli Literature and Language*, pages 3-4 (preface) —Dr. Gaigar
2. *History of Indian Literature*, Vol II, page 604.
3. *Vinaya-pitāka*, edited by Dr. Olden Verga, Vol I. Introduction pages 1 to 56.

was carried on from the soil of Kalinga region for centuries. According to Dr. Verga the language, then used in Kalinga region, had evolved, and came to be known as Pāli after refinement and having undergone change which had an access to Ceylon and adopted as medium of Buddha teachings and propagation of Bodh religion in Ceylon. Another argument advanced by Dr. Olden Verga, is that the language of Stone inscription found in the elephant cave of Khandagiri of Kalinga region was conforming and proximal with Pāli. The stone inscription was possibly in the erstwhile language of Kalinga region, which was but natural.

Mahendra and princess Sanghmitra son and daughter of Emperor Ashoka, had gone to Ceylon for propagation of Bodh religion, This fact is believed to be true generally by all historians now. Dr. Olden Verga, however, does not subscribe to it. In his opinion, the propagation and spread of Bodh religion in Ceylon by the dwellers of Kalinga region was more realistic. According to him, the inhabitants of Kalinga region spared no pains to spread Bodh religion in Ceylon continuously for several centuries.

Views of E. Muler: Like Dr. Olden Verga, E. Muler also belives that Pāli had its origin from the language of Kalinga region. He opines that it was the Kalinga region, wherefrom Indians had moved and settled in ceylon. Thereafter, they propagated Bodh religion in that country.

Critical Review: Certain scholars do not concur with the belief of Ceylonic tradition which considers Māgadhi (native dialect of Magadh region and official language of Magadh dynasty as source of origin of Pāli language. According to them, Magadhi could, in no case, be the source of origin of Pāli. The opinion of Prof. Rāyas Davids is consistent with the belief of Ceylonic tradition to a limited extent only in as much as Lord Buddha had born in Kaushala region. His place of activity and movement was mainly in Māgadh territory. Since he had born in Kaushala, his mother-tongue was, obviously, the language, spoken in that region. It was quite natural on his part to deliver his sermons in Māgadhi dialect, so as to be able to have communication with people at large Being his mother-tongue, it is quite possible that he might have imparted his lectures in the dialect of Kaushala region. However, since he had to deliver his discourses and elaborate his teachings to the people of Magadh, a mixed form of the two dialects might have been accomplished to address the people.

Prof Rayas Davids has stated in this regard that the langage found in the stone inscriptions of Emperor Ashoka was, infact. the developed and modified form of the dialect, used in the territory of Kaushala in sixth-seventh century B.C. Prof. Rayas Davids has also expressed the view that the then standard shape of the language of Kaushala region, obtained during the regime of Ashoka, might have been adopted as official language of Magadh dynasty.

Dr. Winternitz[1] has criticized the mistaken belief of Prof. Rayas Davids and stated that the actual shape of erstwhile language, as was in vogue in 6th-7th century B.C. in Kaushala region, could not be known for definite now. Another ground for refuting the opinion of Prof. Rayas Davids, was that Magadh dynasty was then a celebrated and well-established kingdom. How could one agree that it

1. *History of Indian Literature*, Vol. II. page. 605.

had adopted the language of a neighbouring state. During the reign of Emperor Ashoka, Magadh dynasty was at the peak of its progress and prosperity. Under the circumstances, it was more consistent to believe that the native dialect of Magadh (Māgadhi), might have been adopted as official language of the kingdom. Ofcourse while some other territoral parts are conquered and joined in the central dynasty, the dialects of other territories do have their role in shaping a mixed language to be adopted as state language. The newly accomplished mixed language enjoys the support and recognition of each and everybody and becomes acceptable to all. Hence if was neither rational nor believable that the native dialect of Kaushala region was the source of origin of Pāli. Similarly, the opinions of M/s Wester Guard, Kuhan, Frank and Stain Cono take into account or represent only one aspect of the matter and donot touch all aspects. To believe that the dialect of Vindhya region was the source of origin of Pāli, was as futile as to accept the dialect of Kaushala region as the source of its origin. In the course of their research and investigation the scholars do come across certain characheristics or features of Pāli language which impel them to establish consistency with the dialects of other regions. Thus it transpired that in spite of admitting one specific dialeact as the fundamental source of origin, it had to consider the special characteristics of other dialects as well, in order to accomplish a new language, acceptable by majoity of the people as official language of the dynasty.

Mr. Frank has avanced a typical argument. According to him, the language which is now believed to be Pāli and in which Tripitakas and other allied canonical literature had been accomplished was, infact, literary shape of Pāli. Mr. Frank has considered all those Aryan languages as Pāli. which were the medium of speech in India during the life-time Lord Buddha. However, the said opinion of Mr. Frank is not proper or rational. It was not desirable at all to make any new establishament regarding Aryan languages which were in day today use in India during the era of Lord Buddha. They were known as Prākritas, named in accordance with the names of the territories they were in use. To assume the name of Pāli for all those dialects is absolutely uncalled for and irrelevant. It is equally confusing to add the word literary with Pāli, the language in which Tripitakas had been reduced to writing.

The plea of Dr. Olden Verga and E. Muler that Pāli had been introduced by the inhabitants of Kalinga region in Ceylon is also a fiction. If the languages of Ceylon are compared with the dialects of eastern and western territories in India, they are more close to the dialects used in western territories as against those of eastern territiories.

The scholars have given full consideration to the subject of tracing out the source of origin of Pāli. Different scholars have advanced their own arguments in support of their plea that Māgadhi was the source of origin of Pali language. Buddhist scholars- Bhiksu Sidhartha and Bhikshu Jagdish Kashyapa, as also Western scholars—M/S James Elvis, childers, Windish, Winternitz Griyason and Gāyagar etc. have opined that Magadhi was the source of origin of Pāli, furnishing their own arguments in supoport of there pleas.

James Elvis and Childers have expressed the view that there were 16 regional dialects, as medium of speech in different regions of India during the life-time of Lord Buddha. The dialect which was the medium of exchange in Magadh, was adopted by Lord Buddha for delivering his discourses. Mr. Windish also subscribed to this view. Mr. Winternitz too had lent support to the same theory, with slight variation. According to him, Pali was a literary language. A liberary language is accomplished from co-ordination of several regional dialects. Mr Winternitz, however, admits that ancient shape of Māgadhi was the prominent dialect amongst the regional dialects, from co-ordination of which. Pāli had come into existence.[1]

Although. Sir George Griyason admitted that Māgadhi was the source of origin of Pāli, yet looking to the influence of dialects, pertaining to the western regions, he has remarked that Māgadhi was not the lone and exclusive source of origion of Pāli. According to him, the main source of origin of Pāli was any one of the Western dialects. Mr. Griyason further contrives that the source of origin of Pali was, infact the form of Māgadhi which was recognized by Takṣilā University. As envisaged by him, the edition of Tripitakas had been accomplished there in the aforesaid form of Pāli dialect.[2]

Dr Keith had opposed this view in his article, captioned—'The Home of Pāli', He writes that neither Mr. Griyason nor any other scholar had suggested that Pāli was ever used as medium of instructuon in Takṣilā University. They have also not produced any convincing material in support of their version that Tripitakas had been compiled there.[3]

As a matter of fact, there is considerably long distance between Magadha and Takṣilā. In between Magadh and Takṣila, numerous regional dialects are found in vogue evidently a specified form of Māgadhi was used as medium of instruction in Takṣila University, situated in remote north western part of India, does not appeal to the mind at all. No proof or supporting material is available to substantiate that Tripitakas been compiled in Tākṣila University.

The views expressed by German Scholar, Dr Gayagar on the subject are really investigative and worth consideration. He opines that Māgadhi dialect was the medium of speech of a specific region or district and had acquired an inter-state recognition. It was already undergoing the process of growth and developement even prior to the era of Lord Buddha. Although in an inter-state or inter-regional language which is the medium of expression in different territorial parts, slight changes are bound to take place, yet it does not lose its basic indentity. Lord Buddha had adopted the said popular language as the medium for delivering his religious discourses. It was natural that effects of several regional dialects might have appeared in the inter-state form of Māgadhi dialect. Buddha did not belong to Magadha by birth. Neverthless, major part of his life mission had been accomplished there. It was, therefore, obvious that his own mother-tongue must have been influenced by Māgadhi dialect. In nutshell. Dr. Gayagar viewed that although Māgadhi was not the exclusive source of origin of Pāli. yet it was the popular language of the masses, based on Māgadhi dialect, in which Lord Buddha had imparted his lectures and propagated his message.

On the basis of distinctive features of Māgadhi, as determined by grammarians, could it be claimed that the source of origin of Pāli dialect was Māgadhi or any

---

1. *History of Indian Literature*, Vol. II. page. 13.
2. The article of Dr. Griyason, titled *The Home of Literary Pāli*, published in R.G. Bhandarkar commemoration volume, pages 117-123.
3. *Budhistie studis*, edited by Dr. Law, Page 739.

other distinct form of it (Māgadhi) which is not obtained now? It needs a critical examination. It is a language first that comes into existence, and thereafter its grammar is composed. This fact equally applies to the grammar of Māgadhi. The grammer is a process to regulate and keep within bounds the characteristics of a particular language as against other languages of the same standard. Consequently, the grammarians could not be in a position to ascertain the earlier form of a language prior to the composition of its grammar. The spontaneous flow and viability of a language is interrupted by grammatical constraints. As per critical examination of Māgadhi, carried out by grammarians of Prākritas, the languge in which the Tripitakas and other auxiliary literature had been reduced to writing was different and did not match with Māgadhi. On comparing with Māgadhi used in certain inscriptions and dramatic compositions. it is quite explicit that Pāli is decidedly different from it. The fact remains that the said inscriptions, dramatic compositions and Prākrita grammars came into existence, much after the origin of Pāli dialect.

Chief Characteristics of Māgadhi

In Māgadhi letter 'ra' is turned into 'la' and 'sa' is turned into 'sha'.[1] In words ending in vowel 'a' having masculine gender nominative case, singular number, the last letter 'a' is turned into 'e'[2] or in other words, let us say that in Māgadhi, the word in masculine gender, nominative case, singular number ends in vowel 'e'. The following couplet, given in Sanskrit drama, 'Mrichachhkatika" authored by 'Shūdraka' is illustrative of the characteristics of Māgadhi:

"Kiṁ yāshi Dhāvashi palāyashi pakhalanti vāsu paseed ṇa malishyasi tistha tavat |
Kamen dahyate khalu me hridayaṁ Tapsvi, Angārrāshipatitmiva maskhandam||

However, in Pāli the letter 'ra' remains unchanged. Sometimes it is found to have turned in letter 'la' in an irregular manner. It is however, not found in all cases. It is only rarely found. *For example*, the Sanskrit word तरुण (a young man) is also found used as 'तलुण' in Pāli, although mostly it appears as 'तरुण'. In Pāli, the dental letter स is never changed into a palatal letter श. In Māgadhi the palatal consonant 'श' is frequently used. Besides the dental letter 'स' the cerebral letter 'ष' is also turned into palatal letter श in Māgadhi. Just as 'पुरुष' (a male) 'पुलिशे' [स: (that person) = शे] Like masculine gender, the words ending in vowel 'a' turn in common gender nominative case, singular number, into vowel 'e' in the last. However, in Pāli, neither in masculine gender nor in common gender, the said rule applies. In Pāli, the words in masculine gender end in vowel 'o' and of common gender end in nasal vowel. In certain cases, the last vowel 'a' is found

1. Rasailanshau /8/4/288.
Māgādhyṁ refasya dantyasakārasya cha sthane yathaasankhyaṁ lakārastālathyashākārashcha bhavati
— *Sidhhemshabdānushashāmaṁ.*
2. A ta etsau Māgadhyṁ 11 8 14/28.
Māgadhyṁ Bhashayain say pareakāsrasya ekāran behavate punsi pullige— Same.

ending in vowel 'e' also but it is extremely rare and unbound by any grammatical rule. This is chiefly because Pāli and other Prākritas are not strictly bound by grammatical constraints or rules like Sanskrit. Hence a few deviations are found here and there, which although, inconsistant with grammatical rules, are allowed and considered ignorable.

A dialect, confined to Magadh territory only, could never be exclusive source of origin of Pāli. The source of Pāli could be either a mixed standard form or an inter-provincial form of a language which was probably in use in Central India. The then boundaries of Central India might have been on the west—from western territorial parts of present Haryana to South Bihar (Magadh) on the east and on the North from 'Shrāvāsti' (now identified with Sāhet Māhet, north of Ayodhya in Uttar Pradesh) to Avanti or Ujjaini (It is the western part of Mālva region), on the South, thus covering a very vast and lengthy area. The language which was consistently in use in such a vast area, with only minor variations in different territories, could not belong to any one specific state or region. At best the regional dialect, pertaining to the Capital or a Central place of the kingdom, could have a pre-dominant status. In those days, politically Magadh was a prominent centre of Northern India. Although, prior to Chandragupta there was no emperor, whose empire might have extended to whole of Northern India unchallenged by any other empire yet there were several rulers who had been able to establish their sovereignty on neighbouring territories of Māgadha. Even if they failed to acquire domination they did exercise their influence over them. Hence it would be perfectly relevant to say that there was positively an influence of Māgadhi dialect over the co-ordinated or mixed language of entire Central India. It is quite possible that in order to indicate the influence and supremacy of Māgadhi over all other regional dialects, the name of Māgadhi dialect might have continued.

Ardh Māgadhi Prākrita and Pāli

Ardh Māgadhi is also one of the types of Prākritas. This is the language of Jaina sacred scriptures. A detailed consideration will be undertaken in the next chapter over this dialect. Here we are concentrating over those points only which relate to the origin of Pāli.

Ardh Māgadhi is normally defined to mean the dialect which was the medium of speech in between the area where Māgadhi and Shorseni dialects were spoken. Ardh Māgadhi is also interpreted to mean a language which contains half of the distinctive features of Māgadhi. There are chiefly three special features of Māgadhi. In it the cerebral letter 'ष' and dental letter स are found converted into palatal letter श and the letter र turns into letter 'ल'. The words ending in vowel 'a' in masculine gender, nominative case, singular number, are stuffixed by vowel 'e' in place of vowel 'a' in Māgadhi. The use of palatal letter श is not found at all in Ardh Māgadhi. The use of letter 'la' in place of 'ra' is only occasional. The words ending in vowel 'a' in masculine gender, nominative case, singular number are generally found suffixed by vowel 'e' in Ardh Māgadhi as well. Thus half of the special characteristics of Māgadhi are obtained in Ardh Māgadhi Prākrita. Another special feature of Ardha Māgadhi Prākrita in the formation of case (the relation subsisting between a noun and verb in a sentence or between a noun and verb in a sentence or between a noun and oher words governing it) is that in the locative case, besides suffixes 'ए' and 'म्मि' the suffix 'अंसि' is also found in use. Just as 'वणे' 'वणम्मि' and 'वणसि'. This is further elucidated by the following verse from Dashavaikālik sūtra (Jaina Agamic scripture):

रुक्षवृत्तिः सुमन्तुष्ठः अल्पेच्छः सुभरः स्यात् ।
असुरत्वं न गच्छेत् श्रुत्वा जिनशासनम् ।।

Mr Luders believes that old Ardh Māgadhi Prākrita was the basic source of origin of Pāli. According to him, Tripitakas and other allied literature had been reduced to writing in Ardh Māgadhi Prākrita. Thereafter, it was adapted in Pāli Prākrita. Mr. Luders opines that Pāli is having recourse to a western dialect for its advent. He further states that in Pāli script of *Tripitakas* (Three collections of Buddha teachings) use of Māgadhi Prākrita is also found to a slight degree which is due to the fact that while transforming in Pāli script, certain residual portions of old Ardh Māgadhi had criept in.[1]

Mr. Keith has, however, refuted the said argument of Luders.[2] He probably means that the literary shape of Ardh Māgadhi Prākrita evolve with the passage of time was the same hypothetical old Ardha Māgadhi, as envisaged by Luders, does not appeal to the mind.

Infact, no independent identity of the language, assumed by Mr. Luders as old Ardh Māgadhi Prākrita was available now. Luders seems to have identified old Ardh Māgadhi Prākrita on the basis of stone inscriptions of Emperior Ashoka and remanents of dramatic plays, written by Ashwaghosh. However, they could not be considered as adequate proofs, since they pertain to the subsequent period. The stone inscriptions of Emperor Ashoka will be dealt with elaborately in an ensuing chapter. Eminent linguist of France, Mr. Silvan Levy, has also experessed similar views. He has attempted to prove that the teachings of Lord Buddha, compiled and reduced to writing in the shape of Tripitakas in Pāli script were not the *bonafide* utterances of Lord Buddha.

Infact, the main reason for divergent opinions and suspicions aroused in respect of true identity of Pāli script, was due to manifold characteristics of its own. Lord Buddha had delivered his religious discourses through the medium of a language, known as Māgadhi, a principal dialect of Medium of a language, known as Māgadhi, a principal dialect of Māgadh region but which had been influenced and was an amalgamation of several other dialests, used in Western India. On this point, further consideration is essential from different angles. Certain new facts will come to light on undertaking critical study relating to the era of Lord Buddha, his area of movement, his principal disciples, and erswhile conditions etc.

1. *Buddhistic studies*, page 734.
2. *Ibid* . . . page 734.

Era of Lord Buddha: Contemporary Conditions

Lord Buddha had moved through the territories right from Kurukshetra district (situated in the north of India near about the site of modern Delhi) to Magadh region on the east and from Vindhya region (a range of mountains which separates North from the South of India, forming part of Central India) to Himalalyas *i.e.* in all intermediary states, districts and regions falling in their midst. In Buddhist literature, the vast area has been identified by the words 'Majhimesu' 'Padesu'. It is also well-known that the religious organisation of Lord Buddha was free from the feelings of racial discrimination—high or low. People belonging to all the four castes of Hindus, Brahmanas, Kshatrias Vaishyas and Shudras had been joining his religious organisation irrespective of any consideration. Just as people of all castes and communities were pouring in the organisation of Lord Buddha, similarly, people belonging to differnt states and regions had joined his organisation. Buddha used to deliver his lectures orally. His teachings had been compiled after two or three centuries of his final salvation. They were reduced to writing even much later-say in first century B.C. in Ceylon. Therefore, it is quite probable that a lot of additions and alternations must have taken place in *bonafide* utterances of Lord Buddha in between such a long period.

Dr. Gāyagar has spared no pains to establish with all emphasis at his command that Tripitakas, written in Pāli, contained original utterances of Lord Buddha, keeping in view their languge and contents both. There is a legend in Chūlbagga of Vinaya Pitaka (The book of discipline). There were two Brahman Buddhist monks. One of them was named Yamelu and the other Tekula. They belonged to Vedic tradition before they adopted Bodh religion. Even after joining Buddhist organisation, they were not able to give up Vedic impressions altogether. They found that the mendicants belonging to various tribes, families and lineages, were defiling the teachings of Lord Buddha by way of converting them in their own respective dialect. The said tendency has been signified in Chulbagga in the words "सकाय निरुत्तिया बुद्ध वचनम् दूसेन्ति". The said Brahmaṇa monks approached Lord Buddha and requested him—"Oh Lord! It would be better if you kindly allow us to transform your teachings in Vedic Sanskrit".[1]

Lord Buddha replied—"No! It would be amounting to a sinful act" Therafter, he issued a sacred command and ordered his mendicants to gain complete knowledge of his religious preachings by transforming them in their respective language.[2]

Being under the influence of old Vedic Saṁskārās, Buddhist Brahmaṇa monks had developed a feeling of disliking for Vernacular dialects. Because of their old dispositions, they had been considering the prosodic composition in Vedic Sanskrit as holy and sanctified. Termination of faith and regard for Vedic Sanskrit was not so easy in a short span. Accordingly, they had placed their proposal before Lord Buddha.

Achāry Buddhaghosha has written while explaining the sense of the expression

1. Handa Mayaṁ bhante Buddvachanaṁ chhandaso Āropemati!
2. Anujānāmi Bhikhwe Sakāyaniruttiyā Buddha vachanaṁ Pariyapuṇituṁ.

"छन्दसो आरोपेमाति" as "वेदं विय सक्कटभासाय वाचनामग्गम् आरोपेम्" which means to allow us to transform your teachings in Vedic Sanskrit. Herein Acharya Buddhaghosha has used the words 'Sakkat Bhāshā' which signifies a language adored and treated with honour as well as Vedic Sanskrit.

Dr. Vimalācharan Lā has opined that the literal meaning of 'सक्कट भाषा' is only Sanskrit language and has criticized Āčharāya Buddhaghosha on that account. While commenting upon the views of Dr. Lā, Dr, Bharat Singh Upadhyaya has remarked—'The word Sanskrit' came to be used after the life time of Pāṇini which signifies classical Sanskrit only. The word Chandas (Vedic Sanskrit) actually manifasted that shape of old Aryan language in which the systematically arranged hymnical texts of the Vedas had been written. Lord Buddha had actually meant it. Even in Tripitakas the words "सावित्थी छन्दसो मुख" have appeared. In this expression also, the word 'Chandas' has been used for Vedas or the sacred texts of the Vedic hymns. Hence Lord Buddha had accepted the meaning of Chhandas as that of Vedic Sanskrit.[1]

While elaborating the sense of 'सकाय–निरुत्तिया', Dr. Upādhyāya writes : "Lord Buddha treated disciples of all the four castes of Hindus equally and he had no reservations, whatsoever, as a spiritual head. He therefore, encouraged his follwers to adapt his teachings in their own respective dialect.[2]

Dr. Gāyagar has, however, given a different interpretation of 'सकाय–निरुत्तिया' the words appeared in the religious command of Lord Buddha. According to him, the said words, appearing in the consent given by Lord Buddha, the natural or logical connection of the words 'सकाय निरुत्तिया' is not with the word 'bhikhwe' (religions medicants) but with the words 'Buddha teachings'. Had the words 'सकाय निरुत्तिया' linked to 'भिक्खवे' then the word 'vo' (you) must have appeared for the clarity and relevance of the meaning of the sentence. Then the purport of the words could only be respective dialect of the medicants. However, in the original text of Buddha command, the word 'vo' (you) has not appeard hence it is obviously proved that grammatically, the relation of the words 'सकाय–निरुत्तिया' in the sentence will be with Buddha teachings. Thus the wordings, used by Lord Buddha, in his religious command would mean "Oh Mendicants! I allow you to learn My teachings in the same language in which I have imparted them to you". Therefore, it should be believed that Lord Buddha had allowed his disciples to learn his preachings in Māgadhi dialect alone.[3]

Āchārya Buddhaghosha has explained the words 'सकाय–निरुत्तिया' as 'Here the etymological interpretation of the words 'सका निरुत्ति' (Sanskrit formation 'स्वका–निरुक्ति' means one's own's dialect or language. It is thus clear that highly prudent and deified saint, Lord Buddha had ordered to pick up and learn his teachings in Māgadhi dialect. The language in which he delivered his discourses.[4]

1. *Pāli Sahitya Kā Itihās*, page 24.
2. *Pāli Sahitya Kā Itihās*, page 22
3. *Pāli Literature and Language*, pages 6-7.
4. Ettha Sakā ninutti nām sambhā sambuddhen Vuttapkaro Māgadhko boharo.

Dr. Gāyagar has laid great emphasis on the point that there was an earnest desire for preservation of genuineness and authoritativeness of Buddha utterances in order to retain them intact and unchanged. It is obvious that this policy was followed and pursued even afterwords. According to him neither Lord Buddha nor the mendicants of his organisation could have meant that they (mendicants) belonging to different regions, should obtain Buddha teachings in their respective dialect. Dr. Gāyagar has tried to prove that the definition of 'सकाय–निरुत्तिया' as respective dialect or language was wrong and improper.[1]

Bhikru Siddhartha has subscribed to the view of Āchārya Budhaghosha and Dr. Gāyagar. He has argued that Lord Buddha had declined to allow his utterances to be transformed in Sanskrit a grammatically bound and highly refined language, their how could he have allowed to obtain and transform his religious sermons in ordinary native dialects. As argued by him how would it have been possible to maintain the genuineness and sanctity of Buddha teachings? He has clearly asserted that Buddha had delivered his lectures in the then medium of speech of Māgadha region. His disciples obtained them in the same language and also taught them to others accordingly.[2]

The argument of Buddhist monk Sidhartha, that while Lord Buddha had disallowed transformation of his teachings in a sophisticated laguage like sanskrit how he could have permitted to obtain and record his utterances in an ordinary dialect or local medium of speech, does not appeal to the mind. Sanskrit is grammatically bound and an abstruse language. Only the selected gentry followed it. Thus maintenance of Buddha utterances in Sanskrit language or in an ordinary native dialect were entirely diverse matters. There was no consistency between the two. Besides this, Lord Buddha had a strong preference for local dialects. The main issue, however, was of acquiring Buddha teachings in repective dialect of the mendicants. Buddhist monk, Sidhartha has tried to explain the real intent and to rectify the flaw. However, while discussing the cause and effect, he has failed to devote adequate attention to the minute nature of the point at issue. While summing up his discussion, the inferences drawn by him, had, infact wider sense. Acharya Buddhaghosh, Dr. Gāyagar and Jaina monk, Sidhartha have tried to link the speech of Buddha utterances with the local dialect of Māgadha region was not in conformity with their observations and the inferences drawn by them . The standard shape of Magadhi language and ordinary folk language of Māgadha region could never be one and the same. Lord Buddha had adopted the form of language for delivering his discourses, which was the official language of state polity or the standard (refined) language of of Central India. He obviously, desired that the religious mendicants, belonging to different regions should obtain and record his utterances in the same standard form of the language. Normally a language of the centre of the state polity or a contact language or a national language are easily followed in all states and regions.

Dr. Winternitz has contradicted the views of Dr. Gāyagar relating to the interpretation of 'सकाय–निरुत्तिया'. He did not agree to the inevitability of adding

1. *Pali Literature and Langages*, page 7.
2. *Buddhist Studies*, page 649.

the word 'vo' with 'भिक्खवे' he has stated that it was self-implied when read in its correct perspective. Dr. Vimlacharan Lā and Dr. Keith have shown their inability to support the views of Dr. Gāyagar. Dr. Bharatsingh Upadhayaya too has stated that the views of Dr. Gāyagar could not be endorsed.

Conclusion

Lord Buddha had no persistence or favour whatsoever, for using any specific language. However, it was almost an inevitability for him to adopt a standard language. It might have been deemed in the fitness of things to adopt one single language for obtaining thorough knowledge of Buddha teachings irrespective of the fact that the mendicants belonged to different territorial parts of the country. No doubt there was probability that with the lapse of time, slight changes might take place in the original texts of Buddha utterances as obtained by religious mendicants, belonging to different regions. However, there was only rare possibility of it. Had it been allowed to obtain Buddha teachings in the respective native dialect of each mendicant then it would have been impossible to maintain co-ordination and consistency in the essential characteristics of his preachings.

Special Features of Pāli Phonetics

On comparing with the phonetics of Sanskrit language, several characteristic differences are found in Pāli phonetics. The use of 5 vowels 'ऋ' (ṛ) 'ॠ' (ṝ), 'ॡ' (lṛ), ऐ (e) and औ (ō) are not found in Pāli script. The same was the case with Prakrita dialects. In Pāli, the vowel 'ऋ' (ṛ) is changed to any one of the vowels 'a' 'e' and 'u'. The same applicability of the rule is found in Prākritas. Two additional short vowels 'ए' 'e' and 'ओ' 'o' are also provided in Pāli. In Prākritas also, they are in use. The use of visarga (a symbol in writing representing a distinct hard aspiration and marked by two perpendicular dots : and a characteristic of Sanskrit word formations) is not found in Pāli. In Prākritas also, its use is not found. The cerebral letter 'ष' 'ṣa' and palatal sha are not used in Pāli. Except Māgadhi, cerebral ष 'ṣa' and palatal letter 'श' (sha) are not used in Prākritas also.

The use of 'ळ' (ḷa) consonant is there in Pāli script. Its use is also found in Vedic Sanskrit. However, the use of la consonant is absent in classical Sanskrit. In Prākritas the consonant 'ळ' (ḷa) is used.

It may be worth knowing that on account of artificial and false resemblance of two consonants, the use of consonant 'ḷa is made inadvertantly at some places instead of correct consonant 'La'. In Pāli the consonant 'ह' 'ha' is considered as an independent phonetic sound produced from the clashing of the air or breath against heart region, after rising up vertically from the navel (one of the six ganglions in the human body). However, if the consonant 'ह' 'ha' is joined by the letters य, र, ल, व (ya' ra, la, va) or any nasal consonant, slight variation is noticed in its phonetic sound. In Pāli grammers, the consonent 'ha' is considered to have been produced by clashing of the air or breath with the heart region.

Phonetic Changes

The short vowels 'a' 'i' 'u' 'e' and 'o' are used in Pāli. So they are used in almost all the Prākritas. For instance, formation of Sanskrit word 'मुखम्' 'Mukhaṁ' (mouth is 'मुखं' in Pāli and 'मुहं' in Prākritas. Thus the use of short vowels is there in both Pāli and Prākritas. Similarly, the formation of Sanskrit word 'प्रिय' (dear or affectionate) is 'पिय' in both Pāli and Prākritas.

If the short vowel 'a' precedes a Joint consonant in Sanskrit then in Pāli script it turns into vowel 'e' at certain places. Such as, the formation in Pāli of sanskrit word 'शय्या' (a bed) is 'सेय्या' and 'सेज्जा' in Prākritas. The short vowels 'a' and 'u' inflected at the end in Sanskrit words are turned into long vowels in Pāli. *For example*, the form of Sanskrit word 'Agni' (fire) in instrumental case, plural number will be 'अग्निभि' which will turn as 'अग्गीहि' in Pāli. Similarly, the form in locative case, plural number in Sanskrit will be 'अग्निषु' which well turn 'अग्गीसु' Pāli script.

In Sanskrit, the short vowels 'i' and preceding joint consonants are turned into 'e' and 'o' respectively in Pāli. Just as the word 'पुष्कर' (a blue lotus) in Sanskrit is turned to 'पोक्खर' in Pali.

The letter 'ऋ' (ṛ) in Sanskrit, will turn into short vowels 'a' 'i' and 'u' in Pāli in different words. The Sanskrit lerrer 'ऌ' (lṛ) is also turns into 'u' vowel in Pāli. For instance, the Sanskrit word 'क्लृप्त' will be read as 'कुत्त' in Pāli script.

The long vowel at the end of a word in Sanskrit will trun into a short vowel in Pāli. Such as the form of the word 'देव' (Deva—a deity) in genitive case will be 'देवानाम्' and will turn into 'देवानं' in Pāli.

The long vowels, prior to joint consonants in Sanskrit will turn into short vowels in Pāli. *For example*, the Sanskrit word 'जीर्ण' (old) will turn as 'Jinṇa' 'जियण' in Pāli. The said formation in Pāli is adopted as such in Prākritas as well.

The use of 'Swarbhakti' (a vowel sound phonetically inserted in the pronounciation of र् or ल् when these letters are followed by a sibilant or any single consonant e.g. वर्ष pronounced as वरिष) is abundant in Pāli. As per this rule, when the joint consonants are disjointed or separated, the preceding long vowel before the joint consonant , will turn into a short vowel in Pāli script. *For example*, the form of the word 'चैत्य' (a place of religious worship) will be 'चेतिय' in Pāli. Similarly, the form of the word 'मौर्य' (name of a dynasty of kings, beginning with emperor, Chandragupta Maurya) will be 'मोरिय' in Pāli.

The use of Visarga (A symbol in writing representing a distinct hard aspiration and marked by two perpendicular dots:) is not found in Pāli and Prākritas. A visarga with a sanskrit word, obtains three shapes in Pāli and Prākritas. In case, there is a visarga in the midst of a word, it is associated with the succeeding consonant. Just as, the Sanskrit word 'दुःसह' will turn into 'दुस्सह' in Pāli. The Visarga after the word, ending in short vowel 'अ' will turn into the vowel 'ओ' in Pāli. Such as 'बुद्धः' (a wise or learned man, a sage) is turned into 'बुद्धो' in Pāli. The Visargas, appearing after the words, ending in vowels 'i' and 'u' disappear in Pāli. *For example* 'अग्निः' (fire) =Aggi.

Changes Effected in Consonants

A few rules governing changes obtained in consonants are as follows:

Normally, an independent consonant preceding a Sanskrit word will remain intact in Pāli also. Just as, the form of Sanskrit root 'कृ' (to form or to arrange) in 'लटलकार' (A technical term used by great grammarian Pāṇini to denote the present tense or its terminations), in Ist person, singular number will be 'करोति' which will remain unchanged in Pāli. In Prākritas, however, it will be read as 'करेदि'. The consonant 'क' has remained intact in both Pāli and Prākritas.

Out of five nasal consonants, namely, 'ङ', 'ञ', 'ण', 'न्' and 'म्' only two latter nasal consonants are used initially at the beginning of a Sanskrit word. The same is the practice in Pāli. However, in Prākritas, the nasal consonant 'न' will turn in 'ण'.

The consonants 'य्, र्, ल, व्' appearing initially in Sanskrit words, will remain unchanged in Pāli also. Sometimes, the letter 'र' is found converted into 'ल' which is the general practice or acceptability in Māgadhi Prākrita. *For Exmple*, the word 'राजा' (king) will be found written as 'लाजा' in Māgadhi. However, in Pāli, it is only rare.

The unvoiced or unaspirated consonants 'क', 'त्', 'प' etc. appearing initially in Sanskrit words will turn into hard-sounding or aspirated consonants of the same class in Pāli, such as 'ख्', 'थ्', 'फ्'. For instance, Sanskrit words 'कोलः' (one of a degraded tribe) 'कुब्जः' (hump-backed) and 'परशुः' (a battle axe) will respectively turn into 'खीलो', 'खुज्जो' and 'फरसु' in Pāli.

In a few cases, contrariety to the above rule is also noticed. That is to say. the initial hard-sounding or aspirated consonants, appearing in Sanskrit words are turned into unvoiced and unaspirated (in pronouncing of which little effort is required) consonants of the same class in Pāli. *For example*, for Sanskrit word 'भग्नि' (sister) the use of the forms 'बहिनी' and 'बहिणी' are found in Pāli.

The unaspirated consonant of any of the five classes of letters (from क् to म्) appearing in the midst of Sanskrit words will turn into hard-sounding consonant, of the same class in Pāli, such as 'माकन्दिय' (relating to the city on the Ganges) = 'मागन्दिय' and 'उताहो' (either or) = 'उदाहु' in Pāli.

The unaspirated consonants, appearing in the middle of Sanskrit words will turn into hard-sounding and aspirated consonants of the same class in Pāli. *For example*, the Sanskrit word 'सुकुमार' (a beautifully young or youthful person) will be read as 'सुखुमाल' in Pāli.

The aspirated consonant of any of the five classes of letters in a Sanskrit word is found converted in unaspirated consonant of the same class in Pāli. Such as 'कुशीद' (the profession of usury) = 'कुसीत'.

In certain cases, the dental consonants in Sanskrit turn into cerebral consonants in Pāli. Just as 'दाह' (the sensation of burning) = डाह; 'शकुन' (an auspicious omen) = सगुण; 'प्रथम' (first or foremost) = पठम. The rule applies to the consonants, appearing both initially or in the middle of Sanskrit words.

Intermediary palatal consonant of any the five classes of letters appearing in a Sanskrit word will turn in dental stop consonant of the same class in Pāli, such as 'चिकित्सा' (treatment or administering medicine) = तिकिच्छा.

The cerebral consonant of any of the five classes of letters appearing in the midst of a Sanskrit word, is sometimes changed in dental stop consonant of the same class in Pāli. *For example* 'डिन्डिम' (a kind of small drum) = देन्डिम

Sometimes, the letter 'न्' appearing in a Sanskrit word is found changed in 'र्' or 'ल्' in Pāli. Such as 'नैरंजना' (health) = नेरंजरा; 'एनः' (a kind of black antelope) = एल.

Sanskrit consonant 'ण' is found converted into 'ळ' (la) in some cases in Pāli. Such as 'वेणु' (A bamboo flute) = वेलु. The rule will, however, apply to the consonant, appearing in the middle of a word.

Sanskrit letter 'र्' is geneally turned into 'ल्' in Pāli. However, in some instances, it remains unchanged. For instance, Sanskrit word 'तरूण' (A young man) is found transformed into तलुण in Pāli. The original Sanskrit from is also used in Pāli without any change.

The intermediary consonant 'य' in a Sanskrit word is found converted into 'र' at some places in Pāli. Such as 'आलम्बन' (support) = आरम्भण.

The intermediary letter in a Sanskrit word 'य' is found converted in 'व' in Pāli. Just as 'आयुध' (A weapon, shield etc.) = आवुध।

Similarly, the consonant 'व' appearing in the middle of a Sanskrit word, turns into 'य' in Pāli. Just as "दाव" (forest-conflagration) = 'दाय'! However, this rule does not apply to every such word strictly. In certain cases, the form of Sanskrit word remains unchanged and the same form 'दाव' is retained in Pāli also.

The letter 'व' appearing in a Sanskrit word, will turn into 'म्' in Pāli. Such as 'द्रविड़' (name of the region on the east coast of Deccan or a native of that area) = 'द्रमिल'.

Just in contrast to the above, the letter 'म्' appearing in a Sanskrit word, is found converted in 'व्' in Pāli. *For example*, 'मीमांसा' (One of the six chief Darisanas or systems of Indian Philosophy) = 'वीमांसा'.

Cases of inversion of consonants are too many in Pāli. The consonants, appearing in the middle of a Sanskrit word, are found replacing each other in Pāli. Although this rule does not apply strictly with any specific consonant, yet it generally applies with the consonant 'र्'. Such as 'करेणु' (an elephant) = 'कणेरू'.

The letter 'क्ष' in a Sanskrit word is converted to 'क्ख' or 'च्छ' in Pāli. For instance, 'कक्ष' (A lurking or hiding place) = 'कच्छ'; 'परीक्षा' (Tribal) = 'परिक्खा'; अक्षि (the eye) = 'अक्खि' or 'अच्छि'.

Sanskit joint consonants 'ह्ण' ह्न, ह्म, ह्य, ह्व will revert in Pāli as ण्ह, न्ह,

म्ह्, य्ह् and व्ह् respectively. That is to say the subsequent letters ण्, न्, म्, य् and व् will revert to the position of former letters and *vice-versa*. Such as 'अपराह्ण' = 'अपरण्ह'; चिह्न (mark, symbol) = चिन्ह; 'जिह्वा' (tongue) = जिव्हा. Similarly, joint consonants 'श्न्', 'श्म्', 'ष्ण्', 'ष्म्', 'स्न्', 'स्म्', appearing in sanskrit words, will turn respectively in 'ञ्ह्', 'म्ह्', 'ण्ह्', 'म्ह्', 'न्ह्' and 'म्ह्' in Pāli. For instance, 'प्रश्न' (A query) = पञ्ह; 'अश्म' (A mountain, a rock) = अम्ह; 'उष्ण' (Hot, warm) = उण्ह; 'ग्रीष्म' (summer) = गिम्ह; 'स्नान' (bath) = न्हाण; 'विस्मय' (surprise, astonishment)= विम्हय.

The consonant appearing at the end of Sanskrit words, disappear in Pāli. The same acceptation is found in Prākritas. *For example* भगवान् (God) and सम्यक (Thorough, complete) will turn to 'भगवा' and 'सम्मा' respectively in Pāli.

Pāli Literature

The oldest canonical literature, obtained in Pāli, is in the shape of Tripitakās. The literal meaning of the word Tripitakās is three small boxes or baskets. It may not be inconsistent to believe that while compiling Buddha teachings, they might have been placed in three separate baskets as per subjects dealt with therein. With the passage of time, the literature (collection of Buddhist scriptures) came to be known as Tripitakas.

The period of fifth century B.C. witnessed great revoluationary changes in both spiritual and religious spheres. These revolutions materialised in Eastern territories of India. It appears that Vedic culture with frequency of Yajnas and performances of sacrificial rites might not have been able to keep the masses convinced and satisfied in eastern regions. There must have been an anxiety or inner urge in the minds of the people to attain the path of peace and tranquillity. As a natural consequence, two great luminaries, Lord Mahāvira and Buddha appeared contemporaneously. Although, there were several other spiritual guides. opposing Vedic traditions, and about whom enough has been stated above, yet there is absolutely no material available now, concerning their ideological faiths. The canonical literature relating to Lord Mahāvira and Buddha is available only.

Lord Buddha adopted local dialects as medium for delivering his discourses. He imparted lectures exhaustively on the essence of truth (realisation of the supreme truth) in their own dialects so that each and every member of the audience could be fully benefitted. The scholars used to appear personally before him and get their doubts cleared if any. He used to answer all their queries, in detail and satisfy them. Religious congregations used to take place frequently and he used to address them. Thousands of people used to listen attentively to his lectures. Along with his personal endeavours for his own spiritual advancement, his mission for welfare and upliftment of the people continued uninterruptedly all his life time. All the sermons delivered by Lord Buddha, were oral. His teachings had not been reduced to writing during his life time. Although the science of writing or script-writing was well-known to the scholars by that time yet there was a prevalent tradition of memorizing the religious lectures and retain them in memory. An obvious question arises why such a tradition was followed when the scholars were well aware with the art of writing. No satisfactory reply to the said question was forthcoming. However, it may be added here that there was a usual practice to keep the Vedic texts committed to memory. The same tendency might have prevailed upon Buddhist scholars for memorising Buddha teachings. There were numerous Buddhist monks who were capable to retain Buddha preachings in their memory. In other words, whenever Lord Buddha delivered his discourses, the religious mendicants possessing sharp memories used to learn them by heart. Attributes like 'Vinaydhar', 'Dhammadhar' 'Suttāntik' 'Mātrikādhar' etc. were used for such religious scholars. The scholars who had memorised the lectures pertaining to discipline, modesty and humility, forming part of Vinaya texts (Vinaya pitaka) came to be adored as 'Vinayadhars'. Similarly, those who had acquired knowledge of Buddha religious doctrines or sūtras which formed the subject matter of Sutta-Pitaka, were honoured by the designation of 'Dhammadher' or Suttantika. Those who had specialised themselves with the discourses of Lord Buddha pertaining to Buddhist philosophy and realisation of Supreme Truth, they were laurelled with the attribute of 'Matrikādhars'. The table of contents, showing the successive topics of a work were also called as Mātrikās. Subsequently, Abhidhamma Pitaka was comprehended from the said Mātrikās. There are citations to the said effect in 'Mahāvagga' 'Chūlbagga', Dīgh Nikāya' (Dialogues of Lord Buddha), and Anguttar Nikāya' (The book of gradual sayings) etc.

A question may, obviously, be asked whether all the lectures imparted and sermons delivered by Lord Buddha have been incorporated in Tripitakas (Three collections of Buddha teachings)? However, no such claim has ever been made by the writer of Tripitākas that all the utterances of Lord Buddha were contained in the said Buddhist scriptures. There could be numerous utterances made by Lord Buddha which could not have been retained in memory by his senior disciples. Simultaneously, it also deserved a minute consideration that whatever had been incorporated in the said three collections were Buddha teachings only to the very letter and spirit and nothing beyond. It may be desirable to know as to how the contents came to be compiled before they were reduced to writing. The facts will be self-evident and satisfy our curiosity.

Three Collections of Buddhist Writings

After expiry of three months from final salvation of Lord Buddha, a convention of Buddhist mendicants was held at Rājgraha (Bihar) in the Saptaparṇi cave on the northern side of Vaibhar Mountain with the sole purpose of recitation of Buddha utterances and their compilation so as to be reduced to writing later on. Only after three months of final salvation of Lord Buddha, why was it considered in the fitness of things to collect and compile Buddha teachings? Buddha belonged to a democratic republic. He maintained the same democratic traditions in his religious organisation encouraging openness in day today functioning of the institution. He neither proclaimed his successor nor he issued any directive to the religious mendicants to select his successor. Infact, he did not believe in administering the affairs of the organisation by any specific authority. The religious doctrines-humility, modesty and discipline, taught by him, should act as guidelines for proper conduct of the affairs of the organisation, was his exclusive motive.

There is a context. Gopaka Mogglān enquired from Ānand (the senior-most disciple of Lord Buddha) — "O Blessed Anand! was there any specific learned monk, nominated by Lord Buddha, with explicit command that after his final salvation, he would guide them and the mendicants should obey his spiritual guidance, whenever and necessary ?

Ānand replied "There was no senior monk or theologian who had been nominated by Lord Buddha, an embodiment of perfect wisdom and having attained state of highetst perfection with directive that after his final salvation, he would act as out spiritual guide and we could seek his guidance and support, when necessary.

Gopaka Moggalān again enquired "Respected Anand! was there any senior Buddhist monk who might have been recommended by the organisation as our spiritual guide and who might have been accepted as such by the association of medicants who could be depended upon after final salvation of Lord Buddha and all disputes could be referred to him for his final verdict.

Ānand replied—"There was no learned monk or theologian who might have been granted recognition and pomoted by the organisation to act as our spiritual guide."[1]

None was authoritatively nominated as successor of Lord Buddha after his final liberation, who might have been empowered to administer the affairs of Buddhist organisation. What ought to be done and what ought not to be done by the mendicants, was to be decided in the light of Buddha teachings.

Lord Buddha delivered his sermons orally. His resident pupils used to hear him attentively. The masses also used to listen to his preachings. Probably, his resident disciples were eagre to memorise his teachings and retain them in their memory. Accordingly they must have been quite conscientious and careful in this regard. Infact, the medicants had entirely devoted themselves to religious meditation and spiritual accomplishments. They spared no pains to keep Buddha utterances committed to their memory and take them across in order to embellish their own lives.

When Lord Buddha had attained final liberation, the matured and responsible Buddhist monks were eagre to protect Buddha utterances and keep them intact. During life time of Lord Buddha, they were carefree and thought that they will be able to remove all their doubts or scepticisms after seeking his valuable advice and guidance. However after attainment of his final salvation, they could depend upon his teachings alone for solution of their problems. They very well realised that there were inherent short-comings in human character, which could bulge out any time and subdue the qualities of goodness and morality in them. They degrade human-beings from their right path. The mind has to be controlled and checked with due alertness, correct judgement sincerity and earnestness. Accordingly, the Buddhist mendicants thought it expedient to arrange recitation of Buddha teachings which they had been taking due care of. However, it had also been pricking them

1. *The Middle Length Saying*, Volume III pages 59-60.

that who will be sharing the responsibility to perserve Buddha utterances and keep them intact, after they will be no more in this mortal world.

What has been stated above regarding human weakness is not merely fanciful but a genuine fact. A narrative, appeared in 'Dighnikāya' (Dialogues of Buddha) was worth pondering over in this regard. Hardly, a week had passed after final salvation of Lord Buddha and the condolance tears had hardly dried when an old Buddhist monk named Samudra, remarked—'Oh mendicants blessed with long life ! It was too much No more lamentation and wailing requied. Do not cary we have got rid of that great seer. He used to pinch and torment us. It was a commandment and we were bound to comply with it, or it was contrary to and negation of prescribed religious acts or system and we should abstain from such acts. We shall now be free from all such do's and and don'ts and act according to our sweet will. We shall refuse to do what we did not like to do.

The words spoken by an old Buddhist monk, were, no doubt, highly amazing. The fact remains that as soon as a movement or campaign gains momentum, such people also manage to obtain admission in the institution who have no belief or faith in its ideology. They join it simply to serve their own vested interests and share its achievements. When the number of such opportunists excels in an institution, the movement is bound to weaken. The sense of service to the people is minimized. It appears that such self-centered persons had been successful in gaining entry to the religious organisation of Lord Buddha. The aforesaid monk Samudra, had come out openly to express his feelings but there must have been many more religious mendicants like him who were not dedicated to the ideals of the institution. Such were the conditions when scholarly and highly dedicated mendicants were at their wits end and felt greatly perturbed. In this regard the mental anguish of Ārya Mahākashyapa has been depicted in Chūlbagga in most poignant words. Ārya Mahākashyapa was constrained to make a painful remark- "Unrighteous and irreligious people were having upper hand. Rightanousness and good deeds were being opposed. Impertinence and immodesty were growing. Humility and decency were getting eroded day by day. Oh blessed mendicants- come on, let us make recitation of religious doctrines humility and discipline, taught by Lord Buddha".[1]

Purport Meaning of the Words Collective Recitation

The words Saṁgan or saṁgiti have appeared in the deliberations for carrying out the work of collecting and compiling of Buddha utterances. These words have been used in a specific sense. Lord Buddha had delivered his sermons in inter-regional form of Māgadhi dialect. Hence the mendicants, who had attentively listened to his discourses, had memorised them and retained thim in their memory. Although there was no occasion for an apprehension or likelihood of any major deviations from the original texts of his speeches yet the mendicants belonged to defferent territorial parts of the country and they used to visit different regions to

1. Pūre adhammo dippati, dhammo paṭibāhiyati Avinayo dippati. Vinayo Patibāhayati Hand manyaṁ Āwuso! dhammaṁ cha Vinayaṁ cha sangayam —*Vinaya Pitaka*: Chulbgga.

propagate and spread the religious message of Lord Buddha. Hence the basic texts of Buddha utterances were bound to be influenced by the local dialects of those regions and the dialects of their own native places. Although no deviations occurred in the fundamental body of the texts of Buddha teachings, yet slight variations must have taken place relating to sounds or words in the external appearance of the texts. Under the circumstances, whatever was recollected by various senior scholarly mendicants, having expertise in different texts of Buddha preachings, was compared. The texts recollected were tallied and then they were edited to be given a uniform shape. The final collection of the texts of Buddha discourses, must have been collectively recited with a rhythmic tune or in loud voice amidst the gathering of the medicants and such an assembly might have been termed as concert or symphony. Under Vedic tradition, there was a usual practice of reciting Vedic texts in melodious voice. The use of the word 'Saṁgan' (collective singing) was a pointer to this effect. It is believed that after adopting a uniform shape of the texts of Buddha utterances, they were recited collectively with rhythmic tune and accordingly such a gathering might have been named as a concert or symphony, under Bodh tradition. It means that the texts of Buddha discourses must have been recited in the state of complete self identification alongwith full inspiration. This would apply to both versified and prosaic texts of Buddha teachings.

First Collective Recitation

The first religious assembly or concert was held after 4 months of final salvation of Lord Buddha. The final liberation of Buddha had taken place on 'Vaishakh Shuklā Pūrnimā (full moon day of the latter half of the second month of Hindu Vikrami Calendar). Accordingly, the said religious gathering might have been held probably in the month of Bhādra (sixth month of Hindu Vikrami Calendar). All the senior monks, having expertise in Vinaya texts and religions doctrines of Buddhism were specifically invited. As per Buddhist literature, 500 religious mendicants had participated therein. The symphony was, thus, known as 'Panchshatikā' also (having been attended by 500 participants). The said religious assembly was presided over by Ārya Mahākāshyapa. Ānand, a resident disciple and a close confidant of Lord Buddha was also present in the meeting. Under Buddhist tradition, Anand was adored with the attribute of 'Dhammadhar' which signified that Anand was considered as an authority on religious doctrines of Buddhism. Mahapati Upāli, having expertise in Vinaya texts (relating to moral ethics humility, modesty and descipline) was also present in the said concert. Vinaya was used in a technical sense in Buddhist literature which mainly related to the principles of morality, good behaviour and conduct. Similarly, the technical interpretation of the word 'Dhamma' was religious doctrines. Upāli was considered as the best exponent of Buddhist preachings relating to morality, and manners of conducting oneself.

Ārya Mahākāshyapa posed a number of questions and asked Anand to elaborate about doctrines of Buddhist religion and similarly asked Upāli to explain what he knew about Vinaya texts forming part of Buddha teachings. They repeated what they had heard through revelation by Lord Buddha. Thereupon, Ārya Mahākāshyapa proposed that all the mendicants should collectively recite the texts of Lord Buddha's speeches relating to religious ideology, modesty, humility and discipline. Accordingly, the mendicants collectively recited the texts of religious doctrines and those pertaining to principles of morality, good behaviour and conduct. It would appear that the expositions, made by Ānand and Upāli must have been confirmed by all other scholarly monks, on the basis of their own memory and rememberence. A few modifications, alterations and additions, here and there, might have also been proposed. Therafter, the views and opinions of all the speakers might have been compared, co-ordinated and a final body of the texts relating to religious doctrines, morality and discipline, might have been adopted. Subsequently, all the participants must have collectively recited the approved texts. Infact, it was the initial attempt towards compilation of the texts, forming part of Sutta Pitaka and Vinaya Pitaka.

Historical Veracity of first Collective Recitation

Under Buddhist tradition, the genuineness of organising the first concert is undisputed. There are specific references of the said religious gathering in Buddhist scriptures, Namely—Chūlvagga (Vinaya Pitaka); Deepvansha: Mahāvansh, Nidānkatha of Sāmantpāsādika (Buddhist legends relating to Vinaya Pitaka, written by Acharya Budhaghosha), Mahabodhivansha, Mahavastu and Tibetan Dulva etc. Although, there are slight variations in their contents, yet there is no fundamental difference regarding genuineness of the first concert. There are slight variations in discription of the aims ad objects of convening the said religious gathering, which are however, insignificant. Some of the participants have specifically referred to the ill utterances of the old Buddhist monk, Subhadra in their religious treatises, while others have altogether ignored it, and made no mention of this incident at all. A few others have cited absolutely insignificant grounds that led to convening of the first concert.

There are diverse opinions of the scholars regarding adaptation of the texts relating to good behaviour and conduct, observance of discipline and decency as also doctrines of Buddhism. As narrated in Chūlvagga. The entire work of compiling and editing the texts was done by Arya Mahākashyapa, Ānand and Upāli only. However, as narrated in Deepvansh, certain other Buddhist monks also contributed their humble mite in finalising the texts. Amongst them the names of M/s Anirudha, Vaṁgīsh, Pūrna, Kātyāyan and Koṭṭita are worth mention. No doubt, the main contribution of making the endeavour a success, was of Arya Mahākāshāyapa, Ānand and Upali, yet the contribution of other religious mendicants as well endowed with sharp memory, who had recollected and reproduced the texts of Bodh religion, as revealed by Lord Buddha, could not be ignored. It was because of their constructive co-operatrion that a collective recitation of the texts in rhythmic vioce was possible. Otherwise, it would have been a mere repeating of the texts of Buddha teachings by Arya Mahākāshyapa, Ānand and Upāli. It could not be called a religious concert.

Views of Acharya Budhaghosha

In the first assembly, collective recitation was made of religious doctrines and texts relating to morality and good behaviour. How far the texts of speeches, made by Lord Buddha from time to time and recollected by the scholarly monks, relating to doctrines of Buddhism and ethics of politeness with humility and modesty, had been incorporated in Sutta Pitaka and Vinaya Pitaka respectively is the matter to be discussed later on. No mention is found, whatsoever, regarding collective recitation of Abhidhamma (texts relating to Buddhist philosophy and knowledge of the suprems truth) in the first concert. The question, obviously, arises whether compilation and editing of the texts relating to philosophy of Bodh religion were taken up sometime after the first concert. However, Bodh tradition does not subscribe to this view . It does not agree that the three pitakas had been reduced to wrting at different times. It believes that the texts of all the three Buddhist scriptures were compiled and reduced to writing at one and the same time. Achary Budhaghosha has clearly stated 'Thus, the texts of Buddha utterances, comprising of 84,000 chapters and compiled in the shape of three Budhist scriptures, namely, Vinaya Pitaka, Sutta Pitaka and Abhidhamma Pitaka and after imparting them systematic order, were collectively recited.[1]

Āchāraya Budhaghosha has cited in 'Nidan Katha' of Samantpasadika (Buddhist legends) and Samangalvasini that the texts, relating to the philsophy of Bodh religion and knowledge of Supreme Truth, forming part of Abhidhamma Pitaka, had been compiled and edited in the first concert itself. [2]

Renowned Chinese traveller who stayed in India for several years and served as Āchāyra (principal) at Nalanda University in Bihar, has also subscribed to this view.

The texts finally adopted in the first concert, held at Rajgriha (old capital of Māgadha dynasty in Bihar) and formed part of three Buddhist scriptures is literally the same to the very letter as found now in the shape of three Pitakas, cannot be said for definite. This much, however, can be safely asserted that the contents of the present Tripitakas are based on texts, finally adopted in the first concert.

A reference is found in Chūlvagga, concerning the authenticity of Tripitakas. At the time when the aforesaid concert of Buddhist mendicants was going on, a religious mendicant, named Purāṇa happened to come over there. He was requested to attend the convention. He replied "The Sithaviras (A sthavir is promoted after 10 years of his initiation as a mendicant) had made fine attempt for recitation of the texts, relating to doctrines of Bodh religion and morality. However, what I had personally heard through revelation by Lord Buddha, I would follow accordingly in my life."[3]

---

1. Evametaṁ Savvaṁ pi Buddhvachanaṁ panchasatikasangeetikale Saṁgayantenta idaṁ Vinaya pitakam idaṁ suttanta pitkaṁ idaṁ abhidhamma pitakam imani chabtrasiti dhanmakhandhasahassāni on imam pabhedan vabatheyetwa va sangitaṁ
—*Athasalini*, page 23 (Poona edition 1942)
2. Tato Anantram -dhammasaṁgini vibhanganch kathavatyuncha puggalaṁ dhatu yamak puthanaṁ abidhammāti vuchtiti evaṁ samvinnitaṁ sukhaum nagocharaṁ tanti sangāyikva idam adbhidhamma pitakaṁ namāti vatva panch Arihantstāni sajhyaam.
3. Vinaya Pitaka Chūlvagga, —*Buddhacharya*, page 552.

A few scholars have expressed their apprehension regarding the bonafides of the said religious gathering in the light of the above conversation. According to them, there was a reflection on the authenticity of the texts relating to religious principles of Buddhism and moral ethics, as finally adopted and collectively recited in the concert so far as the comment of old Buddhist monk Purāṇa is concerned. After all, the entire organisation of the religious mendicants could not be expected to concur with the proceedings of the first concert. In the opinion of Dr. Ramesh Chandra Majumdar, the said incident was unfortunate and a danger signal for the entire organisation of Budhist mendicants.[1]

Dr. Bharat Singh Upādhyāya has considered it a mere misapprehension of the scholars and stated. "Purāṇa was a staunch devoted person. Ofcourse, he was more interested in performance of spiritual endeavours in seclusion. He was not prepared to tolerate any distraction in the spirit of his devotion, which he had acquired through revelations of Lord Buddha. What others had heard from the speeches of Lord Buddha. I wish that must remain intact. However, Purāṇa had to get on with what he had been guided and achieved from Lord Buddha and which he rightly deserved. Thus, neither Purāṇa has expressed any feeling of distrust in the genuineness of Buddha utterances nor it was a danger signal in any way, to the organisation of mendicants. The association of Buddhist monks had never barred free expression or manifestation of indepedent views of any of the religious mendicants. It was the singular quality or special characteristic of the institution. The devoted mendicants had collectively recited the texts of utterances made by Lord Buddha, as heard and recollected by them. The same texts of religious teachings of Lord Buddha are found recorded in Sutta and Vinaya Pitakas, written in Pāli script. However, some additional material has also been included therein."[2]

What Dr. Upādhyāya has stated, appears to be true that there were absolutely no constraints on expression of independent views in the Buddhist organisation. However, the comments of Purāṇa—"But what I have heard personally from Lord Buddha, the great spiritual guide and preceptor and obtained, from him personally, I will be retaining the same in my memory and act accordingly. We have to argue and give full consideration to these words. In case, there was no feeling of disagreement with the texts of Buddha teachings as reproduced and recited by the mendicants, they had not been vindicated also. The words of purāṇa, "I will retain the texts in the mind as revealed by Lord Buddha and observe them accordingly" demonstrated his outspokenness. The force with which Purāṇa had asserted the said words, clearly showed a feeling of disregard and aversion to the proceedings of the said convention. Sthavira, Purāṇa could be a true devout, engaged in spiritual accomplishments all alone, but his refusal to participate in the convention, where the texts of Buddha teachings were being compiled inspite of an invitation, extended to him and expression of his firm determination to follow Buddha teachings as he had himself heard, indicated his deep allegiance and faith on one hand, and a feeling of utter disregard for the concert on the other.

There must have been mindicants, contemporary to the time of the convention

1. This was a danger signal for the Church.

— *Buddhistic studies*, edited by Dr. Law, page 44.

2. *Pali Sahitya kā Itihās*, page 91.

who might have attached only casual significance to it. They were satisfied from what they had heard personally through revelation by Lord Buddha. They were, however, not worried for the permanency and perpetuity of Buddha teachings and resultant public good and welfare. Atleast the feeling of compassion and benignity. preached by the great kind-hearted and compassionate Lord Buddha is not promoted in any way by such indifference on the part of other mendicants. Besides this, such disinterestedness towards the valuable work, done by the sponsors of the convention, only leads to the inference that the distinguished and prominent Buddhist Sthaviras might have convened the meeting at their own initiative without obtaining the unanimity, and approval of all other religious mendicants and had taken up the work of compilation and editing of the texts of Buddha teachings on their own. Nevertheless, all this does not harm or adversely affects the *bonafides* of the concert itself.

Second Concert Collective Recitation

Buddha utterances had been collected and compiled in the first concert although they were still verbal and hat not been reduced to writing. The organisation of Buddhist monks continued to carry on its activities, drawing guidance and spiritual inspiration from them. After the lapse of about a century, it was incidentally considered necessary to re-recite Buddha teachings. In Chūlvagga, it is clearly cited that such an occasion arose after 100 years. However, as per calculation of Chinese traveller, Huentsānga the said gap was of 110 years. The second concert was convened to be held at Balukāram of Vaishali Janpada in Bihar. Nearly, 700 Buddhist monks had pariticipated in it. Hence it was also called 'Saptashatikā' (a meeting attended by 700 participants).

The main object of convening the said meeting was to elucidate certain points relating to the morality, good behaviour and conduct which had become confused and controversial. It was alleged that the mendicants of Vaishali had the tendency to violate the guide-lines, prescribed by Lord Buddha, relating to ten ethos to be followed by them but they failed to abide by them:-

1. Singilona-kappa (Sanskrit—Shringi-lavaṇa Kalpa)—To carry the hollow pipe made of stag horn filled with salt.
2. Dwangul-kappa (Sanskrit formation—Dwa-Angul-Kalpa). To take meals even after noon when it had been shadowed equal to two fingers.
3. Gāmanter-kappa (Sanskrit form—Grāmāntar kalpa). To take meals again on the same day after shifting from one village to another.
4. Āvās kappa (Sanskrit form Āvas-Kalpa) to undertake religious endeavours at several places, located in the same vicinity.
5. Anumati-Kappa (Sanskrit form—Anumati-Kalpa). To obtain consent after performance of an act.
6. Achiṇṇa-Kappa (Sanskrit form—Āchirṇa Kalpa)—To follow or emulate an act which was earlier performed by a teacher or spiritual guide.
7. Amathit-Kappa (Sanskrit form—Amathit-kalpa)—To take milk after the meals which might be in the process of coagulation but not turned completely into curd and it was also no longer in the shape of original

milk.

8. Jalogipān—To take toddy wine (Juice of Palm trees.)
9. Adsaka Nisidan (Sanskrit form—Adashaka Nishidan)—To use a square piece of mat which is not stitched with a border or hem.
10. Jātrūp-Rajat:To accept gold and silver in alms.

The mendicants, belonging to Vaishali Janpada, did not consider the above acts as defilement or violation in any way while resorting to the above ten practices. The mendicants were divided in two groups over the above controversy. 1. Mendicants belonging to eastern territories and (2) mendicants belonging to western territories. The mendicants belonging to eastern regions favoured the habits of Vaishāli mendicants while those coming from Western regions strongly criticised the acts of Vaishāli mendicants and censured them guilty. The meeting convened at Balukārām in Vaishāli Janpada was, infact, meant for disposing off the said controversial points. The deliberations of the meeting continued for eight months. At the end of deliberations the conduct of the Vaishāli mendicants was censured and declared against the teachings of Lord Buddha relating to the ethics of morality, good behaviour and conduct.

In the theme of Vinaya-Pitaka, now available, the aforesaid ten practices in respect of which the second convention was organised at Vaishāli Janpada, have been found contrary and violative to the spiritual guide-lines, prescribed by Lord Buddha. From this, it transpires that the present edition of Vinaya Pitāka had been accomplished on the basis of decisions taken in the second concert held at Vaishāli Janpada consistent with the guide lines of Lord Buddha. It is possible that the contents of Vinaya Pitaka prior to the Vaishāli convention, might have been slightly different. Dr. Ramesh Chandra Majumdar and other scholars were of the opinion that the contents of Vinaya Pitaka as available now, could not have been accomplished prior to the convention, held at Vaishāli Janpada.[1]

Had the shape of Vinaya Pitaka been different prior to the convention held at Vaishāli Janpada, in which the ten practices of Vaishāli mendicants, had been declared contrary and violative ot the guide-lines prescribed by Lord Buddha leads us to the only logical conclusion that such activities had not been permitted by Lord Buddha. Otherwise, there would have been no ground for controversy. Had such activities been not forbidden by Lord Buddha, there would have been a floor to stand upon by the mendicants of Vaishāli and their behaviour and attitude would have, obviously, stood vindicated and the Buddhist monks of Western regions would not have dared to declare their conduct as unchaste and immoral. The occasion would not have arisen at all for carrying on lengthy deliberations for a period of eight months continuously and hold the mendicants guilty of immoral acts. After profound consultation and deep study of Buddhist scriptures as also full consideration of the subject and prolonged deliberations for eight months, a decision was taken which must have been supported by scriptural authority. The said sacred authority could be none else but Buddha utterances relating to morality discipline, good behaviour and conduct. There was no doubt or uncertainty at all regarding

1. *Buddhist studies*, edited by Dr. Law, page 62.

the shape of Vinaya Pitaka as it was prior to the arrangement of concert or as it is available now. If minor corrections, modifications, and alterations carried out from time to time were ignored or not attached much signficance, then there were no variations at all in the fudamental shape of Vinaya Pitaka, prior to holding the convention and what was available now. However deserves analytical consideration that in case the aforesaid ten activities of Vaishali mendicants had been forebidden and were against the guide lines relating to the morality and behaviour as contained in Vinay Pitaka, than what were the grounds and support available to the mendicants of eastern regions which prompted them to endorse the immoral activities of Vaishali mendicants?

The three Pitakas (Collections of Buddha utterences) were not reduced to writing for several centuries. They were verbally taught by religious preceptors. There is always an apprehension that the genuiness of religious teachings may not be disturbed. If on deviation from the right path, people try to get their undesirable acts supported, they would not hesitate to reverse and disarray the wordings and carry out additions and alterations therein to suit their vested interests. Such might have been the state of affairs or a situation to warrant determination of the conduct of Vaishāli and other mendicants of eastern regions? In those days, Vaishāli was a prominent political, religious and cultural centre of Eastern India. When the Buddhist monks, belonging to western parts of the country tried to oppose and censure undesirable activities of Vaishāli mendicants it is quite possible that a feeling of regionalism might have developed and overtaken the mendicants, inhabiting eastern territories which is an obvious human instinct. Although, these were petty affairs and had no consistency with the sacred life of Buddhist mendicants. Yet they too formed part of ordinary families and all these vices could creep in them also retaining gold and silver articles with them, drinking of toddy wine and taking liberty with their meals etc. could never be tolerated under strict discipline of Lord Buddha. It should not be considered unfair to believe that such weaknesses might have appeared in Vaisāli mendicants and they might have persisted to either ignore their immoral acts or vindicate their undesirable practices.

Creation of New Buddha Teachings

Vaishāli mendicants and their supporters, residing in eastern regions, were censured for their immoral acts iṇ the convention, held at Vaishāli Janpada. Their ideas and intentions were found contrary to the teachings of Lord Buddha. It had two-fold effects. firstly, the texts of discipline, morality, good behvaiour and conduct were reshaped and secondly the mendicants who had been censured, did not yield to the findings of the convention. They bycotted it and convened a larger convention They fabricated new Buddhist doctrines and declared that they were the real and genuine ones. This was the result of the excitement and provocation faced by the disgruntled mendicants. In *Deepvansha*, holding of the alleged larger convention has been criticized in strongest terms. It is cited therein "The mendicants who had sponsored the larger convention, had infact reverted and completely changed the shape of religious preachings and instructions of great sanctified teacher, Lord Buddha. They created dissention and rift in the original organisation and raised a parallel organisation. They distorted the real intent of Buddhist religion.They collected and compiled altogether different Sūtras and interpreted them differently. They changed the very purport of five collections of Buddha dialogues and the explanation given by Him while elucidating the religious doctrines: [1]

All that happened but with no lasting effect. As against Tripitakas in Pāli script no reliance was placed on the authenticity of their scriptural writings. With the passage of time, no significance was attached to their writings and they were completely ignored.

After the disputed matters had been disposed off in the convention held at Vaishāli Janpada, the edited texts of Buddhist religious preachings were re-recited under the auspices of renowned Buddhist monk, Revata, like first convention, Just as Acharya Buddhaghosh had narrated how the texts of Buddha utterances had been classified in the shape of 3 Pitakas and recited in the first convention similarily, it has been cited by him that the edited texts of Buddha teachings had been re-recited in the second convention. By way of using the words-recitation and re-recitation, Acharya Buddhaghosh has, infact, pointed out how an integrated and an unambiguous shape of Buddha teachings had been accomplished.

Third Concert of Collective Recitation

Bodh religion had taken long strides beyond imagination because of state patronage granted by emperor Ashoka. However, it had an ill-effect also. Many self-seeking and self-centered persons, who had virtually no faith in the ideology of Bodh religion, started pouring in the organisation, having been allured by the facilities and hospitalities, extended by emperor Askoka to the new entrants because of his keen appreciation for the religion and liking for the Buddhist organisation. The religious ideology and doctrines began to be distorted. By the time of emperor Ashoka, Buddhist organisation had already splitted into 18 sects. Then it was considered essential to convene another concert in order to redefine and re-recite the texts of religious principles, moral and ethical values as defined and elaborated by Lord Buddha so that the undesirable element may be expelled from the institution, who had been able to obtain an entry in it. Thus during the reign of emperor Ashoka, after about 236 years from the final salvation of Lord Buddha, the third convention was held in Ashokaram monastery at Patna. Amongst 18 sects "Thervādi (pro senior monks, having completed 10 years after initiation as a mendicant) also called Vibhajyawādi was the principal sect. This sect claimed that it was alone a true representative body of Buddhist religion. The third convention also recognised it as such and was declared the true exponent of Bodh religion.

The literal meaning of the word 'Ther" or Sithavir" is an old man. The word old has not been used in the limited sense of age only. It has been used in the broader sense of superority in spiritual knowledge, philosophy and observance of

1. Mahāsaingitikā bhikkhu Vilomaṁ akaṁsu Sāsanaṁ |
Bhinditwā Mūlsanghaṁ Annan akṁasu Sanghaṁ ||
Aṫtha Sangahitaṁ Suttaṁ Aṇṇtth akarṁsu te |
Atthaṁ Dhammaṁ cha bhindisu ye nikāyesu panchsu ||
— *Deepvansh*, 5, 32-38.

ethical values. The elder disciples of Lord Buddha have been called as Sthavirs (those who had completed more than 10 years after initiation as religious mendicants). Their expositions were final with regard to the ideology of Budha religion. The said Sthavirs were proponents of the philosophy of dividing or disintegrating the essential ingredients ot the matter of substance). Thus, they were also known as 'Vibhajyawādi'. The puport of Vibhajyawādi lay in the philosophy of dividing the matter in its essential ingredients and then elaborate what was existent and real and what was non-existent and unreal. If we penetrate deep into it, there is also a philosophical import. An analytical investigation of entire mental and philosophical import. An analytical investigation of entire mental and physical conditions can be made by dividing the constituent elements in five forms of mundane consciousness, an inner seat (Buddhist consider the five senses with manas as the six Ayatanas) and five essential ingredients.

There is a citation of the aforesaid third convention in Deepvansh, Mahavnsh and Samant-pāsādika (Buddhist scriptures). However, there was no mention of the said convention in the canonical literature belonging to Mahayani sect, nor there was any mention in the memoirs of Huventasāng. There was no citation in any of the stone inscriptions of emperor Ashoka as well. Consequently, the most eminent scholars M/s Miniyefa, Keith, Max Walesar, Barth, Frank, and Sylvalevi etc. have disputed its historic authenticity. However, erudite scholars, namely—Prof Rayas Davids, Mrs. Rayas Davids, Winternitz and Gāyagar etc. have acknowledged the historic genuinness and authoritativeness of the said convention.

Reasons for Avoiding Mention of Third Convention

By the time of emperor Aśoka the organisation had already splitted into 18 sects. It is possible that the followers of other splitted groups might not have accepted it as the representative meeting of all the Buddhist monks and treated it as an assembly of selected few senior Sthavirs only. Hence they might have intentionally avoided its mention. The third convention was held during the reign of emperor Aśoka and it was equally astonishing that he too avoided its mention in his rock inscriptions. However, it must be kept in mind that emperor Aśoka was pro-senior and elderly Buddhist monks. He had great regard for Thervada Aśoka might not have liked that any significance be attached to his support. He might have preferred to keep himself aloof from the said concert so that the decisions taken therein might not be construed to have been influenced by the crown. Presumably Aśoka cherished a desire that unanimous shape of Bodh religion, which should be real and conformable to truth, might emerge after deliberations in the convention. Another reason might be that Aśoka thought it proper to remain aloof and ensure that Sri Moggliputta Tissa, sponsor and president of the aforesaid convention, who was an erudite scholar, a philosopher, having thorough knowledge of superme truth and deeply devoted to spiritual accomplishments must get the entire credit for the success and achievements of the convention. He might have considered it more beneficial to keep himself detached. Nevertheless, the historic significance of the convention could not be denied.

Decisions of the third Convention

Many well informed and highly learned Buddhist monks, belonging to different states and regions, had participated in the said convention. The proceedings of the said concert had continued for a long period of nine months. Attempts must have been made to determine the real texts of Buddha utterances after profound discussion and prolonged delibarations. Certain important decisions were adopted after arguing and giving full consideration to the issues relating to the solidarity of the organisation continuously for a period of nine months. Besides the sect committed to Sthirvāda (Pro-elderly and senior Monks) all the rest seventeen sects were declared as false unreal and untruthful 'Thervādi' to 'Vibhajyavādi' sect was accepted as the true exponent of Bodh religion. The texts of Buddha utterances were edited and given a final shape. Sri Moggliputta Tissa accomplished a canonial book styled *Kathāvathu* in which the ideology of other 17 sects had been dismissed and strongly abrogated which had been declared as false and untruthful at the end of the said convention. The contents of 'Kathavathu' were considered as significant as those of *Abhidhamma Pitaka* (Dealing with Buddhist philosophy and true knowldge of Supreme Truth).

Abhidhamma: Its Background: As a result of incorporation of 'Kathāvathu' in *Abhidhamma Pitaka* (one of the three collections of Buddhist holy writings which primarily deals with buddhist philosophy and knowledge of the supreme truth) a suspicion would, obviously arise in the mind that it must have taken a very long time in final determination of the texts forming part of the said Abhidhamma Pitaka. However, Acharaya Budhaghosh and Chinese traveller, Huentsang, have clearly asserted that the contents of *Abhidhamma Pitaka* were also collectively recited along with the texts of Sutta and Vinaya Pitākas. The texts relating to Buddhist philosophy and supreme knowledge concerning metaphyics were contained in Abhidhamma Pitaka. The era of Lord Buddha demanded propagation of morality, modesty and compassion as also religious tenets, acceptable to all. Manifestation of religious principles and philosophy was sure to create conditions for spiritual advancement of mankind. Under Buddhist tradition, the period of knowledge of philosophical doctrines came much later. Hence it appears more consistent to believe that the subjects relating to metaphysical knowledge might have been partially discussed in the very first convention, and atleast a few texts of philosophical doctrines, must have been edited and finally adopted along with the texts of Buddha utterances forming part of Sutta and Vinaya Pitakas. The process of their composition, additions and refinment must have continued. Inclusion of 'Kathavathu" in *Abhidhamma Pitaka*, provides the ground for such an assumption.

A Significant Accomplishment of the Third Convention

A significant accomplishment of the third convention to send Buddhist Scholars to far off states, territories and foreign lands for propagation and spread of religious message of Lord Buddha for the good and welfare of the common people. For this, a schedule of programme was prepared. The names of scholarly saints appear in Deepvansh, Mahavansh and Samant Pāsādikā who were appointed to move to different regions for spread of religious message.

Tripitakas Reduced to Writing

The magnificent work done by Aśoka for propagation and spread of Bodh religion really deserved to be adored in golden letters. The emperor drew immense satisfaction in rendering this work. It is cited that once emperor Aśoka enquired from renowned Buddhist scholar, Tissa Mogglanputta, whether his contributions to the growth and advancement of bodh relgion were sufficient in his opinion or not? The senior most and elderly monk (Mahasthavira) replied "Your Majesty! you had really done marvellous job for furtherence of bodh religion and you deserved all praise and eulogy for it. However, a significant work had still to be done by you which was lying undone.

The emperor asked "Oh blessed one! please let me know the remaining job to be completed by me, on performance of which. I shall draw complete satisfaction and feel delighted".

Mahasthavirā (A mendicant is promoted to the rank of Sthavira, after having completed 10 years from the date of initiation and to the rank of Mahasthavir, after completing 20 years from the year of initiation) replied "Atleast one member of the Royal family should renounce the world and get initiated as religious mendicant to join Buddhist monastery."

The emperor bowed his head with reverence and added—"Oh blessed one! not one but I would send two members of the Royal family to join the organisation my son and my daughter". Accordingly the son and daughter of emperor Ashoka got initiated as male and female mendicants, who are well known as Mahendra and Sanghmitra historically. In pursuance with the aforesaid resolution to send Buddhist scholars to distant places for propagation and spread of the religious message of Lord Buddha, Mahendra and Sanghmitra were sent to Ceylon (now Sri Lanka). The prince and the princess accompanied by other male and female mendicants, arrived in Ceylon, full of vigour and enthrusiasm to propagate the religious message of Lord Buddha. They carried with them the texts of Buddha utterances in the shape of Triptakās, as revealed and recited in third convention. At that time the ruler of Ceylon was Devānāmpiya Tissa. Indian mendicants, who were messengers of the tenets of Buddhist religion, were accorded warm welcome by him. Besides welcoming them he, himself adopted Buddhism. A great monastery was established in Anurādhāpur town of Ceylon, and systematic studies of Tripitakas were commenced therein. The said system of recitation of the texts of Buddha teachings orally continued for several centuries in the aforesaid monastery.

During the reign of King Vaṭṭhagāmiṇi Abhaya (from 29 to 17 B.C.) the fourth concert was organised in Ceylon. After critical review and collective recitation of the texts of Buddha teachings, it was decided to get the three collections reduced to writing. Accordingly, the three collections of Buddha utterances were written on Palmyra leaves. These were the same texts which prince Mahendra and princess Sanghamitra had committed to their memory and carried them from India to Ceylon. In between the period of arrival of Prince Mahendra in Ceylon and writing of the texts forming part of 3 collections, during reign of Vatthagāmini Abhaya, another two gatherings were held but they were insignificant since no deliberations took place therein to determine the final shape of the texts of Buddha teachings, forming part of the three collections. The texts of Tripitakas as recollected by Prince Mahendra, continued to be recited in Ceylon. Thus the same texts had been merely repeated in the intervening two gatherings. It was why no significance was attached to the said gatherings. The first assembly was held during the reign of Devanām Tissa from 247 to 207 B.C.) in which hearty welcome was accorded to the group of mendicants, who had arrived in Ceylon under the leadership of princess Mahendra and princess Sanghamitra and the King, himself, had adopted Buddhism became a worshipper of Buddha as distinguished from an initiated Bhiku). The other gathering took place during the reign of King Dnṭṭhagamiṇi. He is believed to have ruled from 101 to 77 B.C. Afrer Tripitakas were reduced to writing in Ceylon, their permanent and unchangeable form was finally accomplished. The very contents of Tripitakas, obtained now, are considered genuine and authoritative.

Recent Conventions

After Tripitakas were reduced to writing, there was practically no need to convene the meetings or concerts any longer. Recollecting of texts, their compilation and collective recitation, came to an end as soon as they had been recorded in black and white. However, the work of editing and modification of the texts becomes also necessary with the passage of time which was accomplished in 19th and 20th centuries. The concerts or seminars which took place fulfilment of the said objectives are also called concerts or gatherings in order to provide their continuity with the previous ones. In this way, two concerts were organised and both were held in Burma. Burma also held a significant place amongst countries, following Bodh religion, known as Thervadi. (Pro elderly and senior monks who were adept in Buddhist philosophy) like Ceylon. The first concert was held at Mandley town in Burmah under the patronage of King Bhindan. The Tripitakas written in Pāli script, were edited therein. In order to ensure stability Vinaya, Sutta and Abhidhamma Pitakas were got engraved on marble stone slabs. All the three collections of Buddha teachings were inscribed in Burmese script on 111, 410 and 208 slabs respectively.

Thereafter, another concert was organised at Rangoon, Capital of Burmah, in the year, 1954-56 A.D. for modifications and giving a final shape to the texts of Tripitakas, which was known as sixth concert. In order to achieve this end the texts of Tripitakas written in Pāli script were recited and necessary modifications were carried out wherever needed in order to accomplish a final shape of amended texts. The amended texts of Tripitakas were reduced to writing in Burmese script. The edition of Tripitakas, published in Devangari (Hindi) script under editorship of renowned Buddhist scholar, Bhikṣu Jagdish Kashyapa, is primarily based upon the amended texts modified and published in Burma.

Conclusion

The period of accomplishing final shape of Tripitakas could be classified into two parts. The first part related to the period comprising from the life time of Lord Buddha to the reigning period of King Vathagamini Abhya in Ceylon, when Tripitakas were reduced to writing on Palmyra leaves. The second part ranges from the time of Triptiakas having been reduced to black and white and now when the Tripitakas are finally available in printed form. The first period was most significant in as much as it was during said period when the three conventions were held and final shape was given to the texts, forming part of Tripitakas. Although the system of convening meetings continued even thereafter, yet they were all insignificant and nothing tangible had been achieved therein.

Again a critical review of the circumstances was essential which led to organising the said concerts. Lord Buddha was the prince of Kausala dynasty (A territory situated along the bank of river Saryu in Uttar Pradesh). The principal area of his movement and activities was Magadha in South Bihar. He continued touring about in Magadha region all his life. He continued imparting lectures to acquaint people regarding his spiritual accomplishments. If a person belonging to a certain region, moves or resides in another region, he would like to adopt the same language for his expression which was being used by the civilised gentry of his own territory where he was born as also by the people of the other territory where he was now staying for propagation of his message and enlightening the people. Generally, such a refined language obtains an inter-regional standard. For instance, Rajasthan Madhya Pradesh and Bihar are all Hindi speaking areas, it is called a Hindi belt. Hindi was the exclusive medium of speech and *via* media for all literary pursuits by educated and civilised gentry of these states, which was also called as *Khari Boli* (Standard modern form of Hindi which has been adopted as the official language of the Indian Union and which has become synonymous with modern Hindi). However, the said inter-provincial *via* media or refined shape of Hindi language had numerous dialects which were spoken in different parts of Hindi belt. While conversing an inhabitant of either Madhya Pradesh, Uttar Pradesh or Rajasthan will use Hindi as medium of expression at the time of talking with a resident of Bihar and *vice versa*. Similarly an inhabitant of Bihar will also converse in Hindi with a person either inhabiting Madhya Pradesh, Rajasthan or U.P. and not in his own native dialect or the local dialect of the person with whom he was talking. No doubts, the sub-languages or native dialects, spoken in the said states were all offshoots of Hindi itself but the scope of each dialect was confined to its respective region. Hence two persons, both belonging to Hindi belt will find it difficult to converse in their respective native dialects as they will not be able to follow each other. The era of Lord Buddha will have to be judged from the said angle.

Lord Buddha delivered his discourses in the refined form of Magadha dialect Undoubtedly, he was a great revolutionary of his age. After attaining perfect wisdom and enlightenment he had undertaken an extensive tour with the aim of spreading his religious message for the benefit and enlightenment of the largest number of people, inhabiting entire Northern India. Many males and females belonging to different states attained initiation as mendicants and joined his organisation. They belonged to different states and conversed in their respective dialect. Probably they might have been allotted different territories for their activities. It is also possible that they might have been entrusted with the work of propagating religious message in their respective state to which they belonged. It is most likely that they might have used the regional or local dialect of the area where they moved and conveyed the message of Lord Buddha in order to enable the people to grasp it conveniently. The mendicants were not required to deliver any sermons independently. They were only expected to convey the teachings of Lord Buddha to each and every person in their respective area. Hence they must have been constrained to explain the substance of Buddha message in the local dialects In Nutshell, the mendicants had heard the discourses of Lord Buddha in Māgadhi dialect and accordingly committed them to their memory. However they must have been confronted with the situation of converting. Buddha teachings in the local dialects, may be partially or to a limited extent only so that the people could follow them. From the lengthy durations of the concerts. It sounds that the texts of Buddha speeches, memorised and retained in memory by the mendicants, belonging to different regions, must have been got repeatedly recited and tallied. After setting aside the variations if any, a unanimous shape of the texts must have been decided and approved. It clearly followed that the Buddha utterances must have been modified and refined from time to time without disturbing their originality. Besides minor rectifications, no major alterations took place in the original shape of Buddha teachings. The refined shape of Māgadhi dialect, adopted by Lord Buddha as medium of his discourses, was infact an accomplished mixed form of neighbouring regional dialects.

After about 100 years of the first concert the second concert was convened at Balukaram monastry in Vaishāli Janpada, which lasted for eight months. It appears that the shape of the text, forming part of Tripitakas as determined in the first gathering at Vaibhār mountain at Rājgraha (The erstwhile capital of Māgadha dynasty) must have undergone slight changes may be in wordings only, during the lengthy duration of 100 years was as a result of adaptation in the regions. The scholarly medicants participating from different territories, must have taken a long time in deliberations for coordination of the texts and their final determination to be incorporated in the three collections of Buddhists scriptures. Although the primary aim of convening the second convention was to censure the behaviour and conduct of Vaishāli mendicants, yet everybody could well ask why such a long period of eight months was taken to decide the solitary issue? Seven hundred mendicants, who had participated in the second concert were no doubt primarily concerned with the problem to hold whether the conduct of Vaishāli mendicants was wrong and immoral and, if so to admonish them for their wrong doings. However, the most important job to be done by them was coordination and modification of the texts of Buddha utterances which they nicelly performed with great persevrance.

That was the era of pre-eminence of Buddhist religion. With the passage of time, Buddhism continued to flourish day by day. Buddhist monks and scholars undertook long journeys to propagate and spread the religious message. Vocal recitation of Buddha teachings became common. However, the same evils began to creep in which had crept earlier after the first concert was over. Therefore, besides exposing wrong doers and liars and expelling them from the religious organisation, the historic work of revision and modification of the texts of Buddha teachings was also done in the third concert. It was why the third concert continued for a long duration of nine months.

After critical evaluation of the significance of the aforesaid three conventions. we shall discuss now another important point. Prince Mahendra had lived at Ujjain from his very childhood. In deference to the wishes of his father emperor Aśoka, he attains initiation as a religious mendicant in Buddhist organisation and proceeds to Ceylon carrying the message of the institution. No doubt, Prince Mahendra was the son of Māgadha emperor, Aśoka, yet Māgadhi was not his mother tongue. The medium of speech of Ujjaini, a Prakrita dialect was his mother tongue which had, decidedly been influenced by the dialects of Western regions. Mahendra had memorised the texts of Triptiakas and retained them in his memory which were his asset while he moved to Ceylon. Was it possible that the contents of Tripitakas might have remained uninfluenced by Ujjaini dialect?

Admidst typical conditions, the texts of Buddhist collections were carried to 'Ceylon and there also, oral recitation of the texts continued for quite a long time'. However, after they were brought to Ceylon, nothing warranted for introducing any modifications or changes in their shape. Contrarily, while the texts of Buddha utterances, as recollected by Buddhist monks, were carried to different regions in Northern India, they were, obviously, subjected to various modifications but no such necessity was felt in Ceylon. Two concerts were organised in Ceylon in between the period, the texts of three Buddhist scriptures were carried to Ceylon by prince Mahendra and they were reduced to writing during the reign of King Vaṭhagāmini Abhaya. However, the said concerts were convened merely to maintain the tradition and no significant work was done therein. Infact, there was nothing important to be done respecting the texts of three collections in the said two concerts. Lord Buddha had adopted Māgadhi dialect as medium for delivering his discourses and nothing difinite could be said whether the original language of his teachings had remained infact in the texts of Tripitakas presently available. However, the fact that the originality and genuinness of the ideology, its aboration and wordings of the Buddha teachings are almost intact and it should not arouse any suspicion or disbelief amongst readers of the Tripitakas.

Buddhist Canonical Literature in the Shape of Tripitakas: Brief History

Sutta Pitaka

It forms a significant part of Tripitakas, written in Pāli. The primary aim of the texts of Sutta Pitaka was introduction of religious doctrines as enunciated by Lord Buddha. As appeared in 'Mahaparinivvān-Sutta' (*Dialogues of Lord Buddha* in volumes No.2 and 3).Lord Buddha had addressed his favourite resident disciple, Ānanda — "Oh Ananda ! the religious doctrines, preached by me, and my teachings relating to morality, good behaviour and conduct will illuminate the path and act as spiritual guide after my attaining final salvation". Sutta Pitaka was, no doubt, a unique accomplishment, propounding the religious ideology, as enunciated by Lord

Buddha.

Sanskrit formations of the Pāli word Sutta were both Sūtras (A collection of aphorisms, threads and cords) and Sūktas (Mantras hymns, prayers). In Sanskrit Buddhist treatises, matching aphorisms to Pāli Suttas had been provided. The literal meaning of the word Sutta is an aphorism, thread or cord. The word Pitaka meant a small box or basket. It also meant a methodical arrangement and collection of writings. Both the meanings of the word Pitaka had been indicated in Nidān Kathā of Athashālini (legends) written by Achayra Buddhaghosha. In 'Chanki'[1] and 'Sandaka'[2] Suttas of Majjhim Nikāya (Further *Dialogues of Lord Buddha* in 2 Volumes) the word Pitaka has been used to mean both traditional use of words or in the tradition of works or treatises. Keeping in view the said definitions, the words Sutta pitaka could mean sequence of Buddha teachings arranged systematically and inter-woven like a thread or cord. Just as on unrolling a thread ball, it will go on unfolding automatically. Similarly, Buddha teachings contained in Sutta Pitaka, are manifested on their own with no difficulty at all.

Achāraya Āsanga (4th century A.D.) had defined the word Sutra in his work, 'Mahāyān Sutrālankār' as signifying the subject-matter of any work or treatise. Acharya Buddhaghosh had explained in 'Athashālini'(legendary tales) that what disclosed the purport, gist or substance was a Sūtra.

Under Vedic tradition, the word Sūtra had frequently appeard. The author of 'Shabdakalpadrum' had interpreted the word Sūtra as "what contained limited number of words having distinct and clear sense, being essential and meaningful, having universal application, short or concise in form, used as a memorial rule or precept, flawless in contents such were the characteristics of a Sutra"[3].

The aphoristic style of expression was commonly adopted under Vedic tradition by way of using short or concise formulas, carrying wider sense. However, in Pāli literature, the word Sutta has been used in a much wider and broader perspective which was similar, and corresponding to the above definition of the word Sūtra.

Sutta Pitaka : Subjects discussed therein

Religious sermons, delivered by Lord Buddha, formed part of Sutta Pitaka. The discourses of a few prominent disciples of Buddha, consistent with Buddha teachings, had also been compiled therein. A lively sketch of social and political structure and public life in India in 5th-6th centuries B.C. is also obtained in Sutta Pitaka, in addition to Buddha discourses. An elaborate account is also found of other religious guides, monks, ascetics (of the fourth religious order who had renounced the world) and their ideologies have also been elaborately discussed as per demand of the context. Likes and dislikes of the erstwhile people their occupations, education, achievements in the spheres of art, science, and politics, state of conditions in villages, towns and districts, living standards, problems relating

---

1. *Majjhim Nikāya*, 2,5,5.
2. Same, 2,3,6.
3. Swalpaksaramsandighaṁ, Sārviadivishvato Mukhaṁ.
Astobhabhamanvadyaṁ cha, Sutraṁ sutravido viduḥ.

to agriculture, trade, commerce, social customs, standard of women in society, male and female serfs and family servants etc.—all the significant matters had been discussed. The composition of Sutta Pitaka was in mixed form both in prosaic and poetic form.

Sutta Pitaka comprises of 5 major portions, known as Nikayas namely 1. Digha-Nikāya (Long dialogues of Lord Buddha in 3 volumes); 2. Majjhim - Nikāya (Further dialogues of Lord Buddha in 2 volumes); 3. Saṁyukta Nikāya (Kindred Sayings of Lord Buddha in I and II volumes); 4. Anguttar Nikāya (The book of gradual sayings by Lord Buddha in 5 volumes) and 5. Khuddaka-Nikāya (Small dialogues of the Buddha).

Digha Nikāya (lengthy dialogues of Lord Buddha) is a collection of lengthy discourses. There are 34 suttas (Sūtras or aphorisms) as follows under three categories.

(a) Sīlakhandha Vagga

1. Brahma Jāl Sutta; 2. Samaññphal Sutta; 3. Ambaṭṭha Sutta; 4. Sondanda Sutta; 5. Kūṭdant Sutta; 6. Mahāli Sutta; 7. Jāliya Sutta; 8. Kassapasihanad Sutta; 9. Soṭṭhapād Sutta; 10. Subh Sutta; 11. Kevaḍḍa (kevaṭṭa) Sutta; 12 Lohichcha Sutta; 13. Tevijja Sutta.

(b) Mahāvagga

14. Mahāpadān Sutta; 15. Mahānidān Sutta; 16. Mahāparinirvan Sutta; 17. Mahāsuddassan Sutta; 18. Janvasabha Sutta; 19. Mahāgovind Sutta; 20. Mahāsamaya Sutta; 21. Sakkapañha Sutta; 22. Mahāsatipaṭṭhān Sutta; 23. Pāyāsirajañña Sutta (Pāyāsi Sutta) .

(c) Pātika Vagga

24. Pātika Sutta (Pathika sutta); 25. Udumbariksīhnād Sutta; 26. Chakkavatisīhnād Sutta (Chakkavatt Sutta); 27. Aggañña Sutta; 28. Sampasādini Sutta; 29. Pāsādika Sutta; 30. Lakkhaṇa Sutta; 31. Si Galovāda Sutta; 32. Atānātiya Sutta; 33. Sangiti Sutta; 34.Dasuttar Sutta.

Under category Sīlakkahandha Vagga against serial No.1; Brahmajāl Sutta, have been cited 62 contemporary philosophical tenets or religious beliefs which had great significance for studying of contemporary Indian philosophy and history. Under the same category, against item No.2 in Samaññaphal Sutta there was mention of contemporary spiritual guides who had declared themselves as Tirthankers (sanctified teachers or saints of the Jainas). They were Purana Kassapa; Makkhali Goshāla; Ajitkeshakambali; Pakudhakachchāyan; Nigantha Nātputa and Sanjaya Velaṭhiputta.

Majjhima Nikāya (Further ḍialogues of Lord Buddha) : The four virtues of Aryans Truth, Meditation; Perfect absorption in meditation. Evils of self prowess and final salvation etc. have been elaborately discussed therein. The said Nikāya contained 152 Suttas (sutras) under 15 categories:

(a) Mūlpariyaya Vagga

1. Mūlpariyāya Sutta, 2. Savvāsava Sutta, 3. Dhammadāyāda Sutta,

4. Bhayabhairava Sutta, 5. Anangaṇa Sutta, 6. Ānkkheyya Sutta, 7. Vatthupama Sutta, 8. Sallekha Sutta, 9. Sammādiṭhi Sutta, 10. Satipathān Sutta.

(b) Sihnāda Vagga

11. Chūlsihnāda Sutta, 12. Mahasihnāda Sutta, 13. Mahahukkhanda Sutta, 14. Chūldukkhandha Sutta, 15. Anumāna Sutta, 16. Chetokhil Sutta, 17. Vanpattha Sutta, 18. Madhupindaka Sutta, 19. Dwaidhāvitaka Sutta, 20. Vitakkasanthan Sutta.

(c) Opamma Vagga

21. Kakachūpaya Sutta, 22. Alagaddapama Sutta, 23. Vammika Sutta, 24. Rathavinita Sutta, 25. Nivāpa Sutta, 26. Ariyapariyesana Sutta, 27. Chūlhatthipadopama Sutta, 28. Mahāhatthi padopama Sutta, 29. Mahāsāropama Sutta, 30. Chūlsaropama Sutta.

(d) Mahāyamaka Vagga

31. Chūlgosinga Sutta, 32. Mahagosinga Sutta, 33. Mahāgopālaka Sutta, 34. Chūlgopālaka Sutta, 35. Chūlsachchaka Sutta, 36. Mahāsachchaka Sutta, 37. Chultanhāsañkhya Sutta, 38. Mahatanhāsankhya Sutta, 39. Mahaussapur Sutta, 40. Chūlussapur Sutta.

(e) Chūlyamaka Vagga

41. Sāleyayaka Sutta, 42. Veraññaka Sutta, 43. Mahāvedalla Sutta, 44. Chūlvedalla Sutta, 45. Chūldhammasamādan Sutta, 46. Mahadhammasamādan Sutta, 47. Vīmansaka Sutta, 48. Kosamaviya Sutta, 49. Brahmanimantaṅik Sutta, 50. Bharatajjaniya Sutta.

(f) Gahapatti Vagga

51.Kandaraka Sutta, 52. Atthakanāgar Sutta, 53. Sekha Sutta, 54. Potliya Sutta, 55. Jivaka Sutta, 56. Upāli Sutta, 57. Kukukhatika Sutta, 58. Abhaya Rajkumār Sutta, 59. Bahuvedniya Sutta, 60. Apannaka Sutta.

(g) Bhikkhu Vagga

61. Ambalaṭṭhikarāhulāvād Sutta, 62. Mahārahulovāda Sutta, 63. Chulmalunkya Sutta, 64. Mahamalunkya Sutta, 65. Bhaddāli Sutta, 66. Latthukikopam Suttā, 67. Chātuma Sutta, 68. Nalakpāna Sutta, 69. Gulissani Sutta, 70. Kiṭagiri Sutta.

(h) Parivvājaka Vagga

71. Tevijjakachhagotta Sutta, 72. Aggivañchhagotta Sutta, 73. Mahāvachhagotta Sutta, 74. Dighnakha Sutta, 75. Māgandiya Sutta, 76. Sandaka Sutta, 77. Mahasakuludāy Sutta, 78. Samaṇamaṇḍika Sutta, 79. Chūlsakuludayi Sutta, 80. Vekhnassa Sutta.

(i) Raj Vagga

81.Ghaṭi (Tī) kār Sutta, 82. Raṭhapāla Sutta, 83. Makhādeva Sutta, 84. Madhur Sutta, 85. Bodhi Rajkumar Sutta, 86. Angulimāl Sutta, 87. Piyajātika Sutta, 88. Bahitika Sutta, 89. Dhammachetiya Sutta, 90. Kaṇṇakatthal Sutta.

(j) Brahamaṇa Vagga

91. Brahmāyu Sutta, 92. Sela Sutta, 93. Assalāyan Sutta, 94. Ghotamukha Sutta, 95. Chankki Sutta, 96. Esukāri Sutta, 97. Dhānjāni Sutta, 98. Vāsittha Sutta, 99. Subha Sutta, 100. Sangārava Sutta.

(k) Devadaha Vagga

101. Devadaha Sutta, 102. Pañchtaya Sutta, 103. Kinti Sutta, 104. Sāmagāma Sutta, 105. Sunakkhata Sutta, 106. Avaññasappaya Sutta, 107. Ganakamogglān Sutta, 108. Gopakamogglan Sutta, 109. Mahapunnabha Sutta, 110. Chulpuṇṇabha Sutta.

(l) Anupada Vagga

111. Anupada Sutta, 112. Chhabbisodhan Sutta, 113. Sappurisa Sutta, 114. Sevitavva-asevitavva-Sutta, 115. Bahudhātuka Sutta, 116. Isigili Sutta, 117. Mahachattārisaka Sutta, 118. Ānāpānsati Sutta, 119. Kāyāgatāsi Sutta, 120. Sankhārupati Sutta.

(m) Suññata Vagga

121. Chūlsuññatā Sutta, 122. Mahasuññata Sutta, 123. Achchhāriyabhutdhamma Sutta, 124. Bakkula Sutta, 125. Dantbhūmi Sutta, 126. Bhumija Sutta, 127. Anirudha Sutta, 128. Upakkilesa Sutta, 129. Bālpandita Sutta, 130. Devadūta Sutta.

(n) Vibhanga Vagga

131. Bhaddekarat Sutta, 132. Anandbhaddekarat Sutta, 133. Mahakachchānbhadde Karat Sutta, 134. Lobhāsakingiya Sutta, 135. Chūlkambhvibhanga Sutta, 136. Mahakambhavibhanga Sutta, 137. Salāyatanvibhanga Sutta, 138. Uddesavibhanga Sutta, 139. Arunavibhanga Sutta, 140. Dhātuvibhanga Sutta, 141. Sachchavibhanga Sutta, 142. Dakkhināvibhanga Sutta.

(o) Salayatana Vagga

143. Anāthapindikovāda Sutta, 144. Chhannovād Sutta, 145. Puṇṇevāda Sutta, 146. Nandakovada Sutta, 147. Chūlrāhulovāda Sutta, 148. Chhachhaka Sutta, 149. Mahasalāyatanik Sutta, 150. Nagarvindeyya Sutta, 151. Pindapātipādi Sutta, 152. Indriyabhavana Sutta.

Sanyukta Nikaya (Kindred sayings by Buddha)

It is classified in 5 categories comprising of 56 kindred sayings:

(a) Sanāth Vagga

1. Devata Saṁyutta, 2. Devaputta Saṁyutta, 3. Kosala Saṁyutta, 4. Mar-Saṁyutta, 5. Bhikhuni Saṁyutta, 6. Brahma Saṁyutta, 7. Brāhmaṇa Saṁyutta, 8. Vangīsa Saṁyutta, 9. Vana Saṁyutta, 10. Yakha Saṁyutta, 11. Sakka Saṁyutta.

(b) Nidana Vagga

12. Nidan Saṁyutta, 13. Abhisamaya Saṁyutta, 14. Dhātu Saṁyutta, 15. Anamatagga Saṁyutta, 16. Kassapa Saṁyutta, 17. Lābhasakkār Saṁyutta, 18. Rahula Saṁyutta, 19. Lakkhana Saṁyutta, 20. Opamma Saṁyutta, 21. Bhikkhu

Saṁyutta.

(c) Khandha Vagga

22. Khandh Saṁyutta, 23. Dithi Saṁyutta, 24. Radha Saṁyutta, 25. Okkantika Saṁyutta, 26. Uppāda Saṁyutta, 27. Kilesa saṁyutta, 28. Sāriputta Saṁyutta, 29. Nāg Saṁyutta, 30. Supanna Saṁyutta, 31. Gandhavvakāya Saṁyutta, 32. Valāhā Saṁyutta, 33. Vachchhagot Saṁyutta 34. Gyan Saṁyutta.

(d) Salayatana Vagga

35. Salāyatan Saṁyutta, 36.Vedanā Saṁyutta, 37. Matugama Saṁyutta, 38. Jambukhadaka Saṁyutta, 39. Sāmandaka Saṁyutta, 40. Moggalan Saṁyutta, 41. Chitta Saṁyutta, 42. Mamani Saṁyutta, 43. Askhat Saṁyutta, 44. Avyākat Saṁyutta.

(e) Mahavagga

45. Magga Saṁyutta, 46. Bojjhaga Saṁyutta, 47. Satipaṭhān Saṁyutta, 48. Indriya Saṁyutta, 49. Sammappadhan Saṁyutta, 50. Bala Saṁyutta, 51. Idhipada Saṁyutta, 52. Anurudha Saṁyutta, 53. Gyan Saṁyutta, 54. Anāpana Saṁyutta, 55. Sotapanni Saṁyutta, 56. Sachcha Saṁyutta.

Anguttar Nikaya (Book of Gradual sayings) is classifed in elevan Nipatas. Each nipata is named as per its number. Buddha teachings have been accordingly compiled therein. The names of 11 Nipātas are as follows:

1. Ekak Nipāta, 2. Duka Nipāta, 3. Tika Nipāta, 4. Chatukka Nipāta, 5. Panchaka Nipāta, 6. Chhakka Nipāta, 7. Sattaka Nipāta, 8. Atthaka Nipāta, 9. Navaka Nipāta, 10. Dasaka Nipāta, 11 Ekadasaka Nipāta.

Khudakka Nikaya (Brief sayings by Buddha). There are 15 works as per each independent subject separately as under:

1. Khuddaka Pāth, 2. Dhammapada, 3. Udān, 4. Ittivritaka, 5. Sutta Nipāta, 6. Vimān Vatthu, 7. Peta Vathu, 8. Ther-gāthā, 9. Theri Gatha, 10. Jātaka, 11. Niddesa, 12. Paṭisambhida magga, 13. Apādān, 14. Budhavansh, 15. Chariyāpitaka.

Dhammapada, noted against serial No. 2 above is really a most significant work in Buddhist canonical literature. It has been translated in almost all prominent languages of the world. It contains 423 narratives which were discoursed by way of illustrations by Lord Buddha during his life time. There are excellent teachings relating to the religious ideology, morality, ethics and the way how to lead an auspicious life. It is classified in 26 sections. Each section has been named, conforming with the subject discussed therein with relative illustrations. It deals with profoundly significant topics, sagacious in nature, in a most charming and pleasant style, if Dhammapada is termed as *Geeta* (holy writings which are devoted to the exposition of particular religion and theosophical doctrines) of Bodh religion, it should not be deemed as an exaggeration. It was a prevalent practice even now amongst Buddhists in Ceylon that the religious mendicants who failed to undertake a thorough study of Dhammapada, were considered unfit for being awarded membership of the Buddhist organisation. Even in Burma, Siam, Combodia and Laos, it has been made compulsory for every religious mendicant to memorise Dhammapada, before joining the organisation.

The literal meaning of Dhammapada is religious pada. The word pada here purported to mean a narrative tale, sentence or a line. The narratives, sentences or outlines relating to Buddhism, as discoursed by Lord Buddha, were minutely studied and kept in memory by male and female mendicants during their life time, which is apparent from critical review and constant study of Buddhist literature. Dhammapada appears to be a collection of speeches made by Lord Buddha in his life time and it was incumbent upon each and evey mendicant to memorise it. The word Dhammapada has also appeard in *Saṁyukta Nikāya* (The book of kindred sayings by Buddha), suggesting the same meaning. In two verses of Dhammapada, also, the word has been used to convey the sense of Padas relating to Buddhism. The significance and celebrity of the said scripture is established from the very fact that several of its narratives have been quoted in prominent scriptures, like 'Kathavatthu' and 'Niddesa'. In Milindapanaho (The questions of king Milinda)[1], composed during the period, close to the commencement of Christian calendar, two verses have been quoted from Dhammapada[2] starting with the sentence Bhāsita petṁ Bhagvatā Devātidevena Dhammapade."

Vinaya Pitaka

Vinaya texts (The book of descipline) relating to morality, good behaviour and conduct, have, infact, acquired the status of a constitution (mode of leading life) for Buddhist organisation. Morality and ethical values provided vital strength to the mendicants. Lord Buddha had laid great emphasis for steady observance of religious obligations by all male and female mendicants. Lord Buddha also made a mention of sinful acts, faults and flaws and the austerities to be performed by the mendicants for their atonement in his discourses. Vinaya Pitaka is, in fact, a renowned Buddhist scripture, predominently dealing with in established usages or rules of conduct, prescribed for mendicants to enable them to learn manners of conducting themselves and lead a virtuous life in the organisation. Vinaya Pitaka is primarily a moral code. It is really much helpful in having a glimpse of the erstwhile social and cultural life of the people of India. The said holy scripture is perfect in all respects, yet the contents of the book have been classified under three heads, namely Sutta Vibhanga, Khandhaka and Parivar.

In Sutta Vibhanga there is a description of sinful acts, guilts and faults. There is also a mention of violation of religious obligations, morality or chastity to which the mendicants had committed themselves by repeating the vow thrice in the presence of their spiritual guide for their steady observance on Amavasya (the 15th day of the dark half of every lunar month) and Purnima (the day of full moon) of each month. This was also called Prātimoksa (deliverance). It was held

1. *Milinda Panho*, page |72, 399, published by Bombay University.
2. Verses No.32 and 327 of the same book.

in two parts in the monastery. The male mendicants gathered in a Buddhist monastery and repeated 227 religious obligations to be observed by them on Krishna Chaturdashi (the fourteenth day of) and Purnima (the day of full moon) of each month. Similarly the female medicants gathered in Buddhist monastery and repeated 311 religious obligations to be strictly observed by them on the said days of the month. The violations of the said religious obligations find mention in Sutta Vibhanga. While reciting Pratimokshas, when the chapter listing violations of religious obligations, morality and chastity was read out, it was expected from each male and female mendicant to stand up and acknowledge his/her sin of having violated the prescribed norms. The motive behind this practice was to discourage recurrence of such deviations in future.

Prātimoksha (deliverance of soul) had a significant role in the life of religious mendicants. It had thus been cited in Mahavagga— Prātimoksha (practice of liberating soul) was the foundation, an entrance door (central point) and foremost requirement, of all prominent religions".[1]

An old renowned commentator had defined the word Prātimoksha in most appropriate and suitable words—"If one abided by the religious obligations forming part of Prātimoksha, the latter would help in getting redeemed from many dangers or calamities and immoral acts and finally to be emancipated from the bonds of worldly existence. Hence it is called Prātimoksha (deliverance)."[2]

Khandhaka is comprised of Mahavagga and Chūlvagga. How the religious mendicants should behave and lead their lives in a Buddhist monastery. What are the duties to be performed and religious obligations to be observed by mendicants with similar other requirements find mention in Mahavagga. Sutta Vibhanga was primarily written in a prohibitive style while Mahavagga had been written in a predicative style, what ought to be done and the objects to be accomplished by the mendicents. The details of the events had been elaborately reproduced right from attainment of enlightenment by Lord Buddha to the establishment of first organisation of Buddhist mendicants. The said portion of Mahavagga was most significant from view point of studying ancient historical events. The systematic process and rules governing performance of the ceremony to be ordained in the order of a Buddhist monk after completion of the age of twenty; staying at a place during four months of rainy season; deliverance of the soul from the ill effects of immoral conduct and final emancipation from the bonds of worldly existence; performance of the festivities at the end of the rainy season; and colouring of the dress of a Buddhist mendicant etc. have been elaborately discussed.

Chūlvagga was in a way supplementary to Mahāvagga, and laid down what was fit to be done and what was not desired to be done by Buddhist male and female mendicants in their day today life as also how should they behave; how should they move to walk and how should they address others and converse. Important historic events such as initiation of Anāth Piṇḍaka (son of Suman, president of a mercantile guild, in northern Kośala where Lava is said to have

1. Prātimokkhaṁ ti Ādimetaṁ mukhmetaṁ pāmukhmetaṁ kuslānaṁ dhammanaṁ tena vuchachti patimokhaṁ ti. Gopaka Mojjlana sutta Majjhim nikaya. 3/1/8
2. Yo taṁ Patirakhati taṁ mokheti mocheti apayakadidukhehi tasma patimokhaṁ ti vuchchati —*A Comparative Study of Pratimoksha* p. 4 by Pachova.

reigned); religious gift of Jaitavana (garden of Jait prince which was purchased by Ānath Pinḍaka to be gifted to Lord Buddha); initiation of Maha Prajāpati Gautami (wife of King Shudhodan of Shākya dynasty) at Kapilvastu in Kośala region were found incorporated in Chūlvagga.

Parivār, the last portion of Vinaya Pitaka, is also called Parivār Pāth. It is, as a matter of fact, an index of the subjects dealt with in Vinaya Pitaka. It comprises of 19 chapters. The subjects discussed in Vinaya Pitaka, have merely been repeated in the index, just on the pattern of Abhidhamma Pitaka. Nothing fresh has been added to explain the subjects in Parivār Pāth. However, this portion of Vinaya Pitaka is very helpful in comprehending its texts. In Parivār Pāth, the questions have been raised as to when, to whom and in what connection. Lord Buddha had imparted a certain lecture on humility and modesty, what were the middle and final courses and the nature of various internal conflicts in Buddhist organisation etc. and their answers have been provided. This portion of Vinaya Pitaka had its own significance in providing information how a specific problem, misgiving or a query had been answered in Vinaya Pitaka. According to Mr.Winternitz, Parivār Pāth had the same significance and utility for Vinaya Pitaka as indexes and appendices attached to Vedas. However, there were a few citations in Parivār Pāth which indicated that it had been composed after Vinaya Pitaka had already been accomplished. There was also a mention in it that the Tripitakas had been reduced to black and white. There was a mention in Parivār Pāth that prince (mendicant) Mahendra had arrived in Ceylon. He had established the tradition of reciting Vinay texts regarding moral discipline to be observed and humility and modesty to be displayed by the mendicants of Buddhist organisation. The names of 29 Buddhist monks also appear who had brought out the texts of Vinaya Pitaka on copper plates. It was, obviously, inferred from the above hints that Parivār or Parivār Pāth, as available now, must have been composed in Ceylon much after accomplishment of Vinaya Pitaka.

Abhidhamma Pitaka

Abhidhamma Pitaka was the third collection of Buddha utterances. It is agreed under Bodh tradition that it contained Buddha teachings relating to Buddhist philosophy and the real nature of human soul as being identical with the Supreme Being. It deals with metaphysical knowledge, the realisation of the supreme truth, it was accomplished for scholars and intellectuals only and not meant for ordinary masses. It had been referred to in Athashālini; Manorathpūrṇi and Vibhang Attakathā (books incorporating Buddhist legends) that Lord Buddha, deified religious teacher of both celetial bodies and human beings, had first of all delivered his lecture on the philosophy of Buddhism before his respected mother, Mahāmāya and other divine powers in Trayasitrash heaven (headed by Lord Indra). Thereafter it was repeated by Lord Buddha to his resident chief disciple and a great intellectural, Sāriputta (popularly known as commander of Bodh religion). Thereafter Sāriputta had enunciated the teachings of Lord Buddha to his 500 followers.

In Sutta Pitaka, along with the words Abhivinaya (superior knowledge of texts relating to morality, ethical values, discipline, good behaviour and conduct) the word Abhidhamma (the supreme truth or metaphysics according to Buddhistic doctrines) had also appeared. Both the words had been used to denote superior knowledge of morality and discipline as also of supreme truth, preached by Lord Buddha. Acharya Buddhaghosha had defined the word Abhidhamma in his treatises Atthashālini and Sumangalavilāsini (relating to Buddhist legends) as most superior knowledge of Buddhism or supreme knowledge of Buddhist philosophy. According to him, the sanskrit prefix abhi in the word Abhidhamma signified intensity or superiority (greatness or excessiveness).

Most eminent scholar of Mahayan sect, Asanga[1] had advanced four etymological interpretations of the word Abhidhamma. In his first definition of sanskrit prefix Abhi as 'towards or in the direction of, he said that sermonising face to face by Lord Buddha about Supreme Truth, spiritual enlightenment true happiness and final liberation from worldly existence, led to its naming as Abhidhamma (the Supreme Truth or Metaphysics). In his second interpretation, he described that since Lord Buddha had explained Budhism in many ways by analysing it in various forms, hence it was called Abhidhamma (Supreme Knowledge according to Buddhist doctrines). As per his third interpretation since Lord Buddha had Strongly refuted the ideologies of other sects and contradicted the dogmas of opposite camps, which were antithetical to religious doctrines of Buddhism, hence it was called as Abhidhamma. In accordance with his fourth interpretation, the very Buddhist doctrines, as contained in Sutta Pitaka, had been gone after and regulated. Consequently, it was called Abhidhamma.

The sum and substance of all Buddha preachings was virtually the same. The inevitable requirement of Buddhism was to follow prescribed course of conduct, observance of morality, righteousness, piety, good behaviour manners and morals, as enunciated by Lord Buddha. Thus the difference lay in the mode of its explanation and determination only. What had been incorporated in Sutta Pitaka was in the shape of religious discourses. In Vinaya Pitaka we find Buddha teachings relating to observance of discipline, self redraint, and concentration of mind etc. While Abhidhamma Pitaka contains preachings of Lord Buddha concerning real nature of the human soul, knowledge of truth and Buddhist philosophy etc. The difference lies only whether one was possessed of authorised qualification to pick up and follow the real essence of Buddha teachings. The contents of Sutta Pitaka were meant for each and everybody of average intelligence and were directed towards purifying the mind and heart of the people so that they may distinguish between religious and irreligious actions. The substance of Buddha utterances, forming part of Abhidhamma Pitaka was also the same but they are meant for eminent scholars and intellectuals. Thus the object of Abhidhamma Pitaka was to impart higher metaphysical knowledge to talented persons. Hence the discourses were meant for the highest good of the mankind and for attainment of ultimate salvation. The religious teachings contained in Sutta Pitaka were for the benefit of all and were easily followed. They had been collected and compiled straight away in Sutta Pitaka without any modifications. However in Abhidhamma Pitaka, the views of Lord Buddha have been subjected to critical and minute investigation and explained in different ways from philosophical angle.

Abhidhamma : Its Accomplishment : It was fully believed under Bodh tradition

1. *Mahayān Sūtrālankār*; 11.3

that Buddha utterances relating to Buddhist philosophy and metaphysics were also recited in the first convention side by side with those concerning religious doctrines and texts of discipline, (moral values, politeness and humility) Abhidhamma Pitaka was as old as Sutta and Vinaya Pitakas. Āchāraya Budhghosha is confident that during the life time of Lord Buddha, the texts of Buddhist philosophy and metaphysics were also there along with the texts of Buddha teachings relating to religious principles and those concerning discipline, humility and modesty etc. It was also believed that the word Dhammakathik (The mendicants discoursing on religion) was decidedly used for mendicants, having knowledge of Buddhist philosophy and metaphysics as well.

In the third concert, held at Pātliputra (Patna) Āchārya Moggliputta Tissa had written *Kathāvathu* in which he had strongly repudiated false and incorrect notions based on mere obstinacy. The said work formed part of Abhidhamma Pitaka. Evidently, it was an accomplishment of subsequent period. Its incorporation in Abhidhamma pitaka leads us to believe that the texts of Abhidhamma Pitaka had been subjected to analytical research from time to time before giving it a final shape. However, this argument was not at all acceptable to the followers of 'Thervād'. According to this sect, the outlines of Kathavathu had already been drawn by Lord Buddha himself who was an omniscient and knew well that false interpretations of religious doctrines would be forthcoming and false theories would be invented after his final salvation. Āchārya Budhaghosha had vindicated this view with all emphasis at his command. He had expounded in Nidan Katha of Aṭṭhashālini (Buddhist legends) that although 'Madhupindaka Sutta' and other sūtras had been preached by the disciples of Lord Buddha, yet they had been approved by Lord Buddha and accordingly formed part of his teachings. Similarly, Kathavatthu was part of Buddha teachings and was treated as an essential part of *Abhidhamma Pitaka*.

Because of extreme faith and universal respect for Lord Buddha, the above explanation, which is only a praise and eulogy for him has been advanced. Had the final shape to the texts of Abhidhamma Pitaka been also given during the course of first concert, it must have been stated that the texts of Buddhist philosophy and metaphysics (knowledge of supreme truth) had also been collectively recited along with the texts of religious doctrines and moral values, good behaviour and conduct prescribed for the mendicants. In Chūlvagga[1] where a reference had appeared about recital of Buddha teachings in the first concert, it was cited that only the texts forming part of Sutta and Vinaya Pitakas, had been collectively recited. There was no mention of Abhidhamma Pitaka at all. At the time of second concert, held at Vaishali (Bihar) there was controversy between Sthirvadies (who believed in disintegration of the matter) and Sarvāstivādies (followers of the doctrine that wordly existence was real). On one hand, the followers of 'Sthirvadi' tried to prove that the texts of Buddhist philosophy and metaphysics had been expounded by Lord Buddha himself, while on the other, the followers of other sects had challenged the very genuineness of Buddha utterances relating to philosophy and supreme truth (metaphysics). Thus one is led to believe that the compilation and editing of the texts of Buddha teachings concerning philosophical and metaphysical

1. *Vinaya Pitaka.*

aspects of Buddhism might have started immediately after the first concert was over. The coordination and recital of the texts, forming part of Abhidhamma pitaka is not substantiated to have taken place during the period of first concert. Prior to it, a reference to Mātrikas is found. They were in miscellaneous forms. It appears that Ábhidhamma Pitaka was accomplished with the aid of the said Mātrikas. After the third convention of Buddhist mendicants was over, prince Mahendra had left for Ceylon and he had the texts of Abhdidhamma also in his memory along with the texts of doctrines of Bodh religion and those of morality and discipline to be observed by mendicants. It is beleived that by then the final shape of the texts of Abhidhamma Pitaka had been determined. No material is available to show that further modifications had been carried out in the texts of Abhidhamma Pitaka in Ceylor. Abhidhamma Pitaka was also reduced to writing along with Sutta and Vinaya Pitakas during the reign of Ceylon king, Vaṭṭhagamini Abhaya.

Significance of Metaphysical Knowledge : The followers of Sthirvada or Thervada (The sect believing in division of the matter in its essential ingredients) attached the same significance to Abhidhamma Pitaka as they did to Sutta and Vinaya Pitakas. In Burmah an extensive and profound study of Abhidhamma Pitaka had been carried out. In Ceylon too, the texts of Abhidhamma Pitaka had been greatly regarded. As stated in 'Mahāvansh' the Ceylon kings used to listen to the texts of Abhidhamma Pitāka with perfect concentration and faith. Nay—a few rulers even delivered lectures on Abhidhamma (knowledge of philosophical and metaphysical aspects of the religion). King Kāshyapa I, who lived in 10th century A.D. had got complete texts of Abhidhamma Pitāka engraved on golden plates. Not only this, he got 'Dhammasangini', forming part of Abhidhamma Pitaka, engraved by precious jems. King Vijay Bahu I, (1059 to 1114 A.D.) was, himself, an authority on Abhidhamma Pitāka. He translated Dhammasangini in Singhālese language.

On one hand, Abhidhamma Pitāka was held in great esteem by Sthavira sect and on the other all other sects of Bodh religion even suspected the orginality and genuineness of Abhidhamma Pitāka. Long ago, even a section of mendicants, belonging to Sthavirvadi sect believed that the texts of Abhidhamma Pitāka did not form part of Buddha utterances. The said group reposed its faith in Sutta Pitaka only. A reference appearing in Aṭṭhashālini (Buddhist legends) regarding conversation between two mendicants was really interesting. It read "Oh blessed one! you are quoting such a lengthy line like the height of Susmeru mountain (the mythological mountain of gold). Gentleman ! from where you have quoted it?"

"Blessed one with long life! it has been quoted from Abhidhamma Pitaka".

"Gentleman ! why do you appreciate to quote a line from Abhidhamma Pitaka? would it not have been proper to quote some other extract from authentic teachings of Lord Buddha".

"Blessed one ! who preached metaphysics, contained in Abhidhamma Pitaka?"

"Decidedly not by Lord Buddha".

From the above conversation and discussion, it would not be improper on our part to conclude that the texts of Abhidhamma Pitaka were determined much later as against Sutta and Vinaya Pitakas.

Religious Treatises Forming Part of Abhidhamma Pitaka

Abhidhamma Pitaka, written in Pāli script was comprised of the following components :

1. Dhammasangini, 2. Vibhanga, 3. Puggal Paññati, 4. Dhātu-Katha, 5. Paṭṭhān, 6. Yamaka, 7. Kathavatthupkarṇa.

Dhammasangini was really a superb work, forming part of Buddhist literature relating to philosophical and metaphysical aspects of Buddhism. The exposition of elemental and spiritual world has been so elaborately made in Dhammasangini that a learned scholar gets excellent information of all aspects relating to them. The results of auspicious or inauspicious actions either in this or in a former birth and critical evaluation of mind and mental dispositions as also unmanifested elementary matter or substance from which all things were created and similar other matters have been profoundly discussed therein. Thus it may be added that Dhammasangini was a unique collection identifying moral aspects of Buddhist psychology.

Another Classification of Pali Literature Relating to Tripitakas

Classification of Pāli literafure relating to Tripitakas has been made in several ways in order to make it easy to be understood and retained in the heart. With a view to enable the pupils and scholars to follow all aspects of Buddhist religion in a detailed and systematic manner, numerous classifications, had been made of Pāli Tripitakas and allied literature with critical evaluation, discussion and elucidation of the subjects, dealt with therein. However, on penetrating deep and minutely considering this point, it appears that repeated classification and sub-classification of Buddhist literature exhibited the nature and attitude of Buddhist scholars towards more and more investigation and elucidation of Buddhist doctrines and philosophy.

Besides classification in the shape of three Pitakas and allied literature, the entire Buddha teachings have been divided in five groups, namely-

1. *Digh Nikaya* (Dialogues of the Buddha)
2. *Majjhim Nikaya* (Further dialogues of Buddha)
3. *Saṁyukt Nikaya* (The book of Kindered sayings)
4. *Anguttar Nikaya* (The book of gradual sayings)
5. *Khuddaka Nikaya* (Sutta Nipata)

The five sub-divisions of Sutta Pitaka have also been named as above but with slight variation in their purport. Under the aforesaid classification, the entire literature allied to Tripitakas had been included. The said categorisation had made depending on the significance of the subjects dealt with. The religious treatises and allied literature included in the earlier four groups were the same under both classifications. However under the fifth group, named 'Khuddaka Nikaya', besides 15 treatises relating to Sutta Pitaka, all the treatises allied to Vinaya and Abhidhamma Pitakas had also been included.

Classification of Buddha Teachings in Nine Parts

Another classification of Buddha teachings has been made under nine heads. There was also a reference of the said classification in 9 heads in the scriptures of Mahāyan sect, written in Sanskrit language. As stated in 'Sadharam Pundarika Sutra' Lord Buddha had claimed that his religious commandments were nine-fold.[1]

In Dharma Sangrah it was cited that Buddha utterances could be classifed into nine heads[2] as under:

1. Sutta, 2. Gaiyya, 3. Vaiyākarṇa, 4. Gāthā, 5. Udān, 6. Itivrittaka, 7. Jataka, 8. Avbhutta Dhamma, 9. Vedalla.

1. Sutta: The teachings of Lord Buddha which had been compiled in prosaic form were called sutta (sūtras) and covered under this head. Just as 'Dīgh Nikāya' and 'Sutta Nipata' contained preachings of Lord Buddha in prose.

2. Gaiyya: Collection of Buddha teachings in mixed form versified and prosaic both.

3. Vaiyākarṇa: It was the Pāli version of Hindi word Viyākarṇa. It purported to be a grammar or an explantion or a deliberation upon theology or philosophy of Buddhist religion, the explanatory literature has been included under this category. Buddha teachings forming part of Abhidhamma pitaka and of similar nature were placed under this head.

4. Gāthā: Buddha utterances compiled only in versified form have been placed under this head. The word Gāthā was synonymous with Arya metre[3] (The first and third quarters must each contain 12 Mātras or syllabic instants — one being allotted to a short vowel and two to a long one — the second 18 and the fourth 15.) However, in both Buddhist and Jaina scriptures there has been a tradition to name all verified compositions as gāthās irrespective of the fact that they might have been composed in any form of the metres. Religious treatises such as Dhammapada, composed in versified form and containing Buddha utterances, fall under this category.

5. Udan (Verses of Uplift): The expressions of Lord Buddha in the shape of narratives, full of spiritual knowledge while he was in the state of mental satisfaction, happiness and pleasure which interspersed with emotionalism, friendliness and amity and which were later on composed in versified form were called verses of Uplift.

6. Itivritaka: Its Sanskrit formation is Ituktaṁ, meaning thereby 'it is said so'. Therefore, all preachings of Buddha, starting with the words as explained by Lord Buddha are obtained under this head.

7. Jatakas: The literal meaning of the word Jāta or Jātaka is birth. The tales

---

1. Navāngametanmam Shāsan cha
   Sadharma Pundrika sūtra, page 34 Hindi Edition of Dr. N. N. Dutta.
2. Navangapravachanani
   Mahayansutrasangrah, Ist volume page 332 published by Mithila Vidyapith, Darbhanga, 1961 edition.
3. Yasyāh pāde prathame 12 matrastatha Triteyapi |
   Ashtādasha dwitiye chaturthke panchdasha sārrya ||

of Lord Buddha's previous births have been collected and compiled in Jatakas. Besides, Jatakas, a mention of the said tales is found in Tripitakas as well.

8. Avbhuta Dhamma: Description of outstanding personalities endowed with moral strength, derived through continuous meditation and concentration; or a mention of superhuman powers or supernatural objects is found under this head.

9. Vedalla: After having been satisfied and delighted with Buddha teachings, further clarifications were sought. The quesions put up and answers given by Lord Buddha in the shape of religious discourses are categorised as Vedalla.The scriptures, namely Chūllavedalla Suttant; Mahavedalla Suttant, Sammadithi Suttant and Sakkapāñha Suttant are some of the works, falling under this head.

From the above discussion, relaing to the classification of Buddha preachings under nine heads, it is evident that the difference lay in mere style and way of expression. Accordingly, different portions of one and the same religious treatise could belong to several heads. The classification of Buddha teachings merely reflected that there were such and such types of Buddha utterances which had been compiled in Pitaka literature wherever the context so demanded.

Āchārya Haribhadra, had shown in his commentary on Buddhist treatise in Sanskrit styled 'Abhisamya lankār' that Buddha utterances had been classified under 12 heads as shown hereunder:

1. Sutra (Aphorisms) 2. Geya (In the shape of songs) 3. Vyākarṇa (Grammar) 4. Gāthā (narratives in versified form) 5.Udān (leading to uplift) 6. Avdan (leading to heroic acts and glorious achievements)7. Itivritaka (As enunciated by Lord Buddha) 8. Nidan (purification) 9. Vaipulya (plenty) 10. Jataka (collection of the tales of Lord Buddha's previous births) 11. Updesha (discourses) 12. Adbhut[1] dharma (Excellent religion).

According to another classification, Buddha utterances had been classified in 84,000 chapters on religious knowledge.

Such an extensive classification into divisions or sub-divisions of Buddha utterances, amply indicated the anxiety of Buddhist scholars for making minute investigation and extensive study of his preachings. The fact, however, remains that in practice only Tripitakas and their allied literature formed part of the curriculum, prescribed for religious mendicants.

Division in Multifarious Ways: Its History

Naturally one would like to know since when classification of Buddha teachings in the shape of 3 Pitakas (3 collections of Buddhist sciptures); 5 Nikayas (groups); 9 Angas (parts or portions as of a whole); and 84,00 Skandha (articles or Chapters) had been in force. Regarding accomplishment of three Pitakas (collection of writings after having been collected in three small boxes or baskets), there was a reference in Pikatas themselves. In the rock inscription at 'Bhābru' emperor Aśoka got Buddhist doctrines inscribed so that all the male and female mendicants as well as followers (worshippers of Lord Buddha as distinguished from the Bhikṣhus or mendicants) listened to and abided by them. The portions of Buddha utterances,

---

1. Sutraṁ geyaṁ vijakarnaṁ gathodanaavdanam
Itivritakaṁ nidanṁ vaipuylyaṁ cha sajatkam
Updeshadbhutau Dharmo Dwadeshangmid Vacah

—*Abhisamayalankar*, page 35, Baroda edition.

appearing in the said stone inscription, were in conformity with the names of the aforesaid divisions or sub-division.[1]

The scholars had elucidated the names of respective branch of Buddhist literature where the specific Buddha teachings were to be found Hence their detailed mention here was neither necessary nor desirable.

It is evident from Bhabru rock inscription, got accomplished by Emperer Aśoka that the contents of and classification of Buddha teachings in the shape of Tripitakas as obtained in third century B.C. were exactly the same as they are available now. It could atleast be safely asserted so far Sutta and Vinayak Pitakas were concerned.

Besides Bhabru inscription, in subsequent Buddhistic monuments erected in second centrury B.C. at Sanchi and Bharhuta for keeping sacred relies of Buddha teachings in tact the words 'Panchnekayika (pertaining to five nikayas) Suttantika (relating to Sutta Pitaka) and Pataki (used for a learned scholar, well conversant with the contents of Tripitakas) have appeared. Simultaneously, a few illustration from Jātakas (collections of the tales relating to Lord Buddha's previous births) have also been quoted on the said monumental inscriptions which confirm the genuineness of classification of Buddha teachings in the shape of Tripitakas and Nikayas.

The scholars believe that classification of Buddha teachings in the shape of three Pitakas and 5 Nikayas as available now, had already been determined prior to the age of stone and monumental inscriptions.[2] Subsequent to the said inscriptions, there was an explicit mention of the said classification of Buddha utterances in 'Milindapanho' (The questions of king Milinda); Buddhist legends, written by Āchārya Budhaghosh Deepvansh and Mahavansha etc.

Another classification of Buddha teachings in the shape of 84000 sacred works or articles, as started above, also appears to the quite old. In 'Thergāthā' it is cited that Ānanda (a confidant and senior-most resident disciple of Lord Buddha) had claimed that he was well conversant with 84,000 sermons of Lord Buddha, out of which 82,000 sermons were learnt by him as revealed by Lord Buddha himself and 2,000 from other senior monks of Buddhist organisation. As mentioned by Āchārya Budhaghosh in 'Samantpāsādika' (Buddhist legends relating to Vinaya Pitaka) all the 84,000 religious sermons of Lord Buddha had also been recited in the first concert.[3]

There was a reference to this effect in Mahavansh that emperor Aśoka asked Senior Buddhist monk, Moggaliputta Tissa, "How many religious sermons had been delivered by Lord Buddha. The Buddhist monk replied—"the sermons delivered by Lord Buddha had been incorporated in 84,000 sacred works". Thereupon, the emperor proclaimed that he would get one monastery built up for each sacred sermon and adore them.[4] Thereafter, the emperor started getting the monasteries constructed. Under Buddhist order, great significance is attached to the construction of 84,000 monasteries by emperor Aśoka.

---

1. Imani Bhante! Dhammapaliyayāni Viniayasamukase, aliyavasani, anagaimayāni munigatha moñeyasute upatisapsine e chā laghulovade musauaadaṁ adhigichya budhena bhasite, Etani bhante Dhammapaliyāyāni ichhāmi kiṁ ti bahuke bhikṣuvāye cha bhikhmiye sunyu cha upadhālleyeyu cha! Havaṁ mena upasaka cha upasikā ch etani bhantekhapara abhipietaṁ me janantu tı.
2. *Budhist India* by Royas Davids page 167.
3. *Samant pāsādika*, Ist volume, page 29.
4. *Mahāvansha*, 5, 76.80.

5

INSCRIPTIONAL PRĀKRITAS

In the history of India, Emperor Ashōkā was remembered, not merely on the strength of his armament but he achieved great prominence and success by virtue of pursuing the ideals of friendship and goodwill, tender-heartedness and service to the mankind. Emperor Ashōkā had, no doubt, rendered most valuable service to promote Buddhism but he had due regard for other religions as well. He believed in the progress and well-being of the entire humanity and had spared no pains to serve the people for the whole of his life.

The best testimony for his achievements in the field of religion, good behaviour, his dedication to ethical values, his administration acumen etc. were his inscriptions in Border towns and highly populated internal areas of his empire.

The Languages of Inscriptions: Their Significance

The said inscriptions had played a significant role in enabling to carry out analytical research and investigation of ancient Indian languages and dialectics. The language in which the said inscriptions had been accomplished, was infact, a refined literary form of the language, then in use in Northern India. The territorial parts on the north of Vindhya (Name of the mountain range which separates Northern India from the Deccan or Southern India and which forms the southern limit of Central India) situated in west, east and centre of the country, constituted Northern India. Earlier, the scholars invariably believed that all the inscriptions of emperor Ashōkā had been written in Pāli script but after prolonged research and investigation, the scholars arrived at the conclusion that they had been written in respective Prākrita dialect of each area where the inscriptions had been found.

Classification of Rock Inscriptions

These inscriptions, obtained in Prākrita dialects, were most ancient and a definite source of propagation and spread of Buddha message to the remotest parts of the country. Some of them had been inscribed on rocks, some on the walls of the caves while others on pillars and monuments. They are found right from Himalyan range in North to Karnataka in South and from North-West Frontier (Now in Pakistan) to Bihar and Orissa on the West. The inscriptions could be classified in eight groups, keeping in view the time when they had been inscribed.

1. Two Small Stone Inscriptions: They had been inscribed in about 258 or 257 B.C. Small rock inscriptions of the first type were found at Sidhpur, Jatinga, Rameshwar, and Brahmagiri of Karnataka State; at Roopnath in Jabalpur district and near Gurjarā village in Datia district of the State of Madhya Pradesh; at Sahasrām in Shāhbād district of Bihar; at Vairāth in Jaipur district of Rājasthan; at Māski, Gavimath, Pālkigunda and Irāgudi of Andhra State. Most probably, these inscriptions of the first small type had been written in the 13th year of the rule of Emperor Ashōkā. The scholars had to put in hard labour for deciphering the import of the said first type of inscriptions which they were not required to face while deciphering the inscription of the later era. A short account of the personal life of emperor Ashōkā had also been inscribed in it which had its own historic significance.

The small rock inscriptions of the second type were obtained from three places only — Sidhpur, Jatinga Rameshwar and Brahmagiri of Karnataka state. Practical aspects— how to adhere to the doctrines of Boddha religion—had been elaborated in the said inscriptions by emperor Ashōkā.

2. Bhābru Rock Inscription: It was inscribed in or about the year 257 B.C. and obtained on a rock of hill at Vairāth in Jaipur district of Rājasthan.

As heresaid, Vairāth was the same place, which was the capital of king Virāta, ruler of Matsya dynasty (The region, lying to the west of Dholpur in Rājasthan) where the Pandavās had spent one year in disguise during the era of Mahabharata. The said inscription had a great significance under Bodh tradition. The description of adopting Buddhism and joining Buddhist organisation by emperor Ashōkā has been given in it. Along with it, seven selected portions of Buddhist scriptures had also been incorporated in it, which in the opinion of emperor Ashōkā, deserved to be studied minutely with assiduous application and to be repeated again and again by all the male and female mendicants and worshippers of Buddha (as distinguished from the Bhikshūs). All the seven selected portions, spotted by emperor Ashōkā, in Buddhist-scriptures, are found even now in exactly the same wordings, without any change It is believed that while Bhābru inscription was got inscribed on the rock at Vairāth, emperor Ashōkā was most probably residing in a Buddhist monastery at Vairāth.

3. Fourteen Stone Inscriptions: These rock inscriptions had been got inscribed in or about the year 257 or 256 B.C. They are obtained at eight different places, enumerated below:

1. Shāhbāzagarhi (situated 40 miles away from Peshāwar in North-east direction).
2. Mānserā (District Hāzarā in Pakistan).
3. Kālsi (About 15 miles away in West direction of Mussorrie in Dehradun district of Uttar Pradesh).
4. Girnār (Near Junāgarh in Gujarat).
5. Sopārā (District Thāna in Mahārashtra).
6. Dhōli (in Cuttack district of Orissā).
7. Jaugarh (in Ganjam district of Tamilnādu).
8. Irāgudi (Andhra State).

The religious views and proclamations of emperor Ashōkā relating to the religion, ethics, medical treatment of human beings and animals; public works, obligations to be fulfilled by a ruler; the characteristics of a great ruler; the duties ought to be carried out by regional authorities; contacts with common masses; forbearance in matters of religion, true sense of glory, charities to deserving persons, victory over Kalinga; grounds of conflict; feelings of aversion from battle, winning over countries and states by virtue of propagation and spread of religion in place of creating bitterness and dissentions amongst nations etc., find place in the above inscriptions.

4. Two Stone Inscriptions found in Kalinga Region of Orissa State: They were got inscribed by the emperor in the year 256 B.C. They have been obtained at Dhauli and Jaugarh. Both the said inscriptions related to the administration of newly conquered territory of Kalinga. The royal proclamations issued to his officers by emperor Ashōkā, directing them how to administer the Kalinga territory and exercise control over the savage tribes, inhabiting its border, are found incorporated in them. These rock inscriptions had great significance. As a matter of fact, the said two inscriptions were in the nature of supplements to the above-noted fourteen rock inscriptions. They were like addendums to the 14 rock inscriptions which had already been got inscribed.

5. Three Inscriptions Over Walls of Caves: They were located on the hills near Gayā (Bihar). They were got inscribed during 13th and 20th year of the rule of emperor Ashōkā i.e. in the years 257 and 250 B.C. It was cited in them that emperor Ashōkā Priyadarshi (Dear to the sight) had gifted the said caves to Ājivakās (Jaina nude mendicants). During the era of Lord Buddhā and Lord Mahāvirā, there was a distinct religious sect called— *Ājivakās,* forming part of religious mendicancy. The mendicants belonging to the said fold remained nude with no clothes on their bodies. Makhali Goshala was the supreme head of the said organization. Although, emperor Ashōkā was himself a follower of Buddhist religion yet he had due regard for other religious institutions as well. It was an outstanding example of religious tolerance and submission to other ideologies on the part of Ashoka. Besides this, there was another reason also for having soft corner for Ājivakās. It was cited in 'Mahavaṁsa Satikā' that the name of Ashoka's mother was Dharmā. She had born in a Morya family. She was the principal queen of king Bindusāra. Her parental family was the follower of religious doctrines of Ājivakā sect. The name of their religious preceptor was Janseva. The said queen also reposed faith in the doctrines of Ājivakā sect like her parental family. According to Dr. Radhakumud Mukerjee, it was the reason why emperor Ashōkā had soft corner for Ājivakās. However, in 'Divyāvadān', the name of Ashōkā's mother has been given as Shubhdrāngi and she is stated to be belonging to a Brahman family. Nevertheless, it would be unfair to link the event of gifting Tān caves to Ājivikā sect by emperor Ashoka, simply to oblige his mother who was the follower of the said religious organisation. In the sixth monumental inscription, it is cited that as appeared in 'Satva Pāsandā', the word 'Pūjitā' (worshipful and worthy of reverence), used by Ashōkā, clearly manifested that he had due regard for all religious institutions.

6. Two Pillar Inscriptions Found at the Foothill of Nepal: These two pillar inscriptions have been found in the villages 'Rummandei' and 'Niglivā', situated at the foothill of Nepal. They were believed to have been inscribed in the year 250 B.C. Although, the said inscriptions were short, yet there were several reasons which added to their significance. It was quite evident from the said inscriptions that Ashoka had visited almost all important sacred shrines of Buddhist religion. In the pillar inscription, found in the village, Rummandei, there was a mention of 'Lumbini' forest, the place where Lord Buddha was born. The said place had great significance in the history of Buddha religion. From the pillar inscription of 'Niglivā' village, it has become known that Ashōkā was whole-heartedly devoted to Gautam Buddha on one hand and on the other he had great regard for all preceding Buddhas too. Along with it, the said pillar inscriptions stood testimony to the fact that the boundaries of Ashōkā's empire had extended upto Nepal's foot-hill.

7. Seven Pillar Inscriptions: They are believed to have been got inscribed in between the years 243-242 B.C. These pillars have been found in village Topārā (Near Ambālā in Haryana); Meerut (U.P.). Kaushāmbi (about 30 miles above Allahabad in U.P.); Purvā (District Champaran, Bihar); Lauriyā (Ararāj, Bihar). Lauriya (Nandangarh, Bihar) and Arrah (Bihar).

The monuments at Topārā and Meerut were forcibly removed to Delhi by king Ferozshah which were subsequently brought back to their original places. The pillar inscription found at Kaushāmbi is now lying in the Fort at Allahabad. It was removed from Kaushāmbi to Allahabad. Emperor Ashōkā had got the said monuments inscribed in the later part of his life after having completed 30 years of his rule. Normally, the same matter had been got inscribed on the said seven pillar inscriptions which formed the subject-matter of above noted 14 rock inscriptions. Infact, they could be considered as supplements to the 14 rock inscriptions. In the said pillar inscriptions, there was description of all those measures, ways and means, employed by emperor Ashōkā for propagation of Buddhism during the course of his lengthy rule. The issues relating to Ashōkā's religious policy; ethical values, duties of administrative officers; total ban on slaughter of different animals for selected days in a year and for solemn implementation of the objects of non-violence etc. for universal good have been elucidated in the said pillar inscriptions.

8. Three Small Pillar Inscriptions: It is believed that the said three small pillars had been got inscribed in between the period 248 to 232 B.C. They have been obtained at Sārnāth (Near Varanasi, U.P).

It was cited in the said small pillar inscriptions that the male or female mendicants who would be found creating rift or disunion in the organisation, would be expelled from the religious institution. It appears that the decisions arrived at in the convention, during the ruling period of emperor Ashōkā, to apply brakes to the growing feelings of discord, enmity, hatred and rift in the organisation, were got inscribed on the said pillars so as to give them due publicity. It is obvious that Ashōkā was highly perturbed and anxious to check the rift and disunion in the Buddhist organisation.

There was one more citation on the pillar inscription, now lying in the Fort at Allahabad, which was popularly known as the inscription relating to the queen. The name of the second Queen of Ashōkā was Kāruvāki, who was the mother of prince Tiwar. Her generosity and munificence had been greatly admired in it.

It was thus a brief introduction of the inscriptions of emperor Ashōkā. However, the prime motive here was to make critical evaluation of linguistics in which they had been inscribed. Hence it was essential to reclassify them, keeping in view that they had been inscribed on rocks or pillars in different lands, having different dialects of their own. Accordingly, the said inscriptions could be grossly classified in six groups as per their locations in North-west, West, East, South-east, Central and Southern parts of the country. Ashōkā had got them inscribed in his official state language. The capital of his dynasty was Pātliputra (now Patna) in East India. His state language was the Prākrita, used in eastern regions. The official language has comparatively refined shape as against the medium of speech, commonly used by the masses. Thus during the reign of Ashōkā, his official state language was slightly different, having obtained an accomplished shape. Although, the state language is used in the entire dynastic area in performance of official duties, yet slight variations are always possible in different areas in accordance with regional diversities in native dialects. Emperor Ashōkā, therefore, decided that religious messages and royal commands should be got inscribed in his official state language at all those places where people were in a position to follow it, so that each and every body could be benefited with the teachings and their import.

The inscriptions of emperor Ashōkā, located in eastern regions of the country, had been inscribed in the same language which was in official use. Even in the territories of central India, there was practically no difficulty for the people to grasp it. Of course, minor variations cannot be denied from their local dialects. Thus the language of all inscriptions, located at places right from the valleys of river Ganga and Yamuna to the basin of Mahanadi river in Bihar, was almost the same. The slight variations found here and there were insignificant.

The empire of Ashōkā covered far-off places. There were territories in it where the official language, based on eastern Prākrita, could not be conveniently followed by the people. The native dialects of those areas were altogether different. Hence due care was taken to ensure that rock or pillar inscriptions were got inscribed in their respective native dialect so that common people of these areas might be in a position to understand and take them to heart without least inconvenience. In other words, the language of inscriptions was, obviously, influenced by the local dialect of the respective territory. This fact stands corroborated by the inscriptions found at Shahbāzgarhi and Mānsera in the regions of North-West India (now in Pakistan). Critical evaluation of the variations found in the inscriptions of the said places as against the language of the inscriptions, located in eastern and other parts of the country, shall be carried out later.

Girnār is situated in Saurashtra (Gujarat State). The local dialect of the said area was evidently different from that of eastern territories of the country. Hence it was obvious that the language of inscription at Girnār was in variance with those found in eastern regions. However, its language had been slightly influenced by the medium of speech used in Central India which was apparent from a perusal of the language of Girnār inscription.

South has been beyond the jurisdiction of languages, belonging to Aryan linguistic family. Even during the life-time of Ashōkā, the languages pertaining to Dravadian linguistic group were in vogue in south as is the case now. Of course, the languages of Dravadian linguistic family in those days were like elder sisters of the present languages, belonging to Dravadian group. The language of the inscriptions, found in south, remained uninfluenced by local dialects since they belonged to a different linguistic group. The minor variations observed in the language of inscriptions in south, as against those of eastern territories, were only due to the influence of dialects of Western India. Consequently, there was conformity between the language of inscriptions, obtained in South and those found at Vairāth, Sānchi and Rupnath — may be to a slight degree. Specifically, there was nothing more required to be described in respect of Southern inscriptions from linguistic viewpoint.

Languages of the Inscriptions : Their Comparative Study and Evaluation

The fourteen inscriptions of eimperor Askōkā were located at different places which were far off from each other. Whereas Shāhbāzgarhi was situated in North West, Dhauli happened to be in remote South-East territory of India. Similarly, on one hand Kālsi was situated at the border of Himalayas and on the other Jaugarh stood in far-off Southern territory.

Grossly speaking, there were three linguistic forms obtained in fourteen inscriptions — that of north-west; of eastern and central parts and that of Western India. The language of Shāhbāzgarhi and Mānsera inscriptions had a typical linguistic form which appeared to be influenced by the language of Iran and Western countries, belonging to Aryan linguistic family and was closer to Sanskrit language. The inscription at Girnar seemed to have been influenced by the language of western India. Besides them, the language of other inscriptions had a different form, somewhat resembling with the official language of Ashōkā empire.

The inscriptions of Shāhbāzgarhi and Mānsera existed in the tracts which constituted North-West border of Ashōkā's dynasty. That was the era of Prākrita dialects. The Prākrita dialect of North-West Frontier territory was basically different from Prākrita dialect of eastern parts. The medium of speech of a particular area would always be influenced by the dialects of the neighbouring localities, in as much as the people of neighbouring areas come in contact with each other and exchange their views in day today course of their lives. Hence the language of North-West Frontier region was bound to be influenced by the language of the country situated on the West. The Prākrita used in the inscriptions found at Niya, forming part of Chinese Turkey, popularly known as Niya Prākrita and Dhammapāda Prākrita used in the inscription, obtained at Khaitān, resembled very much with language of the inscriptions of Shāhbāzgarhi and Mānsera.

With regard to the languages of the inscriptions, got inscribed by emperor Ashoka, no final opinion could be given since they needed further study and critical investigation. However, certain points, relating to the languages of the inscriptions are discussed below :-

1. The letter ऋ is found transformed into 'रि' and 'र' For example, the Sanskrit word "मृग" (A deer) is found to have been written as "म्रुगो"[1] in the rock inscription of Shāhbāzgarhi and in that of Mānsera, it is found written as 'म्रिगे'[2]. At a few places, we find the letter 'ऋ' converted into letter 'र'.

In the inscription at Girnār, we find Sanskrīt word 'मृग:' transformed into

1. Mrigo so pi mrugo no dhruvaṁ.
2. Eke mrige se pi chu mrigah no dhruvam !
(Ek ah mrigah sah api cha mrigah na Dhruvah ! — First rock inscription.

'मगो'[1] in place of मुगो or 'म्रिगे' which shows that in Gujrat side, there is a tendency of the letter 'ऋ' converted into letter 'अ'.

In the inscriptions of Kālsi and Jaugarh the Sanskrīt word 'मृग:' is found transformed into 'मिगे'[2]. The language of these inscriptions conforms with the dialect of eastern regions where there is tendency of conversion of the letter 'ऋ' in letter 'इ'.

In the inscription of Shāhbāzgarhi, the letter 'र' forces the following palatal consonant to be converted into cerebral consonant. For instance, the form 'बुढ्रेषु'[3] is obtained for Sanskrit word 'वृद्धेषु' (form in locative case of root word 'वृद्ध' which means grown up persons). However, in the inscriptions of Mānsera, the form 'बुध्रेषु'[4] is obtained for Sanskrīt word 'वृद्धेषु'.

The change of palatal consonants into cerebral consonants is not regularly found as a rule in all inscriptions. For example, in the second inscription, found at different places, the Sanskrīt word 'Aushadhāni (medicinal herbs) has been found transformed into varying farms, such as —'औसुढ़ानि' at Girnār; 'औसुधानि' at Kālsi; 'औसधानी at Jaugarh; 'औषुढ़ानि' at Shāhbāzgarhi and 'औषढ़िनि' at Mānserā[5]. In the fourth stone inscription the Sanskrīt word 'वर्द्धित:'. (Enlarged or magnified) has been found converted in either 'वढ़ितो' or 'वढ़िते'[6].

In North-West Frontier inscriptions, the palatal letter 'श'; cerebral letter 'ष' and dental letter 'स' are found intact as in Sanskrit. Such as — Dosham (fault or sin) 'समजस' (For the society); प्रियद्रशि[7] (affectionate to all — used for emperor Ashōkā); 'अनुदिवस' (Every day, daily); 'प्रणशतसहस्त्रनि' (Large number of lives); 'अरमियिसु' (Engaging in conversation with)[8]; 'पशोपकानि' (For the benefit of animals);

---

1. . . . Eke mrige se pi cha mige no dhruve.
2. Eke mige se pi chu mige no dhruvaṁ.
3. Budheshu hita sukhye dhramyutas aplibodhe Vapata . . .
4. Budhreshu hidaṁ sukhye dhramyut aplibodhaye viyaputa . . .
   (. . .Vridheshu Hitsukhāya dharmayuktasya apariteadhāya Vyapritāh . . .)

   — Fifth inscription.
5. Girnār — Ausudhāni cha yāni manusopgāni cha . . .
   Kālsi — Ausdhāni munisopgāni chā . . .
   Jaugarh — Ausdhāni āni munisopgāni . . .
   Shāhbāzgarhi — Aushudhāni, manushopkāni manushopkāni . . .
   Mānsera — Aushdhini
   (Aushdhāni manushyopgāni cha . . .)
6. Girnār — Atikāntaṁ antaraṁ bahūni Vāsasātāni Vadhito evaṁ prānāraṁbho
   Kālsi — Atikantaṁ antlaṁ bahuṁ Vāsastatāṁ badhite vā pānalaṁbhe . . .
   Dhauli — Atikantaṁ autalaṁ bahūni Vāsastāṁ Vadhite va pānālaṁbhe . . .
   Jaugarh — Atikantaṁ Antalam bahumi
   Vāsastāni Vadhite Va panalambhe
   Shāhbāzgarhi — Atikritaṁ antaraṁ bahūni Vashastāni Vadhito vapranarambho
   . . . Mānsera - Atikritaṁ antaraṁ bahuni vash. shaṁ vadhite va pranaraṁbhe . . .
7. Bahukahi doshaṁ samjas Devan priyo priyadrishi raya dakhati.
   (Bahukān hi doshān Samājasya devānām priya priyadarshi Rājā pashyati)

   —1st Rock inscription
8. Anvdivaso bahuṁ pranashabsahasrini Arabhiyisu . . .
   (Anudivasaṁ bahuṁ prānashatasahasrani ālpasat)

'नस्ति' (Not existing); 'सव्रत्र'[1] (Everywhere) etc.

Exceptions have also been found here and there in stone inscriptions of 'Shāhbāzgarhi'. For instance, in the second inscription, for sanskrit word 'मनुष्य-चिकित्सा' (Treatment of human-beings) the formation 'मनुशचिकिस' and similarly for Sanskrīt word 'मनुष्योपगानि' (for betterment of mankind) the form 'मनुशोपकानि'[2] is obtained.

In the inscriptions of Shāhbāzgarhi and Mānsera, it is found that the letter 'र' has a tendency to change its site. The letter 'र' joins its preceding or succeeding consonant. For example, Sanskrīt word 'धर्मलिपि' (The sacred script), the form 'ध्रमदिपि'[3], for Sanskrīt word 'सर्वत्र' (everywhere), the form 'सव्रत्र'[4] and for Sanskrit word 'प्रियदर्शिन' (Looking kindly upon everything—an epithet of king Ashōkā), the form 'प्रिअद्रशिस'[5] etc. are obtained. Similar tendency of letter 'र', changing its site and joining its preceding or succeeding consonant is not found in the inscriptions of other places.

The letter 'य', appearing in the latter part of the joint consonants of Sanskrit words, disappears in the Prākrita. This tendency is seen in rock inscriptions of North-West Frontier region. For example, for Sanskrit word 'कल्याण' (happiness, fortune), the form 'कलण'[6] and for 'कर्त्तव्य' (obligation) the form 'कटव'[7] are obtained respectively. The said tendency of disappearance of letter 'य' is primarily found in the inscriptions of Shāhbāzgarhi. In stone inscriptions of Mānsera, a few exceptions have also been noticed. Whereas in the 12th and 1st inscriptions of Shāhbāzgarhi, the forms 'कलण' for 'कल्याण'[8] and 'कटव' for 'कर्त्तव्य' have appeared, in those of Mānsera, the forms 'कयण' and 'कटविय'[9] have respectively been found.

---

1. Pashopkāni cha yatra tatra nasti savritra haropita cha . . .
(Pashunpagāṁ cha yatra tatra na santi sarvatra Hāritāni cha . . .)
—2nd inscription
2. Priyadrashisa rao duvi Chikis kit manush-chikish pashuchikisa cha Aushudhani manushopkaṁ ...
(Priyadarshinah Rāgye Chikitse krite manushya chikitsā cha pashuchikitsā cha. Aushdhani manushyopkāni. . .)
3. (a) Yain Dhrandipi devan prias-rao likhpitu.
(Iyaṁ dharmalipiḥ devānāṁ priyeṇa Ragya lekhitā) —Ist inscription
4. Savritra Vijite devanaṁ priyas priyadrishisa ye cha ant—
(Sarvatra Vijite devanaṁ priyasya priyadarshinah. . .ye cha antāh. . .)
—2nd inscription
5. Pur mahnasi devanaṁ prias priadrishasa rao. . .
(Pura mahanase devanaṁ priyasya priya-darshinah Ragyaḥ. . .) —Ist inscription
6. Evaṁ hi devanaṁ priyas ichh kiti Savra prashauḍa bahushrut cha kalaṇa batvo. . .
(Evaṁ hi devānāṁ priyasya ichchha kimiti sarva pashnda bahushrutah cha kalyran wantaḥ. . .)
—12th inscription.
7. Hid no Kichi jive Ārbhit prayuhotviye. Nopi cha sawāja katav.
(Ih na kashchit jivah Alabhya prahotavyah.
Nāpi cha samājah kartavyah) —Ist inscription
8. Evaṁ hi Devanaṁ priyas ichha kiti savra pashaḍa bahushrut cha kayana taviya. . .
9. Hid no ki chi jive Ārbhit prayuhotviye nopi cha sawaja katviya.

In inscriptions of North-West Frontier, the consonants, in which letter 'र' connects, are found intact such as 'प्रज' (Subjects);[1] 'ब्रमण' (A Brāhmana), 'श्रमण' (A religious mendicant)[2] etc. However, exceptions are there. We find for 'द्रयर्थ' as 'दियट'[3].

The letter 'ल्' connecting joint consonants in Sanskrīt words, generally disappears in Prākrita. This tendency is primarily found in the inscriptions of North-West Frontier region only. Elsewhere, it is not found. For instance for the word 'कल्प' (A sacred precept or rule), the form 'कप'[4] and for the word 'अल्प' (Trifling, insignificant), the form 'अप'[5] is found.

In the inscriptions, of North-West Frontier region, the use of 'छ' is found for 'क्ष'. Just as 'मोछये'[6] for 'मोक्षाय'; 'छमितविय' for 'क्षन्तव्य' and 'छमनये' for 'क्षमणाय'[7]

Except North-West Frontier, the tendency for using 'ख' for 'क्ष' is generally found in stone inscriptions of all other places. However, in a few inscriptions of North-West Frontier too, the use of letter 'ख' in place of 'क्ष' has been noticed. For example, in the tenth inscription of both Shāhbāzgarhi and Mānsera, for Sanskrīt word 'क्षुद्रकेण' the form 'खुद्रकेन'[8] has appeared.

In North-West Frontier inscriptions, the use of letter 'ञ' has been found for 'ज्ञ'. Such as 'रञ्ञो'[9] and 'तिकन'[10]

Elsewhere, both forms 'ञ' and 'न' are obtained. The letter 'न' has also appeared in North-West inscriptions but only in rare cases. In North-West inscriptions, the use of 'ञ' is also found for 'न्य'. For example 'अञ्नि'[11] and 'अञे'[12] etc. In Mānsera

1. . . . Tatham cha me praja anuvatatu.
   (. . . तथा च में प्रजा अनुवर्त्तन्वाम्) — 5th inscription
2. (a) Mitrasanistut atikanaṁ cha Bramana shramsanaṁ — 3rd inscription
   (b) Tatra he vasanti Bramana va Shramana va.
   (Tatra hi Vasanti Brāhminā va Shramana va. . . — 13th inscription
3. 13th inscription
4. Imaṁ avakapaṁ dhrame shile cha Tistati dhramaṁ anushashishanti.
   (Idaṁ yāvat kalpaṁ Dharme shile cha tishthantah dharmamanushasishyanti) — 4th inscription
5. Apvayat apmandata sadhu
   (Alpavijayata alpamandatā Sādhu) — 3rd inscription
6 Mochhaya iyaṁ anubadhaṁ —.
   (Mokshaya cha evaṁanubandhaṁ ——) — Vth inscription
7. (a) Yo pi cha apkareya ti chhamitviamte vo devanaṁ priyas yaṁ shako chhamanye.
   (Yoapi cha apakaroti Kshantvyamat eva devanani priyasya yaḥ: Shakya Ksamnāya)
   (b) Ichhati hi devanaṁ priya sabrabhutan achhti ——.
   (Ichhati hi devanaṁ priyah Sarvabhutanachhti . . . . .) — 13th inscription.
8. Dukarṁ tu kho eve khudrakena vagrena usten va . .
   (Dukaraṁ tu Khalu etat Ksudrakena vargena ushta) —Shāhbāzgarhi — Xth inscription
9. Ayaṁ dhramadipi devana prias raño likhyitu.
   (Iyaṁ Dharmalipih devanaṁ priyena Rājā lekhitā) Shāhbāzgarh — Ist inscription
10. Mitra Sanstutañtikanaṁ Sharmaṇa Brāmanānāṁ dānāṁ prānānaṁ anarambho.
    (Mitrasȧustutagyatikanaṁ Shramana Brahmananaṁ danaṁ prnanamanarlabhah) —Shāhbāzgarhi — XI inscription
11. Añani cha divani rūpni drashyitujanas. (—Anyāni cha divūyāni rūpani Darshyitwa janasya) — Shāhbāzgarhi, IVth inscription
12. Eshe añe cha bahnvidhe dhramcharṇe vadhrite (Etat anyat cha bahuvidhaṁ Dharma Charnaṁ vardhitaṁ) —Mānsera, IV inscription

inscriptions, the use of letter 'ण'[1] is also found. At other places, the use of letter 'न' is generally obtained for 'न्य'. The same is the case with Girnār inscription.

In North-West inscription, the inevitability in use of dental and cerebral consonants is not found. For example, in fourth inscription at Shāhbāzgarhi the forms 'तिस्तिति' for 'तिष्ठति' and 'सेठ'[2] for 'श्रेष्ठम्' have been found which means that both dental and cerebral consonants are obtained in one and the same sentence.

In North-West inscription, some forms have been found where the letter 'र' has disappeared. For example, in the sixth inscription, the use of the form 'किट'[3] is obtained for 'कृतम्' (Enough). In fact, the formation should have been 'क्रिट' for 'कृत' as per tendency found in North-West inscriptions as stated above. The letter 'ऋ' is found converted in letters 'रि, रु and र' at certain places.

However, in the inscriptions of eastern territories, this tendency is not found. There the letter 'ऋ' in Sanskrīt words tends to be converted in 'इ', 'उ' or 'अ'. Thus the formation 'किट' in place of 'क्रिट' found in North-West inscriptions (i.e. ommission of letter 'र') appears to be the result of copying eastern Prākrita.

In the inscriptions of North-West Frontier, the tendency of conversion of letter 'आ' into letter 'अ' is repeatedly found. Thus as it is clearly perceived from the appearance of the words 'चिकिस'[4] for 'चिकित्सा' (treatment), Yath[5] for 'यथा' and 'तथ'[6] for 'तथा; 'अधुन' for 'अधुना' (now, at this time); 'पछ' for 'पश्चात्' (afterwards), 'तिव्र'[7] for 'तीव्र' (severe, intense, sharp) and 'अपरधेन'[8] for 'अपराधेन' (offending, guilty) etc.

In North-West inscriptions, nouns ending in last letter 'अ' in nominative case, singular number, tends to convert in 'ओ' and 'ए' both. However, there was no strict adherence to this rule.

In Girnār inscription, the last letter 'अ' is found converted into 'ओ' while in inscriptions of Dhauli, Jaugarh and Kālsi, the last letter 'अ' is seen converted in

1. Imye dhramnushastiye yathaṁ anaye pikramne —Mānsera, III inscription.
2. Dhrame shile cha tistiti dhramaṁ anushishanti. Eta hi Srettsim krmani yaṁ dhramanushashanaṁ dhram charanaṁ picha.
(Dharme Shile cha tishthantah dharmaṁ anshāsiyanti. Etat hi Shreshthaṁ Karma yat dharmanushasnaṁ) — Shāhbāzgarhi, 4th inscription
3. Taṁ maya kitaṁ savra kalaṁ
(Tat maya evaṁ kritain Sarvaṁ kalaṁ. . .) —Shāhbāzgarhi, 6th inscription
4. Priyadrishisa raño duvi chikis kit manushchikis pashuchikish cha.
(Priyadarshinah Rāgyah divi Chikitse manushyachikitsā cha pashu-chikitsa cha.
—Shāhbāzgarhi, second inscription
5. Imim dhramnushasti yath a ye pi Kreṁye
(-Asye dharmanushishtyai yatha anyasmai api karmne) —Shāhbāzgarhi, Third inscription
6. . . . San Cha puna tath kartaṁ badhtaraṁ uphanti ataprashadaṁ
(. . . Sach punah tatha kurvan badhtar supahanti atmapakhande) —Shāhbāzgarhi, 12th inscription.
7. Tato pachha adhuna lagheshu kaligeshu tivre dhramlana. . .
(Tatah pashchāt adhunā labdheshu Kaligeshu Tīvra Dharmapālane. . .)
— Shāhbāzgarhi, 13th Inscription
8. . . . Sankhyekarṇa va alocheti dipikaras va apardhen
(. . .Sanksepkāranam Vā ālochayatu lipikarāparādhen vā)
— Shāhbāzgarhi, — 14th inscription.

letter 'ए' in majority of the cases.[1]

In stone inscriptions of Girnār, the word 'राजा' has mostly appeared for 'राजा' while in stone inscriptions of Kālsi, Dhauli and Jaugarh, generally the word 'लाजा'[2] has appeared for 'राजा'. In shorseni Prākrita, the letter 'र' remains unchanged. However, in Māgadhi Prākritā, the letter 'र' is changed in letter 'ल'.

In inscriptions of Shāhbāzgarhi, both the forms 'रज' and 'रय' are obtained. So is the case in Mānserā inscriptions. But no strict adherence to this rule is found in the inscriptions of both the places.[3]

In the fourth inscription of Mānserā, the form 'रजिने' has appeared for Sanskrīt word 'राज्ञः' (King) while in the inscription at Shāhbāzgarhi, the form 'रञो' has appeared.[4] In North-West inscriptions, generally the letter 'ञ' is used in place of Sanskrīt letter 'ज्ञ'.

In inscriptions of Shāhbāzgarhi and Mānserā, form 'चु' has appeared for 'तु'. However, it is not so in Girnār inscriptions. There the form 'तु' has remained unchanged. But in the inscriptions at Kālsi, Dhauli and Jaugarh, the form 'चु'[5] is found like North-West Frontier rock inscriptions.

In the seventh inscription at Girnār, the form 'तु' has appeared for 'तु'. However, 'चु' at Kālsi; 'च' at Dhauli; 'च'; at Jaugarh चु at Shāhbāzgarhi and also चु at Mānsera.[6] There is no explanation why the form च only has appeared in inscriptions

---

1. Devanaṁ priyo piyadasi Rājā evaṁ āha —Girnār-III inscription
   Devanaṁ piye piyadasi Rājā hevaṁ āhā —Kalsi
   Devanaṁ piye piyadasi Rājā Hevaṁ āhā —Dhauli
   Devanaṁ piye piyadasi laja hevaṁ āhā —Jaugarh
   Devanaṁ priyo priyadrashi rajaahati —Shāhbāzgarhi.
2. Devanaṁ pi. . . Piyadasi Rājā evaṁ āh — Sixth inscription at Girnār
   Devanaṁ piye piyadasi lājā haivaṁ āhā — Kālsi.
   Devanaṁ piye piyadashi lājā hevaṁ āhā — Dhauli
   . . .naim piye piyadasi lājā hevaṁāhā — Jaugarh
3. Devanaṁ piyo priyadarshi raya evaṁ ahati — Shāhbāzgarhi
   Devanaṁ priye priyardrashi rājā evaṁ āhā — Mānsera
   (Devanaṁ priyaḥ priyadarshi Rājā evamāh)
4. Tadishe aja badhite devanaṁ priyas priyadrashish rano
   dhrimanushastiya anaraṁbhe prananaṁ — Shāhbāzgarhi IV inscription
   Tadise aja badhite devana priyasa priya-drashine rejine dramanu
   shastiya anaraṁbhe pranana — Mānsera
   (Tādrishamamajhvardhitaḥ devanaṁ priyasya priyadarshinah Ragyah dharmanushistayā analambhah prānāmām)
5. Yo tu eta desaṁ pi hupesanti so duktaṁ Kāsati — Girnār Vth inscription
   E chu heta desaṁ pi hāpyisanti se dukataṁ kachhati — Kālsi
   E —— heta desaṁ pi hāpyisati se dukataṁ Kachhti — Dhauli
   Yo chu ato —— pi hayeshati so Dukate Kashanti — Shāhbāzgarhi
   Ye chu atra desha pi hapeshati se dukata Kashati — Mānsera.
   (Ye tu atra deshmapi hāpyishyanti te dushkritaṁ Karishyanti).
6. Jans tu Kā uchāvachchhando uchāvachrājo — Girnār
   Jane chu uchāvuchachāndā uchāvuchachhande uchāvuchtāge — Kalsi
   Munisā cha uchāvuchachhandā uchāvuehtāg — Dhauli
   Munisā cha uchāvuchachhandā uchāvuchtāgā — Jaugarh
   Jane chu uchavuchāchhanda uchavuchrage — Shāhbāzgarhi
   Jane chu unchavuchāchhande uchavuchrage. — Mānsera
   (Janah tu uchuhavacha chhandaḥ uchchāvnchrāgah)

at Dhauli and Jaugarh. Might be due to an ommission at the time of scribing. In Dhauli and Jaugarh inscriptions, as cited in the comments given below on the foregoing page, the word मुनिसा has appeared for जनो or जने (People). मुनिसा is, infact, a Prākritā formation for Sanskrit word मनुष्य (mankind). In the inscriptions of Dhauli and Jaugarh only, letter 'च' has appeared for त and not elsewhere. However, in the fourth inscription at Kālsi and Dhauli, prākritā formation चिठितु[1] is obtained for Sanskrīt word तिष्ठन्तः (Staying). In the inscriptions of Shāhbāzgarhi and Mānsera, the form रिपि[2] is obtained for Sanskrīt word लिपि (The art of writing). Elsewhere, the form लिपि or लिपी is obtained.

In the aforesaid inscriptions, three suffixes म्हि, सि and ए are obtained to signify locative case. In the inscription at Girnār, the use of म्हि; in the inscriptions at Kālsi and Dhauli, the use of सि and in the inscriptions at Shāhbāzgarhi and Mānsera, the use of ए is found to denote locative case. For example, in the fourth inscription, for Sanskrit word शीले in locative case, the form सीलम्हि[3] at Girnār; सिलसि[4] in the inscription at Kālsi; सीलसि[5] at Dhauli and 'शिले' in Shāhbāzgarhi[6] and Mānsera[7] inscriptions are obtained.

Languages of Inscriptions : Certain Generalised Facts

Barring the inscriptions of North-West regions, normally dental letter स has appeared in place of palatal letter श and cerebral ष. In stone inscription at Kālsi, the use of both palatal letter श and cerebral ष is also found. In initial nine inscriptions (out of fourteen) at Kālsi, the use of only dental letter स is obtained in place of palatal letter श and cerebral letter ष but in the remaining inscriptions at Kālsi the use of

---

1. Dhamsi silsi chā chithitu dhamaṁ anusāsi-santi — Kālsi
Dhamsi Sīlsi cha chithitu Dhamaṁ anusasi-santi – Dhaulā
(Dharme Shīle cha tishttantah Dharmaṁ anushāsishyomti).
2. (a) Yam dhramdipi devan priyasa——raño likhpitu.
—Shāhbāzgarhi, First inscription
Ayi dramdipi (de) Van (pri) Yena (Priya) द्र (shin) rana (li) Khapit. — Mānsera
(Iyaṁ dharmalipih devānaṁ priyeṇa priyadarshinā Rājā lekhitā)
(b) Etaye athye ayain dhramdipi dipista
Etaye adhrye ayi dhramdipi likhit — Mānsera.
(Etasmai arthaya iyaṁ dharmalipih likhita . . . .)
(c) Ayo dharmdipi devanaṁ priyena prishma dipapito.
— Shāhbāzgarhi, 14th inscription
(Iyaṁ Dharmalipih devānāṁ priyena priyadarshinā Rāgyā lekhitā).
3. . . . . . Dhamamhi Silmihi tistanto dhamani anusasisanti — Girnār fourth inscription.
4. Dhamsi silsi cha chithitu dhamam anusāsisanti — Kālsi.
5. Dhama (si) Silasi cha (Chithi) tu dhamaṁ anusāsisanti — Dhauli
6. Dhrame shile cha tistiti dhramaṁ anushahhishanti —Shāhbāzgarhi
7. Dharme shile cha tistitu dhramani anushashishanti —Mānsera
(Dharme Shile cha tishthantah dharmamanushasishyanti).

mostly cerebral letter ष and at certain places palatal letter श is found.

For instance, the form पियदषी for Sanskrīt word प्रियदर्शी (An epithet of King Ashōkā); यषो[1] for Sanskrīt word यश: (glory, renown); धमसुसुषा for Sanskrīt word धर्म-शुश्रुषा (Service to the religion); सुसुषातु[2] for Sanskrīt word शुश्रुषताम्, अप-पलाषवे for Sanskrīt word अपपरिस्रव: (not flowing); षव[3] for Sanskrīt word सर्वम् (whole, entire, complete); 'षियातिति' for 'स्यात्', इति[4] ऐषे[5] for Sanskrīt word एषा: (Desirable); 'उषुटेन'[6] for Sanskrīt word 'उशता' (Injurious talk); 'हेडिषे' for Sanskrīt word 'ईदृशम्' (of this kind); 'आदिषं'[7] for Sanskrīt word 'यादृशम्' (of which sort or nature); धमषविभागे for Sanskrīt word 'धर्म संविभाग:' (Religious branch); 'धमंषबधे'[8] for Sanskrīt word 'धर्म सम्बन्ध' (To be connected with religion); 'षम्या पटिपति' for Sanskrīt word 'सम्यक् प्रतिपत्ति' (Thorough knowledge or perception); 'षुषुषा' for Sanskrīt word 'शुश्रुषा' (service); 'षंश्रुत'[9] for Sanskrīt word 'संस्तुत' (praised, eulogized); 'षवामिक्येन'[10] for Sanskrīt word 'स्वामिना' (ownership, sovereignty); शे[11] for Sanskrīt word 'स:' (Together with, along with); 'पशवति'[12] for Sanskrīt word 'प्रसूते' (Brought forth); 'पाषंडनि'[13] for Sanskrīt word 'पाषण्डान्' (unbelievers); 'शालवढ़ि' for Sanskrīt word 'सारवृद्धि' (Increase in excellence); 'शिया' for Sanskrīt word 'स्यात' (perhaps, perchance); 'शव पाशंडानं'[14] for Sanskrīt word 'सर्व पाषण्डानाम्' (all hypocrisies).

---

1. Devānaṁ piya piyadashi lājā yasho vā Kiti vā na mahāthāvahā manati.
(Devanaṁ priyah priyadarshi Rājā yashaḥ vā Kirti vā na mahāithvahaṁ manyate.
—Tenth inscription

2. Dhainsusushā susushātu me to Dhaṁvatani vā anuvidhīyatuti.
(Dharmashushrushāṁ shushrustutāṁ mam iti dharmavritmaṇuvidhitamiti
—Tenth inscription

3. . . . . . Ta shavaṁ paltikyaye vā 1
(. . . . . Tata sarvaṁ partrikaya eva . . . . .) —Tenth inscription

4. Kiti Sakle apaplāshve shiyātiti
(Kimti Sakalah apaparisravuh Syat iti)
— Tenth inscription.

5. Eshe chu palinee e apunai
(Esha tu parisravah yat apunyam) — Tenth inscription

6. Ushutena va anata ageuā palakamina shavṁ palitiditu
(——ushta va anyatra aprayat parakrimat sarva paritajya) — Tenth inscription

7. Nathi hedive dāne ādishani dhamshambandhe . . . .
(Nāsti īdrashaṁ dānaṁ yādrashani Dharmadānaṁ) — Eleventh inscriptions

8. Dhamshan vibhāge dhamsambandhe.
(Dharma Samvibhāgah Dharma Sambandaḥ vā) — Eleventh inscription.

9. Mitshainthutnātikyānani Sawanbainbhnāndāne
(. . . . . Mitrasanstut gyatikānām Shramaṇa Brahmaṇani danaṁ) —XI inscription

10. Pitinā pi pute pi bhātinā pi shavāmikyena pi
(Pitrāpi putraināpi bhrātrāpi swaṁena pi). —XI inscription

11. She tathākalant hidlokikye cha āladhahoti. (Sa tathā Kurvan ehlaukikain cha Arādha bhavuti
—XI inscription.

12. . . . . . Palata cha ananta puna pashvati tena Dhamadānenā
(Paratra cha Anantain punyain prasute teur dharmadānena) —XI inscription

13. Devānā piya piyadashi lājā shavā pashandini.
(Devanam priyah priyadarshi Rājā Sarvān Pākhandān . . . . . 1) —XII inscription

14. . . . . . Atha Kita Shalvadhi shiyā ti shavpāshandānaṁ.
(Yatha Kimti Sārvridhih Syāt Sarva pākhandanaṁ) —XII inscription

'Tasha'[1] for Sanskrit word 'तस्य' (belonging to it — genitive case); 'अपकलनशि' for Sanskrit word 'अप्रकरण' (Not the main or principal topic); 'तशि' for Sanskrit word 'तस्मिन' (amongst whom—locative case—singular number); 'पकलनशि'[2] for Sanskrit word प्रकरण (A head or subject of treatment); 'षाधु' for Sanskrit word 'साधु' (A good or virtuous person); 'अंनमनषा'[3] for Sanskrit word 'अन्योन्यस्य' (of one another—Dative case); 'षुनेयु' for Sanskrit word 'श्रृणयुः' (To destroy, to hurt or to goad); 'षषुषेयु' for Sanskrit word 'शुश्रुषेरन्' (Desire to serve); 'देवानं पियषा' for Sanskrit word 'देवानाम प्रियस्य' (for those loved by gods — in dative case); 'अठवषाभिसि-तषा'[4] for Sanskrit word 'अष्टवर्षाभिषिक्तस्य' (After eight years of the coronation of emperor Ashoka); 'पानषतषहशे'[5] for Sanskrit word 'प्राणशतसहस्त्रम्' (living for thousands of years); 'लधेषु'[6] for Sanskrit word 'लब्धेषु' (obtained or attained perfection — in locative case); 'धर्मानुषिधि'[7] for Sanskrit word 'धर्मानुशिष्टि' (Teaching of religious knowledge); 'षं' for Sanskrit word 'तत्' (Extended, spread; covered over); 'अनुषये' for Sanskrit word 'अनुशयः' (Regret, sorrow, repentance); जनषा[8] for Sanskrit word 'जनस्' (A living person—in dative case); 'वषति'[9] for Sanskrit word 'वसन्ति' (They live); 'येशु'[10] for Sanskrit word 'येषु' (To attempt). 'मितषंश्रुतषहायनायतिकेषु' for Sanskrit word 'मित्रसंस्तुत-सहायज्ञातिकेषु' (To render assistance as per recommendation and praise of the friend); 'दाषमतकषि'[11] for Sanskrit word 'दासमृतकेषु' (Dead servant in locative case); तेषं[12] for Sanskrit word तेषाम् (Them-in genitive case—plural number);

---

1. Tasha chu iyaṁ mule a vachguti
   (Tasyain tu idani nūlam ya vachagupti) —12th inscription
2. . . . . . Kiti ta atapāshande puja palapashaudrgalha va no shayā apakalanashi. Lahkā vā shiyā tāshi tashi pakalnashi.
   (. . . . . Kimtiātmapāshānde pūjā parpāshandagarhā vā na syāt aprakarne. Laghuta vā syat tasmin tasmin prakarne) —12th inscription.
3. Samvāye va Sādhu Kiti anamanshā dhamami shyneyu chā shashuheyu chā ti. Hāvvani hi devānāni piyashā ichha . . . . .
   (Samvāya eva Sādhuh, Kimati anyonasya dharmashranusuh cha shushrusheran cha iti. Evam hi devanani priyasb Dehcttā. —12th inscription.
4. Athavasābhisitāshā devānoṁ piyash piyadashinc lājine . . . . . .
   (Ashtavashābhishiktasya devānāṁ priyasya priyadarshinaḥ Rāgyaḥ) —XIII inscription
5. Diyadhamāte pānshatshahshe ye tafā apavradhe. —XIII inscription
   Dvardhamātraṁ prānshatsahasraṁ yat tataḥ apavijudhaṁ.
6. Tatā pachhā adhunā ladheshu Kalisgoshu tivre
   (Tatah pashchāt adhunā labhadheshu Kaligeshu tivram. —XIII inscription
7. Dhamvāyedham Kāmana dhamānushath chā devānāni piyashā
   (Dharmapālanani dharmakāmatā dharmānushishtih cha devanani priyasya. — XIII inscription
8. Tatā vadhaṁ vā malne vā apavahe vā janashā . . . . .
   (Tatra Vadhaḥ vāmarṇaṁ vā apvāhāḥ vā janasya) —XIII inscription
9. Vashati bambhnā vā sham (nā) va . . . (Vasanti Brahmṇāḥ vā shaṁ nā vā —)
   — XIII inscription
10. Yeshu Vihitā esha agabhut shnsushā . . .
    (Yeshu Vihitā eshā agrayabhutshushrushā . . .) — XIII inscription
11. Mitrashaṁthutashāyamātikeshu Dāshmatakashi sham yāpathipati
    (Mitra Sanstut sahāygyāti keshu dasmrit Keshu Samyaka prātipatti) — XIII inscription
12. Teshaṁ tatā hoti upghāte vā badhe vā
    (Teshāṁ tatra bhavati upghātah vā vadhah vā) — XIII inscription.

'षिनेहे' for 'स्नेह:' (Affection, love); 'वियषने' for Sanskrīt word व्यसनं'[1] (A calamity, distress, disaster); 'षिमने[2] for Sanskrit word 'श्रमणेषु' (amongst religious mendicants-in locative case); 'मनुषानं' for Sanskrit word 'मनुष्याणां' (Human beings—in plural number); 'एकतलषि' for Sanskrit word 'एकतरस्मिन' (A mighty person); 'पषादे[3] for Sanskrit word 'प्रसाद:', (Favour, Kindness) : 'षतेभागे' for Sanskrīt word 'शतभाग:' (Hundred pieces); 'षहसभागे[4] for Sanskrit word 'सहस्रभाग:' (A thousand pieces or fractions); 'षयम' for Sanskrit word 'सयंमम्' (Practising self-denial or self control); 'षमचालियं[5] for Sanskrit word 'समचर्या' (Virtuous Conduct). 'आलिक्यषुदहो'[6] for Sanskrit word 'आलिकसुन्दर:' (attractive forehead); 'विशवषि' for Sanskrit word 'विषवाज्रिषु' (Strong poison); 'नामपतिषु[7] for Sanskrit word 'नामपांक्तिषु' (Name of the line or row); 'भोजपितिनिक्येषु' For Sanskrit word 'भोजप्रितिनिकेषुं; 'षवता', for Sanskrit word 'सर्वत्र' (In all places); 'Dhamānuvathi'[8] for Sanskrit word 'धर्मानुशिष्टि' (Religious instructions); 'मनिषु'[9] for Sanskrit word 'मन्येरन' (A state of agitated mind); 'षयकषि' for Sanskrit word 'शराकार्षिण' (Fascination for archery); विजयाषि[10]' for Sanskrit word 'विजये' (Act of conquest) 'लेखपेशामि'[11] for Sanskrit word लेखयिष्यामि' (Shall be writing); 'तषा' for Sanskrit word 'तस्य' (To denote a third person in dative case);' अथषा for Sanskrit word 'अर्थस्य' (Meaning or import — in dative case); 'षिया' for Sanskrit word 'स्यात्' (Perhaps, perchance); 'षंखेपेकालनं'[12] for Sanskrit

---

1. Sinehe avipahine etānaṁ mitashamthut-shahāyanātikya vishna.——
   (. . . स्नेह अविप्रहीण: एतेषां मित्र संस्तुत सहाय ज्ञातिका व्यसनं.) —XIII inscription
2. Yatānathi ime nikāya Ānantā yenesha bahmne chā shamne chā . . .
   (Yatra na santi ime nikāyā anantah Brahmaneshu cha shramneshn cha) — XIII inscription
3. Yatā nathi manushānaṁ ekatalashi pi pāshdashi nau nāmpashāde.
   (Yatra nāste manushyānāmaika tarasmina api pāshaṇḍe nām prasādaḥ) — XIII inscription
4. Tata shate bhāge vā shahashbhāge vā aj Gulumati vā devānam piyashā
   (Tatah Shatabhagah va sahrabhāgah vā gurumat eva devānam priyasya.) —XIII inscription
5. . . . Shayaṁ shamchaliyaṁ madavati (Sayamaṁ Samcharyā mārdavamiti) — XIII inscription
6. Alikyashndale namnichaṁ chauda pandiya avaṁ tambpaniya.
   (. . . Aliksundrah nām nīchā Chauḍah Pāndyā Yavat tāmraparṁiyā. —XIII inscription.
7. Vishavashi Yonkambojesher namke nampantishu ——
   (Nishvajrishu Yavan kāmboje namkesh Nampauktishu ——) —XIII inscription.
8. Bhojpitinikyeshu adhpaldeshu shavatā dēvānaṁ piyasha dhamānuvath anuvatanti
   (Bhojapritinikeshu Āndhrapulindesh Sarvatra Devānām priyasya dharmānushishti manuvartant. —XIII inscription
9. . . . Navaṁ Vijayama Vijyantviya manishu
   (Nawam Vijayam ma vijtevani manyeran) —XIII inscription
10. Shayakavi no Vijayashi Khanti Chalhudandata chā lochetu
    (Sharākarshinah Vijaya Ksānti cha gajhudandatain cha rochyantāṁ) —XIII inscription
11. Bahu cha likhite lekhapeshami chaiva nikyaṁ.
    (Bahu cha likhitaṁ lekhyishyami chawa Nityaṁ) XII inscription
12. Shankheye Kālnaṁ vā Ālochyitu lipikalapatādhena.
    (Sankshepkaranam Va Ālochayatu lipikaraparadhena) —XIV inscription.

word 'संक्षेपकारण' (Brief summary of the grounds); have appeared in Prākritas.

How the situation occurred for an unrestricted use of letters 'ष' and 'श', needs full consideration. It is not found in inscriptions at other places. May be due to flaw in writing. The frequent use of letters 'श' and 'ष' found in inscriptions at Kālsi, is neither systematic nor regulated. These letters do not appear to have consistency with the letters 'श' and 'ष' used in Sanskrit language. It is also explicit from the above extracts that in certain cases both palatal letter 'श' and cerebral letter 'ष' have appeared in one and the same word.

Presumably, those who used the dialect which was the medium of speech in the adjoining area of Kālsi, situated in the vicinity of Himalyan region, near Mussorrie during the life time of emperor Ashōkā, had the tendency to use the letter 'ष' too frequently; comparatively made lesser use of palatal letter 'श' and only nominal or rare use of dental letter 'स'. It is, therefore, logical to believe that emperor Ashōkā might have also got inscribed the letters 'श' and 'ष' in his inscriptions at Kālsi too frequently. The reason could also be found for use of both palatal letter 'श' and cerebral letter 'ष' at different places in one and the same word. It is quite possible that there might have been certain words in the dialect spoken in and around Kālsi, which might be containing both cerebral letter 'ष' and palatal letter 'श'. The argument that it could be due to a flaw in writing is somewhat an extraneous ground which does not appeal to the mind.

There is one more characteristic in the inscriptions of Kālsi and Toprā. Therein the guttural letters 'क' and 'ग' have adopted the form of palatal consonant. This tendency is noticed repeatedly so far as the guttural letter 'क' is concerned. Turning into a palatal consonant means that letters 'क' and 'ग' get joined with letter 'य'. For instance, forms like 'अलिक्य' for 'अलि' (A Black bee); 'कलिंग्य' for 'कलिंग (A region lying to the south of Orissa); 'नातिक्य' for 'ज्ञातिक' (A wise man); 'पालतिक्य' for 'पारत्रिक' (Belonging to the next world; useful in the future life) etc. are obtained in stone inscriptions at Kālsi. Similar illustrations are there in the inscriptions of Toprā as well.

Why the Use of Palatal Letter 'श' is Missing in the Inscriptions of Eastern Region? The inscriptions in Eastern parts were got inscribed by emperor Ashōkā in the official language of Māgadha dynasty without effecting any changes in it, since it was easily understood by the people of eastern regions. It has also been discussed above that official language of Ashoka's dynasty was Māgadhi. In Māgadhi, the use of only palatal 'श' was found in place of cerebral letter 'ष' palatal letter 'श' and dental letter 'स'. It is not because of any change in the modern form of Māgadhi but in the ancient form of Māgadhi also, only palatal 'श' represented all the three 'ष', 'श' and 'स'. This fact is corroborated by the inscription[1] found at

1. Shutnuk nām Devadashikya Tam Kamyitha balansheya Devadine nām lupdakhe.

Jogimārā-Rāmgarh. Although, it is a small inscription, yet it is significant from linguistic viewpoint. It is almost contemporary to the life-time of emperor Ashōkā. All the characteristics of Māgadhi Prākrita are obtained from it. The use of letter 'ल' is found for letter 'र' which is the main characteristic of Māgadhi Prākrita. The letter 'क' has turned into a palatal consonant, after it is joined with letter 'य'. The noun ending with vowel 'अ' in nominative case, singular number, has been replaced by vowel 'ए' at the end in Māgadhi Prākrita. From the Jogimara inscription, it is explicit that letter 'श' has appeared for both palatal letter 'श' and dental letter 'स' which is the chief characteristic of Māgadhi Prākrita.

There has been an obvious tendency of using palatal letter 'श' only in Māgadhi Prākrita. The dramatic plays of Ashwaghosh fully substantiate this tendency. According to Prof. Luders, the language of the plays, written by Ashwaghosh, is ancient form of Māgadhi.

However, the fact that the use of palatal letter 'श' is almost missing from all the inscriptions of emperor Ashōkā, installed in eastern territories, is quite amazing. In all the inscriptions of eastern regions, the use of dental letter 'स' is found for palatal letter 'श' also. Since the refined shape of Māgadhi Prākrita formed the basis for adoption as official language of Ashōkā's empire, the main features of Māgadhi Prākrita ought to have been adopted in it. Accordingly, the use of palatal letter 'श' only ought to have been made to represent palatal letter 'श' cerebral letter 'ष' and dental letter 'स'. There should be a logical explanation for it. According to Dr. Suniti Kumar Chatterjee, it appears that the frequent use of palatal letter 'श', although a chief characteristic of Māgadhi Prākrita, might have been considered uncivil or unfit to be used by a civilized society. It appears that, it might have been treated as part of the language spoken by rural-based public. Since dental letter 'स' is found to have been commonly used in all other prākrita dialects, it might have been considered necessary to use letter 'स' as an essential part of a refined language. Thus, it is possible that the use of palatal letter 'श' might have been avoided in the inscriptions of eastern region. Although, there is no specific standard to judge the civility or uncivility of a consonant, yet the assumption of Dr.Chatterjee also does not appear to be baseless. The fact remains that in the dramatic plays, accomplished later on, the use of Prākrita dialects was prescribed according to the social status of the characters. The use of Māgadhi Prākrita was not recommended for the characters of higher status. The plays, written by Ashwaghosh, are considered oldest as compared to others. A villain character of his play, named 'Dushta' (A wicked person) delivers his dialogues in Māgadhi Prākrita. It is true that Ashwaghosh had written his plays after three to four centuries from the period of inscriptions of emperor Ashōkā and that of Jogimāra-Ramgarh inscription, yet they were worth comparison. No polished or literary language could give up its old standard so soon. A slight refection of its old standard continues for some time. The Māgadhi dialect used by Ashwaghosh in his plays, very much conforms with the language of inscription, installed at Jogimāra-Ramagarh. While delivering his dialogus in Māgadhi Prākrita, the Villain, named

Dushṭa, of the Ashwaghosh play, speaks only palatal 'श' to represent both dental letter 'स' and palatal letter 'श'. Letter 'ल' has been used for letter 'र'. The words ending in vowel 'a' in nominative case, singular number, have been suffixed with vowel 'e' in place of vowel 'a', when written in Māgadhi Prākrita. These are some of the characteristics of old Māgadhi Prākrita which are obtained in the dramatic plays of Ashwaghosh. Of course, Māgadhi used by Ashwaghosh in his plays, has rare similarity with its modern shape, which amply confirms that Māgadhi used by Ashwaghosh in his plays conformed with the ancient form of Māgadhi Prākrita.

Prākrita dialects prescribed by Achārya Bharat in his dramatic compositions signify that those employed in the women's apartments of Royal house-holds; diggers of tunnels; burglars; liquor-dealers, brewers; care-takers of horse stables should converse in Māgadhi dialect in a play. In case, the hero of a dramatic play is confronted with a danger, he is free to speak Māgadhi in order to save his skin and keep his indentity a secret.[1]

As directed by Achārya Bharat, the characters who are required to speak in Māgadhi Prākrita, obviously, belong to the lower strata of the society. The hero belongs to a noble and aristocratic family. In the hour of distress, he needs to conceal his identity. So it is essential for him to hid himself and converse in the dialect, generally used by the lowest in position, which would enable him to save his life and avoid discernment. The above-noted facts lend support to the above version of Dr. Chatterjee. It does not appear merely a falacy that in old days, the scholars might have accommodated the feeling of vulgarity, absence of pleasure or unacceptability towards Māgadhi Prākrita or its constituent part, dealing with unrestricted use of palatal letter 'श'. The arrangement regarding use of Prākrita diaclects by different characters in the plays of Ashwaghosh and use of respective Prākrita, as prescribed by Achārya Bharat, by each character in his dramatic compositions are indicative to this effect.

There is also a probability that the low standard of Māgadhi Prākrita might have been pre-imagined because of frequent use of palatal letter 'श' in it. Even now, if the beauty or ugliness in pronunciation of dental letter 'स' and palatal letter ''श' are considered, frequent utterance of palatal letter 'श' will be found somewhat unpleasant. Another reason may be that the people might be accustomed to the use of letter 'स' Thus, the explanation of Dr. Chattejee does provide an answer to the omission of palatal letter 'श' in the inscriptions of eastern regions.

In the inscriptions of eastern areas, there is abundant use of letter 'क'. Its use is found still greater in stone inscriptions of Kālsi and Toprā.

In the joint consonants, letter 'य' appearing after letters 'त' and 'व' turns into letters 'इय' in Prākritas. For example, in the aforesaid fourteen inscriptions, for Sanskrit word 'प्रहोतव्य:' (pertaining to a yagna to be performed by a household),

---

1. Māgadhi tu narendraṇāmantaḥ purniwasinām. —*Natya-Shāstra*, 17, 50
Surangākhavkādinām Shundakārāshuar akshinaṁ,
Vyasne nāyakānaṁ Syādātmarakshasu Māgadhi —*Natya-Shāstra*, 17, 56

the Prākrita formation in Kālsi inscriptions is 'पजोहितवये'. The same is obtained in the inscriptions at Jaugarh. In Mānsera inscriptions, it is found as 'प्रयुहोतविये'. These formations are not found in Girnār and Shāhbāzgarhi inscriptions. The form 'प्रजूहितइवं' is obtained in Girnār inscriptions for which no explanation is available. The form 'प्रयुहोतवे' appears in inscriptions at Shāhbāzgarhi, which almost conforms with the Sanskrīt word. In the same inscription, for Sanskrīt word 'कर्त्तव्य:' (What ought to be done, an obligation) forms 'कटविये' at Kālsi; the same 'कटविये' at Jaugarh and 'कटविय' in the inscription at Mānsera are obtained.

Amongst aforesaid fourteen inscriptions, in the third inscription, we find the use of form 'अपवियाता' at Kālsi; अपवियति' at Dhauli for Sanskrīt word 'अल्पव्ययता' (economical spending). That is to say the tradition of conversion of letter 'य' appearing in joint consonants after the letters 'त' and 'व' into 'इय' is found in the said inscriptions. However, the same tradition is not found in the inscriptions at Girnār, Mānsera and Shāhbāzgarhi. Prākrita form 'अपव्ययता' has appeared in the inscription at Girnār which shows that in the compound word, the latter portion 'व्ययता' has remained intact. Only the initial component 'अल्प' has changed into 'अप'. In Shāhbāzgarhi and Mānsera inscriptions, the Prākrita formation 'अपवयत' is found. In the first small inscription at Māski, Prākrita forms 'दखतविये' for Sanskrit word 'द्रष्टव्यम्' (Fit to be seen) and 'वतविया' for Sanskrit word 'वक्तव्य' (To be spoken about) are obtained.[1]

In joint consonants, the letter 'व' following the preceding consonant, will turn in 'उव'. In the first stone inscription, for Sanskrīt word 'द्वौ' (Two) Prākrita formations 'दुवे' in inscriptions at Kālsi, Jaugarh and Mānsera and 'दुवि at Shāhbāzgarhi have appeared. It is true that the letter 'व' has converted into 'उव' in all these inscriptions but the vowels, immediately following the letter 'व' differ, which was not an improbability in the context of the said inscriptions, since no consistency or regularity has been maintained completely in the said inscriptions.

In the fourth inscription, the Sanskrit word 'द्वादश' (twelfth), forming part of compound pada 'द्वादशवर्षाभिक्तेन,' the Prākrita formations are 'दुवाडस at Kālsi; 'दुवादस' at Dhauli and दुवदश' at Mānsera. The formation of the said Sanskrit word is, however, not explicit in the fourth inscription at Shāhbāzgarhi. The form 'द्वादस' is found in the fourth inscription at Girnār. For Sanskrit word 'द्वौ' we find no change in the first inscription at Girnār. That is to say, the tendency of conversion of letter 'व' in 'उव', found in the inscriptions of all other places, is not obtained at Girnār. Prākrita formations of above-noted two Sanskrit words in Girnār inscriptions, are either the same or very much resembling them. It appears that the language of Girnār inscriptions is on the pattern of Shorseni Prākrita since

1. Na haivaṁ dakhitviye udālke va ima adhi gadaiyyāti. Khudkā chā udālke cha vativya (Na evani drashtavyasudārā eva ima madhigachchheyuh it, Chhudrakāḥ cha udānkāh cha Vaktavyah.
— Māski, 1st Small inscription

Girnār formed part of the area where Shorseni Prākrita was the medium of speech and conversation. Sorseni Prākrita, having proximity with Sanskrīt language, several of its formations are like those of Sanskrīt.

In the ninth inscription, for Sanskrīt word 'स्वामिकेन' (A Lord or master in instrumental case), the formations are 'सुविमिकेना' at Kālsi; सुवामिकेन' at Dhauli and Jaugarh; At Girnār, the form 'स्वामिकेन' has appeared which conforms with that of Sanskrīt. Prākrita formation 'स्पमिकेन' is obtained in the ninth inscriptions of both Shāhbāzgarhi and Mānsera. Probably, it could be an error of scribing also in these two inscriptions.

In the first, of seven pillar inscriptions, the form 'सुवे'[1], has appeared for Sanskrit word 'स्वस्मिन' (A word of benediction) in almost all the pillar inscriptions at Toprā, Allahabād; Laudiyā Ararāj and Laudiyā Nandangarh. The line, containing the said word, is not conspicuous in the pillar inscriptions of Meerut and Rāmpurvā.

The position in regard to fourth pillar inscription is different. The formation in Prākrita 'अस्वथे'[2] is obtained for Sanskrit word स्वस्था', (Hale and hearty). It is, no doubt, a strange position. Why it was so, could not be readily explained. Would it be irrelevant to believe that at places, where the said pillar inscriptions were got inscribed, dual process of pronunciation might be in practice. According to one of these styles, there might be a tradition to add letter 'अ' initially to each word so as to pronounce it conveniently. However, nothing could be said for definite. It is only an idea conceived in the mind.

Out of three inscriptions of emperor Ashōkā on the walls of the caves, the Prākrita form 'दुवाडस'[3] has appeared for Sanskrit word 'द्वादस' (Twelfth) on the first and second cave inscriptions. However, this rule does not seem to be applying to component 'त्व' forming part of a word. We find that the component 'त्व' of a Sanskrit word is converted to 'त्त' in Prākrita. Such as 'चत्वारि' (Forty) 'चत्तालि' We also find components 'स्म' and 'ष्म' of Sanskrit words changed to 'फ' in the said

---

1. Dhamāpekhā dhamkāmatā chā suve suve Vadhitā — Topra, Ist pillar inscription
Dhamāpekhā dhamakāmtā cha suve suve Vadhita — Allahabad, 1st pillar inscription
Dhamāpekha Dhamakāmtā cha suve suve Vadhitā — Laudiyā Arraj, 1st pillar inscription.
Dhamāpekha dhamakāmtā cha suve suve Vadhita — Laudiya Nandangarh 1st pillar inscription
(. . . Dharmāpekṣā Dharmakāmtā cha Swasmin Swasmina Vardhita . . .)
2. Kimti lajuka aswatha abhita Kammani pavatyevu — —Topra, fourth pillar inscription.
Kimti lajuka aswatha abhita Kammani pavatyevu
—Laudiya Arrāj, IV pillar inscription
Kimti lajuka aswatha abhita Kammani pavahyevu
—Laudiya-Nandangarh, IV pillar inscription
(. . . Kimita Rajjukāh Swasthah abhita Karmam Pravartayeyuh)—
3. Lājinā piyadasinā duvādash Vasạbhisitena) iyam (nigo) ha Kubha di (nā) ā (ji) vikehi
(Raja Priyadarshinā dwadashvarshābhisitenā iyam nyagrodh-guha datta ājivakebhyah)
— Ist cave inscription
Lājina piyadasinā duvādasabhisitenā iyam Kubhā Khaltik pavatasi dinā (ā) jivikehi
(Rāja priyadarshinā dwadasavarshabhishiktena iyam guhā Khaltika parvate datta ājivakebhyaḥ)
— IInd cave inscription.

two cave inscriptions. For example— in the second, inscription of Kalinga, Prākrita form 'तुफेसु'[1] has appeared for Sanskrit word 'युष्मासु' (Second personal pronoun in locative case, plural number); 'अफेसु'[2] for 'अस्मासु'; 'अफाक'[3] for Sanskrit word 'अस्माकम्' (First personal pronoun in ablative case, plural number); 'तुफेनि' and 'तुफे[4] for Sanskrit word 'युष्मान् (Second personal pronoun in accusative case, plural number); and in the first inscription at Kalinga, prākrita form 'तुफेहि'[5] has appeared for Sanskrit word 'युष्मामाभि:' (Second personal pronoun, in instrumental case, plural number).

In small pillar inscription at Sārnāth, Prākrita form 'तुफाक'[6] has appeared for Sanskrit word 'युस्माकम्' (Second personal pronoun, genitive case, plural number). We come across another point, so far as Sārnāth inscription is concerned. Therein, Prākrita form 'तुफे' is obtained for the component 'यूयम्' of Sanskrit word as shown in the note given below. It indicates that the component 'स्म' or 'ष्म' may not be present in a Sanskrit word but they appear to form part of it, there also the tendency of its conversion in letter 'फ' is found.

Although, in the locative case, singular number, the letter 'स्म' is also found in the termination 'स्मिन' yet in Prākrita formation, it does not convert into letter 'फ'. Excluding Girnār, we find that the termination 'सि' has been affixed in Prākrita form in place of 'स्मिन' as in Sanskrit word. For example, in the first small inscription at Brahmagiri, we find Prākrita formation as 'जबूदीपसि'[7]. Similarly, at Bhābru, we find Prākrita forms 'बुद्धसि' 'धंमसि' 'Sanghsi'[8]; in the pillar inscription

---

1. Etasa athasa aṁ tūfesu anus (thi) — Jaugarh
   Etasi uthasi aṁ tufe (su)— Dhauli
   (. . . Etasya arthasya yat yushmāsu anushisti)
2. Siyā antanaṁ avijitānaṁ Kī Chhade su lājā afesu ti — Jaugarh
   Siya antanaṁ avijitanaṁ Kim Chhand sulāj (a) fase — 1-Dhauli
   (Sthāt Antānamvijitanaṁ Kim Chhandaḥ asau Rāja Asmāsu iti)
3. Heva pāpunevū ti Khamisati nedevānam piye afākam —1
   (Evaṁ cha prāpnuyuh iti Ksamishyate naḥ Devānaṁ priyaḥ asmākṁ —1
4. Etāye cha athāye hakaṁ tufeni anusāsūmi — Jaugarh
   Etasi Athasi hakaṁ anusāsāmi tufe—Dhauli
   (Etasmai Cha Arthāya ahaṁ yushman anusāsāmi) —II inscription at Kalinga
5. Tata tufehi ichhitaye kinti majhaṁ patipātyema — Jaugarh
   Tata ichhitviya tufehi Kinti majhaṁ patipādyema ti — Dhauli
   (Tataḥ eshṭavyaṁ yushmābhi Kimti madhyam pratipādyema ti)
   — 1st inscription at Kalinga
6. Āvatke cha tufākaṁ āhāle savata Vivāsyath tufe etena Viyanjnena.
   (Yāvat Cha Ynshmākaṁ Māhāraḥ sarvatra Vivāyat yuyametena Vyanjnena)
   —Small pillar inscription at Sārnāth.
7. Iminā chu Kālena amisā samānā munisa Jambudipsi.
   (Amunā tu Kālena amrishā samānāh manushyāh Jambudwipe mrikhā deveḥ)
   —Brahmgiri; Ist small inscription
8. Vidita Ve bhante āwatke hamā Budhsi dhamsi Sanghsiti galve cha pasāde cha.
   (Viditaṁ Vo bhadantāḥyawat asmākaṁ Budhe dharme Sanghe it Gauravaṁ cha prasādaḥ Cha.

at Sānchi, we find the Prākrita form 'अनाससि'[1]. Amidst 14 inscriptions, we find in the first inscription at Kālsi, Jaugarh, Shāhbāzgarhi and Mānsera that Prākrit form 'महानससि'[2] has appeared while in the seventh pillar inscription at Topra (near Delhi), the uses of 'दानविसगसि' 'सवासि' and 'आलोधनसि'[3] are obtained.

In the second inscription (out of aforesaid 14 inscriptions) of Kālinga, we find Prākrita formations—'खनसि'[4] at Dhauli and 'खने'[5] at Jaugarh for sanskrit word 'क्षणे' (An instant or moment equal to 1/5th of a second). Similarly, in the 12th inscription, we find Prākrita formations 'पकलनसि'[6] at Kālsi; 'प्रकरणे'[7] at Shāhbāzgarhi and 'पकरणसि'[8] at Mānsera. Thus the use of termination 'ए' is also found here and there in locative case, singular number in the said inscriptions.

In the inscription at Girnār, the termination 'म्हि' has been suffixed to denote locative case, singular number. At certain places, the letter 'म्' has turned in nasal sound, marked by a dot above the line ( ) while letter 'हि' has remained intact. Just as 'एकतरम्हि'[9] 'धमम्हि', 'सीलाम्हि'[10] 'महानसहि'[11] 'विजतहि'[12]; are a few of the instances. The use of termination 'ए' is also found suffixed in a few cases to

---

1. Ye Sanghaṁ mokhati bhikhu vā bhikhuni vā audātāni dusāni sananghāpayitu anāsasi visyetviye. (Yaḥ Sanghaṁ bhakṣyati bhikṣu vā bhiksuṇi vā avadātāni dūshyāni saṁnidhāpya anāyāse avāsayitavyaḥ)
2. Pule mahānsasi devānaṁ piyasā priyadasitā lajine anudivasaṁ bahuni pansaṁasāṁi albhiyisu1 — Kālsi
   Puluvaṁ mahānsasi devānaṁ priyas piyadasine tajine anudivasaṁ bāhuni pansatsahasāni ālbhiyisu—1 — Jaugarh
   Pur mahansasi devanaṁ piyas priyadrishasa raö anudivaso bahuṁ praṇashatsahasaini aribhiyisu — Shāhbāzgarhi.
   Pur mahansasi devanaṁ pi. . . sa. . . priya. . . shisa rajine anudivaḥ bāhuni panashatsahasāiṁ ar-su-1 — Mānsera
   (Pura mahanase devanāṁ priyasya priyadarshinah Rajah anudivasaṁ bahuni pranshatsahasrāṁ ālpsat . . . 1)
3. Ete Cha ane cha bahukā mukhā danvisagasi viyapata se mam Chaiva devinam cha Savasi Cha me ālodhansi—1
4. Iyaṁ Cha lipi . . . Khansi antlā pi tisena ekena pi sotiviye 1
5. Iyaṁ Cha lipi . . . Khane antrā pi tisena ekena pi sotiviye. (Iyaṁ cha lipi Ksane antrā api Tishyena ekena api shrotavyā).
6. Lahakā vā shiyā tashi tashi pakalnashi.
7. Lahuka va siya tasi tasi prakaṛne.
8. Lahuka va siya tasi tasi pakaraṇasi (Laghta vā syāt tasmin tasmin prakaṛne)
9. . . Yatra nāsti manusānaṁ ektaramhi Pāsanḍamhi na nāṁ prasādau.. (Yatra nāsti manushyānāmektarasmin api pākhanḍe nāṁ prasādah) 13th inscription (amongst 14 inscriptions)
10. Āva Sankat Kapā dhamamhi sīṁhi tistantau dhamaṁ anusasisanti, (Yavat Saṁvat Kalpaṁ dharme Shile cha tishthantaḥ dharmamanushāsishyanti —Girnar, IV inscription (amongst 14 inscriptions)
11. Purā mahānasaṁhi devānaṁ priyas Priyādasino rā anudivasaṁ bahuṁ prāṇashatsahasrāṁ ārbhisu. (Purā mahānase devānaṁ priyasya priya darshinaḥ Rāgyah anudivasaṁ bahuni prānashatsahasraṁ ālpsat-1 —Girnār, Ist inscription (amongst 14 inscriptions)
12. Sarvat Vijitamhi devānaṁ priyas priyadasino Rājo-1) (Sarvatra Vijitemaṁ yuktāḥ rajjukā prādeshikā Panchsu Panchus varshsu anusaṁyānaṁ nisbkrimantu. —Girnār, 2nd inscription

signify locative case, singular number. For example 'विजिते'[1], 'विजये'[2] and 'प्रकरणे'[3] are a few illustrations of this nature. In other inscriptions of Shābāzgarhi and Mānsera also, the termination 'ए' is found suffixed to denote locative case singular number. Such as 'धमे' 'शिले'[4] etc. However, there are a very few examples of this nature.

In Sanskrit words 'एतस्मै' (For this in dative case, singular number) and 'अमुष्मै' (As now-in dative case, singular number), although the components 'स्म' or 'ष्म' are there, yet they do not convert in letter 'फ' in Prākrita formations in locative case, singular number like the termination 'स्मिन' as discussed above. Prākrita formations 'एताय'[5] and 'एताये'[6] are obtained for Sanskrit word 'एतस्मै' and 'इमाय'[7] for Sanskrit word 'अमुष्मै'. In the said inscription, Prākrita formations —'हमा'[8] for Sanskrit word 'अस्मकम' and हमियाए[9] for Sanskrit word 'मया' (Ist personal pronoun in genitive case, singular number) are obtained. However, the said method of Prākrita formations[10] calls for minute consideration.

---

1. Sarvata Vijitemam yuktaḥ rājuke cha prādesike cha Panchsu
Vāsesu anusaṁyānaṁ niyātu-1
(Sarvatra Vijitemam yuktāḥ rajjukā, prādeshikaḥ panchsu
varshesu anusaṁyānaṁ nishkramantu). — III inscription (out of 14 inscriptions)
2. Saraske eva vijaye chhatiṁ cha . . . 1
(Sharakarshiṇah Vijaye kṣānti cha)
— XIII inscription (Amongst 14 inscriptions)
3. Lahukā va asa tamhi tamhi prakaṛne1
(Laghukā vā syāt tasmin tasmin prakarne)
— XII inscription (Amongst 14 inscriptions)
4. Avakapaṁ dhrame shile cha tistiti dharmam anushashishanti
(Avakapam dhrame shile cha tistiti dharmam anushashishanti)
(Yāvat Kalpaṁ dharme shile cha tishthantah dharmamanushāsishyanti 1)
—Shāhbāzgarhi, IV inscription (Amongst 14 inscriptions)
5. Etāya thāya iyaṁ Sāvane sāvāpite. (Etasmai artha idaṁ Shāvanam shrawitaṁ)
— 1st small inscription at Brahmagiri
Bahakā cha etāya athā —— Vyāpta Dhammahā bhāshāṁ.
(Bahukāḥ cha etasmai arthayaḥ Vyāpritāḥ dharmamahāmātāṁ . . . 1
— Girnār, XII inscription (Amongst 14 inscriptions)
6. Etāye athāye iyaṁ lipi likhit
—Dhauli, 1st inscription (Amongst two Kalinga inscriptions)
Etāye Cha athāye . . . 1
—Jaugarh, 1st inscription (Amongst two Kalinga inscriptions)
(Etasmai arthāya fimaṁ lipih likhita) . . . 1
Etāye me athāye dhama sāvanāni sāvāpitani
(Etasmai arthāya dhrmashrāvaṇāni Shrāvitāni —— 1) —VII pillar inscription at Topra (Delhi)
7. Yi imāya Kālāya Jambuvipsi amisā deva husute Dani misa Kata
(Ye amusmai amushmai Kalaya Jambudwipe amrishadevāḥ abhuvan te idaninimrishā Kritā.
— Ist small inscription at Rupnath
8. Viditaṁ ve mante āvatake hamā budhsi dhamsi sanghsiti galve cha prasāde cha. (Viditaṁ vo bhadantah! Yāvat asmakaṁ budhe dharme sanghe iti gauravaṁ cha prasādaḥ cha)
—Inscription at Bhābru
9. Echu Kho bhante hamiyāye diseyā hevaṁ sanghme chilthitike hosatiti——.
(Yat tu Khalu bhadantāḥ! mayā divyate evam sadharmaḥ chirasthitikah bhavishyati iti ——).
—Inscription at Bhābru
10. Shatruvadadeshaḥ

Various scholars have carried out investigation and analytical research in regard to the dialects of the inscriptions, got inscribed by emperor Ashōkā. The prominent names amongst them are of M/s Frank, Senart and Gune. However, the views of these scholars differ. Certain scholars believe that two types of dialects have been used in the inscriptions of Ashōkā; some believe that three forms of dialects are obtained; a few others suggest that they have been inscribed in four forms of dialects, while the rest opine that 5 forms of dialects have been used in the said inscriptions. However, nothing could be said in a decisive manner. There is still ample scope for further research and investigation in this regard.

Certain words had been picked in different inscriptions and their etymology had been discussed in detail. Before starting critical review, it had been stated that primarily three types of dialects appeared to have been used in the said inscriptions. It could not be claimed that all the three forms of Vernacular dialects were well arranged and systematically used, yet they did have a slight linguistic continuity.

The reason for use of different vocabulary in the inscriptions of North-West Frontier region as compared to inscriptions at other places, has a definite explanation. It would be quite consistent to believe that the Prākrita dialect, used in North-West regions of India had its own characteristics. Possibly, it had been influenced by western languages, belonging to Aryan family spoken in the territories situated adjacent to the North-West frontier territories of the country. It was the same territorial part adjoining Afghanistan. Hence the dialect of North-West Frontier was bound to be influenced by the language of that country as well. Probably, it was the form of Paishachi Prākrita which was in vogue in North-West Frontier. The dialect of the N.W.F.P. inscriptions matched considerably with the Prākrita of the dramatic compositions of Ashwaghosh; Kharoshti Prākrita (an ancient script which was prevalent in north-west frontier of India, roughly between 4th century B.C. and 3rd century A.D.); Dhammapada Prākrita and Nīya Prākrita. This topic will be taken up for discussion later on in the ensuing pages.

There was no distinct variation in the dialects of eastern and central parts of India. The prākrita dialects used in the inscriptions of both territories illustrate that they resembled mainly with Māgadhi Prākrita besides other prakritas of eastern regions. No doubt, there were minor variations in word formations in the inscriptions of eastern and central parts of the country, however, they were insignificant from linguistic viewpoint. Girnār is situated in Saurāshtra (Gujrat) which formed part of erstwhile Shūrsena state (Mediaeval name of the territory lying in and around Mathura). The inscriptions of Girnār give clear or distinct picture of the ancient form of Shorseni Prākrita.

Miscellaneous Names Suggested for Incriptions: The scholars have mentioned the names of Prākrita dialects of Ashokan inscriptions differently. Mr. Senart has named it as petrographic Prākrita. Other scholars have held that it was irrational in as much as the inscriptions of Ashōkā were not confined to the stones or rocks only. Mr. Pischel has named it as 'Lena-vibhasha'. Lena is the prakrita formation of Sanskrit word 'लयन' (A place of rest or a small house). The literal meaning of the word 'layan' is a small room, a small house or a cave. According to Mr. Pischel, Ashokan inscriptions are also inscribed on the walls of the caves. Hence it is the only suitable name for the dialect of his inscriptions. Dr. Gune has, however, disagreed with it and holds that it is not an appropriate name. A few other scholars have attributed the name of 'Lāt Vibhashā' The word 'लाट' is an expanded form of Sanskrit word 'यष्टि' (pillar, pole or a column) just as - (यष्टि - लट्ठि - लाट). Since several Ashokan inscriptions are on pillars or columns, hence it is the only appropriate name as discussed by them. Certain other scholars have named them as Ashokan Prākritas as well. Thus several names have been suggested for the dialects of Ashokan inscriptions. However, they are more popularly known as petrographic Prākritas, and this name appears more consistent and relevant also. Here the word 'शिला' does not literally mean a slab of stone only but it can be a piece of stone, rock or a cave meant for writing or inscribing any thing. This definition appears to be more appropriate and correct.

Other Inscriptional Prākritas

Besides the Ashokan inscriptions, certain more inscriptions are obtained in Prākrita dialects. Some of them are large—sized while others are too small—say only one line inscriptions, pertaining to the period ranging from 400 to 300 B.C. The total number of the said large and small inscriptions is approximately 2000. Most prominent ones are — Mahāsthān Stone plaque inscription; Jogimārā cave inscription in Madhya Pradesh; Sohgaura copper plate inscription of north-west Bihar; Besnagar pillar inscription at Gwalior; Shinkot casket inscription in Kharoshti script of North-West Frontier region in India; Elephant cave inscription of emperor Khārvela in Orissa; petrographic inscriptions of Udayagiri and Khandagiri and rock inscriptions of rulers of Andhra dynasty. They are all large-sized inscriptions.

Inscriptional Prākritas found in Ceylon (Now Sri Lanka)

The inscriptions in Prākrita dialect are obtained in Ceylon also for the period ranging from 100 B.C. to 300 A.D. These inscriptions are found on the walls of the caves and rocks. The petrographic inscriptions are generally found on the banks of the ponds in which there are referances of having gifted ponds for the charitable purposes of the temples.

Linguistic Trend: The Prākritas of the inscriptions, found in Ceylon (Now Sri Lanka), generally conformed with inscriptional Prākritas of eastern and central parts of India. However, they had their own characteristics as well. For example, in words of nominative case, singular number, the termination of vowel 'i' is found suffixed as against vowel 'e' in inscriptional Prākritas of eastern and central parts of the country.

In Singhalese inscriptions — in words of locative case, singular number the letter 'हि' has appeared for letter 'सि'. Similarly, in words of genitive case, singular number, the letter 'ह' has appeared. We find the use of dental letter 'स' in place of palatal letter 'श' as 'अपभ्रंश' is written 'अपभ्रंस' in inscriptional Prākritas of Ceylon. At certain places we find the use of palatal letter 'श' in place of cerebral letter 'ष' also. Mr. Geiger has named the dialects of the inscriptions as Singhalese

Prākritas.

Of course, there is historic significance of inscriptions other than those of emperor Ashōkā also. However, keeping in view the multifarious uses of the words and in so arranging them in a sentence that they may be considered either of Sanskrit or Prākrita and providing adequate material for consideration of various linguistic elements, the Ashokan inscriptions had decidedly greater significance as compared to them.

6

PRĀKRITAS OF TRANSITIONAL PERIOD

Inscriptions in Prākrita Dialects as Obtained Outside India

Canonical literature relating to Tripitakas in Pāli and Jaina Agamas in half Māgadhi dialect was of the similar significance so far as its ancientness and originality are concerned. Their systematic and critical evaluation was desirable here yet it would be better to first examine the shapes of Prākrita dialects, obtained outside the country. They resembled considerably with Ashokan Prākritas, particularly with petrographs of North-West regions.

Transitional Period

The period of Middle Indo-Aryan languages ranges from 500 B.C. to 1000 A.D. The use of vernacular dialects (Derived from or akin to Sanskrit) dominated this era. The said period of domination of the native dialects was, itself classified in 3 parts—(1) Early Middle period of Indo-Aryan languages; (2) Middle period of Indo-Aryan languages; and (3) Later period of Middle Indo-Aryan languages. The initial period of use of Prākrita dialects ranged from 500 B.C. to the beginning of Christian era. The first period covers Pāli and inscriptional Prākritas. The second period deals with evolution of Prākrita dialects and ranges from the beginning of Christian era to 500 A.D. The main dialects, gaining prominence during the said period were half-Māgadhi, Shorseni, Paishāchi and Mahārāshtriyan. The third period of Prākritas ranges from 500 to 1000 A.D. This period witnessed the origin, development, growth and expansion of Apbhransh dialect.

Another Classification: Certain scholars have adopted a different method for classification of the period of Middle Indo-Aryan languages. According to them, the period of early Middle Indo-Aryan languages i.e. the period of Pāli and inscriptional Prākritas is of 500 years ranging from 700 B.C. to 200 B.C. Again the second period of Middle Indo-Aryan languages dates back from 200 A.D. to 700 A.D. The period from 200 B.C. to 200 A.D. remains unaccounted for which has been defined as transitional period. The said transitional period covers the Prākrita dialects, obtained outside India. These Prākritas have been found in three shapes—Prākrita dialects used in the dramatic plays of Ashwaghosh, Prākrita of Dhammapada and Niya Prākrita.

Plays of Ashwaghosh : Use of Prākrita Dialects therein

Buddhist monk, Ashwaghosh, was a philosopher and poet. The period of his dramatic compositions is believed to be first century A.D. Mutilated copies of two Sanskrit Plays, written by Ashwaghosh, were obtained from the territory of Central

Asia. Eminent German Scholar, Prof. Luders, has edited them in a scholarly manner. Certain characters of his plays speak Prākrita dialects. In subsequent dramatic compositions, the use of Prākrita dialects by different characters appears to be artificial and unreal. It is unlike the earlier dramatic plays of Ashwaghosh, wherein, the dialects have been used by the characters in a systematic manner and in their ancient forms and as such they appear to be more real and natural in the course of delivering their dialogues.

Three Ancient Prākrita Dialects: While examining the nature of Prākrita dialects, Prof. Luders has opined that 3 forms of Prākrita dialects have been used in the dramatic plays of Ashwaghosh — (1) Ancient Māgadhi; (2) Ancient Shorseni and (3) Ancient Ardha-Māgadhi. According to Prof. Luders, the low character, known as 'Dushṭa' (A wicked) conversed in ancient Māgadhi; the humorous companion of the hero and the courtesan delivered their dialogues in ancient Shorseni; while that of 'Gomas', (An attendent on Lord Buddha) and 'Tāpas' (A Buddhist monk) was ancient Ardha-Māgadhi. The dialects of the plays of Ashwaghosh conform with the inscriptional Prākritas of emperor Ashōkā.

Ancient Māgadhi Prākrita

From a critical investigation of the dialect, used by the low character, Dushṭa, it is evident that ancient Māgadhi has its own characteristics. the letter 'र' converts into letter 'ल' in Māgadhi. The use of palatal letter 'श' is found for cerebral letter 'ष' and dental letter 'स' also. In words of nominative case, singular number, the termination 'ए' is found suffixed. For Sanskrīt word 'अहम्' (First personal pronoun), the Māgadhi form 'अहकं' is obtained, which is further changed to 'हगे'. In words of genitive case, singular number, the termination 'हो' is found suffixed. These illustrations display the nature of ancient Māgadhi which matches with the Māgadhi used in ancient inscriptions.

Ancient Shorseni Prākrita

The characteristics of ancient Shorseni, spoken by jesters and courtesans are as follows:

For Sanskrit words ending in letter 'अः' in nominative case, singular number the termination 'ओ' is found suffixed in Shorseni Prākrita. Sanskrit letters 'ज्ञ' and 'न्य' are found converted into letter 'ञ'. The use of letter 'इ' is found in Shorseni for Sanskrit letter 'ऋ'. Similarly, the uses of letter 'व्व' for Sanskrit letter 'व्य' and 'क्ख' for Sanskrit letter 'क्ष' are obtained in Shorseni. Uses of 'भवा' for Sanskrit word 'भवान्' 'खु'; for Sanskrit word 'खलु' 'करिय' for 'कृत्वा' and 'तुवब' for Sanskrit word 'त्वम्' are also obtained in Shorseni Prākrita. 'तुवब', a formation in Shorseni for 'त्वम्' (you—second personal pronoun) is comparable with Persian word 'तुवम्' which also means you (Second personal pronoun).

In active voice, the Sanskrit root words which are conjugated with suffixes in order to form present—participles ('शानच - A technical term used by Pāṇini for the Krit affix 'आन' or 'मान' used in forming present—participles) remain unchanged in Shorseni Prākrita as evident from the formations 'भुञ्जमानो' 'पाठयमानो' etc.

In Shorseni Prākrita, the classification of roots in the shape of आत्मनेपदी' (one of two voices in which roots are conjugated in Sanskrit) and 'परस्मैपदी' (one of the two voices in which verbs in Sanskrit are conjugated) like Sanskrit is not made. Hence it is not necessary to consider over formations in Shorseni Prākrita by suffixing 'आन' or 'मान' in order to obtain the forms in present-participle. The form obtained by suffixing 'शानच' termination is 'आन'. It is not affixed by the termination 'श' or 'च'[1].

Ancient shape of Ardha Māgadhi Prakrita

A few of the characteristics of Ardha Māgadhi Prākrita, generally spoken by attendants on Buddha and Buddhist mendicants in Dramatic plays are as follows: Generally in words of nominative case, singular number, the termination 'ओ' is obtained in Ardha-Māgadhi against Sanskrit letter 'अ'. In Jaina Agamas and in subsequent form of Ardha-Māgadhi Prākrita, we find both terminations 'ओ' and 'ए' affixed to denote nominative case singular number. The use of palatal letter 'श' is not found at all in Ardha-Māgadhi Prākrita. The terminations 'क' 'आक' and 'इक' are generally affixed in Ardha Māgadhi. Letter 'र' is found converted in letter 'ल'.

Ambiguity or Slight Clarity: Some of the characteristics of Ancient Māgadhi, Shorseni and Ardha Māgadhi have been mentioned above which are the dialects in which the characters of dramatic plays of Ashwaghosh generally deliver their dialogues. From the above, an elaborate picture of Ardha Māgadhi Prākrita is not obtained as much as we had in the case of Ancient Māgadhi and Shorseni Prākritas. Of course, from the above discussion, the shape of Ardha Māgadhi Prākrita is not very clear. However, it does manifest certain characteristics of Ardha Māgadhi. Briefly speaking, the tendency of conversion of letter 'र' into 'ल' has appeared from Māgadhi Prākrita which is not found in any other Prākrita. The absence of use of letter 'श' in Ardha Māgadhi Prākrita is not very significant in as much as the use of dental letter 'स' is only found in all other Prākritas except Māgadhi.

Kharoshti Script (An Ancient Script Prevalent in North-West Frontier region of India) : Dhammapada Prākrita

A French traveller, Mr. M. Dutreiul De Rhine, happened to trace out certain

---

(1) Tatya lopaḥ
Tasyeto lāpaḥ syāt.

— *Ashthadhyayi of Pāṇiṇi*, 1/3/9

inscriptions at Khotān, a place outside India. Till then, nobody had the knowledge of the said inscriptions. A Russian scholar, Mr. D. Oldenverga, carried out critical investigation of the contents of the said inscriptions and produced some explanations. Another French scholar, Mr. Senart carried out further investigation and declared in 1897 that they were extracts of Prākrita inscriptions. Thereafter, the British and Indian scholars devoted themselves to the study and critical evaluation of the said extracts. As a result of all these concerted efforts, Prof. B.M.Barua and Prof. S. Mitra of Calcutta University got them published in 1921 and held that the dialect used therein was Dhammapada Prākrita. Since the inscriptions had been written in Kharoshti script, the language was named as 'Kharoshti-Dhammapada also. Prof. Jules Block spared no pains to carry out further investigation with regard to the style of composition, language and phonetics etc. and arrived at the conclusion that the said inscriptions had been accomplished in India and carried to Western territory, situated outside India. The inference of Prof. Jules Block appears to be relevant and correct, since by that time, Buddhism had already spread and crossed the national boundaries. It must have gone ahead to neighbouring countries, situated on the West and it could not be considered a sheer improbability. There is enough supporting material for it. After having been brought there, it was a probability that the language of the inscriptions might have been influenced by the language of that area. The language of the said inscription slightly conformed with the language of Ashokan inscriptions obtained in North-West Frontier region. Dhammapada (Buddhist legends with narratives) is divided in 12 volumes. The total number of narratives (legendary tales) is 232. The time of its accomplishment is estimated in or about second century A.D.

Niya Prākrita

Amongst Prākrita dialects found abroad, Niya Prākrita had great significance from philological point of view. Sir Orel Stain travelled thrice to Niya region of Chinese Turkistan, where he happened to trace out a few inscriptions in Kharoshti script. He undertook his first journey in the year 1900-1901; made second trip in 1906-1907 and visited for the third time in 1913-1914. Thus it was the fruit of his constant endeavour for a period of 15 years ranging from 1900 to 1914.

A new fact came to light. The scholars devoted their mind to it. The aforesaid Kharoshthi inscriptions were edited first by Mr. A.M. Bavāyer in 1920; by Mr. E.J. Rapson in 1927 and by Mr.Senart in 1929.

However, it was Mr. T. Baro who carried out profound investigation over the said inscriptions. He declared that the said inscriptions had been written in one of the Prākrita dialects of India. He also expressed the view that the said Prākrita was once the official language of erstwhile 'Shanshan' dynasty during third century.

From minute examination and a critical review of the shape and composition of Niya Prākrita, it transpired that it had its origin from North-West Frontier region, close to Peshāwar, then part of India. This dialect matches with the language of Dhammapada, written in Kharoshthi script. It had considerable similarity with the language of Ashokan inscriptions in North-West Frontier region. This also provided strong support to the belief that it had its origin from India. Since majority of these inscriptions had been discovered from Niya region, hence the dialect in which they had been inscribed, came to be known as Niya Prākrita. The language of Niya inscriptions deserved further investigation and research because of its nearness to the dialect of North-West inscriptions of emperor Ashōkā.

There were certain references in the inscriptions of Niya region which appeared to be in the nature of royal commands issued to their district authorities by the rulers. A few letters relating to purchases and sales were also inscribed therein. A few personal letters also appeared to have been included. Lists of several types had also been provided in the inscripions which made it explicit that the said inscriptions dealt with the affairs relating to the system of administration, trade and commerce.

Some scribing signs or indications were also found in the script of Niya Prākrita, which were, however, absent in the dialects, prevalent in India. These signs have been introduced to denote long vowels, different other vowels, phonetic sounds with voice and elevated accent. It appears to be the effect of foreign languages. Such an effect was inevitable since the aforesaid inscrptions had been removed to a territory situated outside the country. The philologists believe that Niya Prākrita was in use during third century A.D.

Another distinguishing feature of Niya Prākrita is its well accomplished grammar based on phonetic sounds. It might be due to the fact that Niya Prākrita was in use outside India, hence it could not have been influenced by Sanskrit. However, the fate of Prākritas, used in India was different. They continued to be influenced by Sanskrit. Hence they could not retain their original forms like Niya Prākrita so far as their phonetic sounds were concerned.

Morphological Characteristics of Niya Prākrita : Niya Prākrita had its own significance from linguistic view-point. Hence the peculiar features of its morphological construction needed further study and evaluation. Its chief characteristics were as follows:

In Niya Prākrita, letter 'इ' is obtained for Sanskrit letters 'य' 'या' and 'ये'. For instance 'समादाय' (For receiving or accepting)= 'समदि 'भावये' (gist or substance) = 'भवई'; 'मूल्य' (Price or cost) = 'मूलि'; 'ऐश्वर्य' (affluence, wealth) = 'एश्वरि' Leter 'इ' is obtained for letter 'ए' appearing in the middle of a word. Such as 'इमे' (As here, as now) = 'इमि'; 'उपेत:' (Endowed with) = 'उवितो'; 'क्षेत्र' (Soil) = 'छ् इत्र'. For letter 'अ' appearing at the end of a word, we find the use of letter 'उ' in Niya Prākrita—such as 'प्रात:' (Morning) = 'प्रतु'. The ushman sounds 'श, ष, स, ह, appearing in the middle of words and the unvoiced consonants formed by clashing of the breath with vocal chords are found converted in high accented consonants. Excluding Ushman consonants, the low accented consonants disappear and uses of 'इ' or 'य' are found in their place. For instance 'यथा' (such as) = 'यधा' 'सन्तिके' (End, destruction) = 'सदिह;'त्वचा' (Skin) = 'त्वया'; 'प्रथम' (First) = 'पढम'; 'अवकाश' (To get an opportunity or scope for action) = 'अवगजअ'; 'कोटि' (Category) = 'कोडि'; 'गोचरे' (grazed over by cattle) = 'गोयरि'; 'भोजन' (Food) = 'भोयन' etc. In case of a joint consonant, if nasal or ushman sound is included in it, then the consonant of low accent will turn into the consonant of hish accent. For instance 'पंच' (Spread, extended) = पंज' 'सिञ्च' (To sprinkle) = 'सिज'; 'सम्पन्न' (accomplished) = 'सबन्नो'; 'दुष्प्रकृत्ति' (ill-natured) = 'दुबकति'; 'संस्कार' (refinement, perfection) = 'सघर'; 'अन्तर' (Interior) = 'अदर'; 'हन्ति' (Killing or destroying) = 'हदि' etc. Similarly, instances of voiced consonants (of high accent) turning into unvoiced consonants (of low accent) are also found. Such as 'विराग' (Indifference to worldly attachments) = 'विरकु'; 'समागता' (Approached, coming together) = 'समकत'; विगाहा' (plunging or diving into) = 'विकय'; 'योग' (union or combination) = 'योक'; 'ग्लान' (Exhaustion, fatigue) = 'किलेन' 'दण्ड' (punishment) = 'तण्ट' 'भोग' (Enjoyment or pleasure) = 'योग' etc. The use of unaspirated letters (in pronouncing of which little effort is required) in place of aspirated letters (in pronunciation of which hard breathing or aspirate sound is made) as found in Niya Prākrita, appears to be the result of influence of Irānian and non-Aryan languages over it. For instance 'भूमि'(A territory or plot of land) = 'बूम' 'धनानाम्' (Wealth) = 'तनना' etc. The letter 'ख' appearing after a visarga (a colon like sound used in Sanskriīt word formations and resembling letter 'h' in pronunciation) or letter 'क्ष' appearing in a Sanskrit word independently will turn into letter 'ह' in Niya Prākrita. Such as — 'दुःख' (Sorrow, agony) = 'दुह'; 'अनपेक्षिण' (Regardless; indifferent) = 'अनवेहिनो' 'अपेक्ष' (To wish or desire for) = 'अवेह' etc.

On account of pronouncing letter 'ध' in a Sanskrit word with hard breathing or aspirate sound, the use of ushman consonant is found in its place in Niya Prākrita. Such as 'मधुर' (pleasant, charming) 'मसुरु'; 'गाथानाम' (narrative tales) = 'गशन'; शिथिल' (Loose, weak, feeble) = 'शिशिल'; 'मधु' (Sweet, delightful, honey) = 'मसु'; 'अधिमात्रा' (Excess quantity) = 'असिमत्र' etc. The three ushman sounds ('श, ष, स) are there in Niya Prākrita but the use of dental letter 'स' is more commonly found in it. For aspirated ushman sound 'ज' use of letter 'स' or 'झ' is found. The letter 'ऋ' appearing in Sanskrit words stands transformed in either of the letters 'अ', 'इ', 'उ', 'रु' and 'रि' in Niya Prākrita. For example—'मृतः' (Dead, deceased) = 'मुतु'; 'संवृतः' (closed, wound up) = 'सब्वतो'; 'स्मृति': (Rememberance, memory) = 'स्वति'; 'वृद्ध' (old) = 'व्रिद'; 'कृत' (accomplished, done) = 'किड़'; 'पृच्छितव्य' (Inquiry into the future) = 'पुछिदवो' etc.

In case letter 'र' or 'ल' joins or unites with the following letter in a joint consonant of a Sanskrit word, no change will take place in its counterpart in Niya Prākrita. For instance—'प्राप्नोति' (Procuring, providing with) = 'प्रनोदि'; 'कीर्ति' (Renown, glory) = 'कीर्ति'; 'धर्म' (religion) = 'धर्म' or 'धम'; 'मार्ग' (Passage) = 'मर्ग'; 'परिव्रजति' (To turn out a recluse) = 'परिव्रयति'; 'दीर्घम' (Long, large, tall) = 'द्रिघम्'; 'मैत्र' (Belonging to a friend, friendly or amicable) = 'मेत्र etc. In a joint consonant, nasal sound in a Sanskrit word is equalizing with a non-nasal sound in Prākrita. Such as 'पण्डित' (Scholar) = 'पणिदो'; 'दण्ड' (A stick or staff; punishment in general) = 'दण'; 'प्राप्नोति (Procuring) = 'प्रनोदि'; 'गभीर' (Serious, solemn) =

'गभिर'; 'कुंजर:' (An elephant) = 'कुंजरु'; 'प्रज्ञा' (Intellect, wisdom) = 'प्रंभ'; 'शून्य'(Empty, void) = 'शुभ'; 'विज्ञप्ति' (A notification or announcement) = 'विनति' etc. The joint consonant 'श्र' is found altered in letter 'ष' in Prākrita. For example, 'श्रावक' (A Buddhist monk) 'षवक'; 'श्मश्रु' (The growth of a beard) = 'मषु'. The joint consonants 'क्र', 'ग्र', 'थ्र', 'द्र', 'प्र', 'ब्र', 'भ्र', 'स्त', however, remain unchanged in Prākrita. For instance — 'त्रिभि: (The third part) 'त्रिहि'; 'प्रियाप्रिय' (Pleasant and unpleasant) 'प्रिअप्रिअ'; 'संभ्रम' (To be perplexed or confused) = 'सभ्रमु' etc.

The joint consonants 'ष्ट' and 'ष्ठ' in Sanskrit are equated or made even in Prākrita. For example — 'श्रेष्ठ' (Best) = 'शेठी'; 'दृष्टि' (sight, vision) = 'दिठी' 'ज्येष्ठ' (Eldest, most senior) = 'जेठ' etc. In Sanskrit root word 'स्था' the component 'स्थ' is found converted in letter 'ठ' in Prākrita. Such as 'स्थान' (Site) 'ठणेहि–; उत्स्थान' (High place) = 'उठन'; काष्ठ' (Timber) = 'कठ' 'उष्ट्र (camel) = 'उंठ.' If in a joint consonant of Sanskrit, the ushman sound is inherent, then no change will take place in the formations of Niya Prākrita. Just as — 'अस्ति' (Existence) = 'अस्ति''; 'वत्स' (Son) = 'वत्स' etc. The letter 'म्' in words of accusative case, singular number and letter 'स्' in words of nominative case, singular number are dropped and not found in Prākrita. The use of dual number is found in two instances only, such as — 'पदेभ्यां' and 'पदेयो'. The form 'अस' in words of genitive case, singular number in Sanskrit is found inflected in Niya Prākrita.

The verbal formations for determination of present tense, words expressing commands, prescribed rules and future tense etc. are found in Niya Prākrita. The formations in present tense signifying potential mood are obtained in Prākrita, conforming with those of Ashokan Prākritas. For example, for words — 'करेयसि', 'करेयति', 'स्यति' in Niya Prākrita, we find matching words 'उपकरेयति', सियति' etc. in Ashokan Prākritas. The verbal formations in past participle, passive voice, nominative case, masculine gender, plural number have been found suffixed with termination 'न्ति' and the verbal formations for first and second personal pronouns, in present tense, active voice, the inflection 'अस' is found suffixed in Niya Prākrita. For instance — 'श्रुतोस्मि' (I hear) = 'श्रुतेमि'; श्रुत: स्म: (Heard by revelation) = 'स्म' is added in Sanskrit to the present tense of verbs in order to give them the sense of past tense) = 'श्रुतम', 'दत्तोसि' (Sword given away) = 'दितेसि' etc. The nouns in active voice are obtained in Niya Prākrita by suffixing the terminations 'त्वी', 'त्वा' and 'इ' like North-West Frontier Prākritas of Ashokan inscriptions. Just as 'श्रुनिति' and 'अपुछिति etc. The formations in past participle are obtained in Niya Prākrita by suffixing the form of noun 'अन' used in the sense of a verb in dative case, singular number. For instance 'गच्छनाय'; = 'गच्छनए'; देयनए'. Some forms are found in second person also. Just as 'कर्तुं', = 'करनए'; विसजिदुं; = विसर्जनए.

Comparative and Critical Examination

In North-West Prākrita inscriptions, the joint consonants with letter 'र' remain unchanged. The same tendency is found in Niya Prākrita also. However, the tendency of letter 'र' changing its site in North-West Frontier inscriptions, is not found in Niya Prākrita. Even the subsequent inscriptions in Kharoshthi Prākrita do not show this trend. However, this characteristic feature is found in Dhammapada Prākrita.

The letter 'ल' appearing in Sanskrit joint consonants is found deleted in North-West Frontier inscriptions. However, such joint consonants with letter 'ल' are there in Niya Prākrita. For example, Prākrita formations— 'अप' for Sanskrit word 'अल्प' (Insignificant); and 'कप' for Sanskrit word 'कल्प' (Practicable, feasible) are found in the rock inscriptions of Shāhbāzgarhi and Mānsera. However, in Niya Prākrita— similar forms are obtained as appearing in Sanskrit. Just as — 'अल्प' for Sanskrit word 'अल्प' and 'जल्पित' for Sanskrīt word 'जल्पित' (said, spoken) and not 'अप' and 'जपित' as in North-West inscriptions.

Save a few instances, the letter 'छ' is generally found in North-West inscriptions in place of Sanskrit letter 'क्ष'. The same tendency is found in Niya Prākrita. Letter 'स' is found in the aforesaid inscriptions for letter 'त्स' in Sanskrit words. Such as — form, 'चिकिस' is obtained for Sanskrit word 'चिकित्सा' (Treatment). However, it is not so in Niya Prākrita. In the inscriptions of Niya Prākrita, the same formations are there as appearing in Sanskrit. For instance 'वत्स' for Sanskrit word 'वत्स' (son) and 'सवत्सर for Sanskrit word 'संवत्सर' (A year of Vikramaditya's era). Of course, exceptions are there but only a few. For termination 'स्मिन' inflected in Sanskrit words to denote locative case, the use of inflection 'स्म' is found in North-West inscriptions. The termination 'स्म' is changed to 'म्म' in Niya Prākrita. Thus, the termination 'स्मिन' suffixed in Sanskrit words to signify locative case, singular number is replaced by termination 'म्मि' in Niya Prākrita. In Dhammapada Prākrita, the use of three suffixes 'स्म' 'स्व' and 'स' is found for termination 'स्मिन' in Sanskrit. A specific feature is, thus, reflected in the Prākrita dialect of North-West region in as much as there was considerable scope for exercising option to apply one of the alternative forms as termination in order to obtain formation in locative case.

The termination 'त्वी' suffixed for obtaining a verb in past tense or past-participle, as provided in Hindi grammar, has been commonly applied in Vedic Sanskrit. However, it was not so in classical Sanskrit. In Niya Prākrita, the termination 'ति' is obtained for inflection 'त्वी'. For example, Prākrita form 'श्रुनिति' for Sanskrit word 'श्रुत्वा' (That which was heard by revelation) and 'अपुछिति' for Sanskrit word 'अपृष्टवा' (Not inquired or questioned). Similarly, in Dhammapada Prākrita, the formations 'उपजिति' for Sanskrit word 'उपजित्वा' (Conquerable) and

'परिवजेति' for Sanskrit word 'परिवर्जयित्वा' (Act of abandoning and leading the life of a religious mendicant).

In one of Ashokan inscriptions at Haitvartha and in Niya Prākrita, the use of the termination 'नये' is found while in other inscriptions at Haivartha, the use of the termination 'तवे' is seen. In Niya Prākrita, the formations are also found with termination 'तुमन्' inflected at the end, but only a few instances are there. In Ashokan inscriptions of North-West Frontier, we find the use of both suffixes 'अ' and 'ए' to signify nominative case, singular number. In inscriptions of Shāhbāzgarhi, the termination 'ओ' and in those of Mānsera, the inflection 'ए' have generally been used. In Niya Prākrita also, the use of termination 'ए' is mostly found. In Kharoshthi inscriptions of the later period, the use of both suffixes 'ओ' and 'ए' is there. In the inscriptions obtained in the north of Indus river, the use of termination 'ए' has been exceedingly made, while at other places, the use of inflection 'ओ' is found.

However, in *Dhammapada Prākrita*, the termination 'ए' is not found suffixed. Instead, the use of two suffixes 'ओ' and 'उ' is found. Nevertheless, the use of suffix 'उ' is astonishing since the use of letter 'उ' reflected the trend of subsequent age, more so pertaining to the era of 'Apbhransh Prākrita' (one of the middle Indo-Aryan languages). The introduction and use of termination 'उ' could be explained to be the effect of modern trend. From the inflection 'तसिल' affixed to the Sanskrit words, the letter 'इ' and 'ल' get disappeared and for the remaining part of the inflection i.e. 'तस्=त:', the use of letter 'ए' is found in Niya Prākrita. It may be pointed out here that the use of the letter 'ए' at the end of a Prākrita word was the characteristic feature of Māgadhi Prākrita.

In Niya Prākrita, all nouns are obtained, ending in letter 'अ'. To accomplish nouns by suffixing letter 'अ' at the end of a word is consistent with the practice found in Apbhransh Prākrita. In Niya Prākrita, the termination applied for obtaining nominative case and accusative case is the same and the same tendency is found in Apbhransh Prākrita.

It is thus established by virtue of comparative study and detailed discussion that there is considerable resemblance in the distinguishing features of transitional Prākritas—may be to a limited extent in certain cases.

7

THE ORIGIN OF SCRIPT AND ITS DEVELOPMENT IN INDIA

Scripts of Prākrita Inscriptions

The ancient inscriptions obtained in Prākrita dialects were mainly inscribed in Brahmi Script (A widely used ancient Indian script which formed the source of evolution of Devanāgiri and all other indigenous Indian scripts). A few rock inscriptions were found written in Kharoshthi script (an ancient script which was prevalent in north-west frontier of the then India roughly between 4th century B.C. and 3rd century A.D.) Ashokan inscriptions at Shāhbāzgarhi and Mānsera had been inscribed in Kharoshthi script. There are two rock inscriptions, found at Kāngdā in Punjab which have been inscribed in both Kharoshthi and Brahmi scripts. It appears that both these scripts might be in use during those days in that area. It is somewhat extraordinary that a well known petrographic inscription, obtained at Mathura, had been written in Kharoshthi script. There was a similar inscription at Patna also. Hence, it may be desirable to discuss about origin, development and spread of the art of writing in India concisely.

Brahmi Script

Brāhmi Script is most ancient as against other scripts found in India. Just as the religious leaders have laid emphasis that the language of their own religious scriptures and allied canonical literature was of divine and eternal nature, similarly, they have shown equal regard for Brāhmi script. Here the feeling of superlativeness for one's own religion has, no doubt, predominated the real truth. It is an inherent weakness of mankind to apply all adjectives and establish supremacy of their own religion and its sacred books.

Views Under Vedic Tradition

The vedic scholars believe that the source of origin of the word 'Brahmi' is from Brahma (The Supreme spirit). Amongst Trinity of mythological Hindu deities[1], Brahmā is the creator, the first deity to whom is entrusted the work of creating the world. Just as he created the world and all other worldly objects, similarly, the art of writing also came into existence through Him. The script, introduced along with other objects of the universe is Brāhmi script. While relating the significance and utility of script—writing, accomplished by Brāhma, it has been cited in *Nārada-smriti* Had Brahmā not created art of writing or in other words not

1. Brahma = Creator; Vishnu = Preserver of the world; Shiva = Destroyer.

produced an excellent eye in the shape of a script, this world would have been deprived of obtaining bright future.

Narration in 'Lalitvistar'

Lalitvistar is a famous treatise, written in Sanskrīt, relating to Buddhist religion. In its 10th chapter, the topic of script-writing has been dealt with. The names of 64 scripts have been mentioned therein and Brāhmi tops the list.

Out of 64 names of the scripts, there were certain names which were based either on the name of a specific country, state or community. Such as Aṅga Script (Belonging to Anga region, considered to be the same as, or situated very near, the modern Bhagalpur in Bihar); Baṅga script (an Eastern state of pre-partition India including also the sea-coast of Bengal); Māgadh script (A territory in South Bihar. Its capital was Pātliputra — now Patna); Brahamvalli Script; Dravadian script (Name of the territory on the east coast of Deccan); Kanari Script; Dakshin lipi (Region of South India); Darad script (A region bordering Kashmira); Khāsya Script; China Script; Hoona Script; Deva Script; Nāgā Script (A semi-divine Community); Yaksha Script (A class of demi-gods in heaven); Gandharva Script (A class of demi-gods, regarded as musicians of gods); Kinnar lipi (A race celebrated as musicians to please divine gods); Mahoraga Script; Asur Script (demons — A general name for the enemies of gods); Garuda Script (Implying a community here); Uttar Kurudwipa Script (Name of an extensive region or plain near Delhi. It is extended from the South of the Saraswati to the north of Drishadavati rivers); Upper Gaudadi Script (Northern Bengal). Purva Videh Script (Name of the region lying to the north-east of Magadha in Bihar) etc.

There are certain names of the scripts which are probably based on eulogical praise of the deities or utility of the specific objects. Certain other names might have possibly been assigned to the scripts due some other reasons.

Beliefs of Jaina Religion

There is general appreciation and regard for Brāhmi Script in Jaina scriptures too. In the fifth Anga, 'Vyākhyā Pragyapti' (Bhagwati) Sūtra (forming part of Jaina Agamic scriptures). Whereas obeisance has been paid to an 'Arhant' (A superior divinity with the Jainas); 'Sidha' (an accomplished saint, endowed with super-natural faculties); 'Achārya' (A spiritual guide); 'Upadhyaya' (A religious preceptor) and 'Sādhu' (A Jaina Saint) on one hand, a respectful mention has also been made of Brahmi Script on the other.[1] Reverential reference, of Brāhmi script in 'Vyākhyā - Pragyapti', a pre-eminent scripture of Jaina religion, no doubt, signified its ancientness.

Teaching of Various Scripts by Rishabh

Regarding origin of scripts, it is cited in ancient Jaina scriptures that prior to

1. Namo Arhantānaṁ, namo Sidhānaṁ , namo Āyariyanaṁ, namo Uvajṁhāyānaṁ, namo Loe savva Sāhunaṁ, Namo bambhiye liviye.

renouncing the world and adopting asceticism, the initial teacher of Jaina religion, Lord Rishabha, while he was still a ruler, had established all institutions of universal significance. He made arrangements for teaching of all sciences, disciplines and arts. It is stated that Lord Rishabha had arranged for imparting knowledge of 72 Skills, purported for males, to his eldest son, Bharata and also preached for realization of Supreme Being. He got imparted knowledge of symptoms of living organism (Zoology) to his son, Bahubali. He taught 18 scripts to his daughter, Brāhmi[1] and Mathematics to his other daughter, Sundari.

After having obtained perfection in various branches of knowledge, sciences and arts, the sons and daughters of Lord Rishabha further propagated and spread the knowledge to the people at large. Out of 18 scripts, propagated by Brāhmi, the main script was Brāhmi. Hence it came to be called by the name of Brāhmi.

The 18 scripts detailed in 4th Aṅga, 'Samvāyāṅga Sūtra', have been topped by Brāhmi Script. Although, the names of 18 scripts, appearing in the Vth Aṅga, 'Pragyāpna Sutra' do not altogether tally with the names of scripts, produced in 'Samvāyānga Sutra', yet they are identical to a considerable extent, and the initial name, heading the list is the same Brāhmi script. However, the names of scripts narrated in the commentary on 'Vishesha Avashyaka' (forming part of Agamic Scriptures of Jaina religion) and 'Kalpa Sūtra' are, no doubt, different from those, appearing in 'Samvāyānga Sutra' and 'Pragyāpnā Sutra'. It is astonishing that in both the latter sacred treatises, the name of Brāhmi script is missing. The names incorporated in the said lists of 'Visheshā Avashyaka Commentary' and 'Kalpa Sutra', appear to be recent when the use of Brāhmi Script had almost stopped in India and it had lost its significance by then.

Certain names of the scripts, mentioned in the Commentary on 'Visheshā Avashyaka' — such as 'Yavani', 'Turukki', 'Dravadi' 'Singhviya,', 'Mālvini', 'Nāgari', 'Lāt', Pārsi appear to have based on the names of countries and regions. Probably, the names of the scripts had been assigned by the commentator of 'Visheshā Avashyaka', keeping in view the names of territorial parts where they were in vogue. The names of the three scripts (1) Yavani, (2) Parsi, and (3) Turukki are decidedly foreign. Many other names appear to have based on the names of the regions and territories, forming part of India, which had evolved from Brāhmi script. However, no explanation could be offered in respect of certain names of the scripts, such as Hansa etc.

The names of scripts, appearing in 'Kalpa Sutra', such as 'Lāti', 'Chaudi'[2], 'Dāhāli', 'Kānadi', 'Gūjari', 'Saurhathi', 'Marahathi', 'Konkani', 'Māgadhi', 'Hādi', 'Mālvi', etc. seem to have based on the names of different regions and territorial parts of India in the same manner as the commentator of 'Visheshā Āvashyaka' had assigned to the scripts, enumerated in his commentary.

The experts on graphology have carried out detailed investigation and study of Brāhmi and Kharoshthi scripts. They have expressed divergent views. Before taking up critical evaluation of their opinions, it will be in the fitness of things to concentrate the mind on the origin and development of script — writing in India.

---

1. Leha livi Vihānani, jiṇeṇa bambhiye dahina kareṇa.

—*Abhidhan Rajendra Kosh*, Vth Volume, p. 1284.

2. Probably the 'Chaudi' Script was the official script used in the Chol dynasty of South.

Origin of Art of Writing — An Assumption

An Initial Attempt of Primordial Human Race

The scholars believe that the race of primitive mankind had faith in worshipping various deities. They believed in performance of sorcerous acts as well. Till then, their reasoning faculty had not developed. However, the human-beings had imaginative faculty. They might have developed the curiosity to prepare or draw a symbolic picture of their favorite gods, and thus started their attempts to accomplish their aim. Initially, they might have drawn curved and irregular lines. Thus, for attainment of good fortune and personal well-being, as also for prevention of ill-luck and misfortune they might have started practising sorcery and witch-craft. There could be certain other reasons also which might have prompted them to learn drawing lines or other indications for their reference. In order to avoid mixing of their utensils and pitchers etc., collected at the time of certain functions or celebrations, simply because of their similar appearance and to make it easy to identify their respective items, they might have begun marking distinguishing signs. There was no profound thinking at all behind the above contrivance. It was only a spontaneous activation on the part of erstwhile people and the result of their emotional disposition. The process continued. People considered such activities as source of mere fulfilment of their requirements. It is only a concept which will help in examining the factors, leading to the origin of science of writing.

Expressions for Maintaining Mutual Dealings and the Desires and Sentiments for Manifestation of their Feelings

Erstwhile people had already manifested their medium of speech. They had acquired the capability of exchanging their views mutually. Thus they had no difficulty in carrying out their day today activities. The difficulties experienced by human society for want of a medium of exchange in day today course of life, had already been done away with. However, with expansion of their mutual dealings and scope of their activities, they began to feel handicapped. If the people, they were required to deal with, lived in their vicinity with whom they could converse and exchange their views personally, they would have faced no difficulty in maintaining their dealings in as much as they could speak face to face and acquaint themselves with the views of each other. However, it was not practically possible always. Therefore, the people of that age might have become curious to find out any other source for satisfaction of their needs.

Presumably, there could be other grounds as well. With growing intellectual awareness of mankind, the learned persons might have concentrated their mind to carry on further research and investigation. There was an obvious curiosity to provide lasting stability and permanency to their thoughts. From psychological viewpoint, they felt a sort of satisfaction in doing so. Moreover, people could continue to be benefited by the ideas only when they were reduced to writing, especially when the authors of the ideas ceased to exist. Thus the conscious and enlightened persons were anxious to find out a method for stability of their feelings so that this deficiency could be overcome once for all.

A Fundamental Source

People had already started drawing irregular lines and sketches in a symbolic manner — may be still indistinct, in order to give expression to their feelings and satisfaction of their day today requirements. In order to render practical shape to their sentiments, people continued their efforts in that direction. They had mental solace that the method of drawing pictorial lines and sketches would one day enable them to accomplish their target. They were zealous to express their feelings by virtue of symbolic and pictorial drawings inspite of the fact that they were ugly, incomplete and haphazard (unsystematic). In this way, the pictorial script came into existence. Just as drawing of irregular lines and sketches introduced script-writing in its primitive form, the same method led to the origin of pictorial writing.

By whatever study and investigation was carried out by the linguists and research scholars, they arrived at the conclusion that approximately prior to 4000 B.C. there was no systematic form of script-writing in existence. According to the intellects, the learned scholars had started their attempts to find out a medium to put down their views prior to 10,000 B.C. As a consequence of their regular efforts for about 6000 years, they were in a position to introduce initial form of script-writing may be quite vague and unsystematic, which continued evolving with the passage of time.

Pictorial Script

The method adopted to express themselves through pictorial drawings, came to be known as pictography. The initial drawings must have been clumsy and imperfect to look at. The scope of human activity or endeavour was extremely limited at that time. Therefore, the people might have drawn sketches of human-beings, their close associates—animals, tiny creatures, as also plants and vegetables, used by them. In this process, irregular sketches might have been drawn also, somewhat similar to geometrical diagrams.

It was the age of worshipping gods and demi-gods. People might have drawn sketches of gods and goddesses in order to offer them worship and perform corresponding religious rituals. Such paintings might have been portrayed on the walls of the caves, and the murals. It appears that even stones, bones, animal skins, barks of trees, earthen utensils, ivory etc. might have been used for accomplishing these portraits.

Expression

It is an inherent characteristic of mankind to move ahead from an undeveloped stage of life to strive hard in order to obtain a progressive and well-accomplished life. Initially, the human society was familiar with physical world only. Accordingly, whenever people desired to express their feelings in relation to living-beings, animals, creatures, objects and articles, they portrayed their pictures. For instance, if they intended to convey something about a human-being, they painted its picture; if in respect of any bodily limb, the sketch of the limb concerned, if in respect of animals, their sketches; drawing large and small circles for manifesting sun, moon and stars, as also drawing lines all around a large circle to signify the rays of the sun. It was the way, they set about in the beginning. Thus people drew satisfaction in explaining themselves and pick up what others said.

It appears that it might have served the purpose of mankind for some time, by way of portrayal of sketches. However, it was worth knowing here that sketches could be drawn of physical world only. No doubt, there was a sort of universality and cosmopolitanism in it, since the human-beings, animals, mountains and rivers were almost alike everywhere. For instance, their portraits drawn in West Asia would be identical with those drawn in U.S.A. or any other country and they would be understood easily as such, although there was considerable distance in between these countries. Thus the pictorial script, in whatever form it was, it had international and universal shape.

Even Changes in Portrayals did not Yield the Desired Results

Pictorial script was, no doubt, a medium of expression, yet it was not comprehensive. Of-course, one could have the knowledge of physical nature of articles from these drawings but when it was required to convey an abstract idea or a thought of the mind in relation to the physical objects, one felt helpless. Hence it was considered necessary to introduce one more object to form a relation and make the drawing more intelligible. In case a thirsty cow was intended to be painted in a picture, a running cow and a water pool in the vicinity were shown. Similarly, if an impression of famine was to be given, a sketch of a feeble person with his intestines protruded outside was drawn. If a reflection of grief or gloom was to be given, then a face of a person was shown, shedding tears. If an indication of movement was to be made, the feet of a person were painted. All this, however, was not enough to serve the purpose and suffice the day-today requirements.

In ancient China, the art of pictography was in vogue. Expression of inner feelings by way of drawings was also popular there. If an impression of friendship and cordiality had to be conveyed, then two hands were shown in a picture clasping together. If it was desired to give an indication of listening attentively, a person was painted in the picture standing by the side of a door with his ears alert.

Egypt too has been highly rated in the fields of artistic crafts and skills like China. Similar attempts were made there to communicate messages through pictorial drawings but it failed to provide an effective alternative. People carried on their work to a limited extent only and were unable to express all their sentiments and feelings conveniently.

Another difficulty experienced was that only common articles, objects or human-beings could be shown through pictorial drawings. For example, if a person was desired to be shown in a picture, his sketch was drawn with no difficulty. However, when an idea had to be given about a specific person or object, there was difficulty. It was practically impossible to convey the message regarding a proper noun or a person. There could be several persons, having the same name but they had different appearances. Hence it was impossible to convey a massage, relating to them, through pictography.

Lack of Knowledge of Painting or Drawing Pictures —A Problem

After all, pictorial drawing is also an art—even it may be ordinary and unattractive to look at. Everybody could not be expected to be competent in this art. Hence, those who were not capable or accustomed to painting, experienced much inconvenience. Then there could be some people who knew how to make a picture or draw sketch but when they were required to convey their feelings immediately, they found themselves unable to draw pictures with spontaneity. Moreover, only the present views could be conveyed through pictography but there was no medium or source for expression of past and future events.

Thus in the age of pictorial script, people tried to communicate their views some how or other but they did not feel contented. They faced many inconveniences. They were, therefore, on the look out for a better alternative, so as to be able to get rid of day-today discontentment and inconvenience.

Symbolic Script

Drawing pictures was not an easy job. It was time-consuming as well. How long dynamic human-beings could get on with it. In order to make prompt expressions, they used to draw sketches as early as possible without worrying for the quality of their drawings. They kept the work going on for some time by even drawing imperfect sketches. The standard of pictorial drawings continued deteriorating for want of time and skill. Gradually people resorted to drawing some symbolic lines only in place of complete picture. For example, if a mountain was desired to be shown, its sketch used to be drawn and its peaks were specifically projected through lines. However, later on, only symbolic lines were drawn. Thus, the symbolic signs or marks replaced the pictorial drawings. No doubt, it was very easy to pick up the message at the very sight of a picture. But the situation changed and it was not so easy to understand on looking at symbolic signs. People had to memorize that a particular sign or mark symbolized such and such article. There was universality to an extent in pictorial drawings. Hence it was not difficult to explain our views to the people inhabiting different regions or countries. However, the situation on the face of linear drawings was different. Unless people were aware that such and such linear signs had been pre-supposed to convey such and such meanings or expressions, they could not be expected to pick up any message, merely on seeing those signs. Hence the element of universality that was witnessed earlier in pictorial script disappeared and was no longer, existent. It was also not practically feasible for people of different countries to decide the same symbolic signs for different articles.

Abstract Ideas Conveyed by Phonetic Script-Writing

Symbolic sketches were further improved in order to manifest both physical objects and internal feelings. A few symbolic signs in the shape of small pictorial drawings remained in vogue on one hand and on the other a few symbolic signs formed consistency with phonetics and were determined to demonstrate constant change in thoughts and feelings. This method enabled to give an impression of both physical substances and abstract thoughts of the mind in relation to them.

Phonological Script Writing

Symbolic signs were, thus, used for manifestation of physical objects and expression of alstract feelings, relating thereto. People realised the uses and disuses of the method. Presumably, they felt that symbolic signs were more appropriate and consistent for expressing the nature of phonetic sounds. The sign adopted to represent a particular sound was understood as such everywhere. Similar position was, however, not obtained in case of symbolic signs fixed for expression of abstract feelings. Hence this method of symbolic expression was further evolved in purely phonological script-writing.

Classification of Phonological Script Writing

Phonological script was of two kinds — (1) Syllabic; and (2) Alphabetic.

Syllabic Script : There is a difference between an alphabet and a syllable. An alphabet is as much of a sound as can be pronounced atonce, that is, a vowel with or without one or more consonants while a syllable is a combination of more than one phonetic sound. Grossly speaking, no apparent defect was found in the use of syllabic script. However, on penetrating deep into the matter, it was imperfect from linguistic viewpoint. For example, let us take the Hindi word 'प्रिय' (dear). In Hindi or Devanagiri script, it comprises of two components - 'प्रि' and 'य' only. How many alphabetic letters are there in the word 'प्रिय', will not be explicit at a glance. However, if this word was written in Roman Script, five distinct phonetic sounds were there when spelt out as 'PRIYA' Sanskrit scholars will correctly spell out the letters of a Sanskrit word, written in Devanagiri Script. However, from the external shape of the word, one can not discern each letter separately at a glance. For example, let us take Sanskrit word 'वृक्ष' (Tree). Outwardly, it appears that the word is comprised of two letters only but virtually, there are five letters contained in it — 'व', 'ऋ,' 'क्', 'ष', and 'अ' which is not reflected by the outer appearance of the word. Infact, it is the shortcoming in the full-fledgedness of the script. Amongst modern scripts, Bengali, Guajarati, Oriya, Tamil, Telugu, Arabian and Persian etc. are all syllabic scripts like Hindi.

Alphabetical Script : The progress achieved successively in further evolution and improvement of script-writing, infact, culminated in Alphabetical script. Roman script was an excellent example of it. The chief characteristic of alphabetic script is that it has a separate letter for each and every phonetic sound. Therefore, all the letters, contained in a word, will be distinctly written in Roman Script. However, if the words, written in Roman script, have different pronunciations as in the case of English words — 'should', 'could' and 'would' etc. which are not pronounced according to the letters, contained in them, it demonstrates only the draw-back of the language itself and not the script in which they have been written. The script has no shortcoming or flaw, whatsoever.

Scripts of the World : Divided in Two Categories

The scripts, found in use throughout the world, can be classified in two categories on the basis of their shape and appearance. The first category consists of those scripts in which there are no distinct phonetic sounds for each letter or alphabet separately. There is only an independent pronunciation of the word. The second category comprises of the scripts in which there is distinct phonetic sound for each alphabet or letter separately. The philologists have classified the world scripts in two categories as shown hereunder :

First Category : Prominent Scripts

1. Cuniform
2. Hiroglyfic
3. Kreeṭa Scripts
4. Script of Indus Valley
5. Hittite Script
6. Chinese Script
7. Scripts of ancient Central America and Mexico.

Second Category : Prominent Scripts

1. South Semitic Script
2. Hebrew Script
3. Phoenician Script
4. Kharoshthi Script
5. Ārmeika Script
6. Arabian Script
7. Indian Script
8. Greek Script
9. Latin Script.

Origin of Brāhmi Script : Diverse Opinions

A critical evaluation of the diverse opinions of the scholars in regard to the origin of Brāhmi Script is desirable. Many scholars have given full thought and consideration to the subject but it has not been possible to arrive at a unanimous conclusion. The fact remains that each scholar has tried to assert the authenticity of his respective opinion. However, the subject calls for further investigation and analytical research even now.

Origin of Brāhmi from Greek Script

Certain scholars have opined that the source of origin of Brāhmi script is Greek Script. Prominent intellectuals, endorsing this view, are Dr. Alfred Muler, M/s James Princep and Senārt. According to the analysis of Prof. Senārt, the mutual contacts of Indians and Greeks grew rapidly after invasion of Alexander over India. Till then, the art of writing had not begun in India. They learnt it from Greeks and accordingly composed Brāhmi Script.

Infact, the science of writing was in practice in India much before the Indians had come in contact with Greeks. People of this country were well aware with the art of writing. Hence there was no reason, whatsoever, for linking the origin of Brāhmi with Greek script. It is all the more significant that such views had been expressed by noted scholars of the West i.e., Professors Buler and Drizer. In case, the origin of Brāhmi was believed to have taken place during the life-time of emperor Chandragupta Maurya, then was it possible that it had become so refined, well-developed and exalted by the life time of his grand-son, Emperor Ashōkā.

French Scholar, Kupeti : Sometimes, even enlightened scholars make such assumptions which are incoherent and unlikely. French scholar, Mr. Kupeṭi was one who advanced a typical argument in regard to the origin of Brāhmi Script. According to him, the source of origin of Brāhmi script was Chinese script. Linguists and research scholars on science of writing would agree that there was nothing in common between Chinese and Brāhmi scripts. The Chinese script is basically pictorial script, irrespective of the fact that it has undergone a lot of modification from time to time. As aforesaid, there are no syllabic and alphabetic phonetics in Chinese script. Instead, there are pictorial signs representing phonatics pertaining to or related to the words. The number of pictorial signs is enormously large in Chinese script. They could be 40,000 to 50,000 in number . However, the Chinese scholars have now minimised the number considerably and have limited it to about 500 pictorial signs only which have been found in repeated use. These signs have been further simplified and the entire writing work is being done now by virtue of the said limited pictorial signs. The letters of the Brāhmi script are obtained from syllabic phonations or in other words it is a syllabic script. How could it have anything in common with Chinese script.

Of course, Chinese script is most ancient. According to Chinese belief, it had its origin in or about the year 3,200 B.C. According to another version, it came into existence in the year 2700 B.C. However, the mere ground of ancientness is no criteria for attaching so much significance to it. The scholars pay no heed to the view that Brāhmi had its origin from Chinese script and ignore the said view altogether.

North Semetic Script : The two words appearing in linguistic science — 'Semitic' and 'Hemetic' represent two separate and distinct linguistic groups, i.e., Semitic linguistic group and Hemetic linguistic group. There is a Semitic script also.

It is a hearsay that prophet Hazrat Nisha had two sons. Elder one was named Sema and younger one Hema. As per traditional belief, Sema was considered as the creator of the universe and the first or primaeval being of South-West Asian people. The group of languages, widely in use in Sema region, came to be known as Semitic linguistic group. Like the group of languages, the script used in the region, came to be known as Semitic script. The literal translation of the word Semitic was Sami in Hindi. The script used in southern parts of the territory under Semitic linguistic group, was known as Southern Semitic script.

A number of scholars believed that Brāhmi had its origin from Northern Semitic script. Prominent among the said scholars is Buler. Other Western scholars M/s Bewar, Benfe, Westerguard, Whitney, Johnson, William Jones etc. more or less endorsed his views with minor variations, if any, here and there. According to the opinion of Mr. Buler, Semitic alphabets were introduced in India about 800 years before the commencement of Christian era.[1]

Phoenician and Brahmi : An offshoot of North Semitic script was Phoenician language. Since it was in use in the country of Phoenicia, it was called Phoenician. In ancient days, the territory, situated in North-West Asia (modern Syria) was known as Phoenicia. In olden days, Phoenicia was a highly developed centre in the spheres of education, civilization, skills and technology as well as in trade and commerce. The Indian merchants used to visit Phoenicia frequently for business dealings. According to the authors of the above theory, the art of writing was alien to this country. Therefore, the merchant class found it necessary to learn the alphabet of Phoenician script. They did so and removed the hurdle. The said merchant class brought Phoenician alphabet with them to India which was subjected to further alterations, improvements, refinement, expansion and enlargement by the scholars and thus the Phoenician alphabet was given a new shape and an ideal alphabet was obtained. The letters of the said alphabet began to be used easily in writing Sanskrit and Prākrita scripts without least inconvenience. Since the Phoenician alphabet was given a new shape by Brahmana scholars, hence the script came to be known as Brāhmi script. Majority of the scholars endorse this view that the source of origin of Brāhmi script was Phoenician script.

New Founding : Dr. Rajbali Pāndey had advanced a new theory. He expressed the view that the inhabitants of Phoenicia were basically Indians. According to him, many Indians had migrated and settled in Phoenicia. They had carried with them the knowledge of Brāhmi Script. Brāhmi Script was influenced by other scripts and after undergoing various phases of development and growth, it adopted a new shape, known as Phoenician script. According to him, it was why so much similarity was found in these two scripts. Dr. Pāndey had quoted illustrations from Rigveda in support of his plea.

Dr. Pāndey was, no doubt, an erudite scholar. He had tried to establish an altogether new founding in this regard by virtue of his logic and reasoning. However, the facts that Indians had migrated to Phoenicia along with their script and that Phoenician script was the product of Brāhmi script after having undergone various alterations and modifications, were of significant nature and further investigations and analysis were necessary. Mere scriptural illustrations would not suffice.

Southern Semetic Script and Brāhmi

Certain scholars opined that Brāhmi Script had its origin from South Semitic script. The prominent scholars amongst them were M/s Taylor and Saitha etc.

A few scholars believe that the source of origin of Brāhmi Script was from Arabian script, an offshoot of South Semitic branch of linguistics. However, the

1. *Indian Paleography*, p. 17.

fact remained that there was absolutely no resemblance of South Semitic Script or any of its offshoots with Brāhmi script. No doubt, Arabs had close dealings with Indians in the past. But it would be irrelevant to draw an inference on that account that Brāhmi had its origin from Arabian script. It is a historical fact that the relations between Arabs and Indians were not so old that one could rely on the origin of Brāhmi Script from Arabian script. Brāhmi was highly developed script during the period of Emperor Ashōkā.

Dr. Rhys Davids : Dr. Rhys Davids has conceived that there was a script, already in vogue in the valley of Euphretus river, even prior to the origin of Semitic alphabet. According to Dr. Rhys Davids, Brāhmi owed its origin right from the said ancient script of the valley of Euphratus river which was also the source of birth of Semitic scripts. However, there were so many question marks against such an assumption which had no answers. Hence there was no use giving any serious consideration to this view.

India : Place of Origin of Brāhmi Script

Certain Western and Indian scholars strongly refute the above theory and do not agree that Brāhmi had its origin from any foreign script. They opine that it was in India where Brāhmi script had its origin. Amongst the said scholars, the names of M/s Edward Thomas, Gold Stooker, Rajendra Lal Mitra, Lāssen, Dawson and Cunningham were specially worth mention. According to these scholars; the Aryans in ancient India used pictorial drawings or pictorial script for their expression. Most probably, Brāhmi owed its origin to it.

Mr. Buler had, however, opposed this theory. According to him, when there was no trace of any form of pictorial script, alleged to have been used in ancient India, how it could be asserted that Brāhmi had evolved from the said pictography. At the time when Mr. Buler had advanced the said argument, excavations of Mohan-Jo-Daro and Harappa had not been carried out. After the excavations, there was no room for any ifs and buts and all speculations automatically came to an end.

Views of Dr. Chatterji : The views of most eminent philologist of India, Dr. Suniti Kumar Chatterji, deserved full attention and minute consideration. He is quoted here consistently. "Amongst various scripts in India which could be deciphered till now, Brāhmi script was the oldest one. No doubt, it was the most ancient script relating to Aryan linguistics in India. The history of our Hindu Civilization was very old. *Purānās* (Certain well-known sacred works; these are 18; they contain the whole body of Hindu mythology) gave description of events, relating to the times-several thousands of years before Christian era. However, there was no trace of any article, written in an Aryan language, even prior to 300 years B.C. which could have been deciphered. Therefore, Brāhmi Script of Moryan era had to be accepted as primal script amongst all opinions in regard to the origin of Brāhmi script. By that time, almost all scholars believed that Brāhmi had emerged from Phoenician alphabet (which was obtained on the basis of Phoenician language pertaining to 'Shaimiya' linguistic group, used in Phoenicia, a territory of Syria, prior to 1000 B.C.). The Phoenician alphabet was brought to India by Dravadian merchants either via South Arabia or Bay of Iran in or about

900 to 800 B.C. and after having been modified, refined, evolved and enlarged by Brahmaṇa scholars, a full-fledged alphabet in the shape of Brāhmi script had been accomplished. However, a few scholars did not agree with the idea that Brāhmi alphabet had its origin from Phoenician alphabet. They believed that Brāhmi script was obtained from some form of pictography, already in use, by Aryans in India. Now after excavations of Mohan-Jo-Daro and Harappa, a different view is expounded, after deciphering hundreds of coins, recovered therefrom, that the pictorial script, used by ancient Aryans, culminated in Brāhmi Script. Whatever be the reality, the fact remained that Brāhmi script had been founded and brought in use, some time near about 1000 B.C. and which was widely in use during the period of Moryan emperors."[1]

While producing the gist of various concepts, Dr. Chatterji has made certain observations, which will help in arriving at a definite conclusion and critical evaluation of the matter.

Art of Writing in India

Rig Veda and other Vedas : Rigveda enjoyed a unique place in ancient canonical literature of India. Nay — amongst all the literature, accomplished in various languages, pertaining to Indo-European Linguistic group. Rigveda had an extra-ordinary significance from philological view-point. There were references, here and there, in Rigveda which established the existence of writing art in India. For example, there is a recitation in Rigveda 'सहस्र में ददतों अष्टकर्ण्य:' (It meant that a thousand cows, each having eight ears had been gifted). The word `अष्टकर्ण्य' probably referred to those cows, on the ears of which, the figure 8 might have been pricked, either in pursuance of certain religious traditions or as a gesture of certain auspicious achievements. All such cows might have been called `अष्टकर्णी' (having eight ears). Knowledge of writing of figure 8 clearly established that the writing art had been fully accomplished by the time of Rigvedic era.

In Rigveda, the names of metres have appeared as 'Gayatri' (A vedic metre of 24 syllables) and 'उष्णिक (Metres with 28 syllables or 7 syllables in each quarter) which imply that meterical compositions with a fixed number of syllables, proved the existence of writing knowledge.

There were references in *Vajasneyi Samhita* or the *Shukla Yajurveda* (written by the great Sage, Yājnavalkaya) regarding existence of art of writing. In *Kāshka Saṁhita*, *Maitrāyani Saṁhita* and *Taittriya Saṁhita* of Krishna Yajurveda (also known as black Yajurveda), there were references of several types of metres with number of Padas or quarters of each metre together with number of syllabic instants, regulating each pada. Similarly, there were references of total number of metres in Atharva Veda. At one place, we find a clear mention of 11 types of metres.

Upanishads and Brāhmana Treatises

In 'Chhāndogyopnishada', the alphabetical letters, syllables and nouns beginning

1. *Bharat Ki Bhashayen Aur Bhasha Sambandhi Samasyaen*, pp. 170-71.

with vowels 'i', 'u' and 'e' and in 'Taittriya Upnishad', the consonants, vowels, metres and the syllabic instants, regulating them have been produced. In 'Aitreya - Brāhmaṇa', the word 'ओ' (om) is described to have been accomplished by conjugation of letters 'a', 'u' and 'm'. In 'Shatpatha-Brāhmaṇa', there is discussion on singular and plural numbers and three genders etc. In 'Panchavisha Brāhmaṇa' also, there are indications to establish that knowledge of writing was already there. These sacred books are admittedly older than the works of etymologist, Yāsk and Pāṇini, author of 'Ashtadhyayi', (Name of Pāṇinis' grammatical work consisting of 8 chapters). Thus it followed that the art of writing was already in existence in Vedic, Upnishidac and Brahmanic periods.

Other Relative Treatises

The sacred books — *Rāmayanā* and *Mahābhāratā* are believed to be very old. Even if they were not considered to be too old, they had decidedly been accomplished by 500 to 400 B.C. There are citations in the said treatises also that knowledge of writing was already in existence.

The oldest grammatical treatise in Sanskrīt is 'Ashṭadhyāyi', written by Pānini. Mr. Gold-Stooker expressed the view that its period of composition preceded the era of Lord Buddha. Dr. Vasudeva Sharan Agrawal believed that it had been accomplished prior to 430 to 400 B.C. He has also drawn our attention to the renowned treatise 'Bharat', contemporaneous to the period of great grammarian, Pānini, which was really worth reading. The words 'लिपि' (written Characters); 'लिपिकर' (writer) and then parallel forms 'लिबि' (art of writing) and 'लिबिकर' (writer) have appeared in 'Ashṭadhyāyi'. There is also a mention how to form the word 'यबनानी' (The writing of the Yavanas-Greeks). The great commentator, Kātyāyan and Pātanjali, author of 'Mahābhāshya' (great commentary of Pātanjali on Pāṇini's Sutras) have explained the meaning of 'यवनानी' as Greek Script. The word like 'ग्रन्थ' (Religious treatises) have also appeared in the said Commentaries which signifies that the knowledge of writing was already in existence during the era of great grammarian, Pāṇini.

Prof. Maxmuler has presumed that the 4th Century B.C. was the life-time of Pāṇini. According to him, there was no mention, whatsoever, in Ashṭadhyāyi which could substantiate the existence of science of writing during the era of Pāṇini. However, things have become quite clear after publication of *Pāṇini Kalin Bhārat*, written by Dr. Vāsudeva Sharan Agrawal. Infact, the above assumption of Prof. Maxmuler was mistaken and confusing. Probably, he might not have been able to undertake a minute study and critical investigation of 'Ashṭadhyāyi' from the said viewpoint.

There were reflections in Political Economy and Science of Polity, written by Kautilya (the friend and adviser of emperor Chandra Gupta) regarding existence of Knowledge of Writing in India. The period of composition of the said Political Economy is also believed to be 4th century B.C. There were also references regarding existence of knowledge of writing in ancient sacred works such as — 'Vashishtha' 'Dharma Sutra', 'Manusmriti'. (The code of laws ascribed to the first Manu); and 'Vatsāyan Kāmsutra' (a work on erotic subjects).

In Buddhist Canonical Literature

Akhatika : In *Brahamjālsutta* (a scripture forming part of Tripitakas), there was a mention of a game, named 'Akhatikā'. Its formation in Sanskrit will be 'अक्षरिका' (alphabetical letters). The game may be explained like this—A person gives gestural indications of writing a few letters, raising up its hand towards the sky or on the back of another person which were to be discerned and read out by another participant in the game. Writing of letters by raising the hand towards sky meant-forming the letters by movement of the finger in open space. Similar was the purpose of writing letters by the finger by making its gestural movement on the back of another person. The other participant was required to identify the letters formed by raising up the arm towards the sky. Similarly, the person on whose back, the letters were formed by movement of the finger, had to identify them. The victory or defeat in the game depended on whether the participants were able to identify the letters. In case, the forms of letters or art of writing were not known to the people, how they would have been able to play such a game.

'Brahamjāl Sutta', in which there was a mention of the game, called 'Akhatika', was incorporated in the first Sūtra of 'Solakkhandha Vagga', forming part of 'Digh Nikāya' (Dialogues of Lord Buddha) pertaining to Sutta Pitaka (one of the three collections of Buddhistic writings).

Vinaya Pitaka (Vinaya texts—Collection of Buddhistic Writings on Discipline, Ethics and Morality) and Jataka Treatises, (The Rales of Lord Buddha's Previous Births)

In Vinaya Pitaka, an important collection of Buddha discourses and one of the three Buddhist scriptures, references of the words, signifying the art of writing, its eminence, writing in general, and a writer etc. were there. Mr. Olden Varga had assumed the historicity of Vinaya Pitaka to be as old as 400 B.C. or above.

Jatākas are really superb books depicting the social life of human-beings, arts and crafts, educational learning, trade and business professions of ancient India. According to erudite scholar like Mahamahopadhyaya Dr. Gaurishankar Hirachand Ozha, the said Jatākas provided glimpses of day today life of the people in India for the period dating back to sixth century B.C. or even earlier to it. The words like pens, books, schools, writings, articles, writers, alphabetical letters and writing material such as-wooden and bamboo pieces, leaves, golden or yellow leaves, wooden canvas or sheets of papers etc. have appeared in the said Jatāka treatises.

In Jaina Canonical Literature

The name of Brāhmi Script is obtained from 5th Anga, 'Vyākhyapragyapti (Bhagwati) Sūtra (forming part of Agamic Scriptures). The names of 18 scripts have appeared in 4th Anga, Samvayanga and fifth 'Pragyāpna Sūtra'. Other details relating to the names of 18 scripts have been reproduced below in the note at the foot.[1] Besides them, there are hints at other places as well in Jaina Canonical literature regarding existence of knowledge of writing and writing material. There is a reference of 'Sūryābhdeva' in 'Rājprashṇiya Sūtra', wherein the use of the word 'पुस्तक रत्न' (A precious book) is found. Probably, the use of the word 'पुस्तक रत्न' implied that a book was then considered as precious as a costly gem. It is stated in that context : "Then the divine head of the general Council of 'Sūryābhdeva' offered a precious book to Sūryābhdeva who accepted it, opened and looked into it, turned its leaves, undertook recitation of the book, acquired knowledge of religious affairs and thereafter returned the book.[2]

In 'Samvāyanga Sūtra', it is stated that there are 46 characters or alphabetical letters in Brāhmi script.[3] In 'Vrahatkalpabhāshya', the books have been classified into five categories — namely, 'Ganḍi', 'Kachchhvi'; 'Mutthi'; 'Sampuṭaphalaka'; and 'Chhedapāṭi'.[4] In the Commentary on 'Dashavaikālika', written by Achārya Haribhadra, it is stated that ancient religious teachers also believed that there were 5 types of books. A similar mention is found in 'Nishitha Chūrni'. In the commentary on 'Samvāyānga Sutra', it is stated that writing or inscribing of letters of alphabet on copper, iron, wooden, barks of trees, ivory, leaves and silver was already in practice.[5] It is found written in 'Vasudeva Hinḍi' that writing or inscribing a book on Copper plates was common.[6]

It is also obtained under Jaina tradition that 'Chakravartis' (Holders of precious round wheel, most worthy and respectable personalities of their age and exclusive rulers of six parts of India), after having attained the prerogatives of a 'Chakravarty', they get their names inscribed on rocks of a hill or mountain. There is a similar reference in 'Jambudweep Pragyapti' (a Jaina Agamic Scripture) of acting accordingly by emperor Bharat. It is cited therein — "Thereafter, the emperor Bharat, himself, took control of the horses, turned their direction and arrived near Rishabhakūt mountain. He touched the Rishabhakūt mountain with the front portion of his chariot thrice and bridled the horses. Thereafter, he took out a small coin, resembling with the shape of an appliance of a black-smith, having six surfaces, twelve fragments and eight corners. He inscribed with the help of it on a plain surface of eastern side of Rishabhkūt mountain— 'I am a sovereign ruler of India. In the third part of the present wheel of time (When the strength of the people and their figures start decaying, average age of the people and knowledge get reduced and the manhood and sense of dignity gets declined). I am the first emperor. I am the ruler of India. I am the most worthy and distinguished chief of mankind, I have no opposition at all. I have conquered the whole of India. He wrote the said words on the surface of the rock and came back to his Chariot for return journey.

---

1. Please read footnote relating to the topic of 'Jaina beliefs' in this very Chapter.
2. Taenaṁ tassa Sūriyābhassa devassa. Samāniya parisovavamargo devo pothar yaṇaṁ uvaneṇti tatenaṁ Sūryabhe deve potharyaṇaṁ giṇahai pothayaṇaṁ mnai mangyai, potharyaṇaṁ Vrihādei, potharyaṇaṁ vāeti, dhammivaṁ vavasāyaṁ giṇhai potharyaṇaṁ padiṇikha mati.
— *Rājprashniya Sūtra*, Page 167
3. Baṁbhienaṁ liviye Chhāyālisaṁ Māuyakkharā. —*Samvāyānga Sutra*, 46
4. Vrahat-Kalpa-Bhāshya, 3. 3822.
5. Samvāyānga Sutra Tika, p. 78.
6. Vasudeva Hindi, p. 189.

In the commentary on 'Kalpa Sutra' (a Jaina Agamic Scripture), there is a reference in relation to the biography of Lord Mahavira that when he completed eight years of his age, he was admitted to the school by his father, Sidhārtha, after a great celebration. Costly presents were awarded to the teacher and supplied materials, used by the students while reading, such as inkpots, pens and slates etc. in sufficient number.

While putting down in writing 4 projects on 'Avashyaka' (an Agamic Scripture), and explaining the extract 'आगमतः द्रयावश्यक' it had been stated in 'Anuyoga Dwār' that besides using other attributes, three other distinguishing features for accurate pronunciation and recital of texts have been given, namely, (1) Distinct and clear pronunciation of each letter without abandoning or forsaking any letter; (2) Only those letters of the alphabet and syllables forming part of the texts, meant for recitation, should be uttered and no more, or no less; (3) The letters of the texts should not be pronounced in wrong or contrary manner. They should be read correctly. The above features clearly reflected that great emphasis was laid on accurate and correct use of letters. Where the use of the letters was observed so minutely, decidedly, the art of writing must already be there in existence.

The Prākrita words 'पोत्थकम्म' and पोत्थकार' have also appeared in the aforesaid 'Anuyoga Dwar Sūtra'. The word 'पोत्थ' is Prākrita form of Sanskrit word 'पुस्त' (a book or manuscript). After suffixing the termination 'क' to 'पुस्त', the word 'पुस्तक' (A Book) is obtained. According to the author of the gloss, the Prākrita word 'पोत्यकम्म' means 'writing on a palmyra leaf by a small pen or brush and similarly there is the Prākrita form of Sanskrit word 'पुस्तक'. As per Commentator, it means to earn one's living by way of writing the books. Earning a living reflects receiving remuneration after writing a book or reducing it to black and white. Probably, the purport here does not seem writing a new book. In the present sense, he could be called a copyist.

It is thus amply supported by the above references that art of writing was existent in India for a pretty long time. Besides Vedic and Buddhist literature, the references in Jaina canonical literature have their historic significance equally.

Chinese Encyclopaedia

In the well-known Chinese encyclopaedia, named 'Fā-Vān-shu-lin (accomplished in the year 668 A.D.), Brāhmi Script has been defined to mean that it was composed by a religions teacher, named Brāhma or Brahmā. Accordingly, the script came to be known as 'Brāhmi'. Thus, the definition appearing in Chinese Encyclopaedia had its great significance from historic viewpoint.

Amongst the scholars, who advocated that Brāhmi script had its origin in India, Mr. Edward Thomas and others believed that basically Brāhmi script owed its origin to Dravadians. However, Dr. Rajbali Pāndey has strongly refuted this theory. According to him, the basic habitat of Dravadians is South India and not North India. No inscriptions in Brāhmi Script have been found in Southern India. They are obtained in North India only. Had Brāhmi Script been introduced by Dravadians, the inscriptions in Brāhmi Script and relative material ought to have been found in South India, which was, however, not the case.

Dr. Pandey has made a critical review from linguistic viewpoint also. Tamil is most ancient amongst all other Dvavadion languages. He explains that in Tamil language, the pronunciation of only first and the last letters of 'कवर्ग' (first pentad of soft palatal Consonants); 'चवर्ग' (second pentad of palatal consonants) and 'टवर्ग' (The third pentad of Hindi alphabet incorporating the letters ट, ठ, ड, ढ, and ण) is made only while the phonation of intervening consonants remains unvoiced. On the other hand, all the five consonants of each class are voiced in Brāhmi. . . In case, Brāhmi script owed its origin to Dravadians, Tamilian characteristic feature must have been followed in Brāhmi as well, which is, however, not found.

While commenting upon the view of Dr. Pandey, what Dr. Bholanath Tiwari has asserted is quite significant in the present context. He writes: "In the absence of any solid evidence, it is, of course, not possible to assert that Dravadians had introduced Brāhmi Script. Nevertheless, the pleas of Dr. Rāj Bali Pāndey are also not very logical and convincing. It is possible that the bonafide habitat of Dravadians may have been in South but a sizeable number of scholars have expressed the view that they lived in North India as well. Large cities like Mohan-Jo-Daro and Harappa were centers of their great civilization. To obtain 'Brāhmi' language in West Pakistan, which decidedly belonged to Dravadian linguistic group, amply proves that they lived in northern India as well. Later on, they were probably thrashed out by Aryans and they took refuge in South India. Another argument, advanced by Dr. Pandey, that there were lesser number of voiced consonants in Tamil script as against Brāhmi is also not very effective and convincing. Was it not possible that Aryans might have adopted the script of Dravadians or Tamils and modified it to suit their requirements. It is not impossible that the ancient basic shape of a script or its original form may be wanting and incomplete and it is equally possible that attempts might have been made from time to time to improve it and obtain an accomplished shape. Transformation of an imperfect script into a full-fledged and perfect script is quite possible and a natural process."[1]

There were still numerous unanswered questions such as—had the Aryans migrated to India from the territories beyond India? Were the Dravadians original inhabitants of India ? Were the great civilizations of Mohan-Jo-Daro and Harappa, discovered after excavations, representative of thousands of years old culture and civilization of Dravadians ? Was the pictographic material, collected therefrom, indicating that art of writing was already in existence in India and was practised by its original inhabitants ? needed critical study and minute investigation by the scholars. If the scholars spared no pains and made concerted afforts, it is quite possible that new facts may come to light which may enable to diffuse the dark layers of ignorance and answer the above queries. The inquisitives may have fresh enlightenment and be able to satisfy their curiosities. What else can be added or hoped under the circumstances.

Mahamahopādhyāya Dr. Ozha : Mahamahopādhyāya, Dr. Gaurishanker Hirachand Ozha was an erudite scholar and an authority on art of writing. He carried an analytical research and investigation over ancient scripts in India. On

1. Bhāshā Vigyān, Page 502.

this subject, his work 'Prachin Lipimāla' (ancient scripts) was greatly admired. While commenting upon the origin of Brāhmi script, Dr. Ozha writes: "Whatever views are available as a means for arriving at correct knowledge—whether the style of writing on ancient petrographic inscriptions or literary references all indicate that the art of writing was fully developed and had been accomplished in India. However, there is no material available to throw light on its initial development. Therefore, nothing concrete can be added to show how Brāhmi Script came into existence and how it acquired perfection after having gone through various evolutionary phases. Only this much can be confidently stated on the basis of information, available, that Brāhmi Script had already obtained an accomplished form and was extensively used in India. However, its origin from any external source, whatsoever, is not established."[1]

After undertaking minute study and investigation, Dr. Ozha ascertained that only 'ज' of Brāhmi Script and 'गिमेल' of Phoenician script were identical in appearance. On the basis of such trivial ground, no body could say for definite that the two scripts were inter-connected or one was the source of origin of the other. How can such an important conclusion be arrived at on the basis of such insignificant ground. No doubt, Dr. Ozha was an authority on this subject. He made unceasing efforts in this regard. The inferences, drawn by him, cannot be overlooked. They called for further consideration and critical research and investigation.

Two Small Petrographs Existing before the Era of Emperor Ashoka

The inscriptions of emperor Ashōkā were, no doubt, oldest and symbolized the use of Brāhmi script in ancient India. However, two small petrographs were also found, one of which had been located in village Barli or Baḍali in Ajmer district of Rajasthan, and the other had been found in village Piprāvā, situated on the foot hill of Nepal. Although the contents were short, yet whatever they were, the two small inscriptions were older than the Ashokan inscriptions. Hence they provided an opportunity for further consideration of the ancientness of the art of writing.

Dr. Ozha writes : "The first small inscription is a piece of a pillar. In its first line, the words 'वीर' (ा) 'य भगव(त)' and in the second line, the words 'चतुरासिति व (स) are inscribed. The year 84th, appearing in the said inscription, probably points out the 84th year from the samvat or year of salvation of Lord Mahavira, the last Tirthanker (A Jaina Arhant, sanctified teacher or saint of the Jainas). In case, the above inference or calculation is correct, the said inscription might have been written in the year 527-84 = 443 B.C. The script of this inscription appears to be relating to the period prior to Ashokan inscriptions. In the letter 'वी' of the word 'वीराय', the sign for Vowel 'i' is neither found in Ashokan inscriptions, nor in any of the inscriptions, relating to the later period. Hence the said sign for vowel 'i' must belong to the script, which might be in vogue prior to Ashokan inscriptions, the use of which might have stopped by the time of Ashokan era, and a new mark

1. *Prāchin Lipimālā.*

for the vowel ought to have replaced the old mark. From the other small petrograph, found at Piprāvā', it is obtained that the skeletonised bones (the bones of the dead body) of Lord Buddha had been burried under a monument (a kind of Tope erected for keeping sacred relics of Lord Buddha) by the people of Shākya Community (name of the community where Lord Buddha was born). Mr. Buler is of the view that the said small inscription pertained to the period prior to Ashokan era. In fact, it might have pertained to the period, slightly after 487 B.C., the year of salvation of Lord Buddha. Thus it is explicit from the references of the said two small inscriptions that knowledge of writing was already there in India during 5th Century B.C."[1]

In the light of the observations of Dr. Ozha, we again revert to the pictographic material obtained after excavations at Mohan-Jo-Daro and Harappa. Although, detailed study of the said pictorial script has not been carried out yet, so as to be able to declare that Brāhmi Script had been evolved from it, still there is strong possibility of such a likelihood, and drawing such an inference.

Conclusion

A Point at Issue : It is not possible to arrive at any definite and final conclusion in this regard because of diverse opinions and beliefs of the various scholars. However, there are certain aspects which need elaboration and further consideration:

Ashokan inscriptions are clear proofs of ancientness of Brāhmi Script. The aforesaid two small inscriptions of Baḍli and Piprāvā are not factual and do not impart any significant information from viewpoint of graphology. Therefore, it may not be wrong to say that there is no solid material or visible ground to hold that Brāhmi script was in existence prior to Ashokan inscriptions. In case, Brāhmi script had been in use for pretty long time, then why was it so that no rock, cave or pillar inscriptions were found prior to Ashokan era. Besides them, no other article or material had been found to suggest that art of writing was already in existence and Brāhmi script was in use.

It can be safely emphasized in respect of religious scriptures that there was a consistent tradition to retain the texts in memory. Consequently, they had not been reduced to writing nor it was deemed necessary. It might have been believed also that in case each and everybody had an access to the sacred books, they could be misused by undeserving persons for their own selfish ends. Hence scriptural writings might have been forbidden. However, other than religious works, there could be numerous other situations or needs for writing. No material, whatsoever, in the shape of copper, golden and silver coins, stamps or anything of that sort are available. The question repeatedly arises why was it so ?

An idea : There has been a tendency in India that eminent scholars, writers or literateurs always felt reluctant to disclose their names as authors of their accomplishments. This resulted in painful and unpleasant situation from historic viewpoint in the field of literature. There are quite a number of unique compositions, the genuinness of which cannot be verified for want of the names

1. *Prāchin Lipimālā*, pp. 2, 3.

of their authors and period of their accomplishment. Only by collecting scattered and uncertain clues from here and there, it is tried to assume when and by whom they had been written. In fact, by doing so, the learned scholars intentionally avoided self-propaganda, self-praise and to achieve worldly gains. The only desire they cherished for, was their ability to accomplish masterpiece works for the benefit and upliftment of the society.

Will it be an exaggeration to believe that like writers and litterateures, the erstwhile emperors, rulers and eminent personalities might have also developed a tendency to go on with their benevolent acts without worrying to raise any memorials for perpetuating their own name and fame.

Another point is also worth consideration. It was not binding in any way that the language of inscriptions must be eulogical only morality. They could also be the source for recording of series of events and propagation of truth, morality and virtues. What was objectionable in it? Although the question is pertinent, yet its correct answer is not available.

According to Dr. Chatterjee and a few other scholars, Brāhmi Script was in its entirely developed form even as early as 1000 years B.C. Dr. Ozha also endorses the view that Brāhmi Script was fully developed and quite fit to be used even in ancient days.

From the indications found in Regvida regarding existence of writing skill, it could be safely asserted that the last 10th Division of Rigveda had been accomplished prior to 12th Century B.C. and not later than it. Other divisions of Rigveda were comparatively more ancient. Thus the existence of Brāhmi script was there even prior to 12th Century B.C.

On one hand, availability of references, discussed above, and on the other, inability to find any reliable material prior to Ashokan inscriptions regarding existence of writing art in India, does create a feeling of disappointment.

One more Presumption : Is it not feasible that earlier form of Brāhmi script might be in unrefined state, unfit to be used in petrographic inscriptions? As a result of growing business dealings, mutual contacts must have greatly developed between the people of India, Phoenicia and other countries of West Asia. In the context of developing relations, it is obvious that there must have been exchange of mutual specialities or characteristics. In that process, Indians might have attempted to get their script further improved and obtain an accomplished form since they felt concerned to enhance their contacts with foreigners who might be having their own full-fledged script. As a consequence of the said improvement, Brāhmi Script in India must have acquired a refined shape. It might have been further developed and enriched during the course of next few centuries, till it acquired the form, suitable to be used in inscriptions.

In India, those, having blind faith and partiality in excellence of every thing that was old, might not relish the above idea. Probably they could also mistake it to be pro-Western mentality. However, it is not our aim. When there is no solid base to stand upon, probabilities have to be considered and pondered over. They could be multifarious. Hence what has been stated above is only a presumption and is left for the judgment of the scholars. They should argue and have full discussion.

Simply because Brāhmi Script is highly spoken of in our scriptural writings, it should not be deemed sufficient to arrive at any logical conclusion, more so, in the context of present age of scientific investigation. Merely to say that Brāhmi script was in its refined and developed form in primitive India, will not suffice. It will not carry much weight. The path of analytical research and investigation knows no bounds or limits. It remains dynamic and full of activity all along. The rational discussion knows no rigidity nor remains circumstanced. It always calls for new findings and establishments. Hence, it may not be worth-while to use superlative language only while describing the characteristics of Brāhmi script. Only by way of advancing rational and judicious arguments, we can substantiate anything. All these requisites are to be followed for proving excellence of Brāhmi script. Let us believe that the scholars will spare no pains for accomplishment of the task. It is not the task of any single individual but a collecting responsibility of all scholars. More they will concentrate their energies in undertaking critical study and examination, greater chances will be there to come across new findings. It may not be unfair to have such expectations from the learned scholars.

Emergence and Growth of Several Other Scripts from Brāhmi Script

The alphabet of Brāhmi Script was very easy. It was comparatively convenient to write its letters. There was no abundance or unnecessary use of syllabic instants or plurality of vowel marks. The appearance of letters resembled with capital letters of Greek or Latin Scripts. It will be explicit from the forms of the following letters :

Brāhmi	*Hindi*	*Brāhmi*	*Hindi*
𑀅	अ	𑀣	थ
∴	इ	𑀤	द
L	उ	D	ध
𑀏	ए	I	न
≥	ओ	□	ब
+	क	४	म
d	च	𑀬	य
𑀙	छ	2H↑	श
h	त	𑀳	ह

The specific vowel marks joining with the consonants of Brāhmi script were affixed on the head, foot or the body of the consonants, and the effect of the said tradition may be found on the alphabets of the script in India even now.

By the time, the letters of Brāhmi script were inscribed on the surface of rocks and stones by chisels, no change took place in the shape of the said letters since the inscriptional work is possible to be done quite slowly and gently. It cannot be done hastily.

After petrographic inscriptions, the era of writing on the barks or leaves of birch and palmyra trees had started. As compared to rock inscriptions, there was change in the shape of letters was witnessed as a result of rapidity in the speed of writing. Initially, the alphabetical letters of Brāhmi script were straight in form. After they were written by a pin or a wedge, they began to have twists and curves. After coming in contact with regional dialects, in different parts of India, the alphabetical letters of Brahmi script began adopting a new and a bit complicated shape. In case, the alphabets of various dialects spoken and used in different regions of the country, were compared with the alphabet of Brāhmi script the point would be quite clear. In nutshell, all the modern scripts, used in India, have evolved from Brāhmi script. Dr. Suniti Kumar Chatterjee has produced a map of modern scripts in India, having evolved from Brāhmi script in his work "Bharat Ki Bhāshāyan Aur Bhāshā Sambandhi Samasyayen." Being relevant in the present context, the same is being reproduced on the next page.

It is evident from the foregoing map of the scripts, evolved from Brāhmi Script that the latter had even expanded to the countries beyond India. It had influenced the scripts of those countries as well. It was helpful in further growth of the alphabets of old Kuchi, Khotani, scripts of modern Jawa island and Bali island etc. Brāhmi Script was also popular in Gandhar (Name of the Country between India and Persia, the modern Kandhar, comprising of the territories of Peshawar, Rawalpindi, and Kabul (Afghanistan). Many coins had been traced out from the old ruins of the said country which have inscription of the letters of both Brāhmi and Kharoshthi Scripts. In nutshell, there had been a time when Brāhmi was the national script of India and it had influenced the scripts of neighbouring countries as well.

Kharoshthi Script

Kharoshthi Script: Its use : Besides inscriptions in Brāhmi script, there are certain petrographs in Kharoshthi script too. Hence it is desirable to have a brief discussion over this script also as per demand of the context. The oldest examples of the use of Kharoshthi script are the Ashokan inscriptions at Shāhbāzgarhi and Mānsera, territories of North-West Frontier region. A few inscriptions have also been obtained at Kāngrā (Panjab), written in Kharoshthi script. The use of Kharāshthi script has also been found in inscriptions and coins of foreign rulers. It was prevalent in India roughly between 4th century B.C. and third century A.D. That is to say, it remained in use for seven centuries continuously. Kharoshthi script is known by numerous other names, such as — Indo-Vactriyan; Vactriyan; Vactro-Pāli; Vactro-Aryan and Kabulian etc.

Jaina Canonical Literature

While discussing over Brāhmi script, certain extracts were quoted from Jaina religious scriptures. In some of them, there was mention of Kharoshthi script as well along Brāhmi script. For instance, the names of 18 scripts have appeared in Samvayanga Sutra and against serial number 4 appears the name of Kharoshtika which is a synonymous word for Kharoshthi. The name of Kharoshthi script also appears against serial number 4 in Pragyāpnā Sūtra (An Agamic scripture) as shown above. However, in the commentary on

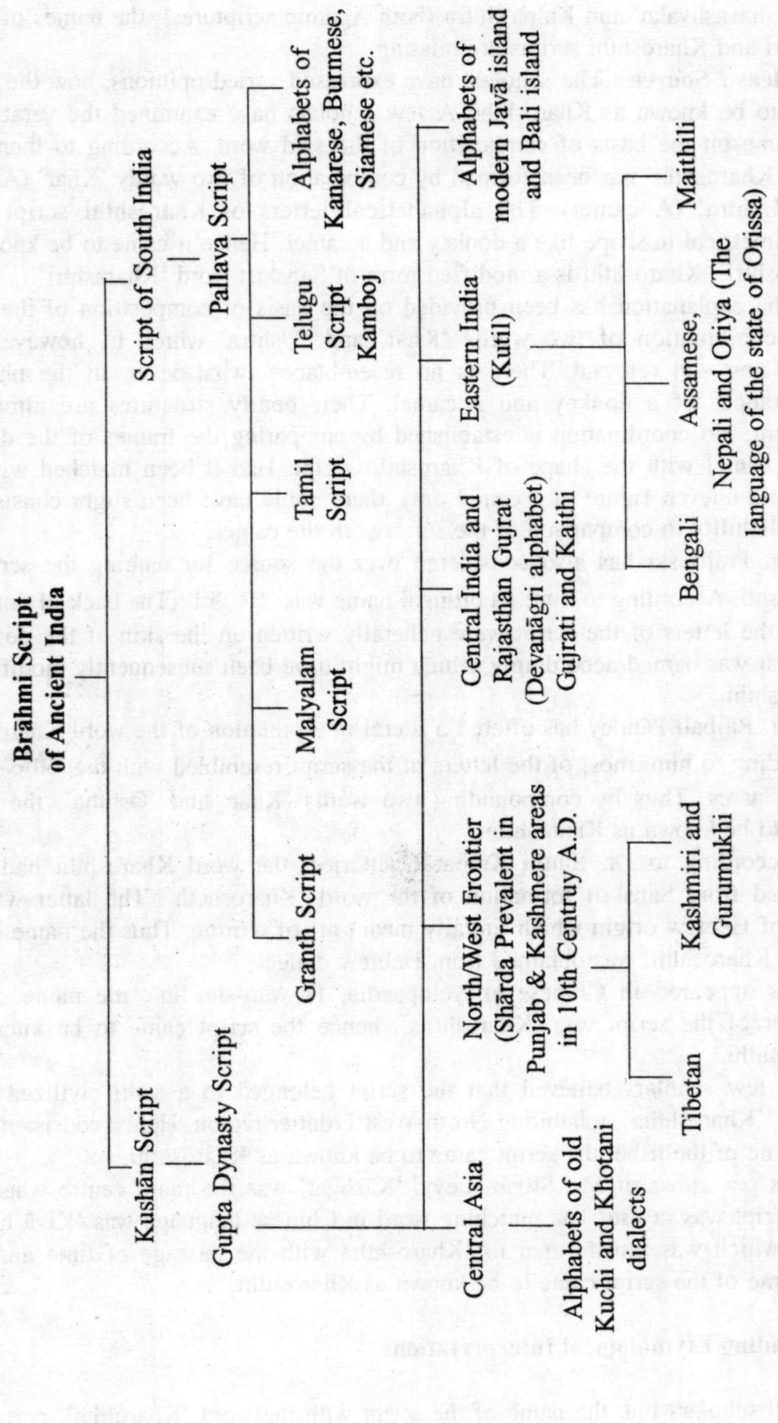
Brāhmi Script of Ancient India
Kushān Script
Gupta Dynasty Script
Script of South India
Pallava Script
Alphabets of Kanarese, Burmese, Siamese etc.
Telugu Script Kamboj
Tamil Script
Malyalam Script
Granth Script
Central Asia
Alphabets of old Kuchi and Khotani dialects
North/West Frontier (Sharda Prevalent in Punjab & Kashmere areas in 10th Centruy A.D.
Central India and Rajasthan Gujrat (Devanāgri alphabet) Gujrati and Kaithi
Eastern India (Kutil)
Alphabets of modern Javā island and Bali island
Tibetan
Kashmiri and Gurumukhi
Bengali
Assamese, Nepali and Oriya (The language of the state of Orissa)
Maithili

'Visheshavashyaka' and Kalpa Sūtra (both Agamic scriptures), the names of both. Brāhmi and Kharoshthi scripts are missing.

Ideas / Source : The scholars have expressed varied opinions, how the script came to be known as Kharoshthi. A few scholars have examined the veracity of the name on the basis of composition of the said word. According to them, the word 'Kharoshthi' has been formed by combination of two words 'Khar' (An ass) and 'Ushtra' (A camel). The alphabetical letters of Kharoshthi script were unsymmetrical in shape like a donkey and a camel. Hence it came to be known as 'kharoshtri'. Kharoshthi is a modified form of Sanskrit word 'Kharashtri'.

The explanation has been provided on the basis of composition of the word from combination of two words 'Khar' and 'Ushtra' which is, however, not convincing and relevant. There is no resemblance, whatsoever, in the physical appearances of a donkey and a camel. Their bodily structures are altogether different. No coordination is established by comparing the frames of the donkey and a camel with the shape of Kharoshthi script. Had it been matched with the ugly and uneven figure of a camel only, there could have been slight consistency and reliability in comparison of the script with the camel.

Dr. Prajiluski has also considered over the source for naming the script as Kharoshti. According to him, its original name was 'खरपृष्ठी' (The back of donkey). Since the letters of the script were generally written on the skin of the donkeys, hence it was named accordingly, which might have been subsequently modified to Kharoshthi.

Dr. Rājbali Pāndey has offered a literal interpretation of the word Kharoshthi. According to him, most of the letters of the script resembled with the 'ओष्ठ' (lips) of the asses. Thus by compounding two words 'Khar' and 'Oshtha', the script came to be known as Kharoshthi.

According to Dr. Suniti Kumar Chatterjee, the word Kharoshthi had been obtained from Sanskrit formation of the word 'Kharosheth'. The latter was the word of Hebrew origin which literally meant art of writing. Thus the name of the script, Kharoshthi, was obtained from Hebrew dialect.

As appeared in Chinese encyclopaedia, Fā-wān-shu-lin', the name of the founder of the script was 'Kharoshtha', hence the script came to be known as Kharoshthi.

A few scholars believed that the script belonged to a semi civilized tribe, called ''Kharoshtha', inhabiting North-West Frontier region. Hence consistent with the name of the tribe, the script came to be known as Kharoshthi.

As per views of Mr. Silvān Levy, 'Kāshgar' was the main centre where the said script was in use. The matching word in Chinese language was 'Kiyā-lu-shu-tā-le' which was transformed to 'Kharoshtha with the passage of time and thus the name of the script came to be known as Kharoshthi.

Misleading Etymological Interpretations

Certain scholars link the name of the script with the word 'Kharottha', pertaining to Armeika language. Sometime, such misleading etymological interpretations merely lead to the state of uncertainty. Finding identical phonetic sounds of two words, one should not erroneously misunderstand them of the same origin and having the same literal meaning. They may have nothing in common. Similarly, it will be a blatant mistake to substitute a word, having an altogether different meaning, only because it appeared more refined in shape and identical in appearance. This is how the word 'Kharottha' of Armeika language was treated. It was alleged to have been modified to 'Kharoshtha' with the passage of time and the script named as Kharoshthi. Varying opinions expressed by different scholars were based on mere conjectures and surmises. They were not corroborated by any historical evidence nor there was any material to support the above inferences.

The misleading etymology of the word 'Kharoshtha', alleged to be the modified form of the word 'Kharottha', belonging to Armeika language, is particularly debatable. While the subject relating to the origin of kharoshthi script will be deliberated upon in the ensuing chapter, the reference of Armeika language will, obviously, be made for elaborating the point.

Source of Origin of Kharoshthi : Dr. Rājbali Pāndey believes that Kharoshthi Script had its origin within India. He has enunciated the idea in his work 'Indian Paleography' (A study of ancient inscriptions in India). His opinion is based on mere guess and conjectures. In order to prove the bonafides of his reasoning, he ought to have produced substantive material, which is, however, missing.

Origin of Kharoshthi from Armaika Script: Quite a number of scholars believe that Kharoshthi had its origin from Armeika script, having two branches (1) Phoenician and (2) Armeika. Several scripts had their origin from Armeika script. Amongst them, the names of Hebrew, Pahalvi and Nebātena were worth mention. Sinetika script had originated form Nebatena and from Sinetika script, old Arabian script came into existence. It is believed that Armeika script was in vogue in the entire empire of Persia, spread over from Asia Miner to Gandhar i.e. almost in the whole of West Asia.

Since ancient days, India had close contacts with the countries of West Asia, more especially with Irān, Cirus was the king of Iran during 5th century B.C. (From 558 to 530 B.C.), who was highly ambitious and powerful ruler. He had a strong will and formidable force to conquer the territories of other countries. He had accomplished his dream and conquered the territorial parts upto Gandhar (a country between Persia and India). Thereafter, the king of Irān (First) had conquered the territories upto Indus river in India. It is possible that the use of Kharoshthi script, originated from Armeika Script, might have been popularised in areas forming part of Iranian dynasty. It might have been enriched and developed with the passage of time till it was considered fit to be adopted as full-fledged Prākrita dialect for inscriptional purposes.

Armeika and Kharoshthi Scripts

Prof. Buler was an expert in graphology. He did a lot of study and investigation on science of writing. He carried out analytical research on Kharoshthi script as well. His attainments on the subject were marvellous. According to Prof. Buler,

Armeika script was older than Kharoshthi. He added that the inscription, written in Armeika script, and found at Taksila (An ancient town of North-West India, known for its famous university) clearly manifested that the people of Armeika had close contacts with Indians. The method of writing in Kharoshthi script is from right to left side. Similar was the case with Armeika Script. While comparing the forms and phonetic sounds of the alphabetical letters (eleven letters) of Kharoshthi script with those of Armika script, Mr. Buler had expressed the view that there was considerable uniformity between both the scripts.

The inferences drawn by Mr. Buler were really authentic and credible. The eminent authority on Graphology. Mahamahopādhyaya Dr. Gaurishanker Hirachand Ozha has also endorsed his views.

Influence of Brāhmi Script

Like Armeika Script and Arabian Script, Kharoshthi Script was also written from right to left side. It came to be used by the people, inhabiting North-West Frontier region of India. Brāhmi was the script of Indian nation. Hence Kharoshthi script was bound to be influenced by Brāhmi. Consequently, Kharosthi also began to be written from left to right side like Brāhmi script.

Mr. Deringer and a few other scholars have drawn our attention to certain modifications in Kharoshthi Script which had taken place as a result of the influence of Brāhmi script. Basically, the vowels had not been provided in Kharoshthi script. The process of affixing signs of dash or circles to the letters to represent short vowels had started in Kharoshthi script which was, obviously, an effect of Brāhmi script. Similarly, consonants, namely, 'भ'and 'घ' etc. which were not found in Armeika scripts, were also absent in Kharoshthi script. They were later provided in Kharoshthi script in accordance with Brāhmi script.

An Imperfect Script : From the above discussion, it is evident that Kharoshthi was not a perfect script from viewpoint of graphology. A script was a source of expression while alphabetical or syllabic phonations were to be expressed. No phonetic sound remains unexpressed in a full-fledged script. However, these were the short- comings of Kharoshthi script. Besides the deficiencies indicated above, there were a few other short comings as well. For example, long vowels were altogether missing in Kharoshthi script. The letters joining consonants in a word were almost rare—rather they were absent. The total number of alphabetical letters did not exceed 37 in Kharoshthi script.

An Inappropriate Script for Writing Sanskrit Words

Kharoshthi Script was totally unfit for writing of Sanskrit language. Conjugated letters frequently appear in Sanskrit. The number of such conjugated words is further enhanced in Sanskrit language by following the rules for conjunction of the constituents in a conjunct word. Kharoshthi script was incapable to illustrate such conjunct words. Consequently, no Sanskrit work was accomplished in Kharoshthi script.

No inscription in Kharoshthi script is found after 3rd century A.D. In other words, after the rule of foreign conquerors in West Asia was over, the use of Kharoshthi script also became restricted. By then (till 3rd Century A.D.), Brāhmi script was having the same fate. However, new scripts had started coming forth from Brāhmi script and they were in the process of replacing it gradually. However, the fate of Kharoshthi was different. Had it been basically an Indian script, its use would have continued unhindered in North-West Frontier region.

There is another important point. As stated above, Kharoshthi script was not suitable for Sanskrit writings. Here the point for consideration is that in case a script had its origin in India, it could never be unfit for writing of Sanskrit language. The sole purpose of a script is to impart concrete shape to a language by way of writing in it. Had Kharoshthi been basically an Indian script, it would have been so formulated that there was no inconvenience in accomplishment of Sanskrit writings, which was then a principal language of this country. Thus it is clear that it owed its origin to an alien source and could be none else but Armeika.

No theological literature by Brahmaṇa scholars is found written in Kharoshthi script. One can understand why no Sanskrit work was written in Kharoshthi script since it was structurally unfit to do so. However, there could be another reason also why no work had been accomplished by a Brahmāṇa scholar in Kharoshthi script. It is quite possible that Brahmāṇa scholars might have felt reluctant to take up writing in a script, which had its origin from an alien source and was considered unholy for scriptural writings. However, the opinion of Budhist and Jaina scholars was different and they had no reluctance, whatsoever, in this regard.

Whatever the reality, Brahmāṇa Scholars were certainly hesitant to adopt kharoshthi script and they were not prepared to impart sanctity to it only because it owed its origin to a foreign source.

In the list of 18 scripts, appearing in 'Samvāyānga Sūtra' (An Agamic Scripture), the initial name, heading the list, is Brāhmi; second 'yavnāni' (Writing script of Greeks) and fourth is 'Kharoshtika' or 'Kharoshthi'. The Yāvāni script signifies here the script of Greece. Similar is the description in 'Pragyāpnā Sūtra' (Another Agamic scripture). Therein also, Brāhmi script tops the list and Yāvani is mentioned against serial No 2. Kharoshthi appears against serial number 4. In the lists of the aforesaid scriptures, there are certain names which apparently owe their origin to foreign countries.

The names of scripts, appearing in 'Samvāyānga Sūtra' and 'Pragyāpnā Sūtra' were not all Indian. A few names of the scripts were decidedly foreign. Other wise, the name of 'Yāvani' script would not have been incorporated in the two lists which was none else but 'Yavnāni Script' of Greece.

Lord Rishabha taught art of writing to his daughter, Brāhmi. It purported to mean that whatever scripts — Indian or non-Indian were in use in India, they were all taught by him to his daughter. In the list of the scripts, appearing in the commentary on 'Visheshāvashyaka' (an Agamic scripture), the name of 'Pārsi Script' is found, which should be the official script of Persian dynasty. It could be a script relating to Armeika Branch of Northern Semitic group of linguistics. Two scripts, mentioned in the list, shown in 'Kalpa Sutra' (an Agamie Jaina scripture), namely — 'Khurāsāni' and 'Parsi' are apparently foreign scripts. The word 'Parsi' has appeared for 'Pārsi'.

In 'Lalit-Vistar' (a Buddhist scripture) a detailed list of 64 scripts appear in which the names of 'Darda'; 'Khāsya' Chinese and Hūṇa scripts are included also. All these scripts appear to be belonging to foreign countries, beyond India.

The source of origin of Kharoshthi script was decidedly from an alien script. The rule of foreign conquerors in certain parts of India, provided special momentum for flourishing and expansion of the said scripts for some period. However, with the end of foreign domination, the use of the scripts was greatly minimised. The script of Kharoshthi, having been patronized by the ruling elite class, was bound to be recognized by the masses governed, by those rulers. Even after the foreign domination comes to an end, a particular system or arrangement, having once enjoyed the patronage of ruling class, is not obliterated overnight. It does take time in getting rid of the prevalent tradition. It might take even a long span of centuries for abolition of the practice. Accordingly, the use of Kharoshthi script had not stopped in India even after an end of the foreign rule of Persian Kings. Finally, its use came to a dead end which was bound to happen.

8

ĀRSHA (ARDHA MĀGADHI) PRĀKRITA AND THE JAINA CANONICAL LITERATURE

Religious Discourses

Tirthankers (Jaina Arhats and sanctified spiritual guides) delivered their religious discourses in Ardha Māgadhi Prākrita. They had a unique style. Miscellaneous listeners picked up their sermons with buoyancy in their own respective dialect. In other words, their teachings used to be transformed in the respective dialect of the listener. The citations to this effect were repeatedly found in Jaina scriptures. In 'Samvāyānga Sūtra', besides 34 super human and divine qualities of a Tirthanker, it has been stated regarding superiority and perfection of the language in which the Tirthankers had delivered their discourses: "Tirthankers delivered their sermons in Ardha Māgadhi Prākrita. The dialect in which they made their utterances was transformed in the respective dialect of Aryans, non-Aryans, bi-footed, four-footed, deers, animals, birds and crawling creatures[1] like serpents etc. so as to impart them all happiness, good fortune and pleasures.

In *Pragyāpnā Sūtra*, while giving multifarious definitions of the word 'Arya', the author has stated: "What are the characteristics of a fine and excellent language? Numerous interpretations of an Aryan language have been given. For instance: "Those who converse in Ardha Māgadhi Prākrita and write in Brāhmi script are nobel Aryan linguists."[2]

There is a citation in *Auppātika Sūtra* (Jaina Agamic scripture): "- - - Thereafter, Lord Mahāvira addressed the emperor Kūṇick (Ajātshatru), son of emperor Shrenika Bimbsār, who was surrounded by councillors of different categories, in a pleasant and deep-sounding voice like roaring sound of newly built clouds of autumnal season; resonant voice of a curlew; in charming voice like that of a kettle drum, which spreaded with the breath towards the heart region; moving spherically to the guttural region and after scattering in the mind, came out in distinct and clear letters of the alphabet; avoiding use of indistinct and inarticulate words, he spoke in *Ardha Māgadhi Prākrita*, having complete and regulated alphabet, having all favourable qualities, popular with all the languages of the world, grammatically regulated, most excellent and auspicious language. He elaborated the religious maxims. Lord Mahāvira imparted religious lectures to all Aryans and non-Aryans without feeling least exhaustion. The said Ardha Māgadhi Prākrita used to be transformed in the respective dialect of both Aryan and non-Aryan audience.

---

1. Crawling creatures like snakes etc.
2. Se Kiṁ taṁ bhāsāriyā? Bhāsāreyā aṇegavihā pannatā. Taṁ - Jahā - Jenaṁ adha. Māghai bhāsāẏe bhāsāi jātha viyaṇam Baṁ livi pavatai.

—*Pragyapna*, Para 1.39.

Achārya Hemchandra has interpreted Jaina medium of speech as none else but Ardha Māgadhi Prākrita in the benedictory Verse (an initial verse in a book meant to invoke divine blessings) of his eminent work 'Kavyānushāshan' (Poetic grammar). He has sung the praise of Ardha Māgadhi Prākrita saying that it has the capability of converting in all other dialects and mediums of speech. Similarly, Sri Vāgbhaṭa, author of *Alankār-Tilak* (A renowned book on figures of speech) has greatly adored Ardha Māgadhi Prākrita as the language of omniscients, the source of origin of all other languages and says "We respectfully bow before Ardha Māgadhi Prākrita which belongs to all and used by omniscients and erudite scholars and has the capability to convert in all other dialects; it is universal in nature and source of origin of all other linguistics."[1]

In order to draw attention to the specific thinking, how the Jaina scholars had developed a feeling of extreme veneration for Ardha Māgadhi Prākrita, being the language of their holy scriptures, the above extracts have been quoted. There may be several devices of using a language. However, where a feeling of respect, eulogy, admiration and reverence abounds all other considerations, the characteristics of a language are too much exaggerated and it is considered superior to all other languages. This practice is not denounced. However, there may be no problem if the mode and purpose of an expression is understood in its correct perspective. Accordingly, the above extracts had been produced which were worth-knowing and called for further elaboration. Lord Mahāvira was the last Tirthanker (sanctified teacher of Jaina religion) of the present age. The Agamic scriptures and other Jaina Canonical literature, now available, have been written in Ardha Māgadhi Prākrita and contain religious preachings and discourses of Lord Mahāvira.

Atthāgama / Suttāgama

Agamic literature has been classified in two groups (1) Atthāgama (Sanskrit formation Arthāgama). They contain interpretations and explanations as given by Lord Mahavira and (2) Suttāgama (Sanskrit formation Sūtragama). His utterances are collected and composed in aphoristic style by his chief disciples, called Gandhers. A Tirthanker imparted lectures on miscellaneous subjects as and when demanded by the occasion and offered explanations. His chief disciples, called Gandhers, compiled his utterances in the shape of aphorisms and reduced them to writing. Achārya Bhadrabāhu has narrated it in his book *Avashyaka Niryukti* (An Agamic Scripture) in the following words: "An Arhat (A Tirthanker) delivered lectures full of reasoning and sense on various topics and offered explanations, wherever necessary, while the Gandhers compiled his discourses and composed them in the shape of aphorisms so as to accomplish a religious jurisprudence. In this way, short and concise technical sentences are used to convey the gist of preachings of a Tirthanker.

---

1. Sarvārdhamāgadhiṁ sarva bhāshāsu parināminīm |
Sārviyāṁ sarvatovāchaṁ Sarvagyiṁ pranidadhmahe ||

—*Alankār - Tilak*, 1.1

Chief Disciples of Lord Mahāvira : Compilation of Jaina Agamic Scriptures

There were eleven Gandhers (Chief Disciples) of Lord Mahavira whose names are given hereunder :

1. Indrabhūti, 2. Agnibhūti, 3. Vāyubhūti, 4. Vyakta, 5. Sudharma, 6. Maṇḍita, 7. Mauryaputra, 8. Akampita, 9. Achalbhrātā, 10. Metārya, 11. Prabhāsa.

The religious organisation of Lord Mahāvira was divided in 9 Ganas (a commune of disciples, headed by two preceptors), namely — (1) Godāsa Gaṇa, (2) Uttar Baliyastaya Gaṇa (3) Uddeha Gaṇa, (4) Chāran Gaṇa, (5) Urdhvavārtika Gaṇa, (6) Vishvavādi Gaṇa, (7) Kāmardhika Gaṇa, (8) Māṇava Gaṇa, and (9) Koṭika Gaṇa.

Gandhers: Their Distinct Characteristics

Gandher is a celebrated and renown word of Agamic literature and has been used with two different meanings. The chief disciples of Tirthankers are known as Gandhers, who compile their discourses in the shape of aphorisms, contained in 12 Angas (forming part of Agamas). Each Gandher heads a Gaṇa (A commune of religious mendicants) who looks after the maintenance of the mendicants and helps in their religious devotion and practice of penance. His important act or duty is recitation of Agamas before the mendicants, belonging to the commune under his supervision.

A Tirthanker elaborates and explains the maxim of his discourses while Gandhers bind them in words in aphoristic style. The entire discourses of a Tirthanker, forming part of Agamic scriptures are consistently same from semantic view-point. However, they are composed, arranged and written by different Gandhers, hence literally and verbally they cannot be uniform and identical. They are bound to differ in verbal constructions. Nevertheless, the gist, sum and substance of all the texts is essentially the same.

Relativity of Gandhers vis-a-vis Tirthankers

To put straight—the obvious meaning of a Gandher is a chief disciple maintaining, administering and reciting the texts of Agamic Scriptures before a commune or group of mendicants which is under his control. A Gandher represents a specific system or order of Jaina institution. The significance of this word is only in relation to a Tirthanker. During the life-time of Tirthankers, their chief disciples are called Gandhers. After the final salvation of a Tirthanker or in case of existence of two Tirthankers simultaneously, there are no Gandhers. Thus the use of the word Gandher is made in a technical sense. It is not used simply to signify a person who was supposed to listen to the teachings attentively as revealed by a Tirthanker and give them a literal shape.

A Specific Attribute Attached to the Office of a Gandher

In the commentary on 3rd Anga, 'Sthanānga Sūtra' appears a specific interpretation of the word Gandher. It is cited therein that it was the primary duty of a Gandher to enlighten the female mendicants.[1] It purports that one of the duties of a Gandher was to create religious and spiritual awakening amongst female mendicants, to inspire them and boost up their morale for spiritual endeavours and practice of austerities. A Gandher was supposed to offer his guidance to the female mendicants, whenever needed. It is clearly reflected that no effforts were spared for mental development and spiritual enlightenment of female mendicants in Jaina institution. Every precaution was taken to ensure that they were not dissatisfied or had any grievance, whatsoever, after exercising control over self and practising austerities. It was, no doubt, illustrative of great awakening and consciousness as also observance of the sacred traditions by Jaina institution.

Eleven Gandhers: Nine Ganas : There is a difference of two in the total number of Gandhers and Gaṇas, headed by them, relating to the religious institution of Lord Mahavira. The fact remains that initial seven Gandhars looked after the affairs of one Gaṇa each and recited utterances of Tirthanker before the mendicants of their respective gana. However, out of remaining four Gandhers, two of them managed the affairs of one Gaṇa each. It transpires that the number of mendicants in the eighth and ninth gaṇas was comparatively smaller. Hence two Gandhers had been entrusted with the responsibility to manage one gaṇa each. Accordingly, Akampita and Achalbhrātā owned the responsibility of eighth gaṇa and Maitārya and Prabhash of the ninth gaṇa.

During Life-time of Lord Mahāvira : Final Liberation of Nine Gandhers

It appears in *Kalpa-Sutra* that all the eleven Gandhers of Lord Mahāvira were well conversant with 12 Angas, 14 Purvas (old sacred texts) and all the Gani Pitakas and retained them in their memory. The sacred texts of 12 Angas were recited by the preceptor or spiritual guide in sweet and charming voice. Hence they are known as Gaṇi Pitākas as well. They attained final salvation after observing fast for one month. They were redeemed from all worldly sufferings and obtained final emancipation. Jaina Acharyaś, Indrabhūti (Gautam) and Arya Sudharmā attained their liberation after final salvation of Lord Mahāvira. After the expiry of Gandhers, their gaṇas joined the association of mendicants under Arya Sudharma.

Compilation of Sacred Texts of Discourses, Delivered by Lord Mahāvira in the Shape of 12 Angas

Tirthankers delivered religious sermons only after attaining omniscience. Thereafter, they were the sole authority on religious matters and possessed exclusive intuitive perception. In other words, they had attained highest truth and spiritual knowledge. In philosophical terms, it could be defined as having realized transcendental knowledge relating to the Supreme Spirit. After becoming an omniscient, Lord Mahāvira delivered religious discourses for the betterment and welfare of entire living-beings. An excellent and methodic system is found in respect of religious lectures imparted by Tirthanker. His most confident and submissive resident pupil, Gautam, although himself an eminent scholar, yet for the

1. Aryikāpratijāgrako Vā Sādhu Visheshaḥ Samayaprisidhah.
— Commentary on *Sthānānga Sutra*, 4.3. 323

benefit and welfare of the people at large, he used to put up questions, covering maximum topics, to Lord Mahāvira and the latter used to answer them with utmost clarity and elaboration.

Religious preachings expounded in *Ardha-Māgadhi Prākrita* by Lord Mahāvira and compiled in aphoristic style by Arya Sudharmā, are available in the shape of 12 Angas[1], may be short and incomplete. Arya Sudharma succeeded to the seat of a spiritual guide after final salvation of Lord Mahāvirā in order to continue imparting sacred knowledge, handed down by tradition and revealing it to his disciples. There is a difference of opinion on this point between two sects of Jaina religion. Arya Sudharma became the supreme head of the religious institution, after final salvation of Lord Mahāvira. Therefore, the subsequent line of succession of spiritual guides, came to be known as lineage of Arya Sudharma. It appears in *Kalpa Sutra* : "All The religious mendicants, free from worldly knots and bondages, who are found now, belong to the lineage of Arya Sudharma, since all other Gandhers had attained final liberation during life-time of Lord Mahāvira without having the distinct lineage of their own disciples.[2]

Arya Sudharma: Establishing Tradition of Carrying Along Sacred Knowledge and Revealing it to his Pupils

While giving an introduction of Arya Sudharma, it appears in *Kalpa Sūtra*: "Arya Sudharma, a Jaina monk and resident disciple of Lord Mahāvirā, belonged to the lineage of Agni Vaishyāyan'. Arya Sudharma had born in or about the year 607 B.C. He led a family—life for 50 years and remained as Jaina monk for 30 years in the institution. After final salvation of Lord Mahāvira and during the period of 12 years of the state of highest perfection, having attained by Gautama, Arya Sudharma was the Supreme head of Jaina institution. After Gautama had attained final liberation, Arya Sudharma remained in the state of perfect isolation for a period of eight years. In this way, his total age is reckoned at 100 years. Under Digamber tradition, his state of highest perfection is believed to have continued for 10 years. In this way, there is a difference of 2 years in the life span of Arya Sudharma under the two traditions.

Although, the main topic dealt with here is Jaina Canonical literature and detailed historic references were not necessary, yet there were certain points connected with religious preachings as revealed by Lord Mahāvira which were to be handed down to the next generation of disciples. It may not be proper to evade discussion on the relative topics. For instance, there are divergent opinions whether the actual successor to the seat of spiritual guide, after final salvation of Lord Mahāvira, was Gautama or Arya Sudharmā. A brief discussion on this point is, therefore, essential.

Beliefs of Digamber Sect : As per belief of Digamber Sect, Gautama had succeeded to the seat of spiritual guide and supreme leader of the religious institution after final salvation of Lord Mahāvira and after the final liberation of

1. The twelfth Anga is still missing.
2. Je ime ajjatāte samanā nigānthā Viharti e e naṁ savve ajja suhamassa aṇagārassa Āhavachchijjā, avalesā gaṇharā nirvachehā Vochhinnā.

Gautama, Ārya Sudharma had succeeded him. In the renowned religious treatise, 'Tiloyapaṇatti', authored by Acharya Yativrashabha and accomplished in 2nd or 3rd Century A.D., which was an authoritative Agamic Scripture of Digamber sect, it is mentioned : "The day, Lord Mahāvirā attained final salvation, Gautama had obtained Kevalya—the state of highest perfection and omniscience. After final liberation of Gautama, Arya Sudharma had attained the state of an omniscient. After having detached himself from all worldly activities and attaining the state of omniscience and after final emancipation by Arya Sudharma, his chief disciple, Jambu Swami, attained the state of perfection and omniscience. After final liberation of Jambuswami, the tradition of successively attaining state of omniscience and highest perfection, came to an end. The period of pioneering religious institution by great seers like Gautama and others totalled to 62 years.

The author of 'Tiloyapaṇatti' has described the period of omniscience of Gautama, Arya Sudharma and Jambu-Swami as the best period when the propagation of Jaina doctrines and spread of the religion was at its climax. According to the details of the total period of omniscience, as appeared in Tiloyapaṇatti, Gautama lived for 12 years after omniscience. Suddharma lived for 12 years and Jambu Swami for 38 years, totalling to 62 years.

Why Gautama did not Succeed to the Seat of Spiritual Guide

Gautam was close confident and a resident disciple of Lord Mahāvira. He enjoyed his confidence and was very close to him. He sought clarifications and the explanations given by Lord Mahāvira are considered to be the asset of Jaina Canonical literature. He was the foremost Gandher of Lord Mahāvira. It was but natural that onus for administering the affairs of the Jaina institution ought to have been shouldered by Gautama, after final salvation of Lord Mahāvira. However, it did not happen. What was the secret behind it? It is to be deliberated upon.

Shwetamber Sect : An Explanation : Shwetāmber sect believes that after attainment of the state of omniscience and highest perfection, an omniscient no longer holds any office or responsibility to administer the affairs of the institution. Of course, if a Jaina monk attains the state of omniscience while holding the seat of a spiritual guide, it will not be incumbent upon him to give up his seat.

The extent of self-perception and spiritual knowledge of an omniscient is so comprehensive and wide-ranging that nothing remains to be known by him. The utterances of an omniscient are based on his intuitive preception and manifestation of self-acquired spiritual knowledge and wisdom. An omniscient will never refer to or quote the teachings of his preceding Kevali (A Jaina saint who has attained the highest perfection). While addressing a religious congregation of the devotees, he will always say that he was explaining what he had self-realized or self-perceived. The spread of religious message and manifestation of sacred knowledge as heard by revelation must go on even after final salvation of a Tirthanker so that the flow of spiritual knowledge and learning is not stopped or obstructed in any way. Accordingly, succession to the leadership of the organisation or to the seat of supreme leadership in favour of Gautama was not agreeable to Shwetāmber sect since Gautama had acquired the state of omniscience immediately after the final salvation of Lord Mahāvira.

A Source of Belief of Digamber Sect : The obstacle in succeeding to the seat of a supreme leader and spiritual guide by an omniscient is not agreed to by Digamber sect. Degambers believe that a Tirthanker never imparts religious lectures in any specific language. He never utters any word or speaks during his discourses. A sound of sacred and mystical syllable 'Om' remains pouring out from the pores of his skin. The same rhythmic sound of 'Om' is converted in the respective dialect of the audience. Thus the listeners find it easy to follow the religious message in their own respective dialect.

Views of Sri Dharmaghosha Sūri

Sri Dharmaghosha Sūri, a religions teacher and renowned scholar of Shwetāmber Sect, writes in the commentary of his work, "Siridusmakālāmaṇa Sanghvayaṁ" (Sanskrit formation "Shri Dushabhakālshramaṇastavaḥ):" On the night of final salvation of Lord Mahāvira, and consequent upon the death of king Chandra Pradyota, his son, Pālaka, was enthroned as a ruler of Ujjaini. On expiry of Udāyi, King of Pātliputra (Patna), without having a male child, king Pālaka also conquered the kingdom of Pātliputra. During the period of his 60 years rule, Gautama, Sudharma and Jambuswami held the title of 'Yuga-Pradhan' (Principal figures and men of the age) for 12 years, 8 years and 44 years respectively."

The figure of 60 years, given in the commentary by the author, does not reconcile with the total period of Supreme leadership of the Jaina organisation by Gautama, Sudharma and Jambuswami (12 + 8 + 44 = 64 years). The commentator has, however, explained the difference, saying that out of total period of supreme leadership of Jambuswami for 44 years, he administered the affairs of the organisation for 40 years during the reign of King Pālaka and 4 years during the rule of nine Nandās. In order to indicate the total period as a spiritual guide by Jambuswami, the figure of 44 years has appeared. Achārya Dharamghosha has also included the name of Gautama along with those of Sudharma and Jambuswami who were considered as principal figures and men of the age. The significance of the word 'Yuga Pradhan' deserves specific consideration.

'Yuga Pradhān': A Most Celebrated Status

Although, it was not a title like those of an Achārya (Spiritual guide); Upādhyāya (Religious teacher or preceptor); Gaṇi (one who is well-versed in the sacred writings); Pravartaka (Pioneer and Promoter of religious doctrines) but the expression of dignity, respect and feeling of exaltation attached to the word 'Yuga Pradhan' signified highest regard for the spiritual guide who was regarded as such.

The lists of succession to the seat of Supreme head of the institution appear in 'Kalpa Sūtra' and 'Nandi-Sūtra both. There is slight variation in the two lists, probably because the list of successors described in 'Kalpa-Sutra' is in due order of the religious preceptors or spiritual guides, succeeding each other, while the names mentioned in the list, appearing in 'Nandi-Sūtra', are in order of succession of each pioneer or predominant personality of the era in the field of spiritualism. Thus the variations found in the two lists is due to the fact that the author of 'Nandi Sūtra' had also incorporated the names of most eminent spiritual guides of their age although constitutionally they were not holding the office of a Guide (Religious preceptor who propounds the doctrines of the religion). The so-called pioneers or chief exponents of the religious doctrines of their age had thrived a lot for elevation, growth and expansion of the religions ideals to the far off places in the country. Those who were holding the office of a guide and were also considered pioneers and chief propounders of the religious doctrines in their era were there in both the lists, appearing in Kalpa Sūtra and Nandi Sūtra.

Chief Attributive Characteristics of a Pioneer or Pre-eminent Spiritual Guide of His Age

The author of 'Nandi Sutra' has described the qualities of the pioneers of the religion in their era in two verses at the end of the list of such principal figures. He writes: "Those who have dedicated themselves to practising penances, adhering to the principles of truth, self-restraint, morality, sublimity, obedience, tranquility and softness in behaviour; those who are known for their virtuous life; possess delicate, graceful and beautiful personalities; who are endowed with excellent qualities of head and heart; who are eloquent and skilful in speech and who are honoured by hundreds of religious devotees and mendicants in general — I bow and pay obeisance to such grand personalities of their age.

When was the Laudatory Attribute of an Eminent Personage of his Time Conferred ?

Under Jaina tradition, highly celebrated, influential, brilliant, splendid, excellent natured Jaina monks possessing great spiritual knowledge and wisdom, having strong character have glittered from time to time. Their grand personalities have been the source of divine vision and they have greatly influenced the people of their age. Such leaders have provided wonderful leadership to remove or check the physical and moral degeneration of the people, living in their age. They have inspired each and everybody to move ahead on the noble and righteous path. Such sober and selected scholars and endowed sages have commanded great respect and highly adored in the Jaina institution. Group rivalries and dissensions have never stood in their way nor weakened their respect and glory in any way. On the contrary, they added to their strength. Such eminent personalities always struggled hard against the evils of their times and were adored with the laudatory attribute of the 'Man of the age'.

What had been the attitude of religious leaders, belonging to different sects relating to Jaina institution to the said pioneers of religion from organisational viewpoint, nothing could be said in a decisive manner. This much, however, could be asserted that the religious teachers, belonging to various sects, held them in high esteem. They acknowledged their superiority unhesitatingly and accepted their spiritual leadership and guidance. Their status was superior-most not only amongst the scholars of any specific sect, community or group but in the entire Jaina institution comprising of male and female mendicants, and Votaries (A class of Jaina followers who led family life and did not renounce the world).

The attribute of 'Man of the Age' was conferred by the Jaina organisation on a most exalted spiritual leader or a highly accomplished saint who possessed extra-ordinary merits and virtues. Although, these principal figures were highly popular, appreciated and respected by all because of their eminence and unique qualities, yet they remained associated with their respective sect or branch for performance of daily austerities for exercising self-control and practising concentration of mind. Obviously, they continued maintaining their contacts with their respective sect or group for obtaining requisite informations through them.

It is evident from the list of successors to the seat of religious guides, including pioneers and supreme exponents of religious doctrines, appearing in 'Nandi Sutra' that this practice might have continued successively in the Jaina institution for quite a long period. On attainment of final liberation by the pioneer and principal religious guide of his time, the jaina organisation might have continued to follow the tradition of nominating a most capable and influential religious leader from amongst all the sects and groups, comprising of four-fold devotees of Jainism to hold the seat of principal or most eminent person of his age. This tradition had continued uninterruptedly or not, could not be said with certainty. An occasion might have arisen when the Jaina organisation, comprising of four-fold devotees, might have failed to find out a highly exalted, dignified and supreme religious guide of his age to take over the seat of his deceased predecessor and the seat might have remained unoccupied for some time for want of a supreme authority and exponent of doctrines of Jainism, suitable to be designated as man of the age.

Views of Āchārya Dharmaghosh : Call for Detailed Consideration

After attainment of final salvation by Lord Mahāvira, Gautama remained alive for 12 years and Sudharmā for 20 years. The day, Gautama obtained final liberation, Sudharmā attained the state of highest perfection. The period of omniscience of Sudharmā lasted for eight years.

However, according to Shwetāmber Sect, Sudharmā continued as a preceptor and spiritual guide for a period of 20 years, since he was designated to the seat immediately after final salvation of Lord Mahāvira, and for 8 years, he held both the seat of a spiritual leader as well as Title of man of the age. During the initial 12 years, while Sudharmā was holding the seat of a religious preceptor, Gautama held the seat of man of the age. This, however, called for minute consideration.

During the life time of Tirthanker, Lord Mahāvira, the name of Gautama has been frequently referred to in Agamic literature. However, after his final salvation, his name is rarely found. Gautama was, no doubt, an eminent personality. He was an erudite scholar and enjoyed excellent reputation. All these characteristics were there in his conduct and behaviour, yet certain other singular qualities, possessed by the man of the age relating to the upliftment and awakening of the masses, religiosity and acting as a pioneer, prompting the people to follow righteous path and rid themselves from the evils, Gautama might be lacking some of the aforesaid characteristics of a man of the age. Possibly, he might have devoted himself towards self-realisation, and identifying himself with Supreme-being. Else, the work of spiritual enlightenment of the people might have continued in a normal way without putting in any extra efforts. Gautama might not have shown due inclination and perseverance for implementing the ideals and objectives attached with the august office of a principal man of the age. On the contrary, the said qualities might have been found in abundance in the splendid character of Arya Sudharmā. After final salvation of Lord Mahāvira, the sacred knowledge as revealed by him through his discourses, was further propounded and spread by Arya Sudharmā by virtue of imparting lectures and encouraging the four-fold devotees and followers of Jainism to adhere to the ethical values and morality for self-exaltation and spiritual upliftment. No doubt, the splendid work done by Arya Sudharmā will remain recorded in golden letters in the history of Jaina religion.

Āchārya Dharamghosh personally had faith and regard for the ideology of Shwetamber sect. How then did he express such a view which was totally inconsistent with the beliefs of Shwetamber sect? It appears that Achārya Dharamghosh was more impressed with the recognitions of Digamber sect regarding succession to the seat of spiritual guide. Since he belonged to Shwetāmber sect, he was clear in his mind that Gautama could not succeed to the seat of spiritual guide after attainment of 'Kevalya' — highest state of perfection. However he could have no hiteh in declaring that during initial 12 years of Sudharmā's spiritual leadership, Gautama had occupied the seat of 'Man of the age.' Possibly, things might have taken shape accordingly.

Arya Sudharma : Twelve Angas (Forming part of Jaina Agamic Scriptures)

Lord Mahāvira had defined and elaborately explained the doctrines of Jainism and Arya Sudharmā had compiled and composed them in aphoristic style in the shape of 12 Angas. The teachings of Lord Mahāvira, which could be retained intact and are available now, is all due to the strenuous efforts of Arya Sudharma and we are all indebted to him for this great obligation. The names of 12 Angas are produced hereunder:-

(1) Āchārānga
(2) Sūtra Kritanga
(3) Sthānānga
(4) Samavāyānga
(5) Vyakhya Pragyapti (Bhagwati)
(6) Gyātri Dharma-Kathānga
(7) Upāsakadashānga
(8) Antkriddishānga
(9) Anuttaropāpatika Dashā
(10) Prashna-Vyakarṇa
(11) Vipāka
(12) Drishṭivāda

Another System or Arrangement Regarding Succession to the Seat of Spiritual Guide

Another description is found regarding order of succession to the seat of a spiritual leader after attainment of final salvation by Lord Mahāvira which slightly varies with the tradition and arrangement, discussed above. There is a petrographic inscription in 'Pārshvanāth Vasati'. The time of its inscription is believed to be near about 522 Shaka Samvat (About 600 A.D.). A portion of the said inscription is as under: "..... Mahavirasavitari parinirvrite Bhagvatparamarshi Gautamgandher sākshathchhiṇyalohārya Jambu Vishnudevaparajita Goverdhan Bhadrabahu-vishakhaproshthilkriti Kāyjayanāg Sidhārth Dhritshnabudhilādi guruparamparina Vakra mābhyagate mahapurash santatisamavadyotitānvaya Bhadrabahuswamino Ujjayanyamashtanga mahanimittatatvagyain Traikalyadarshna nimittena Dwadasawvatsar Kal Vaishamyamuplabhya Kathite Sarvasangha Uttrapathad Dakshināpathaṁ prasthitaḥ."

In the above-noted inscription, the name of Lohārya appears after the spiritual leadership of Gautama came to an end and, thereafter, the name of Jambuswami appears. There is no mention of the name of Sudharma at all. As cited in the inscription, Lohārya succeeded Gautama and Jambuswami succeeded Lohārya. Presumably, Lohārya may have been another name or surname of Sudharmā. If virtually it was so, then there was no likelihood of any discordance with the beliefs of Digamber Sect. However, no distinct clarification is found in this regard.

Names of Āchāryas in Order of Succession Differ: Diversity in Beliefs of Both Sects

Different names shown in the petrograph, in question, do not tally with the names appearing in the list of successors to the seat of supreme religious leadership of Jaina organisation, which is recognised by Digamber Sect. Tiloyapaṇṇatti is considered an authoritative Agamic Scripture, recognised by Digamber Sect. Most probably, it was written in second century A.D. The two parallel lists, containing the names of successive spiritual guides and preceptors as shown in the petrograph and appearing in the sacred book *Tiloyapaṇṇatti* are given hereunder:-

Petrograph	*Tiloyapaṇṇatti*
1. Gautama	Gautama
2. Lohārya	Sudharma
3. Jambu	Jambu
4. Vishnu	Nandi
5. Deva	Nandimitra
6. Aparajita	Aparajita
7. Goverdhan	Goverdhan
8. Bhadrabāhu	Bhadrabāhu
9. Vishāl	Vishāl
10. Proshthil	Proshthil
11. Kritikāya	Kṣatriya

12. Jaya	Jaya
13. Nāg	Nāg
14. Sidhārtha	Sidhārtha
15. Dhritisheṇa	Dhritisheṇa
16. Vijaya	Vijaya
17. Budhila	Budhila

In the two lists, the names appearing against serial nos. 2, 4, 5 and 11 do not tally with each other. In the inscription found at 'Pārasnāthvasti', the name of Budhila appears against serial No. 16 while in 'Tiloyapaṇṇatti', it is cited against serial No. 17. In Tiloyapaṇṇatti, the name appearing against serial No. 16 is Vijaya which is not mentioned in the list, inscribed on the rock. Thus on comparing the two lists, there is difference of one name by the serial No. 17. One name is short in the petrograph. Different names of Achāryās, appearing against the same serial number in the two lists, lead us to believe that the religious preceptors or spiritual guides might have been known by two names. Whether Sudharmā and Lohārya are the two names of the same Acharya, is the matter to be pondered over and decided by the learned scholars. In the light of the above discussion, it may be added here that leaving aside a few exceptions, the great spiritual leader, and omniscient, Arya Sudharmā alone was the successor to the seat of supreme head of the institution after final emancipation of Lord Mahāvira. The sacred knowledge as revealed by Lord Mahavira and heard by his chief disciples, continued to be spread through Arya Sudharma, the great sage and scholar of his age.

Ārya Sudharma : An Introduction

Birth

Ārya Sudharma was born in the territory of Videha (Territory lying to the North-east of Magadha. Its capital was Mithila, the same as Janakpur in Nepal). According to an ancient belief, the region surrounded by Himalaya on North, river Ganges on South, river Kaushiki (Modern Kosi) on east and Gandaki river (now Gandaka river) on West, was known as Videha.[1]

From *Avashyaka Niryukti* (An Agamic scripture by Āchārya Bhadrabāhu), a detailed information is obtained relating to the castes, lineages, parents, physical and intellectual, accomplishments by Gandhers. Accordingly, Arya Sudharma had born in a Brahmana family of 'Agnivaishyāyan' lineage.[2] The name of his father was Dhammila and that of his mother Bhaddilā.[3]

Āchārya Bhadrabāhu, author of *Āvashyaka Niryukti* has stated that Arya Sudharma had born in the twelfth lunar mansion consisting of two stars (having the figure of a bed). He also cited the asterisms in the moons path-lunar mansion,

1. 'Bhārtiya Sanskriti men Jain Dharma Kā Yogdān"— p. 22.
2. Tinni ya Goyamguttā bhāraddā aggivesa Vāsitthā'.
   Kāsava goam hāriya Koḍinnadungaṁ Cha Guttaim

   — *Āvashyaka Niryukti*, Verse 649
3. Vasubhūi dhaṇabhitto dhammila dhandeva moriye chaiva'
   Deve vasu a datte bale a piaro gaṇaharānaṁ

   — *Āvashyaka Niryukti*, Verse 647

at the time of birth of each gandher. It is believed that in those days (During life-time of Āchārya Bhadrabāhu) people might have developed faith in astrological predictions. Else, while writing the biographies of Tirthankers (Jaina sanctified teachers or saints), there might have been the practice to describe the asterisms on the lunar path at the time of their births. By following the same tradition, the author of 'Avashyaka Niryukti' might have found it necessary to describe the lineage of each Gandher also. From historic viewpoint as well, it is always useful to mention the auspicious moments and asterisms on the lunar path of all great persons, whose life-sketches are desired to be displayed. The said astrological details greatly contribute in determination of the chronology of the great spiritual leaders.

Scholarship : Glory and Renown

During the life time of Lord Mahāvira, Videha was quite advanced politically. It was the most ancient territory where in pre-historic times, a republican Govt., had been established. However, in those days, the ideological awareness of the masses was getting weak and they had become accustomed to follow the old traditions and rituals blindly. There was predominance of observing rituals and performing yajnas. Arya Sudharma had been brought up in the midst of such an atmosphere. His father was great intellectual and, therefore, he was fortunate enough to have the opportunity to undertake profound study of Vedas, Vedangas (A certain class of works, regarded as auxiliary to Vedas and designed to help in the pronunciation and interpretation of Vedic texts). The author of the 'Nriyukti' has described the castes and educational accomplishments of Gandhers in a verse[1] in which an attribute of 'Biu' has also appeared along with other laudable attributes. The word 'biu' is Prākrita formation of Sanskrit word "विद:" Acharya Malayagiri has explained the word as under:-

". . . Vidantiti Vidah — Vidvānāh, Chaturdasha Vidyāsthan Pārgamnnāt, Tāni Chaturdasha Vidyāsthānānyamuni — angāni Vedashchatvāro mimānsā nyāyavistaraḥ Dharmashāstram Puranaṁ cha Vidyā hotāschaturdasha, Tatrāngāni' Tadyā shiksha kalpo Vyākarṇaṁ nirukta chhando jyotishaṁ cheti esha grahasthāshram uktaḥ"[2].

Having born in a learned family, Sudharma had the privilege to undertake thorough study of all the four Vedas — Rig Veda, Yajur Veda, Sam Veda and Atharva Veda, Six Vedangas (Name of certain works regarded as auxiliary to the Vedas), namely—(1) Shikshā (the science of proper articulation and pronunciation); (2) Chhandas (the science of Prosody); (3) Vyākaraṇa (grammar); (4) Nirukta (Etymological interpretations of difficult Vedic Words); (5) Jyotish (Astronomy) and (6) Kalpa (Ritual or Ceremonial); Mimānsā (Name of one of the six chief systems of Indian philosophy); Nyāya (A system of Hindu philosophy founded by the great seer, Gautama) Dharam Shāstra (A code of religious laws or jurisprudence,

1. Savve ya mahanā jachcha, savve ujhavayā viu.
Savve duvālsangia, savve Chaudasa Puvvino||
—*Avashyaka Niryukti*, Verse 657.

2. Shri Avashyaka Sūtraṁ, II Volume, p. 339.

especially compiled by sages like Manu and Yajnavalkya etc.) and Purānās (Name of certain well-known sacred works; these are 18; they are said to have been composed by Vyās and Contain the whole body of Hindu mythology) etc. totalling to 14 lores. He was considered an authority over the said lores. People had great appreciation and reverence for those who had mastered the Shāstras and were highly learned scholars and preceptors of sacred books. Hence it is quite possible that he might have earned great name and fame during his life-time.

Of course, there was comparatively less curiosity for any revolutionary or total change, yet they did have a liking for those scholars who had accomplished thorough knowledge of various sacred scripures in a systematic manner from well informed and highly learned teachers. There was a well arranged course amongst Brahmaṇs for studying Vedas, Vedangas, philosophy, religious jurisprudence etc., with steadiness and perseverance. The old system of prosecuting studies in Gurukuls (In older times in India, residential teaching institutions were run by outstanding scholars) was still in vogue, may be partially if not completely. Accordingly eminent intellectuals like Indrabhūti, Sudharma and others had their residential teaching schools. There were 500 resident pupils under Ārya Sudharma in his centre of learning who were acquiring religious knowledge and education from him. They were all residing in his school building. Thus, it may be assumed that their centres of learning, residential arrangements and their social status were all in thriving and flourishing condition.

Inquisitiveness (Desire for leaning) : Source for Attainment of Final Emancipation

Ārya Sudharma was also present with his 500 pupils in the Yajna hall of Somil Brahmaṇa along with Indrabhūtī and other erudite scholars. From there, Ārya Sudharma had left to appear before Lord Mahāvira, and adopted almost a reverse course in the field of religion by adopting religious mendicancy and offering himself at the feet of Lord Mahavira with all sublimity and desire to learn. All these events were indicative of his absolute dedication to attainment of real truth, straightforwardness, objectivity and final emancipation.

At the time, Ārya Sudharma attained initiation as a follower of Jaina religion, he was 50 years of age. At that time, he was 8 years older than Lord Mahāvira which clearly signifies that he was a quite grown up man and a renowned scholar. By then, he had gained considerable prominence. He was well conversant and highly proficient in subjects, he had already gone through. However, he had great curiosity to learn more and he had absolutely an open mind for knowing the real truth.

Therefore, as soon as he became sensible and aware of supreme truth, as enunciated by Lord Mahāvira, he readily agreed to follow the path of virtue without minutest hesitation, with all humility and uprightness like an innocent and simple child. He did not worry at all how to forsake those ideals which he had, hithertso, nourished nor did he bother that his old followers, who had reposed complete faith in him, his dependants and disciples who held him in great esteem, might feel annoyed and reject him because of his supporting the tenets and ideology of a new religion. Would he not fall prey to their disdain utter disregard and contempt? Infact, these were the barriers, impediments and reproachful criticisms which generally did not allow even the great scholars to liberate their minds and go ahead on their path of spiritual growth and development. Arya Sudharma had, infact, risen above these foolish considerations which could only be termed human weaknesses. He had a feeling of self-respect but he was not an egoist. While accommodating a feeling of self-respect, a person does not lose his sense and power of judgment. On the other hand, an egotist loses consciousness and is frittered out of his senses.

Ārya Sudharma realized the insignificance of old religious beliefs which had been recognised and nourished for centuries. He gofrid of them immediately without least hitch. As a matter of fact, those who are enlightened and have not lost their spiritual awareness, hardly worry for what others say or feel about them. They believe in objectivity and support only what is true and correct. Such people are thoroughly honest and remain dedicated to truth.

Effect on his Resident Pupils

Ārya Sudharma had taken a bold step by adopting a new religion. It had favourable reaction on the minds of his disciples, who were equally anxious to realize the truth. His 500 resident pupils who had been pursuing their studies under his able guidance, did not react adversely. They did not feel for a moment that it was a virtual surrender on the part of their spiritual guide and, therefore, they should seek revenge. Where a person blindly supports his own viewpoint or ideology, he droops down and loses his independent power of judgement. He remains bound with stereotyped notions. However, where a person is determined to know the truth, he does not care for such worthless things. The trivial considerations of respect or disrespect, honour or dishonour, regard or disregard lose their significance and have no role to play. It is only stupidity, devoid of reasoning and no enlightened person will like to be involved in such foolish considerations. Obviously, the resident pupils of Ārya Sudharma also adopted religious mendicancy along with their preceptor.

Period of Ārya Sudharma Before Attaining State of Highest Perfection : Busy in Accomplishing Higher Spiritual Knowledge

Ārya Sudharma was an erudite scholar. He utilized his academic knowledge or attainment of spiritual enlightenment. He had the privilege to obtain spiritual guidance from a divine and sanctified teacher, an omniscient and all-seeing celebrated guide, Lord Mahāvira. What else was needed by a devout. He devoted all his energies for accomplishment of spiritual knowledge and pursuance of noble characteristics under his valuable guidance. Soon be acquired most exalted and excellent spiritual knowledge, revealed by Lord Mahāvira, which Ārya Sudharma had compiled in the shape of 12 Angas (Forming part of Agamic Scriptures), after final salvation of his mentor. He became the 5th Gandher (chief disciple of Lord Mahāvira). Inspite of remaining engrossed in self-meditation, he spared no efforts to provide spiritual leadership to enable the religious mendicants of his group to taste the nectar of spiritualism. He continued stimulating each and every body to lead a pious life by adhering to the doctrines of Jainism.

Privilege to have close Contacts with Lord Mahāvira

Ārya Sudharma had the privilege to live close to Lord Mahāvira for a long and continuous period of 30 years. During this period, he gained lot of spiritual knowledge from his sanctified teacher and continued receiving the same. Ultimately, Lord Mahāvira had accomplished his aim by training Ārya Sudharma and imparting him full knowledge of Jaina philosophy to enable him to be true exponent of his teachings. The devout and his devotion to spiritual achievement and his accomplishments had become one and completely identified with each other and there was no distinction, whatsoever. It was the glorious day of Diwali, when the lamp of spiritual enlightenment had finally kindled and Lord Mahāvira had imparted highest spiritual knowledge to his chief disciples which was the ultimate aim of life for each and every devout of Lord Mahāvira.

Ārya Sudharma as Spiritual Guide and Head of Jaina institution

Ārya Sudharma succeeded to the holy seat of spiritual leader and guide after Lord Mahāvira had attained final salvation. The responsibility of management, guidance and providing patronage and protection to the Jaina institution had fallen on his able shoulders. Out of eleven chief disciples of Lord Mahāvira, nine had attained final liberation during his life time. Sincerely believing in the longevity of Ārya Sudharma's life, and that he was more likely to provide leadership to the organisation, they entrusted the leadership and management of their respective Gaṇa (group of mendicants) one by one to Ārya Sudharma before attaining their final liberation.

Two prominent disciples—Gautama and Sudharma had survived after attainment of final salvation by Lord Mahāvira. The very day, Lord Mahāvirā had attained final salvation, his chief disciple, Gautama had obtained the state of highest perfection and omniscience. Resultantly, Ārya Sudharma had to take over the leadership of the organisation. Although, Arya Sudharma was 80 years old then, yet he had an infinite zeal to provide impetus to the cause of growth and expansion of the organisation. He spared no pains to spread the message of the religion and create spiritual awakening amongst the people. He physically lived for 20 years after final salvation of Lord Mahāvira. Out of this period, he spent 12 years as a guide and preceptor and remaining 8 years as an omniscient, after having attained the state of highest perfection.

Before attainment of omniscience, the period of Ārya Sudharma as a guide and leadership of the organisation was also most significant. He toured a number of villages, towns and districts in Northern India. He approached each and everybody and induced them to strive for spiritual achievements. A worthy seer like Jambu and others, who were anxious and striving for final emancipation after freeing themselves from worldly attachments, had attained their initiation as religious mendicants by Ārya Sudharma.

Grand Personality of Ārya Sudharma

Once Ārya Sudharma happened to arrive in the town of Champa (capital of an important Anga kingdom) situated on the right bank of Ganges and its ancient name being 'Angapuri'. It is very near modern Bhagalpur in Bihar. This town was situated near modern city of Bhagalpur. The visit to Champa town led to the composition of sixth Anga, styled 'Ṇayadhamma-Kahāo', wherein certain laudatory attributes for Ārya Sudharma are found mentioned, which clearly manifest that Ārya Sudharma owned a brilliant personality and commanded great respect from his followers.

Ārya: The first attribute is Ārya, preceding his name. The word Ārya is found mentioned in multiforms, having different meanings, sense or purpose. This word widely appears in Agamic literature and has been defined in detail. It has been cited in the commentary on 'Pragyāpna' "आरात् सर्वहेयधर्मेभ्यो यात:-प्राप्तो गुणेरित्यार्य:" which means that those who had dissociated themselves from irreligious paths and activities, fit to be left or abandoned completely, and bound themselves with acceptable doctrines and religious ideologies, are called Āryas.

While defining the word Ārya in 'Pragyapnā Sūtra', its multiple uses have been shown, such as—Regional Ārya; a person of respectable or honourable caste; of worthy family; noble deeds; expert in fine mechanical art; an accomplished linguist; A great scholar; An expert in philosophy' having excellent manners behaviour and conduct; All these are called Arya in their respective field.

The attribute of Arya used for Sudharma is in the sense of a virtuous, blessed and a meritorious person, as defined in the following verse:-

"प्रमाद मिथ्यात्वकषायदोषा दाराद् गत: सद्गुणराशिमाप्त:।
वुद्ध: परेषां प्रतिबोधको य: तमाहुरार्यं विवुधा गुणज्ञा:।।"

Total indifference towards inadvertence, self-delusion, self-praise; abstaining front falsehood and attachment to wordly objects, endowed with excellent qualities, highly-enlightened and imparting spiritual knowledge to others, are some of the characteristics of a person who is called 'Arya' by scholars and intellectuals.

The attribute of 'Arya' has generally been applied to the names of all great scholars and distinguished personalties, in Jaina Agamic literature.

Sthavira: Another attributive word, preceding the name of Sudharma is Sthavira which defines a senior Jaina monk who has completed 20 years after attainment of initiation, who has completed sixty years of age and acquired expertise in 3rd and 4th Angas (forming part of Agamic scriptures). This attribute is indicative of resoluteness in character, firmness and unflinching faith, with unwavering nature.

The Sthaviras not only exercise control over self with steady mind but also encourage others, for observing self-restraints with strong determination. Unless a person is fully developed, numerous evils raise their heads and creep in him from time to time. Sometimes, the persons, striving for spiritual achievements, begin dwindling from their settled path. At that time, if proper, guidance and encouragement is given by a learned and scholarly guide it is bound to be much beneficial. This is the job of a Sthavira. This attribute is prefixed with the names of religions teachers and spiritual guides as well in order to stress their significance and distinguishing characteristics in the institution.

Endowed with Highly Celebrated Caste and Family

Both the maternal and paternal sides of Ārya Sudharma were foremost and were highly accomplished families as is evident from the attributes affixed with his name. Here the words caste and family have been used in a technical sense. It is a hearsay: "कुल पेइयं माई या जाई" which means that the paternal side is called paternal family or lineage and that of maternal side is called caste or class. Lateron, both these words carried with them different meanings which could be termed to be an elaboration or comprehension of their meanings from linguistic viewpoint.

Those who possess noble and excellent personalities, they are endowed with all other distinguishing features or characteristic as well. They own elegant physiques, strength and forcefulness in their nature or character. However, they utilize all these singular qualities in their self-elevation and conquest and overcoming their weaknesses.

Ārya Sudharma possessed all the said distinct qualities. Since he had a strong, well-built and firm body with potentialities, he was in a position to take up all spiritual endeavours and forbear their ferocity.

Endowed with the Virtues of Modesty, Dexterity and Readiness

While describing the attributes, attached with the name of Sudharma, it has been stated that he was endowed with the virtues of humility, modesty, scholarship, elegance, having philosophical outlook, with good behaviour and conduct as also versatility. The word 'Lāghava' is obtained from the word 'Laghu' which literally means-small and light. Again lightness is of two kinds—material and emotional. Being a Jaina saint, Ārya Sudharma had a few articles with him and so he was light. From emotional viewpoint, he had already renounced or resigned from self-ego, vanity or arrogance completely. Therefore, he was light. The attribute, attached with his name is most appropriate from both angles.

Full of Vigour; Brilliance; Energy : Glory

Ārya Sudharma was really endowed with bodily strength, heroic physique, brilliance, beauty and splendour. As a result of performance of severe penances, there is an obvious reflection of lustre, appearing or shining on the face and it is called bodily energy or strength. Similarly, by observing mental and physical austerities, there is brightness and charm on the face which looks like heroic lustre and strength of character. Under Jaina tradition, the Sanskrit word 'तेज' is also used in the technical sense of 'तेजोलेश्या' (A sort of firearm in the shape of missile, highly destructive and annihilating. Here it, means 'endowed with supernatural powers).

After complete attainment of extraordinary faculties, there is propensity and favourable inclination towards acquiring miraculous power. It is called a state-full of vitality and vigour. The Ardha-Māgadhi Prākrita form of Sanskrit word 'वर्चस्वी' is 'वच्चंसी'. In another text, the Prākrita form 'वयसी' has also appeared which literally means—a person who is true to his words, who is not die hard and always inclined to receive or accept, who is always a well-wisher and friendly with everybody, who always speaks innocent and flawless words. The attribute of 'यशस्वी' (Renowned and excellent) signifies a person who is a highly austere and devoted to spiritual endeavours but he never aspires for personal renown and glory. However, he leads the life of self-mortification, exercises strict control over self, exhibits utmost patience and forbearance and is having divine vision, highest spiritual knowledge and perception with similar other distinguishing qualities. The renown and glory of such an accomplished person, automatically spreads all around although he never aspires for it. Ārya Sudharma was the successor to the seat of supreme leadership and spiritual guide of Jaina institution after final salvation of Lord Mahāvira. He was endowed with most excellent qualities and virtues. Thus, it is obvious that his fame and glory had spread far and wide. Consequently, the attribute of 'यशस्वी' is rightly affixed with his name and correctly reflects his significance and abilities.

Triumph Over Anger

Ārya Sudharma had controlled feelings of anger, egotism, delusion, deceit, sensuality, sleep and various physical agonies and sufferings while practising austerities. He had redeemed himself from an inherent allurement for life, and scare of death. Practising of self-denial or bodily mortification had become the primary aim of his life. He was an embodiment of excellent qualities and virtues. Here the word 'qualities' has been used to signify the characteristics relating to concentration of mind, religious devotion and practising of penance. It may be explained thus—self illumination by destroying the ill-effects of the acts done in former lives through observance of religious austerities and efficacy of devotion and by exercising restraint over sensual pleasures, Ārya Sudharma continued moving ahead on the sacred religious path so as to free himself from the bondage of life and death, resulting from one's deeds. Ārya Sudharma was very careful in keeping his body purified in order to derive moral power to be attained through regular meditation and contemplation as laid down in holy scriptures of Jaina religion. He performed great austerities and practised severe penances with a view to attain spiritual force by destroying the ill-affects of inauspicious deeds. He had already subdued his physical and mental adverse pronings and tendencies. He had shed all uncertainties in respect of realisation of Supreme Truth. He had obvious simplicity, sincerity, sweetness, humility, tolerance, endurance and had obtained liberation from physical, mental and conversational impurities and had renounced inauspicious thoughts and greediness. He was an erudite scholar and reciter of sacred texts. He was a celibate and fully engrossed in pursuit of self-realisation and identification with supreme spirit.

Expertise in Vedas: Ordinarily, the word veda literally means-sacred knowledge. What makes one aware with the nature of animate and inanimate objects is a veda. here the word veda implies Agamic scriptures of Jaina religion. In the present context, the word veda has also been used to signify knowledge of one's own settled doctrines and those of others. Ārya Sudharma had acquired expertise in Jaina Agamas, philosophy, religious doctrines of Jainism and the significance of real truth. He had attained perfection in internal and external purification of the body and soul. He was endowed with wisdom, philosophical vision and morality. He was upright in behaviour and conduct.

Noble : Formidable : Ārya Sudharma was really liberal and noble. After having subdued the feelings of anger and wrath, generosity and broadness had invariably become part of his nature. Besides generosity, another laudatory attribute, used for him is his formidable nature. While practising penances and austerities, others felt considerable strain and inconvenience, Ārya Sudharma observed them spontaneously without showing least reluctance. Here the literal meaning of the word 'ghor' is not awful or terrible. Ārya Sudharma was, infact, endowed with noble qualities of uprightness, simplicity, straightforwardness and softness. How could he be cruel or awful? Whereas even the strong-willed and devoted mendicants found it difficult to perform certain austerities and accomplish their spiritual pursuits, Ārya Sudharma practised them with ease and spontaneity. Hence he was adorned with the above attribute. Similarly, he is also called a devoutly austere person with formidable spiritual force.

An Extraordinary Celibate : Dedication of Ārya Sudharma to observance of celibacy was excellent. Accordingly, he was applauded for observing extra-ordinary and extreme celibacy. He was totally indifferent towards his health and physical comforts. He had become totally detached and had given up all care for his body. He had accomplished extra-ordinary and super-natural powers like 'तेजोलेश्या' (a sort of missile obtained after completing prescribed yogic exercises and it is extremely fatal in nature). However, far from utilising his powers, he kept them hidden within himself and never thought of seeking revenge against anybody. Had it not been so, it would have been almost impossible to even look at his highly brilliant and glittering face-shining like radiant rays of the sun. He had four-fold sacred knowledge — intellectual; formal elements experienced by soul (third degree of knowledge); religious texts of discourses by way of hearing to the revelations of Tirthanker, and knowledge of mental dispositions by multiplication of thoughts (penultimate stage in the perception of truth). He was an authority on 14 branches of old sacred texts. Ārya Sudharma is stated to be endowed with all spiritual accomplishments, in 'Avashyaka Niryukti' (by Acharya Bhadrabahu—an Agamic scripture). His bodily frame was sturdy and hard, compact and firm. His physical shape was even, elegant and impressive.

As already stated above, the strength and vigour of the body also plays a determined role in performance of severe penances and forbearance of physical and mental strains while leading an ascetic life. Although it is the spiritual force which enables to endure all the difficulties, yet a firm and strong body is equally essential to face the hostile conditions of the nature-such as impact of cold, heat and rains and violent stormy winds. Well-cultured and noble souls, obtain potential, well—built and perfect bodies because of their pre-accumulated virtues and good deeds. Obviously, all the said virtues were there in Ārya Sudharma.

An Omniscient and Successor to the Seat of a Supreme Religious Teacher

The omniscients never offer themselves to succeed to the hightest seat of a sanctified teacher and leader of the organisation. Hence a question will, obviously, arise that after Ārya Sudharma had attained the state of highest perfection and that of an omniscient, what was his position? When an omniscient declines to accept the succession to the holy seat, how he managed to occupy and continue to hold the seat of the leadership of the organisation?

Succession to the supreme seat of a sanctified religious teacher by an omniscient and after attainment of the state of highest perfection and omniscience while providing leadership to the organisation are clearly two different situations. The situation of declination or hesitation felt in accepting the sacred leadership of the organisation by an omniscient, does not occur in the case of a spiritual guide who attains the state of omniscience while providing leadership to the organisation of religious mendicants. If an omniscient succeeds to the seat of Kevali (an omniscient), the system of imparting sacred knowledge of 12 Angas (forming part of Agamic scriptures) to the chief disciples by revelation, will stop. It may be relevant to assume that Ārya Sudharma had already imparted knowledge of 12 Angas to his resident pupil, Ārya Jambu, during the period of 12 years before attainment of the state of highest perfection and omniscience. There is no bar for a 'Kevali' to deliver religious discourses and enunciate the doctrines of Jainism. Even after attaining the state of an omniscient, Lord Sudharma kept on touring various regions and delivering lectures to explain and elaborate the religious message of Tirthanker. There are numerous references in Agamic scriptures to corroborate this aspect.

Final Salvation : Before attaining final salvation, Ārya Sudharma observed fast unto death for a month (a fast in which the devout, engaged in its observance, remains lying still and motionless like a tree, giving up all bodily movements and refusing service by others). The author of *Āvashyaka Niryukti* has mentioned that similar fast unto death was a must for all Gandhers (chief disciples) of a Tirthanker, for attainment of final emancipation.[1]

Where the meals of all the four types are abandoned for the rest of life, it is known as a fast unto death. As stated above, one specific nature of fast unto death is lying still and motionless like a tree, giving up all physical movements. The said form of observance of fast unto death is called 'Padopgamana' (remaining motionless like the root of a tree). The commentator, Shanti Chand, has stated in his commentary on 'Jambudweep Pragyapti Sutra' (A Jaina religious treatise), while referring to Emperor, Bharat 'Chakravarti' (Most respectable and commendable personality of his time, sovereign ruler of six out of eight principal parts of India), has defined the word 'Pad' as— "The word 'Pad' literally means

---

1. Māsaṁ pāovagyā savvepi ya savvaladhisampannā.
Vajjarisahasanghayaṇā samchauraṁsā ya Saṁdhāṛṇe.

— *Avashyaka Niryukti*, Verse 659

the underground root of a tree. The person who observes fast unto death, remains totally unshaken and firm and this condition of the body is called 'Pādopgata'."

In certain religious treatises, the word '**पादपोगमन**' has appeared in place of '**पादोपगमन**' which has been explained as—"A fast unto death in which the observer adopts a position in which he remains lying absolutely still and motionless, avoiding least movement of the body and this type of the fast is called "Padapogamana fast." In the said fast, the condition of the person, undertaking the fast, becomes still and unmovable. Before observing the fast, he lies down flat on the back and does not allow any of his bodily limbs to move. He is determined to continue in that position by the time he breathes his last. In order to give an exact idea of his remaining still and motionless, avoiding least movement of the body, the immobility of the limbs has been similized with a tree. The nature of the fast has been named accordingly. A tree is the symbol of firmness and stability. The movement that takes place in the twigs or branches of a tree is not on its own but due to blowing of the air. Similarly, the person undertaking fast unto death remains motionless like a tree and does not permit any of his limbs to shake. However, it will be an altogether different matter if he is shaken by somebody else or due to any external object or substance.

The simile of the underground root, given by Sri Shantichandra, commentator on 'Jambudweep Pragyapti' in place of the tree itself, appears to be more relevant here. In order to portray the state of body to be quiet and motionless, the simile of underground root appears to be more appropriate. Since the root is always in the deep underground, the likelihood of its shaking or swinging is not there. On the other hand, there are ample occasions for shaking of a tree. There is either rare or no possibility at all to cause a jolt to the body of a person who is observing fast unto death and lying still like the underground root of a tree. Generally, others also take due care to ensure that the body of the fasting person is not unnecessarily disturbed.

Ārya Sudharma lived a long, pious and accomplished life of 100 years. After renouncing all worldly possessions and pleasures, he had dedicated himself for attainment of ultimate aim of final emancipation which he had duly achieved. He had attained his final salvation at Rajgraha in Bihar (once capital of Magadha dynasty).[1]

Conclusion

Ārya Sudharma was born in the year 607 B.C. It is also believed that Shri Indrabhuti Gautama had his birth in the same year. Sudharma led the house-hold life till he was 50 years old. He remained in ascetic life for 30 years. After final salvation of Lord Mahāvira and attaining the state of omniscience by Gautama, Sudharma had administered the affairs of the institution for 12 years. The day Gautama attained his final liberation, Sudharma had acquired the state of omniscience. The latter continued as such for 8 years. During this period, he

---

1. Parinivvuā gaṇaharā jivānte nāye navajaṇāu
Indabhui suhammo a Rāyagihe nivvue vire.

— *Avashyaka Niryukti*, Verse 658

managed the affairs of Jaina organisation as an omniscient.

Thus Sudharma led the total life of 100 years — 50 years in family life + 30 years as Jaina saint + 12 years as leader of the institution in the state of non-omniscience + 8 years as an omniscient and leader of the organisation. As per Digamber sect, Sudharma is believed to have lived for 12 years after attainment of omniscience.

The poet Veer (11th century A.D.), author of 'Jambusāmichariu' has mentioned that Ārya Sudharma had lived for 18 years as an omniscient, which is, however, contrary, to the beliefs of both Digamber and Swetamber sects. Presumably, poet Veer might have come across a list of successors to show that Ārya Sudharma had lived for 18 years after attainment of the highest perfection and state of omniscience. However, no such list is available now to corroborate his version.

Arya Jambu

Arya Jambu was the last Kevali (omniscient) of the present age. He was the resident pupil of Ārya Sudharma, one of the closest and chief disciples of Lord Mahāvirā. Ārya Jambu deserves all credit and appreciation for regular flow of highest spiritual knowledge, contained in Agamic scriptures, written in Ardha Māgahi Prākrita. Lord Mahāvirā delivered his discourses in the shape of 'Tripadi'. (According to philosophical doctrines of Jaina religion, there are three inherent phases through which each matter or substance has to pass through-origin, protection and destruction. However, the basic elements of the matter remain intact. They donot get destroyed). His chief disciples, known as Gandhers, had later composed them in aphoristic style. Lord Mahāvira also elaborately explained the above philosophical doctrines, while answering to the questions, asked by his closest resident disciple, Gautama, where the context so demanded. All the aforesaid spiritual and philosophical utterances of Tirthanker formed part of 12 Angas (constituent of Agamic Scriptures).

Arya Jambu: Highly Inquisitive and Eagre to Attain Superior-most Knowledge

After attainment of final salvation by Lord Mahāvirā, the successive source for enunciation of religious and philosophical doctrines of Jaina religion, was his chief disciple, Gandher Sudharma. His closest resident pupil, Ārya Jambu was of highly inquisitive nature, sparing no pains to undertake spiritual endeavours. He was a sage, striving after final emancipation. He used to place his curiosities before his revered teacher and spiritual guide, Ārya Sudharma, who used to answer his queries and set his doubts at rest. Generally, he explained on the basis of utterances of Lord Mahāvira, which were heard by him personally when revealed by Tirthanker. Similarly, Ārya Gautama, the principal Gandher and chief disciple of Lord Mahāvirā, used to place his doubts before his propitious teacher and guide. Other prominent Jaina monks and distinguished followers also used to enquire and Lord Mahāvirā used to satisfy all of them. Certain points, relating to Jaina philosophy, though not specifically enquired by any one, were also propounded and explained by Lord Mahāvirā, whenever he found them necessary. Compilation of all the said utterances of Lord Mahāvirā led to the enrichment of unique treasure of sacred knowledge, relating to ideological and philosophical doctrines of Jaina religion. Whenever, Ārya Sudharma used to answer the queries of his intimate resident disciple, Ārya Jambu, he basically used to depend on the disclosures made by Tirthanker and heard by Sudharma. The fact remains that this successive process of revelation and enunciation of ideological and philosophical doctrines of Jaina religion, proved to be the life-line of Agamic scripts (holy scriptures of Jainism). Queries placed by Ārya Jambu and their answers given by Ārya Sudharma provided the base for successive growth and expansion of highest spiritual knowledge like holy water of river Ganges. It was really an unforgettable event of the history of Jaina religion, which was the very source for growth and evolution of Jaina doctrines.

System of Asking Questions and Obtaining Replies Thereof

For elucidation and explaining the significance of this system, an extract from the initial portion as cited in 'Naya-Dhammakahāo' is worth quoting: "At that time, senior disciple of Ārya Sudharmā, Ārya Jambu, born in Kāshyapa lineage, sitting neither too far nor too close to his spiritual guide and kneeling on the ground with bowing head; fully engrossed in abstract contemplation and ecstatic meditation and illuminating himself with the strength and spiritual power attained through self-mortification and by practising of severe penances, used to be present. Having immense faith in his preceptor, he used to getup in order to up to get his doubts and curiosities removed and used to draw near the place where Ārya Sudharmā was sitting. He went round him thrice and paid his obeisance. Ārya Jambu addressed him respectfully with due submissiveness and keeping his forehead on the hollow cup of two palms, joined together; "Lord! you, the chief disciple of Lord Mahāvira, had explained the contents of fifth Anga, 'Vyakhyā Pragyapti'. Now I shall request you to please elaborate the sum and substance of the sixth Anga 'Gayatri Dharmakatha' (Prākrita name— 'Nāya Dhammakahāo')?

Senior Jaina monk, Ārya Sudharmā explained the contents of sixth Anga accordingly. . . . . .

From the nature of the question and humble manner of seeking its reply by Ārya Jambu, it is evident that he had immense faith, regard, devotion and humility towards his mentor and spiritual guide. How a curious student should express his desire to learn before his teacher or spiritual guide, is nicely reflected here. Ārya Jambu had great faith and esteem for Ārya Sudharmā. He was quite sure that he would get true enlightenment from his spiritual leader. The use of the Prakrita adjective 'जायसड्ढे' illustrates the same point here. The process of putting questions continued uninterruptedly with due regard and veneration. There was an extreme curiosity for seeking elucidation on various points and the said disposition of the mind has been reflected by use of the word 'जायसंसए' in the relative sūtra. The use of the said word was in no way a reflection on the lack of faith in philosophical doctrines of Jainism. Ārya Jambu always sought detailed replies to his questions with due clarity and least unambiguity. The word 'जायसंसए' has, therefore, rightly appeared in the sutra.

While analysing the word 'जायसंसए' used as an attribute by Gandher Gautama, as appeared in 'Vyākhyā Pragyapti' (Bhagwati) Sūtra in reference to the explanations sought by him through Lord Mahāvirā, Achārya Abhayadeva Suri, commentator of 'Navāngi' writes:

> "The knowledge which is not correctly remembered or retained in memory, is nothing but illusive and needs to be explained by the religious preceptor and guide. The words 'चलमाणे चलिए' propounded by Lord Mahāvira, have been referred to as an illustration and Achārya Abhayadeva Suri explains that the word 'चलन:' is indicative of present tense while the word 'चलित:' of past tense. How can both formations of the word yield the same sense? Thus the desire to know and seek explanation is nothing but uncertainty of mind."

The object of elaborating the said point is to emphasize here that Ārya Jambu was not confused or unintelligent in any way but he had too much curiosity to learn. The curiosity breeds an ardent desire to acquire knowledge. Infact, an inquisitive person is eagre and zealous to learn more. A wavering mind acts differently. In such a state of mind, the eagerness to know dies and he loses the initiative to work hard.

Ārya Jambu is found interrogating almost in the same manner on other occasions as well, as found, mentioned in 'Nāyādhammakahāo. There was no marked difference in the wordings of the two.

Another Method of Interrogation

There was another style of seeking clarifications and getting the curiosity satisfied by Arya Jambu as cited in second Anga 'Sutrakritanga Sūtra'. Arya Jambu enquires:

Religious mendicants, scholars, theologians house-holders and followers of other sects, enquire from me — who was the solitary saint, having expounded the tenets of true religion for the betterment of the entire humanity? They further ask about the nature and extent of religious perception foreseeing system of philosophy and virtues of Lord Mahāvirā? Oh great religious saint! you are well conversant with his fundamental teachings. Kindly enlighten me what you had personally heard by revelation.

From the above discussion, it is evident that Ārya Jambu was the principal and closest disciple of Ārya Sudharmā. Thus, inquisitives used to place questions to Ārya Jambu and seek elaborations. Similar mentions are found in the above verses. Whatever guidance was sought by religious mendicants, scholars, family men and followers of other sects, the same could readily be provided by Ārya Jambu. However, Ārya Jambu did not straightaway answer their questions. He adhered to the ancient tradition of acquiring knowledge by hearing to the utterances of a spiritual guide. Consequently, he sought answers from his preceptor and spiritual guide, Ārya Sudharmā. From this, it is clear that Ārya Jambu sincerely believed that the teachings of Tirthanker; compiled and composed in the shape of aphorisms by his Gandhers, who had heard them as revealed by Lord Mahavirā, must be carried uninterruptedly for the benefit and welfare of each and everybody.

In 'Sutrakritanga Sūtra', there is a clear citation that Arya Sudharma used to enquire and seek clarifications directly from Lord Mahavirā. The citation reads as under:

> "As stated by Ārya Sudharma, he enquired from the great omniscient and most sanctified saint, Lord Mahavirā as to why did the human-beings suffer the agonies of hell? On what causes or grounds, the ignorant and unwise animates are taken away to hell. "My Lord! I am ignorant, you know it well. Kindly explain. On my request, the super celebrity, having born in the family of kāshyapa lineage, great intellectual, Lord Mahāvira replied who are impudents, ill-informed, ill-mannered, immoral and whose lives are full of onerous deeds, who are sinful and degenerated - I will elaborate the nature of that hell where they are punished for their evil deeds."

It is thus quite clear from the above discussion that whatever Ārya Sudharma desired to convey to Arya Jambu, he was very careful to ensure that it was based on the utterances of Tirthanker, Lord Mahavirā. The citation by Ārya Sudharma—"I enquired from Lord Mahavirā and he answered" clearly reflects that Ārya Sudharma only conveyed the teachings of Lord Mahavirā in their original shape and avoided any additions from his own side.

The assertion of Ārya Sudharma: "I am ignorant and you are a great learned saint, please enunciate"—these words were really manifestations of Ārya Sudharma's extreme humility simplicity, devotion and purity of mind. How could it be believed that a highly accomplished and erudite scholar and holder of illustrious rank of Gandher, Ārya Sudharma was unaware of the sufferings and agonies of hell and why the living beings were taken away to undergo those sufferings. It, therefore, follows that inspite of all awareness, he was eager to hear from Lord Mahavirā, himself, and convey his teachings in their original form without least interference, whatsoever.

As per Jaina philosophy, the means of arriving at correct and true knowledge are of two types-direct and indirect. The self perceived spiritual knowledge, without having any relativity with sense organs or mind, is, infact, a direct perceptibility. The self-realisation or perception is obtained by an omniscient or one who has attained the state of highest perfection only. The deeds, enveloping the soul or obscuring the knowledge of substance or matter is no longer found in an omniscient.

However, the deeds of those who are in know of their mental dispositions through internal impulses and those who know the nature of matter and substratum of properties through their innerself without use of sense organs or mind, their deeds, enveloping the soul, are only partially destroyed. In other words, their knowledge is also self-perceived without having any concern with sense organs or mind. However, their self-perception is only partial since their karmas are destroyed only in part. On the other hand, what is perceived through sensual organs or mind without application of the soul, is not a direct perception but implicit. Nevertheless, in practice, it is considered as direct perception. Consequently, the theologists of Jaina religion treat it as self perception or direct comprehension in practice.

Till then, the Karmās of Ārya Sudharmā, obscuring spiritual knowledge, had not decayed altogether. He had not yet attained the state of omniscience. Hence his true spiritual knowledge was still incomplete as against the authoritativeness of the knowledge of an omniscient. Probably, with this view in mind, he might have expressed his eagerness to know the agonies and tortures inflicted in the hell. Whatever be the reason, the main anxiety might have been to ensure the flow of scriptural knowledge without least interruption.

In texts of Acharanga, Samvāyānga, Sthānānga and Vyākhyapragyapti etc. (The Angas forming part of Jaina Agamic scriptures) it is mentioned that while considering and explaining the subject under discussion. Ārya Sudharma always emphasized that what he was propounding, was entirely in accordance with what he had heard by revelation or as revealed by Lord Mahavirā. The said wordings, used by Ārya Sudharmā, are indicative of the fact that every care was taken to maintain the originality of the utterances, made by Tirthanker and no attempt was made to alter them.

Citation Regarding Jambu

Besides the references, made above, concerning spiritual knowledge, acquired by Ārya Jambu by way of placing questions and seeking replies thereof from Ārya Sudharmā, only this much appears in the list of Sthaviras (List of successiors to the seat of supreme administrator and guide), incorporated in 'Kalpa Sūtra' that Ārya Jambu, born in Kāshyapa family, was resident disciple of Sthavira Ārya Sudharmā who belonged to 'Agni Vaishyan' lineage.

In the list of succession of Sthaviras, as appeared in 'Nandi Sūtra', the name of Ārya Jambu is cited as success or to the seat of Ārya Sudharmā to administer the affairs and to afford spiritual guidance to the mendicants of Jaina organisation.

It is a eulogical formation. In the narrative, the use of the names of Ārya Sudharmā and Ārya Jambu has been made in accusative case with termination inflected at the end. In the latter half of the narrative, the words 'bow to you' have appeared which could be treated to have been used for them.

No more citation is found respecting Ārya Jambu, except what has already been quoted from or referred to in Angas (Twelve in number) and Upāngas (a class of writings, supplementary to the Angas) and other allied canonical literature of Jainism. Under Digamber tradition, the oldest citation regarding Ārya Jambu is found in 'Tiloyapannatti'. Therein, only the name of Ārya Jambu has appeared.

A Charming Personality : Greatly Eulogized by Poets and Authors

Arya Jambu was endowed with most attractive, delicate, amiable, pleasant and blessed personality. His body was really elegant and charming. In young age, he had attained perfection in several disciplines and was skilled in various arts and crafts. In paternal family, he had inherited enormous wealth. He was the only son of his parents. Hence the affection, love and fondness which he received from his parents, was hardly available to even most fortunate persons in the world. Jambu was married with eight girls of distinguished wealthy families who were living embodiments of unparalleled beauty, affection and amiable nature for whom people would generally crave for with strong desire and longing. For what people will put in hard labour and exert themselves day and night, all those riches, wealth and prosperity were at the disposal of Ārya Jambu without putting in least pains. However, Ārya Jambu, being too earger to attain final emancipation, renounced them without least reluctance on his part.

It was a unique example of total detachment and absolute sacrifice, the parallel example of which was difficult to be found on this earth. Inspite of having been endowed with extra-ordinary youthfulness, immense wealth and worldly possessions, he renounced all wordly sensual enjoyments, impelling desires, and attainments without least hitch and dedicated himself to spiritual pursuits for self-realization and attainment of true wisdom. It was really a unique example and a wonderful event of its type.

Ārya Jambu's virtuous acts, spiritual endeavours and absolute detachment greatly impressed the poets, writers and literateurs of his age. Consequently, they wrote extensively over the spiritual accomplishments of Ārya Jambu in various linguistics, dialects and modes of expression. Besides them, there are other works also wherein his biography and life events have been incorporated along with other luminaries. In this way, two types of literature is found concerning important historic events of Jambu's life.

Vasudeva Hindi : Vasudeva Hindi[1] is considered to be the oldest work in the canonical literature of Jaina religion, in which an account of life events of Ārya Jambu also finds place. The author of Vasudeva Hindi is Sri Sanghdās Gani. His life time is believed to be sixth or seventh century of Vikrama era. Vasudeva Hindi is the oldest treatise, composed and written in Jain Mahārāshtrian Prākrita. Later on, whatever books were written, relating to the life-events of Ārya Jambu, they were all based on the said work. In the chapter, styled 'Kathotpatti' (Narrative) of the said book, the life events of Ārya Jambu have been narrated. Since he was the authority and well conversant with Jaina Agamic scriptures, he was the only source for propagation and spread of religious and philosophical doctrines of Jainism. Hence the students must be aware of the biography of Ārya Jambu, and, therefore, his biographical narrative is reproduced below in concise form on the basis of Vasudeva Hindi.

Parents : Birth : Original Residence of Ārya Jambu

The author of *Vasudeva Hindi*, has, first of all, depicted a lively picture of natural beauty, grandeur, riches and prosperity of the people, inhabiting Rajgraha, the then capital of Magadha dynasty. He has also related about the grandeur, magnanimity, his ambition to conquer more territories and glory or great deeds of king Shrenika, ruler of Magadha. A narration is also found of Chelnā, principal Queen of King Shrenika, and his son, prince Konika (Ajātshatru) where the context so demanded.

---

1. In Prākritra dialect, the literal meaning of the word 'hinda' is to move, go about or roam. Accordingly, Vasudeva Hindi contains a travelogue of Vasudeva, father of Vāsudeva Krishna. There is a detailed description of the travels of Vasudeva in the said book. He leaves his home and undertakes excursions, roaming for several years. During his journeys, he is married with a number of girls. A fantastic account of his journeys, day today impressions and experiences has been incorporated in a literary style in the said book.

There was a distinguished wealthy person, named Rishabhdutta at Rajgraha. He owned considerable wealth, inherited by him from his ancestors. He was submissive, prudent, capable, kind-hearted, truthful and generous. He had faith in the doctrines of Jaina religion. His wife's name was Dhārṇi. Her temperament was sweet and unblemished like a crystal gem. She was embellished with virtuous life, full of modesty and ethical values. Once, she happened to visualise five dreams in the state of sub-consciousness. She woke up. The dreams were as follows:

1. Smokeless fire.
2. A pond, full of Lotus and other water-lily flowers.
3. A paddy field, full of paddy crop.
4. A large elephant with four teeth, protruded upwards and crystal white in colour, and
5. Rose apple with fine colour, odour and full of juice.

Dhārṇi described her dreams before her husband, Rishabhadutta. He replied that as per effects of the said dreams, as explained by our sanctified religious teacher and omniscient, you will be giving birth to a son, having extraordinary powers or faculties. Dhārṇi felt greatly delighted and expressed her joy saying that your prediction appears to be true and let it be so if such is the will of God.

A deity, dropped from the heaven, entered her womb. Dhārṇi, the pregnant lady, expressed her desire to worship an omniscient (Jaina spiritual guide) and attend to other Jaina saints. Befitting to the financial status and prosperity of the family, the longings of the pregnant lady were complied with. After nine months of pregnancy, Dhārṇi gave birth to a male child, having loveliness like an autumnal moon and brilliance of the sun. His bodily colour was shining like lotus, made of pure gold, and glittering like the flower of Karṇikāra tree, having the blossom of a lotus or similar other plant. There were auspicious marks on his body, indicative of good fortune and pleasant signs on his hands, feet and face, manifesting peace and happiness. After performance of the fourth ceremony (investiture with the sacred thread) out of 16 major ceremonies, the ceremony of naming the child took place. As a result of seeing a rose-apple fruit in the dream by the mother and appearance of the presiding or chief deity of Jambudweep (one of the seven continents surrounding the mountain Meru), the child was named Jambu. The child gradually grew up, having been looked after by a nurse. Because of the favourable sacraments of the past lives, he attained perfection in several disciplines and skills without putting in much effort.

Coming in Contact with Ārya Sudharma

Jambu attained youth. At the very sight of him, people felt much delighted. They used to admire him with laudable attributes, saying that he was really kind-hearted, sweet-spoken, sagacious and adorer of worthy seers and saints. Jambu was really so nice that he greatly contributed to magnify the dignity and grace of Magadha. His life was full of divine bliss and happiness. Like a Tirthanker, Gandher Ārya Sudharmā happened to pay a visit to Rajgraha (old capital of Magadha dynasty), accompanied by the religious mendicants and a body of his followers. He stayed in a monastery, named 'Gunasheel.' Jambu came to know of the arrival of Ārya Sudharmā. Just as a peacock feels overjoyed and dances on hearing the thunder of clouds, the same boundless joy was experienced by Jambu. He mounted on a chariot and reached there. He got down from the vehicle, slightly away from the monastery. He drew near Sudharmā with detached mind. He went round thrice and after paying his respects, he sat down.

Ārya Sudharmā addressed Jambu and the audience, present there. He elaborately dealt with animate and inanimate substance; atoms attracting Karmas; self-purification from impurities of worldly deeds; close connection of our multiple Karmas with our soul, and spoke on several other topics, relating to final emancipation or liberation of the soul. After listening to the religious discourses of Gandher Sudharma, a feeling of total detachment and renunciation aroused in the mind of Ārya Jambu. Feeling completely satisfied, he got up. He paid his obeisance and prayed: "My Lord! I have heard the sacred knowledge of Jaina religion. After obtaining approval of my parents, and taking refuge at your feet, I shall practise religious austerities for my own good and realization of Supreme Truth."

Gandher Sudharma replied: "It was really worth doing for excellent devouts like you."

An Awakening : After bowing with respect before Ārya Sudharmā, Jambu got into the chariot. After returning by the same route, he arrived at the entrance gate to the city. There he noticed heavy rush of the vehicles. Considering that it was bound to take considerable time to enter the city, he decided to enter the city by another gate. He instructed the driver to turn back and drive the vehicle to another entrance door so that he could reach his place as early as possible. The driver drove the horses and the chariot arrived at the other entrance gate. There Jambu found that a large piece of stone, a weapon used as a missile (supposed by some to be a sort of rocket but described by others as a huge stone, studded with iron spikes) and a sharp circular missile like a disc, were hanging upon with the help of a rope. They were designed to strike against and kill the soldiers of the enemy in order to foil and frustrate their attempt to enter the town. At the sight of them, Jambu began to worry and ponder over the pros and cons. In case, they fell upon his chariot by chance, his end was certain. If he expired, he would not be able to practise the austerities, and would be forced to go to hell. Thus he resolved in his mind to leave the place and instructed his driver to turn back and drive the chariot to Gunsheel monastery where he would be able to meet Ārya Sudharma again. The driver, accordingly, drove back the chariot.

Jambu appeared before Ārya Sudharmā with humility. He expressed his sincere desire to observe celibacy for the whole of his life. Thus, he took the pledge to remain life-long bachelor voluntarily. Thereafter he mounted the chariot and reached his residence.

Submission Before the Parents

Young Jambu got down from the Chariot. He looked quite cheerful. He bowed before his parents and submitted: "I had listened to the religious sermons, delivered by Gandher, Sudharma and was very much impressed. I am anxious to attain the state of highest perfection, in order to avoid all physical sufferings and diseases of grown up age, death and bereavement. I shall seek initiation as religious mendicant. Kindly give me your kind approval."

On hearing the resolve of young Jambu in a decisive tone, the parents had tears in their eyes. They replied—"You heard the preachings, it is alright. Look here, our ancestors too were deeply committed to the ideology of Jainism. However, we never heard that any of them had ever sought initiation. We too have been attending the lectures, yet we never made up our mind to get initiated. We are at our wits end to find that you have decided to attain initiation and renounce worldly life after attending the religious congregation for a day only.

Young Jambu consoled his parents and clarified "There are people who are unable to take a firm decision even after passage of long time, while there are others who are quick in arriving at a decision and proceed accordingly."

In order to acquaint his parents, young Jambu cited an example of the son of a distinguished wealthy person who had likewise taken a prompt decision to attain initiation. Young Jambu again sought the permission of his parents to allow him to obtain initiation. The parents replied—"It will be better to offer yourself for initiation as a mendicant next time when Ārya Sudharma again visits this place."

While citing the illustrations of several friends who had taken bold steps and devoted themselves completely to practising the austerities and attain final emancipation, young Jambu again entreated his parents and said—"Just as his friends had obtained initiation instantaneously at the very place where Lord Mahavirā had delivered his discourses and redeemed themselves from the agony of birth and death (transmigration), similarly, if I failed to obtain initiation immediately, I am afraid I may fall into the trap of sensual enjoyments and lose the inner urge to lead a devout life. I, therefore, pray for your immediate approval."

Father, Rishabhdutta, replied—"you have inherited enormous wealth besides all luxurious articles at your disposal. Therefore, it will be better if you first have full enjoyment of worldly pleasures and only, thereafter, you get initiated."

Thereupon, young Jambu cited the example of a monkey who had died as a result of clinging with the adhesive bitumen, while busy in sexual enjoyment and added—"Because of my young age I am yet confined to the allurement of luxurious eating and drinking only. In other words, I am inclined to taking rich and dainty food only for the present from which I can easily liberate myself. However, when I shall involve myself in all types of sensual enjoyments, and fall prey to the horrors of life and death just like the said monkey, I shall be no where. Infact, I am scared of death. I, therefore, again seek your consent to obtain initiation and renounce the world, besides giving up all worldly attachments."

On hearing the said words of Jambu, his mother started crying and wailing. She said—"Oh my son! it has been my long cherished desire to behold you in the costume of .. bride-groom. However, the decision taken by you totally frustrates my longing. In case, you will carry out my wish, I shall also renounce the worldly life and obtain initiation along with you."

Jambu replied—"Mother! if you are so eager, I shall abide by your wish and act accordingly. However, as soon as the auspicious ceremony of marriage is over, you will not object to my getting initiated."

Mother expressed her complete satisfaction and felt much rejoiced. She said that things would shape as he wished. She further added—"Jambu! you have already been betrothed with eight girls—all belonging to distinguished and well-to-do families. They are all local leading merchants, named Samudrapriya, Samudradutta, Sagardutta, Kuberdutta, Kubersen, Vaishramana Dutta, Vasusen, and Vasupal. They are all followers of Jainism. The names of their wives are Padmavati, Kanakmala, Vinayshri, Dhanshri, Kanakvati, Shrisena, Hrimati, and Jayasena, respectively. The names of their daughters are Samurdrashri, Sindhumati, Padamshri, Padamsena, Kanakshri, Vijayshri, Kamlavati, and Yashomati respectively. These girls really match you. It has long been decided to marry you with them. Hence it is new essential to make their parents aware of the new development."

The message was immediately conveyed to the respective parents of the girls that young Jambu had decided to lead the life of self—denial and mortification as soon as the marriage ceremony was over. Please convey your reactions in this regard.

As soon as the parents of the girls came to know of it, they were sad and dejected. They discussed the matter with their ladies. Their daughters happened to hear what their parents talked about. They took uniform decision and submissively addressed to their parents — "You have already pledged to marry us with Jambu. According to law and from religious point of view, he is our husband. What he will do and the course, he will adopt, we shall follow him." After learning the firm determination and resolve of their daughters, the parents communicated their reply to Rishabhdutta. As per Digamber sect, there were only 4 brides and not 8 as stated above.

Marriages Accomplished : On an auspicious day, yellow ground pulse was applied to the body of young Jambu. The brides were also applied with yellow ground pulse at their respective homes. After performance of all prescribed rites and ceremonies, young Jambu, dressed as a bride-groom, arrived with the marriage party at the residence of each bride, looking as if the moon, was drawing near the stars. After performance of marriage ceremonies, he returned to his home with his wives as if he was accompanied by goddesses of wealth, fortitude, glory and fortune.

Young Jambu was given bath after performance of hundreds of ceremonial rites in a methodical way with full pomp and show. He was adorned with ornaments. Young Jambu was felicitated by the learned citizens. The holy ascetics were duly honoured on this auspicious occasion.

In the evening, a grand feast was arranged in which the local citizens and family members participated. Young Jambu returned home with his parents and newly-wedded wives.

Arrival of Prabhava, a Notorious Thief and Robber

During the same period, there was a notorious robber and dacoit, named Prabhava. He was son of the ruler of Vindhya region and lived at Jaipur. He was well-conversant and expert in several tricks. Consequently, the king of Vindhya region had enthroned his younger son to rule the state. Prabhava felt disgraced and left the home for good. He began to live in inaccessible valleys of Vindhyāchal mountain-range and started to earn his living by committing thefts. He came to know that young Jambu was highly rich and several affluent families, who had participated in the marriage, were staying with him. Prabhava left for his residence. He was well-versed in the trick of opening the locks without keys. He opened the leaves of the main door by using the said trick and entered into the building with the group of his fellow-robbers. He was also conversant with the fraud of hypnotism. He turned the inmates of the building asleep. All of them began to doze. The robbers started to remove their ornaments and clothes. Young Jambu saw to it. Without getting awe-struck, he asked them fearlessly not to harass the guests. By mere utterance of the said words, the robbers turned benumbed and were completely stunned. Prabhava found that young Jambu was sitting comfortably on the luxurious carpet with his newly-wedded wives as if the autumnal moon was surrounded by the stars.

Jambu and Prabhava: Mutual Conversation

On finding his companions benumbed and motionless, the notorious chief of the gang, Prabhava, addressed young Jambu— "I am a robber, named Prabhava, son of the ruler of Vindhya region. A sudden feeling of cordiality towards you has overwhelmed me.

I entreat you to teach me the skills of suppression of the force of feelings by supernatural means and rendering benumbed and motionless as also liberating and freeing therefrom. In exchange, I shall teach the tricks of opening the locks without keys and hypnotizing."

Young Jambu answered—"Prabhava! listen, I shall renounce all worldly pleasures and detach myself from all dear and near ones as also from enormous wealth and attain initiation tomorrow to lead the life of a devout. Virtually, I have already given up all allurements and initiatives. In a way, I have become more vigilant. No trick or superhuman activity can be efficacious in my case. I have got nothing to do with sinful or evil deeds as also foul or dirty tricks. The ultimate result of such foul tricks is bound to be misfortune and indigence. I have already acquired the wisdom from Ārya Sudharmā how to attain salvation or riddance from the circuit of worldly life."

Prabhava heard all this and was highly amazed. He thought in his mind-what a great surprise. Young Jambu was going to renounce all his wealth without least reluctance. He was really marvellous and an excellent youngman. He deserves all appreciation and praise. Prabhava bowed before him with humility. However, he remarked — "Young Jambu! sensual pleasures are also essential in this worldly life. Please enjoy them along with your wives. The sages never support giving up pleasures and comforts that are at our disposal. It is not the opportune time to seek initiation. What made you determined to take such an untimely step? Incase, those who are grown up and mature old persons, choose to adopt such a course for their final emancipation, it is alright. Nobody will censure them."

Young Jambu related several examples like drop of honey falling from a beehive in the mouth of a person who was hanging in a well and facing imminent danger of death by snake-bite and, thus, minutely explained the significance of renunciation of sensual pleasures and leading an absolutely detached life. Resultantly, on one hand young Jambu attained initiation along with his wives and on the other Prabhava, the notorious gangster also obtained initiation along with all other members of his gang.

Just as, Prabhava had earned extraordinary notoriety in committing daring robberies, similarly, he performed miracles in the field of devotion and spiritual performances also. He became chief resident disciple of Ārya Jambu and after his attaining final salvation, Prabhava became the true successor to the seat of spiritual guide, supreme leader of the religious organisation and an accomplished exponent of the sacred texts of 12 Angas (Agamic Scriptures) as revealed by Ārya Jambu.

Under Digamber tradition, the name of the gang leader is stated as 'Vidyuchchar' in place of Prabhava. However, there is no mention, whatsoever, about him of being either a chief resident disciple or successor to the holy seat of Ārya Jambu. According to sacred books of Digamber sect, Vishnu or Nandi was chief disciple of Ārya Jambu and after his liberation, he had succeeded to the seat of a spiritual guide and leader of the organisation.

Chronology of Arya Jambu: The chronology of Ārya Jambu is believed to be as under:

Birth : 543 B.C.

Initiation: In 527 B.C. i.e. at the age of sixteen, slightly after final salvation of Lord Mahavirā.

Obtaining state of omniscience and highest perfection - In 507 B.C.

Final salvation—463 B.C.: Total age 80 yrs.

Another Presumption: In most of the sacred writings of Jaina religion, it is stated that emperor Shrenika, ruler of Magadha dynasty, had enquired from either Lord Mahavirā, himself, or his Gandher Gautama regarding birth particulars of Ārya Jambu. It is, therefore, natural to conclude that Jambu had been during the life time of emperor Shrenika, either earlier or near about his death.

Lord Buddha attained his final salvation in 544 B.C. The coronation of emperor Ajātshatru had taken place 8 years earlier in 552 B.C. Emperer Shrenika is believed to have expired in or about 552 B.C. Accordingly, the year of the birth of Jambu should also be near about that time. If this chronology is believed to be correct, then there is a difference of 10 years as against the old recognition. In that circumstance, the total age of Jambu will be 90 years in place of 80 years, as stated above.

Opinion of Poet Veer: Poet Veer, the author of *Jambusāmi Chariu* (11th century A.D.) and following his line, Brahma Jinadās (13th century Vikrami) and Rājmalla (17th century of Vikram era) have also narrated that young Jambu had attained initiation during the reign of king Shrenika, ruler of Magadha Kingdom. Not merely this, king Shrenika had celebrated the initiation ceremony with great pomp and show, giving it the shape of a grand celebration. Accordingly, the birth of Jambu must have taken place nearly 15-16 years earlier to the death of king Shrenika in 552 B.C. Thus, it appears that he had born in or about the year 568-569 B.C. If it is believed to be more authentic, then the total age of Jambu will accrue to 105 years. Although, the scholars have given enough consideration to this point, yet further critical examination of the issue is very much desirable. It is believed the scholars will go on with their critical investigation in this regard and arrive at a decision which may be more convincing and near truth for all practical purposes.

Final Salvation of Ārya Jambu

Virsena, author of *Dhavala Tika* (commentary) on Shatkhandāgama, written in Shorseni Prakrita (8th-9th century A.D.).[1] Sri Nemichandracharya 'Sidhant Chakravarty', author of 'Gommatsār' (9th Century A.D.); Sri Guṇadhar, author of "Uttar Purāṇa" (Prior to 898 A.D.); Sri Pushpadanta, author of 'Tisatthimahapurisaguṇālankār', written in Apbhransh Prākrita (10th century A.D.)—all the said scholars, belonging to Digamber sect, believe that Gandher Gautama had attained his final liberation after 12 years of the final salvation of Lord Mahāvira and after 12 years of his death, Ārya Sudharma had obtained his final liberation and after another 40 years, Ārya Jambu had attained his final salvation. Thus the period from the final salvation of Lord Mahavirā to the final emancipation of Ārya Jambu totalled to 12+12+40=64 years.

As per Swetamber sect also, the total period of omniscience and the state of highest perfection of Gautama, Sudharma and Jambu had been 64 years. However, the period of omniscience of respective Kevali differs. The period of the state of highest perfection of Gautama ranged to 12 years, that of Ārya Sudharmā to eight years and finally of Ārya Jambu to 44 years totalling to 64 years.

Although, Achārya Yativrashabha, author of *Tiloypaṇṇatti*, belonged to Digamber sect, yet his chronological order is different. He has held that the total period of omniscience of Gautama, Ārya Sudharma and Jambu amounted to 62 years.[2] Poet Veer, author of 'Jambusāmi Chariu', written in Apbhransh Prākrita, has propounded a new theory regarding total period of highest perfection and omniscience of Ārya Jambu. He writes—after 18 years of initiation of Jambu Swami, Ārya Sudharma had attained his final salvation on 7th day of bright half of lunar month Māgh (as per Hindu Calendar) After another 18 years of final salvation of Ārya Sudharma, Jambu had attained his final emancipation.

In *Himvata Therāvali*, it is cited that Ārya Jambu had attained his final salvation in the year 70 after final salvation of Lord Mahāvirā (Jaina Calendar). Thus, the total period of omniscience, of Gautama, Ārya Sudharma and Jambu amounted to 70 years.

Additional Details : Slight Break: While dealing with the traditional history of various religious sects in Braj circle, there is a reference of Ārya Jambu as well. It is stated that Jambu had obtained his initiation at the adolescent age of only 16 years, immediately after his marriage, through his spiritual guide and

---

1. His time is estimated from the last Quarter of 8th century A.D. to the first Quarter of ninth century A.D.
2. Vāsatthi Vāsāṇiṁ godamapahudṁa nāṇavantaṇaṁ|
Dhammapayattankāle parimāṇaṁ pindruveṇaṁ||

— *Tiloyapaṇṇatti*, 1478

preceptor, Ārya Sudharma, a favourite scholar and staunch follower of Lord Mahavirā. Jambu had observed life-long celibacy. After attaining initiation, Ārya Jambu led the life of a religious devout and an ascetic for 20 years. Thereafter, he attained the state of highest perfection. After continuing in the state of omniscience for 44 years, Ārya Jambu had attained his final emancipation at the age of 80 years in the year 62, after final salvation of Lord Mahavirā (Jaina calendar). The year of his final salvation is believed to be Samvat 408 prior to the commencement of Vikrama era. He had accomplished the state of highest perfection at Chaurāsi in Mathura city after practising meditation and self-denial or bodily mortification. He also had his final salvation at Chaurāsi. He is supposed to be the last omniscient of Jain religion.[1]

The citation that Arya Jambu had attained final emancipation in the year 62, after final salvation of Lord Mahavirā (Jaina calendar) after continuing for 44 years as an omniscient and in the state of highest perfection, needs further contemplation. Of course, the figure of 62 years as total period of omniscience of all the three Kevalins is also found in 'Tiloyapaṇṇatti'. However, the period of omniscience of Ārya Jambu for 44 years is not believeable, since this leaves the total period of omniscience of both Kevalins—Gautama and Sudharma to 18 years only (62-44=18) which does not tally and is inconsistent with the beliefs of either sect.

Discontinuance of Several Branches of Sacred Knowledge After Salvation of Ārya Jambu

Ārya Jambu was the last omniscient. Nearly all sects and branches of Jaina religion are unanimous at this point. As believed by Jaina community, several types of sacred knowledge, especially derived from meditation and deep devotion on the higher truths of religion and philosophy had come to an end, after final salvation of Ārya Jambu such as—

(1) Knowledge of mental dispositions pertaining to the soul or spirituality (with Jainas name of the penultimate stage in the perception of truth).
(2) Knowledge of the nature of matter or inherent property by an omniscient through his soul or spirituality without the perception of any object by the senses. (Third degree of knowledge by which what is not within the reach of the senses is perceived).
(3) Knowledge of subtlety of spiritual bodies gained by way of purification of the soul.
(4) Knowledge of one of five bodies, belonging to the soul. It is a minute form issuing from the head of a meditative sage to consult an omniscient saint and returning with the desired information.
(5) Knowledge how to control or restrain the senses and becoming quiet to obtain the inner bliss.
(6) Knowledge how to destroy impurities by fasting and observing abstinence.
(7) Profound devotion and dedication for accomplishment of excellent

1. *Braj ka Sanskritik Itihas*, Pt II, page 55.

character and uprightness. The said spiritual endeavour is very hard and could be practised by a Tirthanker or a Jaina Arhat only.

(8) Shunning of vices for purification of character.
(9) Minutely encountering the evils for refineness of character.
(10) Accomplishment of renowned and reputed character.
(11) Attainment of the state of highest perfection and omniscience, and
(12) Attainment of final emancipation.

Besides other causes, time factor could also be one of the reasons for discontinuation of above-said spiritual endearvours and accomplishments.

A Reference Found in 'Tiloyapaṇṇatti' on the subject under Discussion

The process of attaining the state of omniscience right from Lord Mahavirā to Ārya Jambu finds mention in Tiloypaṇṇatti. It has been further stated that after Jambu Swāmi, Anubaddha was not able to obtain the state of omniscience. Normally, it is believed that after final salvation of Jambu, the process of attaining the state of highest perfection came to an end. However, a list is also found in 'Tiloyapaṇṇatti' in which there are descriptions of the last omniscient, last roaming Jaina saint, last devout, having gained highest knowledge and scholarship, last sage, having acquired knowledge of the nature of matter or inherent property through his spirituality, and last crowned monarch, having attained initiation by an omniscient etc. It is, finally, stated that last omniscient, Shridhar had attained the state of highest perfection on 'Kuṇḍalgiri' (a small mountain).

It may be asked here that Achārya Yativrashabha, author of 'Tiloyapaṇṇatti' had, on one hand, negated the possibility of accomplishing the state of omniscience by any other spiritual leader after final salvation of Jambu Swāmi and on the other, he writes that Shridhar was the last sage who attained the state of highest perfection. How both versions could reconcile with each other? On profound consideration, it appears that the use of the qualifying word अनुबद्ध (constantly flowing) before an omniscient is significant.

It probably means that the process of attaining the state of omiscience after Jambu Swami had come to a standstill. It signifies that the process of attaining the state of highest perfection had stopped after Jambu, which was continuous hitherto. It, therefore, follows that Shridhar had not become an omniscient, immediately after the final salvation of Ārya Jambu but may be after several generations. Nevertheless, this probability is in direct contravention to the earlier version of Achārya Yativrashabha that the process of attaining the state of omniscience had ceased after final emancipation of Ārya Jambu along with other ten spiritual accomplishments.

It, is therefore, essential to have a critical study as to when and where Shridhar had born since it was still believed that Ārya Jambu was the last omniscient. However, the said belief is contradicted by the version of Achārya Yativrashabha that Shridhar had also attained the state of highest perfection after Jambu Swāmi.

Sacred Knowledge Heard and Obtained by Revelation: Retained in Memory: Method Continued

The main reason for calling Vedas as 'Shrutis' (Vedas known by revelation) being that there had been long tradition of hearing sacred or scriptural knowledge through revelation by a spiritual head or a supreme religious leader and retaining the texts thereof in memory. Jaina Agamic scriptures are also called 'Shrutis' in as much as there was similar tradition of learning sacred texts by hearing through revelation by a spiritual guide or sanctified teacher of Jaina religion and retaining them in memory. However, it was not an easy task to retain the sacred texts in memory which had been heard by way of religious lectures, quite intact, without allowing any deviation. This point was well within the minds of ancient seers and scholars. Hence they spared no efforts to take adequate precautions from the very beginning in this regard. The Vedic seers had prescribed a well devised method for recitation of Vedic texts in the shape of 'Saṁhita Pāth' (The continuous texts of the Vedas); 'Pada-Pāth' (An arrangement of the Vedic texts in which each word is written and pronounced in its original form and independently of phonetic changes as against 'Saṁhita Pāth'). 'Krim Pāth' (A particular manner of reciting Vedic texts, leaving at each time one word and taking up another); 'Jatā pāth' (A particular manner of reciting Vedic texts), thus the words 'नमः रुद्रेभ्यः' repeated in this manner would stand thus — 'नमो रुद्रेभ्यौ' 'नमो नमो रुद्रेभ्यः' and 'Ghan-Pāth' (Another method of reciting Vedic texts).[1] As a result of the said scientific method, the basic contents of the Vedas and their glossary have not been disturbed till now.

Jaina seers, who were proficient in Agamic scriptures, were equally conscious that the original texts of the utterances of omniscient should not be allowed to be vitiated in any way. They too prescribed certain constraints and laid down stipulations and conditions for proper recitation of the texts of Agamic scriptures so that the basic form of their contents was not disturbed in any way.

In 'Anuyoga Dwār Sūtra', it has been stated that there were specific methods for correct recitation of the texts of Agamic scriptures, which were as follows:

(1) 'शिक्षित'—To obtain knowledge of Agamic texts in the normal course and to learn how to recite them.

(2) 'स्थित'—Preserving and retaining the texts in the mind which have already been studied and learnt.

(3) 'जित'—Reciting the texts of Agamic scriptures in a systematic manner. It is practicable only when the sacred texts are approved and held authoritative or genuine by an omniscient.

(4) 'मित'—The literal meaning of the word 'mita' is—what has been investigated or examined. The purpose of using the said word is to define how to abide by the constraints, rules and methods of distinct articulation of syllables of the texts under recitation.

1. Kindly refer to the discussion on the topic 'Vedas and their language', appearing in foregoing pages.

(5) 'परिजित'—(Reading well or readily). It is easy to read the texts of Agamic Scriptures in a sequence or systematic order. However, recitation of the same texts in a reverse order is quite difficult. This is possible only when the texts have already been read well and mastered. A student or a scholar must have the practice to recite the texts in an inverted order as well.

(6) 'नामसम' (Remembering anything like one's own name). Each and every body is supposed to remember its name positively under any circumstance. It is thoroughly appropriated to oneself. In the same way, the texts of Agamic scriptures are to be mentally assimilated and thoroughly remembered like one's own name. Only after full practice, a student or a scholar will be able to recite the texts readily and spontaneously.

(7) 'घोषसम' (Phonation with Desired Accent). The literal meaning of the word 'घोष' is phonation or voiced sound. The texts of the Agamic scriptures must be recited in an appropriate manner with desired voiced sound and accent. According to the commentators, the word ghosh (voiced sound) incorporates all the three accents—(1) The acute accent; (2) The grave accent and (3) The mixed accent lying between high and low. It is essential to recite the texts with the same voiced sound or accent as is prescribed by the seers and sages. Every possible care is taken in correct recitation of Vedic hymns or Mantras. It may be equally important to emphasize here that the alphabetical letters should be recited from the same vocal chords or organs to which they belong. The effort of the mouth in the production of articulate sounds[1] is also dealt with under this heading.

(8) 'अहीनाक्षर' : Recital of all letters or syllables of the sacred texts in full without causing to disappear:

While making recital of a saved text, the Phonation of each and every letter or syllable must be distinct and it should be ensured that no letter or syllable is pronounced vaguely or incompletely. The recitation of the text should be manifest and accurate.

(9) **'अन्त्यक्षर' (Letters other than forming part of the word)**

While reciting a sacred text, only those letters or syllables which form part of the text, should be recited. No additional or extra letter should be spoken or mixed therewith.

(10) 'अव्याविद्धाक्षर' (अ+वि+आ+विद्ध) :- The literal meaning of the word 'विद्ध' is pierced, penetrated or wounded. The letter 'आ' as a prefix expresses

1. Slight effort of the mouth and vocal organs in the production of articulate sounds is necessary. It is called an effort in uttering or pronouncing letters. It is of two types. Prior to the utterance of the articulate sound, audible to others, an effort is made to give rise to the vocal sounds inside the mouth which is an initial effort. Without the internal effort which gives rise to the vocal sounds, the external effort is meaningless. Hence internal effort is more significant. It is called the first effort in Sanskrit grammar which is essential for giving rise to the vocal sounds. The significance of the first effort is apparent and is experienced by the person, making recital of sacred texts, since the internal vibrations within the vocal chords, give rise to the vocal sounds. The second effort is made while uttering the words. It is why this is also called an external effort since the audience can have direct cognition and experience while hearing the reciter.

the sense of completely or from all sides. The letter 'वि' as a prefix expresses the sense of intensity or extremity. 'व्याविद्धाक्षर' means broken or affected letters. Recitation of wrong letters or syllables contrary to rules is called vitiation or impairment of the letters. It should be avoided as far as possible.

(11) **'अस्खलित' (Not Stumbling or Slipping—To be careful)**

The sacred text should be recited continuously in an unbroken sequence. There is always deep concentration and a sort of exclusive devotion in continuous recitation which enables manifestation of the true intent of the text clearly. Hence there should be no deviation, whatsoever, in recitation of the text. In an undeviating or careful recitation, the sense (end and aim) of the text is easily understood with no ambiguity at all.

(12) **'अमिलित' (Not mixed)**: There is always an apprehension that alien or unconnected letters other than those, forming part of the text, may not be interpolated or get joined with the original text for want of adequate attention or carefulness. In that case, the correctness of recitation gets vitiated or unpaired.

(13) **'अव्यत्याम्रेडित' (अ+वि+अति+आम्रेडित)** : The literal meaning of the word 'आम्रेडित' is repetition of sound or word. The original form of the word is 'अव्वच्चामेलिय'. If the prefix 'अ' (meaning negation or denoting absence of knowledge) is removed, the remaining form of the word will be 'वच्चामेलिय'. In 'Paiasaddamahannvo' (a work in Prakrita) both forms of the word 'वच्चामेलिय' and 'विच्चामेलिय' are found which have the same meaning. Therein, the word has been defined to mean 'reduplication' (the next word in reduplication).

The word has been defined in the said book to mean that the text, consisting mainly of different ingredients and having been removed because of their being inopportune and re-accomplishing the profundity of meaning after splitting the said ingredients. The commentators of the said book have defined the word to mean-connecting the identical texts of other scriptures with the texts under recitation and obtaining the same meaning as given in the dictionaries. Therefore, there should be no reduplication or repetition of a word in the texts, meant to be recited or passing over them in an inverted order.

(14) **'प्रतिपूर्ण' (In entirety)**: Hastiness or too much hastiness breeds confusion or lack of clarity which might result in omission of certain portion of a text under recitation. Therefore, the recital of sacred texts must be made cautiously and in entirety without leaving out any portion thereof.

(15) **कण्ठौष्ठ विप्रमुक्त (कण्ठ+ओष्ठ+विप्र+मुक्त)** :- The literal meaning of the word 'मुक्त' is 'abandoned or left'. For want of adequate precaution in recitation of the sacred texts, sometimes a word or a syllable is not clearly uttered and its phonation may be held up inside the throat or lips. Therefore, the texts are not recited so neatly and intelligibly as they ought to be.

(16) **'प्रतिपूर्ण घोष' (Recital in completely voiced sound)**

Just as recital of sacred texts in rhythmic tune with exclusive devotion is essential, similarly, utterance of articulate sound of each word or syllable is equally necessary. The recitation of the texts, must not be in such a weak or feeble voice that it may appear difficult to follow them, the words with voiced sound signify that the texts must be recited in proper and audible voice.

What has been stated above relating to the proper recitation of the sacred texts, it is indicative of the sincere efforts to be put in for recitation of the words or syllables in a refined manner and maintaining the continuity of the texts unaffected on one hand and retaining of the sacred texts intact in the memory on the other. The points enumerated above forbid the recital of Agamic scriptures in an improper or reverse order and vague or incomplete production of articulate sounds; mixing of alien or unconnected words other than those forming part of the text, interpolation of the alien words or syllables with the original words of the text etc. They are really significant. Most probably, the motive must have been to ensure that the texts of 12 Angas, forming part of Agamic scriptures obtained by way of revelation and retained in memory, must remain intact and should not be allowed to be disturbed, spoiled or altered.

Supreme Spiritual Knowledge as Enunciated by Omniscients

Why the Omniscients, manifest and reveal spiritual knowledge and how it is compiled and composed in aphoristic style by their chief desciples, has been portrayed nicely in the commentary on 'Visheshavashyaka' (An Agamic scripture). "The author of the commentary writes in a metaphorical language that the great omniscients, possessing endless merits and attaining the state of highest perfection by way of practising severe penance and leading a highly disciplined and regulated life, shower the flowers of spiritual knowledge to enlighten the worthy and sincere devotees. The Gandhers (chief disciples) of omniscients gather the flowers of spiritual knowledge in their minds and retain them in memory. Thereafter, they compile and compose the utterances of the omniscients in aphoristic style for sermonizing and delivering discourses.

While elaborating the illustration of a tree, the scholiast writes: "Just as there is a beautiful, tall tree with large hanging branches, known as 'Kalpa tree' (one of the trees of heaven or Indra's paradise) in the midst of a forest. A bold or adventurous person gets seated over the tree. He plucks sweet-smelling and fragrant flowers. There are a number of persons standing on the ground eager to collect the flowers and they spread their cloth for the purpose. The person, seated on the tree, throws down the flowers on the stretched cloth. The persons standing below, collect the flowers and thread them for the use of others. Similarly, this universe is like a forest in which the aforesaid mythological tree (supposed to grant all desires) in the shape of penances, religious austerities and observances as also true spiritual knowledge, derived from deep meditation, is standing. Thirty-four omniscients with exceedingly superior knowledge are seated on the said tree. They throw down the flowers, simlized with higher truths of religion and philosophy, relating to Jainism on the ground, (compared with imperfect state of mind), to be picked up by the inquisitive chief disciples (Gandhers) for the spiritual growth and advancement of the people.

A Question: Its answer : The scholiast has himself raised a question and discussed it in detail which is worth-reading. According to him an omniscient, having attained state of absolute perfection, is a successful and contented defied saint. Thereafter, nothing is left to be done by him. Why should such saints deliver religious discourses and enunciate their doctrines? They are well conversant with all ills and remedies and an authority on religious jurisprudence. They only address deserving and competent wise men. Why don't they address illusive or unworthy persons?

The scholiast, himself, answers the question and writes, "An omniscient is not bound to lead a solitary and contented life. He is free from love and hatred. However, the generic term "Jina", applied to a chief jaina saint is indicative of religious activity. He is not restricted in any way from religious activities nor he is bound to lead his life without a purpose or object. Even after attaining absolute perfection, he is not unavailing or aimless. In other words, the sun is not bound in any way, yet it is its very nature to illuminate the entire universe. Similarly, an omniscient does not need any favour or obligation from others, yet because of his benevolent nature, he remains anxious to assist and guide other ignorant persons. The lotus flowers are grown and bloomed by the rays of sun. Does it mean that the sun has any specific liking or emotional attachment with the said flowers? On the other hand, the lily flowers are not bloomed by the sun, does it mean that the sun has any disliking towards lily flowers? The sun rays have the same effect everywhere, yet blooming of lotus flowers and withering of lily flowers is the manifestation of their own nature or inherent property of the flowers. Just as the radiant rays of the sun cannot remove darkness for an owl, because of its inherent nature, similarly, a chief Jaina saint or an omniscient cannot create awakening and kindle the hearts of unfortunate and inauspicious persons by imparting spiritual lectures. In other words, just as a doctor, treating a curable disease, cannot be considered to have any special liking for the patient or disliking for a patient of an uncureble disease, similarly, an omniscient who has conquered passions and subdued the senses cannot be blamed to have any special liking for and attachment with auspicious and worthy citizens to whom he has imparted spiritual enlightenment and enabled them to destroy the ill-effects of actions, done in former lives nor he can be called names for showing repugnance to enlighten the unworthy or inauspicious persons because of unredeemable nature of their actions in the former lives. Just as a carpenter who produces beautiful and artistic items from serviceable timber and rejects unserviceable timber, cannot be blamed to have any special liking for usable timber and feeling of repugnance towards unusable timber, in the same way, an omniscient or chief sanctified religious teacher is free to impart lectures and create awakening amongst worthy and deserving persons only and to decline to provide spiritual enlightenment to unfortunate and inauspicious persons. He, however, cannot be blamed to have any special affection for the former or being inimical towards the latter.

Composing of Sacred Texts in Aphoristic Style Like Threading of Flower Wreaths

The Gandhers (Chief disciples of Tirthankers and leaders of the associations of religious mendicants) endowed with the capability of penetrating deep and analysing the basic doctrines of the religion,[1] thoroughly pick up the teachings of their spiritual leaders, heard by them through revelation, and compose the sacred texts in aphoristic style like flower garlands for purposes of discoursing in future.[2]

Just as taking possession of strewn flowers is quite difficult and it is comparatively easier to pick up stitched or threaded flowers, similar is the case with the utterances of a Tirthanker (chief Jaina saint), similized with flowers. If the aphorisms are well arranged by use of suitable words, sentences, divided in smaller heads or topics, fit for studying and imparting lectures, the sacred knowledge, contained therein will be easy to be followed or acquired. In this way, the religious discourses of Tirthankers, composed and threaded in aphoristic style, can easily be picked up, followed, remembered and retained in memory. Consequently, the gandhers compiled the sacred texts of the teachings of Tirthankers in the shape of aphorisms regularly. This much was expected of them and they were destined to do it. It is a part of their duty to obtain proficiency in sacred knowledge and arrange it in aphorisms. All the Gandhers have followed this tradition.

For further elucidation, the aforesaid scholiast explains in the shape of questions and answers; "The Gandhers provide a definite shape to the oral utterances of Tirthankers. However, it may be asked that this does not reflect any distinguishing feature of a Gandher. The fact remains that the Tirthankers deliver their discourses only in elemental form, keeping in mind the scholarly wisdom of their Gandhers. Normally, they donot impart detailed lectures, to be followed by the people at large. In other words, the Tirthankers only reveal the real import in concise form and it is for the Gandhers to elaborate it by arranging in aphorisms. Thus the Gandhers play significant role by composing the teachings of Tirthankers in aphoristic style for propagation and spread of religious doctrines.

1. A scholar having a mind capable of analysing and penetrating deep into the very essential principles, is apt to compose many words from one word. Such a capability is called having an analytical mind. The clear and correct recital of the words by a scholar, is indicative of his wisdom, located in the chamber of his brain or mind. Just as a granary will accommodate huge grain storages, similarly, the brain is capable of retaining innumberable sacred texts in memory and then compiling and composing them in the shape of aphorisms.

2. The literal meaning of the word 'प्रवचन' here is excellent and auspicious texts of the speech or sacred texts of 12 Angas (forming part of Agamic scriptures). In order to teach these texts, the Gandhers compile and compose them in aphoristic style for the benefit and convenience of the religious mendicants so that they may be able to follow them and retain in their memory with out much labour and difficulty. The Gandhers have composed and arranged in aphorisms the texts of utterances of the Tirthankers in the shape of 12 Angas so that they may be explained or expounded comfortably, their significance may be easily realized, they may have total manifestation, easily recollected or retained in memory and conveniently exposed before the audience. The mendicants and followers may seek clarifications which may be answered after analytical discussion by Gandhers which is their sole purpose.

Implicitly of the Real Essence

The aforesaid scholiast further explains the implicitly of meaning or substance. He writes "The meaning is implied and, therefore, incomprehensible. It cannot be explained or interpreted by use of a few words. Consequently, the meaning or essence of a subject cannot be described? The words are a source to accredite a meaning. They enable to have clear perception or appreciation of a subject. The inner meaning or import is entertained in words. Accordingly it has been laid down that Tirthankers only give indication or comprehend the sense and the Gandhers provide it a grammatical wordy form.

He again poses a question— "The Tirthankers speak only sutras, accrediting certain spiritual message and not elaborate them. The Gandhers collect and compile. Then what is the basic difference or distinction between the two?"

The scholiast has, himself, answered the question and stated —"The Tirthankers keep the audience in their mind, they are going to address. They speak only in concise form and donot elaborate the sacred texts contained in 12 Angas. Thus, what the Tirthankers preach is only the essence of the sacred texts of 12 Angas and the Gandhers elaborate them for further propagation in aphoristic style".

Divine Words: Three words, relating to birth, death and eternity, spoken by Tirthankers are called divine words. The scholiast further writes in this connection— "Being unconnected with composition of 12 Angas in aphoristic style, the aforesaid three words, uttered and dealt with by Tirthankers have subtle meanings, the end and aim of religious doctrines. Just as the teaching, relating to the texts of 12 Angas, are beneficial for the entire organisation of religions mendicants, the same is not the case with the aforesaid three words, discussed by Tirthankers. What can be consistently followed by the mendicants is favourable to and likened by them. The 12 Angas, compiled and composed by Gandhers, incorporate sacred texts, as enunciated by Tirthankers in most concise form. The said sacred texts, forming part of Agamic scriptures, are perfect, free from all short-comings or defects, precise and most efficacious. They carry profound meanings.

The scholiast has discussed in detail regarding the object, traditional source, and particular manner of recitation as also the end and aim of compilation of sacred texts in the form of 12 Angas (forming part of Agamas). It appears that he was anxious to establish that the source of flow of the sacred texts was the lectures, imparted by Tirthankers and the only contribution of Gandhers was recollecting, arranging, compiling and composing them in the shape of aphorisms.

Under Vedic tradition, the Vedas have been held as superhuman or of divine origin. The Vedas-Vedic hymns, full of spiritual, knowledge, derived from meditation on higher truths of religion and philosophy, made their appearance in the minds of sages and seers. The seers realized their unique significance from their own intellectual power and wisdom. Hence they revealed them in versified form. The rishis (sages) were only composers of vedic hymns and not their authors or creators. Thus it is evident from the above discussion, made by the scholiast, that the Gandhers were not actually the authors of the sacred texts, contained in Agamic Scriptures, but they had only compiled and composed them in aphoristic style.

They only gave wordy form to what they had learnt from the Tirthankers by revelation or derived from meditation on higher truths of religion and philosophy. It has been the general tendency of all religious cults in India to establish that the canonical literature of their cult alone is divine, eternal, superhuman and most sacred in nature.

Old Sacred Purvas and Twelve Angas

Two categories of intellectuals and scholars are found in Jaina literature. Firstly, those who were well-conversant with the old sacred texts of Jaina religion, prior to the last Tirthanker, Lord Mahavirā, and secondly, these who had specialized themselves with the sacred texts, contained in 12 Angas. The old texts contain complete spiritual knowledge as revealed by earlier omniscients and Tirthankers, prior to Lord Mahavirā. The treatises, containing old sacred texts are 14 in number. Amongst Jaina saints, those who have the expertise of all 14 treatises, hold a prominent place. The Jaina sages who are retaining in their memory the knowledge of entire old sacred texts, are called Shruta Kelvins, possessing highest spiritual knowledge and having attained the state of absolute perfection in the sacred knowledge on higher truths of religion and philosophy.

Traditional belief Regarding Purvas (Old Sacred Texts of Jaina Religion)

According to one specific belief, old sacred texts of spiritual knowledge, prior to the era of Lord Mahāvira, were followed and adherd to. Since the old religious texts, related to the period, prior to the accomplishment of Agamic scriptures, after attainment of final salvation by Lord Mahāvirā, they came to be known as old sacred texts. In order to give literal sense to the literature, the word 'old' appears to have been used.

Composition of Purvas (Old Sacred Treatises) Prior to the Accomplishment of Twelve Angas

According to another opinion, the gandhers had composed 14 sacred treatises on the basis of 3 divine words, relating to birth, death and eternity as discussed and revealed by earlier Tirthankers and omniscients. The said treatises contained the complete spiritual knowledge, derived from meditation on higher truths of religion and philosophy. It is so written in *Avashyaka Niryukti* (An Agamic Scripture).

Since the aforesaid 14 sacred treatises had been composed, prior to the accomplishment of 12 Angas, hence they came to be known as old 14 religious treatises. The tougher and most difficult subjects, relating to the highest truths and philosophical doctrines have been enunciated in an academic and scientific manner, in the said 14 treatises, containing old sacred texts of Jaina philosophy. Consequently, the said religious treatises are meant exclusively for erudite scholars and eminent intellectuals. They are beyond the reach of average people. Hence the aforesaid 12 Angas were accomplished by the gandhers with the support of above said old sacred treatises in simplified form, understandable by common people. What Acharya Malayagiri has written in his comments on 'Avashyaka Niryukta' is really worth consideration.

Incorporation of Spiritual Knowledge, Contained in Old Sacred Texts, in Drishtivāda (12th Anga)

The name of 12th Anga is 'Drishtivāda'. It has been classified in five parts:

(1) Parikarma (A means of purifying the mind),
(2) Sūtra,
(3) Pūrvānuyoga,
(4) Purvagata, and
(5) Chūlikā.

It is admitted that the sacred knowledge, contained in 14 old religious treatises, has been incorporated in the fourth part of 'Dwādshangi' known as 'Pūrvagata'. It is true that the 12th Anga,' Dwādshangi', was accomplished on the basis of old sacred texts. However, it was not considered possible to bypass or ignore the old sacred texts, relating to the highest truths and philosophical doctrines of Jaina religion. Therefore, the old sacred texts were made contiguous part of 'Drishtiwāda'. It is thus, explicitly clear that significant matters, relating to highest truths of Jaina philosophy have been minutely discussed and elaborately explained in 'Drishtivāda'.

It has been cited in the commentary on 'Visheshavashyaka' (An Agamic Scripture) that though the entire canonical literature (sacred texts in a wider sense) or spiritual knowledge has been incorporated in 'Drishtivāda'. The simplified spiritual knowledge as contained in other scriptural treatises, has been derived from it for the convenience and benefit of ignorant and unwise males and females.

Study of 'Drishtivāda' Forbidden for Females

It is evident from the above discussion that the ladies were debarred from studying or having knowledge of 'Drishtivāda'. The citation, appearing in the commentary on Visheshāvashyaka' reads. "The women are worthless, wretched, highly arrogant and full of sensualism by nature. They are comparatively weak in intelligence and retentiveness of memory. Hence the ladies are restricted from studying or obtaining knowledge of Drishtivāda or most superior type of knowledge relating to spiritual resurgence and derived from meditation on the higher truths of religion etc."

The scholiast has pointed out certain inherent weaknesses or shortcomings of ladies. Their frivolous and arrogant nature, sensuality, ignorance and dullness of mind, are some of the disqualifications due to which they are debarred and not entitled to obtain knowledge of 'Drishtivāda'.

While explaining the religious verse No. 55 of the commentary on 'Visheshavashyaka', the Jaina saint, Achārya Hemchandra, writes: "In case, the ladies are allowed to acquire knowledge of 'Drishtivāda', they will develope a vain feeling of arrogance that inspite of having poor intelligibility, they are also conversant with the spiritual texts, as contained in 'Drishtivāda' and will start to humiliate and show disregard to the gents, because of their frivolous nature. Thus they will be forced into a miserable plight. Realizing this, highly compassionate and benevolent omniscients had prohibited imparting knowledge on higher truths of religion and philosophy, as contained in 'Drishtivāda to the ladies, keeping in view that it was bound to create vanity and false proud in them. However, in order to create spiritual awareness amongst ladies, the 11 Angas and other religious works had been accomplished.

The scholiasts Achārya Jinabhadra Gani "Kṣmāshramana' and Achārya Hemchandra have reflected upon the nature, behaviour and faculty of the entire womenfolk, which calls for impartial consideration and discussion for ascertainment of truth. Vanity, fickleness of mind, ignorance, audacity and impudence are the sole disqualifications of ladies only, does not appeal to the mind. However, the popular opinion is going on from ancient times to this effect. Absence of vanity and arrogance, uprightness and honesty in dealings, complete control over sensualism as also strength of intellect and wisdom are both hereditary and attainable through hard labour, perseverance and constant dedication too. How can it be believed that these qualities are inherent in and are essential characteristics of males only? Infact, the ladies have the ability to attain the state of omniscience and deliver spiritual lectures like Tirthankers. They have the capability to acquire the seat of a Tirthanker and attain the state of absolute perfection and highest spiritual accomplishments. How far then it is justified to ascribe such vilified allegations while characterizing the entire womenfolk and hold them unfit to gain knowledge on higher truths of religion and philosophy, as contained in Drishtivāda. It is a controversial or disputed point.

Females and Drishtivāda: Another Argument

There is another consideration of certain intellectuals in this regard. According to them, the old sacred texts relating to the knowledge, derived from meditation or highest, spiritual knowledge as contained in 'Drishtiwāda', is, infact, attainable by all. However , in order to have complete expertise, mere reading or studying the contents of 'Drishtwāda' is not sufficient. Performance of certain spiritual endeavours and observance of total devotion are also essential which call for living in absolute seclusion for some time. It is, however, not convenient for the ladies to live in seclusion and dedicate themselves to spiritual endeavours because of their physical limitations. Consequently the ladies are denied the right to obtain knowledge of the old sacred texts, contained in 'Drishtivāda'. This argument appeals to the mind and is worth consideration.

Accomplishment of Old Sacred Texts: Chronological Sequence

There is a different version in the commentary on 'Achāranga Sūtra' regarding accomplishment of old sacred texts which refutes the foregoing versions. It is cited therein that first of all 'Achāranga Sūtra' had been composed and, thereafter, the sacred treatises in the shape of 12 Angas and allied canonical literature had been accomplished. Whereas on one hand, majority of the scholars were of unanimous opinion that old sacred texts had been collected, compiled and composed prior to the accomplishment of 12 Angas, the narration in the commentary on Achāranga (first Anga) that' Achāranga' had been composed first, is bound to create confusion on the other hand. Since there is no effective means for refutation or rejection of the above statement, we leave the matter for further consideration and analytical investigation by the scholars and arriving at some logical conclusion.

While considering over all the opinions, it clearly transpires that the arrangement for studying old sacred texts was already in existence and they incorporated higher spiritual knowledge, derived from meditation on higher truths of religion and philosophy. This knowledge was virtually meant for erudite scholars and intellectuals who had philosophical pronings and a quest for realizing higher truths. The spiritual knowledge of Jainism and its philosophy was beyond the reach of children, ladies, old and infirm persons as also ignorant and weak-minded persons. Hence for those, who were not competent enough to pick up phenomenal spiritual knowledge, a book titled 'Dharma Sidhānta (religious doctrines) in Prākrita dialect was introduced.

Language of Old Pūrvas (Old Sacred Treatises)

It is not considered feasible to reduce in black and white the entire texts relating to old spiritual knowledge of Jaina religion because of its vastness and magnitude. It is metaphorically stated that there ought to be colossal quantity of ink powder, sufficient to conceal an elephant along with the seat over it. The said quantity of ink powder should be dissolved in water and the old sacred texts should be reduced to writing with that ink. Even then, it may not be possible to thread them in a language and reduce to writing. In other words, the old sacred texts are beyond the scope of expression. It needs strong determination and will to study them and acquire their knowledge. However, whatever be the magnitude of the old sacred texts, they were certainly reduced to writing. Now the only question arises, in which language the old texts of Jaina religion were reduced to black and white.

It is generally believed that the old sacred texts had been accomplished in Sanskrit language. However, certain other scholars hold a different opinion. They do not attach much significance to link them with any specific language. Since it was considered essential for every scholar to undertake study of the old sacred texts and impart their knowledge to others, they could be revealed in any Language with which the spiritual guide was well conversant. It is natural and quite possible. However, there had been a successive decline in the expertise of old sacred treatises, incorporating higher truths of Jaina religion and philosophy. Initially, there were scholars who had expertise in all 14 old sacred treatises which was subsequently reduced to ten old sacred treatises and gradually this expertise continued declining fast and finally, there was hardly any expert in these treatises. The knowledge of old sacred texts, aquired by scholars, must have been communicated or revealed to others by way of lectures and, accordingly, they must have taken recourse to one or other language. In case, they had discoursed in Sanskrit language, then the controversy may arise that Ardha Māgadhi Prākrita was a most primitive language of divine nature, belonging to great sages. Tirthankers always deliver their discourses in Ardha Māgadhi Prākrita which are, obviously, obtained in their own respective dialect by the pupils and students. The celetial bodies also speak in the said dilect. Just as the followers of Vedic school, treat Vedic sanskrit as the most sanctified language of the world, similarly, the followers of Jaina religion believe that Ardha Māgadhi Prākrita is most sacred and of divine nature.

The Prākrita dialects have been the medium of expression in India by common people from primitive days. Most probably, the Vedic Sanskrit was accomplished from any one of the said Prākritas. The era of classical sanskrit followed thereafter. In this view of the matter, how far it was justified to believe that the sacred treatises, containing old spiritual texts of Jaina philosophy, were accomplished in sanskrit language. Probably, it might have occured that the alround superiority of sanskrit language was re-established and Jaina scholars too were tempted to signify that their scriptures, containing sacred knowledge on higher, truths of religion too had been accomplished in sanskrit so that it might add to the significance of their religious scriptures considerably. However, nothing could be said in a decisive manner, yet it does not appeal to the mind that the old sacred treatises of Jaina religion had been decidedly reduced to writing in sanskrit.

The Canonical Literature, falling under the Category of Old Sacred Treatises of Jaina Religion: An Introduction

There is voluminous canonical literature, concerning Jaina religion under the category of Pūrvās. There are 14 Pūravās (sacred treatises, incorporating spiritual knowledge on higher truths of Jaina religion and philosophy), namely—

1. Utpāda Pūrvā :- In this scriptural work the topics relating to the production of elementary matter and sub-stratum of properties as also other allied subjects have been discussed at length. The number of verses, contained in this work, is one crore.

2. Agrāyaniya Pūrvā : This word is accomplished by combination of two words— 'Agra' and "Ayan'. The literal meaning of the word 'Agra' is a measure or size and that of 'Ayan' is—act of going, chapter or section or illustration. In other words the strength and power of all the elementary substances, properties, allied creations and all living organisms have been discussed in the said Pūrvā. The total number of verses (Each verse consisting of four lines), contained in it, are 96 lacs.

3. Viryapravāda Pūrvā : There is critical and minute discussion on strength and efficacy of active and inactive living organisms. This 'Pūrva' comprises of seventy lacs verses.

4. Asti-Nāsti Prāvada Pūrvā : As per Jaina philosophy, there are five categories of predicaments of elementary existence on this earth, namely—living organisms, atoms, religion, irreligion and ether (the subtle and ethereal fluid pervading the whole universe) and non-elementary substances which are not found on this earth, have been elaborately dealt with in this Pūrva. In other words, it has been discussed therein that all articles are known in this world because of their own specific shape or appearance and not as per respective form of other articles. The total number of verses, comprising this 'Pūrva' are sixty lacs.

5. Gyān-Pravāda Pūrva : There is detailed discussion of 5 types of knowledge or perception, obtainable with the help of senses and the mind. The total number of verses, contained in this Pūrva is one crore minus one.

6. Satya-Pravāda Pūrva : The signification or meaning of the word 'truth' also includes concentration of mind, self control and knowledge of truth. These aspects have been elaborately discussed in this Pūrva, which is comprised of one crore and six verses.

7. Ātmā-Pravāda Pūrva : Detailed philosophical and doctrinal discussion regarding the principle of life from different angles and life sensation on one hand and the soul on the other, having regard to the course of conduct or way of life has been made in this Purva which is comprised of 26 crore verses.

8. Karma-Pravāda Pūrva : The Nature and attitude of our actions, said to be of 8 types including those which restrict and shadow our spiritual knowledge or knowledge of our soul which enables us to know the significance of substratum of properties, substances or matter. Specific kinds of atoms are attracted by auspicious and insuspicious manifestations of our soul, resulting in our good or bad actions. The nature and attitude of our actions differ as per variations in conditions of the nature, locations, territories and regions which have been widely discussed in this Purva, which comprises of 1 crore and eighty-six thousand verses.

9. Pratyākhyāu Pūrva : Various types of renunciations, forsaking all worldly belongings and sacrifices have been elaborately discussed in this Pūrva, which is comprised of 84 lacs verses.

10. Vidyānu Prāvada Pūrva : The subjects relating to pursuit of superior and spectacular vidyas and employing suitable means for their accomplishment, have been elaborately discussed in this Pūrva which is comprised of 1 crore and 10 lacs verses.

11. Avandhya-Pūrvā : The literal meaning of the word 'vandhya'is fruitless Accordingly its antonym 'Avandhya' means fruitful. The subjects relating to virtuous and fruitful sacred knowledge, self-mortification, religious austerities, absolute devotion and concentration of mind as also inauspicious acts of negligence and inadvertence in performance of spiritual endeavours, have been discussed and critically examined in this Pūrva, which is comprised of 26 crore verses.

12. Prānāupravāda Pūrvā : The topics relating to the source of life –5 organs of sense; mind, heart and soul, the source of our vitality and strength; inhaling and exhaling of breath and the duration of life, have been minutely discussed in this Pūrva, which is comprised of one crore and fifty-six lacs verses.

13. Kriyā Pravāda Pūrva : The subjects relating to bodily performances, observances of religious obligations, devotion and total concentration of mind as also activities leading to purification of soul and attaining supreme bliss and happiness besides harms of unrestrained actions have been dealt with in this Pūrva, which is comprised of nine crore verses.

14. Lok Bindusār Pūrvā : The topics relating to attainment of sacred knowledge on the higher truths of religion and philosophy, which is most excellent and full of intelligence like a dot above the letter of an alphabet and which is both rational and makes a sense, have been elaborately discussed in this Pūrva which consists of twelve and half crore verses.

Chūlikās : (Crests or Summits)

These Chūlikās are, infact, supplementaries to the 'Pūrvas' (Old sacred treatises, incorporating highest spiritual knowledge of Jaina religion) they are collections of spoken and unspoken (manifest or hidden) explanations, contained in 'Parikarma', 'Sūtra', 'Pūrva-gata' and 'Anuyoga', the constituents of 12th Anga, 'Dishṭivāda'. The subjects, dealt-with in the said sections of Drishṭivāda' which either remained unexplained or called for further explanations, have been elaborately discussed in the said chūlikas. They are considered as most significant part of old sacred treatises of Jaina religion. These chūlikas are like peaks or summits of a mountain of highest spiritual knowledge.

Number of Chūlikas (Auxiliary works for further Explanation and Elucidation of the Texts of 'Pūrvas')

Under 'Pūrvagata', a classification of 14 old sacred treatises, there are chūlikas relating to initial four Pūrvas only. The question may, obviously, arise here that 'Pūrvagata'is one of the branch of 'Drishṭivāda' and the gist of higher spiritual knowledge, forming part of all the 14 Pūrvas, has been comprehended in 'Pūrvagata'. There are Chūlikas relating to four initial Pūrvas, namely-,'Utpāda', 'Agrāniya', 'Virya-Pravāda' and 'Asti-nāsti-Pravāda' only. Then how far will it be relevant to treat the said Chūlikas as collections or compilations of spoken and unspoken (manifest or hidden) explanations, relating to 'Parikarma', 'Sūtra', 'Pūrvagata' and 'Anuyoga', the four components of Drishṭivāda?

For proper arrangement of imparting a systematic order, the sum and substance of 14 Pūrvas, has been incorporated in 'Pūrvagata', one of the components of 'Drishṭivāda' Infact the entire old sacred knowledge of Jaina religion and philosophy as revealed by Tirthankers and omniscients, is contained in the said Pūrvas. Along with it, the sum and substance of other three components of 'Drishṭivāda', namely—'Parikarma', 'Sūtra' and 'Anuyoga', have also been reproduced in Pūrvagata.

The Chūlikas are related to initial four, 'Pūrvas' only. This implies that all the subjects, dealt with in Drishṭivāda, whether enunciated in detail, partly explained insufficiently argued or merely or else inelaboratety expounded, have been compiled in the said chūlikas.

It purports to mean that although all the topics, forming subject-matter of discussion in 'Drishṭivāda', have normally been touched upon in Chūlikās, yet the subjects, dealt with in 4 components of 'Drishṭivāda', namely, 'Parikrama', 'Sūtra', 'Pūrvagata' and 'Anuyoga', which had not been elaborately explained therein, have also been referred to and explained in the said Chūlikas. There are four Chūlikas of the first Pūrva, twelve relate to second Pūrva, eight pertain to the third Pūrva and ten belong to fourth Pūrva. In this way, there are in all 34 Chūlikas (4+12+8+10=34).

Vastus (Auxiliary literature, categorised as Vastus)

Along with the Chūlikas, there is another category of auxiliary literature called 'Vastu' (knowledge of essentials) which helps in further elucidation or augmentation of the abstruse or unintelligible texts of Pūrvas. They are actually meant for the benefit of persons, having limited intelligence, so as to be able to understand the higher truths of Jaina religion and philosophy. The literature which enables to apprehend the knowledge, relating to subtlety of soul, minute living organism, and true disposition of mind as also the elaboration of the real purport, is also designated as 'Vastu'. It is also admitted that there is incorporation of all view-points in the said category of literature.

Number of Vastus Relating to Each 'Pūrva'

There are 10 articles relating to first Pūrva, fourteen articles relating to second Pūrva, eight to third Pūrva, eighteen to fourth Pūrva, twelve to fifth Pūrva, two to sixth Pūrva, sixteen to seventh Pūrva, thirty to eighth Pūrva, twenty to ninth Pūrva, fifteen to tenth Pūrva, twelve to eleventh Pūrva, thirteen articles to twelfth Pūrva, thirty to thirteenth Pūrva and twenty-five to fourteenth Pūrva. In this way, there are in all 225 articles (Two Hundred and Twenty-five articles) 10 + 14 + 8 + 18 + 12 + 2 + 16 + 30 + 20 + 15 + 12 + 13 + 30 + 25 = 225.

There is no occasion for further elaboration of this auxiliary literature. Hence the description of Pūrvas (old sacred treatises containing knowledge on higher truths of Jaina religion and philosophy) has been given in concise form, as demanded by the context.

Revelation of Sacred Knowledge on Higher Truths of Jaina Religion and Philosophy : After Final Salvation of Ārya Jambu

Arya Prabhava : Prabhava came in contact with Ārya Jambu in the shape of an intractable, insolent and untamable robber. However, after listening to the sermons delivered by Ārya Jambu thereby laying emphasis on the significance of virtues—such as endurance, patience and forbearance and also witnessing for himself, the life of Ārya Jambu, full of devotion, dedication, self denial and self-control, Ārya Prabhava was now completely a changed man. He strongly made up his mind to follow the footsteps of Ārya Jambu and lead the rest of his life as an ascetic, full of self-curbs and restraints. The life of a robber or thief was entirely changed to the life of a religious mendicant. Because of his inquisitiveness and strong will-mixed with his lovely nature with good moral conduct and behaviour, his exercising control over self and observance of the path of righteousness in day today course of his life, he attained the state of highest perfection, so much so that after final salvation of Ārya Jambu, the entire responsibility of administering the affairs of the religious organisation of Lord Mahavirā and providing spiritual guidance to the mendicants in general and his pupils in particular, fell upon his able shoulders. Ārya Prabhava had the privilege to succeed to the highest seat of a spiritual leader after final liberation of Arya Jambu. Only a brief reference is found in 'Kalpa Sūtra' (An Agamic Scripture of Jainas) : "Ārya Prabhava, belonging to a

Kātyāyan family was resident disciple of Ārya Jambu of Kāshyapa lineage. The tradition of acquiring spiritual knowledge on higher truths of religion and philosophy, as revealed by Ārya Jambu, continued unabated through Ārya Prabhava, who had obtained perfection and expertise in 14 Pūrvas and was designated as 'Shruta Kevalin' (one having highest spiritual knowledge of Jaina religion and philosophy).

Period of Ārya Prabhava as Spiritual Leader and Preceptor

Ārya Prabhava was the supreme head of the institution as spiritual guide and preceptor for a period of eleven years after his succession to the seat of Ārya Jambu. As per belief of Shwetamber Sect, Ārya Prabhava had attained his final emancipation after 75 years from the final salvation of Lord Mahāvira. The same chronology is found in 'Himvata Therāvali'.[1]

As per reference appearing in relative scripture of Digamber Sect, the name of Vidyuchar (thief) is cited in place of Prabhava (thief). There is no mention of the name of Prabhava at all in the list of succession to the highest seat of spiritual leader and preceptor, following Ārya Jambu. According to the list of succession, identified by Digamber Sect, Vishnu or Nandi succeeded to the holy seat of Ārya Jambu. The period of spiritual leadership of Āchārya Vishnu was of 14 years. In *Tiloyapaṇṇatti* (an Agamic Scripture of Digamber Sect), the name of Nandi appears as successor of Ārya Jambu.

Ārya Shayyambhava

After final salvation of Ārya Jambu, Ārya Shayyambhava was the spiritual leader who carried along and enunciated the sacred knowledge on higher truths of Jaina religion and philosophy, as revealed by his preceptor and guide. He was an erudite and pre-eminent scholar of his age. He was well conversant with Vedic teachings and philosophy. He was an expert in performance of Vedic yajnas and rituals. A reference appears that Ārya Prabhava had an inner urge and accordingly, he directed his two Jaina Munis to contact the eminent scholar, Ārya Shayyambhava and preach doctrines of Jaina religion and philosophy to him, who was then busy in performance of Vedic yajnas. He was filled with spiritual enlightenment and felt

1. According to Muni Kalyānvijayji, Achārya Himvān was a renowned Sthavira (a senior Jaina monk, having completed 20 years as religious mendicant after attaining initiation). Undoubtedly the period of spiritual prominence and exaltation of Achārya Himvān was contemporaneous to that of famous *Anuyoga Pravartaka* (A promoter and propounder of Anuyogas), *Skanditāchārya* and *Nāgārjuna Vāchaka* (A reciter of sacred texts). Since in *Nandi Therāvali,* authored by Achārya Devardhigani, the name of Acharya Himvān appears after the name of Skanditacharya and prior to the name of Nāgārjuna and he has been quoted as disciple of Skanditachārya, which is very difficult to believe in a decisive manner whether *Himvata Therāvali* was authored by Achārya Himvāta or some other scholar. There are certain old citations in *Himvata Therāvali* (prior to the period of Tirthankers and Omniscients or prior to the accomplishment of old sacred texts of Jaina religion and philosophy) which stand corroborated by the ancient inscriptions too. On finding mention of such old 'Theravali' citations, one is led to believe that 'Himvata is probably an ancient treatise. However, there are a few citations which create uncertainty in the mind regarding authorship of Acharya Himvata. Thus, it remains still undecided who is the actual writer of Himvata Theravali and it is for the scholars to carry on further investigation in this regard.

greatly inspired. He came over to Ārya Prabhava and obtained initiation through him. He was already an ardent scholar and by virtue of his prudence, retentiveness of memory and spirit of a genius, he was able to derive knowledge through meditation on higher truths of Jaina philosophy. He made profound study and gained expertise in 14 old sacred treatises, incorporating texts of highest spiritual knowledge of Jaina religion. He came to be known as 'Shruta Kevalin' (Having attained perfection in highest spiriual knowledge of Jainism).

At the time, Ārya Shayyambhava had been initiated, his wife was pregnant. At the scheduled time, she gave birth to a son. He was named 'Manaka'. The son grew up and came to know that his father was an ascetic and a Jaina saint. He approached him and was greatly impressed by his devout life, dedicated to performance of spiritual endeavours and observance of control over self as also leading the life of self mortification. He obtained initiation by his father, who realized and perceived through his extra-ordinary vision that his son, Manaka was destined to live for a short period say for six months only. So that his son may be blessed with long life he composed *Dashavaikālika* (An important Agamic scripture of Jaina religion) by selecting substantial and significant portions from authoritative Scriptural works on higher truths of Jaina philosophy, so that his son may feel inspired to lead the life of a true devout and exercise control over self. He believed that his newly initiated son would he greatly benefited by undertaking critical study of the said sacred book and lead the life of self-denial and control for continuance of the possibility of living for a long time. It was really a marvellous contribution of Achārya Shayyambhava to the students of highest spiritual knowledge.

Composition of 'Dashavaikālika' on the basis of Highest Spiritual Knowledge, Contained in Pūrvas

It is believed that 'Dashavaikālika' had been composed on the basis of highest spiritual knowledge, contained in Pūrvas. For instance, the chapter, styled 'Dharma Pragyapti' of Dashavaikālika had been composed on the basis of the material, derived from 'Ātma Pravāda' Pūrva; the chapter, titled 'Pindaishnā' is based on the contents of 'Karma-Pravāda' and the chapter under the head 'Vākya Shudhi' had been composed on the basis of the contents of 'Satya Pravada' Pūrva and lastly the remaining portion of Dashavaikālika is based on third, Vastu' (The mere outline or skeleton of any subject to be developed afterwards) of Pratyakhyān Pūrva (Relating to the austerities to be observed for expressing regrets and showing repulsion against sinful acts or wrong doings.

Only this much is found mentioned in the list of 'Sthaviras' in succession to the seat of religious teachers and guides appearing in *Kalpa-Sutra* in relation to Ārya Shayyamabhava—"Ārya Shayyambhava was the resident pupil of Sthavira Ārya Prabhava, who belonged to a Katyāyan family while Ārya Shayyambhava belonged to the Vatsa Lineage and was father of 'Manaka'.

The Period of Spiritual Leadership of 'Ārya Shayyambhava'

Achārya Shayyambhava was the supreme head of Jaina organisation for a period of 23 years. In *Himvata Therāvali*, the year of his final emancipation has been cited to be 98, the samvat year after final salvation of Lord Mahāvira, which matches and appears to be correct. However, as believed by Digamber Sect, 'Nandi-Mitrā' had succeeded to the seat of Ārya Shayyambhava, and had provided spiritual leadership to the organisation for a period of 16 years.

Arya Yashobhadra

Ārya Yashobhadra was the resident pupil of Ārya Shayyambhava. In Kalpa Sūtra Sthirāvalli (List of successors to the seat of spiritual leader and guide), he has been introduced as 'Sthavira Ārya Yashobhadra' being resident pupil of Sthavira Shayyambhava who belonged to the lineage of 'Vatsa' and was father of Manaka. Ārya Yashobhadra belonged to the family lineage of 'Tungiyāyan. After final emancipation of Ārya Shayyambhava, the responsibility of revealing highest spiritual knowledge of Jaina religion and philosophy, as also administrating the affairs of Jaina organisation fell upon the able shoulders of Ārya Yashobhadra, who shouldered the said responsibility with efficacy and to the great satisfaction of all. He had gained expertise in 14 Pūrvas (Texts of old spiritual knowledge on higher truths of Jaina religion and philosophy).

Imparting Sacred Knowledge of Jaina Religion to the Kings of Nanda Dynasty

It is believed that Ārya Yashobhadra had imparted spiritual knowledge of Jaina religion to the kings of Nanda dynasty. Accordingly, they turned followers of Jaina religion.

It is cited in 'Himvata Therāvali' that during the period of spiritual leadership of Ārya Yashobhadra, eighth Nanda was the ruler of Magadha dynasty. He was greedy and avaricious. On the ill advice of his Brahmana Minister, Virochan, he attacked the kingdom of Kalinga region (Orissa) and destroyed it altogether. Not merely this, he had also ruined the temple of Lord Rishabha and reduced it to dust, which had been got built up by Magadha emperor, Shrenika, at Kumar Hill and had forcibly brought the golden idol of Lord Rishabba to Magadha along with him[1].

1. In this regard certain points need minute consideration. In case, the rulers of Nanda dynasty were followers of the doctrines of Jaina religion, how they could have dared to wage war with a Jaina king of Kalinga region and totally destroy the temple of Lord Rishabha. As also, why the golden idol of Lord Rishabha was removed from Kumar Hill and brought to Magadha?

   There are diverse opinions of Scholars in this respect. Certain scholars believe that in case the ruler of Nanda dynasty had no faith in the tenets of Jaina religion, he could have easily destroyed the idol of Lord Rishabha instead of bringing the idol of Lord Rishabha to Magadha along with him. According to royal practice and attitude of that period, attacking a ruler, having faith in the same religion, is one thing and propitiating or offending a deity was an altogether different matter. According to the belief of Jaina community, King of Magadha, named Koṇika and subsequently known as Ajāt Shatru, was, decidedly, a follower of Jainism and Chetaka, President of Lichchhavi Republic, was also a Jaina. However, the fact remains, that a fierce battle took place between them and an ideal Republic of those days, called Lichchhvi Republic, unfortunately, had a miserable end and was annihilated for ever.

Period of Spiritual Leadership

Ārya Yashobhadra was the supreme leader of the organisation for a continuous period of 50 years. It is cited in 'Himvata Therāvali' that he had attained his final liberation in the 148th year after final liberation of Lord Mahavirā. His spiritual leadership for 50 years, stands corroborated by the said citation. However, as per Digamber Sect, the third spiritual head after final salvation of Ārya Jambu *i.e.* successor to the seat of Nandi Mitra, was Aparājitā. His period of spiritual leadership is believed to be of 22 years.

Succession to the Seat of Arya Yashobhadra

As described in 'Kalpa Sūtra', after the name of Ārya Yashobhadra in the list of successors, we find that the mode of description is changed and the subsequent citation regarding succession is, sometimes brief and sometimes detailed. It is cited—"The order of succession after Arya Yashobhadra reads — Ārya Yashobbadra who belonged to a family of 'Tungiyāyan lineage', had two resident disciples-Arya Sambhaūtavijaya, belonging to 'Māder' lineage and the other 'Ārya Bhadrabāhu', representing the family of Prāchin lineage. The highest spiritual knowledge of Jaina religion and philosophy, hitherto carried out faithfully to the end by Ārya Yashobhadra, was continued to be revealed by Ārya Sambhuntivijaya and Arya Bhadrabāhu along with administrating the affairs of Jaina organisation.

Two Successors Simultaneously : A New Arrangement

By the time of Ārya Yashobhadra, only one name was nominated to act as supreme leader of the Jaina organisation and as preceptor or spiritual guide. Hitherto the Jaina organisation functioned under the leadership of a single sanctified teacher or saint. After salvation of Ārya Yashobhadara, a new arrangement came into existence. Most probably, Ārya Yashobhadra might have found the aforesaid two dosciples equally fit and capable amongst all other pupils and he might have been confronted with the problem to decide only a single name because of extra-ordinary talents and similar state of worthiness of both of them. When he found it difficult to choose and nominate only one name as his successor, he preferred to declare both, of them-Sambhūtivijaya and Bhadrabāhu as his co-successors. This gave birth to a new tradition. However, it had no adverse effect, whatsoever. Even after appointing two heads of the institution simultaneously, the day-to-day functioning of the organisation and administration of its affairs was not vitiated or rendered ineffectual in any way, since the successorship of both the spiritual leaders was not absolute or unconditional in any way. The senior or the elder leader had an obvious control over the administration of the organisation without the least interference by the junior colleague. After final salvation of the elder colleague, all his rights and titles stood transferred to the junior colleague and he exerccised all those rights for the smooth running of the institution.

The only difference being that earlier only one successor used to be nominated and the right to nominate the next successor remained vested in him. However, as per new convention, immediately after the final liberation of the senior successor, the responsibility for providing spiritual leadership and guidance, automatically fell upon the junior colleague, since he had already been nominated. The new tradition of nominating two spiritual heads simultanaeously had no ill-effect on the day-to-day functioning and administration of the institution. However, it was only an exclusive case of its kind. Virtually, the tradition of appointing or nominating only one successor at a time continued thereafter.

Ārya Sambhūtivijaya

Ārya Sambhūtivijaya was a senior and elder preceptor. Obviously, he was the supreme leader of the organisation and spiritual guide after the final emancipation of Ārya Yashobhadra. Ārya Sambhūtivijaya was expert and fully conversant with highest spiritual knowledge of Jain religion and philosophy as contained in 14 Pūrvas. The period of his spiritual leadership is believed to have continued for 8 years. As cited in Himvata Therāvali, he had attained his final liberation in 156th year after the salvation of Lord Mahāvira. Under the sacred tradition of Digamber Sect, Achārya Goverdhan had succeeded to the seat of Aparājita, the fourth spiritual leader and head of the organisation after final emancipation of Ārya Jambu. The period of spiritual leadership of Achārya Goverdhan had continued for 19 years.

Achārya Bhadrabāhu, Really a Great Dynamic Personality

It is traditionally believed that Achārya Bhadrabāhu was born in a Brahmaṇa family in Southern India in a village, known as Pratishthanpur (Pedhan). He had studied and gained expertise in several Vidyas (disciplines), in consistency with the reputation of his family. He had acquired thorough knowledge of the subjects. It is stated that his financial position was extremely tight. He might have developed interest in the sacred knowledge on the higher truths of Jaina religion and philosophy and accordingly he might have obtained initiation as an ascetic or religious mendicant.

Relation with Vārāhmihir : It is a hearsay that Varāhmihir was a celebrated astronomer and younger brother of Acharya Bhadrabāhu. However, on the basis of information, available, Vārāhmihir is believed to have lived in the sixth century of Vikram era (Hindu calendar). He had died in 587 A.D. On the other hand, Achārya Bhadrabāhu lived in much earlier period, prior to the commencement of Vikram era. Thus, the presumpton of a close relation between Bhadrabāhu and Vārāhmihir is virtually incorrect and incoherent.

Author of Chheda Sutras : There are six Chheda Sutras (works containing aphoristic rules, prescribing religious acts for atonement of sins), forming part of Jaina canonical literature, namely—(1) Nishitha, (2) Mahānishitha, (3) Vyavahār, (4) Dashāshrut-Skandh, (5) Vrahat Kalpa, and (6) Panch-Kalpa (Also known as Jit Kalpa). The complete historic account of India is obtained in a systematic and regular order, described in 'Dashāshrutaskandh'. The scholars are not unanimous and have diverse opinions whether Chandragupta Maurya was follower of Jaina religion or he reposed faith in Vedic philosophy.

'Parishishta Parva' (Authored by Achārya Hemchandra)

It is cited in 'Parishishta Parva' that Chānakya, Prime-Minister of emperor

Chandraguta was follower of Jaina religion. He was keen to persuade Chandragupta to adopt Jaina religion. Once he welcomed and honoured the saint scholars, assembled in two gatherings, who had faith in the tenets of various philosophies or who belonged to various schools of religion and philosophy. In one such meeting, Jaina saints or scholars were also invited. Emperor Chandragupta was greatly impressed by the doctrines of Jaina philosophy and he had adopted Jaina religion also. Almost in the canonical literature of both Shwetamber and Digamber sects, sixteen dreams, visualized by emperor Chandragupta, are well-known and there was a reflection of the possible degeneration in the alround spheres of religion, culture and civilization.

As cited by 'Magasthariza', an ambassador of Greece, in the Royal court of emperor Chandragupta, that the emperor had reposed faith in the doctrines of Jaina religion as against Vedic religion, propounded by Brahmana Scholars. According to renowned scholar, Thomas, not merely emperor Chandragupta but his son, Bindusār and grand-son, Ashōkā were also followers of Jaina religion. Mr. Thomas had tried to substantiate his view by quoting from 'Mudra-Rākshasha (Name of a dramatic play by Vishākhadutta), 'Rāj Tarangini' (Name of a celebrated historical poetry, treating of the kings of Kāshmira by author Kalhaṇa) and Ain-e-Akbari. However, it is apparent from a perusal of Buddhist literature that Bindusār, son of emperor Chandragupta, had faith in Vedic religion.

It may be possible that Ashōkā may have initially been follower of Jaina religion and subsequently, he may have changed his faith. It is cited in 'Himvata Therāvali' that Ashōkā had adopted Bodh religion after 4 years of his coronation. In his royal proclamations, appearing in his inscriptions, he has directed to give alms to the Jaina mendicants as well. It, therefore, follows that even after adopting Bodh religion, the emperor continued to have due respect and reverence for Jaina saints. It is thus possible that emperor Ashōkā may have been initially a follower of Jaina religion. Dr. Leuman, Hornley, Smith, Rāyas Davids, and Jaiswāl, all eminent historians, expressed the view that emperor Chandragupta Maurya was follower of Jaina religion. They also opine that the emperor was the disciple of Achārya Bhadrabāhu.

Association of Chandragupta with Achārya Bhadrabāhu

No strong evidence is available to substantiate the relationship of an Achārya (Religious preceptor) and pupilage between Achārya Bhadrabāhu and emperor Chandragupta. The issue calls for further investigation and research. Renowned historian, Muni Kalyān Vijay also subscribes to this view. According to him, no substantial proof is yet available to establish this view. He further adds that a terrible famine had taken place during the reign of emperor Chandragupta. At that time, there was an old Acharya, named Sutthim or Susthita at Pātliputra. Old citations of this nature are of-course, there, yet no writing or a work, written prior to 10th century, are available to corroborate the above fact. As stated in 'Himvata Therāvali', Achārya Bhadrabāhu had attained his liberation in 170th year and Chandragupta had expired in 184th year, after final salvation of Lord Mahāvirā. Thus, there was a difference of only 14 years in resigning the bodies by Achārya Bhadrabāhu and emperor Chandragupta which was enough to establish that they were contemporary to each other. Inspite of the said sporadic illustrations this matter has received continuous attention of Jaina scholars. However, it needs further contemplation, profound discussion and determination as also consideration of all relative material to arrive at a definite conclusion.

First Recitation of Agamic Texts

It is apparent from various sources that a terrible famine had taken palace, lasting for 12 years, during the reign of emperor Chandragupta Maurya, so much so that people began to pray God to save them from the horrors of famine and there was a sort of disastrous chaos when people were repeatedly praying for deliverance and mercy. Obviously, the mendicants depending on alms, were unable to procure food for their living. It is mentioned in 'Sthiravalli', "The femine was dreadful and terrible like the night of destruction, leading to the end of the world. The group of mendicants shifted to the sea-coast so as to be able to support themselves. The spiritual knowledge, which had been obtained by Jaina scholars by hearing to the utterances of omniscients, was forgotten for want of repitition or repeated recital of the sacred texts. Even the rememberance of highly learned scholars and sages, having extra-ordinary memory, fades or withers for want of regular exercise and repetition. Ultimately, the hard time of famine and scarcity came to an end. The entire association of Jaina saints assembled at Pātliputra (Patna). The 'Angas' (12 Angas, forming part of Agamic scriptures), 'Adhyayans' (auxiliary sacred texts), 'Uddeshakas' (Illustrations), remembered by the Jaina scholars were collected and compiled. However, the 12th Anga, 'Drishtivāda' could not be compiled for want of rememberance of the texts, pertaining to highest spiritual knowledge of Jaina religion and philosophy. Obviously, the Jaina Scholars and sages felt perturbed Achārya Bhadrabāhu was well conversant with the sacred texts on higher truths of Jaina religion, contained in the said 14 'Pūrvas'. He was somewhere on the route to Nepal. The organisation deputed two Munis (Jaina saints) to contact him and persuade him to return". A similar narration is found in *Prākrita Updesha Pada*. It is accordingly stated in *Avashyaka Churni*, (authored by Sri Jiṇadās Gaṇi).

An Assumption that Jaina Monks had moved to Southern India

It has been noted above that the groups of Jaina mendicants had migrated to 'Nirnidhi' or sea coast. This leads us to conclude that the Jaina monks had either shifted to a sea-coast in South or a certain territory in Southern India. However, why it should be taken for granted that it was the sea coast in south. It could be Bay of Bengal also, on the coast of which a long belt of Orissa, joins where the doctrines of Jaina religion had already been propagated and there was a large following of Arhat religion.

Recitation of the Sacred Texts of Pūrvas by Achārya Bhadrabāhu

The message of Jaina organisation had already been communicated to Achārya Bhadrabāhu. He was, however, completely absorbed in undertaking spiritual performances by way of profound meditation and abstract contemplation for accomplishment of tremendous vitality and strength of soul. It was not physically possible for him to move to Pātliputra, since it was bound to obstruct his spiritual attainments. He, therefore, communicated his consent to recite the sacred texts and preach highest spiritual knowledge, contained in the 14 Pūrvas, to the Jaina mendicants who would be arriving at his place for the purpose. It is cited that accordingly 1500 students were sent by the institution to Nepal. Out of them 500 were religious mendicants and two attendants were meant to look after the requirements of each initiated mendicant for making suitable arrangements for its food and attending to other essential duties. Thus there were 1,000 attendants.

Achārya Bhadrabāhu started to recite the old sacred texts of Pūrvas. However, he found it extremly difficult later on to carry on the recitation of holy texts because of the obscure and complicated nature of the sacred texts, containing highest spiritual knowledge and truths of Jaina religion and philosophy more especially forming part of 'Drishṭivāda', for want of adequate prudence and capability to pick up the essence and retain it in memory. Soon the students and scholarly mendicants began to feel bored and highly frustrated. Ultimately, they turned completely nervous and yielded. They could not muster further courage to carry on their studies. Besides Sthūlbhadra, no other mendicant could keep pace or stand its ground. Sthūlbhadra kept his studies continued without losing heart and giving up the initiative. The knowledge of the sacred texts of 10 Pūrvas both in the nature of aphorisms and explanations of the meanings thereof had been obtained by him. While the systematic study of the holy texts was going on smoothly, it so happened that his initiated sisters, who were female mendicants, arrived there to watch how their brother was absorbed in acquiring highest spiritual knowledge of Jaina philosophy, as revealed by Acharya Bhadrabāhu, the great religious preceptor and spiritual guide. Sthūlbhadra came to know of it beforehand through his insight and in order to maker his sisters wonder-struck, he assumed the shape of a lion by his magical skill and spiritual accomplishments. The sisters, obviously, grew frightened and stood highly amazed. Sthūlbhadra, immediately, returned to his original form. The sisters were greatly surprised and struck dumb.

Achārya Bhadrabāhu easily looked through the reality. He was not at all in favour of performing superfluous miracles by misusing spiritual achievements. Obviously, he was very much annoyed. He stopped recitation of the texts and impart spiritual knowledge to Sthūlbhadra. Sthūlbhadra expressed regrets and greatly entreated his precptor to forgive him. Thereupon, Achārya Bhadrabāhu started again to impart knowledge of remaining four Pūrvas to Sthūlbhadra but in the shape of aphorisms only and did not elaborate their meanings. Thus, Sthūlbhadra was able to obtain knowledge of 14 Pūrvas in the shape of aphorisms and 10 Pūrvas with explanations of the meanings thereof. Thus, he is said to have acquired knowledge of the texts of 14 Pūrvas and retained them in memory in aphosistic style and 10 Pūrvas with due explanations and elaborations. In this way, after final liberation of Achārya Bhadrabāhu, there was none to explain and elaborate the meanings thereof and resultantly, the study and teaching of 4 Pūrvas stopped thereafter.

The President or Director, Under whose Guidance, the First Recitation Took Place

The compilation of 11 Angas had been completed at Pātliputra. It is known as first recital. It is not explicitly clear who had presided or directed the proceedings thereof. Achārya Bhadrabāhu was in Nepal, absorbed in yogic or meditative contemplation for higher spiritual accomplishments. Hence his supervision and guidance was out of question. Being next to Bhadrabāhu, the leadership of Sthūlbhadra was accepted because of his superiority and excellence from all view-points. It is also possible that before departing for Nepal Achārya Bhadrabāhu might have himself entrusted the leadership of the institution to Sthūlbhadra.

The maximum possibility appears that the first recitation of Agamic literature and sacred texts had taken place under able guidance of Sthūlbhadra.

Achārya Bhadrabāhu : Beliefs of Digamber Sect

It is traditionally believed by Digamber sect that during the long dreadful period when the horrifying famine had taken place in the entire Magadha region, Āchārya Bhadrabāhu had moved to south along with the groups of Jaina mendicants. Emperor Chandragupta is also believed to have accompanied him, as a Jaina monk. Bhadrabāhu attained his final emancipation at Chandragiri hill near Shravanbelgola in Karnataka State.

It is cited in a petrographic inscription fixed in the monastery of Lord Pārasnāth (The sanctified teacher and guide of Jaina religion) near Shravanbelgola in Karnataka State that in accordance with the advice and direction of Achārya Bhadrabāhu, the organisation of religious mendicants had moved from Northern India to South India, from the said inscription, it is, however, not clear whether Āchārya Bhadrabāhu had also moved to the southern territory along with them. The said inscription dates back to the year 522 of 'Shaka era' (The calendar year, started by king Salivāhana, which commenced 78 years after Christian era).

Vrahatkathā Kosha :This sacred treatise is authored by Āchārya Harishena and was composed and written in the year 853 of Shaka era. The said book reads: Āchārya Bhadrabāhu once happened to reach Ujjaini (The modern Ujjain city in Malwa region of Madhya Pradesh. It is one of the seven sacred cities of Hindus in India), while propagating the doctrines and message of Jaina religion in his tour. He stayed in a garden, located near Siprā river. He entered the city to beg alms. He watched in a house that a young child was having a swing in a cradle—The child cried out-get away. Accordingly, he inferred that a dreadful famine for 12 years was going to occur. He convened a meeting of the association and narrated the incident before the Jaina mendicants. He advised them to move to the south at the earliest possible. He told them that he would stay behind since he was quite an aged man, unable to undertake a long journey.

Visit of Vishākhāchārya to South

There is another significant citation in the said *Vrahat Kathākosha* that emperor Chandragupta had been initiated as Jaina mendicant by Āchārya Bhadrabāhu. He came to be known as Vishākāchārya after attaining initation. As per advice of his sanctified teacher, he moved and arrived in the territory of Pannāta region in south. It is also cited that other heads, namely Rāmilla, Sthulvridha and Bhadrachārya were instructed to proceed to the Sindh region as well as other neighbouring territories. It is also cited in 'Vrahat Kathākosha that Achārya Bhadrabāhu had attained final salvation by undertaking trance meditation and absolute concentration of mind, free from all illusions and by observing prescribed religious austerities at Bhādrapada of Ujjaini region..

Biography of Achārya Bhadrabāhu

In 'Bhadrabāhu Charitra' (a biography of Achārya Bhadrabāhu, accomplished in 16th century of Vikrama era) by Achārya Ratnanandi, there is a similar narration as given in *Vrahat Kathākosha*, which reads "Achārya Bhadrabāhu entered a house begging alms. He found a young infant of 60 days, swinging in a cradle in the said lonely house. He cried out at the right of Jaina monk—go away, go away."

Āchārya Bhadrabāhu asked instantly for how long? The child retorted-for twelve years.

On the basis of the said incident, Achārya Bhadrabāhu apprehended that a terrible famine was bound to take place, lasting for continuously 12 years. He set out to South accompanied by 12000 Jaina mendicants. On specific request of his disciples, he left behind Rāmalya, Sthūlābhadra and Sthulācharya at Ujjain. In the aforesaid biography, it is also stated that the king of Ujjain had been initiated as a Jaina Muni by Āchārya Bhadrabāhu. However, his name is written 'Chandragupti' in place of Chandragupta.

A Voice from Heaven (An Incorporeal Speech)

Āchārya Bhadrabāhu was advancing rapidly towards south. He happened to hear a voice from heaven while crossing a wood. He realised that his time of death was near and his remaining life was too short. He directed Vishākhāchārya to Superintend the affairs of the organisation as his successor, fully knowing and realising that Vishākhāchārya was sobre and sagacious and was well conversant with the texts, contained in 10 Purvas. The newly initiated and most sincere disciple, having intense regard towards his guru, stayed behind to attend him. After some time, Achārya Bhadrabāhu attained final salvation by undertaking trance meditation, free from all illusions and by observing prescribed austerities at that very place.

While moving ahead towards South, Vishākhāchārya reached Chol region, propounding the doctrines of Jaina religion and kindling the hearts of his followers and newly initiated disciples with higher spiritual knowledge and truths of Jaina philosophy, who had accompanied him to save themselves from the ferocity of dreadful famine. The hard time of 12 years famine was passed by undertaking tours in south from one place to another, making temporary sojourns and propagating the message of Jaina religion.Thereafter, the groups of religious mendicants returned to Ujjain under leadership and guidance of Vishākhāchārya. The Jaina monks, who had remained behind and not accompanied to South, were found to have turned slack and sluggish Vishākhāchārya sincerely tried to persuade them to give up the laxity in their temperament and lethargic habits which had been strongly forbidden by the Shāstras but all in vain. However, the easy-going Munis paid no heed and did not mend their life style. When Sthūlachārya also tried to persuade them, they got infuriated and after repeatedly striking him with a stick, pushed him down in a ditch.

Rājāvali, A Work in Kannada Language

There is a production, styled *Rājāvali*, written in Kannada language which incorparates the narrative relating to Achārya Bhadrabāhu and Chandragupta. Rājāvali was accomplished in the year 1751 of shaka era. It was authored by Devachandra. The style of narration is like that of biography of Achārya Bhadrabāhu. However, there are certain fresh incorporations also. For example, the biographer of Bhadrabāhu, had mentioned about visualization of 16 dreams by Chandragupta (Chandragupti), ruler of Ujjaini, while the author of *Rājāvali* writes that the said 16 dreams had been visualized by emperor Chandragupta of Pātliputra.

What has been described above by quoting from various canonical books of Jaina scholars, it is not invariably proved that Achārya Bhadrabāhu, an erudite scholar and a great exponent of jaina philosophical doctrines had really moved to south, stayed there and ultimately had attained final salvation. While the author of *Vrahat Kathākosha* writes that Achārya Bhadrabāhu had attained his final emancipation in the territory of Ujjaini, the biographer of Achārya Bhadrabāhu states that Bhadrabāhu had attained his final salvation by undertaking trance meditation, absolute concentration of mind, free from all illusions and by observing prescribed severe austerities in a wood on the way to South. Similarly, the author of *Vrahāt Kathakosha*, writes that 'Ramilla, Sthūlbhadra and Bhadrāchārya had been directed to proceed to Sindhu region (A territory around Indus river). On the other hand, the biographer of Bhadrabāhu states that they had statyed behind in Ujjain. Not merely this, he has even changed the name of Sthūlvradha to Sthūla-Bhadra and that of Bhadrachārya to Sthūlachārya. It is, no doubt, an important point to be clarified why the biographer of Bhadrabāhu had altered these names when all his preceding writers, had been citing their names as Sthūlvradha and Bhadrachārya.

Another significant point, to be minutely considered is whether Chandragupta, referred to, belonged to Pātliputra or Ujjaini. The mental inclination of scholars, belonging to Digamber Sect, is in favour of assuming that Chandragupta was the ruler of Ujjaini. The author of Kannada work, *Rājāvali*, Sri Devachandra, alone has written that the visionary of 16 dreams, Chandragupta, was the king of Pātliputra.

Although, the message of Jaina religion had already spread far and wide in India, yet it is a historic reality that the main influence of Jaina religion was confined to Magadha and its neighbouring areas. This also leads us to believe that most probably, Achārya Bhadrabāhu too had spent major portion of his life in touring Magadha and adjoining areas and also making frequent sojourns in that region. On this basis, it appears to be more reliable and consistent that emperor Chandragupta, who had come in close contact with Achārya Bhadrabāhu, belonged to and lived at Pātliputra. The trend of Indian and Western scholars too is found generally conforming with this view.

All the scholars and writers, belonging to Shwetamber Sect, are unanimous that Achārya Bhadrabāhu had gone to Nepal for undertaking yogic exercises by way of complete absorption of mind in profound meditation and spiritual endeavours to acquire vitality of soul and possession of great strength with perseverance or steady continuance in devotion. Departure from Pātliputra (Patna) to Nepal not only easy and convenient but also appears to be rational and convincing. Nepal is not very remote from Pātliputra.

It is also feasible that Avanti region (a territory, north of Narmada river; its capital was Ujjain, situated on the Siprā river and western portion of modern Malawā), may have been a constituent of Magadha dynasty. It might be a central place on the West of Magadha dynesty or a State Capital or else Ujjain might be a sub-capital of Magadha empire. It is also possible that emperor Chandragupta, ruler of Magadha dynasty, might have decided to live at Ujjaini in the later period of his life and had come in contact with Achārya Bhadrabāhu and the series of events that took place, might relate to that period.

However, after considering all aspects, it appears that Pātliputra was the main capital of Magadha dynasty, during the reign of emperor Ashōkā, who had appointed his son, Kunāl to live at Ujjaini as state governor of the western territory, forming part of his great empire. It is also mentioned in 'Himvata Therāvali' that Sampriti, the grand son of emperor Ashoka, had moved to Ujjaini in 246th year, after final salvation of Lord Mahāvira. However, Chandragupta had also lived at Ujjaini, is not supported by any definite or tangible proof. Hence the assumption appears to be wrong and unfounded.

As a matter of fact, the version that Chandragupta Maurya was the ruler of Magadha dynasty and lived at Pātliputra appears to be more convincing and relevant. However, it should not be treated as a final verdict. It needs further examination and critical investigation. The topic is closed here with this comment. Achārya Bhadrabāhu may have undertaken a tour to south but, probably, he might have been another Bhadrabāhu. The question of making a trip to south by emperor Chandragupta with Achārya Bhadrabahu No. 1, does not arise.

Spiritual Leadership and Superintendence of Jaina Organisation

The fifth successor to the holy seat of Ārya Jambu and leader of the Jaina organisation, founded by Lord Mahavirā, was Achārya Bhadrabāhu. Both Digamber and Shwetamber Sects are unanimous on this point. In the list of successive holders of the supreme seat, Achārya Bhadrabāhu was the fifth successor to the seat of Ārya Jambu, is agreed upon by both Digamber and Shwetamber Sects. Nevertheless, both sects differ for how long Acharya Bhadrabāhu provided leadership to the organisation. According to Shwetamber Sect, Āchārya Bhadrabāhu, led the organisation for 14 years only. On the other hand, Digamber Sect believes that he continued superintending the affairs of the Jaina organisation for 29 years. As per Shwetamber Sect, the total period, ranging from the final salvation of Ārya Jambu to the final emancipation of Achaya Bhadrabāhu amounts to—(Prabhava-11 years

+ Shayyambhava-23 years + Yashobhadra-50 years + Sambhutivijaya-8 years + Āchārya Bhadrabāhu-14 years =106 years). The total period from final salvation of Lord Mahāvira to the final liberation of Achārya Bhadrabāhu is admittedly 64 years. Thus the total period from final salvation of Lord Mahavirā to the final salvation of Āchārya Bhadrabāhu is reckoned at 170 years (64+106=170).

As per Digamber Sect, the total period from final salvation of Ārya Jambu to the final liberation of Achārya Bhadrabāhu, ranges—Vishnu or Nandi-14 years + Nandi Mitra-16 years + Aparajita-22 years + Goverdhan-19 years + Bhadrabāhu-29 years = 100 years. All the said five religious teachers had attained the state of omniscience and absolute perfection in highest spiritual knowledge of Jaina religion and philosophy, known as 'Shruta Kevalins'. The Digamber Sect is of the view that thereafter no other religious leader had attained the state of omniscience or perfection in sacred texts of Agamas. The total period from the final salvation of Lord Mahāvira to the final emancipation of Arya Jambu is admittedly 62 years. Thus the total period from final salvation of Lord Mahavirā to final liberation of Achārya Bhadrabāhu amounts to 62+100=162 years.

Final Emancipation of Achāraya Bhadrabāhu

The scholars of Digamber tradition have also expressed their views regarding final salvation of Āchārya Bhadrabāhu. However, what has been laid down conventionally by the scholars of Shwetamber Sect, in regard to the final salvation of Achārya Bhadrabāhu is different. The citation in 'Himvata Therawali', appearing in this context, reads. The last authority on 14 Purvas (old sacred treatises of Jaina relgion, the gist of which is incorporated in 12th Anga, 'Drishṭivāda) and 'Shruta Kevalin' (Proficient in highest spiritual knowledge and devoted to the philosophical doctrines of Jaina religion). Āchārya Bhadrabāhu had nominated Sthulbhadra to succeed him, who was the son of famous Prime Minister, Shakṭāl. Thus, after about 170 years from the final salvation of Lord Mahavirā, Āchārya Bhadrabāhu had observed fast unto death, after giving up food completely. He attained final emancipation at Kumar hill in Kalinga region (Orissa) after observing fast for 15 days in the state of total concentration and absorption in abstract contemplation and religious meditation.

Achāraya Sthūlbhadra

It is cited that the first Nanda ruler of Magadha dynasty, had his Prime Minister, Kalpaka, who was Brahman by caste. He was staunch follower of Jainism, Shakṭāl, the celebrated Prime Minister of the ninth Nanda was the descendant of 'Kalpaka'. It appears in *Avashyaka Chūrṇi* (authored by Achārya Jiṇadas Gaṇi) and 'Parishishta Parva' (written by Acharya Hemchandra) that Prime Minister, Shakṭāl had strong faith in the doctrines of Jaina religion. It was why, he had fallen prey to the malice and dislike of Brahmana Community. Sthulbhadra was the son of Prime Minister, Shakṭāl and had seven sisters. Sthulbhadra had attained initiation along with all his sisters.

As per detailed narration, appearing in Kalpa Sūtra Sthiravalli' (A list of successors to the supreme seat as head of Jaina institution) Sthulbhadra had attained by Ārya Sambhutivijaya. It is cited therein Arya Sambhutivijaya, belonging to Madher Community had 12 resident disciples like his own offsprings—1. Nandanbhadra, 2. Upnandan Bhadra, 3. Tishyabhadra, 4. Yashobhadra, 5 Suman Bhadra (Swapanbhadra), 6. Maṇibhadra, 7. Punyabhadra (Purnabhadra), 8. Sthūlbhadra, 9. Rijumati, 10. Jambu. 11. Dirghabhadra, and 12. Pāṇḍubhadra. The name of Sthulbhadra appears against Sl. No. 8. Sthūlbhadra's sisters too had obtained initiation by Arya Sambhutivijya. It is cited in detailed list of successors, contained in 'Kalpa Sūtra', Ārya Sambhutivijya, belonging to Madhar Community, had seven resident female disciples like his own offsprings, namely—1. Yaksa, 2. Yaksaduttā, 3. Bhūtā, 4. Bhūtdattā, 5. Senā, 6. Veṇā , and 7. Reṇā.

After final emancipation of Ārya Jambu, the third successive spiritual head of the organisation, Ārya Yashobhadra had nominated two names to succeed him. After final liberation of Ārya Yashobhadra, Ārya Sambhutivijaya had succeeded him because of his elderliness and being a senior disciple and he was followed by his junior colleague, Āchārya Bhadrabāhu. Sthulbhadra and his seven sisters had attained initiation by Ārya Sambhutivijaya, while he was spiritual head and superintending the affairs.

Final Salvation : As stated in "Dushmakāl Shrishramaṇasanghstotra", written by Achārya Dharamghosh Sūri (Dushamakāl is a long period of downfall with the Jainas. The fifth division of this long period is called 'Dusham', when the morality is at its bottom and there is too much distress). Achārya Sthulbhadra had administered the affairs of Jaina organisation as spiritual leader and guide for 45 years. He attained his final liberation in 215th year after final salvation of Lord Mahāvira.

Time of Discontinuance of the Study of Last Four Pūrvas

As per Shwetamber Sect, the study of last four Pūrvas had ceased after final liberation of Acharya Sthulbhadra, since they had been taught to him by Achārya Bhadrabāhu by recitation of aphorisms only and the elaboration of their meanings or explanations of the precepts had been denied to him as a result of incurring displeasure of his said preceptor. Thereafter, the tradition of teaching sacred texts of 10 Pūrvas only had continued till the spiritual leadership, of Ārya Vajra. According to 'Nandi Sthiravalli, Ārya Vajra was the 18th successor to the holy seat of Lord Mahāvira. He is believed to have attained his final liberation in the 584th year after final salvation of Lord Mahāvira. After final liberation of Ārya Vajra, the study and teaching of 10th Pūrva also came to an end.

The names of the spiritual leaders and successors to the supreme seat of Jaina institution, alongwith the respective period of spiritual leadership of each successor, right from Achārya Sthūlbhadra to Achārya Vajra, who were experts in imparting knowledge of 10 Pūrvas with explanations of the precepts, contained therein, are produced below :-

Name	*Period*
Achārya Sthūlbhadra	45 years
Achārya Mahāgiri	30 years

Achārya Suhasti	46 years
Achārya Guṇasunder	44 years
Achārya Kālaka	41 years
Achārya Skandila	38 years
Achārya Revati Mitra	36 years
Achārya Mangu	20 years
Achārya Dharma	24 years
Achārya Bhadragupta	39 years
Achārya Shrigupta	15 years
Achārya Vajra	36 years
Total	**414 years**
The preceding period of spiritual leadership after final salvation of Lord Mahavirā and upto Acharya Bhadrabāhu	170 years
	584 years

Ārya Rakṣhita succeeded to the seat of Ārya Vajra. The author of the commentary on 'Visheshāvashyaka' (An Agamic Scripture), Jaina Achārya Hemchandra, writes while elabarating the meanings of religious verse No. 2511, that Arya Rakṣita was well conversant with the texts of 9 Pūrvas and only 24 verses of the 10th Pūrva with due clarifications and explanations. The period of spiritual leadership of Ārya Rakṣita and as principal man of the age is believed to be from 584 to 597th year after final salvation of Lord Mahāvira. One of his disciples was 'Durbalika Pushyamitra' who had gained expertise in 9 Pūrvas. However, for want of adequate recitation and remembrance, he began to forget the texts of 9th Pūrva and, thus, after his final liberation, the teaching and revelation of the contents of 9th Pūrva also came to an end. He is believed to have attained his final liberation in the 604th year, after final salvation of Lord Mahāvira. There is alsolutely no mention of 'Durbalika Pushyamitra' in Nandi Sthiravalli. The Nandi Sthiravalli (list of Successors to the holy seat) had, probably, been accomplished on the basis of succession as leading-most men of their age. Most probably, the names of only those spiritual leaders appear therein who had the privilege of succeeding to the seat of the spiritual head and also as leading men of the age. Infact, the teaching and studying of only limited number of old sacred treatises, incorporating highest spiritual knowledge relating to Jaina religion and philosophy, had been carried on for about one thousand years, after final salvation of Lord Mahāvira. Thereafter, the recitation and memorizing the texts of Purvas ceased alogether.

As Per Belief of Digamber Sect

As per traditional belief of Digamber sect the Chronology differs in regard to the discontinuance of teaching and studying of the old sacred texts, containing highest spiritual knowledge of Jaina religion and philosophy in the shape of Purvas. The scholars of Digamber Sect believe that the recitation and rememberance of 11

Angas had also come to an end after the expiry of a specific period. It is cited in *Tiloyapaṇṇatti* that after the final emancipation of Achārya Bhadrabāhu, the practice of acquiring thorough knowledge of all the 14 Pūrvas had ceased. The subsequent precceptors and spiritual guides, namely 1. Vishal, 2. Proshthil, 3. Kṣatriya, 4. Jaya, 5. Nag, 6. Sidhārtha, 7. Dhriteshena, 8. Vijaya, 9. Budhil, 10. Gangdeva, and 11. Sudharma were known for their expertise in the sacred texts of 10 Pūrvas only. As recognized by Digamber Sect, the total period of spiritual leadership of said scholars, ranged to 183 years. After final liberation of the said religious teachers and with the passage of time, the teaching and studying of 10 Pūrvas as also the faculty of memorizing and retaining in the mind of the texts of the said Pūrvas also came to an end.

It is cited in Tiloyapaṇṇatti that there were five Jaina scholars, having expertise in 11 Angas with good retentive memory, in the Jaina institution, founded by Lord Mahāvira, namely 1. Nakṣatra, 2. Jayapal, 3. Pāṇḍu, 4. Dhruvasena, and 5. Kansa, after the tradition of recitation and rememberance of Purvas had ceased. The total period of the spiritual leadership of the said scholars is believed to be around 220 years. However, after they attained final liberation, the practice of gaining expertise in and retaining in the memory of the contents of 11 Angas also stopped.

It is also cited in Tiloyapaṇṇatti that there were 4 scholars who had the proficiency in and were well conversant with the sacred texts, contained in 'Achāranga' (first Anga), namely—1. Subhadra, 2. Yashobhadra, 3. Yashobāhu and 4. Lohārya. After their final liberation, the recitation and revelation of the knowledge of Achāranga also ceased. Thereafter, the spiritual guides had proficiency in only specific portions or limited number of verses, forming part of 14 Pūrvas and 11 Angas. The total period of spiritual leadership of the aforesaid four scholars, having expertise in Achāranga only is calculated to be of 118 years. Thus the total period of spiritual leadership of omniscients = 162 years + Experts in 14 Pūrvas = 183 years + expertise in 10 Pūrvas only = 220 years + those having perfection and conversance in Achārānga only = 118 years =683 six hundred and eighty-three years.

Comparative View and Critical Study

Both Shwetamber and Digamber Sects are unanimous regarding accomplishment of perfection in highest spiritual knowledge and attainment of the state of omniscience by highly sanctified and selected Guides of Jaina religion. Both sects agree that Ārya Jambu was the last Kevalin. The view of both sects regarding expertise in the sacred knowledge on the higher truths of Jaina religion and philosophy, contained in 14 Pūrvas are also identical. According to both traditions, the last authority on 14 Pūrvas was Achārya Bhadrabāhu. Only the difference of eight years is found in chronological calculation. As per tradition of Shwetāmber Sect, the total period, dating back from final salvation of Lord Mahāvira to the final emancipation of Achārya Bhadrabāhu, totals to 170 years, while as per Digamber Sect, it is only 162 years. Thereafter, there are distincit opinions and apparent dissimilarities in the views of both sects. According to traditional belief of Shwetember Sect, the expertise in revelation of the sacred knowledge and elaboration of the meanings of the precepts, contained in 10 Pūrvas, had continued till the life time of Ārya Vājra, who had attained his final liberation in 584th year, after final salvation of Lord Mahāvira. However, Digamber Sect belives that the recitation and rememberance (retaining in memory) of the sacred texts of 10 Pūrvas had continued till 345th years only, after final salvation of Lord Mahāvira. Thus there is difference of 239 years in chronological calculation under both traditions. Under Digamber tradition, the teaching and studying of the sacred texts, contained in 10 Pūrvas, had ceased 239 years earlier. However, the sages and scholars of Shwetamber Sect believe that the proficiency in the sacred knowledge of 10 Pūrvas, had continued even thereafter i.e. upto 584th year from final salvation of Lord Mahāvira. They further believe that the teaching and studying of 9 Pūrvas was in continuance for 20 years, after the life time of Ārya Vājra. Thereafter, the teaching and studying of decreasing number of Pūrvas or their portions, had continued for 396 years. Thus the scholars of Shwetamber Sect are of the view that the recitation and rememberance of the sacred texts of Purvas, though the number rapidly declining, had continued till 1000 years after final salvation of Lord Mahavirā, in one or the other form.

Eleven Angas—Their Existence or Non-Existence

Whereas, under Shwetamber tradition, the continuance of teaching and studying of the sacred texts, forming part of 11 Angas, is acknowledged even now, the Digamber Sect accepts continuance of the teaching and studying of 11 Angas till 565th year only after final salvation of Lord Mahavira. Afterwards, the presence of the scholars, having expertise in the sacred texts of 'Achāranga' only is admitted till 683rd year from the final salvation of Lord Mahāvira. Thereafter, the experts of sacred knowledge of Pūrvas, eleven Angas and Achāranga, ceased to exist. Only partial expertise in Pūrvas and 11 Angas had continued for some more years. There is considerable difference in traditional beliefs of Shwetamber and Digamber Sects regarding pursuance of the practice of imparting and revealing of highest spiritual knowledge of Jaina religion and philosophy after the life time of Achārya Bhadrabāhu. The main difference of opinion lies in as much as the continuance of teaching and studying of sacred texts, contained in 11 Angas, now, is not admitted by Digamber Sect, while it is acknowledged by Shwetamber Sect.

Will the research scholars take pains to find out a rational and logical answer to the above problem in order to remove the difference of opinion and bridge the gap? No doubt, the scholars will have an urge to take greater interest in finding out an answer and will spare no efforts to carry on further investigation in this regard so as to establish new findings.

Combinations in Agamas

Literal meaning of the word 'Anuyoga' (what combines or joins)

The word 'Anuyoga' is comprised of two syllables—'Anu' (It is a prefix to verbs and verbal derivatives) and 'Yoga' (Combination). The prefix 'Anu' here is indicative of 'favourably inclined or conformable to.' An aphorism is always in concise form while its explanation is elaborate. A harmonious or consistent combination, uniting the two, is called 'Anuyoga'. An 'Anuyoga' is like a specific object or thing aimed at and helps in elucidation and elaboration of the sacred texts, contained in Agamic Scriptures.

Types of Anuyogas : The Anuyogas have been classified under four heads : (1) Charaṇakarnānuyoga[1], (2) Dharmakathānuyoga, (3) Gaṇitanuyoga, and (4) Draviyānuyoga[2]. The aforesaid four types of Anunyogas have been discussed, and dealt with in Agamic Scriptures. While in some, they have been comprehensively discussed, in others, they have been dealt with in short or brief only.

Anuyogas : Inseperability : By the time of Ārya Vajra, the method of recitation of the texts of Agamic scriptures was such that there was no applicability of Anuyogas separately. Each aphorism used to be explained by application of all the four types of Anuyogas. It is cited in 'Āvashyoka Niryukti (Authored by Āchārya Bhadrabāhu) : "There is no necessity to apply each Anuyoga separately to obtain explicitness in the interpretation of the sacred texts relating to the religious knowledge or learning in general. In other words, it was not necessary to apply four types of 'Anuyogas'—'Charnakarṇānuyoga' etc separately to obtain elucidation and clarity in the meanings. The sacred texts, relating to the religious knowledge or learning in general and highest spiritual knowledge, pertaining Jaina philosophy, contained in 'Drishṭivāda' were explained by virtue of applying different types of Anuyogas, after the final salvation of Ārya Vajra.

Āchārya Malayagiri writes in this connection that by the time, the Jaina saints and monks had sharp memory and were highly intelligent, there was tradition of elaborating aphorisms by applying all the four types of Anuyogas and not by making segregated use of the Anuyogas.

Āchārya Malayagiri has further emphasized that Āchārya Bhadrabāhu had specifically referred to the religious knowledge or learning in general in his 'Avashyaka Niryukti' because it was primarily imparted in religious discourses, otherwise, all the four types of Anuyogas were applied in exposition of sūtras relating to both religious knowledge in general or highest spiritual knowledge, abounding in philosophical teachings of Jaina religion.

The above point has been discussed in a critical manner in the commentary to *Visheshāvashyaka* (authored by Āchārya Bhadragani 'Kṣamāshramana') : By the time of Ārya Vajra, there was no classification of Anuyogas and each Sutra used to be explained elaborately by applying all the four types of Anuyogas jointly.

In case, the Anuyogas were classified in different types or their application was reduced, as a result of such classification for elaboration of a Sūtra, even then the inherence of all the four Anuyogas in a Sūtra was not disturbed in any way. The commentator, himself, elucidates the point and replies—where as a Sūtra used to be explained earlier by applying all the four types of Anuyogas, now each Sūtra began to be interpreted by applying a particular Anuyoga only.

---

1. The literal meaning of the word 'Charaṇa' is conduct, manner of conducting oneself, showing uprightness and good behaviour. Where there is a discussion or critical examination concerning them, it will be deemed that there was use of *Charaṇakarṇānuyoga.*
2. Where, there is detailed discussion or critical examination in regard to the matter, elementary substances or substratium of properties, it will be deemed that there was use of 'Dravyānuyoga.

Classification of Anuyogas (appropriate and consistent combinations) by Ārya Rakṣita

The classification of Anuyogas had been accomplished by Ārya Rakṣita. He was the successor to the holy seat of Ārya Vajra. He was highly reverred and an eminent religious preceptor. He was greatly honoured by Lords of Heaven. Keeping in view the ensuing odd times, he classified the religious texts, written in aphoristic style, in four types and each Sūtra to be explained by applying one particular Anuyoga.

Durbalikā Pushyamitra was the resident disciple of Ārya Rakṣita and he was endowed with excellent qualities of head and heart—a great religious teacher and guide, a competent reciter of sacred texts and having sharp memory or retentive faculty, yet Ārya Rakṣita realized through his deep insight and meditation that Pushyamitra was finding it difficult to sustain the religious knowledge revealed by him, and retain it confidently in his memory. He, therefore, inferred that learned students of ensuing generation will, obviously, be lacking desired talents and will be devoid of sharp memory and retentive faculty. Consequently with a view to facilitate their work, he classified the sacred knowledge as religious knowledge in general and knowledge, derived through meditation on higher truths of Jaina religion and philosophy. Appropriate and consistent combinations of 4 types were also accomplished by him for proper explanation and elaboration of the sacred texts which were in aphoristic style.

The Jaina scholar, Acharya Hamchandra author of the commentary on 'Visheshāvashyaka' has stated, while explaining the religious verse No. 2511, written in Prākrita dialect, that besides Durbalikā, there were 3 other prominent disciples of Ārya Rakṣita, namely—Vindhya, Falgurakṣita and Goshṭhāmāhila. Āchārya Rakṣita instructed his chief disciple, Durbalika Pushyamitra to recite the sacred texts of Pūrvas before Vindhya. Durbalika started recitation but for want of proper revision, he experienced difficulty in recitation of the texts, contained in ninth Pūrva. Ārya Rakṣita soon realized that although an erudite scholar, Pushyamitra was finding it hard to sustain the knowledge and retain it in memory, the students and scholars of future generation will find it all the more difficult. The said feeling prompted him to systematize the Anuyogas under four heads.

Relevance of Anuyogas with Agamic Scriptures

The Agamic canonical literature has been classified as under in consistency with four types of Anuyogas :

1. Under 'Charṇakarnānuyoga' are covered—11 periodical (to be studied at fixed hours) canonical works, containing doctrinal knowledge of Jaina religion in general; i.e. 11 Angas (forming part of Agamic Scriptures); Mahakalpa Shruta (relating to good conduct and behaviour and observance of the manners, needed for conducting oneself) and Chheda Sutras (concerning expiatory rules).
2. Under 'Dharmakathanuyoga', Agamic Scriptures, containing religious

utterances of omniscients, sages and seers of Jaina religion.

3. Under 'Ganitanuyoga'—"Surya Pragyapti' etc (Astronomical and astrological teachings and informations).
4. Under 'Dravyanuyoga'—'Drishṭivāda' (Matter, relating to highest spiritual knowledge of Jaina religion and philosophy).

Anuyogas : As per Canonical literature of Digamber Sect.

There are 4 types of Anuyogas under Digamber tradition as well. However, their names are different from those shown above, as per Swetāmber tradition :

1. Prathmānuyoga—Covering canonical works concerning places or abodes for attainment of perfect wisdom and enlightenment, i.e. valuable collection of tales, pertaining to ancient legendary history, biographies and other religious or historical narratives or episodes, predominently containing legendary narratives.
2. Karṇānuyoga—Covering under its fold sacred works relating to separation of materialistic and spiritual worlds; four types of salvations (transmigration of soul in infernal regions, lower animal world, the world of mortals and the divine world) and astrological and astronomical books.
3. Charṇānuyoga—Covering religious treatises, which set forth the rules and sub-rules how to build, develope and maintain good moral character, purity of mind and uprightness.
4. Dravyānuyoga—Covering philosophical and doctrinal works, dealing with ascertainment of the real truth, true nature of organic and inorganic worlds; auspicious or inauspicious actions and deliverance of the soul from transmigration or recurring births.

As per belief of Digamber Sect, the Agamic Scriptures are extinct now. Hence the subsequent religious works, which they believe to be authentic and repose their faith in them, have been classified under the above four Anuyogas in accordance with the subjects, dealt with therein as under :-

1. Prathmānuyoga—Ancient sacred works like 'Mahapurāna and Puranas (Names of certain well-known sacred works, containing the whole body of Hindu mythology—ancient legendary history or historical events).
2. Karṇānuyoga—'Tiloyaparṇṇatti' (Its Sanskrit formation is 'Triloka Pragyapti) and Trilok-Sār (authored by Achārya Nemichandra Sidhānt Chakravarty).
3. Charṇānuyoga—Ancient sacred works, incorporating details of 5 great austerities to be observed by Jaina monks and 5 austerities to be observed by household followers of Jainism.
4. Dravyānuyoga—Sacred works like 'Pravachansār and Gommatasār (authored by Achārya Nemichandra Sidhānt Chakravarty) etc.

May be to a slight degree, there is sufficient material for discussion and deliberation in all religious compositions accomplished in aphoristic style, relating, more or less, to all the four types of Anuyogas. It is obvious that in a particular canonical work, there is pre-eminence of a certain topic, while in the other it is insignificant. The manner of proceeding on a subject may, possibly, be like this. It is certain that there was a practice or tradition of elaborating each subject in detail, which may have been referred to in an insignificant or symbolic manner in a Sūtra work. In other words, it may be illustrated like this-that there must have been provision of explanatory material for the benefit of students and scholars so that they could be able to comprehend the Sūtras and the subjects, discussed therein in brief. It could also be treated as supplementary or interpretative literature, helpful in grasping the fundamental subjects, referred to in aphoristic style in Sūtra Works, which the students used to acquire one after the other successively. Earlier, all the four types of Anuyogas used to be applied for elaboration of each Sūtra. However, it was a tough job. Where the original composition is in the shape of a Sūtra, written in concise form in a few technical words, it is always too difficult to remember the detailed explanation and retain it in memory, since it called for extraordinary intelligence, regular presence of mind and continued practice. Hence he classified the Anuyogas under four heads. This made it convenient to classify the Sūtra works, dealing prominently with similar subjects under one type of Anuyoga. For example, the Sutra works, classified under the head of 'Charṇakarṇānuyoga', primarily dealt with the topics, relating to the conduct or behaviour, probity and uprightness. Similarly, under the head of 'Dharmakathā-nuyoga', the Sūtra works, primarily dealing with religious discourses, narratives and tales for exposition of religious doctrines and philosophy, have been incorporated. The 'Ganitanuyoga' covers Sutra works, dealing with astronomical problems and mathematical calculations. In the same way under 'Dravyanuyoga' are covered Sūtra works, dealing with the material to work upon elementary substances and the sub-stratum of properties.

The aforesaid classification of Sūtra works, proved to be very helpful. This enabled the students to follow a consistent course in undertaking critical study of the Sūtras and gain highest spiritual knowledge of Jaina religion and philosophy, more so, when the average intelligence and retentiveness of memory was rapidly diclining day by day. This made it considerably easy to acquire conversancy with the sacred precepts or texts, contained in Shāstras or Sūtra Works. Thus, they were able to have a glimpse of a definite line and a clear indication which of the sacred treatises or works were to be minutely studied by them in order to have the desired knowledge on higher truths of Jaina religion and philosophy.

Second Recitation of Agamic Scriptures

Recitation at Mathura

The first recitation of Agamic Scriptures had taken place at Pātliputra (Patna) under spiritual leadership and guidance of Achārya Sthūlbhadra. As cited in *Avashyaka Churni* (authored by Achārya Jindās Gani), it had been held after 160 years of final salvation of Lord Mahāvira. The texts contained in 11 Angas

(Auxiliary works, forming part of Agamic Scriptures) had been revised and compiled during the first gathering. They continued to be revealed and recited for centuries by religious preceptors to their disciples successively. However, after expiry of about 675 years from the final salvation of Lord Mahāvira, such an odd situtaion arose that arrangements had to be made for inviting the scholars and undertake revision and re-compilation of the Agamic Scriptures for the second time.

Terrible Famine Having Lasted for Tweleve Years

It is stated that a terrible famine had taken place and lasted continuously for 12 years. The day today public life was completely wrecked and it had become too difficult to pull on and protect life. Obviously, it had an unfavourable effect upon the daily routine of religious mendicants as well. The living conditions had become so miserable that it was no longer possible to lead the life of an ascetic and undertake spiritual endeavours. A large number of Jaina mendicants had fallen prey to the jaws of death.

It is cited in *Nandi Chūrṇi* that in the absence of desired capability to acquire higher spiritual knowledge; appreciate its significance and admire its excellence, the treasure of highest spiritual knowledge, as revealed by omniscients and heard by their disciples had become extinct. However, certain other scholars assert that the sacred texts were intact but only the experts who were well-conversant with them were no longer alive. It means the same. Whatever be the case, the fact remains that the tradition of acquiring spiritual knowledge by way of listening to the religious discourses of omniscients and eminent scholars, had been obstructed.

The terrible famine was over and conditions improved. People felt much relieved. The Jaina scholars and sages who had survived, were now worried how to protect the treasure of sacred knowledge? At that time, Achārya Skandila was the principal man of age. The period of his pre-eminance as leading man of his age continued from the year 827 to 840, after final salvation of Lord Mahāvira. In 'Nandi-Sthiviravali (A list showing succession to the supreme seat of the spiritual head), the name of Achārya Skandila appears as 24th successor to the holy seat of Lord Mahāvira. The author of 'Nandi Sthiravalli' writes in his praise that the scientific tradition of explaining and elaborating the meanings of the precepts by applying Anuyogas, is his exclusive contribution. Achārya Skandila was highly celebrated and a renowned figure. His renown and glory had spread all around.

Nandi-Sūtra is believed to have been written by Achārya Devardhi Gani 'Kṣmashramaṇa'. The third or last recitation and recompilation of Agamic texts had been carried out under his auspices. The version of Achārya Devardhigani 'Kṣmashramaṇa' that Achārya Skandila had introduced the practice of explaining and elaboraion of the meanings of Sutra-works by applying Anuyogas, leads us to conclude that although he had kept in mind the proceedings of both conventions, held at Vallabhi and Mathura, yet he had attached greater significance to the Māthuri recitation held under the auspices of Achārya Skandila to treat it as a guide-line for the third recitation. Hence by way of showing regard to Achārya Skandila what he has stated above, seems to be justified.

Mathura was then the principal centre of influence of Jaina religion. A meeting of Jaina scholars was convened to be held there for recitation of Agamic texts under auspices of Achārya Skandila. The holy seers, well conversant with the sacred texts, relating to higher spiritual knowledge of Jaina religion and philosophy had arrived at Mathura from remote places to participate in the proceedings of the convention. Whatever the said seers and scholars recollected and recalled to mind, they recited it which was placed in proper sequence and compiled in the shape of spiritual knowledge of Jain religion in general. At that time Achārya Skandila was alone well versed in application of Anuyogas. He had imparted lecture on the significance and applicability of Anuyogas before the Jaina scholars. Since the said recitation was given at Mathura, it came to be known as 'Mathuri recitation.' The time of the said recitation was way back between 827 and 840 A.D. which is known as the period when Achārya skandila held the position of a principal and most eminent person of the age.

Vallabhi Recital

Almost simultaneously another meeting of Jaina scholars and saints had taken place at Vallabhi in Saurashtra under auspices of Nagārjuna Sūri. The main object of the said gathering was to recollect the sacred texts which had almost been forgotten and to rearrange them in proper sequence. On the basis of old memory, the sacred texts, relating to utterances of omniscients or as revealed by their leading spiritual heads and heard by their disciples were recited by the participants and in this way the rare spiritual knowledge was saved from extinction. The sacred texts, forming part of Agamic Scriptures and other religious treatises, which were in memory of Nagārjuna Sūri and other Jaina scholars, were recited, edited and then compiled in a systematic order. However, the portions of the sacred texts which could not properly be remembered, were minutely looked into and reshaped in consistency with the implied sense. In this way, whatever old sacred texts could be recollected were all compiled edited and arranged in order. Nagārjuna Sūri made recital of the texts, he remembered, before the saints and Jaina scholars, who had attended the gathering.

Achārya Nagārjuna Sūri had presided over the deliberations of the meeting and had provided his valuable guidance. Therefore, it is known as Nāgārjuna recitation also although it is best known as Vallabhi recitation.

Two Recitals Organized at One and the Same Time

It is stated that the two recitals were held at one and the same time. Obviously, it is asked why the meetings at two different places were convened simultaneously. The Jaina scholars who had attended the gathering at Valabhi (Saurashṭra) could have reached Mathura (U.P) as well.

One assumption could be that there were differences amongst the Jaina Scholars of Northern and Western territories of India. Consequent upon the same, the saints who happened to participate in the deliberations at Valabhi might have expressed their unwillingness to join at Mathura. They would have, rather, shown disagreement with the decisions of that convention.

Similarly, it is also possible that the Jaina followers of Western regions might have shown their discord with the goings on, developments, programmes, procedural details and the leadership of the Mathuri recital.

Thirdly, it is also possible that the convention at Vallabhi might have been held after the sittings at Mathura. The Jaina scholars of Western India might not have felt satisfied with the accomplishments of Mathura convention and they might have been eager to undertake another recital for ensuring better co-ordination in editing of the sacred texts, forming part of Agamic Scriptures and allied canonical literature and accordingly, they might have organised a fresh convention to accomplish their aim. Accordingly, besides the sacred texts relating to the spiritual knowledge of Jaina religion, other doctrinal texts were also compiled and edited. The lengthy portions of the texts, which were not intelligible, were systematized by comprehending the explanation and cense thereof.

There could be other grounds as well. However, it is certain that there must have been a substantial cause which impelled them to convene a separate meeting at Vallabhi either simultaneously or with slight interval. It is also cited that religious texts were also reduced to writing in the said conventions.

In the sacred texts compiled in the aforesaid sittings at Valabhi and Mathura, we come across different readings and varying versions. Variations are also found in the manner of compilation in the aforesaid conventions. It is cited in the commentary on *Jyotishkaranṭaka* that Sutra works, namely 'Anuyoga Dwar and others had been compiled on the lines of Mathura recitation. The renowned works, namely, *Jyotishkaranṭaka* and others had been accomplished as per recitation at Vallabhi.

After the two recitals organised under the auspices of Nagārjuna Sūri and Achārya Skandila at Valabhi and Mathura respectively, were over, the two spiritual heads had no meeting at all with the result, the variations in the two versions could not be removed and they are as such even now.

Third Recital

After about 150 years of the aforesaid two recitals,—say during the year 980 or 993, after final salvation of Lord Mahāvira, the third recital[1] had taken place under the auspices of eminent scholar Achārya Devardhigaṇi 'Kṣmashramana'. It is also known as second recital held at Vallabhi.

---

1. Just as the foregoing two recitals were the consequence of terrible effects of the devasting famine, similarly the same horrible effects of the famine prompted to convene the meeting to undertake third recital. It is cited in *Samāchāri Shataka* that many Jaina scholars and seers had fallen victim to the jaws of death as an awful effect of 12 years long famine. Considerable amount of sacred texts, pertaining to higher truths of Jaina religion and philosophy had been destroyed and become extinct. For the benefit of worthy and competent followers and for the purpose of re-manifestation of the holy texts, Acharya Devardhigani 'Kṣmāsharmana' had invited all those learned scholars and saints, who had survived the annihilatory jaws of death, at the instance of Jaina institution, to gather at Valabhi (Saurashtra). He listened attentively to the recital of Agamic texts, whether complete or incomplete short or excess impaired or unimpaired and after getting them compiled in a systematic order, they were reduced to black and white and finally accomplished in the shape of scriptural works (Agamas).

The process of revealing highest spiritual knowledge of Jaina religion and philosophy as done in the past by omniscients, spiritual heads and guides, came to be interrupted, creating state of uncertainty and loss of awareness as also an alround worry in the organisation for preservation of holy texts, forming part of Agamic Scriptures. During the past period of 150 years, major portion of the sacred texts had undergone decline as an ill-effect of adverse conditions and uncertain times. What were the prevailing conditions then, cannot be explained in a decisive manner. However, it transpires from what has been discussed above that the Jaina organisation was really anxious to take up effective steps immediately for preservation of sacred texts to avoid further loss of religious awareness. It is believed that as a consequence of calamitous conditions during past 150 years, major portion of Jaina scriptural texts must have vanished. Various variant versions and different readings of sacred texts were in vogue. Obviously therefore, it may have been found essential to revise, re-compile and re-edit the texts. Consequent upon the same, the scholars were invited to gather again at Vallabhi (Saurashtra) to undertake third recitation of the spiritual texts as remembered by them. The main object of convening the second convention at Vallabhi was to correct the variant versions and readings in correct sequence, to ensure uniformity in the readings and to co-ordinate the texts which remained yet to be compiled. All this was essential to ensure invariability in the contents of Sūtra Works. Obviously it was a most significant endeavour.

The Jaina Scholars, having expertise in recitation of Agamic texts and endowed with sharp memories, gathered at Vallabhi from various regions in India. The variations in texts and differences in readings, found after expiry of two recitals at Mathura and Vallabhi, were re-examined and discrepancies removed. The recitations made by attending scholars and sages as per their memory were mutually tallied. This enabled the spiritual guides to obtain uniformity in the texts. However, the variations in the texts which could neither be removed nor it was found convenient to ensure uniformity in them, they were collected in respective commentaries or Churnis (A selection of unexplained texts or versions). An indication to this effect is found in both original Sūtra works and their commentaries. Miscellaneous other texts which were obtained as per remembrance of the Jaina seers at the time of recital in anyone of the sittings at Mathura or Vallabhi were accepted to be authentic and adopted as such.

Besides the sacred texts which had been compiled and edited in the aforsaid two conventions, some other religious treatises or other miscellaneous contextual items were also minutely edited in the third convention. Thereafter, the entire spiritural texts were reduced to writing. Although compilation, modification and editing of the scriptual writings had been taken up in the thirs convention by way of comparing and co-ordinating the recited texts, obtained in the earlier two conventions, yet it had reposed its reliance on the accomplishments of Mathura convention. The shape of Angas (Agamic Scriptures) and Upāngas (supplementary writings to the Angas), as obtained now, are infact, modified and accurately formed editions of the third convention, under spiritual guidance of Devardhigaṇi 'Kṣmashramana'.

Bodh Religious Concerts : Jaina Recitals

What a strange coincidence ? Whereas three principal concerts had been organised for compilation and editing of *Tripitakas* (A Collection of Buddhist scriptures), in the some way, three recitals had taken place for compilation and accomplishment of modified form of scriptural writings of Jaina religion. However, there is a lot of difference in the chronology of time of holding the said Budhist concerts and Jaina recitals, made by Jaina scholars. While all the three concerts[1] had been held in between 236 years only, after final salvation of Lord Buddha, the Jaina recitals were over in the year 980 or 993 after final salvation of Lord Mahāvirā.

Bodha Pitakas were reduced to writing in Ceylon (now Sri Lanka) in between the period 29 to 17 B.C. on palmyra leaves during the rule of king Vathagāmiṇi Abhaya of that country. A meeting was also held to carry out modifications, if any, yet it appears that no major alterations were made in the body of Pitakas and they were reduced to writing in the same shape as they were carried by Prince Mahendra to Ceylon. For the sake of narration, it may be added here that two meetings had also been held in between the period of Prince Mahendra's arrival in Ceylon and the reign of King Vathagāmiṇi Abhaya, when the Buddhist Scriptures were reduced to writing. Buddha Tripitakas had been compiled and finally accomplished about 750 years earlier and reduced to black and white about 500 years prior to the recitals of Jaina Agamic Scriptures. Keeping in view such a huge chronological gap, it should obviously, be inferred that the Jaina Agamic scriptures could not match with Pali Tripitakas in so far as their ancientness and authenticity from philological viewpoint is concerned. The process of convening meetings of Buddhist scholars, one after the other, had started shortly after the final salvation of Lord Buddha, so much so, that the first concert had been organised only four months, after the final salvation of Lord Buddha. Thus, it should be believed that there was greater originality and consistency in the contents of speeches, delivered by Lord Buddha, forming part of Buddhist scriptures.

Difference in the Situations leading to Spread and Expansion of both Religions

There were diverse conditions at the time of propagation and spread of Bodha and Jaina religions. According to historic scholars, Bodha religion was in favour of following a moderate course to be undertaken for spiritual achievements, avoiding severe penances and absolute self-mortification. Consequently, it had spread far and wide during the life-time of Lord Budḥa, himself. The initiated monks in Budhist organisation, belonged to several states and regions and they spoke different regional dialects. The areas of their activities for propagating and spreading the message of Bodha religion were also different and the said areas were considerably remote from each other, wherein they happened to move from one place to another in order to make people aware of the religious doctrines and tenets of Buddhism. 'Hence it is quite possible that certain amalgamations, alterations and additions must have taken place in the texts of speeches and utterances of Lord Buddha from linguistic viewpoint, since Buddhist monks carried on the religious propaganda

1. Kindly peruse the chapter, dealing with 'Tripitakas' in this book for greater details.

in their own regional dialcets. Consequent upon the same, it was considered essential to gather for recitation and revision of Buddha's preachings, hardly 4 months after the final salvation of Lord Buddha.

The message of Jaina religion had also spread far and wide during the life-time of Lord Mahāvira but not to the extent Buddhism had received acclamation. The main reason being that strict observance of the vows, rules and precepts of Jainism, practising of severe penances and performance of rigorous austerities as also exercising absolute control overself, leading an austere life of self-mortification-were some of the pre-requisites of Jaina religion which were not so easy to be appropriated to oneself. The initiated mendicants of Jain institution generally belonged to neighbouring regions of Videha (lying to the north-east of Magadha. Its capital was Mithilā), Magadha and Kaushala (situated along the bank of Saryu river, signifying a region north of Ayodhya) and other adjoining areas only. Their local dialects were almost similar and were not alien to each other. The areas of movement of Jaina scholars and guides were also limited as compared to those of Buddhist monks. Justifiably, the texts of religious discourses, delivered by Lord Mahāvira, remained intact for a longer period and the need for their revision was felt after a long time from final salvation of Lord Mahāvira.

As a result of terrible long famine and frequent scarce conditions, the texts of religious utterances of omniscients and eminent scholars, as memorized by their senior disciples, had almost vanished or in other words, majority of the jain relgious heads, who were well conversant with those texts, had lost their lives. As an obvious consequence of such calamitous conditions, the recitation and re-compilation of sacred texts, forming part of Agamic scriptures, was carried out. However, the ancientness of Agamic scriptures, from linguistic viewpoint is undisputed. A reflection of those native dialects is clearly found in the spiritual texts of Agamas which were mediums of speech during the life time of Lord Mahāvira and Lord Buddha. The practice being that the Jaina scholars were extremely cautious to memorize the texts of the speeches, delivered by their spiritual guides and retain them in memory word by word besides the explanations of their meanings. It is apparent from the special emphasis laid for pronouncing the sacred texts correctly in Jaina scriptures was made to ensure bonafideness of the words. Although, it cannot be claimed that no modifications were carried out in the original texts at all or they remained totally intact, yet it is a fact that the language of Jaina Agamas did not undergo any significant change as against Pitakas in Pāli Prākrita,which is an ample proof of extreme caution and special endeavours made by Jaina scholars on this account.

Buddhist scriptures had been accomplished at Magadha. From there they had been carried to Ceylon by a prince, who had been brougnt up at Avanti (Another name of Ujjaini, situated along Sipra river). No doubt, he was the royal prince of Magadha ruler, emperor Ashoka, yet his mother tongue was Avanti and not Magadhi dialect. Later on, they were reduced to writing in Ceylon after a span of a few centuries. The said edition of Buddhist scriptures, obtained in Ceylon, formed the basis of all later publications. Thus, it is apparent from the above discussion that the Buddhist scriptures had undergone the process of additions and alterations gradually with the passage of time.

Whereas, Jaina Agmas had been accomplished at Magadha and Videha, they were recited and re-compiled at Magadha, Mathura and Vallabhi in Saurāshtra. They were given final shape in Saurāshtra by the Jaina seers and scholars who were determined to retain the body of Agamic texts intact. Whereas, Jaina Agamas had been accomplished at Magadha and Videha, they were recited, compiled and edited at Magadha Mathura (Uttar Pradesh) and Vallabhi in Saurāshtra. They were given final shape in Saurāshtra by the Jaina seers who were determined to maintain the originality of the sacred texts intact. The Jaina scriptures had been accomplished in the regions where eastern Prākrita dialects were spoken and they were reduced to writing in the territorial parts of Western Prākrita dialects (land of primarily Apbhransh dialects). Thus, there was no long gap between the places where the sittings were arranged in the case of Jaina Scriptures as against Pāli Pitakas which were finalized and reduced to writing in Ceylon. There may have been certain factors responsible for minor additions and alterations here and there in the texts of Jaina Agamas but they were only a few as against Pāli Tripitakas of Buddhist religion. Therefore, there is greater significance of Jaina Agamas from linguistic viewpoint for undertaking study of Prākrita dialects which were the mediums of speech during life periods of Lord Buddha and Lord Mahāvira.

Principal Sacred Texts, Forming part of Jaina Agamas and other Auxiliary Texts—Explanatory in Nature, Treated as other Jaina Canonical Literature

It has been discussed above how the sacred texts of Jaina Agamas had traditionally been handed down by spiritual leaders of one generation to their disciples and so on. From viewpoint of their contents, the Jaina scriptures are divided into two categories:

1. Principal spiritual texts, forming part of Jaina Agamas, and
2. Other supplementary texts, treated as allied Jaina canonical litetature of lesser significance.

Acharya Jinbhadra Gaṇi 'Kṣmashraman has defined in the commentary on 'Visheshavashyaka' that the principal spiritual texts, as revealed by Tirthankers and omniscients and as heard and composed by Gandhers and senior disciples in verses as per Gayatri metre, having six syllables in a quarter, are principal sacred texts, forming part of Jaina Agamas containing highest spiritual knowledge. On the other hand, the texts, composed by Sthaviras, free from grammatical constraints, inconsistent and having no regular or fixed employment of words, forming part of allied Jaina Scriptures, with comparatively lesser significance. The adjectives reading—composed by Gandhers (Chief disciples of Tirthankers); as revealed by Tirthankers and omniscients and the texts of the speeches—of permanent nature and unchangeable—have been used for spiritual texts, forming part of Jaina Agamas and the attributes reading—composed by Sthaviras (Jaina monks, having completed 20 years as religious mendicants after initiation), free from gramatical constraints, inconsistent and of variable nature (having no regular or fixed employment of words) have appeared for sacred texts, forming part of allied canonical works and having lesser significance.

Interpretation by Jaina Scholar, Āchārya Hemchandra

While elaborating the above definition appearing in the commentary on 'Visheshavashyaka', Acharya Hemchandra, a renowned Jaina seer, writes : "The 12 Angas, forming part of Jaina Agamas, having been compiled and composed by Gandhers in aphoristic style are categorized as 'Anga Pravishtha' (principal Agamic Scriptures), while other explanatory works—such as *Avashyaka Niryukti*, authored by Āchārya Bhadrabāhu, a Sthavira and a senior religious teacher of Jain religion, etc. are called as 'Anga Bāhiya' (Auxiliary treatises, having comparatively lesser significance). On making repeated requests thrice by Gandhers and the illustrated texts of speeches, delivered by Tirthankers and omniscients, based on the theory that the elementary substance or the sub-stratun of properities is stable and everlasting. Only the body of an article gets destroyed or vanished. In other words the soul is enternal only the physical frame is mortal-from the theme of 12 Angas and constitute sum and substance of Jaina philosophy. These Angas from part of Jaina Agamas and constitute 'Anga Pravishtha'. All other explanatory and interpretative works, helpful in elaboration of Agamic texts, are called *Anga Bahiya* (Auxiliary canonical literature). The highest spiritual knowledge pertaining to settled doctrines of Jaina religion and philosophy, as imparted by Tirthankers and omniscients to their religious mendicants and house-hold devotees, contained in 12 Angas is categorized as 'Anga Pravishtha' (Forming part of Agamas). Similarly, the utterances not necessarily made in the Jaina organisation and dealing with miscellaneous subjects are contained in 'Anga Bāhiya' (Preliminary and Auxiliary works, having lesser significance).

Comments of Āchārya Malayagiri

Āchārya Malayagiri has defined 'Anga Pravishtha' (Agamic Scriptures) and 'Anga Bahiya' (other allied and auxiliary works) in his commentary on 'Nandi Sūtra' that the fundamental Sūtra works, composed by highly genius and erudite scholars, being chief disciples of Tirthankers, called Gandhers, and which deal with highest spiritual knowledge, derived from meditation on the higher truths of Jaina religion and philosophy, as enunciated from time to time by omniscients as well, are categorized as 'Anga Pravishtha'. All other auxiliary works and allied canonical literature, composed by Sthaviras, having comparatively lesser significance, fall under the category of 'Anga Bāhiaya' (spiritual texts of secondary nature).

The scriptural works, treated as 'Anga Bāhiya' are classified under two heads as follows :

(1) 'Avashyaka Vyatirikta' (Necessary or distinct form of religious works), and

(2) 'Tadvyatirikta' (Derivatives or secondary type of religious treatises).

The canonical literature, categorized as 'Avashyaka-Vyatirikta' is of two types:

(1) 'Kālika' (Depending on time to be studied at fixed hours) and

(2) 'Utkālika (Having no restriction of time).

The sacred texts which are strictly meant to be recited in the initial or last period of the day or night (the period roughly reckoned at 3 hrs.) constitute 'Kālika Shruta', while the spiritual texts which can be studied or recited at any time of the day and night without least restriction of time, form part of 'Utkālika Shruta'. The sacred works, namely *Dashvaikālika* etc. relate to this category. A few names of similar less significant works are produced hereunder :

(1) Kalpa-Shruta'—Sacred texts, prescribing do's and dont's—what was desirable and what was strictly forbidden for Sthaviras (senior Jaina saints, having completed 20 years of religious mendicancy). This type of texts are also of two kinds :

(1) 'Chullakalpa Shruta'—being small treatises, having short explanations, and

(2) 'Maha-kalpa Shruta'—the voluminous and significant works, dealing with manners and morals, prescribed for Jaina saints together with detailed explanations.

(2) 'Pragyapnā'—Sacred texts which deal with organic substances.

(3) 'Pramādāpramāda Adhyayan'—Sacred texts dealing with various types of negligences to be avoided and cautions to be exercised, besides making us aware of calamities and embarrassments, we may have to face on account of our omissions and commissions.

(4) Nandi,
(5) Anuyogadwar,
(6) Devendrastava,
(7) Tandula Vaicharika,
(8) Chandravedhyaka,
(9) Surya-Pragyapti,
(10) Porishimandala,
(11) Mandala-Pravesh,
(12) Vidyāchāraṇa-Vinishchaya'
(13) Gani Vidyā,
(14) Dhyān-Vibhakti,
(15) Maraṇa-Vibhakti,
(16) 'Atma-Vishudhi'
(17) Veetrāg Shruta,
(18) Saṁlekhnā Shruta,
(19) Vihār Kalpa,
(20) Charaṇa-Vidhi,
(21) Ātur-Pratyākhyān,
(22) Maha-Pratyākhyān, etc.

All the above treatises form part of *Utkālika Shruta*; and can be studied any time during day and night without any restriction of time.

The *Kālika Shruta* (To be studied or recited at prescribed hours in the initial or last period of day or night) includes the following works under its category, besides many others :

1. Uttrādhyayan,
2. Dashākalpa,
3. Vyavahār,
4. Vrahatkalpa,
5. Nishītha,
6. Rishibhāshit Granth,
7. Mahanishītha,
8. Jambudweep Pragyapti,
9. Dweep Sagar Pragyapti,
10 Chandra Pragyapti,
11 Kṣullakavimān Pravibhkti,
12. Mahāvimān Pravibhakti,
13. Anga-Chūlikā,
14. Varga-Chūlikā,
15. Vivāha-Chūlikā,

16. Aruṇopapāt, 17. Varuṇopapāta, 18. Garuḍopapāta,
19. Dharṇopapāta, 20. Vaishramṇopapāta, 23. Utthān Shruta,
24, Samutthān Shruta, 25. Nāg Parigyā, 26. Nirýāvalikā,
27. Kalpikā, 28. Kalpāvatansikā, 29. Pushpikā,
30. Pūshpachula, 31. Vrishṇidashā etc.

Nearly 84,000 sacred works, representing miscellaneous subjects, treated under the category of 'Kālika Shruta', were in existence during life-time and spiritual leadership of the first Jaina Tirthankar, Lord Rishabha (founder of a new religious or philosophical school). The religious treatises of the similar type, reckoning up nearly one thousand were existent during the life time of intervening Tirthankers and about 14,000 sacred works were there during the period of Lord Mahāvira (last Tirthanker) covering miscellaneous heads and topics. In other words, each Tirthanker was having the same number of sacred books as the number of his disciples, who had been endowed with all the 4 types of sharp-wit and intelligence, namely, prodigiousness etc. and each disciple multiplied by one thousand. The aforesaid canonical literature formed part of 'Anga Bāhya Shruta', consisting of both 'Kalik-Shruta' (To be recited at definite hours) and 'Utkālika Shruta' (To be recited at any time during day or night with no restrictions at all).

'Anga Pravishthya' : 'Anga Bāhiya' : Their Preciseness

On one hand, knowledge on higher truths of Jaina philosophy, is known for its preciseness, sagacity, clarity and elaborateness; On the other, it has its own unique significance in the philosophical accomplishments of the world and known for its characteristic magnanimity. Under Jaina tradition, the significance of any subject or composition is not only because of its attractive name but because of the stress laid on its proper use or application and the benefit or advantage, derived therefrom. The sacred works of Jaina religion, referred to above, and classified as *Anga Pravishṭya* and *Anga Bāhiya* (Auxiliary or explanatory works of secondary nature) are all authoritative religious books, belonging to Jaina tradition and the Jaina community holds them in high esteem. Their significance, illustriousness and acceptability depends on the endeavour of the devotees, how far they meditate to obtain the sacred knowledge. No doubt, all the above noted scriptural works are highly accomplished and authoritative, yet much would depend upon the nature of a disciple or a devotee, how far he is capable of acquiring sacred knowledge and devotes his mind, or concentrates his energies. Although the Jaina scriptures are highly accomplished and known for their elaboration and illustrativeness, yet their true significance shall have to be judged in perspective of the befittingness of individuals, whether they are apt to acquire their knowledge or not. In case, the learned disciples or students have a thorough insight and precise faith, the Jaina scriptures are most accomplished and incorporate highest spiritual knowledge for them. On the other hand, if the persons acquiring, the knowledge are heretical and have misapprehensions, even the Jaina scriptual works of highest order are illusive. In other words, even the non-Jaina scriptures, which are generally treated as untrue and delusive, if adopted by wise persons, having profound insight and thorough awareness, they would be considered highly significant, containing true knowledge of supreme type. The author of commentaries on 'Visheshavashyaka' and 'Avashyaka Niryukti', Achārya Malayagiri has illustrated this point elaborately.

Why so Much Significance Attached to the Characteristics of a Person, Acquiring, Knowledge

Each substance or property has its own distinct entity. Its utility exists in its substratum, which is self-speaking. The good or bad features of a substance are explained in relativity with another object. An article is perfect or imperfect is judged in relation to different users. It is generally used by a person in accordance with its faith and conviction. In case, the user has a perverted mind and delusive nature, his convictions are unfounded and faith vitiated, he is bound to make use of even the best narratives in a most detestable manner, since the user is unable to appreciate its real significance. If the user of an object is morally upright and possesses a virtuous mind, he is bound to make best use of even heinous and deplorable things for the betterment of entire humanity, since he has moral disposition and is ethically sound.

It is the sum and substance of Jaina philosophy. Under Jaina tradition, there is no hitch or hesitation in even declaring the holy texts of Agamic scriptures as illusive in case they are being studied or their knowledge is being acquired by a perverse or a wicked person. The fact remains that those who are stubborn and possess perverted mind, will always misuse even the most sanctified texts in accordance with their own illusive and wrong convictions. Such vitiated habits will never bring sanctity to their lives. The activities of such illusionists are not directed towards spiritual attainments but towards unethical and materialistic pursuits. In other words, even the highest spiritual knowledge or holiest texts may prove futile to redeem them from false illusions and degeneration of mind. The same principle applies vice-versa to the false and non-spiritual texts, adopted by holy sages, having enlightened mind. The activities of such seers who possess thorough knowledge of religion and philosophy, are always directed towards achievement of self-purification, self-control and self-emancipation. They are always apt to make best use of holy texts for their own upliftment and spiritual enlightenment. It is true that even false and illusive texts are availed of by holy saints for their spiritual upliftment as if they were highly accomplished texts and contained higher truths of religion and philosophy. It is the most distinguishing feature of Jaina philosophy and singularly characteristic for devotion to spiritual accomplishments.

Angās/Upangās/Chheda Sutras/Mūl Sutras/Their Brief Interpretations

Amongst Jaina religious scriptures, classified as above in the shape of 'Anga Pravishtya' (principal Agamic Scriptures) and 'Anga Bāhiya' (other auxiliary and allied works), certain works are no longer available and they have vanished with the passage of time. After including a few commentries or glosses in the available canonical literature, the total number of Authentic Agamic Scriptures is now deemed to be 45 according to Idolaters of Shwetamber Sect. They are classified as Angas, Upāngas Chheda and Mūl Sutra Works.

ANGAS

Why named as Angas ?

The religious teachings as enunciated by a Tirthanker or an omniscient, based on the theory that matter is Supreme and the outer form of an article is destructible or in other words—the soul is eternal and the physical frame is mortal-form the contents of Angas which are Sutra-works, composed by Gandhers (Chief disciples). Why the said Sūtra works were called Angas? It is asked spontaneously and its reply is equally clear and unequivocal. The highest spiritual knowledge of Jaina religion and philosophy, as revealed by Tirthankers and memorized by their chief disciples, has been personified as a human-being. Just as a living being has important bodily limbs, similarly, twelve Angas form significant part of Jaina Āgamas. A person has 2 feet + 2 thighs + 2 eyes + 2 front and rear portions of body + 2 arms + one Neck + one head =12Parts. In the same way, 12 Angas form part of Agamic Scriptures and categorized as 'Anga Pravishtya'. The twelfth Anga 'Drishṭivāda' is now extinct and only 11 Angas are in existence.

1. Āyāranga (Achārānga)

The guide-lines with regard to manners of conducting themselves and observance of moral and ethical values, have been laid down in 'Achārānga', to be strictly adhered to by initiated Jaina mendicants. The said Anga is divided in two sections. Each section is sub-divided in Adhyayans (chapters) and each Adhyayan is further sub-divided in Uddeshyās (Illustrations) or Chūlikas (short commentaries). The first section of Āchārānga comprises of 9 Adhyayans and 44 Uddeshas (illustrations). The second section of Āchārānga consists of 3 Chūlikas (Short commentaries), divided in 16 Adhyayans. From linguistic view point, style of composition and the nature of subjects dealt with, it is evident that the contents of first section of Āchārānga are comparatively more ancient. It has been written mostly in prosaic form. However, a few versified compositions are also found here and there. The contents of first section of Āchārānga are really significant for studying of Ardha Māgadhi Prākrita and ascertainment of its main features from linguistic view-point.

The name of the seventh Adhyayan is cited as 'Mahāparigyā' (Thorough knowledge) which is, however, not available and is believed to have become extinct. It is stated that certain miraculous or extra-ordinary Vidyas (Skills) had been incorporated in the said Adhyayan. As soon as a work is reduced to writing, it becomes accessible to all-whether deserving or non-deserving, entitled or not entitled readers. It is possible that Achārya Devardhigaṇi 'Kṣmashramaṇa' may have preferred to ignore or set aside the said Adhyayan, while reducing Agamic Scriptures to writing, apprehending that undesirable elements may have an access to it and misuse the magical formulas to the deteriment of human society. It is purely an assumption. What was the virtual position, cannot be described in a decisive manner? It is also possible that the said Adhyayan may have disappeared later on due to different reasons.

In the ninth Adhyayan named 'Updhān' (Excellence) there is a thrilling account of severe penances practised by Lord Mahavirā. Besides it, there is a detailed description of his religious tours to the teritorial parts of Lādh (Burdhwan distt.); Vajrabhūmi (Mānbhoom and Singhbhoom districts of Bengal) and 'Shubhra Bhoomi' (Kodarma and areas of Hazaribagh district in Bihar) and how he was subjected to innumberable insults and humiliations as also terrible atrocities committed on him by foolish and stupid persons, having evil nature. The heart-rending narration, appearing in the aforesaid ninth Adhyayan, how he had practised self-mortification and had led the life of an austere devout which is not found elsewhere.

Severe Spiritual Performances by Lord Mahāvira and Physical Hardships Undergone by Him

Indra, King of Heaven, had blessed Lord Mahāvirā by placing a divine cloth over his shoulder which remained with him for more than a year. However, he never intended to use it for covering his naked body in winter season. Immedialety after the expiry of the stipulated period, he had abandoned the colth.

While Staying with Households

Sometimes, he happened to live with house-holds, or came in their contact. While he stayed with families, he came across ladies who were charmed with his stout physique and attractive features. They used to seek sexual union with him. However, he used to remain engrossed in meditation and stick to his path of absolute detachment. He avoided speaking with them even if they tried to talk with him. He maintained his silence even on making reverential salutation or paying respectful obeisance. It is very difficult for ordinary people to follow the suit.

Forbearance of Hardships with Equanimity

Whenever he happened to visit territorial parts, inhabited by non-Aryans, the Knaves or evil-natured persons used to beat him with sticks and pluck his hair forcibly, yet he used to forbear all atrocities with absolutely detached mind.

Avoiding to be Excited by Curiosity and Arrogance

He remained totally detached and showed no excitement at the sight of a gathering wherein religious disputation, dancing or singing was going on, nor he was discomposed at the sight of a fierce fighting with fists or sticks. He expressed no pleasure or displeasure on finding the people busy in amoristic conversation or talks. On the contrary, he showed total reluctance or indifference to all this.

Extremely Averse to Hoardings or Worldly Possessions

Lord Mahāvirā put on very meagre clothes to cover his body and always carried with him a pot in his hand for begging alms. He never accepted the clothes or pots, offered by others.

Non-Attachment with Delicious Foods : Not Easy-Going

He had absolutely no fondness for drinking milk or eating curd. In case, a dust-particle fell in his eye, he never rubbed it to take the particle out. Even on feeling itching sensation in his body, he never scratched.

Following Routine Course in Conformity with the Times

He always followed a right course, consistent with Indian tradition. He never side-tracked the path or looked behind. If somebody unnecessarily interrupted him, he observed silence and made no reply.

Not Scared of Cold : After abandoning the divine cloth, he used to walk in winter season by stretching both hands. He neither contracted his arms nor he placed his hands over his shoulders to avoid restlessness due to cold. While on tour, wherever the fourth period of the day (each priod reckoned at 3 hrs) set in and it grew dark, he used to stop there and pass his night.

Life of a True Recluse, having no Fixed Abode at all

Sometimes by staying in vacant places, having only standing walls; rest houses. water-booths; shops; black-smith workshops; under raised platforms; inns outside villages; lonely houses, erected in a garden; within towns; dilapidated portions or structures and by dwelling beneath the trees, he remained absorbed in practising severe penances with an unwavering mind, day and night leading the life of self-denial with absolute dedication. He was quite vigilant and had devoted himself to intense meditation and remained engrossed in the state of spiritual concentration continuously for 13 years.

Total Vigilance against Drowsiness or Sleep

As and when he felt drowsy, he used to get up and sit upright to be roused from sleep. Lord Mahavirā never lied down, whenever he felt drowsy. He used to get-up and roam in open for a short time at night when it was biting cold. He always shed away lethargy by taming his nerves and winning over bodily hardships.

Torturing in Desolate Places

Finding him engrossed in deep concentration, the immoral and depraved persons, who happened to reach there to seek hiding after committing illegal acts, used to torture him for fear of being identified or that he might inform the police. Else the village guards used to terrify him by hitting him with their weapons and force him to leave the place.

Overcoming Numerous Difficulties and Physical Hardships

Men and women, who were infatuated with charming personalty of Lord Mahavirā, used to torture him. At times, finding him alone in a solitary place, where he happened to be excreting, .the thieves and paramours used to ask him—who was he? Why was he standing there? On having no reply, they used to get annoyed and severely beat him.

However, when Lord Mahavirā was not in the state of meditation, he used to make a reply and say that he was an ascetic. In case, they threatened him to leave the place, he used to quit immediately.

During winter season, when people used to shiver in the biting cold and take shelter in a covered place or used to lit fire to warm themselves or search for warm clothes and blankets to cover their bodies to save themselves from piercing cold breeze. At that time, Lord Mahavirā used to sit in open under a tree and bear the pinching cold.

He used to tolerate the pricking sensation by pungent touch of straw, severity of heat and cold and stinging pain when bitten by large or small mosquitos, with detached mind and showing no signs of morose or displeasure.

Hardships Experienced in Territorial Areas of Lādh etc.

While Lord Mahavirā happaned to tour in difficult terrains of Lādh (District-Burdhwan in Bengal), Vajrabhumi (Manbhoom and Singhbhoom districts) and Shubhrabhoomi (areas of Kodarma and Hazaribagh districts in Bihar), he was allowed to stay in most dirty and inferior places or in disturbed ruins or inside dilapidated structures. The small square pieces of mat, provided to sit upon, used to be rough and full of dirt.

Non-Aryan inhabitants of Lādh region used to beat Lord Mahavirā and rush to bite him. He used to get most inferior and dry food and that too with considerable pains. Dogs often pounced upon him to bite. Hardly one person out of those present there, used to prevent those stray dogs from biting him, rest used to incite the dogs to bite him, merely for fun.

In Vajrabhoomi, other religious mendicants, accompanying him, used to carry small wooden sticks or iron tubes (length equal to four fingers) to keep off the dogs. Still, they were bitten by dogs.

In Lādh region, the Village inhabitances were a few and were very remote from each other, so much so, that even after walking all the day long, no village was noticed to stay in, with the result Lord Mahāvirā used to spend the night in open resting under a tree.

Many non-Aryans used to come out of the village and start beating Lord Mahavirā threatening him to keep off and run away from there atonce.

The non-Aryans, living in Lādh region, used to beat him with wooden sticks, strike him with fists, blows, pointed ends of Lances, bricks and stones as also by cupels of pitchers. Sometimes, they did not hesitate to chop off a part of his flesh, throw dust on him or violently throw him down by lifting him up, so much so that they used to push him down while Lord Mahavirā was deeply absorbed in meditation, sitting in specific postures of 'Godohāsana' or 'Veerāsana'.

Embodiment of Unique Patience and Forbearance

Lord Mahavirā practised abstinence and took extremely light food even when he was in sound health. While he was indisposed, he never underwent treatment, or purification of the body by resorting to purgation, vomiting, application of oil, taking bath, getting the body gently pressed and cleaning of teeth etc. He had given up all physical requirements.

He used to carry out the practice of meditation in open at a cold place in winter season and get heated in sunlight of summer season.

He used to feed himself with insipid and stale food like flavourless dry rice, powder of plums, and urd pulse etc. He spent eight months, depending merely on the said three eatables. Many a time, he had abandoned even drinking water continuously for a fortnight or a month. He used to give up eating and drinking continuously for 2 months, 3 months or 6 months. While concluding a fast, he used to take dry and coarse food. Generally, he used to eat after gap of every 2 days, 3 days and even 5 days.

Whenever, he happened to go for begging, he used to slip away gently from the place, in case he saw any animal, bird or a religious mendicant, awaiting food or begging alms there.

He used to accept with detached mind whatever food was offered to him in alms. Whether liquid in the shape of milk or curd, whether dry and stale food and whether black grams, cooked several days earlier.

While settled in different sitting postures, he used to meditate profoundly with immutable mind. He used to contemplate upon the nature of three worlds-heaven, hades or the organic world of birds, animals and plants etc.

From the above elaboration in regard to the contents of 9th Adhyayan, relating to first section of Achārānga, it is evident that the style of composition, method of critical evaluation and enunciation of the subjects, forming part of Achārānga, are really unique with especial significance, and distinguishing features.

What has been stated above is the true depiction of the life of Lord Mahavirā, engaged in spiritual accomplishments. On one hand, it is a living portrayal of the highest spirituality and absolute dedication to lead the life of renunciation and endurance. On the other hand, it also gives a glimpse of erstwhile conditions of certain regions in India.

Second Section of Āchārānga : Its Style of Composition : Contents

The second section of Āchārānga incorporates the rules and sub-rules, to be adhered to by the Jaina mendicants, details of religious austerities to be performed; manifestation of relative mental dispositions; daily goings of the mendicants; observance of cleanliness in eating and drinking; using a bed of leaves for sleeping; scheduled religious trips; staying at a specified place for four months of rainy season; medium of expression; clothes and pots; excretion of urine and faces etc. It is believed that 'Nishithādhyayan' (The texts containing instructions of prohibitive nature to be followed by Jaina mendicants in order to avoid doings of wrong acts), pertaining to'Mahākalpashruta' (Another name for Āchārānga) had been composed on the lines of 20th chapter of third 'Āchārvāstu' (article relating to morality-manner of conducting oneself) relating to 'Pratyakhyan Pūrva' (One of the 14 Pūrvas containing old texts of Jaina religion and philosophy). Truly speaking, Āchārānga is considered as most significant amongst all the 12 Angas (forming part of Agamas).

Interpretative Literature

For elaboration of the texts of Āchārānga an annotation by Achārya Bhadrabāhu, a Chūrṇi (short commentary on the sutras of Achārānga) by Achārya Jinadas Gaṇi; a critical review by Shilānkāchārya' and an elucidation by Shri Jinahans had been written.

Dr. Hermon Jacobi, a noted scholar of Jaina cononical literature, had translated 'Āchārānga' in English and wrote its Foreword in an analytical style. The said translated English version of Āchārānga was published in the 22nd volume of the famous series of 'Sacred Books of the East', printed at Oxford, and edited by renowned scholar on Indology, Prof. F. Maxmuler. The first section of Āchārānga Sūtras was edited by great German scholar, Prof. Walter Shūbing and published in 1910 at Lipzig. Āchārānga was also published in 1935 by 'Āgmodaya Samiti', Bombay, alongwith commentaries of Achārya Bhadrabāhu and Achārya Shilānka.

2. Suyagadanga (Sanskriṭ formation Sutrakritanga)

Various Prākrita Transformations Obtained for Sutrakritanga

Various Prākrita names are found as—'Suyagada', 'Suttakada' and Sūyāgaḍa' etc. for second Anga Sūtakritanga Sanskrita transformation for Prākrita words—'Suyagaḍa' and 'Sūttakaḍa' is 'Sūtrakrita. The literal explanation of this Sanskrit word is—Tirthankers elaborated the meanings of the texts of their speeches which were memorized by their Gandhers and they compiled and composed the said texts in Sutra-works. Thus the sanskrit word 'Sūtrakrita' means (composition in aphoristic style) or the Sutra-works composed in the shape of aphorisms. In other words a Sūtra-work which contains the true philosophy of religion, is called 'Sūtrakrita'. Else, a creation in which the established rules of conduct, relating to oneself and others have been incorporated is called 'Sūyāgaḍa' or 'Sūtrakritā. However, as stated above, the definition that a Sūtra-work which enunciates the philosophical beliefs of one's own and others is more significant. Elaborate discussion of such philosophical notions is found in 'Sūtrakritānga' only and in no other Anga, and this is its speciality.

Nature of Sūtrakritānga : Its Contents

It is divided in two sections. The first section is comprised of 16 Adhyayans and the second section consists of 7 Adhyayans. The first section of 'Sūtrakritānga' is mostly in versified form. Only one Adhyayan is found to have been composed in prose. However, the second section of 'Sūtrakritānga' has been composed in both poetic and prose forms. The said Agamic Scripture has been composed in metres of various types. Besides 'Gatha metres' (Arya metre), 'Indra Vajra' (metres with eleven syllables in each quarter), 'Vaitālika' (Each stanza is of 4 quarters, the first and third of which contain the time of 14 short syllables and the second and fourth sixteen syllables) and a few other metres such as 'Anushthapa' (metre with 8 syllables in a quarter) have also been used.

Discussion of various Doctrines or Isms

The doctrines or theories relating to 5 elements (Earth, water, light, air and sky); knowledge of the Supreme Spirit (Supreme being regarded as impersonal and divested of all quality and action—an all pervading spirit); Monotheism (Knowledge of the identity of the universe and the Supreme Spirit—Non-dual identity especially that of Brahma with the universe or with the soul); Materialism; spiritual ignorance (which makes one consider his self as distinct from the Supreme Spirit and the material world as reality); Abstention from spiritual endeavours (Abstaining from religious performances); Fatalism (Dependance on destiny or fate); Self sub-ordination; Moral disposition; Five forms of mundane consciousness (Under Jaina philosophy); Essential ingredients (Theory of Elementary Substance); have been elaborately discussed in the first section of 'Sūtrakritānga'. There is only a symbolic or vague method of establishing or rejection of a doctrine, found in the said part. It is not specifically clear which of the doctrines had received philosophical recognition and if so, to what extent. It is also possible that these ideologies might not have developed enough to acquire the shape of full fledged philosophical thoughts. The various schools of philosophy, based on the said ideologies might be only in their preliminary process of development. Various expressions of technical nature have been explained with illustrations and metaphorical descriptions, relating to precautions to be taken while begging and after being granted alms; tolerance to be shown against physical hardships experienced or faced in ascetic life; tortures inflicted in different infernal regions, characteristics of a Jaina saint, the fourth stage in the religious life of a Brahmaṇa, when he quits his home and family and lives only on alms; Jaina mendicants; a Jaina mendicant in general and a saint or devotee who has renounced all worldly attachments, wanders about naked and lives on alms as a hermit. Various religious doctrines and creeds, enunciated above are also found to have been elaborately expounded in relative commentaries or explanatory literature.

In the second section of 'Sūtrakritānga', different opinions or doctrines of other sects have been negated and various expressions of technical nature have been defined, such as oneness of human body and soul, enshrined in it and imparting to its life, motion and sensation; omnipotence of Supreme God; fatalism etc. The subjects specifically elucidated in the said section relate to harms of impure food and violation of norms, while begging alms. Incidentally technical terms like earth planet; the dreams of a pregnant women, vowels and consonants as also female characteristics have also been elaborately explained. The name and style of last 'Adhyayan' is 'Nālandiya'. The mutual conversation between Chief

Gandher, Gautama and his close relation, Udaka Pedhālputta at Nālanda (Bihar) has been reproduced in it. Finally, there is a mention of adopting five austerities (Non-Violence, truth, not stealing, celibacy and renunciation of worldly possessions) by 'Udaka Padhālputta' in place of four austerities (During intervening period in between the first and last Tirthankers, there were only 4 austerities required to be observed by religious mendicants).

Besides the significance of 'Sūtrakritānga' for ascertainment of different ideologies, religious doctrines or creeds, it is also unique from linguistic point of view in as much as the ancientness of the said Anga is well established beyond doubt. There is plenteous material in it which calls upon the philologists also to undertake critical study and further investigation.

Other Explanatory Treatises : Achārya Bhadrabāhu had written an annotation on 'Sūtrakritānga'. Achārya Shilanka had written a commentary on it with active co-operation of another scholar, 'Bāharigani'. A gloss had also been written. Its elucidations or explanations had been composed by Harsh, Kula and Sādhuranga. Dr. Herman Jacobi had translated it into English which had been published in the 45th volume of renowed Series "Sacred Books of the East" from Oxford in England.

3. Thānānga (Sthānānga)

The said Anga is classified into 10 'Adhyayans' containing 783 aphorisms. Its contents are different as against the previous two Angas. The number of articles dealt with in each Adhyayan is consistent with the number of said Adhyayan. For instance, in first Adhyayan, the topics relating to one terrestrial world (earth), one immaterial or spiritual world (Having no people); one religion; one irreligion; one established rule of conduct; one convention etc have been discussed. Similarly, in second Adhyayan, there is discussion on subjects or articles which are two in number, such as two performances etc. In the same manner, the number of topics or subjects dealt with in each Adyayan is in uniformity with its number and thus finally, in the tenth Adhyayan, only those articles or objects have been comprehended which are ten in number. The said style of elucidation is really consistent with that of Buddhist treatise 'Anguttar Nikaya' (The work of Gradual Sayings) in Pāli script.

The aforesaid style of dealing with specific items is really excellent. For example, three vedas-Rigveda, Yajurveda and Sāmveda, three types of knowledge religious, material and sensual and trees of three varieties have been discussed. The topic relating to seven prohibitive measures to counteract betrayal of prescribed codes of conduct by religious mendicants of the Jaina organisation founded by Lord Mahavirā. There is also a mention of nine chief disciples of Lord Mahavirā, who had made appropriate endeavours for accomplishment of supernatural faculties, finally leading to the attainment of Tirthankerism (A state of highest perfaction). In this manner, the same number of topics have been discussed as per number of each Adhyayan, which is unique and superb from numerous considerations.

Explanatory Works : Achārya Abhayadeva Suri had written a commentary on 'Sthānānga' in 1063 A.D. He had written glosses on nine. Angas besides the initial two Angas, namely—'Achārānga' and 'Sūtrakritānga' and last one

'Drishṭivāda' (which is no longer available now). He is popularly known as commentator of nine Angas. Achārya Abhayadeva Sūri has speicified the practical difficulties, experienced by a Commentator in doing justice with his comments and with the expectations of learned people from a commentator. It is a reflection on the state of affairs, then prevailing, with regard to sacred treatises. He writes : 'Traditional system of religious teachings having vanished; lack of talents, needed for proper examination and determination; for want of proper prudence and wisdom; advancing of sound reasoning and arguments; lack of Shastras, covering all religious matters, helpful for undertaking critical evaluation and examination; paucity of sharp memory or rememberance; diversification and multiplicity in recitations; incorrect pronunciation or recitation of sacred texts; obscurity and ambiguity of aphorisms; besides variations found here and there, are some of the short comings experienced while writing commentaries. In nutshell, the interpretations of spiritual texts, as adopted and approved by our 'learned scholars or guides are alone acceptable to us and none-else.

4. Samvāyānga

The literal meaning of the word 'Samvāya; is aggregate or collection. The style of composition of this sacred work is some what similar to that of 'Sthānānga. Whereas, 'Sthānānga' is comprised of ten Adhyayans, 'Samvāyānga' consists of 12 Adhyayans. There is description of all 12 Angas and the subjects, dealt with in the said Angas. In accordance with the style of dealing with the same number of topics in consistency with the number of each Adhyayan as in 'Sthānānga', there is reference of 9 Adhyayans relating to the first section of 'Achārānga'; 16 Adhyayans pertaining to the first section of 'Sūtrakritānga' 19 Adyayans of first section of 'Nāyādhamma Kahāo', composition of certain aphorisms relating to Drishtivāda', according to rule of three a deoctrine of Goshalaka, 36 Adyayans concerning 'Uttrādhyayan' 44 Adhyayans, containing religious discourses of Jaina Rishis or Seers; 55 Adhyayans containing utterances of Lord Mahavirā on the night of attaining final salvation and 84,000 Padas or Quarters, relating to 'Vyakhyāpragyapti' (5th Anga). There is reference of Nandi Sūtra as well. It appears from the above narration that 'Nandi Sūtra' had been composed after accomplishment of 12 Angas in aphoristic style.

Order of Narration : In 'Samvāyānga' there is description of 24 Heads (founders of communities or guilds), 24 Tirthankers (Jaina Arhats-sanctified religious teachers); 'Chakravartis'; (Universal monarchs; highly venerable and most adored personalities of their age and holders of 14 precious divine symbols) Baldevas (Elder step-brothers of Vasudevas 9 in number) Vāsudevas (They have dark colour and soverign rulers of 3 Parts of India and holders of 7 precious divine symbols—They are nine in number) alongwith names of parents of each and their places of birth in alphabetical sequence. Thus, the total number of highly respected and most excellent personalities of their age is 54 (Tirthankers 24 + Chakravarties 12 + Vāsudevas 9 + Baldevas 9=54) as detailed in Samvāyānga and not 63. In the above list, appearing in 'Samvāyānga', 9 'Prati-Vāsudevas' (Subordinate or less significant Vāsudevas) have not been included. It appears that the said subordinate Vāsudevas might have been considered as distinguished personalities of their age much after the accomplishment of 'Samvāyānga Sūtra'. The portion of 'Samvāyānga Sūtra' which contains the above narration may be considered as short legendary history of Jaina religion. Undoubtedly, the said portion of 'Samvāyānga' is really unique on which are based the mythological scriptures of Jaina philosoply. In Samvāyānga Sūtra. Lord Rishabh (First Tirthanker of Jaina religion) is stated to be belonging to Kaushala (Name of the region, situated near banks of Saryu river) and Lord Mahavirā to Vaishali (An important and prosperous town in Bihar which was the centre of Lichhavi Republic). It is thus confirmed that Lord Mahavirā belonged to Vaishāli.

There is reference of 72 arts or skills in Samvāyānga Sūtra, including arts of writing; reckoning and calculating; using metaphorical expressions; dramaturgy; lyrical compositions; and playing on musical instruments etc. Besides them, there is reference of 18 Scripts including Brāhmi script and its 46 diagrammatic alphabets. Achārya Abhaya Deva Sūri has written the commentary on 'Samvayanga Sūtra.

5. Vivāhā Paṇṇatti (Vyākhya Pragyapti)

Since there is vivid description of the world of organic and inorganic creation in the said Anga, hence it has been named as 'Vyākhyā Pragyapti' (Detailed elaboration or explanation). Summarily, it is known as 'Bhagwati Sutra' as well. It contains 41 collections of one hundred stanzas each and each collection is further divided in a number of illustrations. There are ten illustrations relating to each shataka numbering first to eight, twelth to fourteenth, and eighteenth to twentieth. Besides them, there are varying number of illustratives of remaining shatakas. Fifteenth shataka of 100 stanzas has no illustratives. The said collection contains biographical sketch of Goshālaka, son of Makhli. It appears as an independent work in itself. We also find 'Sūtra-wise classification of 'Vyākhyā Pragyapti'. It contains 867 Sūtras (aphorisms) in all.

Style of Composition : The style of composition of Vyākhyā Pragyapti is in the shape of questions and answers. Chief Gandher, Gautama, used to ask and Lord Mahavirā used to reply his questions. According to Achārya Abhaya Deva Sūri, author of the commentary on Anga in question, the number of such questions and answers is 36,000. He writes that 'Vyākhya Pragyapti' is comprised of 2,88,000 verses. As against it, the total number of verses on 'Samvāyānga Sūtra' is 84,000 and in 'Nandi Sūtra' is 1,44,000.

At certain places the questions and their answers are in extremely concise form such as :

Q : Your Holiness! What is the shape of knowledge or consciousness?
Ans : Knowledge derived from wordly experience.
Q : What is the fruit of wordly experience?
Ans : Self denial.
Q : What is the effect of self-refutation?
Ans : Self-control.

On the other hand, there are very lengthy answers to certain questions" Fifteenth shataka of 100 stanzas (Verses) is its example which exclusively contains the life-sketch of Goshālaka only.

Encyclopaedia of Jaina Religion

By way of questions and answers, the interpretations and explanations relating to Jaina philosoply, metaphysics, historical accomplishments, many eventful occurrences and description of individuals together with multiple allied matters, have grown so extensive and voluminous that it may not be an exaggeration to treat 5th Anga, 'Vyākhyā Pragyapti' as an encyclopaedia of Jaina religion.

Other Sacred Works also Referred to

In order to summarize the lengthy discussions and give them the shape of authentic versions, repeated references of the relevant extracts, appearing in 'Pragyāpnā Sutra'; 'Jiwabhigama', 'Auppātika Sūtra', (An Agamic Scripture) and 'Nandi Sūtra' have been made and quoted wherever found necessary. The author of 'Nandi Sūtra' is believed to be Achārya Devardhigaṇi 'Kṣmashramana' who was the convenor and President of Vallabhi Convention in Saurashtra. The achievements of Vallabhi convention are also found recorded in 'Vyākhyā Pragyapti' which leads us to infer that the said Anga had been accomplished in the present shape sometimes by the year 527 A.D., approximately after expiry of 1000 years from the final salvation of Lord Mahāvirā. The same inferance can be drawn in respect of other Angas as well. However, the contents of 'Vyakhyā Pragyāpti' are decidedly too old and handed down traditionally as revealed by religious preceptors having been heard and retained in memory by their disciples.

Historicity of the Contents

The topics relating to biographical sketch of Lord Mahāvira, his principal disciples and followers including household devotees as well as other ascetics have been elaborately dealt with in the said Anga and all these contents are most significant from historic viewpoint. In the seventh collection of 100 stanzas, there is reference of two fierce battles fought between emperor Ajātshatru of Magadha dynasty on one side and his maternal grandfather King Chetaka on the other. Emperor Ajātshatru had performed severe penance for 3 days and acquired supernatural powers. Accordingly, on the first day even the small pieces of stones, straw and leaves, thrown by the army of Emperor Ajātshatru struck the soldiers of King Chetaka as if attacked by huge rocks or large pieces of stones, killing the soldiers instantaneously. On the first day, nearly 84 lacs soldiers were killed. Next day, emperor, Ajātshatru got seated in a chariot, built by celetial bodies. Emperor Ajātshatru and his soldiers attacked the army of king Chetaka by swirling round their pestles and brandishing them like swords, butchered nearly 96 lacs soldiers of Chetaka's army on the second day. These battles are unparallel and unique from historical, political and military technological (strategic warfare) viewpoints. Mention of various regions in Vyākhayā Pragyāpti, namely, Anga (Territory situated on the right bank of river Ganges, very near the modern Bhagalpur in Bihar)' Banga (Territory of East Bengal including Tripura and Gāro hills); Malaya (One of the seven principal chains of mountains in India. It is to be identified with the Southern portion of the Ghats running from the south of Mysore and forming the eastern boundary of Travancore); Mālvaya (The modern Mālvā in Central India); Achchhā; Vachchha; Kochchha; Dādh; Lādh; (Territory lying to the west of Narmada river including Baroda and Ahemdabad)' Mauli; Kāsi; Kaushal (Territory situated along the banks of river Saryu); Abāha; Sumuttar etc. pointed out the erstwhile geographical regions in India. There is elaborate information regarding biographical and life events, ideology, religious activities and performances of Goshālaka, son of Makhali, founder of 'Ājivakā' Sect and an arch rival of Lord Mahāvirā which is not available in such an exhaustive manner elsewhere. There is a repeated mention of the subsequent followers and disciples of Lord Pārshwanath and the four great austerities (non-violence, truth, celibacy and renunciation), observed by them. It is thus evident that an independent sect, following the tenets of Jaina religion known as 'Nirgranth Sect' was already in existence right from the age of 23rd Tirthanker, Lord Pārshwanath, to the era of Lord Mahavirā. The said 'Nirgranth Sect' had started following 5 great austerities (Total renunciation of violence, falsehood, theft, unchastity or non-celibacy and worldly possessions etc.) in place of four and the followers of Nirgrantha sect had begun joining the religious organisation of Lord Mahāvirā).

Besides commentary, written by Achārya Abhaya Deva Suri, there is an annotation and a small gloss or exposition, written by Dān Shekhar.

6. 'Nāyādhammakahāo' (Gyāta Dharmakathā or Gyātri Dharmakathā in Sanskrit)

Interpretation of the name : There can be 3 adaptations in Sanskrit of Prākrita word, 'Nāyādhammakahāo'—'Gyatā Dharmakathā', 'Gyatridharmakathā' and 'Nyāya Dharmakathā'. The words 'Gyatā' Dharmakathā' have been defined in *Abhidhān Rajendra Kosh* that the literal meaning of the word 'Gyāta' is illustration. The religous discourses with illustrations are given in this Scripture. It may also be elucidated that in the first section of this Agamic Scripture are given illustrations while the religious discourses are found in the second section of the said Anga.

The words 'Gyātri Dharmakathā' also signify that the scripture in question contains religious discourses, delivered by Lord Mahavirā, belonging to a highly learned family. The sacred Anga under reference is generally known by this name.

The third adaptation in Sanskrit is 'Nyāya Dharmakathā' which means that this scripture contains religious sermons, relating to morality or prudent conduct with sacred rules or precepts, duly illustrated with examples.

Shape of the SAID Scripture : Its Contents

The said Agamic Scripture is classified in two sections. The first section consists of 19 Adhyayans and the second section is sub-divided into 10 Adhyayans. The first Adyayan of first section of the 6th Anga, under reference, contains the story of Prince Meghkumār, given birth by Queen Dhārini, wife of Emperor Bimbsār, ruler of Rajgraha. As soon as the prince grew to be a young man, having acquired the knowledge of several arts and disciplines consistent with his royal grace and splendour, it so happened that the prince listened to religious sermons delivered by Lord Mahavirā. He developed a feeling of indifference towards worldly pleasures. He attained initiation. However, while leading the life of an ascetic, he had entertained slight weakness. He was perplexed and thought that he had committed grave blunder by forsaking royal pleasures and adopting the life of a religious mendicant. However, when Lord Mahavirā narrated the history of his previous birth, he regained strength and exercised control over self with greater resoluteness of mind. There are similar episodes in other Adhyayans as well in order to provide stimulation to practice severe penances, to lead the life of self-denial and total renunciation and to exercise control over-self. In eighth Adhyayan, there is short story of Malli, the princess of Videha (the region lying to the north-east of Magadha. Its capital was Mithila) and in 16th Adhyayan, there is a narrative of Draupadi of her previous birth. Both the tales are most important from historical viewpoint.

The second section of 6th Anga in question is classified in 10 chapters or sub-divisions. These chapters generally incorporate legendary tales of chief or principal Queens of divine kings, Indras, reigning over different heavens.

Achārya Abhaya Deva Sūri has written its commentary, which was modified by Dronachārya. From what has been written by Abhaya Deva Sūri in appreciation of the said scripture (Sixth Anga), it is explicit that the sacred texts were recited in many ways in those days.

7. Upāsaga Dasāo (Upāsaka Dashā)

Name : Its Interpretation

The literal meaning of Sanskrit word 'Upāsaka' is a house-hold votary (as distinguished from a Bhikṣu) and that of 'Dashā' is a state or condition of mind, dedicated to observe as far as possible all the five austerities, namely, abnegation of violence, falsehood, stealing, unchastity and hoarding.

Contents : The said Anga is comprised of ten Adhyayans, which contain the episodes of ten votaries or house-hold worshippers. The religious precepts or observances to be adhered to by Jaina votaries have been elaborately explained with the help of the said narratives. It has also been stressed that the devotees or followers are bound to be confronted with numerous difficulties, obstacles and seductions in the course of discharging their religious obligations. However, they never get frustrated or give up their religious pursuits. At the end, the gist of the main subjects, discussed by way of production of 10 episodes, cited above, has been incorporated in last 12 verses.

A Supplement to Āchāranga : The texts of the seventh Anga, in question, supplements Achārānga. Whereas, in Āchāranga, the religious obligations of Jaina Bhikṣus have been discussed, in 'Upasakadashā', the religious performances to be made by family devotees or houshold votaries of Jaina religion, have been discussed. The topics relating to the life style of Ananda and similar other devotees, belonging to highly rich and prosperous families as also the financial conditions of the common masses have been dealt with at length in the said Agamic Scripture. Achārya Abhayadeva Sūri has written a commentary on it.

8. Antagadadasāo (Antakriddashā)

Name : Its Interpretation

The great Jaina saints who had attained final salvation after practising severe penances, and self meditation. They had ended their lives and redeemed themselves from the vicious circle of repeated births and deaths or transmigration. They came to be known 'Antakrit' (having gone to the end of or were thoroughly conversant with). Since there is description of such sanctified religious teachers or divinities in the 8th Anga, in question, it is styled 'Antakriddashā'. It is divided into eight parts. The first part is further sub-divided into 10 Adhyayans, the second part into 8 Adhyayans, the third part has 13 Adhyayans, the fourth part comprises of 10 Adhyayans, the fifth part consists of 10 Adhyayans, the sixth part contains 16 Adhyayans, the seventh part is sub-divided into 13 Adhyayans and the 8th part has 10 Adhyayans. In the said scripture, the episodes are not complete. Therefore, it has been advised to refer 'Vyakhyā Pragyapti' (5th Anga) or 'Gyatridharmakathā' (6th Anga) for fuller details of the said stories.

A Problem : The comments appearing in 'Sthānaga' (3rd Anga) on 'Antakriddasha' do not conform with its present form. Therein it is stated that the said scripture is classified into ten Adhyayans, namely:—1. Nami Adhyayan; 2. Mātanga Adhyayan; 3. Somila Adhyayan; 4. Rāmgupta Adhyayan; 5. Sudarshan Adhyayan; 6. Jamāli Adhyayan; 7. Bhagāli Adhyayan; 8. Kiṁ Karmapallita Adhyayan; 9. Fālita Adhyayan and 10. Manditaputra Adhyayan.

It is quite possible that originally the scripture, in question, may have been classified into 10 Adhyayans only alike 'Upāsaka Dashā' and later it might have multiplied with the passage of time and assumed its present form. Just as there are small episodes of house-hold votaries or devotees in 'Upāsakadashā', similarly, the narratives of highly sanctified religious teachers and guides might have been incorporated in 'Antkriddashā' and style of composition of said narratives is almost identical.

In the eighth Adhyayan of third part of 'Antakriddashā, the tale of Gajasukumāl, son of Devaki, is given which is specifically worth mention. The said episode has been brought forth in subsequent writings in an enlarged and lengthy form. Similarly, in third Adhyayan of sixth part of the said scripture, the story of Arjuna, gardener appears which is considered as most important in canonical literature of Jaina religion. Several Commentaries have been written on the said episode. The eighth part of the said Anga deals with several types of penances, fasts (abstaining from every kind of sensual gratification) and austerities to be performed by Jaina monks.

9. Anuttarovāviyadasāo (Anuttaropātika Dashā)

Name : Interpretation

In the above-noted scripture, there are small legendary stories of certain distinguished personages who had secured birth in a class of gods in heaven and had attained final salvation through spiritual exercises, performance of severe penances and observance of trance meditation. The Sanskrit title *Anuttaropātika* is a compound of two words 'Anuttar' (A Class of Gods in heaven with Jainas) and 'Uppāt' (birth, origin). Thus the name of 9th Anga is true to the meanings of the words and true to the sense thereof.

The said Agamic Scripture is classified into three parts. The first part comprises of 10 Adhyayans; second part consists of 13 Adhyayans and the third part contains 10 Adhyayans. The portrayal of the characters (Life sketches of distinguished personages) is not complete or exhaustive in the said Adhyayans. Only short narratives have been given with an indication to find out detailed stories elsewhere. However, the portrayals of 'Jāli', son of 'Dhariṇi' in the first part and 'Dhanya' son of 'Bhadra' in the third part have been reproduced more elaborately. All the austerities, prescribed for religious mendicants and performed by Dhanya as also his declining health as a consequence thereof, are some of the topics, discussed therein which remind us how Lord Buddha was reduced to a skeleton after practising severe penances, the detailed description of which apears in Buddhist Pali scriptures, namely, 'Mahasīhnādasuatta' and 'Kassapasihnādasutta'.

Present Form : Incomplete : Erroneous : It appears that the present appearance of ninth Anga is incomplete and erroneous. There is also a reference of its ten chapters in Sthananga' (3rd Anga). It appears that originally, it may have its sub-divisions in the shape of 'Adhyayans like earlier seventh and eighth Angas as discussed in foregoing pages, while now it is found classified in 3 parts only.

10. Paṇhavāgarṇāiṁ (Prashna Vyākarana)

Whether Consistent with its Name

Two words 'Prashna' (Questions) and Vyakarṇa (Grammatical analysis or exposition) have been compounded to constitute the name of the holy work, under discussion, which literally means-analytical replies or explanations of the questions placed. However, the contents, as available now, are not consistent with the name of the scripture. They are not in the form of questions and their answers.

Its Present Shape : The edition of the sacred treatise, as available now, is classified in two parts. The first part deals with the impulse called yoga or attention which the soul participates in the movement of its various bodies; it is defined as the 'action of the senses which impels the soul towards external objects'. These objects may be good or evil as per direction of the soul. Five entrances of the senses which impel the soul to fall prey to transgression and self-tormenting acts, namely-violence; falsehood; stealing, unchastity and hoarding of worldly possessions, have been dealt with at length. The second part deals with five particular religious observances, such as non-violence, truth, not stealing, celibacy and absolute renunciation, which have been discussed in detail. Besides the commentary of Achārya Abhaya Deva Suri, Achārya Nayavimal has also written an annotation on it.

Its Present Form : A Critical Review : In 'Sthananga Sūtra' (The third Anga), there is reference of ten Adhyayans as sub-divisions of 'Prashna-Vijākaraṇa' (10th Anga under discussion), namely—'Upamā' (Similes-expressive of); 'Sankhya' (Reckonings); 'Rishibhāshita' (Utterances of Jaina sages); 'Achāryabhashita' (Speeches of spiritual guides or preceptors); 'Mahavir-bhāshita (Utterances of Tirthanker, Lord Mahavirā); 'Kṣomaka Prashna' (Questions relating to a specific Vidya, meant for invoking a deity on cloth); 'Komal Prashna' (Questions relating to delicate subjects); 'Adarsha Prashna, (model questions); 'Bāhuprashna' (Questions with regard to specific vidyā, by application of which, the deity is invoked on arm).

In 'Nandi Sutra', the subjects as dealt with in 'Prashna Vyākarna' have been cited as 108 questions placed by senior disciples or devotees; 108 answers, given by omniscients without actually, putting forward any questions; 108 answers of both questions and without questions, 'Angushtha Prashna' (Quesions relating to thumbs); 'Bāhu Prashna' (Questions concerning Arms) 'Adarsh Prashna' (Questions with regard to the specific Vidya for invoking deties on mirror glass); Divya Vidyas (Super human Vidyas for application of spells by enchanting Mantras) and subduing of divine powers like 'Nāgkumar' and 'Swarna Kumar' and how to establish communion with them to obtain their divine bliss.

The nature of questions and answers as discussed in 'Sthananga' and 'Nandi' Sutras is nowhere found in 'Prashna Vyakarna', now available. Hence it may not be wrong to infer that its original form, as cited in 'Sthānānga' and 'Nandi' Sūtras did not survive. Probably, it had vanished with the passage of time.

11. Vivāgsuya (Vipāka Shruta)

The good or bad results of auspicious and inauspicious or sinful acts done in this or previous births, have elaborately discussed in the above-noted scriptural work. Accordingly, it is titled as 'Vipākshruta' or 'Vipāka Sūtra' (sacred knowledge concerning results of actions in present or past (births). It is classified in two parts. The first part deals with adversities and calamities befalling as a result of evil acts and the second part incorporates pleasures and happiness, obtained by us as a consequence of our auspicious and virtuous acts. Each part consists of 10 Adhyayans which contain an analytical description of sorrowful and joyful results of actions performed by living beings in their present and past lives.

In Jaina philosophy, the religious theory that auspicious or inauspicious propensities of our soul attract the small particles of the body and activate them into actions as also pleasant and unpleasant results of our actions in the present or previous births, have been elaborately discussed which is really unique and considered most significant in the philosophical literature of the world. The 11th Anga 'Vipaka Shruta' is extremely useful so far as the theory of 'Karmas' as per Jaina philosophy is concerned that one has to face the consequences of ones actions good or bad, has been enunciated in it with illustrations. Here and there, we find references in it of blind persons, walking with the support of lathis for begging alms as also of patients, suffering from terrible diseases like Asthma, catarrh, cough, fistula, itching sensation and leprosy etc. Similarly, some people are found cruelly admonished, beaten and crying with pain or distressed at the hands of State officials with cruelty. Narratives concerning longings of pregnant women, human sacrifices, acts of seducing by prostitutes, numerous meat and sweet-meat preparations also appear in the scripture, under reference. It also deals with primitive beliefs, human tendencies, customary practices, crimes and offences etc. The said scripture is highly useful for critical study of social order of that period.

The above scripture has been named in'Sthānānga' as 'Kammavivāgaḍasāo. Alike 'Upāsaga Dasāo' (7th Anga); 'Antagada-dasāo (8th Anga) and 'Paṇhāvāgaraṇadasāo' (10th Anga), the 11th Anga is also comprised of 10 Adhyayans, namely—1. Mrigāputra Adhyayan. 2. Gotrās Addyayan; 3. Aṇḍa Adhyayan; 4. Shakaṭa Adhyayan; 5. Brāhmana Adhyayan; 6. Nandishena Adhyayan; 7. Saukarika Adhyayan; 8. Udamber Adhyayan; 9. Sahasdāh Āmalak Adhyayan and 10. Kumār Laxmi Adhyayan.

However, ten Adhyayans relating to first section of 'Vipāka Sūtra', now available, are as follows :

1. Mrigāputra Adhyayan; 2. Ujjhita Adhyayan; 3. Abhagga (Abhagna) Sena Adhyayan; 4. Shakaṭa Adhyayan; 5. Brahaspati Adhyayan; 6. Nandi Adhyayan; 7. Umber Adhyayan; 8. Shauryadatta Adhyayan; 9 Devadutta Adhyayan; and 10. Anju Adhyayan.

The Adhyayans relating to the second part of the said scripture are as under :

1. Subāhu Adhyayan; 2, Bhadra Nandi Adhyayan; 3. Sujāta Adhyayan; 4. Suvāsava Adhyayan; 5. Jina Das Adhyayan; 6. Dhanpati Adhyayan. 7. Mahābala Adhyayan; 8. Bhadra Nandi Adhyayan, 9. Mahāchandra Adhyayan and 10. Vardatta Adhyayan.

The first Adhyayan incorporating the tale of Subahu Kumar, relating to the second part of the Scripture in question is comprehensive while remaining nine Adhyayans are extremely concise. There are mere references of various characters. After making the name of the character known, its story has been abreviated in each Adhyayan. The study of the characters is only in name with nominal description. The names of the following Adhyayans, relating to 'Kammavivāgadasāo', as appeared in 'Sthānānga' and those pertaining to the first part of 'Vipaka Sutra', under reference, are somewhat similar in name :

Sthānānga Sūtra	*First Part of Vipāka Sūtra*
1. Mrigaputra Adhyayan	Mrigaputra Adhyayan
4. Shakaṭa Adhyayan	Shakaṭa Adhyayan
6. Nandishena Adhyayan	Nandi (Nandishena) Adhyayan
7. Umber Adhyayan	Udambar Adhyayan

On having a comparative view it may not be deemed difficult to believe that the shape of 'Vipāka Sūtra' might have partly remained intact while partly disturbed or changed in words or contents. There might have occurred slight variation in seriatim of Adhyayans also.

12. Dithvāya (Drishtivāda)

Synonyms of Drishtivāda as Given in 'Sthanānga'

While dealing with Pūrvās (Old texts of highest spiritual knowledge and philosophy of Jaina religion), it had been stated that the 12th Anga 'Drishtivāda' had vanished with the passage of time and it was no longer available. Ten synonymous names are found in 'Sthanānga', namely :

1. Drishtivāda; 2. Hetuvāda; 3. Bhūtvāda; 4. Tatvavāda; 5. Samyakvāda; 6. Dharmavāda; 7. Bhāshāvijaya; 8. Purvagata; 9. Anuyoga gata and 10. Sarvapranabhūt Jiva Satva Sukhāvaha. In Samvāyānga (4th Anga) Dristhivāda is stated to be classified into 5 distinct parts : 1. Parikarma, 2. Sūtra; 3. Pūrvagata; 4. Anuyoga and 5. Chūlika.

As appeared in 'Sthānānga Sūtra', the eighth synonym of Drishtivāda is 'Pūrvagata'. At the same time, the third part of Drishtivāda is 'Pūrvagata'. Thus the word 'Pūrvagata' has appeared as synonym of 'Drishtivāda' on one hand and as one of its constituents on the other. It appears that this word has been used in a different sense, when used as both a synonym of Drishtivāda and as one of its divisions. The word 'Drishtivāda' is to be seen in its totality. Thus, where the word 'Pūrvagata' has been used as synonym of 'Drishtivāda' it carries the same sense as the latter. However, where the word 'Pūrvagata' has appeared as one of its constituent parts, it means a part or component of Drishtivāda which is indicative of old spiritual and philosophical knowledge of Jaina religion, contained in 14 Pūrvas.

Literally, Drishtivāda and Pūrvagata (old spiritual texts incorporated in 14 Pūrvas) do not appear to have identical meaning or sense. We shall, therefore, be required to consider over it minutely. As a matter of fact, the true and highest spiritual knowledge, forming part of 14 Pūrvas, is so exhaustive that the entire religious and philosophical knowledge of Jaina religion is covered thereunder. Nothing remains uncovered. Consequently a scholar, well conversant with the texts of 14 Pūrvas, having retentive memory is considered at par with an omniscient. Besides Pūrvagata, Drishtivāda has been divided in other parts as well for specific study and pursuit of knowledge, relating to any other knowledge, made by critical investigation. Certain prominent subjects, specific wings of knowledge, which have greater relivance with our life require more application and steady pursuit. It appears that in order to categorize the religious learning into an average or superior one, the above classification of Drishtivāda has been made. In other words, although the entire spiritual and philosophical knowledge of Jaina religion is contained in 'Pūrvagata', even then the subjects dealt with in other branches of Drishtivāda are also to be studied minutely.

Further Classification of Drishtivāda : It is stated above that 'Drishtivāda' has five components. However, further sub-divisions have been made of those branches for better comprehension. It is learnt from the study of 'Parikarma' a branch of 'Drishtivāda' that subjects, relating to 'art of writing' and mathematics have been discussed therein. Under 'Sūtra' branch of Drishtivāda, the various traditions of deliberating and analytical, discussions, namely—'Chhinna Chhedanaya' 'Vichchinnachhedanaya' and 'Chaturnaya' were adopted. While the lines of 'Chhinna Chhedanaya' and 'Chaturnaya' were followed by Jaina scholars, the method of 'Achhinnachhedanaya; was adopted by the scholars of 'Ājavaka Sect'. However, with the passage of time both lines came to be amalgamated and became part and parcel of Jaina philosophy.

Purpose of Anuyogas : The fourth constituent of 'Drishtivāda' is Anuyoga. It is of two types 'Prathmānuyoga' and 'Gandikānuyoga'. The Prathmanuyoga contains narratives relating to pregnancies, births, practising of severe penances and attainment of sacred knowledge, derived from meditation on higher truths of religion and philosophy by Tirthankers and omniscients while 'Gandikānuyoga' contains brief life sketches of 'Kulkars' (Heads of noble families) 'Chakravarties' (Highly respected monarchs of 6 parts of India and holders of 14 gems-first gem in the shape of a wheel). Baldevas (Elder step motherly brothers of Vasudevas. They are nine in number) and Vasudevas (They get incarnated on earth from heaven or hell as per their Karmās of previous biths. They are dark in colour and are absolute rulers of 3 parts of India. They are nine in number) and similar other eminent or distinguished personages. From the nature of subjects, dealt with in Annyoga, it may be treated as the body of Jaina mythology or philosophy. Under Digamber tradition, it is generally known as 'Prathmānuyoga' only.

While defining the word 'Chūlika', being 5th constituent of 'Drishtivāda', it is cited that Chūlika literally means a crest or top. Just as there are crests of Meru mountain (Name of a fabulous mountain, round which all the planets are said to revolve and which forms the centre of several islands). Similarly, the Chūlikas are collections or compositions of explained or unexplained meanings or explanations of the subjects dealt with in 'Parikarma', "Sūtra, Pūrvagata; and Anuyoga, the four constituents of 'Drishtivāda. According to the annotator, the texts of 'Parikarma', 'Sūtra'; 'Pūrvagata' and 'Anuyaga', which could not be properly explained, have been commented upon elaborately in the said Chūlikas (commentaries). The Chūlikas relate to four constituents of Drishtivāda. According to Digamber Sect, Chūlika the fifth constituent of 'Drishtivāda' has been sub-divided in five parts—1. Jalgata; 2. Māyāgata; 3 Rūpagata; 4. Sthalgata; and 5. Akāshagata. It is presumed that the subjects, dealt with in the said 5 types of Chūlikas, probably related to conjuring, magical tricks, spells and incantations which were basically wrong on or inconsistent with the philosophical doctrines of Jaina religion and its stress on undertaking thorough investigation or making a critical appreciation of spiritual matters before relying faith on or following them. Therefore, such irreligious beliefs or tricks could not last long, since they were alien to the ideology of spiritual advancement and attainment of final emancipation requisits of Jaina religion.

Twelve Upāngas (Supplementary Writings to the main Angas)

Supplementary Writings (Upāngas)

From ancient days the spiritual texts of Jaina religion have been categorized as 'Anga Pravishtha' (Spiritual texts in the shape of 12 Angas, compiled and composed by Gandhers and forming part of Agamic Scriptures) and 'Anga Bāhya' (Other spiritual texts, composed by Sthaviras and having lesser significance as compared to 12 Angas, which contain highest spiritual knowledge). In 'Nandi Sūtra', Anga Bāhiya has been further sub-classified into 'Kalika' (which is studied or recited during fixed hours only—say during initial three hours and last three hours in day and night) and 'Utkālika' (Which is studied any time without restriction of fixed hours). The scriptural treatises which are of auxiliary nature and supplement 12 Angas, form part of 'Anga Bāhya'. The supplementary works to 12 Angas are also 12 in number. There is no explanation as to what led to the composition of auxiliary works to supplement the main Angas. Agamas—Vedas of Jaina religion, have been personified as a living person. Just as 12 Angas were accomplished by Gandhers in aphoristic style to meet the requirements of bodily limbs of Agamas personified, similarly, it might have been found essential to compose supplementary texts to elucidate the texts of 12 Angas. No more explanation or historical evidence is available to corroborate the point. The word 'Upānga' has appeared in 'Tatvārtha Bhāshya' (Commentary on Jaina philosophy), written by Achārya Umāswāti.

Angas : Upangas : No Similarity or Resemblance

Twelve Angas were composed by Gandhers (chief disciples of Tirthankers). They have their own texts of highest spiritual nature. Upāngas were composed by Sthaviras and the texts, contained therein, are different. The Angas and Upangas have no similarity or resemblance at all so far as the subjects, dealt with therein, are concerned. For instance, the first Upanga ought to have been related to first Anga so far presentation and critical evaluation of the subjects is concerned. However, it is not so. Similar position is there in respect of all other Upāngas. In case, they had any consistent relation with Angas, they ought to have been their supplements, which is, however, not the case. How these writings came to be known as Upāngas, is not clear and no distinct and viable explanation or answer is available.

Vedāngas : Vedas hold a unique place in all ancient scriptural writings of India. In order to help in the correct pronunciation and interpretation of Vedic texts, it was considered necessary to compose auxiliary works, known as Vedāngas. The Vedāngas are six in number, namely—1. Shikṣha (the science of proper articulation and pronunciation); 2. Vyakarṇa (grammatical analysis regarding etymology of a word); 3. Chhandas (the science of prosody); 4. Nirukta (etymological explanation of difficult Vedic words); 5. Jyotish (Astronomy) and 6. Kalpa (ritual or ceremonial). Without apprehending the Vedāngas, it may not be easy to pick up and comprehend Vedic texts as also to follow the rituals, prescribed for performance of Yajnas. Hence the study of Vedāngas is considered essential in order to understand the vedic texts.

Composition of Upāngas (Supplementaries) to Vedas

Besides the aforesaid six Vedāngas, it was found necessary to compose another four auxiliary works, known as Upāngas, for comprehension and making it easy to follow the true meanings of the Vedic texts by people of average intelligence. The said auxiliary works include Purāṇās (Sacred works—these are 18; they are supposed to have been composed by Vyāsa and contain the whole body of Hindu mythology); 'Nyāya' (The philosophical system of Nyāya school founded by sage 'Gautama', Mimāmsā (one of the six chief Darshanas or systems of Indian philosophy) and 'Dharma Shāstra' (Theological or religious jurisprudence). The said 'Upāngas' had been accomplished, because of their inevitability and they met the desired object as well. Obviously, the study and apprehension of Vedic texts became considerably easy.

Upvedās (A class of writings, subordinate to the Vedas)

The four Up-Vedas were, also accomplished, namely—'Ayurveda' (Indian Medicinal system); 'Gāndharva Veda' (The science of music); 'Dhanurveda' (The part of Yajurveda which dealt with the art and science of archery) and 'Arthashāstra' (Political Economy). Each Upveda is attached to each of the four Vedas. Thus Āyurveda is attached to Rigveda; 'Dhanurveda' to 'Yajurveda', 'Gandharva Upveda' to Sāmveda and Arthashāstra to Atharva Veda.

The significance of six Vedāngas and four Upangas is established beyond doubt. However, how far four Upvedas supplemented the Vedas is not very clear. For instance, Gandharva Veda can be considered to be attached to Sāmveda. Similarly, the consistent relationship with other Upvedas can also be proved with their respective main Veda. It is never difficult to establish remote relationship or consistency between two objects but it may at best amount to aptness in argumentation and shrewdness in presentation here. Infact, there is no anxiety there to observe or ratify any truth. The prefix 'Up', when applied to a word, must necessarily show that it is supplementing the original and how far this aim is being accomplished is to be examined here. For example, 'Gandhara Upveda' may be treated to be attached to Samveda but how it supplemented Samveda or for want of which Samveda would have been incomplete does not appeal to the mind. The relationship between 'Gandharva Upveda and 'Samveda is established to an extent. However, it is not so in case of other Upvedas. Why then the said Upvedas had been accomplished? No satisfactory answer is found to this question. Probably, there might have been intense anxiety amongst the scholars to establish consistency of popular scriptures like 'Dhanurveda' etc. with main divine Vedic texts.

Upāngas (Auxiliary Sacred Works of Jaina Agamic Scriptures) : Their Critical Review in the Light of above Discussion

'Anga Pravishtha' (12 Angas, forming part of Agamic scriptures), containing highest spiritual and philosophical knowledge are, the most authentic scriptures of Jaina religion. The contents of 12 Angas are in accordance with the utterances or teachings of Tirthankers and omniscients. The authenticity of other canonical works, distinctly separate from 12 Angas (which had been composed by Sthaviras) depended on how far they were consistent with the sacred texts of 12 Angas. The supplementary writings or works, called Upangas, having lesser significance as compared to highest spiritual knowledge, contained in 12 Angas, are treated as 'Anga Bahya' (spiritual texts of secondary nature). However, it is not explicit whether it was at all necessary to accomplish 12 Auxiliary works in the shape of 12 Upāngas and how for they helped in elucidation of Agamic texts. Attention has already been drawn towards the points discussed already in this regard.

It appears that erudite Jaina scholars might have also been allured to name their own religious treatises of secondary significance as Upāngas alike six Vedangas and four Upangas (Suplementaries to Vedas) which had been accomplished for expounding Vedic texts. Besides systematization of spiritual texts and impressiveness in naming their auxiliary spiritual works as Upāngas, was there any other impellent as well is the matter to be investigated and critically examined by our young scholars. These are somewhat scattered and unconsolidated views in regard to Jaina Upangas (Supplementaries to Agamic texts). Accordingly, responsibility now rests upon young talented scholars of Jaina religion to undertake further investigation in this regard.

1. Uvavaiya (Ovāiya) (Aupapātika in Sanskrit)

Literal meaning of the word 'Aupapātika'

The literal meaning of the word 'upapāta' is manifestation or appearance. It also means obtaining another life or birth. This word is also found to signify moving vertically upward or attaining salvation. The Upānga in question contains the stories of those taking rebirths in hell or heaven and also those attaining final salvation. Hence the Upānga has been named as 'Aupapātika'.

Contents: In the Agamic Scripture, noted above, it has been discussed in an attractive manner, how the living-beings attain repeated births in other existences, as a consequence of their miscellaneous acts, ideas, feelings and spiritual endeavours, quoting numerous instances and illustrations. The main features or significance of the said upānga being that it incorporates vivid accounts of towns, gardens, trees, large earthen slabs, kings, queens, human-gatherings, assemblies of celetial bodies, excellent merits of Lord Mahāvira, elaborate description of his physical charm, 34 superhuman qualities, attributed to him, virtues of Jaina monks, illustrations of meritorious Jaina saints, 354 types of penances, undergone by Jaina Sādhus to mortify their bodies, Specific Yogic exercises for elevation and accomplishment of highest perfection, highly sanctified spiritual teachers and guides, their exquisite qualities, yielding intuitive happiness. The said Upānga has been recommended to be consulted for obtaining elaborate description relating to the above topics, since they have not been reproduced elsewhere. The said Upānga holds a unique place amongst all works or compositions, written in narrative style. The mode of expression and elaboration is unique.

2. Rāyapaseniya (Raj Prashniya)

The said Upānga has been classified into 5 heads, namely —Deva Adhikār, Devaviman Adhikār; Deva-Ridhi Adhikār; Pardeshi Rājā Adhikār and Dridhaprategue Kumār. Under initial three heads, the description of Sūryabhi Deva, an exalted celetial body in Heaven, his abode and affluence of his divine life are given; the fourth head relates to `Rājā Pardeshi' and the fifth head concerns with the narrative of `Dridh Pratigua Kumār'.

Contents: Gandher Gautama, chief disciple and administrator of a group of Jaina mendicants, enquired from Lord Mahavirā about the previous existence of 'Sūryabhi Deva', a highly accomplished divine entity, having great affluence and magnificence with unparalleled radiance and elegance, splendour and beauty. Lord Mahavirā answered the question of his chief disciple, Gautama, and informed him that Sūryabhideva was King Pardeshi in previous birth. From here onwards, the narrative account of King Pardeshi appears which is, impact, a significant part of the said Upānga. King Pardeshi was totally materialistic. He happened to come in contact with Keshikumar. They had wide discussion on the topic of materialism versus spiritualism. King Pardeshi, a materialist and non-believer in doctrine of-repeated births places questions one after another and Jaina monk, Kesi Kumar sheds away his inhibitions by answering all his questions comprehensively in a most rational and convincing style. King Pardeshi feels contented and finally bows before truth. He attains initiation and adopts religious mendicancy. He begins leading an ascetic life with devotion and religiosity. His queen poisoned him. However, without least malice or agitation in mind, he observed fast unto death and finally attained salvation. With the said description, the narrative ends.

The said portion of Upānga is most significant in so far as the old method of discussion, deliberation or debate on scriptures is concerned. On further questioning by chief disciple, Gautama, Lord Mahavirā replied that the name of Sūryabhideva in his next birth will be 'Dridh Pratgua Kumār'. In this way, the last chapter relates to the future life sketch of Dridha Pratigua Kumār.

Significant Contents

While describing the artistic structure of the palace or heavenly abode of Suryabhi Deva, it is stated that it was magnificent, equipped with all amenities and riches, highly comfortable and well decorated portion of the celetial world. We also find mention that it was adorned with festoons, dolls and puppets, pillars, quadrangular spot in the court-yard of a palace, consecrated Idol, the pericarp of a lotus, a small box made of bamboo, conch-shell, a theatre or play-house, musical instruments, acting or performance on the stage etc. Infact, the above narration is significant for undertaking study and critical appreciation of ancient architecture, art of singing with music and dancing etc. There is a reference of displaying 32 types of dramatic performances before Lord Mahavirā by celestial young damsels and boys in the shape of ancient dance performances — `Nritta',[1] Nritya'[2] and `Nātya'[3] which provides sufficient material for contemplation and investigation.

A Reasoning: In `Nandi-Sūtra', the name of the above upānga has appeared as `Rayāpaseṇiya'. The renowned scholar, Dr. Jagdishchandra Jaina has written the word as `Rāyapaseṇia' while Achārya Malayagiri has opined that the correct name

---

1. `Nrittaṁ Tāllayāshrayaṁ'. From rhythm to the measure of time and from rhythmic tune to the pauses in music and dance which can be fast, mediocre, and slow. For instance—Folk dances and 'Garba' dance of Bhil tribe in India.
2. 'Bhavāshrayaṁ Nrityaṁ-Nritya'—Expression of emotions by physical movements while dancing. For example, two classical styles of Indian dancing, popularly known as 'Bharat Nātyaṁ' and 'Kathaka'. Dances of renowned Kathaka dancer, Udaishanker.
   Note:- There are two modes of each type of dancing — 'Nritta' — Lāsya-Madhur (A dance in which emotions are represented by various gesticulations and attitudes with melodious tunes).
   'Nritya'—Tanḍava-uddhata (The mythological annihilatory dance of Lord Shiva which is majestic and stately.
3. `Avasthānukriti nātyaṁ'. While dancing to make physical gestures, verbal expressions, indications of feelings or emotions while dancing in order to copy the gestures or appearances of somebody.

of the upānga is `Rāyapaseṇia'. However, there is no unanimity regarding the chief character or hero of the story. Traditionally it was believed that the hero of the said tale was none else but King Pardeshi. However, according to Dr. Winternitz, it was basically the tale of King Prasenjita, ruler of Kaushala (presently Ayodhya). Subsequently, the scholars tried to link the story with the name of King Pardeshi.

No doubt, the words 'Rāyaprasenạia' and 'Rāyapaseṇiya' could be identified with King Prasenjita, ruler of Kaushala, yet the episode, as available now, cannot be linked with King Prasenjita from viewpoint of history. How the plot of the episode changed with the passage of time or what were the conditions that led to the alteration of the theme of the story, nothing can be said for definite. Therefore, for want of concrete or consistent evidence, it cannot be assumed that there was relevance in identifying the name of King Prasenjita with the name of Upānga.

3. Jīvājivābhigama

As is evident from the very name of the Upānga in question, it contains vivid description of the world of organic and inorganic creation and their types etc. Briefly, it is named as `Jivābhigama' also. Traditionally, it was believed that initially the Upānga was comprised of 20 chapters. However, its edition, now available, contains only 9 chapters, comprising of 272 Sūtras. It is possible that the said 20 chapters, or major part of the scripture or the surviving portion of the scriptural work may have been recompiled and re-classified into 9 chapters, after obsolescence or disappearance of the rest. However, they are all mere conjectures and no appropriate information or indication is there for arriving at any other tangible result.

In the process of questions placed by chief Gandher, Gautama, and replies given by Lord Mahavirā, the conversation covered miscellaneous topics or subjects, namely—identities with forms or formless; ordinary mortal beings; those accomplished saints who had attained the state of highest perfection; communities of the males, females, and eunchs i.e. the description of human origin; the head of organic creatures and plants; seven infernos; supernatural spirits or beings; shining peak of Meru mountain; Jambu Dweep (one of the seven continents, including India surrounding Meru mountain); Salt sea or ocean; Uttar Kuru (The region, situated with north of India, near about the site of modern Delhi); Neelvant deep lake and others; Black Sea; Mānnshottar hill; Earth; other continents and islands; and oceans etc. At certain places, the explanations are extensive. As justified by the context, the topics relating to public festivals; vans and vehicles; ornaments; gardens; water reservoirs; ponds, buildings; thrones; sweets, liquors; and metals etc. have also been discussed therein. The said upānga is really significant, in so far as studying of various aspects of social life of the people in India, is concerned.

Explanatory Literature: Achārya Malaygiri has written the commentary on it. He has given indications that the texts of the said Upānga have varied at numerous places. He has also pointed out that many Sutras of the said Upānga are no longer available. Brief glosses have also been written by Achārya Haribhadra and Deva Suri. An annotation (small gloss) is also stated to have remained unpublished yet.

4. Pannavaṇā (Pragyāpnā)

Name: Meaning

The literal meaning of the word is to make known, to teach or to communicate. The name of the said Upānga is true to the etymology of the word.

It is an excellent sacred work, expounding philosophical doctrines of Jaina religion. It contains 36 verses, dealing with the topics, relating to place of knowledge or teaching; multifarious speeches or utterances; regions; locations; changing shape of matter; exhalation and inhalation (respiration); consciousness; generating source; linguistics; the body of animate or inanimate objects, providence; attachment to worldly objects; organs of sense; performance or practice; yogic attainments, corporeal or bodily actions; the faculty of seeing; bodily actions, confinement to repeated births, as the consequence of religious acts—good or bad (by which the soul is attached to worldly pleasures); two states of Karmās; Perception of Karmās; Nature of Karmās; food; knowledge on higher truths of religion and philosophy; spiritual consciousness ; A technical word, often used by the sect of Ajivakas ; Abstract knowledge of matter or stratum of properties through one's soul attending or waiting upon. Knowledge or perception obtained after continuous endeavours; artificial arrangement of words in such a manner as to make different parts of a stanza correspond in sound or thought, etc.

It is explicit from the very names of verses, as stated above, that many important aspects of spiritual knowledge of Jaina religion have been enunciated which will, undoubtedly, be much helpful in undertaking critical study of Jaina philosophy. It is most comprehensive and illustrious amongst all the twelve Upāngas. It holds the same unique place amongst Jaina scriptures as `Vyākhyā Pragyapti' (5th Anga) amongst twelve Angas. Pragyāpnā upānga can also be considered as an exhaustive dictionary of Jaina philosophy.

Its Composition: It is believed that Ārya Shyām, 'Vāchakavanshiya' (belonging to the family of reciters of holy scriptures) had composed the texts of said Upānga. He was held to be an authority on only a portion of the texts of Pūrvas. Two verses (narratives) are found, composed by an unknown writer, in support of the above facts. The purport of these verses reads: "We bow and pay our reverence to Ārya Shyām, belonging to 23rd generation of 'Vāchakavandhiya' Ārya Sudharma with a calm and composed personality and an erudite scholar and a true genius of his age who gifted to his disciples the gem of spiritual knowledge in the shape of 'Pragyāpnā' Upānga."

The mention that Ārya Shyām belonged to 23rd generation of Ārya Sudharma, is not supported by any Pattāvali (List of successors to the supreme seat of a sanctified religious teacher) or Sthvirāvalli (List of such successors in seriatim of senior disciples, known as Sthaviras). In Sthvirāvalli appearing in 'Nandi Sūtra', the name of Achārya Shyām is there but he belongs to 12th generation in the list of successors after Ārya Sudharma. Name of Achārya Brahma Deepak Singh is cited against serial No.23 of the said list. He has been cited as well conversant with `Kalika Shruta' (The sacred texts which are recited at fixed hours only-say in initial three hours or last three hours during day and night); an expert in all the 4 Anuyogas (what-combine or unite the texts), having committed them to memory and holder of the title of an excellent reciter of holy scriptures. The serial number against which the name of Ārya Shyām appears in Sthirāvalli, appearing in `Kalpa-Sūtra' (A Jaina Agamic Scripture) does not tally with that of `Nandi Sūtra'.

Basis for Composition : An Assumption

There are two eulogical verses initially in `Pragyāpnā Sūtra', which are really significant. He writes: "The treasure of highest spiritual knowledge and source of divine bliss and happiness for worthy and excellent persons. Lord Mahavirā, had manifested the feelings of all living creatures. The manner in which, the spiritual texts, forming part of `Drishtivāda, have been enunciated by Lord Mahavirā, similarly I shall interpret them accordingly in `Pragyāpnā Sūtra', comprising of miscellaneous Adhyayans."

The Pada (a quarter of a stanza) `Dithināyaṇisandaṁ', used in composition of the two initial eulogical verses, needs special attention. 'Drishṭivāda' is deemed to have ceased to exist and is no longer available. After final liberation of Achārya Bhadrabāhu, known for his proficiency in 12 Angas (Agamas and their explanatory works), the tradition of gaining expertise in all the 12 Angas and memorizing them, came to be stopped. However, expertise in limited portions of Angas (Jaina Agamas) may have continued. While eulogising in aforesaid two verses, Ārya Shyām is attributed to have gained perfection in 14 Pūrvas (old sacred texts, representing highest spiritual and philosophical knowledge of Jaina religion). It is also possible that Ārya Shyām may have acquired only partial expertise in Pūrvas which is evident from the words used in the said verses.

Explanatory Literature: Achārya Haribhadra Sūri had written a short commentary on it. He had interpreted the words which required comprehension. Achārya Malayagiri has written an annotation on the Upānga, in question. Shri Kulmaṇḍana has written a gloss on it for further elaboration.

The commentators have also drawn our attention to different readings found in the texts of the said Upānga. They have also detected certain words which, according to them, were inexplainable. They left such words unexplained, branding them as sectarian words. It is possible those words may have been found too abstruse to be explained, making no explicit sense. Or they might have found no other way out but to abandon such words, declaring that they should be understood by way of their traditional usage. Upadhyaya Yashovijayji has expounded it in a critical manner.

5. Sūryapannati (Sūrya Prajyapti)

Name: Consistency with its Etymology:

As per Jaina philosophy, the topics, relating to the theory of two suns, sun-rise, sun-set, its shape, energy and courses of movement etc. have been dealt with elaborately in the Upānga, under reference. Besides them, there is detailed discussion on the subjects concerning shape, movement and location of moon and other stars as well. The Upānga has been classified into 20 chapters and comprises of 108 Sūtras. The word `Prābhrita' is adaptation in Sanskrit from `Pāhuda', a word of Prākrita dialect.

Definition of Sanskrit word `Prābhrita' : The use of the word 'Prābhrita' is generally made in the sense of a topic or chapter of a holy scripture. Its literal meaning is — a present, gift, an offering to a deity or to a king. Its etymological interpretation is: "when a rare or precious article, difficult to be acquired or accomplished, lovely and beautiful as also befitting to the occasion is gifted to our dear and near one, whose satisfaction and happiness is sincerely cherished, it is popularly called a 'Prābhrita'.

With regard to the use of the word 'Prābhrita' in the sense of a chapter or topic of a sacred work, it is cited: "The proper course advised for studying religious treatises to the meritorious, humble and obedient pupils by their gurus (spiritual guides) is also popularly called a `Prābhrita'. The productivity of the brains of Jaina scholars is obvious so far as selection of appropriate words is concerned. The use of the word `Prābhrita' in the sense of a topic or a chapter, certainly reflects a sort of literary taste or charm.

Explanatory Works: As generally believed, Achārya Bhadrabāhu, well conversant with Agamic scriptures, had written a commentary on the Upānga, under reference. However, it is not available now and has ceased to exist with the passage of time. Achārya Malayagiri has commented upon it. As a matter of fact, the contents of the said Upānga are so abstruse that it is not possible to follow them without the aid of a commentary. The said Upanga has attracted scholars of the country and abroad since it deals with the subject of a specific nature, relating to the study of planets—sun, moon and stars etc. and providing material to the scholars for further investigation. Prof. Bevar had written an article on the said Upānga in German language, which was published in Germany in the year 1868. It is also a hearsay that Dr. R.Shām Shāstry had translated the Upānga, in question, under the style "A Brief Translation of Mahavira's Sūryaprajnapati." However, the same is not available now. Dr. Thibo had written an essay on `Sūryaprajnapati' in which he had referred to the theory of two suns and two moons, propounded in Jaina ideology. According to him this was also the belief of Greeks before their arrival in India. The said article had been published in *Journal of the Asiatic Society of Bengal*, volume No. 49.

6. Jambuddivapannatti (Jambudweep Prajnapati)

Its Characteristic

The topic of Jambudweep (one of the seven continents, surrounding the mountain Meru) has been discussed miscellaneously in the above Upānga. The said scripture has been classified in two parts—initial half and latter half. The former portion consists of 4 chapters while the latter portion is comprised of 3 chapters. The entire scripture contains 176 Sūtras.

Purported meaning of the word `Vakṣaskār'

The word `Vakṣaskār' has been used here in the sense of a section, chapter or any smaller division of a work. However, the fact remains that there are a few large mountains in Jambudweep bearing the name of `Vakṣaskār' which are considered significant in many ways from viewpoint of Jaina geography. The use of the word `Vakṣaskār', made by the author of the Upānga, in question, to mean a chapter, section or a small division of the book, while discussing about Jambudweep, appears to be relevant and quite in order.

Contents: The Upānga, under reference, contains a detailed description of Indian territory, forming part of Jambudweep. Many inaccessible spots — various mountains, rivers, caves and forests, situated in India, have been referred to and discussed therein.

The wheel of time as per Jaina ideology (Time represented as a wheel, always moving), is very very long. According to Achārya Hemachandra, it is equal to twenty crores or crores of oceans of years. There are six successive stages of this long period of 'Avasarpanikāl' (in which the life-span of human-beings is reduced; auspicious sentiments are minimial and inauspicious feelings get increased), namely, 'Susham-Shushmā' (the first stage in which there is no grief but happiness); 'Sushmā' (second stage in which there is lesser amount of pleasure as compared to the first stage); 'Susham-Dushmā' (third stage in which there is grief also to a slight degree alongwith happiness); `Dusham-Sushmā' (fourth stage in which there is excess of suffering and less happiness); `Dushmā' (fifth stage in which there is pain and affliction); and `Dusham-Dushmā' (sixth stage in which there is extreme sorrow and unhappiness and no pleasure, whatsoever). Similarly, in 'Utasarpini Kāl' (a long transcendental period of elevating upwards as per Jaina philosophy) which has also six stages— `Dusham-Dushamā' (The first stage in which there is extreme sorrow and distress); `Dushmā' (second stage in which there is comparatively lesser woe); `Dusham-Sushmā' (third stage in which along with grief there is happiness also-may be to a slight degree); `Susham-Dukhmā' (fourth stage in which there is more happiness or pleasure and lesser grief); `Sushmā' (fifth stage in which there is divine bliss and happiness) and `Susham-Shushmā' (In Sixth stage, there is abundance of pleasure and no unhappiness at all). There is thus detailed narration of various stages of downfall and elevation. In the said context, there is mention of 14 Kulkars (distinguished heads of the families); 24 Tirthankers (Supreme sanctified teachers and philosophers of Jaina religion); Lord Rishabha; 72 arts — as music and dancing etc; and 64 arts, mainly for ladies besides numerous other skills and crafts etc. There are similar other significant topics, dealt with therein. The Upānga `Jambu-Prajnapati' is really useful for undertaking study of geography and brilliance of India of pre-historic times from viewpoint of Jaina religion and philosophy.

7. Chandapannatti (Chandraprajnapati)

As Mentioned in 'Sthānānga' (3rd Anga)

In `Sthānānga Sūtra', alongwith the names of `Sūryaprajnapati', `Jambudweep Prajnapati', `Dweepsāgar-Prajnapati', the name of `Chandra-Prajnapati' also appears as part of `Anga-Bāhya' (Scriptural works of Secondary Nature, composed by Sthaviras). It is thus evident that both Sūryaprajnapati' and `Chandra-Prajnapati' are ancient scriptures. Initially, they were two distinct sacred works, each dealing with its own independent subjects.

Present edition of 'Chandraprajnapati': A Mystery

The edition of `Chandraprajnapati', now available, is a true copy of `Sūrysprajnapti' with the only exception that the former contains an initial verse, meant to invoke divine blessing and 18 other verses, giving summary of 20 chapters. The said verses are given initially in `Chandraprajnapati' and, thereafter, the discussion on the topics begins as specified in the Table of contents of the book. The said verses are not there in `Sūryaprajnapati', signifying that the contents of the book start without initial benedictory verse and Table of subjects to be discussed. Rest of the contents are the same from begining to the end. When they are two independent and distinct scriptures, why such resemblance? It is a mystery and in order to solve it, different explanations have been offered.

Mysteriousness : An Answer: There are traditionalists and orthodox religionists who will never like to budge an inch from their old convictions and are not prepared in any way to change their thinking and adopt an independent attitude. Inspite of uniformity of the contents in toto, they do not agree that `Sūryaprjnapati' and 'Chandra-prajnapati' are one and the same and there are no apparent dissimilarities in them. They argue that there are many topics relating to the course and movement of sun, moon and stars which are identical and have been discussed in both the scriptures. Hence question does not arise of any variation in their details or contents. On the other hand, there are points, which differ in both treatises, yet their wordings are almost similar. A word may have different meanings. People are generally aware with the customary meaning of a word only. The sense of a word, in which it is not commonly used, remains unknown to the people. Only a limited number of persons could be aware with the unprevailing sense of a word. Similar situation appears to be here.

The fact remains that there are many words, appearing in both scriptures, which are identical but carry different meanings. It might have been done so knowingly, and in accordance with a decided policy. There are topics or subject-matters which are treated and discussed before deserving persons only and not in the presence of incapable or unworthy people. Hence it was in the fitness of things to keep such matters unmanifested by use of mystic words. The deserving hands are always able to comprehend the sense of mystic words and attain knowledge. No wonder, the scholars might have come across with the situation of this type. The learned scholars who were conversant with the mystic vocabulary, must have been able to impart knowledge by disclosing the true sense of mystic words to the deserving hands. However, this practice might have ceased with the lapse of time and manifestation of mysterious vocabulary might have come to an end. Consequently the suspicions are raised again and again why the contents of the too distinct scriptures are similar. Infact, the paucity of adequate knowledge is mainly responsible for it. The fact remains that both the Upāngas are distinctly genuine and totally undisturbed. They must be taken as two distinct and independant scriptures.

Any argument may be advanced to support a conventional plea, yet it is the basic right of prudent scholars to examine the authenticity of the prevailing orthodox views and arrive at a logical conclusion. Hence it should not be treated as a repudiation of the traditional theory when it is stressed that the pleas of mysteriousness of vocabulary or plurality of their meanings were not sufficient to establish that they were two separate and distinct scriptures. No more reasoning is called for to emphasize this. As soon as the scholars will be allowed to ponder over the matter freely, majority of them will not be convinced with the pleas of mysterious vocabulary and plurality of their meanings. It should not be taken otherwise if it is emphatically argued that both Upāngas, now available, are not only identical in their contents but also have the same purpose and intent.

An Indecisive Reflection : A Presumption

Possibly, in old days, two hand-written manuscripts of *Sūryaprajnapati* might be lying in a library. The title page of one of the manuscripts might be there with the name of the holy book *Sūryaprajnapati* written over it while the title cover of the other manuscript might have been missing, lost or destroyed. The first page of the former manuscript, having the title cover, and containing initial benedictory verse (an auspicious introduction in the form of a prayer at the beginning of any work or composition) as also table of contents might also be missing. In other words, the shape of both the manuscripts should be considered like this—in one of the manuscripts, there is title page, bearing the name of the sacred book but the first page, containing the initial verses, is missing. The matter starts straight away. In the other manuscript, there is no title-cover, bearing name of the sacred book. The first page starts with the verses—the initial verse meant to invoke divine blessing and others discuss table of contents. Thus the minor distinction between the two manuscripts being that in one of them, the title cover was missing but the first page, containing the verses, was there. However, in the other, the title cover, bearing the name of the sacred treatise was there but the first page, containing the verses was missing. At the first glance, the start of the two manuscripts looked different, and anyone, having no knowledge of Jaina scriptures was bound to feel at its wits end. It is also possible that somebody might have undertaken screening of the library books while placing them in a systematic order or preparing their inventory. He might have come across the said manuscripts, while scrutinizing the lot of Jaina scriptures—say Angas or Upāngas. He might not have felt uncertainty in respect of the manuscript, having title cover and bearing explicitly the name of the holy scripture. However, he must have been at his wits end to find that the title cover of the other manuscript, bearing the name of the book, was missing. He might have pondered over the matter but for want of conversance with the Jaina scriptures, he might not have been able to decide. He could be an ordinary employee or a supervisor of the liberary with scant knowledge or average intelligence.

It appears that he might not have interfered with the former manuscript, bearing the name of the holy scripture on the title page and the contents of which had started right from the first page. However, in case of the other manuscript, which did not have the title page or bear name of the sacred work and because of the verses, appearing on the starting page, he might have mistaken it to be a different book. He might have presumed its name to be 'Chandraprajnapati' and written it accordingly on the manuscript. He was not supposed to have examined the contents and compare the texts of the two manuscripts with an analytical mind.

Probably, the original manuscript or volume of `Chandraprajnapati' might have vanished and it could not have been traced out. Thus, on the basis of the assumed name, put down on the manuscript by the librarian or the library clerk, the two manuscripts, having the same contents, might have been treated as two distinct scriptures, bearing different names and they continued to be dealt with as such for centuries to come. Hundreds of years have passed since then and the two volumes, containing the same texts, are still considered as two distinct sacred treatises.

Religious teachings inculcate faith and create awakening in us. Blind faith always lacks judgment and wisdom. However, it is there and generally found in religious institutions, which should be discarded and condemned outrightly. Because of extreme religious faith, the eminent Jaina scholars, having expertise in Agamic scriptures, were unable to gather strength to acknowledge the truth although they were fully aware of the fact that the texts of both the Upāngas are similar in all respects. As soon as the followers of Jaina religion, happened to know the reality, the Jaina scholars began to advance irrational arguments in support of their fallacy, as cited above, in foregoing pages.

In any view of the matter, it should not be considered as offending the religion or deviation from the righteous path that the matter calls for further investigation and study in order to arrive at the truth and for satisfaction of the followers of Jaina religion.

Variations in Serial Numbers: There is slight difference in placement of Jambudweep-Prajnapati, Sūrya-Prajnapati and Chandraprajnapati in serial order. Amolaka Rishi (A poet and sage), who was the first scholar to translate 32 Agamic scriptures in Hindi, has held Jambudweep Prajnapati as fifth, Chandraprajnapti as sixth and Sūryaprajnapati as seventh Upānga in seriatim. Mr. Winternitz is of the view that basically Chandraprajnapati was considered to have been composed earlier than Sūryaprajnapati. Mr. Winternitz also believes that the present shape of Chandraprajnapati is certainly different from its original contents. The subjects treated in the initial composition were clearly of different sort.

On the contrary, I have discussed Sūryaprajnapati at serial No. 5, Jambudweep-prajnapati and Chandraprajnapati at serial Nos. 6 and 7 respectively. The main reason being that the volume of Sūryaprajnapati is intact and available in its original form. Consistent with the name of the said Upānga, the descriptions regarding sun and the subjects relating thereto are more extensive. No doubt, there is citation regarding moon also but comparatively in much concise form. The existing edition of Chandraprajnapati is doubtful and cannot be taken as original composition. Hence I have dealt with it after Jambudweep Prajnapati. Achārya Malayagiri has written commentary on 'Chandraprajnapati'.

Five Niryāvalias (Sanskrit-Niryavalikās)

Remaining five Upāngas have been incorporated in five Niryāvaliyas (Niryavalikās) as under:

(1) Niryāvaliyā or Kappiyā (Kalpikā)
(2) Kappavadansiyā (Kalpāvataṁsikā)
(3) Pupphiyā (Pushpikā)
(4) Pupphachūliyā (Pushpachūilikā), and
(5) Vahi-nadakṣā (Vrishṭi-Dashā)

It is possible, all the remaining five Upāngas might have been earlier included in a single Niryāvalikā Sūtra. However, when it was decided to accomplish 12 Upāngas i.e. to supplement each Anga separately, it followed that each of the 5 Upāngas formed part of a separate Niryāvalikā.

8. Niryāvaliyās (Niryāvalikās) or Kappiyās (Kalpikās)

Classification

The eighth Upānga comprises of ten Adhyayans (Chapters), namely—1. Kālkumār Adhyayan; 2. Sukāl Kumar Adhyayan; 3. Mahākāl Kumar Adhyayan; 4. Krishna Kumar Adhyayan; 5. Sukrishna Kumar Adhyayan; 6. Mahākrishna Kumar Adhyayan; 7. Vir Krishna Kumar Adhyayan; 8. Rāmkrishna Kumar Adhyayan; 9. Priyasena-Krishna Kumar Adhyayan; and 10. Mahāsena-Krishna Kumar Adhyayan.

The princes in whose names, the aforesaid Adhyayans have been styled, were the sons of king Shrenika, ruler of Magadha dynasty and brothers of Koṇika (Later king Ajātshatru) who had been killed one by one by the arrows of Chetaka, Supreme Head of Vaishali Republic, during the battle fought between him and King Ajātshatru.

Theme: The first Adhyayan contains the narrative of Kālkumār. His mother, Kāli, enquires from Lord Mahāvira about the welfare of his son who had gone to fight in the battle for king Konika (Ajātshatru). On being informed that her son had been killed by the arrow, shot by Chetaka, she is overwhelmed with grief and sorrow. On being consoled, she returns to her residence. Thereafter, Gandher Gautama enquires from Lord Mahavirā about the events of previous and succeeding births of Kāl Kumar. The answer, given by Lord Mahavirā, portrays a detailed sketch of King Ajātshatru, how pregnant Chelna, queen of king Shreṇika, visualises in her dream to eat the fried pieces of flesh[1] from the heart of her husband and tasting of the wine; deftness shown by Abhaya Kumar in fulfilment of the longings of the pregnant queen; birth of `Koṇika' and getting him thrown out on the heap of refuge by his mother, Queen Chelna; picking him back by King Shreṇika; and rearing him up most affectionately; on growing into a powerful young prince, how he got himself enthroned forcibly after imprisoning his father; committing of suicide by king Shreṇika for fear of excessive torture; and how king, Ajātshatru had invaded Chetaka, the administrative head of Vaishāli Republic, after the latter had refused to return `Sechnaka' elephant to side with Bohillakumar, younger brother of Ajātshatru. There is only symbolic mention of the two fierce battles, known as

1. In the original text, Prākrita word `Silehi' has appeared, the substitute of which in Sanskrit will be `Shaula'. Since the pieces of flesh might have been fried with a prong or pointed instrument, called Shūla, the word `Shaula' was probably used for the fragments of the flesh.

`Mahashila Kantaka' and `Rathmūsala', fought between king Ajātshatru and Chetaka. For detailed version of these wars, a reference of 'Vyākhyāprajnapati' has been made.

It only transpires from the contents of the second Adhyayan that there was a big town, named Champā (Also called Angpuri. This town stood on the Ganges). Purnabhadra was the name of Jaina temple, located in the said town. King Koṇika (Ajātshatru) was then the ruler and his principal Queen was Padmavati. Earlier, Sukāli Rāni, charming queen of King Shreṇika and younger step-mother of prince Koṇika, lived in Champā town. Sukāli Rāni had given birth to a beautiful son, named Sukāl Kumar. Similar to the story of Kāl Kumar, who had joined with 3000 elephants and was killed in the battle, a detailed narrative of Sūkāl Kumar appears in the said Adhyayan. It is also cited at the end that Sukāl Kumar will attain final emancipation and the state of highest perfection (by way of penance) in the territory of `Mahavideha' (lying to the north-east of Magadha). The contents of the second Adhyayan end there.

Regarding the contents of remaining eight Adhyayans from third to tenth, it is cited: "The narratives contained in remaining 8 Adhyayans are also similar to that of Kāl Kumar, given in the first Adhyayan. The names of mothers and their sons are almost similar. Thus the eighth Niryavaliya Sutra (Upānga) ends here.

9. Kappavaḍaṁsiya (Kalpāvatansika)

The literal meaning of the compounded word `Kalpavitaṁsa' means the abodes of celetial bodies, decked with ornaments. The name of the above Upānga is thus a derivative therefrom. It consists of 10 Adhyayans (Chapters) which contain brief episodes of 10 grand-sons of king Shreṇika, who had been killed in the great battle. Each Adhyayan is styled conforming with the name of the respective hero or the main character of the episode. For example — 1. Padam Kumar Adhyayan; 2. Mahāpadam Kumār Adhyayan; 3. Bhadra Kumār Adhyayan; 4. Subhadra Kumār Adhyayan; 5. Padambhadra Kumār Adhyayan; 6. Padamasena Kumār Adhyayan; 7. Padam Gulmakumār Adhyayan; 8. Nalini Gulmakumar Adhyayan; 9. Ānand Kumar Adhyayan and 10. Nand Kumar Adhyayan.

Each was the respective grandson of king Shreṇika and sons of Kāl Kumar and others, as mentioned in the earlier `Niryāvaliā Sūtra' (eighth Upānga). The first Adhyayan contains the brief tale of Padam Kumar, son of Kāl Kumar, covering four or five pages, relating to his birth, initiation, final emancipation after obtaining rebirth in `Mahāvideha region' and having accomplished the state of highest perfection. The second Adhyayan contains extremely brief account regarding birth of Mahāpadam Kumar, son of Sukāl Kumar, say in six or seven lines and it had been added that the rest of the details are similar to that of first Adhyayan. Regarding the contents of remaining eight Adhyayans, it had been stated in a few words only that they should be read as appeared in first Adhyayan. It has also been pointed out that the name of each grand-prince of king Shreṇika, conformed with the name of his respective mother. At the end, after laying the respective period of ascetic life, led by each prince, and the divine abode obtained by him in heaven, the matter of the ninth Upānga has come to an end. Thus the contents of the Upānga, under reference, are extremely short.

There was antocratic rule of kings in Magadha dynasty during the era of Lord Mahavirā and Lord Buddha. `Kalpika' (8th Upānga) and `Kalpavataṁsika' (9th Upānga) are really significant for having an idea of the social conditions of pre-historic age.

10. Puppхiā (Pushpikā)

The Upānga in question, is comprised of 10 Adhyayans (Chapters) which contain the episodes of such male and female devotees who had attained a place in heaven by virtue of their devotion to religion and spiritual performances. They came to offer their obeisance to Lord Mahavirā by their heavenly cars after being dressed elegantly with full glory and magnificence.

Description of Various Devoutly Austere Persons

In the course of narrating the tale of Somila Brahmana, there is mention of 40 types of ascetics or devouts, some of whom are as under :

(a) Holder of one water-pot (earthen or wooden) only;
(b) Subsisting on fruits only;
(c) Those coming out of water immediately after taking a single dip only;
(d) Those taking repeated dips in water;
(e) Those who kept standing in neck-deep water;
(f) Those keeping all their clothes, utensils and bodies cleansed;
(g) Those taking their food after blowing conch-shell;
(h) Those who keep themselves in standing posture at all times;
(i) Those subsisting on venison:
(j) Feeding themselves by taking meat of an elephant;
(k) Always keeping their sticks raised high from the ground;
(l) Those wearing bark-garments.
(m) Those standing inside water perpetually;
(n) Those residing under the trees permanently;
(o) Those depending on water only;
(p) Those pulling on by eating moss only;
(q) The ascetics who depended only on air;
(r) Those living exclusively on roots of the trees only;
(s) Those depending on bulbous roots of the trees only:
(t) Feeding themselves by taking leaves of the trees only;
(u) Those eating barks of the trees only;
(v) Those depending on sap of flowers only;
(w) Those eating seeds and sprouts only;
(x) Those feeding themselves by taking leaves, flowers and fruits, fallen from the trees spontaneously;
(y) Feeding themselves by articles, thrown away by others;
(z) Those exposing themselves to the heat of the sun;
(aa) Those enhancing the severity of their bodies by practising hard penances;

(bb) Those who undertake the severest penance by warming themselves amidst five fires (one each of the east, west, north and south; the sun overhead being the fifth);

(cc) Those tormenting their bodies by heating themselves on hot pots.

Instances of miscellaneous types of devout Sādhus, shown above, are, infact, illustrative of practising multiforms of spiritual performances and severe penances. Evidently, some of the ascetics appeared committed to practising abstract meditation. It may be performed in several ways, such as by standing on one leg, holding up the arms or inhaling smoke etc. a sort of forced meditation by undergoing physical hardships during the course of their exercises, is called 'Hathyoga'. What was the consolidated shape of the said spiritual endeavours, forming part of forced meditation? Were they practised in accordance with the doctrines of any philosophical sect or the tenets of a religious group? Were there other modes of self-mortifications also, practised in India, besides these, referred to above? Were there other modes of self-mortification too, practised in India, besides those, discussed above, and what was the philosophical thinking or ideology to support such hardships in yogic exercises? Thus the said Upānga may be found useful for undertaking study of these subjects.

11. Puppha Chūlā (Pushpa-chūlā)

The above Upānga consists of 10 Adhyayans, namely—1. Sri Devi Adhyayan; 2. Hridevi Adhyayan; 3. Vriti Devi Adhyayan; 4. Kīrti Devi Adhyayan; 5. Buddhidevi Adhyayan; 6. Laxmi Devi Adhyayan; 7. Iladevi Adhyayan; 8. Surādevi Adhyayan; 9. Rasadevi Adhyayan; and 10. Gandhdevi Adhyayan. The first Adhyayan contains the narrative of Sri Devi. The said goddess visits Lord Mahavirā in her heavenly car with full glory and elegance of a divine lady to pay her obeisance. Gandher Gautama enquires her life events in previous birth. Lord Mahāvira answers and provides the desired information. In this way, the narrative, concerning the previous birth of Sri Devi is contained in the first Adhyayan. Only token reference is found of remaining nine goddesses in Adhyayans, numbering two to ten which reads: "Just as the first Adhyayan contains the legend of Sri Devi, similarly, the stories of other goddesses are incorporated in remaining nine Adhyayans. All the goddesses lived in `Saudharma Lok' in heaven. The names of towns, temples, parents and their own names in their previous births are in accordance with `Samgrāhini Gāthā'. All the goddesses had come in contact with `Lord Pārshvanāth' in their previous birth. They were all initiated by `Pushpachūlā Āryā'. All of them were particular in keeping their bodies cleansed and by nature they observed perfect cleanliness. They will all drop down from heaven and take rebirth in `Mahāvideha' region and attain final emancipation. Thus, the contents of 11th Upānga came to an end.

12. Vahindashā (Vrishṇidashā)

Name: As stated in `Nandi Churṇi', originally the full name of the, above Upānga was 'Andhaka Vrishṇidashā'. The word 'Andhaka' became extinct with the lapse of time and now it is named as `Vrishṇidashā' only. It consists of 12 Adhyayans which contain the narratives of 12 princes, belonging to `Vrishṇi' family (Vrishṇi was the name of an ancestor of Lord Krishna). The name of each Adhyayan conforms with the respective name of the prince, such as—1. Nishadha Kumār Adhyayan; 2. Anīk Kumār Adhyayan; 3. Prahna Kumār Adhyayan; 4. Vedhkumar Adhyayan; 5. Pragati Kumār Adhyayan; 6. Mukti Kumār Adhyayan; 7. Dashrath Kumār Adhyayan; 8. Dridha Rath Kumār Adhyayan; 9. Mahādhanush Kumār Adhayayan; 10. Saptadhanush Kumar Adhyayan; 11. Dashdhanush Kumar Adhyayan; and 12. Shatdhanush Kumar Adhyayan.

Contents:- The first Adhyayan contains the story of Nishadh Kumar, son of Baldeva (elder brother of Krishna) and his wife, Revati. The narrative relates about his birth, his growing into a youngman, his attaining initiation as a religious mendicant by Lord `Arishthanemi'. The narrative also contains the events of his previous birth and succeeding two births and his attaining final emancipation in `Mahāvideha region' at the end of his second birth.

Although, the reference of Lord Vāsudeva Krishna appears only incidentally as per demand of the context in the first Adhyayan, yet it is significant. There is vivid description of his riches, pre-dominance in all fields; his well-equipped army, affluence, dignity, excellence and military strength etc. The first Adhyayan is really useful for having knowledge about the rule of Vrishni or Yādava community, mammoth clan of Yādavas and pre-historic details of Saurashṭra region. Remaining eleven Adhyayans contain only symbolic information and read as: "The remaining eleven Adhyayans should also be deemed to have incorporated story of respective prince as in first Adhyayan. The name of each prince in his previous birth, may be obtained from `Saṁgrahni Gātha'. The description of each of the remaining 11 princes neither exceeds nor is less as compared to that of prince Nishadhkumar. In this way, the 12th Upānga ends with the above information.

An Important Information

After concluding the narration, forming part of the 12th Upānga, `Vrishnidashā', it has also been added "Niryāvalikā', a branch of Jaina Agamic literature ends here. The briefings pertaining to 12 Upāngas have concluded here. `Niryāvalikā' is, infact, a consolidated form of spiritual knowledge, sub-divided in 5 chapters and each chapter containing the contents of an upānga. Each chapter or upānga was preached daily and completed in 5 days. The first to fourth branches of Niryāvalikā consist of 10 Adhyayans each while the fifth branch contains 12 Adhyayans. Thus `Niryāvalikā', a consolidation of sacred texts, forming part of last 5 Upāngas, ends here. From the said narration, it is explicitly clear that 5 separate branches of Niryāvalikā (Kalpia; Kalpavataṁsikā; Pushpikā; Pushpachulā and Vrishṇidashā) were earlier in the shape of one consolidated treatise, Niryāvalikā.

Chheda Sutras (Conduct Rules for Kindlings)

The same significance is attached to Chheda Sūtras in Jaina institution as given to `Vinaya Pitaka' in Buddhist writings. The rules of conduct for regulating the lives of Jaina male and female mendicants, as enunciated by Lord Mahāvirā and successively revised and redetermined from time to time, are contained in the said Chheda Sūtras. On violating a conduct rule, it was binding on the erring mendicant to perform expiatory acts for atonement of the sins and these reformatory measures have been elaborately discussed in the said Sūtras.

In order to maintain the sanctity of religious mendicancy, the said sūtras are highly essential and exceedingly superb. Hence the Chheda Sutras form part of most sacred type of knowledge, contained in Jaina Agamic scriptures. It is, therefore, recommended that only erudite scholars of Jaina philosophy should be allowed to have deep penetration into the subject. It has also been emphasized that no spiritual leader or preceptor be permitted to move from village to village with his group of disciples without having profound knowledge of or grip over Chheda Sūtras.

It is cited in `Nishitha Bhāshya' (A commentary on Sūtras pertaining to the expiatory acts for atonement of sins, committed by mendicants at night) that the Cheeda Sūtras tend to disclose real essence of philosophical teachings, enunciated by Tirthankers. Accordingly, they are of extremely secret and confidential nature. Only well accomplished scholars are entitled to obtain their thorough knowledge. Average students or pupils should not be allowed to have an access to them. According to the author of the said commentary, just as the water, stored in an unripened pitcher, may destroy it, similarly, the mystic doctrines, forming part of Chheda Sutras, may bring ruin to incapable persons, not entitled to or strictly forbidden to go through them. In the same way, it has been equally stressed that the Sūtras of Vinaya Pitāka (A collection of writings in which the rules of conduct have been elaborately discussed to be followed by Buddhist mendicants) are mystic and of secret nature. It is cited in `Milinda-prashna' (The questions of king Milinda) that Vinaya Pitaka should be kept at a hidden place to deny access by undesirable persons so that it may not be the cause of any ill-repute to the Budhist institution. It purports to lay emphasis on the point that in the chapter, dealing with prescribed religious acts to be performed for atonement of sins, various ills committed by male and female mendicants, during the darkness of night, as a result of their sheer ignorance, negligence or intense desire for worldly enjoyments, have also been discussed at length. It is always detrimental to the interests of an institution if the common masses come to know about actual state of things. Those who are not well conversant with the psychic attitude, they are prone to scepticism and diffidence and develope lackness of faith and reverence towards young male and female mendicants. Most probably, maintaining strict confidentiality of Chheda Sūtras has been stressed on this very account.

There are six Chheda Sūtras, namely--

(1) Nisīha (Nishītha); (2) Mahānisīha (Mahānishītha); (3) Vavahār (Vyavahār); (4) Dasāsuyakhandha (Dashāshrutaskandh); (5) Kappa (Kalpa or Vrhat Kalpa) and (6) Pancha Kappa or Jiva Kappa (Panch-Kalpa or Jiva Kalpa).

1. Nisiha (Nishitha)

Literal meaning of the word Nishitha

The literal sense of the word Nishītha is midnight; the time of sleep or the night in general. The word `Nishītha' has been defined in `Nishītha-bhāshya' to mean darkness, indistinctness and secrecy etc. The undisclosed part of religious doctrines or what is mysterious and secretive are also covered under this definition. Just as mysterious lores, spells and incantations are not explained in the presence of incompetent and immature persons and secrecy is maintained in regard to them, similarly, Nishītha Sūtras are also confidential and they cannot be taught to each and everbody.

Shape : Theme : Nishītha is believed to have drawn its theme from second section of `Achārānga Sūtra' (First Anga, dealing with established rules of conduct or manners of conducting oneself). It is also considered to be fifth Chūlā of second section of Achāranga Sūtra. It is also named as `Nishītha Chūlā Adhyayan'. `Nishītha Sūtra' is also treated to be 'Achār-Prakalpa' (established rules of good conduct and behaviour).

Both methods of applying general rules as well as particular rules or exceptions have been discussed at length in `Nishītha Sūtra' with regard to the conduct and behaviour of male and female religious mendicants and in case of deviations from the right course, the religious acts to be performed for atonement of sins have also been prescribed therein. The related subject has been discussed minutely and in a critical manner, which is worth studying by each male and female mendicant who has a sincere desire to exercise control over self. It is admitted that if a Jaina saint fails to retain the texts of `Nishītha Sūtra' in memory, he is disentitled to succeed to the seat of a religious preceptor or spiritual guide for the whole of his life.

Composition : Author: When the sacred texts of *Nishītha Sūtra* had been accomplished and by whom is still disputed. The author of the commentary on `Nishītha Sūtras' believes that the Jaina scholars, who were well conversant with Pūrvas (old spiritual and philosophical texts), had composed `Nishītha Sūtras'. In other words, they were accomplished on the basis of highest spiritual knowledge, contained in the Pūrvas of jaina religion. It may also be laid down that Nishītha Sūtras were composed on the basis of conduct rules, prescribed for religious mendicants, as contained in 20th chapter of third section, relating to ninth Pūrva 'Pratyākhyān' (renunciation, abnegation).

The annotator, Jinadas Mahattar, has expressed the view that `Vishākh Maṇi Mahattar' had composed Nishītta Sūtras, for the exclusive benefit of future disciples and their pupils. However, it has been laid down in the commentary on `Panchkappa Sutras' that Achārya Bhadrabāhu was the author of Nishītta Sūtras.

Nishitha Sūtra is comprised of 20 'Uddeslakas' (Illustrations) and each Uddeshaka contains varied number of Sūtras.

Explanatory Literature: The etymological commentary (which explains a Sūtra or an aphorism word by word with comments of its own) had been written on Nishītha Sūtras. Traditionally, Achārya Bhadrabāhu was known for his aptness in writing etymological interpretations of the words, contained in aphorisms of religious treatises. Sri Sangh Das Gaṇi had written `Panchakalpa Bhāshya' for elaborating the etymological commentary, written on Nishitha Sūtras. Sri Jinadas Mahattar had written a critical annotation on etymological commentary, Panchakalpa Bhashya and Sūtras. The disciple of Shri Pradyumn Sūri had further written a small annotation on them for further elucidation. An extensive or voluminous commentary was also written on Nishītha Sūtras but the same is not available now. `Nishītha Sūtras' with commentary and gloss have been published by `Sanmati Gyānpith', Agra which were edited by erudite scholars, Upadhyaya Sri Amar Muniji and Muni Sri Kanahaiyalalji 'Kamal'.

2. Mahānisiha (Mahānishītha)

'Mahānishitha' is considered to be the essence or essential part of all fundamental doctrines of Jaina religion, as enunciated by Lord Mahāvira. However, the fact remains, that the original manuscript of `Mahanishītha' could not be preserved to be safe. Its pages had been eaten away by termites and destroyed. It was further processed and reproduced by leading Achāryas, Vridhvādi, Sidhasena, Yaksasena, Devaguna, Yashovardhan, Ravigupta, Nemichandra, and Jinadasgani etc. Generally, `Nisitha' (1st Chheda Sūtra) is named as `Laghu Nishītha, and the book, under reference is known as `Mahānishītha'. However, this argument is not tenable since the original volume of `Mahānishītha' is no longer available now, as stated above.

Body : Contents:- Mahānishitha' is comprised of 6 Adhyayans and 2 Chūlās. The name of the first Adhyayan is `Shalyodharṇa'. While censuring the sinful acts (which are like extraneous substances, lodged in the body and causing it a great pain), there is mention of 18 entry points of the sins in our body. The results of actions either in this or in a previous birth and three kinds of miseries which human-beings have to suffer in this world as a result of their actions as also desirability of refuting actions, causing physical and mental afflictions have been discussed in second Adhyayan. In third and fourth Adhyayans, it is strongly preached that we should avoid indulging in any association or have any contact with Sādhus of vile and immodest nature. Incidentally, a reference has also been made to `Navakār Mantra' (Sacred text of 5 prayers) and it is also cited that Ārya Vajra had restored the significance of the said `Navakār Mantra' and held it as fundamental sacred text of Jaina religion. The significance of reciprocal relationship between religious Acharyas and their pupils has been evaluated in a critical manner in fifth Adhyayan, styled `Navanīt Sār'. In the said context, the affairs of Jaina organisation of religious mendicants have also been discussed. It appears that the chapter, styled `Gachhāchār' has been written accordingly. Ten types of self-acknowledgments and self-criticisms in the presence of religious preceptors and elderly monks, about sins, committed by mendicants and four types of religious acts for atonement of sins have been laid down in the sixth Adhyayan.

There is also citation of devoted women who burn themselves willingly on the funeral pyres with their dead hausbands and after the expiry of issueless king their widowed daughters are enthroned.

Historicity of the Contents: Keeping in view the language and nature of subjects, dealt with in `Mahānisītha Sūtra', it will not appear consistent to include it in the category of ancient Agamas of Jaina religion. The topics relating to mystical practices for attainment of super-human faculties are also found to have been discussed therein. There is mention of other various treatises as well besides Jaina Agamic Scriptures. In addition to the above, there are other references as well which confirm the possibility of its being a recent composition.

3. Vavahār (Vyavahār)

'Vyavhar Sūtra' holds a significant place in Jaina canonical literature. It has been held to be the essence or substantial part of 12 Angās, forming part of Jaina Agamas. Although, the Chheda Sūtras are six in number, yet only three Chheda Sutras are more significant so far as the subjects treated, their elaboration and style of composition are concerned. `Vyavahār' Sutra holds a unique place amongst them. Remaining two important Sūtras are `Nishitha' and `Vrahat Kalpa'.

Its Shape : Contents: It consists of ten illustratives and each illustrative has distinct number of Sūtras. The body of its contents is smaller than `Nishitha' and bigger than `Vrahat-Kalpa'. There is an effective and vital mention of the vices and sins, committed knowingly or unknowingly, by male and female mendicants of Jaina organisation as also self-acknowledgement of their sins in the presence of a spiritual leader and observance of religious performances for atonement or propitiation of their sins. For instance, it is cited in the first illustrative that in case, a Jaina mendicant starts moving all alone by dissociating himself from other mendicants of his group, and, thereafter, desires to rejoin the group, it will be binding upon him to appear before the Acharya or religious head of his group to make self-confession of his guilt and after expressing regrets for his ommissions and commissions, he should perform religious acts, prescribed for indemnification and self-purification. However, if the Acharya or spiritual head of his own group is not available, he should confess his guilt in the presence of any other senior monk or a scholar of his group. In case, they too are unavailable, the author of the Chheda Sūtra has advised to do so in the presence of a senior monk or a scholar of any other group. However, if they too are not available, the author has allowed options of other distinguished persons before whom he should appear, confess his fault, censure himself and atone for self-purification. In case, none of the above alternatives are available, the author has specified that the sinner should sit at a place on the east or north of a village, town, corporation, capital, a tiny hamlet, on a piece of garment or a mat, in a city or a capital of 400 villages etc. and after placing the two palms together on his forehead, he should make self-introspection by admitting that he had committed a sin and was guilty of violating the sanctity of the institution. He should make self-confession and address Tirthankers and omniscients that he was censuring himself and was ready to perform prescribed religious acts for propitiation of his sin or sins.

It is really a unique process for attainment of self-purification and refinement of inner-self and which inspires for maintaining the dignity of religious mendicancy.

There are numerous illustrations in `Vyavahār Sūtra' which are significant for appropriately conducting the affairs of Jaina organisation and preserving its sanctity.

Certain Signiticant References: The second illustrative, relating to the above

Sūtra, is also important from viewpoint of practising atonements for expiation of sins. Many relative points concerning propitiatory acts to be performed, such as—obtaining re-initiation after completion of prescribed austerities as also to make self-confession and censure oneself for the sin, committed by it, amongst general people after removing the apparel and relinquishing external appearance of a Sādhu for a stipulated period etc. It is cited therein — "A Jaina Sādhu who is afflicted with disease; highly agitated on account of excess formation of wind or flurried as a result of typical causes (say fever of love or passion); who is feeling sick for fear of wrath of a Yakṣa (a demi-god); is seized considerably with the terror let loose by a horse; who is frenzied or hysterical; who is disturbed on account of any calamity forced by a divine power; whose mind is unstable because of attachment to worldly objects or intense emotion of anger, who is feeling perturbed for fear of undergoing severe penances for atonement of sins; it will be undesirable to expel them from the organisation of Jaina mendicants unless they recover fully from their physical or mental ailments. There are similar other illustrations governing the behaviour of Jaina Sādhus.

Requisite qualifications or potentialities needed for attainment of the office of Gandhers (who have acquired true knowledge of God and Jaina philosophy; own sterling qualities of head and heart; who are chief disciples of Tirthankers and compose their teachings in aphoristic style, as heard by them and retained in their memory); do's and don'ts while touring; rules for holding a seat or office; routine how to beg alms; rules for and against sexual enjoyments; information regarding one's own study etc. are some of the points discussed in the above Chheda Sutra which are really significant for having thorough knowledge of routine life of Jaina Sādhus.

The seventh illustrative is worth studying since it signifies reciprocal behaviour of male and female mendicants and their status in the jaina organisation. It is cited that a male mendicant, irrespective of the fact that he had attained initiation hardly three years ago, can act as a spiritual guide or teacher to dictate to a female mendicant who may have even completed thirty years after initiation. Similarly, a male mendicant, having been initiated only 5 years back, can deliver sermons to an old female mendicant as Achārya or preceptor, irrespective of the fact that she had been initiated sixty years ago. These provisions are in conformity with the directions, contained in Vinaya Pitaka (Vinay texts relating to the conduct and behaviour of Buddhist monks or Sādhus) to the effect that the females who had been ordained and received into the order of Buddhist monks even a hundred years ago, were bound to greet, get up to welcome and pay obeisance to male Sādhus by folding the hands together and raising them to the head, irrespective of the consideration that they (males) were ordained and received into the order of ascetics that very day. Thus the consistencies or inconsistencies of such a policy of discrimination between male and female mendicants in a holy organisation, need to be reviewed and re-examined in a critical manner.

The ninth illustrative deals with the religious vows and pledges taken by Jaina Sādhus and the tenth illustrative contains the procedures for observing gradual fasts during the moonlit half of the lunar month and dark half of waning moon:

(1) Beginning from the first day of the moonlit half of the lunar month by taking only one large spoonful barley corn and enhancing the quantity by one spoonful daily—thus taking 15 spoonfuls on 15th day of lunar month and again reducing the quantity by one spoonful daily i.e. taking 14 spoonfuls on 1st day of the dark half of the waning moon and then to go on reducing it by one spoonful daily so as to take only one spoonful on the 14th day and observing complete fast on the 15th day of waning moon (last day of the dark fortnight);

(2) Beginning from the first day of the dark half of the waning moon by taking 15 large spoonful sesame preparation and then to go on reducing the quantity by one spoonful daily—thus taking only one spoonful on the last day of the dark fortnight and again enhancing the quantity by taking two spoonfuls on first day of the moonlit half and then go on enhancing the quantity by one spoonful daily so as to take 15 spoonfuls on fourteenth day and observing total fast on the full moon day (fifteenth day of the bright half of a lunar month).

The tenth Adhyayan incorporates the fixed usage or rules of propriety to be observed by male and female mendicants, while undertaking study of holy scriptural works. Accordingly, they are entitled to study the following religious treatises in accordance with the period of their initiation:

Expiration of time after initiation	*Name of sacred treatises, allowed to be studied:*
Three years	Āchār-Kalpa (Sacred precepts relating to good conduct or behaviour)
Four years	Sutrakritānga (2nd Anga)
Five years	Dashāshrutaskandh (Jaina Agamic scripture) Kalpa and Vyavahār (Chheda Sūtras)
Eight years	Sthānānga (Third Anga) Samvāyānga (Fourth Anga)
Ten years	Vyākhya Prajnapati (Fifth Anga)
Eleven years	Kṣullikā-Vimān-Pravibhakti, Mahati-Vimān-Pravibhakti, Anga Chūlikā, Varga Chūlikā Vrjākhyā-Chūlikā.
Twelve years	Aruṇepapāta, Garuḍopapāta, Varunopapāta, Vaishramaṇopapāta; Velgharopapāta.
Thirteen years	Utthān-shruta, Samuthān Shruta, Devendro-papāta, Nāgpariyapanikā.
Fourteen years	Swapna-Adhyayan
Fifteen years	Chāraṇa-Bhāvanā-Adhyayan
Sixteen years	Veda-Nisarga
Seventeen years	Ashivisha-Bhāvanā-Adhyayan
Eighteen years	Drishṭi-Vish-Bhāvanā-Anga
Nineteen years	Drishṭivād-Anga
Twenty years	Each and every scripture. (All scriptural works)

Rendering of physical service to Acharyas, Preceptors; Sthviras (Senior monks, having spent 20 years after initiation and having acquired systematic knowledge of Agamic scriptures); devoutly austere persons; newly initiated pupils; Sick monks due to infirmity of old age; family priest or teacher; Sādhus of Jaina community or organisation and aged colleagues, has been stressed in the tenth illustrative.

Author : Commentator: `Vyavahār Sūtra' (3rd Chheda Sūtra) is believed to have been written by Achārya Bhadrabāhu. He has also commented upon it. However, it is not clear whether the author and commentator—both named Bhadrabāhu, are one and the same person. It is quite possible that the author and commentator, having a common name, may, however, be distinct scholars. A Bhāshya (a commentary which explains a Sutra or aphorism word by word with comments of its own) is also available but the Bhashya and Niryukti (Etymological interpretation of words or explanations of their derivatives) have almost amalgamated. Achārya Malayagiri has also written an exposition (explanatory note) on Bhashya as well. Other explanatory works have also been written in the shape of Churṇi and Avachūri. It is also believed that an encyclopaedic commentary was also written on Vyavahār Sūtra' but the same is not available now.

4. Dasāsūkhandha (Dashāshrutaskandh)

It is a fourth Chheda Sūtra. It is also called as `Dashā' (State or condition of mind); `Āchār Dashā' (Condition of mind relating to established usages or rules of conduct) or `Dashā Shruta' (holy learning pertaining to different states of mind or vicissitudes of life). It is classified into ten parts and each such division is termed as `Dasha'. For eighth part, the word Adhyayan has appeared.

The first part of Dashā deals with twenty situations of lack of total concentration or devotion to penance. Twenty-one situations of vitiated life (corrupt practises) have been taken up in second part of Dasha. The literal meaning of Sanskrit word 'Shabal' is spotted, variegated, or objectionable. Here the word `Shabal' has been used in the sense of vitiated conduct. In the third Dashā (Chapter), 33 types of insubordinations (disregards to the preceptors) have been discussed.

Characteristics of an Excellent Religious Preceptor

It is cited in fourth part of `Dashā' that spiritual guides or teachers are endowed with eight characteristics or accomplishments, namely:

1. Excellence in manners and morals;
2. Perfection in highest spiritual knowledge or philosophical doctrines;
3. Excellence of body (good health);
4. Art of speech and perfection in mode of utterance;
5. Eloquence in recitation;
6. High intellectualism;
7. Perfection through experiments or practice; and
8. Competence in making collections.

The above-noted characteristics or excellent qualities of religious preceptors have been further classified so as to give clear perception of magnificent ascetic culture. Hence the said classifications are being discussed below:-

Four types of excellence in manners and morals:

(1) To be firmly established in practising self-control or self-denial;
(2) To be free from egoism and vanity;
(3) Having no fixed employment or regular income; and
(4) To have a stable or unwavering mind.

Four types of perfection in highest spiritual knowledge:

(1) Well-versed in Jaina Agamic literature;
(2) Familiarity with Jaina scriptures;
(3) Well-conversance with characteristic Jaina Canonical literature; and
(4) Perfect accuracy in utterance or voiced sound.

Four types of physical elegance:

(1) Uniform physique with proportional length and height;
(2) Having undisgraceful body;
(3) Firm and steady constitution; and
(4) Perfection of sensual organs and their capability of fully responding.

Four types of perfection in speech or utterance:

(1) Speech or language fit to be grasped;
(2) Sweet-speaking;
(3) Avoiding use of unconditioned or unrestricted speech; and
(4) Use of distinct and confident speech.

Four types of accomplishments in reading and recitation:

(1) After due consideration, the purpose should be specified why it was desired to recite the texts;
(2) To recite in a proper manner;
(3) To elucidate an appropriate subject only; and
(4) To explain or elaborate the substance in an explicit manner.

Four types of Intellectualism:

(1) Disintegrated intellect (A sort of knowledge);
(2) Desire for acquiring knowledge;
(3) The knowledge to be imparted or given away to others; and
(4) Possessing of knowledge and preserving it in memory.

Four types of wisdom for practising:

(1) Practising of ideology with self-knowledge or realisation;
(2) Practising of religious doctrines as enunciated in an assembly or synod;
(3) Practising of Jainism as propounded in a regional assembly; and
(4) Practising as per knowledge of the essentials.

Four types of competence in making arrangements or collection of anything:

(1) To find out and examine carefully a suitable site for stay of all religious mendicants, in rainy season;
(2) To arrange for bed-spreads with support for all Jaina monks for meditation etc.
(3) To perform each and every duty at scheduled hours; and
(4) To adore and pay respects to senior guides or elderly men of reputation.

Details of total concentration or absorption of mind for profound meditation and its ten forms are contained in the 5th Dashā (chapter or portion). In sixth Dashā, ten gradual stages of spiritual endeavours or performances by a house-hold devotee, follower or votary of Jaina religion have been explained in detail. In this regard, the author of above-noted Chheda Sūtra has comprehensively dealt with about inactivism or habit of abstaining from spiritual performances as a result of false illusions and in the process of referring to the various sinful acts or deeds and vices, creeping in as a consequence of malice, malevolence, worldly illusions, rancour, voluptuousness, worldly pleasures, prosperity and craving for popularity etc., the author has portrayed a thrilling picture of hellish punishments.

The seventh `Dashā' deals with how a devout mendicant must move through 12 stages of spiritual advancement. While discussing about conduct rules to be adhered to by a mendicant during first stage of his religious performances, ranging for a period of one month, it is cited that during his month-long tour, if he happens to visit the territory where people are familiar with him, he must move ahead after staying during the night only. However, where there is none to recognize him, he is free to stay for a night or two and, thereafter, he must leave. In case of violating these guide-lines, the mendicant shall be liable to expiate in the same manner as he will have to atone in case of committing the sin of foresaking the penance or spiritual performance or deviating from observance of the obligations after attainment of initiation. Each stage of devotion and mortification, to be practised by a Jaina mendicant, has been extensively dealt with in the seventh Chapter, which are essential to be studied by each and every mendicant, engaged in spiritual pursuits for self-realisation.

The eighth 'Dashā' contains detailed version regarding removal of foetus from the womb of a Brahmaṇa lady and re-establishing it in the womb of a brave woman of Kshattriya clan; birth of Lord Mahāvira; his initiation in ascetism and his attaining state of omniscience and highest perfection and finally, attaining his salvation or emancipation. The eighth Chheda Sūtra is also styled as `Pajjosaṇa-Kappa' or `Kalpa-Sūtra'. A number of scholars and Achāryas have written commentaries on the said Sūtra. Amongst the said commentators, the prominent ones are Jinapriya, Dharmasāgar, Vinaya-Vijaya, Samaya-Sunder, Ratna-Sāgar, Sangh-Vijaya, and Laxmi-Vallabh etc. During observance of `Parynshan' festival (Performance of certain rituals and delivering discourses on its significance), the Jaina Sādhus quote from `Dashāshrutaskandh' Sūtra at the time of delivering sermons before their disciples and followers. Traditionally reading or quoting from Chheda Sutras publicly in religious gatherings is forbidden, since they contain remedial measures for the omissions and commissions, made knowingly or unknowingly by male and female mendicants of Jaina organisation, and they are meant to be known by the sinners only who are liable to expiate for their sins. `Paryūshan Kalpa' is although one of the Chheda Sūtras, yet it has its own distinct utility and significance for obtaining knowledge of historic events relating to the life of Lord Mahavirā, the last Tirthanker of Jaina religion. It is a hearsay that in Samvat year 523 of Vikram era. the prince of King Dhruvasena, ruler of Ānandapur, had expired. In order to console and for bestowing of peace to the bereaved family, the practice of quoting from the said Sūtra had started, in the course of delivering a consolatory speech.

Author : Explanatory Literature : The author of `Dashāshrutaṣkandh' (Fourth Chheda Sūtra) in believed to be Achārya Bhadrabāhu. He is also believed to have written commentary upon it. However, while dealing with `Vyavahār' (Third Chheda Sūtra), it has already been stressed that the composition of original Sūtra and comments upon it cannot be made by one and the same person. A gloss has also been written on it. A small commentary or exposition, written by Brahamarshi Pārshvachandra, is also available on the said Sūtra.

5. Kappa (Kalpa or Vrahat Kalpa)

While discussing about the contents of, eight Adhyayan of `Dashāshrutaṣkandhi', it has been stated above that the said Chheda Sūtra is also known and styled as `Paryushan Kalpa'. However, the subject-matter of the fifth Chheda Sūtra, also styled as `Kalpa or Vrahat-Kalpa' is evidently different from the above. The literal meaning of Sanskrit word `Kalpa' or `Kalpya' is proper, fit or right. It also means a prescribed rule to be observed in preference to all others. The rules of conduct to be observed for leading the life of self-denial or abstinence are known as `Kalpa' or `Kalpya'. On the contrary, the acts which hinder our spiritual endeavours are known as `Akalpa' or `Akalpya' (Not fit to be followed). There is an elaborate discussion regarding nature of clothes, pots and places for residence or halt, to be used by male and female mendicants, in order to enable them to lead a well regulated and restrained life. It is believed to be most ancient moral code to be followed by Jaina mendicants for the purpose of leading a true saintly life. The Chheda Sūtra, in question, is highly important like `Nishitha' and `Vyavahār' (First and third Sūtras) so far its language and the subjects dealt with, are concerned. The language of the Chheda Sūtra, under reference, is decidedly more ancient. However, the commentators or interpreters have carried out modifications (alterations and additions) here and there which have changed its shape as had been the fate of other Jaina Agamas.

Shape : Contents: The above Sūtra is classified into six illustratives. The topics relating to the social relationship between Jaina mendicants have been extensively discussed, namely—their manner of eating and drinking; mode of their living and their movements or performance of tours to other regions etc. Incidentally, it has been laid down in the first illustrative of the above Chheda Sūtra, that the male and female mendicants are permitted to move on the East upto Anga region (The territory situated on right bank of Ganges, called Angapuri. This territory is situated very near the modern Bhagalpur) and upto Magadha territory in South Bihar; On South upto Koshambi (It is near the modern Kosam, about 30 miles above Allahabad); On west upto Thaneshavar region (Lying to North of Kurukṣetra on Delhi-Ambāla road) and on North-East upto Kuṇāl territory. This is the area, inhabited by Āryans. It is not advisable at all to move beyond the said regions. However, it has been further laid down that in case the Jaina monks do not apprehend any hostile opposition in spreading the message of their religion or else they perceive possibilities of enriching the spiritual and philosophical knowledge pertaining to Jainism, in that case it may be worth-while to tour the places beyond the above territories as well.

The third illustrative contains prohibitive rules in regard to moving freely in each others places of rest without maintaining propriety of conduct in relation to their sitting, sleeping, eating, studying and practising meditation etc. Besides the above, many other issues relating to performance of prescribed acts at the time of attaining initiation; obtaining possession of articles, necessary to lead the day-today life of mendicancy; knowledge of the nature of clothes to be put on during four months of rainy season and remaining eight months of the year, have been elaborately dealt with in the third illustrative. The said guide-lines help in adhering to the path of self-denial and mortification as also in maintaining spiritual awareness precisely.

The fourth illustrative deals with conduct rules and atonements to be practised by Jaina mendicants for expiation of their sins. In that connection, the following modes of atonements have been analytically discussed:

(1) **Anndhatika**—Performance of exterior austerities by observing fasts etc.
(2) **Pāranchika**—A religious mendicant, expelled from the Jaina organisation, will renounce his/her garment and paraphernalia of ascetic life for a scheduled period and censure himself/herself openly before each and every person. Thereafter, he or she will be entitled to obtain re-initiation; and
(3) **Anvāsthāpya**—Attaining re-initiation after completion of prescribed austerities.

A Few Significant Citations: Incidentally, it has been stated, where the context so demanded, that a male or female mendicant was forbidden to cross any of the leading holy rivers more than once in a month, namely—Ganges, Yanuna, Saryu, Kosi and Māhi etc. Simultaneously, it is also cited therein. "In Irāvati (Rāvi) river in Kuṇāla region, there is always scanty water, hence it is advised to cross the river by keeping one leg inside the water and the other leg above the level of water and move ahead step by step cautiously by decanting the water. It may not be undesirable on the part of a mendicant to cross the said river even twice or thrice a month. However, where it may not be found feasible on account of excessive water, the right course will be to cross the river only once in a month.

Incidentally, it is mentioned in the sixth illustrative of the above Sūtra that if a nail, thorn or sharp-edged piece of a glass pierces in the foot of a Jaina mendicant and he is not able to pull it out as also there be no other male mendicant nearby to help him, the female mendicant could extract it with a clear conscience which will not be, in any way deemed to be an infringement of the directives of a Tirthanker. Similarly, if an insect, maggot, germ or dust particle falls in the eye of a Jaina mendicant and he, himself, may not be able to remove it and at the same time, there be no other male Sādhu nearby to help him, the female mendicant can rub it out with a clear heart and in any view of the matter, it may not be a violation of the conduct rules or directive issued by a Tirthanker.

If a female mendicant happens to face the similar situation, the male Sādhu may pull out the nail, thorn or a sharp-edged piece of a glass from the foot of the female mendicant and similarly, he may remove or rub out the insect, germ or dust particle from her eye with a clean heart and the same may not be offending the directions of a Tirthanker, in any way.

There is another assumption. In case, a female mendicant may be found slipping from a rough terrain or a rock and she may not be in a position to balance herself. At the same time, there be no other female mendicant, nearby to rescue her, then the help may be sought of a male mendicant to provide her support and save her from falling down which will not be deemed to be an infringement of the conduct rules, enunciated by a Tirthanker. Similarly, if a male Sādhu rescues a female mendicant by pulling her out of a river, reservoir or mud-deposit, it will not be a violation of the guide-lines issued by a Tirthanker. In the same manner, if a female mendicant happens to stumble down while ascending or descending a boat or fails to balance herself due to physical disorder, caused by the excess of wind within the system or feels prone to end her life after getting hysteric as a consequence of excessive joy or affliction due to intense grief or is perturbed under the ill-influence of super-natural powers and evil spirits, a male Sādhu may save the female victim by catching hold of her hand and providing physical support. The author of the Chheda Sūtra, in question, has cited many other examples to specify that on the face of such extraordinary events, a male mendicant will be perfectly justified to extend his help and save her form impending disaster. He will be absolutley committing no fault or defying the guide-lines of a Tirthanker.

It is thus evident that the author has spared no pains to analyse various aspects, relating to mutual behaviour of male and female mendicants in the organisation and specified a system for maintaining effective purity in the day-today life of jaina mendicants. It was essential to do so to enable them to act more humanely and to eusure that they did not ignore their obligations towards each other.

Composition and Comments: The author of `Kalpa' or `Vrahat Kalpa' (fifth Chheda Sutra) is believed to be Achārya Bhadrabāhu. It is cited by Achārya Malayagiri that the Chheda Sūtra, in question, was composed on the basis of the material, contained in 20th chapter of 3rd section, titled `Āchār' (conduct), relating to ninth Pūrva, styled Pratyākhyān'. In order to avoid extinction of expiatory rules or prescribed religious acts to be practised for atonement of sins and which were essential to be learnt by each and every male and female mendicant, Achārya Bhadrabāhu had composed *Vyavhār* and *Kalpa Sutras* (3rd and 5th Chheda Sūtras).

The author of the commentary on `Kalpa' is also believed to be Achārya Bhadrabāhu, which is, however, disputed. A brief commentary has been written by Sri Sanghdās Gaṇi. Achārya Malayagiri has stated that etymological interpretation, written by Achārya Bhadrabāhu and bhāshya (A commentary which explains each Sutra word by word with comments of the author), written by Sanghdās Gaṇi, have so amalgamated with each other that it is almost impossible to segregate them and obtain their distinct identities. Achārya Malayagiri had composed a briefing on the Bhāshya of Sanghdās Gaṇi. However, it was incomplete and after about two centuries, Achārya Kṣemakirti Sūri had given it a final shape. An extensive commentary is also available on *Vrahat-Kalpa* but it is not complete. It covers only upto 3rd illustrative. A characteristic small commentary has also been written on Vraḥat-Kalpa.

6. Pancha Kappa (Panch-Kalpa)

The above Chheda-Sūtra in known by two names—`Panch-Kalpa Sūtra' and `Panch-Kalpa Bhāshya'. At a glance, it appears that they are two distinct works but, infact, it is not so. They are only two names for one and the same scripture. According to Achārya Malayagiri and Kṣemkirti Sūri, Panch-Kalpa Bhāshya is only a component of Vrahat-Kalpa Bhāshya. It is a similar case like `Pinda-niryukti' and `Augha niryukti'. *Piṇḍa-Niryukti* is basically not an independent treatise. It is only a component of `Dashvaikālika Niryukti'. Similarly, Augha-niryukti' is not an independent work but only a component of `Āvashyaka-Niryukti (authored by Achārya Bhadrabāhu). Since they dealt with distinct subjects, they were categorized as independent compositions for the convenience of the readers.

Since Panch-Kalpa Sūtra' or `Panch-Kalpa-bhāshya is derived from `Vrahat-Kalpa bhāshya, hence it should also be believed to have been written by Achārya Sanghdās Gaṇi. A brief commentary had also been written on Panch-Kalpa Sūtra.

Jiyakappasutta (Jitkalpa-Sūtra)

Here the traditional meaning of the word `Jia' or 'Jiya' or `Jita' is a sort of practice relating to old manners and morals; propriety of conduct; and adherence to settled rules for atonement of sins and maintenance of purity etc. The said Sūtra contains expiatory rules, meant for Jaina mendicants to enable them to atone for their sins accordingly. The said scripture consists of 103 verses. The issues relating to the significance and usefulness of expiatory acts by observance of religious austerities, meant for purification and refinement of the inner-self. Ten types of expiatory acts have been elaborately explained in it--

(1) Confession of the alleged sin before the preceptor without concealing anything;

(2) The expiator should, himself express his/her repentence and pray 'let my sin be turned out to be baseless and false';
(3) Expiating in both ways combinedly as shown above;
(4) Rejection of defiled food obtained unknowingly;
(5) Renunciation of unnecessary concern or attachment for physical comforts by way of intense concentration and resoluteness;
(6) Observance of fasting etc. being external forms of penance;
(7) Reduction in order of seniority amongst initiated monks. The junior mendicants get the advantage of seniority over the monk, having committed the sin, for the period, he has been down-graded;
(8) To make amends and get re-initiated;
(9) Obtaining fresh initiation after completion of prescribed penance; and
(10) The Jaina mendicant, having been expelled from the organisation, must put off the Sādhu garment and censure, himself before each and every person, he meets.

It is believed that the practice of observing ninth and tenth atonements came to an end after final salvation of Achārya Bhadrabāhu.

Composition : Interpretative Literature

Pre-eminent Jaina scholar and author of `Visheshavashyaka Bhāshya', Sri Jinabhadragaṇi Kṣmāshramaṇa, (Seventh Century of Vikram Era) is believed to have accomplished `Jita Kalpa-Sūtra Bhāshya' also. However, the said commentary is in no way an independent composition. It is merely a collection of various verses from `Brahat-Kalpa-bhāshya', Vyavahār Bhāshya; Panchkalpa bhāshya; and Piṇḍa-Niryukti etc. Achārya Sidhasen has made a briefing on it. Srichandra Sūri has written an annotation, styled `Visham-pada Vyākhyā' (Complex formations requiring explanations). Sri Tilkāchārya has written a gloss on it. The compositions titled `Yati Jitakalpa' and `Shradha Jitakalpa' are also believed to form part of `Jita Kalpa Sūtra'. The ethical values prescribed for Jaina Sādhus have been dealt with in `Yati Jita Kalpa' while the conduct rules to be followed by Jaina saints or Votaries (as distinguished from the Bhikshus or initiated mendicants) have been explained in `Shrādha Jitakalpa'. `Yati Jitakalpa' was written by Somprabhasari and Sri Sādhuratna has written a gloss on it. Shrādh Jitakalpa was accomplished by `Achārya Dharamghosha and Sri Somtilaka has written an exposition on it.

Principal Scriptures

`Uttrādhyayan', `Dashavaikālika', `Āvashyaka', `Pinda-Niryukti' and `Augha Niryukti' are generally acknowledged to be basic scriptures of Jaina religion. However, it is not a unanimous opinion. A few scholars express the view that only `Uttradhyayan'; `Dashvaikālika' and `Āvashyaka' are principal works, forming part of Jaina Agamas. They do not agree that `Pinda Niryukti' and `Augha Niryukti' are also basic scriptural works of Jaina religion. Certain scholars include `Pinda Niryukti' also amongst fundamental scriptures besides the aforesaid three sacred works. As discussed initially, there are scholars who include `Augha Niryukti' also amongst fundamental scriptures of Jaina religion. However, there are a few other scholars who exclude `Avashyaka' from the list of three basic scriptures and include `Anuyoga Dwār' and `Nandi Sūtra'—thus in all four basic scriptures. A few others also include `Pāksika Sūtra' as fifth fundamental scripture alongwith the said four.

Significance of Fundamental Scriptures, Referred to Above

`Uttradhyayan' and `Dashavaikālika' Sūtras' have, infact, great significance in Agamic scriptures of Jaina religion. The scholars treat them as most ancient works in the entire canonical literature of Jaina religion. From linguistic point as well, their ancientness is undisputed. They are highly accomplished holy books keeping in view the nature of the subjects discussed therein. They may be compared with pre-eminent Buddhistic, writings, namely—'Sūtra Nipāta' and `Dhamapada'. An analytical study of the said two scriptures by the student-disciples and research scholars will enable them to make an evaluation of Jaina philosophical and ethical doctrines as also to assess the living conditions of Jaina mendicants, governed by the said ethics.

Why Called Principal or Basic Scriptures

How and when the term 'principal or basic Sūtras' came in vogue for the first time, no definite answer is available. The use of these words are nowhere found in Jaina Agamas. Even in later compositions, we find that the words `basic or fundamental Sūtras' have appeared in the exposition of 30th couplet of `Jaina-dharmavarstotra', written by Achārya Bhāvdeva Sūri. It is cited therein that `Uttradhyayan', Āvashyaka, "Pinda-Niryukti-Ogha Niryukti" and `Dashavaikālika' are four basic or fundamental Sūtras.

Views of Western Scholars: It is certainly praise-worthy that a few scholars of western countries have, infact, done a tremendous job with exemplary dedication and perseverance, undeviated by hard labour, so far as making deep study of Indian canonical literature and undertaking critical investigation thereon is concerned. How far they were able to accomplish their work and what were the attainments in the field of their research and investigation, are some of the points to be debated upon independently, yet their straneous efforts, sense of enthusiasm, constant zeal and endeavour are, no doubt, exemplary for Indian scholars. The intellectuals of Germany and other Western countries have specifically done considerable research work on Jaina canonical literature and Prākrita dialects. The diverse views expressed by the Western scholars relating to Jaina Agamas are produced hereunder:

Views of Prof. Charpantier: The renowned German orientalist, Prof. Charpantier has written in his prologue on `Uttradhyayan Sūtra' that since it contained Lord Mahavirā's own utterances, hence it came to be known as fundamental Sūtra. It means that it is a collection of the words of Lord Mahavirā, himself, uttered by him, while delivering his discourses.

Opinion of Dr. Walter Schubring

Renowned research scholar of Jaina canonical literature, German Professor, Dr. Walter Schubring, has commented in his book *Lax Raligion Dyaina* on page 79 (Published in German language) that since the said scriptures contained the basic guide-lines, to be followed by Jaina male and female mendicants while practising mental concentration and undertaking other spiritual pursuits, the sacred texts came to be known as basic or fundamental Sūtras of Jaina religion.

Views of Prof. Guerinot: Renowned Italian Prof. Guerinot, a research scholar of Jaina scriptures, has explained it differently. While doing so, it appears that he had in his mind two shapes of a holy book — the main Sūtra-work and the commentaries, written upon it. Accordingly, he stated that the words `basic scriptures' were consistent with `Traites original' in Italian language. That is to say, professor Guerinot believed that the words `Mūl-Sūtras' had appeared for `basic or original compositions'. In various commentaries, annotations, etymological interpretations, expositions and, glosses etc, written to explain the `Mūl Sūtras' the words `Original Sūtra' have appeared for the original composition on which the commentaries have been written. A lot of explanatory literature is found to have been accomplished on `Uttradhyayan' and `Dashavaikālika'—more than any other scripture of Jaina religion. Thus, the tradition of referring to the original productions as `Mūl Sūtras' may have started.

Critical Review

The arguments of Western scholars are, no doubt, objective, yet they do not bear examination when tried on factual considerations. The assumption of Prof. Chārpantier that the words `Mūl Sūtras' had been used since they contained the original utterances of Tirthanker, Lord Mahavirā, holds good, to some extent so far as `Uttradhyayan' is concerned. However, it has no relevance, whatsoever, with `Dashāvaikālika' etc. In case, the word `Mūl' had any consistency with the original utterances of Lord Mahavira, it could be more appropriately used for `Acharanga' and `Sūtrakritānga' (the first and second of the twelve sacred books of the Jainas, forming part of Agamas), which contain religious sermons and discourses, delivered by Lord Mahavirā, and composed in Sūtras (aphorisms) by his Gandhers, who had heard and retained them in their memory. However, it is not correct so far as `Dashāvaikālika' etc. are concerned. Hence the assumption of Prof. Charpantier with regard to the purport of the word `Mūl' cannot be accepted.

The contention of Dr. Walter Schubring that as the `Mūl Sūtras' contained initial guide-lines with regard to the manners of action, mutual behaviour, traditions and methods to be followed by Jaina mendicants, hence the word `Mūl' (original) was used for the said Sūtras. However, this argument is also ineffective since all other fundamental scriptures of Jaina religion donot deal with manners and morals to be followed at the initial stage of religious mendicancy. The said argument does have relevance with `Dashāvaikālika' to certain extent but the case of other Agamic scriptures is different `Uttradhyayan' holds a unique place amongst all other Mūl Sūtras, referred to above, yet it deals with numerous other subjects relating to the philosophical ideology of Jaina religion, besides rules and bye-rules, methods and manners to be followed by Jaina mendicants during the long course of their religious mendicancy, a number of illustrations, stories, themes and series of events, having historical significance, are also found incorporated in it, which are connected with many facets of ascetic culture or renunciation and philosophical doctrines of the religion. Therefore, the argument of Dr.Walter Schubring is also faulty and one-sided. All what has been discussed in Mūl Sūtras, is not fully reflected in the explanation offered by Prof. Schubring. It does not impress that the scholar has expressed his opinion after minute consideration and profound thinking. The fact remains that there are other important scriptures as well on which many scholars have commented upon. They could, of course, vary in number. No definite inferences can be drawn from such vague comments. Hence the futility of such vague assumptions is evident.

After pondering over the above discussion, it transpires that since the said scriptures deal with fundamental principles, ideological and philosophical doctrines of Jaina religion, they are known as `Mūl Sūtras'. If we look into the nature of subjects dealt with in Uttrādhyayan and Dashāvaikālika, this fact may be amply evident.

Uttarajjhayaṇa (Uttrādhyayan)

Name:Appropriateness: Uttrādhyayan is literally a combination of two words—Uttar and Adhyayan. The meanings of Uttar are—(a) later-latter, following or subsequent, and (b) superiority, excellence or characteristic. Besides, it is used normally in the sense of an answer or reply.

So far its meaning as latter or subsequent in concerned, it may be explained here that Uttrādhyayan was always studied after recitation of Achārānga (The title of the first of twelve sacred books of Jainas, dealing with the ethics to be adhered to by mendicants).

After final salvation of Achārya Shayambhava, an authority on Jaina Agamas, a change occurred in the traditional way, meant for recitation of Uttrādhyayan. It began to be recited after Dashavaikālika. However, no necessity was felt for effecting, any change in its name, since `Uttrādhyayan' was recited subsequently in both cases.

The literal meaning of the word 'Uttar' is also superior and excellent. Therefore, certain scholars have interpreted that the ideological and philosophical doctrines of Jaina religion have been discussed in Uttrādhyayan in an excellent manner, hence its name is quite appropriate and consistent with the nature of the subjects dealt with therein.

Prof. Leumann centered his mind straightly on the literal meanings of the words `Uttar' and `Adhyayan' and inferred that `Uttrādhyayan' means later readings. According to Prof. Leumann, the said readings or Agamic Scripture had been composed after accomplishment of 12 Angas (Twelve sacred books of the Jainas, forming part of Agamic literature). Therefore, the said scriptural word came to be known as Uttrādhyayan.

It is cited in `Kalpa Sūtra' and various other commentaries that Lord Mahavirā had answered 36 self-posed (unasked) questions, covering almost all points, relating to ideological and philosophical doctrines of Jaina religion, prior to attaining his final salvation. Accordingly, the collection and compilation of the said readings came to be known as `Aprashta-Vyākarṇa' (self expounding or analysis). The said sacred book, containing replies to self-posed or unasked questions was titled as "Uttrādhyayan". The reference of `Aprashta-Vyākarṇa' is also found in `Trishṭishlākāpurushcharita', authored by Achārya Hemchandra, an erudite Jaina scholar.

Examination : The explanation furnished by the authors of `Kalpa Sūtra' and various explanatory writings and the argument of Prof. Leumann basically differ. Replying of 36 self-posed questions by Lord Mahavirā, prior to his final salvation and their compilation in the shape of a book later on by his chief disciples is true. However, to infer that the said book came to be known as `Uttrādhyayan' does not appeal to the mind. In place of asserting that Lord Mahavirā had answered self-posed questions, prior to his attaining final salvation, will it not be more consistent to say that he had delivered his last sermons to enrich spiritual knowledge of his disciples and followers. Besides this, the word `Vyākarṇa' (analysis) has appeared for the answers given by Lord Mahavirā which means he had expounded his last, spiritual message. In case, the word `Uttar' would have been defined to mean `last or in the final phase', there could have been slight consistency. However, the use of the word `Uttar' in the sense of answer has no relevance[1] with the actual contents of `Uttrādhyayan'. Illustrations, legendary tales and series of events are incorporated in the said `Sūtra', which cannot be defined as answers in any view of the matter. From literary viewpoint also, there could be no answer without placing a question. It could be a religious lecture, discussion, analysis or evaluation of earlier teachings but not an answer. What the commentator has stated about the nature of the contents of Uttradhyayan, the view of Prof. Leumann only contradict it.

However, what Prof. Leumann has commented, is not illogical. According to the findings of philologists, the language of Uttrādhyayan is quite old. Prof. Leumann has nowhere established its recency. On the other hand, he has commented that it was a subsequent composition after accomplishment of 12 Angas which could not be treated as impossible.

There is one more point. There are numerous other sacred books which were accomplished after composition of 12 Angas. The question arises why the said sacred book alone was titled as `Uttrādhyayan' because of its subsequence to the Angas. In reply, it may be stated that Uttrādhyayan is equally rich in contents and matches in significance with 12 Angas. Therefore, the said accomplished book was named as Uttrādhyayan. However, it may be a mere surmise. No other solid argument or explanation is available, in its support.

In nutshell, it is a unique accomplishment in entire Jaina canonical literature so far enunciation of philosophical and ethical doctrines are concerned. Just as *Bhagvada Gita* is the very essence of Vedic philosophy, Uttrādhyayan enjoys the same significance in relation to Jaina philosophy. Its poetic and pleasant style; sweet, soft, delicate and lovely dialogues; use of spontaneous and rhetorical language

1. Lord Mahavirā had given his answers or delivered his sermons at the last stage of his life.

etc. besides several other characteristics have greatly impressed the critics and research scholars. Dr. Winternitz has highly spoken of it, admiring that it was, infact, poetic expression of ascetic culture and was having the same significance as Mahābhārata in Vedic literature; Sūtra-nipāta and `Dhammapada' in Buddhistic writings.

The significance and usefulness of `Uttrādhyayan' has not been appreciated for a few centuries only but since very long time. The annotator has demonstrated its importance in three verses which read: "The persons who have liberated their souls from worldly bonds; who are really worthy and excellent and who are completely satisfied, are entitled to study 36 Adhyayans (Chapters) of Uttrādhyayan. On the other hand, the mortal-beings who have not liberated their souls from worldly bonds; who are crooked and perverse; who have not got rid of their knots; who are inauspicious and unfortunate; who have not been able to overcome worldly attachments and are plunged in worldly pleasures over head and ears, who are sinful and source of affliction and distress for others, they are not entitled to study Uttrādhyayan. Hence the student-disciples, devoted to spiritual, accomplishments, should undertake study of `Uttrādhyayan', containing fundamental teachings, imparted by Jaina Arhats or omniscients and perfect in all respects after performance of prescribed austerities etc. and obtaining blessings of religious guides or Achāryas.

Uttrādhyayan is comprised of 36 Adhyayans. The titles of 36 Adhyayans, relating to Uttrādhyayan, are cited in 36th annexure to `Samvāyānga Sūtra' (title of the fourth Anga or sacred book out of the 12 scriptures of Jaina religion) which conform with the names of 36 Adhyayans of Uttrādhyayan. At the end of 36th Adhyayan of Uttrādhyayan, appearing under the style of `Jivājivavibhakti' (classification of organic and inorganic creations), it is cited: "After manifesting highest spiritual knowledge, meant for excellent and worthy scholars, who had liberated their souls from worldly bonds and which is contained in 36 Adhyayans of Uttrādhyayan, Lord Mahavirā, a supreme divinity and an omniscient, and son of distinguished parents had attained his final emancipation." It has already been discussed above how Lord Mahavirā had delivered his last sermons by way of self-posed questions and their answers at the time of his final phase of life,[1] which formed the theme of 36 Adhyayans of Uttrādhyayan.

Views of Etymologist, Acharya Bhadrābahu

However, the views of etymologist, Achārya Bhadrabāhu differ from the traditional belief. He has written in his commentary:—"The contents of a few chapters of Uttrādhyayan have been derived from 12 Angas (12 sacred scriptures of Jainas); a few of them are based on the religious discourses, delivered by Tirthanker, himself; while a few of them have been accomplished as per directives of Budhas (highly prudent scholars to whom the highest truths of religion and philosophy are revealed automatically without help of any spiritual guide); a few Adhyayans are on the basis of mutual dialogues or debates; In this way, 36 Adhyayans were accomplished for redeeming mankind from shackles of worldly bonds."

1. It is traditionally believed by Jainas that Lord Mahavirā had delivered his last sermons on the night of Dipavali, prior to attaining his final emancipation, in the shape of 36 questions and answers.

The author of gloss, Jinadas Mahattar, and Vādivetal Shānti Sūri, author of an extensive commentary, have subscribed to the views of etymologist, Achārya Bhadrabāhu. According to them, the second Adhyayan deals with physical afflictions and extreme hardships borne by Jaina saints, while practising religious austerities. Its contents have been derived from 70th Chapter of Pūrva, styled `Karma Pravāda', relating to 12th Anga `Drishttivāda'. The eighth Adhyayan, styled `Kāpilya' is based on the teachings of Kapila, an erudite and highly intelligent scholar. The tenth Adhyayan titled `Drumpushpika' contains the utterances of Tirthanker, Lord Mahavirā. The 23rd Adhyayan, styled `Keshi Gautmiya' is in the shape of mutual conversations and dialogues.

Literal sense of the words `Bhadrabāhunā Proktāni' (elaborately explained by Achārya Bhadrabāhū)

A citation is also found to the effect: "Bhadrābahuna Proktāni Bhadrabāhbāni Uttrādhyayanāni" from which a few scholars wrongly infer that Achārya Bhadrabāhu was the author of Uttrādhyayan. The foremost point to be debated here is that Achārya Bhadrabāhu is the author of the commentary on Uttrādhyayan and not the main Sūtra. It has been already discussed above that according to Achārya Bhadrabāhu, the contents of 36 Adhyayans of `Uttrādhyayan' have been derived from various sources—from 12 sacred Angas; discourses and utterances of Tirthanker, himself; as enunciated by Buddha (highly accomplished scholar, needing no guidance from any other spiritual leader) as well as based on debates and dialogues.

In the above phrase, the verb `Proktani' appears with the subject in instrumental case, `Bhadrabāhuna'. The literal meaning of the word `Proktani' is not composition. The formation of the word `Proktāni'—`Prokarshena-uktāni' which means to elaborate, enunciate or to instruct. The word has been defined accordingly in grammars of `Shākṭāyan' and `Sidhhema'. Thus in accordance with the said interpretation, Achārya Bhadrabāhu could be an excellent interpretator, exponent or an expert on Uttradhyayan but not its author in any view of the matter.

Certain scholars are of the opinion that 18 Adhyayans of the initial half portion of Uttrādhyayan are comparatively older while 18 Adhyayans of the latter portion are recent. However, no authoritative or circumstantial proofs are available to substantiate this view or make any demarcation between alleged two portions of Uttrādhyayan.

Examination : Comments: If we care to examine minutely, we find that the writings of the said scripture are neither based exclusively on the religious utterances of Lord Mahavirā nor it has been accomplished by one single individual. It is explicit that the language throughout is not identical but varies. On one hand, we find the use of ancient form of Ardha-Māgadhi Prākrita and on the other, we observe that uses of recent forms of words, pertaining to Ardha Māgadhi Prākrita are also available. From this, it is obvious that the entire scripture had not been accomplished at a single stretch of time. It appears that new portions have been added from time to time, resulting in accomplishment of a complete scripture, forming part of Jaina Agamas. However, no indisputable evidence is available to establish when and by whom such additions and modifications had been carried out. In nutshell, it may be more logical to assert that different sages and philosophers had contributed to the accomplishment of Uttrādhyayan and they did not belong to the same era.

Contents: The subjects relating to transient nature of life; vicious consequences of malevolent acts; attitude of a stupid person; wretched life; ill consequences of sensual enjoyments; comparison of a person, indulging in sensual pleasures with a goat; specific features of living-beings, attaining lowest existences; rarity in attainment of human-life; sacred texts of Jains Agamas; religious faith; significance of leading an austere life; capability of house-hold devotees and nature of austerities to be performed by them; destiny of a noble and virtuous person; pleasures of divine life; features of wise and ignorant persons; delightful effects of knowledge; worthlessness of sectarian outlook; demoralizing effects of communalism; an ideal Sadhu; conditions for devotion to perance by religious students; wicked mendicants; minute deviations, defiling flaws of religious mendicants; 8 types of guide lines for delivering religious discourses; A true devotional act; A priest; nature of fire meant for performance of yajna; daily routine prescribed for religious mendicants, engaged in performance of spiritual endeavours, valiant features of devotees, determined to attain perfection; course for attainment of self-conquest and development; understanding to judge what was to be attained, what was to be refrained from and what was to be rejected or ignored; lack of vigilance, carelessness and mistaken judgments are the prime causes of vices, creeping in our mind such as greed, illusion, insensibility anger, worldly attachments and rancour etc. details of Karmas (acts done in our present and former births); self-realisation by multiplication of atoms, attracted in our bodies by practising deep meditation and concentration of mind; sense of absolute detachment; worldly objects; death without achieving spiritual enlightenment and death after accomplishment of spiritual gains etc., have been elaborately dealt with and profoundly discussed in different Adhyayans (Chapters) of Uttrādhyayan.

Illustrations : Episodes : Its another significant part consists of metaphorical descriptions, illustrations, similes, and short stories or tales. Philosophical and ethical doctrines of Jaina religion have been elaborately discussed in Uttrādhyayan, which is really unique from various viewpoints. Twenty-fifth Adhyayan is exemplary in as much as it vividly deals with spiritual endeavours, their forms, methods and modes etc. There are several chapters which demonstrate beautiful combinations of similies and metaphoric expressions which help in elucidation of the points so nicely that they are easily understood by the students and disciples. The legendary tale, relating to Indra, king of heaven and princely sage, Nami really presents a lively portrayal of characters who are absolutely detached, having enduring patience and how they strive to attain final emancipation is incorporated in the ninth Adhyayan. The 12th Adhyayan of Uttrādhyayan, styled "Hari Keshiya", contains revolutionary and progressive views wherein effectiveness of an austere life and dignity of a devout, engaged in spiritual pursuits—a holy saint, Harikeshbala, born in a Shudra family (lowest in the traditional Hindu caste hierarchy) is well established as against false arrogance, vanity and vain glory of a higher caste or family.

The 22nd Adhyayan, titled `Rathnemiya' is unique from various viewpoints in as much as it endorses the supremacy of self-prowess and creation of spiritual awareness etc. There are exciting discussions about the life events of Tirthanker Arishṭanemi; absolute renunciation of worldly desires and passions by him; self-destroying weaknesses of a Jaina Bhikṣu, Rathnemi's internal mental infirmity rising of intense sexual desires in him; rousing of his conscience by Rājmati etc., are most significant from viewpoint of emotional and intellectual exaltation.

The 23rd Adhyayan, styled `Keshi-Gautmiya' incorporates valuable information regarding meeting of holy monk, Keshi, belonging to the era of Tirthanker Lord Parshvanath, with Gandher Gautama, a devout and chief resident disciple of Lord Mahavirā, their mutual conversation and exchange of views in the shape of questions and answers. How spiritual attainments relating to the era of Lord Pārshvanāth were getting absorbed in the spiritual doctrines of the era of Lord Mahavirā so harmoniously, is sufficiently established, after perusal of the said Adhyayan. The said Adhyayan also provides a comparative study, how the Jaina monks practised 5 great austerities, as enunciated by the first and last Tirthankers and four austerities prescribed during the era of intervening 22 Tirthankers.

Explanatory Works: The commentaries and interpretative notes on Uttrādhyayan are too many. Achārya Bhadrabāhu had accomplished a commentary, giving etymological derivations of its words; Jinadass Mahattar had composed a `Chūrṇi' (A brief gloss) on it; Shri Shānti Sūri, connected with `Dhārāpadra' branch of Jaina mendicants and adorned with the title `Vādivaitāl' (An accomplished musician) had written a commentary over it, namely `Paiya' or `Shishyahita' which is also popularly known as `Vrahada Vritti' (an exhaustive commentary on Uttrādhyayan). Shānti Sūri is believed to have expired in the year 1040 A.D. On the basis of the said extensive exposition, Achārya Devendragaṇi, who subsequently, came to be known as `Nemichandra Sūri', had written an annotation, styled `Sukhabodhā', which was completed in 1073 A.D. There are many other Jaina scholars too who had commented upon Uttrādhyayan. The prominent names amongst them are : Laxmi Vallabha, Jayakirti, Kamal-Saiyaṁ, Bhāvavijaya etc.

Western scholars have also made their contribution. For instance, Prof. Charpantier has translated the basic texts of Uttrādhyayan in English with his own introduction. Jacobi, a renowned scholar, who is known for his tremendous research on Jaina Agamas, had also translated it in English which was edited by Prof. Maxmuler and published in 45th chapter of the famous work "Sacred books of the East" in 1875 at Oxford.

Āvassaya (Āvashyaka)

Name : Its Relevance: The word `Āvashyaka' has been derived from Sanskrit word 'Avashya' which means—to be necessarily done—what is inevitable and to be done at all costs. Accordingly, the word `Avashyaka' specified those religious austerities which had to be essentially and inevitably performed by Jaina mendicants for observance of purity and avoiding any deviations in day today conduct of their affairs. The number of such religious austerities, is six. The holy scripture `Āvashyaka' is classified into six parts, in which the topics relating to `Sāmāyika' (customary);`Chaturtrishati-Stava' (eulogium to 24 Tirthankers); `Vandana' (Paying obeisance); `Pratikramana' (confession); `Kāyotsarga' (Abandonment of physical impurities); and `Pratyākhyān' (Renunciation).

Sāmāyika: Appearance of the feeling of impartiality, equability or homogeneity in the core of hearts of the Jaina mendicants is called `Sāmāyika'. For obtaining the said state of mind, a devout will have to keep itself away from vices or sinful acts done/caused to be done/or effected either mentally, physically or orally. The devout remains indifferent towards attaining inauspicious powers by yoga practices. All this has been discussed in the first part of `Āvashyaka' (An Agamic scripture).

Chaturthvinshati-Stava (Eulogizing 24 Tirthankers)

In the second portion of `Āvashyaka', 24 Tirthankers have been eulogized for enlightening the people with divine knowledge which fills the hearts and souls with noble and pious feelings.

Vandan (Paying Obeisance): The third part of `Avashyaka' deals with how to pay obeisance to the spiritual guide. A disciple bows at the feet of preceptor to pay its respects and seeks his blessings. The pupil enquires about the welfare of its teacher since the latter had remained engrossed in deep meditation and practised severe penances.

Pratikramaṇa (Stepping towards)

`Pratikramaṇa' has been elaborately dealt with in the fourth part of `Āvashyaka'. Pratikramaṇa literally means showing aversion towards external things and stepping towards attainment of self-realisation. For instance, in case a devout goes astray or deviates from an austere life and adopts inauspiciousness through its sheer carelessness, it can again revert to lead a virtuous life. In case, knowingly or unknowingly, a religious mendicant has offended or acted against moral values or it has injured the feelings or sentiments of somebody or instead, it has deviated from usual study of sacred texts, then the said bhikṣu, anxiously wishing to return to its old sacred way of life, must be filled with the feeling of repentance and censure itself for having violated the code and acted against prescribed ethology. The purpose of the said confession is to repent and strive again to lead the same austere and prinicpled life.

Kāryotsarga (Abandonment of Physical Attachments)

The fifth portion of `Āvashyaka' elaborates the significance of leading an altogether detached life. The literal sense of `Kāyotsarga' is to abandon physical attachments or bodily cares and to strive for attainment of self-realisation. It is virtually a state of profound dedication wherein a devout bhikṣu will be anxious to subdue physical instabilities and establish itself in a state of absolute concentration of mind.

Pratyākhyān (To Renounce): The sixth part of `Āvashyaka' lays down that the Jaina mendicants should abstain from practising mystical exercises, leading to the attainment of three kinds of power`Sāvadya'; `Nirvadya' and `Sūkṣam' and they should avoid tasty foods, drinking of liquors, dainties and delicacies.

Explanatory Literature: Achārya Bhadrabāhu had written etymological interpretations of the words; a Bhāshya (a commentary which explains a sūtra or aphorism word by word with comments of the author) was also composed on it; Achārya Jnabhadragaṇi `Kṣmashramaṇa' had authored an exhaustive commentry on it with profundity, styled "Visheshāvashyaka Bhāshya which is a unique accomplishment in Jaina canonical works. Shri Jinadass Mahattar had written a brief gloss on it. Acharya Haribhadra Sūri had composed an exposition on it, known as `Shishyahita', wherein six subjects, forming part of `Āvashyaka' have been discussed at length in 35 Adhyayans. Incidentally, many ancient historical tales have also been incorporated therein from Prākrita books. Āchārya Malayagiri had also composed an annotation on it. Achārya Māṇakya Shekhar Sūri had written `Dipikā' (an elucidation) on the etymological interpretative notes of Achārya Bhadrabāhu. Sri Tilkachārya had also composed a brief gloss on `Āvashyaka'.

Dasaveyāliya (Dashavaikālika)

Name : Its Relevance: `Dashavaikālika' is a combination of two words `Dasha' and `Vaikālika'. The word `dasha' signifies ten Adhyayans and the word `Vaikālika' means composition, projection or preachings. The meaning of the word—`Vikāl' is evening, twilight or the close of day. `Vaikālika' is an adjectival formation from it. It is believed that since the texts of the said sacred book are recited in the evening, hence it has been named accordingly. It is also assumed that the said scripture was either composed or discoursed in ten evenings, hence it came to be known as `Dashavaikālika'. It had been accomplished by Achārya Shayambhava for the benefit and convenience of his son, manak, a young Jaina bhikṣu. `Dashavaikālika' is considered foremost in all other holy scriptures, the texts of which are recited without any restriction of scheduled hours.

The Sūtra, in question comprises of 10 (ten) Adhyayans and two Chūlikās. The contents of ten Adhyayans have been compiled on the basis of discourses, delivered by Tirthanker while two Chūlikās appear to be independent productions. There are two diverse opinions regarding composition of Chūlikās. According to certain scholars, they appear to have been written by Achārya Shayambhava, himself. It is possible, the Chūlikas may have been written by the author after compilation of 10 Adhyayans. The language of the main Sūtra and two chūlikās is not so dissimilar that they should be treated to have been composed by two separate authors. However, a few others donot subscribe to this opinion. According to them, chūlikās have been composed by a separate author and then attached to ten Adhyayans.

Compilation : Source : Pūrvās (old Texts of Highest Spiritual and Philosophical Doctrines of Jaina Religion): As appearing in `Niryukti' (commentary with etymological interpretations) on `Avashyaka', written by Achārya Bhadrabāhu, that the contents of fourth Adhyayan of `Dashavaikālika' are based on `Atma-Pravāda Pūrva' (seventh Pūrva); fifth Adhyayan is based on `Karma Pravāda Pūrva (Eighth Pūrva). The contents of seventh Adhyayan are based on `Satya-Pravāda Pūrva' (sixth Pūrva) and the theme of remaining Adhyayans has been derived from 3rd `Vastu' of `Pratyākhyān Pūrva' (ninth Pūrva).

Another Assumption — Contents Based on Other Agamic Scriptures

Achārya Shayambhava, an authority on Jaina Agamas, had drawn out an essence of the said holy scriptures and accomplished `Dashavaikālika' from the substance thereof. If the issues, dealt with in Dashavaikālika are minutely examined, it may be explicit that they are closely connected with or have been discussed in various Agamas. The title of second Adhyayan of `Dashavaikālika is `Shrāmaṇyapurvaka', in which the Jaina Sādhus have been instructed to keep away from allurement of sensual pleasures. In the said context, the story of Jaina monk, Rathnemi, has been concisely given. The contents of the said Adhyayan are almost similar with those appearing in 22nd Adhyayan of Uttrādhyayan, styled as `Rathnemiya'. However, in Uttrādhyayan, the narrative of Rathnemi and Rājimati has been produced more elaborately. Nevertheless, the implied tone of both is one and the same.

The title of fourth Adhyayan of Dashavaikālika is `Shaḍajivanikāya'. After briefly describing the six types of living beings, their killing has been forbidden. In this way, the first great austerity of non-violence has been propounded. Thereafter, five austerities have also been discussed therein. From the beginning, emphasis has been laid on abstaining from sinful deeds and keep the mind free from the influence of worldly desires. The contents of the said Adhyayan are almost similar with those contained in the latter part of 15th Adhyayan, pertaining to 2nd section of `Āchārānga Sūtra' (title of the first out of 12 sacred Angas of the Jainas). In the former half portion of 4th Adhyayan of Dashavaikālika, the detailed biography of Lord Mahavirā has been given while in the latter half portion details about six types of living beings are given. It is quite possible that the material of fourth Adhyayan of `Dashavaikālika' may have been derived from the 15th Adhyayan of Achārānga Sūtra.

The title of the fifth Adhyayan is `Pindaishnā' (begging of alms). All aspects relating to begging of alms by Jaina *bhikṣus* have been elucidated in it. How to go about begging or avoid going, when and where to accept alms or refuse—all these topics have been elaborately discussed. The contents of the Adhyayan, in question, are presumably based on the contents of first Adhyayan, pertaining to second section of Āchārānga Sūtra. The title of the said Adhyayan is also `Pindaishnā'.

The title of the seventh Adhyayan is *Vākya-shudhi* (accuracy of language). Besides laying emphasis on the significance of language worth being used or to be avoided by Jaina bhikṣus, the topics, relating to good manners and morals, purity of character etc. to be observed by devout Jaina monks have been discussed in detail. The knowledge of the various styles of conversation and the knowledge of the ways of the world (how to behave) to be acquired by Jaina mendicants are, infact, indicative of their detached, uninvolved, sensible, conscious, vigilant and spiritualtistic lives. The title of the fourth Adhyayan, relating to second section of `Achārānga Sūtra' is `Bhāshājāt'. The nature of the language to be used or to be avoided by Jaina mendicants has been minutely discussed therein. It is believed that the same analysis or finding appears in seventh, Adhyayan of `Dashavaikālika' with a view to benefit the Jaina Bhikṣhus or for their attainment of the desired objective.

The title of ninth Adhyayan of Dashavaikālika is `Vinaya-Samādhi'. The attitude of a religious student or pupil must be humble and polite towards his/her preceptor. The significance of humility and politeness as also disadvantages of impropriety of conduct have been explained with illustrations. The contents of the said Adhyayan are almost similar with those appearing in first Adhyayan, styled `Vinaya-Shruta' of Uttrādhyayan, wherein the significance of polite behaviour of a disciple towards his/her spiritual guide and inhibition of disrespect to him, have been elaborately discussed.

The title of tenth Adhyayan of `Sashavaikālika' is `Sa bhikṣu'. It deals with day-today goings and performances of Jaina bhikshus, their conduct and behaviour, religion—oriented resoluteness and determination, abandonment of worldly attachments, and total indifference to sensual objects. These are some of the characteristics that have been discussed therein in an enlivened manner. Infact, it is a lively sketch of a true Jaina devout and highly inspiring to all these who are determined to undertake spiritual endeavours. The title and contents of 15th Adhyayan of `Uttrādhyayan' are almost identical with it. There is considerable uniformity between the two. Not only in essence but in wordings and poetical composition too, there is remarkable similarity. Consequently, it may not be wrong to infer that tenth Adhyayan of Dashavaikalika is only a modification of 15th Adhyayan of Uttradhyayan.

Chūlikās (Crests)

Rati-Vākyā: At the end of tenth Adhyayan, there are two Chūlikas relating to the said Dashavaikālika Sūtra. The title of the first Chūlika is `Rati-Vākyā'. The Sādhus, engaged in spiritual accomplishments, derive great pleasure and happiness. However, from physical viewpoint, there are innumerable hardships at every step. They have to face opposition from hostile elements at every moment. Sensual enjoyments are strictly forbidden. All these contingencies are bound to create psychological problems. If a specific bhikṣu is confronted with such an adverse situation, when he/she may find himself/herself unable to carry on with the hard life of mendicancy and may feel tempted to re-adopt family life, then in order to provide stimulation and keep him/her determined to go on with the life of a devout, it may be highly in the fitness of things to feed him/her with enlightening and inspiring views. All these points have been dealt with in the said Chūlikā.

The issues, relating to tragic consequences of worldly enjoyments, adversities of life, worthlessness of sensual objects, their transient nature, unpleasant effects, uncertainties, fruitfulness of leading an ascetic life, sacredness and acceptability of virtues, have been elaborately discussed in the said Chūlikā. The feelings have been inculcated for observance of the religious obligations and moral code of conduct even at the cost of one's life. After cautioning the mendicants against sensualism, sexual pleasures, worldly attachments, physical contentments and other mundane allurements, they have been instilled with confidence to re-engage themselves in self-realisation and attainment of eternal happiness, observance of self-constraints and re-dedication to the life of renunciation and forbearance. All these issues have been discussed objectively. The above discussion is not only interesting but highly stimulating too. Since in the process of composition of the said Chūlikā, the words—engagement in self-realization, dedication to a life of devotion, identification with the life of self-denials, have frequently appeared, hence the said Chūlikā has most probably been rightly styled as 'Rati-Vākya'.

'Viviktachariyā' (Observance of austerities leading to renunciation of the world)

The title of Chūlikā No. 2 is 'Viviktācharyā'. The literal meanings of the word 'Vivikta' are — separated from, detached, liberated from, lonely, solitary place, discreet or judicious etc. The contents of the said Chūlikā are of attributive character in appreciation of the life of complete detachment from worldly pleasures, i.e., of one whose mind is free from the influence of passions. Hence such a mind is always discreet and judicious. Aiming at improving the life of religious mendicants, the Chūlikā deals with do's and do'nts, how Jaina Sādhus should avoid adopting the life of convenience, they should face hostile conditions and float against the current; display courage and consistency in observance of moral values; retain with them only limited number of items, essential for day today use; absolute retirement from family life; not to accept physical service or assistance from others; keeping the mind composed and exercising control over all sensual organs; leading entirely an austere life etc., on pursuance of which, a mendicant will be highly enlightened and celebrated.

Speciality : Significance: Along with its unique significance in elaboration of Jaina philosophy and ethology, it is equally important in grammatical constructions, style of composition and its richness from philological viewpoint. The linguistic form and uses of sentences in the Chūlikā are apparently quite old and they conform with the language of ancient Jaina sacred books, namely, Achārānga and Sutrakritānga Sūtras. Similar compositions and uses of words, signifying ancientness of the language, as witnessed in Uttrādhyayan, are also found in Dashavaiklika. However, it is an altogether independent subject and relates to the significance of Ardha Māgadhi Prākrita, which is not desirable to be taken up here. According to Dr. Pischel, both 'Uttrādhyayan' and 'Dashavaikālika' are unique from the viewpoint of studying Prākrita dialects.

Explanatory Literature: Achārya Bhadrabāhu had written etymological interpretative notes on Dashavaikālika. Brief glosses were written by Agastya Singh and Jinadas Mahattar. Achārya Haribhadra Sūri had composed an annotation on it. Sri Samaya Sundar Gaṇi had composed 'Dipikā' (a small exposition); M/S Tilkāchārya alias Tilaka Suri, Sumati Sūri and Virnaya Hans had written 'Vrittis' (explanations). Shri Aparajita Sūri of Yāpniya Sangh, alias Vijaychārya had also accomplished an annotation on Dashavaikālika, styled 'Vijyodayā'. He has made a mention of it in another composition, 'Bhagwati Arādhanā'. Sri Gyānsamaraṭa and Rajhans Mahāmahopadhyaya had written commentaries on it in Gujrāti. The commentary of Sri Gyānsamarata is known by the name and style of 'Bālāvabodh'.

Its First Publication: In the course of making research on orientology, the western scholars were very much interested in having critical study and investigation on Jaina scriptures as well. They have spared no pains in accomplishing this objective. This fact is fully supported by the fact that Dr.Ernest Leumann, an erudite German Scholar, had arranged publication of `Dashavaikālika' for the first time in the *Journal of the German Oriental Society* in 1892. Prior to it, the sacred book was available in the shape of hand-written copies of manuscript only. It had not been got printed till then. Thereafter, it was also published in India and, subsequently, several editions had been published one after the other. In 1932, it was got published in Germany by eminent German scholar Dr.Walter Schubring, who had undertaken intensive studies of Jaina canonical literature and Prākrita dialects in India with his own comments and Introduction.

Pinḍnijjutti (Pinda Niryukti)

Name : Explanation: The word `Pinda' is used in a technical sense in Jaina vocabulary and means food, fit to be eaten. There are fixed standards regarding quality of food articles, their preparation and their fitness or unfitness for eating etc. Various aspects relating to the purity or impurity of eatables, meant for Jaina mendicants, their defective cooking and style of eating etc. have been elaborately dealt with in the above sacred book. Since the said scripture primarily deals with the suitability or unsuitability of prepared food for Jaina mendicants, the theme and substance of many of its verses are identical and very much conform with the contents of the verses of `Mūlāchār' (Key-points relating to ethology), written by renowned Jaina scholar, Vattaker, belonging to Digamber sect.

Contents : Shape: The said scripture contains 671 verses in all. Truly speaking it is not an independent accomplishment. The name and style of fifth Adhyayan, pertaining to `Dashāvaikālika' is `Pindaishna'. Niryukti (etymological interpretative commentary), written by Achārya Bhadrabāhu on the said Adhyayan is so lengthy and exhaustive that it began to be admitted as an independent Agama of Jaina religion. The verses, contained in the said Niryukti and `bhāshya' (a commentary which explains each sūtra or aphorism word by word with comments of the author), written on the said Adhyayan, have become so intermingled that it is practically very difficult to distinguish them.

Pinda Niryukti deals with eight topics, namely — `Udgama' (origin); `utpādana' (Output); `Eshṇā' (Desires); `Saṁyojnā' (Preparation); `Pramāṇa' (Standard) `Angār' (Charcoal, fire); `Dhūm' (Smoke) and `Kāraṇa' (motive, object). Many issues relating to begging alms have been discussed in an exciting manner. There is mention of 16 types of violations of prescribed standards respecting eatables and their preparations respectively and ten types of violations pertaining to striving to get. Violations of prescribed guide-lines relating to begging for alms have been repeatedly discussed with illustrations, citing examples of Jaina monks who were found guilty of consuming damaging type of food and violating prescribed standards. They had to perform expiatory religious acts for atonement of their sins.

There are important guide-lines when and how the mendicants should beg for alms from house-holds. It has been stated that if a house-lady be busy in taking her meals; churning curd; grinding flour; crushing rice or combing cotton, a Jaina mendicant should refrain from begging food from her. Similarly, begging food has been strictly forbidden from infants or very young children; infirm and aged persons; drunks; delirious persons; those suffering from high fever; blinds and leprous etc. Begging for alms has also been prohibited by making astrological predictions; pretending to cure; influencing house-holds by practising spells and incantations or enchanting them into submission.

Certain Significant References

Incidentally, it has been specified that the Jaina monks should apply clay of termite-infested houses to alleviate the poisonous effects of snake-biting; make use of fly-dungs to check vomiting; to use the bones of other living-beings to set their dislocated bones and to drink cow-urine for successful treatment of leprosy etc.

The guide-lines, how a Jaina mendicant should refrain from having allurement for delicious food; and gladly accept the food in alms with absolutely detached and sensible mind, so that the house-holder may not be put to any inconvenience on that account. The mendicant should not be instrumental in causing any hardship or unfavourableness to him and avoid creating any untoward situation amongst family members of the house-hold etc. have been laid down and treated in such a psychological and judicious manner that they are really worth going through for undertaking investigation of routined life of Jaina Sādhus.

Achārya Malaygiri had written an extensive commentary on Pinda-Niryukti and Sri Virāchārya had composed a short gloss on it.

Ohnijjutti (Ogha-Niryukti)

Name : Its Appropriateness: The literal meaning of the word `Ogha' is current, continuity, tradition or traditional religious instructions. The guide-lines, pertaining to observance of proper conduct and behaviour is day-today course of religious mendicancy, have been laid down in it. Most probably, it has been named and styled accordingly. Just as all relevant instructions and guide-lines, relating to permissible food for Jaina mendicants, have been incorporated in `Pinda-Niryukti', similarly, the matters of general character, pertaining to observance of good behaviour and conduct by Jaina Sādhus in day-today course of their ascetic life, have been dealt with in `Ogha-Niryukti'.

Just as `Pinda-Niryukti' is treated to be a part of `Dashavaikālika Niryukti', similarly, `Ogha-Niryukti' is believed to be a component part of `Avashyaka-Niryukti', authored by Acharya Bhadrabāhu, which contains 811 verses. The versified compositions of `Niryukti and `Bhashya' have become so intermingled that it is not practically possible to distinguish them.

Ogha-Niryukti has been classified into eight chapters, namely—`Pratilekhan Dwār (Transcription); `Pinda-Dwār' (Regarding food); `Upadhi-nirupana' (Determination of Fraud and dishonesty); `Anāyatan-Varjan' (Forbidding unrestrained or unsupported activities); `Pratisevanā dwār' (Service to others); `Ālochana Dwār' (self censuring); and `Vishudhi Dwār' (self purification). It is explicit from the very names of the chapters that all aspects relating to the day today routine and behaviour of Jaina Sādhus have been discussed therein.

A Unique Reference: There is an issue of universal nature, debated again and again and which has been dealt with in `Ogha-Niryukti' as well. It is with regard to protection of self—whether safety of one's own life is more essential or preservation of spiritual attainments even at the cost of one's own life is necessary. In case, an occasion arises when ruin of one is imminent then to which of the two we should attach priority to save? There have been diverse opinions on the point. While some of the scholars have given their precedence for preservation of spiritual values at all costs, others are in favour of saving one's own life first and then to atone for omissions and commissions.

It has been emphasized in `Ogha-Niryukti' that a Jaina saint should adhere strictly to the values of religious mendicancy with purity and perfection of mind. However, when danger to one's life may appear imminent, then precedence must be given to save the life first. If a devotee is able to survive, he/she will be in a position to perform prescribed austerities to atone and to re-establish its position and worth. Honesty of purpose and purity of heart are the characteristics of saintly life as well as observance of spiritual values.

It has been laid down with all emphasis that the sole aim of the life of a true devout is absolute dedication to spiritual pursuits and exercising control over self. It is not meant for sensual enjoyments. However, if a devout loses its life and there is no physical existence, how it will be able to carry on with its spiritual pursuits, and perform its obligations. Hence saving the life and protection of the body is a must and should not be misconstrued as having any fondness for this mortal body. It is only a device or means to go on with spiritual endeavours. Therefore, care and protection of the body is highly essential. The issue has been discussed in "Nishitha Chūrṇi" as well, wherein it is cited that every possible precaution be taken not to allow occurrence of any intervention in spiritual endeavours. However, if there is no other way out, one can temporarily suspend its spiritual performances in order to save the life, the very source of physical existence.

Determination of Essential items to be used by a Jaina mendicant

The minimum possible articles, essential for day-today use and performance of austerities by Jaina mendicants, are called `Upadhi'. The topic has been elaborately dealt with in the said chapter. It has been a controversial issue between Digamber and Shwetamber sects of Jaina religion whether the religious mendicants are entitled to keep with them essential items like clothes and utensils etc. or not. Explanations and clarifications have been offered by both sects in support of their ideological convictions which have been incorporated in the said chapter of `Ogha-Niryukti' and may really be helpful to research students to have a comparative view of the opinions of both sects. There is an elaborate description of the items (clothes and utensils etc.) to be possessed by each category of Jaina Sādhus—a `Jina-Kalpi' (A Jaina monk, engaged in the practice of most exalted type of penances—those practised by Tirthanker himself, after having attained state of highest perfection a 'Sthavira-Kalpi' (A Jaina Sādhu performing austerities, while living in the association with other mendicants and preaching them religious, philosophical and ethological doctrines of Jainism); as also ordinary male and female mendicants.

The items to be possessed by Jina-Kalpi and Sthavira-Kalpi Sādhus

The items approved for a `Jina-Kalpi' Sādhu, appearing in the said chapter are—

1. Pot for drinking water; 2. A piece of cloth to cover the pot; 3. A stand for placing the utensil; 4. A saffron cloth to cover the mouth of the pot; 5. A veil or covering; 6. Chappals; 7. A whisk, made of peacock feather; 8, 9, 10. Three cloth pieces to cover the limbs of the body; 11. A dirt remover to cleanse the floor and 12. A small piece of cloth to cover the mouth. It is also cited that the piece of cloth against item No. 5. is also used to conceal the secret parts of the body besides covering the food pot, when recessary.

For Sthavira-Kalpi Sādhus, besides the above 12 items, there are two additional items as well, namely— (1) `Cholpatta' (A garment reaching the feet) and (2) Mātraka (A measuring unit). In this way, there is provision of 14 items for them.

The Items Permissible for Female Mendicants

Besides, 12 items, allowed for use of Jinakalpi Sādhus and only one of the two additional items, provided to Sthavira Sādhus i.e. Mātraka (A measuring unit), another 12 items have been specified to be used by female mendicants. In this way, 25 items are permitted to be possessed by female mendicants in all, namely — 14. `Kamdhaga'; 15. `Uggahaṇaṁtaga' (A small garment in the shape of a boat to cover the secret part of a female); 16. `Pattaka' (A small garment, having the shape of an underwear to hide item No. 15 from both sides); 17. `Adhoruga' (A garment to be put on by female mendicants to cover items No. 15 and 16); 18. `Chalnikā' (An unsewn cloth, worn to cover thighs upto knees); 19. `Avabhitar niyaṁsaṇi' (The garment hanging upto half thighs so that no one be tempted to laugh at the female mendicants while changing their clothes); 20. `Bahir-Niyaṁsaṇi' (The garment hanging upto knees and tied on the waist with a cord); 21. `Kanchuka' (A piece of garment like a brassier to cover the breasts); 22. 'Ukkachhiya' (It is also like item No. 21 to cover the breasts); 23. `Vekachhiya' (A garment to cover both the above brassieres — items No. 21 and 22.); 24. `Saṁghādi' (They are four garments to be worn by female mendicants on different occasions - (1) while at residence or living place; (2) and (3) to be put or while going out for begging alms and (4) while attending the gathering where a Tirthanker deliveres his sermons); 25. `Khandhakarni' (A piece of cloth-about 2 yards in length for protection of the body from severity of wind etc. It was also used to be placed on the back of a beautiful and attractive lady to look like a hump of a hunch—backed lady like Kubja).[1] The issues relating to the nature of above cloth pieces or garments, their uses, appropriateness, modifications from time to time and improvements etc. are really worth studying to appreciate how the Jaina mendicants were leading the life of renunciation and were using basic minimum in day-today course of their mendicancy.

Explanatory Works: Amongst explanatory literature on Ogha-Niryukti, the commentary, written by Sri Droṇāchārya, is rated, very high. It has been composed

---

1. Niryukti, 674-77 and Bhāshya pages 313-320.

like a `Chūrṇi', having abundance of Prākrita words. In other words, it is a mixed composition of both Sanskrit and Prākrita words. A gloss had been written by Achārya Malayagiri. A small exposition is also found to have been accomplished on 'Ogha-Niryukti'.

`Pakhiyasutta' (Pākṣika-Sūtra)

While explaining the significance of `Āvashyaka Sūtra' and undertaking an evaluation of it, a reference had been made how to return to the path of self-realisation, once having been illusioned by worldly pleasures. The process of stepping back towards attainment of self-realisation; observance of austerities for re-purification of the soul and acquiring true wisdom, is highly conducive for spiritual achievements. Under Jaina tradition, the act of `Pratikramana' (The process of returning to the path of) is of five type—(1) During day time; (2) During night; (3) Fort-nightly; (4) Four monthly and (5) Yearly. The basis for composition of `Pākṣika-Sūtra', under reference, is fortnightly process of undertaking religious austerities and stepping back towards attainment of self-realisation. It is a component part of `Avashyaka Sūtra' itself, or a special supplement to the said component. Issues, relating to observance of five great austerities, namely — non-violence, truth non-stealing, celibacy and renunciation along with sixth austerity of relinquishment of night meals or how to arrange to end the austerity, have been dealt with in the above-noted sacred work. Paying obeisance to highly sanctified spiritual leaders (omniscients) has also been discussed therein. Incidentally, the names of 12 Angas, 37 sacred treatises to be studied during fixed hours and 28 scriptural-works to be studied at one's will without any restriction of time, have been referred to in the above `Pākṣhika Sūtra'. Achārya Yashodeva Sūri has written a commentary on it under the name and style of `Sukhavi-bodha'.

'Khāmṇā-Sutta' (Kṣhāmṇā Sūtra)

The above sacred book is also known as `Pākṣhika Kṣāmṇā Sūtra'. There is no significant material in it. It is traditionally believed that Pākshika Sūtra' and Kṣamṇā Sūtra are one and the same by certain scholars while others take them as independent compositions.

Vandittu-Sutta

The above Sūtra starts with an initial verse — "Vandittu Savvasidhe" (We bow to you. You enable us to accomplish all our spiritual pursuits). The said Sūtra has been styled accordingly. It is believed that the said scripture had been composed by Gandhers. Various scholars have commented upon it, prominent names amongst whom are of Deva Sūri, Pārshva Sūri, Jineshevar Sūri, Shri Chand Sūri and Ratan Shekhar Sūri. A gloss had also been written which is considered oldest amongst all interpretative literature. It had been authored by Shri Vijay Singh in the year 1183 of Vikrama Era (Hindu calendar). The Sūtra, in question, has also been styled as 'Shrādh Pratikramaṇa Sūtra'. It should be deemed as a component part of `Avashyaka Sūtra'.

Isi Bhāshiya (Rishi Bhāshita)

The word `Rishi' (Sage) here has appeared for a highly sanctified seer to whom true or essential nature of supreme knowledge (Philosophy of a religion) becomes manifest without guidance of any spiritual head. The contents of the above-noted Sūtra are believed to be based on the utterances of the said seers. Hence, it has been styled as `Rishi-bhāshita'. It is comprised of 45 Adhyayans in which the biographies of the aforesaid Budhās (Seers or sages) have been incorporated. The contents of some of the Adhyayans are in versified form, while others are in prosaic form. It is believed that a `Niryukti' (Commentary with etymological interpretations of each and every word of Sutras) has also been written on it. However, the same is not available now.

Nandi-Sūtra and Anuyogadwār

**`Nandi-Sūtra': Its Author**: The author of `Nandi-Sūtra' is believed to be Devāvāchaka, disciple of Dūshyagaṇi. According to a few scholars, Deva Vāchaka was only an alias of `Devardhigaṇi' `Kṣmāshramaṇa', Deva-Vāckaka and Devardhigaṇi Kṣmashramaṇa were not two separate personalities. They were one and the same. However, it is not established beyond doubt from the material available. There is definite evidence to the effect that both belonged to separate associations of religious mendicants.

Body : Contents: Initially, there are fifty verses in it. In the first three verses, the author has paid obeisance to last Tirthanker, Lord Mahāvira, to seek his blessings for successful completion of his work. Thereafter, in the subsequent verses from Nos. 4 to 19, he has eulogized and paid tributes to the Jaina organisation, in the shape of a lovely metaphoric expression. In 20th and 21st verses right from the first Tirthanker, Lord Rishabh, to last Tirthanker, Lord Mahāvira, rich tributes have been paid to all the 24 Tirthankers collectively. In the following verses Nos. 22, 23 and 24, there is narration of all the eleven Gandhers of Lord Mahāvira and his religious institution. In verses Nos. 25 to 47, there is a reference of the list of successors of Sthaviras (senior guides) right from Ārya Sudharmā to Dūshyagaṇi with eulogy. In the verses Nos. 48 to 50, rich tributes have been paid to most renowned and distinguished religious leaders of their age and the great scholars, who had specialized themselves in exposition of highest spiritual knowledge, contained in Jaina Agamas and other fundamental scriptures. From this, it is evident that while framing the list of successors to the supreme seat of Jaina institution, the leading spiritual guides, considered as principal men of their age (attributed with title of Yug-Pradhān) were taken into account. Thereafter, the actual contents begin in aphoristic style. The narrative tales have also been repeatedly produced in elucidation of the points.

While elaborating the sacred knowledge, especially derived from meditation on the higher truths of religion and philosophy, various stages have been defined such as `Mati' (Knowledge acquired with the help of mind and organs of sense); `Shruta' (highest spiritual knowledge, revealed by omniscients and heard by their chief disciples and retained in their memories and then communicated to others by way of compilation and composition of the texts in aphoristic style); 'Avadhi' (third degree of knowledge by which what is not within the reach of senses is percevied). 'Manaḥ Paryava' (Name of the penultimate stage in the perception of truth) and `Kevalya Gyān' (State of highest perfection, detachment of the soul from the matter and complete identification with the Supreme Spirit — a state of final beatitude). Topics pertaining to these various types of spiritual knowledge, their heads and sub-heads, growth and development etc. have been profoundly discussed in a philosophical manner. While deliberating upon highest spiritual texts (forming part of Jaina Agamas), a reference has been made to `Dwādshānga' (12 sacred scriptures of Jainas) or `Gaṇi-Pitakas' (collections of sacred texts accomplished in aphoristic style by Gandhers-Chief disciples of a Tirthanker), namely—Achārānga, Sūtrakritānga, Sthānananga, Samvāyānga etc. Incidentally, the matter of false, untrue and perverted type of spiritual texts, has also been dealt with. The spiritual texts in the shape of those, accomplished by Gandhers, Agamas, based on religious sermons and discourses, delivered by Tirthankers; precepts, composed by Gandhers, which are of permanent nature and those, composed by Sthaviras which are free from grammatical constraints and are of lesser significance, have been elaborately defined and discussed. The said chapter of Nandi-Sūtra is worth studying in order to have knowledge of the factors that led to the growth and expansion of Jaina Agamas. Jinadass Mahattar had composed a Chūrṇi (a brief explanation) on Nandi Sūtra while Achārya Haribhadra and Achārya Malayagiri had written commentaries on it.

Anuyoga Dwār: Alike the Contents of Nandi-Sūtra, Anuyoga Dwār is also a recent accomplishment which is quite evident from the style of its language and expression. Ārya Raksita is believed to be its author. The subjects relating to various Anuyagās have been comprehended in it. Especially, the topic of numerals, forming subject-matter of Gaṇita Anuyaga, has been elaborately dealt with in it. The contents of the said book are mostly in the shape of questions and answers.

Seven Notes or Tunes: Incidentally seven notes or tunes of Indian musical gamut, namely—`Shaḍaja' (fourth Note); `Rishabha' (second note); `Gandher' (third note); Madhyam (fifth note); `Panchama' (seventh note); Dhaivata' (sixth note) and `Nishada' (1st note) have been vividly described. Regarding sources of the origin of above tunes, it has been stated that `Shadaja' (fourth note) is produced from the front part of the tongue; the source of production of `Rishabha tune' (second note) is heart, `Madhyam' (fifth tune) is articulated, from middle of the tongue; `Gandher' (third tune) is produced from the tip of the tongue; `Panchama' (seventh note) is produced from the nasal cavity; `Dhaivata' (sixth tune) is created by joining of the upper and lower jaws, and `Nishada' (first tune) is created by movement of eye-brows.

While differenciating between the tunes, produced by animate and inanimate objects, it is cited that the peacocks produce sound in `Shadaja' tone (fourth note); cocks in `Rishabha' tone (second note); Swans in `Gāndher' tone (third note); animals like cows and sheeps etc. in `Madhyama' tone (fifth note); Cuckoos in `Panchama' (seventh note) in spring season; the cranes and curlews in `Dhaivata' tone (sixth note) and the elephants trumpet in `Nishada' tone (first note). The good and evil consequences of tonal set-up, made by mankind, have also been discussed. Incidentally, the topic relating to the scale in music and intonation (a duly regulated rise and fall of sounds, conducting the air and the harmony through the keys in a pleasing manner by passing from one key to another) has also been discussed.

Eight case terminations have also been defined. It is cited therein that an order or directive is in nominative case; delivering of discourses or sermons in objective case; the act of giving or handing over is in dative case; cause or motive is in instrumental case; taking away or removal of a thing is in ablative case; relation as the essence of genitive case; location or place—the sense of the locative case and addressing or calling out somebody is in vocative case.

Topics relating to grammar, such as—`Prākriti' (The root or crude form of a word to which case terminations and other affixes are applied); `Agama' (An Augment in grammar); `Lopa' (elision or dropping); `Sāmasa' (Euphonic combinations—compounding of words to obtain brevity); `Tadhita' (An affix added to primary bases in order to form derivatives or secondary bases from them); and `Dhātu' (roots arranged according to Pānini's grammatical system) have been dealt with in detail. Incidentally nine sentiments in poetic compositions (Rasās are more or less a necessary factor of every poetic composition) have also been discussed where the context so demanded.

`Palyopama' (Method to measure a fixed time under technical sense of Jaina religion); `Sāgropama' (larger period than `Pālyopama') etc., their magnitudes, innumerability or numerability; the infinity of time etc. have been widely discussed. Infact, the said information is quite significant to know the method of measuring or reckoning the time under technical sense of Jaina religion.

Valuable Informations: The topics relating to undesirable preachings; illusory knowledge, heretics, `Kāpālikas' (followers of a certain Saiva Sect, characterised by carrying skulls of human beings in the form of garlands and eating or drinking from them); religious devouts; wandering mendicants, after having renounced the world; defiled saints, etc., depending for their livlihood on religion; bearers of straw, wood or leaves on their heads or shoulders; those earning their livelihood by selling cloth, yarn and utensils etc., weavers, carpenters, painters, manufacturers of ivory items, parasols etc. have been dealt with, as demanded by the context.

Means of Arriving at Correct Knowlege

While deliberating upon the means of arriving at correct knowledge, four means, namely—`Pratyakṣa' (obtained by direct perception); `Anumān' (obtaining knowledge by conclusions from given premises); `Upmān' (Analogy, recognition of likeness, considered as a mean of arriving at correct knowledge); `Agams' (by studying of Shāstras or sacred scriptures—the last of the four kinds of proof, recognized by the followers of Nyāya system of philosophy) have been discussed. Knowledge obtained by direct perception has been further classified in two types—(1) knowledge perceptible to the senses, and (2) non-perceptible to the organs of sense, further, knowledge perceptible to the senses is of 5 kinds — (1) knowledge obtained by hearing; (2) perceptible to the eyes; (3) through the sense of smelling; (4) preception through the organ of taste, the tongue (5) and the knowledge perceptible through touch.

While explaining the knowledge, not perceptible to the organs of the sense, it is stated to be of three types — (1) third degree of knowledge by which what is not within the reach of the senses is perceived, (2) Manaḥ Paryava Gyān (Name of the penultimate stage in the perception of truth), and (3) Kevalya Gyān (Attainment of highest spiritual knowledge by an accomplished and highly sanctified teacher, devoted to the doctrine of absolute unity of the Spirit).

While dealing with Anumān' (knowledge obtained by drawing conclusions from given premises), it has also been classified into (1) Pūrvavata (As contained in Pūrvas-old Sacred texts of Jainas); Drishṭi (Drishṭivāda — 12th Anga) and Sadharmma (Being of the same religion). Along with dealing about the means of arriving at correct knowledge, the topic of political wisdom or statesmanship has also been discussed in detail. From the nature of the subjects argued, it is established that the work is not very old-rather it is ạ recent composition. Jinadass Mahattar has written a `Chūrṇi' (brief exposition) on it. Achārya Haribhadra and renowned Jaina scholar, Achārya Hemchandra have commented upon it.

Dasa Paiṇṇaga (Dasha Prakirṇaka)

The literal meaning of the word — `Prakirṇaka' is the material scattered or strewn about. It is a miscellany or a collection of miscellaneous writings under the technical sense of Jaina religion, Prakirṇakas are those sacred treatises which have been accomplished from time to time on various topics concerning spiritualism and Jaina metaphysics by highly learned seers and chief disciples of Tirthankers.

Tradition of Writing Sacred Books on different Topics of Religious Significance

As appeared in `Nandi-Sūtra', the chief disciples of first Tirthanker, Lord Rishabha, had composed 84000 books on topics of religious significance; the learned disciples of Tirthankers from Nos. 2 to 23, had written innummerable books on different topics while the disciples of last Tirthanker, Lord Mahavirā, had produced 14,000 books on spiritual matters.

It is also cited in `Nandi-Sūtra' that under Jaina tradition, each type of disciples, endowed with either prodigy, modesty, discipline, workmanship, prudence or far-sightedness have produced as many thousand books as they are in number. Similarly, the enlightened sages, who need no guidance of any other spiritual leader for self-illummination and realisation of supreme truth, have also accomplished as many thousand sacred books as per their own number and strength.

Achārya Malayagiri, author of the commentary on `Nandi-Sūtra' has further elaborated the point and writes that the learned disciples of Tirthankers also accomplish books on religious and philosophical matters, as enunciated by Trithankers and heard by them through revelation and retained in their memory. All these sacred writings of learned disciples are called `Prakirṇakas'. Alternately, Achārya Malayagiri writes that the disciples of a Tirthanker listen attentively to the utterances of Jaina Arhat on highest spiritual knowledge and philosophy of Jaina religion and, thereafter, convey the sum and substance of his speeches to the religious mendicants and devouts in their own dexterous speeches. These lectures of chief disciples, when compiled in the shape of sacred treatises, are known as

`Prakirṇakas'. While it is believed that the `Prakirṇakas' are written by chief disciples of Tirthankers on the pattern of preachings of Arhats how this explanation could apply to `Buddhas' (highly enlightened sages of their age) who neither get initiated nor they submit to the religious leadership of any other senior guide or spiritual head). It is true Buddhas donot accept discipleship of any other spiritual head, yet in view of the supremacy of spiritual knowledge, taught by Jaina Arhats and their overall command on the religious institution as a deified teacher of Jainas, they can also formally be treated as learned disciples of Tirthankers. Thus the relevance of composition of `Prakirṇakas' by Buddhas, can not altogether be rejected.

Names of Prakirṇakas, available Now

At present, there are only ten `Prakirṇakas' available, namely—

(1) Chausaraṇa (Chatuḥ Sharaṇa);
(2) Āura-Pachchakkhāṇa (Ātur-Pratyakhyān);
(3) Mahā-Pachchakkhāṇa (Mahā-Pratyākhyān);
(4) Bhatta Parishṇā (Bhakta-Parigyā);
(5) Tandulavaiyāliya (Tandul-Vaichārika);
(6) Saṁthāraga (Saṁstāraka);
(7) Gachchhāyār (Gachchhāchār);
(8) Gaṇi-Vijjā (Gaṇi-Vidyā);
(9) Devindra-Thaya (Devendra Stava); and
(10) Maraṇa-Samāhi (Maraṇa-Samādhi).

1. Chausaraṇa (Chatuḥ Sharaṇa)

Under Jaina tradition, Arhats (Super divinities with Jainas); Sidhs (Accomplished Jaina saints, having attained the state of perfection); Sādhus (Jaina monks) and religious ideology (as enunciated by Tirthankers and omniscients) are considered as four fundamental supports or pillars of Jaina religion. Since the said `Prakirṇaka' deals with the said four main components of Jaina philosophy and culture, accordingly, it is styled as `Chatuḥ-Sharaṇa' Prakirṇaka.

The sinful acts are to be forsaken and good-deeds to be performed — this is the sum and substance of every religion. Good deeds always help in attainment of serenity and evil acts to anxiety and restlessness, which means that people should always desist from doing evil deeds and ready to undertake performances of noble deeds. The said `Prakirṇaka' is also titled `Kushlānubandhi Adhyayan' which means that it directs towards performance of good deeds. The said treatise is worth studying and to be minutely contemplated in all the three divisions of the day i.e. before noon, at noon and after-noon. It, therefore, follows that it is an excellent composition. In the last verse of `Chatuḥ-Sharaṇa', the name of `Virbhadra' has appeared who is believed to be its author. Shri Bhuvantunga has written an annotation and Sri Gunaratna has written a brief gloss on it.

2. Āura-Pachchākhāṇa (Atur Pratyakhyān)

Name : Purport : Contents: The literal meaning of the word `Atur' is suffering from, sick or diseased. During the state of sickness, a person generally confronts two situations. Those who have fondness for their bodily comfort, physical pleasures and worldly attachments, they suffer from delusion of mind and remain steeped in ignorance. They are at a loss to understand what to do. They crave for the sensual enjoyment which they have been unable to derive hitherto. Consequently, they are not in a position to show any reluctance towards worldly pleasures even during last moments of their life. Such a death is, however, not appreciable in any view of the matter.

People of an altogether different category are those who remain conscious of the fact that they are mortal beings and the physical or worldly enjoyments are entirely of transient nature. Hence they keep themselves engrossed in spiritual concentration for self-réalization. They endure all physical ailments and bodily hardships by virtue of their spiritual force. They gradually abandon taking meals finally leading to observance of fast unto death, which is, infact, manifestation of great moral power. They identify themselves with Supreme spirit and finally end their lives without showing least remorse. Under technical sense of Jainas, it is treated as a highly cherished and adorable death.

In the *Prākirṇaka*, under reference, wise or unwise deaths, as interpreted above, have been discussed elaborately. Infact, they are manifestations of different mental dispositions, and accordingly the said `Prākirṇaka' has been styled as `Ātur Pratyakhyān'. It has been explained that by showing utter disregard or disapproval for worldly pleasures alone, one can attain true salvation and eternal peace. Alike `Chatuḥ-Sharaṇa' first Prākirṇaka, it is also believed to have been authored by Sri Virbhadra and, like-wise, Sri Bhuvantunga has written an annotation and Sri Gunaratna has composed a small gloss on it.

3. Mahā-Pachchākhaṇa (Mahā-Pratyākhyān)

Name : Purport: Renunciation of immoral path, uncharitable deeds and improper acts alone lead to true happiness. This is, infact, the real path for attainment of piety and devoutness for the people. In the above-noted `Prakirṇaka', all sinful acts have been strongly deprecated. The great ideals of relinquishing all worldly pleasures and significance of absolute renunciation have been highly adored which lead to attainment of final emancipation. Presumably, on that very account, it has been styled as `Mahā-Prātyākhyān'.

Contents: Worldly illusions and allurements for sensual pleasures, donot let a person move on the path of piousness and self control. A person never feels contented even after enjoying all sorts of worldly pleasures. They donot lead us to final emancipation from worldly life. Instead, they are the source of transmigration and repeated births in this mortal world. While dealing with the relative subjects, the topics concerning abandonment of worldly illusions and attachments; putting up with the life of endurance and absolute indifference towards sensual enjoyments; five great austerities and spiritual accomplishments etc. have been elaborately discussed in the above `Prakirṇaka'. Finally, it has been stressed that total renunciation and showing reluctance towards worldly pleasures, is the only way for attainment of the state of perfection and final emancipation. The Prakiraṇaka, in question, consists of 142 verses.

4. Bhatta Parishṇa (Bhakta-Parigyā)

Name : Purport : The literal meaning of the word `Bhakta' is cooked food and that of `Parigyā' is `To be aware of' To find out or ascertain or to know. In `Sthānānga Sūtra' (Third Anga or title of third of the twelve sacred books of Jainas), the word `Parigyā' has been defined to carry a specific sense of renouncing and/or showing total disregard to worldly objects with full awareness. Under Jaina tradition, `Bhakti Parigyā' is one of the kinds to achieve final salvation by observing fast unto death. It has already been explained above, while dealing with second Prakirṇaka, `Ātur Pratyākhyān', that a true devout, when ailing seriously, should observe fast unto death to go into eternal trance and attain final emancipation. However, the method of `Bhakta-Parigyā' (renunciation of food or taking only a mouthful of boiled rice) is slightly different and has nothing to do with physical ailment. A Jaina Sādhu observes fast unto death with full awareness in order to end its life with noble feelings and righteousness. There is an elaborate description to this effect in the third chapter of `Dharma-Sangraha', dealing with morality and ethical values to be observed by Jaina devouts. Besides other topics, the subject of `Bhakta-Parigyā' has been explained with great precision in the Prakirṇaka, in question. Accordingly, the said Prakirṇaka has been named and styled as `Bhakta-Parigyā'.

In addition to the topic of `Bhakta-Parigyā', other two methods—'ingani' (Movement of bodily limbs allowed to a limited extent) while observing fast unto death and `Padopagamana' (lying firm like a tree without least movement) during fast unto death, have also been discussed therein. Thus, these three are the methods of attaining final salvation by observing fast unto death.

Certain Significant Discussions: In the said Prakirṇaka, great significance has been attached to absolute faith with knowledge of truth as essential ingredients of Jaina religious philosophy. It is laid down that those who fail to preserve the said qualities, they are bound to degenerate and they cannot attain final emancipation. Several illustrations of Jaina Sādhus have been produced who had to undergo immense hardships and bodily sufferings. However, they endured them with exemplary courage and spiritual force and finally attained the state of perfection.

Great stress has been laid on exercising self-control. It is cited that absolute control over self is highly essential in order to concentrate the mind in spiritual endeavours. Here the mind has been compared with unsteadiness and agility of a monkey who cannot remain calm even for a moment. It is a tough exercise for the mind to keep off from sensualism.

In the said Prakirṇaka, harsh and unpleasant words have been used for the females. They have been illustrated by comparison to female serpents and applied humiliating names as—root cause of all sorrows; distrustful and unreliable; wicked-minded as also full of hypocritical behaviour. The author of the above Prakirṇaka is believed to be `Virbhadra' and shri Guṇaratna had written a brief commentary upon it.

5. Tandulavaiyāliya (Tandul-Vaichārika)

Name : Purport: The name has been accomplished by way of combination of two words `Tandula and Vaichārika'. The literal meaning of the word `tandula' is rice and that of `Vaichārika' is ideological. There is an assumption regarding the name of the above Prakirṇaka. It is cited that the Prakirṇaka has been styled, keeping in mind the numeric quantity of rice eaten daily by an aged person of 100 years.

The purport of the above assumption is not very clear. Probably, it may have been the idea that the number of rice grain, eaten in a single day by an old person, aged 100 years, can be counted easily. Obviously, the quantity of food, taken by an old man' is limited and reflects that only nominal quantity of rice can be eaten by an aged man of 100 years, the grains of which may not be difficult to count.

The above Prakirnaka contains 586 religious verses. The topics relating to the nutrition of embryos while in wombs and their nature; breathing in and out; various joints in the body, their locations and shape; the number of pulse-vilerations; the pores on the surface of the skin; bile, blood and semen etc. have been discussed therein in detail. Besides the important topics, referred to above, a few other related topics, namely—the period of pregnancy; the bodily limbs of the parents, different stages of life such as childhood, sports of children and ignorance etc.—ten stages of human life; devotion and perseverance in spiritual pursuits etc. have also been dealt with.

A Perverted Version of Females

In the Prakirṇaka, in question, a despicable and horrible description of womenfolk has, incidentally, appeared. It is stated that the ladies are living embodiments of all vices, evils and misconduct, she has been compared with a river, flowing out of a mountain, similized with false and hypocritical behaviour. She is full of corrupt tactics and mean habits. She is the source of mental agony for ascetics. She is cruel like a beast. Just as a black cobra cannot be tamed or taken for granted, similarly, a female cannot be trusted. Just as a wild horse cannot be controlled easily, in the same way, a lady is indomitable and too difficult to be sub-dued.

A Few Typical Etymological Derivations

While using despicable expressions for the ladies, a few typical derivations of the words have appeared, showing their analogy or likeness with females. For instance, while defining the Sanskrit word `Pramada' (A young handsome woman), it is cited that since the ladies turn the males amorous and impassioned in love, hence they are called `Pramdās'.

The etymological interpretation of the word `Mahila' (A woman) has been given thus—`Since the ladies are skilled in the art of infatuating males, hence they are called `Mahilas' (Ladies).

In Prakrita dialect, the use of the word `Mahiliyā' is also found besides `Mahilā' in the sense of a woman. While analysing the word `Mahiliyā', it is cited that since the ladies are fond of prompting quarrels, they are called `Mahiliyās'.

While defining the word `Rāmā' (A charming young woman) etymologically, it has been stated—`Since the ladies' appear quite charming and they attract males by their amorous gestures and dalliance, they are called `Rāmās' (young beautiful women)'.

The word 'अंगना' (A beautiful woman with well-rounded limbs) has been etymologically defined thus—`Since they make external gestures for expression of love and create impassioned feelings amongst males, hence they are called 'अंगना'.

While giving etymological interpretation, of the word `Nāri (A female), it is stated that since there is none other so hostile or damaging to menfolk, as females, hence they are called `Nāris'.

From a perusal of the above etymological interpretations appeared for womenfolk, it is explicitly clear that the author had tried to establish that the females were only instrumental in satisfaction of sexual urges. Most probably, by depicting the ladies merely as a source of sexual enjoyment in such a despicable and humiliating manner, the motive of the author may have been to frighten the menfolk to the extent that they are overawed and terribly scared of beautiful women so that they may turn indifferent towards them and keep themselves engaged in their spiritual pursuits. No doubt, it could be a plea of the author to assert his views, yet it could prove to be an irritant and counter-productive. Rather its efficacy is very much doubtful and controversial from psychological viewpoint as well. An annotation has been written on the said Prakirṇaka by Vijayavimala.

6. Samthāraga (Sanstāraka)

What is spread out on the floor is called `Saṁstāraka'. It is also used in a technical sense under Jaina tradition. The devouts who are determined to end their lives by observance of fast unto death after absolute concentration and self-realisation, they prepare a bed of Kusā grass, spread it on earth and lie down over it. By attaining final emancipation on the said `Saṁstārakas', they are able to accomplish their cherished goal for which they had carried out life-long spiritual endeavours, aspiring for an end. While lying firm on the earthly bed, they easily cross the ocean of the world and attain final salvation. Thus, if we consider a `Saṁstāraka' as the source to cross over the worldly ocean, it may not be wrong, irrelevant or illogical. In the said Prākirṇaka, the process how a true devout, engaged in self-realisation or self-conquest should end its life and attain final emancipation, has been elaborately discussed.

The said Prākirṇaka contains 123 verses. Herein, the significance of `Sanstārakas' (earthly beds) has been described in an attractive and metaphoric language. Just as a `Vaidurya Mani' shines like a cat's eye and Sandalwood is considered most fragrant amongst all other aromatics, and just as a diamond is costliest amongst all other precious stones, similarly, lying down on `Sanstārakas' for undertaking fast unto death and aspiring for final emancipation is considered to be most excellent, amongst all other spiritual endeavours. It is further laid down in most exciting words that a Jaina Sādhu, lies on an earthly bed of Kushā grass, undertakes fast unto death and aspires for true happiness by way of attaining final emancipation. In the said Prākirṇaka, the stories of many Jaina Sādhus have been produced as illustrations, who had lied down on `Sanstārakas' and after having undertaken fast unto death and absorption in profound meditation, had gone in eternal trance and finally, attained deliverance of the soul from transmigration. Sri Guṇaratna had composed a brief gloss over it.

7. Gachchhāyār (Gachchhāchār)

The word `Gachchha' is used to signify an association or community of followers, who observe certain enforced rules or a fixed tradition and which are administered by religious preceptors or spiritual heads. When a large number of people live a collective or community-based life, they are, obviously, required to adhere to certain norms, traditions or arrangements so that the collective living could go on smoothly, properly and peacefully. The same criteria applies to the organisation of Jaina mendicants. The male and female mendicants belonging to a certain group or association, are required to observe specific norms, traditions or ethical code, concerning ascetic culture, discipline, mutual cooperation and reciprocal sense of service as also maintenance of friendly relations with each other. In modern vocabulary, it can be termed as federal moral code. All these topics have been dealt with in this Prakirṇaka.

The Prakirṇaka, in question, contains 137 verses, a few of which have been composed in Anushtapa' meters (eight syllables in each quarter) and certain of them have been cast in `Ārya' meters (The first and third quarters must each contain 12 Mātrās or syllables—one being allotted to a short vowel and two to a long vowel—the second quarter 18 Mātrās and the fourth 15 Mātrās or syllables). the Chheda Sūtras, namely—`Mahā-Nishitha', `Vrahatkalpa' and `Vyavahār' etc. have already been discussed in the foregoing pages, relating to the moral laws, prescribed for male and female mendicants, knowingly or unknowingly violations thereof and the atonements prescribed therefor etc. It is believed that after having collected the relevant portions from the said Sūtrās, the above `Prakirṇaka' has been written in the interest and for the benefit of male and female Jaina mendicants, living collectively in a group or association. The topics relating to moral laws, governing reciprocal behaviour of male and female mendicants along their religious preceptors, belonging to an organisation, as also how to regulate their conduct have been dealt with extensively in the said work."

While discussing about the spiritual heads or guides of an organisation of Jaina mendicants, it is cited at a place in the said Prakirṇaka that if the gurus or Achāryas, themselves, are immoral and donot restrain those who are depraved or avoid taking drastic steps against erring Sādhus, they, themselves, are guilty of going wrong and frustrating the very ideals of a religious institution. The topics relating to mutual accommodation, humility and modesty, sense of service, respect, goodwill and kindly feelings between senior Jaina Sādhus on one hand and junior or young mendicants on the other, have also been taken up in the said Prakirṇaka.

The Jaina mendicants have been prompted to observe celibacy strictly. It has been laid down that even the grown up or aged Sādhus should avoid indulgence in conversation with female mendicants. The company of female mendicants is the root of all evils for male Sādhus.

While further elucidating the point, it is emphasized that a Sthavira (Senior Jaina Sādhu) may be a strong-minded and resolute person, yet just as the butter is melted, if placed near fire, similarly, it is quite possible that a female mendicant may develope a feeling of attachment and love for him. In that case, if the male Sthavira loses control over self, he will be seized by misfortune in the same manner as a fly is caught or entrapped in mucus. Finally, it is laid down with all emphasis that a male Sādhu must avoid the company of young girls, old ladies, sisters, daughters and even daughters' daughters.

Explanatory Literature: Sri Vjaya-Vimal Gaṇi, disciple of Shri Ānand Vimal Sūri, has written commentary on `Gachchhāchār'. In the course of his comments, the author writes that `Varahamihir' (A celebrated astronomer, author of 'Brihat-Saṁhita'. He is believed to have died in 587 A.D.) was the real brother of Achārya Bhadrabāhu. However, while discussing the biography of Achārya Bhadrabāhu, it has been stated above that it is not corroborated by historical facts. Probably, for want of anxiety to prove the authenticity of historical disclosures, there might have been a tradition to lay down such unauthentic versions without any hitch.

The commentator also writes that `Vārāhamihir' had accomplished `Brihat-Saṁhitā', a voluminous book on astronomy, after making profound study of `Sūrya Pragyapti' and `Chandra Pragyāpti' (5th and 7th upāngas-supplementaries to Angas).

8. Gaṇi-Vijjā (Gaṇi-Vidyā)

At a glance, it appears that the word `Gaṇi', appearing initially in the name and style of the above `Prakirṇaka', may have been used in the sense of a head of a gaṇa (a group or association of religious mendicants), since in Prākrita language, the word `Gaṇi' is generally used in the similar sense. In Sanskrit as well, the word `Ganina' literally means a teacher (having a class of pupils). While compounding two words, the last letter `na' disappears and only the word `Gaṇi' survives. Infact, the initial word `Gaṇi', appearing in the name of the above Prakriṇaka, has not been used in the sense of a religious head or incharge of a group of mendicants. There is another etymological derivation of the word `Gaṇi' also. The suffix `in' is applied to the root word `Gaṇa' and the resultant word-- 'Gaṇin' is obtained which means counting or reckoning. Here the word `Gaṇi' has been used in the same sense, since the subjects, relating to calculation or reckoning have been dealt with in the Prakirṇaka, in question. The said Prakirṇaka contains 82 verses. The astronomical matters, concerning lunar days, days of a week, motion of planets, a period of 48 minutes (any short portion of time, calculated in astronomy), auspicious conjunction of planets, the moment of the sun's entrance into a zodiacal sign, an asterism in the lunar mansion, knowledge of good or bad omens etc. have been discussed therein at length. The word `hora' has appeared to mean an hour.

9. Devindra-Thaya (Devandra-Stava)

A Jaina votary (devotee), while paying his obeisance to all 24 Tirthankers, eulogizes Lord Mahāvira, the last Tirthanker. At this, his wife expresses her eagreness to know about Indra (the lord of gods in heaven) and other divinities, enjoying higher or highest status in paradise. All this forms the subject-matter of the above Prakirṇaka.

Like several of the earlier Prakirṇakas, this Prakirṇaka is also believed to have been written by Sri Virbhadra. There are 307 verses contained in it.

10. Maraṇa-Samāhi (Maraṇa-Samādhi)

Death is imminent for every living-being, and it must be welcomed as and when it overtakes. However, people are greatly scared of death and the very idea of it creates shivering in their bodies. Under Jaina philosophy, this matter has received profound consideration with a view to turn the incident of death into a pleasant experience so that the death is rejoiced by the people in place of getting afraid and, it is observed as a great celebration. Infact, ending the life by observing fast unto death and devoting to intense meditation are the undertakings to that effect.

Perfect stability of mind, firm determination, absolute concentration, being disposed towards self conquest, realisation of purity of thoughts, giving up all worldly attachments and ending the life with total detachment are some of the characteristics needed for attaining final emancipation. As a result of intense meditation, the fondness for eating and drinking altogether stops. The devout is no more vulnerable to the idea of spiritualism or non-spiritualism. Highly intellectual sages of Jaina religion and philosophy have laid down guide-lines for the devotees after undertaking profound study of religious scriptures and having identified themselves with Supreme Truth. In this way, the topics relating to attainment of final emancipation by observing fast unto death and its various forms have been fundamentally and minutely dealt with in the said Prakirṇaka.

Body : Contents: The Prakirṇaka, under reference, contains 663 verses. It is voluminous as compared to all other Prakirnakas. The topics, dealt with in earlier Prakirṇakas, `Bhakti-Parigyā' (Taking of simple boiled food consciously); `Ātur-Pratyākhyān' (Renunciation of worldly pleasures in order to attain final emancipation); `Mahā-Pratyākhyān' (Total rejection of immoral path and renunciation of sensual pleasures). `Maraṇa-Vibhakti' and `Maraṇa-Vishodhi' (other types of final liberations) and `Arādhanā' (Serving and propitiation) etc. have also been extensively discussed in the above Prakirṇaka.

The Prakirṇaka, in question, starts in the shape of mutual conversation-between an Achārya and his pupil. The Jaina disciple is curious to know the significance of ending the life by observing fast unto death. His preceptor explains 14 means adopted to attain the state of total concentration and intense meditation after observance of fast unto death and ultimately to end the life. The teacher expounds the significance of `Ārādhanā' (worshipping); Ālochanā (self-censuring); `Saṁlekhanā' (Performance of severe penance after having exercised complete control over self both physically and mentally and renouncing all worldly attachments); `Utsarga' (abandonment of belongings—An act of discipline to be observed in the course of excretion so that no living creature is hurt); `Avkāsh' (not swayed by malice); `Saṁstāraka' (Spreading of Kushā grass bed to lie down for undertaking fast unto death); `Nisarga' (a voiding excrement); `Padopgamana' (Lying down firmly, controlling all physical movements and giving up meals altogether); are the means to end life without having least allurement and attachment to worldly objects.

Enunciation of how to observe fast unto death; performance of severe penance after having exercised absolute control over self both physically and mentally and renouncing all worldly objects, and the forms of austerities to be practised while ending life and attaining final emancipation, have been discussed at length in the above Prakirṇaka which are not only worth going through by Jaina devouts but fit to be given intuitive consideration also. As per demand of the context, a few illustrations of Jaina seers have been given who had endured all physical hardships with absolute detachment and had attained final emancipation after lying down motionless like a tree; having abandoned food altogether and practising severe penances. Many more illustrations have been given while expounding doctrines of Jaina philosophy. The above Prakirṇaka closes after describing 12 feelings of devotion of past perceptions.

The above are the precise details of the topics discussed in the foregoing ten Prakirṇakas. Besides them, there are a few other Prakirṇakas also, namely—`Rishi-bhāshita'; `Tirthodagār Parigyā'; `Ajiva-Kalpa'; `Sidha-Prābhrita'; `Ārādhanā-Pratākā'; `Dweep-Sāgar Pragyapti'; `Jyotish-Karaṇḍaka'; `Anga-Vidyā and `Yoni-Prābhrit' etc.

Conclusion: According to Shwetāmber Sect, there are 45 Agamas which have been analytically discussed in earlier chapters, namely—Angas-11; Upangas-12; Chheda Sūtras 6; Mūl Sūtras-4; Nandi-Anuyagdivar-2; and Prakirṇakas 10 — totalling to 45. In case, other Prakirṇakas are also added, the number of Agamas will enhance to 84. It is cited that the total number of groups of mendicants, constituting the organisation of Shwetāmber Sect was also 84. It is assumed that the total number of Agamic scriptures might have prompted to form the same number of groups of the religious mendicants.

However, `Sthānak-Vasi' and `Terapanthi' sects of Swetāmbers recognize only 32 Agamas to be authoritative as against 45 Agamas accepted by Shwetāmber idolaters. Which are as follows:

Angas	11	
Upangas	12	
Chheda Sūtras	4	(Nishitha, Vyavahār, Vrahat Kalpa and Dashāshrutaskandh)
Mūl Sūtras	4	(Dashāvaikālika, Uttrādhyayan, Anuyoga, Dwār, Nandi)
Avashyaka	1	
Total	32	

Explanatory Works to Help Understanding of the Texts of Agamas

Necessity: While dealing with the auxiliaries to the vedas of Aryan linguistic group and explanatory works, relating to Jaina Agamas, we had discussed about 6 Vedangas and 4 Upāngas (Purāṇās, systems of Hindu philosophy and jurisprudence etc) Besides them, Brahmāṇas and Sūtrās[1] and Bhāshyas (commentaries which explain Sūtras or aphorisms word by word with comments of their authors), written by leading Vedic Achāryas, namely `Sāyaṇa' and others. Without undertaking minute study of the auxiliaries, it may be found impossible to grasp the real essence of Vedic texts.

Atta-Kathās (Buddhist legends), written by Achāryas Budhaghosha. Budhadutta and Dharmapāl, have the same significance in relation to Tripitākas (collections of Buddhist scriptures), written in Pāli Prakrita as the Vedāngas, upāngas, upvedās and commentaries etc. to grasp Vedic texts. Knowledge and profound study of Buddhist legends is equally important for picking up the texts of Buddhist writings.

The auxiliaries to Jaina Agamas in Prākrita language have the same significance in order to pick up the exact meanings of their texts.

The style of expression is highly technical in Jaina Agamas. The subjects, dealt with in many of these holy scriptures, are of critical and sagacious nature, difficult to be followed or easily understood without the help of commentaries. Besides it, there is one more reason for unintelligibility of Agamic texts. Because of several recitations, held at different places and under auspices of different spiritual heads, the variations in the texts were bound to take pláce. Hence it is very difficult to harmonize the subjects, discussed therein, and pick up the substance thereof without aid of the auxiliary works. The interpreters have repeatedly offered explanations of abstruse portions so that the scholars and the students may find it easy to undertake critical and minute study of the texts and pick up their essence.

Nature of Explanatory Works: It has been a persistent effort of Jaina Achāryas that the contents of Agamic texts may be picked up correctly by the prospective readers. Accordingly, they spared no pains in composition of more and more interpretative works. Consequently, plenteous literature is found in the shape of `Niryuktis' (commentaries with etymological interpretations); `Bhashyās' (Word by word explanation of each Sūtra with comments); `Chūrnios' (brief, expositions); `Tikās' (glosses); `Vrittis' (Explanations of complex formations); `Dipikas' (Illustratives); `Vyākhyās' (Enlargements upon the subjects); `Vivechan' (Critical investigations); `Avachuries' (Elucidations); `Panjikās' (commentaries which explain and analyse every word); `Vachnikās' (The signification or meanings of words with explanations) and `Tabba' (Brief expositions). A major portion of the said auxiliary literature has already been published while the rest in lying locked in liberaries, boxes or spines etc.

Amongst the aforesaid categories of auxiliary works, the Niryuktis and Bhāshyas have generally been written in Prākrita dialects. Although, the Chūrnis are found to have been composed in mixed form of Sanskrit and Prākrita words,

---

1. Sūtras have been classified in four calegories — 1. Shrot Sūtras; 2. Grahya Sūtras; 3. Dharma Sūtras and 4. Shulva Sūtras.

yet they have been composed primarily in Prākrita vocabulary. A few `Tikās' are found exclusively in Prākrita language alone or in mixed vocabularies of Prākrita and Sanskrit both, yet majority of the Tikas are found written in Sanskrit language. Besides the Jaina Agamas, the above four types of explanatory works are also found in Prākrita language. Thus, combinedly they are called 5-fold sacred treatises.

Profound and critical study of 5 fold Jaina canonical literature is extremely necessary in order to have knowledge of various stages and processes of growth and development of Prākrita dialects and analytical study of Prākrita language from linguistic viewpoint and with a view to have true knowledge of Jaina philosophy and ethics.

Nijjutti (Niryukti)

According to Jaina Achāryas, erudite scholars and interpretaters, what is contained in Sūtras or aphorisms or what has been specified in Sūtras, wherein the glossarial explanation of obscure words is properly incorporated and what is desired to be correctly specified, is called `Niryukti'. The etymologists are always keen to explain the texts word by word, especially those occurring in Agamas so that the devotees and the followers may be in a position to conceive the substance of the sacred texts correctly. However, the Niryuktis have generally been written in symbolic style with the result the explanations or etymologists interpretations, offered therein, cannot be easily followed and need further elucidations. Although, numerous examples, illustrations and narratives have appeared, wherever necessary, yet they have been referred to only symbolically and have not been quoted in an elaborate manner. It is believed that Niryuktis have, primarily, been written on the basis of Pūrvas (old spiritual texts, incorporating ideological and philosophical doctrines of Jaina religion) as revealed from time to time by omniscients and heard or retained in their memory by their chief disciples.

Probably, one of the prime motives may have been that with the aid of Niryuktis, the Jaina mendicants or Sādhus will be able to pick up the meanings of Agamic texts without much difficulty and commit them to their memory. Niryuktis have been composed in Ārya Meters (In Ārya Metres, the first and third quarters must each contain 12 Matrās or syllable instants, the second quarter 18 and the fourth 15). Hence, it is comparatively easy to memorize such verses and retain them in memory. The narratives and illustrations are also there—may be only in symbolic manner, with the soothing effect that the religious preceptors are able to communicate their message more effectively by repeating them elaborately before their audience.

Historical Genuineness: Niryuktis are oldest amongst all auxiliaries. Piṇḍa Niryukti and Ogha Niryukti are considered as significant as Jaina Agamas. It is thus explicit that composition of Niryuktis had already been taken up prior to recitation, compilation, editing and final determination of Agamic texts at Valabhi (Saurashtra) in 5th century A.D. The prominent Jaina logician, Achārya Mallavādi, author of `Dwādshāranayachandra' had quoted the verse from a Niryukti in his book for elucidating his point which is sufficient to uphold that the composition of Niryuktis had already started before the life-time of Achārya Mallavādi which is believed to be in fifth century of Vikarmi Era.

Authors of Niryuktis: Niryuktis (commentaries with etymological interpretations of the words) have been written on ten prominent scriptural works, namely—(1) `Achārānga'; (2) `Sūtra-Kritānga'; (3) `Sūrya-Prajnapati'; (4) `Vyavahār'; (5) Kalpa Sūtra'; (6) `Dashāshrutaskandh'; (7) `Uttrādhyayan'; (8) `Āvashyaka'; (9) Dashvaikālika and (10) `Rishibhāshita'. The Niryuktis, composed on `Sūrya-Prajnapati' and `Rishibhāshita' are not available now. The author of the above Niryuktis is popularly known as Āchārya Bhadrabāhu. However, Āchārya Bhadrabāhu, the last authority on all 14 Pūrvas (old sacred treatises, containing highest spiritual and philosophical knowledge of Jaina religion) and author of `Chheda Sūtras' (Prescribing expiatory measures to atone for sins by Jaina mendicants) and Achārya Bhadrabāhu, author of Niryuktis, are considered being two separate identities. Here, it may also be mentioned that the verses of Niryuktis and those of bhashyās have so intermingled at many places that it is very difficult to distinguish them. Even the authors of Chūrṇies have not been able to avoid quoting of those verses in their compositions.

Incidentally, numerous topics, relating to manners and morals, prescribed for Jaina mendicants; doctrines of Jaina philosophy; mythological legends and traditions as well as historical events (partly historical and partly legendary tales) have been detailed in the said Niryuktis. They are really significant for acquiring knowledge of Jaina philosophy and culture; manners of action or manners of conducting themselves and ideological contemplations and reflections etc. Niryuktis have, primarily, been composed in Ardha-Māgadhi Prākrita and they are worth studying for carrying on analytical research of Prākrita dialects from philological viewpoint as well.

Bhās (Bhāshyās)

In order to elucidate further the substance of Agamic texts, bhāshyās (commentaries which explain the texts word by word with comments of the author) had been composed. The style of their composition is almost the same as of Niryuktis. The said bhāshyās have been written in Prākrita dialects. Just like Niryuktis, the explanations of Sūtras given in Bhāshyās are also concise. Whereas, Niryuktis have primarily been written in Ardh-Māgadhi dialect, in Bhāshyās, we also find uses of expressions in Māgadhi and Shorseni Prakritas besides Ardha-Māgadha.

Composition : Author: Bhāshyās have been accomplished on 1. Nishitha; 2. Vyavahār; 3. Vrahatkalpa; 4. Panch Kalpa; 5. Jita-Kalpa; 6. Uttrādhyayan; 7. Āvashyaka; 8. Dashavaikālika; 9. Pinda-Niryukti and 10. Augha Niryukti.

The Bhāshyās, written on `Nishitha'; `Vyavahār' and `Vrahat-Kalpa' are considered most significant from various angles. They are believed to have been accomplished by Sri Sanghdās Gaṇi `Kṣmashramaṇa'. It is stated that he was contemporary to Yākini-Mahattar-Sunu-Āchārya Haribhadra Sūri.

On `Avashyaka' (Mūl Sūtrā-forming part of Jaina Agamas), one Laghu-bhāshya (A short commentary); `Mahā-bhāshya (Detailed commentary) and one `Visheshāvashyaka bhāshya' (A special excellent commentary). Since multifarious topics have been discussed at, length in `Visheshāvashyaka bhāshya', hence greater significance is attached to it and holds a unique place in Jaina canonical literature. It has been composed by Āchārya Jainabhadradas Gaṇi `Kṣmāshramaṇa'. Jita-Kalpa (Sixth Chheda Sūtrā) and `Swopagya-bhāshya', written on it, are also believed to have been accomplished by Jinabhadradās Gaṇi `Kṣmashramaṇa'.

Many significant and detailed informations with regard to saintly life of old Jaina Sādhus, are found in the aforesaid Bhāshyās (commentaries). Study of these bhāshyās on `Nishitha', `Vyavahār', and Vrahat-Kalpa Sūtras may be much helpful in having authoritative informations of old manners and morals, observed by Jaina Sādhus, their reciprocal behaviour, mode of life, old customs and traditions, performance of religious austerities for expiation of sins and purification of self etc. After undertaking critical and analytical study of these bhāshyās, many significant clues are found with respect to old traditions and manners of conducting themselves by Jaina Saints.

Chuṇni (Chūrṇi)

Characteristics of Chūrṇis : Their Inevitability

The Niryuktis and Bhāshyas were accomplished in Prākrita dialects in the shape of verses in concise form. By virtue of the said commentaries, it was not possible to offer elaborate explanations of Agamic texts. The detailed commentaries or expositions can only be written in prosaic form, which are, obviously, more intelligible and can be followed easily by readers of average intelligence. Niyuktis and bhāshyas are in concise form which are of better use to religious teachers, preceptors, discoursers and spiritual guides for delivering their discourses in brief. However, they donot fulfil the requirements of young students or pupils who are eagre to apprehend knowledge of Agamic texts more clearly and elaborately. Thus the system of expounding Agamic texts in prosaic form, already in vogue in the shape of Chūrṇis (A style of prose composition for better conceivability of abstruse texts).

The author of `*Abhidhan Rajendra*' (A dictionary or vocabulary of words) has thus defined a Chūrṇi. The words in which have multiple meanings in the shape of `Pravritti' (Acceptation of a word in accordance with a grammatic rule); Apravritti (absence of application of a grammatic rule); `Vibhāsha'[1] (with optionality of a rule) which has the characteristic in enunciation of words acceptable or to be used in composition and those which are fit to be abandoned; wherein the roots have been prefixed by prepositions or suffixed by indeclinables, in which the flow of language is uninterrupted and free from terminations or stops and there is continuity like poetic verses and in which the sacred writings are philosophical with foresight and wisdom. Such an accomplished composition is called `Chūrṇi'.

Language of Chūrṇis: The authors of Chūrṇis have adopted a unique style in their compesitions. As per belief of Jaina community, Ardhā-Māgadhi Prākrita is a divine language, used only by holy sages. Thus, on one hand, they have used Ardh-Māgadhi Prākrita and on the other, they have used Sanskrit language also. Sanskrit is known for its richness and profundity in expression or exposition of

1. Settled grammatical rules for acceptation of words —*Abhidhān Rajendsa* III Volume page 1995.

philosophical and mythological discussions in an elegant style, fit to be grasped by highly accomplished and erudite scholars. The vocabulary of Sanskrit language is exhaustive from philological viewpoint and has the characteristic of formation and adaptation of new words to be added to its glossary. It has its own characteristic vocabulary, fit to explain even abstruse texts in brief and with clarity. Sanskrit enables to discuss a subject in depth and effective style. Sanskrit has its own significance in expounding even technical words or phrases with ease. The authors might have considered it worth-while to accomplish their churnis (Commentaries in prosaic form) by making use of both Sanskrit and Ardh-Māgadhi dialect and they might have decided to draw advantage of the said characteristics of Sanskrit language.

The use of both Ardh-Māgadhi dialect and Sanskrit in accomplishment of Chūrṇis, has been similzed with the popular maxim--`Obtaining fair justice by segregating Jewels and corals'. Even if the jewels and corals are blended together, the distinct identity of each is easily perceivable. Similarly, both languages do not lose their respective identity even though used combinedly in composition of Chūrṇis.

Primacy of Ardha Māgadhi Prakrita in Chūrṇis

Although the use of both Sanskrit and Ardh Māgadhi dialect was made while composing Chūrṇis, yet main use was there of Ardh Māgadhi Prākrita. The narratives or small tales, wherever necessary, have been produced in Ardh Māgadhi Prākrita, concerning various spheres of life — religious social and political. The authors of Chūrṇis have also explained obscure words of the Sūtras and given their etymological interpretations in Ardh Māgadhi dialect only.

Relative verses have been quoted from various scriptures of both Sanskrit and Ardh Māgadhi Prākrita to substantiate the discussion on the points under consideration.

Chūrṇis : Their Authors: Chūrṇis have been written on numerous Sutras, namely—Āchārānga, Sutra Kritānga, Vyākhya Prajnapati, Vrahat Kalpa, Vyavahār, Nishitha, Panch-Kalpa, Dashāshrutaskandh, Jita Kalpa, Jivābhigama; Jambudweep Prajnapati, Uttrādhyayan, Āvashyaka, Dashavaikālika, Nandi and Anuyoga-Dwar.

The great Jaina scholar, Sri Jinadass Gaṇi Mahattar, undoubtedly, made enormous contribution to enrich not only Jaina canonical literature but glorified the entire theocratic treasure of India. He was born in a family of traders. He belonged to Vajra branch under `Kotika gaṇa' of Jaina mendicants. According to historians he is believed to have lived in sixth century A.D.

An ancient manuscript of Chūrṇi on `Dashāvaikālika' has been discovered in a library at Jaisalmer (Rajasthan). It has been written by Sthavira Agastiya Singh, who is believed to have lived in third century of Vikrama Era. It is, therefore, obvious that the said Chūrṇi had been accomplished two or three centuries earlier to the recitation and editing of the Agamic texts, carried out at valabhi (Saurashtra) gathering under auspices, of Sri Devardhi Gaṇi `Kṣmashramaṇa'. The said Chūrṇi was got published by `Āgam-Mahodadhi', Late Muni Sri Puṇyavijayaji. The famous Chūrṇi on `Dashāvaikalika, accomplished by Achārya Sri Jinadas Gaṇi Mahattar, has been named and styled as `Vridha-Vivraṇa' (a mature exposition) by Achārya Haribhadra Sūri.

Most Significant Chūrṇis: Although, valuable material concerning knowledge of mankind and folk life is available here and there in the Chūrṇis, yet the Chūrṇis, written on `Nishitha' and `Āvashyaka' (Chheda Sūtras) are treated as excellent. Considerable informative material is contained in them, pertaining to erstwhile Jaina traditions, antiquities of archaeological significance and social values. Many knowable subjects have been dealt with in the said Chūrṇis concerning social relationships, modes and manners of living, eating and drinking, apparels and ornaments, used by the people, social, religious and political beliefs, customs and practices under vogue, prescribed moral standards, melās and functions organised on festive occasions, festivals and celebrations held by the people, mercantile conditions, trade routes, caravans of traders, sailing to distant coasts for procurement of business, agricultural and mercantile products, famines, robbers and thieves etc. The said topics have been extensively discussed which may be very helpful in having knowledge of erstwhile public life and popular mind of those days.

From the above, it is evident that Jaina scholars were always anxious to enlighten each and everybody with regard to the ideological and philosophical tenets of their religion. Accordingly, they had carried out indepth study of day today values, observed by the people and vices that had crept in the erstwhile social life. It is why they were in a position to portray a lively picture of day today public life in India. It is also evident from the above discussion that besides establishing contacts with the people, they came across, they were quite tactful and worldly wise. They knew well the ways of the world. No doubt, the Jaina seers had profound knowledge, derived from meditation, on higher truths of their own religion and its philosophical doctrines but they had similar perfection in the ideologies of other religions or beliefs as well. Infact, they possessed vast knowledge, covering almost all topics. They were universal in their outlook. The said Chūrṇis are highly significant for having critical and investigative study of erstwhile people as well as their folk life and literature. The practice of writing churnis (commentaries in prose) had continued on other allied scriptures as well other than Agamas. For instances, Chūrṇis had also been composed on important Sūtras like `Karma Granth' and `Shrāvaka-Pratikramaṇa'.

Tikās (Commentaries or Glosses)

Purport: Agamas are true exponents of religious ideology and philosophy of Jaina religion, manners and morals--in, nutshell, they are very foundation of Jaina culture. Consequently, the Jaina seers have spared no pains to elaborate and explain the contents of Jaina Agamas to the maximum extent possible, so that the maxim of the Sūtras could be more explicit and intelligible. Therefore, on on hand, Niryuktis, Bhāshyās and Chūrṇis had been accomplished and on the other, the process of writing Tikās (Annotations) had also continued. While, Niryuktis and Bhāshyās had been composed in Prākrita verses, the Chūrṇis were written in the style of prose compositions in both Sanskrit and Prākrita languages combinedly and the Tikās (Annotations) were primarily written in Sanskrit only. There are certain distinguishing features and clear-cut advantages of Sanskrit language in so far as accomplishment of new words, providing etymological interpretations and derivation of words, with unique capability of expression and elaboration of a subject are concerned. These special characteristics of Sanskrit language allured Budhist and Jaina scholars to adopt the language as medium for expression of their views and writing of their books. Accordingly, in ensuing period when Jaina and Budhist scholars were eagre to enunciate their respective ideologies and philosophical doctrines, mainly to meet the requirements of learned and scholarly people, they preferred to take up writing of their books in Sanskrit language. Besides renowned treatise, styled `Sanmati Tark Prakarna' (True knowledge gained by reasoning a philosophical system of arriving at truth), written by Āchārya Sidhsena, almost all other important works, forming part of canonical literature of Jaina religion, have been accomplished in Sanskrit language. Due to extreme regard for Ardh-Māgadhi Prākrita, since it was the exclusive medium of expression, wherein Tirthankers had delivered their religious sermons, the tales and narratives had been quoted in original Prākrita dialect in Tikās, wherever considered necessary, as per demand of the context. A few of the Tikās have also been written in Ardh-Māgadhi Prākrita but their number is extremely limited.

Composition of Tikas — An Ancient Practice

The system of writing Niryuktis, Bhāshyās, Chūrṇis or Tikās, various forms of commentaries, have not been attempted in consistent with any tradition. Instead they have been written as per independent will of the commentators. The system of writing Tikās was already in vogue even prior to holding of Valabhi recitation and editing of Agamic texts. The author of Chūrṇi on `Dashavaikālika' Sūtra, Jaina scholar, Agastya Singh, who is believed to have lived in third century of Vikrama era, has repeatlly given references of certain Tikas in his Chūrṇi.

A Mention in Himvata Theravali

As stated in `Himvata Therāvali', Ārya Gandhhasti, author of `Tatvārth Mahābhāshya' (An extensive commentary with explanation of each Sūtra word by word) and resident pupil of Ārya Madhumitra, had written a gloss on `Dwadshanga' on the advice of Ārya Skandila, which is, however, not available now. According to `Agam Mahodadhi', Muni Puṇyavijayji, a gloss on `Āchārānga (Tittle of the first Anga) had been, probably, written after two centuries of the commencement of Vikrama era. A `Vivarna' is also a form of commentary, written in Sanskrit. Thus the process of writing Tikas had actually started even earlier.

Prominent Authors of Tikas

Āchārya Haribhadra Suri: An erudite scholar, `Adhyatma yogi' (An accomplished yogi), Achārya Haribhadra Sūri, was most distinguished author of Tikas on Agamic texts. He is believed to have lived in eighth century A.D. He has written Tikas on `Avashyaka', `Dashāvaikālika', `Nandi', `Annyaga Dwar' and `Pragyāpnā Sutra'. There is a clear reflection of his abilities, profound study and vast knowledge on having perusal of his Tikas. He has reproduced small tales and narratives in Prākrita dialect in his Tikas. The subsequent authors have also followed this tradition in their Tikas, amongst whom the names of `Vādivaitāl' Shānti Sūri; Nemichand Sūri and Āchārya Malayagiri etc. are worth mention.

Shilankāchārya: Shilankāchārya had written Tikās on 'Achāranga' and 'Sutrakritānga' (Titles of first and second Angas) forming part of 12 sacred books of Jainas, in which many truths relating to Jaina philosophy and ethology have been expounded for enlightenment of its followers. Sri Shilankāchārya is believed to have lived in ninth century A.D.

Shāntyāchārya and Nemi Chandrāchārya

In the eleventh Century A.D., there were two eminent Jaina scholars, namely—`Ādivaitāl' Āchārya Shānti Sūri and Āchārya Nemichandra Sūri. The former had written a Tikā on `Uttrādhyayan', styled `Paiya' or `Shishyahitā' which also came to be known as `Uttrādhyayan Vrahat-Vritti'. Sri Nemichandra Sūri had also composed a Tika, styled `Sukhbodhā', basing his comments on the lines of the Tika of Āchārya Shānti Sūri.

Whereas, Āchārya Shānti Sūri has reproduced Prākrita tales or narratives in his `Tikā' with assertory propositions like as per 'established tradition or the views of ancient sages' 'This is what other elders say' The said narratives or tales may be found very helpful by the research scholars. It also leads us to the conclusion that there was a long tradition to quote such tales or narratives in support of the comments. The said extracts are really significant for undertaking a critical or analytical study of old traditional tales. A few narratives quoted in `Paiye' and `Sūkhbodha' Tikās are so lengthy that they can constitute an independent volume. The narratives, written by Sri Brahma Dutta, are of similar type.

Subsequent authors of Tikās, namely—Achārya Abhaya Deva and others

During 12th-13th century there were several accomplished authors of Tikas who had made significant contribution towards creation of explanatory and interpertative literature in the shape of Tikas (annotations). Āchārya Abhayadeva Sūri had composed authentic Tikās on 'Sthanānga', 'Samvāyānga', 'Vyākhyā-Prajnapati', 'Gyātri-Dharmakatha', 'Upāsaka Dashā', 'Antkriddashā', 'Anuttaraupātikadashā', 'Prashna-Vyākaraṇa' and 'Vipāka-Shruta' (Titles of 9 Angas out of twelve, forming part of Jaina Agamas) which are greatly valued in entire Jaina Canonical literature. Because of having composed Tikas on nine Angas, he is more popularly known as author of `Navāngi' Annotations (pertaining to nine Angas-sacred scriptures of Jainas). He is believed to have lived in 12th century A.D.

Specialities : Significances:- The said Tikās had, on one hand, served a magnificent purpose by expounding obscure Agamic texts, containing highest spiritual knowledge and philosophical doctrines of Jaina religion and on the other, had enriched the treasure of Jaina canonical literature which is highly accomplished one and has great significance. The learned authors have produced an anlytical description of various departments of knowledge, concerning human life. These Tikas have covered almost all aspects—whether psychological, philosophical, literary or social.

The said explanatory works provided great stimulation to the ensuing generations of scholars for accomplishing new sacred books to enrich Jaina canonical literature. Not merely this, even the literature of other religious sects or groups was equally influenced which is a matter, requiring further investigation and study.

9

SHORSENI PRAKRITA AND ITS CANONICAL LITERATURE

Present Topic : In the foregoing pages, while referring to 45 Agamas, accomplished in Ardh-Māgadhi Prākrita, it had been pointed out that they were not all recognized authoritative ones by Digamber Sect. According to them, the texts of 12 Angas (Twelve sacred books of Jainas), based on spiritual utterances of Tirthankers and composed and edited by their Gandhers on the basis of what they had heard by revelation and retained in their memory, popularly known as 12 Angas, have ceased to exist and they are no longer available.

The Agamic Scriptures which are identified as authoritative ones by Digamber Sect and which were accomplished in Shorseni dialect (A regional variation of Prākrita and the Apbhransh languages), will be dealt with in this Chapter since they are deemed to have great significance in Prākrita literature from various angles. However, it may be worth-while to discuss how Jaina religion came to be divided into Digamber and Shwetamber Sects prior to above discussion.

Nihnavavād (The Practice of Contradicting True Meanings and Setting Forth Hostile or Offending Interpretation)

Under Jaina tradition, there have been certain scholars who have always shown scant regard to the prevalent meanings of sacred texts, as propounded by Trithankers and set forth their own inauspicious interpretations. Such scholars are called as `Nihnavas'. The word `Nihnava' here represents both the offending theories or conclusions and also the persons, propounding them.

Literal Meaning of the Word 'Nihnava'

The word `Nihnava' literally means—denial or concealment of true knowledge. It is thus generally used in the sense of secrecy or concealment in general. However, the said word is used in a technical sense under Jaina tradition. Achārya Malayagiri has given critical explanation of the word `Nihnava', while elaborating the texts of *Avashyaka Niryukti* (authored by Achārya Bhadrabāhu) thus—The scholars who out of ignorance, instinctively cling to worldly life and bodily enjoyments or out of sheer and strong attachment with worldly objects, deny or conceal true knowledge as revealed by a Tirthanker and distort it to their own liking, are called `Nihnavas' since they make concealment of truth and propound their own perverse conclusions. It is further stated that if a person shows least disregard or faithlessness towards even a single word of sacred text, he is said to have illusory knowledge with false vision, since the utterances of Tirthankers are alone considered true and authentic by Jainas.

The said `Nihnavas' are only partly illusive or detractors. In their external appearance, they donot look differently from other Jaina saints.

In the same context, there is reference of `Botika nihnavas' also who are believed to hold adverse views in almost each and every matter, concerning Jaina religion.

Summary: It is evident from the above discussion that as per belief of Shwetamber Sect, a few persons are always there who donot repose their faith on all principles or ideological doctrines of a religion. They revolt against the official line and start propagating their own independent doctrines and raise a separate organization of their followers. They only disagree with a specific portion of the ideology and are unanimous on all other tenets or philosophical doctrines of the religion. There was no apparent difference also in their external appearance and looked very much similar to other Jaina monks. Accordingly, they were neither ex-communicated from the religious fold nor treated as such. They were only considered `Nihnavas' who disowned certain fundamentals of the religion and propagated their own doctrines. The words `Botikas-Nihnavas' have appeared for followers of Digamber Sect as well which will be discussed in detail later on as per demand of the context.

Citation in Sthānānga Sūtra and 'Avashyaka Niryukti'

In the seventh chapter of `Sthānānga Sūtra' (Title of the third out of 12 Angas), there is reference of seven `Nihnavas' (Those who disown the real truth as propounded by a Tirthanker and preach their own perverse doctrines). However, in *Avashyaka Niryukti*, they have been referred to with greater details. As laid down in it, the perverse doctrines of seven types were actively advocated and preached in the organisation of Lord Mahāvira (comprising of male and female religious mendicants and household devotees), by `Nihnavas', namely—`Bahuratavāda' by Jamāli in the area of Shrāvasti (It is now identified with Sahet, Mahet north of Ayodhya); `Jiva-Pradeshavāda' by Tishyagupta, in the area of `Rishabhpur'; `Avayakta-Vāda' by Āsādh, from the area of `Shwetvikā'; `Samuchhedavāda' by Ashwamitra from the area of Mithilā (Name of the territory, lying to the north-east of Magadha in Bihar); `Dwaikriyavāda' by Ganga from the territory of `Ullukātir'; `Trairāshikavāda' by Rohagupta from the territory of `Antraujika'; and `Abadhikavāda' by Goshthāmāhila from the territory of Dashapur (on the north of Ujjaini in Malvā region, lay another principality with its capital at Dashpur on the `Chārmāṇvati' river, which now appears to be the modern town of Dholpur in Rajasthan). There is also a reference of the place of origin of `Botika-Vada' (Digambers) in the commentary, written by Achārya Malayagiri on *Avashyaka Niryukti*.

The approximate period when the above perverse doctrines began to be propagated by `Nihnavas' in the religious organisation of Lord Mahāvira also finds mention in the said commentary i.e., `Bahuratavāda' began to be advocated after 14 years of attaining `Kevalya' (the state of highest spiritual perfection) by Lord Mahāvira; `Jivapradeshavāda' after sixteen years; `Avyaktavāda' after 114 years;

`Samuchhavāda' after 220 years; `Dwaikriyavāda' after 228 years; `Trairāshikavāda' after 544 years and `Abadhikavada' after 584 years. `Botikavada' was preached after 609 years of attainment of `Kevalya' by Lord Mahavira.

Botika Nihnava: As per Shwetamber Sect, besides seven defiants, referred to above, there was one more defiant also, called `Botika'. As already pointed out, the basic difference between seven other defiants and Botika being thus—Whereas the above-noted seven defiants were in disagreement with only one specific point or portion of the ideology, while `Botikvāda' contradicted almost each and every doctrine, that was followed. As per Shwetamber Sect, the said `Botikavāda' (total disagreement) gave birth to Digamber Sect.

Just as Shwetamber Sect considers the emergence of Digamber Sect being a deviation from the true path, in the same way, Digamber Sect considers vice-versa, which will be discussed where the context will so demand; what is purported to be emphasized here is that each Sect considers itself as true exponent of the ideology and philosophy of the religion, enunciated by Lord Mahavira and the other as having strayed from the real path.

Before commenting on the subject, it may be more appropriate to first discuss the opinions of both sects and their respective viewpoints.

As per Belief of Shwetamber Sect

As appeared in 'Āvashyaka Niryukti'

While commenting upon verse No. 146, contained in the original Sūtra of `Avashyaka Niryukti', Āchārya Malayagiri has stated: "There was a garden, called `Deepak' in the town of Rathvirpur. Once Achārya Ārya Krishna happened to visit that place. The said preceptor was delivering lecture on the significance of `Jinakalpik' perfection (As per concept of Jaina religion, a devout, after dissociation from the religious organisation, is required to practice prescribed spiritual exercises for atttainment of strong will and determination. The exercises are as stringent as severe acts of the penances, practised by Tirthankers. Hence called Jinakalpik). At that time, one Shivabhūti enquired from the Āchārya about Upadhi (Belongings allowed to the religious mendicants to be kept for day-today use). Necessary reply was given by the preceptor but Shivabhuti did not feel satisfied. He developed faithlessness in the tenets of Jaina religion because of lack of intution. He put off his clothes and came out of the abode of Jaina mendicants. His sister, Uttrā, was female mendicant. She came to the garden to pay respects to her brother. After seeing her brother in naked condition, she also cast off her clothes as a mark of her illusive attachment for him. Thereafter, both left the place and moved to the town for begging alms. A prostitute happened to watch Uttra in absolute naked condition. She pondered over in her mind and thought that if the people would see the ladies entirely naked, they would feel disgusted and turn averse to the entire womenfolk. The prostitute helped her to put on clothes on her body which Uttra did not appreciate. She again threw off her clothes. Thereafter, the pros covered her breast and lower portion of her body with two pieces of cloth. However, Uttra tried to remove them also. At that time, her brother had a look on her and advised not to remove them, accepting them as divine gift ....."

The commentator, Āchārya Malayagiri, has further stated in the course of his comments on verses No. 147 and 148 of `Avashyaka Niryukti' that thus, Shivabhūti and Uttra had given birth to an utterly false notion by defying established usages of Jaina religion, at Rathvirpur, merely on the basis of fallacious arguments and irrational reasoning. In nutshell, Shivabhuti was founder of Digamber ideology, supporting absolute nudity of the Jaina monks. After him, his disciples Sri Kaundilya and Kottavira continued this tradition.

Citation in 'Visheshāvashyaka Bhāshya'

As cited in `Visheshāvashyaka Bhāshya' (authored by Āchārya Jinabhadra Gaṇi `Kṣmāshramaṇa'), Digamber Sect, believing in total nudity of the Jaina monks, came into existence after 609 years of final salvation of Lord Mahāvira. Thereafter, the two verses No. 147 and 148 have been discussed which had earlier been referred to while commenting on `Āvashyaka Niryukti'.

Narrative Produced by Jaina Scholarly Saint, Āchārya Hemachandra

Jaina seer, Āchārya Hemachandra, author of the commentary on `Visheshāvashyaka Bhāshya', has quoted the tale of Shivabhūti in detailed form which reads: "Once upon a time, Āchārya Ārya Krishna, a spiritual guide and philosopher, happened to visit Rathvir town. There lived a Govt. servant, named Shivabhūti, in that town. He was also named `Sahasramalla'. He enjoyed the favour and patronage of his king. He was a mirthful and whimsical person, and used to roam about in the night, enjoying the life in a capricious mood. He used to return home at late night after whiling away time in aimless loitering. His wife was completely tired and felt much unhappy over his daily routine. One day, she complained to her mother-in-law, who had great affection for her, and brought to her notice that her son (own husband) was habitual to return considerably late at night and never came back at proper time. She had to wait for long hours at night and missed her evening meals. She had to keep awake till he arrived. So she was very much distressed. Her mother-in-law consoled her and said—daughter! why did you not inform me earlier? However, you don't worry now. You go to your bed and I shall keep awake in place of you and take the impertinent boy to task and teach him a lesson for ever."

At the instance of her mother-in-law, she went to sleep and the old lady kept on waking. As usual, Shivabhūti returned after mid-night and knocked at the door. Mother was already much enraged. She annoyingly answered — "you guilty boy! you insolent son! you have returned so late after moving aimlessly at night? You go wherever you like or where you find the door open. I shall neither follow you to appease in any way nor shall I die without you."

Such wrathful and hauty words of his mother greatly pinched him and he immediately returned from his house. He began to loiter about in the town. While roaming here and there, he happened to find the door of an Ashrama (Dwelling place of Jaina mendicants) lying open. Shivabhūti drew close to the monks and after paying obeisance, he prayed for his initiation so that he could lead the life of a devout. The Jaina Sādhus listened to his story and after having come to know that he was in the good books of the ruler and his mother and other family members had not given their approval, they declined to initiate him. Thereupon, Sahasramalla (Shivabhūti) himself plucked out his hair with the help of ash, lying there. At this, the Jaina Munis initiated him as a religious mendicant.

Next day, all the Munis left this place to live at another convent. After passage of some period, it so happened that the Jaina Sādhus again returned to that town. On having come to know of their arrival, the ruler arrived at the convent and gifted a precious blanket, ornamented with Jewels to Shivabhūti since he had great affection and liking for him. The spiritual head had noticed it. He addressed Shivabhūti and told him that it was not desirable on his part to accept such costly apparel, being a Jaina Sādhu. Any misfortune could overtake him on the way. Hence it was not at all advisable to keep it with him. However, Shivabhūti did not relish the idea and he retained it with him inspite of instructions of the Achārya to the contrary. Not merely this, he had so strong fondness for it that he used to take it out to make sure that it was in perfect condition as soon as he came back after begging alms. Ofcourse, he did not use it to cover his body. When the Achārya watched his folly, he knew that Shivabhūti had developed spiritual ignorance and delusion which should be strictly checked and done away with.

One day, when Shivabhūti was away, the Achārya tore the blanket into small pieces and delivered one piece to each of the mendicants to wipe off their feet. As soon as Shivabhūti came to know of it, he was reddened with anger but kept mum.

Once it so happened that Achārya Ārya Krishna was imparting lecture on Jina-Kalpik performances while dealing with the topic of belongings allowed to be kept by a religious mendicant. Shivabhūti raised some queries in that connection which were duly answered by the spiritual head. However, since Shivabhūti was mentally agitated because of his strong attachment for the blanket, how could he feel agreed and satisfied?

Questions : Answers : Unsatisfied

The author of the bhashya on `Visheshāvashyaka' writes : "Shivabhūti enquired from the Guru — "Why the Jinakalpik state could not be accomplished now? The spiritual head replied--"Practising of severe penance as done by Tirthaṇkers or omniscients had ceased after final salvation of Ārya Jambu."

Shivabhūti remarked—"Practising of Jinakalpic penance could stop for immorals or spiritless devotees only. How could it altogether be stopped for capable or resolute-minded devotees?

Shivabhūti was much offended because of his strong liking for blanket, ornamented with precious jewels which had been torn into pieces without his knowledge. He, therefore, added—"Many ill-consequences have been found with the habit of storing. Hence there is a sacred provision for absolute detachment and renunciation. Infact, the severe penances of a Jinakalpa alone are worth practising."

The Sādhus are generally supposed to be free from shyness, aversion, feelings of hot and cold etc. as a result of maintaining nudity or nakedness of the body. It is why they donot put on clothes. Hence nakedness alone is propitious and conducive to happiness.

Jaina Guru replied—"If possession of clothes was considered a sin and source of worldly attachment then the maintenance of the body could also be a curse. If a particular object was found to be the cause of attachment why should it be possessed at all? If such an argument prevailed then the religion itself will be disowned."

Those who are against the teachings and religious philosophy, as enunciated by Tirthankers, for them even the Jaina religion, Jaina Sādhus and religious utterances of Jaina Arhats (compiled in the shape of 12 Angas by their Gandhers), all can be the source of worldly-illusim. For Goshālaka and Sangam etc. even Lord Mahāvira was the cause of astringency. Since the human bodies are the source for performance of the austerities for attainment of final emancipation, they cannot be considered as property or belongings. Similarly, if the clothes are put on to cover the bodies for undertaking spiritual endeavours, they can not be considered as worldly possessions?"

"Every attempt was made to satisfy Shivabhūti, but he was labouring under delusion. He was highly agitated and had lost faith in the teachings of Jaina Arhats. He abandoned the clothes altogether. As a gesture of affection for her brother, his sister, Uttra, a female mendicant, also put off her clothes. As soon as a prostitute happened to see her completely naked, she helped her to put on clothes. However, she again cast them off. Thereafter, the pros tied a piece of cloth to cover her breasts. While she was about to throw it off also, her brother, Shivabhūti advised her to let it remain. Thereupon, she did not remove the cloth.

Shivabhūti had initiated Kaundilya and Kottavira as his disciples. Through them, his independent sect came into existence."

Conclusion: As per Shwetamber Sect, the above episode is generally repeated regarding advent of Digamber Sect. However, under Digamber tradition, there are several legendary tales narrated regarding birth of Shwetamber Sect, which will be taken up later on.

There is not much difference in the narratives, appearing in the gloss on `Avashyaka Niryukti' and commentary on `Vishāvashyaka Bhāshya' except that Achārya Malayagiri has stated that the prostitute had tied pieces of cloth on both—the breast and around the loins (the lower region of the female body) while the author of the commentary on `Visheshāvashyaka Bhāshya' has stated about tying the cloth on breast only. Covering the lower region has been ommitted by him.

In regard to Uttra, it may be inferred that the female mendicant was, no doubt, allowed admission in Digamber Sect with minimum cover on the body. If it is believed to have been followed by Digamber Sect, how the ladies were subsequently allowed to put on adequate clothes on their bodies. As a matter of fact, such legends have no historical significance. They are merely fictional. Why such fictions are invented, will be taken up for discussion as and when demanded by the context.

As Per Digamber Sect

Citation in 'Darshan Sār' (Written by Achārya Devasena): *Darshan Sar*[1] composed by Achārya Devasena, is highly accredited sacred book under Digamber tradition. Regarding origin of Shwetamber Sect, it appears therein:

"After 136 years of the expiry of emperor Vikramāditya, the `Shweta Pat' (those who put on white clothes) Shwetamber Sect came into existence at Valabhi[2] in Saurāshtra. Shri Shāntāchārya was the disciple of Sri Bhadrabāhu Gaṇi and the name of his disciple was `Jina Chandra', who was of loose and defiled character. He laid foundation of Shwetamber Sect and he was the proponent of the theory that the females could attain final emancipation in the same feminine body. The Tirthankers, after attainment of Kevalya (The state of highest perfection) take their food by their mouth as well and they get diseased also. A Jaina mendicant, having superiority of intellect, can accomplish spiritual perfection even if he wears apparel on his body. It was also expounded by him that the embryo of Lord Mahāvira had been removed (Initially, he had appeared in the womb of a Brahmana lady, Devanandā and, thereafter, the embryo was again established in the womb of a Kṣatriya lady, Trishta, by a divine power). The Sādhus can attain final emancipation even in a dress or appearance other than what has been prescribed by the Arhats of the Jainas. A religious mendicant can accept food in alms from any place or source which may be inconceivable or thought unfit. He had, thus, propounded theories against the very spirit and essence of Jaina Agamas and had written books, full of illusions and inversions. After his death, he was thrown in first infernal region out of seven by way of punishment for his sins."

Advent of Shwetamber Sect as Appeared in 'Bhāva - Sangraha'

Besides Achārya Devasena, author of *Darshan-Sār*, referred to above, there was another Achārya Devasena, who was the author of *Bhāva-Sangraha*, also considered significant under Digamber Sect. Regarding emergence of Shwetamber Sect, the following is cited therein:

"After 136 years of the death of emperor Vikramāditya, the Shwetamber Sect came into existence at Vallabhi in Saurashtra. Achārya Bhadrabāhu was staying in Ujjaini Town (Malwa region) those days. He was an astrologer of repute. Through his predictive knowledge, he got an inkling. He informed the mendicants of his religious organisation that he was apprehending a severe famine to last for 12 years. He, therefore, advised the Jaina monks to leave the place as early as possible and move to distant regions with their respective groups to avoid the melancholic situation."

---

1. Composed in Vikrama samvata 990.
2. In East Gujarat, an ancient city was located near modern Bhābhānagar. It was a flourishing and prosperous city in olden days. Renowned Chinese Tourist, Huentsānga, who had toured India in 7th century, A.D. has made a mention of this town in his travelogue. During those days, it was a magnificent and beautiful town. It is believed that Valabhi town was situated near the modern village `Valā' in Saurashtra. The 12 sacred books of Shwetamber Sect forming part of Agamas, had been recited, compiled and edited at Valabhi.

"On listening to the advice of Achārya Bhadrabāhu, all the group-leaders managed to shift immediately to safer regions."

"A group leader, named Shānti, happened to arrive at Valabhi town with attractive surroundings in the state of Saurashtra."

"As the luck would have it, the said region too was under the grip of terrible famine—so much so-that the poors and destitutes, afflicted by hunger, were rendered so heartless that they even did not mind killing comparatively resourceful persons and cut open their abdomens to collect whatever eaten food was found therein to satiate their own hunger. It was really a horrible plight."

"On the face of such duress, all the Sādhus, under leadership of Acharya Shanti; were compelled by the irony of circumstances to cover their bodies with white pieces of cloth and get equipped with a blanket, stick, a pot either made of scooped gourd or bottle gourd each."

"They abandoned manners and morals, prescribed for Jaina Sādhus and started begging alms (food) in a humiliating manner. As and when, they felt hungry, they did not hesitate to approach house-holds and even to take their food by sitting inside the houses. Thus, somehow, maintaining themselves, they were able to pass that miserably long period. The period of famine was ultimately over and normal days restored. Thereafter, Achārya Shanti invoked all the Sādhus of his organisation and directed them to get rid of past despicable practices. They should express remorse for what they had done by censuring themselves and atone for their sins. They should readopt the manners, conducive to their ascetic life."

"On hearing it, the first and leading most disciple of `Achārya Shanti, reluctantly replied as who can dare to undertake such severe spiritual endeavours these days which include observance of fasts; avoidance of meals; interference or obstructions created for those who are engaged in seeking deliverance and consequent preventing them from accomplishment of it; sticking to one place; nakedness with no clothes on; tranquil-mindedness; to live strictly as celibate; sleeping over open ground; plucking out of hair after every two months, causing unbearable pain; and 22 other awsome physical performances—all these are extremely diffcult exercises which we are unable to carry out. The present way of life, adopted by us, is more practical and comfortable. We cannot afford to give up this type of life at this hard time."

"At this, Achārya Shanti retorted that there was no use to lead such sort of depraved life. It was a mark of disgrace and utter distortion of the tenets of Jaina religion, as enunciated by Arhats. A saint or devotee who has renounced all worldly attachments, wanders about naked and lives as a hermit, is considered of the highest order and most excellent amongst all devouts. This way of life is consistent with the teachings of Jaina Arhats. Any deviation from it or denunciation of the said path is nothing but sheer delusion and reliance in any other creed or ideology is perversion."

"Hearing all this, the chief disciple of Achārya Shanti grew enraged. He picked up a long stick and struck it against the forehead of Sthavira Achārya Shanti. The blow proved fatal and the Achārya succumbed to the injuries. Thereafter, he was reborn as `Vyantar Deva' (a supernatural spirit or being in Heaven)."

"The said assessin and chief disciple of Achārya Shanti, became the spiritual head of the organisation. He, thus, founded Shwetamber Sect, which was only a hypocritical act on his part. He began to preach that even a devotee who is not freed from all ties or attachments and possesses clothes and pots etc. can also attain final emancipation."

"He and his disciples composed such religious books which were full of hypocritical views. They started preaching their own manners and morals. They used to find faults with the ideology of Digamber Sect which preached that a devotee must be free from worldly ties or knots and renounce all worldly attachments. They started collecting fat amounts from their ignorant followers by way of deluding and cheating them."

The soul of Achārya Shanti was existent in the body of `Vyantar Deva', and the latter began creating hurdles in his way and censure him for adopting a wrong path. The Deva smeared him for deviating from the true ideology of Jaina religion.

Although, it was not feasible for them to give up comfortable life, yet they got very much frightened. They began to offer worship of all eight kinds to please `Vyantar Deva' and seek his blessings.

In this way, the mode of worship, introduced by Shri Jinachandra, principal disciple of Achārya Shanti, is prevalent even now. First of all, the said `Vyantar Deva' (Heavenly re-birth of Achārya Shanti) is offered worship. He is, infact, tutelary deity of `Shwetambers'. This is how the misguided Shwetamber Sect came into existence.

Summary: The name of the author of `Darshan Sār' and that of `Bhāva-Sangraha' is Achārya Devasena. However, they are decidedly two distinct scholars. The 11th verse of `Darshan Sār' and 52nd verse of `Bhāva-Sangraha', wherefrom the narration starts regarding emergence of Shwetamber Sect, is almost identical in both. There is only slight variation in descriptive words and their placement in the latter half portion of each narrative.

It cannot be asserted whether the story had been borrowed by the author of `Bhāva-Sangraha' from `Darshan-Sār' or vice-versa. According to certain scholars, the story was most, probably borrowed from `Bhāva Sangraha' which leads us to infer that `Bhāva-Sangraha' may have been accomplished prior to `Darshan-Sār'. However, there is no credible evidence at our disposal to substantiate the inference.

The source and substance of both the narratives donot appear any different with the only exception that the description in `Darshan-Sār' is in concise form while in `Bhāva-Sangraha', it is comparatively in more elaborate form. The names of Achārya Bhadrabāhu, his disciple, Achārya Shanti and his pupil, Jina Chandra, are found identical in both narratives. However, in `Darshan-Sār', it is ommitted that Achārya Bhadrabāhu was a renowned astrologer. Probably, it may have been done to summarize the description. According to `Darshan-Sār', Jinachandra was languid and demoralised person and he gave birth to Shwetamber Sect. There is, however, no detailed mention of this fact.

In `Bhāva-Sangraha', while making a mention of severe famine, lasting for 12 years at a stretch, its lamentable effects in demoralising Jaina Sādhus and turning them lethargic and easy-going. Since they were not prepared to atone far their sins, it is described how the Shwetamber Sect came into existence.

In both narratives, the specification of the period is the same i.e. the advent of Shwetamber Sect had taken place in the year 136 of Vikrama era, equivalent to the year 606 after final salvation of Lord Mahāvira which means that Achārya Bhadrabāhu may have predicted about likelihood of severe, famine for twelve years before the said period of Vikrama year 136 i.e. in the Vikrama year 124 or in the year 594 after final salvation of Lord Mahāvira.

There is a difference of three years only. Digambers believe that the said schism in Jaina organisation had taken place 3 years earlier as against the assertion of Shwetāmbers.

Story Appearing in 'Vrahat Kathākosha'

In narrative verse No. 131, appearing in *Vrahat Kathākosha*, authored by Achārya Harishena[1], there is an enumeration how the Shwetamber Sect had come into existence. While producing the biographical sketch of Achārya Bhadrabāhu in the foregoing pages, it had been stated that Achārya Bhadrabāhu had visited Ujjaini town in Mālwa region. While he was moving about in the town, begging food, Achārya Bhadrabāhu found how a child gave an impression of an inauspicious omen (occurrence of an event portending evil) and on the basis of the same, the Achārya predicted that a terrible famine was likely to take place for a continuous period of 12 years. He advised his followers to shift immediately to safer places. Thereupon leaving by a group of Jaina mendicants to Punnāta region in South under leadership of Vishākhāchārya and moving of other groups of Sādhus under respective leadership of Rāmilla, Sthūlvridha and Bhaḍrāchārya to Sindh region; obtaining final emancipation by Achārya Bhadrabāhu with total detachment and disillusionment after observance of fast unto death in a garden, known as `Bhādrapada' at Avanti (Name of modern Ujjaini—one of the seven sacred cities of Hindus); and returning of the said groups of mendicants as soon as the famine was over, have been dealt with at length in `Brahatkathakosha'. Therefore, detailed repetition of the said events has been avoided, being unnecessary. They have only been symbolically referred to here.

According to the above version, the division in the organisation took place only after return of Vishākhāchārya from South. The following appears therein:—

"Rāmilla, Sthūlvridha and Bhaḍrāchārya, who were totally indifferent to the worldly desires and attachments, immediately contacted Visākhāchārya on his return. They were too scared of transmigration; coming and going in new births. They cast off ragged garments from their persons and re-adopted the life of total renunciation and living naked without clothes.

Those who failed to relish the teachings of their spiritual guides or have deep penetration into their revelations; those who believed that there were austerities of two types—Jina Kalpic (severe penances, meant to be practised by Arhats only) and Sthavira-Kalpic (comparatively less severe austerities to be practised by Sthaviras—senior monks), continued wearing garment covering their half bodies. Such feeble-minded devotees, having no spiritual force, had laid foundation of

1. Year of accomplishment being 853 of Shākā era.

Shwetamber Sect.

Purport: The author of *Vrahat Kathakosha* has tried to link the above story with Achārya Bhadrabāhu, known for his expertise in Agamic texts. According to Dıgamber tradition, Achārya Bhadrabāhu had attained his liberation in the year 162 after final emancipation of Lord Mahāvira while under Shwetamber tradition Achārya Bhadrabāhu is believed to have expired after 170 years of final salvation of Lord Mahāvira. In case, the event of schism in Jaina organisation is connected with the life time of Achārya Bhadrabāhu, it will transpire that the division had occurred about 450 years earlier, since it has been clearly specified in both `Darshan-Sār' and `Bhāva-Sangraha' that Shwetamber Sect had come into existence in the year 606 after final emancipation of Lord Mahāvira. However, before taking up this point, we shall like to produce a few more assumptions under Digamber tradition to this effect.

Spilt in Jaina Organisation: Another Assumption

In fifteenth Century A.D.[1], there was a poet of Apbhransha Prākrita (one of the middle Indo-Aryan dialect), named `Rayadhu' or `Raidhu'. Traditionally, he was a follower of Digamber Sect. He has enumerated the said story of split in the Jaina organisation in his sacred book `Mahavira-Charit. He has incidentally referred to about enthronization of emperor Chandragupta, by his guru Chānakya (celebrated writer on civil polity; also known as Kautilya); as also his successors Bindusār, Ashoka and Kuṇāl. It is also found mentioned how the innocent prince Kuṇāl was cruelly blinded as a result of treachery, played by his jealous step-mother. The author, Rayadhu has named Kuṇāl's son as Chandragupti. It is believed that Chandragupti was another name of `Sampriti'.

Raidhu writes in his book that Ashoka had enthroned Chandragupti with great fanfare. Chandragupti (Sampriti) had spared no pains for expansion and extensive propagation of tenets of Jaina religion.

Thereafter, the author, Raiyadhu, makes a mention of Achārya Bhadrabāhu and asserts that the repeated version of sixteen dreams, found in Jaina canonical literature, alleged to have been visualized by Chandragupta, were, infact, dreamed by Chandragupti, (Sampriti). Apprehending a great mishap in the shape of terrible famine in near future, Chandragupti renounced all worldly desires and attained initiation by Achārya Bhadrabāhu. Thereafter, the events described are almost the same as detailed above i.e. indication of bad omen by the child; prediction of severe famine to last for 12 years; migration of Jaina Sādhus to South to save themselves from the severity of famine; wearing of clothes and adoption of pots and sticks etc in their hands by Sthulāchārya and other senior monks; re-union of various migrant groups of Sādhus as soon as the famine was over; Splitting of Jaina organisation into Shwetamber and Digamber Sects etc.

The Points to be Deliberated Upon

There appears to be no well-reasoned consistency between Achārya Bhadrabāhu

1. Year 1439 A.D.

and Chandragupti alias Sampriti as held by leading poet, Raidhu. As laid down in *Dushmākālshrishramana-Sangh-Stava*, written by Achārya Dharmaghosh Sūri, nine Nandas ruled over Magadha dynasty till the year 215 after final salvation of Lord Mahāvira. Thereafter, the Morya dynasty ruled for 108 years. Which means till the year 323 after final salvation of Lord Mahāvira. Had Achārya Bhadrabāhu been contemporary to Chandragupti alias Sampriti then chronologically, he could not have lived prior to the year 300 after final salvation of Lord Mahāvira. On the contrary, he would have lived even after the said period, which would have, obviously, meant repudiation of the beliefs of both Digamber and Shwetamber sects in regard to the lifetime of Achārya Bhadrabāhu and with a view to coroborate the said assumption, there is no effective or substatial evidence, available.

Scepticism that prevails in regard to the correct life-time of Achārya Bhadrabāhu is mainly due to the fact that there have been several Acharyas with name-sake of Bhadrabāhu. This issue will be taken up in ensuing pages as per demand of the context.

Views of Āchārya Ratnanandi

As appeared in *Bhava-Sangraha* and *Vrahat Kathakosha*, as soon as the dreadful period of famine was over, the group of Jaina Sādhus gathered again at a place to assess the situation. Thereafter, the Jaina institution had splitted into two branches—Digamber and Shwetamber Sects.

Achārya Ratnanandi[1] has described the said incident of schism in Jaina organisation with greater detail and elaboration. According to him, after Jaina Sādhus had returned from the places of their migration and gathered again at one place to discuss and chalk out future course of action, there was dissension amongst them over the issue of total nakedness or semi-coverage of the bodies with pieces of cloth by Jaina Sādhus. However, Shwetamber Sect had not come into existence immediately thereafter. Achārya Ratnanandi has made a mention of an additional story which is produced below.

Advent of Shwetamber Sect as per 'Ardha-Phālaka' Doctrine (Keeping half body covered by a piece of cloth and remaining half quite naked)

After the dreadful famine came to an end, a new theory of semi coverage of the body with a piece of cotton cloth and maintaining nakedness of the rest had been propounded which has been produced by Achārya Ratnanandi as under :

"The said typical doctrine of semi-coverage of the body with cotton cloth had come to light in the same manner as oil is found floating over the water."

The followers of `Ardha-Phaláktā' doctrine, infact, made distortion of true preachings of Jaina Arhats and started misguiding the ignorant persons to follow vile course.

They were fond of all types of sensual pleasures and were arbitrary in their

---

1. In the above-noted sacred book of Achārya Dharmaghosh Sūri, the reference of Achārya Ratnanandi and his accomplished book *Bhadrabāhucharita* also appears while mentioning the life-history of Achārya Bhadrābahu.

behaviour. They had introduced new austerities to be observed by them and reduced them to writing in the shape of Sūtras (aphorisms)."

"In this way, quite a long time had passed since introduction of the doctrine of semi nudity and semi coverage of the body with a piece of cloth. The story, thus, runs—once, there lived a celebrated king, named Chandrakirti, enjoying great reputation and glory like a shining moon as ruler of Ujjaini. The name of his Queen was Chandrashri. She had given birth to a daughter, named Chandralekha.

The said girl happened to study the holy scriptures of Jaina religion under spiritual guidance of the said Sadhus who had propounded the theory of semi coverage of the body."

She possessed rare qualities of beauty and wisdom.

"There was a well-known town of Valabhi in Saurashtra State which was ruled by a great politic and sagacious king, Prajapāl. All the kings had been subdued by him. His queen was Prajāvati who had been endowed with excellent qualities of head and heart.

He had a beautiful prince, named Lokpal. He was too gentle and amiable. He was also fortunate having favourable stars. The prince, was well-versed in miscellaneous branches of knowledge.

The king, Prajapal, delightfully sought the hand of princess Chandralekhā, beautiful daughter of king Chandrakiriti, for his son. The prince was happily married with the said princess. Just as Indra, king of Heaven draws extreme pleasure while having union with his wife, Shachi, similarly, the prince drew maximum happiness and greatly enjoyed married life with his wife. In due course of time, he inherited the great kingdom of his father. He recognised Chandralekha as his principal Queen."

"Lokpāl began to rule and nurture his great kingdom, in consistence with the significance of his name. He was powerful and exercised immense influence upon all other kings who bowed their heads before him. On a fateful day, while the king was in a delightful mood, his principal Queen, entreated him—my dear husband! my spiritual guide and mentor lives in the town of `Kānyakubja'. He commands universal respect. Kindly invite him to visit your palace. The request was gladly acceded to by the king."

"The king directed his attendants to proceed immediately and bring Jaina Sādhus with them. Accordingly, they reached there and after repeatedly bowing before leading gurus, entreated them to accompany them. Thereupon, Jinachandra arrived at Valabhi with other Sādhus.

The king came to know of the arrival of Jaina monks. He, accompanied by his courtiers (Feudal Lords), Ministers and prominent citizens, started immediately to pay his obeisance to Sādhus, humming up all directions with tunes of musical bands."

"The king happened to watch the monks from a distance. He was shocked at the sight. He thought he had never come across such Sadhus who were half naked and only semi clad. They could not belong to an adorable sect. He, therefore, felt reluctant to approach them and pay his respects.

The king returned to his palace from there and appeared sad. The Queen, however, realized the agitation going on in the mind of the king."

Because of her extreme faith and regard for the Sādhus, the Queen immediately arranged clothes to be put on by Sādhus before arriving at the palace.

When the king found them properly clad, he offered them his best respects. Thus the king who had great fondness for his Queen, could lower down to do anything.

Since the clothes, supplied by the Queen and put on by Sadhus were white, the sect, subsequently, came to be known as Shwetamber Sect in place of 'Ardha-phālakas' (semi-clad)."

"In this way, Shwetamber Sect came into existence after 136 years of the death of king Vikramāditya. Jinachandra was the founder of the sect. He was the first spiritual head. The stupid fellow propounded illusory doctrines against the very spirit of Jaina Agamas, namely--Jaina Arhats or omniscients, after having attained Kevalya (the state of highest perfection), took food by their mouths; the females attained final emancipation in their feminine forms; the Sādhus who had fondness for eating and were pleased to gather worldly possessions, were also entitled to attain final liberation."

Reasoning and Full Consideration of the Subject

It appears from the above narration of Ratnanandi that after the famine was over, the Sādhus, who were adamant to cover their bodies with a piece of cloth, did use it but they were only semi-clads. The partial nakedness was still there. They only placed an outer garment over their bodies or wrapped themselves with a piece of cloth only. It was why, Lokpal, king of Valabhi, was highly perplexed and was at his wits end. He must have reasoned in his mind and thought what a typical sect it was. The Sādhus were semi covered and semi naked. In other words, they were neither totally naked nor they had adequate covering over their bodies.

After, white clothes furnished by the Queen, were worn by the Sādhus, the king developes regard for them and pays his respects. From the said narration, it clearly sounds that the partial nudity and partial coverage of the bodies by the Sādhus, did not appeal to the king. He was at a loss to understand to which sect they belonged and which ideology they represented.

From what has been stated above, it may not be wrong to believe that the king might have come to know about two types of Jaina Sādhus only either totally naked or fully clad. However, in case the king had preference for nude Sādhus only he would not have accorded such warm welcome to the Sādhus as soon as he found that they had properly covered their bodies with white clothes and they were no longer semi nudes and semi covered.

Although, Achārya Ratnanandi has tried to defend himself by arguing that a person can do anything and lower down to any extent out of sheer indulgence for his wife. That is to say, the king warmly welcomed the Sādhus only to appease his queen. However, the argument is not sound in as much as he would not have shown reluctance to entertain the Sādhus, finding them half naked and half covered, if he was guided only by the love, he had for his queen.

Moreover, 'Bhadrabāhu Charit', authored by Sri Ratnanandi, is not-considered authentic nor any significance is attached to it from historic viewpoint. It is, therefore, not necessary to scrutinize its contents and verify them. Of course, Ratnanandi has tried to connect his story with Achārya Bhadrabāhu. However, the timing in his story that Shwetamber Sect came into being in 136th year of Vikram Era can have nothing to do with the life time of Achārya Bhadrabāhu who is believed to have died after 170 years of final salvation of Lord Mahavira.

Bhadrabāhus More Than One : The events, prominently referred to under Digamber Sect, have been produced above. From perusal of the above stories, it is apparent that various scholars, belonging to Digamber tradition, have tried to link their tales with Acharya Bhadrabāhu, although there is absolutely no consistency between them with regard to his exact life-time. They donot appear to have made any serious attempt to prove the historicity of his life-time. Thus the readers have to remain contented with the utopian stories since no effort has been made to establish their authenticity. However, there is one more reason for suspense in this regard in as much as there have been several Achāryas, bearing the same name. The scholars who fail to pay proper heed or attach due significance to the historicity of their tales, are bound to be confused on this account as well.

Hence, it may be worthwhile to consider over the spiritual heads, bearing the same name—`Bhadrabāhu' under both Digamber and Shwetamber traditions.

Bhadrabāhus Under Digamber Tradition

On perusing canonical literature, belonging to Digamber tradition, it is evident that there have been several Achāryas, bearing the same name—`Bhadrabāhu'. Their brief account is given hereunder:

First Bhadrabāhu: Achārya Bhadrabāhu, having expertise in Jaina Agamic scriptures, was the first one, already discussed above. As appearing in `Tiloyapaṇṇatti', an authoritative sacred book, recognized under Digamber tradition, he had attained his final liberation in 162nd year of final salvation of Lord Mahavira. He was eighth in succession to the supreme seat of Lord Mahāvira. These facts are believed to be unanimously true under Digamber tradition.

Second Bhadrabāhu: In `Tiloyapaṇṇatti', while describing how the knowledge of expertise in Jaina Agamas was getting diminished with the passage of time, the names of Acharyas have been indicated[1] with the respective names of Agamas they had mastered. As cited therein, Sri Subhadra, Yashobhadra, Yashobāhu and Lohārya were experts in Achāranga only.

---

(1) (a)			
	Omniscients	— 3 Time	62 years
	Experts in Jaina Agamas	— 3 Time	100 years
	Expertise in 10 Purvas (out of 14 old sacred treatises of Jainas)	— 11 Time	183 years
	Having proficiency in 11 Angas (Forming part of Jaina Agamas)	— 5 Time	220 years

(Contd. . .)

As appearing in `Tiloyapaṇṇatti', the experts in 11 Angas were there upto samvat year 565 after final salvation of Lord Mahāvira. Thereafter, there were proficients in Achāranga (Title of the first Anga) only, who had their supremacy for 118 years as cited in `Tiloyapaṇṇatti' in between Samvat years 565 to 683 after final salvation of Lord Mahavira. That is to say, four religious heads who were experts in Achāranga only dominated during the said period of 118 years, namely—Subhadra, Yashobhadra, Yashobāhu and Lohārya.

Out of the above-noted 4 experts in `Achāranga', third Achārya Yashobhadra has also been named as `Bhadrabāhu' under Digamber tradition. In `Prākrita-Pattāvali', written by Achārya Nandi, the name of Achārya Bhadrabāhu appears in place of Yashobhadra, with the only difference that in Tiloyapaṇṇatti, he has been described as an authority on Achāranga only while in Pattavali (List of successors to the seat), he has been shown as an expert in 8 Angas. However, it is certain that both designations have been used for one and the same Achārya. Whereas, the name of `Yashobhadra' appears in Ṭiloyapaṇṇatti' against Sl. No. 27, the name of Bhadrabāhu has also been shown in the `Pattavali' against Sl. No. 27 certain

---

(*Contd. . .*)

Dexterity in Achārānga (Title of the first out of 12 sacred books of Jainas)	— 4 Time	118 years
Total period upto expertise in 11 Angas	Total time	683 years
		565 years

(b) Omniscients -- 3 =	1. Gautama 2. Sudharma 3. Jambu
Experts in Jaina -- 5 = Agamas	1. Nandi 2. Nandimitra 3. Aparājitā 4. Goverdhan 5. Bhadrabāhu
Experts in 10 = Purvas -- 11	1. Vishākh 2. Prosththila 3. Ksatriya 4. Jaya 5. Nāga 6. Sidhārtha 7. Dhrishtishena 8. Vijaya 9. Budhila 10. Gangadeva 11. Sudharma.
Proficient in 11 - 5 Angas	1. Naksatra 2. Jayapal 3. Pāṇdu 4. Dhruvasena 5. Kansa
Expertise in -- 4 Achārānga only	1. Subhadra 2. Yashobhadra 3. Yashobāhu 4. Lohārya

points concerning `Pattavali' of Nandi, relate to next chapter and they will be discussed accordingly where the context will so demand.

Bhadrabāhu : Guptagupti : Chandragupti

In Sanskrit `Gurvāvali' of Nandisangh, the name of Sri Guptagupti appears as successor to the seat of Achārya Bhadrabāhu. However, on having a critical study of preceding and following observations on the point, it clearly transpires that he is the same Bhadrabāhu who has been named as Yashobāhu, one of the four experts on Achāranga only in `Tiloyapaṇṇatti'.

There is a point needing special attention here. In the foregoing narratives, the name of Sri Chandragupti, king of Ujjaini, has appeared side by side with the name of Achārya Bhadrabāhu. It is quite likely that the king's name could be Guptagupti in place of Chandragupti. The author of `Gurvāvali', has used an attribute with the name of Guptagupti as "Asheshanarnāyakavanditānghiḥ" (meaning that the entire princely class bowed at his feet) which supports the view that Guptagupti was a king and he adopted saintly life after renouncing royal pleasures. The word `Gupti' appears in latter part of both names, from which it may not be out of place to infer that the king Chandragupti may be none else but Guptagupti. Hence it is worth further investigation that the earlier stories ought to be connected with the name of Guptagupti and not Chandragupti. It is possible that the original texts of the stories may have changed with the passage of time.

Third Bhadrabāhu: After obliteration of 11 Angas (sacred treatises of Jainas) in the Samvat year 683 after final salvation of Lord Mahāvira, the name of another Achārya Bhadrabāhu appears who is stated to be a great astrologer. In the foregoing narratives, the attribute of `expert in the science of astrology' has also been used with the name of Achārya Bhadrabāhu at a few places which appears probably due to sheer misconception. How could Achārya Bhadrabāhu, who is linked with the events of Samvat year 136 of Vikrama era, be an astrologer? As cited in `Tiloyapaṇṇatti', he was an authority on Achārānga only and preceded `Lohāchārya'. Navertheless, because of namesake, the misunderstanding, continued unchecked for a long time. It has already been emphasized above that least attention has been paid towards chronological and historical accuracy.

Bhadrabāhus Under Shwetamber Tradition : First

Under Shwetamber tradition, the first Achārya Bhadrabāhu was a great scholar and an authority on Jaina Agamas. He had composed Chheda Sūtras, incorporating guide-lines to atone for sins, committed by Jaina Sādhus. As per Shwetamber belief, he had breathed his last after 170 years of final salvation of Lord Mahavira. Achārya Hemchandra, a renowned Jaina scholar, has also signified the same year in his book `Parishishta—Parva' with regard to the final liberation of Achārya Bhadrabāhu.

Second Bhadrabahu: Under Shwetamber tradition, the second Bhadrabāhu was the same Achārya who had composed 10 Niryukits on various Sūtras (commentaries with etymological interpretations of obscure words) and had authored

`Upsarga-Har-Stotra'. He is also believed to be the author of `Bhadrabāhu Saṁhita' (An astrological guide). He was an astounding scholar of astrology. He is also popularly known as Bhadrabāhu, the astrologer. It is also a hearsay that the great astronomer, Vārāhmihir has signified the year 427 of Shaka era at the end of his accomplished book on astrology `Panchsidhāntikā'. Accordingly, Vārāhmihir was alive in the Samvat year 562 of Vikrama era (equivalent to the Samvat year 1032 after final salvation of Lord Mahāvira). If the hearsay of his being real brother of `Vārāhmihir' is believed, the life time of astrologer Bhadrabāhu should also be treated contemporaneous to him.

Achārya Bhadrabāhu : Certain Historical Facts

From historic viewpoint, the contemporaneity of Achārya Bhadrabāhu and Chandragupta Maurya is still undecided. A few scholars are of the opinion that they were contemporary to each other. In this regard, there are certain historical facts appearing in Jaina canonical literature, belonging to Shwetamber Sect, which may be helpful in arriving at any truth.

'Titthogālipainnā' : It is cited in `Titthogālipainnā' that on the very night, Lord Mahāvira had attained final salvation, Pālaka had been coronated as king of Ujjaini. He had reigned for 60 years. Thereafter, Nandas ruled for 155 years. After the end of Nanda dynasty, Mauryas came to power. They had ruled for 108 years. Subsequent to the rule of Mauryas, king Pushyamitra was enthroned who had ruled for 30 years. Thus, as per the said chronology, the Maurya dynasty had started ruling with effect from the year 215 after final salvation of Lord Mahāvira.

Chronological Order as per 'Dushmākālshrishramana-Sangh-Stava'

According to *Dushmākālshrishramana-Sangh-Stava*, written by Achārya Dharamaghosh Sūri, the chronological period of each kingdom has been given almost in the same order. He states that Pālaka had ruled for 60 years; Nandas for 155 years; Mauryas for 108 years and Pushyamitra had reigned for 30 years.

Establishment of the chronology of each kingdom appears to have been done, keeping in mind how long they exercised their central authority over their entire kingdom. Although, Pālaka was basically the ruler of Avanti (It is the western part of Mālwa, on the north of Narmada river and its capital was Ujjaini) but as laid down by Achārya Dharmsghosha Sūri in his book, when king Udāi had died issueless, Pālaka had invaded Magadha dynasty[1], once ruled by emperor Ajātshatru (Koṇika) and conquered it. He had thus extended his kingdom and established his authority over Northern India as well.

Achārya Dharmaghosha Sūri has also specified the names of spiritual heads of Jaina organisations in erstwhile states. As laid down in the aforesaid `Sangh-stava' of Achārya Dharmaghosha Sūri, during the rule of king Pālaka and nine Nandās, the spiritual heads of Jaina organisation were Achārya Jambu (for 40+4

---

1. Here the word Patliputra (modern Patna) signifies Magadha dynasty, the capital of which was Patliputra during the rule of king Udāi.

years); Achāya Prabhava (11 years); Achārya Shayambhava (23 years); Achārya Yashobhadra (for 50 years); Achārya Sambhutivijaya (8 years); Achārya Bhadrabāhu (14 years); and Achārya Sthulabhadra (for 45 years). Further, as mentioned in the said `stava', during the rule of Mauryās, the supreme heads of Jaina organisation were—Ārya Mahagiri (for 30 years); Ārya Suhasty (46 years) and Achārya Guṇasunder (for 32 years). Achārya Dharmaghosha Sūri has also reconciled the period of leadership of each spiritual head with the period of reigning by various rulers. According to the said chronological order, Achārya Bhadrabāhu lived during the reigning period of Nandas over Magadha. Achārya Dharmaghosha Sūri has mentioned the period of rule of each Nanda separately. Accordingly, the period of reigning of the seventh Nanda had come to an end in Samvat year 156 after final salvation of Lord Mahāvira. Achārya Bhadrabāhu was the spiritual leader of Jaina organisation for 14 years, who had attained his final liberation in samvat 170 after final salvation of Lord Mahāvira. Evidently, he led the organisation for four years during the reign of eighth Nanda and remaining ten years during the rule of ninth Nanda. Thereafter, Achārya Sthūlbhādra succeeds him and administers the affairs of Jaina organisation for 45 years till the end of Nanda dynasty.

The dynasty of Nandās comes to an end in Samvat 215 after final salvation of Lord Mahavira when Achārya Sthūlbhadra also attains his liberation. Thereafter, Chandragupta Maurya establishes Mauryan Dynasty under able guidance and direction of Achārya Chānakya. Evidently, the rule of Mauryan dynasty had commenced not only after final liberation of Achārya Bhadrabāhu but also after the death of Achārya Sthulbhadra.

A Cause of Misunderstanding

Chandragupta Maurya is treated as contemporary to Achārya Bhadrabāhu, only due to the confusion, arising from the version of Achārya Hemchandra appearing in his sacred book `Parishishta Parva', wherein it is cited that Chandragupta Maurya had been coronated after 155 years of attainment of final salvation by Lord Mahāvira. However, the chronology, as specified above, is considered most reliable and authentic under Shwetamber tradition.

Full Consideration made by Scholars

The Research scholars have argued at length and given their full attention to the above citation of Achārya Hemachandra. However, they have not been able to trace out any historical support to the version of Achārya Hemachandra, wherein it is cited that Chandragupta Maurya was coronated in samvat 154 after final salvation of Lord Mahāvira. Achārya Bhadrabāhu had attained final salvation in the year 170 and Chandragupta Maurya had breathed his last in samvat year 184 after final salvation of Lord Mahāvira. However, the authenticity of `Himvata Therāvali' is disputed as against `Tithogāmi Painnā' and `Dushmākāl-shrishramaṇasanghstava'.

The scholars believe that the year of coronation of king Chandragupta, shown in `Parishishta Parva' is wrong and miscalculated. On the very night of final salvation of Lord Mahāvira, Pālaka had been enthroned and he ruled continuously for sixty years. This period appears to have been ommitted through oversight at the time of calculation by Achārya Hemchandra.[1] It appears that straight away he counted 155 years of the rule of nine Nandas and, thereafter, he made a mention of coronation of Chandragupta Maurya.

Epitome: Chandragupta Maurya had found his kingdom after having finished the dynasty of Nandas in the year 215 after final salvation of Lord Mahāvira, equivalent to the year 312 B.C. as per Christian era. Chandragupta Maurya's grandson, Ashōkā, the great, was enthroned in the year 269 B.C. which is an established fact from historic viewpoint. There is a gap of 43 years in between the reigning period of Chandragupta Maurya and enthronement of emperor Ashoka. Chandragupta had admittedly ruled for 18 years and his son, Bindusār for 25 years. In this way, the rule of Chandragupta Maurya had ended in the year 233 after final salvation of Lord Mahāvira (coronation in the year 215+18 years of his rule = 233).

As per `Dushāmkalshrishramanasanghstava', the period of spiritual leadership of Jaina organisation by Achārya Mahāgiri, had lasted for 30 years during the rule of Mauryas. Accordingly, he had administered the affairs of Jaina organisation from the year 215 to 245 after final salvation of Lord Mahavira. The period of Chandragupta Maurya's rule is covered by the said period of leadership of Achārya Mahāgiri and, therefore, Chandragupta Maurya was contemporary to Achārya Mahāgiri and not Achārya Bhadrabahu.

Two Points of View: While dealing with the split in the Jaina organisation into Digamber and Shwetamber Sects, the ideas and narrations of both Sects had been presented in the foregoing pages. However, it has been repeatedly emphasized that the convictions and beliefs of both sects are not free from bias or prejudices.

It may be worth-while to discuss the matter more elaborately in the light of canonical literature of both sects, now available.

The main controversy arises when Digambers invariably plead that absolute nakedness is a must for a Jaina Sādhu. If an ascetic has even a thread on his person, he does not deserve to be a Jaina Muni, since it is nothing but possession of a worldly article irrespective of its size or volume. Contrarily, Shwetambers believe that spiritual heads who are undertaking Jinakalpik penances (After having dissociated from the Jaina institution, they perform austerities by leading a lonely life in a forest or a solitary place for accomplishing state of highest perfection. The said austerities are as harsh as severe penances practised by Arhats themselves without worrying for physical inconveniences, arising out of inclement weather or natural disasters), might put off clothes and live naked altogether. However, the elderly monks, practising Sthavira Kalpa (They continue in the institution to practice and preach about the significance of austerities to their disciples and help in the growth of their religious and philosophical knowledge and development of their character. In old age, while they are physically unable to undertake tours, they live at one place and provide spiritual guidance to their pupils). They are free to

---

1. Hemchandra must have ommitted by oversight to count the period of sixty years of king Pālaka after Mahavira. — *Epitome of Jainism*, Appendix A, Page IV.

put on clothes and keep their bodies covered. The saintly life of Jaina Sadhus is not spoilt in any way by putting on meagre clothes with sense of absolute detachment. In the sacred books of Shwetamber Sect, it is mentioned that putting on prescribed clothes to cover the bodies, cannot be deemed to be an act of acquisition or hoarding in any way. The said argument of Shwetamber Sect is significant and calls for critical examination and further discussion on the point.

We are discussing below on the effectiveness of this argument, quoting from the Agamic scriptures, wherever necessary.

Achāranga : Nominal clothing : Total Nudity

It is cited in Achārānya conspicuously : "A Jaina mendicant, who lives half and half covered with a piece of cloth naked is not required to worry whether his cloth has become wornout; seek for another change or ask for thread and needle to stitch the torn cloth; else shorten or lengthen it in order to make if fit for wearing again. Those who tolerate all physical hardships and bodily afflictions with absolutely detached mind as a result of coming in contact with sharp-edged and pungent articles, such as straw, grass etc., cold and hot inclement weather, biting on the naked body by large or small mosquitos and germs etc and tolerating similar other inconveniences, they add to the elegance of saintly life.

It 'appears that the author of Achāranga Sūtra has laid stress on two points. Firstly, as soon as an article is possessed, one is bound to be burdened with worry for its proper upkeep. In case, there is no belonging at all, one is free from all worries. Therefore, if the Jaina Sādhus adopt absolute nudity, they are redeemed from all worries about the maintenance and upkeep of clothes. Thus the main benefit of remaining completely naked is freedom from all care. Contrarily, the Sādhus who even put on minimum clothes on their person without having least attachment for them, they are bound to be worried and remain careful for their upkeep and carry out repairs as and when necessary.

The author of Achāranga Sūtra also appeard to be emphasizing that a nude Sādhu is expected to bear all physical hardships and afflictions with equanimity. To bear all sufferings on naked bodies needs great stamina and resoluteness of the mind. The Jaina Sādhus who are able to bear all pains and sufferings with detached mind without least strain on their mind and taking things easy. They remain dedicated to spiritual achievements which provide them great stimulus to go on with their severe penances.

To put on a Cloth Girth round the Waist in order to Overcome Feeling of Shyness and to avoid Disgrace

While discussing about nudity to be adopted by Sādhus, it appears in 'Achāranga'— "There could be Jaina Sādhus who could forbear bodily sufferings on account of coming in contact with sharp-edged straw, pungent grass, inclement weather, biting by small or large mosquitos as also similar other adversities. However, they cannot afford to give up shyness altogether, in that case, they should not mind wearing loin cloth around their waist. Subsequently, as soon as they are able to overcome shyness, they should remove the loin cloth and boldly face bodily afflictions as a result of coming in contact with sharp-edged grass, excessive hot and cold weather, biting by small or large mosquitos on their naked bodies without exhibiting least aversion. In this way, they should carry on with their spiritual endeavours and practise severe penances for illumination and conquest of the self.

Implied Sense: What an astonishment that a Jaina Sādhu may be able to tolerate all bodily sufferings but may find it difficult to discard the feeling of shyness. Infact, there is always an element of ego combined with shame—may be due to spiritual ignorance. How he would outwardly appear—whether he would look ugly and despicable so that others might dislike him. These are the feelings which might haunt a Sādhu and demoralise him to the extent that he might develope feeling of contemptibility for himself although he is able to endure all physical hardships easily without showing least sign of remorse. The author of Achāranga Sūtra believes that later on a time may come when the Jaina Sādhu may be in a position to overcome his shyness and again adopt total nudity. However, he had again stressed the point that a Jaina Sādhu must be prepared to bear all bodily sufferings, consequent upon coming in contact with pungent straw of grass, severity of cold and hot weathers, biting by mosquitos etc. with a strong will and spiritual force.

The implied sense of what the author intends to convey, seems to be that a true devout must develope moral strength to treat the soul singularly independent from the mortal body which is liable to undergo physical strains and miseries in day-today course of life.

Using A Piece of Cloth: It is cited in Achāranga Sūtra : "A Jaina Sādhu, who is determined to retain with him only a single pot and a single garment to be placed on his body, never intends to beg or ask for another garment. In case, he decides to part with the said single cloth as well, he may ask for a flawless piece of cloth to be placed on his body. Else, he should give up the garment altogether and adopt total nudity. In this way, he should go on performing religious austerities and magnifying his life of renunciation and detachment from all worldly objects."

Wearing of two Garments: In connection with Jaina Sādhus who are accustomed to wearing two garments on their body, it is cited in Āchārānga Sūtra: "The Jaina saints who adhere to their voluntary observance of possessing only one pot and two pieces of garments to cover their bodies, they donot care to beg or ask for a third piece for change or replacement. However, if they happen to lose both the pieces of garment, they may beg and accept similar type of pieces. It is perfectly in line with established rules of conduct, meant to be observed by Sādhus. As soon as they find that the cold season is over and summer has set in, they shall get the worn out pieces turned over and retain with them the usable piece. if they find that any of the pieces is lengthy, they may get it shortened. In this way, either they should get accustomed to wear only single garment or adopt total nudity. Thus, the Sādhus will be adding to the grace of their austere life by conducting themselves with spontaneity, ingenuity and smartness."

Placing of Three Pieces of Cloth on the Body : In connection with Jaina Sādhus, using three pieces of cloth to cover their bodies, it is mentioned in `Āchāranga' Sūtra; "The Sādhus who are adhering to a vow of possessing one pot and 3 pieces of garment, they donot show anxiety to ask for or beg the fourth piece of garment. However, if they find that they no longer possess 3 pieces of cloth, consistent with their pledge, they may beg to make up the deficiency. They should not be reluctant to wear whatever made available to them. In no case, they should wash or colour them. They should decline to wear washed or coloured garments. At the time of moving about from one village to another, they should not hide their clothes.[1] It is perfectly in accordance with the manner and morals, prescribed for Jaina Sādhus. As soon as, the Sādhus realise that the cold season is over and the hot season has commenced, they must get the worn out pieces turned over they should retain with them only those pieces which are serviceable. Alternatively, they may retain with them only two garments or only one, whichever usable. Else, they should live naked. By doing so, they would be glorifying their devout life."

Longing for Clothes: The title of 5th Adhyayan, relating to II section, of Achāranga Sūtra' is `Vastraishṇā'. There are various do's and don'ts (prescription and negation) regarding clothes to be put on by male and female mendicants. The types of garments have been detailed at the beginning of 5th Adhyayan which are worth putting on by the religious mendicants. It reads: "As soon as male or female mendicants long to have a garment, they should beg a suitable one, befitting to their saintly life either made of wool, jute, hemp, silk or Āk (a medicinal plant) cotton. The Jaina Sādhus who are young, healthy, free from all bodily afflictions with a strong physique, they should use only a single garment and not two. The female mendicants should use four pieces of cloth -- one piece a yard long; two pieces of one and a half yard length and fourth piece of two yards length. In case, the pieces of cloth, having desired length, are not available or it may not be possible to obtain them, the female mendicants should stitch smaller pieces to obtain desired length."

Citation of Both Nude and Clothed Mendicants in "Uttrādhyayan"

While discussing about Jaina Sādhus with or without clothes, it is cited in *Uttrādhyayan Sūtra* (An Agamic Scripture): "It is found that a Jaina monk does not put on clothes while practising severe penances of a Jina-kalpa'. However, the Sādhu puts on clothes while practising less severe penances of sthavira-kalpa. Those who are well conversant with the penances of a Jina-Kalpa or Sthavira-Kalpa, glorifying their austere and devout life, such dedicated Sadhus never feel gloomy or make any repent."

Substance: The prescriptions and negations in respect of number, size and nature of clothes to be used in day-today course by Jaina mendicants or adopting total nudity by them, have been discussed at length in Achāranga Sūtra which is evident from a few illustrations, cited above.

After going through the said citations, no feeling of propriety or impropriety arises in the mind with regard to true saintliness of Jaina Sādhus, irrespective of

1. Here it purports to mean that Jaina Sādhus must put on garments of ordinary quality, and value so that they may not feel constrained to hide them for fear of being stolen by thieves.

the fact they wear clothes or remain naked. Clothing or no clothing makes absolutely no difference in universally accepted norms, prescribed for true Sādhus. However, Jaina religionists predominantly believe in observance of absolute renunciation and practising of self-mortification for attainment of final emancipation. A true devout is always dedicated to acquire the pleasure of self-realisation for which he spares no pains, after putting an end to humilities on account of low acts or deeds, performed by him in his past and present births. (complete annihilation of the Karma). After all, his ultimate goal of final emancipation is going to be accomplished only after absolute decay of his Karmās. Thus, the purpose of showing excellence of Jaina Sādhus, adopting nudity is only to emphasize that such Sādhus are obviously, detached and carefree. They are in a position to dedicate themselves to spiritual performances and practising severe penances. A Jaina devout is known for his exemplary forbearance of most awesome and heart-rending agonies without expressing least uneasiness while practising hard penances and self-mortification for attainment of final emancipation. After all, such a devout deserves all appreciation for his extreme endurance and deep devotion.

Although, there are clear guide-lines to be observed by Jaina Sādhus, pertaining to maximum limit of clothings permitted as also the number, size and measurement of such clothings, yet the observations, made above, in respect of one piece, two pieces or three pieces of garments, allowed to be retained, only meant to demonstrate that inspite of clear provisions, the Jaina Sādhus exercised maximum restraint in use of such clothings, because of their feelings of extreme detachment and total renunciation. Only a few mendicants used 3 garments. Others put on two garments or one garment only. However, the author of `Achāranga Sūtra' has not hesitated to advise them to forsake wearing of clothes altogether with the exclusive aim that the Jaina devouts must eventually move on the path of absolute renunciation and practising self-denial or mortification for self-realisation.

There is a reference of Jaina Sādhus, covering their bodies with one piece of cloth only in the book of Gradual Sayings.[1] Keeping in view the contemporaneity of Lord Mahāvira and Lord Buddha, there are references in their respective sacred books of both religions in respect of the followers of the other religion which are really significant for undertaking critical investigation by scholars. From the said appearance in the book of *Gradual Sayings*, it is evident that under spiritual leadership of Lord Mahāvira, the Jaina Sādhus were proned to use minimum covering on their bodies with a view to have perfect concentration on their spiritual pursuits.

Tradition of Lord Pārashvanāth Versus Tradtion of Lord Mahāvira

The learned scholars have given profound consideration to the ethical side of the problem i.e. observance of total nudity on one hand and keeping the body covered with minimum clothing on the other. A few scholars believe that nudism had gained momentum during or after the era of Lord Mahāvira. Earlier, the Jaina

1. *Anguttar Nikāya* (The book of Gradual Sayings), Volume III, Page 383.

Sādhus used to wear clothes as per practice prevalent under the tradition of Lord Pārashvanāth. According to them, the word `Nirgranth' (freedom from worldly ties or knots), appearing for Jaina monks, was, infact, manifestation of superiority of nakedness as against wrapping round the body with pieces of cloth since the latter amounted to acquisition of belongings.

Meeting of Keshi with Gautama

There is an important reference in `Uttrādhyayan Sūtra', respecting controversies between the followers of the tradition of Lord Pārashvanāth and those, belonging to the tradition of Lord Mahāvira. We are producing below the relevant portion of the said citation, which reads: "Lord Pārashvanāth, a highly sanctified teacher of Jaina philosophy, an omniscient, supreme leader of the Jaina institution and 23rd Tirthanker, had preceded the last Tirthanker, Lord Mahāvira. Keshi was a great scholar, an expert on Jaina Agamas and he perceived through his third degree of knowledge what is generally not within the reach of sensual organs. He was a leading luminary and a celebrated disciple of Lord Pārashvanāth. He was endowed with excellent qualities of head and heart. While moving from one village to another, Keshi happened to arrive at `Shrāvasti' (Region, now identified with Sahet-Mahet, north of Ayodhya) along with a group of his followers. There was a garden, named `Tinduka', in the suburban part of that town. The Jaina Sādhu, Keshi stayed there with his followers, enclosed with barbed wires to avoid entry of small or big animals."

"It was the era of last Tirthanker, Lord Mahāvira, who was a great spiritual leader of universal repute, founder of a large organisation of both male and female mendicants and household followers, absolutely free from emotions of love and hatred. His chief disciple was Gautama, an erudite scholar, a great luminary, and a man of high ethical values. He was an authority on 12 Angas (Twelve sacred books of Jainas) and highly enlightened. Gautama also happened to visit Shravasti along with his group of followers."

"There was a garden, known as Koshthaka close to that town. Gautama stayed therein with his disciples in a barbed portion. Both Keshi and Gautama, who had completely sub-dued their passions and attained self-realisation, began to move about in that town. The disciples of both spiritual leaders who were true devouts, austere and full of virtues, started conversing and arguing with each other."

"What are the religious beliefs and doctrines of our sect and what are theirs? What are the specific points of their ideological interpretations and what are ours? Lord Pārashvanāth had preached for performance of four great austerities while Lord Mahāvira based his reliance on 5 great austerities, namely, absolute renunciation of violence, untruthfulness, theft, unchastity and acquisition of any belongings."

"Under the tradition of Lord Mahāvira absolute nakedness of Jaina mendicants is desired while under Lord Pārashvanāth tradition, covering of the body with pieces of cloth finds acceptability. Although, the Sādhus, belonging to both traditions, are engaged in performance of the similar austerities and accomplishing the same goal of final emancipation, yet there are diverse beliefs—why? As soon as the leaders, representing both traditions, Keshi and Gautama came to know of the scepticisms, creeping in the minds of their respective followers, they decided to meet and exchange views."

"Whereas, Gautama was an embodiment of humility, modesty and discipline, as enunciated by Lord Mahāvira, the last (24th) Tirthanker, Sri Keshi represented the tradition of Lord Pārashvanāth, 23rd Tirthanker. Hence Gautama proceeded to Tinduka garden, where Sri Keshi was staying with his followers. As soon as, Keshi saw Gautama, arriving at his place, he hastened to receive Gautama and his followers, accompanying him, with due honour and regard, befitting to his grace, fame and dignity. Keshi immediately managed to get the mats spread out to cover the straw, grass and husk etc., lying on the floor."

"Highly celebrated Jaina saints, Keshi Kumar and Gautama, sitting together, looked so bright and graceful as if they were like a sun and a moon. Many followers, belonging to various sects, curious spectators, onlookers and spiritually ignorant persons along with thousands of local citizens had assembled there to watch and hear the religious debate. The divine bodies demons, mythological celetial musicians, demi-gods-living in heaven, monsters and invisible evil spirits had also gathered at the site."

"Addressing Gautama, Keshi eagerly enquired—Oh fortunate one! Will you allow me to place a few questions to you to set my curiosity at rest?

Gautama answered — Oh brother! you are free to ask any question, you like. Thus, after obtaining sanction from Gautama, Keshi Kumar enquired "— Although, we have faith in the tenets of the same religion, yet nudity is a must for Jaina Sādhus, as preached by Lord Mahāvira. On the other hand, covering of the body with nominal clothing is essential as per teachings of Lord Pārashvanāth — why so?"

"The devouts, belonging to both traditions, are engaged in the same spiritual pursuits — why the said diversity then? Oh enlightened one! donot you feel sceptic on finding the followers of the same religion living differently? On hearing the words of Keshi Kumar, Gautama replied—By virtue of their highly exalted knowledge, the Arhats had decided that such and such articles are necessary as means of supporting life by devouts of Jaina religion."

"Infact, external appearance or outer mode of living is only meant for cognition and knowledge of the people and for enabling the devouts to excercise control over self. As a matter of fact, both Tirthankers—Lord Pārashvanāth and Lord Mahāvira, had preached that sacred knowledge, derived from meditation, on the higher truths of spiritualism and philosophy of Jaina religion are alone needed or are the exclusive source for attainment of final emancipation. (Expression of gratefulness by Sri Keshi Kumar).

Oh Gautama! you are really blessed one. The scepticism in my mind has come to an end. Let no further —."

Examination : Comments

From the aforesaid chapter of Uttrādhyayan, numerous factors have come to be known. From the said extract, it is explicitly clear that the followers of Lord

Pārashvanāth tradition were there during the life-time and era of last Tirthanker, Lord Mahāvira. While roaming about, the Sādhus, belonging to the lineage of Lord Pārashvanāth appeared differently from the followers of Lord Mahāvira. The very fact that Jaina saint, Keshi Kumar, had stayed with his group of followers in Tinduka garden while Gautama had sojourned with the team of his disciples in Koshthaka garden at Shrāvasti, is sufficient to support the above inference. Although, there was no diversity on basic fundamentals of the religion amongst both sects, yet the followers, belonging to the two traditions, differed on assumption of external appearance and performance of prescribed austerities. There was, no doubt considerable effect of the severality found in their outward appearance and spiritual performances on the mind of the general public. As soon as the news spreads of a religious debate between leaders of two different sects i.e.—Keshi Kumar and Gautama, thousands of people gathered at the spot to watch the proceedings and listen to the discussion. Whereas, there was a sort of anxiety to learn amongst religious-minded and learned persons, there was a bit excitement and slight feeling of curiosity amongst others.

Inspite of the above, there was no unpleasantness, whatsoever, amongst the followers of both sects. On the other hand, there was perfect harmony, good-will and kindly feelings for each other. Since Sri Keshi Kumar belonged to the lineage of 23rd Tirthanker, Lord Pārashvanāth, Gautama had an obvious feeling of great appreciation and regard for him. Consequent upon the same, Gautama takes the initiative and moves to Tinduka garden with his followers, where Keshikumar was staying with his team of disciples. Keshikumar equally responds to the gesture of humility, shown by Gautama, and accords him warm welcome by setting up a proper seat, befitting to his status.

The author of Uttrādhyayan has depicted Keshikumar as an inquisitive interrogator and Gautama an answerer to his queries. Most probably, it was done since Gautama represented the tradition of last Tirthanker and he was considered as the authoritative and reliable exponent of the doctrines of Jaina philosophy, as enunciated by Lord Mahāvira.

The devouts, representing the tradition of Lord Pārashvanāth, appeared to be in favour of putting on clothes to cover their bodies while the Sādhus, following the tradition of Lord Mahāvira had a liking to live naked. The fact that Lord Pārashvanāth had directed his devouts to keep their bodies covered while Lord Mahāvira had preached to his followers to observe nudity, calls for further research and investigation.

While both traditions were already existent in Jaina institution, why Lord Mahāvira is singled out to have preached for observing nudity and Lord Pārshvanāth is singularized to have directed his followers to keep their bodies covered? Lord Mahāvira belonged to the family which had faith in the teachings of Lord Pārashvanāth. His parents were staunch followers of the lineage of Lord Pārashvanāth. Therefore, the feasibility that the line of teaching of Lord Mahāvira was in contrast with that of Lord Pārashvanāth does not appeal to the mind. It is fundamentally believed by the Jaina community that all Arhats basically preach the same philosophical doctrines of the religion. However, because of obvious variation in the nature of the people — some of them being ignorant and stupids, while others being intelligent and wise; some being crooked and dishonest, while others being simple-minded, honest and sincere, they interpret the philosophical teachings of Arhats differently with the result they are diverse in their opinions in regard to the prescribed austerities to be practised by their followers. Infact, there is no fundamental difference in their utterances. The difference may lie in their wordings which is only external. The sum and substance is, however, same.

The curiosity regarding two sets of followers—those putting on garments and those observing absolute nudity by Jaina Sādhus was also set at rest by Gautama, explaining that external appearance only helped in proper identification of the followers and for accomplishment of spiritual pursuits conveniently. Finally, he has ended his reply by emphasizing that true saintliness depended on knowledge of truth, religious philosophy and uprightness in behaviour. Although, the author of Uttrādhyayan has tried to show that the curiosity was set at rest by Gandher Gautama, yet his answer does not appear to be convincing. It appears that the basic question is still unanswered.

In case, the practices of observing nudity while performing severe Jinakalpic penances and wearing clothes in Sthavira-Kalpic performances were already in vogue as per sacred tradition of Jaina religion, why did the mendicants, belonging to the organisation of Lord Pārshvanāth develope uncertainty in their minds on finding the nude mendicants, accompanying Gandher Gautama?' Similarly, why the followers of Lord Mahavira's tradition were at their wits end to watch the dressed Sādhus, belonging to the lineage of Lord Pārshvanāth. Had there been both Jinakalpic and Sthavira-Kalpic Sādhus together in the organisation of Lord Mahāvira, there would have been absolutely no occasion for any uncertainty and the Sādhus, belonging to the tradition of Lord Pārashvanāth would have antomatically been satisfied.

There is likelihood of another reason also. Lord Mahāvira exercised great spiritual influence those days. Religious—minded people seemed to be very much impressed by him. The followers of the tradition of Lord Pārshvanāth may have felt inclined to join the organisation of Lord Mahavira. Thus, the situation may have arisen, necessitating mutual co-ordination, amongst the followers of both the lineages. Possibly, a number of Sādhus, belonging to the tradition of Lord Pārshvanāth may have expressed their willingness to adopt nudity. Rest of them, may have still preferred to wear the clothes for want of adequate courage and resoluteness. In order to alleviate the situation, it appears that Jinakalpic and Sthavira-Kalpic penances may have been prescribed for Sādhus, belonging to both categories. Thereupon; the majority of the followers of Lord Pārshvanāth may have joined the organisation of Lord Mahāvira. The Sādhus adapted themselves to take up Jinakalpic or Sthavira-Kalpic exercises as per congeniality of their nature and forbearance of the hardships. Accordingly, both methods of penances have been endorsed by Shwetamber Sect. However, the said assumption is contrary to the belief that the philosophical tenets of Jaina religion, as enunciated by Arhats, are uniform in substance and they donot vary in any way.

On one hand, Digambers believe that 12 sacred books of Jainas, accomplished on the basis of religious discourses of Lord Mahāvira, have ceased to exist. On the other, Shwetambers are of the view that no scriptural works, pertaining to the period, prior to the era of Lord Mahāvira, are now found. Hence in order to know the actual state of affairs, going on, prior to the life-time of Lord Mahāvira and the condition of Jaina institution, we have to draw our inferences on mere surmises. Presumably, Lord Mahāvira might have laid greater emphasis on the significance of Jina Kalpic penance in order to elevate moral strength of Jaina devouts and to encourage them to practise self-denial, absolute detachment from worldly objects and self-mortification for attainment of higher perfection. At the time, when Sādhus, belonging to the tradition of Lord Pārshvanāth, happened to come in contact with the Sādhus, belonging to the organisation of Lord Mahāvira, at Shrāvasti, the latter might have held Sthavira-Kalpic Jaina Sādhus in lower esteem. In the same way, the said argument could equally apply to the followers of Lord Pārshvanāth, who were all accustomed to wear clothes. There was, obviously, no appreciation for nudism amongst them. Obviously, they could not be supposed to have any knowledge of Jinakalpic exercises, or understand the significance of nudity in saintly life.

In nutshell, it may be stated that observance of Jinakalpic performances was not in practice during the era of Lord Pārshvanāth, prior to the life time of last Tirthanker, Lord Mahāvira. Lord Mahāvira had laid much emphasis on undertaking Jinakalpic performances in order to develope the spirit of forbearance and tolerance of physical strains, to exercise self-restraint and lead the life of self-mortification so as to be able to cope with the hardships of severe penances. However, with the lapse of time, it might have been realised that each and every Jaina monk was not able to carry on such severe penances. Hence it might have been found in the fitness of things to allow both types of spiritual performances—Jinakalpic and Sthavira-Kalpic, to be undertaken by Sādhus, belonging to the tradition of Lord Mahāvira, consistent with the perseverance and energy of each. Thereafter, both types of penances might have gained momentum amongst followers of Lord Mahāvira.

Continuance of Both Traditions by the Time of Leadership of Ārya Jambu

Decidedly, leading of naked life by Jaina monks is comparatively more harsh and onerous. Undoubtedly, it needs lot of courage to forbear physical hardships, adversities of weather and natural disasters with equanimity. However, there is an important aspect of the matter which cannot be lost sight of. There are established rules of morality and minimum limit of decency and decorum, with which a nude monk is bound to put up with while coming in contact with various people of the society. He may have to be confronted with certain practical difficulties even in the noble cause of propagation of ideology and spread of religious message in day-today course of life while observing nudity. Of course, the staunch followers may not be averse because of their extreme faith and regard for them. They pay no heed to their nakedness. On the other hand, they hold them in great esteem, keeping in view their spirit of total renunciation and self-denial. However, where the place is alien and there are no firm believers in their doctrines, they do come across practical difficulties in establishing liaison with the people. Contrarily, the dressed Sādhus find it easy to have rapport with the public and deliver discourses to expound their message to create religious awakening and spiritual enlightenment amongst them. They donot face any difficulty in mixing up with the audience, Possibly, it might have been the practice that the Jaina monks who were keen to be engrossed in deep meditation and undertake severe penances, they were allowed to live nude and take up Jinakalpic austerities. They remained detached from the society and kept aloof from general public. The responsibility of creating religious awareness lay on dressed Sādhus. On one hand, they devoted reasonable time for their own spiritual advancement and on the other, they used to impart lectures to popularise ideals of Jaina religion and explain doctrines of Jainism and its philosophy.

Thus, there were two categories of Jaina Sādhus-each entrusted with distinct responsibilities, which they continued to carry out with utmost dedication and devotion. While one category of Sādhus were engaged in practising tapashchariya and self-mortification for attainment of spiritual perfection, which called for exceptional courage and dedication; the other category of Sādhus moved from one place to another creating religious awareness and spreading the message of Jaina Arhats side by side performing prescribed austerities with a view to exercise self-control and reḍeem themselves from self-delusion. Hence it was immaterial which category of Sādhus were required to face greater hardships and which led an easier life. Both categories of Sādhus commanded respect and were adored by the society. The said system continued uninterruptedly for a long time during the spiritual leadership of Lord Mahāvira uptil the era of Ārya Jambu. However, after his final liberation, there was slight change in the situation.

Change : An Assumption : For want of maturity in mind and certainty in thoughts, there is always an equal likelihood of rising up and adopting a Virtuous path in life on one hand and going downwards or getting degenerated on the other. Until a devout is able to overcome its worldly attachments, there is every possibility of increase in self-ego, concept of individuality and spiritual ignorance.

Possibly, some sort of misunderstandings or dissensions might have crept in the institution after final liberation of Ārya Jambu. It is possible that the nude Sādhus might have developed a feeling, why should they allow themselves to be treated at par with dressed Sādhus since they led the life of self-mortification and endured all physical hardships? Why should not the said category of Sādhus be allowed higher status and held in greater esteem as against dressed Sādhus, since the former had to undergo extreme physical and mental strains and control the feelings of nervosity and shyness.

Action breeds reaction. The reaction of hostile attitude and showing disregard to others is bound to result in greater hostility, disdainful contempt and strong opposition. Accordingly, the expressions of hostility and contempt, shown by Jinakalpic Sādhus must have created an adverse reaction on the minds of Sthavira-Kalpic Sādhus. They might have argued that the activities of dressed Sādhus in creating religious awareness and spreading the message of Jaina Arhats amongst the masses, was no less significant as against the physical hardships, borne by nude Sādhus. Probably, they donot realize or appreciate how much efforts, they are required to put in for fulfilment of their object. In case, the naked Sādhus are subjected to bodily afflictions and disasters on account of severe penances and inclement weather etc. the clothed Sādhus have to endure both favourable and unfavourable conditions and adapt themselves to numerous hardships and inconveniences. While they could easily afford a life of affluence, and happiness, they chose the life of absolute detachment and renunciation of all worldly objects. It is not an ordinary task.

Presumably, the learned scholars of both sides might have advanced their arguments accordingly and insisted on their respective stand which might have culminated in further widening of the gap, ultimately, leading to the split of the Jaina institution in two distinct sects of Digambers and Shwetambers.

Differences Cropped on Surface after Final Liberation of Ārya Jambu

The traditional method of functioning of ooth camps—Digambers and Shwetambers was almost identical save minor differences, if any, till the life time of Ārya Jambu. While Digambers believe that Lord Mahāvira was succeeded by Gautama, Loharya and Jambu respectively—thus Ārya Jambu was the third spiritual head of the organisation in succession, Shwetambers are of the view that Lord Mahāvira was succeeded by Ārya Sudharmā and Ārya Jambu which transpires that Jambu was second in succession to the Supreme seat of Lord Mahāvira.

The issue regarding entitlement of Gautama to the seat of Lord Mahavira, has already been discussed at length in foregoing pages of this book. Hence it is absolutely unnecessary to repeat it again, Gautama is held in highest esteem under sacred tradition of Shwetambers as well, irrespective of the fact that he is not admitted to have succeeded to the supreme seat of Lord Mahāvira.

After final salvation of Gautama, the name of his successor appears as Sudharma in certain holy books of Digamber Sect while Lohārya in certain others. For example, the name of Ārya Sudharma appears in `Tiloyapaṇṇatti'; `Prākrita-Pattāvali', authored by Nandi; `Harivansh Purāṇa'; `Shrutāvtār' and in petrographic inscription No. 105 at Shravenbelgolā in Karnataka.

The author of Dhavalā Commentary on `Shatkhaṇḍāgama', Achārya Virsena, has mentioned that Lohārya had succeeded to the seat of Gautamā in the intial portion of the chapter, styled `Sat-Prarūpnā' and again in the chapter, styled `Vednā'. Similarly, in stone inscriptions Nos. 1 and 2 at Shravanbelgola in Karnataka state, the name of Lohārya is found after Gautama. However, the author of the commentary `Jayadhavalā' has mentioned the name of Sudharma in place of Lohārya.

Infact, Sudharma and Lohārya are not two distinct personalities. Lohārya is an alias or an alternative name of Ārya Sudharma. Under Shwetamber tradition, only one name Sudharma appears in all holy scriptures, while under Digamber tradition, the use of both names is found. From the citation, appearing in `Jambudweep Paṇṇatti Sūtra' (a Jaina Agama under Digamber tradition), it is evidently clear that both names have been used for one and the same person.

Ārya Jambu had succeeded to the seat of Ārya Sudharma or Lohārya which is admitted by both sects. Thus, there were no apparent points of contention between the two camps till the life-time of Ārya Jambu. There was a sort of co-ordination and both camps followed established usages. Till then, the differences on account of observance of nudity by Digambers and covering of bodies by Shwetambers had not appeared on the surface. Subsequently, the situation changes which is apparent from variations, found in the lists of successors to the Supreme seat under both traditions.

Right from Ārya Jambu to Achārya Bhadrabāhu, the last authority on Jaina Agamas, there have been five authoritative scholars, having expertise in Agamas, namely—Nandi (alias Vishnu); Nandi-Mitra, Aparajita; Goverdhan and Bhadrabāhu as per list of successors to the seat, recognised by Digamber sect. However, under Shwetamber tradition, the names of five authoritative scholars of Jaina Agamas, after final liberation of Arya Jambu are — Phabhava, Shayambhava, Yashobhadra, Vijaya and Bhadrabāhu.

Under the two traditions, leaving aside Achārya Bhadrabāhu, the names of other four spiritual heads are different. Therefore, it may not be wrong to infer that dissensions must have cropped up in the Jaina institution on certain issues after final liberation of Ārya Jambu and the main controversial issue could be with regard to observance of absolute nudity or covering the bodies with minimal clothing by Jaina Sādhus. Needless to emphasize that the lists of successors to the supreme seat after Achārya Bhadrabāhu, entirely differ.

Two Fold Technique Adopted

By the time, the scholars are hopeful of continuance of a tradition, they spare no pains to carry on their investigation and convince the people of their significance. However, when serious differences come to the fore and the scholars find themselves unable to patch them, the organisation is bound to split and each splitted group innovates its own ideology and assumes credit of all gains and achievements for itself, accomplished by the old institution. However, the ill-effects of the said mentality get reflected in several ways. Each group claims to be the real inheriter of the old values and concepts and censures the other to have deviated from the real path. The imaginary stories, fabricated by both Digambers and Shwetambers regarding the circumstance that led to the division and emergence of the other sect are sufficient to substantiate the argument.

The ideological base of each sect is its canonical literature. The sect, obviously thrives and draws inspirations from its sacred books. Hence no organisation or sect can afford to give up anxiety for preservation and manitenance of the holy works which are the source of its growth and expansion. The congregations of both Buddhist and Jaina scholars, held to recite, compile and edit the texts of speeches, delivered by Lord Buddha and Lord Mahāvira, from time to time, are sufficient to indicate how anxious they were to preserve the utterances of their sanctified religious heads.

The holy scriptures which fail to vindicate the ideology or view-points of a particular religious sect- nay—on the other hand, they rather repudiate them, the said organisation is bound to ignore them or attach least significance to them. The sect will decry them to be false, imaginary or interpolated and will not repose faith in them. In other words, it will be just like saying—no bamboo—no flute, which means every attempt will be made to avoid religious debates on the basis of the said scriptures. The motive in declaring by Digambers that 11 Angas (sacred books of Jainas) and considered highly authentic under Shwetamber tradition, had already become obliterated and were no longer in existence. Their contention that in case, any of the said Angas or portions thereof are now found, they are absolutely false and unauthoritative, is, infact, nothing but reflection of the same state of mind. This is the matter which calls for further consideration and needs to be deliberated upon.

Both types of spiritual endeavours—Jinakalpic penances by nude Sādhus and Sthavirakalpic by Jaina monks, putting on minimum clothing, have been dealt with and characterised in Agamas, accredited by Shwetambers. Accordingly, Shwetambers supported both types of penances, practised by Digamber Sādhus as well as Shwetamber Jaina Munis. However, the scant respect, shown by Digamber Sect to their authentic Agamas, was bound to react adversely. Consequent upon the said reaction, it is quite possible that Shwetambers too might have declined to continue one-sided support to the Jinakalpic penances and observance of nudism by Digambers. Shwetambers also might have declared that Jinakalpic penances had ceased after final salvation of Ārya Jambu and they were no longer practised. This might have neutralized the support, received by Digambers as per holy books of Shwetamber Sect. The research students are very well aware that such incidents are not uncommon in the history of religious organisations.

Achāraya Mahāgiri : A Reference

Even after declaring by Shwetambers that Jinakalpic penances had come to a stop after final salvation of Ārya Jambu, there is an illustration of Shwetamber Muni, having undertaken Jinakalpic performances. He was Achārya Mahāgiri. He had succeeded to the seat after Achārya Sthūlbhadra. It has already been pointed out in foregoing pages, where the context so demanded that Sthūlbhadra had attained liberation in Samvat year 215 after final salvation of Lord Mahāvira. Thereafter, Achārya Mahāgiri had taken over the leadership of Jaina organisation. It is cited that after some time, he had entrusted the leadership to a fellow religious student (A pupil of the same preceptor), named Suhasti and engaged himself in practising Jinakalpic penances. The fact that Achārya Mahāgiri had done so even after it had already been declared by Shwetamber Sect that Jinakalpic penances were no longer in practice, must have created confusion amongst Jaina monks. It is a problem and needs an answer.

Achārya Hemachandra writes that Achārya Mahāgiri had resorted to practising Jinakalpic penances, yet he acted in consistency with the beliefs of Shwetamber sect that Jinakalpic penances were no longer in practice. He has stated: "Achārya Mahāgiri had entrusted the leadership of Jaina organisation to Suhasti. As soon as he made up his mind to start performing Jinakalpic austerities he adopted solitude, moving about all alone. Since practising of Jinakalpic penances had already been discontinued as per Shwetamber tradition, he did not totally dissociate himself from the activities of Jaina institution. He only began taking a walk alone, which was in consistency with the course of conduct, prescribed for a Jinakalpic devout.

Although, Achārya Hemachandra has justified the Jinakalpic performances, taken up by Achārya Mahāgiri, while continuing his association with the institution, yet the argument does not appeal to the mind. Had he performed Sthavira Kalpic austerities, he had ample scope to attain the state of highest perfection. He could have accomplished his pious aim of attaining final emancipation.

From the illustration of Achārya Mahāgiri, it is apparent that even amongst Shwetambers, an allurement was there for practising Jinakalpic penances and observing nudity which was essential for such devouts.

Summary: As incidentally stated earlier, Achārya Mahāgiri had administered the affairs of Jaina organisation for 30 years. His tenure as its religious head, came to an end in Samvat year 245 after final salvation of Lord Mahāvira. The year of his final liberation is also believed to be Samvat year 245, which means that Achārya Mahāgiri had provided his spiritual leadership to the organisation only for a limited number of years. However, it cannot be asserted in a decisive manner for how long he had continued as such. Meanwhile, Achārya Mahāgiri might have made up his mind to practise severest penances, prescribed for only Jinakalpic devouts and after be eutrusted the responsibility of administering the affairs of Jaina organisation to his colleague, Suhasti, who happened to be his fellow student, he might have started his spiritual performances, aspiring to acquire the state of highest perfection. Suhasti might have carried on his duty as leader of the Jaina organisation, yet Achārya Mahāgiri might have continued as an Achārya to initiate the mendicants and propound the religious and philosophical doctrines of Jainism during his entire life till Samvat year 245 after final salvation of Lord Mahāvira and, thereafter, Suhasty was promoted to the office of a spiritual preceptor and an initiator.

An Epilogue: The process of alienation that had started in the Jaina organisation, after final liberation of Ārya Jambu, continued widening day by day. The fact has been discussed at length in earlier pages. By the time, it was samvat year 600 after final salvation of Lord Mahāvira, the rivalry in between two camps had considerably gone up, finally culminating in two sects of Digambers and Shwetambers. Even Jaina Agamas in which Shwetambers had reposed their faith, had been disowned and rejected by Digambers.

A Novel attempt for Harmonizing Relations: There was a split in the Jaina institution in the shape of Digambers and Shwetambers. The gulf between the two sects was so deep that it was not an easy task to bridge it even at its earlier stage or may not be possible now or in future. Undoubtedly, it was not a healthy sign and proved suicidal for the rapid growth and expansion of Jaina cult. However, nothing tangible could be done. Obviously, a few Sādhus must have felt anguished at the state of affairs, and realised that the two ideologies or currents of thoughts, that led to a split in the cult, may not be easy for both the sects to shed their institutions and differences and reunite. According to them, they were like two parallel straight lines which could never meet. One of the main dissensions between two sects was outright rejection of 11 Angas which are greatly regarded by Shwetambers and treated as part of Jaina Agamas, based on utterances of Arhats and composed in aphoristic style by their Gandhers. Digambers have declared them false and unauthentic. Similarly, Shwetamber sect had declared that Jinakalpic performances, directed towards profound meditation and connected with the practice of self-denial and bodily mortifications, were no longer relevant and had ceased to be practised.

After considering over the matter, a few Jaina scholars might have decided to ease the situation by removing superfluities. The deliberations to the said effect might have continued for some time and others might have also been induced to follow a middle course.

The Birth of Yāpniya Sangh

The said ideology finally led to the origin of Yāpniya Sangh. The founders of the said institution adopted a novel method to bring forth mutual harmony and create understanding and to pacify the extermists in both camps. They accepted nudity of Digambers as way of life i.e., they began to live naked and at the same time expressed their full faith in majority of the Agamas, relied upon by Shwetambers, and readily declared that they contained the utterances of Arhats and were authentic and reliable. They must have felt that adoption of a middle course alone could pacify the extremists at both ends. On one hand, the holy scriptures, traditionally handed down, will be saved from ruin and complete decay and on the other, the Jinakalpic austerities, symbolic of forbearance, total renunciation and endurance of extreme bodily hardships due to exposure to inclement weather and natural disasters, will be saved from extinction. It is believed that the new organisation might have been shaped, shortly after the split of Jaina institution into two sects.

The new organisation preferred to borrow and take up certain ideological beliefs of both camps, with the result both sects were displeased and did not welcome its emergence and vehemently opposed it. Digambers were agitated that the new Sangh reflected the ideological concepts of Shwetambers while the latter viewed that apparently they did not find any distinction in the living style of the members of new Sangh with that of Digambers. Consequently, the comments of both sides in regard to the emergence of the new Sangh are not healthy and free from prejudicial attitude. There is tinge of sectarianism as well.

It is, however, worth noting that although the followers of Yāpniya Sangh looked different in their external appearance from Shwetambers and yet they reposed their faith in majority of the Agamas, relied upon and treated as authentic by Shwetamber Sect. The Sādhus of Yāpniya Sangh considered that the said Agamas were the source of their inspiration to obtain initiation and lead the life of mendicancy. Hence it may be worthwhile to discuss about the activities of the said Sangh in greater details.

A Reference in Darshan Sār

As appeared in *Darshan Sār*, authored by Achārya Devasena, Yāpniya Sangh was founded by a Shwetamber Sādhu, named Shri Kalasha in Kalyan town in Samvat year 205 of Vikrama era.

It clearly reflects that Yāpniya Sangh owed its origin to a Shwetamber Sādhu. Although, the initiated Sādhus of Yāpniya Sangh observed nudity, yet it is equally significant that its ideology was very much in conformity with philosophical doctrines of Shwetamber Sect. As laid down earlier, according to Achārya Devasena, Shwetamber Sect had come into existence in Samvat year 136 of Vikrama era. It, therefore, follows that the period of another 69 years may have been taken in shaping the ideology and finalizing it, which ultimately led to the origin of a new distinct body.

In another copy of `Darshan Sār' the words "Sat Sae Panch Uttare Jāde" appear in the second line of the verse, already referred to in fore-going pages which means that Yāpniya Sangh had born in Samvat year 705 of Vikrama era and not Samvat 205, as stated above. However, it does not appear to be reliable as several well-known scholars and spiritual heads of Yāpniya Sangh, namely `Shāktāyan' and others had lived long before Samvat year 705. Hence it will be more appropriate to believe that Yāpniya Sangh had come into existence in Samvat year 205.

Birth of Yāpniya Sangh as per Ratnanandi

Immediately, after completing his story regarding origin of Shwetamber Sect, in his sacred work `Bhadrabāhu Charita' Achārya Ratnanandi starts giving an account of the circumstances that led to the birth of Yāpniya Sangh. While continuing his story, Ratnanandi writes: "King Lokpal and his queen, Chandralekha, were the staunch followers of Shwetamber Sect. A princess had born to them who was extremely handsome and endowed with excellent qualities. She was named `Nakulā Devi'. Under supervision of his religious preceptor, she had the privilege to acquire thorough knowledge of several Shāstras. In due course, she grew to be a young woman in her full youthful bloom. She had an attractive physique with gold-like brightness. She even surpassed celetial damsels in beauty. She was perfect and well accomplished in various arts and skills."

"There was a prosperous town named `Karhātāksha' (Karhātaka)[1] King Bhupal ruled over there. He was an irresistible warrior with an overwhelming influence all around. He got married with the said princess with great pomp and show. Because of her extra-ordinary abilities and auspicious nature, she soon became the principal Queen of that king who enjoyed all pleasures of life in the company of his beloved queen."

"One day, when she found the king well-disposed and agreeable, she entreated the king—My Lord! my great spiritual leader, mentor and guide lives in my father's town. Kindly invite him with his followers to deliver sermons and for adding to our spiritual enlightenment.

The king listened to the request of his queen and immediately sent for his minister, Budhisāgar. The king directed him to proceed atonce and bring with him the guru and spiritual guide of the queen along with his followers. The minister reached the place of the said guru and paid his obeisance, eulogizing him with utmost humility and submissiveness.

The minister made repeated requests to the guru and his disciples to accompany him to his king's palace, which they acceded to. They accompanied the minster and came to the town of his king. The king felt much rejoiced as soon as he came

1. It is identified with modern Karādha town in Satarā district of Maharashtra state.

to know of their arrival.

The king left to greet the guru and his followers and to pay his best regards to them. However, he was amazingly shocked on watching the guru and his associates. Contrary to his expectations, they were nudes yet holding a pot and a stick each against those who observed absolute nudity with no possessions at all. He was at his wits end whether they represented any other creed or sect for whom, he had no regard. Consequently, he was reluctant to contact them.

The king returned to his palace and bewared his queen of his deep anguish at the sight of her guru and his followers. They did not appear to be true Sādhus and, obviously, they had taken an evil course. They appeared to have faith in an alien ideology in contravention to the teachings of Jaina Arhats. They are caught in worldly possessions and he had no faith in such Sādhus.

"The queen appreciated the sentiments of her husband and immediately approached her spiritual guide. After paying her best regards, she bowed her head and humbly submitted. My Lord! I entreat you to renounce all worldly possessions and adopt the appearance of nude Sādhus (with his followers), who are absolutely free from all knots and revered even by heavenly gods."

The guru and his disciples accepted the wise suggestion of the queen and atonce renounced all worldly possessions. They only held a wooden pot and the feathers of a peacock's tail, tied in a bunch, each. Thus they adopted the appearance of Digamber nude Sādhus.

Thereafter, the king appeared before the Sādhus and paid his best respects. After respectfully bowing before them, he brought them to his palace. They were greatly honoured and admired by the king and the residents of the town. Their external appearance was that of Digamber Jaina Munis while their manners, morals and doctrinal beliefs were those of Shwetamber Sect. They were observing nudity and acting like trained acrobats, dancing to the tune of their masters without proper guidance and spiritual enlightenment. Thus, the said depraved persons, after assuming false appearance had given birth to Yāpniya Sangh".

According to Ratnanandi, the followers of Yāpniya Sangh had their external appearance like that of Digamber Munis, while their religious faith and spiritual performances conformed with those of Shwetamber Sect. In other words, they were depravedes, having deviated from the right path and adhering to the perverted ideology of Shwetamber Sect. According to him, the followers of Yāpniya Sangh were devoid of basic knowledge of fundamental doctrines of Jainism. They had only assumed the external appearance of Digamber Sādhus.

As Per Views of Indranandi

Indranandi, who had lived in 11th century A.D., has referred to five sects in his book—`Niti Sār', namely—`Gopuchchhaka', `Shwetamber', `Dravidas'., `Nishpichchhaka' and `Yāpniya', which are having semblance with or claiming to be followers of Jaina doctrines. According to Indranandi, just as Shwetambers did not represent a body of true Jainas, they bore only unreal or fallacious appearance of Jainas and had nothing in common with the tenets of Jaina ideology and philosophy. Similarly, Yāpniya Sangh did not represent a body of true Jainas.

Analysis by Shrutasāgar

Shrutasāgar, who lived in 16th century of Vikrama era, has analysed the views of Indranandi regarding existence of 5 fake bodies which claimed to be followers of Jainism and has made his own comment from which it is evident that he was more anxious to hold Kalpasūtra (A Jaina Agama) worthless or attach least significance to it. The literal meaning of Sanskrit word `Vesar' is mule with which he has similized the Yāpniya Sangh.

Comments of Guṇaratna: Shri Guṇaratna, who had lived from 1400 to 1475 of Vikrama era, had written a commentary styled `Tark Rahasya Dipika' on `Shatdarshansamuchchaya', authored by Achārya Yākini Mahattara Sūnū (He lived from 750 to 827 of Vikrama era). The annotator has commented on the views of the author of `Shaddarshansamuchchaya', appearing at the beginning of 4th chapter of his book, relating to the genders, external appearance and ethology etc. pertaining to Jainas.

According to Guṇaratna, the words 'Gopya' (of undivulging nature) and `Yāpniya' (Fit to be removed, expelled or rejected) are almost synonymous. The doctrines of Yāpniya Sangh are consistent with those of shwetamber sect in as much as both sects believe that the females can attain their final emancipation while in their existing feminine bodies and Kewalies (Arhats) take their meals by way of their mouth even after attainment of Kevalya (a state of highest perfection). Such fallacies are not approved at all by any branch or sub-branch of Digamber Sect. According to Guṇaratna, these are the two main conflicting issues amongst all other diversities found under the traditions of Shwetambers and Digambers. However, it is astonishing that Achārya Guṇaratna has held that Yāpniya Sangh is very much a branch or offshoot of Digamber Sect. It appears that Guṇaratna is led to form his opinion on the basis of external appearance (nakedness) of Yāpniyas. Probably, he has failed to pay proper heed to the ideological differences of the two sects. Simply because the Sādhus of Yāpniya Sangh also observed nudity like Digambers, he might have reasoned to hold that Yāpniya Sangh was also an offshoot of Digamber Sect. However, as pointed out earlier, Digambers never recognised Yāpniya Sangh as an offshoot of their sect. The standard or line of thinking of all religious institutions or sects is almost identical. Unless, the two organisations conform in all respects, they donot accord even a partial recognition to the other. In other words, it restricts the scope of the principle of pluralism, which is an important aspect of Jaina philosophy. The matter certainly deserves assiduous application of the mind by the scholars.

Various Other Alternative Names or Substitutes for Yāpniya Sangh

Dr. A.N. Upādhye, an erudite scholar of Prākrita dialects and Jaina philosophy, has suggested various synonyms of the word `Yāpniya' as appeared in `Annals of Bhaudārkar Oriental Research Institute, Volume LV. Poona, 1974, Page 12 such as Yāpniya (Yapni); Jāpniya; Yāpni; Āpniya; Yāpuliya; Āpuliya; Jāpuli; Jāvuliya; Jāviliya; Jāvaligeya; etc. In the process of defining the said words, he arrived at the conclusion that the said words had been derived from the root words—`Yām' or `Jām', which in turn appeared to have a link with four austerities performed under the tradition of Lord Pārshvanāth.

Another Assumption: Primarily, there are two major branches of Buddhist religion—Mahāyān and Hīnayān. How they came to be known as such is really interesting. One of the sects which laid emphasis not only for self deliverance and emancipation but pleaded for abounding in tender-heartedness, compassion and benignity for all and dedication to the entire humanity, called itself `Mahāyān'. On the other hand, the sect which advocated for self-deliverance and emancipation only, was considered a group of selfish people. Considering them to be insignificant and of frivolous nature, the sect came to be known as `Hinayān'. The name of the sect was adopted as such which ultimately became synonymical to it. The word `Hīnayān' once suggested to show despise against the shortsightedness of its founders, became synonymous with nature and name of the sect.

The similar tendency appears to have influenced in naming the sect as Yāpniya Sangh. Yāpya is a Sanskrit word which means—to be removed, expelled or rejected. Low, contemptible, trifling, unimportant etc. Hence what is contemptible, trifling or unimportant—can be defined as `Yāpniya'. As already discussed above, the religious sect, called Yāpniya Sangh was not only rejected but reprehended by both Digambers and Shwetambers Sects. Hence it is possible that both sects might have started calling it with that name in order to express their indignation and resentment. The said name might have become synonymous and adopted as such with the lapse of time. There are numerous instances of this type in linguistics science.

Yāpniya Sangh : Its Following and Influence: The followers of Jaina religion must have reacted differently as a result of split in Jaina institution in the shape of Digambers and Shwetambers. Presumably, those believing in the maxim of `Forbearance of physical hardships in spiritual pursuits, is bound to yield greater fruits' must have shown their liking for nude Sādhus as against those covering their bodies. On the other hand, there must have been certain scholars who would have advised that Jaina Sādhus should undertake tours to establish contacts with the people and spread the message of Arhats. Such Sadhus would have, obviously, preferred to put on clothes to avoid obscenity and vulgarity. Besides them, there must have been some people who might have disapproved or rejected the ideologies of both sects.

In this way, numerous debates might have been held on one hand and on the other, people might have continued to take part in religious activities in accordance with their own beliefs. Meanwhile, within a short span of less than hundred years, a new movement might have emerged in the shape of Yāpniya Sangh. Those who were tired of rigid dogmatic views of both sects, might have welcomed the emergence of the new sect and reposed their faith in its doctrines. They would have joined Yāpniya Sangh along with their associates and those who might be under their influence.

As soon as, a new sect is founded, its protagonists are too enthusiastic to propagate the ideals and spread the message of the new organisation as early as possible. It should be believed that similar course was adopted by Yāpniya Sangh also. It was easy too since the new Sangh represented the ideals of both Digamber and Shwetamber Sects and if had an obvious access to the followers of both creeds. Consequent upon the same, the following of Yāpniya Sangh rapidly increased day by day. Yāpniya Sangh had comparatively better response from South than Northern India. It had gained so much popularity in South that it was treated as sole representative body of Jaina religion and philosophy.

From the very beginning, Digambers were immensely popular in South. It explains why Yāpniya Sangh acquired recognition and eminence so early. Ofcourse, Digambers strongly criticized the followers of Yāpniya Sangh, alleging that they had only external resemblance with Digambers, otherwise, they were Shwetambers in disguise. However, in addition to the external appearance, the followers of Yāpniya Sangh also worshipped naked idols of Tirthankers and performed rituals, similar to those of Digambers. Yāpniya Sangh reposed its faith in majority of the Jaina Agamas, relied upon by Shwetambers and held similar views with regard to attainment of final emancipation by females in their existing feminine form and eating by Kevalis by way of mouth even after attainment of Kevalya (The state of highest perfection). Only a selected few scholars and educated persons dare to study and pick up the abstruse philosophical doctrines of religion which call for profound knowledge and intelligence. Mostly, people are influenced by external appearance, ways and means and performances of the followers of a sect. In this way, they might have found that it was quite conducive to make an approach to Digamber dominated areas in South. The followers of Yāpniya Sangh might have found South a congenial area for propagation and spread of their ideological doctrines. They might have whole—heartedly started the work and spared no pains.

Inspite of the fact that Digambers were already popular in South, Yāpniyas must have taken all pains to establish contacts with the masses and enlarge the area of their influence. Digamber Sādhus were generally inclined to maintain status quo whereas Yāpniyas were progressive in their approach and revolutionary in outlook. It was not an easy task for Yāpniyas to declare in Digamber dominated areas that Jaina Agamas, relied upon by Shwetambers, were also believed by them to be authoritative. Undoubtedly, it was a challenging job in those days. There is a peculiar liking and sense of respect for such bold propagators of a religious sect, more especially amongst conscious and enlightened persons. It is very likely that the followers of Digamber Sect might have welcomed the Yāpniyas, considering the new Sangh as part and parcel of Digamber sect itself and being representative body of progressive ideology. It is possible, the Yāpniyas might have received greater welcome and treated as visionary seers by Digamber community.

Popularity : Royal Patronage

Numerous indications are there to establish that Yāpniya Sangh was in existence in Southern parts of the country during the period, ranging from 5th century to 14th century of Vikrama era, commanding great following and enjoying royal patronage in Karnataka for a long time Modern districts of Dhārwār, Belgaum, Gulbarg and Kolhapur were prominent areas wherein the Sangh had gained great popularity.

A Few Important Gift-Deeds

Dr.A.N. Upādhye has referred to certain important gift-deeds, granted to Yāpniyas in one of his articles which are indicative of great popularity and influence of Yāpniya Sangh in South Dr. Upadhye writes: "King Mrigesh Verman, belonging to `Kadamba' lineage, (475 to 490 A.D.) had granted landed property to Yāpniya Digambers, Jainas, Kūrchakas (Holders of a bunch of peacock feathers). The name of spiritual head, appearing in the said gift-deed is of Achārya Daṁkirti. Thereafter, king Mrigesha Verman's son (497-537A.D.) had granted a village in order to provide regular source of income to meet the expenses of daily worshipping and feeding the Sādhus of Yāpniya Sangh, mainly during four months of rainy season while they had sojourn at a place. In the said gift-deed, the names of Achāryas Dāmkirti, Jayakirti, Budhsena and Kumar Dutta are found mentioned. Presumably, they were all spiritual guides of Yāpniya Sangh.

King Krishna Verman, son of King Deva Verman, (475 to 480 A.D.) had granted a village to meet the day-today expenses of Yāpniya Sangh temple.[1]

From the said references, it is explicit that the rulers of Karnataka had great reverence for the Sādhus of Yāpniya Sangh. The Yāpniyas had their own temples which were managed and looked after by Yāpniya ascetics. The rulers were particularly anxious to ensure that Yāpniyas faced no trouble in management of their temples and the sādhus were fed during four months of rainy season. In order to enable the Yāpniyas to meet their requirements, the rulers used to make donation of a village (Rent-free grant) to the members of Yāpniya Sangh.

Although, it is not very significant, yet it needs mention how the said grants were acceptable to Yāpniya Sādhus, which were sanctioned by the rulers to enable the Yāpniyas to maintain their temples and feed themselves which appears to be odd and somewhat contrary to the very spirit of Jaina ideology. It, obviously, implies that the ascetics of Yāpniya Sangh were gradually losing their spirit of tolerance and endurance of physical strains in day-today course of their ascetic life.

Stone Inscription at Kāgwāda

There is a grand idol of Lord Nemināth, installed in a cellar underground of a Jaina temple at Kāgwāda in Belgaum district. There is an inscription on the stone of the rectangular seat of the idol. The year of the installation of the stone as inscribed thereon is 1394 A.D. There is a mention of Yāpniya Sangh and its Achāryas, namely, Nemichandra, Dharmakirti and Nāgchandra, all belonging to

1. Mrigesh Verman (475 to 490 A.D.) of the Kadamba dynasty has given a grant to Yāpniyas, Nirgraṇthas and Kūrchakas. The teacher mentioned in the plate is Daṁakirti. Further his son (497 to 537 A.D.) also made a grant of village, out of the income of which the pūja etc. were to be performed and the Yāpniya ascetics to be fed for four months. The teachers mentioned here are Dāmakirti, Jayakirti, Budhsena and Kumardutta, possibly all of them Yāpniyas. Further, Deva Verman, the son of Krishna Varman (475-480 A.D.) made a donation of a village to the members of Yāpniya Sangh in favour of their temple for its maintenance.

—*Annals of Bhandarkar Oriental Research Institute*, Vol. LV, Poona 1974, Page 12.

Punnāga genealogy on the said inscription. Achārya Nemichandra, spiritual head of Yāpniya Sangh has been attributed with the designation of founding Achārya and guide of "Tuluva dynasty". It is explicit from the said version that Achāryas (Religious preceptors) of Yāpniya Sangh used to exercise great influence upon the Kingdoms of South and commanded great respect from the rulers thereof. The said spiritual heads used to play significant roles in shaping the destiny and giving final shape to the principal events of the said dynasties. The designation of "founding father ôf Tuluva dynasty", attributed to Achārya Nemichandra, amply reflected that the said spiritual guides of Yāpniya Sangh exercised great influence upon the rulers of their Age.

Infact, the description that the Achāryas belonged to `Punnāgavriksamūlgaṇa' only meant to show that it was one of the branches of Yāpniya Sangh itself.

Expansion of Yāpniya Sangh in Various Groups called Ganas

As soon as a religious institution gains popularity and its following is considerably enlarged, it is bound to be divided in various branches or groups and sub-groups. In this connection, Dr.A.N. Upadhye writes — "The Yāpniya Sangh is associated with Gaṇas like Kumuligaṇa (or Kumudigaṇa) (Koti); Maḍuvagana; Kandurā or Kānūragaṇa; Punnagavriksamūlgaṇa (also linked with Mūl Sangh), Vandiyūargaṇa, Kāreyāgaṇa; Nandigachchha and Mailapānvya. This contemination with different gaṇas indicates that the Sangh gradually got itself expressed through Gaṇas which shows that Yāpniya sect was becoming more and more prominent in Karnataka and roundabout.

It is not decidedly clear whether the gaṇas were under administration of a central authority of Yāpniya Sangh or they were independent in conducting their affairs. Whether the Sangh was divided into ganas with a view to ensure smooth administration only or as a result of ideological or ethological differences, having crept in the Sangh,—nothing definite can be stated in this regard. However, this much can be emphatically stated that the field of activities of the Sangh must have considerably expanded, necessitating its division into gaṇas.

Yāpniya Achāryas: Their Literary Pursuits: Agamas Relied upon By Shwetambers

The Achāryas of Yāpniya Sangh had greatly contributed to the enrichment of Jaina canonical literature. Having deep insight into the subjects, they had accomplished illustrious books, on religious matters. As already pointed out, it was the era when they had fully established their supermacy in religious affairs especially in Southern India and had won the favour of erstwhile rulers, well to do persons and the public at large. They were held in great esteem by the rulers as well as the masses of that period. The spiritual heads of the Sangh were sanctioned rent-free grants of lands for maintenance of their temples and for the subsistence of Yāpniya Sādhus, who being carefree, had dedicated themselves to the pursuit of knowledge. Consequent upon the same, the temples of Yāpniyas had turned into prominent centres of learning. Thus, a fine tradition of studying renowned spiritual works and production of fresh canonical literature had continued for centuries under auspices of Achāryas of Yāpniya Sangh.

We shall now discuss how the Achāryas and literateurs of Yāpniya Sangh had made use of Jaina Agamas, relied upon by Shwetambers, in accomplishment of their new compositions so that the readers may be enlightened to this effect.

Shivārya : Shivakoti: Shivārya, also popularly known as Shivakoti, had written `Ārādhanā', believed to be an ancient and authentic sacred treatise under Digamber tradition. The said book, is styled as *Bhagwati Ārādhanā* as well. It specifically deals with ethics, prescribed for Yāpniya Munis. It incorporates guide-lines for four types of spiritual pursuits—namely to undertake thorough study of philosophical doctrines; precise knowledge derived from meditation on higher truths of religion; observance of good behaviour and moral conduct and practising of self-denial and self-mortification for attainment of final emancipation.

Jaina scholar, Jinendra Varṇi has mentioned in his work *Jaina Sidhānt Kosha* (A dictionary of Jaina religion) that Shivakoti (Shivarya) had lived in the middle of first century A.D.[1]. Although, there is no reliable evidence in support of definite chronology of Shivārya yet he is, undoubtedly, believed to be most ancient scholar Most probably, he lived during the period after the split of Jania institution in the shape of Digamber and Shwetamber sects and emergence of Yāpniya Sangh.

Ārādhanā : A few Controversial Points?

Although, Ārādhānā or Bhagwati Ārādhanā belongs to Digamber tradition, yet on having a minute study of the subjects, dealt with, it is found that the views expressed are, not in consistency with the doctrines, enunciated in canonical books of Digamber Sect. Dr. Jagdish Chandra Jain writes in this regard —. "It is worth noting that several concepts of the ideology of Yāpniyas, as detailed in *Bhagwati Ārādhanā*, are inconsistent with the manners and morals, laid down to be observed by Digamber Munis. For example, providing food and water by other Sadhus to the diseased ones has been justified in *Bhagwati Ārādhanā*. Similarly, in the chapter, styled `Vijhana' of Bhagwati Ārādhanā, the method how to abandon the dead body of a Jaina Sādhu in the forest, has been advised. There are also references therein of `Kalpa', `Vyavahar' and `Jītakalpa' and `Acharanga etc., Agamic Scriptures, relied upon by Shwetambers. Many narratives of Bhagwati Ārādhnā, resemble with those, appearing in `Avashyaka Nirayukti' and `Vrahat-Kalpa-bhāshya', ancient holy scriptures of Shwetamber Sect.[2]

From the above, it clearly transpires that Shivārya was attached with and had equal faith in both traditions of Digambers as well as Shwetambers. Presumably, he had alliance with Yāpniya Sect, otherwise, he would not have referred to the Jaina Agamas, relied upon by Shwetambers.

Shivārya, Referred to by Shāktāyan

Shāktāyan, who himself was a Yāpniya, and will be dealt with extensively in the

1. *Jainendra Sidhant Kosha*, volume I, page 335.
2. *Prākrita Sāhitya Kā Itihās*, page 304.

following pages has quoted Shivārya, showing great regard for him, which is self-evident from the following extracts:

Shāktāyan writes in his exposition of Sutra No. 2/1/1 of his grammar:

> "Iti Shivaryam! Tachchhivāryaṁ. Aho Shivārya vartate Shivāryo Shabdo Loke Sushṭhu Prakrita ityarthaḥ."

In his gloss of Vyakarṇa Sutra No 1.3.168, Achārya Shāktāyayan writes:

> "Shobhanaḥ Sidhevinishchayaḥ Shivāryasya Shivāryeṇa Vā."

On the topic of attainment of final emancipation by females in their present birth (feminine form), Shāktāyan has reproduced two verses from Shivāryas book — *Sidhi Vinishchaya*.

> "Yat Saṁyamopakārāya Vartte Prokta Metadupkarnaṁ.
> Dharmasya hi Tat Sādharmatanya adhikaranamaharhana ||
> Astainyabahirvyutsargavivekaishṇa dismitinām.
> Updeshanmupadesho hyupathera parigrahatwasya ||"

Wearing of a garment and covering the body is only a medium to save the limbs so as to be able to undertake spiritual performances and it is in no way an act of acquisition of property. This aspect of the matter has specifically been dealt with in the said two verses. According to Shivārya, covering of the body with nominal clothing is not an act of acquisition in any view of the matter but only a source for accomplishing spiritual objectives.

It is the doctrine of Shwetamber Sect which finds support from the above verses. These are a few examples which lend support to the view that Shivārya was a Yāpniya Sādhu.

The renowned Scholar, Aparājita Sūri has written a commentary on `Ārādhanā' in which we find several references, testifying that Shivarya was a Yāpniya Sādhu or belonged to Yāpniya Sect.

Arguments of Aparajita Sūri'

Aparājita Sūri is believed to have lived in or about 7th century A.D. He was also known as Vijayachārya. On one hand, he had written a commentary on `Ārādhnā' and on the other, he had accomplished an exposition on `Dashavaikālika Sūtra'. While discussing about Dashvaikālika Sūtra, a mention is found to this effect. Both commentaries had a common title of `Vijyodayā'.

`Bhagwati Ārādhanā' is primarily an accomplishment, relied upon by Digamber Sect, while `Dashvaikālika' Sūtra is treated as one of the Jaina Agamas by Shwetamber Sect, upon which Aparājita Sūri has composed a commentary. From all this, it is believed that Aparājita Sūri belonged to Yāpniya Sangh. For instance, how Aparājita Sūri has defined the following verse of `Ārādhanā' is enough to support the point :

"Āchelakkuddesiyasejjāhar Rāyapindakiar Kasme |
Vayajethapadikakamne māsaṁ pajjosavaṇakappo ||421||

While defining the above verse of `Ārādhanā', Aparājita Sūri has quoted from Achāranga'; `Sutrakritānga, and Nishitha Sūtras—all relied upon by Shwetambers as Jaina Agamas in support of acceptability of clothing and a pot by a Jaina Sādhu, clearly reflects that he had complete reliance on the said Agamas. It equally sounds that Shivārya must have Shwetamber Agamas in his mind, while composing the above verses, contained in Ārādhanā, since the prominent scriptures, relied upon by Digambers, do not lend support to the advisability of acceptance of a garment and a pot by each Sādhu or they help them in any way to carry on their spiritual pursuits.

In practice, adopting nudity by Jaina Sādhus and ideologically supporting the theory of Shwetambers that Jaina Sādhus ought to keep their bodies covered -- is it not a strange co-ordination between diverse view-points which, obviously, leads us to the conclusion that Shivārya and Aparājita Sūri were decidedly Yāpniyas or they belonged to Yāpniya Sangh.

There are certain mentions in `Ārādhnā' which are neither supported by Shāstras of Digamber tradition nor those, relied upon by Shwetambers. It, thus, transpires that they neither belonged to Digamber sect nor they were followers of Shwetamber Sect. They were connected with any other tradition which could be none else but Yāpniya Sangh.

Shāktāyan : A Foremost Leader of Yāpniyas

Shāktāyan was a renowned grammarian, philosopher and an authority on Jaina Agamas. His another name was 'Pālyakirti'. He is believed to be contemporary to king Amoghavarsha, ruler of 'Rashtrakūta' dynasty. This fact stands corroborated by his own version, appearing in his commentary, styled `Swopagya' on Sūtra No. 4.3.208 of his grammar. He defines the Sūtra with illustration that the enemies of king Amoghavarsha had been completely destroyed.

Most celebrated scholar, Late Dr. Mahendra Kumar `Nyāyāchārya' (The philosophical system of the Nyāya School) has stated with regard to the life time of Shāktāyan. He writes in his preface to the second volume of his book *Nyāyakumudachandra* that king Amoghvarsha is believed to have lived from 814 to 877 A.D. Accordingly, he has reckoned the period of Shāktāyan to be in between 800 to 875 A.D.

Shāktāyan was, undoubtedly, an eminent teacher and a spiritual leader of Yāpniya Sangh. The noted commentator, Achārya Malayagiri, belonging to 12th-13th century of Vikrama era, has greatly eulogized Shāktāyan in his commentary on `Nandi Sūtra' by attributing him the title of *Yāpniyayatigrāmāgraṇi* (A foremost Leader of Yāpniya Sangh).

References of Shwetamber Agamas in the Grammar of Shāktāyan

Shāktāyan commands a unique position amongst all the grammarians of Jaina community. His impact is clearly found on the grammar, namely, `Sidhahem-ashabdānushāshan', written by Āchārya Hemchandra, which is self-evident from a minute study thereof. Shāktāyan grammar enjoys greater recognition amongst followers of Digamber tradition for coaching newly initiated disciples of the sect.

While explaining various Sūtras of his grammar, Shāktāyan has repeatedly referred to the relevant illustrations, contained in Jaina Agamas, relied upon mainly by Shwetambers which proves beyond doubt that he extremely reposed faith on Jaina Agamas. Had he belonged to Digamber Sect, it would never have been possible for him to do so. Hence the attribute of `Yāpniyayatigrāmāgriṇi', used by Āchārya Malayagiri for Shāktāyan, appears to be perfectly in order.

While emphasizing that certain texts of religious sacred books, relied upon by Shwetambers, are to be studied or revised at stipulated hours only, Shāktāyan suggests that there ought to be intermittents for not studying the holy texts during lunar and solar eclipses; noise of a whirlwind; an earth-quake; roaring thunder; a flash of lightning; a fiery phenomenon in the sky (falling of a meteor); practising on a machine; in mourning; a festive occasion; in morning or evening twilight. These are called ten off periods when studying of holy texts should be ceased. The said intermissions in study are consistent with Shwetamber tradition. The above-cited explanation is really important to have a glimpse of the views and beliefs of Shāktāyan—how far they are in conformity with the philosophical system of Yāpniya Sangh.

The Topics of Attainment of Final Emancipation by Females in their Existing Birth and Taking of Food as a Mouthful by Kevalins

Amongst several other controversial topics between Digambers and Shwetambers, the twin issues, relating to the attainment of final emancipation by females in their existing birth and taking of food as a mouthful by Kevalins after attainment of Kevalya (the state of highest perfection) are most significant. As already discussed above, Shwetambers believe in both of them while Digambers disagree and hold diverse views. The ideological beliefs of Yāpniya Sangh are perfectly in consonance with those of Shwetamber Sect.

The said topics have been discussed as per demand of the context, in Jaina Agamas, yet Shāktāyan was the first and foremost scholar to enunciate these points effectively in his own philosophical style in Sanskrit language. The title of his composition is *Stree-Nirvan-Kevali-Bhukti Prakarṇa.*[1] The author has written his own commentary as well on the book. The said topics have been nicely dealt with by Shāktāyan by exercising his superb talents and making use of his deep insight and wielding his pen effectively. It has no parallel.

However, it does not mean that prior to Shāktāyan, no one else had attempted to define and elaborate these issues. Prior to him, a few Yāpniya sages too have expressed their views over these issues. In `Lalit-vistrā',[2] written by Achārya

1. The said treatise was published in Samvat year 2030 of Vikrama era by Atmanand Jaina Society, Bhāvnagar (Gujarat), after having been edited by renowned Jaina scholar, Jambu-Vijayji.
2. The title of commentary, written by Achārya Haribhadra Sūri on Sūtras of 'Chaitya-Vandana' is `Lalitvistarā'.

Haribhadra Sūri, an extract of `Yāpniya Tantra' (A religious treatise of Yāpniyas) has been produced in regard to the topic of attainment of final emancipation by females. It is enough to signify that an old treatise—'Yāpniya Tantra' was already in existence, belonging to Yāpniyas, in which the ideological doctrines of Yāpniya Sangh might have been comprehended. It had been reduced to writing in Prākrita language which is, however, no longer available now.

Distinguishing Features of Shāktāyan's Book

The treatise — *Stree-Nirvan-Kevali-Bhukti-Prakarṇa*, authored by Shāktāyan, has its unique features. It has been written in refined form of Sanskrit, which is known for its capacity of expressing even philosophical matters in a logical style most effectively in a concise form. Shaktāyan has spared no pains in making full use of the characteristics of Sanskrit in his book. Rebuttal or rejection of the earlier concepts on one hand and establishment of the new doctrines on the other and for that matter, presentation of relevant portions from Jaina Agamas and quoting references from commentaries with explanations of Sūtras, word by word along with the comments of the author and substantiation by virtue of advancing rational and forceful arguments, Shāktāyan has comprehended the subjects, relating to attainment of final emancipation by females in their existing feminine forms and taking of food as a mouthful by Kevalins in a most logical and effective manner, with the result, the said work of Shāktāyan continued to be regarded as a unique composition for centuries.

Not only Yāpniyas but learned scholars of Shwetamber Sect as well drew inspiration from the said book of Shāktāyan. It continued its guiding role for the seers and authors of Shwetamber Sect, who referred to it frequently while attempting their own productions on the said topics.

Religious Debate Held in Between Vadi Devasūri and Kumudchandra

King Sidhrāj Jaisingh (Dating back 1143 to 1199 of Vikrama era) had great fondness for learning and realisation of the Supreme Truth. A religious debate was arranged in his royal Court. Amongst the topics to be discussed, the issue of attainment of final emancipation by females in their existing life was most predominant one. On one side, Achārya Vādi Devasūri represented Shwetamber Sect and on the other Achārya Kumudchandra belonged to Digamber tradition. There is a reference of the said religious debate in `Prabhāvaka Charit'. It is cited therein: "The illustrations from the commentary on `Uttrādhyayan', authored by Achārya Shanti Sūri, enabled to make the opposite party spell-bound, just like the snakes are charmed by playing on flute. By advancing the arguments, relating to attainment of final emancipation by females in their existing feminine forms, obtained from the said commentary, Deva Sūri, disciple of Achārya Munichandra, had prevailed upon Digamber Seer, Sri Kumudchandra, in the presence of King Sidhrāj Jaisingh."

Muni Jambuvijayji, editor of *Stree-Nirvan-Kevali-Bhukti-Prakarṇa*, authored by Shāktāyan, believes that possibly Shanti Sūri, who lived in 11th century A.D., may have referred to the chapter-concerning attainment of final emancipation of females in their existing forms, as expounded by Shāktāyan in his book `Stree-nirvan-Kevali-Bhukti-Prakarna', while writing his commentary, styled `Paiya' on `Uttrādhyayan' which enabled Vādi Devasuri (12th century A.D.) to defeat Kumudchandra in the religious debate. Such a probability cannot be denied.

The object of above assertion is only to emphasize that the said work of Shāktāyan provided a stable base for quite a long time to all those who brought out their own productions and undertook to elaborate the topics, concerning attainment of final emancipation by females and taking of food as a mouthful by Kevalins.

Amongst Shwetamber scholars, Abhaya Deva (11th century A.D.); Vādi Devasūri (12th century A.D.) and Yashovijaya (17th century A.D.) have primarily advanced the same pleas, as given by Shāktāyan in his book, in support of the theories that females could attain final emancipation in their existing feminine forms and Kevalins took food as a mouthful, after attainment of the state of Kevalya.

Whereas, on one hand, the scholars of Shwetamber tradition have taken recourse to the said accomplished work of Shāktāyan to advance pleas in vindication of their own stand and on the other, the seers of Digamber Sect have also illustrated from the said book in repudiation of the theories that females could attain final emancipation in their existing life and Kevalins fed themselves through their mouth. Thus the recourse was taken to the work of Shāktāyan for corroboration and negation of the viewpoints by Shwetambers and Digambers both. For example, the renowned logician and Digamber Seer, Achārya Prabhāchandra, (Lived between 925-1023 A.D.) author of *Prameya-Kamal-Mārtanda* and *Nyāya Kumudchandra* had taken recourse to the relevant chapters of Shāktāyans book while arguing about twin topics of attainment of final emancipation by females in their existing birth and taking of food as a mouthful by Kevalins, after attainment of Kevalya, (the state of highest perfection).

A Few Significant Points Worth Knowing

The relevant illustrations, referred to from Agamas, by Shāktāyan, in support of his comments, are found slightly varying here and there as against the original texts, contained in the said Agamas. Besides him, other Yāpniya scholars too have quoted relevant portions from Agamas in support of their pleas. It is very likely that variations may be witnessed on comparing with the original texts of the Jaina Agamas, relied upon by Shwetambers, in their case also. The matter is really pursuable by research scholars. It is also possible that the editions of Jaina Agamas, which were then in possession of or relied upon by Yāpniyas, might have contained varied texts—both in contents and spirit as against the editions of Agamas, available now with Shwetambers. It may be worthwhile to keep this aspect in mind by the research scholars on Shwetamber Agamas to arrive at the truth. It is quite possible that the research scholars may be able to trace out the cause of the said variations in the texts which are bound to throw light on several facets, still undisclosed.

Shāktāyan has also dealt with certain other topics in his book which have nothing in common with the traditional beliefs of both Shwetambers and Digambers.

They are exclusive beliefs of Yāpniya Sangh.

While dealing with `Upadhi' (Foundation), Shāktāyan has classified it in three parts—(1) `Ogha' (The whole, continuity) (2) `Anu' (Atomic particle), and (3) Aupagrahik' (eclipsed). The second ingredient `Anu' seems to be connected with Yāpniya philosophical doctrine only. It is the peculiar characteristic belief of Yāpniyas only. There are similar other topics, dealt with by Shāktāyan in his book which deserve the minute attention of the Jaina research scholars.

Shruta-Kevali : Deshiyāchārya

Shāktāyan has applied two attributives with his name in the concluding paragraph of his grammar, namely—`Shruta-Kevali' (An expert scholar of Jaina Agamas) and `Deshichārya' (Native Achārya or religious preceptor). In this way, the leaders of Yāpniya Sangh signified their distinct identity as against those, belonging to other sects.

Dr. Upādhye has opined that Achārya Sidhasena Diwākar (5th century of Vikrama era) was also a spiritual leader of Yāpniya Sangh[1]. According to Dr. Upādhye, Achārya Haribhadra Sūri might have used the attribute of Shrutakevali for Sidhasena Diwākar.

Religious Beliefs of Umāswāti

In a petrographic inscription, connected with Digamber Sect, Umāswāti has been attributed with designations of `Shruta-Kevali' and `Deshiya'. It is assumed that Umāswāti probably belonged to Yāpniya Sangh. The late Pt. Nathu Ramji `Premi' has given some valid reasons why Umaswāti must have belonged to the Yāypniya Sangh in his book, styled "Jaina Sahitya Aur Itihās' and has elaborately expressed his views in this regard.

Views of Pt. Sukhlalji: Pt.Sukhlalji Sanghvi does not subscribe to the view that Umāswāti was a Yāpniya. He refers to the article styled `Bhartiya Vidyā', annexed with `Tatvarth Sūtra', authored by him, and comments as under:

"An article of Late Pt. Nathu Ramji `Premi' has appeared in the issue of Shudhi Souvenir under the Style" Vāchaka Umāswāti Ka Sambhāshya Tatvarth Sūtra Aur Unkā Sampradāya.' After long consideration and determination Pt. Nathu Ramji Premi has expressed the view that Vachaka Umāswāti was an Achārya and spiritual leader of Yāpniya Sangh. Hence in order to make critical examination of the grounds, advanced by Premiji, Pt. Sri Dalsukh Mālvania undertook profound study of *Bhagwati Arādhāna* along with its commentary. After deep application of the mind, he classified the information and prepared brief notes, on which I also deliberated upon and exchanged views with Mālavnia. I went through relevant portions of *Bhagvati Ārādhāna*, its commentaries and `Vrahat-Kalpa Bhāshya' etc. Throughout, we had an open mind and spared no pains to arrive at the truth. Finally, we came to the conclusion that Vachaka Umāswāti had nothing to do with Yāpniya tradition.

---

1. Dr. Upādhye's *Introduction to the Sidhasena Diwakar's Nyaya Vatara* and other works. Published by Jaina Sahitya Vikasa Mandala, Bombay, 1971.

1. In case, the author of *Bhagwati Ārādhnā*, Shivārya and its commentator, Aparājita Sūri are agreed to be Yāpniyas, their distinguishing features ought to be as under:

   (a) The inherent characteristic of a Yāpniya is that he must observe nudity and live naked.

   (b) According to Yāpniya ideology, female Munis can also attain final emancipation in their existing form alike Male Sādhus. Under specific circumstances, they are also entitled to observe nudity as soon as they are able to cultivate a feeling of complete detachment.

   (c) Under Yāpniya tradition, there is a usage to accept and hold the food on the palm of the hand and feed oneself. The Sādhus are not allowed to possess any other article except earthen or wooden waterpot and a bunch of the feather of tail of peacock.

The above distinguishing features of Yāpniyas do not conform with the citations, appearing in the commentary of Umāswāti and a renowned sacred book, styled `Prashmarti' in as much as it is considered essential to hold a pot only and keep the bodies covered by Jaina Sādhus and there is no obligation for them to observe nudity at all. There is no mention of a waterpot and a feather bunch of the tale of peacock to be possessed by a Sādhu.

2. One of the arguments of late Pt. Nathu Ramji Premi is that the views of Umāswāti in regard to efficacy of virtues appear in the commentary of Aparajita. However, the history is a mute witness to the fact that diverse opinions are found on trivial and insignificant matters under the same tradition and similarly, uniformity is noticed on such trivial and minor issues in two separate organisations, having diverse ideologies and traditions. Under the circumstances, it should not be viewed anomalous that Umāswāti, having supported the idea that Jaina Sādhus must hold a waterpot and keep their bodies dressed should have agreed with Yāpniya Sangh which is fundamentally opposed to the idea that the Sādhus should keep their bodies covered and hold a waterpot."[1]

Examination: To prolong discussion on the said point may be considered a sort of digression from the actual subject. Hence it may be in the fitness of things to give a few indicatory references only. The authenticity of *Tatvartta Sūtra* is admitted by both Digambers and Shwetambers. However, there are slight variations in the texts of Tatvārth Sūtra, relied upon by each sect. Similarly, the number of Sūtras[2] (aphorisms) in each chapter also differs. The variations in the texts of Tatvarth Sūtra are mainly observed where there is diversity in views and ideology

1. Comments of the author of this book on 'Tatvarth Sūtra' with commentary on pages 14-15.
2. Total number of aphorisms in all 10 chapters of Tatvarth Sūtra', relied upon by Digambers:- 1/33, 2/53, 3/39, 4/42, 5/42, 6/27, 7/39, 8/26, 9/47, 10/9 = Total number of aphorisms-357.
   Total number of aphorisms in each chapter of Tatvarth Sūtra, relied upon under Shwetamber tradition:- 1/35, 2/52, 3/18, 4/53, 5/44, 6/26, 7/34, 8/26, 9/49 and 10/7 = Total number of aphorisms - 344.

of each sect.

According to Shwetamber Sect, the author of *Tatvārth Sūtra* and its commentator is one and the same person while Digambers believe that the authors of *Tatvārth Sūtra* and its commentary are two separate scholars.

As per Digambers, the initial commentator of Tatvarth Sūtra is Achārya Pujyapada alias Devanandi. He is believed to have lived between the latter half of 5th century and the first half of the sixth century A.D.[1]

The texts of Tatvārth Sūtra, relied upon by Achārya Pujyapāda in his commentary `Sarvārth Sidhi' have been endorsed by Achārya Akalanka, author of the commentary `Tatvārth Rajvartika' (7th century A.D.) and Achārya Vidyanand (who lived from 775 to 840 A.D.) in his commentary `Tatvarth Shloka-Vārtika'. Other learned scholars of Digamber tradition have followed the suit. Shwetamber scholars, however, believe that the texts of Tatvarth Sūtra, as expounded in the `Bhāshya' are genuine.

Owning to their Respective Side

The scholars, belonging to Digamber tradition who have written expositions on `Tatvarth Sūtra', generally hold that its author, Umāswati (Umaswami)[2] belonged to Digamber Sect. Similarly, Shwetamber scholars have owned him to be a follower of Shwetamber Sect. Probably, it is also one of the causes, leading to the variance in the texts of *Tatvārth Sūtra*, as relied upon by each sect.

Originally, the texts of `Tatvārth Sūtra' might have been identical. However, as a result of their sectarian biases, they failed to carry on with the original texts and keep them intact. Those which were not offending to them in any way, or were consistent with their ideological beliefs, they were not disturbed. However, the texts which were found incongruous or against their convictions, they might have been removed, altered or rectified accordingly. If we make a critical review of Tatvārth Sūtra with an open mind, we feel inclined to believe that Achārya Umāswāti was eagre to establish ideological harmony between both sects by virtue of his accomplished book, *Tatvārth Sūtra*. If a spiritual guide and an erudite scholar like him is believed to be connected with Yāpniya Singh, it should not be considered an improbability. Hence it is quite desirable that research scholars should undertake critical investigation in the light of the assumptions of Late Pt. Nathu Ramji Premi and reflections of Dr. Upādhye,[3] made by him in this regard.

Saidhantika: Traividha : Another Two Attributes

Besides the titles of *Shrutakevali* and *Deshiyāchārya*, certain Yāpniya Achāryas are found to have applied another two attributes with their names. According to

1. Preface to *Sarvarth Sidhi*, Page 88.
2. Umāswāmi is also popular amongst Digambers.
3. ---- The Sutras and Bhāsya show some clear cut difference with the Ardhamagadhi canon and Pujyapāda is not very happy with the text of the Sutras in Onany places. That late Pt. Premi has given some valid reasons why Umāswāti must have belonged to the Yāpniya Sangh ----
—*Annals of Bhandarkar Oriental Research Institute*, Vol. LV. Poona 1974 p. 20

Dr. Upādhye-titles like Saidhāntika, Traividha, used by some Yāpniya Achāryas indicate their profound study of Shatkhandāgama etc. The point needs further investigation.

Epitome : Yāpniya Sangh had one time greatly flourished and spread far and wide in India. Under its auspices, extensive canonical literature had been accomplished by Yāpniya Achāryas. For several centuries, the Sangh continued to be held in great esteem in India. However, it is quite amazing that such renowned and esteemed organisation lost its identity and survived only in name with the passage of time. Neither a single Sādhu or a follower of Yāpniya Sangh is found anywhere nor there is any trace of that organisation now. There could be several causes for the downfall of the institution. Possibly, the rare zeal, devotion and dedication with which the scholars of the Yāpniya Sangh initially worked day and night for the growth of their organisation might have considerably gone down as soon as they found that the Sangh had earned great name and fame and was held in great esteem by the people. The rent-free grants of landed properties, cash and kind, gifted by the royal and well-to-do devotees must have considerably accumulated, with the consequence, Yāpniya Sādhus must have turned easy-going and started leading a comfortable life in place of life of absolute detachment, self-denial and perseverance. Resultantly people might have started losing faith and respect for them. Under the circumstances, Digambers and Shwetambers both might have resolved to uproot Yāpniya Sangh, in as much as both were opposed to Yāpniya traditions. Many such assumptions could be made. Infact, it is a matter of historical significance and calls for further investigation and research on the subject by the scholars of history.

It is an undisputed fact that Yāpniyas owned several temples in Southern India which have vanished and lost their separate identity. They have completely merged with Digamber temples during the said transitional period, so much so that it is not possible now to identify them separately. With religious bias, Digamber Scholars used to preach that no respect be shown to the idols installed and worshipped by Yāpniyas at all.

The trend of history is such that nobody can claim with certainty what turns and twists be taken by human psyche (mind and heart). Its spirit of diligence and perseverance had disappeared with the lapse of time.

An Epilogue

While deliberating upon the topic of versatile study and constant pursuit of Jaina Agamas relied upon by Shwetambers, we had discussed how the bifurcation took place of Jaina institution into Digamber and Shwetamber Sects and how the Yāpniya Sangh came into existence. Although, the discussion has been lengthier, yet in our opinion, it is equally important to obtain critical information and knowledge about the existence of Agamas, their nature, diminution, comprehension, preservation, explanatory and auxiliary literature produced for easy understanding of the texts of Agamas, spiritual accomplishments with their help and religious movement launched and built up therefor etc. Agamas and other holy scriptures are meant for enlightening the people. How the public psyche is built and life moulded is a significant chapter of the annals of our social life-on one hand and on the other it is manifestation of our ability to implement the teachings of Arhats, contained in Jaina Agamas and other sacred books. This fact should not be ignored.

Angas (Title of the twelve sacred books of the Jainas): Their Non-Availability Now : Truth

As per Digamber tradition, the gradual discontinuance of 12 Angas had already started which ultimately ceased to exist after the year 683 of final salvation of Lord Mahāvira. The matter has been dealt with by us in the foregoing pages, as per demand of the context. In this connection, a few additional points are being discussed hereunder:

Discontinuance of 12th Anga also accepted by Shwetambers

Swetambers also agree that *Drishtivāda* (Title of 12th Anga) is no longer found. After final liberation of Devardhigaṇi `Kṣmashramaṇa', the expertise in Pūrvas (old sacred treatises of Jainas) had come to an end. There is a specific mention in this regard in Prākrita production `Titthogalipaiṇṇā' etc.

Regarding other 11 Angas, while disagreeing with Digambers that they have absolutely ceased to exist, Shwetambers too believe that they are in the process of decadence and ultimately may cease to exist.

It is cited in *Titthogālipaiṇṇā* "After final liberation of Diṇṇagaṇi Pushyamitra, *Vyākhyā-Pragyapti Sūtra* (Title of the 5th Anga) shall cease to exist in Samvat year 1250 after final salvation of Lord Mahāvira.

While describing the virtues of Pushyamitrā, the last authority on `Vyākhyā Pragyapti', the author of *Titthogalipaiṇṇā* writes: "Pushyamitra is highly accomplished Jaina Sādhu with great spiritual force. He is destined to be the last authority on `Vyākhyā-Pragyapti'.

On falling down and destruction of the fruits-laden tree, similized with `Vyākhyā-Pragyapti', comprising of 24000 verses, a highly accomplished sacred book, people and scholars will feel orphaned in the absence of this holy treatise and deprived of the virtues of "Vyākhyā Pragyapti."

After liberation of Achārya Sambhuti, belonging to the lineage of `Madar', the expertise in *Samvayanji Sutra* (Title of the 4th Anga) shall come to an end in Samvat year 1300 of final salvation of Lord Mahāvira. Again the expertise in *Sthanānga Sūtra* (Title of the 3rd Anga) will cease in Samvat year 1350 of final salvation of Lord Mahavira after the death of Ārjava) a Jaina saint. It has thus been predicted by Jaina Arhats."

"After the death of Jaina saint, Phalgumitra, belonging to Gautama lineage and endowed with great spiritual force with expertise in *Dashāshrutaskandha* (Title of 4th Chheda Sūtra, forming part of Jaina Agamas), in samvat year 1500 of final salvation of Lord Mahāvira, Dashāshrutaskandha shall cease to exist."

"Subsequent to the death of Jaina saint, Mahashramaṇa, born in Bharadwaj lineage, in Samvat year 1900 after final, salvation of Lord Mahāvira, Sūtrakritānga (Title of 2nd Anga) shall cease to exist."

"Similarly, after the expiry of Jaina Sādhu, Vishnu, belonging to Hāritalineage in Samvat year 2000, after final salvation of Lord Mahāvira, *Acharanga Sutra* (Title of the first Anga) shall stand terminated.

"Thereafter, slightly prior to the end of the 5th part of the wheel of time, namely `Dushmā' (a long period of time with the Jainas when the virtuous and auspicious manners will be constantly on decrease and inauspicious tendencies will be rapidly increasing), there will be one renowned Achārya, Duḥprasaha. He will be endowed with sterling virtues of submissiveness and dedication. In India, he will be the last authority on Acharanga Sūtra. After his death, Acharanga Sūtra, laying down ethics and virtues to be observed by Jaina Sādhus will finally disappear and cease to exist.[1]

It is believed that the said incident will take place near about Samvat year 21000. It is also cited that the day on which the 5th part of `Avasarpaṇi Kāl' (It is a long period of time with the Jainas. According to Achārya Hemchandra, it is equal to 2000,000,000,000,000 Sāgaras of years) Achārya Duḥprasaha will breathe his last in first part of the day (The day is divided in 8 Pahars of 3 hours each) and after his death Achāranga Sūtra will cease to exist completely.

Thus all the 12 Angas will cease to exist one by one in due course of time. The author of *Titthogalipaiṇṇā* writes: "Infact, it is Achārānga alone which lays down true guide lines concerning ethics to be observed by Jaina Sādhus and which alone teaches them how to behave and conduct themselves morally.

After discontinuance of Achāranga Sutra, impropriety will prevail every where as a result of non-observance of customary duties and departure from established usages. Even the very existence of Jaina mendicancy will be at stake."

It is also cited in respect of remaining Agamas and allied scriptures, surviving the process of elimination in *Titthogalipaiṇṇā*: "Till Samvat year 21000 after final salvation of Lord Mahāvira `Dashvaikālika' will serve the purpose of Jaina Sādhus. Thereafter, with the expiry of Achārya Duḥprasaha, Dashāvikālika will also stand obliterated.

Similarly, till Samvat year 2,1000, after final salvation of Lord Mahāvira, and by the time, the Jaina institution will remain in existence, `Avashyaka Sūtra' (forming part of Jaina Agamas) will continue to meet our requirements.

Import: From the above citation, appearing in *Titthogālipaiṇṇā*, it is quite explicit that Shwetamber scholars too have accepted the elimination of Jaina Agamas. Whereas Digamber Achāryas contend that Agamas had been eliminated completely, Shwetambers believe that they had been partially eliminated and partially remained in existence. What ever portions of 11 Angas (Shwetamber Achāryas also agree that 12th Anga is no more in existence) are now found, they constitute only a very small portion of the entire lot. So that the learned readers have a comparative view of the actual position, the sum-total of the contents and the portions, now available, are given hereunder:

1. The substance of what has been cited in verses No. 816 and 817 of Titthogālipaiṇṇā is that in Samvat year 2000 after final salvation of Lord Mahāvira, with the death of Jaina Scholar, Vishnu, born in `Hārit' lineage, Ācharanga will stand partially discontinued and in Samvat year 21000 after death of Jaina scholar `Duhprasaha', the recitation of Acharanga will completely cease.

Agamas : In Totality : Available Portions

1. It is believed that Achāranga contained 18000 verses. The portion, now available, has only 2500 verses. It has already been stated in foregoing pages that the seventh Chapter, styled `Mahāparigyā' is altogether missing.
2. Total number of verses, contained in original `Sūtrakritanga' is believed to be 36,000. The texts, now available, comprise of 2100 verses only.
3. Total number of verses in original Sthānanga Sūtra is believed to be 72,000. The portions, now available, contain only 3770 verses.
4. It is believed that the original `Samvāyānga Sūtra' contained 1,44000 verses. However, now the serviving portion has only 1667 verses.
5. There are two different opinions regarding total number of verses contained in the original *Vyākhyā-Pragyapti Sūtra*. As laid down in Nandi Sūtra the said Anga consisted of 2,88,000 verses while as per `Samvāyānga Sūtra', the total number of verses in original `Vyākhyā-Pragyapti' was 84,000. However, the surviving portions contain only 15,752 verses. The said Anga was classified into 101 `Shatakas' (A collection of 100 stanzas each). However, the total number of Shaktas, now available, is only 41.
6. As per `Samvāyānga Sūtra' and `Nandi Sūtra' the total number of verses, contained in `Gyātridharmakatha' (Title of the sixth Anga) is reckoned at thousands. However, in the commentaries on the said Sūtras, the total number of verses is 5,76,000. The total number of verses in the surviving portions is only 5,500. Thus it is explicit that many narratives or tales have become extinct with the lapse of time.
7. Similarly, as per `Samvāyānga Sūtra', and `Nandi Sūtra', the total number of verses, appearing in `Upāshaka-Dashā' (Title of seventh Anga) is calculated at thousands. However, as cited in their commentaries the total number of verses in `Upāshaka-Dashā' is 11,52,000. The existing portion contains only 812 shlokas.
8. The total number of verses, contained in original `Antkriddashā' (Title of 8th Anga) is estimated at thousands. However, in the commentaries of `Samvāyāng Sūtra' and `Nandi Sūtra', the number of verses is slated to be 23,04,000. Now only 900 verses are found in the surviving portion.
9. The total number of verses, contained in original `Anuttaropātika-Dashā' (Title of the ninth Anga) is reckoned to be in thousands. However, as cited in the commentaries of Samvāyānga Sūtra and Nandi Sūtra, the total number is 46,08,000, while there are only 192 verses in the surviving portion.
10. In `Prashnavyākarnā Sūtra' (Title of the 10th Anga), the number of verses is reckoned to be in thousands. However, it appears in the commentaries on Samvayanga Sūtra and Nandi Sūtra that the number of verses is 92,16,000. At present, only 1300 verses are found in the surviving portion.

    As discussed earlier, the appearance of `Prashṇa-Vyākarṇa Sūtra', described in `Nandi Sūtra' is totally different from the one, available now.
11. The total number of verses in `Vipāka Sūtra' (Title of the eleventh Anga) is estimated to be in thousands. However, as cited in the commentaries

on Samvāyānga Sūtra and Nandi Sūtra, the number of verses is 1,84,32,000. Now only 1216 verses are found in the surviving portion.

`Tiloyapaṇṇatti' : A Specific Mention

It is firmly believed under Digamber tradition that the 12 Angas (12 sacred books of Jainas) had become extinct in Samvat year 683, after final salvation of Lord Mahāvira. The process of extinction of the 12 Angas has been specified in stanzas No. 1482 to 1492 of Tiloyapaṇṇatti, which had been dealt with earlier as per demand of the context. Besides the said reference, it is also cited by Achārya Yati Vrashabha : "For pioneering the Jaina institution and expounding the religious and philosophical doctrines, the sacred knowledge as revealed by Tirthankers and compiled by their Gandhers in the shape of 12 Angas will continue to guide till Samvat year 20317, after final salvation of Lord Mahāvira (Slightly before the expiry of 5th part of `Avasarpini Kāl', namely `Dushmā'—a long period of time with the Jainas). Thereafter, the said Angas will become extinct as a result of anachronism."

The above point has been further expounded in `Mahapurāṇa'. It is cited therein: "Although the tradition of practising the life of self-mortification and austerities by Jaina devouts and undertaking profound study of Jaina Agamas, based on the utterances of Tirthankers and Jaina Arhats, will stop, yet Achārya Virasena and his pupil, Jinasena and others will continue to have expertise in any one portion or branch of holy learning as revealed by Tirthankers till the time of expiration of Dushmā, the fifth part of `Avasarpani Kāl'—namely Sushmā (A long period of time with the Jainas when the virtues will be constantly on decline and inauspicious tendencies will be rapidly increasing).

Inspite of the above version in *Mahāpurāna*, it is emphatically asserted under Digamber tradition that the aforesaid 12 Angas had undergone complete extinction. The point calls fc- further investigation and explanation.

Anga Pravishta and Anga Bāhya Under Digamber Tradition

Just as Jaina Agamas and other allied scriptures are believed to be classified into two categories under Shwetamber tradition, namely, *Anga Pravishtya* (Based on religious discourses, delivered by Jaina Arhats; compiled by their Gandhers and the contents are of lasting nature) and *Anga Bāhya* (Teachings of spiritual heads; compiled by their Sthaviras; free from grammatical constraints and the contents are of secondary nature). In the same way, under Digamber tradition too, it is believed that Agamic scriptures are classified into two, parts namely, `Anga Pravishtya' and `Anga-Bāhya.' Thus the type of classification and the names of works relating to two groups are identical to a considerable extent identical.

Comments of the Author of Dhavalā Commentary

The author of *Dhavalā Tikā* on `Shatkhanḍāgama', Acharya Virasena, has commented regarding Anga Pravishtha and Anga Bāhya. "From semasiological viewpoint, the Jaina canonical literature is classified into two groups—(1) Anga Bāhya and (2) Anga Pravishtya. Again there are 14 types of Anga Bāhya from semasiological viewpoint—1. Samayika, 2. Anga Chaturvinshatistāva, 3. Vandanā, 4. Pratikramaṇa; 5. Vainyika; 6. Kritikarma; 7. Dashavaikālika; 8. Uttrādhyayan; 9. Kalpa-Vyavahār; 10. Kalpyākalpya; 11. Mahakalpya; 12. Punḍrīka; 13. Maha-Punḍrīka; and 14. Nishidhikā.

Regarding Anga Pravishtya, Acharya Virasena comments as below:-

"Anga Pravishṭya has also been classified into 12 categories, namely — 1. Achar; 2. Sūtrakrita; 3. Sthān; 4. Samvāya; 5. Vyākhya Pragyapti; 6. Gyātridharmakathā; 7. Upasakādhyayan; 8. Antakriddashā; 9. Anuttaraupapātka Dashā; 10. Prashna-Vyākarna; 11. Vipāk Sūtra; 12. Drishtivāda. (Twelvth sacred book of Jainas).

In 18,000 verses of 'Achārānga Sūtra' are laid down guide-lines as to how the Sādhus should move or walk; how they should get seated; how they should get asleep; how to address and converse with others and how to get redeemed from the consequences of inauspicious acts by which the soul is attached to worldly pleasures? As enquired by Gandhers and replied by Jaina Arhats it is cited that the Sādhus should move with care; sit carefully; sleep cautiously; take food in a proper manner and hold talks with others attentively. Thus by behaving and conducting themselves properly, the sādhus will be redeemed from confinement to repeated births as a result of impious acts, (verses No. 70-71 of Achāranga Sūtra).

In 36,000 verses, Sūtrakritānga deals with sacred knowledge, especially knowledge derived from meditation on the higher truths of religion and philosophy which teaches a Sādhu how to understand his own nature and behave with others; modesty and discipline; teaching and enlightening others; austerities which are feasible and which are nonfeasible for Sādhus; determination of propitiatory rules for expiation of sins, committed knowingly or unknowingly by Jaina Sādhus; performance of any religious act or duty or observance of any moral or religious act etc It also deals with religious doctrines of Jainas as well as those of other religions.

In 42,000 verses of Sthānānga Sūtra, starting from situation No. 1 to varying situations of heart and soul, a noble-souled *Sanyasi*, protector of spiritual values — an Arhat of the Jainas—is only one. Whereas, religious and philosophical doctrines represent two separate branches of knowledge and a Mahatma is endowed with the knowledge of both the branches, hence his significance is two-fold. Further, a Sanyasi is blessed with inner vision and is determined to attain awareness of the significance of past actions or the fruits and rewards of the past actions. In other words, there are three stages of Karmas—their rise, decline and duration. With that distinction in view, a Mahatma is also of three types. Since a Sādhu is destined to pass through four stages in life, hence he is of 4 types. Again, there are five states of the soul (with Jainas) when actions arise and exert an inherent influence on the future. With that classification in view, a Sanyasi is of 5 types. Since a living being is to pass from one existence to another (previous or future) on East, West, North, South, upwards and downwards in six directions, hence a Saint is of six types. Because of knowing how to speak in seven roundabout ways regarding existence or non-existence of God, he is of seven types. The impulse called yoga or attention with which the soul participates in the movement of its various bodies, it is defined as the `action of senses which impels the soul towards external objects', it is good or bad accordingly as it is directed towards good or evil objects, it is of eight types. The dravyas are nine. The earth, ether, time etc. as nine substances considered by Vaiseshikās. Thus the living-beings are stated to be of 9 kinds. There are ten somatic forms of living creatures belonging to earth, water, fire, wind, all types of vegetations, ordinary classes of vegetations, belonging to the breed, possessing two sensual organs. Three organs, four organs and five sensual organs. They are, thus, described of ten types "72-73". (contained in verses No. 72 and 73).

In 1,64,000 verses of Samvāyānga Sūtra, the elementary substances and properties have been dealt with combinedly, having constant and inseparable connection or inseparable inherence of existence of one thing in another. In other words, the Sutra enlightens us with the organic world from what they are normally visible to us to other analogic factors, namely the nature of substance and its ingredients, region, time and existence, forming part of seven categories of the vaiseshikās. The aggregation of the factors is of 4 types—that of organic substance, area, time and existence. So far as the ingredients of Dravya or matter are concerned, `Dharmastokāya' (existence of Virtues); `Adharmastikaya' (existence of unrighteousness); `Lokākāsh' (The subtle and ethereal fluid pervading the whole universe). They are like a territory or region of organic world. From viewpoint of the area, the hole or a big cavity, called `Simantaka' on the first layer of the first inferno (Ratanprabhā is the name of the first inferno according to Jainas); the earth equal to two and a half times of an island and heavenly living place of Vaimantika semi-gods, called `Riju' situated in the first' part of the first heaven and like the abode of Sages or Sidhas. From viewpoint of time, a minutest indivisible portion of time is equal to another minutest indivisible part of time. Simultaneously, a Mahurat (A period of 48 minutes or any short portion of time) is equal to another short period of 48 minutes. From viewpoint of fundamental ideology, the highest spiritual knowledge, revealed by Jaina Arhats and omniscients is worth learning in the same manner and to the same extent as that of Jaina philosophy thorough knowledge of truth as enunciated by Tirthankers), since by undertaking study of real truth alone, one can attain real awareness.

In 2,28,000 verses of `Vyākhyā-Pragyapti (5th Anga) are contained answers to sixty thousand questions relating to the world of organic and inorganic creation.

In, 5,56,000 verses of `Nathdharma-Kathā' or `Gyatridharmakathā', it is laid down that arrangements must be made for systematic study of holy scriptures and with that end in view, the significance of religious discourses of Tirthankers, the answers given by Arhats to the queries of Gandhers and how their suspicions and fears were dispelled, have been discussed in detail with numerous illustrations stories and tales, incorporated as per demand of the context.

In 11,70,000 verses of `Upāskadhyayan' (7th Anga), the characteristics of 11 types of followers or votaries of Jaina religion are given, namely, those who are mere spectators or anxious to have only broad outlines of the activities going on in Jaina institution; those who practise spiritual performances; those who are averse to attainment of any yogic powers; practising total renunciation of meals of all the four kinds for a fortnight and forsaking of all inauspicious tendencies for that period; abstaining from all attachments; desisting from taking meals at night; observance of celibacy; desisting from false pride; indifference to acquire and hoard wealth; those desisting from showing intense desire for anything; those who desist from any particular desire etc. In this way, the characteristics of the aforesaid 11 types of followers or votaries of Jaina religion (other than initiated mendicants); the methods how to observe the prescribed austerities and the manner how the said devotees should behave and conduct themselves have been dealt with at length in the said Sūtra.

In 23,28,000 verses of `Antkriddashā' Sūtra (8th Anga) are contained the narrations of 10 Kevalins in the religious organisation of each Tirthanker who had obtained final emancipation after undergoing agonizing pains, misfortunes, calamities and bodily affections and after attaining highest perfection. It is also cited in *Tatvārth Bhāshya*: "Those who put an end to the circuit or course of worldly life and redempt themselves from worldly illusions, are known as `Antakrit Kevalins (Those having attained absolute perfection and final salvation from mortal life). In the religious organisation of Tirthanker, Lord Vardhmān, there were 10 omniscients, namely Nami, Matanga, Somila, Rāmputra, Sudarshan, Yamlika, Balika Kishkavila, Palamba and Ashtaputra. Similarly, there were ten vagrant ascetics (Homeless) of each of the remaining 23 Tirthankers, right from Lord Rishabhadeva, who had practised severe penances and attained the state of highest perfection after forbearance of all agonizing pains, physical hardships and with the decay of past Karmas. The Anga in which the description of all such Kevalins has been incorporated, is known as `Antakriddashā'.

In 92,44,000 verses of `Anuttaroupapadikadasha' (9th Anga) are contained Stories of ten omniscients in the religious organisation of each Tirthanker who had obtained best heavenly abodes after they had practised severe penances and endured great mental and physical agonies. It has been explained in `Tatvārth Bhāshya' that whose aim is to be reborn in `Anuttar' heavenly abodes, are called `Anpapādikas'. There are 5 Anuttar heavenly abodes namely `Vijaya, Vaijyanta, Jayanta, Aparājita and Sarvārthasidhi'. Those who obtain their rebirth in the said Anuttar heavenly abodes, they are called `Anuttaropādikas' —Ten Anuttaropadikas, belonging to the religious organisation of Lord Vardhmān (Lord Mahāvira) are— Rishidas, Dhanya, Sunakṣatra, Kārtikeya, Ānanda, Nandan, Shālibhadra, Abhaya, Vārishena, and Chilātaputra. Similarly, there were ten `Anuttaropādikas' in the religious organisation of each Tirthanker — right from Lord Rishabhadeva and onward upto 23rd Tirthanker who had obtained rebirth in Anuttar heavenly abodes namely Vijaya and others after practising severe penances and undergoing great physical hardships and calamitous conditions. Thus the Anga which contains the description of ten omniscients, belonging to the religious organisation of each Tirthauker, who had obtained rebirth in Anuttar heavenly abodes, is known as `Anuttaraupapādikadasha' Sūtra.

In 93,16,000 verses of `Prashṇa-Vyakarna' Sūtra (10th Anga), are contained discourses and disputations in the shapes of `Ākṣepṇi'; `Vikṣepaṇi' `Samvedṇi' and `Nirvedaṇi' as also answers to the questions concerning all-round prosperity, profit and loss (advantages and disadvantages); life and death; victory and defeat etc. relating to the past, present and future times and remedies, if any.

The disputation which strongly refutes the unitarian doctrine (monotheism) and after abrogating and rectifying the erroneous principles of other religions as also endorsing the theories of seven categories of Visheshikas and nine dravyās, namely earth, ether, time and animate world etc., the roots of Jaina philosophy, is called *Ākṣepaṇi Kathā*. Similarly, what initially describes the flaws of Jaina religion as against the doctines of other religions and , thereafter, what negatives the theories of other religions and improves upon them and establishes the supermacy of Jaina philosophy so far as its fundamentals of six Dravyās and nine Padārthas (Elementary substances) are concerned, is called *Vrkshepaṇi Kathā*. The discourse which propounds the fruits of virtuous actions is called *Saṁvedaṇi Katha*.

Question: What are the fruits of virtuous deeds?

Answer: Spiritual accomplishments of Tirthankers (highest sanctified teachers of Jaina religion); Gandhers, Sages, Chakravartis (They are most accomplished personalities of their times and sovereign heads of six parts of India); Baldevas (Elder step brothers of Vāsudevas and after practising severe penances, they attain final emancipation); Vāsudevas (Accredited personalities and exclusive rulers of 3 parts of India; Devas (divine bodies); Vidyadhers (A class of demigods or semi-divine beings) are the fruits of righteous acts.

What enumerates the ill consequences of sinful acts is called `Nirvedaṇi Kathā'.

Question: What are the ill-effects of evil deeds?

Answer: Living in hell; transmigration in the forms of animals; attainment of re-birth in the lives of low and degenerate creatures; infirm and old age; death; ailments; pain and agorny; poverty and indigence are some of the ill-consequences of evil deeds.

In other words, the religious discourse which helps in creation of total aversion to worldly attachments, is called *Nirvedaṇi Kathā*. It is said that the religious discourse which propounds the philosophical doctrines and real truth of the religion is called *Ākṣepaṇi Kathā*. The Kathā which reflects upon the wrong notions and convictions of other religions and strongly repudiates the theories — mainly that of monotheism, followed by other religionists and enunciates the theory of pluralism, the very root of Jaina philosophy, is called *Vikshepaṇi Kathā*. The *Kathā* which explains the fruits or rewards of auspicious acts is called *Saṁvedaṇi Kathā*. On the contrary, the Kathā which signifies the ill effects of inauspicious acts and helps in creation of the spirit of absolute detachment from worldly pleasures, is called *Nirvedaṇi Kathā*.

While explaining the significance of all the 4 types of Kathās (religious discourses) it should be kept in mind that in no case Viksepaṇi Kathā should be recited before the persons who have no knowledge of the religious precepts, as enunciated by Jaina Arhats or who have not been able to have an access to them. Those who are not aware of the fundamentals of their own religion, are bound to be misguided by the false and illusionary doctrines of other religions. Therefore, narration of *Viksepaṇi Katha* must be avoided before such persons who have failed to acquire knowledge of the sacred precepts of their own religion. They are, ofcourse, entitled to listen to the other Kathās which could be discoursed before them. Those who have grasped the true essence of their own sacred precepts, after listening to the discourses of remaining three types; those who have acquired knowledge of the good or bad effects of the auspicious or inauspicious acts; those who have full reliance and dedication to the teachings of Jaina Arhats and are indebted to them over head and ears; those who have no reluctance, whatsoever, in paying obeisance to the Tirthankers; those who are averse to worldly enjoyments; who are well conversant with the methods how to practice penances and perform great austerities; who are humble, modest and endowed with moral values — such devouts are entitled to be revealed with `Vikṣepaṇi Kathā'. In this way, the Kathā which was denied to be discoursed before the persons, unworthy to hear it, becomes fit to be narrated before the persons, possessing the above qualities. Hence the Jaina scholars must ensure that only deserving persons had the access to Vikṣepaṇi Kathā'.

The said `Prashna-Vyakarṇa Sūtra' also elaborates the points, relating to death (Killed); destruction, fist-blow, anxiety, advantage and disadvantage, pleasure and pain, life and death, victory and defeat, names, Dravyās, age and numerals etc.

Vipāka Sūtra (11th Anga) is comprised of 1,84,00,000 verses and elaborately describes the fruits of Virtuous acts and ill effacts of unrighteous deeds. The total numbr of verses, contained in the above-noted 11 Angas, thus comes to 4,15,02,000.

In the commentary, styled "Sarvārthasidhi' on `Tatvārtha Sūtra' Achārya Pūjyapāda has also expressed his views on `Anga Bāhya' and `Anga Pravishthya'.

Size of Each Anga as Illustrated in `Anga Pannatti'

In *Anga Paṇṇatti*[1] the number of quarters along with the number of shlokas (couplets) and syllables contained in each Anga have been specified. The same are produced hereinbelow for the information of learned research scholars:

1. Achārānga	Number of quarters	18,000
	Number of shlokas	9,19,59,23,11,87,000
	Number of syllables	29,92,69,54,19,84,000
2. Sūtrakrita :	Number of quarters	36,000
	Number of verses	18,39,18,46,37,4,000
	Number of syllables.	58,85,39,08,39,68,000
3. Sthānānga	Number of quarters	42,000
	Number of verses	2,14,57,15,41,03,000
	Number of syllables	68,66,28,93,12,96,000
4. Samvāyānga	Number of quarters	1,64,000
	Number of verses	8,37,85,07,79,26,000
	Number of syllables	26,81,12,24,93,63,2,000

1. The name of its author is Achārya Shubhchandra. He was an outstanding scholar. Under Digamber tradition, he is known for his expertise in various Shāstras (namely Grammar, Philosophical system of the Nyāya School and `Parmāgama' etc.) and as a poet in six different languages, adorned with the title of `Chakravarty'. There is detailed discussion on 12 Angas and 14 Pūrvas (old sacred treatises of Jainas) in *Anga-Paṇṇatti*.

5. Vyākhyā Pragyapti	Number of quarters	2,28,000
	Number of verses	11,64,81,69,37,02,000
	Number of syllables	3,72,74,14,19,84,64,000
6. Gyātridharma Kathā	Number of quarters	5,56,000
	Number of verses	28,40,51,84,95,54,000
	Number of syllables	98,96,59,18,57,28,000
7. Upāskādhyayan	Number of quarters	11,70,000
	Number of verses	59,77,35,00,71,55,000
	Number of syllabls	19,12,75,20,22,89,60,000
8. Antkridashā	Number of quarters	23,28,000
	Number of verses	1,18,93,39,39,88,52,000
	Number of syllables	38,05,88,60,76,32,34,000
9. Anuttaraupapadikaddashā		
	Number of quarters	92,44,000
	Number of verses	47,22,61,74,41,46,000
	Number syllables	15,11,23,75,81,16,67,000
10. Prashna-Vyākarṇa		
	Number of quarters	93,16,000
	Number of verses	4,75,94,01,13,38,94,000
	Number of syllables	1,52,30,08,36,28,46, 08,000
11. Vripāka Sūtra		
	Number of quarters	1,84,00,000
	Number of verses	9,40,02,77,03,56,00,000
	Number of syllables	30,08,08,86,51,39,20,0000
12. Drishtivāda	Number of quarters	10,86,85
	Number of verses	5,55,25,80,18,73,94,27,107
	Number of syllables	17,76,82,56,59,96,61,66,16,67,440

Summary

From the names of sacred treatises, categorized as `Anga Bāhya' and Anga Pravishṭya and the discussion relating to them, it is established beyond doubt that the Agamic Scriptures and allied canonical literature relied upon under Digamber and Shwetamber traditions are almost the same. Besides, it is also proved that the sources of origin of the series of sacred treatises, belonging to both the sects are almost the same.

Similarly, the topics dealt with and the relevant illustrations produced in their support in successive literature of Digamber Sect, namely, `Bhagwati Ārādhanā' and `Mulāchār' etc. are very much identical with those quoted in sacred books of Shwetamber Sect, namely—`Vrahat-Kalpa-Bhashya'; `Avashyaka Niryukti'; `Pinda-Niryukti'; `Maraṇa-Samādhi'; `Bhaktā-Parigyā' and `Sanstāraka' etc.

Shatkhandāgama : Its Significance

After presentation of the views and beliefs of Digamber Sect with respect to 12

Angas, we shall now deal wih renowned holy scripture of Jainas, known as `Shatkhanḍāgama'. As per Digamber Sect, it owes its origin to 12 Angas (12 sacred books — forming part of Jaina Agamas). It has been composed in aphoristic style in Shorseṇi Prākrita.

The entire community of Jaina Digambers has immense faith, feelings of great respect, admiration and adoration for `Shatkhanḍāgama', which primarily deals with the theory of good or bad acts done as per auspicious or inauspicious tendencies of our mind and soul, being a fundamenal doctrine of our Jaina philosophy.

Name of the Scripture: No reference of the said scripture is found in Jaina Agamas. However, Achārya Virasena, author of `Dhavala Tika' on Shatkhandagama, has named it as `Khanḍa-Sidhānt.' He writes therein that Shatkhanḍāgama is classified in six sections. In this way, Achārya Virasena named it as `Shatkhanḍā-Sidhānt.

With the passage of time, it came to be known as an Agama, Parmagama and finally as `Shatkhanḍāgama'.

Sri Pushpadanta, a renowned poet of `Apbhransha' dialect and author of `Mahapurāna', has named it as `Agama Sidhānt'. In the commentary on `Gommatsār', it has been named as `Parmāgama'. However, Indranandi has referred to it as `Shatkhanḍāgama' in his sacred book `Shrutavtār'.

The use of the word Agama is significant in as much as it carries a specific sense. An Agama contains authoritative utterances of Jaina Arhats only. Their veracity cannot be questioned. A rational or a settled view may be termed as a doctrine of the religion but not an Agama. The contents of an Agama are revealed by Kevalius and compiled and composed by their chief disciples. Thus, under Jaina terminology, only those sacred treatises which contain religious discourses and utterances of omniscients are called Agamas. In other words, the source of the contents of an Agama are the sermons and discourses, delivered by Arhats. Hence the name of Agama proposed for the above scriptural work appears to be perfectly justified, keeping in view, the reliance placed by Digambers on it.

An Event Worth Remembering

More than six centunies had elapsed after final salvation of Lord Mahāvira. As believed under Digamber tradition, the time of obliteration of Agamic scriptures had arrived. A major portion of the Agamas had already become extinct and only a small portion was in existence. In those days, Achārya Dharsena alone was the exponent of the surviving Agamic texts.

In `Prākrita-Pattāvali' of Nandi Sangh, Achārya Dharsena has been shown as an authority on Āchārānga (The title of the first of 12 sacred books of Jainas). The author of `Dhavala' commentary has described him to be partially conversant with Angas and Pūrvas (old sacred treatises of Jainas). Whatever be the truth, the fact remains that he was an eminent scholar and a great devout. He was deeply absorbed in meditation at Chandra cave in 'Girinagar.'[1] He was, obviously, worried

1. What is now popularly known as 'Girnār'.

that the highest spiritual knowledge, lying in his memory, might not become extinct after his death. So he was eagre to teach all, what he remembered, to a capable and deserving Jaina scholar. He sent a message to the conference of Jaina sādhus, which was in session at Mahimānagri those days. Achārya, Virasena, author of *Dhavata Tikā* has narrated the said event as under:

"Having been worried that the highest spiritual knowledge, obtained by him, as revealed by omniscients, and retained in his memory, may not get obliterated after his sudden demise Achārya Dharsena, who was an authority on 8 Angas and a great astrologer, was seated in Chandra cave at Girinagar (Saurashtra), absorbed in profound meditation, sent a communication to the Jaina Achāryas, of South India who were holding a conference at Mahimanagari. After going through the message of Achārya Dharsena, two scholarly mendicants were directed to proceed from the coast of Venā river in Andha Pradesh to Girinagar in Saurashtra. The said two Sādhus were quite competent to acquire the knowledge of sacred texts, remembered by Achārya Dharsena, and were known for their submissive and modest nature. They were endowed with good manners and moral conduct. The order of their preceptor had given them the similar feeling of contentment as food provides satability to a hungry person. They were blotless and belonged to respectable families. They were accomplished artists and well-versed in various disciplines. They were accustomed to solicit instructions from their gurus by entreating thrice."

What the author of *Dhavalā Tikā* has mentioned about the capabilities of Achārya Dharsena — his presaging always indicative of auspiciousness, his profound knowledge of Jaina Agamas, his ability trying the competence of pupil mendicants, how the pupils displayed their dexterity and finally, undertaking commencement of the studies etc. are really worth going through. Hence the details are being produced hereunder:

Visualization of Dream by Acharya Dharsena: As cited in Dhavalā commentary, both the mendicants, having undertaken their journey from Mahāminagari, were about to reach their destination. Meanwhile, Achārya Dharsena happened to visualize a dream in the last hours of the night (A pahar equivalent to three hours). He visualized that two bulls with shining white colour like a Jasmine flower, moon or a conch-shell with attractive appearance, were drawing near him. They went round him from left to right as a mark of respect and submissively prostrated at his feet.

Achārya Dharsena felt satisfied after dreaming and spontaneously paid obeisance to the god of learning, a personification of most exalted type of spiritual knowledge. The same day, both the mendicants reached the cave where Achārya Dharsena was seated and appeared before him. They bowed with reverence and paid their best respects. They took rest for two days and, thereafter stood with folded hands before Achārya Dharsena and humbly submitted — we are at your feet to undertake study of Agamic texts. Achārya Dharsena replied — it is nice. He encouraged the students by cheering up their spirits.

Agitation in the Mind of Achārya

Achārya Dharsena visualized an auspicious dream and next morning he realized its fruits. Achārya was feeling agitated in his mind whether the mendicants, who had arrived, actually deserved to acquire knowledge of Agamic texts or not. He sincerely believed that ethically sound knowledge ought to be imparted to the worthy or virtuous students only. Even the highest spiritual education, imparted to an evil-minded person, cannot lead to happiness. In this way, the Achārya was feeling much agitated on this score.

If out of sheer delusion, a religious preceptor elaborates the texts of highest spiritual knowledge before foolish and immature audience similized with clouds over hills, broken pitchers, serpentines, sieves, buffaloes, rams, parasites, parrots, dirt and mosquitoes, etc, he is bound to fall prey to arrogance, poisonous effects of sensual pleasures, deviation from the right path, and deprivation from the precious jems in the shape of sacred knowledge on higher truths of religion, philosophy and ethical values. He is bound to move to infernal regions and suffer agonies for a long time. Thus Achārya was feeling agitated and he was pondering in his mind that imparting of spiritual knowledge to wanton students might prove to be a horrifying experience, inevitably leading to recurrent births and deaths.

Although, Achārya Dharsena was fully aware of the purpose of arrival of the two Jaina scholars, yet he contrived to test their worthiness. He knew it well that judging the capabilities in right earnest will be a delightful experience and quite pleasuresome.

Test : A Success: After having decided accordingly, Achārya Dharsena put the two mendicants to test, who had arrived there to undertake study of the sacred texts under able guidance of the said Guru. He imparted two Vidyas (Exercises). One of them exceeded in syllables and the other was deficient. He instructed the two students to practice them after observing fast six times for every two days as an expiatory act and by virtue of constant devotion and profound dedication, they should attain total accomplishment in the said Vidyas. The Munis started accomplishing the said Vidyas. The chief goddesses of the said Vidyas graced them by making an appearance. The teeth of one of the said female deities, were visibly out and the other was one—eyed. The Jaina monks were highly amazed to watch such deformities in heavenly bodies. No deformity is possible in celetial bodies. Both of them were apt in recitation and application of Mantras. Hence, after adding adequate number of syllables in the Mantras of the Vidyā in order to make up the deficiency and setting aside the additional syllables from the Mantras of the other Vidyā, they again repeated the performance for successful culmination of the endeavour and accomplishment of the desired ends. This time they were successful in their spiritual attempt. They were very much delighted to find that both the chief goddesses had made their appearance in their natural charming and auspicious forms. Both the scholars came over to Achārya Dharsena and related the whole story how they had wielded the Mantras of the Vidyās effectively after making necessary amends and how they had been graced by the goddesses with their auspicious appearance. Achārya was completely satisfied and started imparting knowledge of the sacred texts with effect from an auspicious week day occasioned by lucky stars.

Imparting of Spiritual Knowledge After Self-Satisfaction: It is obvious from above citation that Achārya Dharsena was convinced of the capabilities of the two pupils. He was fully satisfied that both the students were competent and worthy to acquire perfection in the sacred texts. He, energetically, began imparting knowledge to the students. The obliging nature of a guru and total dedication, perseverance and hard labour on the part of the students are bound to culminate in successful completion of the studies and attainment of true perfection. The same happened. Pushpadant and Bhūtbali started learning and acquiring knowledge of the spiritual texts with profound devotion, dedication, obedience and sense of reverence. Achārya Dharsena gladly imparted highest spiritual knowledge of Agamic texts that were in his memory and, in this way, the two aspirants successfully completed their course or religious studentship and attained perfection in spiritual texts, they had aspired for.

The author of Dhavalā commentary writes that it was at forenoon on the 11th day of the latter half of the month of Asārh (According to Hindu calendar) when the study of desired texts was over. The students, having accomplished their studies, were eagre to stay for some more time with their guru and serve him. However, things were to take their own shape. Achārya Dharsena instructed them to return immediately. However, Indranandi writes in his book that they were asked to leave next day. Although, it was not relished by the two disciples, yet they could not dare to act against the wishes of their mentor. They left the place.

Sojournment of journey during four months of rainy season was near at hand. Under Jaina tradition, the period starts from 14th day of the lunar fortnight of Asārh month. Jaina Sādhus generally stop undertaking any journey during 4 months of rainy season. They make a sojourn in a specified village or town till the end of rainy season. Here a very pertinent question arises why Achārya Dharsena was so anxious to make them leave at the earliest possible irrespective of the fact that rainy season was to start shortly after.

Departure of Munis : Probabilities

There could be several likelihoods why Achārya Dharsena felt constrained to instruct his resident pupils to leave his place immediately.

Achārya Dharsena had sent a written message to the organisers of the conference of Jaina Munis at Mahimānagri to nominate two learned students to reach his place so that he could impart knowledge of Agamic texts, retained in his memory. Most probably he might have got an inkling in his mind that his life span was extremely short and his end was quite near. Otherwise, there was no impelling ground for him to take the initiative himself. After he had imparted the knowledge of the highest spiritual texts to the students, he must have imagined that his end was near and he could breathe his last any moment. He might have considered that the students had completed their studies and they were required to return ultimately. The students to whom he had imparted knowledge with such keenness and affection, must not be allowed to witness his death and feel agonized on that account. Probably also, he might have thought that in case he allowed his students to stay with him and serve him while he was on death bed, he might develope fancy for them. They were so dear, humble and obedient to him that he could have feeling of affection and attachment for them. Such feelings were in contrast with the basic characteristics of saintly life—a life of absolute renunciation, forbearance and detachment.

Presumably also, Achārya Dharsena was a true ascetic, devoutly austere, leading life of self-mortification and practising severe penances. He was a true Yogi. As soon as he found that he had already imparted spiritual knowledge to his pupils and accomplished his aim, he might have decided to get absorbed in meditation again and thought why he should permit his students to stay with him any longer.

However, the said assumption does not appeal to the mind. There was no occasion, whatsoever, for such a haste to instruct the students to leave his place as soon as they could. He could go on with his meditative concentration even in their presence. There was no likelihood of any disturbance in his spiritual performances even if they decided to stay for a few more days.

Another presumption could as well be that Achārya Dharsena might have thought that why he should be instrumental in delay of propagation of the highest spiritual knowledge even for a day after he had imparted to his resident pupils. Accordingly, he might-have instructed them to leave immediately. However, the said presumption too is not very appealing.

Reflections of Indranandi and Shridher

Indranandi and Shridher both have reflected in their respective composition, styled `Shrutavatār' that Achārya Dharsena did have an inkling in his mind that his end was near ashand. His disciples might not be unnecessarily grieved to see him dead. Therefore, he asked them to leave as early as possible without least delay.

Making Sojourn at Ankleshwar during four Months of Rainy Season

Pushpadant and Bhūtbali departed immediately, considering that they were bound to carry out the instructions of their guru. They came over to Ankleshwar. Indranandi has mentioned the name of the town as `Kurishwar' in his book. It is also cited that both the Munis had arrived there after travelling for nine days. It follows that in case they left Girinagar on 11th day of the lunar fortnight of Asārh month, they reached Ankleshwar on the fourth day of the dark half of the month (the fortnight of the waning moon) of Shrāvan and in case they had started their journey on the 12th day of the latter half of Asārh month, they arrived at Ankleshwar on fifth day of the first fortnight of Shrāvan month that is to say, the Munis reached there after six or seven days of the start of Chaturmas (A period of 4 months, reckoned from the 14th day in the bright half of Asārh to the 14th day in the bright half of Kartika). Although, their journey for a period of one week after the start of 4 months of rainy season was against the tenets and moral code, prescribed for Jaina mendicants, yet they had to do so under exceptional circumstances. They had hardly 3 days at their disposal for movement and it was well-nigh impossible for them to arrive at a suitable place for making a sojourn during four months of rainy season. Hence they had, practically, no other alternative but to make a sojourn at Ankleshwar during rainy season.

Acharya Dharsena : Attainment of Final Liberation

Only a small part of biographical sketch of Achārya Dharsena, an eminent scholar and a true yogi, profoundly devoted to spiritual accomplishments, is manifest before us. No other description, relating to the earlier or later period of his life, is available. His ardent desire to impart knowledge of highest spiritual texts to competent and deserving hands; availability of really capable, inquisitive and competent resident disciples, imparting of spiritual knowledge and, thereafter, attainment of final liberation is all what is known about him. After instructing Pushpadant and Bhūtbali to leave his place without unnecessary delay, he departs for ever. What happened, thereafter, is completely in dark. Generally, it has been the fate of each and every leading scholar and devout in India.

However, in the light of the material available, citations and inferences, we shall further like to discuss about Achārya Dharsena in ensuing pages where the context may demand.

Production of Shatkhaṇḍāgama

Jaina Munis, Pushpadant and Bhūtbali made a sojourn during rainy season at Ankleshwar. It appears in Dhavalā commentary : "After completing the period of sojourn, Achārya Pushpadant moved to `Vanvāsa' region along with Jinapālita, a new disciple, Bhūtbali `Bhattaraka' (A title of respect or distinction used with the names of highly respected and learned scholars) shifted to `Dramika' region. Subsequently, Achārya Pushpadant granted initiation to Jinapālita. Achārya wrote `Sat-Prarūpṇā' Sūtra in 20 chapters in aphoristic style and taught the Sūtras to his new disciple, Jinapālita. Thereafter, he sent his composition to Bhūtbali "Bhattāraka."

Several new facts are disclosed to us from the citation in Dhavalā commentary. A new mendicant, Jinapālita, is referred to us. After meeting him, Achārya Pushpadant moves to Vanvāsa region along with him is, somewhat confusing. There is apparently no relevance of this version. Where does Achārya Pushpadant come across Jinapālita and why he decides to move to Vanvāsa region along with him, is slightly intriguing and calls for the preceding and the following sequence, which is, however, missing.

Dr. Hiralal Jaina, an erudite scholar of oriental languages—Prākritas and Apbhransha etc. and editor of Shatkhaṇḍāgama has referred to a word `Datthūna' of Prākrita dialect, which appears in `Dhavalā' Commentary in order to provide an explanation. In Prākrita dialect, the word `Datthūna' is normally used to denote past tense, thereby meaning `after having seen'! However, Dr. Jaina points out that he has also found the use of the said word in the sense of Sanskrit word `Drishtum' which literally menas `for seeing'. He has also quoted a few illustrations from `Paumchariyaṁ', showing similar inflected forms of root words.

Indranandi writes that Jinapālita was nephew (sister's son) of Achārya Pushpadant. It is quite possible that Jinapālita might have been a well-mannered and accomplished boy and Achārya Pushpadant might have developed a keen inclination to initiate him as his disciple since he was eagre to make over the knowledge of rare spiritual texts which had been revealed to him by Achārya Dharsena, a great seer and an accomplished sage of his age. As a matter of fact, competent hands are rarely available. Because of his close family relations and personal knowledge of his talents and capabilities, Achārya Pushpadant must have appreciated that Jinapālita was the right choice to be imparted knowledge of the scarce texts and that he will be doing full justice with what he was considered fit for. Thus, with a view to meet Jinapalita and persuade him to adopt saintly life, after renouncing all his attachments with worldly objects, he might have decided to move to Vanvāsa where Jinapālita was residing and which was also the birth place of Achārya Pushpadant. Therefore, it was quite natural on his part to go there.

The possibility of going to Vanvāsa, in order to meet Jinapālita, stands corroborated by the fact that he was initiated by Achārya Pushpadant and he composed a sacred treatise, containing the rare texts of highest spiritual knowledge, revealed by his guru, Achārya Dharsena, so that the latter could have their first hand knowledge and retain them in his memory to teach the texts to his disciples.

After obtaining knowledge of the Sūtras from his spiritual guide and mentor, Achārya Pushpādant, Jinapālita moves to the place of Achārya Bhūtbali who examines Jinapālita and finds that he was well aware with `Vīsadi Sūtras', composed by Achārya Pushpādnat. However, Achārya Bhūtbali is very much worried to learn that the life span of Achārya Pushpādant was too short. He, obviously, feels concern that it was his moral duty to complete the sacred treatise, partially composed by his colleague, Achārya Pushpādant.

The above version also lends support to the belief that Achārya Pushpādant might have come to know of his short life and been worried on that account to find out a competent and deserving resident pupil whom he could impart knowledge of the rare texts and save them from obliteration. He might have then centered his mind on his nephew, Jinapālita.

Accomplishment of Shatkhandāgama

It is cited above that Achārya Pushpādant was able to compose only 20 chapters of Shatkhaṇḍāgama in his short span of life. The author of Dhavala commentary on Shatkhaṇḍāgama writes that Achārya Bhūtbali was, obviously, worried to ensure completion of the holy scripture for the benefit of entire Jaina community. He, therefore, started writing the sacred book from the next chapter, styled `Dravyapramānānugama' and completed Shatkhaṇḍāgama.

At the very start of the chapter, `Dravyapramānānugama' it has been pointed out that it was the creation of Achārya Bhūtbali. For example "— The mendicants who have learnt regarding existence of 14 kinds of animate objects are further enlightened about the strength of each sentient being."

In this way, accomplishment of Shatkhaṇḍāgama, a large voluminous scripture is, undoubtedly, the result of combined understanding and co-ordinated efforts of the two great seers, Achārya Pushpādant and Bhūtbali.

Indranandi describes in his book `Shrutāvtār' how the great scripture `Shatkhaṇḍāgama' had been accomplished: "Achārya Bhūtbali attentively listened to

`Sat-Prarupṇa', recited loudly by Jinapālita. From the said narration, it was manifestly clear to him that Achārya Pushpādant was eagre for creation of Shatkhaṇḍāgama for the benefit of Jaina Sādhus and the people of average intelligence. He realized through religious contemplation that the life span of Achārya Pushpādant was too short. He took the onus upon himself and composed 5 sections of Shatkhaṇḍāgama, comprising of 6,000 Sūtras (aphorisms), including those, written earlier by Achārya Pushpādant. Thereafter, he composed sixth section, styled `Mahabandh', comprising of 30,000 verses.

It follows that 20 paragraphs of 1st section of Shatkhaṇḍāgama, styled `Jivasthān', comprising of 177 aphorisms had been written by Achārya Pushpādant. The remaining portion of 1st section; second section titled `Kṣullaka-Bandh'; third section, titled—`Bandh'-Swāmitiva-vichaya'; 4th section, styled `Vedanā' and 5th section titled `Vargaṇā' in all comprising of 5823 aphorisms, had been written by Achārya Bhūtbali. In this manner, five sections of Shatkhaṇḍāgama contained 6000 aphorisms. The sixth section of Shatkhaṇḍāgama, written by Achārya Bhūtbali, incorporates 30,000 verses. It is also cited in `Dhavala' and `Jayadhavala' commentaries that the sixth section, titled `Maha-Bandh' had been composed by Achārya Bhūtbali. In this way, Achārya Pushpādant and Achārya Bhūtbali are believed to be joint authors of Shatkhaṇḍāgama.

The sanctity of Shatkhaṇḍāgama is established in `Dhavala' commentary, which reads : "The contents of the said religious scripture are based on the utterances and preachings of Lord Mahāvira, himself, the sacred texts, heard through revelation by Gautama were compiled by him and subsidiarily written by leading Jaina Achāryas—Pushpadant and Bhutbali, free from worldly illusions and delusive feelings of love and hatred.

The commentator further elaborates that in order to establish the sanctity and significance of a religious treatise, it is essential to indicate that its contents are based on the authoritative utterances of a Jaina Arhat or an omniscient. It is perfectly justified."

The wordings used by Achārya Virasena, in his commentary on Shatkhaṇḍāgama to the effect that the contents of the holy scripture are in perfect consonance with the preachings of Tirthankers, are self-speaking.

Worship of Shatkhaṇḍāgama : Ceremony on Shruta Panchmi

As soon as Achārya Bhūtbali had finished all the six sections of Shatkhaṇḍāgama, it is believed there was great jubilation all around in the Jaina institution. The author of Dhavalā commentary has made no other comment except what has been cited above in regard to the completion of the holy scripture. However, Indranandi has made a mention in his renowned composition `Shruta-Avtār' which reads: "Achārya Bhūtbali, after having accomplished Shatkhaṇḍāgama, worshipped the holiest treatise (forming part of Jaina Āgamas) on the 5th day of lunar fortnight of Jyeshtha month (As per Hindu calendar) alongwith all the followers of four categories, constituting Jaina organisation. Accordingly, the said day came to be known as `Shruta Panchmi', the day on which the Jainas worship their Agamas and other sacred treatises even now."

Achārya Bhūtbali was happy to send the accomplished manuscript of

Shatkhanḍāgama to Achārya Pushpādant through his resident pupil, Jinapālita. Achārya Pushpādant was, obviously, too glad to find that his cherished dream had materialized. He exhibited no less zeal to worship the holy book along with all the members of his Sangh.

From the above citation, it is obvious that Achārya Pushpādant whose life span was believed to be too short, was alive by the time of completion of Shatkhanḍāgama. It also reveals that Achārya Pushpādant was decidedly elder in age to his colleague, Achārya Bhūtbali. Accordingly, as a mark of respect towards him, he had arranged to forward the manuscript through his resident pupil, Jinapālita, for his approval. The author of Dhavalā commentary has paid his obeisance firstly to Achārya Pushpādant and, thereafter, to Bhūtbali, in the benedictory verse, appearing at the start of his commentary. which also lends support to the view that the initial portion of Shatkhanḍāgama had been composed by Achārya Pushpādant and subsequent portion by Achārya Bhūtbali.

Dhavalā Commentary : Really a Unique Creation

From the very beginning, great significance is being attached to Shatkhanḍāgama under Digamber tradition. Consequently, many scholars have made comments on it. The prominent names of the commentators are—Srikund Kund (2nd Century of Vikrama era); Shamkunḍa (third century of Vikrama era). Tumbulūr (fourth century of Vikrama era); Samant Bhadra (fifth century of Vikrama era) and Bappadeva (Between sixth to eighth century of Vikrama era).

In the ninth century of Vikrama era, Achārya Virasen, an erudite scholar of his age, had written Dhavalā commentary on Shatkhanḍāgama which is comprised of 72,000 verses. Achārya Virasena was an outstanding scholar. It appears that he had undertaken profound study of all grammatical and allied compositions, relating to Shatkhanḍāgama which is explicit from his repeated references and analytical discussion, made in his annotation. On one hand, his commentary is voluminous in size and on the other, it is a unique creation in as much as the author spared no pains in undertaking minute study and critical evaluation of divergent views and ideologies of various Achāryas, intellectuals and sages before making comments on the rare text of Shatkhanḍāgama. No doubt, it is unparallel so far as elaboration of Indian philosophical and religious doctrines are concerned. Achārya Virasena deserves all appreciation for the tremendous work, he has done.

The said commentary has been greatly commended by learned scholars and scholarly persons because of its clarity and elaborateness in expression and style. The said commentary began to be used unhesitatingly by scholars for reading and studying. Presumably, after accomplishment of Dhavalā commentary, the use and consultation of other commentaries almost came to a stop. No other commentary is available now. Possibly, a copy of any other commentary may be lying under lock in any one of the ancient liabraries of Southern India.

Kāshai — Prābhrita

There is another accomplished scripture under Digamber tradition, namely `Kashāi-Prābhrita', which incorporates highest spiritual and philosophical texts, based on the teachings of Jaina Arhats or omniscients. It has been written by Achārya Guṇadher. Whereas Shatkhaṇḍāgama is treated as the first doctrinal composition, `Kashāi-Prābhrita' is the second accomplishment on the higher truths of Jaina religion and philosophy, based on the utterances of Jaina Arhats and omniscients. From the very beginning the said book too has been held in great esteem immediately after its accomplishment. It has also been written in Shorseni dialect. Several explanatory works and commentaries came to be written on Kashāi-Prābhrita' as well but none of them are available now.

Achārya Virasena, the renowned author of `Dhavalā commentary, also undertook to write a commentary or gloss on `Kashāi-Prābhrita'. He intended to write an exhaustive commentary on it like that on Shatkhaṇḍāgama. He was able to write a small portion of the desired extensive annotation, comprising of 20,000 verses only when he breathed his last. However, the work did not remain suspended. His learned successor and an erudite scholar, Jinasena, made up his mind and undertook to complete the work. He too was a studious scholar and well-informed. He took up the challenge and devoted himself to complete the job with dedication, zeal and perseverance. Accordingly, the commentary on `Kashāi-Prābhrita' was accomplished which comprised, of 60,000 verses, out of which 40,000 verses had been composed by Achārya Jinasena. We shall discuss about the nature of its contents in the ensuing pages, as per demand of the context.

Shatkhaṇḍāgama : Taken out from the Lock and Key of the Library

Shatkhaṇḍāgama is treated as a most authentic and dignified scripture under Digamber tradition, which forms the subject-matter of the present discussion. The only manuscript of Shatkhaṇḍāgama on palmyra leaves, was lying intact in an ancient-library of South India. Digamber ideology of Jaina religion was highly popular in South. Therefore, it may not be out of context here to mention in brief how Digamber ideology impressed and gained momentum in South. On the contrary, it may prove helpful in comprehending the subject. Hence a few important points are being discussed herein below :

Expansion of Jaina Religion in South

Jaina religion had its origin in North India. First Jaina Tirthanker, Lord Rishabh Deva, belonged to Ayodhya and last Tirthanker, Lord Mahāvira to Vaishāli. Ayodhya is located in almost central part of North India while Vaishāli is situated in eastern territory of India.

Jaina religion came into existence in Northern India and spread far and wide upto Indian ocean in extreme South. For thousands of years, it continued to gain prominence and win immense popularity in South. Jainaism was held in great esteem and veneration by both the rulers and the people at large.

It is traditionally believed that initial Tirthanker, Lord Rishabh, and last Tirthanker, Lord Mahāvira, had paid visits to South which provided great impetus

1. Kshatrā Chudāmani by Odeyadeva Vadībhsimitra; the legend is retold in the Kannada Jeevandhārā Charite of Bhaskara and the Tamil Jeevkā Chintamani of Tiruthukka-devar.

to the spread of Jaina religion in Southern territories. In this connection, Prof. S.K. Ramchandra Rao writes: "There is a legend, appearing in a Sanskrit book[1] of eleventh century that Lord Mahāvira himself came to the South, to the Kannada region more specifically, known at that time as Hemangada desh, during the reign of King Jivendhra, whom Lord Mahāvira met and admitted him into the ascetic fold. There is a belief that even during the days of the very first Tirthankara Rishabha, presumably several thousands of years before the arrival of the twenty-fourth Tirthanker, Lord Mahāvira, (599 B.C.), there were several South Indian princes in the entourage of Lord Rishabha and that they finally, retired to the Satrunjaya hills in Pālitānā (Saurashtra).

However, it is only a legend of the past. Nevertheless, it is a fact that Jaina religion had greatly influenced the people in South for very long time.

A Large Religious Congregation, Sponsored by Emperor Khārvel

It is essential to refer to an important event, having taken place in Kalinga region. Khārvel was a mighty king of Kalinga dynasty in modern Orrisa. He is believed to have acceded to the throne in the year 143B.C. He was a true follower and devout of Jaina religion. Just as emperor Ashoka had spared no pains in contributing his best for spread of Buddhist religion, similarly, his grand-son, Sampriti, had made enormous contribution to propagation and spread of Jaina religion in Northern India. Likewise, Khārvel, ruler of Kalinga region, had concentrated all his energies in propagation and spread of Jaina religion in whole of South India.

Emperor Khārvel was, undoubtedly, a great warrior. He was conqueror of many realms in all directions—such as `Shunga' and `Satvāhan' dynasties and Greeks in parts of Northern India. Nearly, all irrepressible powers had been subdued and thrown out of their kingdoms. Thereafter, he arranged to sponsor a large congregation for extensive propagation, revealing of doctrines and flourishing of Jaina religion in remote areas in which eminent scholars, Sādhus, seers, kings, avowed to Jaina philosophy, and distinguished persons gladly participated. There were detailed discussions and lengthy deliberations on many topics, relating Jaina religion.

A ceremonious reception was accorded to emperor Khārvel by large gathering of participants and laudatory attributes were applied such as—`a great conqueror'; `a propitious king; a Sanyasi King, detached from worldly pleasures and a great religioner king' etc. It is cited that the king of Pāndya (Name of a dynasty in the extreme South of India, lying to the South-West of `Choladesa'. It may be identified with the modern Tinnevelly in Kerala) had supplied a ship-load consignment of rice for feeding the participants.

In nutshell it will be sufficient to say that Jaina religion had spread in Southern India, prior to the commencement of Christian era.

With the pious and active co-operation of emperor Khārvel, and other kings of South, the message of Jaina religion spread far and wide in Southern India.

Although, Jaina religion had its sway in Tamilnadu and Andhra Pradesh as well, yet its impact was great in Karnataka. It was whole-heartedly welcomed there. The story how the followers and religious mendicants under spiritual leadership of Achārya Bhadrabāhu in Northern India, were forced to move to

Karnataka State as a result of terrible effects of continous famine, lends credence to the fact that Jainas had great influence there. Obviously, thousands of Sādhus, moving to South in Karnataka, were confident and were free from worries of feeding themselves. They were sure that they would not have to starve after reaching Karnataka and they would be in a position to pass the unfortunate period happily.

A Curiosity : Satisfaction: Only Digambers gained popularity in south and not Shwetambers. Even now, all the followers of Jainism in South are Digambers and none of them belongs to Shwetamber Sect. Primarily, they are the traders or businessmen who had shifted from Rajasthan and Gujarat to South and established their businesses there. However, it is a moot question why Digamber ideology alone had been adopted in South. Presumably, at the time of split in the Jaina institution in North, there was very little impact of Jaina religion in South. Possibly, Digamber scholars and learned seers must have been too zealous to carry the message of Digamber Sect. Alongwith it, they might have cherished a desire to nourish an independent area for settling and expanding their organisation. Accordingly, they might have made up a firm mind to propagate their religious doctrines extensively in South. Else, they might have realized that the people in South were comparatively more prolific and conscious. For leading the nude life they might have found the climate of South more congenial since it was located under tropical zone. There could be a few other reasons as well which might have prompted the religious mendicants of Digamber Sect to move to South. The efforts, put in by Digamber scholars, in consistency with their perseverance and zeal while propagating their ideology, yielded favourable results. The impact of Digamber ideological and philosophical doctrines is clearly established on undertaking critical examination of literary, cultural and sculptural accomplishments in South.

Certain Leading—Most Intellectuals of Digamber Sect in South

No doubt, South proved to be highly prolific for production and growth of canonical literature, relating to Digambers. Eminent Digamber Acharyas and scholars, born in South, greatly contributed to the accomplishment of multifarious literature on Jaina philosophy, metaphysics and spiritualism, covering almost all important topics, which goes a long way in enriching Indian literature thoughts and reflection. It should not be deemed an exaggeration to add that highly accomplished or superb type of religious books, belonging to Digamber tradition, had been composed or reduced to writing in south. By virtue of their unique and creative books, they had greatly enriched Jaina canonical literature. Achārya Kund-Kunda (who lived near about the beginning of Christian era) was the key author of several significant religious books, namely—`Samaya-Sār'; `Pravachan-Sār'; `Panchāstikāya' and `Niyamsar' besides several other compositions. He was highly esteemed and considered a celebrated Achārya—so much so—that he was treated next to Gandher Gautama (First and foremost disciple of Lord Mahāvira). Achārya Umāswami, author of `Tatvarth Sūtra', a highly', celebrated accomplishment on Jaina philosophy (1st century A.D.); Achārya Samantabhadra, really a great genius, an influential preacher, author of several authoritative books, including `*Āpta-Mimāṁsa*'. He lived from 120 to 185 A.D.; Achārya Devanandi Pujyapāda, a great thinker, author, grammarian; an expert in observance of Yoga (meditative contemplation) a devout, poet, author of highly spoken commentary, styled `Sarvārtha Sidhi' on `Tatvārtha Sūtra'; writer of *Jainendra Vyakarṇa* (a grammatical composition); Achārya Akalaṇka (Seventh century A.D.), a prominent teacher and founder of `Philosophical system of Nyāya School of Jaina religion', a wise thinker, author of several highly accomplished books, such as—*Tatvārtha-Rajvātika*, *Ashṭashati*, *Nyāya-Vinishchaya* etc. These are a few leading Acharyas and seers of Digamber Sect whose names are worth to be written in golden letters. Achāryas Virasena, Jinasena, Gunabhadra, Nemichandra etc. and several other outstanding scholars, literatures and writers had taken birth on the auspicious land of South India, who had left great impact in their respective field of activity.

Influence of Jaina Religion in South

Infact, the Jaina religion and its canonical literature had greatly influenced the people in South. The spread of Jaina ideology in South was not confined to religious sphere only but it had a wide impact on the day-today life of the people. How far the public life was guided in South by the ideology of Jainism, will be apparent from the following assertion of Prof. S.K. Ramchandra Rao:

> "The history of Jainism would altogether be incomplete without a consideration of Southern developments. Similarly, the history of South India will equally be incomplete without treating of the part played by Jainism".

Intuitionism, ideological and philosophical doctrines, their impact on day-today public life and ceaseless cultural and literary pursuits—are the criterions to judge the attainments of Jainism in South and on examination we find that they hold water and are no less impressive.

Influence of Jain Religion in Karnātaka

Jainism had spread far and wide in South, more especially in Karnataka which was really astounding.

Kadamba Dynasty: A few characteristic-features of Jainism—politeness, simplicity, piousness and sense of endurance found in its propagators and propounders greatly attracted several dynasties in South to either embrace the religion or provide backing and incentive for its propagation. Even the kingdoms, which were primarily staunch followers of Vedic religion, readily contributed for growth and spread of Jaina religion in South. The initial centuries of Christian era had witnessed the advent and rise of Kādamba dynasty. The rulers of the said dynasty were basically followers of Vedic religion. However, they extended every possible assistance for spread of Jainism in South. By the end of the fourth century, king Kākutsya was the ruler of the said dynasty who extended full support to the preceptors of Jaina religion. King Mrigesh Verma had two princes, namely, Bhānu Vermā and Ravi Vermā. Both of them too spared no pains to patronize the religion.

Ganga Dynasty: Right from latter half of fourth century to tenth century, there was reign of Ganga dynasty over major part of Karnātakā. The said dynasty had lent full support to the propagators of Jaina religion in Karnātakā. The founding head of Ganga dynasty in Karnātakā was king Konguṇi Verma. It is believed to have been founded in the year 350 A.D. Majority of the rulers of the said dynasty were devotees of Lord Vishnu. However, it is found that they reposed full faith in the ideals of Jainism as well. In this regard, there is a hear-say. At the time of establishment of the said kingdom, Sri Singhnandi was the spiritual head of Jaina organisation. He had made substantial contribution in founding and establishment of the said dynasty. Resultantly, the rulers of the said kingdom had an obvious regard for Jaina religion.

It is cited in the Gazetteer of Mysore that Ganga dynasty was the pillar of Jainism in South. Nandgiri (Nandi hills) was its fort and Kūvālal (identified with modern Kolar) was its capital. Jaina Tirthankers were their gods and Jainism their religion.[1] The grandson of the founder of the said dynasty was Hari Verma. During the reign of king Hari Verma, Talkudu was adopted as capital in place of Kuālal. Thereafter, the said dynasty came to be known as `Gangas of Talkudu'.

In the year 475 A.D., Avinita ascended to the throne of Ganga dynasty. He was the renowned king of the said kingdom. He took active interest in the growth and expansion of Jaina religion. His guru and spiritual mentor was Achārya Vijaykirti. He issued grants of rent-free lands for upkeep of Jaina monasteries. Although, king Avinita was a devotee of Shaivism, yet he equally reposed faith in ideals of Jainism too and provided all possible support for its growth and expansion.

Durvinita succeeded his father, Avinita. He was a great warrior stoic and completely detached. He was enthroned in the year 482 A.D. On one hand, he was a great warrior and on the other, a staunch devout. In petrographic inscriptions, he has been adored with the attributes of `Dharmaraj Yudhishthirā' (The latter was known for his truthfulness and righteousness than for any military achievements; He was formally crowned emperor of Hastinapur in the epic age of *Mahābhārata*) and `Vaivasta Manu' (a celebrated personage regarded as the representative seventh Manu and father of human race according to Hindu mythology). Achārya Devanandi `Pujyapāda', an eminent scholar and author of the celebrated commentary `Sarvārtha Sūtra' on `Tatvārth Sūtra', as already discussed in the foregoing pages, was his guru and spiritual guide. The king greatly contributed to the growth of Jaina religion.

Durvinita was himself an eminent scholar. It is said that the epic poet, Bhārvi, author of the renowned Sanskrit treatise `Kirātārjuniya', had received patronage of his royal court for some time. King Durvinita has written a commentary, on the 15th Chapter of `Kiratarjuniya' in Kannada language. The king is considered as one of the best prosers of Kannada language.

Durvinita is also believed to be originally a Vaishnavite (devotee of Lord Vishnu). However, he extended full support for boosting up Jainism in Karnataka during his reign. His ardent faith in Vaishnavism did not hinder in his moral support to the growth of Jaina religion in any way. Undoubtedly, he was an extremely liberal and noble-minded king.

Mushkar was the prince of King Durvinita. He was having immense faith in Jainism. He exhibited great enthusiasm is spread of the ideals of Jaina religion. He saw to it that several Jaina monasteries were constructed during his reign. His

1. Lewice Rice, *Mysore Gazetteer*, 1, page 388.

successors also further augmented their efforts in continuing the said tradition.

The last king of Ganga dynasty was Mārsingh II. He was a great warrior and extremely religious. He was eulogized with laudatory attributes of `Ganga Vajra' and `Dharmāvtār'. During last phase of his life, he attained initiation by Achārya Ajitasena. He attained final emancipation after observance of total detachment from worldly objects and exercising self-mortification by way of physical and mental concentration. He is believed to have obtained final salvation in the year 974 A.D. With his death, the rule of Ganga dynasty also came to an end. The status of subsequent successors, belonging to Ganga dynasty, was no better than feudal lords.

Chāmundarāya, A Staunch Devotee of Jaina Religion in Karnātaka

In the line of feudal lords, belonging to Ganga clan, an outstanding personality appeared on the scene who spared no pains to enhance the following of Jaina religion and enrich its culture. He was Chāmuṇḍārāya, a military general and minister of feudal Lord, Rajmalla IV, of Ganga dynasty. The period of reigning by feudal Lord, Rajmalla, is believed to be 974 to 984 A.D. Chāmuṇḍarāya was a great warrior. He did his best to add to the prestige and glory of Rajmalla. The said army commander has been highly eulogised in a stone inscription of Shravanbelgola in Karnātaka. He has been adored with eulogical attributes of a `staunchly devout'; `a distinguished hero'; `a valient fighter like a lion', an excellent hero in all three worlds; all powerful and a fearful like a death sting for the army of the foe; strictly truthful like king Yudhishthira and an excellent soldier etc., which are illustrative of his overwhelming influence, gallantry and renown.

The other aspect of his glorious life was his religiosity and literary pursuits. His grip in these matters was also exemplary. He was an outstanding scholar. He had composed *Trishashtishalākāpurushmahāpurāṇa* in Kannada language which was a unique creation of Kannada literature Chamuṇḍrāya had also written `Charita-Sār' in Sanskrit. Thus, long strides were taken in the fields of enriching Jaina canonical literature, art and culture during the life time of the distinguished warrior and intellectual. Achārya Nemichandra, `Sidhānt--Chakravarty' had written a significant book under the style *Gommata Sār*, basing his composition over the said book, which is held in great esteem under Digamber tradition and its contents are evalued at par with those of `Shatkhaṇḍāgama and Dhavalā commentry.

Chāmuṇḍārāya is accredited for getting erected a huge statue of `Gommateshwar-Bāhubali', installed at Indragiri (a hill) at Shravanbelgola in Karnataka, which is no less than a wonder of the world. A legend goes that great emperor Bharat had got a huge statue of Lord Bāhubali erected in an arch shape, being 525 ft. high at Poḍanpur. It is believed that Chāmuṇḍarāya had drawn inspiration from the said story for getting a similar grand statue raised. Chāmuṇḍarāya is believed to have lived in between the latter half of tenth century and the first half of the eleventh century A.D.

Rāshtrakūta Dynasty: Amongst the dynasties which had lent whole-hearted support in propagation of the ideals of Jainism and accomplishment of canonical works for spread of Jaina religion, the rulers of Rāshtrakūta dynasty had played a significant role. The said dynasty had ruled over Karnataka from eighth century to tenth century A.D.

Hoyasala Dynasty: Hoyasala dynasty had reigned over Karnataka from 11th century to 13th century A.D. The kings of the said dynasty were devouts of Jaina religion. Just as Jaina Achārya Singhnandi, had played a predominant role in founding and establishment of Ganga dynasty rule over Karnataka, similarly, Jaina Achārya Shantideva had extended his blessings and cooperation in establishment of the said dynastic rule. The rulers of the said kingdom were quite enthusiastic to lend their whole-hearted support for spread of the ideals of Jaina religion and philosophy. Several splendid Jaina monasteries and statues were got raised during the rule of the said dynasty.

Besides the above important dynasties, the rulers of Vijaynagar and several other kingdoms had made tremendous contribution to the growth and expansion of the said religion in Karnataka.

Summary

In this way, tremendous influence exercised by the Kings and their courtiers, holding exalted positions and with the active cooperation and the faith reposed by the people in Jaina Achāryas and as a soothing consequence of extreme curiosity, longing and excessive zeal and devotion of the public, long strides were taken in the growth and spread of religion, accomplishment of Jaina canonical literature and progress of Jaina arts and culture in South, particularly in Karnataka which is certainly a glorious chapter of the history relating to the religions in India and has great significance even now from numerous viewpoints.

Mūdabidri, A Divine Place of Jainas in South like Vedic Kashi in North

The credit for preservation of Shatkhaṇḍāgama certainly goes to Karnataka state. The said scripture remained safe and intact in a small town, named Mūdabidri, situated in South of Karnataka.

Mūdabidri is considered a sacred centre of Jaina religion in South by Jaina community, having the same significance as Kashi for Vedic Hindus in North India. Thus, it should be believed that the said town of Mūdabidri enjoyed great repute amongst Jaina followers so far as the spread and growth of Jaina religion, its impact on the people, undertaking minute study, critical appreciation, evaluation, preservation and enrichment of Jaina philosophy are concerned. Especially in Karnataka State, Mūdabidri was the most renowned centre of Jaina religion, arts and culture. Extremely precious and valuable statues are lying installed here which really attract the attention of entire Jaina population throughout the world.

A Historic Account of Mūḍabidri

It may not be out of context to mention here the legendary and traditional history of Mūdabidri on the basis of reports and hearsays as also petrographic inscriptions, found here and there. In South, Jaina temples are technically known as `Vasadis'.

There are such 18 Vasadis at Mūdabidri. One of them is popularly called `Guru Vasadi' which is considered as most sacred and sanctified amongst all others. Manuscripts on palmyra leaves of 'Dhavalā', 'Jaya Dhavalā' and 'Maha Dhavalā' commentaries are lying safe here in a library under lock and key, insdie Guru Vasadi. Since the said books deal with the established principles and settled doctrines of Jaina religion, the place is also known as `Sidhānt'-Vasadi.

Rise and Progress of Mūdabidri

In 11th century A.D. or near about, there was a king, named Vallāladeva I, belonging to Hoyasala dynasty. During his reign, the town of Mūdabidri had greatly flourished. `Ālupa' kings of Tuluna dynasty, had further enhanced the dignity of the town in 13th century A.D. They happened to grant state recognition to the Tirthanker temple of Lord Pārashwanāth.

Again, during the reign of Vijayanagar dynasty in 15th century A.D. the rulers had further added to the grandeur of the said town. Although, the rulers of Vijayanagar were basically followers of Vedic religion, yet they had immense regard for Jaina temples as well. There is a stone inscription, got inscribed by King Devarāya II of Vijayanagar dynasty, relating to the year 1429 wherein there is also a mention of the said town. The town was identified by the name of `Venupur' also. It is cited in the said inscription that the habitants of Venupur or Mūdabidri are really excellent. They are pure-minded and honest. They observe purity in their performances and are ardent followers of Jaina ideals. They listen to the discourses of Jaina Acharyas with perfect attention and dedication.

One of the Vasadis, located in the town, is named `Hos-Vasadi'. It is also called `Tribhuvan Tilak Chūḍāmani'. Its main pavillion (a hall or a portion of the building consecrated to the deity) was got built up during the reign of `Mallikārjuna Immadidevarāya', king of Vijayanagar dynasty. Rulers of several other Kingdoms along with their distinguished wealthy courtiers contributed their best in adding to the grace and dignity of the town.

Late Dr. Hiralal Jain, an eminent scholar of Apbhransha Prākrita and the reputed editor of Shatkhanḍāgama, has made a mention of Mūdabidri in his preface of Satkhanḍāgama. It is stated that Pt. Loknath `Shāstry, resident of Mūḍabidri had furnished the requisite information in that regard. According to the said information, the literal meaning of the Kannada word, Mūdabidri," and its relative history are cited in the preface.

Analysis of the Word Mūdabidri

`Mūdabidri' comprises of two words—Mūda and bidure. In Kannada language, the word `Bidir' literally means bamboos. There was a time when `Sidhānt Vasadi' of Jaina religion was lying hidden under a cluster of bamboos. The temple was traced out after piercing through the said cluster. Accordingly, the place came to be known by the name of `Bidure'. In Kannada, the word `Mūda' means East and the word `Padu' signifies west. There is an ancient village, named Mulki, in West which is called `Padu-bidure'. Since the village, where Sidhānt Temple was found, is located on the east of the said village, it came to be called as `Mūdabidure'. The word `Mūdabidri' is only an adaptation of the word `Mūdabidure'. While analysing the word, it is amply evident that main emphasis has been laid on the word `Bidir', meaning bamboos, Probably on that very account, the said inhabitance also came to be known as `Vanshapur' or `Venupur'. The place is also named as `Vritpur' or `Vritipur', signifying that some time it had been the habitat of Jaina Sādhus, engaged in observance of religious austerities.

Sidhant Vasadi — An Anecdote

It is evident from the above description that the said place was like a forest, surrounded by bamboos. It is believed that about one thousand years ago, a Jaina Muni had visited the site from Shravanbelgola. He stayed in `Paḍuvasadi' temple. The said ancient temple exists in Mūdabidri even now. Several ancient manuscripts were found in the temple which were placed together in a Jaina monastery. One day, it so happened that the said Muni went out in the forest for evacuation of excrement. He noticed a lion and a cow mixing freely at the place where the temple of `Guru Vasadi' is now located. The Jaina Sādhu was highly amazed and thought that the site must have spectacular significance. He probed the matter and was greatly delighted to find a majestic idol of Lord Pārshvanāth, carved out of black stone in a standing posture, measuring nine arms in length and hidden in a cluster of bamboos. The entire Jaina community was full of joy.

They got the idol renewed and got a temple built up. The said temple is popularly known as `Guru Vasadi'. On the foot-stool of the idol of Lord Pārashvanāth, the date and year of its consecration has been inscribed. According to it, the initial installation of the Idol was carried out in Samvat year 636 of Shaka era, equivalent to the year 714 A.D. The front pavillion, known as Laxmi Mandapa was got constructed by a wealthy merchant of Chol dynasty. It was built up in the year 1535 A.D. It is believed that the total expenditure, incurred in construction of `Guru Vasadi' temple, amounted to Rs. 6 crores. Imagine the total cost of the temple at current rates. Presumably, the figure of total expenditure might also be including the cost of precious jem-studded idols, installed in the temple.

Mūdabidri : Establishment of an Institute for Bhattaraks (An epithet Applied to Great and Learned Jaina Scholars)

There was a king, named Vishnuvardhan belonging to Hoyasal dynasty. In the year 1117 A.D. he separated himself from Jaina religion and adopted Vaishnavism. On one hand, there is a long list of kings who, fundamentally, were followers of either Vaishnavism or Shaivism yet they extended all possibly help for spread of Jaina ideals in their kingdoms so much so that they deserve to be mentioned in golden letters and on the other, there is a black spot in history in as much as the king, belonging to Hoysal dynasty, who was originally a Jain, bade good bye to Jainism and turned Vaishnavite. He had started to destroy Jaina religion, its philosophy and culture altogether. The new religious converts are generally overwhelmed with surcharged emotions and they often turn out to be highly intolerant and dogmatic.

There was great influence of Jaina religion, its art and culture on the habitants of Holevidu. Several grand and magnificent temples of Jaina Tirthankers were in existence there. The said jealous king got them destroyed. He committed unbearable atrocities on the followers of the religion. The Jaina community was, obviously, too scared and agitated on this account. As per hearsay, there was divine wrath because of his excesses. A terrible earthquake rocked the territory. There were explosions on the oceanic land of Dor sea, resulting in a vast pit. King Vārsingh, succeeding King Vishnuvardhan and thereafter King Vallal Deva realised the mishap. They found that the people of their kingdom were growing restless and were in a revolting mood. With a view to calm down the growing commotion and mental disquietness, they got many temples of Jaina community renovated and several new temples erected. They granted rent-free lands for maintenance and upkeep of the temples. King Vallardeva did one more favour. In those days, Chāru Kirti was the Bhattarak (An epithet applied to a highly learned Jaina scholar) in Jain temple at Shravanbelgola in Karnataka. It is stated that he was well conversant with mystical formulas and Mantras for attainment of super-human faculties. He had been adorned with the attribute of `Panditāchārya' (A great scholar). King Vir Vallardeva invited him to the capital. Bhattāraka Chāru Kirti acceded to the request of the king and came over to Dor sea. He calmed down the riotous conditions by virtue of his mystical powers and pacified the agitated minds. The king felt greatly delighted to find that the glory of Jaina religion had re-established Bhattaraka Chārukirti `Panditacharya' moved to Mūdabidri along with the team of his disciples from the territory of Dor sea. Obviously, he must have found Mūdabidri more suitable place for propagation and revealing of Arhat doctrines by way of delivering discourses. There he laid foundation of Gurupith — Bhattaraka Institute. In nutshell, it is the brief account how Bhattaraka Pith came to be established at Mūdabidri. It is believed to have been founded in the year 1172 A.D. All subsequent Bhattarakas in Jaina temples also came to be known by the name of Chāru Kirti. After the death of initial Bhattaraka, Chāru Kirti began to be used as symptomatic name for each Bhattaraka.

It is believed that manuscripts of Shatkhanḍāgama and Dhavalā, Jayadhavala and Mahādhavala commentaries, written on palmyra leaves were brought over to the said Institute at Mūḍabidri from Bankāpur, district Dhārwār (Karnataka). Shifting of such eminent religious treatises to the Pith at Mūdabidri and placing them together reflects that the said Institute was held in great esteem amongst Jainas in South. Especially in Karnataka, it had earned great name and fame for coaching and studying of highest spiritual knowledge, relating to Jaina ideology. Consequent upon the same, it might have been found essential to bring over the holy manuscripts and keep them in the institute with due care. Accordingly, they were fetched from Bankapur or wherever they were available and brought to Mūdabidri. The authorities or those at the helms of affairs there might have handed them over without least reluctance. Else, how could it have been practically feasible?

Fundamental Religious Treatises of Jaina Religion at Mūdabidri

It is quite astonishing that only one maunscript of each of the above noted fundamental treatises of Jaina religion, highly accredited under Digamber tradition, could survive. There was a time when Digamber Munis were very much eagre to go through the rare texts of these celebrated books. Infact, it was considered inevitable to study the said holy books for gaining knowledge of theoretical aspects of Jaina ideology. Only those scholars were considered to be knowing the real truth, who were well conversant with the texts of Shatkhaṇḍāgama. However, it is very likely that the situation might have reversed later on. It has already been suggested earlier that after accomplishment of Dhavalā commentary on Shatkhaṇḍāgama, all the preceding commentaries had lost their significance and thrown out. They were completely ignored. Only the teaching and studying of Dhavalā commentary started exclusively. After writing of `Gommata Sār' by Achārya Nemichandra `Sidhant-Chakravarty', probably Dhavalā commentary had the same fate *i.e.* the scholars might have lost charm to study Dhavalā commentary and started to meet their purpose by going through `Gommat Sār' only which incorporated the essence of Shatkhaṇḍāgama and its allied compositions. By their very nature, the human-beings are easy-going. However, irrespective of the circumstances, such a tendency to follow a short cut must be avoided as far as possible.

The scope of thorough knowledge on the higher truths of religion and philosophy is too vast. One needs life-long dedication to be absorbed in it. Merely a make-shift policy to keep the work going will not yield any fruitful purpose. An easy-going person generally believes in stop-gap policy which is suicidal. The fact remains that the knowledge acquired by undertaking minute study of Shatkhaṇḍāgama and its commentary, will never be possible to be obtained by merely going through Gommat-Sār.

There are two sides of knowledge. Infact, it is a means and an end both. Hence, no significance be attached to what is easily attainable without putting in much strain or efforts to be secured. Constant devotion and dedication are the key to success. Any way, the said rare manuscripts were placed together in the library of Mūdabidri temple under lock and key. They were then the objects of merely having a look at or paying respects.

The flow of knowledge is like the flowing water of sacred Ganges. It must always keep flowing as knowledge is not like the stationary water of pool. The rare holy scriptures, containing highest spiritual and philosophical knowledge of Jaina religion were, unfortunately, confined to the precincts of the Temple library. They had the same fate like that of stagnated water in a small pond or pool.

Mūdabidri is the holiest place of Digambers in the country. Every year, thousands of Jainas pay a visit to the said centre of pilgrimage and have a view of the highly precious, jems-studded statues of Arhats and rare manuscripts, explaining ideals of Jaina religion. The same ritual is repeated every year.

Certainly, the use of the word—a prison house is not relishable, yet its use should neither be regarded as an expression of contempt in any way nor a mere coloured description of the truth. The fact, however, remains that the said rare treatises are lying under lock and key and nobody is allowed an access to them. They appear to have no greater utility than the idols of Tirthankers—merely objects of worship.

Late Dr. Hiralal Jain, the celebrated editor of Shatkhaṇḍāgama, overwhelmed with emotion, has remarked. "The priceless treasure of highest spiritual knowledge is practically of no avail than lifeless objects, meant for veneration only. Had the said rare treatises been at the disposal of our eminent literateurs, they would have been able to compose highly accomplished books, enriching our religious literature, and imparting it a distinct place and shape. Many doctrinal issues which had consumed lot of energy and time of our intellectuals, are still lying unsolved. Really, it is a pity that we could not be able to make use of the rare texts, incorporating vast treasure of spiritual knowledge and continued to remain deprived of it....."[1].

Shatkhaṇḍāgama : Story How it was Removed from Lock and Key

No doubt, the eminent scholars, religious preceptors and learned sages had been pleading for a long time for removal of the holy scriptures from the lock and key of the library so that the students and scholars could have an access to them and undertake minute study of the texts, comprehending the ideological and philosophical truths of Jaina religion. There is really an interesting story how the said manuscripts were taken out and I think it will be appropriate to enlighten the readers by relating the said story.

Anxious Thought Given to the Matter During Life Time of Pt. Todarmalji

Under Digamber tradition, Pt. Todarmalji (from Vikrama Samvat 1797 to 1824) is known for his excellence on highest truths of Jaina philosophy. The attribute of `Achārya-Kalpa' (An expert on Jaina ethology) is an enough indication to this effect. During his life time, there were significant deliberations between Jaina followers of Jaipur and Ajmer in Rajasthan to remove the said maunscripts so that the Jaina scholars and pupils be benefitted by going through them minutely. However, even after anxious deliberations, the matter could not materialize into action since Pt. Todarmalji had, unfortunately, an extremely short span of life. Had he lived long, he would have been able to persuade the Jaina organisation to step forward in this direction.

Journey by Seth Mānikchand : Who Felt Agitated and Shaken

Late Seth Manikchand, J.P. of Bombay was a renowned social worker, a noble person and a devout Jaina, belonging to Digamber Sect. It so happened that he undertook journey to Mādabidri in Samvat year 1940 of Vikrama era, accompanied by other Jaina followers. He was pleased to have a view of priceless statues of Arhats and holy manuscripts, containing highest spiritual knowledge while he was having a glimpse of the manuscripts, he was shocked to find that the palmyra leaves were getting time worn. He was, obviously, worried that in case, the holy manuscripts were left to decay gradually, it may not be far when they might get

1. *Shatkhaṇḍāgama*, volume I, Part I, Section I on page 6 of the foreword.

destroyed completely and be no longer available for a reference even. Sethji talked to the Bhattaraka of the temple and local heads. He asked them whether they could follow and explain the contents of the said manuscripts. They replied in negative and added they remained content on having a look at them daily and offer their prayers. Sethji was very much perturbed on hearing it and felt disturbed on that account. He thought that those who were at the helms of affairs were totally ignorant and were unable to read them even. On enquiry, the Seth was informed that one Pandit Brahmasuri resident of Shravanbelgola alone was capable to read them. Seth was, obviously, unhappy. However, for want of time, he could not take any steps and returned from there to Bombay with a sore heart.

Attempts Made by Sethji in This Regard

Because of his pre-occupations in business, it was not practically possible for him to take effective steps into the matter immediately. However, the issue was constantly pricking his mind and after returning to Bombay, he had started consultations with his close associates. Seth Hirachand Nemichand of Sholapur was his friend. The latter was also a veteran social worker and a staunch devout as also follower of Digamber Sect. Seth Manikchand wrote a letter to him and conveyed his anxiety on account of deteriorating condition of the rare manuscripts. He urged him to pay a visit to Mūdabidri and have a look at the holy treatises for himself. He prevailed upon him to devise a plan how to save the sacred manuscripts from total ruin and how to restore them to their original condition. The letter greatly moved Seth Hirachand Nemichand and he managed to leave for Mūdabidri next year. He contacted Pt. Brahma Sūri at Shravanbelgola and persuaded to accompany him to Mūdabidri. On the entreaty of Seth Hirachand Nemichand, Shāstriji (A learned scholar of Shāstras) recited the auspicious introduction in the form of a prayer, written at the commencement of Dhavala Commentary before him and in the presence of other devotees. Everybody was overwhelmed by joy. Sethji felt inspired and made up his mind to spare no effort for getting the rare manuscripts taken out from the lock and key of the temple library. He also discussed with Pt. Brahma Sūri whether it would be convenient for him to get each manuscript copied out. Thereafter he returned to Bombay and personally conversed with Seth Manikchand J.P. that efforts must be made for getting the manuscripts copied. In this way, it was firmly determined to proceed accordingly. However, they were leading traders and remained awfully busy with their occupations. Time passes quickly and another ten years elapsed before they could take any action in this regard.

Copying Work Started and Again Postponed

While the above delebrations were in progress, one Seth Mūlchand Soni of Ajmer set about on pilgrimage to Mūdabidri alongwith Pt. Gopaldas Barāiyā, an erudite scholar of Digamber Sect. Sethji managed to obtain the consent of the Bhattaraka of the temple and local managing body for preparation of the copy of each manuscript. It was decided to get them copied out by Pt. Brahma Sūri. The work of copying, thus, started. Pt. Brahma Sūri had hardly copied 300 verses of Shatkhaṇḍāgama when the work had to be dispensed with. There was a controversy between Seth Mūlchand on one hand and Temple Bhattaraka and local heads on the other. Seth Soni was eagre to carry the said copies with him to Ajmer which was strongly resented by Bhattaraka of the temple and local managers. They were unanimous on the point of getting the manuscripts copied but were reluctant to allow their removal to anyother place outside Mūdabidri. Thus, the work of copying was suspended.

Copying Recommenced : Completed

Seth Manikchand of Bombay and Seth Hirachand of Sholapur had already made up their minds, yet they could not be able to implement their plan earlier due to their pre-occupations in their businesses. They renewed their attempts. Finances were arranged. They decided to persuade Pt. Brahma Sūri to carry on the job and accompany them to Mūdabidri. It was a gigantic task. Hence Pt. Gajapati Shāstry of Miraj was also appointed to assist him. Both the learned scholars came over to Mūdabidri and commenced their copying work w.e.f. the year 1896 A.D. 15 leaves of Jayadhavalā commentary, incorporating 1500 verses had hardly been copied when Pt. Brahma Sūri breathed his last after brief illness. Thereafter, only one copier, Gajapati Shāstry was there to finish the job. He remained engaged in the work with full force and with whole hearted dedication. After unceasing hard labour for 16 years, he was able to accomplish the copies of the manuscripts of Dhavala and Jayadhavalā commentaries in Devanāgiri script from Kannada script. The work, thus, taken up in the year 1896 A.D. could be accomplished in the year 1912 A.D. after 16 years.

Copies Prepared in Kannada Script as well

While the work of copying the manuscripts in Devanāgri script was in progress, the work of obtaining one copy in Kannaḍa script was also taken up. Pt. Devaraj Sethi, Shāntāppā Upadhyāya and Brahmaiyā Indu—all of Mūdabidri were appointed to copy the manuscripts in Kannaḍa script. In this way, copies of Dhavalā and Jayadhavalā commentaries were prepared in both Devanāgri and Kannaḍa scripts. However, the copies were retained in `Sidhānt-Vasadi' (A Digamber Jaina temple at Mūdabidri).

Preparation of Copies of Mahādhavalā Commentary

Seth Hirachand of Sholapur who had been sponsoring the project, came over to Mūdabidri. Dhavalā and Jayadhavalā commentaries had already been copied out. He expressed his sincere desire that in his opinion it would be much better if the third manuscript of `Mahādhavalā commentary' was also allowed to be copied. Simultaneously, Seth Hirachand also stressed the need for preparation of several copies of each manuscript to be placed at different centers for reference and guidance of research scholars on Jaina philosophy. However, the local body, at the helms of affairs, was reluctant to allow it. Only this much was agreed that a copy of Mahadhavalā commentary be made out in Kannaḍa script and placed in the temple at Mūdabidri. Pt. Nemiraj Sethi was deputed for the job who accomplished it prior to the year 1918 A.D. In this way, a copy of Mahadhavalā commentary in Kannaḍa script was ready. However, Seth Hirachand was eagre for preparation of its copy in Devanāgiri script too. The proposal of Sethji was accepted and Pt. Loknath Shastry was appointed to complete the job. He accomplished the work within a period of 4 years. Thus, the work of copying the manuscripts was taken up in 1896 and was over in 1922 within a period of 26 years in all.

An Extra Copy Prepared by Pt. Gajapati Shāstry

As stated above, the entire job of copying Dhavalā and Jayadhavalā commentaries in Devanāgiri script was exclusively done by Pt. Gajapati Shāstry, leaving aside a small portion of 1500 verses only which had been accomplished by Pt. Brahma Sūri. He knew it well that the copy in Devanāgiri script, made by him, will be retained in Mūdabidri temple and will not be allowed to be removed to any other place outside Mūdabidri. He was giving an anxious thought to the matter. His wife, Laxmi Bai, was a highly learned woman. She too pondered over and assessed the situation. Both of them decided to prepare an extra copy each of Dhavalā and Jayadhavalā commentaries in Kannaḍa script secretly. Laxmi Bai persuaded her husband to proceed accordingly. Finally, both of them made up their mind to prepare an extra copy each secretly in Kannaḍa script.

They prepared the copies in Kannaḍa script simply because it was their mother tongue and they found it easy to finish the work promptly. Possibly also, Laxmi Bai may be lacking adequate practice of copying in Devanāgiri script and she was afraid, she might not be able to lend her cooperation in preparing copies in Devanāgiri script. On the other hand she could offer all assistance to her husband in preparing copies in Kannaḍa script. Thus the leaves of the manuscripts, copied in Devanāgiri script during the day, used to be carried by Pt. Gajapati Shāstry to his house secretly in the evening. At night, he used to copy them at home with the help of his wife in Kannaḍa script. Whereas, on one hand, the copy in Devanagiri script was ready of each manuscript and on the other, the extra copies in Kannaḍa script were also ready. Both husband and wife had put in strenuous efforts to complete the job.

Of course, the said action of Pt. Gajapati Shāstry may not be held justified from ethical viewpoint nor he had done it with a broader outlook to help in spread of the message of Jaina Arhats. Even then, it must be admitted that in case Pt. Gajapati Shāstry and his learned wife had not taken the bold step, the rare scriptures would not have become public. If at all they were ever taken out from the lock and key of the Temple library, it would have taken lot of time and strain.

Removal of Copies of Manuscripts in Kannaḍa Script from Mūdabidri

Pt. Gajapati Shāstry was anxious to deliver the copies to a really capable and worthy person so that they were placed at a suitable site for reference, whenever necessary. He aspired for a suitable reward also in lieu of them. He reached Sholapur and requested Seth Hirachand to accept the copies. However, Seth was reluctant to accept them. He also wrote a letter to Seth Manikchand at Bombay, advising him not to accept the copies of Dhavalā and Jaya-Dhavalā commentaries since it was immoral in his view. As stated earlier, Seth Hirachand was himself anxious for wide publicity of the rare treatises and had pleaded for preparation of several copies of each manuscript, yet he felt he was bound to abide by the undertaking, he had given to Bhattaraka of Mūdabidri temple and local heads that he would not be a party in removal of the manuscripts or their copies outside Mūdabidri without their explicit consent. Hence he considered it somewhat unethical on his part to accept the copies.

Thereafter, Pt. Gajapati Shāstry left for Saharanpur. Where one Seth Jambu Prasad was a well-to-do person and a key figure of Jaina community. He accepted the copies and suitably rewarded Shāstriji. The copies were placed in a Jaina temple at Saharanpur.

Lala Jambu Prasad Seth was, obviously, keen for preparation of the copies in Devanāgiri script as well so that the students and scholars in North India be benefited. Pt. Gajapati Shāstry assured him to do the job to his satisfaction but things could not materialize. Owing to the sudden illness of his son, he was constrained to return to his native town immediately. As the luck would have it, his wife fell seriously ill and expired after a short illness. Under such unfavourable circumstances, he was rendered helpless and could not move to Saharanpur. He also breathed his last in 1923 A.D. Hence the extra copies could not be prepared by Shāstriji in Devanāgiri script from his Kannaḍa copies.

Transcription from Kannaḍa Script into Devanāgiri Script

Seth Jambu Prasad was sparing no pains for getting the copies transcribed into Devanāgiri script as early as possible. For completion of the work, it was essential that the desired copiers must be conversant with script-writings in both languages. They should also possess adequate knowledge of Prākrita and Sanskrit languages. Lalaji succeeded in coming across Pt. Vijay Chandraiyyā and Pt. Sita Ram Shāstry, who were competent and possessed desired qualifications. They started the work of transcribing with effect from the year 1916 A.D. and were able to accomplish the work in the year 1923 A.D. after 7 years. L.Jambu Prasad and others were of the opinion that the copies in both scripts must be tallied attentively to avoid lapses, if any. The copies must be identical in both scripts and tally in all respects. Pt. Loknath Shāstry was requested to come over to Saharanpur. He tallied the copies in both scripts.

Preparation of a few Additional Copies

The copies of Dhavalā and Jayadhavalā commentaries, obtained in Devanāgiri script were also placed together with copies in Kannaḍa script in Jaina temple at Saharanpur. The copying work was over. However, there was repetition of an almost similar incident what had taken place at Mūdabidri. Pt. Sita Ram Shāstry had prepared an extra copy of each and retained them with him. Presumably, he might have thought to transfer the copies to any other significant or well-known centre of Jaina community for the benefit and use of the students and scholars and on the other to be rewarded suitably in lieu of handing them over.

There is also one more assumption in this regard. It is stated that while Pt. Vijay Chandraiyyā and Pt. Sita Ram Shāstry were carrying on the work of transcribing in Devanāgri script, the procedure, adopted by them for convenience sake, was that Pt. Vijay Chandraiyyā used to read out Kannaḍa version while Pt. Sita Ram Shāstry used to put down its Devanāgiri version on a rough sheet so that the fairing work could go on smoothly without any inconvenience or delay later on. Accordingly, Shri Sita Ram Shastry prepared a fair copy of each book in the size and shape of a religious treatise from the rough sheets and handed over the fair copies in Devanāgri script to L.Jambu Prasadji. However, the copies on rough sheets were retained by Pt. Sita Ram Shāstry.

Under Digamber tradition, Shatkhanḍāgama is held in great esteem. As soon as the learned persons of different places happened to know of accomplishment of copies in Devanāgri script of commentaries on Shatkhanḍāgama, they approached Pt. Sita Ram Shāstry to prepare extra copies of both commentaries in Devanagri Script to be placed in the temple of their respective place. Thus, a few additional copies were got prepared by Pt. Sita Ram Shāstry from the rough sheets, already in his possession, which were placed together in Jaina temples at Ajmer, Amraoti, Arrah, Indore, Kāranjā, Jhālrāpātana, Delhi, Bombay, Beavar, Saugar, Sivani and Sholapur.

Thus, it is the brief description how the copies of the rare manuscripts of Dhavalā and Jayadhavalā commentaries came to be prepared and how they were removed from Mūdabidri. It is no doubt a thrilling story. There are two significant aspects of every religion—its ideological side and worshipping. If there is a balanced endeavour for attainment of both ends, then only it should be deemed that one is a true devout engaged in pursuit of spiritual knowledge on one hand and religious meditation and worshipping on the other. However, if the pursuit is confined to mere rituals of worshipping and prostrating before the idols, the very propose of spiritual endeavour is frustrated. Whenever, such rituals become common they lose their significance. Instead, ignorance and insensibility overtake the followers of a religion. Only the mechanical way of Idol worshipping becomes the routine of their day-today life. The act of only incensing manuscripts of Shatkhanḍāgama and its allied literature amounts to the same idiocy on the part of worshippers. The true respect to be offered to the religious treatises is in their minute studying, contemplation and reflection thereon. In case, the pursuit of sacred knowledge on higher truths of religion and philosophy by going through religious books is given up or altogether abandoned and only the religious treatises are worshipped daily in the morning or in the evening by incensing them or by making circular movements of a lighted lamp and applying saffron colour or sandalwood paste etc., can it be considered a true worship? It should not be difficult for the learned intellectuals to find out its answer.

Publication of Shatkhaṇḍāgama

Highly celebrated writer and thinker, Late Dr. Hiralal Jain spared no pains so as to be able to get Shatkhaṇḍāgama published. He and his colleagues had to face lot of hurdles and difficulties. In those days, there were dogmatics who alleged that publication of religious scriptures amounted to utter disregard to the religion and disobedience to the spiritual guides and preceptors. They considered it more blissful to keep the sacred treatises under lock and key within the four walls of a temple or its library. However, as they say: "Persons of resolute will and strong determination never care for the favourableness or unfavourableness of the circumstances". Accordingly, Dr. Hiralal Jaina and his associates did not lose heart and continued pursuing their aim with full enthusiasm. Consequently, the rare manuscripts which were once inaccessible were now available for reference to the scholars.

The difficulties experienced by Dr. Hiralal Jain and his associates could be judged from the fact that when they expressed their eagreness to get the rare treatises published, none appeared to be willing to hand over the copies at all. Dr. Jain has, himself, described—our primary object was to obtain copies of Dhavalā and Jayadhavalā commentaries. It was the time when religious-minded persons were annoyed at the very idea of getting them printed and none agreed to part with the copies Amidst such hostile conditions, Shri Singhai Pannalalji and local managing body at Amraoti were bold enough to hand over the copies, placed in the temple there.

Press copies were prepared from the copies, obtained from Amraoti which had been transcribed from the copies, lying in the temple at Saugar. The copies, placed in Saugar temple, had been prepared by Pt. Sita Ram Shāstry.

The copies placed in the temples of Arrah and Kāranjā were made available for correction of the proofs. The said copies had been prepared by Pt. Sita Ram Shāstry. However, question did not arise for tallying the proofs with the copies, lying in the library of Mūdabidri temple, since those, at the helms of affairs at Mūdabidri, considered it an irreligious act to get the religious treatises published. Dr. Hiralal Jain has, thus, related his anguish: "The copies with which we were trying to compare and carry out corrections in the proofs, were themselves full of errors and ommissions, so much so that we had to tax our brain for correction of each and every word, found wrong in the said copies. We had to prolong our sittings late at night—sometimes upto 2 a.m. to be completely exhausted. Even then, we were not sure whether the words substituted by us, tallied with the words, contained in the copies, lying at Mūdabidri temple. We had to bear with it for want of authentic copies. Had they been at our disposal, we would have felt least embarrassed. It occurred to us that we were really unfortunate like those whose parental wealth was taken forcible possession of and who were left to loiter from door to door to beg for filling their bellies. After all who suffered on that account? In case, the authentic copies of the commentaries were at our disposal much time, and energy could be saved to be better utilized in accomplishment of other religious treatises for the benefit of Jaina followers. From sheer wastage of time and energy like this, the progress of the society is greatly impeded. By slow moving like this, it is bound to consume lot of time and energy in extraction of the rare scriptures from the lock and key of Mūdabidri temple library. It is, no doubt, a critical period so far as accomplishment of new literary productions, art and culture are cancerned. Political unrest or insurgency leads to total destruction of the accomplished arts and culture within no time. Let Almighty bless! If, however, the country is overtaken or is in the grip of a crisis who will be able to take care of the existing rare texts in the shape of 12 Angas, based on the utterances of Jaina Arhats and omniscients. The instances of Hassh, China and other countries are fresh in our mind. In case, ancient idols or statues get broken, they may be got replaced or re-installed at an opportune time. Similarly, if the old temples dilapidate and collapse, they can be got re-built as soon as convenient. In the same manner, if the number of followers or devotees of a religion falls short, it can be got enhanced by accelerating the speed of propaganda and expansion of its message. However, the teachings of ancient gurus or religious Achāryas, once destroyed, cannot be restored or re-accomplished. Is it practically possible to restore the rare texts of 12 Angas and its allied literature, even after incurring billions of rupees? No—never. Consequently, the vigilant nations, societies or conscious people spare no pains to save the precious collection of their ancient scriptures at all costs. It may, however, be borne in mind that the methods employed earlier for the safety of religious treatises or other rare texts, are no longer effective now. There is a huge stock-pile of highly destructive weapons and no safeguard is possible against such formidable force of annihilation. Thus there is no other effective remedy except arranging to get thousands of copies published of each important holy book to be placed at different remote centers so that even on the face of worst calamitous conditions, they may not get obliterated altogether and the possibility or existence of atleast one copy of each treatise may not be ruled out. It is really a foolish act on our part to turn a deaf ear or remain indifferent from providing security to our finest treasure of rare texts, containing highest spiritual knowledge, so much so that we are sitting quiet even after hearing a danger signal and smacking the danger of total annihilation."

Dr. Hiralal Jain received excellent cooperation from Pt. Phool Chandra `Sidhānt Shāstry' and Pt. Hiralal Shāstry `Nyaya Tirth', erudite scholars of Jain Digamber sect. Similarly, he received valuable cooperation from Dr. A.N. Upādhye, renowned scholar of Prākritas and Jaina canonical literature as also from `Vyakhyān-Vāchaspati' Pt. Devakinandan `Sidhānt Shāstry', celebrated intellectuals and thinkers for correction of the proofs.

Publication of Initial Part of Shatkhaṇḍāgama : A Novel Reaction

A human-being is a strange creation of the universel. What it contemplates and how it acts or reacts is always a mystery. Whether it will continue to hold the same views tomorrow or day after or it will adopt a new course, nobody knows.

After publication of the initial portion of Shatkhaṇḍāgama, the reaction of the learned students and scholars of Jaina community was highly soothing. For the first time, they realised that they would have an access to the holiest scripture with its Hindi version which was hitherto beyond their reach. On one hand, the intellectuals who were anxious and keenly aspiring for its publication, were, obviously, happy and on the other, those who were earlier reluctant even to handover the manuscript of Shatkhanḍāgama and allow its transcription in Hindi, had a sigh of relief. They too realised for the first time the great significance and need of publishing such rare scripts for the benefit of the Jaina followers.

Orientation in views is quite natural. At times, mankind is impelled to get rid of emotional craze and step on the solid foundation of wisdom and prudence. The same thing happened here. The Bhattaraka of Mūdabidri Jain temple, its managing body and local eminent persons were greatly delighted on its publication. According to Dr. Hiralal Jain, there was an obvious change in the trend of thinking of those who were at the helms of affairs. He writes: "After publication of `Dhavalā Sidhānt', the first part of Shatkhanḍāgama what was expected by us, came to be cent percent true. We are happy to disclose that after the copies in Kannaḍa and Hindi Scripts were published, they were gifted by us to Mūdabidri temple in form of books, duly bound. As soon as the printed books were received at Mūdabidri, they were placed in a decorated Chariot and were carried in the shape of a procession. They were worshipped like Jaina Agamas. A meeting was held, comprising of local distinguished citizens in which the arrangements made by us for correction of the proofs, editing and publication of the holy treatises were highly admired and praised and it was pleaded that full facilities must be provided for tallying with the original manuscripts to avoid unnecessary delay and handicap in correction, editing and printing of the remaining books, otherwise, maintenance or rare texts would be difficult. The said meeting was presided over by Shri Charukirti, Bhattaraka of the temple.

After the said inauguration proceedings, Bhattārakaji himself communicated the decision and invited us to reach Mūdabidri for tallying of the proofs with the original manuscripts."[1] Initial part of Shatkhanḍāgama had already been published. Approval was also received for tallying the proofs of next portions with the original manuscript of Shatkhanḍāgama. The assent for preparation of the copy of Mahadhavalā commentary was also received for purpose of publication.

Manuscripts at Mūdabidri: It is known from the eulogy of Dhavala commentary, written in mixed languages of Sanskrit and Kannaḍa and from minute study of the stone inscription at Shravanbelgola that a pious and religious-minded lady, Demmiyakka, Demati, Deyawati or Devamati, wife of a distinguished Seth Chāmunda, sister of Buchirāj, and father's sister of Bhujabaligangpermādideva had presented the said manuscripts on palmyra leaves to her guru, Shri Shubhchandradeva on completion or conclusion of her religious observance at the auspicious occasion of Shent-Panchmi. As appeared in the inroductory benediction and inscription at Shravanbelgolā, Sri Shubhchandradeva had breathed his last on Friday, the 10th day of lunar fortnight of the month of Shravan in Samvat year 1045 of Shākā era (The era of king Sālivahan in 78 A.D. — equivalent to 1123 A.D.). Sri Shubhchandradeva belonged to the organisation of Sadhus, namely, `Mūlsanghdeshiganạpustaka'.

1. *Shatkhanḍāgama*, section I, Pt.I, volume I, Foreword page 2.

There is a detailed account in the stone inscription No. 49 (129) at Shravanbelgola (Karnataka) in appreciation of her austere death (By way of devotion to intense meditation with comletley detached or disillusioned mind for attaining final salvation). Her numerous virtues, namely-generously offering eatables, religious treatises, medicines and granting assurance of security from fear or danger; dedicated worshipper of Jaina Arhats, observing perfect chastity, having virtuous disposition and endowed with beauty and charm. Finally, it is cited in Kannaḍa script that she had attained her final liberation on Thursday, the 11th day of dark fortnight of Phalguna month of Samvat year 1042 of Shāka era.

It is believed that Demati had presented the manuscripts on palmyra leaves to her guru, Sri Shubhachandradeva in between Samvat years 1037 to 1042 of Shaka era.

Dr. Hiralal Jain concludes on the basis of related events, articles, writings and incidental references that the aforesaid rare manuscripts on palmyra leaves were probably written in or about Samvat year 950 of Shākā era.

Acharya Dharsena in Historical Perspective

No authoritative historical or biographical data is available even now regarding ancient scholars, literateurs and writers. Whatever information is found, it is vague and ambiguous. Hence one has to depend on mere surmises to draw its conclusions. The tendency of ancient scholars and intellectuals had been strange in as much so they exhibited perfect vigilance and care in respect of the project undertaken by them but they were always reluctant to furnish information regarding their own biographical data. Whenever, the writers of the subsequent era decided to produce the life history of their predecessors, the desired data was not at their disposal. If at all, they were able to collect some material it was totally insignificant and did not meet their requirements. It is obvious that the relative events, occurrences and narrative tales are forgotten with the lapse of time. Oral rememberance is always short-lived.

Nothing is elaborately known regarding Acharya Dharsena who was a motive force in accomplishment of Shatkhanḍāgama, incorporating the real essence of 12 Angas, held in highest esteem under Digamber tradition, except that he had imparted knowledge of rare texts to Pushpadant and Bhūtbali. Achārya Dharsena was an authority on Āchrānga (Title of the 1st Anga) and conversant with other Angas and Purvās. Certain conclusions can be drawn on the básis of the material, collected from here and there regarding traditionalist notion, then in practice, how the religious instructions were handed down through a series of spiritual guides and preceptors, from one generation to another.

Name of Achārya Dharsena not Found in the List of Successors to the Seat of Spiritual Head of Jaina Organisation

The list of successors to the highest seat of a spiritual head of Jaina institution, right from Achārya Gautama to Achārya Lohārya, as recognized under Digamber tradition, appears in `Tiloyapaṇṇatti'; `Harivansh Purāṇa', `Dhavalā', `Jayadhavalā commentaries and `Shrutavtār' etc. as already discussed above, where the context demanded, 28 Gurus had succeeded to the highest seat right from Achārya Gautama to Lohārya, out of whom 3 were Kevalins, (Having attained the state of highest perfection), 5 Shruta-Kevalins (who had attained perfection in Jaina Agamas), 11 had acquired expertise in ten Pūrvas (Title of the old sacred treatises of Jainas), 5 experts in 11 Angas and 4 had expertise in Acharanga Sūtra (Title of the first Anga, dealing with ethical values to be observed by Jaina Sādhus). After the name of Achārya Lohārya, no mention is found of next successors to the highest seat in the above list.

However, it should be assumed that after Lohārya, Achārya Dharsena might have succeeded to the seat. Only this much appears in list after the name of Achārya Lohārya that at the time of attaining the proficiency of a spiritual teacher, better known as an Achārya (an initiator), Dharsena had partial expertise in Angas and Pūrvas.

From the above description, no definite inference can be drawn with regard to the time of spiritual leadership of Achārya Dharsena. Indernandi has made a mention of four Achāryas collectively in `Shrutavtār' after the name of Sri Lohārya, namely Vinayadatta, Shridutta, Shivdutta and Arhaddatta who had acquired partial expertise in Angas and Pūrvas. After them, Indernandi has mentioned the name of Achārya Arhadbali, commenting that he was an outstanding spiritual leader and administrator of Jaina institution. His birth-place was `Puṇḍavardhan' in Eastern India. He was anxious to give a new shape to the Jaina organisation, befitting to the times. He convened a conference of Jaina seers and scholars on the auspicious occasion of `Yuga-Pratikramana' (A ceremony, meant for confession), held after every, five years. It is cited in `Shrutavtār' that Jaina Munis, residing in the vicinity of about 800 to 900 miles, had participated in the conference. After minute assessment of the prevailing conditions, Achārya Arhadbali thought that Jaina Sādhus could no longer be expected to lead a detached life, free from feelings of partisanship. The Jaina institution was quite large, having spread far and wide in India. Hence it may be found difficult by the Sādhus to adjust with each other and live amiably without any bitterness. Consequently, it would be better to split the organisation into several constituents. Achārya Arhadbali opined that at least the ideological unity of the Sādhus would not be disturbed and remain intact. Each constituent may have its own constitution and style of functioning. This would certainly provide impetus to the feelings of mutual cordiality; affection and co-ordination amongst the religious mendicants. Accordingly, he splitted the organisation into several constituents, prominent amongst them being-Nandi, Veer, Aparajita, Deva, Panchslip, Sena, Bhadra, Gurudher, Gupta, Singh, Chandra etc.

Indranandi has written in `Shruta Avtār' that Achārya Meghnandi had succeeded Achārya Arhadbali. He has held him to be a great sage. Finally, Achārya Meghanandi had attained final emancipation, after having devoted to intense meditation and acquiring the state of total disillusionment. The name of Achārya Dharsena appears in `Shrutavtār' after the name of Achārya Meghanandi, who was residing in Chandra cave of Urjayant hill near Girnar town in Saurashtra, absorbed in meditation.

Thus, Indranandi has described names of four Achāryas (Initiators) and 3

Munis after the name of Achārya Lohārya. However, he has given no indication with regard to their order of succession nor whether they were connected with each other as spiritual preceptors and disciples. No reliable information is available, whatsoever. It appears that Indranandi might have come to know the names of the said Achāryas and Munis and made a mention in `Shrutavtār' without caring to find out their chronological sequence. Whatever brief information or data, he might have gathered about them, he might have produced in his book along with their names. It is cited in a casual manner by Indranandi himself that he was not aware with the preceptorial relationship or affinity between Achāryas Gandher and Dharsena, since he was unable to trace out the desired information either from any ancient religious treatise or from any aged Jaina Muni.

Name of Achārya Māghnandi, Appeared in Sanskrit Gurvāvali of Nandi Sangh

Whereas there is citation regarding origin of Nandi Sangh and `Balātkargaṇa' in Sanskrit `Guruvāvali' (List of successors to the Supreme Seat) of Nandisangh from the main organisation on one hand and the name of Achārya Māghnandi on the other. The author of Gurvāvali further adds that Māghnanadi was partially expert in old Pūrvas and he was held in great esteem and paid due regards by both mortals and immortals.

Achārya Arhadbali had splitted the main institution into several constituents for better administration and for better care of the mendicants. It is quite possible that he might have entrusted the supreme leadership of Nandi Sangh to Achārya Māghnandi. However, there is no mention of the name of Achārya Dharsena in the said `Guruvāvali'. As appeared therein, Achārya Jinachandra had succeeded Achārya Māghnandi and, thereafter, the name of Achārya Padmanandi Kundakunda is cited as successor to Achārya Jinachandra.

Here the question may, obviously, arise whether the name of Achārya Māghnandi, appearing in `Shrutavtār' and the one cited in `Gurvāvali' of Nandi Sangh are one and the same person or they are two distinct personalities, since the name of Achārya Dharsena appears as successor to Achārya Māghnandi in Shrutavtār while there is no such mention in `Guruvāvali'.

Presumably, both Jinachandra and Dharsena were virtualy disciples of Achārya Māghnandi. Dharsena might have devoted himself to the pursuit of higher spiritual knowledge, absorption in intense meditation, attainment of perfection in Mantrās, practising of severe penances and exercising absolute control overself. The story of his remaining engaged in spiritual endeavours in Chandra cave of Urjayant hill, amply supports the said presumption. Under the circumstances, it appears feasible that Achārya Māghnandi might have entrusted the responsibility of administering the organisation to Achārya Jinachandra. Consequent upon the same, the name of Jinachandra appears as successor to the supreme seat in place of Dharsena.

The attributive of `Purvapadānashvedi' (Partial expertise in the sacred texts, contained in Pūrvas—old spiritual treatises of Jainas, incorporating highest preceptorial knowledge is significant in as much as Achārya Dharsena was also partially expert in old Pūrvas. Hence both can be placed at equal footing so far knowledge of old Pūrvas is concerned. Therefore, Achārya Māghnandi, appearing in Gurvāvali of Nandi Sangh and the one named in `Shrutavtār' of Indranandi, in all probability, appear to be one and the same person.

The name of Achārya Māghnandi also appears in `Jambudivapaṇṇatti" (relating to Digamber Sect). It is cited therein: "Māghnandi had completely subdued worldly illusions, namely-hatred and love, affection and attachment. He was a great scholar of Jaina Agamas and was an eminent intellectual. The name of disciple of Māghnandi is shown Sakalchandra who had made profound study of Jaina philosophy and shed away impurities and foulness of the soul. He voluntarily adhered to the moral ethics, performed religious austerities and led virtuous life. Thus, he was endowed with sterling qualities of head and heart. Shri Nandi was the disciple of Achārya Sakalchandra and he had imbibed qualities of pure heartedness, brightness of character and intellectualism. He had attained complete purification and acquired knowledge of higher truths on Jaina religion and philosophy.

The attributive of `Shruta-Sāgar-Pāraga' (Having acquired complete expertise in Jaina Agamas and other Agamic Scriptures), used here for Māghnandi, appears to be truly significant in as much as he had also been highly spoken of for his singular qualities and excellent scholarship in both `Shrutavtār' and Sanskrit `Gurvāvali' of Nandi Sangh which clearly reflects that Māghnandi, referred to in all the above three treatises is one and the same Achārya.

It is true that the name of Achārya Māghnandi's disciple in Sanskrit Gurvāvali is Padmanandi while the names of successive disciples, found in `Jambudivapaṇṇatti' are Sakalchandra and Shri Nandi. However, it is possible that both names might have been used for one and the same person.

Pottery and Māghnandi: There is a popular legend. Once Māghnandi, the pre-eminent scholar, happened to visit the town for begging alms. A young pretty daughter of a potter met him. She felt infatuation and entreated him to respond favourably for her love. The young Muni also felt strongly attached to her. In this way, he started indulging in sensual pleasures in place of leading the life of self -- denial and absolute renunciation. He began living with her and manufacturing earthen utensils.

It is cited that once there was a controversy on an important ideological point in Jaina organisation. The scholars failed to solve the problem and arrive at a unanimous decision. The Supreme leader of the organisation pondered over the matter and looked around to find out a suitable guide for mediation. Finally, it occurred to him that Māghnandi was the only suitable person to remove uncertainty. He was confident of his talents and scholarship on ideological matters. He advised the Jaina Munis to approach Māghnandi and request him to mediate and offer his valuable guidance. Accordingly, the Munis arrived at the site of the potter and contacted Achārya Māghnandi. They referred the controversial issue to the eminent scholar and guide for consideration and imparting his valuable opinion to remove uncertainty.

The Munis asserted that because of his supremacy in Jaina ideology and his knowledge on higher truths of Jaina philosophy and religion, he will continue to receive best regards from the organisation. Maghnandi again realized his worth and significance which he had, unfortunately, lost sight of due to his sheer indulgence in worldly enjoyments. Atonce, he gave up the company of the potter's daughter and again picked up his earthen pot and the bunch of peacock feathers. He was allowed to perform necessary atonements in order to purify himself and join the Jaina organisation.

There is another story concerning pottery life of Māghnandi. It is cited that at the time of baking the unfinished earthen pitchers, he used to sing poetic compositions in mild tone since he had a poetic convention. The murmuring used to take the shape of poetic compositions. A prayer in prosodic form, comprising of 16 verses was published under the style *Etihasik Stuti* (Historic prayer) in a magazine, titled *Jaina Sidhānt Bhāsker* which is believed to have been composed by Māghnanadi, while he was leading the life of a potter. There is also the above story, being related concerning pottery life of Maghnandi.[1]

Although, nothing can be stated with certainty regarding true identity of Maghnandi, since there have been several Achāryas, bearing the name of Māghnandi under Digamber tradition, yet the attributives of `Expert in Jaina Agamic Scriptures' and `his excellence on higher truths of Jaina philosophy' used for him, clearly establish that Māghnandi, disciple of Achārya Arhadbali, and the one referred to above, are one and the same person. In the petrographic inscription at Shravanbelgola (Karnataka), the attributive of `Sidhānt Vedi' (Well conversant with the settled doctrines of Jaina ideology) has been used.

Consideration of Strong and Weak Points

The total period of spiritual leadership of the organisation right from Achārya Gautama to Achārya Lohārya has been reckoned at 683 years as appears in `Tiloyapatti', Dhavalā and Jayadhavalā commentaries and`Shrutavtār', all accredited scriptures, under Digamber tradition.

Indranandi has quoted the names of 4 Achāryas—Vinaydutta, Shridutta, Shivdutta and Arhadutta collectively at a stretch without pointing out their chronological sequence and, thereafter, names of two Achāryas—Arhadbali and Māghnandi who administered the affairs of the organisation in between the tenures of Achārya Lohārya and Achārya Dharsena. Pt. Jugal Kishore Mukhtār, an eminent Jaina scholar under Digamber tradition, has given his full consideration to the chronology of earlier 4 Achāryas. According to him, the aggregate period of their spiritual leadership is of 20 years. Pt. Jugal Kishore Mukhtār has further reckoned the period of Achāryas Arhadbali and Māghnandi at 10 years each. In this way, Achārya Dharsena is believed to have succeeded to the Supreme Seat in Samvat year 723 after final salvation of Lord Mahāvira i.e. after 40 years of the spiritual leadership of Lohārya.

Mention of Achārya Dharsena in 'Prākrita Pattāvali of Nandi Sangh

`Prākrita-Pattāvali' of Nandi Sangh provides significant information with regard to succession to the Supreme Seat which needs to be considered from various angles.

1. *Jaina Sidhānt Bhāsker*, 1993, Issue 4, on page 151.

In the said Pattāvali; the names of successive spiritual heads-right from Achārya Gautama to Lohārya or Lohāchārya are exactly the same as appearing elsewhere. However, the author of the Pattāvali has mentioned the names of another five Achāryas, namely-Arhadbali, Māghnandi, Dharsena, Pushpadant and Bhūtbali and has assessed the total period of spiritual leadership of 28 Achāryās plus 5 Achāryās in all 33 Achāryas to be 683 years. Thus the difference lies in the chronology of Achāryas in as much as elsewhere the total period of spiritual leadership upto Lohārya has been reckoned at 683 years.

The main characteristic of the above Pattavali is that the chronological period of spiritual leadership of each Achārya has been shown separately, unlike Tiloyapaṇṇatti etc. wherein only aggregate period of `Kevalins' (omniscients), `Shruta-Kevalins' (having attained perfection in Jaina Agamas) and scholars, having expertise in ten Pūrvas (old sacred treatises of Jainas), eleven Angas (sacred books of the Jainas) and Achāranga (Title of the first Anga) only has been given. The said categorization appears to have been made on the basis of successive fall in specialization of the sacred texts. For example — the total period of five `Shruta-Kevalins' has been combinedly given to be 100 years. The respective period of each `Shruta-Kevalin' has not been revealed distinctly.

Tallying of Both Chronologies

The aggregate period of 3 Kevalins, five `Shruta-Kevalins' and eleven scholars, having expertise in 10 Pūrvas, has been shown at 62 years, 100 years and 183 years respectively in `Tiloyapaṇṇatti' etc. and the same figures are found in *Prākrita-Pattavali* as well. The aggregate of the period of each category of experts will amount to 62+100+183=345 years which also appears in the said Pattavali. However, the respective period of spiritual leadership of experts in 10 old Pūrvas is given as—Vishakhacharya - 10 years; Proshthil - 19 years; Ksatriya - 17 years; Jayasena - 21 years; Namsena - 18 years; Sidhartha - 17 years, Dhritisena - 18 years; Vijaya - 13 years; Budhilinga - 20 years; Deva - 14 years and Dharmasena - 14 years, totalling to 181 years. Thus, it does not tally with the aggregate period of 183 years as shown in Tiloyapaṇṇatti etc. Probably, it is due to miscalculation by the author of *Prākrita Pattavali*. He has noted 2 years less against the name of any one of the Acharyas.

Now, let us take the period of spiritual heads, having supremacy in eleven Angas. The authors of Pattavali and Tiloyapaṇṇatti are unanimous so far as the number of such experts is concerned. Both agree that they were five. Whereas, in Tiloyapaṇṇatti etc. the aggregate period of spiritual leadership of the said 5 experts is 220 years, it is reckoned at 123 years only in `Pattavali', namely - Nakṣatra - 18 years; Jayapal - 20 years; Pāṇḍava - 39 years, Dhruvasena - 14 years and Kansa 32 years = Total - 123 years.

Similarly, the period of spiritual leadership of four experts in Achāranga only as appeared in Tilopaṇṇatti etc. has been calculated at 118 years, whereas in Pattavali they have been held to be experts in ten, nine and eight Angas respectively. Their respective period of spiritual leadership has been shown in `Pattavali' as - Subhadra - 6 years; Yashobhadra - 18 years; Bhadrabāhu - 23 years and Lohācharya

- 52 years - totalling to 99 years. Herein also, the author of 'Pattānali' seems to have made mistake in calculation. The author has totalled the period of the said four Achāryas to 97 years inspite of citing the respective period of each spiritual head separately which total to 99 years. Infact, if the total period of all the four Achāryas is taken at 97 years, then alone the aggregate of total period of spiritual leadership of each category of Acharyas will tally correctly. It is, therefore, concluded that 2 extra years appear to have been inadvertently added in the respective period of anyone of the said four Achāryas.

It should be assumed that the four spiritual heads, stated to be well-versed in ten, nine and eight Angas respectively in *Prākrita Pattavali* could possibly be — Subhadra in 10 Angas; Yashobhadra in nine Angas and Bhadrabāhu alias Yashobāhu and Lohācharya alias Lohārya in 8 Angas respectively.

The lists of successors to the supreme Seat, appearing in other sacred books of Digamber sect end with the name of Lohārya while in *Prākrita Pattavali*, the names of Arhadbali, Māghnandi, Dharsena, Pushpadant and Bhūtbali also appear after the name of Lohārya. As detailed therein, the period of leadership of Achāryas Arhadbali is 28 years; that of Māghnandi is 21 years; Dharsena - 19 years; Pushpadant - 30 years and Bhutbali - 20 years = totalling to 118 years.

In this way, the total period of spiritual leadership of the organisation by Kevalins - 62 years; that of `Shruta-Kevalins - 100 years; of those being well-conversant with 14 old Pūrvas - 183 years; of those having expertise in 11 Angas - 123 years; of those being well-versed in 10, 9 and 8 Angas respectively-97 years and of those having perfection in one Anga only - 118 years = Aggregate being - 683 years.

Critical Examination: From the above discussion, it is explicit that there are different versions, mainly on three points in between *Prākrita-Pattavali* on one hand and the lists of successive heads of Jaina institution, appearing in other holy treatises of Digamber sect on the other, namely — (1) difference in the chronological period of five experts on 11 Angas; (2) those who have been described to be an authority on `Acharanga' only under Digamber tradition, they have been declared to be experts in ten, nine and eight Angas respectively in `Prākrita-Pattavali', and (3) incorporation of names of 5 additional Achāryas in Pattavali after the name of Lohārya alias Lohāchārya, namely—Arhadbali and others.

Generally, the scholars, belonging to Digamber tradition, have accepted the succession of spiritual heads, pertaining to each academic category and their relative period of spiritual leadership, as specified in Tiloyapaṇṇatti etc. Then the question arises wherefrom did the author of *Prākrita-Pattavali* obtain the varying figures of chronology of various spiritual heads? Presumably, the author of `Pattavali' might have come across some other reliable evidence, beyond reach of other scholars, on the basis of which, he might have compiled a different list of successive heads with varying chronology.

The author of *Prākrita-Pattavali* has laid down the respective period of spiritual leadership of each Achārya separately which is really significant in as much as he could not dare to produce a different list of successors unless he had reliable evidence at his disposal, more particularly in view of the fact that no other scholar, right from `Yativrashabha' to Indranandi could dare to differ.

In case, we minutely examine the chronological figures of the Achāryas, having expertise in 11 Angas, we are constrained to conclude that the figures shown by the author of `Pattavali' appear to be more reliable and consistent. Moreover, if the total period of spiritual leadership of five Achāryas, having well-conversance in 11 Angas, aggregating to 220 years, is not absolutely wrong, it is also not very convincing and pertinent.

In `Tiloyapaṇṇatti' etc. immediately after describing the chronology of Āchāryās, having expertise in 11 Angas, there is a mention of those Āchāryās who are well-versed in Achāranga (Title of the first Anga) only. That is to say there is obliteration of 10 Angas at one stretch. On the contrary, in `Pattāvali' after mentioning the Achāryas, having excellence in 11 Angas, there is description of those Achāryas who were considered an authority on ten, nine and eight Angas respectively. Thus, the process of regular decline in the expertise of Jaina Agamas, as appeared in Pattāvali, seems to be more rational and believable.

Incorporation of 5 Achāryas, namely—Arhadbali, Māghnandi, Dharsena, Pushpadant and Bhūtbali in *Prākrita-Pattavali* without disturbing the total chronology of 683 years, is, somewhat, confusing and needs further investigation.

A Likelihood: It is quite, possible that the author of `Pattavali' might be belonging to the same group or constituent of Jaina organisation to which Achāryas Arhadbali; Māghnandi and Dharsena etc. belonged. Accordingly, he might have felt allured to insert the names of the said five Achāryas after the name of Lohārya to signify that they were eminent scholars, having specialization in Achāranga, however without disturbing the aggregate of the chronological period, accepted unanimously by all other authors. There was unanimity till the entries of the name of Lohārya alias Lohāchārya in the lists of succession to the supreme seat, appeared in various treatises under Digamber tradition. However, after the split of the organisation in several groups or constituents for ensuring better administration, the situation was, obviously, different. That is to say, each splitted group was anxious to include the names of Achāryas, belonging to it to draw an authoritative list. Thus, in all probability, the author of `Pattavali' might have manipulated changes in the chronological period of various Achāryas so as to be able to incorporate the names of, the aforesaid five Achāryas in the `Pattavali' while retaining the total time limit of 683 years. The author of `Pattavali' has also reduced the respective period of leadership of each spiritual head so that the chronology of successive heads to the supreme seat of the organisation may not appear unreal or unconvincing.

Another Probability: After the institution had splitted in several groups or constituents, pre-eminent Jaina scholars or sages, irrespective of their group affiliations were highly adored and paid obeisance by all Jainas. However, it might not have been found feasible to include their names in the unanimously approved lists of Achāryas, appeared in various religious treatises of Digamber Sect. Resultantly, in subsequent lists of succession, the names of Achāryas, belonging to different groups, began to differ after the name of Achārya Lohārya. Hence, it is very likely that the names of highly accredited and accomplished Jaina scholars, namely—Acharyas, Arhadbali, Māghnandi and Dharsena etc., who did belong to the category of those Achāryas who had gained expertise in one or more Jaina

Agamas, might have been knowingly abandoned or ignored. It is also equally possible, that the list of successive spiritual heads, drawn on the basis of declining efficiency in Jaina Agamas, might have extended upto the name of Achārya Bhūtbali and the aggregation of the chronological period might have been obtained at 683 years upto the name of Bhūtabli. However, when a unanimous shape was determined to be given to the list of successive Achāryas, how they could afford to include the names of those who happened to belong to any specific group or branch of the Jainas. In this way, they would have preferred to restrict the names of Achāryas upto Lohārya and adjusted the chronology of each Achārya accordingly. This might have been done in order to obtain a unanimous list of successive heads to the supreme seat without being challenged from any quarter, whatsoever.

Nevertheless, the above presumption does not appear to be sound or convincing. Except `Pattavali', there is no mention of the names of five Achāryas in any other list of successors, appearing in various other holy books of Digamber tradition. Hence neither `Pattavali' can be taken for granted nor it can be rejected out night, believing that it was a mere imagination of the author, since many of the disclosures, made by him, are not vague and appeal to the mind.

Further investigation in this regard is called for and highly essential for disclosure of the truth.

According to `Pattāvali', the aggregate period of spiritual leadership upto Māghnandi has been reckoned till 614 years after final salvation of Lord Mahāvira. Thereafter, the total period upto Achārya Bhūtbali ranges to 69 years which is to be apportioned amongst three Achāryas, namely—Dharsena, Pushpadant and Bhūtbali. Thus, the period of spiritual leadership of Achārya Dharsena is calculated from Samvat year 615 to 633; that of Achārya Pushpadant from Samvat 634 to 663 and that of Achārya Bhūtbali from Samvat 664 to 683 after final salvation of Lord Mahāvira.

Authenticity of `Prākrita Pattāvali'

The language found in *Prākrita-Pattāvali* is inaccurate and mixed, so much so that the standard of Prākrita dialect has gone down to Apbhransha (one of the lowest forms of Prākrita dialects, generally used by cowherds etc.) and finally, use of Hindi words in found. However, from minute examination of its contents, it appears that it is not an authentic copy from the original one. When copies after copies are transcribed by scholars who are not well-conversant with the Prākrita dialects, the process of incorrect-transcription is bound to go unchecked. `Pattāvali' in question, also appears to have faced the same lot. Besides figures, the standard of the language in `Pattavali' has continued to vitiate and changed considerably with the passage of time. The body of Pattāvali has undergone drastic changes and it is far removed from the original shape of Pattavali by now. On the basis of its existing form, it may not be possible to determine the exact time of its accomplishment, yet it can be safely assumed that it is not a recent composition. Late Dr. Hiralal Jain has laid reliance on it for determination of the chronology of Achārya Dharsena. He was, in fact, curious to form a definite opinion on this point and, therefore, he did his best to procure the original copy of Pattāvali which was lying under custody of `Jaina Sidhant Bhavan' at Arah (Bihar). The contents had been publishęd in *Jaina Sidhānt Bhasker*' from the said original copy. However, it could not be traced out in the temple library at Arrah inspite of best efforts and, thus, there was no occasion for further investigation into the matter. The notable informations, provided by the said pattavali, with regard to the chronological order of various spiritual heads, under Digamber tradition are really significant. Further research and investigation is essential in this regard since it is quite possible that many important clues or supporting evidence be found on the basis of which, the author of *Prākrita-Pattāvali* was able to produce the list of successive Digamber Achāryas with such authenticity.

'Jonipāhuda' — Acreation of Acharya Dharsena in Prākrita

Jonipāhuda is an ancient collection of mystical formulas or spells and Mantras in Prākrita dialect. Achārya Dharsena is believed to be its author. The possibility of accomplishing a book on the science of spells and magic by Achārya Dharsena was not something unworthy on his part. While narrating how Pushpadant and Bhūtbali; the two disciples, had come in contact with Achārya Dharsena for attainment of spiritual knowledge of the rare texts which were in his rememberance, it, was stated that in order to judge their worthiness, Achārya Dharsena had imparted two mystic formulas for successful culmination of their endeavour to wield the Mantras effectively. It establishes that Achārya Dharsena had attained perfection in the science of magic and spells and he had an aptitude also for the subject. Accordingly he had preferred to judge the potentialities of his would-be disciples by virtue of practising magical formulas.

Jonipāhuda contains 800 verses in Prākrita dialect. It is cited that Achārya Dharsena had acquired the material through the grace of `Kusumāndini Mahādevi' and had accomplished `Jonipāhuda' for the guidance of his deserving resident-pupils, Pushpādant and Bhusbali. A reference of `Jonipāhuda' is also found in Dhavala commentary. It has been commented therein that `Jonipāhuḍa' elaborately deals with the science of spells and incantations as also with a chapter on atoms and their division etc.

Reference Also Found in 'Vrahadtippiṇikā

A Jaina scholar of Shwetamber Cult had prepared an exhaustive inventory of all scriptural-works, accomplished by Jaina scholars of all shades, including those belonging to both Digamber and Shwetamber sects. He spared no pains to include the names of all the books, covering almost all subjects, concerning Jaina religion, which had been written by ancient as well as modern scholars of his age. *Jonipāhuda* has also been referred to therein, written by Achārya Dharsena. According to the author of *Vrahadtippinikā*, it had been accomplished in Samvat year 600 after final salvation of Lord Mahāvira. There is no occasion for suspecting the authenticity of `Vrahada-Tippiṇika', in as much as a shwetamber scholar has referred to the book, written by a Digamber scholar.

As per `Prākrita Pattavali' of Nandi Sangh, elaborately dealt with in foregoing pages, the tenure of spiritual leadership of Achārya Māghnandi had ended in Samvat year 614 after final salvation of Lord Mahāvira. From a perusal of`Vrahadippinika' and `Prākrita-Pattavali', it appears that Achārya Dharsena had accomplished his book *Jonipahuda* nearly 14 years prior to his succession to the supreme seat of Jaina organisation. By the time, he had undertaken to produce a book on a complicated subject of mystical spells and incantations, he must have attained his full youth, if not turned into a grown up and mature person.

There is a hand-written maunscript of *Jonipahuda*, lying in the library of Bhandarker Oriental Research Institute, Pune (Maharashtra) which is believed to have been written in Samvat year 1582 of Vikrama era.

Joṇipāhuda : A Unique Accomplishment in the Field of Spells and Magical Formulas

Joṇipāhuda is a unique creation in so far as it elaborately deals with the science of spells and magic. The remarkable book is held in great esteem under both Digamber and Shwetamber tradition. The facts related by Dr. Jagdish Chandra Jain with regard to the significance of the book, are being reproduced here: As appeared in *Nishitha Chūrṇi*, (Vol. IV, page 375, cyclostyled copy), Achārya Sidhsena had caused the horses to live by complying with the mystical formulas, given in `Jonipahuda' and by virtue of applying the Mantras, specified in the book, the he-buffaloes could be turned unconscious. The Mantras enabled to make fortunes. It is cited in *Prabhavaka Charit* (Volume 5, pages 115-117) fish and lions could be produced. In the commentary, authored by Achārya Hemchandra on *Visheshavashyaka Bhashya* (Verse No. 1775), it is laid down that animate objects like snakes and lions and inanimate articles such as jems and gold etc. can be obtained by dissolving different substances and alien properties. According to the author of *Kuvalaya Mala*, if the guide lines, contained in `Jonipahuda' are correctly followed, they are bound to yield desired results. Achārya Jineshwar Sūri has also referred to `Joṇispāhuda' in the chapter `Kathakosh' of his book, comprising of 800 verses. Kulmanḍan Sūri has agreed in his book *Vicharamrita Sangrah*, written in Samvat year 1473 of Vikrama era (equivalent to 1416 A.D.) on page 9 A. that the chapter of `Yoni-Prābhrita' is based on old sacred treatises of Jaina religion.

From the above, it is explicit that Achārya Dharsena had given a new shape to `Jonipāhuda' by adding some portion from `Agrayani Pūrva'. The book originally contained 28,000 verses, the sum and substance of which was summarised and incorporated in `Yoni-Prābhrita'.

Conclusion

In the light of what has been discussed above, there are two inferences regarding chronology of Āchārya Dharsena. On the basis of `Tiloyapaṇṇatti', `Harivansh Purāna', `Dhavalā', `Jayadhavalā' commentaries and `Shrutavtār', the chronology of Āchārya Dharsena is established after Samvat year 681 of final salvation of Lord Mahāvira. However, if it is determined on the basis of *Prākrita-Pattāvali* and *Joṇipāhuda* the chronology of Achārya Dharsena will have to be fixed slightly before Samvat year 600 after final salvation of Lord Mahavira. That is to say, he lived in the first century A.D. According to `Tiloyapaṇṇatti' etc. his chronology is established after expiry of the 1st century A.D. In any view of the matter, be must have lived prior to the commencement of 2nd century A.D. and on this very basis, the chronology of Achāryas Pushpadant and Bhūtbali is also to be determined.

Dhavalā and Jayadhavalā

Achārya Virsena deserves full credit for enlightening the followers of Jaina religion with rare spiritual texts, contained in Shatkhanḍāgama by writing `Dhavala' (Bright) commentary on it.

The exhaustive nature of Dhavala commentary has already been emphasized above. It is, infact, bewildering to imagine that a single individual undertook to explain and elaborate the substance of 72,000 Shlokas, incorporated in Shatkhanḍāgama. Achārya Virsena is to be highly admired for writing 20,000 verses of Jayadhavala commentary also in addition to his voluminous Dhavala commentary inspite of his indisposed health. Thereafter, he could not sustain his mortal frame and breathed his last.

In this way, Achārya Virsena had composed 92,000 verses in his life time. It appears that after undertaking profound study of holy scriptures, he devoted his life to literary attainments. Accordingly, he was able to accomplish his desire.

Mahābhārata is a voluminous and large-sized epic, having universal significance. It is comprised of one lac verses. However, it was not the exclusive accomplishment of Vyasdeva only. None could say with certainty, how many poets or seers had made their contribution to its achievement. Contrarily, Dhavalā commentary is comprised of 72000 Shlokas, slightly lesser in volume as compared to *Mahābhārata*, yet it is an exclusive production of a single author, Achārya Virasena. It adds to its significance. The wise and learned men like Achārya Virasena are only rare in this world who absolutely concentrate their energies is acquisition of true spiritual knowledge. They are, infact, knowledge incarnate.

A Brilliant Scholar : Endowed with Genius Character

The wisdom and intelligence of Achārya Virasena was exemplary. His faculty of rememberance and understanding was extra-ordinary. His profound knowledge of holy scriptures was immense. He was well-conversant with the ideals of his own religion as well as of others. His perfection in grammar, philosophy, prosody and astrology etc. was unique. He was a true dynamic figure.

According to Jinasena, Achārya Virasena was highly prudent with great far-sightedness, as if he was a true Kevalin and an imbodiment of omniscience. On finding that he was a genius, enlightening the Jainas, the scholars treated him to be an authority on Jaina Agamas and a real sage with outstanding abilities.

By having profound knowledge of philosophical doctrines of Jaina religion, he had attained the state of perfection like Buddhas who need no help of any other philosopher or guide.

Jinasena has remarkably added that Achārya Virasena had spared no pains in undertaking profound study or Jaina Scriptural works. According to him, Achārya Virasena had studied old Jaina sacred treatises minutely and had added to their glory. That is to say, he had made study of old scriptures, containing highest spiritual knowledge of Jaina philosophy with full devotion and imparted knowledge thereof to others with absolutely detached mind.

It follows that Achārya Virasen had made comprehensive study of all important Scriptures, that were available to him in his life time. Consequently, he was able to incorporate the gist of all accredited holy books in his Dhavala commentary to make it a unique accomplishment.

Jinasena has described in the preface of his book *Ādi Purāṇa* that Achārya Virasena was a great orator, an excellent expounder of the tenets of Jaina religion, a noble soul, a popular scholar, an accomplished poet and a true spiritual guide. He was an eloquent speaker like Achārya Brahaspati, the preceptor of gods.

Jinasena has emphasized the significance of Dhavalā commentary in highly emotion-filled language. He says that Dhavala commentary, styled `Dhavalā Bhārti' has established a record and has illuminated the whole universe. That is to say, its name and glory has spread far and wide and its brilliance has manifested in both Lokas (Earth and Heaven).

Accomplishment of Dhavalā Commentary

Indranandi has dealt with Achārya Virasena and his Dhavalā Commentary in `Shrutāvtār'. In the said context, Indranandi writes that Virasena had acquired the knowledge of ideological doctrines of Jaina religion from guru Elāchārya. The said Achārya directed his disciple to proceed to `Vāṭagrām'. He stayed in a Jaina temple, got erected by one Seth Antendra. There he happened to come across an old commentary on `Vyakhya Pragyapti-Shatkhaṇḍāgama. Thereafter, he accomplished Dhavalā commentary in the said temple premises.

In the same perspective, Indranandi has described the total number of verses, composed by Virasena, forming part of Dhavalā and Jayadhavalā commentaries. He also writes that Dhavala commentary has been accomplished in mixed vocabulary of Prākrita and Sanskrit. Indranandi also adds that Jayadhavalā commentary had been completed by Achārya Jinasena which comprises of 60,000 Shlokas.

Name : Its Significance: Why Achārya Virasena had titled his commentary as Dhavalā, no satisfactory answer is found. Dhavalā is a Sanskrit word which literally means white, handsome, clear, pure, spotless and shining. The lunar fortnight of a month (Hindu Calendar) is also called `Dhavalā'. It is quite possible that the author of the commentary might have found the word `Dhavalā' capable to communicate all the characteristics of his commentary by use of a single word to signify comprehension of the sense; clarity in expression of a feeling from the bottom of the heart; beauty in arrangement and analysis of the words; brilliance in revelation of the contents and lucidity in style etc. with the lapse of time, the name of Dhavalā turned to be so popular and agreeable that Shatkhandāgama and its allied literature, came to be known as *Dhavalā Sidhant* (Brilliant doctrinal literature of Jaina religion).

Finally, it is cited in the praise of Dhavala commentary that it was completed on the 13th day of bright fort-night of Kartika month (According to Hindu Calendar). Since the commentary was completed in the lunar fortnight of the month, it is quite possible that the author might have felt inclined to name it as Dhavalā commentary.

There is one more explanation as well. The commentary had been accomplished during the reign of king Amoghvarsh I, a highly accredited ruler, belonging to Rashtrakūṭa dynasty. The king was endowed with rare qualities of head and heart. He possessed brilliant character; owned pious nature and was highly religious-minded. An attributive of `Dhavalā' (Exceedingly handsome) is also found to have been applied to him. Although no decisive explanation can be offered why the said adjective was applied to his name, yet it is possible that keeping in view his accomplished character and purity of his heart, people might have felt inclined to use the adjective of `Dhavala' for him. The king had elegant physique with beautiful complexion and used to pay his best respects to the eminent scholars, recluses and meritorious persons. He treated them with utmost devotion. Hence it does not appear to be irrelevant that the said attributive, used for King Amoghvarsh I, might have prompted the author to name his commentary on Shatkhandāgama as Dhavalā.

Whatever be the truth, Dhavalā commentary is held in greatest esteem not only under Digamber tradition but in the entire literary circles of India — more so in the field of metaphysics and philosophy. It appears that the outer beauty of the name might have amassed the emotive beauty as well.

Characteristics of Dhavalā

As cited above, Dhavalā commentary has been composed in mixed dialect of Prākrita and Sanskrit languages. The composition in mixed dialect his been similized with the maxim of precious and ordinary stones, when mixed do not lose their distinct identities. They never get mingled with each other. In the same way, though Dhavalā had been composed in mixed dialect of Prākrita and Sanskrit language, yet the words of both the languages are conspicuous and have not lost their identities.

The use of both languages in accomplishment of the commentary by the author, has its own significance. Sanskrit has an aptitude for presentation of metaphysical and philosophical subjects in a most logical and lucid style. It has its own specific and technical glossary with grammatical style of composition, which has no parallel. On the other hand, Prākrita is a popular language of the masses which was once commonly used by the people in India. With a view that the use of the commentary was not restricted to learned scholars and a selected gentry only, hence Prākrita vocabulary was also used in composition of Dhavalā Commentary so that even the average people could be able to follow it conveniently. In order to do justice with the people, possessing average intelligence, use of Prākrita vocabulary cannot be considered to be an unseasoned act in any view of the matter.

The author of the commentary has consulted multifarious books, belonging to both Digamber and Shwetamber Sects without least reservation in mind. In nutshell, he has spared no pains to add to the utility and significance of his production by turning it more and more beneficial for its readers. His style of composition is marvellous and his accomplished commentary is bound to render great assistance to research scholars.

Completion of Commentary : Time

There is no uncertainty at all regarding the life-time of Achārya Virasena. In the concluding chapter of his commentary, the author has given certain significant clues in predictive style. Late Dr. Hiralal Jaina has carried out minute study of the relevant position and has signified that Dhavalā commentary came to be finished on the 13th day of lunar fortnight of the month of Kartik of Samvat year 738 as per Shāka era (equivalent to 816 A.D.).

Achārya Jinasena, worthy disciple of Achārya Virasena, had completed Jaya Dhavalā commentary, already started by his guru, on 10th days of lunar fortnight of the month of Phalguna of Samvat year 759 of Shaka era (equivalent to 837 A.D.). It was during the reigning period of King Amoghvarsha.

The intervening period between completion of Dhavalā and Jayadhavalā commentaries is 21 years. It is the first and the last time limit when Achārya Virasena had breathed his last, i.e. it took place in between the said period.

Late Dr. Nāthu Ram Premi, a prominent scholar of Jaina history and philosophy, has opined that Achārya Virasena had lived from Samvat year 665 to 745 of Shaka era which is based on a number of preceding and following references and testimonies.

Shatkhandāgama : Sources for its Material

The fourth head of the 12th Anga `Drishtivāda' is styled `Purvagata' which is classified into 14 Pūrvas (old sacred treaties of Jainas). The title of the second Pūrva is `Agrāniya' which is further classified under 14 heads, as shown below:

1. Pūrvānt	2. Aprāutā	3. Dhruva
4. Adhruva	5. Chayanlabdhi	6. Ardhopama
7. Pranidhikalpa	8. Artha	9. Bhaum
10. Vratādika	11. Sarvarth	12. Kalpaniryāṇa
13. Atitasidhabadha	14. Anāgata.	

The fifth head `Chayanlabdhi' is divided in 20 sections. The title of the fourth section is `Karma Prākriti' which consists of 24 `Anuyaga Dwārs', named as below:

1. Kriti	2. Vedanā	3. Sparsh
4. Karma	5. Prakriti	6. Bandhan
7. Nibandhan	8. Prakrima	9. Upkrima
10. Udaya	11. Moksa	12. Saṁkrim
13. Leshyā	14. Leshyā Karma	15. Leshyā Pariṇām,
16. Sātāsata,	17. Dirghā Hrasva,	18. Bhavadhārṇiya

19. Pudgalātma 20. Nidhattānidhatta 21. Nikāchitā-Nikāchita,
22. Karma Sthiti, 23. Paschim Skandha, 24. Alpabahutva.

Thus, the sources of composition of Shatkhaṇḍāma were classified or sub-classified portions or chapters of Jaina Agamas, as shown above.

Shatkhaṇḍāgama — An Introduction

Shatkhaṇḍāgama is comprised of six sections. The title of the first section is `Jīvaṭṭhāṇa'. The major part of the said section has been composed on the basis of sixth `Anuyag Dwār', styled Bandhan' and its sub-head `Bandha-vidhan'.

The First Section `Jīvaṭṭhān' consists of 8 Anuyoga Dwārs and 9 `Chūlikās'. The names of 8 Anuyoga Dwārs being —

1. Sat, 2. Saṁkhyā, 3. Kṣetra, 4. Sparshana,
5. Kāl, 6. Antar, 7. Bhava, and 8. Alpabahutva.

The names of 9 `Chūlikās' are as under:

1. Prakirtisamutakīrtanā, 2. Sthān-smutakirtaṇā,
3-5. Three Mahadanḍakas, 6. Jaghanya Sthiti,
7. Utkrishtha Sthiti, 8. Samyakatvotpatti, and 9. Gati-Agati.

The subjects, dealt with in the aforesaid Anuyoga Dwārs' and `Chūlikās' have been elaborately discussed and critically investigated on the basis of merits or excellent points, found therein.

Second Section: The second section of Shatkhanḍāgama is titled `Khudda-Bandh'. Its transformation in Sanskrit is Ksullaka Bandh'. It has been composed on the basis of sub-classification `Bandhaka' of Anuyoga Dwār `Bandhan', relating to Karma Prākriti' Pahuḍa. The said section of Shatkhandāgama' has been sub-classified into 11 chapters, namely —

1. Swāmitva; 2. Kāl; 3. Antar;
4. Bhagvichaya; 5. Dravyapramāṇānugama; 6. Kṣetranugama;
7. Sparshānugama; 8. Nānājivakāl; 9. Nānājivantar;
10. Bhāgābhāgānugama, and 11. Alpabahutvānugama.

In the aforesaid second section of Shatkhanḍāgama, the topics relating to living-beings, facing the bond of life and death as well as various types of bondages, resulting from one's deeds, have been minutely discussed under 11 heads, specified above.

Third Section: The third section of Shatkhanḍāgama is styled `Bandh-Swāmitva-Vichaya'. `Bandh-Vidhān', a sub-classfication of Anuyoga, Dwār, `Bandhan', under `Karma-Prākriti' Pāhuda is of four types--`Prākriti' (nature); `Sthiti' (A state, position or situation); `Anubhāg' (portion or branch); and `Pradesh' (A region or territory) The nature is of two kinds-original and secondary. The secondary nature is of two kinds — `Ekaikottar', and (2) Avvōgārh'. Again, `Ekaidottar' nature has been sub-classified into 24 parts as under:

1. Samutkirtanā; 2. Sarvabandh; 3. Nosarva;
4. Utkrishṭa; 5. Anutkrishṭa; 6. Jaghanya;
7. Ajaghanya; 8. Sādi; 9. Anādi;
10. Dhruva; 11. Adhurva; 12. Bandh-swamitva-vichaya;
13. Bandhkāl; 14. Bandhāntar; 15. Bandhsannikarsh;
16. Bhangavihaya; 17. Bhāgābhāg; 18. Parimān;
19. Kṣetra; 20. Sparshan; 21. Kāl;
22. Antar; 23. Bhāva and 24. Alpabahutva.

The third section of Shatkhanḍāgama has been composed primarily on the basis of 12th part — Bandh-swamitva-vichaya. The following topics have been primarily dealt with in the third section:

Which of the living-beings are guided by their souls while performing deeds and which of them have no direction or guidance by their souls.

The nature of vices which are totally destroyed as a result of moral upliftment.

What are the fetters, falling under the categories `Swodayabandhātmaka' and `Parodayabandhātmaka', that bind the souls of living-beings.

Fourth Section: The fourth section of `Shatkhandāgama' is styled `Vedna'. It has been accomplished on the basis of two Anuyogadwārs, namely, `Kirti' and `Vedana' under `Karma-Prākriti' Pahuḍa. The topic of Vednā has been dealt with at lenght. Accordingly, the section in question has been styled as `Vednā'. It contains numerical description of 5 types of bodies, guided by their souls, namely — `Audārika' (The gross body which envelopes the soul); `Vaikriya' (yogic); `Ahārikā' (According to Colebrook, it is a minute form, issuing from the head of a meditative monk to consult an omniscient and returning with the desired information) `Tejas' (Heat or light considered as the third of the five elements of creation) which grants vital power or strength and `Karmana' (Body—performing a work well or completely); the striking and peaceful dispositions of the aforesaid 5 types of bodies, performances and non-performances of living-beings in initial and final stages of life as also indistinct and non-manifested instincts of the body.

There are seven parts of a performance:

1. `Nām' (Name);
2. `Sthāpnā' (Establishment);
3. `Drivya' (Matter);
4. `Ganṇā' (Calculation);
5. `Granth' (A religious of literatory treatise);
6. `Karaṇa' (An instrument or means or an action); and
7. `Bhāva' (Inclination or disposition of mind).

Out of the above, the significance of `Ganṇā' has been established at length.

The `Vednā' section of Shatkhandāgama is comprised of 16 chapters, namely—

1. Nikṣepa; 2. Naya; 3. Nāām;
4. Dravya; 5. Kṣetra; 6. Kāl;
7. Bhāva; 8. Pratyaya; 9. Swāmitva;
10. Vednā; 11. Mati; 12. Anantar;
13. Sannikarsha; 14. Parimāṇa; 15. Bhāgabhāgānugama, and
16. Alpabahutvānugama.

The fourth section `Vednā' has been discussed, keeping in view the above topics.

Fifth Section: The fifth section of Shatkhanḍāgama is styled `Vargaṇā' (Multiplication). It has been accomplished on the basis of Anuyagadwārs titled `Sparsha'; `Karma' and `Prākriti' and `Baudh', a sub-classification of Anuyoga Dwār `Baudhan' under `Karma-Prākriti Pāhuda'.

While dealing with the topic of `Sparsh' (contact) it has been found of 13 types as laid down in 16 Chapters of Vednā (Fourth section of Shatkhanḍāgama) and in the instant case the applicability of `Karma-Sparsh' (influencing of Karmas — auspicious or inauspicious acts attracted as per nature of the particles of matter, atom or Dravya, inherent in the body, as per Jaina philosophy) have been discussed.

Under the aforesaid 16 heads of Vednā section of Shatkhanḍāgama, the ten forms of Karmas have been elaborately dealt with, namely—

1. Naam; 2. Sthāpnā; 3. Dravya; 4. Prayoga;
5. Samvadhān; 6. Adhaḥ;
7. Iryapāth (The observances of a religious mendicant to obtain knowledge);
8. Tapa (Religious austerities);
9. Kriyā (Accomplishments) and
10. Bhāva (Devotion and meditation).

While dealing with Prākriti (nature), the topics of `Shila' (good nature and morality and `Swabhāva' (one's state of mind) have been discussed which are, infact, essential constituents of nature-rather its synonyms. The nature has been classified into four parts — `Naam' (Name); `Sthāpnā' (Establishing); Dravya (The substratum of properties — elementary substance) and `Bhāva' (Disposition of mind). The nature of matter, prompting Karmās has been elaborately discussed under 16 heads of `Vednā' section, referred to above.

The main topic of 5th section of Shatkhanḍāgama is `Bandhniya', a sub-classification of Anuyoga Dwār `Bandhan'. Under the said topic, 23 types of `Vargṇās' (multiplications) mainly relating to `Karma-baudh' (consequences of religious acts-good or bad) have been discussed at length.

Sixth Section: The said section of Shatkhanḍāgama is styled `Mahabandh'. It has already been stated above that Achārya Bhūtbali was its author. In continuation of the portion, already composed by his senior fellow student, (Pupils of the same preceptor), Achārya Pushpadant, Achārya Bhūtbali first completed 5 sections of Shatkhanḍāgama and, thereafter, composed sixth section, styled `Mahabandh', comprising of 30,000 Verses. What has been cited in `Shrutavatar' by Acharya Indranandi, has already been referred to above, while making a brief analysis of Shatkhanḍāgama.

Achārya Virasena has commented in his `Dhavalā commentary'. "After completion of the 5th section of Shatkhaṇḍāgama, styled `Vargaṇā', Achārya Bhārtbali had dealt with 4 types of attachments in his sixth section, styled `Mahābandh'. He has discussed in detail about `Prākritibandh' (Attachment to false illusions); `Sthitibandh' (Attachment to a region or territory) and `Pradeshbandh' (Attachment to an area). Hence their repetition is unnecessary here. Accordingly, the topic of `Bandh-Vidhān' is closed here.

In this way, Achārya Bhūtbali has profoundly discussed all the four types of `Bandhans' (Attachments) with their further classifications and sub-classifications in the sixth section of Shatkhaṇḍāgama, titled `Mahabandh'.

Summary

From the brief account of all the six portions of Shatkhaṇḍāgama, it is explicit that it is a unique accomplishment in Indian philosophy so far theory of Karmas (Performance of deeds — good or bad as per nature of particles, inherent in the body as per Jaina philosophy) is concerned.

Kasai--Pāhuḍa (Kashāya-Prābhrita)

While making a mention of Achārya Dharsena, a reference has also been made to Achārya Guṇadher in earlier pages. Just as for want of biographical particulars of Achārya Dharsena, nothing conclusively can be said about his life events. Similarly, no biographical history of Achārya Guṇadher is available. The name of Achārya Dharsena has appeared as successor to Achārya Māghnandi in *Prākrita Pattāvali* of Nandi Sangh. However, there is no reference about Achārya Guṇadher's order of succession.

As already stated above, Indranandi has expressed his ignorance of the biographical datas of both Achāryas Dharsena and Guṇadher in his famous book *Shrutāvtār*.

It is true that biographical details of Achārya Guṇadher are missing. However, his unique accomplishment in the shape of `Kasai-Pāhuda' is no less contribution to the enrichment of Jaina philosophy and which is sufficient to immortalize his name. The mortal remains are destroyed but the views of an author continue for ever and as such the author cannot be deemed to have expired.

Sources of Contents: Alike Shatkhaṇḍāgama, Kasai-Pāhuḍa is also known to have its source of origin from 12 Angas. Amongst 14 Pūrvas (old sacred treatises of Jainas, containing highest spiritual knowledge), the title of the fifth Pūrva is `Gyān-Pravāda Pūrva'. The third Pāhuda of its 10th Chapter is styled `Pejjadospahuḍa'. `Kasaya-Pāhuda' has been composed on the basis of the said `Pāhuḍa'. Accordingly, it is also styled as `Pejjadospāhuḍa'. The Sanskrit transformation of the Prākrita word `Pejjados' is `Preyash-Dwesh' which literally means love and hatred. It is key note to know the absolute truth. Without fully grasping it, it is not possible to break the fetters of worldly attachments.

Subject-matter: In the said book, the causes of worldly attachments such as anger etc and their vicious consequences in the shape of sheer attachment and malevolence, have been discussed minutely in a critical manner.

Composition: Kasaipāhuḍa has been composed in versified form. The total number of Sutras is 233. Although, the Sutras are concise in form, yet they carry deep sense with profound knowledge. Decidedly, Achārya Guṇadher made great contribution towards spread of philosophical doctrines of Jaina religion and enrichment of spiritual knowledge, earlier manifested through Shatkhanḍāgama.

It is believed that after accomplishment of `Kasāya-Pāhuḍa', Achārya Guṇadher had narrated it to Achārya Nāghasti and Ārya Mankṣu and the said tradition had continued even thereafter.

Explanatory Literature: Achārya Yativrashabha had written a Chūrni (gloss), comprising of 6,000 Verses in Prākrita dialect on `Kasaipāhuḍa'. It is believed that Achārya Yativrashabha had explained the said Chūrṇi-Sutras to Shri Uchchārṇā-chārya who in turn had composed 12,000 Uchchāraṇa Sūtras. However, the said explanatory literature is no longer available now.

The most renowned commentary on `Kasāyapāhuḍa' which greatly added to its significance is `Jayadhavalā' commentary, initially written by highly celebrated author, Achārya Virasena and completed by Acharya Jinasena, after the death of his guru. The matter has been referred to in earlier pages also where the context so demanded. It is really an exhaustive commentary in sixty thousand verses. The initial 20,000 verses of the said commentary had been composed by Āchārya Virasena and next 40,000 verses were composed by Āchārya Jinasena, after the death of the former.

The significance of `Jayadhavalā' commentary can be judged from the very fact that just as five sections of Shatkhanḍāgama are titled as `Dhavala' and the sixth section as `Maha-dhavala', similarly, `Kasāya-pahuḍa' is also popularly known as `Jayadhavalā' because of the title of its commentary.

Body of Kasāya-Pāhuḍa:- Kasāya-Pāhuḍa consists of 15 chapters or heads namely—1. Pejjadosvibhakti; 2. Sthiti-Vibhakti; 3. Anubhag-Vibhakti; 4. Pradesh-Vibhakti—Jhiṇājhiṇasthityantika; 5. Bandhaka; 6. Vedaka; 7. Upyoga; 8. Chatuḥ-sthan; 9. Vyanjan; 10. Darshanmohopashāmnā; 11. Darshan Mohkṣapṇā; 12. Saṁyamāsaṁyam-labadhi; 13. Saṁyam-labhdi; 14. Chāritra-Mohopa-shāmnā; and 15. Chāritra-Mohakṣapṇā.

It is evident from the very titles of the Chapters of Kasaipahuḍa that the sacred book is highly significant in so far as it helps in the growth of spiritual enlightenment and self-purification.

Language of Shatkhanḍāgama

There was a time when the territory, adjoining the town of Mathura, was popularly known as `Shorsena Janpada'. The native dialect of the said area was called `Shorseni-Prākrita'. Besides Shrosena Janpada, the said dialect was used in an extensive territory, spreading out on the east upto the area, ahead of which Ardha-Māgadhi Prākrita was the medium and on the west upto the region, ahead of which `Paishāchi Prākrita' was the medium of expression. In nutshell, Shorseni Prākrita was popular in central territory of Northern India.

The Prākrita dialect, primarily used by Digamber scholars and authors in accomplishment of their canonical literature, appears to be very much close to Shorseni Prākrita. The following points need to be contemplated upon in this regard.

The principal centre of activities of Digamber Sect was South India which is amply reflected in relative tales. It was the period when a terrible famine, lasting continuously for 12 years, had overtaken the country, consequent upon which, a few unfortunate incidents had taken place, leading to the virtual split in Jaina institution in two distinct sects. The wing, sustained in Northern India, was primarily of Shwetambers, who believed in existence of old Agamas and allied scriptures — may be partially, if not entirely. Shwetambers spared no pains in ensuring safety of Jaina Agamas or Agamic texts by convening meetings of Jaina scholars and intellectuals who undertook recitation of spiritual utterances of Jaina Tirthankers, revised and edited the texts to be reduced to writing which were, hitherto, in the memory of the scholars only. Consequently the texts could remain intact for the benefit of the people.

However, the views of Digamber Achārya were different. They believed that 12 Angas had become obliterated. Resultantly, they might have lost their grip on Ardha-Māgadhi Prākrita and found it more congenial to accomplish their writings in Shorseni Prākrita, since it was the popular medium of expression in the entire central territory of Northern India. Every author or writer aspires that his works are widly acclaimed and they continue to get lasting appreciation of their readers. It, obviously, depends upon more and more awareness of the dialect. Shorseni was a popular dialect and an effective source of expression in those days. Naturally, Digamber scholars might have found it safe to write in Shorseni Prākrita for wider recognition of their books.

Probably also, whatever contacts, Digambers had with Northern India, they might have been confined to in and around Mathura and, accordingly, the Digmber authors might have found it convenient to take up their spiritual writings in Shorseni Prākrita (A regional variation of the Prākrita and Apbhransh languages).

Shorseni Prākrita, adopted by Digamber authors in writing of their religious treatises came to be known as Jaina Shorseni Prākrita, mainly because the Jaina scholars were the foremost in adopting Shorseni for composition of their scriptural works who had then own accomplished style and tradition. Thus, the language developed, polished and enriched by Jaina sages, was bound to have its own identity which came to be popularly known as Jaina Shorseni Prākrita.

Presumably also, at the time when Jaina institution was still a compact body and it had not splitted nay even much earlier say from the life time of Lord Mahāvira, all religious discourses were delivered in Ardha Māgadhi Prākrita. Infact, Ardha Māgadhi was the official language of Jaina religion. Whether Lord Mahāvira made his utterances verbally in Ardha Māgadhi Prākrita or expressed, his feelings through phonetic sound, emitted by his body, ultimately, they had been compiled and co-ordinated in Ardha Māgadhi Prākrita. It has been emphasized above that Digambers had great regard for Ardha Māgadhi Prākrita, since it was a divine language and medium of speech used by Tirthankers. Besides this, they were also aware that all their old sacred treatises, containing ideological and philosophical truths, had been reduced to writing in Ardha Māgadhi Prākrita. Hence although, they had adopted Shorseni for their writings, it had an impact of Ardha Māgadhi and developed a new shape which, with the passage of time, came to be known as cherished language of Jaina Scholars for accomplishment of Scriptural works or as Jaina Shorseni language, distinct from Shorseni Prākrita.

From minute examination of the characteristics of Jaina Shorseni Prākrita, it is obtained that it does not represent the true nature and form of Shorseni Prākrita. There are numerous examples to show that the vocabulary used by Digamber Jaina scholars is more close to the glossary of Ardha Māgadhi Prākrita.

The renowned grammarian of Prākrita dialect, Dr. R.Pischel has named it as Jaina Shorseni Prākrita. The intention appears to be the same.[1] However, Dr. Denecke, learned student of Dr. Walter Schubring, does not subscribe and holds that the hypothetical name of Jaina Shorseni, suggested by Dr. Pischel is not consistent. In his opinion, it will be more appropriate to name the language as 'Digambari language'. Dr. A.N. Upādhye and other intellectuals disagree and donot subscribe to this view. They are right in as much as Digamber scholars have also written religious books in Kannaḍa and Tamil languages as well which are highly accomplished books and have added to the richness of the said languages. Thus, grossly speaking, naming of the language as Jaina Shorseni Prākrita appears to be more consistent.

The uses of Deshi Prākrita dialect words are almost absent in Jaina Shorseni Prākrita, since the forms thrived and prospered in the area, belonging to Dravaḍian linguistic group and as such the words of Deshi Prākrita could not be included in Jaina Shorseni Prākrita, used by Digamber scholars.

Shorseni, used by Digamber scholars, was not influenced by the languages of Dravaḍian linguistic group in as much as the phonics, morphology and syntax of languages, pertaining to the said group are distinct from those of Aryan linguistic group. No doubt, Sanskrit is found to have an impact on Jaina Shorseni. Firstly, Shorseni was under influence of Sanskrita from the very outset. Varurichi has advocated that Shorseni had its origin from Sanskrit.[2] and secondly, Sanskrit has its own characteristics, a glimpse of which is found in the writings of eminent Digamber scholars, namely—Sumant Bhadra, Pūjyapāda, Anant-Virya, and Aklanka etc.

It is a brief account of Shorseni Prākrita, used by Digamber scholars in their writings. Although, certain dissimilarities are also found in the language, used by various Digamber scholars in accomplishment of their books, yet they are obvious, keeping in view the diversities in the places of their living, times and conditions etc. and they are not very significant. Thus, the language of Shatkhanḍāgama is Jaina Shorseni Prākrita. Whatever, dissimilarities are there in the languages of the original Sūtras and the commentaries on Shatkhanḍāgama they may be due to the diversities in territorial and living conditions of the authors.

Chief Features of Shorseni Prākrita

The main features of Shorseni Prākrita are as under:

---

1. Comparative grammar of the Prākrita languages, pages 20-21.
2. Prakriti : Sanskritaṁ.

—*Prākrita Prākash,* 12.2.

Letter `ga' is used in place of `Ka', appearing in the middle of a word. Similarly, letters `ta' and `tha' are found converted in letters `da' and `dha' respectively.

Letter `di' is prefixed in a verb, signifying present tense, first person and singular number.

Generally, suffixes of `ua', `tu' and `dūṇa' are applied in indeclinables, used as verbs, signifying past tense.

Conclusive and Thorough Investigation

A lot of discussion has already been made, wherever, it was so necessary, in regard to norms and substances, linguistics and styles of composition of both Jaina Agamas and Tripitakas (Three collections of Buddhist writings). There can be numerous similarities in uses of words and expressions in Jaina Agamas and Tripitikas which call for minute research and examination. It may not be desirable on our part to elaborate them in the present volume keeping in view its largeness or voluminosity in size.

I have only referred to the points and it will be for the coming generation to answer them in greater details. For me, it will not be practical to do so even in the third volume since fresh topics have been dealt with therein and it will be no less voluminous in size as against first and second volumes.

Pitaka: The word Pitaka has been used under both Jaina and Bodh traditions to mean a shastra or a collection of holy writings. It literally means a large basket or a box for storage and preservation of sacred writings, generally used by a scholar or a religious preceptor. The use of the word `gani' (one who is well-versed in sacred writings) is generally found in Buddhist scriptures to have been made for Lord Mahāvira, Lord Buddha and pioneers of other religious sects besides propounders of different ideological doctrines.[1] Possibly, the word `Gaṇi Pitaka' might have been adopted under Jaina tradition to denote spiritual utterances of Lord Mahāvira.

Nigantha: It is a Prākrita formation of Sanskrit word `Nirgranth' (free from knots of the soul) which means absolute freedom from both internal and external material attachments or worldly pleasures. In Tripitakas (Buddhist scriptures) the word `Nirgranth' appears repeatedly for Jaina community and `Nirgranth Gyātputra' for Lord Mahāvira. The use of the word `Nirgranth' is also found for Jaina monks as also religious utterances of Lord Mahāvira.

Puggal: (Sanskrit formation `Pudgal'). The use of the said word is found under Jaina and Bodh traditions only. While it purports to mean `matter' (Elementary substance) under Jaina tradition, it is used in the sense of soul under Bodh tradition.[2]

The word `Pudgal' also appears in Jaina Agamas to mean elements of life or living organism.[3] While replying to a question of Gandher Gautama, Lord Mahāvira had used the word `Pudgal' for soul.[4]

---

1. Sanyuktanikāya, Dahar Sūtta (3.1-2), page 68; Dighnikāya, Samaujaphal Sūtta 1/2; Sūtta Nikāya, Samīya Sutta, pages 108-11 etc.
2. Majjhim Nikāya (114).
3. Bhagwati Sutra Shataka, 20-3-2.
4. Bhagwati Sutra Shataka, 8-3-10.

Arhat and Buddha: At present, the word Arhat is commonly used to mean Lord Mahāvira or a Tirthanker and the word Budha to mean Lord Buddha under Bodh tradition. The two words have become conventional and acquired specific meanings. The fact, however, remains that the words Arhat and Budha have appeared in Jaina Agamas for their highly enlightened divinities. Tirthankers and Omniscients and similarly, they have appeared in Buddhist scriptures for their highly respectable and celebrated preceptor of Baudha religion.

There is a well-known verse, appearing in Jaina Agamas, reading as under—

"Jeya Budha Atikanta
Jeya Budha Anāgayā"[1]

Similarly, there is a well-known verse found in Buddhist scriptures which reads as under:

"Ye Budha Atitā cha ye cha Budhā Anāgatā
Pachuppannā va ye Budhā ahaṁ Vandāmi te sadā

In Jaina Agamas, the uses of the words `Budha'; `Sambudha' and Sanyabudha (Jaina defied saints) have appeared at several places, as shown below:

Tithagarāṇaṁ sayaṁ Sambudhanaṁ[2]
Tivihā Budhā-ṇāṇ Budhā Dansaṇa Budhā Charitta Budhā.[3]

Samānenaṁ bhagvayā Mahāvireṇa Aigarenaṁ tithayareṇaṁ Sayaṁ Sambudhenaṁ[4]
Budhehi evan paveditaṁ[5]
Sankhāi thamma ya Viyāgaranti Budha hu te Antkarā bhavanti[6]

Similarly, under Buddhist tradition, the word `Arhat' is found to have been used for highly reverred spiritual heads. For Lord Buddha himself, the attributives of `Arhat', `Samyaka' (All whole, entire) and `Sambudh' (a deified saint, Lord Buddha).[7] After final salvation of Lord Buddha, a convention of 500 Budhist monks was held in which 499 monks except Anand were addressed as Arhats. By the time, the proceedings of the convention started, Ananda had also attained Arhatship (a qualified and competent spiritual guide).[8] Besides the above, the uses of the word `Arhat' in Jaina Agamas and Budha in Buddhist writings are found time and again.

1. Sutra Kritānga Sūtra, 1-1-36.
2. Rāyapasenaiyaṁ, 5.
3. Sthānānga Sūtra, 3.
4. Samvāyānga Sūtra 2/2.
5. Achāranga Sūtra, 4/1/340.
6. Sutrakritanga Sūtra, 1-14-18.
7. Dighnikāya, samanjjaphal Sūtta 1/2.
8. Vinaya Pitaka, Panch Shatikā Skandhak.

Thera: The word `Sthavira' has appeared under both traditions to signify an elder or senior monk. Under Jaina tradition, the rank of Sthavira Sādhus has been further classified and sub-classified, keeping in view their spiritual knowledge, age and the seniority or juniority after attainment of initiation. Under Budhist tradition, the designation of There or Thero is prefixed with the names of all those Sādhus who have completed 12 years after attaining initiation.

Bhante: While addressing respectable and elderly persons, the salutation or Bhante or Bhadant (a term of respect applied to address senior Jaina and Buddhist monks) is found to have been used under both traditions. For instance, use of phrases, `Se Kantthena bhante'; `Ṇuṇaṁ bhante'; `Seva bhante'; and `Savvaṁ bhante' is found in Jaina Agamas.[1] Similarly, the use of the salutation 'bhante' (bhadant) is found abundantly in Budhist writings.

Aouso: The use of the address `Aouso' (Ayushmān) is found for persons of equal age or youngers under both traditions to denote a wish for the addressee to be blessed with longevity of life. Even Lord Buddhā was addressed as `Aouso Gautama'. Goshālaka (A pioneer of a different religious ideology -- Head of Ajivakas) also addressed Lord Mahāvira as `Aouso Kāsvā'[2].

'Shrāvaka'; `Upasaka'; `Shramnopāsaka'

The use of the word `Shravaka' is found under both traditions. Under Jaina tradition, the Shravaka represents a devotee, leading a family life.

However, under Buddhist tradition, the said word has been used to represent both categories of devouts—those having renounced the worldly attachments and those leading household life.[3] `Upāsaka' (a worshipper as distinguished from a bhikṣu who has renounced the world) and a `Shramṇoupāsaka' (Aṇ ascetic) appear frequently under both traditions.

`Asrava' (Pain, affliction or distress) and `Sanvar' (Control over ideas inviting actions) are used in the same sense under both traditions[4] According to Jainas, action of the senses which impells the soul towards external objects is called `Asrava'. It is good or evil accordingly as it is directed towards God or evil objects.

A similar phrase is found in sacred books of each tradition. In Jaina Agamas, it reads --

`Āgārāo Aṇagāriyaṁ pavvaittaye'.[5] In Buddhist scriptures, it reads — `Agārammā' Angāriyaṁ Pavvajjanti'.[6]

**`Samyakadrishti'** (Having thorough and perfect vision) and `Mithyadrishṭi' (having false and illusory vision). The said words are found to have been used in the same sense under both traditions.

Jainas and Budhists both consider that their own followers are having perfect and true vision, while those following other ideologies are having false and illusory vision.

1. *Bhagwati Sūtra*, Shataka 7/3/279.
2. *Bhagwati Sūtra*, Shataka 15.
3. *Anguttar Nikāya,* Ekkaniyat, 14.
4. Jaina Agama Samvāyānga Sūtra No. 5, Majhim Nikāya (Further dialogues of Lord Buddha), 2.
5. *Bhagwati Sūtra*, 11/12/431.
6. Mahāvagga.

**`Uposatha'**. The use of the said word is found under both traditions. However, as cited in `Digh Nikāya' (Dialogues of Lord Buddha — 3 volumes) Lord Buddha had criticised the performances of `Upasatha' as carried out amongst Jainas.

`Vairamna'. The use of the said word is found under both tradition in the sense of observance of austerities.

Tathāgata. Although, the said word has been primarily used for Lord Buddha under Buddhist tradition, yet it appears at certain places in Jaina Agamas as well. For example—

"Kao Kaie mehāvi upajjanti tahāgay Tahāgayā uppadikkantā chakkhu Logassanuttarā."[1]

**`Vinaya' (Humility):** The significance of discipline and humility is accepted under both traditions. The Budhist scripture `Vinaya Pitaka" (Book of Discipline) primarily deals with the moral code to be observed by Bodh Sādhus. In Jaina Agamas too there are several chapters, exclusively dealing with Vinaya texts, prescribed for Jaina monks. The title of the ninth chapter of `Dashvaikālika Sūtra' is `Vinaya Samādhi'. Its first sentence reads—"Thamā Va Kohā Va Mayappa Māyā guru sagase Vinayaṁ na sikhe". The title of the first chapter of `Uttrādhyayan Sūtra' is `Vinayashruta' and the sentence reads therein -- "Viṇayaṁ pān Karissāmi, aṇupivviṁ suṇeha me."

Prohibited Discourses: Narration of tales or events relating to females, devotees, homeland and king's exploits are found prohibited in Jaina Āgamas. Similarly, in chapters, styled `Brahmajāl and `Sāmanjaphal' of Digh Nikāya (Dialogues of Lord Budha), it has been stressed to avoid narration of such stories. It reads—"Tirachchhān Kathaṁ, Anuyukto Viharit Saiyyadhadaṁ Raj kathaṁ, Chorkathaṁ, Mahānat Kathaṁ, Senā Kathaṁ, Bhaya Kathaṁ, Yudha Kathaṁ, Annakathaṁ, pān kathaṁ."

Three Submissions — Four Submissions

Under Buddhist tradition, the three submissions are generally popular while as per Jaina Agamas four submissions are very important. The submissions under both traditions are as below:

I submit to Lord Buddha.	I submit to Lord Tirthankers.
I submit to Buddhist organisation	I submit to the highly accomplished sages of Jaina religion who have subdued worldly pleasures and attained perfection.
I submit to Bodha religion	I submit to holy saints of Jaina religion.
	I submit to the ideals of Jaina religion as enunciated by Kevalins.

Prayer: The popular eulogical sentence, appearing in Jaina Agamas reads -- "Namotthuṇaṁ samṇassa Bhagwao Mahāvirassa" (I bow to Lord Māhavira and holy saints of his institution). Similarly, the eulogical sentence, under Buddhist

1. *Sūtrakritanga Sūtra* 2/15/120/625.

tradition reads "Namotthuṇaṁ samaṇassa bhagwao Samyak Saṁbudhassa." (I bow to Lord Buddha, having accomplished thorough enlightenment as also his learned disciples).

Towns and Regions: The names of the towns—Nālandā, Rajgraha, Kayangalā and Shrāvasti and names of the regions—Anga (The region on the right bank of Ganges and popularly called Angapuri, which is considered to be the same or situated very close to modern Bhāgalpur). and Magadha (The territory in South Bihar) are found in holy books of both traditions.

It is cited in Jaina Agamas that a person can never pay off the obligations of three types of benefactors in life—Gurus, employers and parents.[1] It is also added that even if very superior type of services are rendered, he will still remain indebted and will not be able to fulfil his obligations towards them. Almost a similar saying is found in Buddhist scriptions. While addressing his mendicants, Lord Buddha observes — that even if a son bears his father on one shoulder and his mother on the other and even if he applies or massages a cosmetic paste over the bodies of his parents continuously for 100 years and regularly gives them bath with temperate water, he will not be deemed to be obliging them in any way nor he will be considered to be fulfilling his obligations since a son has unlimited obligations to his parents, which he cannot pay off during his whole life. However, as per Jaina Agamas, a person can redeem itself from obligations if he assists his benefactors in spiritual performances.

Two Tirthankers: As cited in Jaina Agamas, it is firmly believed that there can never be two Tirthankers at a time and within the same region or country-say India. Similarly, while delivering sermons before his mendicants, Lord Buddha emphatically states that there is not the slightest possibility that two highly enlightened Buddhas could live at one and the same time and within the same territory.[2]

Female Tirthanker, Chakravarty

It is firmly believed by Jainas that a female in her present birth can never become a Jaina Arhat (Tirthanker), a Chakravarty (A most celebrated individual of its age who holds 14 precious gems in the shape of most outstanding symbols. A Chakravarty is an exclusive ruler of 3/4 part of the country-say India) and Indra (Lord of heaven). In the same manner, Lord Buddha emphatically denies the probability of any female becoming a thorough enlightened Budha, Chakravarty or Indra.[3] However, according to Shwetambers, a female, named Malli, had attained the status of Tirthanker, although it was a wonder in itself and there is no possibility of its recurrence.

1. *Sthānanga Sūtra*, Tha-3.
2. *Anguttar Nikāya* (The book of Gradual sayings of Lord Buddha).
3. *Ibid.*

APPENDIX - I

Glossary of Jaina Technical Terms

Abhigama : Knowledge; Five duties to be observed by the votary, when he enters into the monks' residence. These duties are : (i) renunciation of animate materials, (ii) limitation of inanimate materials, (iii) folding of hands on seeing a monk, (iv) concentration of mind, and (v) wrapping of scarf round the face.

Abhigraha : Specific secret mental resolve.

Abhijati : Effect.

Abhīkṣaṇa Jnānopayoga : Perpetual pursuit of knowledge.

Acelaka : Devoid of clothes; Naked; Few clothes.

Acitta : In-animate matter, non-sterilised.

Acyuta : Twelfth heaven; *See* Deva.

Adhyavasāya : Thought, mental effort.

Aghātī-karma : Non-destructive karmas. The karmas, which do not destroy the inherent attributes of knowledge etc. of the soul, are called non-destructive karmas. There are four such karmas : (i) feeling producing, (ii) life-span, (iii) physique-making, and (iv) status-determining. *See* Ghati-karma.

Agurulaghu : Neither heavy nor light, Neither greatness nor smallness.

Akalpanīya : Prohibited, Faulty.

Akevalī : A state before acquiring omniscience; Non-omniscient.

Akṣiṇa-mahānasa Labdhi : A supernatural or divine power acquired through specific austerities. The foods prepared could be served for hundreds or thousands of people until the austerite does not eat.

Amarśauṣadha Labdhi : A supernatural power acquired though observance of specific austerity. Just as all the diseases are pacified by the bath in elixir, all the diseases are destroyed only by the touch of this type of austerite; Supernatural power of tactile medication.

Anagāra Dharma : The monastic religion; Observance of vows without any transgression or exception.

Anaśana : Life-long renunciation of four-fold food; Fasting.

Anga : Primary canon, *See* Dvādaśāngī.

Anīka : Army and Army commander; They have to fight in the form of dancers and musicians during war.

Antarāya Karma : Obstructive karma; A karma which obstructs the gains etc. on its fruition.

Aṇuvrata : The partial renunciation of violence, falsity, stealing, non-celibacy or sex and possessions as per capacity. This is the conduct of householder votaries. Minor vows.

Apaścima : Māraṇāntika Sanlekhanā : A fast unto death devoid of attachment with body after subsiding the passions at the time of death.

Apavartana : Attenuation; Loss in fruitioning power of duration and intensity of karmas.

Apratikarma : Absence of physical activities like raising up, sitting, sleeping and walking etc. during fasting. This occurs during the tree-like steadfast fasting.

Arhat : *See* Arihanta.

Arihanta : A person, victor of the enemies of attachment and aversion and enriched with specific grandeur; A paragon of the Jainas; Venerable; Enlightened.

Arthāgama : The scriputres in the form of meaning.

Asankhya-pradeśī : Innumerable-pointed; The point (pradeśa) is defined as the indivisible part of an entity. The entity is called innumerable-pointed which has innumerable number of points. Every living being is innumerable-pointed.

Aticāra : Transgression, Infraction. It is to partially violate the vow or arrange factors for violation of a vow.

Atiśaya : Excellence; Excessively extra-ordinary specificity of the qualities found in human beings in a normal way.

Atthama Tapa : An austerity of fasting of three days, Telā.

Auddeśika : Particularised; Food, clothes or residence specially meant for offering to the wandering monks, striver monks, passionless monk and others.

Autpātiki Buddhi : Inborn intellect; An intellect grasping the matters unseen, un-heard and un-analysed and materialising it.

Avadhijnāna : Clairvoyance; Knowledge of perceptiple substances through the soul without the help of senses and mind; Limiting knowledge.

Avasarpiṇī kāla : Devolution cycle of time; The division of time cycle where the bone-joints and configurations of the living beings gradually get weakened, the life-span and size decrease, and there is a gradual loss of rise, activity, valour, potency, self-exertion and prowess. During this period, the colour, smell, taste and touch also get dull. The auspicious volitions go on decreasing and inauspicious volitions go on increasing. There are six spokes of this devolution epoch :
1. Extreme Plentitude; 2. Plentitude; 3. Plentitude-cum-penury; 4. Penury-cum-plentitude; 5. Penury; 6. Extreme penury.

Ava-svāpini : Deep sleep.

Āgāradharma : Acceptance of vows with exceptions, Householders' religion.

Āgāra-dharma-praiṇdhi : Prominently managing the external dress and ornaments.

Ākāśātipātī : Divine power of (i) getting rains of desired materials like silver etc. or undesired entities or (ii) moving in sky by learnings or smearing of feet.

Ārā : Section; Spoke of time.

Ārta-dhyāna : To be anxious about the separation of the desired and non-separation of the undesired; A kind of meditation; Sorrowful meditation.

Ārogya : Heaven of the Buddhas.

Āśatanā : Disrespect; To level false charges on teachers; To dishonour them or feel superior to them.

Āsrava : Door of influx of karmas; Influx; The karma-attracting volitions of the self.

Ātāpanā : An austerity of putting the body in distress by heat and cold etc.

Ātma-rakṣaka : Body-guards of Indra. They have to be ever-ready for the protection of Indra.

Āyambila vardhamāna Tapa : An austerity, in which a kneaded or parched grain (or its powder) is eaten once a day by steeping it in water, is called 'Āyambila' (tasteless food). The gradually increasing level of this austerity is called by this name. In this austerity, there is one fasting after an Āyambila, one fasting after two Āyambila, one fasting after three Āyambila .... fasting after 100 Āyambilas. This austerity takes a time of 20 years, 9 months and 20 days.

Bādara Kāya-yoga : Gross physical activity.

Bādara Mana-yoga : Gross mental activity.

Bādara Vacana-yoga : Gross vocal activity.

Bāla Maraṇa : Fools' death; Death under non-restrained or ignorant state.

Bāla -tapasvī : An ignorant austerite; Undertaking austerities with ignorance.

Baladeva : The elder step-brother of Vāsudeva. There are nine Baladevas born in each of the evolution and devolution epoch. Their mothers see four dreams. After the death of Vāsudeva, they get initiated and undertake hard austerities, for spiritual progress. Some of them get liberation while others take rebirth in heavens.

Bandha : Bondage; Karmic bonding, Intimate contact of karmic mattergies with the soul.

Belā : Two day fasting.

Bhadra Pratimā : A kind of austerity with meditation; Undertaking meditation for four Praharas each facing in eastern, western, southern and northern direction.

Bhakta-pratyākhyāna : Life-long renunciation of three or four kinds of food under inflictions or without inflictions.

Bhāva : Mode; Thoughts.

Bhava-siddhika : Liberatable beings; Living beings having a capacity for liberation.

Bhāvitātmā : Purified soul; Purified soul enganged in restraint; Monastic mental resolves.

Bhavya : Liberatable beings; *See* Bhavasiddika.

Bhikṣu-pratimā : The practice of austerity by the monks with specific mental resolve; There are twelve monastic mental resolves. The first mental resolve has a period of one month. The second mental resolve has a period of two months; The third has a period of three months; the fourth has a period of four months, the fifth one has a period of five months; the sixth one has a period of six months and the seventh one has a period of seven months. The period of the eighth, ninth and tenth mental resovles has a duration of one week each. The eleventh mental resolve has a period of one fortnight. The twelfth mental resolve has a period of one night.

There is one delivery of food-intake in the first resolve. The second, third, fourth, fifth, sixth and seventh resolves have two, three, four, five, six and seven deliveries respectively. The eighth, ninth and tenth resovles have alternative four-fold food renunciation and intake of Āyambila on completion. The eleventh resolve has 3-day fasting with four-fold food renunciation as an essentiality. The 4-day fasting is essential in the twelfth mental resolve. Please, see the description of 8th, 9th, , 10th, 11th and 12th mental resolve under the descriptions of first seven-day, second seven-day, third seven-day, single day and single night mental resolves respectively. While undertaking and observing these mental resolves, the monk renounces the total attachment with the body and he is always engrossed in the attachment with his soul alone. He endures all the sufferings and afflictions due of gods, humans and animals with equanimous attitude while alleviating his dejected mentality.

Bhūta : One-sensed beings-trees etc.; A synonym of 'Jīva' .

Bhuvanapati : Mansional gods; *See* Deva.

Brahmaloka : Fifth heaven, *See* Deva.

Caccara : Chwk; A place where more than four roads meet or cross together.

Cakra-ratna : Gem-wheel. The first jewel out of fourteen jewels of cakravartī. It has a golden edge. Its spokes are made of red gem (Lohitākṣa). Its centre is made up of diamond gem. It is complete in all respects and it is also divine. The army of cakravartī follows the direction in which this gem-wheel moves. The distance of Yojana is the distance it moves in one day. Due to the effect of this wheel, many kings surrender the carkravartī without fighting while some others surrender him after fighting.

Cakravartī : Most praiseworthy and excellent man of his era. He bears a gem-wheel. There are 63 torch-bearers in every evolution and devolution epoch — 24 Ford-builders, 12 Cakravarties, 9 Vāsudevas, nine Baladevas, and nine anti-Vāsudevas. The Cakravartī is the soverign ruler of the six sections of Bharata region. There are fourteen jewels of a Cakravartī : (i) wheel, (ii) umbrella, (iii) royal staff, (iv) sword, (v) gems, (vi) leathers, (vii) Kakiṇī gem, (viii) army commander, (ix) house lords, (x) carpenters, (xi) royal priest, (xii) women, (xiii) horses, and (xiv) elephants.

Carama : Ultimate, Last.

Cāraṇa-ṛddhi-dhara : Proficient in the prodigy of sky-movement; see Janghācāraṇa, Vidyācāraṇa.

Cāritra : The best practices performed with the objective of the purification of the soul.

Caturdaśa-pūrva : The fourteen pre-canons (Pūrvas). They are included in the twelfth primary canon of Dṛṣtivāda (Discourses on Doctrines). The fourteen pre-canons are as below :

(1) The Pre-canon on Origination; (2) The Pre-canon on the Top Tenets; (3) The Discourses on Potency; (4) The Discourses of Relativism; (5) The Discourses on knowledge; (6) The Discourses on Truth; (7) The Discourses on Soul; (8) The Discourses on Karma; (9) The Discourses on Renunciation; (10) The Discourses on Learnings; (11) The Discourses on Welfare and Auspicious Events; (12) The Science of Vitality or Health; (13) The Pre-canon on performing Arts and Crafts; and (14) The Essence of the Universe.

Caturgati : Four destinities; Wandering of soul in four destinities or four kinds of birth-states like infernal, peripatetics, astral and celestials.

Cāturyāma : Four Major vows; The five major vows are included in the four major vows during the periods of 22 ford-builders excluding the first and the last out of 24 ones.

Caubīsī : The twenty-four ford-builders in the evolution or devolution epochs.

Caudaha Ratna : *See* Cakravartī.

Caudaha Vidyā : Fourteen kinds of learnings : (1) six Vedangas (components) : 01 phonetics, (2) rituals and conduct, (3) grammar, (4) metrology, (5) astrology, (6) etymological commentaries. (7-10). Four vedas : Rg, Yajuh, Sāma and Athārva, (11) Mīmāṁsā, (12) Nyāya, (13) Religions, (14) Legends (Purāṇas).

Chadmastha : Non-omniscient; The term 'Chadma' is the fruition of destructive karmas.

The soul under this kind of state is called 'chadmastha'. The Jīva is called chadmastha until he acquires the omniscience.

Chattham Tapa : Austerity of two-day fasting (Belā).

Darśana : Intuition; Conation; Grasping of general attributes of a general-cum-specific entity overlooking the specific attributes.

Daśama Tapa : An austerity of 4-day fasting.

Deśavratī : Partial observer of vow (not total).

Deva : Special-bed-born living beings; Gods; Celestials; There are four kinds of celestial :

1. Mansional gods; 2. Peripatetic gods; 3. Astral gods; 4. Empyrean gods.

1. '*Mansional gods :* The thickness of Ratnapraphā hell has 12 layers. The first two are empty. The rest ten have residents. The ten kinds of mansional gods— fiendish youths, serpentine youths, vulturine youths, lightning youths, oceanic youths, directional youths, areal youths, elcetric youths reside there. They have bright shine like a child. That is why, the term 'youth' (Kumāra) is used with their names. Their residences are called 'Mansions' (Bhuvana). It is due to this that these gods are called mansional gods.
2. *Peripatetic gods :* There are eight kinds of peripatetic gods— Kinnara, Kimpuruṣa, Rākîasa, Bhūta and Piśāca, Mohoraga, Gandharva etc.
3. *Astral gods :* There are five classes of astral gods : moon, sun, planets, asterisms and stars.
4. *Empyrean gods :* There are two kinds of empyrean gods : (i) Born-in Kalpas, (ii) Born-in beyond-Kalpas. The 'Kalpa' term means permissible conduct, empyrean-size earth, a system-having the categories or greats of Indra, Indra-equivalents etc. There are twelve kinds of Kalpa : (i) Saudharma, (ii) Īśāna, (iii) Sanatkumāra, (iv) Māhendra, (v) Arahma, (vi) Lāntaka, (vii) Śukra, (viii) Sahasrāra, (ix) Ānata, (x) Prāṇata, (xi) Āraṇa, (xii) Acyuta. The Kalpas of Saudharma and Īśana are situated parallely in the south and north of Meru at a height of 1½ Rajju above it. The Kalpas of Sanatkumāra and Māhendra are also situated parallel on the upper side of Saudharam and Īśāna Kalpa, Brahma, Lāntaka, Śukra and Sahasrāra are also above them one over the other. The Kalpas of Ānata and Prāṇata are both parallel. The Kalpas of Āraṇa and Acyuta are also parallel to them but above them. The life-span of Kalpa empyreans are as below :

Kalpa	Min-Life-span	Max life-span
1.	1P	2 Sāgaras
2.	1P	> 2 Sāgaras
3.	2 Sāgaras	7 Sāgaras
4.	2 Sāgaras	> 7 Sāgaras
5.	7 Sāgaras	10 Sāgaras
6.	10 Sāgaras	14 Sāgaras
7.	14 Sāgaras	17 Sāgaras
8.	17 Sāgaras	18 Sāgaras
9.	18 Sāgaras	19 Sāgaras
10.	19 Sāgaras	20 Sāgaras
11.	20 Sāgaras	21 Sāgaras
12.	21 Sāgaras	21 Sāgaras

The term 'Beyond-Kalpas' (Kalpātita) means the heavens where there is no difference of senior or junior. All are Indras (Ahamindras—I am Indra). They are divided into two categories : (i) Graiveyaka (neck of the Jaina universe) and (ii) Anuttara (Incomparable).

According to Jaina canons, the shape of the universe is like a man with spanned feet. The Graiveyakas are positioned near its neck. That is why, they are so-called. There are nine of them : (i) Bhadra (virtuos), (ii) Subhadra (Pious), (iii) Sujāta (well-bred), (iv) Saumanasa (Mind-pleasing), (v) Priya-darśana (lovely-sight), (vi) Sudarśana (well-sighted), (vii) Amogha (Unfailing), (viii) Su-prati-buddha (well-enlightened), and (ix) Vanśīdhara (Flutist). They have three triads each of which has three heavens.

The Anuttara (incomparable) heavens are the best of all the empyrean planes. They are five in number : (1) Vijaya (Victory), (2) Vaijayanta (Banner), (3) Jayanta (Moon), (4) Aparājita (Invincible), and (5) Sarvārtha-siddhi (All-accomplished). The four of them are in four directions and the fifth-Sarvārtha-siddhi is in the center of them.

The graded heavens are 12 and non-graded heavens are 14. Thus, their total number is 26. All of them have a gradual increase in seven characteristics and gradual decrease in four charcterisitcs.

The seven characteristics are as below :

1. Life-span.
2. *All the four kinds of powers* : (i) Infliction of pain when angry, (ii) infliction of pleasure when kind, (iii) prodigies of miniaturisation etc., and (iv) get others work forcefully are gradually increasing. But they do not utilise them because of the retardation of passions. The magnanimity, impartiality and seriousness is also gradually increasing these.
3. *Happiness* : The pleasure due to experience of desired sensual objects.
4. *Brilliance* : The great shine of body, dress and ornaments.
5. *Purity of Aureoles* : Piety in volitions.
6. *Capacity of Senses* : The power of grasping the desired sense-objects like beauty and sounds from a distance.
7. *Clairvoyance* : The range of power of knowing through right and wrong clairvoyance.

The following are the four characteristics which gradually decrease :

1. *Motion* : Power of movement and movement in practice from one place to another place.
2. *Occupancy of Body* : Height of the body.
3. *Family* : The family of gods and goddesses and empyrean planes.
4. *Pride* : The pride of residence, family, power, sensualism, splendour and life-span.

Devādhideva : The highest of the deities; *See* Arihanta.

Dig-virati Vrata : Vow of limitation of directional movement; This is the sixth vow of a Jaina votary. Under this vow, the votary limits the movements in all the ten directions.

Dik-kumariyān : Goddesses engaged in the delivery of the ford-builders. There are 56 of these goodesses. Their residences are also different. There are eight residences in lower world, eight in the upper world on Meru mountain, eight on eastern

Rucakādri, eight on southern Rucakādri, eight on western Rucckādri, eight on Northern Rucakādri, four on Intermediate Rucaka mountain and four on Rucaka island.

Diśācara : Degraded or derailed disciple.

Dravya-lingī : Having physical or outer signs; only external garb.

Duṣama-suṣama : The fourth spoke of the devolution epoch which has more penury than plentitude; Penury-cum-plentitude.

Dvādaśa Pratimā : Twelve Mental Resolves; *See* Bhikṣu-pratimā.

Dvādaśāngī : Twelve-limbed Jaina scripture; The term 'Anga' (limb) is defined as the collection of the sermons of the ford-builders by the chief disciples in the form of scriptural texts. They are twelve in number. This total collection in known as twelve-limbed or 'Dvādaśāngī'. Just as there are twelve main parts — 2 feet, 2 thighs, 2 breasts, two sides, 2 arms, 1 neck and 1 head — in the body of human beings, there are tweve limbs of the scripture-man. Their names are :

1. *Āyaro* : (Monastic Conduct).
2. *Sūyagadānga* : (Limb of Tenets).
3. *Thānanga* : (Numerated Stationings).
4. *Samavāyānga* : (Numerated Categories).
5. *Viyaha-paṇṇatti* : (Enunciation of Explanations).
6. *Ṅāyā-dhamma-Kahānga* : (Religious Stories of Jnātṛs).
7. *Uvāsaga-daśānga* : (Decad of Votaries).
8. *Antagada-daśānga* : (Decad of Worldly Terminators).
9. *Aṇuttarova-vāiya daśānga* : (Decad of Anuttara-borns).
10. *Panhāvagaraṇa* : (Interpretation of Prognositics).
11. *Vipāka-suttānga* : (Doctrine of Fruition).
12. *Ditthi-vāya* : (Discourses on Doctrines).

Dvimāsikī to Sapta-māsikī Pratimā : The mental resolves of the monk in which he accepts the foods in the form of two, three, four, five, six and seven deliveries of foods upto two to seven months as the case may be.

Dvitīya-sapta-ahorātrika-pratimā : A specific mental resolve in which a monk undertakes alternate fasting with renunciation of four-fold food. The monk undertakes physical detachment postures like sitting on hands-on-knees (utkatuka), sleeping like bent-stick (Laganda-śāyī), lying like a straight staff (Dandāyata) outside the village etc.

Eka Ahotātra Pratimā : It is the practice of posture of detachment with body (kāyotsargā) with hung arms outside the village when he is undertaking four-fold food-renunciation for three-days.

Eka-rātri-pratimā : It is to undertake the posture of detachment with body, with hanging arms, unblinking eyes, sight on single object and standing in Jina-posture—(standing even with a distance of four Angulas between the feet) and bent body outside the village for a night while undertaking four-days fasting with four-fold food-renunciation.

This mental resolve can be undertaken only when permitted by the preceptor with purified soul possessed of specific bone-joints, patience and prowess.

Ekā-daśāngī : Eleven primary canons; They do not include Dṛṣtivāda (Discourses on Doctrines); *See* Dvādaśāngī.

Ekā-satikā : A single untailored cloth which was used by the votaries for curbing the violence to living beings, during speaking.

Ekavalā Tapa : It is a kind of austerity based on a specific immaginary figure. It is run on the basis of a diagram (*See* the figure). It takes 1 year, 2 months and 2 days for a single step. There are a total of four steps. Thus, the whole austerity takes a period of 4 years, 8 months and 8 days. The renunciation of denatured foods is not necessary in the first breaking up of the austerity. But there is renunciation of denatured foods in the breaking up of fasting in the second step. There is renunciation of smearing in the third step and breaking up of fasting but Āyambila in the fourth step.

Gaccha : Group of monks.

Gaṇa : Group of multitude; Group of dissciples of two Ācāryas.

Gaṇadhara : Chief disciples of the ford-builders possessing a number of attributes like super-knowledge and intuition. They compile the sermons of the ford-builders in the form of texts.

Gaṇipitaka : The tewlve-fold scripture is a treasure of the Ācārya. Hence, it is also called as Basket of the Ācārya.

Gāthāpati : Lord of house; Lord of a great and rich family. A person who has both the professions—agriculture and trade.

Ghāti-karma : According to Jainism, the cause of worldly cycle is the karmas. When there are vibrations in the space-points of soul due to wrongness, non-abstinence, non-vigilance, passions and activity, the infinite-times-infinite karma-convertible mattergies associate with the space points occuring in the specific areas of the soul like the water and milk. These mattergies are called 'karmas'. The karmas are divided mainly in two classes : (i) Destructive and (ii) Non-destructive. The karmas which destroy the inherent attributes of knowledge etc. of the soul, are called 'destrucive karmas'. There are four of them : (i) Knowledge-obscuring, (ii) Intuition or conation-obscuring, (iii) Deluding and (iv) Obstructive.

Gotra-karma : Status-determining karma; A karma whose fruition leads one to be designated as high and low. The high-status determining karma is earned by not being proud of caste, family, power, beauty/personality, austerity, scriptural knowledge, gains and splendour etc. The pride about them earns low status, determining karma.

Graiveyakas : Empyrean planes above the heavens. They are nine in number.

Guṇaratna (Rayaṇa) Samvatsara Tapa : It is a specific austerity resulting in a large amount of karmic shedding or an asuterity in which the yearly time is spent with the enrichment of the quality of karmic shedding. This austerity lasts for more than a year. That is why, it is called a year-round austerity. In undertaking this austerity,

(i) There is alternate fasting in the first month.

(ii) There are two-day fastings in the second month.

Similary, there is sixteen day fasting in the sixteenth month.

During the period of austerity, there is endurance of heat in the sun in the day with a posture of sitting-on-hands-on-knee (utkatukāsana). In the night, there is nakedness with heroic posture (virāsana). This austerity takes 13 months and seven days. There are 76 days of breaking the fast. (*See* the figure in the end.)

Guṇavarta : Supplementary vows of votary; The three vows-sixth, seventh and eighth-of votary are called supplementary vows, Reinforcing vows, *See* Bāraha-vrata.

Guru - laghu : Heavy-cum light; Smallness and greatness.

Guru Cāturmāsika Prāyaścitta. A kind of expiation, in which there is suspension of monkhood for four months.

Guru Māsika Prāyaścitta : A kind of expiation in which there is suspension of monkhood for a month.

Gyāraha-Pratimā : Eleven mental resolves; The metnal secret resolves of the votaries are called mental resolves. The votary moves towards spiritualism through their observance. They are given below :

(i) *Mental Resolve of Faith :* Period of observance : 1 month; To have predilection in religion; to alleviate related flaws while having pure faith.

(ii) *Mental Resolve of Vows :* Period of observance : 2 months; Acceptance of the vows of five minor vows and three suplementary vows (Guṇavratas), undertaking of fasts.

(iii) *Mental Resolve of Equanimity :* Period of observance : 3 months; Acceptance of the vows of equanimity and limitation of movement in directions.

(iv) *Mental Resolve of Fasting :* Period of observance : 4 months; Undertaking fastings on eighth, fourteenth, dark and bright fifteenth days of the month.

(v) *Mental Resolve of Posture of Physical Detachment :* Period of observance : 5 months; Undertaking the posture of physical detachment in the night, not to eat in night. Not to pass *dhoti* between the legs and tuck it in the waist; To be celibate in the day and limitation of sex in the night.

(vi) *Mental Resolve of Celibacy :* Period of observance : 6 months; Observance of total celibacy.

(vii) *Mental Resolve of Renunciation of Animate Things :* Period of observance : 7 months; Renunciation of animate food.

(viii) *Mental Resolve of Renunciation of Domestic Violence or Sinful Activities:* Period of observance : 8 months; Not to undertake any sinful activities or got done by others.

(ix) *Mental Resolve of Renunciation of Service by Others :* Period of observance : 9 months; Not to get the sinful activities done through servants and other persons.

(x) *Mental Resolve of Renunciation of the Particularised :* Period of observance : 10 months; Renunciation of partcularised foods; During this stage, the votary tonsures his hairs by razor or keeps the hair-crest or top-knot. He does not say anything except, "I know or I do not know" on being asked about the household problems.

(xi) *Mental Resolve of Remaining Monk-like :* Period of observance : 11 months; During this period, the votary tonsures his head by razor or hand-plucks the hairs. He accepts the garb of a monk, conduct of a monk and accessories of a monk. The attachment with his family members, however, remains. Hence, he goes to persons of his family for alms-begging.

Hallā : A specific insect having a shape similar to the grass of Govalika creeper.

Iccha-parimāṇa Vrata : The fourth vow of the votary, in which he limits the possessions; Vow of limiting possessions.

Īryā samiti : Carefulness in walking (*See*, Samiti).

Jallauṣdha Labdhi : A supernatural power acquired through specific austerity. Due to this prodigy, all the diseases of patients are alleviated by the dirt of ear, nose and body of the austerite.

Jambūdvīpa : There are innumerable island-continents and oceans in the middle universe. Every island-continent is surrounded by the ocean and each ocean is surrounded by the island-continent. Jambūdvīpa is in the centre of all of them. It is 1 lac Yojana wide from east to west and south to north. There are seven regions located in it : (i) Bharata, (ii) Haimavata, (iii) Hari, (iv) Videha, (v) Ramyak, (vi) Hairanyavata and (vii) Airāvata. The Bharata region is in the south, Airāvata region is in the north, and the Videha (Mahā-videha) region is in the east and west.

Janghācāraṇa Labdhi : The supernatural power or prodigy of sky-movement through patting of thighs. The prodigy can be acquired by the monk practising the austerity of 3-day fasting (Telā). By patting the thighs, the monk can fly away upto the thirteenth continent of Rucakavara in a single flight in oblique direction. While returning, he can have his first pace at the eighth continent of of Nadiśvara and, then, reach the same place in Jambūdvīpa where from he started in his second pace. If the sky-movement refers to upper direction, he can reach the Pānduka Forest of Meru mountain in a single leap, and while returning, he can reach the place where from he started by placing one foot at Nadana forest.

Jātismaraṇa jnāna : The knowledge of earlier birth. Due to this knowledge, a man can know from one to nine earlier births. According to an opinion, one can know about 900 earlier births.

Jina : The soul-victor of the enemies of attachment and aversion. The terms 'Arhat', Tīrthankara' etc. are its synonyms.

Jina-kalpika : Jina-modelled; To engage one-self in practising the best of the conduct after dissociating from the monk-group. This conduct is as difficult as that of the ford-builders. That is why, it is called 'Jina-modelled'. The practitioner does not make any effort to pacify the disease. He is not distrubed from the natural pains due to cold and heat etc. He does not change his line of action due to the inflictions by the deities, human beings and animals. He accepts alms with secret mental resolve. He is always absorbed in meditation and posture of physical detachment. The practice of this conduct could be undertaken by a person who is enriched with specific knowledge and bone-joints.

Jīna-mārga : The path or religion propounded by the Jinas.

Jītācāra : Traditional conduct.

Jīva : Five-sensed living being.

Jnāna : Knowledge; To grasp only the specific attributes or entities irrespective of their general attributes.

Jnānāvaraṇīya Karma : Knowledge-obsuring karma; A karma which covers the attribute of knowledge of the soul.

Jṛmbhaka : They are self-willed or unrestrained gods. They are always delightful, sportive, sexy and ill-conducting. They defame the person on whom they get angry. They glorify the person who keeps them satisfied. They have ten classes : 1. Food supplier; 2. Drinks suppliers; 3. Dress/fabric supplier; 4. Residence supplier; 5. Bedding suppliers; 6. Flower suppliers; 7. Fruit suppliers; 8. Flower and fruit suppliers; 9. Learnings teachers; and 10. Non-manifest gods.

These gods function to reduce or increase the quantities of food etc., to increase or decrease any entity and to make a thing tasteful or tasteless. They reside in large

Vaitādhya, Citra, Vicitra, Yamaka, Samaka and Kancana mountains. Their life span is one Palyopama years. They circle around Jamūdvīpa three times a day on the commands of the guardian gods. They also protect and preserve the grains, water, clothes, metals like gold etc., residences, flowers and fruits, learnings and many other common materials. They are peripatetic gods.

Jyotiṣka : The Astral gods; *See* Deva.

Kalpa : Prescribed conduct, sanctions, rules.

Kalpa-Vṛkṣa : Wish-fulfilling tress; The specific trees through which the supplies of the means of foods and drinks, residence and accessories, light and fire, sports and recreations are easily satisfied. There are ten kinds of wish-fulfilling tress.

Kanakāvali Tapa : A specific austerity based on a specific imaginary figure of ornament made of golden gems. It is run on the basis of the diagram (*See* the figure at the end of this appendix). It takes 1 year, 5 months and 12 days for a single step. It has also four steps. The renunciation of denatured food is not essential in the breaking of fast in the first step. However, it is essential in the second step. The renunciation of smearing food in the third step and there is Āyambila in the fourth step.

Karaṇa : Volitions; Activities related with self-done, got-done and approval-based functions.

Karma : The specific aggregates of mattergy transformed into karmas and attracted by the good and bad propensities of the living beings; Karma; Deeds; Actions.

Kārmikī Buddhi : The intellect developed through the regular practice and thoughts; Experience-based intellect.

Khādima : Edible materials like dry fuits and sweets.

Kilviṣika : The gods who belong to the inferior class; Sinful gods.

Kṣira-Samudra : This is the fifth ocean surrounding Jambūdvīpa. It is this ocean where the hand-plucked hairs of the ford-builders were cast of by the Indra; Milky ocean.

Kutnkāpaṇa : Universal supermarket; A place where all kinds of materials including living and non-living ones are available. In this shop, rich person is charged rupees one thousand and the cakravartī etc. are changed a lac of rupees for a thing for which a common man is charged only five rupees.

The shop-keeper used to accomplish some peripatetic god. The same god managed for every material of the shop. However, some other people say that these shops were without owner or keeper. The peripatetic gods only were running them and were accepting the price of the materials sold.

Labdhi : Supernatural power; Prodigy; Superattainment; Specific powers acquired through the purificatory processes of the soul.

Labdhi-dhara : Endowed with specific supernatural power.

Laghu-caturmāsika Prayaścitta : A kind of expiation, through which the flaws are purified through the austerities etc.

Laghu-sinha-niṣkrīdita Tapa : A kind of austerity; Minor austerity of lion-like pastime : Just as a lion looks behind while moving forward, similarly, this austerity involves gradual increase and decrease in the austerity (of fasting) in a serial order. It has two varieties : (i) Minor and (ii) Major. In the minor austerity, there is a maximum of 9-day penance and, then, gradual decrease of the period of penance. The period for the whole undertaking is 6 months and seven days. There are also four traditions of this austerity which can be judged from the diagram later.

Lāntaka : The sixth heaven; *See* Deva.

Leśyā : The volitions of the soul occurring due to the mattergies of yoga-variforms; Aureole; Colouration.

Loka : The place of existence of the realities of (i) medium of motion, (ii) medium of rest, (iii) extensive space, (iv) time, (v) mattergy, and (vi) the living being.

Lokāntika : There are five layers of the fifth heaven. These layers are equivalent to the storeys of the houses. There are eight black rows in four normal and four intermediate directions in the mobile channel in southern direction near the third layer named Ariṣta (Unhurt). There are nine empyrean planes of initiation-promoter gods. The eight planes are there in the eight rows and the ninth one is in the centre of them. Their names are as below :

(i) Arci (Flame), (ii) Arcimāla (Group of flames), (iii) Vairocana (Creator), (iv) Prabhankara (Lustre), (v) Candrābha (Moon-shine), (vi) Sūryābha (like sunshine), (vii) Śukrābha (like venus-shine), (viii) Superatiṣthā (well-located), (ix) Riṣtābha (wine-ḷike shine-central plane).

The gods are called 'lokāntika' as they live in the end of the fifth heaven-Brahmaloka. They are normally free from sensualism. Hence, they have been called as 'deital miraculous monks' (Devarṣi). As per ancient tradition, they encourage the ford-builders for initiation.

Lokapāla : Guardians gods of boundary. Every Indra has four guardians goods each. They are highly prodigied. They are lords of many gods and goddesses.

Mahābhadra Pratimā : A kind of austerity proceeded with meditation; To undertake physical detachment posture (Kāyotsarga) for a day facing each of the four directions.

Mahākalpa : A specific time built; Bhagavati Sūtra describes the value of Mahākalpa in the following way : "The river Gangā is 500 Y long, ½ Y wide and 500 D deep. Seven such Gangās make a Mahāgangā, seven Mahāgangās make a Sādīna Gangā, seven Sād+īna Gangās make a Mṛtyu-gangā; seven Mṛtyu-gangās make a Lohita gangā (Red Gangā); seven Lohita Gangās make a Avanti-Gangās and seven Avanti-gangās make a Pramā-vanti Gangā. Thus, there are 1,17,649 Gangā rivers.

The sand-particles of these rivers have two varieties : (i) fine and (ii) gross. The fine particles are not desirable here. Out of the gross sand-particles, one particle is taken out every hundred years. Thus, the time required for emptying the sand-particles of these Gangās is called the time-unit of Mānasa-sāra. The three lac Mānasa-sāras make a period of Mahākalpa. 24 lac Mahākalpas make a unit of Mahāmānasa. The unit of Mānasa-sāra has three varieties. Maximal, medial and manimal Majhhima-Nikāya sandak suttanta 2.3.6 has given the value of 84000 Mahakalpas in a little different way. Accordingly, there are 80 Antar-kaplas (interrupted Kalpas in a Mahākalpas.)

Mahānirgrantha : Ford-builder; Tīrthankara.

Mahā-pratimā Tapa : An austerity of great mental resolve; *see* Eka-rātri-pratimā.

Mahā-sinha-niṣkrīdita Tapa : A kind of Austerity; A major austerity of lion-like pastime; Just as a lion looks behind while moving forward and, similary, this austerity involves gradual increase and decrease in austerity (of fasting) in serial order. This austerity has two varieties : (i) Major and (ii) Minor. In the proposed austerity, there is a maximum of 16-day austerity of increasing fasts followed by 16-day decreasing fasting. It takes 1 year, 6 months and 18 days for the complete austerity. There are four traditions of this austerity. The order of this austerity runs as per the diagram.

Mahā-videha kṣetra : A region in Jambūdvīpa; *See* Jambūdvīpa.

Mahāvrata : Major vows; Finer vows; life-long physical, vocal and mental renunciation of violence, non-truth, stealth, non-celibacy and attachmental possession. The total renunciation of all these five sins leads them to be called as major vows or 'Mahāvratas'. This is the good conduct for those moving towards spiritual practices after renouncing the householdership.

Manah-paryaya Jnāna : Telepathy; Mind-reading knowledge; The knowledge of mental states according to mind variforms.

Mandalika Rājā : The ruler of a mandala or territory.

Mankha : Alms-beggars eking out their livelihood through paintings.

Manthū : Powder of dried plums etc.

Mānuṣottara Parvata : Name of a mountain in Jaina Universe beyond which human beings can not go. There is Lavaṇa ocean surrounding Jambūdvīpa. Dhātaki Khanda Dvīpa surrounds this ocean which is surrounded by Kālopdadhi ocean. There is Puṣkara dvīpa surrounding Kāloadhi ocean. The Māunuṣottara mountain is in the centre of Puṣkara dvīpa. It divides this dvīpa in two parts. This mountain forms the boundary of human universe and time-zone. No person except the monks with supernatural power of moving through the touch of things or specific learnings can go beyond this mountain.

Mārga : Path; The path of liberation in the form of right knowledge etc.

Māsiki Bhikṣu Pratimā : The mental resolve of taking one delivery of food and one delivery of water daily for a month,

Mati-jnāna : Sensory knowledge; a knowledge occuring through the instrumentality of senses and mind.

Meru-parvata ki cūlikā : Summit of Meru mountain; There is Meru mountain in the centre of Jambūdvīpa which is 1 lac Yojanas high and has a golden shine. There is 40 Y summit on this mountain. There are four forests also on this mountain : (i) Bhadraśāla, (ii) Nandana, (iii) Saumanasa and (iv) Pānduka. The Bhadraśāla forest surrounds the mountain equial to the surface of the earth. The Nandana forest is 500 Y high above it where even the gods go for their pastimes. There is the Saumanasa forest 62,500 Y above this forest. And there is the Pānduka forest spread around the summit. There are four golden rocks in this forest where the birth celebrations of the ford-builders are held.

Mithyātāva : Wrong faith; Reverse belief about the reality or knowledge.

Mokṣa : Liberation; Salvation; The positioning of soul in its own nature after the total destruction of all the karmas.

Mūlaguṇa : Basic attributes; The vows which are like the root of the tree of conduct. There are five minor vows for the votary and there are five major vows for the monks.

Nāgendra : The Lord of serpentine youths of the mansional gods.

Nairaujika Bhava : Mode of infernals.

Ṇamotthuṇam : The Prākṛta eulogy of the Enlightened and the Salvated ones.

Nandiśvara Dvīpa : The eighth island-contiment from Jambūdvīpa.

Naraka : Hells; Those places in the Jaina lower world where the inimense sinners are born to bear the fruits of their sins. They are seven in number :

1. *Ratna-Prabhā* : (gem-shine, Full with terrible black gems).
2. *Śarkarā-prābha* : (stone-shine, full with stones edged with bears and spears).
3. *Bālukā-prabhā* : (sand-shine, highly hot sand hotter than the sand of the oven of the grain-parcher).
4. *Panka-prabhā* : (mud-shine, full of mud like that of blood, flesh and pus).
5. *Dhūmra-prabhā* : (smoke-shine, full of sour smoke like that of smokes form burning chillies and mustards).
6. *Tamah-prabhā* : (darkness-shine, full of deep darkness).
7. *Mahātamah-prabhā* : (deep-darkness shine, full of deepest darkness.)

Nidāna : A mental thorn of future desires; *See*, Nidāna śalya under 'śalya'.

Nikācita : Incapacitation; It is a state of incapacitation of factors leading to the fruition of karmas as per their duration of bonds.

Ninhava : Concealment, Denial of doctrines of the ford-builders.

Nirgrantha Pravacana : Jaina scriptures sermonised by the ford-builders.

Nirjarā : Karmic shedding; The purity of the soul due to the shedding of karma through austerity.

Nirhārima : Taking-out of dead-body from the hermitage; *See* Pādopagamana.

Nitya-pinda : Intake of food daily from one house.

Padānusāri Labdhi : A supernatural power acquired by observance of specific austerity; Syllable-based prodigy; Accordingly, one knows the text in full on listening or knowing any one syllable of the text from the beginning, middle or end.

Pādopagamana : Fasting under tree-like-steadfast state; A kind of fasting in which the monk stays steadfast like a tree and does neither help himself nor seeks help from others and renounces all kinds of efforts and activities. It is essential that all the four kinds of food is renounced. It has two varieties :

1. *Nirhārima* (Taken-out after death) : The dead body of the monk who died in the hermitage under the vow of tree-like steadfast fasting, is taken out of it for ritualisation. The term ' Nirhāra' means to 'take out' the abandoned body in this way.
2. *Anirhārima* (Lonely death) : The abandonment of body under tree-like steadfast fasting in a lonely place like forest is not taken out to other places for ritualisation. This type of body-abandonment is called 'lonely death'.

Palyopama : A pit- 1Y deep, 1Y long and 1Y wide- is densely filled with hairs of beings born-in-pairs in uttarakuru and having a life of 1-7 days and cutting each of them into innumerable parts. It should be so packed that no fire could burn it, no water could enter in and it should not show any flexibility even when all the army of a universal monarch passes over it. One hair-piece should be taken out form the pit after each hundered years. The time taken to remove all the hair-pieces in this way and, thus, emptying the pit, is the Palyopama time (in years).

Pānca Divya/Āścarya : Five splendours manifesting at the time of food-intake by the omniscients :

1. Rains of variety of gems.
2. Divine clothes.
3. Sacred fragrant water.
4. Shower of fragrant flowers.
5. Divine sounds or drum beating by the gods.

Panca-muṣtika luncana : Plucking of hairs by dividing the head in five portions.

Pandita-maraṇa : Prudents' death; Death under meditation while observing vows in full.

Pāpa : Inauspicious karmic mattergy; Sin; The causes of sin are also called 'sin' formally.

Pāriṇāmikī Buddhi : The intellect devolped due to long experience.

Parīṣaha : Afflictions; Variety of physical troubles during the ascetic life.

Pārśvanātha-santānīya : Belonging to Pārśvanātha tradition.

Pārśvastha : Slack monks; Those monks who have only the garb of monk but who do not observe the conduct properly.

Paryāya : Mode; The changing nature of the substances.

Pauṣadha (Povāsa) : 1-day fasting; Renunciation of the four-fold food and sinful activities for a day and night.

Prajnapti ādi Vidyā : There are sixteen goddesses of learning as below :

1. Prajnapti, 2. Rohiṇī, 3. Vajra-śṛnkhalā, 4. Kuliśānkaśā, 5. Cakreśvarī, 6. Naradattā, 7. Kāli, 8. Mahākāli, 9. Gaurī, 10. Gāndhārī, 11. Sarvāstra-mahājālā, 12. Mānavī, 13. Vairotyā, 14. Acchuptā, 15. Mānasī 16. Mahāmānasika.

Prāṇa : 2-4-sensed living beings; A synonym for the living beings in general; vitality.

Prāṇata : The tenth Kalpa or heaven; *See* Deva.

Prathama-sapta-Ahorātra Pratimā : Alternate fasting for seven days with renouncing of four-fold foods : undertaking of physical detachmental posture like squatting, one-sided sleeping or supine-sleeping.

Prati-codanā : Contrary preceptual injunction

Prati-sāraṇā : Remembrance of contrary doctrines.

Pratyākhyāna : Renunciation; Abandonment.

Pratyupadhāra : Disrespect.

Pravacana-prabhāvanā : Glorification of the religious order through many ways.

Pravartinī : The chief nun promoting the other nuns to undertake selfless service and other religious activities as directed by the head of the group.

Pravṛtta-Parihāra : Entry into the interior of the body.

Pravṛtti-vāduka : Specific messenger to receive and acquire new (of the group).

Prayaścitta : Expiation; Atonement, To repent internally for purification of flaws occuring during spiritual practices. It is undetaken ten-foldly :

1. *Ālocanā* : Confession; To request the senior monk or preceptor about the defects/flaws during the spirtual practices.
2. *Pratikramaṇa* : Penitential retreat; Expression by the aspirant 'Let my sins be annulled' while undertaking sel-expiation for the transgressions or offences.
3. *Tadubhaya— Both of (1) and (2)* : Confession and penitential retreat.
4. *Viveka* : Discrimination; Renunciation of foods after learning about its particularisation.
5. *Kāyotsarga* : Physical detachmental posture; Renunciation of attachment with the body with due concentration.
6. *Tapa* : Austerity; Penances; External austerities like fasting etc.
7. *Cheda* : Reducing the standing of the monk. According to this expitation, the junior monks become senior to the transgressor monk during that period of reduction in rank.

8. *Mūla* : Re-initiation.
9. *Anavasthapya* : Temporary expulsion; Re-initiation after specific austerities.
10. *Pārāncika* : Re-inititation after reproach; Self-condemnation in public after changing the garb of monkhood for a specific time after expulsion form the group.

Prītidāṇa : Awarding the person conveying good news.

Puṇya : Auspicious karmic mattergy; Sacred; The causes of earning sacredness are also formally called 'Sacred'.

Rajoharaṇa : Whisk-brooms of Jina monks; An accessary of Jaina monks which is used for cleaning the ground etc.

Rāṣtriya : The officer, who is appointed to administer the province or nation.

Rju-Prājna : Simple and intelligent.

Rju-jada : Simple and ignorant; Simple but unable to understand the meanings of scriptures.

Rucakavara Dvīpa : The thirteenth island-continent from Jambūdvīpa.

Sāgaropama, Sāgara : A larger unit of time. It is equal to 10 crore r̄ crore = 10^{15} Palyopama years.

Sahasrapāka Taila : A thousand-times digested oil made from many medicinal substance or the oil whose preparation has cost 1000 gold coins.

Sahasrāra Kalpa : Eighth heaven; Thousand-faceted kalpas; *See*, Deva.

Śaileśī Avasthā : Rock-like steadfast state; The state of the monk in the fourteenth spiritual stage—when there is cessation of mental, vocal and bodily activities— is called the rocklike-steadfast state : This state is the highest state of meditation which causes Meru-like steadiness and non-trembling.

Śrīdevī : Name of the chief queen of Cakravartī. She is 4 Angulas lesser in height than Cakravartī. She is always ever-young. The diseases are pacified by her touch only. She does not have any issue.

Śalya : Stings or thorns (which cause pains). It has three varieties :

1. *Deceit* : Having a volition of deception. To confess a transgression deceitfully or request it to the teacher in a different way; Charging others falsely.
2. *Future Desires* : To think about acquiring the splendour of kings, gods etc. in the next birth due to spiritual practices like austerities, celibacy etc. on seeing their grandeur.
3. *Wrong-faith* : To have faith in perversity.

Samācārī : Essential monastic conduct.

Samādhi-danā : Provision of mental equanimity; Affording mental health by serving the minister, preceptor, seniors, novices, ailing and austerite monks.

Samādhi-maraṇa : Death under meditation; Death under detachmental volition while observing the scriputral conduct.

Sāmānika : Co-chiefs; Indra-equivalents; These gods have the same life-span etc. as the Indra. But they are not Indra's. These gods are like ministers, parents, and teachers etc. for the Indra.

Samavasaraṇa : The place of Holy assembly where the ford-builders sermonise; Assembly of the ford-builder.

Samaya : The smallest unit of time.

Samāyika Cāritra : Total abstinence from sinful activities; Conduct of equanimity.

Sambhinna-śrotṛ-labdhi : A supernatural power of all-sensing through one sense; A specific divine power acquired by specific austerity. Due to this power, one could grasp objects of all the five senses simultaneously through one sense only. The sounds of conch and drum etc. in the army of Cakravartī can be separately identified through this power.

Samiti : Carefulness; Propensities favouring restraint; There are five carefulnesses : (1-5) Carefulness in walking, speaking, examining the purity of foods, picking and placing and excretions.

1. *Īryā (Walking)* : Walking with forward looking a couple of paces ahead for success in observance of right knowledge, faith, conduct and self-study and excluding sensuals.
2. *Bhāṣā (Speaking)* : Speaking sinless, beneficial, limited and doubtless speech avoiding the defects of language.
3. *Eṣaṇā (Examination of purity of foods)* : Search for the general essentials like foods and drinks etc. and supporting essentials like bed, blankkets while avoiding the defects of various types.
4. *Ādāna-nikṣepaṇa (Picking and Placing)* : To pick and place clothes, vessels etc. carefully.
5. *Excretion (utsarga)* : Excretion of urine, feces, spittings, and phelgm etc. on inanimated and pre-observed ground.

Samucchinna-kriyā-nivṛtti : Cessation of subtle activity; The fourth variety of pure meditation; Where all the activities are stopped. *See* Śukla dhyāna.

Samvara : Stoppage; Control of volitions of the soul causing influx of the karmas.

Samyak-darśana : Right faith; Righteousness.

Samyak-dṛṣti : Right-faithed; Right visioned; A person having accurate faith in spiritual entities.

Samyaktva : Righteousness; Accurate belief in realities.

Samyaktvī : Right-faithed; Enriched with right faith/righteouness.

Sanhanana : Bone-joints; Tight bonding of bones of the body; Physical strength.

Sacelaka : Having clothes; Having costly clothes.

Sanjnī-garbha : The place of birth of the human beings; A specific term of Ājīvika sect.

Sankramaṇa : Transition; Mutual change of homologous karmic species.

Sangha : Gathering of monk-groups; The group of disciples of more than two heads of monk.

Sanlekhanā : Austerity of leaning and thinning the passions etc. with austerity and physical and mental concentration.

Sanniveśa : Suburb.

Sansthāna : Configuration; A specific shape.

Santhārā : Renunciation of foods etc. at the last stage of life.

Sanyūthā Nikāya : The group of infinite living beings. A specific term of Ājīvikas.

Sa-pratikarma : Activities during fasting; Activities of walking, sleeping, sitting and standing etc. during fasting. These activities are there during the fasting by gradual rejection of foods.

Sapta-saptamikā Pratimā : Seven-septadic mental resolves; This mental resolve lasts for 49 days. There are septads of seven day each. In the first septad, there is intake of one delivery of each of food and drink which gradually increases upto seven deliveries of each of them. This austerity involves posture of physical detachment alongwith the deliveries.

Sarvārtha-siddha : Last of the Anuttara empyrean abodes; All-accomplished empyreans; Penultimate liberated; *See* Deva.

Sarvato-bhadra Pratimā : All-welfare mental resolve; Two methods of this resolve are found in literature. According to one method, there is undertaking of posture of detachment with body for one day (24 hrs) each facing in each of the ten directions. It is mentioned that Bhagvan Mahāvira followed this method only. According to the second method, there are two varieties of this mental resolve: (i) Minor, (ii) Major.

1. *Minor Sarvato-bhadra Pratimā* : The 'Sarvatobhadra' is the method of placing the numbers in a square in such a way that addition of horizontal and vertical direction is the same as shown in the figure. This austerity of mental resolve, in the first stage, begins, with a fast which gradually increases upto 5-day fasting. In the second stage, the middle number is taken as the number of days of fasting and the fastings are, then, completed in full five sections. Similar order of fasting continues next time. As per one system, the total period of this mental resolve is 3 months and 10 days (100 days). There are four systems of this austerity. Their order is as given in the diagram below in Table 1.
2. *Major Sarvato-bhadra Pratimā* : This austerity starts with fasting of a day and it goes on increasing gradually upto 7-day fasting. The order of increase in fasting is as per the minor type. The only difference is that there is the longest fasting period of 5 days while in this case, it is 7 days. The period of this austerity is 1 yr., 1 month and 10 days (i.e. 405 days). There are four systems of this austerity which follow the diagram as shown below in Table 2.

1	2	3	4	5
3	4	5	1	2
5	1	2	3	4
2	3	4	5	1
4	5	1	2	3

Table 1 :
Minor Sarvatobhadra Pratimā

1	2	3	4	5	6	7
4	5	6	7	1	2	3
7	1	2	3	4	5	6
3	4	5	6	7	1	2
6	7	1	2	3	4	5
2	3	4	5	6	7	1
5	6	7	1	2	3	4

Table 2 :
Major Sarvatobhadra Pratimā

Sarvauṣadha Labdhi : A supernatural power of medication through all parts of the body; A supernatural power acquired by a specific austerity. The rain water, river water and air, if touched by the body of this austerite, become eliminators of disease and curer of poisons. If any material mixed with poison is there in his utensils or mouth, it becomes depoisoned. Even the memory of this austerite depoisons the most poisonous substance. His body-parts like nails, hairs and teeth etc. also serve as divine medicine.

Śatapāka Taila : A hundered-times digested oil made from many medicinal substances or the oil which has been prepared by spending 100 gold coins.

Ṣat-Āvaīyaka : Six essential duties; Six dis-passionation devices; The essential duty (Āvaśyaka) is defined as those duties to be performed by the living being or soul for acquiring right faith, knowledge and conduct. There are six essential duties :

1. *Eqanimity (Sāmāyika)* : To live with equanimity; To have equanimous behaviour with all.
2. *Eulogy of Twenty-four (Catur-vinśati-stava)* : Eulogisation of qualities of thē ford-builders with devotion.
3. *Veneration (Vandanā)* : The three-fold auspicious activity through which the venerable and respectable persons are offered devotion and regards.
4. *Penitential Retreat (Pratikarmaṇa)* : To move towards sacred activities after having gone in reverse direction non-vigilarntly. Thus, gradual movement towards auspicious activities after abandoning the inauspicious activities. It is the confession of one's own offences in brief.
5. *Postures of Abandonment of Bodily Attachment. (Kāyotsarga)* : To abandon attachment with the body with due concentration.
6. *Renunciation (Pratyākhyāna)* : Renunciation of specific item for a specific period.

Sattva : Living beings of earth, water, air and fire class; A synonym of Jīva or the living being.

Saudharma : Righteous; The first heaven; *See* Deva.

Sāvadya : Sinful.

Śayyātara : Owner of monk residence.

Śeṣa-kāla : Time after the Rainy residence of the monks.

Siddhi : Accomplishment; Salvation; The state acquired by the destruction of all the karmas.

Śikṣā vrata : Educative vows : The educative vows are defined as those vows which are repectitively practiced and, therefore, practice-prominent.

Śleṣmauṣadha Labdhi : A supernatural power of medication by phelgm; A divine power acquired by specific austerity. Accordingly, the rubbing of a small amount of phelgm of the austerite could completely remove the leprosy of the person.

Snātaka : Bodhi-sattva.

Śruta-bhakti : Scriptutral devotion; Devotional hymn of scriputres; The constant promotion of scriptural knowledge with devotion and removal of dis-interest about it.

Śruta-jnāna : Vocable knowledge; Scriptural knowledge; A sensory knowledge capable of making others understand through of physical vocables like words, gestures, symbols etc.

Sthāvara : Non-mobile beings; One-sensed beings; Living beings incapable of movements for beneficial propensities and aviodance of non-beneficial propensities.

Sthavira : Senior monks; Stabilisers of lax monks in their spiritual practices. There are three kinds of senior monks : (i) senior-by-initiation, (ii) senior-by birth and (iii) senior-by-scriputral knowledge.

1. *Senior-by-inititaion (Pravṛjyā-sthavira)* : The monks whose initiation period has been twenty years or more.
2. *Senior-by-birth (Jāti-sthavira)* : The monks who are aged sixty years or more.
3. *Senior-by-scriptural knowledge (Śruta-sthavira)* : The monks who have mastered over the primary texts of Sthānānga (Numerated Stationings), Samvāyānga (Numerated Categories) and others.

Sthavīra-kalpika : Commune-dweller monks; Spiritual practice while living in the group of monks; Promotion of Jina scriptures and austerities; Improving the qualities of knowledge, faith and conduct in the monk-disciples; Reside in one place only due to weakened body and old age avoiding defects of foods and supporting accessories there.

Sthiti-patita : A 10-day birth (of a son) ceremony as per family tradition.

Śukla-dhyanā : White, pure or absolute meditation; Pure reflective meditation; It has four varieties :

1. *Pṛthaktva-vitarka-savicāra* : (Meditation on differential conceptual thinking with shifting).
2. *Ekatva-vitarka-savicāra* : (Meditation on mono-aspectual conceptual thinking with shifting).
3. *Sūkṣma-kriyā-apratipāti* : (Infallible subtle activity).
4. *Samucchinna-kriyā-nivṛtti* : (Cessation of subtle activity).

Sūkîma-kriyā-apratipâti : State of infallible subtle activities; The third stage of pure meditation where other kinds of activities are stopped except the subtle involuntary activities like respiration etc.; *See* Śukla-dhyāna.

Suṣama : Plentitude; The second spoke of the devolution epoch where there is some lesser plentitude than the first spoke.

Suṣama-Duṣama : Plentitude-cum-penury; The third spoke of devolution epoch (or the fourth spoke of the devolution epoch) where there is some penury also alongwith plentitude.

Suṣama-suṣama : Extreme plentitude; The first spoke of the devolution period where there is alround plentitude.

Sūtra : Scriptures; Aphorism.

Sūtrāgama : Basic scriptures.

Svādima : Relishable edibles; Mouth-purifying materials like betel-nuts, cardamums etc.

Tāla-puta viṣa : Name of a poison effecting death in a time of clapping the hands.

Tamah-prabhā : Name of a hell (smoke-shine); *See* Naraka.

Tattva : Meaning; Essence; Reality; Real.

Tejo-leśyā : Red Aureole; A supernatural power of destruction associated with heat. This power can be acquired through specific austerity. One should undertake two-day fastings for six-months. During breaking of fast, the aspirant should eat a handful of fried cake of black gram (urda) and a handful of water. He should practise endurance of intense heat in the sun with face upward in the place set for this austerity. After this practice, one acquires the power of destruction associated with heat. It is called 'brief' when it not practised. It is called 'detailed or extended' when it is practiced. The person with this supernatural power achieves capablity to destroy, kill, root out and inflame the sixteen countries of (1) Anga, (2) Banga, (3) Magadha, (4) Malaya, (5) Mālava, (6) Accha, (7) Vatsa, (8) Kautsa, (9) Pātha,

(10) Lata, (11) Vajra, (12) Mauli, (13) Kāśī, (14) Kośala, (15) Avādha, (16) Sambhuttara and others. The power which is used to counter this power is called 'cold supernatural power of Red aureole.'

Tīrtha : A ford through which the worldly ocean can be crossed; The four-fold order of right sages, nuns, votary and votaress; The sermons of ford-builders and their chief-disciples are also called as ford. The ford-builders sermonise only after acquiring omniscience. It is on the basis of their sermons that people become sages, nuns, votary and votaress.

Tīrthankara : The attained person enforcing the religious fords; Ford-builders.

Tīrthānkara Gotra-Nama-Karma : The physique-making karma of Ford-buildership; A physique-making karma whose fruition leads one to be born as ford-builder.

Tiryak Gati : The sub-human destinity.

Trāyastrinśa : Empyreans serving as ministers or guides to the Indras.

Tridandī Tāpasa : Three-staffed specific Ascetics; An ascetic penalised by three kinds of violence of mind, speach and body.

Tṛtiya-sapta-ahorātra-pratimā : Alternate seven-day fasting with renunciation of four-fold foods by a monk, and to undertake detachmental postures of cow-milking, heroic or mango-like curved type outside the village etc.

Udiraṇa : Pre-maturation, Fruition of karmas prior to regular duration.

Udvartanā : Delayed fruition of karmas; The increase in fruitional power of the duration and intensity of karmas.

Upānga : Subsidiary/secondary canons; Canonical sub-limbs; The post-canonical scripture composed by scripture-ominiscient or pre-canonist Ācārya to elaborate the contents of primary canons. There are twelve of these secondary texts :

(i) Uvavāī, (ii) Raya-paseṇiya, (iii) Jivābhigama, (iv) Paṇṇavaṇā, (v) Sūriya-paṇṇattī, (vi) Jambūdīva-paṇṇattī, (vii) Canda-paṇṇattī, (viii) Nirayā-valiā, (ix) Kalpāvatansikā, (x) Pupphiyā, (xi) Pupphacūliya, (xii) Vanhi-dasā.

Upayoga : Functional consciousness; Applied consciousness-knowledge and conation/ Intuition. There are five knowledges :

(i) Sensory, (ii) Vocable, (iii) Clarivoyance (iv) Telepathy or mind-reading, and (v) ominiscience/absolute.

There are four kinds of conations :

(i) ocular, (ii) Non-ocular, (iii) Clarivoyant and (iv) Absolute.

Utsarpiṇī : Evolution epoch; It is that division of time where the living beings have gradually increasing in auspicious bone-joints and configurations. The life-span and size gradually increase. There is gradual increase in rise, activities, valour, potency, self-exertion and prowess. During this period, the colour, smell, taste, and touch of mattergies also get auspicious. The most inauspicious volitions become gradually less inauspicious, auspicious, better and best auspicious.

During the devolution period, there is the worst state in the end of the epoch while there is the best state during the evolution period in the end.

Utsūtra-prar̄paṇā : Enuncation against the rule or actuality.

Uttara Gaṇa : Subsidiary/secondary qualities; Propensities to protect primary qualities. They are purity of foods, carefulness, reflections, austerities, mental resolves, secret resolves etc. for monks and direction-binding vow etc. for the votary.

Uttarāsanga : Scarf.

Vaimānika : Empyrean gods; *See* Deva.

Vainayikī Buddhi : Reverential intellect; Intellect acquired through the service or teachings of the teachers.

Vaiśravaṇa : God of wealth; Kubera.

Vaiyāvṛtti : Selfless service; Service of ministers, preceptors, novice, ailing austerite and senior monks and co-religious persons, family, group and four-fold order of the religion through foods etc.

Vajra-madhya-candra Pratimā : A one-month long mental resolve with the thounderbolt-like fasting order. It starts with the first day of dark fortnight and has the food-intake of deliveries according to the rise and fall of the phases of moon for a month. At the beginning, there is a food-intake of 15 deliveries gradually decreasing upto one delivery on the fifteenth dark day. It is, then, followed by two deliveries on the first day of bright fortnight with a gradual increase upto 15 deliveries on fourteenth day. There is fasting on bright fifteenth day.

Vakra-Jada : Crooked-cum-foolish; A person who disregards the real spiritual knowledge despite teachings and showing his foolishness as a form of skill-fulness through his outwitting due to crookedness.

Varṣā-dāna : Year-long daily donation by the ford-builders.

Vāsudeva : A category of Torch-bearers; Those persons appear on earth as Vāsudeva who take birth on the basis of their future desires in earlier birth in heavens or hells. There are nine Vāsudevas each in evolution and devolution epochs. When they are concieved, their mothers have seven dreams. Their colour of the body is black. They are rulers of three sections of Bharata region. They acquire this position by killing their enemies-anti-Vāsudevas. They have seven gems :

1. Sudarśana cakra (Handsome discus).
2. Amogha khadga (Unfailing sword).
3. Kaumodikī gadā (Moonlight-like mace).
4. Amogha vāṇa (Unfailing arrow).
5. Garuda-dhvaja ratha (Eagle-flagged-chariot).
6. Puṣpa-mālā (Flower garland).
7. Kaustubha mani (Kaustubha gem).

Vibhanga Jnāna : Wrong clairvoyance; The clarivoyance is defined as the knowledge of mattergic objects by the soul without the assistance of senses and mind. The knowledge of the wrong-faithed one is called wrong clairvoyance.

Vidyācāraṇa Labdhi : A supernatural power of desired movement through learnings or magic. This power is acquired by the monk undetaking the austerity of 3-day fasting. One can reach the eighth Nandiśvara Dvīpa in two-fold sky-movement with a small support as per scriptural prescriptions. One can move upto Mānuṣottara mountain in the first step, and one can reach the starting point in a single step while returning. Similarly, one can reach Meru in two steps of flight while moving in upper direction and reach the starting point in a single step while returning.

Vijaya Anuttara Vimāna : Beyond-kalpa Anuttara plane-named Vijaya; *See* Deva.

Vikurvaṇa Labdhi : Supernatural power of protection; A specific divine power acquired through a specific austerity. Due to this, many kinds of form can be created. The body may be made as fine as a thread which could pass through the hole of a needle. The body can be made so high that even the Meru mountain may look upto his knees. The body can be made lighter than air and heavier than diamond. There could be walking on water like that on earth and dive in the earth like water.

One can pass through the mountain without hindrance like passage through the hole and there can be invisiblisation like air everywhere. One can fill the universe with many kinds of form, one can subjugate even the cruel animals.

Vipruṣauîadha Labdhi : A supernatural power of medication by excretions; A divine power acquired by a specific austerity. The drops of feces and urinary excretions serve as divine medicines for the patients.

Vītarāgatā Virādhaka : Non-practitioner in toto; A person not practicing the accepted vows in toto; Dying even before undertaking atonement of his evil deeds or sins.

Vyantara : Peripatetic gods; Forest-residing gods; *See* Deva.

Yaugalika : Born-in-pairs; The period of civilisation prior to the human civilisation when the human beings were born in pairs. All their necessities were satisfied through the wish-fulfilling trees.

Yava-madhya Candra Pratimā : A one-month long mental reslove; This resolve is completed by taking deliveries of food in increasing and decreasing order like the shape of the barely grain according to loss or gain in the phases of the moon and starting with the bright first day of the month. For example, one has an intake of one delivery on the bright first day, two deliveries on the second day and so on upto 15 deliveries on the fifteenth bright day. Now, one has 14 deliveries on the dark first day and so on gradually decreasing upto one delivery on the dark fourteenth day and, have fasting on the dark fifteenth day of the month.

Yoga : Propensities/activities of mind, speech and body.

Yojana : A unit of distance equal to 4 Kroras ~8 miles ~13.28 km. When Cakravartī Bharata started for his victory mission, the gem-wheel was moving ahead of his army. The Yojana was designated as a distance travelled by the gem-wheel on the first day.

चित्र 1

एकावली तप

की परिभाषा से संबंधित

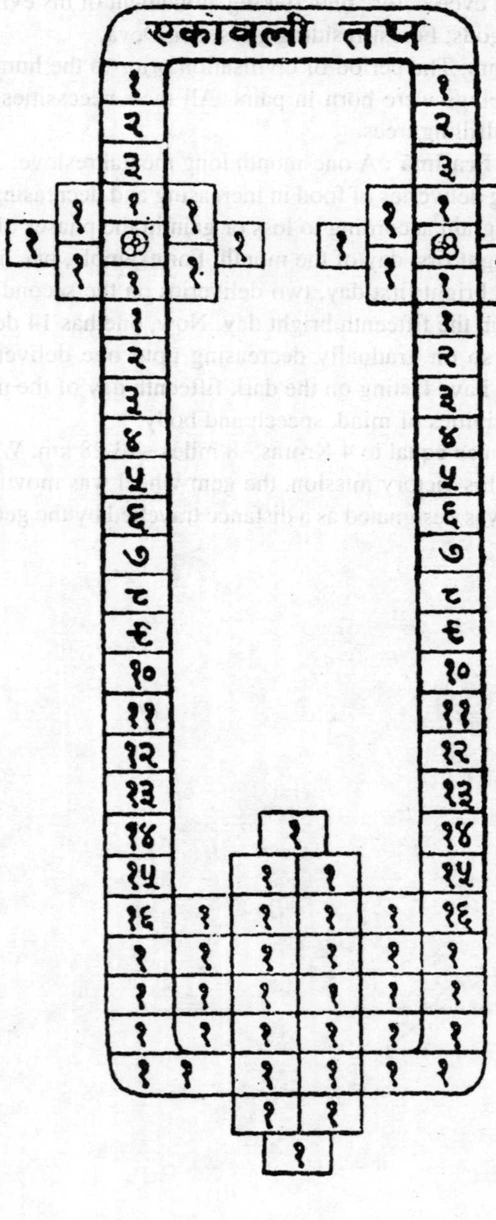

चित्र 2

कनकावली तप

की परिभाषा से संबंधित

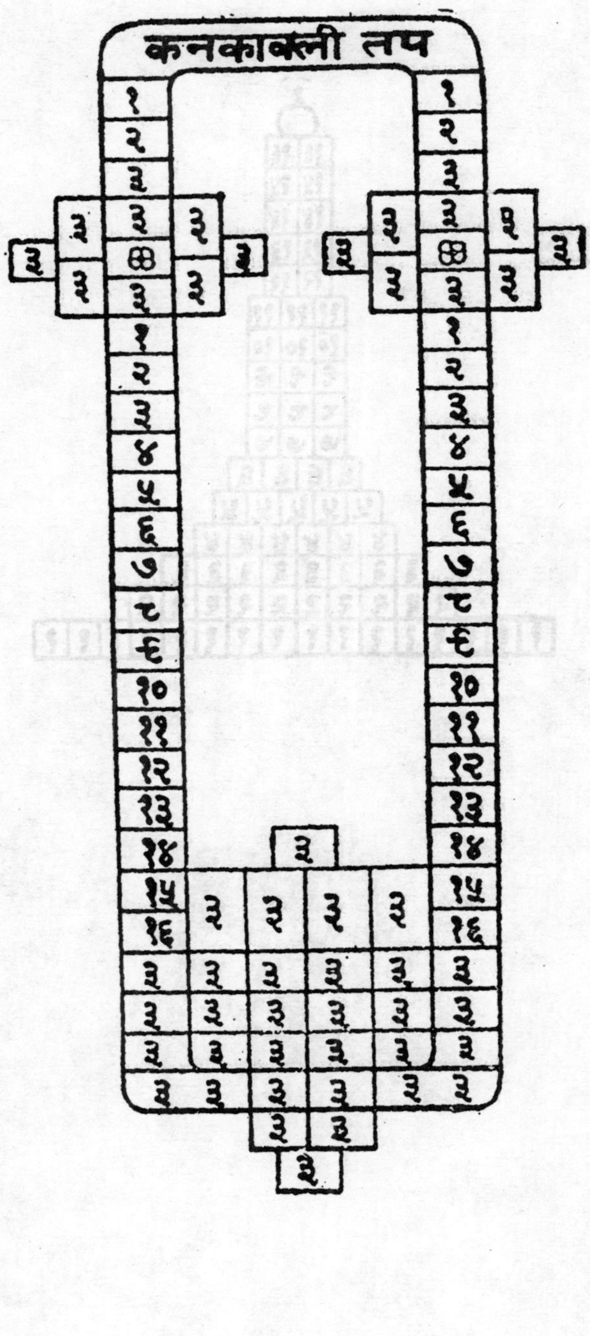

चित्र 3

गुणरत्न (रयण) संवत्सर तप

की परिभाषा से संबंधित

चित्र 4

महासिंह निष्क्रीड़ित तप

की परिभाषा से संबंधित

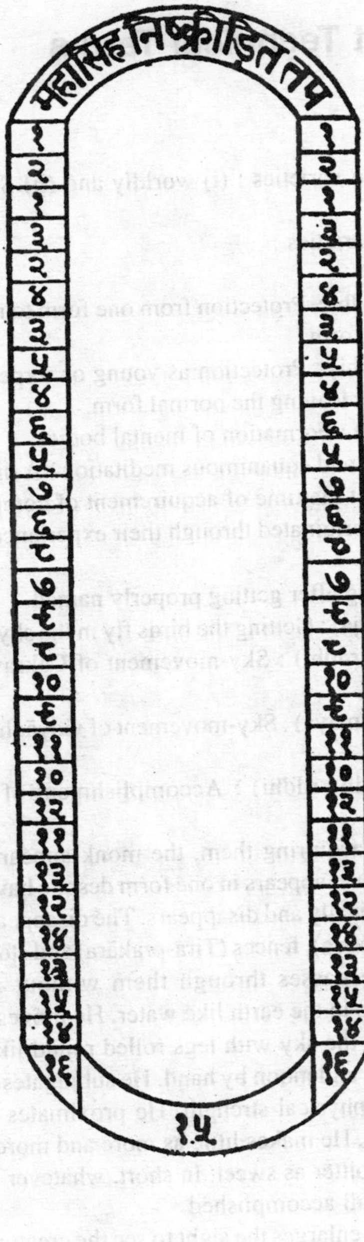

चित्र 5

लघुसिंह निष्क्रीड़ित तप

की परिभाषा से संबंधित

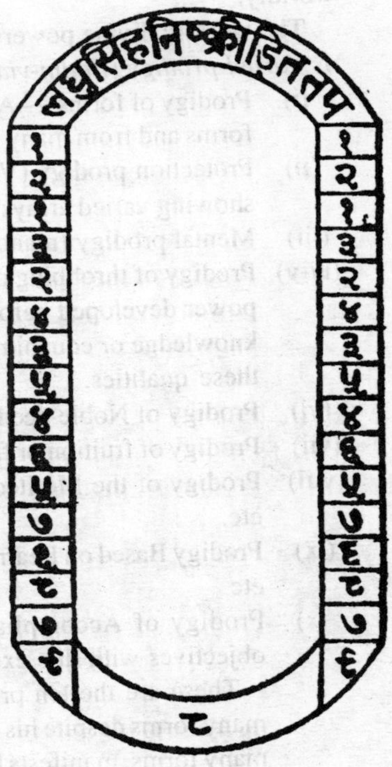

Glossary of Buddhist Technical Terms

Abhijāti : Birth.

Abhijnā : Divine power; Basically, it has two varieties : (i) worldly and (ii) Super-worldly.

The worldly divine powers have five varieties :

1. *Varied-prodigy (Ṛddhi-vidha):*

(i) Prodigy of forms — Adhiṣthāna ṛddhi : Protection from one form to many forms and from many forms to one form.

(ii) Protection prodigy (Vikurvaṇa ṛddhi) : Protection as young or serpent or showing varied arrays of army after leaving the normal form.

(iii) Mental prodigy (mano-maya ṛddhi) : Formation of mental bodies.

(iv-v) Prodigy of throbbing of knowledge and equanimous meditation : A divine power developed before, after or at the time of acquirement of complete knowledge or equanimous state or originated through their experiences of these qualities.

(vi) Prodigy of Noble deeds : Wandering after getting properly named.

(vii) Prodigy of fruition or flying (vipakāja) : Getting the birds fly in the sky etc.

(viii) Prodigy of the Merited (Puṇyavān ṛddhi) : Sky-movement of Cakravartī etc.

(ix) Prodigy Based on Learnings (Vidyā-maya) : Sky-movement of vidyādharas etc.

(x) Prodigy of Accomplishment (Siddha-ṛddhi) : Accomplishment of the objectives with due exertion.

These are the ten prodigies. On acquiring them, the monk appears in many forms despite his form being one, appears in one form despite having many forms, manifests himself physically and disappears. The disappeared monk passes through walls (Tirah-kadya), fences (Tira-prakāra) and stones or mountains (Tirah-parvata). He passes through them without any obstruction like that in sky. He dives in the earth like water. He moves on water like the ground. He moves in the sky with legs rolled round like a bird. He touches and rubs the hot sun and moon by hand. He subjugates the Brahmalokas with the force of his physical strength. He proximates the distance and distances the proximity. He makes little as more and more as little. He makes sweet as bitter and bitter as sweet. In short, whatever the monk with this prodigy wishes—is all accomplished.

The endowment of these prodigies enlarges the sight to see the creator of the universe-Brahma. It qualifies him to listen to his words and mind. He transforms the body into mind and mind into the body.

2. *Prodigy of Perceptible Divine Hearing (Divya-śrotra-dhātu)* : The monk endowed with this pure and supernatural power of divine hearing can listen to the near and distant sounds or words like the gods. The monk possessed of this prodigy can identify the sounds like 'this is the sound of conch or kettle-drum' out of many kind of sounds, being created even in Brahmaloka.

3. *Prodigy of Mind-reading (Metoparya Jnāna)* : The monk endowed with this prodigy knows the minds of others. He knows one as having attachmental mind when he has this type of mind. He knows others' mind in the same way as it exists at the moment such as detached mind, mind with aversion, mind devoid of aversion, deluded, mind, undeluded mind, distracted mind, abridged mind, intelligent mind, mind devoid of intelligence, inferior mind, superior mind and absorbed mind (concentrated mind), non-concentrated mind, detached and non-liberated mind.

4. *Prodigy of Memory of Earlier Births (Pūrva-nivāsa-anusmṛti-jnāna)* : The monk endowed with this prodigy remembers many kinds of earlier births. He can remember one, two, hundred, thousand, hundred thousand etc. births. He can remember many periods of duration of dissolution, creation and destruction-cum-origination of the universe. He remembers that at that time, he was in a particular place, state of birth, species, destinity and state of knowledge. I was in a specific state of birth. I had this name, lineage, life-span, food and experience of pleasure and pain. I was born in a specific place after death from there where I had this name ..... etc. After death there, I am born here in this Kṣatriya or Brahmin family. The heretics remember their earlier births upto 40 Kalpas (a unit of time equivalent to 20 Antar-Kalpas). The natural votary remembers earlier births upto 100 or 1000 Kalpas, the great/senior votaries remember earlier births upto 80 lacs of Kalpas, the topmost votaries remember the earlier births upto innumerable lacs of Kalpa years the self-enlightened one remembers the earlier births upto two innumerable lacs of Kalpa yeas and the Buddha remembers the earlier births upto a period without measure.

5. *Prodigy of Departure and Arrival (Cyutotpādana Jnāna)* : A monk endowed with the superhuman divine sight can know and see the different living beings while dying, taking birth, in good state and in bad state. He can also know the living beings with good or bad colours, acquiring good or bad rebirth, and achieving the birth state according to his own karmas. The living beings behaved badly with body, speech and mind. They condemned the noble people. They had wrong-faith. They acted as wrong-faithed. Now, they have acquired the infernal destinity and misfortune after their death. Some others behaved well bodily, vocally and mentally. Some praised the noble people. They had right faith. They acted as right-faithed. They have now acquired good destinity and heavens. Thus, he knows all ... through his divine eye.

6. *Prodigy of Destruction of Causes of Karmic Influx (Āsrava kṣaya)* : The monk endowed with this prodigy wanders in the world with self-realisation

after knowing the self in this same birth by acquiring influx-less supreme mind and wisdom.

Adhikaraṇa Samaya : The violation of conduct for pacifying the quarrels is also a default.

Adhiṣṭhāna Pāramitā : Perfection in resolve; Steadiness; Remaining totally steady in one's resolve like a mountain which does not tremble and waver, and which remains steady in its own place/position.

Adhvanika : Permanent.

Agniśālā : Water-heating room.

Akuśala Karma : Sinful activities; Activities always resulting in bad effects.

Anagāmī : Not taking birth again; The yoga-practicing mendicant becomes as not-taking birth again after totally destroying the desire for lust for sensuals and doing undesirable for others.

Anāśvāsika : Mentally non-satisfying.

Anavasrava/Anāsrava : Non-influx of karma; Devoid of karmic fruition.

Aniyata : Unspecified; Uncertain; A mendicant proposes for one of the three defaults of 'Pārājika, Sanghādidesa, and Pācittiya before a believer votaress in solitude. When the incident is presented before the monk-assembly, the default of the mendicant is decided on the basis of the statement of the votaress, the mendicant is awarded expiation. As the offence is not pre-decided, this is called unspecified or uncertain.

Anuprajnapti : Address.

Anuśāsanīya prātihārya : Discipline Keeping; The mendicant has the discipline : "Think thus, do not think thus; Think thus in your mind, do not think thus in your mind; Do not do this, leave it, accept it."

Anuśrava : Scriptural tradition.

Anuśrāvaṇa : Post-promulgation query; After disciplinary promulgation, one asks the mendicant group : 'Whosoever accepts the order, please keep silence; whosoever do not accept, please express their mind.'

Apāyika : Moving to the evil destinity/state.

Arhat : The mendicant alleviates the attachment in perceptibles, non-perceptibles, pride, arrogance and ignorance (ne-science) and becomes the Enlightened or Venerable (Arhat) one. All his bad karmas get off and all his influxes are destroyed. After death, his worldly cycle is totally terminated. The causes of his worldly life are removed and his worldly pains are permanently over. This is the state of the liberated while living and supreme position.

Aṣṭangika Mārga : The eight-fold noble path :
(i) Right vision, (ii) Right resolve, (iii) Right speech, (iv) Right action, (v) Right livelihood, (vi) Right conduct, (vii) Right memory, and (viii) Right meditation.

Aupapātika : The infernal and celestial beings.

Avici Naraka : The lowest of all the eight hells (of Buddhists) where there is fierce fire always burning in the area of 100 Yojanas.

Avicīrṇa : Not performed.

Avitarka-vicāra- samādhi : The mendicant acquires the state of uni-channeled thought on scriptural knowledge who finds flaws in scriptures and does not find flaws in shifting process and, therefore, crosses the first stage of meditation with a desire to leave even that knowledge. Out of the four meditations, the concentration on first, second and third meditation is known as this form of concentration.

Avyākrta : Indescribalde.

Ācāryaka : The religion.

Ādeíanā Prātihārya : Miracle of sermons; Accordingly, one can express the resolves of the minds of others after knowing it through one's own mind.

Ājāniya : Belonging to excellent/noble caste.

Ākāśānantyāyatana : The third out of the four form-less Brahmalokas ?

Āknicanyāyatana : The fourth out of the four formless Brahmoloka ?

Ānantarya Karma : Sinful karmas; Post-actions-fruition karma; There are five such karmas — (i) Murder of mother, (ii) Murder of father, (iii) Murder of Arhat, (iv) Causing blood flow from the body of the Buddha, (v) Creation of dissension in the group. These five sins are called 'Post-action fruition karmas'. By performing these acts, the human being does never get liberation after destroying the causes influx in the same birth. The result of these sins follows them.

Ānupūrvī Kathā : Story narrated in succession. Accordingly, the stories related with donation, good conduct (śila) and heavens are narrated. The bad affects of sensualism are described and the importance of renunciation of sufferings and detachment is illustrated.

Āpatti : Penalty of offences.

Ārya-satyā : Noble Truth : (i) Suffering, (ii) Cause of suffering, (3) Alleviation of suffering, and (iv) Methods of alleviation of suffering.

Āsrava : Karmic influx; Mental impurities; There are four kinds of mental impurities : (i) Desire, (ii) Birth, (iii) Vision and (iv) Ne-science.

Āssa-santa : Assuring.

Bala : Virtues; Capacities. There are five virtues : (i) Faith, (ii) Potency, (iii) Recall or memory, (iv) Mental concentration, (v) Supreme wisdom.

Bhakta-ccheda : Non-availability of food.

Bhavāgra : End point or pinnacle of the world; The practitioner of meditation and yoga enters the subtle world from the gross world due to his meditation. He moves into this world with such a speed that he reaches a point where the world ends. This point is known as the pinnacle of the world.

Bhinna-stūpa : Foundation-less structure.

Bodhi-manda : The compound of Buddha temple in Buddha-Gayā.

Bodhisattva : An individual who accumulates such a knowledge and sacredness through his efforts during many earlier births that he may become Buddha any time in future.

Bodhi-vṛkṣa : The Tree of Enlightenment.

Bodhyanga (Seven) : Factors of Enlightenment : There are seven factors : (i) Memory, (ii) Potency, exertion or internal energy, (iii) Affection or delight, (iv) Mental concentration, (v) Dis-interestedness and (vi) Pacification of body and mind (Praśrabdhi).

Brahmacarya vāsa : Initiation; Celibacy.

Brahmacarya-phala : Effect of Celibacy : The Religion of Buddha.

Brahma-danda : Supreme punishment; The mendicant, who is awarded supreme punishment, may speak to other mendicants at his will, but they can neither speak to him nor address or exert control over him.

Brahma-loka : World of Brahma; The best among all the seventeen worlds of gods. Their residents are called Brahmas.

Brahma-vihāra : Supreme wanderings/Reflections; The reflection on four virtues : (i) Friendship, (ii) Compassion, (iii) Delight-ness and (iv) Dis-interested-ness.

Buddha Kolāhala : Proclamation about the birth of the omniscient Buddha, thousand years before his birth. The guardian gods wander with proclamation, "Thousand years from now, the Buddha will take birth in this world."

Buddha-bīja : The future Buddha.

Buddhāntara : Interval between the liberation of one Buddha and appearance of another Buddha.

Buddhaśrī : Excellence of Buddha.

Caitya-garbha : The main sanctuary of the temple.

Cakra-ratna : Gem-wheel; The first gem of Cakravartī out of the seven ones. It has 1000 spokes, the centre or nave of the wheel is ring-shaped. It is completely symmetrical and divine. The army of Cakravartī moves in the direction of its movement. The army stops wherever this wheel stops. Due to the effect of this wheel, the kings become sub-ordinates of Cakravartī without any fight and he instructs them about the five good conducts (Panca-sāla).

Cakravāla : Circular system of universe; There are innumerable circular systems in this universe. A circular system is like a world in itself whose length and width is 12,03,450 Yojanas and whose circumference is 36,10,350 Yojanas. The thickness of each circle is 2,40,000 Yojanas and it is surrounded by a layer of 4,80,000 Yojanas of deep water. There is an air-layer, of 9,60,000 Yojanas thickness surrounding this water. In the center of each circle, there is a Sinerū mountain whose height is 1,68,000 Yojanas. Half of its height is under sea and half is on the surface. There are seven series of mountain surrounding the Sinerū mountain — (1) Yugandhara, (2) Isadhara, (3) Karavikā, (4) Sudassana, (5) Semidhara, (6) Vinataka and (7) Assa-kaṇṇa. The lord of gods (Mahāraja devas) and their attendant yakṣas (demons) reside over these mountains. There is Himavān mountain in the circle which is 100 Y high and which has 84000 peaks. The circular rock is surrounding the whole circular system.

Every circular system has one sun and moon with a width of 49 and 50 Yojanas respectively. Every circular system has palaces for Trāyastinía gods, asura gods and Avici-infernals.

There are four great islands or continents named Jambūdvīpa, upper-goyāna, eastern Videha and Uttarakuru. Each continent is surrounded by 500 small islands. There is the Lokantarika Niraya (intra-mundane hell). The light of the suns brightens only one circular system. However, the radiance of Buddha can brighten all the circular systems.

Cakravartī : Wheel-turning monarch; Universal monarch; A great person possessed of seven gems — (i) wheel, (ii) elephant, (iii) horses, (iv) Jewels, (v) wife, (vi) Lord of businessman or citizens and (vii) gem-leader (according to Majjhima Nikāya etc.) or son-(according to Dīgha-Nikāya etc.) and four prodigies — (i) supreme beauty, (ii) long-life, (iii) Diseaseless-ness (Nirātan-katā) and (iv) dearness to all Brahmanas and businessmen or citizens.

Cāra dvīpa : Four islands; Four islands in the four directions of Sumeru mountain. There is Pūrva Videha in the east, Upper-goyāna in the west, Uttarakuru in the north and Jambūdvīpa in the south.

Cāra-Rddhipāda : Four methods of acquiring accomplishment of concentration :

1. Concentration acquired through good karmas (chanda).
2. Concentration acquired by potency or inner energy.
3. Concentration acquired by meditation (mental).
4. Concentration acquired by mental deliberations.

Cārikā : Wandering for teaching the religion. It has two varieties : (i) Immediate (tvarita) and (ii) Normal. The accidental wandering to enlighten a distant votary is the immediate wandering. In contrast, the normal wandering is to walk daily for a Yojana or half-a-Yojana in order of villages or towns with intake of foods and for the purpose of the beneficiation of the public.

Catu-madhura snāna : Bath in four-pleasant things : Butterfat, Butter, honey and sugar.

Cātūrdvīpika : Simultaneously raining cloud on all the four-continental earth.

Cātūr-mahā-rātrika devatā : (i) Dhṛtasāṣra (ii) Virūdha (iii) Virūpakaṣa and (iv) Vaisravaṇa are called the four catur-maharajika gods. Their one day is equal to 50 years of human beings. The thirty such days make up a month and 12 months make up a year. Their life-span is 500 such years. (App 90 lac of years).

Catuṛyāma : The four-fold doctrine of Mahāvira :

1. The knotless restrains the use of (unsteriled) water.
2. The knotless instructs to restrain all the kinds of sin.
3. The knotless becomes sin-free by restraining himself from all the sins.
4. The knotless is always engaged in restraining himself from all kinds of sin.

According to Dīgha-nikāya Sīhanada sutta, the four-fold doctrine is as follows :

1. Not to do violence to the living beings, not to get it done, nor to approve it (Non-violence).
2. Not to steal, not to get it done, nor to approve it (non-stealing).
3. Not to speak false, not to get false spoken, nor to approve false speaking (truth).
4. Not to involve in five-fold sensual gratification, not to get others involved in them and not to approve them.

Chanda : Attachment.

Cīvara : Reddish dress of mendicants which is prepared by jointing many pieces of cloth. According to Vinaya (Text of Monastic Conduct), the mendicants are prescribed to have three reddish dresses :

1. *Antara-vāsaka* (cloth to be wrapped below the waist). It is wrapped like a lungi.
2. *Uttarāsanga (upper garment)* : A 5 H long and 4 H wide (1 h = 1.5 ft) cloth used for wrapping the upper part of the body like a cover.
3. *Sanghātī (Folded cloth on shoulders)* : A cloth whose length and width is similar to the upper garment but it is doubly stitched. It is kept on shoulders with folds. It is used to cover the head and body during cold or other occasions.

Dākṣiṇeya : Presentable; Present or gift is the donation capable of awarding the other-world (heavens). The person capable of receiving presents is called presentable.

Dāna-Pārmitā : Perfection or fullness in donations; Offer of desired materials to the beggars or mendicants without caring for wealth, riches, sons, wives or body etc. just like the water-pitcher which becomes empty by turning it down.

Daśa-bala : Ten virtues :

(i) To know as proper what is proper and improper what is improper.

(ii) To know the position and causes of fruition of karmas done in present, past and future.

(iii) To know properly the superb intelligence (gāminī pratipadā).

(iv) To know the universe and manifold elemental universes properly.

(v) To know the living beings with different thoughts properly.

(vi) To know the weakness and strength of senses of other living beings.

(vii) To know the raise, cleansing, defilements of attachment, concentration, meditation and liberation properly.

(viii) To know the things about the earlier births properly.

(ix) To see the living beings taking birth, dying and going to the heavens through the pure and divine eyes.

(x) Realisation of supreme wisdom and liberation of influx-less mind due to destruction of influx.

Daśa-sahasra-Brahmānda : Ten thousand circular systems of the world which are Buddha areąs in the form of his birth.

Deśanā : Acceptance of one's own guilt or fault; Teachings.

Dhāraṇā : Holding; To say after looking the public or monks on listening to the sermons, "I hold that the public accepts what I have said; That is why, it is silent."

Dharma : Religion; Teachings of Buddha on religion and philosophy to different people at different places, and under different circumstances. It is also called as 'Sūtra'.

Dharma vinaya : Opinion.

Dharma-cakra-pravartana : Enforcement of the wheel of teaching the religion. The first teaching of religion to the five mendicants is know aṣ 'Dharma-cakra-pravartana Sūtra'.

Dharma-cakṣu : Knowledge of religion.

Dharma-dhātu : Object of mind.

Dharma-kathika : Teacher of Dharma.

Dharma-paryāya : Teachings of religion.

Dharmatā : Specificity.

Dhūtavādī : Detachment or renunciation-based life-style. The term 'Dhūta' means the one who has combed the defilements. It also means the religion of carding off the defilements. A person who combs his defilements off by the mental or other components and teaches others to do the same, is called 'cleansed' or 'follower of cleansing'. There are 13 components of cleansing (Dhūtangas or Resolves of cleansing) :

(i) Resolve for wearing reddisḥ clothes made of rags found on sands, rubbish, crematorium and sandy roads.

(ii) Resolve for wearing three reddish clothes, shoulder-cloth, upper garment, and waist-wrapping garment.

(iii) Resolve to subsist on begging.

(iv) Resolve for begging without gap of houses; Begging round from houses from one corner to the other corner without gap.

(v) Resolve for single-dieting.

(vi) Resolve for taking foods only from a single container despite having many containers having foods but refusing to take from them.

(vii) Resolve for no-food after taking it once like the khalu bird.
(viii) Resolve for residing in the forest.
(ix) Resolve for living under the tree.
(x) Resolve for living under open space.
(xi) Resolve for living in the crematorium.
(xii) Resolve for sitting and sleeping on particularised bed, "it is for you". The resolve is in the form of as it is.
(xiii) Resolve for taking rest or sleep without lying.

Dhyāna (Cāra) : Four-fold meditation; In the first meditation, there are five components— (1) discursion, (2) thought, (3) affection, (4) happiness and (5) concentration. The deep engagement of mind in the object is called discursion. This is the propensity of not allowing the object out of mind. The term 'affection' means mental pleasure. One gets delight by subduing the five hindrances (Nīvaraṇas) of desire, sinful activity, somnambulism, arrogance and disgust. The delightness creates affection. The term 'happiness' means physical joy. The affection causes the body to be pacified which gives pleasure. The concentration means 'samādhi'. Thus, the affectionate pleasure due to desirelessness, bereft of sinful karmas, discursion, and thought leads to the first stage of meditation.

In the second meditation, there is no discursion and thought. In their absence, one gets concentration and vigilance. In this stage, faith gets stronger and the affection, pleasure and concentration become prominent.

In the third meditation, there is no component of affection even. There is prominence of concentration and pleasure. The thought of pleasure does not create deviations in mind. However, there is specific attribute of forbearance and concentration during this meditation.

In the fourth meditation, there is even no fourth component of pleasure. There are two propensities of disinterestedness and memory developing in this meditation alongwith concentration. There is the forsaking of physical pleasure of pain in this stage and there is bereavement of attachment and aversion. During this best meditation, the mind becomes totally cleansed and pure due to the forsaking of pleasure and pain and mental satisfaction and dis-satisfaction.

Dīgha-bhāṇaka : Ancient teachers learning Dīgha-nikāya by rote.

Divya Cakṣu : Divine sight; Engagement of one's mind to learn about the birth and death of the living beings by acquiring concentrated, pure and steady mind.

Droṇa : A measure for measuring the grains in olden times. This is bigger than Nāli :
4 Prasthas = 1 Kudava
4 Kudava = 1 Droṇa
1 Prastha is nearly equal to 0.25 Seer, hence 1 Droṇa is app. equal to 4 Seers or is 3.20 kg [Abhidhāna Cintamaṇi Kośa 3.50].

Dukkata kā doṣa : Offence of sin.

Gamika : Departing mendicant.

Ghatikāra : Mahābrahmā; God of Creation.

Ījjhāna : Burrnese year : Mynmar year.

Indra-kīla : A colossal iron-pillar or rock near the entry gate of the city to check the attack of the enemy.

Jambūdyīpa : An island 10,000 Yojanas wide, whose 4000 Yojana area is filled with water and is called as ocean. The human beings reside in an area of 3000 Yojanas.

The rest of the 3000 Yojana area consists of the Himavān mountain (Himālaya) which is 500 Yojanas high adorned with 84,000 peaks and which has 500 rivers flowing around it.

Janghā-vihāra : Walking.

Jantā-ghara : Bath-room.

Jāti-sangraha : Collection of relatives and followers for their enlightenment.

Jnāna-darśana : Realisation of realities.

Jnapti : Information; To inform the group of mendicants in proper order : "If the groups feels proper, it should follow it."

Kalpa : A Time unit of innumerable years. There are four kinds of Kalpa :

1. *Samvarta Kalpa* : Kalpa of world-dissolution.
2. *Samarta-sthāyī Kalpa* : Kalpa of duration of dissolution.
3. *Vivarta Kalpa* : Kalpa of creation.
4. *Vivarta-sthāyī-kalpa* : Kalpa of duration of world creation.

In the Samvarta Kalpa, there is dissolution of the creation and there is the birth of the creation in the Vivarta Kalpa. They are gradually occuring in the world. The life-span of celestials are measured in Kalpas. The Kalpa-unit has a higher value than the time to take out all the mustard seeds densely filled in a $1Y^3$-pit at the rate of one seed per 100 years.

Kalpika-kutiyā : Store house, Store.

Kārṣapaṇa : A copper coin of that period; (app. 10 gms of today).

Karuṇā : Compassion; The attitude of compassion towards all the living beings of the world.

Kathā-vastu : Discussion, Dispute.

Kāya-smṛti : Recollection of respirations of body; The mendicant sits in a forest, under a tree or an empty house. He undertakes postures and keeps his body straight. He inhales with recollection, he exhales also with recollection. He experiences while inhaling and exhaling long breath. When he inhales and exhales short breath, he also experiences it. The mendicant, then, practices the process of inhaling and exhaling while experiencing the position of his whole body. He practices the inhaling and exhaling after suspending or retaining the breath for some time. This practice leads him to be vigilant, alert and restrained. Thus, while wandering, his greedy attitudes are destroyed. The mind is instilled inside and becomes concentrated and absorbed.

Kleśa : Defilements of mind.

Kriyāvādī : Actionist; One who sermonises actions only.

Kṣānti-pāramitā : Perfection of forbearance; Just as the earth endures all the materials—pure and impure—thrown over it, does not show anger but always has delightful mind; similarly, the mendicant should always bear the respect and disrespect equally and acquire the highest stage of forbearance.

Kṣīṇāsrava : A state of Arhat-hood; Destroyed-desires.

Kuśala Dharma : Pious activities; Ten auspicious moral latencies or pre-dispositions which are always there at every moment during the observance of good activities.

Kutūhalaśālā : Hall of religious discussion; A place where followers of different religions discuss their religion and the audience listens to them curiously.

Loka-dhātu : The Realm of universe.

Madhyama Pratipadā : Middle path; A path between the extreme sensualism and extreme detachment.

Mahā-abhijnā-cārikā : Nun with great divine powers; *See* Abhijnā.

Mahābhi-niṣkramaṇa : Great going out after leaving home by Bodhisattva for initiation.

Mahāgocara : Resident of densely populated area near a pleasant garden.

Mahā-brahmā : Gods having a life-span of one innumerable Kalpas residing in the world of Brahma; *See* Brahmaloka.

Maitrī : Friendship towards all.

Maitrī-ceto-vimukti : Reflective release of friendship-ful mind in the form of, "May all the living beings live without enmity and violence. May all the living beings enjoy their lives with happiness."

Maitri-pāramitā : Perfection of friendship; Just as the water cools every body-sinner and the sacred and cleanses the defilements of both, similarly, the perfection of friendship means to expand this attitude with equanimous views towards all-the well-wishers as well as bad wishers.

Maitri-sahagata citta : Mind associated with the attitude of friendship.

Māṇavaka : Son of Brāhmana.

Manomaya Loka : The world of gods; Mental world.

Māra : The term has many meanings : (i) Death in general, (ii) Suffering or defilement which leads man to take birth in deathful world. (iii) Name of the son of the Vaśavarti god who presumed himself as the ruler of the world of desires. Whosoever undertook the spiritual practices on leaving sensualism, was taken as his enemy. He tried to deviate him from his path.

Muditā : Satisfaction; Delight.

Naigama : An official post like the wealthy person of the city, but a little higher in status.

Nairyāṇika : One who ferries over the sufferings.

Naiṣkarmya Pāramitā : Perfection or fullness in desirelessness; Just as a prisoner does neither have any attachment with the prison even after long stay there, nor he is ever eager to reside there, similarly, this fullness means to take all types of birth as prison and to wish for getting away from them.

Naiva-sanjanā-sanjnāyatana : The fourth non-perceptible world of Brahmā out of four : Non-perception-cum-non-non-perception.

Nāli : A measure of measuring grain in ancient times. It was app. equal to 1.5 Seers or 1.25 kg (as per '*Buddha-kālina Bhāratiya Bhūgola*', p. 552).

Nidāna : Cause; Desire for future.

Nirmāṇarati devatā : Gods with power of multiplication; These gods change their forms on their own will. They feel joy in this action. Their one day is equal to 800 years of human world. Thirty days are equal to one month and twelve months make a year. Their life-span is eight thousand such divine years.

Nissaggiya Pācittiya : A kind of expiation; Requital of offence occurs when the mendicant leaves the order after accepting the offence before the group, single monk or many monks.

Pānca Mahātyāga : Five-great renunciations : (i) wealth, (ii) body, (iii) life, (iv) offspring and (v) wife.

Pānca Mahāvilokana : Five objects of great thinking; While residing in the Tuṣita world, Bodhisattva thinks about his (i) time, (ii) island, (iii) country, (iv) family, (v) mother and (vi) life-span related with his birth.

Panca-śīla : Five good conducts :

(i) Abstinence from violence or killing.
(ii) Abstinence from taking not-given (non-stealing).
(iii) Abstinence from non-celibacy (celibacy).
(iv) Abstinence from false speech (truth).
(v) Abstinence from taking intoxicating materials.

Pānṣukūlika : Resolver of wearing reddish clothes made of rags.

Pārājika : Expiation of expulsion; When there is a grave default, the mendicant is expelled from the order.

Paramārtha-pāramita : Completely resolute in meditational practices; Not to deviate from practice even at the death-point. There are ten perfections of such practices.

Pāramitā : Perfection; Sitting with resolve for practices where the care for body is completely renounced. There are ten such resolves.

Paranirmita-vaśavartī devatā : Goods controlled by others; Their abodes are ruled by the Māra-evil destroyer. Their one day is equal to 1600 human-years. Thirty such days make a month and twelve months make a year. Their life-span is 16000 such divine years.

Pariveṇa : Hall of studies : A hall where the monks gather and study. This place is surrounded by walls and there is an open courtyard.

Pati-bhāna : Explanation of variegated questions.

Pāti-desanīya : Forgiveness for defaults; The defaulter monk requests the order of monks : " I have done an improper and condemnable offence. I beseech pardon for this".

Pinda-pāta : Food-in-alms; The mendicant stands at the door of a householder with his begging bowl. He stands pacified with his eyes down there. A member of the family drops the alms in his bowl and bows before him. The mendicant moves ahead with blessings to him. When the begging bowl is full, he returns to his monastery. The food served to the mendicant with invitation is also included in the term.

Pinda-pātika : A mendicant having black-bee-like alms or food collecting.

Prajnā : Supreme wisdom of emptiness ; Destruction of ne-science.

Prajnā Pāramitā : Perfection of supreme wisdom; Just as the mendicant subsists on alms and does not leave any one of excellent, medium or low families during his alms-begging, similarly, he should acquire the highest wisdom through questionings from wise men.

Prajnapti : Enunciations; Prescription, religious code.

Prātihārya : Miracles.

Pratimokṣa : Monastic Rules of conduct : The Vinaya Pitaka (Basket of Mendicants, Code of Conduct) has two independent chapters — one on the conduct of male mendicants and the other on the conduct of nuns. They contain 227 and 311 rules respectively. All the mendicants and nuns gather in the vow-observance hall on the dark fourteenth and bright fifteenth day and recite and repeat these rules.

Pratipāda : Path; Knowledge.

Prati-samvit-prāpta : Acquirement of distinct knowledge is called 'Prati-sambhidā'. There are four such distinct knowledges :

(i) *Distinctive knowledge of objects (Artha-prati-sambhidā)* : The five points- cause- based effect, Nirvāna (Nirukti), meanings of what has been said, fruition and action- are called 'objects' (arthā). The distinctive knowledge of these objects is called 'Distinctive knowledge of objects.'

(ii) *Distinctive knowledge of Buddha Sermons (Dharma)* : There are five Dharmas (1-2) Cause and (resulting in) effect, (3) the sermonised noble path, (4) good actions and (5) bad actions. The deep looking into these Dharmas is called the Distinctive knowledge of 'Dharma'.

(iii) *Distinctive knowledge of Etymology (Nirukti)* : The distinctive knowledge through Māgadhi— the basic language of all the living beings about the derivative nature of the objects and sermons and their behaviours, statements about them and ascertaining their true nature is called Distinctive knowledge of etymology or derivation. The person proficient in this kind of knowledge knows the meanings of the words like 'touch' experience (vedana, pain) etc. They do not have any nature.

(iv) *Distinctive knowledge of explanations (pratibhāga)* : The support of the knowledge looking into the knowledge of all the objects is the knowledge itself or the objects and duties conveyed by it is called the Distinctive knowledge of explanations.

Pratītya-samutpāda : Relative causality; Origination of an entity after destruction of another one. The material causes of aggregates are : (i) Form, (ii) Feeling, (iii) Instincts (iv) Pre-disposition and (v) Intellect or cognition.

Pratyanta : Boundary.

Pratyaya : Cause (Primary and secondary); Permissible articles of mendicants. There are four such articles : (i) Reddish dress, (ii) Food-in-alms, (iii) Beds and seats and (iv) Medicines for curing ailment.

Pratyeka-buddha : Self-enlightened; A person who self-realises the essence of religion. He does not need any teacher for learning the religion.

Pṛthak-Jana : Common man who has not acquired the state of noblehood. There are eight noble states of noble-hood of the path of liberations :

(1-2) Path of resolute movement (srotāpanna) and its effect.

(3-4) Path of ultimate arrival (saṛkdāgāmī) and its effect.

(5-6) Path of non-arrival (anāgāmī) and its effect.

(7-8) Path of enlightened-hood (Arhat) and its effect.

Pudgala : Individual; Living being.

Pūrvalakṣaṇa : Pre-signals; Presentation of an oldman, diseased man, dead corpse and initiated saint by the Sahampati Brahma to promote initiation of the Bodhisattva while going to see the garden before renouncing the house.

Ṛddhi-prātihārya : Miraculous deeds due to yogic power; Accordingly, the mendicant can transform himself into many forms, and many forms into one form. He can manifest himself and he can also disappear. He can cross through the walls, stone-rocks and mountains like that in the sky without any strike. He can dive in earth like in water. He can move on water like that on the earth. He can fly in the sky with rolled legs like the birds. He can touch the mighty sun and moon and rub them with his hands. He can go to the Brahmaloka associated with his body.

Sa-brahmacārī : Fellow disciple; Śramaṇa initiated in the same order.

Samādhi : Rightful concentration of mental activities on a single substratum; Purification of mind.

Sahampati Brahmā : The great Brahmā (a god) on whose request, Buddha preached his religion. On many occasions, he secret-visited Buddha. He was the mendicant named Sahaka during the time of Kāśyapa Buddha. He was born as Mahābrahmā in the world of Brahmā as a result of his observance of five qualities (indriyas) of faith, potency, memory, meditation and wisdom.

Śaikṣya : Novice; Learner; The novice learner is defined as that who has acquired four paths (out of five except the Arhat one), and three effects (out of four, fruition, exertion, similar to cause and control). He has to learn about others. The mendicants who have acquired the Arhat-hood, are called Non-novices.

Sakṛdāgāmī : Coming only once in future. The mendicant, in his first stage, moves on to the path of liberation after winning over the five obstructions of lust for senses and thoughts of evil on others. At this stage, the main activity is to destroy karmic influx. If he does not acquire Arhat-hood in this birth, he may acquire it in the next birth by taking birth once again.

Sallekha-vṛtti : Propensity of renunciation; An austerity; The person is said to have the best renunciation tendency who observes all the conducts even at the time of his imminent death without doing and getting the splendours, attendants and state of activities on the basis of his qualities of few desires and overlooking the enunciations of Bhagavan Buddha.

The term 'nimitta' means a servant who takes care of residence, beds and seats. When the householders ask, "What is being done? Who is getting it done", one should say, 'no body' or say anything like this.

The term 'avabhāsa' means 'splendour'. It is illustrated like, "O worshippers, where do you live ?"

"We live in a palace".

"O worshppers, the mendicants should not need the palaces". The statement like this or similar should be made.

The term 'parikathā' means the state of affairs. It is illustrated by stating like "There is difficulty of residence for the mendicants" or any other statement with reference to specific states.

Samādhi-bhāvanā : A reflection which leads to Buddhahood in the same birth.

Sambodhi : Buddha-hood.

Samgati : Destiny, Future eventuality.

Samyak-sambuddha-pravedita : Perceived by the Buddha.

Sāndṛṣtika : Symbolic; Worth looking into; The term 'sandṛṣti' means to see. The term here, thus, means worth looking into. The extraordinary religion, while being observed checks the cycle of birth and death. That is why, it is called "worth looking into".

Sanghādi-sesa : Short-period expulsion of the defaulter mendicant for purification of his default.

Sanghāta : Net, Web.

Sanjnā : Preliminary knowledge; Instinct. The knowledge like 'this is this object' after the contact of sense and the object is called instinct or sanjnā.

Sanjnā-vedayita-nirodha : A kind of samādhi where there is non-existence of knowledge and experiencing. The mendicant under this samādhi does not feel, 'I will acquire the state of suppression of knowledge and experiencing,' "I am acquiring this state of samādhi," "I have acquired this state of samādhi". The mind of aspirant gets accustomed in such a way that he acquires this state of samādhi. In this samādhi, there is, first, the suppression of speech, followed by body and mind.

Sannipāta : Gathering, Assembly.

Sansthāgāra : Meeting Hall.

Santuṣita : Son of gods in the Tuṣita world.

Sarvārthāka Mahāmātya : Private secretary.

Satya-pāramita : Perfection of truth; Just as the star of Venus does not deviate from its path in any season, similarly, this perfection means not to deviate from the path of truth despite hundreds of troubles and allurements of riches etc.

Saundika Karmakara : Brewer, Distiller.

Sekhiya : Commandments whose violation is a fault.

Śikṣāpada : Monastic rules.

Sīla : Good conduct; Abstinence from fully prohibited activities like violence etc.; Purity of body.

Śīla-pāramitā : Perfection in good-conduct; Just as the camari (deer or cow) protects her tail disregarding even her life, similarly, the mendicant should always be resolute for the protection of his good conduct even at the cost of his life.

Smṛti-samprajanya : Consciousness and experience.

Sramaṇa Pariṣkāra : Four kinds of things acceptable by the mendicant :

(i) Reddish clothes made of rags,

(ii) Food-in-alms,

(iii) Seats, beds and residence, and

(iv) Medicines for ailments.

Śrāmaṇera : Wearing of reddish clothes after getting initiated. Under this condition, the Buddhist scripture is taught. The aspirant has to live with the initiator and to undertake ten vows of good conduct : abstinence from violence, stealing, illicit sex, false speech, intoxication materials, evening meals, amorous disposition, cosmetisation, high seat and gold and silver.

Srotā-patti : Coming into the stream of liberation; To be on the path of liberation where from there is no possibility of downfall. The mendicant is called to be on the path of liberation when he crosses over the three obstacles of disgust, existencial attitude and faith in wrong conduct. The mendicant on the path of liberation attains liberation in a maximum of seven rebirths.

Sthavira : Senior monk; One becomes sthavira after ten years of initiation and becomes 'Mahāsthavira' after twenty years of initiation.

Styāna-gṛddha : Somnambulist; Laziness of body and mind.

Su-ākhyāta : Well-narrated; Well-said.

Su-nirmita : Son of the gods of Nirmāṇa-rati heavenly world.

Su-pravedita : Well-realised; Well-proclaimed.

Su-yāma : Son of the gods of Yāma heavenly world.

Thallaccaya : Big offence.

Tīna Vidyā : Three learnings : The following are the three learnings :

(i) Memory of earlier birth.

(ii) Knowledge about birth and death.

(iii) Knowledge of destruction of mental defilements.

Trāyastrinśa devatā : These are the empyrean gods whose lord is Śakra. Their one day is equal to 50 years of human world. Thirty such days make up a month, 12 such months make up a year. Their life-span is 1000 such years (~1,80 lac years.)

Tuṣita devatā : The Bodhi-sattvas live in the palaces of Tuṣita (satisfied) gods. They take birth in the world after completing their life-span there. They, then, get Nirvāṇa after acquiring enlightenment. Their one day is equal to 400 years of human beings. Thirty days make up a month, twelve months make up a year. Their life-span is 4000 such divine years.

Udāna : Breathing upwards; Words from the mouth of the mendicants out of delightful mood.

Unnīsa-vidyāyen : Nineteen learnings : (i) Scripture, (ii) Smṛtis-books on canonical code of law, (iii) Sānkhya, (iv) Yoga, (v) Nyāya (logic based), (vi) Vaiśeṣika (Specificists), (vii) Mathematics, (viii) Music, (ix) Vaidyaka : Science of life-span, (x) Four Vedas, (xi) All Legendary, Books, (xii) History, (xiii) Astrology, (xiv) Incantationolgoy, (xv) Logic, (xvi) Mystical formulary of worship (tantra), (xvii) Military science, (xviii) Meterology, and (xix) Palmistry.

Upa-pāramitā : Secondary Perfections : Renunciation of external materials with great resolution in the objective. There are ten secondary perfections.

Upaśama-samvartanlka : Propitiator of peace.

Upa-sampadā : Ritual of initiation; A person desirous of monkhood is ritually initiated after he has learnt and understood the religion. When the monk assembly is there, the novice presents himself before it, and he is examined by the assembly. When he passes the test, he is taken into the group of monks, and he is, then, called 'Bhikṣu' (mendicant). He has to observe 227 rules under the laws of Buddhist monastic conduct. A person can be initiated only after he is twenty years old.

Upasthāka : Accompanying attendant.

Upasthāna-śālā : Meeting Hall.

Upekṣā : Dis-interested-ness towards the world.

Upekṣā pāramitā : Perfection in Disinterested-ness; Just as the earth overlooks on the good or bad materials thrown over it without any pleasure or pain, similarly, the perfection-in-disinterestedness means to be equanimous in the state of pains and pleasures and to move towards the highest state of indifference.

Uposatha : Vows; A votary or worshipper, with clean dress, goes to the Buddhist-monastery. He kneels down before the mendicant and requests him, "O venerable, I speech you to award me eight vows of good conduct with three refuges (of Buddha, Religion and order)". The votary repeats his request thrice. The mendicant awards him one vow each time and stops for a moment; the votary respects the vow every time. The votary, then, resides in the monastery for the whole day, observes all the eight vows of good conduct and spends his day in pious thoughts. Many votaries observe these vows for the whole life. The eight vows of good conduct are as below :

1. I will live by renouncing the violence or destruction of vitalities.
2. I will live by renouncing the things not-given (or stealing).
3. I will live by renouncing the sensual desires.
4. I will live by renouncing the falsity.
5. I will live by renouncing the use of intoxicating materials.
6. I will live by renouncing the foods in the evening.

7. I will live by renouncing the use of dance, songs, instrumental music, amorous pastimes, garlands, cosmetics, smearing pastes, and beautification of body.
8. I will live by renouncing the high seat and decorated bed.

Uposathā- gāra : Hall for observing vows.

Uttara-kuru : An island among the four islands.

Uttara-manuṣya-dharma : Divine powers.

Vārṣika Śātikā : A loin or waist-wrapping cloth used during the rainy season because of non-drying of clothes in this season.

Vaśavartī : Son of gods born in the palace of Paranirmita Vaśavartī gods.

Vidarśanā/Vipaṇyanā : Insight introspection; Knowledge of wisdom or truth which accrues due to the realisation of momentariness, sufferabillity and non-soulness of entities.

Vihāra : Monastery; Hermitage.

Vijnanānantyāyatana : Thought on infiniteness of cognition/perception; The second of four formless abodes of Brahmaloka.

Vimukti : Liberation.

Vināya : Scripture on monastic rules, A text in which the monastic rules for monks and nuns are detailed. (Vinaya-pitaka).

Vīrya Pāramitā : Perfection of potency or exertion; Just as the lion is always vigilant, active and mentally resolute while sitting, standing or walking, similarly, the mendicant should acquire the highest potency by being active in all the birth-states.

Viśvakarmā : God of Architecture; A god resident of Trāvatinśa heaven who is the architect among the gods. He is present before the Buddha for architectural work on the command of Íakra at different times.

Vyākaraṇa : Forecast, Grammar; Explanation.

Vyāpāda : Mischief; Treachery.

Yāma-devatā : Tutelary deity of village; There is one day of 200 years of human world. Thirty such days make a month, and 12 such months make a year. The life-span of these tutelary gods is 2000 such divine years.

Yaṣṭi : A measure of length :
20 Yaṣtis = 1 Vṛṣabha.
80 Vṛṣabha = 1 Gāvuta.
4 Gāvuta = 1 Yojana Ī 8 miles.

Yojana : 2 miles : 3.32 kms.

BIBLIOGRAPHY

	Name	Author
1.	*Anga Paṇṇatti*	Achārya Shūbhchandra
2.	*Anguttar Nikāya*	Translated by Shri Bhadant Anand Kaushalyāyaṇ Published by Mahabodhi Sabha, Calcutta in 1957-63.
3.	*Alankār Tilak*	
4.	*Anuyoga Dwār Sūtra*	
5.	*Aṭṭhasālini*	Pune edition, 1942
6.	*Ashtadhyāyi Vriti*	Author Pāṇini
7.	*Abhisamalyankar*	Baroda Edition.
8.	*Abhidhan Rajendrā Kosha*	Acharya Vijayā-Rajendra Suri Ratlam, 1913-34. (seven volumes)
9.	*Amar Kosha*	Nānārtha Varga. (Third volume)
10.	*Ashoka Ke Dharmalekha*	Edited by Janardan Bhatt. Published by Publication division, Ministry of Information and Broadcasting, Old Secretariat, Delhi-1957.
11.	*Achārānga Niryukti*	
12.	*Acharanga Sūtra (Jaina Agama)*	With commentary by Shīlankāchārya, published by Āgmodaya Samiti, Surat, 1935.
13.	*Ādi Purāṇa*	Acharya Jinasena edited by Pt. Pannalal Jaina, Published by Bhartiya Gyānpith, Kāshi, 1963.
14.	*Ārādhanā*	Aparājita Sūri
15.	*Ārādhanā Vijyodayā*	Aparājita Sūri
16.	*Āvashyaka Niryukti*	Āchārya Bhadrabāhu with commentary by Achārya Malayagiri and published by Āgmodaya Samiti, Bombay, 1928.
17.	*Āvashyaka Niryukti*	Āchārya Bhadrabāhu with commentary by Āchārya Haribhadra and published by Āgmodaya Samiti, Bombay, 1916.
18.	*Aupapātika Sūtra*	With commentary by Abhayadeva Sūri and published by Devachand Lalbhai preservation of Manuscripts Fund, Surat, 1937.
19.	*Bāl-Ramayana*	Rajshekhar.
20.	*Bhadrabāhu Charitra*	Āchārya Ratnanandi
21.	*Bhagwati Sūtra (Jaina Agama)*	With commentary by Abhayadeva Sūri and published by Rishabhadevaji Kesari Malji Jaina Shwetamber Sansthā, Ratlām, 1937.
22.	*Bharat Ki Arya Bhashayen*	Dr. Indrachandra Shastri
23.	*Bharat Ki Bhashayen Sambandhi Aur Bhāshā Samasyayen*	Dr. Suniti Kumar Chatterji

	Name	Author
24.	*Bhāsha Vigyān*	Dr. Bholanath Tiwari
25.	*Bhatri Harikrita Nīti Shataka*	Achārya Sidharshi
26.	*Bhāva-Sangraha*	Āchārya Devasena Edited by Shri Pannalal Soni and published by Manikchand Digamber Jaina Granthmālā Samiti, Hindi Granth Ratnāker Karyālaya, Bombay, 1921.
27.	*Braj Ka Sanskritik Itihas*	
28.	*Chhāṇdogyopanishad*	
29.	*Chūlvagga Parichchheda*	
30.	*Chūlvansh Parichchheda*	
31.	*Darshan-Sār*	Devasenāchārya. Edited by Pt. Nathuram Premi and published by Jaina Granth Ratnaker Kāryalaya, Bombay, 1920.
32.	*Dashavaikalikā Vriti*	
33.	*Deep Vansh*	(Ceylonic Pāli Granth, Edited and translated by Older verga and published by Williams and Norget, London, 1906-1915.
34.	*Dharma Sangrah with Tika*	
35.	*Dhavalā*	
36.	*Digh Nikaya*	(Hindi version) Translated by Rāhul Sānkritāyan and published by Mahabodhi Sabhā, Sārnāth, Benaras, 1936.
37.	*Dwatrishad Dwātrishika*	Āchārya Sidhasena Divakar.
38.	*Gauḍavaho*	Vākpati Rāj
39.	*Gommat Sār*	Nemichandrāchārya Sidhant Chakravarty R/o Pāḍham with commentary by Pt. Manohar Lal and published by Shri Paramshrutā Prabhāvaka Maṇḍal, Bombay, 1913.
40.	*Gopaka Maggalān Sutta*	
41.	*Gyatridharma Katha*	
42.	*Gyatri Dharma Katha Sūtra*	
43.	*Himvata Therāvali*	
44.	*Jaina Agama*	Pt. Dalsukh Mālvaniyā, published by Jaina Sanskṛiti Shodh Mandal, Varanasi, 1947.
45.	*Jaina Sidhant Bhāsker*	Published by Jaina Sidhānt Bhavan, Arrah, 1913.
46.	*Jainendra Sidhant Kosh*	Kṣullak Jinendra Varṇi.
47.	*Jambudweep Paṇṇatti*	With commentary by Shantichandra Gaṇi (Pts 1 and 2) and published by Devachand Lalabhai Preservation of Manuscripts Fund, Surat, 1920
48.	*Jaya Dhavalā Prashasti*	
49.	*Jyotishkarandaka Tikā*	
50.	*Kachchāu Vyakarṇa*	

	Name	Author
51.	*Kalpa Sūtra*	Published by Sārābhai Maṇilal Nawab, Ahmedabed, 1941
52.	*Kalpa Sūtra Tikā*	
53.	*Kalyān*	Published by Geeta Press, Gorakhpur
54.	*Kām Sūtra*	
55.	*Karpūr Manjari*	Acharya Rājshekhar
56.	*Kāvyādarsha*	Daṇḍi
57.	*Kavyālankar Vriti*	
58.	*Laghu Sidhant Kaumudi*	
59.	*Lalit Bistar*	Edited by Dr. P.L. Vaida, (Budhist treatise in Sanskrit). published by Mithila Vidyapitha, Darbhanga (Bihar) 1958
60.	*Lalit Bistrā*	Āchārya Haribhadra
61.	*Mahaparinirvān Sutta*	
62.	*Maha-Purāṇa*	Published by Manikchand Jaina Granthmālā, Bombay.
63.	*Mahābhārat*	
64.	*Mahābhāshya*	Mahirshi Patanjali Edited by Bhargavā Shastri, Published by Nirṇaya Sāgar Press, Bombay, 1951.
65.	*Mahāvansha*	Translated by Bhadant Anand Kauslāyayan (Hindi version) and published by Hindi Sahityā Sammelan, Prayāg.
66.	*Mahāvagga*	Mahāvir Jaina Vidyalaya Golden Jubliilee Souvenir, Volumes 1-2, Bombay, 1968.
67.	*Mahavira Charitā*	Rayadhu
68.	*Mahayan Sūtra Sangraha*	Published by Mithila Peeth, (I volume) Darbhanga (Bihar) Edition 1961.
69.	*Mahāyān Sutra Alankār*	
70.	*Majjhim Nikaya*	Translated by Rahul Sānkritāyan (Hindi version) and published by Mahabodhi Sabhā, Sārnath Banares, 1933.
71.	*Manusmriti*	
72.	*Milind Panho*	(The questions of king Milinda) (Pali version) Edited by Shri R.D. Vadekar and published by Bombay University, Bombay, 1940.
73.	*Mundkopnishada*	
74.	*Nandi Sūtra*	
75.	*Nandi Sūtra Sthvirāvaḷi*	
76.	*Nārada — Smriti*	
77.	*Nātya Shastra*	Āchārya Bharat.
78.	*Nāyādhamma Kāhāo*	Chief Reciter, Achārya Tulsi, Edited by Muni Nathmal and published by Jaina Vishwa Bharti, Lādnu, Vikram Samvat 2031.

	Name	Author
79.	*Niruktā*	
80.	*Nirya-Valika*	(With commentary and Hindi Gujrati versions) Ghasilalji Maharaj. Published by All India Shwetamber Sthanak Jaina Preservation of old manuscripts Samriti, Rājkot, 1960
81.	*Niryukti*	Āchārya Bhadrabāhu.
82.	*Nishith Bhāshya*	
83.	*Niti Sār*	Āchārya Indranandi
84.	*Paiasadda mahashnavo*	Pt. Hargovind Das Seth Edited by Dr. Vāsudeva Sharan Agrawal and Pt. Dalsukh Malvaniyā Published by Prākrita Granth Parishad, Vārānasi - 5 (Second Edition) 1963.
85.	*Pāli-Maha-Vyakarṇa*	Bhikṣu Jagdish Kāshyapa.
86.	*Panch Sidhantkā*	Āchārya Vārāhmihir
87.	*Pāli Sāhitya Kā Itihas*	Dr. Bharatsingh Upādhyāya and Published by Hindi Sāhitya Sammelan (Second Edition) Prayāg, 1963.
88.	*Paṇini Shiksha*	
89.	*Paṇiniya-Ashtadhyāyi*	
90.	*Parshishṭa Parva*	Āchārya Hemchandra, edited by Dr. Hermon Jacobi, and published by Asiatic Society of Bengal, Calcutta, 1932.
91.	*Prabhāvaka Charita*	Prabhachandra and published by Sindhi Granthmala, Calcutta, 1940.
92.	*Prāchin Lipimālā*	Dr. Gaurishankar Hirachand Ozha
93.	*Pragyāpnopāngama Pūrvārdhama*	
94.	*Pragyāpnā Sūtra*	Translated by Amolak Rishi
95.	*Prākrita Updesh Pada*	Achārya Haribhadra
96.	*Prākrita — Pattāvali*	
97.	*Prākrita-Prakash*	Achārya Varruchi
98.	*Prākrita Lakshan*	
99.	*Prishishṭa Parva*	Achārya Hemchandra, Edited by Seth Hargovind Das, Published by Jaina Dharma Prachāraka Sabha, Bhāvnagar, 1957.
100.	*Raipasenaiyaṁ*	Edited by Pt. Bechar Das Dosi, (Jaina Agama) Published by Gurjar Ratna Granth Kāryālaya Ahmedabad, 1939.
101.	*Rajprashniya Sūtra*	
102.	*Rigvedā*	
103.	*Rāmāyaṇa*	Geeta Press, Gorakhpur.
104.	*Ratnakarandashravakā Chār*	Published by Mānakchand Digamber Granthmala Samiti, Bombay.
105.	*Shākṭāyana*	

	Name	Author
106.	*Shākṭāyan Vyākarṇa*	
107.	*Shravanbelgola inscription*	
108.	*Shri Avashyaka Sūtra*	Āchārya Malayagiri (IInd Volume)
109.	*Shri Dushmākāl-Shraman-Sangh-stava*	Āchārya Dharmaghosh Sūri
110.	*Shrutāvtār.*	
111.	*Shrutavtār*	Indranandi
112.	*Shat Khanḍāgama*	Āchārya Virasena (Dhavala commentary), Edited by Dr. Hiralal Jaina, and published by Sitābchand Laxmichand, Amraoti (Gujrat) 1941-57.
113.	*Shatprābhrita Tikā*	
114.	*Shaddārshan Samuchaya with commentary*	Yakini Mahattarā Sūnu Āchārya Sūri
115.	*Samyukta Nikāya (The Book of Kindred sayings) (Pali version)*	Edited by Bhikṣu Jagdish Kashyapa and published by Pali Prakashan Mandal, Nāv Nālanda Mahavihār, Nālanda (Bihar), 1959.
116.	*Sanskrit-Hindi Kosha*	Āpte Vāman Shivarām.
117.	*Sadharma Pundarīka Sūtra*	Dr. N.N. Dutta (Hindi Edition)
118.	*Samant-Pāsādikā*	Achārya Budhghosh, Edited by J.Yakākusu, Makoto Nagai, and published by Pāli Texts society, London, 1947.
119.	*Samvāyānga Sūtra*	(Jaina Agama) with commentary by Abbaya Deva Sūri, Edited by Māster Nagindas Nem Chand, Published by Seth Maneklal Chunni Lal, Kantial Chunnilal, Ahmedabad, 1938
120.	*Saraswati Kanthābhrana*	Ājaḍa
121.	*Sāmānya Bhāsha Vigyān*	Dr. Babu Ram Saxena.
122.	*Sāmveda*	
123.	*Sāhitya Darpana*	Mahamahopādhyāya Pt. Durga Prasad Dwivedi.
124.	*Sidhahema-Shabdānu-shāshan*	Hemchandracharya and published by Sidhchakra Sāhitya Prachāraka Samiti, Bombay.
125.	*Sumangla Vilāsini*	Āchārya Budhghosha and published. by Pali Texts Society, London, 1886-1932.
126.	*Sūtrakritānga Sūtra*	(Jaina Agama) with commentary by Āchārya Shilankācharya and edited by Shrichandra Sāgar Gaṇi and published by Shri Gaudiji Pārshvanāth Jaina Derasar Pedhi, Bombay.
127.	*Sūtrakritānga Niryukti Chūrṇi*	
128.	*Sthirāvali Charitam*	
129.	*Sthānānga Tika*	Āchārya Abhayadeva Sūri, 1063.
130.	*Sthananga Sūtra*	(Jaina Agama) with commentary by Achārya Abhayadeva Sūri, and published by Agmodaya Samiti, Surat, 1920.

	Name	Author
131.	*Sthananga Sūtra Vritti*	
132.	*Stree Nirvān-Kevali Bhukti Prakarṇa*	Edited by Muni Jambu Vijayji and published by Atmānand Jaina Sabhā, Bhāvnagar, Samvat 2030.
133.	*Thānānga Sūtra*	
134.	*Tatwārth Sūtra*	Umaswati and published by Raichand Jaina Shāstramālā, Hirābāgh, Bombay, 1906.
135.	*Tāndya Maha-Brahmaṇa Pachvṁsha Brahmaṇa*	
136.	*Tatvārth Sūtra Sarvartha Sidhi*	Acharya Pujajapād
137.	*Tithogalipaiṇṇa*	(Jaina spiritual treatise) still unpublished.
138.	*Tiloyapaṇṇatti*	Āchārya Yativrashabha, edited by Dr. Hiralal Jaina and A.N. Upadhye Published by Jaina Sanskriti Sankvakshakā Sangh, Sholapur, 1951
139.	*Taitriya Saṁhita*	
140.	*Uttrādhyayan Sūtra*	With commentary by Bhāvavijaji and published by Atmānand Jaina Sabhā, Bhāvnagar.
141.	*Upmiti Bhava Prapanch Kathā*	Āchārya Sidharshi
142.	*Vrahat Kathākosh*	Āchārya Harishena Edited by Dr. A.N. Upadhye and published by Sindhi Jaina Granth- mālā, Bombay, 1943.
143.	*Vrahat Kalpa-Bhāshya*	
144.	*Vasudeva Hindi*	
145.	*Vinaya Pitaka*	Edited by Bhikshu Jagdish Kashyapa (Pāli Version) published by Pāli Prakashan Maṇdal, Navnālanda, Mahāvihar, Nālandā (Bihar) 1956.
146.	*Vinaya-Pitaka* (Introduction)	Edited by Dr. Olden Verga.
147.	*Vipāka Sūtra*	
148.	*Vipāka Shruta*	
149.	*Visudhimagga*	Āchārya Budhghosh
150.	*Visheshāvashyaka Bhāshya*	Āchārya Jinabhadra Gaṇi Komashramana, (with commentary) commentary by Kotyāchar, Published by Rishabhdeva Keshri Mal Shwetamber Sanstha Ratlam, 1936-37.
151.	*Vrahdaraṇya Kopnishada*	
152.	*Vrishṇi Dasha Sūtra*	
153.	*Vaiyākarṇa Sidhānt Kaumudi*	
154.	*Vyakhya Pragyapti*	(Bhagwati) Sūtra, with commentary by Abhaya Deva Sūri, Published by Rishabhdeva Keshari Mal Jaina Shwetamber Sansthā, Ratlam, 1947
155.	*Yāgya Valkya Smriti*	

Name of the Book	Name of Author
1. *A Comparative Study of Pratimoksha*	Pachova.
2. *An Introduction to Linguistic Science*	Prof. Adager Sturvint, New Haven, 1948.
3. *Annals of Bhaudārkar*	Oriental Research Institute, Poona, 1974.
4. *Budhist India*	Rayas Davids.
5. *Buddhistic Studies*	Edited by Dr. Law.
6. *Comparative Grammar of Prakrita language*	Dr. Pischel.
7. *Dr. Upādhyāya's Introduction to Siddhasena Divākar's Nyaya Vatara and other works*	Published by Jaina Sāhitya Vikās Mondala, Bombay, 1971.
8. *Epitome of Jainism Appendix*	
9. *History of Pali Literature*	By Dr. Law.
10. *History of Indian Literature*	Dr. Winter Nitza, Calcutta, 1933.
11. *Indian Historical Quarterly*	December, 1928.
12. *Indian Palaeography*	Dr. Bular.
13. *J. Bendryes Language*	J. Bendryes, London, 1952.
14. *Jainism in South India*	Prof. S.K. Ramchandra Rao.
15. *Language*	Dr. Blum Field.
16. *Lax Religion Dyaina*	Dr. Waltter Schubring.
17. *Linguistic Survey of India*	Sir Jorj Abrāham Griyorsan, 1927.
18. *Manu Smriti*	M.Monior Williams.
19. *Mysore Gazetteer*	Laws Rice
20. *Pāli Literature and Language*	Dr. Gaiger.
21. *Rajasthan District Churu Gazetter*	
22. *R.G. Bhandarker Commemoration*	
23. *Sanskrit English Dictionary*	By Sir Monier Williams, M.W.A. K.C.I.E.
24. *The Middle Length Saying*	
25. *The Pali Literature of Burma*	London, 1909.
26. *The Story of Language*	Mosiyo-Pai, London, 1952.

Index

OTHER WORKS OF THE AUTHOR

1. *Agama Aur Tripitaka Ek Anushilan Volumes I and III*
2. *Ahiṁsa Vivek*
3. *Ahimsā Paryavekṣan*
4. *Anuvrit Jiwan Darshan*
5. *Ahimsa ke Anchal men.*
6. *Acharya Shri Bhiksu Aur Mahatma Gandhi*
7. *Aṇn Se Purṇa Ki Or.*
8. *Anuvrit Vichār*
9. *Acharya Tulsi : Ek Adhyayan.*
10. *Anuvrit Krānti Ke Badhte Charan*
11. *Anuvrit Āndolana Aur Vidyārthi Varga*
12. *Anuvrit Digdarshan*
13. *Anuvrit Āndolan*
14. *Anuvrit Drishti*
15. *Bāl Dikshā : Ek Vivechan.*
16. *Jaināgama:Digdarshan*
17. *Jaina Darshan aur Adhunik Vigyān*
18. *Mati Mādhurya*
19. *Maryādā Mahostsava : Itihās Aur Parichaya*
20. *Mahavir Aur Budh Ki Samsāmyikta.*
21. *Manjil Ki Or.*
22. *Man Ke Dvanda : Shabdon Ki Kārā.*
23. *Nayā Yuga: Naya Darshan*
24. *Naitik Vigyān*
25. *Navin Samāj Vyavsthā men Dān Aur Dayā.*
26. *Prerṇā Deep.*
27. *Sarva Dharma Sadbhāva*
28. *Satya Manzil Samikṣha Rāh*
29. *Terāpanth Digdarshan*
30. *Tera Panth Shashan Praṇāli*
31. *Yuga Pravartaka Bhagwān Mahāvira.*
32. *Yuga Dharma Terāpanth*
33. *Yathārth Ke Paripārshva men.*

(In Sanskrit)

34. *Āshuka Vyāni*
35. *Bhikṣhu Charitraṁ*
36. *Bhakte Ruktayaḥ*
37. *Lalitānga Charitram.*
38. *Mātherān Shushmā*
39. *Nīti Nilotpalāni*

(In English)

1. *Agama Aur Tripitaka:Ek Anushilan Vol. I.*
2. *Anuvrata Ideology.*
3. *A Pen-Sketch of Achārya Tulsi.*
4. *Contemporaniety and Chronology of Mahāvira and Buddha.*
5. *Glimpse of Anuvrata.*
6. *Glimpse of Terāpanth.*
7. *Jaina Philosophy and Modern Science.*
8. *King Bimbisāra and King Ajātshatru in the age of Mahāvira and Buddha.*
9. *Light of Inspiration.*
10. *New Age: A New Outlook*
11. *Pity and Charity in the New Pattern of Society.*
12. *Strides of Anuvrata Movement.*
13. *Theory of Relativity and Syādvād.*